Handbook of Emotion Elicitation and Assessment

Series Editors
Richard J. Davidson
Paul Ekman
Klaus Scherer

Series in Affective Science

Handbook of Emotion Elicitation and Assessment

EDITED BY

James A. Coan

John J. B. Allen

UNIVERSITY PRESS

2007

OXFORD
UNIVERSITY PRESS

Oxford University Press, Inc., publishes works that further
Oxford University's objective of excellence
in research, scholarship, and education.

Oxford   New York
Auckland   Cape Town   Dar es Salaam   Hong Kong   Karachi
Kuala Lumpur   Madrid   Melbourne   Mexico City   Nairobi
New Delhi   Shanghai   Taipei   Toronto

With offices in
Argentina   Austria   Brazil   Chile   Czech Republic   France   Greece
Guatemala   Hungary   Italy   Japan   Poland   Portugal   Singapore
South Korea   Switzerland   Thailand   Turkey   Ukraine   Vietnam

Published by Oxford University Press, Inc.
198 Madison Avenue, New York, New York 10016

www.oup.com

Oxford is a registered trademark of Oxford University Press

Library of Congress Cataloging-in-Publication Data
Handbook of emotion elicitation and assessment / [edited by] James A. Coan, John J. B. Allen.
     p. cm.—(Series in affective science)
ISBN 978-0-19-516915-7
1. Affect (Psychology)   2. Emotions.   I. Coan, James A.   II. Allen, John J. B.   III. Series.
BF511.H355 2007
152.4072—dc22   2006014136

9 8 7 6 5 4 3

Printed in the United States of America
on acid-free paper

Contents

Contributors

Ralph Adolphs
Department of Neurology, University
of Iowa, and
Humanities and Social Sciences,
California Institute of Technology

John J. B. Allen
Department of Psychology
University of Arizona

Zara Ambadar
Department of Psychology
University of Pittsburgh

David M. Amodio
Department of Psychology
New York University

Jo-Anne Bachorowski
Department of Psychology
Vanderbilt University

Margaret M. Bradley
NIMH Center for the Study of
Emotion and Attention
University of Florida

Hermann Brandstätter
Johannes-Kepler-University of Linz,
Austria

Lynlee Campbell
School of Psychology
University of Western Australia

James A. Coan
Department of Psychology
University of Virginia

Jeffrey F. Cohn
Department of Psychology
University of Pittsburgh

John J. Curtin
Department of Psychology
University of Wisconsin, Madison

Eric Eich
Department of Psychology
University of British Columbia

Paul Ekman
Department of Psychiatry
University of California, San Francisco

Nathan A. Fox
Department of Human Development
University of Maryland

Katalin M. Gothard
Department of Psychology
University of Arizona

John M. Gottman
Relationship Research Institute,
Seattle

Elizabeth K. Gray
Psychology Department
North Park University, Chicago

Irina Grebneva
Department of Psychology
University of British Columbia

James J. Gross
Department of Psychology
Stanford University

Eddie Harmon-Jones
Department of Psychology
Texas A&M University, College Station

Heather A. Henderson
Department of Psychology
University of Miami

Marc W. Hernandez
Department of Psychology
University of Chicago

Tom Johnstone
Waisman Center for Brain Imaging
    and Behavior
University of Wisconsin, Madison

Takeo Kanade
Robotics Institute
Carnegie Mellon University

Alfred W. Kaszniak
Psychology Department
University of Arizona

James D. Laird
Department of Psychology
Clark University

Peter J. Lang
NIMH Center for the Study of
    Emotion and Attention
University of Florida

Robert W. Levenson
Department of Psychology
University of California, Berkeley

David L. Lozano
Mindware Technologies, Gahanna,
    Ohio

Dawn Macaulay
Department of Psychology
University of British Columbia

Colin MacLeod
School of Psychology
University of Western Australia

David Matsumoto
Department of Psychology
San Francisco State University

Lis Nielsen
National Institute on Aging
National Institutes of Health

Joycelin T. W. Ng
Department of Psychology
University of British Columbia

Catherine J. Norris
Waisman Center for Brain Imaging
    and Behavior
University of Wisconsin, Madison

Arne Öhman
Department of Clinical Neuroscience
Karolinska Institute, Stockholm

Michael J. Owren
Department of Psychology
Cornell University

Lisa A. Parr
Yerkes National Primate Research
    Center

Alexandra D. Percy
Department of Psychology
University of British Columbia

Rebecca D. Ray
Department of Psychology
Stanford University

Nicole A. Roberts
Department of Psychology
University of Wisconsin, Milwaukee

Edmund T. Rolls
Department of Experimental
    Psychology
University of Oxford

Jonathan Rottenberg
Department of Psychology
University of South Florida

Anna Marie Ruef
Boston Veterans Administration
    Medical Hospital

Nancy L. Stein
Department of Psychology
University of Chicago

Sarah Strout
Department of Psychology
Clark University

Jeanne L. Tsai
Department of Psychology
Stanford University

David Watson
Department of Psychology
University of Iowa

Stefan Wiens
Stockholm University and Karolinska
    Institute

Edward Wilson
School of Psychology
University of Western Australia

Seung Hee Yoo
Department of Psychology
San Francisco State University

Leah R. Zinner
Department of Psychology
University of Wisconsin, Madison

Handbook of Emotion Elicitation and Assessment

James A. Coan
John J. B. Allen

Introduction

Organizing the Tools and Methods of Affective Science

Affective science—the scientific study of emotion and emotion-related processes—is now a mature domain of inquiry, with its own standardized measures, induction procedures, data analytic challenges, subdisciplines, core theoretical debates, and so on. Though long associated with psychology, researchers in the affective sciences can now be found in a variety of disciplines. Psychologists, biologists, sociologists, geneticists, neuroscientists, ethologists, economists, behavioral ecologists, and even physicians each contribute their specific expertise like pieces of a puzzle, because emotions distribute their echoes and effects at every one of these levels and more.

A cursory scan of titles in the Oxford University Press Series in Affective Science bears this out. By 2003, the mammoth *Handbook of Affective Sciences* (Davidson, Scherer, & Goldsmith, 2003) offered as near an exhaustive overview of the field as we are likely to see soon, making it clear that emotions are implicated in domains of inquiry as broad and diverse as brain-behavior relationships, behavior genetics, personality, social bonding and interaction, evolution, culture, decision making, psychopathology, and health. To date, both the series and the *Handbook of Affective Sciences* have focused on overviews of results and explications of theoretical developments in this diverse field. Few texts devote space to explicit discussions of the empirical tools and methodological challenges that collectively allow emotion research to proceed, despite the fact that the study of emotion often requires highly specialized designs, instruments, and strategies. Indeed, new techniques are proliferating at an impressive rate, often without heed to the specific incremental advantages they may or may not offer. Well-validated and substantially understood measures are frequently neglected in favor of expeditious progress, convenience, or both. The field is now at a point at which a large number of excellent elicitation procedures and assessment approaches exist, and the broader application of these procedures and approaches stands to increase interlaboratory standardization and, by doing so, to increase the speed and accuracy with which emotion research can be communicated among peers. In short, it is time for a handbook that organizes and details the major methodological accomplishments of this multifaceted field, and that is what we hope to provide with the *Handbook of Emotion Elicitation and Assessment*.

In publishing this handbook, however, we emphatically do *not* wish to stifle the creative development of innovative methods. On the contrary, our hope is that this book will *accelerate* the development of new elicitation and assessment procedures by discouraging researchers from reinventing approaches for which sufficient resources currently exist. In advocating the expanded use of standard and well-researched methods and techniques, we, in fact, hope to encourage current and future emotion researchers to cast their collective gaze with greater creativity and determination toward domains that lie beyond the field's current reach.

It is also our intent that this handbook serve as something more than a mere collection of tools. Some chapters address broad methodological problems (e.g., working with infants and children, measuring subjective emotional experience). Others seek to assist the broader community of affective scientists in being critical and conversant on topics still beyond the scope of many laboratories (e.g., comparative research, functional neuroimaging). Still others review and recommend general methodological orientations and strategies (e.g., thinking like a social psychologist in designing emotion elicitations). Ultimately, this collection should serve as a pragmatic resource for emotion researchers in need of both specific guidance and general advice. Scales are presented and described, stimuli are reviewed in a methodological context, coding systems and detailed assessment tools are suggested, innovative methodologies are proposed, current methodological problems are highlighted, and general recommendations are expressed. It is a book of resources—a kind of bookshelf consultant—for the affective scientist, or for the scientist whose foray into the affective sciences may be in its beginning stages.

The volume is organized into three general sections. The first addresses the laboratory *elicitation* of emotion, the second discusses the *assessment* of emotion, and the third focuses on methods that support research on emotion's potential biological underpinnings.

Part I: Emotion Elicitation

Section I (chapters 1–10) covers a diversity of strategies for eliciting emotion in the laboratory. The selection of topics under elicitation procedures reflects our view that no single sensory domain is paramount—that indeed emotions can arise through a variety of modalities and that these modalities (even some that can be controversial) need to be well understood and properly implemented if comparable results across laboratories can be achieved.

Opening this section, Rottenberg, Ray, and Gross (chapter 1) offer detailed instructions on the acquisition and use of standardized emotional film clips, and Bradley and Lang (chapter 2) discuss the proper use of their well-known International Affective Picture System (IAPS). Other chapters provide detailed instructions and recommendations for using emotional *behavior*. Ekman (chapter 3) provides detailed recommendations for using his Directed Facial Action (DFA) task, and Laird and Strout (chapter 4) review the implementation of what they refer to as a "family" of elicitation techniques that utilize emotional behaviors. Wiens and Öhman (chapter 5) clarify the often murky methodological waters surrounding the elicitation of "unconscious" emotion via masking techniques and provide invaluably specific recommendations for their use.

Of course, although essential (especially when implemented properly), films, images (perhaps especially masked ones), and emotional behaviors can be limited in their ability to elicit *intense* forms of emotion in the laboratory or,

indeed, some forms of emotion altogether. Famous among the elicitation-resistant laboratory emotions is anger, but the elicitation of intense or "authentic" emotional responses in the laboratory is, in general, challenging. Harmon-Jones, Amodio, and Zinner (chapter 6) offer recommendations for the use of strategic laboratory social interactions in the elicitation of emotion with high levels of both experimental control and ecological validity. In chapter 7, Roberts, Tsai, and Coan review a specific strategy for eliciting emotional reactions that are not only authentic but often quite intense. Their *dyadic interaction task* offers the possibility of studying emotional processes in social contexts and at levels of intensity that are often beyond what is achievable—either methodologically or ethically—using ordinary laboratory challenges.

Eich, Ng, Macaulay, Percy, and Grebneva (chapter 8) describe their *MCI technique,* a theoretically based elicitation procedure that places music (M) and contemplation (C) in an idiographic (I) context, such that individuals are not subjected to other experimental procedures until they are *known* (via occasional measurements) to be sufficiently induced into a target mood. Their instructions include lists of widely available pieces they have used for this purpose, and with the advent of online music stores (e.g., iTunes), acquisition of this music has become inexpensive and convenient.

Rolls (chapter 9) reviews the use of primary reinforcers in the elicitation of emotion and emotional processes (e.g., physiological processes associated with emotion). In providing his recommendations, he also outlines a broad model of emotions as reflecting brain systems that respond to rewards and punishments. In this way, Rolls invokes fundamental evolutionary processes that foreshadow later chapters on the biological underpinnings of emotion and emotional responding. Similarly, Levenson (chapter 10) reviews methodological issues in the elicitation of emotion in neurological patients. The reader is particularly referred to this chapter for Levenson's excellent review of a broad array of elicitation techniques, many of which do not receive dedicated chapters in this volume.

Part II: Emotion Assessment

Emotion elicitation is of little use if we are incapable of reliably measuring emotional responses. Leading off this section, Gray and Watson (chapter 11) describe the history and proper use of a variety of paper-and-pencil scales designed to assess both state and trait affect, with particular emphasis on the widely used Positive and Negative Affect Schedule (PANAS). It would be hard to overestimate the impact of such scales, especially because the reliable and valid measurement of subjective experience is such a formidable task (as noted by Nielsen and Kaszniak later in chapter 22). Wilson, MacLeod, and Campbell follow this in chapter 12 with a discussion of information-processing approaches to understanding emotion and emotional effects. This work offers a new and fruitful heuristic for understanding the role of emotion in a variety of cognitive contexts, with a specific focus on our conceptual understanding of cognitive vulnerabilities to affective disorders such as depression and anxiety.

Cohn, Ambadar, and Ekman (chapter 13) introduce behavior coding with their review of the Facial Action Coding System (FACS). Their chapter discusses the major facial elements associated with emotional expression and describes procedures for extended training and certification in FACS coding. In chapter 14, Cohn and Kanade describe their important ongoing work in the domain of automated facial analysis (AFA), an emerging technology that holds the promise of automating FACS coding. Owren and Bachorowski (chapter 15) present methods for measuring a complimentary mode of emotional expression in their comprehensive discussion of vocal acoustics associated with emotional responding, and, synthesizing across channels of expression, Coan and Gottman (chapter 16) describe the Specific Affect (SPAFF) Coding System for coding emotional behavior at the construct level. This system trains coders to be constantly mindful not only of emotional facial expressions but also of vocal acoustic properties and verbal content.

Experience sampling and the analysis of time are of increasing interest to affective scientists, and with good reason. Technical and data analytic advances in recent years have made the study of these important variables—long neglected as they have been—more available and affordable. Ruef and Levenson (chapter 17) describe a device for continuous, fluid reporting of emotional responding through time called the *affect rating dial*. The basic design and implementation of this tool offers a host of advantages to researchers interested in the chronotropy of emotional responding, the study of psychophysiological coherence in emotional responding, and the synchrony of emotional responding among interacting dyads. Stein and Hernandez (chapter 18) then describe the Narcoder, a program that allows researchers greater access to the richness of emotional thoughts and language, as well as the ways in which verbal content can indicate emotional understanding and subjective well-being. In chapter 19 Brandstätter brings the analysis of time together with a detailed look at subjective emotional experience in his discussion of the time sampling diary (TSD). Brandstätter has been a pioneer in applying methods of frequent experience sampling across time and situations. His chapter offers clear instructions for implementing his particular approach, including innovative data analytic methods for use with TSD data, once collected. Researchers will find his approach broadly applicable, as well as a useful foundation for future iterations of time sampling methodologies.

Practical methodological concerns associated with special populations and problems are highlighted in the next three chapters. In chapter 20, Matsumoto and Yoo walk the reader through the myriad methodological issues that frequently arise in the study of emotion across cultures. Matsumoto and Yoo take the reader beyond simple two-culture comparison studies, offering descriptions of different types of cultural comparisons, as well as recommendations for maximizing the interpretability, repeatability, and impact of such studies. Similarly, Henderson and Fox (chapter 21) offer a host of pragmatic and theoretical recommendations for the sound study of emotion in infants and children. Developmental milestones (e.g., in social-cognitive development and attentional control) hold implications for the kinds of questions that can likely be asked in such populations, and the validity of parental reports of child and infant emotionality raise additional methodological and pragmatic concerns. Ethical issues also come to the fore in dealing with infants and children in ways that are not as common with adult populations. Finally, Nielsen and Kaszniak (chapter 22) raise a number of vexing questions about the nature and measurement of subjective emotional experience. These questions range from how well such reports actually capture the richness of experience to whether such reports are capable of providing insights about underlying emotional events, especially at the level of physiology. Rather than cautioning affective scientists to shy away from measuring emotional experience (as, they note, so many have done), Nielsen and Kaszniak celebrate the "rich phenomenality of emotion" and call on researchers to expand their notions of experience measurement to include dimensions of motivational, perceptual, and cognitive awareness and to explore alternative reporting methodologies.

Part III: Methods for Understanding the Biological Bases of Emotion

When first considering a section on methods for understanding the biological bases of emotion, we quickly realized that the section could easily expand into a book of its own. In fact, several related books currently exist (e.g., Cacioppo, Tassinary, & Berntson, 2000), few or none with an explicit emphasis on emotion. We heartily recommend these books to affective scientists intent on exploring the biology of emotion. We also note, however, that emphasis on the biological bases of emotion—and of virtually every other domain of psychological science —is on the rise, both in the media and as a function of funding priorities at most granting agencies. At the very least, affective scientists now need to be conversant on a variety of topics related to the physiology and evolution of emotion. Chapters in this section thus satisfy a number of practical goals.

Parr and Gothard (chapter 23) introduce readers to the assumptions, general methods, and ethics of conducting research on emotion in nonhuman primates. Much of what they have to say is applicable to a wide range of animals. Their chapter sets the tone for many in this section in that its function is to acquaint readers with what they will need in order to gain access to and become proficient with nonhuman primate populations, as well as how to become better consumers of the literature in this area. In chapter 24, Curtin, Lozano, and Allen provide readers with a quite comprehensive introduction to the psychophysiological laboratory. This pragmatic chapter approximates a manual for readers, assuming sufficient funding, to actually set up a psychophysiological laboratory of their own. The authors note that psychophysiological equipment continues to become both cheaper and better with each passing year, thus making it easier for the relative novice to break in.

The two final chapters introduce readers to two broad domains of affective neuroscience: work with lesion patients and intracranial recording and functional magnetic resonance imaging (fMRI). Both provide sufficient methodological knowledge that interested readers should become significantly better consumers of this literature, but both may also serve as excellent introductions to these domains for individuals intending to actually commence research in these exciting areas. Moreover, as more affective scientists forge collaborations with individuals who have access either to rare neurological patient populations or hugely expensive neuroimaging facilities, these chapters can serve to provide a depth of understanding of these approaches that exceeds the level of relatively informal meetings and conversations but foregoes very steep investments in formal training and time.

Adolphs begins, in chapter 25, with descriptions of types of lesion studies while noting that lesion methods in humans are absolutely vital for the establishment of causal links between neural activity and behavior. Indeed, he asserts (and we agree) that other methods, such as fMRI, are as sole measures *incapable* of identifying causal links between neural structures and emotional behaviors. (This alone is an important methodological lesson, worthy of a great deal of emphasis.) As Adolphs makes abundantly clear, lesion methods have grown extremely sophisticated and stand to make powerful contributions to our understanding of the neurobiology of emotion. Norris, Coan and Johnstone (chapter 26) follow with their discussion of functional neuroimaging in the study of emotion. With their chapter, Norris and colleagues strive not only to provide methodological information critical to the design, analysis, and understanding of fMRI research but also to place fMRI in a broader conceptual context, commenting on the impact fMRI has had on the field of affective science. They note that although fMRI has provided unprecedented access to neural processes, inferential overreaching and misunderstanding has frequently occurred. They discuss the reasons for such misunderstanding and make recommendations for avoiding it in the future.

Our Core Assumption: Methods Follow Questions

In assembling a book that emphasizes tools and methods, we were gratified to have one of our core assumptions confirmed by our contributing authors: that the great diversity of methodological approaches represented here reflects the fact that affective science is highly theory-driven. Although some have argued—and it is doubtless true—that the tools of science themselves often serve as powerful heuristics for new theoretical developments in the sciences (Gigerenzer, 1991), we find this to be somewhat less true (but not entirely untrue) of the study of emotion. Perhaps because "grand theories" of emotion have existed for some time, tools have often been adapted, co-opted, and developed for the purpose of settling contentious debates or disconfirming commonly held notions; that is, with prespecified propositions in mind. It is perhaps for this reason that the study of emotion has long served as a magnet for interdisciplinary collaboration. It is increasingly apparent that a complete understanding of any emotional process is going to require attention paid to multiple levels of analysis, from the cultural to the behavioral, psychological, experiential, physiological, and molecular. This practice will increase in frequency in the coming years and decades, with significant progress coming from the use of a wide variety of approaches, within and across studies. We find this prospect exciting and hope that readers of this volume will begin to enjoy a greater familiarity with a diversity of methods, all the while maintaining a focus on questions they are interested in answering as opposed to the specific methods they are interested in using.

Conclusion

We said earlier that we hoped, with the *Handbook of Emotion Elicitation and Assessment,* to provide a volume that organizes and details the major methodological achievements in the affective sciences. We feel that this mission has been very nearly accomplished—"very nearly" because there are so many more methods and approaches that we would like to have included (e.g., quantitative and molecular genetics, statistical methods for affective scientists, etc.) but that took us a step or two too far from our original purpose. Nevertheless, our sincere hope is that readers will discover a substantial trove of practical assistance between these covers and that this assistance will prove useful for years to come.

References

Cacioppo, J. T., Tassinary, L. G., & Berntson, G. G. (Eds.). (2000). *Handbook of psychophysiology.* New York: Cambridge University Press.

Davidson, R. J., Scherer, K. R., & Goldmsith, H. (Eds.). (2003). *Handbook of affective sciences.* New York: Oxford University Press.

Gigerenzer, G. (1991). From tools to theories: A heuristic of discovering in cognitive psychology. *Psychological Review, 98,* 254–267.

Emotion Elicitation

Jonathan Rottenberg

Rebecca D. Ray

James J. Gross

Emotion Elicitation Using Films

Research on emotion has undergone explosive growth during the past few decades, marked by new theories (e.g., evolutionary analyses; Tooby & Cosmides, 1990), methods (e.g., anatomically based systems for coding facial expressive behavior; see chapter 13, this volume), and findings (see Cacioppo & Gardner, 1999). Some of the research in this area has been correlational, focusing on factors that naturally covary with emotional processes, such as chronological age, physical health, or social status. However, experimental research also has flourished, focusing on emotional processes in the context of relatively well-controlled laboratory environments. Our chapter on the use of emotion-eliciting films, like many of the contributions to the *Handbook of Emotion Elicitation and Assessment,* lies squarely within this second, experimental tradition.

Scientists who take an experimental approach have had at least two distinct motives for eliciting emotion. First, emotion has been used as an independent variable in manipulations that demonstrate the important contribution made by emotion to a diverse array of phenomena, ranging from aggression (Zillman & Weaver, 1999) to helping behavior (Isen, Daubman, & Nowicki, 1987). Second, emotion has been used as a dependent—or outcome—variable in work that has illuminated several emotion-related phenomena, such as self-reported experience (Duclos & Laird, 2001), facial expressive behavior (Ekman, Friesen, & Ancoli, 1980), autonomic or central nervous system activation (LeDoux, 1996; Levenson, 1988), and individual differences in emo-

tion responding (e.g., Gross, Sutton, & Ketelaar, 1998; Rottenberg, Kasch, Gross, & Gotlib, 2002).

Whatever their motivation for studying emotion, experimentalists have required a reliable means of eliciting emotion in an ethically acceptable fashion. Happily, investigators have made vast improvements over the buckets of frogs (Landis, 1924) and other ad hoc measures of the past, moving toward more tightly controlled and replicable emotion elicitation procedures. Indeed, as the other chapters in this volume attest, many different emotion elicitation techniques have now come to fruition, including images and sounds (Bradley & Lang, chapter 2; Wiens & Öhman, chapter 5, this volume), expressive behavior (Ekman, chapter 3; Laird & Strout, chapter 4, this volume), scripted and unscripted social interactions (Harmon-Jones, Amodio, & Zinner, chapter 6; Roberts, Tsai, & Coan, chapter 7, this volume), and music (Eich, Ng, Macaulay, Percy, & Grebneva, chapter 8, this volume).

The development of films as emotion elicitors has paralleled this wider maturation of emotion science. For much of the past half-century, researchers have selected individual film clips using relatively informal criteria, often to elicit a diffuse state of anxiety or stress (e.g., Lazarus, Speisman, Mordkoff, & Davison, 1962). In fact, until recently, the empirical record concerning films was scanty, prompting reservations about the reliability and validity of film-based emotion induction procedures (Polivy, 1981). There have been two notable efforts to build a scientific database concerning films by formalizing film selection criteria and assembling a standardized library of emotion stimuli capable of eliciting specific emotional states. Philippot (1993) presented normative viewing data ($N = 60$) from a set of 12 film clips that elicited six emotional states and reported success for stimuli that elicited amusement, sadness, and a neutral state. Gross and Levenson (1995), also working from a discrete emotions perspective, presented normative viewing data ($N = 494$) from 16 films targeting eight emotions and reported success for stimuli that elicited amusement, anger, contentment, disgust, sadness, surprise, a neutral state, and, to a lesser extent, fear.

As emotion science has matured, the palette of viable emotion elicitation techniques has grown. Increasingly, investigators face a baffling array of techniques to elicit emotion. Unfortunately, the published literature offers little explicit guidance on these issues, forcing investigators to base their decisions on informal rules of thumb, idiosyncratic training experiences, or personal communications. With these needs in mind, we intend this chapter to be a guide for investigators contemplating the use of short film clips to elicit emotion. In the sections that follow, we first outline the general task of eliciting emotion in a laboratory. Second, we compare the properties of films to other laboratory emotion induction procedures. Third, we discuss how to use films in different experimental contexts and avoid potential pitfalls. Fourth, we offer examples of films that have worked well in our own research applications. Finally, we close with reflections on the future evolution of films as an emotion elicitation procedure.

Eliciting Emotion in the Laboratory

Historically, the task of eliciting emotion in the laboratory has been made all the more difficult because emotion itself has been such an elusive construct. With different investigators employing their own idiosyncratic and often widely discrepant definitions of emotion, it is no wonder that there has been considerable confusion as to which procedures reliably elicit emotion. Fortunately, affective scientists have increasingly moved toward a consensual understanding of key affective processes, a move that has greatly facilitated the systematic study of these processes (Ekman, 1992; Russell, 1991).

Here we follow common usage and view emotions as a transient but coordinated set of responses that occur when an individual faces a situation (real or imagined) that is relevant to salient personal goals. Like others, we view emotions as being *multicomponential,* typically involving changes in cognitive, experiential, central physiological, peripheral physiological, and behavioral response systems (Lang, 1978). For example, anger may be reflected by thoughts concerning revenge, feelings of great distress, an elevated heart rate, and an attack on the source of one's anger. Finally, like other contemporary researchers, we distinguish emotions from other affectively laden concepts. For example, compared with

an emotion, a *mood* is a longer, slower moving state that is less tied to specific objects or elicitors (Watson, 2000).

Guided by this conception of emotion, laboratory emotion elicitation procedures include a broad array of efforts to evoke a brief affective response in one or more emotion response systems via some type of stimulus. Figure 1.1 highlights several of the key features of the emotion-generative process as it unfolds during a laboratory elicitation procedure (whatever that procedure may be).

The left of the figure draws attention to the fact that emotions elicited in the laboratory usually are not created *de novo* but rather arise from preexisting affective states. Indeed, affect has been understood as a stream with a continuous, or tonic, output (e.g., Russell, 2003). Emotions occur as bursts of activity, or waves, superimposed against the backdrop of this affective stream. The interaction between phasic emotion and tonic affect is not well understood and is clearly an important avenue for future research (Neumann, Seibt, & Strack, 2001). Indeed, an inspection of Figure 1.1 suggests that it is quite difficult to distinguish the waves of emotion from background affective tone, as there are no nonarbitrary criteria for deciding when one phenomenon ends and the other begins. Finally, the different "peaks" within Figure 1.1 illustrate a related complexity—that emotional impulses have no uniform signature and instead exhibit a variable duration and morphology. The notion of affective chronometry (Davidson, 1998) signals the emerging scientific interest in characterizing the variability of the emotion waveform by decomposing it into a number of temporal subcomponents, such as latency, rise time, magnitude, duration, and offset.

It should be noted that Figure 1.1, although useful for heuristic purposes, simplifies the emotion-generative process in many ways. For example, emotional responses are plotted with a single line, a representation that assumes that different emotion response elements (e.g., emotion experience, behavior, and physiology) exhibit synchrony during emotion activation. Theoretically, a high degree of synchrony between emotion response systems has been seen as essential in helping an organism mobilize a response to a challenge (e.g., make a fast getaway when a bear charges; Levenson, 1999). Em-

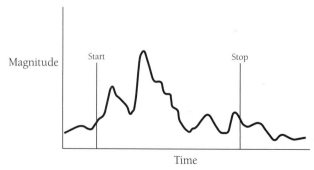

Figure 1.1. Affective responding over the course of a laboratory emotion elicitation procedure.

pirically, however, it is clear that emotional response systems do not covary perfectly in their activity (Gross, John, & Richards, 2000; Lang, 1978), with modest intercorrelations between emotion response systems often obtained (Mauss, Wilhelm, & Gross, 2004; Ruch, 1995), and even dissociated activity observed in some settings (e.g., Lacey, 1967).

Another limitation of Figure 1.1 is that it does not acknowledge the role of individual differences. A growing body of findings demonstrates that individual differences influence emotion generation at every stage of the process. These influences occur as a function of affectively toned traits such as dispositional mood (Watson, Clark, & Tellegen, 1988), emotional reactivity (Kagan & Snidman, 1999), emotion regulatory styles (Gross, 1998), and metaemotions (Salovey, Mayer, Goldman, Turvey, & Palfai, 1995), as well as personality traits (Larsen & Ketelaar, 1991; Gross et al., 1998), physical health status (Ritz & Steptoe, 2000), and other subject characteristics such as gender, race, class, and culture (e.g., Vrana & Rollock, 2002). Individual (and group) differences represent an important theme to which we return later.

Because emotion is a multifaceted process about which so much is still unknown, no single technique can serve all purposes for eliciting emotion in the laboratory. Thus the very same properties of a given induction procedure that make it a valuable procedure to probe emotion in many contexts may represent liabilities in others. With an eye to helping investigators decide whether and how films might serve their research aims, we now compare films with other common elicitation procedures.

Using Films to Elicit Emotions

A nonexhaustive list of procedures that have been used to elicit emotion in the laboratory includes: images, sounds, self-statements, facial and body movements, scripted and unscripted social interactions, hypnosis, drugs, relived or imagined scenes, music, and odors (see Martin, 1990). These procedures differ from one another in a large number of ways. To facilitate comparisons, we highlight seven key dimensions that are salient to the selection and use of these procedures. The approximate location of films along these seven dimensions is presented in Figure 1.2.

Intensity

Emotional intensity can be viewed in several ways. For present purposes, we consider the intensity of emotional responses in terms of the two conceptually separable (but often correlated) dimensions of (1) response strength and (2) response breadth.

Experimentalists face important ethical constraints regarding the strength of the emotional responses they may elicit, even when participants are carefully selected and debriefed. The experience of intense negative emotions can be

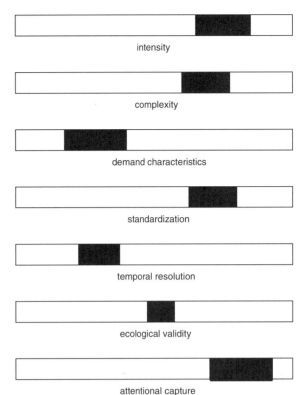

Figure 1.2. Films as an emotion elicitation procedure.

painful and traumatic, and even the experience of intense positive emotions can be associated with a loss of control that is aversive. Films are capable of eliciting mild or strong emotional responses. For a number of positive and negative emotions, films rival or exceed the response strength that can be elicited ethically with other procedures.

The relative potency of films may be due in part to the intrinsic power of carefully crafted, external, and dynamically varying stimuli. We suspect it is also due to the relatively permissive cultural mores that surround film emotion. In the United States and other Western countries, cinema and television traffic widely in graphic and emotionally explicit material, and it is likely that the presence of these media gives experimenters who use films a somewhat freer hand to elicit strong responses (even negative ones) without creating a sense of harm or ethical violation. By contrast, other procedures, such as hypnosis or confederate procedures that elicit strong negative states, may be readily perceived as deceptive or manipulative, and the effects of these induction procedures may be quite difficult to remove via debriefing (Ross, Lepper, & Hubbard, 1975).

There is also good evidence that films are capable of eliciting activations across many of the response systems associated with emotion (e.g., experience, behavior, autonomic and central physiology; Averill, 1969; Gross & Levenson, 1993; Karama et al., 2002; Palomba, Sarlo, Angrilli, Mini, & Stegagno, 2000). To the extent that investigators want to elicit broad, multisystem responses, films may hold advantages over other procedures. Anecdotal evidence suggests that self-statements have somewhat weaker effects on behavior and physiology; facial movement has relatively weaker effects on experience; and music has relatively weaker effects on physiology. Published data indicate that, whereas some film clips are capable of generating multi-system activations (e.g., Rottenberg, Gross, Wilhelm, Najmi, & Gotlib, 2002), many film clips will not. One difficulty in sorting out this issue is that films, like many elicitation procedures, are generally normed only on the basis of self-reported emotion experience (a limitation of film validation procedures that is discussed more fully later). In light of the relatively loose coupling among emotion response systems, even the most robust self-reported norms provide no guarantee that a film will generate behavioral and physiological activations.

Complexity

When considering the complexity of films, what is perhaps most striking is the variability of film clips on this dimension. A film can be a still, silent image, such as a fixation cross or test pattern, or a dynamic visual and auditory sequence that depicts complex themes. In their traditional incarnation, the film clips that are used for emotion induction tend to be dynamic, multimodal, and reliant on meaningful narrative. Given these features, therefore, most emotion-eliciting films will be relatively high in cognitive complexity. Indeed, even a very simple film, such as a sequence depicting an arm being amputated (e.g., Gross & Levenson, 1993) likely requires considerably more appraisal (Frijda, 1988) than competing procedures to elicit disgust, such as ingesting a bitter taste (reliant on a primitive reflex). On the one hand, films share with other narrative-based procedures (e.g., relieved emotion tasks) the ability to elicit cognitively sophisticated emotional states such as nostalgia. On the other hand, films impose relatively high levels of cognitive demand on participants—potentially a drawback when testing special populations, such as young children, infants, or cognitively impaired adults (e.g., those with schizophrenia).

Attentional Capture

Emotion elicitation procedures also vary in how much of participants' attention they require to operate. Masked stimuli make limited demands on attention and operate on emotion almost totally outside of participants' conscious awareness (see Wiens & Öhman, chapter 5, this volume). By contrast, the Velten (1968) procedure directs participants to read a series of emotional self-statements, a task with high attentional requirements that preclude performance of most other concurrent tasks (e.g., filling out questionnaires, answering interview questions). As a dynamic display that engages both visual and auditory modalities, film clips are also typically fairly high in attentional capture. In fact, film effectiveness can be degraded by competing demands placed in either modality (e.g., gradient coil noise). Therefore, films may be a suboptimal proce-

dure in experimental settings in which participants must carry out a secondary task (e.g., mental arithmetic).

Demand Characteristics

Films are embedded in experimental contexts that vary considerably in their level of demand. Some experimental cover stories are more likely to provoke demand (e.g., the film is part of a neuroticism test) than others (e.g., the film is part of a memory test). Likewise, the specific instructions that accompany film viewing also influence demand. For example, before showing a sad film, Marston, Hart, Hileman, and Faunce (1984, page 128) presented the instructions, "Let yourself experience whatever emotions you have as fully as you can, don't try to hold back or hold in your feelings." In part out of demand concerns, we (for this film, *The Champ*, and for others) use the simpler instructions to "please watch the film carefully." Finally, film demand characteristics are also film-content-dependent. A film depicting a man eating dog feces suggests a fairly transparent intent to elicit disgust, whereas the intent of a film depicting landscape scenery is relatively opaque.

Bearing all of these caveats in mind, film clips can elicit emotion with relatively low levels of demand. Furthermore, films often generate effects in response systems that are typically seen as being outside of participants' volitional control (e.g., heart rate). By contrast, procedures such as self-statements, relived emotion, and hypnosis almost invariably contain strong cues concerning the targeted affective state. These cues may be less obvious for directed facial movement or confederate procedures; these procedures are thus probably lower in demand than films.

Standardization

Although threats to standardization are present in any laboratory procedure, the stimulus content, presentation apparatus, and viewing conditions can all be tightly controlled with film clips. The standardization of films is therefore high, allowing for the potential replication of effects across laboratories (Gross & Levenson, 1995). Films share this high degree of standardization with other normative media, such as slides and music. Confederate interaction procedures tend to be less standardized than films because experimenters cannot totally regiment the dynamic interplay between human participants. Relived emotion procedures are less standardized than films simply because by-person idiographic variation is the source of their power. The high standardization of films does not, of course, guarantee that films will be effective equally for all participants (see later section on individual and group differences).

Temporal Considerations

Emotion researchers differ widely in their requirements for temporal resolution, or granularity. For example, phenomena that are modified by emotion over seconds or milliseconds (such as the startle reflex, event-related brain potentials, or brain activations) require data collection techniques that accommodate a high degree of temporal resolution. Still-picture paradigms (see Bradley & Lang, chapter 2, this volume), in which stimuli are presented in relatively short trials (approximately 6 s) that are averaged together to increase measurement reliability, have been used for this purpose. Films, in their prototypical use, are much lower in temporal resolution and range from about 1 to 10 minutes in length. Because emotions are a relatively rapid phenomenon, with onsets and offsets over seconds, films (and other low-resolution procedures such as confederate interactions) will produce epochs of data that are heterogeneous in emotional activation. Experimenters who use films must consider procedures to extract the emotional phenomena of interest from these longer epochs (e.g., a priori criteria, whole period averages), an issue also discussed in more detail later.

Ecological Validity

Like many of the stimuli that make us emotional in real life, film clips represent a dynamic display of prototypic situations relevant to well-being and survival (e.g., loss, danger; Tooby & Cosmides, 1990). From this standpoint, films appear to be high in ecological validity. At the same time, both theoretical and empirical uncertainty surround this issue (e.g., Ritz & Steptoe, 2000). On the one hand, film emotion appears to be real and robust. For example, about one-third of female participants overtly weep in response to a sad film we have used (e.g., Rottenberg, Gross, et al., 2002), and our best films in other emotion categories produce similar results (e.g., visible gagging to disgust films, convulsive laughter to amusing films). On the other hand, film emotion is a kind of aesthetic emotion (Frijda, 1989) that requires a "willing suspension of disbelief" for its operation. That is, participants become emotional in response to films in spite of (or because of) the fact that film images are an *illusion* of reality.

In sum, although some questions remain concerning the ecological validity of films, films are probably more naturalistic (and hence more generalizable) than a number of other techniques such as directed facial movement or hypnosis, which resemble very few everyday life situations. In situations in which high ecological validity is required, one might do well to employ scripted or unscripted social interaction procedures, as they elicit emotions that are as real and robust as film emotions while requiring no willing suspension of disbelief.

General Considerations When Using Films

Thus far, we have focused on *whether* films are the right emotion elicitation procedure to use in a given research context. In the following section, we consider *how* to use film procedures once one has decided that films are appropriate.

With films, as with many techniques used in experimental psychology, the devil is in the details. With this in mind, we discuss several factors that influence how well films work in different settings and offer suggestions for avoiding common pitfalls.

How Should Emotion Be Measured?

Not surprisingly, judgments regarding the success or failure of film-based emotion elicitation efforts often hinge on how emotion itself is measured. Here we discuss two issues relevant to the measurement of emotion when using films: (1) proximity of activation and measurement periods and (2) the extraction of emotion.

Emotions are evanescent. Therefore, delays, even short ones, between the activation of emotion by a film and the assessment of emotion by an experimenter can introduce measurement error. Further compounding this error is the prospect that the time course of an emotional response varies by emotion response system (e.g., facial expressive behavior may have a faster offset than emotion experience). The costs of delay are well illustrated by the common practice of assessing self-report responses to films retrospectively using questionnaires. As time elapses between the film's end and the questionnaire's completion, the elicited affect is likely to fade and/or be distorted by errors or systematic biases in recall (Levenson, 1988). To avoid problems associated with delayed retrospective reports and to obtain continuous measures of experience that parallel continuous measures of other response domains (e.g., behavior and autonomic psychophysiology), there has been a growing interest in rating dial methodologies, which afford continuous measures of emotion experience, in either online or cued-review rating formats (Fredrickson & Kahneman, 1993; Gottman & Levenson, 1985; Ruef & Levenson, chapter 17, this volume)

One concern about frequently assessing emotion experience is that the act of repeated measurement can potentially alter the emotional response itself, a concern that does not apply as strongly to the physiological and behavioral response systems, which may be monitored continuously without interfering substantially with emotional responses. Decisions regarding when and how to assess emotion experience require that the experimenter balance the desire for valid and perhaps even continuous emotion experience reports against the competing desire not to interfere with emotional responding during film and postfilm (recovery) periods. In our own work, we typically assess central and peripheral physiological responses, videotape expressive behavior, and—depending on the study—use a mix of retrospective and real-time emotion experience ratings.

A second measurement issue concerns the extraction of emotion from film viewing periods. Many researchers—ourselves included—have relied on overall period averages to measure experiential, behavioral, and physiological reactivity during a film clip. Overall average response is a useful summary statistic and provides an important starting point for data analysis. At the same time, we have alluded to the fact that films have relatively low temporal resolution and typically create heterogeneous epochs of data. This means that the period average strategy will almost invariably include nonemotional epochs and/or epochs in which nontargeted emotions were elicited, effectively "watering down" the emotion data of principal interest. Furthermore, an exclusive focus on overall averages may detract from other potentially informative parameters of emotion (e.g., threshold, rise time, variability). One promising alternative to period averages is to extract time windows of data based on a priori response criteria—such as rating dial measures of emotion experience, facial movements that match intended prototypes (Rosenberg & Ekman, 1994), or behavioral or physiological profiles indicative of the target emotional state (Davidson, Ekman, Saron, Senulis, & Friesen, 1990).

What Kind of Baseline Should Be Used?

However one measures emotion, and whichever way one extracts particular periods of interest, it is necessary to estimate the impact of a film compared with some point of reference. In fact, because acute emotional responses are usually superimposed on some prior affective state, it is difficult, if not impossible, to draw inferences about the nature of a film effect without a relevant baseline period. Thus another basic issue for implementing film procedures is establishing a proper point of comparison, or baseline, against which to assess the effects of a given film clip.

What type of baseline should one use? Historically, a resting state has been a major workhorse. In our experience, however, there are drawbacks associated with resting baselines: (1) rest may not be a representative state of the organism; (2) it may create a floor that precludes detection of deactivation effects; (3) rest instructions may introduce unwanted variability, as participants differ radically in their ability to comply (see also Christoff, Ream, & Gabrieli, 2004; Levenson, 1988). To avoid these drawbacks, we have in our own work moved toward use of neutral-emotion-film baselines (e.g., Rottenberg, Gross, et al., 2002). In addition, a film baseline also has the desirable feature of controlling for the effects of viewing a dynamic external stimulus (Piferi, Kline, Younger, & Lawler, 2000). Specific relatively neutral film clips are recommended for baseline later in this chapter.

Even when a baseline has been well constructed, it will not be useful as a comparison condition unless it is timed appropriately. Levels of responding in experiential, behavioral, and physiological channels are never static but drift, or fluctuate, throughout a laboratory session. Delays between baseline and activation periods introduce the confounding effects of time. Therefore, it is often useful to have multiple baseline periods, and baselines must be positioned temporally proximal to the emotion film (ideally in a contiguous position). In designs that employ multiple emotion films, the

issue of response drift is acute and strongly militates for the use of multiple baselines.

How Can Film Clips Be Matched?

A related consideration is how to best match films to allow strong inferences about emotion effects. That is, when two (or more) emotion film conditions are compared, emotion researchers will usually want to infer that observed condition effects are due to emotion rather than film differences. The complexity of films complicates this inference: Films differ from one another on a large number of potentially confounding characteristics (e.g., length, intensity, complexity, core themes, presence and number of human figures, color, brightness, picture motion; see Detenber, Simons, & Bennett, 1998). Moreover, investigators usually have few degrees of freedom in matching stimuli on these characteristics because: (1) the pool of effective films available for any given target emotion is often small (i.e., 2–5 films); (2) the number of possibly relevant dimensions of difference among films is so large; and (3) even slight variations in the editing of film clips can dramatically alter their effectiveness as emotion elicitors.

Because it is rare that films can be matched across all characteristics, investigators must match along a few characteristics that have the highest priority. In our own work we have matched films based on length, theoretically important dimensions (e.g., activation level), known effects in the literature, and study-specific aims (e.g., an investigation of stimulus meaning matched films on thematic content; Rottenberg, Gross, & Gotlib, 2005). Decisions about matching should be made explicitly, with reference to the goals of the particular study.

How Many Film Clips Should Be Used?

Our discussion of baseline and of film stimulus confounds have suggested several noise sources that can obscure the "signal" of emotion. How can one boost this signal? One approach is to sample emotion for extensive periods by using several film exemplars for a given emotion and/or very long stimulus presentations. Indeed, psychometric theory argues that aggregation over multiple film exemplars (and long films) should increase measurement reliability (Epstein, 1983).

However sensible this approach to sampling emotion may be, it is often problematic to carry out in practice because: (1) different films designed to target a particular emotion do not always generate equivalent responses; (2) the risk of habituation, sensitization, or fatigue effects increases with more film presentations; (3) longer films are more heterogeneous and often less effective than shorter films (e.g., long neutral films can become aversive); and (4) practical constraints related to participant availability and attention span often make it impossible to use multiple exemplars for each target emotional state. For these reasons, we have used a compromise sampling strategy in our own research: For each target emotion we use one (or two) relatively short film stimuli that are typically between 1 and 3 minutes in length and that are as homogenous as is possible. Our strategy to boost the signal of emotion therefore places a heavy burden on stimulus selection (and reducing sources of noise).

What Is the Psychological Context During Film Viewing?

The sensitivity of emotion to psychological context is an interesting (and bedeviling) aspect of emotion that can disrupt the standardization of film elicitations of emotion. Films are often shown in the context of complex, multisession studies, in which participants complete questionnaires, have sensors attached, are videotaped, and interact with one or more experimenters. Although an investigator may be particularly interested in participants' emotional responses to one aspect of this complex experience (i.e., the films), it is important to remember that several aspects of the experimental protocol may trigger emotional responses that compete with (and even supersede) participants' emotional responses to the film clips. Of course, it is impossible for an investigator to control (or even to be aware of) *every* aspect of the psychological context. Nevertheless, three aspects of the psychological context stand out as threats to standardization and can be controlled and/or monitored: (1) timing, (2) order, and (3) prior viewing.

A first consideration is timing, or *when* a film is presented in the course of a laboratory session. It would be unwise to assume that a sad film presented at the end of a grueling 2-hour laboratory session will be evaluated in the same way as it would at the beginning of the session, given the greater likelihood of increased participant fatigue (Morgan, 1920) and reactivity to repeated laboratory tasks (Thompson & Spencer, 1966). A second consideration is the order in which a film is presented within a laboratory session. For example, certain orders of film presentation may be more susceptible to carryover effects than others. Several studies indicate that residual affective states that match the valence of a new emotion stimulus will enhance the response to the new stimulus (e.g., Branscombe, 1985; Neumann et al., 2001), suggesting that carryover effects are most probable when films of like valence are presented in blocked order. A third element of the psychological context that poses a threat to standardization is the film-viewing histories of participants. Participants often have previous experience with films used in laboratory procedures, simply because many of the best emotion film clips are edited segments of commercially available entertainments. Prior viewing has been associated with a heightened report of the target emotion (Gross & Levenson, 1995), and it may influence the experience of viewing film clips in other ways (e.g., expectation effects)

In our own work, when emotion-specific effects are important to us, we make a point of ensuring that each film

occurs in each position within the experimental protocol. We also try to limit carryover from one film to the next using temporal spacing (e.g., with self-report assessment periods), as well as nonemotional distractor tasks (e.g., copying geometric figures; Gross, et al., 1998). With respect to the issue of prior film viewing, we routinely ask participants (both during pilot testing of the films and during the experiment itself) whether they have seen the film before. We then use this information to control for the effects of prior viewing.

Does the Physical Context Matter?

One important determinant of participants' responses to film stimuli is the physical setting in which films are presented. Emotional reactivity to films has been associated with mundane aspects of the experimental situation such as room lighting (Knez, 1995), larger display size (Detenber & Reeves, 1996; Lombard, 1995), warmer room temperature (Anderson, Deuser, & DeNeve, 1995), and color (as opposed to black and white; Detenber, Simons, & Reiss, 2000). Physical setting also includes participants' proximity and access to other people. Laboratory film procedures (like all emotion procedures) are socially embedded phenomena. Individuals may report differing reactions to films as a function of the group size (e.g., whether films are viewed in group or individual session formats), and these effects may differ by emotion (Jakobs, Manstead, & Fischer, 2001). Even within the context of single-subject paradigms, subtle changes in the physical arrangements may influence reactivity via the implied social presence of others (Fridlund, 1992). For example, the presence of video recording equipment in a participant room may increase self-consciousness that dampens or enhances behavioral responses. In our own work, we have used a 20-inch monitor positioned about 5 feet from the participant in solitary film viewing sessions conducted in a living-room-like laboratory room with dimmed lights. Throughout experimental sessions, participants and experimenters are in contact via an intercom. Cameras used to record participants' expressive behavior are discreetly hidden behind darkened glass panels in order to minimize participants' self-consciousness.

What Is the Role of Individual and Group Differences?

A dramatic example of the power of individual differences to influence the outcome of emotion elicitation procedures is hypnotic emotion inductions, which are not usable in the majority (70–75%) of people who not highly hypnotizable (Bower, 1981). Individual differences also influence reactivity to emotion film clips. For example, variations in self-reported neuroticism and extraversion have been shown to influence negative and positive reactions to films, respectively (e.g., Gross et al., 1998). Likewise, biological traits, such as resting electroencephalographic (EEG) asymmetry in anterior regions of the brain, have also been shown to predict film reactivity (Wheeler, Davidson, & Tomarken, 1993). How one proceeds in the face of these individual differences depends largely on one's research aims. Some researchers (e.g., personality researchers) welcome variation on these factors because these differences are the focus of study (e.g., Berenbaum & Williams, 1995). In other cases, such as work on basic emotion processes (e.g., forms of self-regulation), these individual differences may constitute nuisance variance that interferes with the detection of other subtle yet important effects.

The influence of group membership (e.g., linguistic, gender, racial, or socioeconomic) on emotion film reactivity is at an early stage of investigation and is an important area for future research. Preliminary evidence, however, indicates that the Gross and Levenson (1995) films generalize to other linguistic groups (e.g., German-language speakers; Hagemann et al., 1999). Emotion film effects have also generalized across different ethnic groups in some samples (Gross & Levenson, 1995; Tsai, Levenson, & Carstensen, 2000), but additional study of this issue is needed. Other findings suggest that gender may be a particularly important influence on film reactivity: Women, relative to men, have been shown to exhibit stronger reports of emotional experience (Gross & Levenson, 1995; Hagemann et al., 1999), to be more expressive (Kring & Gordon, 1998), and to exhibit differential neural activations to emotion elicitors (Karama et al., 2002). Treatment of these group differences, we believe, should hinge on one's wider research aims: where group differences are the object of study, individuals with certain group memberships can be oversampled (Canli, Desmond, Zhao, & Gabrieli, 2002); where group differences represent confounds, they can be addressed by screening (e.g., studying each sex separately; Gross & Levenson, 1993) or by using post hoc statistical controls.

In our own work, we are cautious about assuming that film reactivity will generalize across groups in the absence of strong normative data. We have found that the successful use of film clips entails extensive piloting of films and attention to sample composition, and we regularly report the gender and ethnic composition of study participants so as to allow others to better compare our results with their own. If we believe (as we often do) that there may be important gender effects, we may conduct an initial study with a single gender (often women) and then replicate and extend results of this initial study by using a mixed-sex sample. Likewise, for treatment of individual differences, we recommend the use of instruments to screen out participants who have individual difference profiles that might contaminate results and/or collecting data on these individual difference variables to enable post hoc statistical control (e.g., Wheeler et al., 1993). In our own work, we typically obtain a wide array of individual difference measures, most often via the Internet, before the experimental session.

Recommended Film Clips for Eliciting Discrete Emotional States

In this section, we first discuss the process of finding, editing, and validating film clips. We then recommend a number of film clips that meet our criteria for eliciting specific target emotions, drawing in part on the film library described in Gross and Levenson (1995). Toward the end of this section, we consider other film clips that may be useful but that do not target discrete emotions. The number of proven emotion elicitors remains relatively modest. We remark on some of the stumbling blocks that have stood in the way of developing and validating a larger library of films and present recommendations for overcoming these obstacles in future stimulus development.

Developing and Validating Film Clips

Clearly, it would be desirable to have an extensive database of valid film stimuli that rivals those of other normative emotional stimuli (e.g., pictures, words, and sounds). Perhaps most enviable in this respect is the International Affective Picture System (IAPS; Lang, Bradley, & Cuthbert, 1995), a database of hundreds of colored pictures that have been standardized on large normative participant samples for judged pleasure and arousal, distributed internationally to scores of researchers, and used extensively in cognitive, social psychological, and biobehavioral studies. The comparatively modest size of the library of well-validated film clips prompts a consideration of obstacles that often arise in the course of developing new stimulus films.

First, films are complicated to develop because, unlike slides, they are embedded within another source. For the foreseeable future, at least, in-house production of emotion films falls beyond the technical, dramaturgical, and financial means of most laboratories. Extracting emotion films from a candidate source is an iterative process that involves a number of steps, including nominating candidate sources, informally screening scenes from candidate sources, frame editing clips taken from candidate sources, collecting pilot data on edited clips, reediting clips on the basis of the pilot ratings (assuming that the initial ratings look promising), and, finally, collecting normative data from participant samples based on the final edited version of the film clip.

In our experience, we have been repeatedly surprised at the fragility of the film extraction process. Often, film segments that are powerfully emotionally evocative in the context of the larger film fail to elicit emotion when the film clip is viewed on its own, particularly if the participant has not seen the film. We also have found that even if a film segment survives its surgery, the emotional impact can vary as a result of relatively minor variations in the editing of either the music, the image, or both.

A second factor that has hindered the development of a large library of films has been a lack of systematic communication among scholars. Whereas still pictures and other materials are shared widely, uncertainty concerning the fair use of commercial films for scholarly purposes has slowed the development of a centralized repository where film clips might be stored, copied, and distributed. The development of the Internet, however, has made it easier for scholars to develop centralized locations that post frame-editing instructions for generating stimulus films (which does fall under fair use). As we move forward into the future, we expect the Internet will remain an important resource for building the community of researchers who develop and use emotion films.

A third factor that has made it difficult to build a large library of film clips is the disparate (and often incommensurate) film validation procedures. In our own research, we have followed the practice of carefully pretesting each of the films we are thinking of using with a sample that is matched to the intended research population. We collect validation data on 8–10 films at a time in group-format sessions that last approximately 1 hour (fatigue and the duration of films lim-

its the number of films that can be validated). We obtain a broad range of emotion experience reports immediately after each film clip is shown. As is evident from the other contributions to this volume, there are many different ways to assess emotion experience.

The specific emotion terms we usually use span a broad range of theoretically important discrete negative and positive emotional states. We typically also include the term *confusion* to assess how easy it is for the participant to understand the film clip outside the original film context. The use of a wide range of terms allows us to compare films we employ to elicit different target states. Within a given study, we often find it useful to use several terms that converge on a target emotional state so that we may create target composites. For example, in a study of amusement and sadness, we used the rating form shown in Figure 1.3. On the form, participants rate the greatest emotion that was experienced during the preceding film, using both discrete emotion (specific) and dimensional (pleasant vs. unpleasant) terms. Participants rate each term on 9-point Likert (0–8) scales that for discrete

Figure 1.3. Postfilm questionnaire used in film validation.

POST FILM QUESTIONNAIRE

The following questions refer to how you *felt while watching the film.*

0	1	2	3	4	5	6	7	8
not at all/ none				somewhat/ some				extremely/ a great deal

Using the scale above, please indicate the greatest amount of EACH emotion you experienced while watching the film.

_____ amusement	_____ embarrassment	_____ love
_____ anger	_____ fear	_____ pride
_____ anxiety	_____ guilt	_____ sadness
_____ confusion	_____ happiness	_____ shame
_____ contempt	_____ interest	_____ surprise
_____ disgust	_____ joy	_____ unhappiness

Did you feel any other emotion during the film? O No O Yes
    If so, what was the emotion? _____
    How much of this emotion did you feel? _____

Please use the following pleasantness scale to rate the feelings you had during the film. Circle your answer:

0	1	2	3	4	5	6	7	8
unpleasant								pleasant

Had you seen this film before? O No O Yes

Did you close your eyes or look away during any scenes? O No O Yes emotions are anchored by *not at all* and *extremely* and that for the dimensional valence item is anchored by *unpleasant* and *pleasant.* We also allow participants to rate any other emotion they may have felt during the film and ask whether they looked away during the film (in which case they may not have seen important parts of the film).

When deciding whether or not a film is efficacious (including the films we recommend here), we have relied on *intensity* and *discreteness* as the two primary metrics. That is, *intensity* refers to whether a film receives a high mean report on the target emotion relative to other candidate films. *Discreteness* refers to the degree to which participants report feeling the target emotion more intensely than all nontargeted emotions. One way to formalize the *discreteness* metric is to use an idiographic "hit rate" statistic that is the percentage of participants who indicated that they had felt the target emotion at least 1 point more intensely than other, nontargeted emotions. Different films that putatively elicit the same target state can be compared statistically by combining intensity and discreteness scores into a success index, in which each intensity score represents a z score derived by normalizing intensity scores for all comparison films and in which each discreteness score represents a normalized discreteness value relative to all comparison films. We have recently added to these metrics for judging the success of a film the recommendation that films have high alphas for the target composites and be low in reports of confusion.

We emphasize that our reliance on retrospectively assessed self-reports of emotion (obtained in group-viewing sessions) for film validation is practical, not philosophical. We do not view any of the major emotion response systems (i.e., experience, behavior, physiology) as the "gold standard." Given the loose coupling between emotional response systems, self-report ratings will not perfectly predict which films will produce behavioral or physiological activations. We encourage researchers to collect validation data from as many response systems as possible to afford more precise statements concerning the effects of a given film. We acknowledge, however, that resource limitations often make it impossible to validate film materials using the full range of behavioral and/or physiological measures and the same viewing contexts (e.g., individual sessions) as will be used in the experiment itself.

Our Film Recommendations

Both our emotion film recommendations and the criteria on which they are based build on and extend our past efforts (Gross & Levenson, 1995). In this work, we have generally wanted to elicit specific discrete emotional states (e.g., anger, sadness) rather than more diffuse states of positive or negative activation (Watson, 2000). Therefore, in stimulus development we have searched for films that are relatively high on discrete emotions (the target) and as low as possible

on other related emotions. We should note that frequently we have found that our initial intuitions as to how a film clip would work have been wrong, and a film clip that we believed would elicit a discrete state produced what might best be characterized as a diffuse state of positive or negative activation and was hence discarded. We illustrate this point by contrasting self-report profiles of two films that were both developed to elicit disgust. Unexpectedly, a film depicting an employee wounded in an industrial accident (Figure 1.4, panel A) was far less successful from the standpoint of discreteness than a film depicting the surgical amputation of an arm (e.g., Figure 1.4, panel B).

In the following sections, we offer our current recommendations regarding film clips that will elicit neutral or relatively discrete emotional states. We organize these recommendations according to target emotion. One point of difference from Gross and Levenson's set of target emotions should be noted: Mild levels of contentment that were previously considered separately are now considered under Neutral. Table 1.1 presents validation data for these films across a core set of items to facilitate comparisons. In appendix 1, frame instructions are presented for creating many of these stimuli from commercially available sources. Additional film instructions, as well as copies of noncommercial films, are available at http://www.cas.usf.edu/psychology/fac_rottenbergJ.htm.

A. Amputation of Arm Film Clip

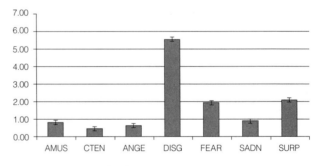

B. Industrial Accident Film Clip

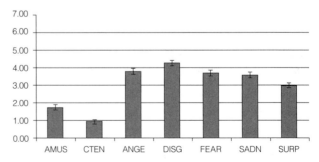

Figure 1.4. Different response profiles obtained for two films targeting disgust. Participants could report Amusement (AMUS), contentment (CTEN), Anger (ANGE), disgust (DISG), Fear (FEAR), Sadness (SADN), or Surprise (SURP).

Table 1.1

Recommended Films for Eliciting Discrete Emotional States

Target Emotion Film Clip	Sex	Mean (SD) Self-Reported Emotion									
		AMUS	ANGE	CFUS	DISG	EMBA	FEAR	HAPP	INTE	SADN	SURP
Amusement											
Harry	M (N = 29)	5.45 (1.23)	0.39 (0.72)	0.55 (0.85)	0.74 (1.32)	2.55 (2.01)	0.23 (0.82)	3.39 (1.71)	4.45 (1.43)	0.13 (0.43)	1.90 (2.33)
	F (N = 41)	5.61 (1.28)	0.24 (0.62)	0.22 (0.53)	0.22 (0.73)	2.10 (2.07)	0.35 (0.98)	3.32 (1.82)	3.63 (1.93)	0.17 (0.67)	1.27 (1.72)
Robin	M (N = 28)	5.89 (1.17)	0.32 (0.67)	0.71 (1.18)	0.50 (0.92)	0.82 (1.44)	0.07 (0.26)	4.68 (1.96)	4.79 (1.34)	0.14 (0.45)	2.07 (2.12)
	F (N = 34)	5.82 (1.99)	0.21 (0.49)	0.70 (1.67)	0.91 (1.71)	0.53 (1.02)	0.06 (0.24)	4.59 (2.09)	4.50 (2.29)	0.18 (0.46)	1.94 (2.23)
Cosby	M (N = 14)	5.21 (2.36)	0.07 (0.27)	0.21 (0.58)	0.57 (1.40)	0.79 (1.53)	0.07 (0.27)	3.71 (2.43)	3.64 (1.87)	0.07 (0.27)	1.14 (2.41)
	F (N = 24)	5.20 (1.76)	0.08 (0.27)	0.31 (0.68)	0.38 (0.90)	0.35 (0.89)	0.04 (0.20)	4.23 (1.66)	4.62 (1.88)	0.04 (0.20)	1.77 (2.05)
Whose Line	M (N = 13)	7.23 (1.01)	0.62 (1.12)	0.54 (1.13)	1.85 (2.79)	0.92 (1.44)	0.31 (0.85)	5.92 (1.93)	6.08 (1.89)	0.08 (0.28)	3.38 (2.27)
	F (N = 15)	6.87 (1.19)	0.07 (0.26)	0.87 (1.46)	2.07 (2.58)	1.80 (2.91)	0.20 (0.56)	5.27 (2.60)	5.47 (2.64)	0.47 (1.81)	3.47 (2.47)
Anger											
Bodyguard	M (N = 27)	1.34 (1.61)	5.03 (1.82)	1.21 (1.11)	4.69 (1.61)	1.10 (1.76)	1.62 (1.57)	0.76 (1.33)	3.66 (2.02)	3.07 (2.12)	1.66 (1.97)
	F (N = 33)	0.61 (1.12)	5.36 (1.39)	1.82 (2.21)	4.94 (1.80)	0.61 (1.25)	2.15 (2.00)	0.42 (0.90)	3.15 (1.62)	4.21 (2.13)	1.21 (1.76)
Cry Freedom	M (N = 21)	0.78 (1.62)	5.87 (1.96)	3.09 (2.73)	5.74 (1.76)	1.78 (2.58)	3.00 (2.92)	0.83 (1.64)	4.09 (2.11)	5.22 (2.17)	2.86 (2.75)
	F (N = 36)	0.14 (0.42)	6.17 (1.68)	2.28 (2.25)	5.33 (2.48)	0.72 (1.65)	3.69 (2.41)	0.22 (0.72)	3.22 (2.26)	5.56 (1.93)	2.42 (2.56)
Disgust											
Pink Flamingos	M (N = 20)	2.40 (2.39)	0.95 (1.50)	1.85 (2.13)	6.60 (1.39)	0.85 (1.76)	0.45 (1.05)	0.55 (1.61)	1.20 (2.12)	0.90 (1.77)	3.05 (2.56)
	F (N = 31)	2.47 (2.56)	0.47 (1.22)	1.87 (2.27)	6.34 (1.54)	1.12 (2.08)	0.38 (1.13)	0.34 (0.83)	1.88 (1.86)	0.29 (1.10)	3.72 (2.43)
Amputation	M (N = 74)	1.23 (1.72)	0.68 (1.17)	2.22 (1.94)	5.00 (2.22)	0.51 (1.15)	1.74 (1.84)	0.27 (0.63)	2.65 (2.12)	0.93 (1.46)	2.12 (2.27)
	F (N = 71)	0.42 (1.20)	0.66 (1.50)	2.30 (2.43)	6.19 (1.92)	0.32 (0.88)	2.15 (2.36)	0.15 (0.73)	2.68 (2.37)	0.76 (1.56)	2.00 (2.34)
Foot Surgery	M (N = 11)	0.45 (0.82)	0.18 (0.41)	1.82 (2.27)	4.91 (2.30)	0.36 (0.81)	0.45 (1.04)	0.09 (0.32)	3.00 (2.57)	0.27 (0.91)	0.82 (1.94)
	F (N = 18)	0.56 (1.15)	0.39 (0.78)	2.00 (1.94)	4.44 (2.62)	0.39 (1.20)	1.78 (2.44)	0.17 (0.51)	2.44 (2.28)	0.28 (0.75)	1.50 (2.04)
Fear											
Shining	M (N = 23)	1.39 (1.37)	0.65 (1.27)	2.91 (2.26)	0.39 (0.78)	0.22 (0.42)	3.26 (2.03)	0.96 (1.22)	4.61 (1.27)	0.70 (1.26)	1.74 (2.05)
	F (N = 36)	0.83 (1.23)	0.17 (0.38)	1.92 (2.25)	0.00 (0.00)	0.00 (0.00)	4.61 (2.07)	0.19 (0.75)	3.89 (1.72)	0.17 (0.45)	1.08 (1.65)
Lambs	M (N = 31)	2.65 (2.36)	1.74 (1.53)	1.61 (1.54)	2.39 (1.96)	0.48 (0.81)	3.87 (2.46)	1.70 (1.97)	4.81 (1.52)	0.74 (1.13)	2.19 (2.04)
	F (N = 40)	1.07 (1.39)	0.80 (1.14)	0.88 (1.52)	1.80 (2.08)	0.28 (0.68)	4.45 (2.23)	0.60 (1.01)	4.32 (1.95)	0.53 (1.38)	1.88 (2.14)
Neutral											
Sticks	M (N = 19)	1.05 (1.65)	1.37 (1.71)	3.58 (2.52)	0.84 (1.26)	0.21 (0.42)	0.16 (0.38)	0.79 (1.62)	1.11 (1.56)	0.53 (1.26)	1.16 (1.68)
	F (N = 36)	0.83 (1.21)	0.92 (1.46)	1.92 (2.31)	0.39 (0.80)	0.14 (0.49)	0.33 (1.37)	0.75 (1.16)	0.92 (1.32)	0.11 (0.52)	0.62 (1.02)
Denali	M (N = 12)	2.33 (2.06)	0.00 (0.00)	0.58 (1.08)	0.00 (0.00)	0.08 (0.29)	0.25 (0.45)	3.75 (1.91)	4.54 (1.50)	0.67 (1.50)	0.42 (1.16)
	F (N = 12)	2.25 (2.09)	0.00 (0.00)	0.00 (0.00)	0.00 (0.00)	0.08 (0.29)	0.00 (0.00)	3.00 (1.91)	3.58 (2.47)	0.67 (1.23)	0.63 (1.72)

(continued)

Table 1.1
(continued)

Target Emotion Film Clip	Sex	Mean (SD) Self-Reported Emotion									
		AMUS	ANGE	CFUS	DISG	EMBA	FEAR	HAPP	INTE	SADN	SURP
Sadness											
The Champ	M (N = 28)	0.82 (1.19)	1.75 (1.78)	1.50 (1.71)	1.07 (1.49)	0.57 (1.07)	1.14 (1.58)	0.36 (0.68)	2.86 (1.69)	5.18 (1.47)	1.18 (1.39)
	F (N = 24)	0.38 (0.71)	1.21 (1.35)	1.42 (1.72)	0.54 (0.78)	0.29 (0.86)	1.63 (2.23)	0.17 (0.48)	3.46 (2.21)	6.33 (1.31)	1.08 (1.59)
Lion King	M (N = 14)	1.79 (1.89)	2.14 (2.48)	0.64 (1.50)	0.79 (1.48)	0.29 (1.07)	1.50 (2.14)	0.29 (0.61)	4.14 (2.71)	6.79 (1.12)	0.64 (1.39)
	F (N = 15)	1.40 (2.20)	2.53 (2.29)	0.07 (0.26)	1.00 (1.93)	0.60 (1.24)	1.80 (2.68)	0.67 (1.11)	4.67 (2.23)	6.93 (1.53)	0.27 (0.59)
Return to Me	M (N = 15)	2.00 (2.04)	1.73 (2.19)	4.20 (2.70)	0.80 (1.32)	0.33 (1.05)	2.40 (2.26)	2.27 (2.79)	4.73 (2.58)	7.00 (1.20)	4.33 (2.79)
	F (N = 15)	1.40 (2.53)	2.20 (2.54)	3.07 (2.96)	0.67 (1.18)	1.27 (2.19)	2.27 (2.55)	2.47 (2.56)	6.00 (1.96)	6.93 (1.58)	3.40 (3.11)
Surprise											
Capricorn	M (N = 25)	1.12 (1.72)	0.40 (1.00)	3.64 (2.23)	0.63 (1.21)	0.20 (0.50)	2.36 (2.52)	0.56 (1.04)	3.04 (2.46)	0.52 (0.96)	5.04 (1.74)
	F (N = 37)	0.59 (1.01)	0.32 (0.82)	3.97 (2.51)	0.22 (0.53)	0.00 (0.00)	2.76 (2.36)	0.08 (0.28)	2.81 (2.03)	0.32 (0.82)	5.05 (2.24)
Sea of Love	M (N = 20)	1.60 (1.64)	0.20 (0.52)	2.15 (1.87)	0.20 (0.52)	0.15 (0.49)	2.90 (2.40)	0.70 (1.59)	2.85 (1.76)	0.20 (0.52)	3.80 (1.85)
	F (N = 34)	1.35 (1.65)	0.24 (0.89)	1.29 (1.73)	0.26 (0.90)	0.44 (1.46)	2.97 (1.96)	0.62 (1.33)	2.68 (1.82)	0.15 (0.56)	4.47 (1.97)

Column key: AMUS = Amusement, ANGE = Anger, CFUS = Confusion, DISG = Disgust, EMBA = Embarrassment, FEAR = Fear, HAPP = Happiness, INTE = Interest, SADN = Sadness, SURP = Surprise.

Row key: *Harry* = *When Harry Met Sally*: Discussion of orgasm in café (Reiner, Scheinman, Stolt, & Nicolaides, 1989); *Robin* = *Robin Williams Live*: Comedy routine (Morra, Brezner, & Gowers, 1986); *Cosby* = *Bill Cosby, Himself* Comedy routine (Cosby, 1996); *Whose Line* = *Whose Line Is It, Anyway?* Helping hands comedy routine (McCarthy, Forrest, Gowers, & de Moraes, 2001); *Bodyguard* = *My Bodyguard*: Bully scene (Devlin & Bill, 1980); *Cry Freedom* = *Cry Freedom*: Police abuse protesters (Spencer, Briley & Attenborough, 1987); *Pink Flamingos* = *Pink Flamingos*: Person eats dog faeces (Waters, 1973); *Amputation* = *Amputation*: Amputation of arm (Ekman & Friesen, 1974); *Foot Surgery* = *Leg Surgery*: Surgery on a foot (Courtesy of Paul Ekman); *Shining* = *The Shining*: Boy playing in hallway (Kubrick, 1980); *Lambs* = *Silence of the Lambs*: Basement chase scene (Saxon, Utt, Bozman, & Demme, 1991); *Sticks* = *Abstract Shapes* (ScreenPeace screen saver); *Denali* = *Alaska's Wild Denali*: Summer in Denali (Hardesty, 1997); *The Champ* = *The Champ*: Boy with dying father (Lovell & Zeffirelli, 1979); *Lion King* = *The Lion King*: Cub with dead father (Hahn, Allers, & Minkoff, 1994); *Return to Me* = *Return to Me*: Dog and man after death of wife (Tugend & Hunt, 2000); *Capricorn* = *Capricorn One*: Agents burst through door (Lazarus & Hyams, 1978); *Sea of Love* = *Sea of Love*: Man is scared by pigeon (Bregman, Stroller, & Becker, 1989).

Amusement

There are a number of film clips that reliably elicit reports of amusement and associated facial signs, such as smiling and laughing behavior. Two of the films we currently recommend were comedy segments validated in Gross and Levenson (1995). We also present validation data for two new films, *Cosby,* and *Whose Line Is It, Anyway?*

Anger

Anger is one of the more difficult emotions to elicit with film clips. Several researchers have had reported difficulty eliciting high levels of reported anger (e.g., Gross & Levenson, 1995; Philippot, 1993). Moreover, films designed to elicit anger states often turn out to elicit a blend of negative emotions, including related states such as disgust and sadness. We present data for two reasonably successful anger films, *My Bodyguard* and *Cry Freedom,* which revolve around themes of injustice. Although we welcome further efforts to develop anger films, we suspect that film procedures are at a disadvantage relative to techniques that induce anger through interpersonal situations (e.g., confederate or marital interaction), perhaps because anger requires high levels of personal engagement and/or immediacy that are difficult to achieve with a film.

Disgust

Several films reliably elicit reports of disgust and associated facial signs, such as grimacing. Two of the disgust films we currently recommend were validated in Gross and Levenson (1995). We also present validation data for one new film, *Foot Surgery,* which depicts surgical incisions made to the bottom of a patient's foot.

Fear

Fear is also a difficult emotion to elicit with film clips. As with anger, fear films tend to elicit a blend of emotions (e.g., interest, tension). Furthermore, fear stimuli that produce robust experience reports have had often disappointing effects on behavior and/or physiology (Rottenberg, Kasch, et al., 2002). Moreover, we have found that the fear films that we have piloted are accompanied by substantial gender differences on the target emotion (higher ratings for women than for men). With these caveats, we recommend two fear films.

Neutral

As we have worked with film clips over the years, we have been increasingly impressed by the heterogeneity of "neutral" as a category. We have developed two main types of neutral film clips, which might be termed *plain neutral* and *pleasant neutral.* The plain neutral type of film clip provokes very little emotion report of any kind. It is exemplified by an abstract visual display taken from a screen saver display baseline, described in Gross and Levenson (1995). This film clip has the advantage of eliciting little report of emotion. It has the disadvantage that with long (or multiple) presentations of this film clip, participants may sometimes report feeling annoyed or bored. For this reason, we have developed a second type of neutral film that is more pleasant in hedonic tone (e.g., elicits low levels of contentment). A good exemplar of a pleasant neutral film clip is *Denali,* which depicts nature scenery, animals, and uplifting music. We now favor this type of film for most purposes (e.g., our baseline) because it is well tolerated by participants, it is relaxing, and it fully engages participants' attention.

Sadness

We have also had success eliciting reports of sadness and associated facial signs, such as an upturned inner eyebrow and tearfulness. One film we currently recommend, *The Champ,* depicts a death scene. It was validated in Gross and Levenson (1995) and has been extensively used (e.g., Gross et al., 1998). We also present validation data for two new films, *Lion King* and *Return to Me.*

Surprise

Despite relatively good agreement among emotion researchers that surprise is an emotion, there has been relatively little research on surprise. One consideration in studying surprise is that it has distinct temporal properties—namely rapid onset and offset. In fact, we suspect that films that elicit reports of surprise (including the two we recommend) elicit at most only a few seconds of this emotion. Therefore, careful data extraction is a critical issue in the study of surprise.

Special-Purpose Film Stimuli

We have recommended a number of emotion film clips that we endorse as effective elicitors of relatively discrete emotional states. At the same time, we think it is critical for the field to continue to develop emotion stimuli that elicit other kinds of affective states. This is appropriate because many questions about emotion are best probed with film stimuli that are highly tailored to answer them. For example, we welcome efforts to generate stimuli that induce mixed emotional states (e.g., bittersweet; *Do You Remember Love*), broad negative states (e.g., *Hiroshima;* Butler et al., 2003), or oscillating emotional states (see Figure 1.5 for an example of an amusement-sadness-amusement sequence: *Steel Magnolias*).

The Future of Emotion Elicitation Using Film Clips

Film clips are now—and will continue to be—an important tool for eliciting emotion in the laboratory. As the scientific database concerning films expands, researchers will have many opportunities to use film clips to learn more about emotion. Here we highlight three directions that we think will shape the future use of films.

Use of Films to Study Affective Chronometry

The dynamism of films is well adapted to studying the unfolding of the emotion waveform over time as it is manifested in each emotional response system. We believe that researchers will want to capitalize on films' dynamic quality to develop the emerging theme of affective chronometry (Davidson, 1998). That is, in addition to studies that focus on the overall magnitude of emotional responses, researchers will use films to conduct studies to clarify aspects related to emotion's latency, rise time, duration, and offset (e.g., Hemenover, 2003; Rottenberg, Wilhelm, Gross, & Gotlib, 2003).

Use of Films to Study Emotional Coherence

In addition to clarifying how emotion unfolds over time, researchers may wish to use films to clarify the *organization* of emotional responses. One major postulate of many contemporary theories of emotion is that emotion imposes coherence across multiple response systems (e.g., experiential, behavioral, and physiological). Surprisingly, few studies have tested this core hypothesis, and those that have done so have yielded mixed results. In Figure 1.5, we display data from a recent study of 60 women who viewed a 5-minute film clip constructed from segments drawn from *Steel Magnolias*. Segments were sequenced so as to target amusement, then sadness, then amusement. Throughout the film viewing period, continuous measures of emotion experience, expression, and physiology were obtained in order to examine the conditions under which response coherence is evident (Mauss, Levenson, McCarter, & Gross, 2005). As is evident from Figure 1.5, behavioral, experiential, and physiological responding were all correlated during film viewings, but the correlations between behavioral and experiential response systems were higher than the correlations between either of these and physiological responding. In future work, it will be important to employ films to study emotion coherence in other samples varying in age and mental health.

Use of Related Dynamic Presentation Technologies

We continue to be excited by the emergence of related dynamic presentation technologies that will expand the repertoire of emotional stimuli that can be presented to participants. Perhaps most notable is the emergence of interactive presentation technologies such as virtual reality, which allow a participant to interact with objects and other individuals within a simulated environment that is presented in 3-dimensional computer graphics (Loomis, Blascovich, & Beall, 1999). Furthermore, these interactive technologies will be reinforced by the development of Internet-based display and rating procedures that will allow researchers to collect larger amounts of emotion data. The use of interactive technologies will allow exploration of many aspects of emotion that are difficult to probe with an emotion film (e.g., the effects of emotion on

Panel A

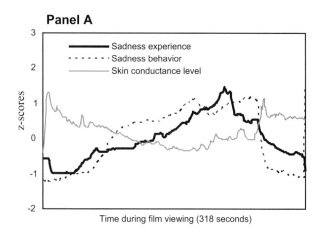

Panel B

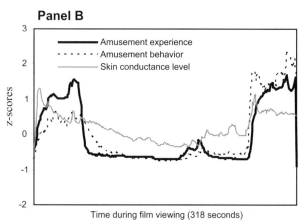

Figure 1.5. Coherence between emotion response systems during an amusing-sad-amusing film sequence.

mutual gaze). At the same time, precisely because of films' highly standardized and noninteractive quality, we are confident that films will continue to have an abiding utility in the field, even as novel emotion elicitation techniques are refined.

Appendix: VHS and DVD Instructions for Creating Emotion Films

This appendix contains information about creating 12 of our recommended films. Most of these stimuli were developed from full-length commercial films, all of which are currently available in videotape or DVD format. For these commercial films, we have provided detailed frame editing instructions for creating the same excerpt that we evaluated in this chapter. For those of you who have editing equipment, we have provided precise timing information in terms of hours, minutes, seconds, and frames. If you have a conventional VCR that tracks time in hours, minutes, and seconds, you can use the counter on your VCR to locate the excerpts to the nearest second, and, if possible, you can use the pause mode and frame advance to locate the exact frame (there are 30 frames per second in VHS [NTSC] format). In recognition that our field is becoming more digital and computer based, we have also included frame editing instructions (in parentheses) for films that are currently available in DVD format. If your equipment does not have this kind of timing capability, you will need to use a stop watch. In any event, we recommend that you follow our editing instructions as closely as possible, because relatively small editing variations can produce somewhat different emotional reports.

Some of the film stimuli are derived from noncommercial sources. These are available for download as noted.

Amusement Films

Harry

Film: *When Harry Met Sally*
Target emotion: Amusement
Clip length: 2'35"

Instructions: Advance to the first frame, in which an elderly couple is visible (the first scene after the opening credits). Reset the timer to 00:00:00:00 (hours:minutes:seconds:frames). Begin the clip at 00:42:39:29 (00:44:49:17). At this point, a man and a woman are sitting in a restaurant. The clip begins five frames after the camera angle switches from a view of the man and woman at the table to a view (over the man's shoulder) of the woman fixing the sandwich on her plate and saying "You know, I'm so glad I never got involved with you. . . ." End the clip at 00:45:15:12 (00:47:25:07). At this point, an older woman who is ordering her meal has just said "I'll have what she's having."

Robin

Film: *Robin Williams Live*
Target emotion: Amusement
Clip length: 7'59"

Instructions: Advance approximately 2 minutes into the film, to the point at which the comedian first comes onto the stage. When the camera switches from a view of the audience (a woman is descending the stairs to her seat) to the first frame of a close-up of the comedian's torso and head, reset the timer to 00:00:00:00 (hours:minutes:seconds:frames). Begin the clip at 00:03:13:01. At this point, the camera has just moved from a back view of the comedian to a front view of him as he looks down at his cup of water. End the clip at 00:11:11:10. At this point, the comedian has just said, "you're still there!" and the camera has gone to an upper-balcony view of the theater. End the clip 73 frames after the camera has gone to the upper balcony.

Robin Short (Short version of validated film clip)

Film: *Robin Williams Live*
Target emotion: Amusement
Clip length 3'25"

Instructions: Advance approximately 2 minutes into the film, to the point at which the comedian first comes onto the stage.

When the camera switches from a view of the audience (a woman is descending the stairs to her seat) to the first frame of a close-up of the comedian's torso and head, reset the timer to 00:00:00:00 (hours:minutes:seconds:frames). Begin the clip at 00:06:41:01. At this point the comedian is holding a cup of water and stepping off the step with his right foot, saying "I'm fine now. . . ." Stop recording at 00:08:00:01. At this point, the comedian has just talked about a dog who says, "I've just learned to lick my own genitals, leave me alone! Don't do this to me!" The camera has switched to a faraway shot from the upper balcony. Stop recording at this point, 26 frames into the shot from the upper balcony, just before the comedian says, "And your dog. . . ." Begin recording at 00:08:51:12. At this point, the comedian has his mouth open, his head slightly back, and his left hand open. Begin recording 17 frames before the comedian closes his hand, just before he says, "And you're inside stoned going, 'Oh God help me now!'" End the clip at 00:10:56:19. At this point, the comedian has just said, "his face turns into a cheeseburger, you lunge!" and lowered his arms and looked slightly off to his left.

Anger Films

Bodyguard

Film: *My Bodyguard*
Target emotion: Anger
Clip length: 4'06"

Instructions: Advance to the first frame in which a growing circular form has the words "Magnetic Video" written under it in full. Reset the timer to 00:00:00:00 (hours:minutes:seconds:frames). Begin the clip at 01:12:23:05 (01:12:15:01). At this point, two men are visible, one wearing a red tank top and the other wearing an army jacket. A fight is about to begin. Several people are in the background, including a blond-haired boy in the lower right-hand corner of the screen. Begin the clip at the first frame in which the blond-haired boy's hand covers both his mouth and nose. End the clip at 01:16:29:27 (01:16:20:20). At this point, a man dressed in a gray muscle shirt and black pants is exiting the scene, with trees, a wall, and a fence in the background. This comes two frames before a shot of a man with a bloody nose on all fours.

Cry Freedom

Film: *Cry Freedom*
Target emotion: Anger
Clip length: 2'36"

Instructions: Advance to the point at which "Cry Freedom" is typed across the screen. At the first frame in which the "m" is visible, reset the timer to 00:00:00:00 (hours:minutes: seconds:frames). Begin the clip at 2:24:56:11 (02:25:56:07). At this point, there is a shift from a view of protesters in the distance to a close-up of a bald girl with a pink skirt and a boy crossing just in front of her. Begin the clip with the first frame of this close-up. Stop recording at 2:25:16:07 (02:26:15:05). At this point, a boy in a dark gray sweater is jumping up and down. Stop recording at the last frame in which he is visible before the camera shifts to the two groups of protesters joining into one group. Begin recording at 2:25:32:06 (02:26:32:06). This is the point at which the camera switches to a view of the three groups of protesters who have just joined into one big group that is advancing straight toward the camera. End the clip at 2:27:49:10 (02:28:49:10). At this point, a man in a car has just shot a boy who was running away. Stop recording after the boy falls, at the first frame in which he is completely still.

Disgust Films

Pink Flamingos

> Film: *Pink Flamingos*
> Target emotion: Disgust
> Clip length: 0'30"

Instructions: Advance to the first frame in which the words "Dreamland Studios" are visible with a mobile home behind them. Reset the timer to 00:00:00:00 (hours:minutes:seconds:frames). Begin the clip at 1:31:08:08 (1:31:28:11). At this point, three people have just seen a woman walking her dog. They begin to smile and lick their lips. The dog lowers its head towards the ground slightly. Begin recording 2 seconds and 22 frames (82 frames) after the camera switches from a close-up of the woman to the dog defecating. End the clip at 1:31:38:08 (1:31:58:11). At this point, the woman has her teeth together in a smile after having stuck her tongue out. (This is a little more than a second before "The end" appears.)

Amputation

> Film: Noncommercial surgery film
> Target emotion: Disgust
> Clip length: 1'02"

Film available for download at http://www.cas.usf.edu/psychology/fac_rottenbergJ.htm

Fear Films

Shining

> Film: *The Shining*
> Target emotion: Fear
> Clip length: 1'22"

Instructions: Advance to the first frame of the film, which shows a body of water surrounded by mountains. Reset the timer to 00:00:00:00 (hours:minutes:frames). Begin the clip at 00:56:51:15 (00:57:03:08). At this point, a boy's hands are visible (one flat on the floor and the other in a fist).

There are toy trucks and cars on a red, brown, and orange carpet. End the clip at 00:58:12:18 (00:58:24:01). At this point, an open door with a key in the lock is visible, and one full second has passed since the boy has said "Mom, are you in there?"

Lambs

> Film: *Silence of the Lambs*
> Target emotion: Fear
> Clip length: 3'29"

Instructions: Advance to the first frame of the film in which the words "A STRONG HEART DEMME PRODUCTION" appear. Reset the timer to 00:00:00:00 (hours:minutes:seconds:frames). Begin the clip at 01:40:16:29 (01:40:56:01). At this point, a dirt road and trees are in the forefront and a mint green trailer is in the background. Stop recording at 01:43:44:23 (01:44:24:10). At this point, the profile of a dark-haired woman is visible. There is a metal wire hanging from the ceiling that appears to almost (but not quite) touch her nose and chin. Begin recording at 01:46:36:24 (01:47:16:01). At this point, hands holding a gun are moving rapidly into the scene from the right of the screen. In the background, there is dirty yellow wallpaper. End the clip at 01:46:38:19 (01:47:18:01). At this point, the dark-haired woman has her back to the yellow wallpaper and has pointed her gun between the upper middle and the upper right-hand portions of the screen. Her right hand obscures most of the left half of her face and we hear her exclaim as the lights go out.

Neutral Films

Sticks

> Film: Noncommercial screen saver
> Target emotion: Neutral
> Clip length: 3'26"

Instructions: Film available for download at http://www.cas.usf.edu/psychology/fac_rottenbergJ.htm

Denali

> Film: "Alaska's Wild Denali"
> Target emotion: Neutral
> Clip length: 5'02"

Instructions: Reset the timer to 00.00.00:00 when the credits for the Alaskan production company come up. Begin the clip at 00:33:28:00 (00:33:15:00), right after a person plays a guitar. Start as the music is still playing and fading and the visual is a silhouette of a mountain and the midnight sky; the narrator talks about the Alaskan midnight sky. End the clip at 00:38:30:00 (00:38:17:00). At this point, a buck is eating little grasses, and there is a shot of a mountain stream.

Sadness Films

The Champ

Film: *The Champ*
Target emotion: Sadness
Clip length: 2'51"

Instructions: Advance past the title, "Metro-Goldwyn-Mayer Presents," to the first frame in which the title is no longer visible. Reset the timer to 00:00:00:00 (hours:minutes:seconds:frames). Begin the clip at 01:50:29:02 (01:54:23:01). At this point, a boxer is lying on a table in a locker room. The boxer says "Where's my boy?" Another man answers, "He's right here." Begin recording as a blond-haired boy walks out of a darkly lit area, just before you hear the boxer ask "Where's my boy?" for the last time. Stop recording at 01:50:52:05 (01:54:45:20). At this point, the boxer says "TJ," and then says "Annie was here tonight, TJ." Stop recording after he says "TJ" and before he says "Annie was here tonight, TJ." Begin recording at 01:51:56:14 (01:55:54:01). Begin recording immediately before the child says "Yeah. . . . The champ always comes through. . . ." Stop recording at 01:52:26:04 (01:56:18:20). At this point, the boxer has just closed his eyes and died. Begin recording at 01:53:15:21 (01:57:13:15). At this point, we see a side view of the dead boxer lying on the table. The camera then goes to the boy who is standing in front of a tall man. Only the man's torso is visible. He is wearing a towel around his neck and is holding the boy's shoulders. The boy is crying and saying, "Champ." End the clip at 01:55:11:03 (01:59:08:20). At this point, the boy is crying, saying "I want Champ." The man replies, "Please, TJ, listen to me. He's gone. He's gone, son. He's gone." The child, still crying, replies, "No. No. He's not gone, he's not, he's not." Stop recording at the frame in which the boy backs away from the man.

Surprise Films

Capricorn

Film: *Capricorn One*
Target emotion: Surprise
Clip length: 0'49"

Instructions: Advance to the first frame in which the words "Sir Lew Grade Presents" are visible. Reset the timer to 00:00:00:00 (hours:minutes:seconds:frames). Begin the clip at 01:32:58:18 (01:33:07:06). At this point, a man is sitting on a bed in an apartment. Begin recording at the first frame after the camera switches from a close-up of the man's face to a shot from down the hall. End the clip at 01:33:47:27 (01:33:56:17). At this point, men have just burst through the door. Stop recording at the frame after the third agent has left the screen (from left to right) and the man can be seen on the bed.

Sea of Love

Film: *Sea of Love*
Target emotion: Surprise
Clip length: 0'9"

Instructions: Advance to the first frame in which the words "A Martin Bregman Production" are visible. Reset the timer to 00:00:00:00 (hours:minutes:seconds:frames). Begin the clip at 01:19:05:15 (1:19:26:01). At this point, a man has gotten out of an elevator and begun walking down the hall toward an exit door. Begin recording as he turns the corner, at the frame in which he first turns his back completely to the wall and is looking toward the left. End the clip at 01:19:16:00 (1:19:35:03). At this point, the last bird has just flown out of view.

References

Anderson, C. A., Deuser, W. E., & DeNeve, K. M. (1995). Hot temperatures, hostile affect, hostile cognition, and arousal: Tests of a general model of affective aggression. *Personality and Social Psychology Bulletin, 21,* 434–448.

Averill, J. R. (1969). Autonomic response patterns during sadness and mirth. *Psychophysiology, 5,* 399–414.

Bartz, G., Ronder, P. (Writers), & Barnouw, E. (Producer). (1970). *Hiroshima-Nagasaki, August 1945* [Motion picture]. United States: The Video Project.

Berenbaum, H., & Williams, M. (1995). Personality and emotional reactivity. *Journal of Research in Personality, 29,* 24–34.

Bower, G. H. (1981). Mood and memory. *American Psychologist, 36,* 129–148.

Branscombe, N. R. (1985). Effects of hedonic valence and physiological arousal on emotion: A comparison of two theoretical perspectives. *Motivation and Emotion, 9,*153–169.

Bregman, M., Stroller, L. (Producers), & Becker, H. (Director). (1989). *Sea of love* [Motion picture]. United States: MCA/Universal Home Video.

Butler, E. A., Egloff, B., Wilhelm, F. W., Smith, N. C., Erickson, E. A., & Gross, J. J. (2003). The social consequences of expressive suppression. *Emotion, 3,* 48–67.

Cacioppo, J. T., & Gardner, W. L. (1999). Emotion. *Annual Review of Psychology, 50,* 191–214.

Canli, T., Desmond, J. E., Zhao, Z., & Gabrieli, J. D. (2002). Sex differences in the neural basis of emotional memories. *Proceedings of the National Academy of Sciences of the USA, 99,* 10789–10794.

Christoff, K., Ream, J. M., & Gabrieli, J. D. E. (2004). Cognitive and neural basis of spontaneous thought processes. *Cortex, 40,* 1–9.

Cosby, W. (Producer/Director). (1996). *Bill Cosby, himself* [Motion picture]. United States: Twentieth Century Fox.

Davidson, R. J. (1998). Affective style and affective disorders: Perspectives from affective neuroscience. *Cognition and Emotion, 12,* 307–330.

Davidson, R. J., Ekman, P., Saron, C. D., Senulis, J. A., & Friesen, W. V. (1990). Approach-withdrawal and cerebral asymmetry: Emotional expression and brain physiology. *Journal of Personality and Social Psychology, 58,* 330–341.

Detenber, B. H., & Reeves, B. (1996). A bio-informational theory of emotion: Motion and image size effects on viewers. *Journal of Communication, 46,* 66–84.

Detenber, B. H., Simons, R. F. & Bennett, G. G. (1998). Roll 'em!: The effects of picture motion on emotional responses. *Journal of Broadcasting and Electronic Media, 21,* 112–126.

Detenber, B. H., Simons, R. F., & Reiss, J. E. (2000). The emotional significance of color in television presentations. *Media Psychology, 2,* 331–355.

Devlin, D. (Producer), & Bill, T. (Director). (1980). *My bodyguard* [Motion picture]. United States: Fox Hills Video.

Duclos, S. E., & Laird, J. D. (2001). The deliberate control of emotional experience through control of expressions. *Cognition and Emotion, 15,* 27–56.

Ekman, P. (1992). An argument for basic emotions. *Cognition and Emotion, 6,* 169–200.

Ekman, P., & Friesen, W. V. (1974). Detecting deception from the body or face. *Journal of Personality and Social Psychology, 29,* 288–298.

Ekman, P., Friesen, W. V., & Ancoli, S. (1980). Facial signs of emotional experience. *Journal of Personality and Social Psychology, 39,* 1125–1134.

Epstein, S. (1983). Aggregation and beyond: Some basic issues on the prediction of behavior. *Journal of Personality, 51,* 360–392.

Fredrickson, B. L., & Kahneman, D. (1993). Duration neglect in retrospective evaluations of affective episodes. *Journal of Personality and Social Psychology, 65,* 45–55.

Fridlund, A. J. (1992). The behavioral ecology and sociality of human faces. In M. S. Clark (Ed.), *Emotion* (pp. 190–221). Newbury Park, CA: Sage.

Frijda, N. H. (1988). The laws of emotion. *American Psychologist, 43,* 349–358.

Frijda, N. H. (1989). Aesthetic emotions and reality. *American Psychologist, 44,* 1546–1547.

Gottman, J. M., & Levenson, R. W. (1985). A valid procedure for obtaining self-report of affect in marital interaction. *Journal of Consulting and Clinical Psychology, 53,* 151–160.

Gross, J. J. (1998). The emerging field of emotion regulation: An integrative review. *Review of General Psychology, 2,* 271–299.

Gross, J. J., John, O. P., & Richards, J. M. (2000). The dissociation of emotion expression from emotion experience: A personality perspective. *Personality and Social Psychology Bulletin, 26,* 712–726.

Gross, J. J., & Levenson, R. W. (1993). Emotional suppression: Physiology, self-report, and expressive behavior. *Journal of Personality and Social Psychology, 64,* 970–986.

Gross, J. J., & Levenson, R. W. (1995). Emotion elicitation using films. *Cognition and Emotion, 9,* 87–108.

Gross, J. J., Sutton, S. K., & Ketelaar, T. (1998). Relations between affect and personality: Support for the affect-level and affective-reactivity views. *Personality and Social Psychology Bulletin, 24,* 279–288.

Hagemann, D., Naumann, E., Maier, S., Becker, G., Lürken, A., & Bartussek, D. (1999). The assessment of affective reactivity using films: Validity, reliability and sex differences. *Personality and Individual Differences, 26,* 627–639.

Hahn, D. (Producer), Allers, R., & Minkoff, R. (Directors).

(1994). *The lion king* [Motion picture]. United States: Walt Disney Pictures.

Hardesty, T. (Producer). (1997). *Alaska's Wild Denali: Summer in Denali National Park* [Motion picture]. United States: Alaska Video Postcards.

Hemenover, S. H. (2003). Individual differences in rate of affect change: Studies in affective chronometry. *Journal of Personality and Social Psychology, 85,* 121–131.

Isen, A. M., Daubman, K. A., & Nowicki, G. P. (1987). Positive affect facilitates creative problem solving. *Journal of Personality and Social Psychology, 52,* 1122–1131.

Jakobs, E., Manstead, A. S. R., & Fischer, A. H. (2001). Social context effects on facial activity in a negative emotional setting. *Emotion, 1,* 51–69.

Kagan, J., & Snidman, N. (1999). Early childhood predictors of adult anxiety disorders. *Biological Psychiatry, 46,* 1536–1541.

Karama, S., Lecours, A. R., Leroux, J., Bourgouin, P., Beaudoin, G., Joubert, S., et al. (2002). Areas of brain activation in males and females during viewing of erotic film excerpts. *Human Brain Mapping, 16,* 1–13.

Knez, I. (1995). Effects of indoor lighting on mood and cognition. *Journal of Environmental Psychology, 15,* 39–51.

Kring, A. M., & Gordon, A. H. (1998) Sex differences in emotion: Expression, experience, and physiology. *Journal of Personality and Social Psychology, 74,* 686–703.

Kubrick, S. (Producer/Director). (1980). *The shining* [Motion picture]. United States: Warner Home Video.

Lacey, J. I. (1967). Somatic response patterning and stress: Some revisions of activation theory. In M. H. Appley & R. Trumbull (Eds.), *Psychological stress: Issues in research* (pp. 14–42). New York: Appleton-Century Crofts.

Landis, C. (1924). Studies of emotional reactions: 1. A preliminary study of facial expression. *Journal of Experimental Psychology, 7,* 325–341.

Lang, P. J. (1978). Anxiety: Toward a psychophysiological definition. In H. S. Akiskal & W. L. Webb (Eds.), *Psychiatric diagnosis: Exploration of biological criteria* (pp. 265–389). New York: Spectrum.

Lang, P. J., Bradley, M. M., & Cuthbert, B. N. (1995). *International Affective Picture System (IAPS): Technical manual and affective ratings.* Gainesville, FL: University of Florida, Center for Research in Psychophysiology.

Larsen, R. J., & Ketelaar, T. (1991). Personality and susceptibility to positive and negative emotional states. *Journal of Personality and Social Psychology, 61,* 132–140.

Lazarus, P. (Producer), & Hyams, P. (Director). (1978). *Capricorn One* [Motion picture]. United States: CBS/Fox Video.

Lazarus, R. S., Speisman, J. C., Mordkoff, A. M., & Davison, L. A. (1962). A laboratory study of psychological stress produced by a motion picture film. *Psychological Monographs, 76,* 553.

LeDoux, J. E. (1996). *The emotional brain: The mysterious underpinnings of emotional life.* New York: Simon & Schuster.

Levenson, R. W. (1988). Emotion and the autonomic nervous system: A prospectus for research on autonomic specificity. In H. Wagner (Ed.), *Social psychophysiology: Perspectives on theory and clinical applications* (pp. 17–42). London: Wiley.

Levenson, R. W. (1999). The intrapersonal functions of emotion. *Cognition and Emotion, 13,* 481–504.

Lombard, M. (1995). Direct responses to people on the screen: Television and personal space. *Communication Research, 22,* 288–324.

Loomis, J. M., Blascovich, J. J., & Beall, A. C. (1999). Immersive virtual environments as a basic research tool in psychology. *Behavior Research Methods, Instruments, and Computers, 31,* 557–564.

Lovell, D. (Producer), & Zeffirelli, F. (Director). (1979). *The champ* [Motion picture]. United States: MGM/Pathe Home Video.

Marston, A., Hart, J., Hileman, C., & Faunce, W. (1984). On the laboratory study of sadness and crying. *American Journal of Psychology, 97,* 127–131.

Martin, M. (1990). On the induction of mood. *Clinical Psychology Review, 10,* 669–697.

Mauss, I.B., Levenson, R.W., McCarter, L., Wilhelm, F.H., & Gross, J.J. (2005). The tie that binds? Coherence among emotion experience, behavior, and physiology. *Emotion, 5,* 175–190. .

Mauss, I. B., Wilhelm, F. W., & Gross, J. J. (2004). Is there less to social anxiety than meets the eye? Emotion experience, expression, and bodily responding. *Cognition and Emotion, 18,* 631–662.

McCarthy, M. C. (Writer), Forrest, A., Gowers, B., & de Moraes, R. (Directors). (2001). Episode 119 [Television series episode]. In D. Breen, J. L. Ehrman, M. Leveson, T. Park, R. Phillips, & A. M. Thorogood (Producers), *Whose line is it, anyway?* Culver City, CA: Warner Brothers Television.

Morgan, J. J. B (1920). The effect of fatigue on attention. *Journal of Experimental Psychology, 3,* 319–333.

Morra, B., Brezner, L. (Producers), & Gowers, B. (Director). (1986). *Robin Williams live* [Motion picture]. United States: Vestron Video.

Neumann, R., Seibt, B., & Strack, F. (2001). The influence of mood on the intensity of emotional responses: Disentangling feeling and knowing. Cognition and Emotion, *15,* 725–747.

Palomba, D., Sarlo, M., Angrilli, A., Mini, A., & Stegagno, L. (2000). Cardiac responses associated with affective processing of unpleasant film stimuli. *International Journal of Psychophysiology, 36,* 45–57.

Philippot, P. (1993). Inducing and assessing differentiated emotion-feeling states in the laboratory. *Cognition and Emotion, 7,* 171–193.

Piferi, R. L., Kline, L. A., Younger, J., & Lawler, K. A. (2000). An alternative approach for achieving cardiovascular baseline: Viewing an aquatic video. *International Journal of Psychophysiology, 37,* 207–217.

Polivy, J. (1981). On the induction of emotion in the laboratory: Discrete mood or multiple affect states? *Journal of Personality and Social Psychology, 41,* 803–817.

Reiner, R. (Producer/Director), Scheinman, A., Stolt, J., & Nicolaides, S. (Producers). (1989). *When Harry met Sally* [Motion picture]. United States: New Line Home Video.

Ritz, T., & Steptoe, A. (2000). Emotion and pulmonary function in asthma: Reactivity in the field and relationship with laboratory induction of emotion. *Psychosomatic Medicine, 62,* 808–815.

Rosenberg, E. L., & Ekman, P. (1994). Coherence between expressive and experiential systems in emotion. *Cognition and Emotion, 8,* 201–229.

Ross, L., Lepper, M.R., & Hubbard, M. (1975). Perseverance in self-perception and social perception: Biased attributional processes in the debriefing paradigm. *Journal of Personality and Social Psychology, 32,* 880–892.

Rottenberg, J., Gross, J. J., & Gotlib, I. H. (2005). Emotion context insensitivity in major depressive disorder. *Journal of Abnormal Psychology, 114, 627–639.*

Rottenberg, J., Gross, J. J., Wilhelm, F. H., Najmi, S., & Gotlib, I. H. (2002). Crying threshold and intensity in major depressive disorder. *Journal of Abnormal Psychology, 111,* 302–312.

Rottenberg, J., Kasch, K. L., Gross, J. J., & Gotlib, I. H. (2002). Sadness and amusement reactivity differentially predict concurrent and prospective functioning in major depressive disorder. *Emotion, 2,* 135–146.

Rottenberg, J., Wilhelm, F. H., Gross, J. J., & Gotlib, I. H. (2003). Vagal rebound during resolution of tearful crying among depressed and nondepressed individuals. *Psychophysiology, 40,* 1–6.

Ruch, W. (1995). Will the real relationship between facial expression and affective experience please stand up. The case of exhilaration. *Cognition and Emotion, 9,* 33–58.

Russell, J. A. (1991). In defense of a prototype approach to emotion concepts. *Journal of Personality and Social Psychology, 60,* 37–47.

Russell, J. A. (2003). Core affect and the psychological construction of emotion. *Psychological Review, 110,* 145–172.

Salovey, P., Mayer, J. D., Goldman, S. L., Turvey, C., & Palfai, T. P. (1995). Emotional attention, clarity, and repair: Exploring emotional intelligence using the Trait Meta-Mood Scale. In J. W. Pennebaker (Ed.), *Emotion, disclosure, and health* (pp. 125–154). Washington, DC: American Psychological Association.

Saxon, E., Utt, K., Bozman, R. (Producers), & Demme, J. (Director). (1991). *Silence of the lambs* [Motion picture]. United States: Orion Pictures.

Spencer, N., Briley, J. (Producers), & Attenborough, R. (Director). (1987). *Cry freedom* [Motion picture]. United States: MCA/Universal Home Video.

Thompson, R. F., & Spencer, W. A. (1966). Habituation: A model phenomenon for the study of neuronal substrates of behavior. *Psychological Review, 73,* 16–43.

Tooby, J., & Cosmides, L. (1990). The past explains the present: Emotional adaptations and the structure of ancestral environments. *Ethology and Sociobiology, 11,* 375–424.

Tsai, J. L., Levenson, R. W., & Carstensen, L. L. (2000). Autonomic, expressive, and subjective responses to emotional films in older and younger Chinese American and European American adults. *Psychology and Aging, 15,* 684–693.

Tugend, J. L. (Producer) & Hunt, B. (Director). (2000). *Return to me* [Motion picture]. United States: Metro-Goldwyn-Mayer Pictures.

Velten, E. (1968). A laboratory task for the induction of mood states. *Behaviour Research and Therapy, 6,* 473–482.

Vrana, S. R., & Rollock, D. (2002). The role of ethnicity, gender, emotional content, and contextual differences in physiological, expressive, and self-reported emotional responses to imagery. *Cognition and Emotion, 16,* 165–192.

Waters, J. (Director). (1973). *Pink flamingos* [Motion picture]. United States: Lightning Video.

Watson, D (2000). *Mood and temperament.* New York: Guilford Press.

Watson, D., Clark, L. A., & Tellegen, A. (1988). Development and validation of brief measures of positive and negative affect: The PANAS scales. *Journal of Personality and Social Psychology, 54,* 1063–1070.

Wheeler, R. E., Davidson, R. J., & Tomarken, A. J. (1993). Frontal brain asymmetry and emotional reactivity: A biological substrate of affective style. *Psychophysiology, 30,* 82–89.

Zillman, D., & Weaver, J. B. (1999). Effects of prolonged exposure to gratuitous media violence on provoked and unprovoked hostile behavior. *Journal of Applied Social Psychology 29,* 145–165.

Margaret M. Bradley
Peter J. Lang

2

The International Affective Picture System (IAPS) in the Study of Emotion and Attention

In this chapter, we discuss the development and use of picture stimuli incorporated in the International Affective Picture System (IAPS, pronounced "eye-aps"; Lang, Bradley, & Cuthbert, 2005), a large set of emotionally evocative color photographs that includes pleasure, arousal, and dominance ratings made by men and women. The IAPS is currently used in experimental investigations of emotion and attention worldwide, providing experimental control in the selection of emotional stimuli, facilitating the comparison of results across different studies, and encouraging replication within and across psychological and neuroscience research laboratories. Numerous studies in our laboratory over the past 15 years have explored subjective, psychophysiological, behavioral, and neurophysiological reactions when viewing these affective stimuli. Basic findings from these studies, which will be informative for researchers considering or using the IAPS stimuli, are briefly summarized in this chapter.

The Problem

If scientists wish to study the effects of background noise on the efficiency of factory workers, it is fairly easy for them to control the type of noise by using accepted physical scales for determining loudness and frequency. Because these established scales are widely used, results can be exactly evaluated by retest (even in another laboratory), confirming or disconfirming the original results. In this systematic manner, science progresses in many of its fields of endeavor.

Unfortunately, researchers in psychology, neuroscience, and psychiatry have, in the past, lacked recourse to similar standards for specifying the emotionality of stimuli. In fact, there are no obvious physical parameters that can be used to organize emotional stimuli. Stimuli that are visually similar, for example, such as a snake and a garden hose, can differ widely in emotional impact across individuals or prompt affect in one context and yet fail to do so in a slightly different setting. One person may fear cats, whereas her neighbor can't get enough of them. The anticipated beefsteak that makes one diner glow with pleasure disgusts the vegetarian. There is great diversity of emotional reactions to physically equivalent events.

Nonetheless, the emotion researcher needs standards and metrics in order to reach a scientific understanding of the issues fundamental to emotional health—to provide timely information on disturbances in emotional development, to assess the physiological impact of stress, to evaluate emotional psychopathology, to determine the degree of emotional impairment in brain-damaged patients, and to construct more efficient treatments for fear, anxiety, and depression. Historically, investigators have dealt with this problem by developing unique stimuli for study in each emotion experiment. Stimuli used in one laboratory, however, were seldom available to other laboratories. And attempts at recreating the same experimental materials from descriptions in the literature often resulted in stimuli that were quite disparate, rendering replication problematic and undermining the communal effort that is essential to a cumulative science.

In recent years, we have begun to address the seemingly intractable problem of emotional stimulus standardization. To begin this effort, we collected photographs that depict the people, objects, and events that represent human experience. We elected to begin by using pictures as affective stimuli for a number of reasons: their clear evocative ability; the relative ease of editing, cataloguing, and distributing these stimuli; and the fact that pictures are static cues. A static (i.e., unchanging) cue is particularly desirable in the initial investigation of emotion, as other affective cues (e.g., films, stories, etc.) can contain movement, narrative development, or other dynamic changes in the information array that can complicate interpretation of the measured affective response. For instance, a number of psychophysiological measures of emotion (e.g., heart rate, event-related potentials, etc.) are sensitive to dynamic changes in the sensory array, making it more difficult to assess modulation that is specifically due to affect. Controlling these parameters in dynamic stimuli is more complex than with static pictures, whose physical parameters are relatively easy to control—including, for example, image size, duration, brightness, luminosity, color, and so forth. This ease of control is useful for both stimulus selection and experimental manipulation. In this digital age, pictures are also easy to edit and manipulate, as well as to catalogue and distribute, a primary goal when creating the IAPS.

The IAPS (Lang et al., 2005) currently includes more than 1,000 exemplars of human experience—joyful, sad, fearful, angry, threatening, attractive, ugly, dressed and undressed people; houses, art objects, household objects; housing projects; erotic couples; funerals; pollution; dirty toilets; cityscapes, seascapes, landscapes; sports events; photojournalism from wars and disasters; medical treatments, sick patients, mutilated bodies; baby animals, threatening animals, insects; loving families; waterfalls; children playing—a virtual world of pictures. Each picture in the IAPS is rated by a large group of people (both men and women) for the feelings of pleasure and arousal that the picture evokes during viewing. The pictures are then numbered (4 digits) and catalogued according to the mean and standard deviation of these affective ratings and distributed freely to academic researchers. Using these ratings, scientists can select and/or match pictures on the basis of the average reported emotional impact of that picture and are able to control for emotional arousal when investigating effects of hedonic valence and vice versa. Most important, the IAPS encourages replication and extension of published experimental reports using the same or similar stimulus material, promoting a cumulative increase in scientific knowledge.

Evaluative Judgment and the Motivation Organization of Emotion

The IAPS stimuli are standardized on the basis of ratings of pleasure and arousal. This decision reflects both theory and data. In the nineteenth century, Wundt (1896) first proposed a dimensional model of affect as part of his theory concerning mental chemistry, arguing that affect resulted from variations in basic dimensions of pleasure and arousal. Later, based on factor analyses of evaluative language, Osgood and coworkers (e.g., Osgood, Suci, & Tannenbaum, 1957; see also Mehrabian & Russell, 1974; Russell, 1980) developed a dimensional theory of semantic meaning after finding that the most variance in semantic judgments was accounted for by a single factor, hedonic valence, which ranged from unpleasant (unhappy, annoyed, despairing, etc.) to pleasant (happy, pleased, hopeful, etc.). The fundamental role of hedonic valence in emotions received further support from studies of language categorization (Ortony, Clore, & Collins, 1988; Shaver, Schwartz, Kirson, & O'Connor, 1987), which proposed that human knowledge about emotions is hierarchically organized with a superordinate division between positivity (pleasant states: love, joy) and negativity (unpleasant states: anger, sadness, fear). A second dimension resulting from Osgood's factor analytic work also accounted for substantial variance in evaluative judgments; this was a dimension he labeled *arousal*. This dimension reflects the activation parameter in affective experience and ranges from an unaroused state (calm, relaxed, sleepy, etc.) to a state of high arousal (excited, stimulated, wide awake, etc.).

We have previously proposed that two motive systems exist in the brain—appetitive and defensive—that account for the primacy of the hedonic valence and arousal dimensions in emotional expression (Lang, 1995; Lang, Bradley, & Cuthbert, 1990). These neural systems are evolutionarily old, shared across mammalian species, and have evolved to mediate the behaviors that sustain and protect life. The defense system is primarily activated in contexts involving threat, with a basic behavioral repertoire built on withdrawal, escape, and attack. Conversely, the appetitive system is activated in contexts that promote survival, including sustenance, procreation, and nurturance, with a basic behavioral repertoire of ingestion, copulation, and caregiving. These systems are implemented by neural circuits in the brain, presumably with common outputs to structures that mediate the somatic and autonomic physiological systems involved in attention and action (see Davis, 2000; Davis & Lang, 2003; Fanselow, 1994; LeDoux, 1990). Thus motivational activation is associated with widespread cortical, autonomic, and behavioral activity that varies in its intensity. Judgments of hedonic valence indicate which motivational system is engaged; judgments of arousal index the intensity of its activation.

Emotional engagement relies on the activation of neural circuits, subcortical and cortical, that mediate the expressive, autonomic, and somatic changes typically associated with affective expression. Pictures are particularly good cues for this associative activation, as they share sensory features with the actual object—a picture of a snarling dog shares a number of perceptual features with an actual dog (e.g., teeth, eyes, mouth open, etc.), making it more likely that this cue will match and activate visual representations that include associations to the subcortical structures that mediate defensive behavior. Other types of cues, such as language ("the dog growls menacingly"), do not share sensory/perceptual features, making it less likely that these cues will strongly engage the fundamental motivational systems. Particularly for humans, who are highly visual creatures, pictures are able to accurately represent many of the most arousing affective events (e.g., sexual, nurturing, threatening).

According to this motivational view, the diversity of specific expressed emotions (e.g., fear, anger, disgust, etc.) evolved from different *tactical* reactions to a broad context of stimulation. Thus, for example, a rat shocked on its footpads may attack a companion animal (an anger prototype) or, if alone, may become immobile and freeze (a fear prototype). When given an escape path, the rat may flee the field (fear prototypes). The *contextual tactics* of approaching or withdrawing have become much more varied in humans. Nevertheless, the *strategic frame* of appetite and defense remains fundamental in emotional experience (Lang et al., 1990). Thus, although the tactical demands of the specific context may variously shape affective expression, all emotions are organized around a motivational base. In this sense, appetitive and defensive motivation can be considered to be the strategic dimensions of the emotion world.

SAM Ratings of Pleasure and Arousal

To measure the pleasure and arousal of IAPS stimuli, we use a rating instrument called the *self-assessment manikin* (SAM;

Lang, 1980). As Figure 2.1 illustrates, SAM is a graphic figure that ranges from smiling and happy to frowning and unhappy in representing the hedonic valence dimension. For the arousal dimension, SAM ranges from excited and wide eyed to relaxed and sleepy. Participants indicate feeling *neither* happy nor unhappy (i.e., neutral), or neither calm nor aroused, using the midpoint of each scale. In this version of SAM, the participant can fill in any of the five figures depicting each scale or the box between any two figures, resulting in a 9-point rating scale for each dimension. (In addition to the paper-and-pencil version, a 20-point SAM scale exists as a dynamic computer display on a variety of different systems [Cook, Atkinson, & Lang, 1987] that is highly correlated with ratings on the 9-point SAM scale.)

To determine whether SAM ratings are comparable to the factor analytic scores of pleasure and arousal derived from the relatively longer semantic differential scale devised by Mehrabian and Russell (1974), we compared SAM ratings and judgments made using the semantic differential scale (Bradley & Lang, 1994). Each participant viewed a set of IAPS pictures and made judgments using the 18 bipolar-adjective pairs in the semantic differential for each picture. The resulting matrix of correlations was factor analyzed (see table 2.1), and the solution indicated two factors that accounted for the most variance—pleasure and arousal. Most important, the correlation between SAM ratings of IAPS pictures and factor scores derived from the semantic differential was very high, indicating that SAM is able to quickly assess these fundamental dimensions of emotion.

A third dimension, accounting for much less variance in semantic evaluation research, was termed *potency* or *dominance* by Osgood et al. (1957). The SAM instrument represents this dimension using a figure that ranges from small (not dominant) to large (dominant). When rating static picture stimuli, dominance ratings are highly correlated with ratings of hedonic valence, with pleasant pictures rated as higher in dominance than unpleasant pictures. We have

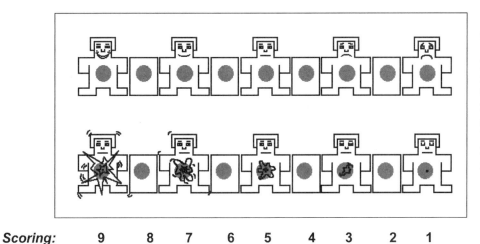

Figure 2.1. The self-assessment manikin (SAM; Lang, 1980) used to acquire ratings of pleasure and arousal for pictures in the IAPS. Each dimension is represented by five graphic figures, and participants can select any of the figures or between any of the figures, making a 9-point scale. See color insert.

Scoring: 9   8   7   6   5   4   3   2   1

Table 2.1

Factor analysis for ratings on the bipolar pairs of the semantic differential when viewing IAPS pictures resulted in two factors of pleasure and arousal that correlated highly with SAM pleasure or arousal rating (Bradley & Lang, 1994)

Semantic Differential	Factor 1 "Pleasure"	Factor 2 "Arousal"	Correlation with SAM pleasure rating
Unhappy-Happy	.91	.06	.98
Annoyed-Pleased	.88	.07	.99
Despairing-Hopeful	.86	.06	.97
Unsatisfied-Satisfied	.87	.14	.96
Melancholic-Contented	.73	.10	.96

Semantic Differential	Factor 1 "Pleasure"	Factor 2 "Arousal"	Correlation with SAM arousal rating
Unaroused-Aroused	.05	.83	.90
Sleepy-Wide Awake	−.05	.81	.91
Dull-Jittery	−.21	.79	.92
Calm-Excited	−.18	.79	.91
Relaxed-Stimulated	−.21	.77	.94
Sluggish-Frenzied	−.27	.77	.90

speculated that the dominance dimension, which is relatively weak in accounting for variance in evaluative judgments of symbolic stimuli, is perhaps more potent (pun intended) in social interaction. For instance, dominance usually characterizes differences in unpleasant arousing events, with anger characterized by somewhat higher dominance than fear. Nonetheless, both are rated lower in dominance than highly pleasurable events. For symbolic sensory stimuli (e.g., pictures, sounds, words), there is no actual personal interaction in which social potency can play a role. In this case, dominance covaries highly with hedonic valence. Nonetheless, for more event-like stimuli, dominance will clearly account for some portion of variance in evaluative reports.

Normative Rating Procedure

In each IAPS rating study, approximately 60 new exemplars, varying in pleasure, arousal, and semantic content, are presented to approximately 100 participants, half women and half men. Rating sessions are conducted in small groups ranging in size from 8 to 25. For each rated picture set, three different picture orders are used that balance the position of a particular exemplar within the entire series of pictures. In each rating study, pictures are selected that are in color, that have high resolution (e.g., 1024 x 768), and that communicate affective quality relatively quickly.

In addition to the new IAPS exemplars rated in each picture set, three practice pictures are viewed prior to the experimental ratings. These pictures illustrate the range of contents that will be presented and serve to anchor the emo-

tional rating scales. Common anchor points used are: #4200 (woman at beach), #7010 (basket), and #3100 (a burn victim). Each trial begins with a 5 s preparatory cue ("Get ready to rate the next picture"), followed by a 6 s presentation of the to-be-rated picture. Immediately *after* the picture leaves the screen, the participant is given 15 s to make ratings of pleasure, arousal, and dominance using SAM.

Thus far, 16 different rating studies have been conducted. In the first 6 studies, a paper-and-pencil version of the 9-point SAM instrument (Lang, 1980) in booklet format was used to acquire affective ratings; in the last 9 studies, a newer, computer-scorable SAM instrument was used (see Figure 2.1). The list of anchor adjectives from the semantic differential scale for each factor (e.g., stimulated, excited, frenzied, jittery, wide awake, aroused for the SAM "arousal" dimension) are routinely used in the instructions we use (see the appendix to this chapter) to define the concepts of "pleasure" and "arousal" (and "dominance") for the participant. Note that, although we, as researchers, describe the two fundamental dimensions as "pleasure" and "arousal," the SAM scales are not introduced to participants using these umbrella terms. Rather, by using the range of adjectives that the semantic differential provides, one avoids reliance on a single, specific adjective which may be used more frequently in a context associated with a specific hedonic valence.

Affective Space

Figure 2.2 illustrates the *affective space* that results when each picture is plotted in the 2-dimensional space defined by its mean pleasure and arousal rating. There are several characteristic features of this affective space, which appears to be shaped as a "boomerang" when pleasure ratings are plotted on the Y axis or as a U-shaped function when pleasure ratings are plotted on the X axis. The shape of affective space results from the empirical facts that (1) as pictures are rated as more pleasant or more unpleasant, arousal ratings increase as well, and (2) pictures that are rated as neutral tend to be rated low in arousal. These observations are supported by the statistics. Across the entire set of pictures, the linear correlation between pleasure and arousal rating is relatively weak ($r = .28$), whereas the quadratic relationship is stronger (.54) and captures the relationship: Emotional arousal increases as hedonic valence ratings become increasingly more pleasant or unpleasant. These relationships are stable and reliable (Greenwald, Cook, & Lang, 1989).

We have interpreted this space as consistent with the idea that judgments of pleasure and arousal reflect the level of activation in fundamental appetitive and defensive systems. Figure 2.2 (top) illustrates the trajectories through affective space associated with activation of the appetitive motivation system and the defensive motivation system. When neither motivational system is active, judgments anchor the neutral, calm position in affective space. As pictures activate either appetitive or defensive systems more highly, they fall farther

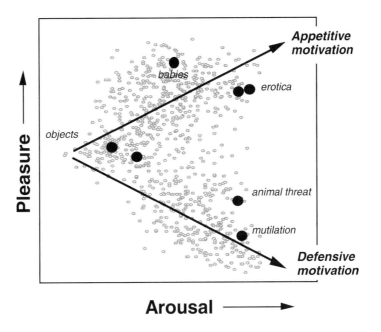

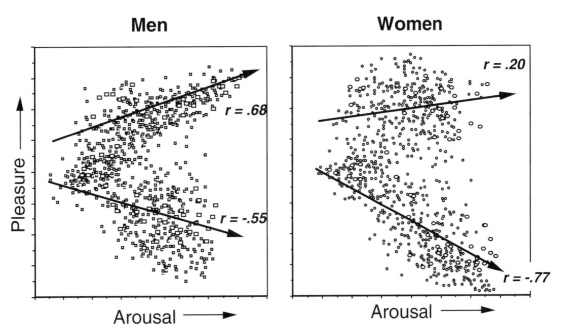

Figure 2.2. Top panel: Each picture in the IAPS is placed in a 2-dimensional affective space on the basis of its mean pleasure and arousal rating. Bottom panel: The affective space for IAPS pictures for men and women are slightly different, with men showing tighter coupling (higher linear correlation) between pleasure and arousal ratings for pleasant pictures, whereas women show a tighter coupling between pleasure and arousal (higher linear correlation) for unpleasant pictures.

along the appetitive and defensive trajectories illustrated. Thus pictures of erotica highly activate the appetitive system, whereas threatening stimuli highly activate the defense system.

For picture stimuli, the unpleasant, calm quadrant is the least inhabited sector. The types of contents that currently reside here include pictures depicting pollution, starving children, and cemeteries. Assuming that this portion of space

remains difficult to fill, reasonable hypotheses concern the specific type of emotional stimuli (i.e., static visual images) and/or the underlying function of emotion (e.g., extremely aversive stimuli may require high mobilization). As Tellegen (1985) suggests, high negative affect may necessarily involve a high level of arousal.

Whereas the mean ratings for each picture clearly produce a boomerang-shaped affective space, the degree of coupling between pleasure and arousal ratings varies for individuals. A *negative* linear relationship between pleasure and arousal ratings characterizes individuals who tend to primarily rate unpleasant events as arousing; we call this a *negative bias* here. On the other hand, a predominantly *positive* linear relationship characterizes individuals who primarily rate pleasant events as arousing; we call this a *positive bias*. The distribution of intra-subject correlations across studies is quite stable: Typically, half or more of the sample show no significant bias, with approximately 30% showing a negative bias and about 20% showing a positive bias.

Gender affects these distributions in consistent ways. More men (40%) then women (16%) show a positive bias, whereas more women (30%) than men (15%) show a negative bias. Interestingly, men and women do not differ in the proportion of those showing no bias. The inference is that, if deviating from linear independence, men will tend to find pleasant pictures more arousing than unpleasant pictures but that women will tend to find unpleasant pictures more arousing than pleasant pictures. These gender differences are also apparent when separate affective spaces are derived for men and women (see Figure 2.2, bottom). For pleasant pictures, men show a stronger correlation between pleasure and arousal ratings (.68) than do women (.20); conversely, for unpleasant pictures, women show a stronger correlation between pleasure and arousal rating (−.77) than do men (−.55). Thus men are more likely to report high arousal (and pleasantness) when looking at pleasant pictures, whereas women are more likely to report high arousal (and unpleasantness) when looking at unpleasant pictures.

Cross-Cultural Consistency

The shape of affective space is cross-culturally consistent, at least in Western cultures. A significant quadratic relationship between pleasure and arousal was obtained for a subset of IAPS pictures rated in Germany, Sweden, and Italy. One difference among these countries is worth noting—the distribution of *arousal* ratings. Compared with the United States and German samples (which did not differ in mean arousal ratings), Swedish participants generally assigned lower arousal ratings to the pictures, indicating calmer emotional reactions, whereas the Italians rated pictures as significantly more arousing overall. Surprisingly, these data tend to support the general cultural stereotypes that exist for these countries. More important, these data indicate that the IAPS might reliably index cultural differences in emotional disposition, which renders it a potent set of stimuli for investigating cross-cultural affective experience. More complete and current IAPS norms exist for Spain (Molto et al., 1999; Vila et al., 2001) and for Belgium (Verschuere, Crombez, & Koster, 2001), in both of which a similarly shaped affective space was also found. Because SAM is a culture-free, language-free measuring instrument, the picture rating methodology is suitable for use in many different countries and cultures.

Age and Affective Space

Because pictures do not rely on verbal or reading skills, they are also an excellent stimulus for studying emotion in children. In one study, we developed a picture set suitable for viewing by children and compared ratings of pleasure and arousal acquired from young children (7–9 years old), adolescents (13–15 years old), and college students (McManis, Bradley, Berg, Cuthbert, & Lang, 2001). As expected from previous studies, the pleasure and arousal dimensions were linearly independent for adults. A very similar relationship was found for the children and for the adolescents. As in adults, the relationship between pleasure and arousal ratings was significantly quadratic for both the younger children ($r = .64$) and the adolescents ($r = .68$). Strong positive correlations between the children's and adults' ratings were found for both pleasure and arousal, suggesting that children rated the pictures similarly to adults. Given the high correlations between the ratings and the similarity of the relationships between the affective dimensions, the conclusion is that children, adolescents, and adults used SAM in similar ways to organize their emotional experience.

In another laboratory study (Cuthbert, Bradley, Zabaldo, Martinez, & Lang, 1994), women from the ages of 18 to 60 viewed a subset of pictures from the IAPS. Whereas the younger, college-age women produced a typically low and nonsignificant linear correlation between pleasure and arousal, the mature women in this sample (i.e., 45 and older) showed a strong negative bias, with a linear correlation of -.73. Clearly, these mature participants were viewing the emotional world differently (at least as defined by these stimuli). For these women, pleasant events were those that were nonactivating; on the other hand, events that were arousing tended to be rated as unpleasant. This finding (which should be assessed in older males as well) suggests that age may result in fundamental changes in affective space.

IAPS and Picture Content

Although the pictures in the IAPS vary widely in terms of semantic content, they have been selected primarily for their ability to evoke affective reactions. Not surprisingly, the pictures that evoke the most emotion in humans involve those depicting human agents, activities, and events, with the result that over half of the pictures in the IAPS depict people engaged in pleasant, neutral, or unpleasant activities. Figure 2.3 illustrates the proportion of pictures in four basic semantic categories of people, animals, objects (nonliving), and scenes. Overall, unpleasant pictures involving people are rated as more unpleasant (2.6) than are unpleasant pictures of animals (3.4), but both pictures of unpleasant people and animals prompt high arousal ratings (5.7 and 5.8, respectively), suggesting that any mobile agent that threatens human life is viewed as an arousing event.

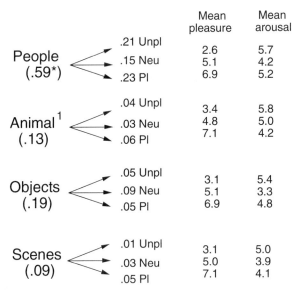

		Mean pleasure	Mean arousal
People (.59*)	.21 Unpl	2.6	5.7
	.15 Neu	5.1	4.2
	.23 Pl	6.9	5.2
Animal[1] (.13)	.04 Unpl	3.4	5.8
	.03 Neu	4.8	5.0
	.06 Pl	7.1	4.2
Objects (.19)	.05 Unpl	3.1	5.4
	.09 Neu	5.1	3.3
	.05 Pl	6.9	4.8
Scenes (.09)	.01 Unpl	3.1	5.0
	.03 Neu	5.0	3.9
	.05 Pl	7.1	4.1

Figure 2.3. The proportion of pictures in the IAPS that occur in each of four basic semantic categories for pictures rated as pleasant, neutral, and unpleasant and the average pleasure and arousal ratings from the normative IAPS ratings (Lang, Bradley & Cuthbert, 2000) for each picture content. *Note:* *proportion of pictures in IAPS in each content; [1]fish and insects included.

For pleasant pictures, those involving people (e.g., erotica, sports, adventure) tend to be rated higher in arousal (5.2) than are pleasant animals or objects (4.2 and 4.8, respectively), although objects are rated as more arousing than pleasant animals (e.g., puppies, bunnies, deer, etc.). Among the most arousing pleasant objects are pictures depicting things that humans either need (e.g. food) or desire (e.g., money, sports cars). Neutral pictures are more likely to involve objects than people or animals, and, indeed, neutral animals and people are rated as more arousing than nonliving neutral objects.

Figure 2.4 illustrates the affective space for a variety of different picture contents for men and women. Overall, the shape of affective space is again similar for men and women. On the other hand, it is also clear women rate *all* of the unpleasant content as more unpleasant and more arousing than do men, and men tend to rate erotic stimuli (either couples or opposite-sex erotica) as more arousing and more pleasant than do women (Bradley, Codispoti, Sabatinelli, & Lang, 2001). These data are consistent with the individual biases found in reports of pleasure and arousal (as mentioned earlier), as well as with the gender differences in affective space. Importantly, they indicate that women tend to rate all unpleasant contents as more arousing and unpleasant than do men (rather than just specific unpleasant contents), whereas the bias in men for pleasant events is more pronounced for explicitly erotic materials. Taken together, the data support an interpretation of greater defensive reactivity for women and greater appetitive activation—specifically, by erotic materials—for men.

Specific Emotions

As we noted earlier, discrete emotional states—fear, anger, sadness, joy, and so forth—can be understood as specific tactical responses in appetitive and defensive contexts. To determine whether and how IAPS pictures differ in prompting specific emotions, we asked participants to circle the emotions elicited during picture viewing from the following list: Happy, Loving, Sexy, Excited, Romantic, Satisfied, Comfortable, Free, Amused, Playful, Nurturing, Bored, Confused, Irritated, Sad, Angry, Afraid, Anxious, Pity, Disgusted, Impatient (see Bradley, Codispoti, Sabatinelli, & Lang, 2001). An effort was made to include a wide range of both pleasant and unpleasant emotional states, despite the fact that unpleasant states often dominate in basic lists of emotion.

Across participants, many different emotion labels were selected for the same picture, suggesting no clear one-to-one relationship between picture content and discrete emotion. Table 2.2 lists the two most frequently selected emotion labels for each picture content, together with the proportion of participants who selected that label. The highest agreement was obtained for pictures depicting contamination (e.g., spoiled food, dirty toilets, etc.) and mutilation, which were both rated as evoking disgust by men and women. Threatening contents were often labeled as eliciting fear, but more so among women. Similarly, women were more likely to indicate feeling "happy" when viewing pictures of families and nature scenes than were men.

Men and women were most different in the specific emotions they indicated feeling when viewing erotica. Whereas both men and women rated erotic couples as making them feel "romantic" and "sexy," men indicated feeling "sexy" and "excited" when viewing erotic women, whereas women showed much less agreement among themselves, with the most frequent reports indicating feeling "amused" and "embarrassed" when viewing erotic men. These data agree with the SAM pleasure and arousal ratings, in which men tend to rate opposite-sex erotica as more pleasant and more arousing than women do. On the other hand, whereas women also rate erotic couples as less pleasant and less arousing than do men, they selected similar labels (e.g., "sexy" and "romantic") when describing their affective experience. These data are consistent with the idea that intensity of appetitive or defensive motivation is the foundation of emotion, with different discrete emotions used to describe different tactical responses in similar motivational states.

Psychophysiology and the Motivational Organization of Emotion

Evaluative reports are clearly sensitive to dimensional variations in the IAPS pictures. On the other hand, these subjective judgments are just one way of tapping a person's affective experience. Indeed, the inherent plasticity in language and

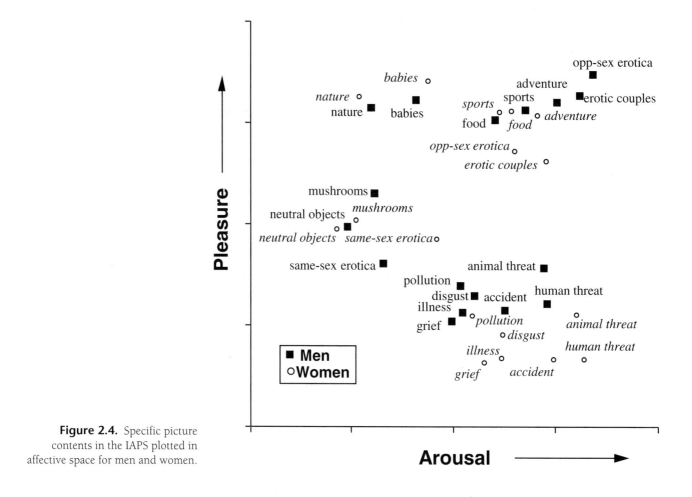

Figure 2.4. Specific picture contents in the IAPS plotted in affective space for men and women.

Table 2.2

List of the most frequent specific emotion descriptors selected when viewing different picture contents in the IAPS and the proportion of men and women selecting that specific emotion to describe their affective experience

Picture Content	Women	Men
Erotica		
Erotic couples	Romantic (.41), Sexy (.37)	Romantic (.47), Sexy (.44)
Opposite-sex erotica	Amused (.36), Embarrassed (.22)	Sexy (.50), Excited (.40)
Same-sex erotica	Bored (.56), Confused(.26)	Bored (.56), Confused (.17)
Adventure	Excited (.63), Free (.66)	Free (.61), Excited (.55)
Sports	Excited (.69), Free (.60)	Excited (.55), Free (.52)
Food	Happy (.37), Satisfied (.17)	Happy (.27), Excited (.17)
Families	Happy (.79), Loving (.78)	Happy (.58), Loving (.58)
Nature	Free, (.76), Happy (.60)	Free (.56), Happy (.41)
Pollution	Disgust (.56), Irritation (.43)	Disgust (.34), Irritation (.26)
Loss	Sad (.79), Pity (.56)	Sad (.61), Pity (.59)
Illness	Pity (.67), Sad (.69)	Sad (.51), Pity (.58)
Contamination	Disgust (.88), Irritation (.50)	Disgust (.78), Irritation (.40)
Accidents	Sad (.63), Pity (.55)	Sad (.49) , Pity (.50)
Mutilation	Disgust (.81), Sad (.47)	Disgust (.75), Pity (.42)
Animal Threat	Afraid (.69), Anxious (.31)	Afraid (.42), Anxious (.23)
Human Threat	Afraid (.67), Angry (.42)	Afraid (.37), Angry (.35)

List of emotion descriptors included: Happy, Loving, Sexy, Excited, Romantic, Satisfied, Comfortable, Free, Amused, Playful, Nurturing, Bored, Confused, Irritated, Sad, Angry, Afraid, Anxious, Pity, Disgusted, Impatient (Bradley, Codispoti, Sabatinelli, & Lang, 2001).

its sensitivity to experimental cues raise the possibility that participants may primarily rate the pictures in a socially appropriate manner. If this were the case, one might expect to find a divergence between evaluative judgments and other indices of emotional response. As Lang (1968) originally noted, correlations between measures of emotion are typically modest. Part of the problem may be related to the lack of standardized stimuli for assessing concordance to the same emotional cues in different response systems.

Physiology and the Individual's Ratings

Using the IAPS stimuli, covariation between an individual's evaluative judgments and other relevant emotional responses can easily be assessed. One method is to rank the pictures on the basis of the pleasure or arousal ratings made by each individual. Once the pictures are ranked for each person, affective responses in other systems (e.g., skin conductance) are averaged at each rank across participants. Note that the picture rated as most unpleasant (or pleasant) will vary across individuals—it might be an attacking dog for one person, a car accident for another. This method recognizes the diversity in affective experience across individuals and allows one to assess the covariation between evaluative judgments and other affective reactions, providing a metaphorical "emotional psychophysics" that parallels Stevens' (1961) classic method relating subjective reports of stimulus magnitude to the physical intensity of the stimulus.

In two experiments that examined the relationships between evaluative judgments and physiology (Greenwald et al., 1989; Lang, Greenwald, Bradley, & Hamm, 1993), clear, reliable relationships emerged, as Figure 2.5 illustrates. First, the pattern of facial corrugator supercilii muscle activity strongly parallels reports of *pleasure*. As pictures are rated as increasingly unpleasant, activity in the corrugator ("frown") muscle, located just above the eyebrow, also increases. Moreover, pictures rated as most pleasant prompt decreased corrugator EMG activity, providing a bidirectional change from neutral pictures. Identical relationships between corrugator EMG activity and pleasure ratings were found by Larsen, Norris, and Cacioppo (2003) for IAPS pictures, as well as when listening to affective sounds or reading affective words. Changes in the zygomaticus major ("smile") EMG activity also covary with reports of pleasure, although less strongly than for corrugator EMG activity. Moreover, for the most unpleasant pictures, EMG activity measured over this zygomatic muscle shows a slight increase. These relationships were also replicated by Larsen et al. (2003) for pictures, as well as for sounds and words. Skin conductance changes, on the other hand, strongly covary with reports of emotional *arousal*, as does the magnitude of a late positive potential that begins around 400 ms in the event-related potential measured at picture onset (see Figure 2.5, bottom left). These relationships suggest that IAPS pictures prompt measurable emotional engagement that relates to evaluative judgments and

that the dimensional organization of emotion is well captured by systematic variations in autonomic, somatic, and cortical activity.

Physiology and Normative Ratings

In addition to assessing how bodily reactions covary with each individual's judgments of pleasure and arousal, a second, and perhaps more typical, method for using the IAPS to study emotion is to select sets of pleasant, neutral, and unpleasant pictures based on the normative IAPS ratings of pleasure and arousal (Lang, Bradley & Cuthbert, 2004). The pattern of affective modulation in facial EMG, cardiovascular, electrodermal, and electrophysiological activity elicited by standard sets of affective pictures mirrors those obtained when assessing individual covariation.

Facial EMG

Again, a very reliable measure of hedonic valence (pleasure) is the amount of activity measured over the corrugator muscle (see Figure 2.6, top left). Compared with viewing neutral pictures, activity in this muscle increases (compared with a baseline immediately preceding picture onset) when viewing unpleasant pictures and decreases for pleasant pictures. Moreover, both men and women show significant changes in this facial muscle when viewing unpleasant pictures (Bradley, Codispoti, Sabatinelli, & Lang, 2001). Among unpleasant pictures, corrugator EMG activity is enhanced for the most unpleasant contents (see Figure 2.6, top right), with the largest changes prompted by pictures of mutilated bodies and contamination (Bradley, Codispoti, Cuthbert, & Lang, 2001). The least corrugator EMG activity is found when viewing pleasant, calm stimuli, such as nature scenes and babies or families.

Activity measured over the zygomaticus major or "smile" muscle (see Figure 2.6, bottom left) also varies with hedonic valence, but somewhat more weakly. A few specific pleasant contents seem to prompt the most EMG activity over this muscle (see Figure 2.6, middle left), including pictures of babies, puppies, families, and, to some extent, food, particularly among female participants (Bradley, Codispoti, Cuthbert, & Lang, 2001). For men, little activity is found over the zygomatic muscle when viewing any pleasant content. Moreover, for both men and women, measurable activity in this muscle is obtained when viewing some unpleasant contents, including human or animal threat and contamination, as the zygomatic muscle can also be part of a more widespread facial grimace.

Based on Duchenne's work, Ekman (1993) suggested that an authentic smile involves activity around the eyes, as well as in the lower face, whereas a faked smile involves only the mouth region. When activity over the orbicularis oculi muscle (i.e., beneath the eye) is measured during picture viewing, together with zygomatic EMG (and corrugator EMG), specific patterns of facial activity result (Bradley, Codispoti, Cuthbert,

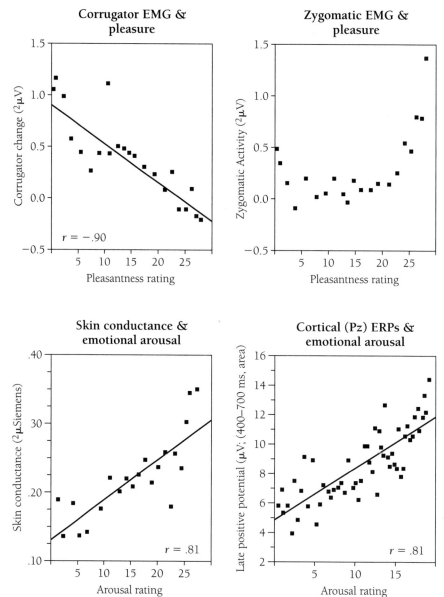

Figure 2.5. Covariation between evaluative judgments and specific psychophysiological responses. Facial EMG activity (measured over the corrugator "frown" and zygomatic "smile" muscles) covary with changes in pleasantness ratings, whereas skin conductance change and the magnitude of a late (400–700 ms) positive component in the event-related potential are more closely associated with changes in rated arousal (Cuthbert et al., 2000; Greenwald et al., 1989).

& Lang, 2001). Pleasant pictures of babies and families prompt heightened activity over both the zygomatic and orbicularis oculi muscles, consistent with the notion that these contents elicit an authentic "Duchenne" smile. Activity over the orbicularis oculi muscle is also enhanced when viewing unpleasant contents, together with increased corrugator EMG activity, but particularly for those contents that people tend to label as "disgusting" (e.g., mutilation and contamination). Taken together, these data suggest that coactivation in the zygomatic and orbicularis oculi muscles indicates an authentic smile, whereas coactivation of the corrugator and orbicularis oculi muscles is linked to a facial expression of disgust. On the other hand, all unpleasant contents were associated with increased corrugator EMG activity, suggesting that facial muscle is reliably engaged during aversive picture viewing.

Skin Conductance

Skin conductance responses are reliably enhanced when viewing pleasant or unpleasant, compared with neutral, pictures (see Figure 2.7). Thus, this phasic sympathetic activity is a good index of the arousal dimension of motivation. On the other hand, these electrodermal responses habituate quite rapidly and are typically engaged by only the most arousing pleasant and unpleasant contents. For pleasant pictures, as Figure 2.7 illustrates, skin conductance responses are significantly elevated primarily for pictures of erotica (Bradley, Codispoti, Cuthbert, & Lang, 2001). Although men typically show *larger* conductance responses when viewing erotica than do women, reliable increases in skin conductance when viewing erotic pictures are obtained for women as well (Bradley, Codispoti, Sabatinelli, & Lang, 2001). For unpleasant

Corrugator EMG

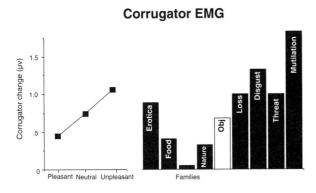

Zygomatic EMG

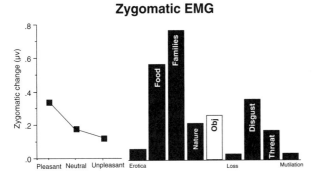

Figure 2.6. Facial EMG changes (rectified, integrated EMG) for sets of pictures selected on the basis of normative ratings of pleasure (left panel) and for specific picture contents (Bradley, Codispoti, Cuthbert, & Lang, 2001).

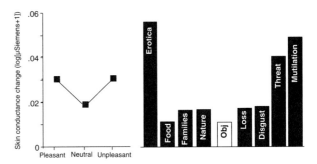

Figure 2.7. Skin conductance activity for sets of IAPS pictures selected on the basis of normative ratings of pleasure (left panel) and for specific picture contents (Bradley, Codispoti, Cuthbert, & Lang, 2001).

contents, skin conductance activity is again heightened for the most arousing contents—pictures of human threat, animal threat, and mutilated human bodies (see Figure 2.7).

These data suggest that eliciting a measurable electrodermal response depends on relatively high motivational activation. Given the association between electrodermal reactivity and sympathetic nervous system activity, one hypothesis is that measurable sympathetic ("fight or flight") activation depends on relatively intense motivational activation. More important, the data suggest that experiments that do not include highly arousing erotic and mutilation/threat contents will prompt little differentiation in skin conductance activity. In addition, whether pleasant or unpleasant pictures result in similar electrodermal magnitude will depend on the specific content and proportion of highly arousing pictures in each hedonic valence category in the study. For instance, experiments that include few erotic but many threatening stimuli will find increased skin conductance for unpleasant, compared with pleasant, pictures rather than equivalent responses for both pleasant and unpleasant stimuli.

Heart Rate

When viewing pictures for a 6 s duration, a typical triphasic pattern of heart rate response is obtained, with an initial

deceleration (usually taken as an index of orienting, or intake; Graham, 1973) followed by an acceleratory component and then by a secondary decelerative component. Figure 2.8 illustrates this cardiac pattern. Hedonic valence contributes to the amount of initial deceleration, as well as to the initial acceleratory activity, with unpleasant stimuli producing more initial deceleration and pleasant stimuli producing greater peak acceleration (Greenwald et al., 1989). As Figure 2.8 illustrates, greater initial heart rate deceleration is associated with viewing all unpleasant contents (Bradley, Codispoti, Cuthbert, & Lang, 2001), suggesting that, regardless of arousal, unpleasant material prompts greater initial orienting and attention. Overall, pleasant pictures tend to modulate the second, acceleratory component of the cardiac response to pictures, with increased peak acceleration, compared with viewing unpleasant pictures (Greenwald et al., 1989).

Cardiac reactions to pleasant pictures can, however, show substantial initial deceleration, especially when viewing arousing pleasant contents. Figure 2.8 illustrates data from a study in which participants viewed 24 pictures (8 pleasant, 8 neutral, 8 unpleasant) on one day and returned a week later to view 24 new pictures. For unpleasant pictures, initial deceleration is consistently obtained on both occasions. For pleasant pictures, on the other hand, initial deceleration is enhanced during the second session, with the most arousing contents, for example, erotica and adventure, prompting clear deceleration during the second viewing. One hypothesis is that, following exposure to the range of picture contents, participants voluntarily direct attention (orient) to pleasant stimuli, whereas this type of orienting is relatively more automatic for unpleasant contents. We have found that experiments that present a large number of pictures (i.e., allowing familiarity with picture contents), or that explicitly cue picture content, will tend to obtain sizable initial heart rate deceleration for highly arousing pleasant pictures. On the other hand, significant cardiac deceleration is a hallmark of affective processing for unpleasant pictures in all experimental contexts.

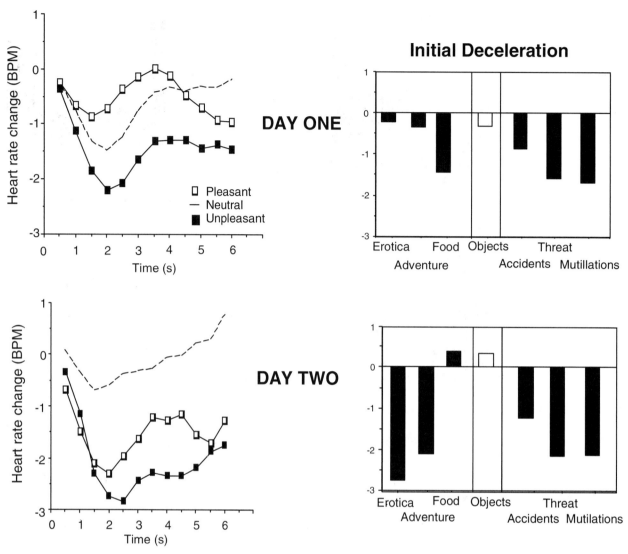

Figure 2.8. The triphasic cardiac waveform prompted by a 6 s presentation of IAPS pictures selected on the basis of normative ratings of pleasure (*left*) and for specific picture contents (*right*) for two sets of novel pictures viewed 1 week apart (first visit, *top*; second visit, *bottom*).

The modulation and shape of the cardiac waveform during picture viewing is highly dependent on the duration and presence of a sensory foreground. Pictures shown briefly for 500 ms result in a very brief decelerative response that does not differ as a function of hedonic valence (Codispoti, Bradley, & Lang, 2001). Thus cardiac activity during picture viewing appears to be tightly coupled to sensory information processing (i.e., orienting) and does not vary reliably with affect when picture presentation is brief and the stimulus no longer perceptually available. Consistent with this hypothesis, initial deceleration decreases quickly and ceases to be modulated by affective valence when the same pleasant, neutral, and unpleasant pictures are shown repeatedly in an experiment (Bradley, Lang, & Cuthbert, 1993), a context in which information intake is presumably low following repetitive exposure.

Cortical ERPs and Slow Wave Activity

When electrophysiological measures are assessed during picture viewing, specific event-related potentials and sustained positive slow wave activity are observed in response to emotionally arousing picture stimuli, irrespective of hedonic valence (Crites & Cacioppo, 1996; Cuthbert, Schupp, Bradley, Birbaumer, & Lang, 2000; Palomba, Angrilli, & Mini, 1997). Perhaps the most common finding, illustrated in Figure 2.9, is the modulation of a late positive potential, starting 300–400 ms after picture onset, that is larger when viewing either pleasant or unpleasant, compared with neutral, materials. Using a slow time constant, a sustained positive slow wave can additionally be seen that is maintained until the picture is terminated (Cuthbert et al., 2000). Topographically, the difference in the late positive potential due to affect is maximal over centroparietal cortex and is often more pronounced over the right hemisphere, as illustrated in Figure 2.9.

The magnitude of the late positive potential is greatest for pictures that are rated as most arousing, including, for pleasant pictures, erotica (and romance) and, for unpleasant pictures, mutilated bodies and human or animal threat (Schupp et al., 2004). Thus in a number of ways modulation of this ERP component is similar to that obtained in the skin conductance response—enhanced for the most arousing picture contents. The late positive potential is similar in topography to the P3 component that is obtained slightly earlier (i.e., starting around 300 ms) for simpler stimuli (e.g., letters, words, simple visual figures) and that is often interpreted as reflecting differences in attention or resource allocation (see Naatanen, 1988, for a overview). Assuming a slight delay in the timing of this component due to the relatively higher information load in the IAPS pictures, the late positive potential can be interpreted as reflecting increased attention for motivationally relevant stimuli (Lang et al., 1997). Consistent with the interpretation, emotionally arousing pictures are rated as more interesting than neutral stimuli, are voluntarily viewed for a longer period of time, and show inhibition of reaction time (RT) to simple or startling probes, all of which suggest that emotionally engaging pictures may elicit more attention or require additional resources (Bradley, Cuthbert, & Lang, 1999; Greenwald et al., 1989).

Blood-Oxygenation-Level-Dependent Neural Activity

Consistent with the ERP data, emotional pictures, whether pleasant or unpleasant, prompt greater blood-oxygenation-level-dependent (BOLD) changes than neutral pictures in occipital (particularly right hemisphere) cortex (Lang et al., 1998), including fusiform cortex, lateral occipital cortex, and medial parietal cortex, when pictures are shown to participants in the MRI scanner. Interestingly, BOLD signal changes vary directly with the rated level of arousal of different picture contents (Bradley et al., 2003) and are strikingly similar for both men and women (Sabatinelli, Flaisch, Bradley, Fitzsimmons, & Lang, 2004). The largest changes in the BOLD signal in visual fusiform cortex are obtained for highly arousing contents of erotica, threat, and mutilation, with significantly lower activity for pictures of babies, happy animals, and neutral objects. One hypothesis is that increased activation in these secondary visual cortex structures reflects reentrant processing from subcortical structures, particularly the amygdala. Indeed, Amaral, Price, Pitkanen, and Carmichel (1992) describe substantial input and output connections linking visual cortex to amygdaloid nuclei in the primate.

In a recent study (Sabatinelli, Bradley, Fitzsimmons & Lang, 2005), we measured BOLD activity in the amygdala and in the fusiform cortex for a variety of different picture

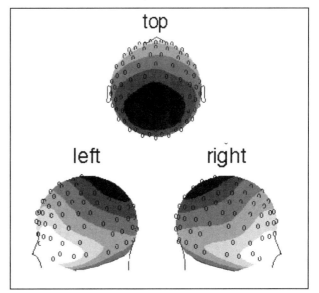

Figure 2.9. The event-related potential measured at Pz, Cz, and Fz during a 6 s presentation of IAPS pictures selected on the basis of normative ratings of pleasure, and the scalp distribution of the difference in a late positive potential (400–700 ms following picture onset) illustrating its centroparietal maximum (Keil et al., 2002).

contents, expecting significant covariation if these structures reflect motivational engagement. As Figure 2.10 (left) illustrates, significant activation was found in both the amygdala and the fusiform cortex when viewing affective pictures. Overall, the magnitude of BOLD signal change during picture viewing was higher in visual cortex, as might be expected for these sensory stimuli. Nonetheless, in both structures, emotionally arousing pictures prompted greater signal change than pictures rated lower in arousal. When BOLD activity was normalized within each structure, the pattern of activity was impressively similar across picture contents, with increases in fusiform activity clearly related to increased amygdala activity, and vice versa. Although correlational in nature, these data are consistent with the hypothesis that increased sensory activation during affective picture viewing is related to the amount of activation in subcortical, particularly amygdalar, regions. Moreover, highly arousing *pleasant* contents, as well as unpleasant pictures, prompted clear, measurable signal change in the amygdala, suggesting that this structure is not solely reactive to aversive cues.

Additional Affective Responses

A host of other affective reactions have been investigated in the context of viewing IAPS pictures, including modulation of the startle reflex (see Bradley, Cuthbert, & Lang, 1999,

for an overview), neuroendocrine reactions (e.g., Blake, Varnhagen, & Parent, 2001; Codispoti et al., 2003), respiratory changes (Ritz, 2004), metabolic brain changes (e.g., Lane, Reiman, Ahern, Schwartz, & Davidson, 1997), memory performance (Bradley, Greenwald, Petry, & Lang, 1992) and others. Many of the basic findings summarized in this chapter have been replicated and extended by researchers investigating both basic and applied issues in the study of emotion, which should encourage new researchers to consult the database regarding affective reactions to IAPS pictures prior to designing new studies In this way, the field can make systematic progress in understanding emotion, rather than producing parallel lines of research that do not benefit from existing knowledge.

Some IAPS Issues

Safety and Effectiveness

In order to study emotion, it is first necessary to induce an emotional state or reaction in the laboratory context. The IAPS picture stimuli are designed to do so in a safe, noninvasive manner, eliciting affective reactions in a controlled setting with the mental health of the participant in mind. Typically, insti-

Bilateral amygdala activation

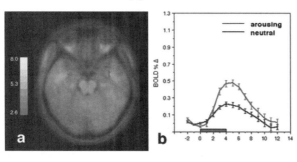

Bilateral fusiform cortex activation

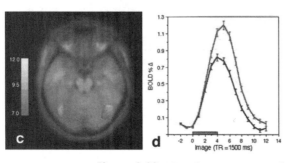

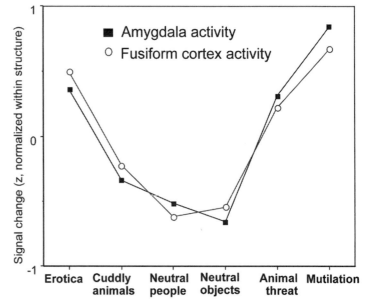

Figure 2.10. Neural activity measured in the amygdala (top left) and fusiform cortex (bottom left) using fMRI is increased when viewing emotionally arousing, compared with neutral, pictures, and both covary similarly with specific picture contents (Sabatinelli et al., 2004). See color insert.

tutional review board panels are often concerned with whether presenting IAPS pictures to participants is safe, asking: Are IAPS pictures *too strong* for inducing emotion in the lab? On the other hand, scientists and researchers are more likely to wonder whether IAPS pictures are effective, often asking: Are pictures *strong enough* to induce emotion in the lab? Similar responses apply to both queries.

The IAPS pictures vary in emotional provocation, from none or very little to those that are judged to evoke pleasant or unpleasant arousal. The pictures in the IAPS do not exceed in provocation the types of images that can be found on television or that are routinely seen in magazines and newspaper headlines (e.g., people brandishing guns at the viewer or dead victims of war as seen on a news program; the bloody organs in an open-heart operation on a medical channel; the erotic pictures in advertisements and on cable television stations). In fact, the most evocative IAPS images represent the sexual and violent content that people often actively seek out in both television viewing and in printed matter.

The intensity of affective responses to pictures is less than that elicited by the anticipation of real pleasures or actual dangers, as well as by actual pain or real erotic encounters. Compared with the anticipatory physiological reaction when a physician approaches a patient with a hypodermic needle, for instance, physiological reactions induced when viewing unpleasant pictures are quite small. Pictures are, after all, symbolic, rather than actual, stimuli. No matter how frightening a picture is, it cannot physically threaten; no matter how enticing an erotic or a food picture is, it will never satisfy. Nonetheless, it is indeed fortunate that, despite reduced reactions, these relatively small-scale responses are significantly correlated with judgments of pleasure and arousal, varying, presumably, in type and intensity with the more extended reactions caused by actual emotional events. Using pictures, emotion can be probed and studied in the laboratory with relative safety.

Of course, prior to picture presentation, participants should be informed about the range of content that may be presented (e.g., "Some of the pictures may include content that can be considered objectionable, such as sexually explicit pictures and violent pictures [threatening people, disfigured human bodies]."). And, with the possible exception of certain studies with clinical populations, participants should be discouraged from participating if they are apprehensive about some specific content (e.g., a small percentage of normal people are blood phobic). The participant's option in this case should be exactly the same as when one chooses not to turn on a particular television program, see a particular movie, or buy a particular magazine. It is well to keep in mind, furthermore, that even if one is eventually surprised by the impact of a picture, one can always close one's eyes—a simple option that is not often available in real life when emotionally provoked and a reason, perhaps, to monitor eye movements during picture viewing if possible.

After more than a decade of study, the research and clinical communities now have vast experience with these mate-rials. At the University of Florida alone, more than 3,000 normal participants have viewed a range of these picture stimuli. The IAPS has been used widely in clinical settings with a great variety of patients, including those with neurological disorders (e.g., Siebert, Markowitsch, & Bartel, 2003), PTSD and other anxiety disorders (e.g., Amdur, Larsen, & Liberzon, 2000; Shapira et al., 2003), drug abuse and dependency issues (e.g., Geier, Mucha, & Pauli, 2000; Gerra et al., 2003;), depression and anhedonia (e.g., Dichter, Tomarken, & Baucom, 2002), psychopathy (Patrick, 1994), food-related disorders (e.g., Drobes et al., 2001), and schizophrenia (e.g., Quirk & Strauss, 2001). Although emotionally arousing pictures prompt affective reactions, these evaluative and physiological responses are relatively transient—present during and shortly after viewing, but subsiding rapidly thereafter. Importantly, there have been no reported instigations or exacerbations of psychiatric conditions attributable to mere picture viewing.

Physical and Perceptual Characteristics

Because they are natural photographs, IAPS pictures can differ in perceptual characteristics, including color composition, brightness, contrast, luminosity, spatial frequency, and so forth. These physical differences can be controlled for in specific picture sets by using the many different digital editing software packages currently available (e.g., Photoshop). Pictures selected for use in specific studies can be adjusted to remove purely physical differences among stimulus sets. Importantly, whether pictures are presented in color or in gray scale has proven to have little or no effect on many indices of affective engagement, including autonomic, somatic, and BOLD neural activity (Bradley, Codispoti, Cuthbert, & Lang, 2001; Bradley et al., 2003), suggesting that presentation in gray scale might be a useful method for removing differences due sheerly to color composition. Differences in brightness and contrast, which together relate to luminosity, are easy to adjust using existing digital photo software, and spatial frequency (a measure of visual complexity) can be calculated and balanced across stimulus sets (e.g., Sabatinelli, Flaisch, Bradley, Fitzsimmons, & Lang, 2004).

Distribution and Access

The IAPS is currently distributed by the NIMH Center for the Study of Emotion and Attention (at the University of Florida) in digitized form on CD-ROM disks, together with files containing pleasure and arousal ratings for men and women. Over a thousand researchers worldwide have requested and received copies of the IAPS since its inception. It has been used in nearly every area of emotion science—psychophysiology, cognitive psychology, neuroscience, social psychology, neuropsychology, psychiatry, clinical psychology, and so forth. The IAPS continues to be distributed free of charge to academic investigators for their private use in nonprofit research; the IAPS is not available to corporate or other nonacademic research enterprises. And, the IAPS continues in its development; new experiments consistently require a larger number of pictures, both in terms of providing appropriate controls and in attaining appropriate cell sizes for experimental manipulations. We therefore continue to seek and to add new exemplars to the IAPS, routinely conducting new rating studies to provide additional norms for pleasure and arousal. We have noted that researchers will often add new exemplars of their own to the IAPS in order to increase the number of pictures in a particular category or to target a particular category (e.g., alcohol-related cues). Continued development of the IAPS would benefit greatly from a communal effort in which emotion scientists who develop new materials would send them to us (via CD) for possible inclusion in the IAPS. The only requirements for appropriate stimuli are that the pictures are in color and at least 1024 x 768 pixels in resolution.

Conclusion

Pictures may *truly* be worth a thousand words—certainly, in the alacrity with which they elicit emotional engagement. As visual cues, the perceptual information in pictures match many features of the actual objects they represent. Thus emotionally arousing contents capture attention promptly and activate the motivational systems on which human emotion is founded. With brief exposure, human participants report emotional experiences that vary reliably in pleasure, emotional arousal, and even in reports of specific emotional states. Importantly, the pictures also prompt autonomic and somatic reflexes of defense and appetite that confirm affective engagement. Moreover, electroencephalographic and neuroimaging studies clearly show enhanced activation to emotional pictures—increasing with emotional arousal—in visual cortex and in subcortical circuits implicated in attention and action. Thus the goal is well met: Experiments using pictures in the IAPS provide an increasingly sophisticated database regarding affective reactivity. Furthermore, the picture-viewing context has shown itself to be a powerful yet eminently controllable methodology that advances understanding of mechanism in normal emotion and potentially in pathological states. Finally, the availability of a large set of standardized affective stimuli to emotion researchers, each identified by number and with accompanying evaluative data, provides a foundation for exact replication and a true accumulation of knowledge across laboratories and paradigms—a distinct need for our young science.

Appendix: Instructions for Using SAM to Rate Pleasure and Arousal

The first SAM scale is the happy-unhappy scale, in which SAM ranges from a smiling figure to a frowning figure. At one extreme of this scale, you feel happy, pleased, satisfied, contented, hopeful. If you feel completely happy while viewing the picture, you can indicate this by filling in the bubble in the figure on the left. The other end of the scale indicates that you feel completely unhappy, annoyed, unsatisfied, melancholic, despairing, bored. You can indicate feeling completely unhappy by filling in the bubble in the figure on the right. The figures also allow you to describe intermediate feelings of pleasure. If you feel completely neutral, neither happy nor unhappy, fill in the bubble in the figure in the middle. If, in your judgment, your feeling of pleasure or displeasure falls *between* two of the figures, then fill in the circle between the figures. This allows you to make more finely graded ratings of how you feel when viewing the pictures.

The excited-versus-calm dimension is the second type of feeling that SAM represents. At one extreme of this scale, you feel stimulated, excited, frenzied, jittery, wide awake, aroused. If you feel completely aroused while viewing the picture, fill in the bubble in the figure at the left of the row. On the other hand, at the other end of the scale, you feel completely relaxed, calm, sluggish, dull, sleepy, unaroused. You can indicate that you feel completely calm by filling in the bubble in the figure at the right. As with the happy-unhappy scale, you can represent intermediate levels by filling in the bubble in any of the other figures. If you are not at all excited nor at all calm, fill in the figure in the middle. Again, if you wish to make a more finely tuned rating of how excited or calm you feel, fill in the circle between any of the pictures.

Acknowledgments

This work was supported in part by National Institute of Health grants DE 13956 and P50–MH072850 aa NIMH Behavioral Science grant to the Center for the Study of Emotion and Attention (CSEA), University of Florida, Gainesville, Florida. The many colleagues (faculty, post-doctoral associates, graduate and undergraduate assistants) who have contributed to the research described in this chapter over the years are too numerous to mention—many are cited in published research reports in the reference section. All have contributed importantly to the work summarized in this chapter and have energized this endeavor with their passion, their time, and their scholarly efforts.

Please send requests for reprints to either author at: NIMH Center for the Study of Emotion and Attention (CSEA), Box 112766 HSC, University of Florida, Gainesville, FL 32610–0165.

References

Amaral, D. G., Price, J. L., Pitkanen, A., & Carmichel, S. T. (1992). Anatomical organization of the primate amygdaloid complex. In J. Aggleton (Ed.), *The amygdala: Neurobiological aspects of emotion, attention, and mental dysfunction* (pp. 1–66). New York: Wiley.

Amdur, R. L., Larsen, R., & Liberzon, I. (2000). Emotional processing in combat-related posttraumatic stress disorder: A comparison with traumatized and normal controls. *Journal of Anxiety Disorders, 14*, 219–238.

Blake, T. M., Varnhagen, C. K., & Parent, M. B. (2001). Emotionally arousing pictures increase blood glucose levels and enhance recall. *Neurobiology of Learning and Memory, 75*, 262–273.

Bradley, M. M., Codispoti, M., Cuthbert, B. N., & Lang, P. J. (2001). Emotion and motivation: I. Defensive and appetitive reactions in picture processing. *Emotion, 1*, 276–298.

Bradley, M. M., Codispoti, M., Sabatinelli, D., & Lang, P. J. (2001). Emotion and motivation: II. Sex differences in picture processing. *Emotion, 1*, 300–319.

Bradley, M. M., Cuthbert, B. N., & Lang, P. J. (1999). Affect and the startle reflex. In M. E. Dawson, A. Schell, & A. Boehmelt (Eds.), *Startle modification: Implications for neuroscience, cognitive science and clinical science* (pp. 157–183). New York: Cambridge University Press.

Bradley, M. M., Greenwald, M. K., Petry, M. C., & Lang, P. J. (1992). Remembering pictures: Pleasure and arousal in memory. *Journal of Experimental Psychology: Learning, Memory and Cognition, 18*, 379–390.

Bradley, M. M., & Lang, P. J. (1994). Measuring emotion: The self-assessment manikin and the semantic differential. *Journal of Behavioral Therapy and Experimental Psychiatry, 25*, 49–59.

Bradley, M. M., Lang, P. J., & Cuthbert, B. N. (1993). Emotion, novelty, and the startle reflex: Habituation in humans. *Behavioral Neuroscience, 107*(6), 970–980.

Bradley, M. M., Sabatinelli, D., Lang, P. J., Fitzsimmons, J. R., King, W. M., & Desai, P. (2003). Activation of the visual cortex in motivated attention. *Behavioral Neuroscience, 117*, 369–380.

Codispoti, M., Bradley, M. M., & Lang, P. J. (2001). Affective reactions to briefly presented pictures. *Psychophysiology, 38*, 474–478.

Codispoti, M., Gerra, G., Montebarocci, O., Zaimovic, A., Raggi, M. A., & Baldaro, B. (2003). Emotional perception and neuroendocrine changes. *Psychophysiology, 40*, 863–868.

Cook, E. W., III, Atkinson, L., & Lang, P. J. (1987). Stimulus control and data acquisition for IBM PCs and compatibles. *Psychophysiology, 24*, 726.

Crites, S. L., & Cacioppo, J. T. (1996). Electrocortical differentiation of evaluative and nonevaluative categorizations. *Psychological Science, 7*, 318–321.

Cuthbert, B. N., Bradley, M. M., Zabaldo, D., Martinez, S., & Lang, P. J. (1994). Images for all ages: Women and emotional reactions. *Psychophysiology, 31*, S37.

Cuthbert, B. N., Schupp, H. T., Bradley, M. M., Birbaumer, N., & Lang, P. J. (2000). Brain potentials in affective picture processing: Covariation with autonomic arousal and affective report. *Biological Psychology, 52*, 95–111.

Davis, M. (2000). The role of the amygdala in conditioned and unconditioned fear and anxiety. In J. P. Aggleton (Ed.), *The amygdala* (Vol. 2, pp. 213–287). Oxford, UK: Oxford University Press.

Davis, M., & Lang, P. J. (2003). Emotion. In M. Gallagher &

R. J. Nelson (Eds.), *Handbook of psychology: Vol. 3. Biological psychology* (pp. 405–439). New York: Wiley.

Dichter, G. S., Tomarken, A. J., & Baucom, B. R. (2002). Startle modulation before, during and after exposure to emotional stimuli. *International Journal of Psychophysiology, 43*, 191–196.

Drobes, D. J., Miller, E. J., Hillman, C. H., Bradley, M. M., Cuthbert, B. N., & Lang, P. J. (2001). Food deprivation and emotional reactions to food cues: Implications for eating disorders. *Biological Psychology, 57*, 153–177.

Ekman, P. (1993). Facial expression and emotion. American Psychologist, *48*, 384–392.

Fanselow, M. S. (1994). Neural organization of the defensive behavior system responsible for fear. *Psychonomic Bulletin and Review, 1*, 429–438.

Geier, A., Mucha, R. F., & Pauli, P. (2000). Appetitive nature of drug cues confirmed with physiological measures in a model using pictures of smoking. *Psychopharmacology, 150*, 283–291.

Gerra, G., Baldaro, B., Zaimovic, A., Moi, G., Bussandri, M., Raggi, M. A., et al. (2003). Neuroendocrine responses to experimentally induced emotions among abstinent opioid-dependent subjects. *Drug and Alcohol Dependence, 71*, 25–35.

Graham, F. K. (1973). Habituation and dishabituation of responses innervated by the autonomic nervous system. In H. V. S. Peeke & M. J. Herz (Eds.), *Habituation* (Vol. 1, pp. 163–218). New York: Academic Press.

Greenwald, M. K., Cook, E. W., & Lang, P. J. (1989). Affective judgment and psychophysiological response: Dimensional covariation in the evaluation of pictorial stimuli. *Journal of Psychophysiology, 3*, 51–64.

Keil, A., Bradley, M. M., Hauk, O., Rochstroh, B., Elbert, T., & Lang, P. J. (2002). Large-scale neural correlates of affective picture-processing. *Psychophysiology, 39*, 641–649.

Lane, R. D., Reiman, E. M., Ahern, G. L., Schwartz, G. E., & Davidson, R. J. (1997). Neuroanatomical correlates of happiness, sadness, and disgust. *American Journal of Psychiatry, 154*, 926–933.

Lang, P. J. (1968). Fear reduction and fear behavior: Problems in treating a construct. In J. M. Schlien (Ed.), *Research in psychotherapy* (Vol. 3, pp. 90–103). Washington, DC: American Psychological Association.

Lang, P. J. (1980). Behavioral treatment and bio-behavioral assessment: Computer applications. In J. B. Sidowski, J. H. Johnson, & T. A. Williams (Eds.), *Technology in mental health care delivery systems* (pp. 119–137). Norwood, NJ: Ablex.

Lang, P. J. (1995). The emotion probe: Studies of motivation and attention. *American Psychologist, 50*, 371–385.

Lang, P. J., Bradley, M. M., & Cuthbert, B. N. (1990). Emotion, attention, and the startle reflex. *Psychological Review, 97*, 377–395.

Lang, P. J., Bradley, M. M., & Cuthbert, M. M. (1997). Motivated attention: Affect, activation and action. In P. J. Lang, R. F. Simons, & M. T. Balaban (Eds.), *Attention and orienting: Sensory and motivational processes* (pp. 97–135). Hillsdale, NJ: Erlbaum

Lang, P. J., Bradley, M. M., & Cuthbert, B. N. (2005). *International Affective Picture System (IAPS): Affective ratings of pictures and instruction manual.* Technical Report no. A-6. University of Florida, Gainesville, Fl.

Lang, P. J., Bradley, M. M, Fitzsimmons, J. R., Cuthbert, B. N., Scott, J. D., Moulder, B., et al. (1998). Emotional arousal and activation of the visual cortex: An fMRI analysis. *Psychophysiology, 35,* 199–210.

Lang, P. J., Greenwald, M. K., Bradley, M. M., & Hamm, A. O. (1993). Looking at pictures: Affective, facial, visceral, and behavioral reactions. *Psychophysiology, 30,* 261–273.

Larsen, J. T., Norris, C. J., & Cacioppo, J. T. (2003). Effects of positive and negative affect on electromyographic activity over zygomaticus major and corrugator supercilii. *Psychophysiology, 40,* 776–785.

LeDoux, J. E. (1990). Information flow from sensation to emotion plasticity in the neural computation of stimulus values. In M. Gabriel & J. Moore (Eds.), *Learning and computational neuroscience: Foundations of adaptive networks* (pp. 3–52). Cambridge, MA: Bradford Books/MIT Press.

McManis, M. H., Bradley, M. M., Berg, W. K., Cuthbert, B. N., & Lang, P. J. (2001). Emotional reactivity in children: Verbal, physiological, and behavioral responses to affective pictures. *Psychophysiology, 38,* 222–231.

Mehrabian, A., & Russell, J. A. (1974). *An approach to environmental psychology.* Cambridge, MA: MIT Press.

Molto, J., Montanes, S., Poy, R., Segarra, P., Pastor, M. C., Tormo, M. P., et al. (1999). Un nuevo metodo para el estudio experimental de las emociones: El International Affective Picture System (IAPS): Adaptacion Espanola. *Revista de Psicologia General y Aplicada, 52,* 55–87.

Naatanen, R., (1988). Implications of ERP data for psychological theories of attention. *Biological Psychology, 26,* 117–163.

Ortony, A., Clore, G. L., & Collins, A. (1988). *The cognitive structure of emotions.* Cambridge, UK: Cambridge University Press.

Osgood, C., Suci, G., & Tannenbaum, P. (1957). *The measurement of meaning.* Urbana, IL: University of Illinois Press.

Palomba, D., Angrilli, A., & Mini, A. (1997). Visual evoked potentials, heart rate responses and memory to emotional pictorial stimuli. *International Journal of Psychophysiology, 27,* 55–67.

Patrick, C. J. (1994). Emotion and psychopathy: Startling new insights. *Psychophysiology, 31,* 319–330.

Quirk, S. W., & Strauss, M. E. (2001). Visual exploration of emotion eliciting images by patients with schizophrenia. *Journal of Nervous Mental Disorders, 189,* 757–765.

Ritz, T. (2004). Probing the psychophysiology of the airways: Physical activity, experienced emotiona nd facially expressed emotion. *Psychophysiology, 41,* 809–821.

Russell, J. (1980). A circumplex model of affect. *Journal of Personality and Social Psychology, 39,* 1161–1178.

Sabatinelli, D., Bradley, M. M., Fitzsimmons, J. R., & Lang, P. J. (2005). Parallel amygdala and inferotemporal activation reflect emotional intensity and fear relevance. *NeuroImage, 24,* 1265–1270.

Sabatinelli, D., Flaisch, T., Bradley, M. M.,. Fitzsimmons, J. R., & Lang, P. J. (2004). Affective picture perception: Gender differences in visual cortex. *NeuroReport, 15,* 1109–1112.

Schupp, H. T., Cuthbert, B. N., Bradley, M. M., Hillman, C. H., Hamm, A. O., & Lang, P. J. (2004). Brain processes in emotional perception: Motivated attention. *Cognition and Emotion, 18,* 593–611.

Shapira, N. A., Liu, Y., He, A. G., Bradley, M. M., Lessig, M. C., James, G. A,. et al. (2003). Brain activation by disgust-inducing pictures in obsessive-compulsive disorder. *Biological Psychiatry, 54,* 751–756.

Shaver, P., Schwartz, J., Kirson, D., & O'Connor, C. (1987). Emotion knowledge: Further exploration of a prototype approach. *Journal of Personality and Social Psychology, 52,* 1061–1086.

Siebert, M., Markowitsch, H. J., & Bartel, P. (2003). Amygdala, affect and cognition: Evidence from 10 patients with Urbach-Wiethe disease. *Brain, 126,* 2627–2637.

Stevens, S. S. (1961). To honor Fechner and repeal his law. *Science, 133,* 80–86.

Tellegen, A. (1985). Structure of mood and personality and their relevance to assessing anxiety, with an emphasis on self-report. In T. A. Hussain & J. D. Maser (Eds.), *Anxiety and anxiety disorders* (pp. 681–706). Hillsdale, NJ: Erlbaum.

Verschuere, B., Crombez, G. Z., & Koster, E. (2001). The International Affective Picture System: A Flemish validation study. *Psychologica Belgica, 41,* 205–217.

Vila, J., Sanchez, M., Ramirez, I., Fernandez, M. C., Cobos, P., Rodriguez, S., et al. (2001). El sistema internacional de imagines afectivas (IAPS): Adaptacion Espanola (Segunda parte). *Revista de Psicologia General y Aplicada, 54,* 635–657.

Wundt, W. (1896). *Lectures on human and animal psychology* (J. E. Creighton & E. B. Titchener, Trans.). New York: Macmillan.

Paul Ekman

The Directed Facial Action Task

Emotional Responses Without Appraisal

In this chapter I first describe how my colleagues and I came up with the idea that voluntary facial actions could generate other emotional responses. Then I discuss the experiments we performed and how we attempted to rule out artifacts that might have been responsible for the phenomena. In a set of studies we showed the generality of our findings over age, sex, and culture. Next I discuss two theoretical issues: (1) whether voluntarily moving our facial muscles actually generates emotion and (2) three alternative explanations of the way voluntary actions generate emotional responses. Last, for those who might want to use the Directed Facial Action Task (DFA), I include the nuts-and-bolts information about how to administer it.

Wallace Friesen and I discovered this phenomenon by accident in the course of developing the Facial Action Coding System (FACS; Ekman & Friesen, 1978; Ekman, Friesen, & Hager, 2002). In order to verify which specific muscles generate each change in the appearance of the face, we systematically contracted all of the single muscles and then all the possible combinations of two, three, four, and five muscles and videotaped the expressions we each produced. Each of us found (before telling the other) that sometimes we experienced very strong physical sensations and sometimes also the imagery associated with an emotion.

Once we focused our attention on this and repeated the combinations of facial actions, which generated often quite unpleasant feelings, we noted that this happened only when we performed the muscular configurations that resembled the universal expressions of emotion we had identified a few years earlier. Not knowing how to measure the physiology of emotion, we were not able to study this until a few years later when Robert Levenson spent his sabbatical in our laboratory. Combining his expertise in measuring changes in autonomic nervous system (ANS) activity with our specification to the participants about which muscles to contract, we performed our first experiment.

The Experiments

We found that different patterns of ANS activity were generated by the muscular configurations for the expressions of anger, fear, and disgust. We asked the same participants to also attempt to relive emotional experiences. In the publication of our findings in *Science* (Ekman, Levenson, & Friesen, 1983), we noted that the anger-versus-fear differences we found with the DFA also occurred with the relived-emotions task. This consistency in the emotion-specific patterns of ANS activity generated by the DFA and the more conventional relived-emotions task was later replicated and extended to differences among anger, fear, disgust, and sadness (Levenson, Carstensen, Friesen & Ekman, 1991).

We believe that the consistency in the emotion-specific ANS patterns found in these two very different tasks argues that specificity is not task specific but emotion specific. It supports my (Ekman, 1999) proposal that there are many ways to access emotion but that, once emotions are switched on, there are similarities in the response patterns (facial expression and ANS at least) regardless of the access route.

Before going further, it is important to note that we did not ask our participants to pose emotions. For example, instead of asking a participant to pose anger, we gave the following instruction:

- Pull your eyebrows down and together.
- Raise your upper eyelids.
- Now tighten your lower eyelids.
- Narrow, tighten, and press your lips together, pushing your lower lip up a little.

Another set of four experiments (Levenson, Ekman, & Friesen, 1990) ruled out many possible artifacts and refined our findings. The DFA produced significant autonomic distinctions among the emotions and significant subjective experience of emotion. These distinctions were stronger when the participants reported experiencing the emotion associated with a facial configuration; the distinctions were also stronger when the facial configurations the participants produced most closely resembled the universal expressions that the instructions requested them to make. Additionally, in this and another set of experiments (Levenson et al., 1991), we showed that the findings were not limited by:

- the participant's sex;
- the participant's age;
- the participant's background (in the original study we examined actors; in later studies we examined college students and retired persons);
- group as compared with participant-by-participant analyses;
- the fact that we did not require that participants see their faces in a mirror or on the experimenter's face (other features of the original study).

To show that our findings could not be attributed to differences in the difficulty of making the various facial configurations, we reported (1) the participants' ratings of how difficult it was to make each facial expression, (2) the results of other studies that had identified how difficult it was to deliberately perform each facial action (Ekman, Roper, & Hager, 1980), and (3) measures of the pattern of physiology shown on a trial in which the participants produced a non-emotional face. Nevertheless, a few years later Boiten (1996) performed an experiment that suggested to him that our findings were due to differences in the difficulty in making the various facial contractions. In a reanalysis of Boiten's data and further analyses of our own data we showed this was not the case (Levenson & Ekman, 2002).

We were concerned that the participants might have inferred from the muscular instructions which emotion we were trying to generate on each trial. Perhaps it was such knowledge rather than the muscular movements per se that produced the emotion-specific changes in ANS activity. To check on this, we had participants in one of our experiments read the instructions for making the faces without making the facial movements. Instead, they were asked to guess the associated emotion for each set of instructions. Almost no one could identify fear from the instructions for making that face, and more than half of the participants failed to identify anger or disgust from their instructions, suggesting that this was not the means by which the emotion-specific ANS activity was generated.

In another experiment, we (Levenson, Ekman, Heider, & Friesen, 1992) replicated our DFA findings in a culture as different from our own as we could find at that time. We studied the Minangkabau of Western Sumatra, a matrilineal, Muslim, agrarian culture.

In one more experiment, I collaborated with Richard Davidson in examining central nervous system activity generated by the DFA. For theoretical reasons, we focused on just the comparison between two voluntarily made facial configurations. Earlier we (Davidson, Ekman, Saron, Senulis, & Friesen, 1990) had found different patterns of regional electroencephalography (EEG) when participants who were watching motion picture films had shown just the action of the muscle producing the smile and the action of that muscle plus one of the muscles orbiting the eye. This fit with the findings from many other studies that it is only the latter expression that signals enjoyment. I have called this smile of enjoyment involving zygomatic major and orbicularis oculi, pars lateralis (in FACS terms 6+12) the Duchenne smile, for it was the French neurologist who first observed this phenomenon (Ekman, Davidson, & Friesen, 1990). We gave the participants the instructions to make each type of smile and replicated the finding with spontaneous behavior. Only the DFA instruction for the Duchenne smile generated the pattern of regional brain activity observed in many other studies for enjoyment (Ekman & Davidson, 1993). The point for us here is that this study showed that the DFA generates not only different patterns of autonomic activity but also different patterns of central nervous system activity.

Is It Emotion?

Despite these findings, replicated in a half-dozen experiments across cultures, sex, and age and examined in ANS and CNS measures, the question remains as to whether the DFA is generating emotion or just the physiology of emotion. The answer depends on whether one believes that there is a gold standard for emotion that is missing in these studies. For some that gold standard is the very physiological changes we have obtained.

Nearly all emotion theorists agree (Ekman & Davidson, 1994, chapter 1) that emotion incorporates phenomenological experience, a distinctive expression in the face and/or voice, cognitive appraisal, physiological activation, and some form of coping. I (Ekman, 1977) have argued that the presence of any one of these elements is not sufficient to establish that an emotion has occurred, nor is the absence of any one sufficient to establish that an emotion has not occurred. Instead, confidence that an emotion has occurred increases with the number of elements present.

In the DFA studies, facial expression (voluntarily performed) and physiological activation have been achieved. Although I do not believe that self-report is the gold standard, we found that most participants reported experiencing emotion during the DFA and that it was the emotion that we intended to target in the instructions for each trial. Interestingly, these self-reports increased when the facial configuration most closely conformed to the facial configurations the instructions called for.

For those still worried that it was demand characteristics—knowledge of the label from the muscle-by-muscle instructions—that produced the self-reports, our rejoinder (mentioned earlier) is that less than 3% of our participants could identify fear from the instructions, yet we obtained a report of feeling fear from a substantial proportion of those who made the muscular movements.

What is missing is the events that typically precede an emotional experience and appraisal of those events. I do not argue that that is not an important part of emotional experience. Instead, I suggest that it is not essential to generate some of the elements of emotional experience. That is interesting in and of itself—that elements of emotion can be generated without appraisal. Note that I am not saying that there is no cognition, for certainly the individual is thinking hard to try to get the facial muscles to contract. But it is not appraisal as it has been conceived of by those who have written about it.

This capacity for the physiology of emotion (at least some important parts of it; the full extent we do not yet know) and subjective experience to be generated by making a face, when combined with Ulf Dimberg's (1982) findings that we often unwittingly imitate faces we see, suggests that the phenomena we have substantiated may play a contributing role in empathy. Those who imitate the expression they see may feel at least some of what the expresser is feeling on the inside. If I see someone suffering, for example, and my face unwittingly assumes the sufferer's expression (Dimburg, 1982), our research suggests that I will begin to experience the physiology of suffering.

"Put on a happy face," the song goes, and you will feel happy. That is what we have found. Can you use voluntarily performed facial actions to change an emotional state, to help get out of a mood saturated with a different emotion? We were unable to get funding to support research on those matters. I suspect that making an emotional face will not overcome a contrary mood or emotion, because I think that when the involuntary system has a grip on our emotion system, it is not easy to interfere with it. But that is conjecture, untested.

Let me turn now to a discussion of the mechanisms that might explain how making an expression generates physiological and subjective emotional responses.

Explanations

There are three quite different explanations of how voluntary facial actions generate emotion-specific physiology (Ekman, 1992). The first explanation, which I endorse, posits a central, hardwired connection between the motor cortex and other areas of the brain involved in directing the physiological changes that occur during emotion. Usually, when emotions are aroused by perception of a social event, a set of central commands produce patterned emotion-specific changes in multiple systems, including (but not limited to) such peripheral systems as facial expressions, vocalizations, skeletal muscular settings, and ANS activity. When there is no emotion operative, as in our experiments, but one set of those commands is generated deliberately, the established emotion networks transmit the other emotion-specific response changes. The initiating action need not be a facial expression; emotion-specific vocalizations or respiration patterns, for example, should do just as well. (We have preliminary data to support the idea that deliberately made vocalizations generate emotion-specific ANS changes.)

A second group of alternative explanations propose that any connection between expression and physiological change is learned, not hardwired. The extreme version of this viewpoint sees emotions as totally socially constructed and has no reason to expect that there always will be both an expression and a unique pattern of physiology in every emotion, let alone any connection between the two. Emotion-specific ANS activity might be learned only in those cultures that teach their members specific adaptive behaviors for an emotion, and there would be no reason for every culture to do so or, if they did, to teach the same adaptive pattern. If anger exists in two cultures, and it certainly need not in every culture, there would be no necessary reason for anger to be associated with fighting and the physiology that subserves such actions in any two cultures. Nor would there be any reason for expressions to be learned and associated with any physiology.

Our findings, reported earlier, of the same emotion-specific ANS physiology and the capability for voluntary facial action to generate that activity in a Moslem matrilineal Indonesian culture challenge such a radical social constructivist view. A more moderate social learning position, which allowed for universals in both expression and physiology, might still claim that the link between the two is learned, not hardwired—established through repeated co-occurrence.

A third set of alternative explanations emphasizes peripheral feedback from the facial actions themselves rather than a central connection between the brain areas that direct facial movements and other brain areas. This view includes variations in terms of whether the feedback comes from the muscles, skin, or temperature changes and whether such feedback is hardwired or requires learning. This explanation is consistent with the views of Izard (1977), Laird (1974), Tomkins (1962), and Zajonc (1985).

We had hoped to challenge the second and third explanation in our studies of a dozen individuals with Moebius syndrome, a congenital absence of the facial nerve. Never able to make a facial movement because nothing connects their motor cortex to the facial muscles, they nevertheless have an intact motor cortex. It is likely that the part of the motor cortex responsible for directing facial movement has been largely taken over by other motor areas, but something should remain. If these people tried to make an expression, the first explanation, the one we endorse, would suggest that because the commands would register in other brain areas, we would be able to observe the emotion-specific physiology.

It didn't work. The people with Moebius syndrome found it very hard and very frustrating to try to make facial movements they had never been able to bring into action. My encouragement, "it doesn't matter that your face won't move, just send the message for the movements," either baffled or frustrated them. And we had no way to determine whether they were succeeding in issuing the motor commands, as their faces could not move.

For now there is no clear empirical basis for a definitive choice among these three explanations. Now let's turn to the practical section of this chapter: how to administer the DFA.

Administering the DFA

Pretest, Practice, Selection of Participants

Some of the movements required in the DFA are difficult for many people to make. Raising just the inner corners of the eyebrows (part of the sadness configuration), pulling the lip corners down (another required movement for the sadness configuration), raising the entire eyebrow and drawing the brows together (part of the fear configuration), raising the cheeks (required for the happiness configuration), and lowering the eyebrows while at the same time raising the upper eyelid and tightening the lower eyelids (required for the anger configuration) cause the most trouble. Although there is a tendency for those who have difficulty with one set of movements to have difficulty with other facial movements that are not easy to make, that is not always the case. The movements for the disgust and surprise configurations are easy for nearly everyone to make.

One approach we have taken is to screen participants in advance of scheduling them for the actual experiment and rejecting those who can not make all of the difficult movements. Because attaching the leads for the physiological measures takes much time and ties up a lab, we found such screening to be useful. Another approach was to provide potential participants with a practice document, which described and visually depicted every one of the movements that would be required. We asked them to practice trying to make the movements, looking in a mirror to compare their performance with the ones shown in the provided illustrations. Those who succeeded after practice then contacted us to be scheduled for participation in the experiment. (The facial movement practice instructions are included in appendix A).

Instructing the Participants

A coach provides the instructions over an intercom, observing the participants as they attempt to conform to the instructions, giving them feedback if they succeed, and telling them what they are doing wrong if they do not succeed. The coach might say, for example: "You are raising the entire eyebrow, we want you just to raise the inner corners of the eyebrow"; "when you raised your upper eyelids you relaxed your eyebrows; you have to keep the eyebrows lowered when you raise your upper eyelids"; and so forth. We believe the coach must be experienced in using the Facial Action Coding System (FACS; Ekman & Friesen, 1978; Ekman, Friesen, & Hager 2002) in order to provide such feedback and encouragement, but we never tried using an inexperienced person as a coach.

In most of our studies, participants could not see their faces in a mirror. Participants do find it much easier and less frustrating, but sometimes embarrassing, if they can observe in a mirror or on a video monitor their attempts to follow the instructions. And we found no difference in the physiological findings between the groups who saw and those who did not see themselves in a mirror. (We have not analyzed the data to determine whether the subjective reports are influenced by the presence of a mirror).

A trial is composed of the following segments:

- A standard set of movements unrelated to emotion to provide a comparison against each emotion configuration performance. ("Close your mouth and puff your cheeks out gently and close your eyes"). Once the movements are made, the individual is asked to hold the configuration for 15 seconds.
- The emotional configuration instructions (discussed shortly). Once the performance is achieved, the participant is asked to hold the configuration for 15 seconds. If the person does not achieve the required configuration within 3 seconds (or earlier if the coach becomes convinced the person will not be able to make the movements), he or she is told to hold whatever configuration he or she has produced.
- A 30-second rest.
- Asking the participant, "What emotions did you feel?" If the free responses do not obviously fall into one of the emotions targeted by the instructions, participants are asked to provide more information about the emotion they experienced.
- If a participant reports feeling an emotion, he or she is asked, "Using a scale of 0 to 8, with 0 being no emotion and 8 being the most [reported emotion] you

have ever felt in your life, and 4 being moderate, how much did you feel just now when you made the face?"

- Asking the participant, "Did you feel any bodily sensation? Any memories?"
- Asking for a difficulty rating: "Using a scale of 0 to 8, with 0 being very easy, 8 being extremely difficult, and 4 being moderate, how difficult was it to make the face?"
- A 2-minute rest period.

The instructions for the facial configurations are:

- "Pull your eyebrows down and together. Raise your upper eyelids. Now tighten your lower eyelids. Narrow, tighten, and press your lips together, pushing your lower lip up a little." Once the configuration is achieved: "Now hold that face." (This is the instruction for anger, but the emotion is never mentioned to the participant.)
- "Wrinkle your nose, let your lips part. Pull your lower lip down. Let your tongue move forward in your mouth but you don't need to stick it out." Once the configuration is achieved: "Now hold that face." (This is the instruction for disgust.)
- "Raise your eyebrows as high as you can and pull the inner corners of your brows together. Raise your upper eyelids and tighten your lower eyelids. Let your mouth drop open and stretch your lips horizontally. It may help to use a muscle in your neck to pull your lip corners horizontally." Once the configuration is achieved: "Now hold that face." (This is the instruction for fear.)
- "Raise the inner corners of your eyebrows and pull them up and together in the center of your forehead. Pull the corners of your lips down. Raise your cheeks and pull your lip corners up against the downward pull. Glance down." Once the configuration is achieved: "Now hold that face." (This is the instruction for sadness.)
- "Raise your cheeks. If it is hard to do try squinting a little. Part your lips and let your lip corners come up." Once the configuration is achieved: "Now hold that face." (This is the instruction for happiness.)

In order to obtain a measure of the physiological activity produced by making difficult facial configurations, we always included also the following set of instructions for a nonemotional facial configuration: "Raise your eyebrows. Tighten your lower eyelids. Close one eye. Pucker your lips. Puff your cheeks out gently."

In our experiments, we always used two different orders for presenting the instructions.

Other Data Recorded About the Facial Performances

The coach recorded his or her judgment about the quality of the performance on a 4-point scale, from worthless to excellent. The coach also noted the presence of signs of embarrassment, amusement, or relief.

A trained FACS coder viewed each videotaped performance and, following very exact instructions, rated each performance on a 4-point scale of perfect, good (specific actions that must have been shown are specified for each configuration), minimal (specific actions that must have been shown are specified for this rating for each configuration), or disqualified (the failure to provide the minimal actions and/or the addition of specified actions that could involve the evocation of another emotion). A copy of this rating procedure is provided in appendix B. It is important to note that we did *not* find emotion-specific ANS activity in those trials that were rated as disqualified or minimal. Furthermore, the higher the quality rating, the more pronounced the emotion-specific activity.

Appendix A: Screening for the Directed Facial Action (DFA) Task

Paul Ekman and Wallace V. Friesen

The tape for training you to screen subjects for inclusion in a study that includes the DFA contains:

- A rehearsed portrayal of each of the muscle contractions or combination of muscle contractions that are to be requested during the screening.
- Actual screening sessions of subjects who varied in their ability to perform the requested actions.

In addition to the tape you will need 10 copies of the screening form that you will be using when actually seeing potential subjects.

Instructions

Study the rehearsed portrayals of the first section carefully. Be sure that you can recognize each requested action.

If possible, ask your friends to be subjects and have them perform each requested action as you rate their performance.

View each requested action for the actual screening sessions and rate the quality of each performance. View each performance only once and in real time.

SUBJECT #_____ NAME:_____DATE: _____
VIDEOTAPE # _____
EXPERIMENTER:_____

In this experiment we are going to ask you to perform several muscle actions on your face. Use the mirror to help you perform each of the actions that I instruct you to make.

Don't be discouraged if you can't make the action at first. I will be coaching you when you have difficulty and will be offering hints about how to make each action.

*** EYEBROWS ***

EASY	DIFF	NO	EMBAR.	
2	1*	0*	E	Raise your eyebrows. Raise them as high as you can. (PHOTO Action Units (AU): 1+2)
2	1*	0*	E	Lower your eyebrows and draw them together. (PHOTO AU: 4)
2	1*	0*	E	Combine both of the movements you have made. Raise your eyebrows up and also pull them together. (PHOTO AU: 1 + 2 +4)
2	1*	0*	E	This time raise just the inner corners of your eyebrows and pull them together. (PHOTO AU: 1+4) IF PROBLEMS, THEN REVERSE THE ORDER OF THE ACTIONS. Pull your eyebrows together and then lift the inner corners.

*** EYES ***

EASY	DIFF	NO	EMBAR.	
2	1*	0*	E	Raise your upper eyelid, trying to expose the white above your eyeball. (PHOTO AU: 5)
2	1*	0*	E	Raise your eyelid as high as you can, exposing as much of your upper eyeball as you can. (PHOTO AU: 5E)
2	1*	0*	E	Raise your eyelid just a little bit, exposing very little of your upper eyeball (PHOTO AU: 5A)
2	1*	0*	E	Tighten your lower eyelid (PHOTO AU: 7)
2	1*	0*	E	Combine the last two actions. Raise your upper eyelid and then tighten your lower eyelid. (PHOTO AU: 5E + 7)
2	1*	0*	E	Glance down, but don't close your eyes. (PHOTO AU: 64)
2	1*	0*	E	Close your eyes. (PHOTO AU: 43)
2	1*	0*	E	Now close just one eye. (PHOTO AU: U43) LEFT RIGHT

*** LOWER FACE ***

EASY	DIFF	NO	EMBAR.	
2	1*	0*	E	Push your lower lip up while pressing your lips together. (PHOTO AU: 17 + 24)
2	1*	0*	E	Pull the corners of your lips down: just do it slightly, while slightly pushing your lower lip up. (PHOTO AU: 15B + 17A)
2	1*	0*	E	Wrinkle your nose, letting your lips part. (PHOTO AU: 9)
2	1*	0*	E	Pull your lower lip downwards, exposing the roots of your lower teeth. (PHOTO AU: 16)
2	1*	0*	E	Let the corners of your lips come up. (PHOTO AU: 12E)
2	1*	0*	E	Do the same thing but just on one side of your face (PHOTO AU: U12C) RIGHT LEFT
2	1*	0*	E	Tighten your lip corner on just one side of your face. (PHOTO AU: U14) RIGHT LEFT
2	1*	0*	E	Stretch your mouth horizontally, pulling your lip corners back toward your ears. (PHOTO AU: 20)
2	1*	0*	E	Let your mouth drop open. (PHOTO AU: 26)
2	1*	0*	E	Raise your cheeks. (PHOTO AU: 6) IF PROBLEMS THEN: Try closing your eyes and squeezing them shut. Then do it less severely with your eyes open.
2	1*	0*	E	Let your tongue move forward in your mouth, but you don't need to stick it out.
2	1*	0*	E	Pucker your lips. (PHOTO AU: 18)
2	1*	0*	E	Close your mouth and puff your cheeks out gently. (PHOTO AU: 34)
2	1*	0*	E	Tilt your head back and to the side a little. (PHOTO AU: 55 + 58 or 56 + 59) LEFT RIGHT

* DISQUALIFY IF ANY RATING CIRCLED THAT IS ASTERISKED.

Appendix B: Criteria for Rating DFA Performances

Paul Ekman

0 = WORTHLESS . . . The subject couldn't do any of the critical Action Units (AUs); or the subject did the wrong emotion; or the subject included AUs which would almost certainly make it a blend with another emotion.

1 = POOR . . . About the worst performance you could see and still not want to throw it away. It could be bad because they had such a hard time doing it and couldn't hold it for more than a second. Or it could be that not all of the critical AUs were included (and by that I don't mean all of the AUs we asked for, but the ones that we think are most important). Or it could be that they included some other AUs which might cause a blend, but you can't be absolutely sure.

2 = FAIR . . . No real problem other that it isn't great. There is no problem of a blend, and it might include the most important AUs, but it isn't really good. It might have taken a long time to get it or not be held the whole time. An important AU like AU5 might drop out after a second or two. If a face with all critical AUs is performed with no blend AUs, the rating should be at least a 2, even if the AUs fade before the end of the trial.

3 = GOOD . . . All the critical AUs are performed, and it wasn't an ordeal getting him or her to do it, and it held most of the time. Nothing wrong with it but it isn't the best you have seen.

4 = EXCELLENT . . . One of the best performances. Done readily, held throughout, all of the AUs asked for. Convincing job.

ANGER:

REQUESTED AUs:	4CDE + 5CDE + 7CDE + 17 + 23 + 24
CRITICAL AUs:	4 + 5 + 23 or 4 + 5 + 24
BLEND AUs:	1, 2, 6, 9, 11, 12, 13, 14CDE, 20CDE, 43

CONTEMPT:

REQUESTED AUs:	R12 + R14 + [55ABC OR 56ABC] + 58ABC L12 + L14 + [55ABC OR 56ABC] + 58ABC
CRITICAL AUs:	U12 OR U14
BLEND AUs	1 ALONE, 2 ALONE, 1 +2 + 4, 4CDE, 5CDE, 9, 10, 11, 13, 15, 16, 17BCDE, 18, 19, 20, 21, 22, 23, 24, 25, 26, 27, BILATERAL 6, 7, OR 12BCDE

(The combination of 1 + 2 would not create a blend.)

DISGUST:

REQUESTED AUs:	9 + [10 AND/OR 16] + 19 + 26
CRITICAL AUs:	9
BLEND AUs:	1, 2, 11, 12, 13, 14, 15, 20CDE, 22, 23, 24

FEAR:

REQUESTED AUs:	1+ 2 + 4 + 5ABCDE + 7 + 20ABCDE + 26

CRITICAL AUs: 1 + 2 + 4
BLEND AUs: 9, 10DE unless 20 within one intensity point, 12BCDE[1], 13, 14CDE[1], 15VCDE[1], 17CDE, 18, 22, 23, 24, 43

[1] If 20CDE, then 12A, 14AB or 15A will not disqualify. If 20ABCDE, then 14A will not disqualify.

HAPPY:
REQUESTED AUs: [6 AND/OR 7] WITH 12CDE
CRITICAL AUs: 6 + 12
BLEND AUs: 1, 2, 4, 9, 10>=12, 14BCDE, 15, 17BCDE, 18, 19, 20>12, 21, 22, 23, 24BCDE.

SAD:
REQUESTED AUs: 1 + 4 + [6 AND/OR 7] + 15ABC + 64
CRITICAL AUs: 1 + 4 + 6
BLEND AUs: 2, 9, 10, 12>15, 13, 14, 16CDE, 17DE, 20>15 (by 2 intensity points), 22, 23, 24, 27.

SURPRISE:
REQUESTED AUs: 1CDE + 2CDE + 5AB +26
CRITICAL AUs: 1ABCDE + 2ABCDE + 26
    or 1ABCDE + 2ABCDE + 5AB
    or 5AB + 26
BLEND AUs: 1>2 BY more than intensity points, 4, 5CDE, 6, 7, 9, 10, 11, 12, 13, 14, 15, 17, 19, 20, 21, 23, 24, 43

EFFORT FACE:
REQUESTED AUs: 1 + 2 + 7 + 18 + 34 + U43
CRITICAL AUs: 1 + 2 + 18 + 34
BLEND AUs: 5, 6, 9, 10, 11, 12, 13, 14, 19, 23

References

Boiten, F. (1996). Autonomic response patterns during voluntary facial action. *Psychophysiology, 33,* 123–131.

Davidson, R. J., Ekman, P., Saron, C., Senulis, J., & Friesen, W. V. (1990). Emotional expression and brain physiology: I. Approach/withdrawal and cerebral asymmetry. *Journal of Personality and Social Psychology, 58,* 330–341.

Dimburg, U. (1982). Facial reactions to facial expressions. *Psychophysiology, 19,* 643–647.

Ekman, P. (1977). Biological and cultural contributions to body and facial movement. In J. Blacking (Ed.), *Anthropology of the body* (pp. 34–84). London: Academic Press.

Ekman, P. (1992). Facial expressions of emotion: An old controversy and new findings. *Philosophical Transactions of the Royal Societ., 35,* 63–69.

Ekman, P. (1999) Basic emotions. In T. Dalgleish & T. Power (Eds.), *Handbook of cognition and emotion* (pp. 45–60). Sussex, UK: Wiley.

Ekman, P., & Davidson, R. J. (1993). Voluntary smiling changes region brain activity. *Psychological Science, 4,* 342–345.

Ekman, P., & Davidson, R. J. (Eds.). (1994). *The nature of emotion: Fundamental questions.* New York: Oxford University Press

Ekman, P., Davidson, R. J., & Friesen, W. V. (1990). Duchenne's smile: Emotional expression and brain physiology II. *Journal of Personality and Social Psychology, 58,* 342–353.

Ekman, P., & Friesen, W. V. (1978). *Facial Action Coding System: A technique for the measurement of facial movement.* Palo Alto, CA: Consulting Psychologists Press.

Ekman, P., Friesen, W. V., & Hager, J. C. (2002). *The Facial Action Coding System.* Salt Lake City, UT: Research Nexus eBook.

Ekman, P., Levenson, R. W., & Friesen, W. V. (1983). Autonomic nervous system activity distinguishes between emotions. *Science, 221,* 1208–1210.

Ekman, P., Roper, G., & Hager, J. C. (1980). Deliberate facial movement. *Child Development, 51,* 886–891.

Izard, C. E. (1977). *Human emotions.* New York: Plenum.

Laird, J. D. (1974). Self-attribution of emotion: The effects of expressive behavior on the quality of emotional experience. *Journal of Personality and Social Psychology, 29,* 475–486.

Levenson, R. W., Carstensen, L. L., Friesen, W. V., & Ekman, P. (1991). Emotion, physiology, and expression in old age. *Psychology and Aging, 6,* 28–35.

Levenson, R. W., & Ekman, P. (2002). Difficulty does not account for emotion-specific heart rate changes in the directed facial action task. *Psychophysiology, 39,* 397–405.

Levenson, R. W., Ekman, P., & Friesen, W. V. (1990). Voluntary facial action generates emotion-specific autonomic nervous system activity. *Psychophysiology, 27,* 363–384.

Levenson, R. W., Ekman, P., Heider, K., & Friesen, W. V. (1992). Emotion and autonomic nervous system activity in the Minangkabau of West Sumatra. *Journal of Personality and Social Psychology, 62,* 972–988.

Tomkins, S. S. (1962). *Affect, imagery, consciousness: I. The positive affects.* New York: Springer Verlag.

Zajonc, R. B. (1985). Emotion and facial efference: A theory reclaimed. *Science, 228,* 15–21.

James D. Laird
Sarah Strout

Emotional Behaviors as Emotional Stimuli

Smile at the approaching friend and feel happy. Scowl into the blinding, setting sun, and rage at the drivers ahead. Race up the stairs and fear the impending meeting. When we think about the elicitors of emotion, we think immediately of events in our lives—the arrival of our friend, the tedious crawl of traffic, the threatening boss—and we imagine that the causes of our emotions are events that preceded them. Sometimes, though, the emotional feelings may arise by a different route. In this chapter we describe a family of techniques for eliciting emotional reactions, techniques that arise from a particular theoretical understanding of emotional processes. This theory suggests that often the smile is the proximal cause of happiness, the scowl causes the anger, and the pounding heart of the stair climber causes anxiety. The techniques we describe in this chapter all involve manipulating the target person's behavior, or his or her understanding of that behavior, in order to change his or her feelings. As one might expect, these different techniques have both advantages and disadvantages in comparison with the techniques that focus on eliciting circumstances. We begin with a brief description of the background theory that is just sufficient to provide an explanation of the reasons this family of elicitation techniques can be successful. Then we discuss some of the advantages and disadvantages of these techniques relative to others, so that readers can get some idea of how useful those techniques might be for their purposes. After a fuller description of these techniques, we return to the question of advantages and disadvantages in more detail.

A Brief Theoretical Excursion

Both common sense and many psychological theories of emotional processes assume a sequence of events that begins with some eliciting stimulus, which in turn produces an emotional feeling; the feeling then causes changes in autonomic responses, expressive behaviors, and actions. In the famous example, a bear enters the room, we feel fear, and our fear feeling makes our hearts pound, our face and body fall into "fearful" patterns of movement, and we run away. The commonsense model runs roughly as depicted in Figure 4.1.

Of course, more sophisticated psychological theories include a number of further complexities. Most important is undoubtedly the need for some sort of interpretative or "appraisal" process to give meaning to the eliciting stimulus. Unless we know that real bears have powerful muscles, sharp claws, and crabby dispositions, we would have no reason to fear the larger version of our childhood toy.

Over a century ago, William James (James, 1884) proposed that the sequence of events in an emotional episode was importantly different: The immediate result of the eliciting circumstances was not the feeling but rather the array of emotional behaviors; the feeling actually occurred at the end of the sequence, as a result of the behaviors. Indeed, he said that emotional feelings are actually the experience of the emotional behaviors as they were occurring. The sequence as James outlined it is depicted in Figure 4.2.

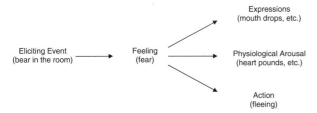

Figure 4.1. The commonsense "theory"/assumption about the sequence of events in an emotional episode.

As the figure makes clear, one way to elicit emotional feelings is to manipulate the behaviors. Despite this obvious implication, for almost 80 years after James' 1884 statement of the theory, relatively little supporting evidence was available. Some groundbreaking but much-criticized studies by Schachter and his colleagues (Schachter & Singer 1962) had shown that manipulating arousal changed the intensity of some emotional feelings, but little, if any, research on the effects of other kinds of emotional behavior on feelings had been conducted. Indeed, when one of us (JDL) first began studying the effects of emotional behaviors on feelings (Laird, 1967, 1974), most psychologists were very skeptical about James's basic idea, especially in regard to expressive behavior and action. They just did not believe that being induced to smile would make a person feel happier or that frowning would make people feel angrier. The inclusion of this chapter in this handbook is a sign of how "mature" the science concerning that issue has become. In the past few decades, literally hundreds of studies have manipulated various kinds of expressive behavior and demonstrated corresponding changes in emotional feelings (for a review, see Laird, 2006). A small but substantial number of studies of emotional actions have been equally supportive, and despite a number of well-founded criticisms of the early Schachter work, a role for arousal in producing feelings is also well established. In sum, using behaviors to elicit emotions has developed from a mildly preposterous curiosity to a useful tool. In this chapter, we try to make it clear how that tool may be used to the best effect.

A number of different theoretical models have been proposed to explain the effects of behavior on feelings. Deciding which is most appropriate seems to be quite complicated and perhaps as yet unsettled. We prefer self-perception theory (Bem,

1972) and believe it is the best fit with the data (Laird, 2006; Laird & Bresler, 1992). Self-perception theory is in effect an extension of James' theory of emotion to include all feelings. Self-perception theory asserts that all of our feelings are "perceptions" of our behavior as it is occurring. As Bem explained, we are in the same position as an outside observer of our behavior and must "infer" our feelings from our own behavior.

Whatever the final resolution of the various theoretical disagreements, self-perception theory has the particularly helpful empirical implication that any behavior that we might use to infer someone's emotional state could, in principle, be manipulated to produce that state. Consequently, the whole gamut of expressive behavior becomes a potential toolbox for the production of emotional feelings, and thus far the research supports that happy assumption.

Among the behaviors that have been manipulated and that have produced corresponding emotional feelings are facial expressions (Laird, 1974; Schnall & Laird, 2003), postures (Duclos et al., 1989; Flack, Laird, & Cavallaro, 1999a), patterns of gaze (Kellerman, Lewis, & Laird, 1989; Williams & Kleinke, 1993), tone of voice (Hatfield, Hsee, Costello, & Weisman, 1995), and gestural movements (Foerster & Strack, 1997, 1998). Among the feelings that have been produced by these manipulations are anger, fear, sadness, joy, liking and loving, confidence, pride, guilt, and boredom. Subsequent sections are organized around the kinds of behaviors that have been manipulated. We briefly sketch the kinds of studies that have been done, the effects of different kinds of manipulations, and, when possible, include any relevant "lab lore" about how to produce these effects. Before describing the various techniques, we discuss some of the particular advantages and limitations of the various behavioral manipulation tasks relative to some other procedures that are commonly used to elicit emotional feelings.

Relative Costs and Benefits of Behavioral Manipulations

Compared with other emotion elicitation techniques, behavioral manipulations have both advantages and disadvantages, arising from differences in the ease of manipulation and from the nature of the outcomes.

The Complexity and Difficulty of the Manipulations

The basic manipulation of emotional behavior can be extremely simple, consisting of no more than a simple request, such as, "Please disguise your feelings so that the observers won't know what you are feeling." (See Kleck et al., 1976; and Lanzetta, Cartwright-Smith, & Kleck, 1976, for examples of this kind of manipulation.) Or it can be no more than, "Please smile in the way you usually do." (e.g., Duclos & Laird, 2001). In contrast to these very simple manipulations, in most experiments conducted until recently the behavioral

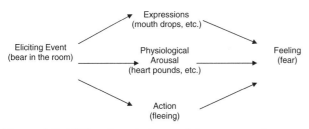

Figure 4.2. William James's theory of the sequence of events in an emotional episode.

manipulations have been quite complicated and demand attention and skill from the experimenter. However, the principal motivation for complexity has been the need that most experimenters have felt to disguise the nature and purpose of the manipulations in order to ensure that the induced feelings are not due to experimenter influence or participant's compliance. Early in this research tradition, skeptics often tried to attribute the results to experimenter influences, but large amounts of evidence have rendered that possibility extremely unlikely (Laird, 2006). Consequently, elaborate deceptions are often unnecessary.

In sum, for many applications emotional behaviors can be manipulated very easily. For others some degree of disguise may be necessary, and we describe some successful cover stories and manipulation techniques later.

Range of Possible Target Emotional Feelings

The "basic" emotions that all have distinctive facial expressions or postures are quite easy to produce. For example, people can be induced to smile, and they report feeling happy (Laird, 1974); to sit in a slumped posture to produce a feeling of sadness (Duclos et al., 1989); and to speak in a harsh tone to produce anger (Hatfield et al., 1995). Feelings that do not have characteristic behaviors are more difficult or perhaps impossible to produce through behavioral manipulations. For example, we would not expect to be able to produce feelings of nostalgia or awe by behavioral manipulations.

On the other hand, when they work, behaviors produce quite specific effects. Facial expressions or postures of a specific emotion will produce changes in that emotion and in those that are closely associated, but they will not affect emotions that are different in kind. For example, both facial expressions and postures of anger produce changes in anger feelings and also in the closely related feeling of disgust, but they do not induce fear or sadness (Duclos et al., 1989; Flack et al., 1999b; Flack, Cavallaro, Laird, & Miller, 1997). By contrast, our experience has been that other techniques, such as music, film clips, and guided imagery, often produce changes in generally positive or negative feelings but that within those categories people vary considerably in how specific their emotional responses become.

Size of Effects

Certainly the effects of behavioral manipulations in experiments do not approach the intensity of some real-life emotional episodes. On the other hand, most other experimental manipulations of feelings also produce effects that are only moderately strong. For example, expressions and postures produce effects that are similar in scale to those produced by film clips (Laird et al., 1994) and guided imagery (Duclos & Laird, 2001). Furthermore, more intense effects can be produced by combining different manipulations, such as expressions and postures (e.g. Flack et al., 1999b), although

even these stronger effects fall short of the strongest of natural emotional experiences.

Variations in Effects Across Persons

Perhaps the largest weakness of behavioral manipulations is that they appear to affect the emotional feelings of only a portion of the population. When people are induced to adopt facial expressions such as smiles and frowns, some people report strong feelings of happiness and anger, but others are relatively unaffected (Laird & Crosby, 1974). These differences seem to reflect the degree to which people are focused on their own bodies and actions (personal cues), as opposed to social and situational expectations (situational cues). People who are more responsive to personal cues change their feelings to match their facial expressions (Laird, 1984) and their emotional postures (Duclos et al., 1989; Flack et al., 1999b) and also to respond to their own appearance (Kellerman & Laird, 1982). They also report feeling more romantic attraction to a stranger with whom they have shared mutual gaze (Kellerman, Lewis, & Laird, 1989; Williams & Kleinke, 1993). In contrast, people who are less responsive to personal cues from their bodies and behaviors are more likely to accept suggestions about how they should feel (Kellerman & Laird, 1982) and are more affected by the social meaning of their circumstances (Duclos & Laird, 2001; Kellerman et al., 1989). For example, in a placebo administration, people who are unresponsive to personal cues show conventional placebo effects, feeling relaxed if told a placebo would relax them and aroused if told the pill was arousing. In contrast, those who are strongly responsive to personal cues show reverse placebo effects, such that receiving information that a pill will make them relaxed leads to increased tension (Duncan & Laird, 1980). The latter effect appears to occur because people interpret (of course, not at all consciously) their unchanged bodily responses, despite the pill effects, as indicating that they are especially aroused (Storms & Nisbett, 1970).

In sum, these and many other studies show that manipulations of emotional behaviors do produce robust changes in feelings, but not in all people. Obviously, one would prefer an emotion elicitation technique that was sure to affect everyone. However, note that the research on many other elicitors, such as still photos, film clips, and music, does not seem to have explored the question of individual differences in impact. Thus these other techniques may also fail to affect every participant. As a trivial example, in one study in which we employed film clips (Laird et al., 1994), we observed that whether people had seen the original movie or not made a large difference in how they responded. As another example, our impression is that the impact of music on mood depends significantly on one's musical experience. In sum, behavioral manipulations may not be that different from other kinds of elicitation in how universally they affect participants.

One important variation between individual differences in the behavioral manipulations and in other tasks deserves underlining. Many of the reasons that people are unaffected by other emotion elicitation techniques are essentially random, unrelated to the kinds of issues that are often the targets of emotion research, and hence theoretically trivial. For example, having seen a movie before or being familiar with a piece of music may affect people's emotional responses, but not in some way that would interact with effects of mood on other variables. These differences can very reasonably be considered to be "error variance." In contrast, the differences between participants who are responsive to personal and to situational cues are precisely differences in the processes that generate emotional feelings. Thus they may have some theoretically significant implications for the outcome of studies.

At any rate, we believe that whenever people use behavioral techniques to manipulate emotional feelings, they should consider also assessing individual differences in response to personal versus situational cues. Later in this chapter we describe a relatively easy technique for doing so, which requires little time and no deception.

Effects on Other Psychological Processes

When the research question concerns the effects of emotional feelings on cognitive processes, such as memory (Blaney, 1986; Bower, 1980), behavioral manipulations have special advantages. Many other emotion elicitation techniques, such as directed recall, films, or the Velten technique (discussed later), contain cognitive material that may have effects on other processes through purely cognitive routes, such as priming. In contrast, behavioral techniques can produce emotional reactions without much verbal interaction and without the kind of talk that might prime other cognitions. Thus the effects of the feelings can be observed relatively "purely" (e.g., Laird, Cuniff, Sheehan, Shulman, & Strum, 1989; Laird, Wagener, Halal, & Szegda, 1982).

Although we have emphasized the impact of behavioral manipulations on feelings, other aspects of emotional processes are also affected, sometimes even when feelings are not. For example, sometimes suppression of expressive behavior affects feelings (Duclos & Laird, 2001; Laird et al., 1994), but sometimes only psychophysiological responses such as heart rate and skin conductance are affected (Gross, 1998; Gross & Levenson, 1993).

In the next few sections we discuss specific techniques for eliciting emotional feelings, beginning with the most widely studied and used, facial expressions. Table 4.1 provides an overview of the kinds of behaviors that have been manipulated and the kinds of feelings that have been produced by these manipulations.

Facial Expressions

Two major groups of techniques for manipulating facial expressions have been employed. In the "muscle by muscle" procedure (Laird, 1984), the researcher induces an emotional expression by instructing the participant to contract and relax different facial muscles. The major alternative has been to induce participants to minimize or exaggerate their natural emotional expressions (Laird, 1984). Within these two groups are a variety of more or less subtle and clever ways to induce or restrict the facial expressions.

Muscle-by-Muscle Manipulations

In one of the first studies using this technique (Laird, 1967, 1974), the participants were recruited for an experiment on "electromyographic (EMG) measurement of facial muscle activity." When the participants arrived at the laboratory, they were told that the researchers would be investigating the ef-

Table 4.1
Feelings induced by specific emotional behaviors

Feelings Produced	Behaviors Manipulated					
	Facial Expressions	Postures	Tone of Voice	Eye Gaze	Action	Arousal
Happy	x		x			
Angry	x	x	x			x
Sad	x	x	x			x
Afraid	x	x			x	x
Disgusted	x	x				
Surprised	x	x				
Loving				x	x	x
Liking				x		
Pride		x				
Confidence		x				
Boredom					x	
Familiarity					x	

fects of looking at different kinds of pictures on this "EMG activity," using electrodes attached to their faces. It was explained that two kinds of recordings were needed, one from muscles that were relaxed and one from muscles that were contracted. Actually, these contractions and relaxations were the way in which the researcher produced the facial expressions without the participant's being aware of the purpose of the manipulations. Then, almost as an afterthought, the researcher mentioned that there was one kind of error in the electrical measurements that needed to be statistically factored out, and that was the effect of moods on brain activity. So that the participants would feel free to report changes in feelings for which they would have no explanation, they were told that "we all have moment-to-moment fluctuations in mood that we ordinarily don't pay much attention to, but in this experiment they may be important, so be careful to notice how you are actually feeling during each trial, and then afterwards tell us." The reports were on rating scales that asked them how strongly they felt various emotions.

Two kinds of trials were run in this experiment. In one, the participants were asked to contract the muscles between their eyebrows by drawing their eyebrows down and together and at the same time to contract the muscles at the corners of their jaw by clenching their teeth. This produced an intense frown. On the other kind of trial, the participants were asked to contract the muscles under the electrodes on their cheeks, by drawing the corners of their mouth back and up to produce a smile (Laird, 1967, 1974).

Notice that in the participants' minds, the EMG was the important measurement in the experiment, and the important manipulation was the kind of picture that they looked at during each trial. The actual experimental manipulations, the contractions of facial muscles, had been presented as simply a means for obtaining the correct kinds of EMG measurements. The measure of emotional feelings had been almost dismissed, as a way to get rid of a small source of error.

In subsequent studies we have used similar muscle-by-muscle manipulations to produce feelings of disgust, sadness, and fear, in addition to anger and joy. Somewhat unexpectedly, we also produced feelings of surprise with the fear expression and reduced feelings of happiness with the sad expression (Duclos et al., 1989; Flack et al., 1999a; Flack et al., 1999b).

The Facial Action Coding System

A somewhat different, but conceptually identical, technique for manipulating expressions was used in a number of more recent studies by Levenson, Ekman, and their colleagues. Ekman and his colleagues have developed a very precise system (the Facial Action Coding System, or FACS; Ekman & Friesen, 1978) for identifying emotional expressions by coding the movements of individual facial muscles. In a series of studies (e.g. Levenson, 1992; Levenson, Carstensen, Friesen, & Ekman, 1991; Levenson, Ekman, & Friesen, 1990; Levenson, Ekman, Heider, & Friesen, 1992), they instructed participants how to contract the muscles identified by the FACS

to form specific expressions of six emotions. In each of these studies, the corresponding emotional feeling was induced. (See especially Ekman, chapter 3, this volume.) In some of these studies, the participants were aware of the emotional nature of their expressions, but in others, they were not. The awareness of participants does not seem to have a large effect on the results of these types of studies.

The FACS-driven technique also affects psychophysiological responses, producing distinctive patterns of heart rate, skin temperature, and skin conductance for each of the specific emotions.

The FACS-guided manipulations are much more elaborate and detailed than those we have used. Our experience has been that if the major muscle groups of a particular expression are engaged and if the participant is told that the facial position should feel comfortable and not strained, the remaining muscles of the expression are rapidly recruited. For example, when we manipulate muscles to produce a smile expression, we do not mention the contractions of the *obicularis occuli* that Ekman (Ekman, Davidson, & Friesen, 1990) has identified as necessary for a genuine smile. We find that within moments, the eye contractions begin to occur as well, especially if participants are relaxed and the expression appears unstrained. Probably this occurs because facial expressions are organized, integrated patterns of muscle movements that are generated as wholes, rather than in parts.

In these two muscle-by-muscle techniques, participants are often unaware of the emotional purposes of the manipulations and often even unaware that the muscle contractions form a facial expression. However, they are certainly quite aware of the experimenter's focus on their facial activity. A different group of techniques induces facial expressions by some clever manipulation that leaves the participants unaware that movements of the facial muscles were interesting to the experimenter.

Using Pencils to Induce Emotional Affect

Examples of this technique include two studies done by Strack, Martin, and Stepper (1988). In this research, participants were recruited for a study of the best techniques for teaching writing to handicapped people. The participants held a pencil in their mouths, either with their lips tightly clamped around it or with their lips drawn back. The latter position (see Figure 4.1) produces an expression like a smile, whereas the former produces a kind of unpleasant, disgust-like expression. The participants spent some time trying to write in these expressions and then judged a series of cartoons for their funniness. The results were just as expected: the participants who had assumed smile-like expressions judged the cartoons to be funnier and to evoke more amusement than did participants who had assumed the other expression. None of the participants in this research recognized that the "writing positions" created expressions of emotion or that the purpose of the research involved their emotional feelings.

Using Golf Tees to Induce Emotional Affect

In another experiment, Larsen, Kasimatis, and Frey (1992) attached golf tees to their participants' foreheads between their eyebrows. Under the guise of studying "divided attention," they asked the participants to perform a number of tasks while manipulating the golf tees with their forehead muscles. On some trials they were instructed to make the tips of the tees touch, which they could only do by drawing their eyebrows down and together. The effect was to create an expression like sadness. On comparison trials they kept the tees separated. One of the other tasks involved rating the sadness of pictures that had already been found to elicit some sadness. However, when the golf-tee manipulation had produced a sad expression, the participants rated these pictures as significantly sadder.

Using Pronunciation to Induce Emotional Affect

A third, extensive series of studies showed the effects of another subtle manipulation on emotional feelings (Zajonc, Murphy, & Inglehart, 1989). In these studies participants were induced to pronounce various sounds, which produced facial expressions. The best known example in the United States is the "ee" sound, used by photographers who ask their sitters to say "cheese" before the picture is clicked, thereby producing a smile. Another was the German sound "ü," which is pronounced somewhat like the English sound "eu" and produces an expression very much like disgust. When participants were saying "ü," they reported much less pleasant feelings than when they were saying "ee." Once again, the participants were completely unaware of the purposes of the experiment. A similar result, using the same techniques, was obtained with native Japanese speakers (Yogo, 1991).

Mimicry

Another use of deception to induce facial expressions involves mimicry. Many studies have had participants mimic pictures of emotional stimuli, mostly emotion expressions, and shown that this mimicry leads to emotional contagion (e.g., Bush, Barr, McHugo, & Lanzetta, 1989; Hess, Philippot, & Blairy, 1998; Wallbott, 1991). The research reports that participants copy the emotion expressions and may also report feeling the emotion that corresponds to the stimuli.

Note that in all three of these last techniques, participants were induced to produce emotion-like expressions, but in every case they were unaware of the "shape" of their faces. Manipulations of this sort provide especially strong evidence against experimenter bias explanations of the emotional effects but are generally somewhat weaker in impact, probably because to maintain the deception the experimenter loses some degree of control over the expressions.

Exaggerating and Minimizing Expressions

A second strand of research employs a quite different methodology. Rather than trying to directly create the expressions from scratch, in these studies the goal was to modify the natural, ongoing expressions of emotion. In one example of this approach (Lanzetta et al., 1976), participants were asked to endure a series of uncomfortable electric shocks. On some trials they were asked to intensify their expressive reactions to the shock, on others to inhibit them. During each shock and pretense trial, recordings were made of the participants' skin conductance. (Skin conductance normally rises much higher after painful or unpleasant events than after non-painful events.) After each trial, the participants also were asked how painful the shock had been.

The intensity of the shocks had the expected effects: participants reported that the more intense shocks were more painful, and their skin conductance rose higher. Their behavior had similar although smaller effects: If the participant acted as if the shock was more intense, he or she reported more pain, and his or her skin conductance was higher. If he or she acted as if the shock was mild, then his or her pain reports and skin conductance reflected his or her actions. So, in these studies, feelings of pain seem to have been due at least in part to the participants' facial expressions of pain, at least when they were receiving actual shocks (Kleck et al., 1976).

A number of other studies of this general form were carried out, with consistent results (e.g. Kraut, 1982; Vaughan & Lanzetta, 1980, Vaughan & Lanzetta,1981; Zuckerman, Klorman, Larrance, & Spiegel, 1981). For example, in one study the participants were induced to exaggerate or minimize their facial expressions in order to fool a supposed audience (Kleck et al., 1976). As we would expect, minimizing their facial expressions produced less intense feelings, and exaggerating made the feelings more intense.

In our lab, we (Laird et al., 1994) induced participants to inhibit their expressive behavior by a different ruse. We attached electrodes to their faces and, as we did, we explained that the electrodes were very subject to movement artifacts. Therefore, on the trials in which we were recording from those electrodes, it was important that they not move their facial muscles. As a comparison, we told them that on other trials we would record from their fingers, so they should not move their hands. Then the participants watched brief segments of funny movies. Inhibiting their facial expressions did reduce the participants' enjoyment of the movies, whereas inhibiting finger movements had no effect.

In a more recent study, Sandra Duclos (Duclos & Laird, 2001) explored the effectiveness of deliberate inhibition of expression on feeling. In contrast to the many studies of college students, the participants in Duclos' study were adults recruited from a mainstream church who were unacquainted with recent psychology and were very dubious about the potential benefits of controlling their expressive behavior. Nonetheless, inhibiting expressive behavior was quite effective in reducing the intensity of both sadness and anger.

Measuring Individual Differences in Response to Personal Cues

Once we were sufficiently confident that expressions did indeed affect at least some people's feelings and that the results were not due to experimenter bias, we began to look for economical ways to identify those people who responded to personal cues from their expressive behavior. Few, if any, questionnaire measures identify those who respond to personal cues, so the only recourse was to perform one sort of self-perception manipulation to use as a predictor for others. The expression manipulation procedure became the standard tool for this purpose, using simply a frown and a smile manipulation. Participants were manipulated into a smile, then a frown, and then another pair of a smile and frown. In the most effective version of this procedure, participants were asked to examine a "black and white reproduction of a modern painting, by the artist Oshenberg." The pictures were random rectangular shapes, and each was given a caption that implied a contrasting emotional feeling. So during a smile, the participants would be looking at a picture entitled *Betrayal,* and during a frown the title would be *Dancing.* After each expression, they described their feelings on 6-inch linear scales, labeled *Don't feel at all* at one end and *Feel very strongly* at the other. The feelings rated were Anger, Sad, Happy, Fear, Disgust, Tired, and a few others that varied from study to study. For each pair of one smile and one frown, an index was calculated by subtracting people's anger and sadness while smiling from their anger and sadness while frowning and subtracting their happiness while frowning from their happiness while smiling. The resulting scores were added, yielding an index that was positive if people were happier when smiling and angrier and/or sadder while frowning. If the index was negative, their feelings corresponded more strongly to the picture titles. People whose index was positive on both pairs of trials were assigned to the personal-cue group and the remainder to the situational-cue group. Numerous studies demonstrated that the personal-cue group identified in this way was also affected by various other manipulations of their emotional behavior, whereas the situational-cue group was usually unaffected (e.g. Laird, Cuniff, Sheehan, Shulman, & Strum, 1989; Duncan & Laird, 1977, 1980; Edelman, 1984).

Undisguised Manipulations of Expressive Behavior

Most studies that manipulated expressive behavior also disguised the purposes of the manipulations through elaborate cover stories and deceptions. However, some studies did not employ disguises (e.g., Levenson, 1992; Levenson et al., 1990; Levenson et al., 1991; Levenson et al., 1992). We developed an undisguised version of our expression manipulation task that seems to work reasonably effectively in separating personal- and situational-cue groups (Duclos & Laird, 2001; Laird et al., 1994; Schnall, Abrahamson, & Laird, 2002; see appendix). In this procedure, people are told that previous

research has shown that some people feel happier when smiling and angrier when frowning, that we have no idea which sort of person they are, and that we would like them to try smiling and frowning and then report their feelings on the same sets of rating scales as were used in the disguised procedures. When scored in the same way as the disguised procedure, the resulting scores are skewed toward positive, probably reflecting two factors. First of all, there are no opposing situational cues from the picture labels. Second, the instructions may contain some bias toward perceiving oneself as responding to the expressions. However, a split at the median, or at the saddle in the common bimodal distribution of scores, creates groups that predict other self-perception responses quite reasonably.

Posture

Manipulating postures has been used to produce feelings of anger, sadness, disgust, and fear (e.g., Duclos et al., 1989; Fazio, 1987; Flack et al., 1999b) and feelings of confidence and pride. Postures have generally been manipulated in much the same way as have been facial expressions and seem to produce approximately the same size of effects.

The kinds of emotions that can be evoked by facial expressions and postures closely parallel our everyday recognition of specific corresponding expressive behaviors. For example, there seems to be no distinctive happy posture, and attempts to produce happiness through posture have not been successful (Flack et al., 1999a, 1999b; Flack et al., 1997). On the other hand, everyday speech does not describe facial expressions of pride and confidence but does recognize prideful postures, and these have been successfully manipulated (Laird, Kuvalanka, Grubstein, Kim, & Nagaraja, in press; Stepper & Strack, 1993).

Eye Gaze

Two emotions have particularly characteristic patterns of gaze associated with them, and both patterns have been used to induce emotional feelings. One of these is gaze aversion—avoiding meeting the eyes of the person to whom one is talking. In everyday life, we often assume that someone who will not meet our eyes is feeling guilty, and two studies have shown that if people are induced to avoid another's eyes, they do indeed feel guilty (Schnall et al., 2000).

An even more distinctive pattern of gazing occurs between lovers. Only lovers hold the long, unbroken gaze into each other's eyes. In at least four studies, opposite-sex strangers have been induced to gaze into each others' eyes; later they report increased feelings of attraction to each other (Kellerman et al., 1989; Williams & Kleinke, 1993).

These are particularly useful potential manipulations, because very few other ways of creating feelings of either love or guilt exist. The feelings evoked by the gazing do not seem particularly strong, although we know of one instance in which participating in a shared-gaze experiment led to a year-long romance. Furthermore, romantic attraction was also induced by asking strangers to hold hands (Williams & Kleinke, 1993), an effect that could probably be combined with gazing to produce even stronger feelings.

Tone of Voice

The harsh tones of rage and the gentle, soothing coos of motherly love are certainly as distinctive as any other expressive behaviors, and they have also been used to induce emotional feelings. For example, people induced to read passages while using the pace, rhythm, and pitch of emotions reported emotional feelings that matched the speech patterns (Hatfield et al., 1995; Siegman & Boyle, 1993). Participants who were asked to speak in a loud, harsh tone reported feeling more angry, whereas when they spoke in a soft, low tone, they reported feeling more sad. Flack has replicated this basic procedure with both normal and psychiatric patient populations (Flack et al., 1999a; Flack et al., 1997).

Breathing

In standard lie detection procedures, one measure is breathing rate, because changes in breathing rate are presumed to reflect emotional reactions to lying. If so, then self-perception theory would predict that inducing people to breathe in emotional ways would produce the feelings, and indeed that is the case (Bloch, 1985; Philippot, Chapelle, & Blairy, 2002). These effects seem to be a bit weaker than those of other manipulations, but they are particularly unlikely to be recognized by participants in research.

Emotional Actions

Emotional actions such as fleeing and attacking are relatively difficult to arrange in the laboratory, and perhaps they are too complicated to be useful ways to evoke emotions, but a few variants have promise. One study examined the impact of escape on the perception of pain (Bandler, Madaras, & Bem, 1968). Participants placed their hands on a plate that delivered electric shocks. Half were instructed to leave their hands there for the whole period of the shock, whereas the others were asked to lift their hands as rapidly as they could when they felt the shock. The result was that the first group endured much greater durations of shock, but the second group described the shocks as more painful. Pain, of course, is not usually thought of as an emotion, but in fact, a portion of pain experience seems to be emotional. The pain experience seems to consist of a sensory component and an emotional fear component.

An even more skeletal kind of action manipulation was created by Manfred Clynes (Clynes, 1976). He asked people to place their fingers on a button connected to strain gauges that measured pressures in three dimensions. They were then asked to "press out" a pattern of movement to represent a specific emotion, such as anger or joy. He discovered that the patterns that people produced were specific to the emotions and very similar across people. In a subsequent procedure, he asked them to press patterns for a particular emotion over and over and found that the pressing behavior produced the emotional feeling in his participants.

Freud and many others have proposed that emotional feelings may be a bit like fluids that need to be "expressed" lest they build up pressure until they explode. The process of expressing emotions, especially anger, to avoid rupturing the hypothetical container is called *catharsis*. Unfortunately for the catharsis hypothesis, but fortunately for those of us who wish to elicit emotions, inducing people to act angrily does not reduce subsequent anger. Instead, it increases it (Tavris, 1984). For example, people who were angered and then given a chance to punch a bag to "use up" their anger were actually more aggressive when given an opportunity later (Bushman, Baumeister, & Stock, 1999). Indeed, probably the single most effective way to induce anger through behavior may be to ask people to act angrily (e.g., Duclos & Laird, 2001).

In sum, when one can contrive an opportunity for people to perform emotional actions, these may be particularly effective ways of eliciting the emotion.

One classic technique for inducing emotional feelings involves verbal behavior. Velten (Velten, 1968) asked people to read a long series of sentences with emotional content. For example, people might read a long series of sad sentences, such as "It isn't worth going on," and "Everything seems hopeless." Not surprisingly, reading these sentences did produce changes in mood.

A group of easily manipulated actions has been found to affect feelings of agreement, liking, and belief. Of course, these feelings are not usually considered to be emotions, but the manipulations are so easy and effective that we have included them because they may suggest useful applications by emotion researchers. Examples of these manipulations include head nods and shakes. If people are induced to nod their heads, they agree more with material they have encountered, whereas shaking their heads negatively produces less agreement (Brinol & Petty, 2003; Wells & Petty, 1980). Similarly, when people are induced to push something away, they are less attracted to whatever they are attending to than if they pull something toward themselves (Cacioppo, Priester, & Berntson, 1993; Foerster & Strack, 1997, 1998).

Summary

A considerable variety of emotions can be elicited by manipulating emotional behaviors, including at least all of the most "basic" emotions: anger, fear, sadness, joy, disgust, and surprise; as well as guilt, romantic love, liking and disliking, pride, and confidence. Most of the behavioral manipulations—facial expressions and postures, gazing, speech and tone of voice, pulling and pushing objects, nodding and shaking—produce quite specific effects. The size of these effects is not overwhelming, but the usual results are not trivial, either, and they compare favorably with the magnitude of effects produced by other techniques that can be employed in the laboratory. In general, these manipulations do not require too much time; nor are elaborate methodologies necessary. And no equipment at all is required. Almost all of the potential objects of these manipulations, the participants, believe that feelings cause the behaviors, not the reverse; so the effects of participants' expectations are significantly reduced in most applications. In short, it seems to us that these techniques are a relatively untapped resource for future research on emotion.

Appendix: Expressions and Feelings Instructions

A great deal of research has demonstrated that when people adopt facial expressions of emotion, some people feel the emotions they are expressing. For example, some people feel happier when they smile and angrier when they frown. Other people are unaffected by their expressions. Most of us have not noticed whether we respond to our expressions or not, probably because we are too busy living our lives. However, recent research has demonstrated that if people sit quietly, deliberately adopt their normal expressions, and focus their attention carefully on their feelings, they can report their responses quite accurately.

So what we would like you to do is to adopt facial expressions and then report what you are feeling by filling out four sets of mood rating scales, beginning with the one on the next page. When you fill it out, please try to describe as accurately as possible how you actually felt. If you felt happier when smiling, or angrier or sadder when frowning, we need to know that, but if you felt nothing, or felt happy while frowning, it is equally important that we know that. People who are affected by their expressions and those who are not are about equally common, and the only way we can know what sort you are is what you tell us here. So please try to be as accurate as possible.

Each trial starts with an instruction about which expressions to adopt. You need only maintain the expressions for 10 or 15 seconds, or whatever seems right to you, so that you can be reasonably confident about your reactions. Notice that we would like you to repeat the two expressions, for a total of four trials.

It will help if you close your eyes while you are "expressing" to avoid distractions.

Trial 1

On this trial, we would like you to adopt a smile. Smile as you naturally do, and then notice how you are feeling. Then please describe your feelings by making an "X" on the line that best describes how strongly you felt each of the emotions. For example, if you felt an emotion somewhat, but not too strongly, you would put your mark somewhere in the middle of the line.

Anxious

/————————————————————/
   Did not feel at all   Felt very strongly

Interested

/————————————————————/
   Did not feel at all   Felt very strongly

Angry

/————————————————————/
   Did not feel at all   Felt very strongly

Sad

/————————————————————/
   Did not feel at all   Felt very strongly

Happy

/————————————————————/
   Did not feel at all   Felt very strongly

Disgusted

/————————————————————/
   Did not feel at all   Felt very strongly

Afraid

/————————————————————/
   Did not feel at all   Felt very strongly

Surprised

/————————————————————/
   Did not feel at all   Felt very strongly

Trial 2

On this trial, we would like you to adopt a frown. Frown as you naturally do, and then notice how you are feeling. Then please describe your feelings by making an "X" on the line that best describes how strongly you felt each of the emotions. For example, if you felt an emotion somewhat, but not too strongly, you would put your mark somewhere in the middle of the line.

Anxious

/————————————————————/
   Did not feel at all   Felt very strongly

Interested

/————————————————————/
   Did not feel at all   Felt very strongly

Angry

/————————————————————/
   Did not feel at all   Felt very strongly

Sad

/————————————————————/
   Did not feel at all   Felt very strongly

Happy

/——————————————————————————/

    Did not feel at all   Felt very strongly

Disgusted

/——————————————————————————/

    Did not feel at all   Felt very strongly

Afraid

/——————————————————————————/

    Did not feel at all   Felt very strongly

Surprised

/——————————————————————————/

    Did not feel at all   Felt very strongly

References

Bandler, R. J., Madaras, G. R., & Bem, D. J. (1968). Self observation as a source of pain perception. *Journal of Personality and Social Psychology, 9,* 205–209.

Bem, D. J. (1972). Self-perception theory. In L. Berkowitz (Ed.), *Advances in experimental social psychology* (Vol. 6, pp. 1–62). New York: Academic Press.

Blaney, P. H. (1986). Affect and memory: A review. *Psychological Bulletin, 99,* 229–246.

Bloch, S. (1985). Modèles effecteurs des émotions fondamentales: Relation entre rythme respiratoire, posture, expression faciale et expérience subjective. *Bulletin de Psychologie, 39,* 843–846.

Bower, G. H. (1980). Mood and memory. *American Psychologist, 36,* 129–148.

Brinol, P., & Petty, R. E. (2003). Overt head movements and persuasion: A self-validation analysis. *Journal of Personality and Social Psychology, 84*(6), 1123–1139.

Bush, L. K., Barr, C. L., McHugo, G. J., & Lanzetta, J. T. (1989). The effects of facial control and facial mimicry on subjective reactions to comedy routines. *Motivation and Emotion, 13,* 31–52.

Bushman, B. J., Baumeister, R. F., & Stock, A. D. (1999). Catharsis, aggression, and persuasive influence: Self-fulfilling or self-defeating prophecies? *Journal of Personality and Social Psychology, 76,* 367–376.

Cacioppo, J. T., Priester, J. R., & Berntson, G. G. (1993). Rudimentary determinants of attitudes: II. Arm flexion and extension have differential effects on attitudes. *Journal of Personality and Social Psychology, 65,* 5–17.

Clynes, M. (1976). *Sentics: The touch of emotion.* Oxford, England, Anchor Press.

Duclos, S. E., & Laird, J. D. (2001). The deliberate control of emotional experience through control of expressions. *Cognition and Emotion, 15*(1), 27–56.

Duclos, S. E., Laird, J. D., Schneider, E., Sexter, M., Stern, L., & Van Lighten, O. (1989). Emotion-specific effects of facial expressions and postures on emotional experience. *Journal of Personality and Social Psychology, 57,* 100–108.

Duncan, J. W., & Laird, J. D. (1977). Cross-modality consistencies in individual differences in self-attribution. *Journal of Personality, 45,* 191–206.

Duncan, J. W., & Laird, J. D. (1980). Positive and reverse placebo effects as a function of differences in cues used in

self-perception. *Journal of Personality and Social Psychology, 39,* 1024–1036.

Edelman, B. (1984). A multiple-factor of body weight control. *Journal of General Psychology, 110,* 99–114.

Ekman, P., Davidson, R. J., & Friesen, W. V. (1990). The Duchenne smile: Emotional expression and brain physiology: II. *Journal of Personality and Social Psychology, 58,* 342–353.

Ekman, P., & Friesen, W. V. (1978). *Facial Action Coding System.* Palo Alto, CA: Consulting Psychologists Press.

Fazio, R. H. (1987). Self-perception theory: A current perspective. In M. P. Zanna, J. M. Olson, & C. P. Herman (Eds.), *Social influence: The Ontario Symposium* (Vol. 5, pp. 129–150). Hillsdale, NJ: Erlbaum.

Flack, W. F., Jr., Cavallaro, L. A., Laird, J. D., & Miller, D. R. (1997). Accurate encoding and decoding of emotional facial expressions in schizophrenia. *Psychiatry, 60,* 222–235.

Flack, W. F., Laird, J. D., & Cavallaro, L. A. (1999a). Additive effects of facial expressions and postures on emotional feelings. *European Journal of Social Psychology, 29,* 203–217.

Flack, W. F. J., Laird, J. D., & Cavallaro, L. A. (1999b). Emotional expression and feeling in schizophrenia: Effects of expressive behavior on emotional experience. *Journal of Clinical Psychology, 55,* 1–20.

Foerster, J., & Strack, F. (1997). Motor actions in retrieval of valenced information: I A motor congruence effect. *Perceptual and Motor Skills, 85*(3, Pt. 2), 1419–1427.

Foerster, J., & Strack, F. (1998). Motor actions in retrieval of valenced information: II. Boundary conditions for motor congruence effects. *Perceptual and Motor Skills, 86*(3, Pt. 2), 1423–1426.

Gross, J. J. (1998). Antecedent- and response-focused emotion regulation: Divergent consequences for experience, expression, and physiology. *Journal of Personality and Social Psychology, 74,* 224–237.

Gross, J. J., & Levenson, R. W. (1993). Emotional suppression: Physiology, self-report, and expressive behavior. *Journal of Personality and Social Psychology, 64*(6), 970–986.

Hatfield, E., Hsee, C. K., Costello, J., Weisman, M. S., & Denney, C. (1995). The impact of vocal feedback on emotional experience and expression. *Journal of Social Behavior and Personality, 10*(2), 293–312.

Hess, U. U., Philippot, P., & Blairy, S. (1998). Facial reactions to emotional facial expressions: Affect or cognition? *Cognition & Emotion, 12*(4), 509–531.

James, W. (1884). What is an emotion? *Mind, 19,* 188–205.

Kellerman, J., & Laird, J. D. (1982). The effect of appearance on self-perception. *Journal of Personality, 50,* 296–315.

Kellerman, J., Lewis, J., & Laird, J. D. (1989). Looking and loving: The effects of mutual gaze on feelings of romantic love. *Journal of Research in Personality, 23,* 145–161.

Kleck, R. E., Vaughan, R. C., Cartwright-Smith, J., Vaughan, K. B., Colby, C. Z., & Lanzetta, J. T. (1976). Effects of being observed on expressive, subjective, and physiological responses to painful stimuli. *Journal of Personality and Social Psychology, 34,* 1211–1218.

Kraut, R. E. (1982). Social presence, facial feedback, and emotion. *Journal of Personality and Social Psychology, 42,* 853–863.

Laird, J. D. (1967). *William James and the role of the face in emotional feelings.* Unpublished doctoral dissertation, University of Rochester, Rochester, New York.

Laird, J. D. (1974). Self-attribution of emotion: The effects of expressive behavior on the quality of emotional experience. *Journal of Personality and Social Psychology, 33,* 475–486.

Laird, J. D. (1984). The real role of facial response in experience of emotion: A reply to Tourangeau and Ellsworth, and others. *Journal of Personality and Social Psychology, 47,* 909–917.

Laird, J. D. (2006). *Feelings: The perception of self.* New York: Oxford University Press.

Laird, J. D., Alibozak, T., Davainis, D., Deignan, K., Fontanella, K., Hong, J., et al. (1994). Individual differences in the effects of spontaneous mimicry on emotional contagion. *Motivation and Emotion, 18,* 231–246.

Laird, J. D., & Bresler, C. (1992). The process of emotional experience: A self-perception theory. In M. S. Clark (Ed.), *Review of personality and social psychology: Vol. 13. Emotion* (pp. 213–234). Newbury Park, CA: Sage.

Laird, J. D., & Crosby, M. (1974). Individual differences in self-attribution of emotion. In H. London & R. Nisbett (Eds.), *Thinking and feeling: The cognitive alteration of feeling states (44–59).* Chicago: Aldine-Atherton.

Laird, J. D., Cuniff, M., Sheehan, K., Shulman, D., & Strum, G. (1989). Emotion specific effects of facial expressions on memory for life events. *Journal of Social Behavior and Personality, 4,* 87–98.

Laird, J. D., Kuvalanka, K., Grubstein, L., Kim, T. H., & Nagaraja, T. (in press). Posture and confidence: Standing (and sitting) tall makes you feel good. *Journal of Nonverbal Behavior.*

Laird, J. D., Wagener, J. J., Halal, M., & Szegda, M. (1982). Remembering what you feel: The effects of emotion on memory. *Journal of Personality and Social Psychology, 42,* 646–658.

Lanzetta, J. T., Cartwright-Smith, J., & Kleck, R. E. (1976). Effects of nonverbal dissimulation on emotional experience and autonomic arousal. *Journal of Personality and Social Psychology, 33,* 354–370.

Levenson, R. W. (1992). Autonomic nervous system differences among emotions. *Psychological Science, 3,* 23–27.

Levenson, R. W., Carstensen, L. L., Friesen, W. V., & Ekman, P. (1991). Emotion, physiology and expression in old age. *Psychology and Aging, 6,* 28–35.

Levenson, R. W., Ekman, P., & Friesen, W. V. (1990). Voluntary facial action generates emotion-specific nervous system activity. *Psychophysiology, 27,* 363–384.

Levenson, R. W., Ekman, P., Heider, K., & Friesen, W. V. (1992). Emotion and autonomic nervous system activity in the Minangkabau of West Sumatra. *Journal of Personality and Social Psychology, 62,* 972–988.

Philippot, P., Chapelle, G., & Blairy, S. (2002). Respiratory feedback in the generation of emotion. *Cognition and Emotion, 16*(5), 605–627.

Schachter, S., & Singer, J. E. (1962). Cognitive, social and physiological determinants of emotional state. *Psychological Review, 69,* 379–399.

Schnall, S., Abrahamson, A., & Laird, J. D. (2002). Premenstrual tension is an error of self-perception processes: An individual differences perspective. *Basic and Applied Social Psychology, 24,* 214–227.

Schnall, S., & Laird, J. D. (2003). Keep smiling: Enduring effects of facial expressions and postures on emotional experience and memory. *Cognition and Emotion, 17,* 787–797.

Schnall, S., Laird, J. D., Campbell, L., Hwang, H., Silverman, S., & Sullivan, D. (2000). *More than meets the eye: Avoiding gaze makes you feel guilty.* Paper presented at the annual meeting of the Society for Personality and Social Psychology, Nashville, TN.

Siegman, A. W., & Boyle, S. (1993). Voices of fear and anxiety and sadness and depression: The effects of speech rate and loudness on fear and anxiety and sadness and depression. *Journal of Abnormal Psychology, 102,* 430–437.

Stepper, S., & Strack, F. (1993). Proprioceptive determinants of emotional and nonemotional feelings. *Journal of Personality and Social Psychology, 64,* 211–220.

Storms, M. D., & Nisbett, R. E. (1970). Insomnia and the attribution process. *Journal of Personality and Social Psychology, 16,* 219–228.

Strack, F., Martin, L. L., & Stepper, S. (1988). Inhibiting and facilitating conditions of facial expressions: A non-obtrusive test of the facial feedback hypothesis. *Journal of Personality and Social Psychology, 54,* 768–776.

Tavris, C. (1984). On the wisdom of counting to ten: Personal and social dangers of anger expression. In P. Shaver (Ed.), *Review of personality and social psychology* (Vol. 5). Beverly Hills, CA: Sage.

Vaughan, K. B., & Lanzetta, J. T. (1980). Vicarious instigation and conditioning of facial expressive and autonomic responses to a model's expressive display of pain. *Journal of Personality and Social Psychology. 38*(6), 909–923

Vaughan, K. B., & Lanzetta, J. T. (1981). The effect of modification of expressive displays on vicarious emotional arousal. *Journal of Experimental Social Psychology, 17,* 16–30.

Velten, E. (1968). A laboratory task for induction of mood states. *Behaviour Research and Therapy, 6,* 473–482.

Wallbott, H. G. (1991). Recognition of emotion from facial expression via imitation? Some indirect evidence for an old theory. *British Journal of Social Psychology, 30*(3), 207–219.

Wells, G. L., & Petty, R. E. (1980). The effects of overt head movements on persuasion: Compatibility and incompatibility of responses. *Basic and Applied Social Psychology, 1*(3), 219–230.

Williams, G. P., & Kleinke, C. L. (1993). Effects of mutual gaze and touch on attraction, mood and cardiovascular reactivity. *Journal of Research in Personality, 27,* 170–183.

Yogo, M. (1991). Self-regulation of affects: Effects of facial expressive behavior on psychosomatic states. *Doshisha Psychological Review, 38,* 49–59.

Zajonc, R. B., Murphy, S. T., & Inglehart, M. (1989). Feeling and facial efference: Implications of the vascular theory of emotion. *Psychological Review, 96,* 395–416.

Zuckerman, M., Klorman, R., Larrance, D. T., & Spiegel, N. H. (1981). Facial, autonomic, and subjective components of emotion: The facial feedback hypothesis versus the externalizer-internalizer distinction. *Journal of Personality and Social Psychology, 41,* 929–944.

Stefan Wiens

Arne Öhman

Probing Unconscious Emotional Processes

On Becoming a Successful Masketeer

Have you ever had an unconscious emotion?[1] As conscious beings, humans might consider this question absurd. Because everyday experience suggests that all important mental events are accompanied by consciousness, humans are convinced that consciousness is critical in mediating and controlling these events and behavior. Accordingly, emotion is commonly equated with emotional experience (feeling), and the notion of unconscious emotion seems either contradictory in terms or not worth discussing, as unconscious emotions would play only a trivial, if any, role at all in mental life. William James (1884), one of the forefathers of modern psychology, supported this notion by stating that "our feeling . . . IS the emotion" (p. 190). This discussion of emotion in terms of conscious experience (feeling) has a long tradition in psychology (e.g., Damasio, 1994; Frijda, 1986; Schachter & Singer, 1962). Thus Clore's (1994, p. 290) statement that "emotions cannot be unconscious because they must be felt, and feelings are by definition conscious" is endorsed by many contemporary emotion researchers.

However, other researchers have challenged this notion of equating emotions with feelings. In fact, this alternative view has a tradition that is at least as long. For example, according to Sigmund Freud (1916–1917/1959), a contemporary of William James's, unconscious emotion plays an important role in mental life. However, although Freud's ideas were developed further in psychoanalysis, other researchers have conceptualized unconscious emotions in ways that have little in common with Freud's theorizing (e.g., Kihlstrom, 1999; LeDoux, 1996; Öhman, 1986).

The purpose of this chapter is to review conceptual, methodological, and technical issues in studying unconscious emotion. We begin with a historical overview of research on unconscious emotion and outline an information-processing model of emotion that illustrates different approaches to studying unconscious emotion. That is, unconscious emotion occurs either when people are not consciously aware of the emotional stimulus or when they show signs of emotion (e.g., psychophysiological changes) even though they do not report any accompanying changes in emotional experience. Then we describe backward masking, which is considered to be the most prominent method for blocking conscious awareness of visual stimuli. In backward masking, a brief visual stimulus (target) is followed immediately by another visual stimulus (mask). Because people often report that they are consciously aware only of the masks but not the targets, masking allows one to reduce, if not eliminate, conscious awareness of masked targets to study their unconscious effects. Based on an example study (Öhman & Soares, 1994), we describe the method and general rationale for using backward masking. Then we discuss technical issues of masking, followed by methodological and conceptual issues in the assessment of awareness. These include the distinction between subjective and objective thresholds, the definition of unawareness in terms of a statistical criterion, and the timing of measuring awareness. Finally, we describe two paradigms that might represent potential solutions to many conceptual problems. Whereas findings of qualitative differences support the distinction between conscious and unconscious emotional processes, a psychophysical approach offers a more eclectic perspective, as dose-response relationships with awareness can be studied and the use of complementary measures of awareness is advocated. Thus the demonstration of qualitative differences and the study of dose-response relationships between awareness and emotional measures of interest might provide useful tools in probing unconscious emotional processes.

A Historical Sketch of Unconscious Emotion

Sigmund Freud

In contrast to our everyday experience and traditional conceptualizations of emotion, Sigmund Freud (1916–1917/1959) argued that unconscious processes play an important role in emotion, in that people can be influenced by unconscious emotional and motivational states. For example, emotions might be isolated from their real sources through displacement or projection, as when one's own anger is attributed to one's partner. Similarly, people might be influenced by emotional processes even though defense mechanisms such as denial, intellectualization, and reaction formation might prevent people from experiencing feelings. Thus emotions have to be inferred from their effects on behavior rather than from self-reports of emotional experience. Because feelings can be distorted, if not eliminated, conscious experience is not a necessary component of emotion.

Whereas culture and art of the twentieth century embraced these ideas, academic psychology was skeptical. When psychology became an independent discipline in the nineteenth century, introspection was used to study consciousness, which meant that unconscious processes were neglected. Because behaviorism replaced consciousness with behavior as the object of study, concepts of unconscious, as well as conscious, processes became irrelevant. Further, attempts to introduce psychodynamically inspired notions into mainstream psychology—such as the New Look in perception (Bruner & Goodman, 1947)—were subjected to rigorous criticism (e.g., Eriksen, 1960; Holender, 1986; see Öhman, 1999, for review).

The Cognitive Revolution

The cognitive revolution of the 1960s and 1970s reintroduced mental phenomena as a primary object for psychologists to study. However, researchers in cognition accepted the behaviorist dictum that mental phenomena had to be studied in behavioral terms (e.g., Mandler, 1975). Accordingly, rather than asking their participants directly to report on mental experience, the cognitive movement sought to reconstruct the architecture of the mind from observing behavioral responses in experimental settings. Thus introspec-

tive experience and insights were irrelevant to cognitive theory.

However, with the maturing of cognitive science, the problem of consciousness could be addressed with experimental data (e.g., Posner & Snyder, 1975; Tulving & Schacter, 1990). In this research, consciousness was presumed to have limited resources in that it is slow and can process only one thing at a time (e.g., Posner & Snyder, 1975). However, in addition to the capacity-limited processing of consciousness, another level of information processing was necessary to explain how organisms can process the vast input of external and internal stimuli. For the system to function efficiently, this other level had to process information in an automatic, parallel mode (e.g., Schneider, Dumais, & Shiffrin, 1984). Without this automatic level of information processing, no one would be able "to walk and chew gum at the same time" (to paraphrase a U.S. president's remark about a colleague). In fact, this perspective challenges the commonsense idea that consciousness plays a critical role in initiating and controlling action. For example, Gazzaniga (1998) argued that the brain works mostly automatically and leaves it to consciousness to interpret and make sense of what is going on after actions have already been executed (see also Roser & Gazzaniga, 2004)

Because information-processing models assign a limited role to consciousness, Shevrin and Dickman (1980) argued that the existence of unconscious mental activity seems to be necessary in all psychological models. Indeed, cognitive theories implied unconscious processing stages (Erdelyi, 1974), and, eventually, notions of a *cognitive unconscious* were introduced (Kihlstrom, 1987). Although most research focused on cognition, researchers began to study unconscious processes in emotion. For example, Zajonc (1980, p. 151) argued that "preferences need no inferences," suggesting that immediate and automatic emotional reactions to stimuli can occur with a minimum of cognitive processing and can shape subsequent cognitive activity. Similarly, Öhman (1986) proposed that emotional responses to evolutionary fear-relevant stimuli could occur unconsciously. In most of this research, the method of visual masking was used to probe unconscious emotional processes.

Delineating Unconscious Emotion

Beyond Emotional Experience

Whereas psychologists interested in cognition accepted that their primary goal was not to elucidate conscious experience but to develop a theory of mental processes that would account for a wide variety of data, including, eventually, conscious experience, most emotion researchers have focused on the experience of emotion (e.g., Ellsworth & Scherer, 2003; Frijda, 1986). However, LeDoux (1996) argued that the science of emotion would profit from following research on cognition. Accordingly, emotion research should opt for theories that account for systematic bodies of data rather than giving primacy to accounting for subjective experience of emotion. Indeed, a definition of emotion that includes but is not limited to conscious experience is necessary for linking emotion research to other domains of science. For example, an evolutionary perspective on emotion (Öhman & Wiens, 2003; Tooby & Cosmides, 1990) provides a functional scenario in which commonalities and differences between humans and nonhumans can be used to further a general understanding of emotion and to elucidate brain-behavior relationships in emotion (e.g., LeDoux, 1996).

Inferring Emotion From Four Indicators

Peter Lang (1968) argued that emotion can be inferred from three different response systems: verbal reports, psychophysiological responses, and behavior. However, these response systems should not be viewed as alternative indicators of a unitary emotional state (presumably mirroring experience) but rather as a loosely coupled ensemble of partially correlated outputs that may show discordant changes to experimental manipulations (Lang, 1993). Indeed, because each response system reflects many sources of variance in addition to emotionally relevant ones, there are limits to their possible covariation. As a result, dissociation between them is a mathematical necessity (Öhman, 1987).

Although an emotion incorporates changes in verbal, psychophysiological, and behavioral components, it also requires an eliciting stimulus, the evaluation of which (as good or bad) is the essential function of the emotion (e.g., Oatley & Jenkins, 1996). Accordingly, we are angry about something, afraid of somebody, and happy because of some event. Theorists of widely different orientations agree that the perceived (or attributed) cause of the emotion is a central determinant of emotional experience (e.g., Damasio, 1994; Schachter & Singer, 1962; Smith & Ellsworth, 1985). Therefore, an emotional stimulus appears necessary for inferring emotion. Indeed, affective changes that either occur in the absence of a stimulus or last longer than a few minutes are commonly referred to as changes in mood.

Converging Operations

Although stimulus, emotional experience, behavior, and psychophysiology are important components of emotion, none is necessary per se to infer emotional processing. For example, expressive outputs in behavior or physiology might be voluntarily edited or concealed (display rules; Ekman, 1972), and for well-learned emotional responses, the peripheral physiological component might simply be short-circuited (Damasio, 1994; Harris & Katkin, 1975; Mandler, 1975). Also, observations of panic attacks without anxiety (Kushner & Beitman, 1990) suggest that emotional processing might occur without any effects on emotional experience. Similarly,

whether a stimulus is emotional often depends on appraisal processes that can be idiosyncratic for the individual (e.g., Ellsworth & Scherer, 2003). Also, if the eliciting stimulus is internal, such as a thought or a memory, it will be hard for an observer to measure. A possible solution to this problem is to adopt a convergent operations approach (Campbell & Fiske, 1959; Kihlstrom, Mulvaney, Tobias, & Tobis, 2000). According to such a perspective, emotion is inferred from the convergence of several indicators, and the inference is particularly persuasive if the indicators come from diverse domains (Campbell & Fiske, 1959).

A Model of Unconscious Emotion

Figure 5.1 shows an information-processing model of emotion to illustrate different approaches to the study of unconscious emotion. As shown, conscious and unconscious mechanisms evaluate and appraise the stimulus input. These emotional (core) mechanisms produce changes in emotional experience (feeling), behavior, and psychophysiology. Although the emotion is not directly observable, it is inferred from the properties of the stimulus, as well as from changes in emotional experience, behavior, and psychophysiology (shaded areas in figure). As indicated by the bidirectional arrows among experience, behavior, and psychophysiology, these different components might interact among each other. For example, as stipulated by psychophysiological theories of emotion (e.g., James, 1884), psychophysiological changes might affect emotional experience (for review, see Wiens, 2005).

Although figure 5.1 suggests that conscious and unconscious evaluator mechanisms receive equal input, the relative proportion of conscious and unconscious processing might vary for different emotions. For example, in fear, unconscious processing might dominate conscious processing. Also, although the figure suggests that conscious and unconscious evaluator mechanisms have separate effects on emotional output, they might share similar pathways on emotional output. However, whereas the depicted scenario (with separate pathways) allows conscious and unconscious mechanisms to have qualitatively different effects on emotional output, a model with identical pathways for conscious and unconscious mechanisms could not account for qualitatively different effects.

As further illustrated in Figure 5.1, unconscious emotion might be indicated in at least two ways. In a stimulus-focused approach, the input is manipulated so that conscious awareness of the stimulus is eliminated (as represented by X). Because participants are not consciously aware of the emotional input, any emotional responses are due to unconscious mechanisms. As such, these changes in experience, behavior, and psychophysiology would be evidence for unconscious emotional processing or simply unconscious emotion (e.g., Öhman, 1999). In contrast, in an experience-focused approach, the critical evidence for unconscious emotion is that participants show convincing signs of emotional pro-

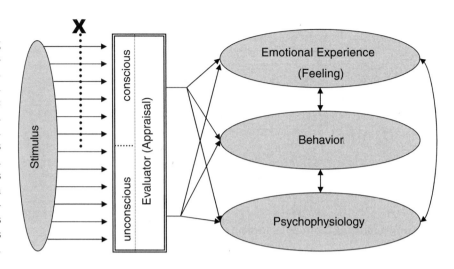

Figure 5.1. Information-processing model of emotion. Note that emotion is inferred from the stimulus, emotional experience (feeling), behavior, and psychophysiology (shaded areas). The purpose of a stimulus-focused approach to unconscious emotion is to eliminate all conscious processing of the stimulus input (X). Accordingly, backward masking is used to study unconscious emotional processing. In contrast, in an experience-focused approach, unconscious emotion is conceptualized as emotional processing without any effects on emotional experience.

cessing without reporting any changes in their emotional experience (feeling). Thus, because it is irrelevant whether the stimulus input is processed consciously or unconsciously, emotional processing can be fully intact except for any effects on emotional experience (Kihlstrom et al., 2000). This approach is discussed in a recent review by Berridge and Winkielman (2003). In a study by Winkielman, Berridge, & Wilbarger, 2005, thirsty and nonthirsty participants were shown masked emotional faces (happy, angry, or neutral) and were asked to indicate the gender of the neutral masking faces. Afterward, they were asked to rate their moods and were also given a pitcher of a fruit-flavored drink, which they could pour into a glass and consume. Results showed that although thirsty participants reported no changes in their emotional experience (mood), their consumption behavior was affected by the emotional faces. Participants who were shown masked happy faces poured and consumed more than participants who were shown masked neutral faces. In contrast, participants who were shown masked angry faces showed the opposite pattern. These data suggest that emotional responses (as inferred from the emotional stimuli and the drinking behavior) can occur without any effects on conscious experience (Winkielman & Berridge, 2004). Because it appears irrelevant for the experience-focused approach whether or not the stimulus input is processed outside of awareness, similar conclusions would be drawn for results obtained with nonmasked pictures. Although some research has employed this experience-focused definition of unconscious emotion, the stimulus-focused approach has been employed more commonly. These studies have mainly used backward masking to degrade visual input.

Backward Masking and the Dissociation Paradigm

The method of *backward masking* is considered to be the most promising method for studying unconscious processes

(Holender, 1986). When a visual stimulus (target) is shown briefly and followed shortly by another visual stimulus (mask), people often report that they are consciously aware only of the mask, not of the preceding target. Thus the target is backward masked. For example, if a picture of an angry face is shown briefly and followed by a neutral face, participants might report being aware only of the neutral, not the angry face; that is, the angry face is masked. Aside from backward masking, other masking methods are available. For example, in sandwich masking, the target is both preceded and followed by masks, and in energy masking, a light flash serves as the mask. However, we do not consider these further because backward masking is used most commonly. Also, because these methods have been used for a similar purpose, the central issues in masking apply to all methods.

The masking method has been commonly used in the context of the *dissociation paradigm*. The basic rationale of this experimental design is as follows: In order to test whether awareness of the target pictures is a necessary condition for responding, awareness has to be completely eliminated. If masking parameters are manipulated so that participants are completely unaware of the masked target pictures (i.e., awareness is eliminated), any emotional responses to the masked pictures would have to be unconscious, as they would occur without any direct involvement of consciousness. In contrast, if conscious awareness of the masked pictures were necessary for their processing, then no responses could be observed in the absence of conscious awareness. Therefore, to rule out the possibility that responding could be potentially due to residual conscious processing, awareness has to be completely eliminated (as illustrated by the X in Figure 5.1). But this approach is conservative, as awareness could well be an epiphenomenon in many cases of emotional processing. That is, although awareness might accompany many responses, it might not play a causal role in these processes.

When the dissociation paradigm is used, it has to be demonstrated that participants are completely unaware of the masked pictures. Typically, unawareness is indexed by null sensitivity of the measure of awareness. That is, if participants perform at chance levels on the awareness measure, they are considered unaware of the masked pictures. If these participants, however, respond better than chance on the emotion measure, the dissociation between the measures of awareness and emotion is interpreted to indicate that the emotional effects were unconscious, as they occurred without participants being aware of the masked pictures (Figure 5.1).

Example Study: Öhman and Soares (1994)

Öhman and Soares (1994) adopted the dissociation paradigm to study unconscious fear processes in participants afraid of either spiders or snakes. In this research, awareness was indexed by self-report and performance on a forced-choice classification task, and emotional processing was indexed by skin conductance and emotional ratings. In the first of two experiments, fearful and nonfearful participants were presented with masked pictures of spiders, snakes, flowers, and mushrooms at various stimulus-onset asynchronies (SOAs) between target and masking pictures. On each trial, participants responded if the masked target picture was a spider, snake, flower, or mushroom and also rated their confidence. Figure 5.2 shows results from fearful participants. As shown, classification performance and confidence ratings varied over SOA. A similar pattern was observed for nonfearful participants (not shown). Because at an SOA of 30 ms or less, fearful and nonfearful participants performed at chance levels in classifying the masked pictures, Öhman and Soares concluded that participants were unaware of the masked pictures at these masking parameters. Nonetheless, when the same masking parameters were used with other participants who reported themselves to be highly fearful of either spiders or snakes (1994, experiment 2), they showed greater skin conductance responses to masked pictures of feared animals (either spiders or snakes) than to pictures of nonfeared animals (either snakes or spiders) and flowers and mushrooms. These findings are shown in Figure 5.3. Also, when participants were presented with examples of masked pictures, they rated feared pictures as more negatively valenced and arousing than nonfeared pictures. In contrast, nonfearful participants did not differentiate among the pictures in their skin conductance responses and emotional ratings. Also, when asked to identify the content of the masked pictures, both fearful and nonfearful participants were generally unable to do so. Because the masking parameters apparently prevented participants from becoming aware of the masked pictures (as indexed by self-report and chance performance on the forced-choice classification task), these results suggest that participants can show fear (as indexed by skin conductance and emotional ratings) even when they are not consciously aware of the feared pictures.

The Öhman and Soares (1994) study illustrates the use of masking in the dissociation paradigm to study unconscious emotional processes. Although some readers might consider

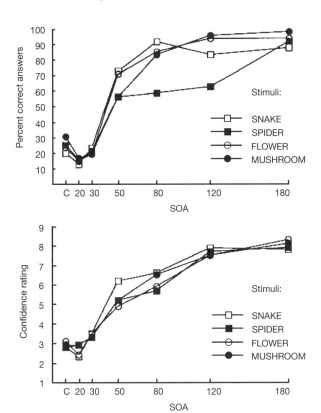

Figure 5.2. Percent correct (top) and confidence ratings (bottom) for different pictures at various stimulus onset asynchronies (SOAs) for fearful participants in the Öhman and Soares (1994) study. Note that in the control condition (C), a masking picture served as the target. Adapted from Öhman and Soares, 1994.

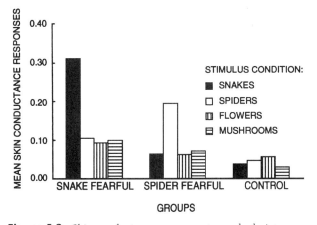

Figure 5.3. Skin conductance responses to masked pictures for snake-fearful, spider-fearful, and nonfearful participants in the Öhman and Soares (1994) study. Adapted from Öhman and Soares, 1994.

the findings to be convincing data for unconscious emotions (fear), other readers might be more critical. In fact, there is an ongoing debate on a number of issues that are relevant to this type of research. However, before we delve into this discussion, we describe the main technical challenges in masking research. We have long experience with masking in our lab, and these comments and suggestions are intended to be helpful to other researchers who want to use masking in their labs. However, readers who want to go directly to the discussion of conceptual and methodological issues can skip the following section (and go to the section titled "Being aware of awareness, exhaustively and exclusively"). Also, Table 5.1 provides a summary of the main conceptual, methodological, and technical issues in masking, together with comments and suggestions.

The Nuts and Bolts of Masking

CRT Monitors

Masking requires that pictures be presented briefly and in short order. Also, valid masking requires that picture duration is stable over repeated trials. Because research suggests that small changes in picture duration can have strong effects on awareness (e.g., Esteves & Öhman, 1993), variability in picture duration over trials confounds changes in picture duration with changes in awareness. Indeed, this potentially confounding effect can seriously threaten the validity of masking results. For example, a performance index across trials is invalid if individual trials vary substantially in duration (and thus awareness). In fact, with substantial variability in picture duration and awareness, it appears hard to maintain perceptual processing at a particular performance level or threshold (e.g., unconscious perception). Hence, unless the reliability of masking set-up is demonstrated, the potential variability in picture durations over trials creates risks for confounded results (Wiens & Öhman, 2005). At first, reliable presentation of brief pictures might not seem to be a problem. For example, with common computer monitors (the bulky type), even film clips can be viewed without any flickering. In fact, because common monitors are cathode-ray tube (CRT) monitors, pictures can be presented for less than a few milliseconds. In a typical CRT monitor, a CRT beam moves rapidly across the screen and activates a thin phosphor layer that covers the entire screen. Typically, the beamer starts in one of the upper corners, continues horizontally to the end of the line, and then writes the next line below. When all lines are written, the beamer jumps back to the starting position. This whole cycle is called a *refresh cycle*. As an illustration, imagine that you try to write on a screen with a laser pointer. Because you can draw only a small part of the screen at a time, you have to move your pointer quickly across the screen to fill the screen. As part of a recent study, we conducted photodiode measurements to

assess the accuracy of a common CRT monitor in presenting pictures at short durations (Wiens et al., 2004). In this study, a photodiode was placed in the middle of the monitor to detect luminance changes in response to picture presentations. The target picture was a white rectangle filling the entire screen. As shown in Figure 5.4, the pattern of luminance changes resembled a waveform. Each wave corresponded to a refresh cycle. Before the beamer reached the location of the photodiode (middle of the screen), luminance was zero; when the beamer swept over the location of the photodiode, luminance increased rapidly; and afterward, luminance dropped back to zero within a few milliseconds. However, luminance decreases occurred more gradually than luminance increases. This occurred because the phosphor remained activated even after the beamer had moved on.

Although our measurements showed that timing accuracy was excellent, the CRT technology has several limitations for masking purposes. First, interpicture intervals are rather long and can be manipulated only in large steps. Because it takes some time for the beamer to sweep over the whole screen (refresh cycle), the interval between two updates is determined by the time it takes for the beamer to complete a refresh cycle. This interval can be calculated from the *refresh rate,* which is the number of refresh cycles per second. For modern CRT monitors, refresh rates typically range from 60 to 160 Hz. Thus the interval between two consecutive screen updates (refresh cycles) varies from 16.7 ms (= 1/60 x 1,000) down to 6.3 ms (= 1/160 x 1,000), respectively. However, for most monitors, there is an inverse relationship between screen resolutions and supported refresh rates. That is, because the numbers of individual screen locations (i.e., pixels) increase at higher resolutions, supported refresh rates tend to decrease, as it takes longer to update all pixels. Therefore, before purchasing a monitor, we recommend checking which refresh rates are supported by particular screen resolutions. For example, although some monitors may allow refresh rates up to 160 Hz, their software drivers may be limited to 100 Hz. Further, although interpicture intervals of 6–17 ms might seem to be adequate SOAs between targets and masks, our own observations suggest that, depending on the type and size of the pictures, participants might report seeing the masked targets. Also, because common software does not allow one to change refresh rates during an experiment, the SOAs can be manipulated only in multiples of refresh rates. Thus, if the refresh rate is set to 60 Hz, the SOA can be manipulated only in intervals of 16.7 ms, from 16.7 to 33.4 to 50.1 ms, and so forth. From our experience, these changes in SOAs are too coarse, as they can result in dramatic changes in participants' perception of the masked targets.

A second limitation of CRT monitors is that picture duration is not continuous but a function of phosphor persistence and number of refresh cycles (Bridgeman, 1998). Pictures are not presented at once but are built up during a refresh cycle. Although this presentation is not ecologically

Table 5.1

Summary of the main conceptual, methodological, and technical issues in masking together with comments and suggestions

Topic	Issues	Comments and Suggestions
Conceptual/methodological		
Stable picture presentation	For each condition, picture duration must be stable over trials, otherwise, variability in picture duration might confound changes in duration with changes in awareness.	Our research suggests that displays based on LCD/TFT technology do not fulfill this requirement whereas CRT and mechanical shutters do (Weins et al., 2004; Wiens & Öhman, 2005).
Dissociation paradigm	Purpose is to eliminate awareness and test whether emotional responding remains. If so, this suggests that awareness is not necessary for emotional activation (cf. Holender, 1986).	A drawback is the requirement of null sensitivity on the awareness measure (see below). The study of qualitative differences and the psychophysical approach avoid this problem (see below).
Defining unawareness in terms of null sensitivity	Because unawareness is typically indexed by null sensitivity on the awareness measure, it depends on a statistical criterion and thus on power (e.g., alpha, number of trials).	The study of qualitative differences and the psychophysical approach avoid this problem (see below).
Defining a valid measure of awareness	A valid awareness measure has to capture all aspects of awareness (exhaustive) without capturing also unaware processes (exclusive; Merikle & Reingold, 1998; Reingold & Merikle, 1990).	Researchers have yet to agree on a valid measure of awareness. Whereas some favor objective measures (i.e., discrimination performance), others favor subjective measures (i.e., self-reported awareness; Wiens & Öhman, 2002).
Measures assess thresholds	It is often assumed that an objective measure assesses the objective threshold. However, factors such as motivation, number of trials, and response bias can affect results. Hence, an objective measure might actually measure the subjective threshold (Merikle & Daneman, 2000).	Because there is no generally accepted measure of awareness, research reports need to include sufficient detail about task and performance.
Qualitative differences	If observed effects differ qualitatively for two masking conditions, these findings support the notion of independent processes for unaware and aware processes and also provide evidence for the validity of the awareness measure (for a review, see Merikle & Daneman, 2000).	Claims for qualitative differences need to be carefully examined.
Psychophysical approach	Determine the dose-response relationship between awareness and emotional processing.	Provides quantitative information about emotional processing at various levels of awareness. Advocates the use of comprehensive measures of awareness. Minimizes risk of missing critical masking parameters. Avoids proving null sensitivity of awareness measure (as for dissociation paradigm).
Technical		
CRT monitor	Because CRT monitors write the screen on each refresh cycle, picture updates are limited by the refresh rate (e.g., 60 Hz = 16.7 ms), and the number of refresh cycles determines picture duration (Figure 5.4; Bridgeman, 1998; Wiens et al., 2004). Note that phosphor persistence in a single refresh cycle determines minimum picture duration.	CRT monitors exhibit excellent accuracy, and most experiment software allows synchronization with refresh cycles (Wiens et al., 2004). However, picture duration is limited to multiples of refresh cycles, and CRT monitors cannot be used in MRI because of interference.
TFT/LCD displays	Individual screen locations can be updated independently from each other. Because refresh cycles are not generated as for CRT monitors, experiment software has difficulties with synchronization. Also, picture presentation shows poor accuracy (Wiens et al., 2004).	Our results (Wiens et al., 2004) argue against the use of TFT/LCD displays. However, a notable feature is that pictures can be shown in steady state (i.e., no rewriting of the screen with each refresh cycle). This permits the use of LCD data projectors (instead of slide projectors) together with mechanical shutters in masking (see below).
Mechanical shutter	Mechanical shutters show excellent accuracy and can be controlled in milliseconds (independent from refresh cycles) (Wiens et al., 2004). Our research suggests that displays based on LCD/TFT technology do not fulfill this requirement, whereas CRT and mechanical shutters do (Wiens et al., 2004; Wiens & Öhman, 2005).	Because data projectors (based on TFT/LCD technology) can display pictures in steady state, a shutter can be placed in front of the projector to control picture duration (Wiens & Öhman, 2005) Therefore, we recommend the use of a mechanical shutter that is mounted in front of a data projector (for each target and masking picture; Figure 5.6).

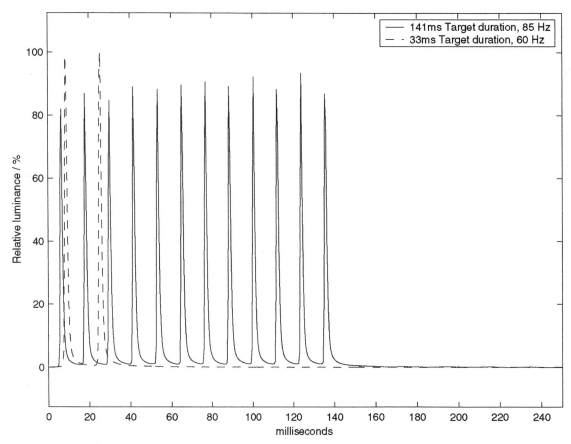

Figure 5.4. Luminance changes over time for the CRT monitor at two arbitrary target durations. Note that at a refresh rate of 60 Hz, a 33-ms picture corresponds to two refresh cycles (16.7 ms each), whereas at 85 Hz, a 141-ms picture corresponds to 12 refresh cycles (11.8 ms each). From Wiens et al., 2004.

valid, few vision researchers have discussed its implications (Krantz, 2000). However, even if this fact is ignored, it is important to keep in mind that picture duration is not the same as the duration of a refresh cycle. As illustrated in Figure 5.4, picture duration depends on phosphor persistence rather than on the refresh cycle. Therefore, even if a picture is nominally shown for only a single refresh cycle, its actual duration depends on phosphor persistence, which typically lasts 4 ms. Thus, whether a refresh cycle lasts 6.3 or 16.7 ms (at 160 or 60 Hz, respectively), the duration of a picture for a single refresh cycle would be about 4 ms. As further shown in Figure 5.4, actual picture duration is more difficult to determine if a picture is shown for several refresh cycles (Bridgeman, 1998).

LCD/TFT Displays

Although the CRT monitor has these limitations, its timing accuracy is outstanding compared with a modern flatbed monitor. This newer type of monitor is based on liquid crystal device (LCD) and thin-film transistor (TFT) technology. Simply stated, this type of monitor consists of a filter (LCD or TFT) that is placed in front of a light source. In contrast to CRT, this technology allows one to manipulate pixels in the filter individually so that it might be possible to update all pixels at once. Also, because the pixels can be held stable until they receive a new signal, picture duration can be continuous (this is illustrated in Figure 5.5C). However, although the LCD/TFT technology seems promising, our tests suggested that it might not be suitable for masking at this stage of technological advancement. That is, our photodiode measurements indicated that parameters such as onset latency, rise time, duration, and maximum luminance showed poor reliability for the panel, particularly so for short picture durations. Because small changes in picture parameters tend to have strong effects on perception (e.g., Esteves & Öhman, 1993) and thus may confound results, these data argue strongly against the use of LCD/TFT monitors in masking.

Similar results were obtained for a data projector with LCD technology. A data projector functions similarly to a flatbed monitor, except that the light source is stronger. Although Figure 5.5B illustrates that picture duration can be continuous, our photodiode measurements found that presentation parameters showed poor reliability. These results argue against the use of data projectors in masking.

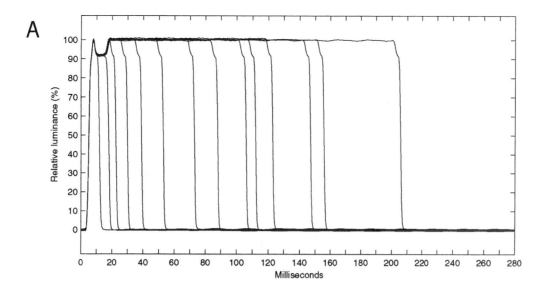

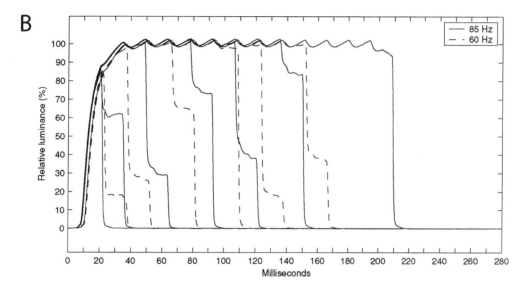

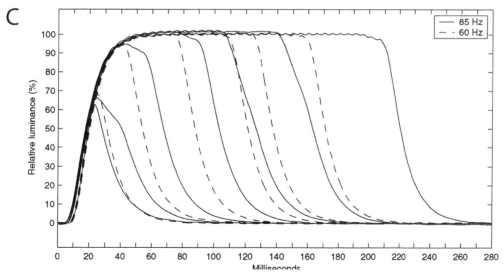

Figure 5.5. Luminance changes over time for mechanical shutter (A), LCD data projector (B), and TFT panel (C) at picture durations of 8 (only for shutter), 12, 17, 24, 33, 47, 67, 82, 100, 106, 117, 141, 150, and 200 ms. Note that for projector and panel, durations at a refresh rate of 60 Hz are indicated by a dashed line. From Wiens et al., 2004.

Mechanical Shutters

Although these data support the use of CRT monitors, the drawbacks of CRT monitors (see preceding discussion) are reduced, if not eliminated, with mechanical shutters. As part of our study (Wiens et al., 2004), we also tested the timing accuracy of a mechanical shutter that was mounted on a data projector. A mechanical shutter resembles a metal screen that functions like the shutter in a camera; that is, a brief opening of the shutter controls exposure duration. In our lab, we mount the shutters in front of data projectors. Although mechanical shutters have traditionally been used together with slide projectors, we use data projectors. This is possible because pictures on a data projector are not rewritten as for CRT monitors (see Figure 5.5B and Figure 5.4). To test the accuracy of the shutter, a presentation screen was placed in front of the shutter, and the photodiode was fastened in the middle of the screen area that was illuminated by the data projector when the shutter was open. The data projector presented the target picture continuously, and the shutter controlled target durations. As shown in Figure 5.5A, the shutter showed outstanding precision. Further, because the duration of shutter opening is not limited by refresh rates at all, picture durations can be manipulated in steps of milliseconds. Therefore, the shutter permits excellent control over picture durations.

Recommendations

These features favor the use of mechanical shutters over CRT monitors. However, researchers might be concerned that the use of mechanical shutters requires a more demanding setup for masking than CRT monitors. On CRT monitors, it is possible to present target and masking pictures in short order, with a minimum SOA corresponding to a refresh cycle. In contrast, a setup with shutters requires a shutter and projector each for target and mask, as data and slide projectors do not allow one to change pictures within a few milliseconds. However, although hardware demands might be lower for CRT monitors than for shutters, the software demands for CRT monitors can cause difficulties of their own. The main problem is that the software needs to synchronize picture presentation with the refresh rate of the CRT monitor. That is, the software needs to know when a refresh cycle starts in order to update the screen only at the beginning of the new refresh cycle. If this is not done, pictures might be shown for either fewer or more refresh cycles than intended. Some available software synchronizes picture presentations with the refresh cycles of the CRT monitor.[2] However, it appears that this software cannot control the exact onset of individual refresh cycles and is limited by particular refresh rates. In fact, even if it were possible to switch refresh rates within an experiment, our findings (see Figure 5.4) suggest that overall luminance levels might differ for different refresh rates, probably because there is less time for the beamer to illuminate the phosphor at higher refresh rates. In contrast, software demands for the use of mechanical shutters are much simpler, as they require only a simple on/off signal (e.g., a TTL signal from the parallel port). Because shutters permit excellent control over onset and duration of pictures in steps of milliseconds, their use is recommended.

Figure 5.6 shows a schematic of a possible setup involving two mechanical shutters, two data projectors, and two computers (Wiens & Öhman, 2005). Both target and mask require their own data projectors and shutters to allow for immediate switching between target and mask. Figure 5.7 shows a picture of the setup in our lab with two cased VS25 shutters that are mounted in front of two data projectors. As further shown in Figure 5.6, a master computer displays the target picture on the target projector and sends a signal (e.g., TTL via parallel port) to the slave computer to display the mask. The master computer also controls target and mask shutter durations (e.g., TTL via parallel port). Because data projectors (unlike CRT monitors) present pictures in steady state, they can be used in combination with mechanical shutters that control picture duration. However, because data projectors need some time to reach steady state for each picture (e.g., Figure 5.5B), pictures ought to be shown only after steady state is reached. For example, in our lab shutters are opened only at least 200 ms after picture onset to guarantee steady state.

Taken together, our findings do not support the use of monitors and projectors based on LCD/TFT technology in masking. In contrast, both CRT monitors and mechanical shutters showed excellent timing accuracy. However, mechanical shutters permit a more ecologically valid method of picture presentation than CRT monitors. Also, they permit exact control over picture onset and duration in steps of milliseconds rather than in steps of refresh cycles. Because our own experiences indicate that small changes in masking parameters can have strong effects on participants' perception of the masked pictures, the advantage of greater control over stimulus parameters recommends the use of mechanical shutters in masking. But, because our results might not apply to all available and future displays (e.g., plasma displays, displays with digital light processing technology, LCD goggles), we encourage researchers to test their equipment for accuracy. Indeed, Mollon and Polden (1978) tested tachistoscopes and demonstrated that accuracy was generally poorer than claimed by manufacturers and assumed by researchers. Because our observations confirm that the validity of presentation parameters cannot be taken at face value, we recommend that researchers provide evidence for the accuracy of their display equipment in their publications. Photodiode measurements might be ideal for that purpose (for details, see Wiens et al., 2004). Although evidence for accuracy is particularly important for displays based on LCD/TFT technology, even studies that use shutters and CRT monitors should provide this evidence. For example, studies with CRT monitors should include information regard-

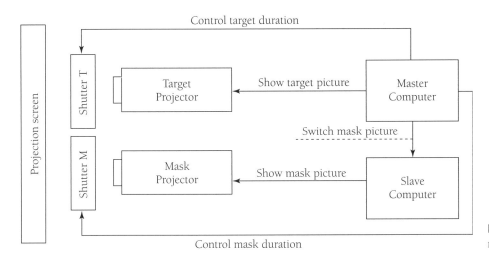

Figure 5.6. Schematic of the masking setup used in our lab.

ing refresh rate and ensure that picture presentation was synchronized with the refresh cycle.

Being Aware of Awareness, Exhaustively and Exclusively

Aside from these technical aspects of masking, there are a number of conceptual issues that continue to be debated in the literature. The extensive use of the dissociation paradigm (e.g., Öhman & Soares, 1994) might be due to the fact that it was advocated in a widely cited review (Holender, 1986). Unfortunately, it has a number of problems, most of which

stem from two basic requirements: to find a valid measure of awareness and to demonstrate that this measure shows null sensitivity (i.e., that participants perform at chance levels).

Exhaustiveness: Measuring All Aspects of Consciousness

As discussed by Reingold and Merikle (1990), a valid measure of awareness ought to be exhaustive in that it measures all conscious aspects of awareness. The distinction between a nonexhaustive and an exhaustive measure is illustrated in Figure 5.8. In this figure, solid lines represent conscious input, and dashed lines represent unconscious input. Further,

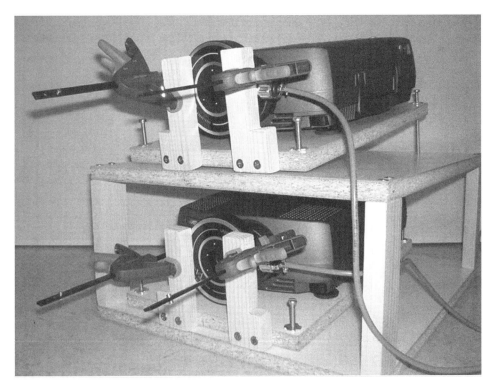

Figure 5.7. Picture of the masking setup used in our lab with two VS25 shutters (Vincent Associates, Rochester, New York) that are mounted in front of two data projectors. Because our system needs to be mobile, clamps are used to hold the shutters in place.

thick lines highlight input that is captured by the awareness measure. As shown in Figure 5.8A, if a measure is not exhaustive, it does not capture all aspects of conscious input. Hence, any purported unconscious effects might be due to the residual conscious input that is not captured by the measure (i.e., the thin lines in Figure 5.8A). In contrast, an exhaustive measure (Figure 5.8B) measures all aspects of conscious processing.

For example, Lovibond and Shanks (2002) criticized the awareness measure used by Öhman and Soares (1994), claiming that this forced-choice classification task is not sensitive enough to index awareness. That is, participants might be able to discriminate among the masked pictures without being able to *identify* (i.e., verbally label) them as spiders, snakes, flowers, and mushrooms. Accordingly, participants might have been aware of curly features of the masked snakes without being able to identify these pictures as snakes. This argument implies that the classification task in the Öhman and Soares (1994) study was not an *exhaustive* measure of awareness. Thus, because Lovibond and Shanks (2002) argued that the classification task was invalid, the findings in the Öhman and Soares (1994) study cannot be taken as evidence that participants responded to feared masked pictures of which they were unaware.

Exclusiveness: Measuring Only Consciousness

Another central requirement for a valid measure of awareness is that it ought to be an *exclusive* index of only conscious, not unconscious, processes (Merikle & Reingold, 1998). Therefore, if unconscious, as well as conscious, processes affect a measure, it would violate this requirement, as it would not be an exclusive index of only conscious processes but would also be affected by unconscious processes. This is illustrated in Figure 5.8C. Although a measure might be exhaustive, it might not be exclusive. If so, this measure would not only be sensitive to all aspects of conscious processes but

would also be partly sensitive to unconscious processes. Thus it would not allow one to determine whether performance is due to conscious or unconscious processes or both. Therefore, a valid measure has to be both exclusive and exhaustive, in that it measures all conscious processes but no unconscious processes.

For example, it is unclear whether the awareness measure proposed by Lovibond and Shanks (2002) fulfills the requirement of exclusiveness (Wiens & Öhman, 2002). If participants' ability to discriminate among the masked pictures without being able to identify them is not an exclusive measure of conscious processes, discrimination could be due to unconscious and/or conscious processes (Figure 5.8C). If so, the awareness measure suggested by Lovibond and Shanks (2002) would be invalid.

Subjective and Objective Thresholds

The debate about the validity of different measures of awareness has a long history (Eriksen, 1960). In general, this debate centers on a distinction between awareness measures that index either objective or subjective thresholds (Cheesman & Merikle, 1984, 1986). Originally, Cheesman and Merikle (1984) defined the *subjective threshold* as the "level at which subjects claim not to be able to discriminate perceptual information at better than chance level" and the *objective threshold* as the "level at which perceptual information is actually discriminated at a chance level" (p. 391). During the past decade, however, these terms have been used more generally to distinguish between people's (subjective) self-reported or claimed awareness and their actual (objective) discrimination performance (e.g., Merikle & Daneman, 2000). Therefore, in the present context, people would be subjectively unaware of the masked pictures if they reported that they could not tell what was depicted in the pictures. In contrast, people would be objectively unaware of the masked pictures if they could not discriminate among the masked pictures. Based on this dis-

Figure 5.8. Schematic of effects of exhaustiveness and exclusiveness on measuring awareness. Solid lines represent conscious input, and dashed lines show unconscious input. Further, thick lines highlight the input that is captured by the awareness measure. Note that a measure that is not an exhaustive measure (A) is not sensitive to all aspects of conscious processes, whereas a measure that is not exclusive (C) is sensitive also to unconscious processes. An ideal measure of awareness is both exhaustive and exclusive (B).

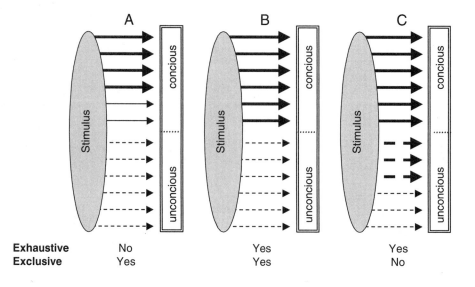

	A	B	C
Exhaustive	No	Yes	Yes
Exclusive	Yes	Yes	No

tinction, tasks that measure participants' ability to discriminate among the masked pictures are commonly called *objective measures,* whereas tasks that measure participants' self-reported awareness are called *subjective measures.* For example, the classification task in the Öhman and Soares (1994) study was an objective measure, as participants' ability to recognize masked spiders, snakes, flowers, and mushrooms was assessed with a forced-choice classification task in which participants chose among all possible picture categories. In contrast, presenting participants with masked pictures and asking them to report what was depicted would be a subjective measure of awareness, as participants' self-reported awareness is measured. Research suggests that objective and subjective measures yield different results; objective measures typically require stronger masking (e.g., shorter SOA) than subjective measures for participants to be classified as unaware (Cheesman & Merikle, 1984, 1986).

Objective measures have generally been favored over subjective measures (Holender, 1986). The most important reason is that objective measures do not leave the response criterion to the participant (Eriksen, 1960). As captured in signal detection theory (Macmillan & Creelman, 1991), participants' responses on a discrimination task are affected by their discrimination abilities (e.g., indexed by d'), as well as their response biases (e.g., indexed by *beta;* e.g., Wiens, Emmerich, & Katkin, 1997). Response bias reflects participants' predisposition to respond that the target was present. Whereas objective measures often allow one to separate discrimination ability from response bias, subjective measures might not allow this. To illustrate with a simple example, if the subjective measure described earlier is used, participants might differ in their willingness to speculate on what was depicted in the masked pictures. Because the conservative participants would perform less well on a subjective awareness measure than the liberal participants, it would seem that conservative participants are less aware of the masked pictures than liberal participants. Thus, even if conservative and liberal participants do not differ in their discrimination abilities, differences in response bias would result in confounded subjective measures of awareness.

Several factors can affect response bias. Whereas one common factor is demand characteristics (Eriksen, 1960), Merikle (1992) pointed out that subjective measures also reflect participants' notions of the value of their own awareness. For example, some participants might report that they are aware of a snake picture if they can detect something curly, whereas other participants might report that they are aware of a snake picture only if they can clearly identify all aspects of the snake. However, because the experimenter has little control over the participant's criteria and response biases, "we are in fact using as many different criteria of awareness as we have experimental subjects" (Eriksen, 1960, pp. 292–293). Also, because research has shown that participants tend to underestimate their performance in difficult perception tasks (Björkman, Juslin, & Winman, 1993; Cheesman

& Merikle, 1984, 1986), participants in masking studies might be biased toward being less willing to report that they were aware of masked pictures. As a result, subjective measures might well underestimate participants' awareness of the masked pictures. Consistent with this expectation, subjective measures of awareness tend to be less sensitive than objective measures (e.g., Cheesman & Merikle, 1984). In sum, because objective measures typically allow one to separate discrimination ability from response biases, they can control for the confounding influence of performance underestimation.

The Subjective Nature of Awareness: Noticing Versus Perceiving

Although objective measures of awareness allow one to assess participants' discrimination ability objectively, this feature is also their greatest drawback. In contrast to subjective measures, objective measures transfer the responsibility of deciding about awareness to the experimenter. However, as elaborated by Bowers (1984), awareness is basically of a subjective nature, a fact that is completely ignored by objective measures of awareness. Because awareness is a process that is closer to the process of "noticing" than "perceiving," a valid measure of awareness ought to capture what participants notice rather than what they can perceive. Therefore, the critical issue is whether self-reported awareness or objectively measured discrimination ability is a better index of awareness. Adherents of objective measures rely on discrimination ability (e.g., an experimental psychologist's perspective) and dismiss participants' self-reports as confounded by response biases. However, because objective measures index only participants' ability to discriminate (i.e., to perceive instead of notice), they ignore the inherently subjective nature of awareness and thus cannot be viewed as valid measures of awareness per se (Wiens & Öhman, 2002). Therefore, findings that objective measures tend to be more sensitive than subjective measures might be due to their violation of exclusiveness rather than to response biases.

Are Unaware Processes Logically Impossible?

In fact, whereas proponents of objective measures of awareness generally accept that performance at chance levels indicates that people are unaware of masked pictures, they infer that performance better than chance demonstrates necessarily that people are actually aware of the masked pictures. This reasoning has been challenged by studies of brain-damaged patients. In these studies, objective measures were used to demonstrate that people can perform a task although they are unaware of the target stimuli, as indexed by subjective measures. The most famous example is blindsight. As reported by Weiskrantz (2000), patients with damage to the primary visual cortex report that they are completely unaware of visual stimuli presented to their damaged visual field.

Further, when instructed to respond to these stimuli, patients report that they are purely guessing and need to be urged to respond anyway. Nonetheless, the patients show evidence that they can discriminate among the stimuli. Thus the patients exhibit blindsight in that they can discriminate stimuli in their damaged visual field although they report that they are unaware of the stimuli. Because objective measures (i.e., discrimination tasks) were used to index performance outside of awareness, these data challenge the notion that above-chance performance on objective measures necessarily shows that people are aware of the target stimuli. In fact, the notion that greater-than-chance performance demonstrates awareness implies that blindsight, as well as similar perceptual phenomena in unilateral neglect and prosopagnosia, does not exist, as greater-than-chance performance on objective measures would necessarily indicate that patients are aware of the target stimuli. Accordingly, if this reasoning were taken to the extreme, then any kind of discriminative response to masked pictures would necessarily indicate awareness. If so, it would be logically impossible to demonstrate performance without awareness (Bowers, 1984), as any form of discriminative responding would, by definition, indicate that participants were aware of the masked pictures (Wiens & Öhman, 2002).

Awareness as a Statistical Criterion

Aside from requiring a valid measure of awareness, the dissociation paradigm also requires that this measure show null sensitivity. In fact, even if researchers can agree on how to measure awareness, the requirement for demonstrating null sensitivity represents a problem of its own. If unawareness were defined in terms of an absolute performance level, then unawareness would not depend on any other factors aside from the absolute performance level. To illustrate, imagine a task that requires participants to recognize masked pictures of spiders and snakes, in which half of the pictures are spiders and half are snakes. On each trial, either a masked spider or snake is presented, and participants respond by forced choice whether the masked picture was a spider or a snake. If unawareness were defined in terms of an absolute performance level of 50%, which would be expected if participants responded randomly, then unawareness would not depend on any other factors. Accordingly, individual participants would be unaware if their performance levels were at 50%.

Individual Testing: You Must Be Aware (*p* < .05)!?

However, because null sensitivity is commonly defined in terms of chance performance, unawareness is based on a statistical criterion. Therefore, in order to determine whether an individual participant performed at chance (and was unaware of the masked pictures), awareness must depend not only on the absolute performance level but also on the sig-

nificance level (i.e., alpha) and the number of trials. As a result, awareness depends on the statistical power of the awareness test. Regarding effects of alpha, imagine that the forced-choice classification task of masked spiders and snakes consisted of 20 trials. Then a one-tailed alpha of .20 would correspond to a performance level exceeding 60% correct (> 12 trials), whereas a one-tailed alpha level of .10 would correspond to a performance level exceeding 65% correct (> 13 trials). That is, at an alpha of .20, individual participants would be unaware if they identified 60% or fewer of the masked spiders and snakes, whereas at an alpha of .10, participants would be unaware at up to 65% correct identifications. Thus the choice of alpha affects whether or not participants are classified as unaware. Further, although it might seem that alpha levels of .10 and .20 are odd and that the traditional alpha of .05 would do, the choice of the standard alpha of .05 might not be appropriate. Because most research is interested in rejecting the null hypothesis, an alpha of .05 allows for a low probability of only 5% of rejecting the null hypothesis even though it is true (i.e., Type I error). However, although a low alpha reduces the risk for a Type I error, it increases the risk for a Type II error. That is, although an alpha level of .05 reduces the risk of falsely concluding that participants who perform better than chance are aware of the masked pictures even though they are not (i.e., Type I error), it increases the risk for falsely concluding that participants who do not perform better than chance are unaware of the masked pictures even though they are (i.e., Type II error). In our example with 20 trials, participants would have to identify more than 70% correct to perform significantly above chance at a one-tailed alpha of .05. Thus participants who perform at or below 70% correct would be unaware of the masked spiders and snakes. However, the validity of this conclusion might be questionable, particularly so for performance levels at or close to 70% correct. Therefore, if the purpose of the research is to show that participants are unaware of the masked pictures, a big alpha level (at least .10) ought to be selected to reduce the risk for a Type II error. However, because there is no standard alpha level in masking research, researchers have set alpha levels arbitrarily.

Also, issues of directionality need to be considered when alpha is set. Because alpha can be one-tailed or two-tailed, it can be determined if individual participants perform worse than chance, as well as better than chance. In terms of the example, participants might perform significantly above chance in recognizing spiders and snakes but might, alternatively, perform significantly below chance in recognizing spiders and snakes. In the former case, participants correctly label spider pictures as spiders and snake pictures as snakes, whereas in the latter case, they reverse label spiders and snakes. Performance below chance levels is hard to interpret, as it suggests that participants could apparently discriminate among the masked pictures. Nonetheless, because such reverse labeling can happen, it is important to clarify whether the choice of alpha is one-tailed or two-tailed.

Further, when unawareness for individual participants is determined based on a statistical criterion, it depends not only on the alpha level but also on the number of trials. In the above example with 20 trials, individual participants performed better than chance at a one-tailed alpha of .10 if they correctly identified more than 65% (> 13 trials). However, if the task were based on 40 trials, individual participants would already perform better than chance (at one-tailed alpha = .10) if they correctly identified more than 60% (> 24 trials). In short, as proportionally fewer trials are sufficient to obtain a statistically reliable estimate, an increase in number of trials increases statistical power.

Group Testing: Everybody Is Aware!?

Whereas the preceding examples referred to the situation of determining whether individual participants performed better than chance, many studies tested whether a group of participants performed better than chance. These studies typically reported that participants in the study were unaware of the masked stimuli, because they did not perform better than chance as a group. However, it is questionable that a global significance test is sufficient to demonstrate unawareness for the whole sample. For example, if participants vary substantially in their performance (i.e., high variance), it is unlikely that a global performance test will turn out significant. If so, the sample could contain a number of participants who performed quite well. Because this would be consistent with the idea that some participants were aware of the masked pictures, it would be erroneous to conclude, based on a global significance test, that all participants were unaware of the masked pictures.

Also, similar problems to those discussed for significance testing of individual participants apply to significance testing of a group of participants. Accordingly, the choice of both size and directionality of alpha are important, as well as statistical power. Whereas testing of individual participants varies with the number of trials in the awareness measure, testing of a group varies with the number of participants. For example, if a group of participants went through the spider/snake classification task and obtained overall 52.7% correct (SD = 5.2), mean group performance would not differ significantly from chance performance (50%) with a sample size of 10, $t(9)$ = 1.63, p = .137. In contrast, with a sample size of 20, group performance would differ from chance, $t(19)$ = 2.37, p = .027. In this example, the additional participants in the larger group obtained identical scores to the first group. Therefore, if unawareness is determined for the whole sample, then these findings would lead to the nonsensical conclusion that participants become aware as sample sizes increase. To conclude, problems in defining unawareness based on a statistical criterion are apparent at a group level, as well as an individual level, of statistical testing.

The difficulties in using a statistical criterion in defining unawareness affect mostly objective rather than subjective measures of awareness, as objective measures rely on behavioral performance data rather than on self-report. As subjective measures assess participants' self-reported awareness, statistical testing is of minor importance in determining whether participants are unaware of the masked pictures. In contrast, as objective measures assess participants' discrimination performance, statistical testing is commonly used to decide whether participants are unaware of the masked pictures. Taken together with the conceptual problem that objective measures are insensitive to the subjective nature of awareness, these issues question the validity of indexing awareness with objective measures.

Measures Versus Thresholds

When an Objective Measure Indexes the Subjective Threshold

In fact, it is commonly believed that the use of objective measures ensures that the objective threshold is assessed; however, this assumption is challenged by several problems. First, even if awareness is measured with an objective task, it is possible that the performance measure used might be confounded by response bias. As such, it would not be a pure (objective) index of participants' discrimination ability but might represent a measure of participants' subjective awareness. For example, although detection tasks are objective measures, the commonly used performance measure of percent correct is affected by response bias, as well as discrimination ability. That is, if participants are instructed to detect whether or not a target was shown, percent correct will be affected by their predisposition to respond that a target was shown. In fact, due to changes in response bias, a participant with stable discrimination ability might score anywhere from 50–95% correct on detection tasks (Azzopardi & Cowey, 1997).

Second, if a statistical criterion is used to define unawareness, the classification of participants as aware or unaware depends on the statistical power of the objective task. For example, if the objective task consists of only a few trials, participants could perform almost perfectly and still be classified as unaware (Merikle, 1982). To illustrate, if the example task involving masked spiders and snakes (discussed earlier) consisted of 10 trials, individual participants could identify correctly 70% of the pictures without performing significantly better than chance (at one-tailed alpha = .10). However, the conclusion that the participants were unaware of the masked pictures at the objective threshold appears to have questionable validity.

Third, when masking parameters are chosen so that the masked pictures are barely, if at all, visible, participants might have no motivation to perform a discrimination task (Duncan, 1985; Merikle, 1992). Because participants would report being unaware of the masked pictures, a forced-choice classification task that requires participants to indicate whether a masked picture was a spider or a snake might be perceived as meaningless, as none of the pictures are noticed. If so, participants might not see a point in trying to classify spiders and snakes and, therefore, might push buttons randomly. As a result, they would perform at chance. Thus the objective measure (i.e., identification task) would not necessarily index the objective threshold but might reflect the subjective threshold (i.e., participants' self-reported unawareness). Our own observations from pilot studies support this argument. When pictures were masked well and participants were instructed to indicate whether a masked picture was a spider or a snake, some participants stopped responding because they thought that the projector was broken, as they did not notice any spiders and snakes. Therefore, in our experiments in which we attempted to assess the objective threshold, we explained to participants that it might appear to them that no target pictures are shown at all but that they should attend to all pictures and decide whether a spider or snake was presented. Thus participants' subjective sense of guessing on the classification task did not undermine their motivation to perform well on this task. However, this discussion highlights the issue of whether or not the use of objective measures guarantees that the objective threshold is assessed. For example, Merikle and Daneman (2000) suggested that factors such as an insufficient number of trials on the objective measure, as well as insufficient motivation of the participants, could explain why many reports of unconscious processes have been comparable in studies in which unawareness was assessed with either an objective measure (purportedly indexing the objective threshold) or a subjective measure.

To conclude, the use of an objective task does not guarantee that the objective threshold is assessed. However, if a performance measure is used that is unaffected by response biases (e.g., d' instead of percent correct), if the task has sufficient statistical power (e.g., sufficient number of trials, large alpha), and if the participants are motivated to perform the task, then the finding that participants performed at chance would support the conclusion that participants were unaware at the objective threshold. However, in order to decide about the validity of claims regarding unawareness, these matters ought to be addressed in every research report. For example, one suggestion is to include confidence intervals, as these depend on statistical power. However, because there are no generally accepted criteria (e.g., size of alpha), any conclusion regarding awareness might be questioned by researchers with different criteria.

Measuring Thresholds

Although we believe that the concepts of subjective and objective thresholds are helpful, they provide only rough guidelines in distinguishing different levels of awareness.

In general, the subjective threshold refers to whether participants notice the masked pictures, whereas the objective threshold refers to whether participants can discriminate the masked pictures on a behavioral task. However, because the definitions are rather vague, it is unclear which specific measures ought to be used to capture these thresholds. In fact, Cheesman and Merikle (1986) measured thresholds in terms of performance on either a detection task (experiment 2) or an identification task (experiment 3). That is, performance was indexed by participants' subjective or objective ability to detect whether or not a word was presented (detection task) or which word was presented (discrimination task). However, because research suggests that these tasks can yield different results (e.g., Haase, Theios, & Jenison, 1999), it is unclear whether these two tasks measure the same process. To give another example, the task used by Öhman and Soares (1994) to measure participants' ability to classify masked spiders, snakes, flowers, and mushrooms appears to provide an index of the objective threshold. However, as Lovibond and Shanks (2002) argued, participants might be able to discriminate among the masked pictures without being able to verbally label the masked pictures. Because both measures assess different kinds of discrimination abilities, it is unclear which measure is the correct one to index the objective threshold. Similarly, if participants are shown masked spiders and snakes, but they report that they did not see any spiders or snakes, it might be concluded that they were unaware (subjective threshold). However, if participants also reported that they noticed that masked pictures were shown even though they could not tell whether the pictures were spiders or snakes, these findings would suggest that participants had some subjective awareness of the masked pictures (similar to Weiskrantz's [2000] notion of type 2 blindsight). Therefore, it is unclear whether it can be concluded that participants were unaware at the subjective threshold. So, unless one postulates that there are as many thresholds as there are tasks, conclusions regarding whether the subjective or objective threshold is assessed depend on the specific task that was used to index awareness. However, this decision might be particularly difficult for tasks that combine subjective with objective features. For example, Kunimoto, Miller, and Pashler (2001) introduced a measure that combines (objective) discrimination ability with (subjective) confidence. On each trial, participants choose a response and indicate their confidence (high or low). Then a signal-detection analysis is performed in which correct responses with high confidence (*hits*) are contrasted with incorrect responses with high confidence (*false alarms*). Because participants' predisposition to indicate high confidence (response bias) affects both hits and false alarms, participants' ability to discriminate correct responses from incorrect responses in terms of confidence can be assessed independent of response bias.

Taken together, these points indicate that concepts of measurement and threshold need to be distinguished to avoid potential misunderstandings in the discussion of measuring awareness. Thus they illustrate the need to distinguish between empirical measures and theoretical constructs, a distinction that has often been blurred in the study of unconscious processes (Reingold & Merikle, 1990).

When to Measure Awareness

Because masking research on emotional responses that uses the dissociation paradigm includes two measures, one to index awareness and the other one to index emotional processes, a final issue is when these measures ought to be taken. We recommend that both measures be taken in the same participants (i.e., within-subjects design). Because awareness is best tested at the level of individual participants, it is advisable to measure awareness of all participants in the study. However, if factors such as time restrictions do not permit obtaining both measures from the same participants, performance data from other participants are helpful in characterizing awareness for the participants in the study. For example, before their actual experiment, Öhman and Soares (1994) conducted an experiment in which they found that participants showed little, if any, evidence that they could classify masked spiders, snakes, flowers, and mushrooms at the particular masking parameters. These findings supported the notion that the masking parameters were generally effective in preventing participants from recognizing the masked pictures.

Further, when awareness and emotional processes are assessed in a within-subjects design, both measures can be collected concurrently or separately. In our research, we have used both approaches. For example, in the Wiens, Katkin, and Öhman (2003) study, a separate forced-choice classification task was used, whereas in the Öhman and Soares (1998, experiment 2) study, some participants completed a classification task while emotional processes (i.e., skin conductance) were monitored. If awareness is assessed in a separate task, it is best measured in the same session as the emotional measures, as performance might not remain constant between sessions (e.g., Wolford, Marchak, & Hughes, 1988). However, although a concurrent measure of awareness might be most sensitive in indexing awareness, it is likely that the measuring process affects the variables of interest. Therefore, emotional processing might depend on the task that participants perform during the experiment. For example, when participants were shown emotional faces and had to decide either which other face or which verbal label matched the emotional expression, they showed amygdala activation only when they matched the faces to other faces, not when they verbally labeled the expressions (Hariri, Bookheimer, & Mazziota, 2000). Because concurrent and separate measurements of awareness represent different experimental contexts that might engage different processes (e.g., passive viewing versus active search), this discussion suggests that the timing of measuring awareness needs to be carefully considered.

Measuring Emotions

Clearly, the main issues with masking research have to do with the assessment of awareness. However, because the purpose of using masking in emotion studies is to study emotional processes that occur outside of awareness, emotional measures need to be included as dependent variables. In our own research, we have mostly used psychophysiological measures of emotion with an emphasis on sweat gland activity. The study by Öhman and Soares (1994) is a typical example (see Figure 5.3). As described earlier, results showed that participants who were afraid of spiders (but not of snakes) showed greater skin conductance responses (SCRs) to masked spiders than to masked snakes, flowers, and mushrooms. Similarly, participants afraid of snakes (but not spiders) showed greater SCRs to masked snakes than to other masked pictures. In contrast, participants who were unafraid of spiders and snakes did not show elevated SCRs to these masked pictures. Because these data are consistent with reports that people with phobias show elevated SCRs to fear-eliciting pictures (Globisch, Hamm, Esteves, & Öhman, 1999), the findings by Öhman and Soares (1994) suggest that fear was elicited unconsciously by the masked spiders and snakes. However, research has found that people show elevated SCRs to arousing stimuli, whether negative or positive (for a review, see Bradley et al., 2001). For example, when people rated pictures on dimensions of valence and arousal, they showed elevated SCRs to pictures that they rated as unpleasant and arousing (e.g., accidents, mutilations), as well as to pictures that they rated as pleasant and arousing (e.g., nudes). Thus elevated SCRs were not specific to negative emotions but depended on how arousing the pictures were. Therefore, findings of elevated SCRs to masked spiders and snakes (Öhman & Soares, 1994) might reflect processes associated with the arousing properties of the spiders and snakes, rather than negative valence. Further, it is possible that such responses might represent attentional, as well as emotional, processes (Öhman & Wiens, 2003). Although findings of amygdala activation to nonmasked and masked phobic pictures in people with spider and snake phobias (Carlsson et al., 2004) provide evidence for emotion, this example illustrates that researchers need to be aware of the limitations of their emotional measures.

Masking: Too Many Problems?

At this point, critical readers of this chapter might conclude that the masking method has too many problems to be useful in studying unconscious emotional processes. The technical demands seem quite tedious. Also, given that there is no generally accepted measure of awareness, the choice of an awareness measure seems to be arbitrary. Further, when the dissociation paradigm is used, unawareness is commonly demonstrated with null sensitivity. However, because null sensitivity is typically defined based on a statistical criterion, it depends on a number of factors (e.g., alpha, number of trials) that also seem to be arbitrarily chosen by researchers. In fact, whether or not significant results are obtained, critics with different criteria will probably challenge the data. If null findings are obtained, the study might never get published. With this "file-drawer problem," the generalizability of significant findings will be overestimated. Also, as discussed by Eriksen (1960), dissociations between two measures might occur due to chance. Thus the dissociation paradigm does not rule out the possibility that, even though the awareness measure shows null sensitivity, significant findings on an emotional measure might be due to chance (Type I error). Indeed, because the dissociation paradigm combines two statistical tests (i.e., null sensitivity for awareness measure and significance for the emotional measure), the actual probability of a Type I error is not readily apparent. Null findings are also problematic because there is no manipulation check for the perceptual processing of masked pictures. That is, although participants should be unaware of the masked pictures, they should be able to process them perceptually. Otherwise, no effects at all would be expected. For example, if masked pictures are shown for 1 nanosec, they would probably not be processed at all, and neither nonemotional perceptual nor emotional processes would be expected. Therefore, without a manipulation check for nonemotional perceptual processing to masked pictures, null findings for emotional processes are hard to interpret.

Two Potential Solutions: Qualitative Differences and the Psychophysical Approach

Although these problems might appear insurmountable, there are at least two solutions to these issues: demonstrating qualitative differences and taking a psychophysical approach.[3] Merikle and his colleagues have developed and applied the approach of demonstrating qualitative differences to memory and perception (for review, see Merikle & Daneman, 2000). The central aspect of their approach is that obtaining effects that differ qualitatively for conscious and unconscious processes validates the distinction between these processes. That is, results that show that conscious processes differ in direction (i.e., qualitatively) and not just in size from unconscious processes make the distinction between both processes valid and interesting. Also, if a measure of awareness can index these qualitative differences between unconscious and conscious processes, it receives support as a valid measure of awareness.

Although it is challenging to find experimental contexts in which conscious and unconscious processes would be postulated to differ qualitatively, Merikle and his colleagues have identified several examples in independent areas of research (Merikle & Daneman, 2000). For example, in a study by Merikle and Cheesman (1987), participants were presented with a modified version of the Stroop task. In a typical Stroop task, participants are shown color words (e.g., green, red) that are printed in color (e.g., green, red). When the color words are printed in matching colors (e.g., green in green ink, red in red ink), participants have no difficulties in naming the ink colors. However, when the color words are printed in nonmatching colors (e.g., green in red ink, red in green ink), participants' performance in naming the ink colors is impaired (Stroop effect), as it is difficult to ignore the semantic content. In the Merikle and Cheesman (1987) study, only the words green and red and the corresponding ink colors were used. On each trial, a word was shown, followed by a color patch. Participants were instructed to name the color of the patch as quickly as possible. In addition, they were informed that on 80% of the trials, word and color would not match, but on the remaining 20% of the trials, word and color would match. Thus, when participants saw a color word, they could anticipate that, for the majority of trials, the color of the patch would not match the color word (e.g., if they saw green, the color of the patch would most likely be red). To study unconscious and conscious processes, the color words were masked at either short or long SOAs. Merikle and Cheesman (1987) argued that when participants can consciously perceive the color words (at long SOA), they can use the information from the color words intentionally in anticipating the nonmatching ink. That is, when participants are aware of the words (at long SOA), they can use the relative frequency of matching and nonmatching events to improve their performance. Hence, participants should respond faster on nonmatching trials and more slowly on matching trials. In contrast, when participants are not aware of the words (at short SOA), they cannot use the information from the color words to counteract automatic processes. Hence, participants should respond faster on matching trials and more slowly on nonmatching trials. Thus participants would show a typical Stroop effect when words are masked (short SOA) but a reverse Stroop effect when words are not masked (long SOA). Consistent with these predictions, results showed qualitatively different effects for masked and nonmasked color words. When words were masked, reaction times were faster on matching than on nonmatching trials. In contrast, when words were not masked, reaction times were faster on nonmatching than matching trials. These results have been replicated (Daza, Ortelli, & Fox, 2002; Merikle & Joordens, 1997). Because effects on reaction time were in the opposite direction for masked and nonmasked words, these findings provide evidence for qualitatively different processes. Thus they validate the distinction between conscious and unconscious processes. Because research further suggests that participants were unaware of the masked words at the subjective threshold (Cheesman & Merikle, 1984), the findings of qualitative differences suggest that the subjective threshold is a valid index of awareness.

Qualitative Differences

The approach of demonstrating qualitative differences could be useful in studying emotional conscious and unconscious processes. Unfortunately, to our knowledge, there is no study that has explicitly used this approach. However, the results of a study by Morris, Öhman, and Dolan (1998, 1999) might qualify as an example of qualitative differences (Wiens & Öhman, 2002). In this study, participants were fear conditioned to two nonmasked angry faces. That is, for each participant, it was randomly determined which of two angry faces was paired with a loud noise. At the beginning of the experiment, participants were shown both angry faces and were instructed that they would perform a detection task during the experiment. On each trial, if they saw either angry face, however fleetingly, they should push one button, and if they did not see either angry face, they should push another button. After conditioning, participants were shown masked, as well as nonmasked, examples of the angry faces. When angry faces were masked, neutral faces served as masks, and when angry faces were not masked, the angry faces were shown after the neutral faces. Results for the detection task showed that participants indicated that they saw all of the nonmasked angry faces but none of the masked angry faces. Further, results from positron emission tomography (PET) brain imaging indicated that, after conditioning, differential amygdala activation occurred for masked and nonmasked presentations of the angry faces. In nonmasked presentations, the left amygdala was activated, whereas in masked presentations, the right amygdala was activated. Because this pattern of results yielded a significant interaction between masking and laterality, the findings suggest qualitatively different effects for masked and nonmasked presentations on amygdala activation. These data replicate and extend prior research that demonstrated a critical role of the amygdala in conditioned fear (LeDoux, 1996).

Also, because the qualitative differences were indexed by the awareness measure used by Morris et al. (1998), these findings support the validity of the awareness measure. Thus these data challenge Lovibond and Shanks's (2002) criticism of this type of awareness measure (Wiens & Öhman, 2002). However, it is unclear whether the awareness measure used by Morris et al. (1998) assessed the subjective or objective threshold. In the study, participants responded that they saw all of the nonmasked angry faces and none of the masked angry faces. However, because participants were allowed to respond only yes or no to indicate their awareness, they may have reserved the *yes* response only for the nonmasked angry faces even though the masked angry faces might have been partly detectable. That is, although participants might have been able to discriminate the masked angry faces, they responded *no* (i.e., unawareness) to masked angry faces because these fell below their subjective criterion of visibility. Thus the 0% correct on the (objective) detection task might be an index of the subjective threshold rather than the objective threshold. This issue is further complicated by the fact that the detection task might index a task dimension that is independent from the dimension of interest (Duncan, 1985). Whereas the detection task assessed participants' ability to detect either angry face, the dimension of interest referred to the difference between the angry face paired with noise versus the angry face not paired with noise. So, even if participants responded that they did not detect either masked angry face, they might have been able to discriminate between the two masked angry faces. Consistent with this idea, Haase et al. (1999) showed that even though participants responded that they did not detect either masked stimulus (*CCC* or *ZZZ*), they were able to discriminate between them. Therefore, although the findings of qualitative differences in the Morris et al. (1998) study support the validity of the awareness measure, further research is needed to clarify questions regarding participants' awareness.

When Are Differences Qualitative?

Although findings of qualitative differences for masked and nonmasked emotional pictures provide strong evidence for unconscious processes, it seems difficult to identify emotional processes that are predicted to differ qualitatively for masked and nonmasked pictures. For example, findings that effects are significantly stronger for nonmasked than masked pictures are insufficient for qualitative differences, as effects for masked and nonmasked pictures would merely differ in size, not qualitatively. Although effects that differ in direction are the strongest evidence for qualitative differences, there are scenarios that are less obvious. For example, the findings by Morris et al. (1998, 1999) regarding differential activations in the left and right amygdala suggest that effects were qualitatively different for masked and nonmasked pictures. Similarly, counterintuitive findings of significantly stronger effects to masked pictures than to nonmasked pictures might also represent a qualitative difference (e.g., Rotteveel, de Groot, Geutskens, & Phaf, 2001). However, any claims for qualitative differences need to be carefully examined. For example, Cheesman and Merikle (1986) reported that participants were able to use a predictive strategy in a Stroop priming task when words were not masked but were unable to do so when words were masked. The authors concluded that these data provided evidence for qualitative differences. However, because there was no significant effect for masked words and a significant effect only for nonmasked words, these results might represent not qualitative but quantitative differences. Similarly, the findings by Morris et al. (1998) are consistent with the notion of qualitative differences. However, they might also be conceptualized as quantitative differences. For example, the right and left amygdalae might differ in their relative activation functions to degraded and nondegraded input. If so, this phenomenon might be similar to sensitivity differences to frequency for hair cells in the cochlea. Because hair cells vary in their sensitivity to different frequencies depending on their location within the cochlea, cells at one end of the cochlea are mostly sensitive to low frequencies, whereas cells at the other end of the cochlea are mostly sensitive to high frequencies. Although these sensitivity differences depending on location can be conceptualized as qualitative differences, they might be more parsimoniously described as relative (quantitative) differences. Accordingly, the right amygdala might be relatively more sensitive to degraded input, whereas the left amygdala might be relatively more sensitive to non-degraded input. Even if this alternative explanation might seem unlikely, it illustrates the need to consider whether findings of apparent qualitative differences can be interpreted more parsimoniously in terms of quantitative differences.

The Psychophysical Approach

An alternative to the search for qualitative differences is the psychophysical approach. The main purpose of this approach is to determine the dose-response relationship between awareness and the emotional measure of interest. Thus awareness is not necessarily treated as a dichotomous phenomenon (i.e., participants are either aware or unaware of the masked pictures) but can vary in degree. To manipulate awareness, masked pictures are presented at various masking parameters. Then the relationships between effects of masking parameters on participants' awareness of the masked pictures and the emotional measure can be assessed. Hence, given that issues relating to the concept of thresholds (subjective vs. objective) and the measurement of awareness are far from resolved (as discussed previously), the psychophysical approach allows a more eclectic approach.

The psychophysical approach has several notable features. First, the psychophysical approach provides information about the shape of the response function across a range of masking conditions. Thus, instead of trying to prove that unconscious processes exist,[4] the psychophysical approach provides quantitative information about relative changes in emotional processes as awareness is varied. So, even if the underlying relationship resembles a step function, results from a study covering a range of masking conditions could provide good evidence for this step function. For example, results might show that effects on the variable of interest remain unchanged across the short range of masking intervals, increase in a steplike fashion at the middle intervals, and remain stable for the longer masking intervals. This pattern would support the idea that the underlying relationship follows a step function. In contrast, even if a study with two conditions included the two critical middle intervals, results would not allow one to conclude anything about the effects of short and long intervals, as findings of a step function for the middle intervals would also be consistent with other relationships (e.g., U-shape) across intervals. In fact, as illustrated in Figure 5.9, the relationship between awareness and emotional activation might not be linear, as suggested by some models of unconscious perception (e.g., Snodgrass, Bernat, & Shevrin, 2004). If so, studies that sample only two points (unconscious vs. conscious) will not detect

these relationships. Hence, they do not allow one to draw strong conclusions about the underlying relationship between awareness and emotional activations. In contrast, the psychophysical approach can capture the exact nature of the relationship between awareness and emotional activation.

Also, because the psychophysical approach aims at studying the shape of the relationship across a range of conditions, it advocates the use of complementary measures of awareness. As described earlier, there is an ongoing debate on how to measure awareness. Even if awareness is simply classified in terms of subjective and objective thresholds, it is unclear which measures are best at assessing these thresholds. However, because research suggests that the thresholds differ, research that studies effects below and above these thresholds could provide evidence to support either or both concepts. For example, because research suggests that stronger masking (e.g., shorter SOA) is necessary for participants to be unaware at the objective rather than the subjective threshold, a study that covered both thresholds could be useful in determining whether changes in the variable of interest occur when participants become aware at the objective or subjective threshold or both. To illustrate, Figure 5.10 shows hypothetical emotional activation at different levels of unawareness. As shown, in a strong model of unconscious processing, emotional responses occur already below the objective threshold. Alternatively, in a weak model of unconscious processing, emotional responses occur above the objective but below the subjective threshold (for an example regarding amygdala activation to masked fearful faces, see Pessoa, 2005).

Last, because the psychophysical approach covers a range of masking parameters, it minimizes the risk of missing the critical range of masking parameters. Because unawareness effects might occur only within a small range of masking parameters, an experiment with only a single unaware con-

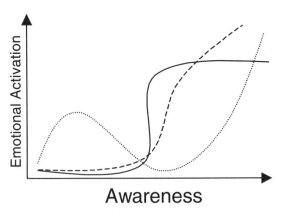

Figure 5.9. Hypothetical dose-response functions between awareness and emotional activation. Because emotional responding might not be linearly related to awareness, manipulation of target duration in small steps permits the study of the nature of the relationship (i.e., dose-response function) between awareness and emotional activation.

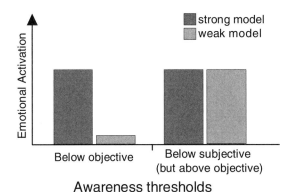

Figure 5.10. Models of emotional activation for different levels of unawareness. In a strong model of unconscious processing, emotional responding occurs already below the objective threshold. In a weak model of unconscious processing, emotional responding occurs below the subjective threshold but above the objective threshold.

dition is likely to miss this critical range. If masking is too effective, no perceptual or emotional processing is expected. As explained earlier, this is a potential problem, as there is typically no manipulation check for perceptual processing of masked pictures. Similarly, if masking is ineffective, participants would be rated as aware on the measure of awareness, and the data would seem useless. Because our observations suggest that there is no gold standard for effective masking parameters (e.g., SOA of 30 ms) and that masking is sensitive to small changes in lab conditions (e.g., background illumination), the constant requirement to fine-tune and test masking parameters is reduced in psychophysical experiments that cover a range of masking conditions.

Inferences About the Role of Awareness

Although the psychophysical approach is useful in characterizing the relationship between emotional processing and awareness, it does not allow one to draw inferences about the causal nature of this relationship. Because changes in awareness are associated with accompanying changes in masking parameters, it cannot be distinguished whether changes in emotional processing result from changes in either awareness or masking parameters or both. Thus, even if conscious and unconscious perceptual states might be associated with qualitatively different effects, consciousness per se might not necessarily play a causal role in the observed pattern of differences (cf. Kunimoto et al., 2001). Therefore, if the purpose of a study is to determine whether changes in awareness per se are associated with certain effects, masking parameters have to remain constant, whereas awareness changes. For example, if masking parameters remain constant and if participants report being aware of the targets on only half of the trials, then trials on which participants reported

awareness of the masked targets (hits) can be contrasted with trials in which participants reported no awareness of the masked targets (misses) to study effects of awareness per se. Of course, this assumes that mere reporting of awareness (false alarms) has no effects (e.g., for amygdala activations for false alarms to fearful faces, see Pessoa, Japee, Sturman, & Ungerleider, 2006). However, although this design can help identify processes that are correlated with awareness, it is also insufficient to prove the causal nature of the relationship between awareness and obtained findings, as awareness could be an epiphenomenon (Frith, Perry, & Lumer, 1999). Nonetheless, because masking research has been mostly interested in determining whether emotional processing can occur in the absence of awareness, effects of awareness per se are irrelevant for this question. Thus, to study which degree of emotional processing can occur at different levels of awareness, the psychophysical approach is a valid strategy.

Example Study of the Psychophysical Approach

A current study in our lab using functional magnetic resonance imaging (fMRI) illustrates the psychophysical approach (pilot results were presented by Wiens, Fransson, Ingvar, & Öhman, 2004). The purpose of this study is to further our understanding of the relationship between awareness and amygdala activation to fearful faces (Whalen et al., 1998). In the study, target pictures were fearful, neutral, and scrambled faces. To manipulate awareness, targets were presented for durations of 15, 20, 30, and 60 ms and were followed immediately (masked) by scrambled faces that were shown for 500 ms minus target duration (so as to have the same picture duration in all conditions). As part of the study, participants ($N = 15$) performed two recognition tasks in the fMRI scanner. One task was a two-interval forced-choice (2IFC) face detection task. On each trial, a masked fearful or neutral face and a masked scrambled face (lure) were shown with a 1.5-s interval between them. Then participants decided whether the first or the second masked picture was a face and whether they actually saw a face or were just guessing. The other task was similar (also 2IFC) except that a masked fearful face and a masked neutral face (lure) were shown on every trial. In this fear-recognition task, participants decided whether the first or second masked face was fearful and reported whether or not they actually saw a fearful expression. The present study used 2IFC tasks instead of simple (yes/no) detection tasks for the following reason. Because participants often report little, if any, awareness of masked pictures, their subjective sense of unawareness might undermine their performance on simple (yes/no) detection tasks. For example, participants might lose motivation and respond *yes* and *no* randomly. As a result, performance would be underestimated. In contrast, 2IFC tasks tend to avoid this problem because a target is actually presented on every trial (Macmillan & Creelman, 1991). Hence performance estimates can be expected to be more accurate for 2IFC than detection tasks.

Figures 5.11 shows preliminary results for the face-detection task (A and B) and the fear-recognition task (C and D) for the four target durations. Panels A and C are based on signal detection analyses of the data. Panel A shows mean percent correctly detected faces for fearful and neutral faces, and panel C shows mean percent correctly recognized fear, expressed as adjusted maximum percent correct (PCmax). Panel B shows mean percent of reported faces for fearful and neutral faces, as well as for scrambled faces (i.e., false alarms), and panel D shows mean percent of reported fear for correct and incorrect responses. Results in panels A and C are presented in PCmax rather than raw percent correct because the latter measure can be confounded by response biases. Also, PCmax was used instead of the signal detection index d' because readers tend to be more familiar with percent correct. Accordingly, the signal detection index d' was computed first. However, because sensitivity (d') cannot be computed for null or perfect performance, half a response was either added or subtracted, respectively. Because in these 2IFC tasks, participants could decide based on two intervals, sensitivity estimates (d') were adjusted (divided by $\sqrt{2}$). Then, for each participant, PCmax was defined as percent correct for a given

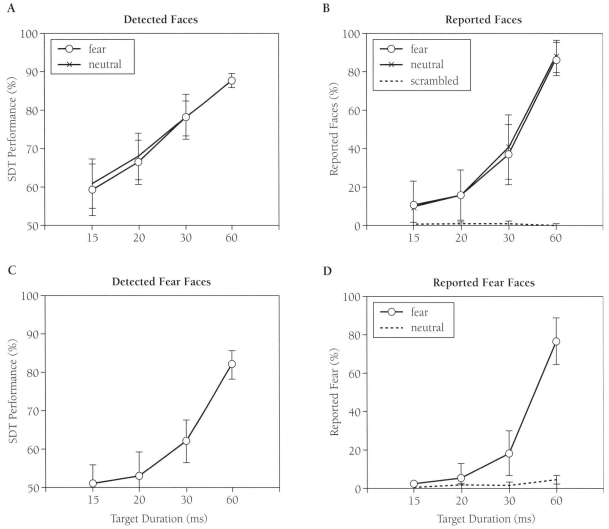

Figure 5.11. Performance on the two-interval forced choice (2IFC) tasks across four target durations ($N = 15$). Panel A shows mean (with 95% confidence intervals) percent correctly detected faces for fearful and neutral faces in the face-detection task, as expressed in maximum percent correct (PCmax) from signal detection (SDT) analyses. Panel B shows the mean (with 95% confidence intervals) percent reported faces for fearful, neutral, and scrambled faces in the 2IFC face-detection task. Panel C shows mean percent of fear that was correctly recognized in the 2IFC fear recognition task (as adjusted PCmax). Panel D shows mean percent reported fear for fearful and neutral faces in the fear-recognition task. Note that PCmax is the maximum percent correct without any response biases and adjusted (divided by $\sqrt{2}$) for the fact that participants could decide based on two intervals.

sensitivity (*d'*) in the absence of any response biases (Macmillan & Creelman, 1991).

As shown in Figure 5.11, as target duration increased, percent of detected and recognized faces increased gradually rather than in a steplike fashion. This was true also for psychophysical curves of individual participants (not shown). However, as shown in Figures 5.11A and B, there was no difference in face detection for fearful and neutral faces. Also, across target durations, participants performed better on the face-detection task (A) than on the fear-recognition task (C). These findings indicate that face detection was easier than fear recognition. Also, findings suggest that manipulation of target duration was successful in affecting participants' reported awareness and recognition performance of masked faces.

However, when discussing the data across participants in terms of objective and subjective thresholds, the following conclusions might be drawn. Because participants did not perform beyond chance in discriminating between fearful and neutral faces at target durations of 15 and 20 ms (Figure 5.11C) these findings suggest that fear recognition was below the objective threshold at these intervals. However, because face detection was much greater than chance even at 15 ms (Figure 5.11A), the objective threshold for face detection was exceeded in all target durations. In contrast to conclusions about objective thresholds, inferences about subjective thresholds are harder to draw. If the subjective threshold were defined as the target duration at which the percent of reported faces differs significantly from zero (or from the false alarm rate), the subjective threshold would not differ from the objective threshold (because both would be based on discrimination performance). Therefore, a definition of the subjective threshold cannot rely on discrimination performance. One possibility is the use of an empirical threshold (e.g., 50%). If so, participants would be considered unaware below the subjective threshold (50%) at target durations shorter than 60 ms, as they reported less than 40% of the faces in the face-detection task and less than 20% of the fearful expressions in the fear-recognition task (Figure 5.11B and D).

Because fMRI was also measured in a separate part of the study, we can study brain activations to masked faces at different levels of awareness. Results from this study will address whether amygdala activation occurs to masked fearful faces below both objective and subjective thresholds or whether it occurs only above the objective but below subjective threshold (see Figure 5.10). Also, because, contrary to previous research, scrambled faces rather than actual faces served as masks, we can study activations to masked faces per se. Further, although it was not feasible to include more than four masking conditions, we can study dose-response relationships between awareness and emotional processing (see Figure 5.9). That is, instead of dichotomizing awareness in terms of subjective and objective thresholds, performance measures can be used to index awareness on a continuum. Thus the debate about concepts of thresholds can be avoided.

Conclusions

This chapter reviewed conceptual, methodological, and technical challenges in the use of masking to study unconscious emotional processes. Traditionally, the approach has been to try to eliminate awareness to assess effects of masked target pictures of which participants are not consciously aware (i.e., dissociation paradigm). Unfortunately, there is no definition and measure of awareness that researchers agree on (i.e., issues of exhaustiveness and exclusiveness). Also, because unawareness has been indexed as null sensitivity of the awareness measure, it has been defined in terms of a statistical criterion. Thus it depends on statistical power and is also affected by difficulties in proving the null hypothesis (i.e., participants are unaware). Further, because masking requires that pictures be shown briefly and in short order, it places great demands on display technology. Unfortunately, our research suggests that commonly used displays based on TFT and LCD technology do not recommend themselves for masking. Therefore, although some displays can handle masking, each setup needs to be validated. Hence we urge researchers to provide evidence for the validity of their display equipment in their publications. Also, because there is no gold standard for masking parameters and because perceptual processes are affected by small changes in masking parameters, researchers need to focus on assessing awareness in their participants rather than on reporting only the masking parameters.

Because of its focus on conceptual, methodological, and technical aspects involved in masking, this chapter has discussed findings from masking studies on emotional activations only if relevant. For example, there are a number of recent imaging studies on awareness and amygdala activation (for review, see Wiens, 2006). Although we are enthusiastic about this surge in research, we would like to encourage researchers to employ the psychophysical approach described here in their studies. Also, because all of these studies used displays (TFT, LCD) that might have questionable validity for masking, we invite researchers to use a setup similar to ours involving shutters (see Figure 5.6). Because shutters are not limited by refresh cycles, they permit manipulation of picture duration in milliseconds. Thus they provide an excellent means to study the relationship between awareness and emotional activation.

One reason that researchers disagree on how to define and measure awareness might be that it is an oversimplification to treat awareness as a unitary concept. Awareness might have to be conceptualized in terms of processes such as detecting, discriminating, identifying, and noticing. If so, comprehensive measures (e.g., objective and subjective) should be used to characterize these processes. Although findings of qualitative differences represent strong evidence for the distinction between conscious and unconscious processes and for particular measures and concepts of awareness, the psychophysical approach provides an alternative strategy for studying the dose-response relationships between awareness and emotional processes. When used with masking, these approaches allow researchers to study the role of awareness in emotional processes and thus to probe unconscious emotional processes.

Acknowledgments

We thank Ed Katkin for helpful comments. Stefan Wiens would like to thank his family in Södervika for a relaxing writing environment during the summer of 2003. The authors' research was supported by grants from the Bank of Sweden Tercentennial Foundation and the Swedish Council for Research in the Humanities and Social Sciences to Arne Öhman.

Notes

1. *Unconscious* simply means *not conscious.*
2. Examples are Presentation (Neurobehavioral Systems), E-prime, ERTS (Beringer, Frankfurt am Main, Germany), and DMDX (http://www.u.arizona.edu/~kforster/dmdx/dmdx.htm).
3. Reingold and Merikle (1988) proposed an approach in which *direct* and *indirect* measures are compared in their relative sensitivity. If participants perform better on the indirect measure (e.g., of emotional processes) than on the direct measure (of awareness), then this would be evidence for unconscious processing. Although this is an interesting design, it requires that both measures be assessed under comparable conditions, including the same response metric. Unfortunately, this requirement is unlikely to be met by most measures of emotion.
4. As Cohen (1994, p. 1001) put it: "Go build a quantitative science with *p* values!"

References

Azzopardi, P., & Cowey, A. (1997). Is blindsight like normal, near-threshold vision? *Proceedings of the National Academy of Sciences of the USA, 94,* 14190–14194.

Berridge, K. C., & Winkielman, P. (2003). What is an unconscious emotion? (The case for unconscious "liking"). *Cognition and Emotion, 17,*181–211.

Björkman, M., Juslin, P., & Winman, A. (1993). Realism of confidence in sensory discrimination: The underconfidence phenomenon. *Perception and Psychophysics, 54,* 75–81.

Bowers, K. S. (1984). On being unconsciously influenced and informed. In K. S. Bowers & D. Meichenbaum (Eds.), *The unconscious reconsidered* (pp. 227–272). New York: Wiley.

Bradley, M. M., Codispoti, M., Cuthbert, B. N., & Lang, P. J. (2001). Emotion and motivation I: Defensive and appetitive reactions in picture processing. *Emotion, 1,* 276–298.

Bridgeman, B. (1998). Durations of stimuli displayed on video display terminals: $(n-1)/f$ + Persistence. *Psychological Science, 9,* 232–233.

Bruner, J. S., & Goodman, C. C. (1947). Value and need as organizing factors in perception. *Journal of Personality, 16,* 69–77.

Campbell, D. T., & Fiske, D. W. (1959). Convergent and discriminant validation by the multitrait-multimethod matrix. *Psychological Bulletin, 56,* 82–105.

Carlsson, K., Petersson, K. M., Lundqvist, D., Karlsson, A., Ingvar, M., & Öhman, A. (2004). Fear and the amygdala: Manipulation of awareness generates differential cerebral responses to phobic and fear-relevant (but nonfeared) stimuli. *Emotion, 4,* 340–353.

Cheesman, J., & Merikle, P. M. (1984). Priming with and without awareness. *Perception and Psychophysics, 36,* 387–395.

Cheesman, J., & Merikle, P. M. (1986). Distinguishing conscious from unconscious perceptual processes. *Canadian Journal of Psychology, 40,* 343–367.

Clore, G. L. (1994). Why emotions are never unconscious. In P. Ekman & R. J. Davidson (Eds.), *The nature of emotion: Fundamental questions* (pp. 285–290). New York: Oxford University Press.

Cohen, J. (1994). The earth is round ($p < .05$). *American Psychologist, 49,* 997–1003.

Damasio, A. R. (1994). *Descartes' error: Emotion, reason, and the human brain.* New York: Putnam.

Daza, M. T., Ortelli, J. J., & Fox, E. (2002). Perception without awareness: Further evidence from a Stroop priming task. *Perception and Psychophysics, 64,* 1316–1324.

Duncan, J. (1985). The techniques for investigating perception without awareness. *Perception and Psychophysics, 38,* 296–298.

Ekman, P. (1972). Universals and cultural differences in facial expressions of emotion. In J. K. Cole (Ed.), *Nebraska Symposium on Motivation 1971* (Vol. 19, pp. 207–283) Lincoln: University of Nebraska Press.

Ellsworth, P. C., & Scherer, K. R. (2003) Appraisal processes in emotion. In R. J. Davidson, H. Goldsmith, & K. R. Scherer (Eds.), *Handbook of affective sciences* (pp. 572–595). New York: Oxford University Press.

Erdelyi, M. H. (1974). A new look at the New Look: Perceptual defense and vigilance. *Psychological Review, 81,* 1–25.

Eriksen, C. W. (1960). Discrimination and learning without awareness: A methodological survey and evaluation. *Psychological Review, 67,* 279–300.

Esteves, F., & Öhman, A. (1993). Masking the face: recognition of emotional facial expressions as a function of the parameters of backward masking. *Scandinavian Journal of Psychology, 34,* 1–18.

Freud, S. (1959). Introductory lectures on psycho-analysis. In J. Strachey (Ed.), *The standard edition of the complete psychological works of Sigmund Freud* (Vols. 15–16). London: Hogarth. (Original work published 1916–1917)

Frijda, N. H. (1986). *The emotions.* Cambridge: Cambridge University Press.

Frith, C., Perry, R., & Lumer, E. (1999). The neural correlates of conscious experience: An experimental framework. *Trends in Cognitive Sciences, 3,* 105–114.

Gazzaniga, M. S. (1998). *The mind's past.* Berkeley: University of California Press.

Globisch, J., Hamm, A. O., Esteves, F., & Öhman, A. (1999). Fear appears fast: Temporal course of startle reflex potentiation in animal-fearful subjects. *Psychophysiology, 36,* 66–75.

Haase, S. J., Theios, J., & Jenison, R. (1999). A signal detection theory analysis of an unconscious perception effect. *Perception and Psychophysics, 61,* 986–992.

Hariri, A. R., Bookheimer, S. Y., & Mazziota, J. C. (2000). Modulating emotional responses: Effects of a neocortical network on the limbic system. *Neuroreport, 11,* 43–48.

Harris, V. A., & Katkin, E. S. (1975). Primary and secondary emotional behavior: An analysis of the role of autonomic feedback on affect, arousal, and attribution. *Psychological Bulletin, 82,* 904–916.

Holender, D. (1986). Semantic activation without conscious identification in dichotic listening, parafoveal vision, and visual masking: A survey and appraisal. *Behavioral and Brain Sciences, 9,* 1–66.

James, W. (1884). What is an emotion? *Mind, 9,* 188–205.

Kihlstrom, J. F. (1987). The cognitive unconscious. *Science, 237,* 1445–1452.

Kihlstrom, J. F. (1999). The psychological unconscious. In L. A. Pervin & O. P. John (Eds.), *Handbook of personality: Theory and research* (2nd ed., pp. 424–442). New York: Guilford Press.

Kihlstrom, J. F., Mulvaney, S., Tobias, B. A., & Tobis, I. P. (2000). The emotional unconscious. In E. Eich, J. F. Kihlstrom, G. H. Bower, J. P. Forgas, & P. M. Niedenthal (Eds.), *Cognition and emotion* (pp. 30–86). New York: Oxford University Press.

Krantz, J. H. (2000). Tell me, what did you see? The stimulus on computers. *Behavior Research Methods, Instruments, and Computers, 32,* 221–229.

Kunimoto, C., Miller, J., & Pashler, H. (2001). Confidence and accuracy of near-threshold discrimination responses. *Consciousness and Cognition, 10,* 294–340.

Kushner, M. G., & Beitman, B. D. (1990). Panic Attacks Without Fear: An Overview. *Behaviour Research And Therapy, 28*(6), 469–479.

Lang, P. J. (1968). Fear reduction and fear behavior: Problems in treating a construct. In J. M. Shlien (Ed.), *Research in psychotherapy* (Vol. 3, pp. 90–102). Washington, DC: American Psychological Association.

Lang, P. J. (1993). The three-system approach to emotion. In N. Birbaumer & A. Öhman (Eds.), *The structure of emotion: Psychophysiological, cognitive and clinical aspects* (pp. 18–30). Seattle: Hogrefe & Huber.

LeDoux, J. E. (1996). *The emotional brain.* New York: Simon & Schuster.

Lovibond, P. F., & Shanks, D. R. (2002). The role of awareness in Pavlovian conditioning: Empirical evidence and theoretical implications. *Journal of Experimental Psychology: Animal Behavior Processes, 28,* 3–26.

Macmillan, N. A., & Creelman, C. D. (1991). *Detection theory: A user's guide.* New York: Cambridge University Press.

Mandler, G. (1975). *Mind and emotion.* New York: Wiley.

Merikle, P. M. (1982). Unconscious perception revisited. *Perception and Psychophysics, 31,* 298–301.

Merikle, P. M. (1992). Perception without awareness: Critical issues. *American Psychologist, 47,* 792–795.

Merikle, P. M., & Cheesman, J. (1987). Current status of research on subliminal perception. In M. Wallendorf & P. F. Anderson (Eds.), *Advances in consumer research* (Vol. 14, pp. 298–302). Provo, UT: Association for Consumer Research.

Merikle, P. M., & Daneman, M. (2000). Conscious vs. unconscious perception. In M. S. Gazzaniga (Ed.), *The new cognitive neurosciences* (2nd ed., pp. 1295–1303). Cambridge, MA: MIT Press.

Merikle, P. M., & Joordens, S. (1997). Parallels between perception without attention and perception without awareness. *Consciousness and Cognition, 6,* 219–236.

Merikle, P. M., & Reingold, E. M. (1998). On demonstrating unconscious perception: Comment on Draine and Greenwald (1998). *Journal of Experimental Psychology: General, 127,* 304–310.

Mollon, J. D., & Polden, P. G. (1978). On the time constants of tachistoscopes. *Quarterly Journal of Experimental Psychology, 30,* 555–568.

Morris, J., Öhman, A., & Dolan, R. J.(1998). Modulation of human amygdala activity by emotional learning and conscious awareness. *Nature, 393,* 467–470.

Morris, J. S., Öhman, A., & Dolan, R. J. (1999). A subcortical pathway to the right amygdala mediating "unseen" fear. *Proceedings of the National Academy of Sciences of the USA, 96,* 1680–1685.

Oatley, K., & Jenkins, J. M. (1996). *Understanding emotions.* Oxford, UK: Blackwell.

Öhman, A. (1986). Face the beast and fear the face: Animal and social fears as prototypes for evolutionary analyses of emotion. *Psychophysiology, 23,* 123–145.

Öhman, A. (1987). The psychophysiology of emotion: An evolutionary-cognitive perspective. *Advances in Psychophysiology, 2,* 79–127.

Öhman, A. (1999). Distinguishing unconscious from conscious emotional processes: Methodological considerations and theoretical implications. In T. Dalgleish & M. Power (Eds.), *Handbook of cognition and emotion* (pp. 321–352). Chichester, UK: Wiley.

Öhman, A., & Soares, J. J. F. (1994). "Unconscious anxiety": Phobic responses to masked stimuli. *Journal of Abnormal Psychology, 103,* 231–240.

Öhman, A., & Soares, J. J. F. (1998). Emotional conditioning to masked stimuli: Expectancies for aversive outcomes following nonrecognized fear-relevant stimuli. *Journal of Experimental Psychology: General, 127,* 69–82.

Öhman, A., & Wiens, S. (2003). On the automaticity of autonomic responses in emotion: An evolutionary perspective. In R. J. Davidson, K. Scherer, & H. H. Goldsmith (Eds.), *Handbook of affective sciences* (pp. 256–275). New York: Oxford University Press.

Pessoa, L. (2005). To what extent are emotional visual stimuli processed without attention and awareness? *Current Opinion in Neurobiology, 15,* 188–196.

Pessoa, L., Japee, S., Sturman, D., & Ungerleider, L. G. (2006). Target Visibility and Visual Awareness Modulate Amygdala Responses to Fearful Faces. *Cerebral Cortex, 16,* 366–375.

Posner, M. I., & Snyder, C. R. (1975). Attention and cognitive control. In R. L. Solso (Ed.), *Information processing and cognition: The Loyola Symposium* (pp. 55–85). Hillsdale, NJ: Erlbaum.

Reingold, E. M., & Merikle, P. M. (1988). Using direct and indirect measures to study perception without awareness. *Perception and Psychophysics, 44,* 563–575.

Reingold, E. M., & Merikle, P. M. (1990). On the interrelatedness of theory and measurement in the study of unconscious processes. *Mind and Language, 5,* 9–28.

Roser, M., & Gazzaniga, M. S. (2004). Automatic brains,

interpretive minds. *Current Directions in Psychological Science, 13*(2), 56–59.

Rotteveel, M., de Groot, P., Geutskens, A., & Phaf, R. H. (2001). Stronger suboptimal than optimal affective priming? *Emotion, 1,* 348–364.

Schachter, S., & Singer, J. E. (1962). Cognitive, social, and physiological determinants of emotional state. *Psychological Review, 69,* 379–399.

Schneider, W., Dumais, S. T., & Shiffrin, R. M. (1984). Automatic and control processing and attention. In R. Parasuraman & D. R. Davies (Eds.), *Varieties of attention* (pp. 1–28). New York: Academic Press.

Shevrin, H., & Dickman, S. (1980). The psychological unconscious: A necessary assumption for all psychological theory? *American Psychologist, 35,* 421–434.

Smith, C. A., & Ellsworth, P. C. (1985). Patterns of cognitive appraisal in emotion. *Journal of Personality and Social Psychology, 48,* 813–838.

Snodgrass, M., Bernat, E., & Shevrin, H. (2004). Unconscious perception: Model-based approach to method and evidence. Perception & Psychophysics, 66, 846–867.

Tooby, J., & Cosmides, L. (1990). The past explains the present: Emotional adaptations and the structure of ancestral environment. *Ethology and Sociobiology, 11,* 375–424.

Tulving, E., & Schacter, D. L. (1990). Priming and human memory systems. *Science, 247,* 301–306.

Weiskrantz, L. (2000). Blindsight: Implications for the conscious experience of emotion. In R. D. Lane & L. Nadel (Eds.), *Cognitive neuroscience of emotion* (pp. 277–295). New York: Oxford University Press.

Whalen, P. J., Rauch, S. L., Etcoff, N. L., McInerney, S. C., Lee, M. B., & Jenike, M. A. (1998). Masked presentations of emotional facial expression modulate amygdala activity without explicit knowledge. *Journal of Neuroscience, 18,* 411–418.

Wiens, S. (2005). Interoception in emotional experience. *Current Opinion in Neurology, 18*(4), 442–447.

Wiens, S. (2006). Subliminal emotion perception in brain imaging: Findings, issues, and recommendations. *Progress in Brain Research, 156,* 107–123.

Wiens, S., Emmerich, D. S., & Katkin, E. S. (1997). Response bias affects perceptual asymmetry scores and performance measures on a dichotic listening task. *Neuropsychologia, 35,* 1475–1482.

Wiens, S., Fransson, P., Dietrich, T., Lohmann, P., Ingvar, M., & Öhman, A. (2004). Keeping it short: A comparison of methods for brief picture presentation. *Psychological Science, 15,* 282–285.

Wiens, S., Fransson, P., Ingvar, M., & Öhman, A. (2004). Activation of fusiform gyrus to masked neutral faces at brief (10–60 ms) durations. Paper presented at the 10th annual meeting of the organization for human brain mapping, Budapest, Hungary.

Wiens, S., Katkin, E. S., & Öhman, A. (2003). Effects of trial order and differential conditioning on acquisition of differential shock expectancy and skin conductance conditioning to masked stimuli. *Psychophysiology, 40,* 989–997.

Wiens, S., & Öhman, A. (2002). Unconsciousness is more than a chance effect: Comment on Lovibond and Shanks (2002). *Journal of Experimental Psychology: Animal Behavior Processes, 28,* 27–31.

Wiens, S., & Öhman, A. (2005). Visual masking in magnetic resonance imaging. *NeuroImage, 27*(2), 465–467.

Winkielman, P., & Berridge, K. C. (2004). Unconscious emotion. *Current Directions in Psychological Science, 13,* 120–123.

Winkielman, P., Berridge, K. C., & Wilbarger, J. L. (2005). Unconscious affective reactions to masked happy versus angry faces influence consumption behavior and judgments of value. *Personality And Social Psychology Bulletin, 31,* 121–135.

Wolford, G., Marchak, F., & Hughes, H. (1988). Practice effects in backward masking. *Journal of Experimental Psychology: Human Perception and Performance, 14,* 101–112.

Zajonc, R. B. (1980). Feeling and thinking: Preferences need no inferences. *American Psychologist, 35,* 151–175.

Eddie Harmon-Jones

David M. Amodio

Leah R. Zinner

6

Social Psychological Methods of Emotion Elicitation

Social psychology has long embraced the study of emotion. In an early experiment, Schachter (1959) induced anxiety to examine its effects on affiliation. Schachter's original description of the anxiety manipulation illustrates many of the methodological features of social psychological experiments:[1]

> In the high anxiety condition, the subjects, all college girls, strangers to one another, entered a room to find facing them a gentleman of serious mien, horn-rimmed glasses, dressed in a white laboratory coat, stethoscope dribbling out of his pocket, behind him an array of formidable electrical junk. After a few preliminaries, the experimenter began:
>
> Allow me to introduce myself, I am Dr. Gregor Zilstein of the Medical School's Departments of Neurology and Psychiatry. I have asked you all to come today in order to serve as subjects in an experiment concerned with the effects of electrical shock.
>
> Zilstein paused ominously, then continued with a seven- or eight-minute recital of the importance of research in this area, citing electroshock therapy, the increasing number of accidents due to electricity, and so on. He concluded in this vein:
>
> What we will ask each of you to do is very simple. We would like to give each of you a series of electric shocks. Now, I feel I must be completely honest with you and tell you exactly what you are in for. These shocks will hurt, they will be painful. As you can guess, if, in research of this sort, we're to learn anything at all that will really help humanity, it is necessary that our shocks be intense. What we will do is put an electrode on your hand, hook you into apparatus such as this [Zilstein points to the electrical-looking gadgetry behind him], give you a series of electric shocks, and take various measures such as your pulse rate, blood pressure, and so on. Again, I do want to be honest with you and tell you that these shocks will be quite painful but, of course, they will do no permanent damage. (Schachter, 1959, pp. 12–13)

Social psychology is noted for its use of psychologically meaningful and involving experimental manipulations. These high-impact manipulations are combined with cover stories that mask the deception that is employed. Indeed, this methodology of inducing emotion distinguishes social psychological methods from other methods. Like other types of experimentation, social psychological experiments use random assignment to conditions, and they control extraneous variables and manipulate only the variables of interest. However, unlike other types of psychological experiments, social psychological experiments often use high-impact manipulations designed to create realistic, emotion-eliciting situations, and they typically employ cover stories to mask any deception needed to manipulate a variable.

Designing a Social Psychological Experiment

Planning a social psychological experiment that involves deception requires five basic stages. Excellent, detailed discussions of how social psychological experiments are planned and conducted have been presented previously (e.g., Aronson, Brewer, & Carlsmith, 1985; Aronson & Carlsmith, 1968). The present discussion builds on these past discussions and applies them to the field of emotion research. However, as Aronson and colleagues have noted, it is impossible to specify a set of guidelines that will make someone a *good* experimenter. To become a skilled experimenter, one needs to observe good experimenters and conduct experiments under their guidance (see also Festinger et al., 1959).

Constructing the Cover Story

The first stage involves the construction of the cover story, or the rationale for the experiment, that distracts participants from the experiment's true purpose. A good cover story sets the stage for the entire experiment and smoothly incorporates the manipulation of the independent variable and the collection of the dependent variable. Because participants in experiments are often curious, and sometimes suspicious, adults, the context must make sense to them. In other words, the experimental manipulation and the measurement of the participants' responses must be presented in a situation that is sensible and internally consistent or that tells a logical story. These design elements enhance the impact of the experimental manipulation and provide justification for the collection of data.

As mentioned earlier, social psychological experiments often involve deception. Thus, in experiments employing deception, the experimental situation must include a sensible, logically consistent rationale for conducting the research. It must also include a plausible reason for the collection of the dependent variable(s). Both of these elements of the design should make it almost impossible for participants to detect the true purpose of the experiment.

In addition to explaining all aspects of the experiment in a plausible manner and thus preventing participants from attempting to detect the true (or another) purpose to the experiment, the cover story should capture the attention of the participants so that they will be alert and responsive to the experimental events. If, because of a poor cover story, participants believe that the experiment is concerned with something trivial, they may not be attentive to the experimental manipulation and thus it may have little impact on them. At their essence, good cover stories are like good movies—they actively involve the participant in a kind of drama and thus maximize the impact of the experimental manipulation.

For cover stories to successfully convince participants and for manipulations to have impact, they need to be fully comprehended by participants. To accomplish this, instructions often need to be presented in different ways, for example, both orally and in written form. Key portions of instructions (for both cover stories and manipulations) need to be repeated or paraphrased. In addition, the tasks used in experiments must attentionally engage the participants, although this should not be much of a problem in a well-designed high-impact experiment.

The ability of a cover story and manipulation to have the intended experiential effects should be ascertained in pretests. Often, readers fail to appreciate the amount of pretesting that went into fine-tuning a good cover story and manipulation. Pretesting is necessary to ensure that the independent variable is manipulating what is intended. For example, it would be impossible to assess the effects of anger on information processing without first assessing whether the anger manipulation was indeed evoking the emotion of anger.

The fine details in the presentation and delivery of the cover story make all the difference in whether or not participants become suspicious. The experimenter must know his or her lines and convey a sense of confidence in the value of the experiment.

The Experimenter's Behavior

In addition to delivering the cover story in a convincing manner, the experimenter also needs to behave consistently over the duration of the months of data collection and to treat each participant equivalently to how others are treated. Moreover, the experimenter should act in a relatively neutral manner toward participants and avoid being too friendly and chatty, so that participants are in a relatively neutral emotional state when the intended emotion manipulation is presented. Experimenters should also avoid drastically altering their appearance during the running of an experiment (e.g., hair color or length should probably not be altered). Experimenters should be encouraged to avoid wearing clothing that is out of the ordinary or that would prime certain ideas (e.g., shirt with skull and crossbones, concert t-shirts, school t-shirts). Such attire could add error variance, as much research has demonstrated the effects of subtle primes on behavior (e.g., see the review by Bargh & Ferguson, 2000) and experimenter attire has been found to alter participants' behavior (e.g., Simon et al., 1997). Moreover, if more than one experimenter is used on a given experiment, steps needs to be taken to ensure that the two or more experimenters behave consistently with each other. All of these steps should be taken to reduce error variance.

Constructing the Independent Variable

The third stage of social psychological experimentation involves the design and construction of the independent variable. The independent variable is the experimental manipulation, and it should be independent of all sources of variation except the one that is being manipulated. A particular conceptual (or theoretical) independent variable may be operationalized in multiple ways. Ideally, replications of experimental results are obtained with a variety of manipulations of the abstract conceptual variable. For example, the abstract concept of anger may be induced through a variety of manipulations, such as goal blocking or the receipt of insults. The manipulation should occur seamlessly in the experiment so that participants are oblivious to the fact that the experimental manipulation is taking place.

Manipulations can be accomplished using within-subjects designs, whereby each participant is exposed to each level of the independent variable, or they can be accomplished using between-subjects designs, whereby each participant is exposed to only one level of the independent variable. In between-subjects designs, participants should be randomly assigned to conditions. Although within-subject designs are preferable for many reasons (e.g., each participant serves as his or her own control and thus reduces unwanted variance), it is often not plausible to use within-subject designs in high-impact/deception experiments, for a few reasons. First, the effects of the emotion induction may be so intense that they would contaminate subsequent manipulations. Second, it may not make sense to participants to respond to a different situation under slightly different conditions, for example, receiving both an insulting and a neutral evaluation of one's performance on a task.

Avoiding Participant Awareness Biases

One important issue that arises in developing the independent variable is the need to avoid participant awareness biases. That is, the design of the manipulation should ensure that participants respond just as they would if they confronted the stimulus or situation outside of the experimental laboratory, in their everyday lives. Participant biases can take many forms—participants may respond in a socially desirable (or undesirable) manner, or in such a way as to confirm (or disconfirm) what they believe are the experimenter's hypotheses. These potential participant biases are the reason that social psychological experimenters frequently use deception and elaborate cover stories.

Experimenter Should Be Blind to Condition

Another potential problem in experiments is that the experimenter's own behavior may provide subtle (or not so subtle) cues that influence the reactions of the participants. The idea that an experimenter who is not blind to condition can influence the participants' behavior has been repeatedly demonstrated (Rosenthal, 1994). Indeed, these experimenter expectancy effects are quite dramatic and can occur even when the experimenter does not intend them. In a profound demonstration of this point, Rosenthal and Lawson (1964) found that rats learn mazes more quickly when the experimenters are led to believe that the rats are good learners, whereas rats learn mazes more slowly when the experimenters are led to believe that the rats are poor learners.

To prevent experimenter expectancy effects, several steps must be taken. The experimenter can be made unaware of the research hypotheses. However, doing such assumes that the experimenter will not form his or her own hypotheses, which, in turn, may affect the participant's responses. Because experimenters are typically members of the research team, participating in the research process for educational purposes, they are likely to form their own hypotheses and may correctly guess the true hypotheses. Making them unaware of the hypotheses would prevent them from participating fully in the research processes and is therefore undesirable. In addition, for experimenters to conduct adequate debriefings (discussed later), the experimenters need to be fully aware of the hypotheses. For these reasons, it is preferable to keep the experimenter aware of the hypotheses but to keep him or her unaware of the condition to which the participant is assigned. However, this may be impossible to do, depending on the nature of the experiment. In such cases, the research should employ two experimenters, one who delivers the manipulation and immediately leaves the participant's room and another who collects the dependent variable while remaining unaware of the condition to which the participant had been assigned. Even in this type of situation, the first experimenter must remain unaware of the condition until the manipulation is delivered, so that his or her premanipulation behavior is constant across conditions. A remedy to this issue is the use of instructions or manipulations delivered via computer or tape recordings. However, in employing this remedy, the researcher should ensure that the participants attend fully to the manipulation. Another possibility is to make the experimenter blind to one variable but not another when an interaction between two or more variables is predicted.

The Dependent Variable

When assessing the effects of an emotion induction, behavioral or physiological measures are preferred, although self-reports are often used because of convenience. The use of self-reports may be disadvantageous, however, because they may not produce veridical reports of experience (e.g., because the participant may be unaware of or unable to report an emotional experience or because they may give false responses). Moreover, completion of self-reports of emotional experience can bias later behavior and cognition (e.g., Berkowitz, Jaffee, Jo, & Troccoli, 2000). That is, completing an emotion questionnaire immediately after an emotion induction (and prior to collection of cognitive or behavioral measures of interest) might make participants aware of the hypotheses and/or cause heightened awareness of their feelings, which might alter the subsequent reactions. For example, Berkowitz and colleagues (2000) have found that the simple completion of an emotion questionnaire immediately following a negative affect induction can reduce hostile reactions, as the individuals become more aware of their negative affect and attempt to prevent it from biasing later cognition and behavior.

In addition, participants may not respond honestly to questions, because of a need to respond in a socially desirable way or because they want to respond in a manner consistent with what they expect the experimenter might want. Disguising the fact that a particular measure is the critical dependent measure can prevent these problems. One way to disguise the measure is to collect it in a setting that seems completely removed from the experiment. This can be accomplished by telling participants that they are participating in multiple studies; in this case, the dependent variable can be collected in a "different" study from the one in which the independent variable was manipulated.

Another way of disguising the measurement of the dependent variable is to use measures over which participants have relatively less cognitive control. For example, Hass, Katz, Rizzo, Bailey, and Moore (1992) used an indirect measure of emotional experience by presenting "words" quickly on a computer monitor and having participants guess which word was quickly presented from a short list of words. In fact, nonsense words were actually presented, and the short list of words included some descriptors of various emotional states. Hass et al. found that participants induced to feel negative affect selected negative-affect words more often than participants not induced to feel negative affect. Measures of recognition, reaction time, and accuracy of recall can also be used as relatively less controllable measures. Finally, measures of behavior and physiological responses also provide means of obtaining valuable information from participants, and many of these responses often occur relatively automatically (see, e.g., in this volume, Coan & Gottman, chapter 16; Cohn, Ambadar, & Ekman, Chapter 13). We often study emotion because we are interested in its effects on behavior and cognition. As such, it is important to measure these outcomes, as well as more traditional measures of emotion, in such studies.

Postexperimental Interview

An experiment does not end abruptly when the last dependent variable is collected. Instead, the experimenter needs to interview the participant, for several important reasons, which are discussed here. Throughout the interview, the experimenter must show sensitivity to and respect for the participant.

Checking for the Clarity of Instructions and Suspicion

The first goal in the interview is to ascertain whether the participant fully understood the instructions, manipulations, and tasks, so that the experimenter can redesign the experiment if needed (early in the conducting of the experiment) or to decide whether the participant's data should be excluded from data analysis (such data loss should be reported in the write-up of the experiment). The experi-

menter needs to learn whether the deception was effective or whether the participant became suspicious in a way that would invalidate the data collected. If, for example, a particular participant did not believe that he or she was going to be shocked in Schachter's (1959) experiment, then the data from that person would be invalid and excluded from analysis.[2]

Often, in a postexperiment interview, the cover story is maintained for a few minutes. That is, the experimenter asks general, open-ended questions about the experimental events. For example, the experimenter might begin by asking, "What did you think about the questionnaires you completed? What did you think about the essay you wrote? What did you think about the evaluation of your essay? What did you think about the other participant involved in the study— how did you decide how to evaluate the other person? Did everything go smoothly? Did anything about the study seem unusual? Do you have any questions?" Then, after a few general questions, the experimenter will ask whether the participant was doubtful of any part of the experiment. For instance, the experimenter might ask, "Based on what has happened thus far, can you think of something that we might be interested in other than what I told you to begin with?" Asking this type of question after the more general questions can assist in determining how suspicious the participant was and whether the participant's affirmative response to the more direct question might have been due to prompting during the interview. By beginning with very general and nonleading questions about reactions to the experiment and gradually moving toward more specific and leading questions, the researcher is able to assess whether persons had genuine reactions to the experimental situation, whether they doubted the realism of it, and whether they could guess the hypotheses being tested.

Regardless of whether or not the participant was suspicious, the experimenter needs to treat the participant with respect and with sensitivity. If an individual was not suspicious, then she might believe she was duped and might feel bad about herself for being foolish. On the other hand, if an individual was suspicious, he might feel bad about ruining the experiment. Although participants involved in deception experiments are told that the experiments were designed in such a way that they would not know the actual purpose of the research, and although it logically follows that participants should experience no shame in being deceived, it is important to be sensitive to the participants' concerns, as individuals do not always respond rationally (e.g., Epstein, 1994).[3]

Educating the Participant About the Purpose of the Experiment

After determining whether the participant understood the instructions and whether he or she was suspicious, the experimenter should ensure that the participant understood the experimental procedures and hypotheses at a level that enhances his or her understanding of the scientific process. By actively participating in the research and then learning about it, participants have an opportunity to experience and learn about meaningful and interesting research firsthand. The experimenter should thoroughly explain why deception was needed to address the experimental hypotheses. See appendix A for an example of a debriefing.

Ensuring That the Participant Leaves in a Good State of Mind

Finally, and most important, the experimenter must ensure that the participant leaves the experiment in a good mood and that he or she feels relatively positively about his or her experience in the experiment. If the experimental procedures were particularly stressful, it would be wise for the experimenter to contact the participant a few days later to make certain that there are no residual effects.

Ethical Issues

The use of high-impact experiments involving deception raises questions about the ethics of conducting such research. A complete discussion of ethical issues in research is beyond the scope of this chapter (see Aronson, Ellsworth, Carlsmith, & Gonzales, 2000, for a more complete discussion). However, we offer a few brief comments. When research questions can be adequately answered without the use of deception, such methods should be employed. However, there are times when deception is necessary. The experimental arousal of certain negative emotions—anger, fear, disgust—is an area of research about which many scientists and laypeople express ethical concern. However, understanding of these emotions is very important in improving mental health and society, and deception may be necessary to effectively evoke valid emotions. Moreover, these emotions are routinely experienced in everyday life; thus the experimental evocation of them does not cause reactions that depart from everyday experiences and occurrences. In fact, our participants in high-impact negative emotion studies often say that they found the experience interesting and worthwhile. Then they complain about participating in boring research studies. Might such boring studies be considered more ethically questionable than high-impact negative emotion studies? Individuals often pay to go to movies where negative emotions are aroused, but they rarely pay to be bored. With care and sensitivity, ecologically valid studies on these emotions can be conducted, without harm to participants. Although the methods described here have emotional impact, there is no reason to suspect that they would cause lasting distress. Because other methods of examining emotion may produce invalid results (e.g., hypothetical scenarios that ask how an individual would feel), it is also ethically questionable to conduct such research, as the participants' time would be wasted and the data would be meaningless and misleading. See Table 6.1 for a summary of the preceding information.

Table 6.1

Requirements for a successful social psychological emotion manipulation

Cover Story

- create a context that makes sense
- provide good rationale for the study
- capture the attention of the participant
- ensure participant understands the story
- pretest to confirm effectiveness

Experimenter's Behavior

- behave consistently over duration of data collection
- treat each participant equivalently to how others are treated
- act in relatively neutral manner toward participants
- do not drastically alter physical appearance during experiment
- avoid wearing unusual clothing
- two or more experimenters should behave consistently with each other

Independent Variable

- keep independent variable free from all other sources of variation
- assign participants randomly to condition
- keep experimenter blind to condition
- avoid participant awareness biases
- manipulate independent variable seamlessly so participants are unaware

Dependent Variable

- measure behavior or physiology if possible
- if self-report, disguise the dependent variable
- be careful about placement of self-report emotion measure

Postexperimental Interview

- check for clarity
- check for suspicion
- educate the participant
- ensure participant leaves in a good state of mind

Why Use Social Psychological Manipulations of Emotion?

As is now evident, social psychological methods of inducing emotion are difficult to carry out. They require lots of planning, creativity, and interviewing. They also require that researchers spend lots of time and effort training experimenters to act in a convincing manner. So, one might ask, why should one go through these difficulties to induce emotion? There are a number of answers to this question.

The use of social psychological methods, as described earlier, provides a means of inducing emotions and assessing their consequences that avoids many problems often encountered using other methodologies. For example, social psychological methods assist in preventing responses that are due to demand characteristics, the phenomenon by which the participant responds in a way that confirms (or disconfirms) the experimenter's hypothesis. Moreover, these methods are designed to elicit realistic responses, that is, responses the participants would make outside the laboratory, unaffected by self-presentational biases or social desirability concerns. These concerns are greatly minimized by masking the purpose of the experiment, the manipulation of the independent variable, and the assessment of the dependent variable.

Another reason to use social psychological methods to evoke emotion is that certain emotions may be impossible to evoke effectively using other methods. Anger, for instance, is an emotion that may be quite difficult to evoke using standardized sets of photographs or films. As is evidenced later in this chapter, anger can easily be evoked using social psychological methods.

The use of cover stories, deception, and the like also permits researchers to evoke emotions that are psychologically real and similar to the emotions that occur outside of the laboratory.[4] For social animals, emotions are often evoked in social contexts. Thus, to fully understand emotion processes, emotions need to be evoked in the context in which they often naturally occur—the social environment. The use of cover stories, deception, and other social psychological methods allows the researcher to evoke emotions in a controlled manner inside the laboratory. Social psychological methods may be complemented by other methods when researchers want to test the generalizability of their emotion effects.

Examples of Social Psychological Methods of Emotion Evocation

To illustrate the social psychological method of emotion induction, we describe a few examples. We have chosen examples with which we are familiar; we are in no way attempting to provide a comprehensive review of social psychological methods of emotion induction, as such would exceed the space limitations for this chapter (see appendix B for a short list of additional publications that report experiments using social psychological methods to evoke emotions). In what follows, we provide highly detailed descriptions of the experimental procedures in order to convey the depth and detail of the manipulations and cover stories. Details that may seem trivial are included because it is these minor details that give realism to the experimental situation.

Anger

The emotion of anger has been induced in a variety of ways by social psychologists (e.g., Berkowitz, 1962, 1993). In fact, anger is an emotion that typically requires high-impact manipulations and the use of deception to elicit. Whereas other emotions can be induced using film clips or photographs, anger is difficult to induce using such stimuli.

Using Interpersonal Insult to Induce Anger

As an example of an experiment using social psychological methods to induce anger, consider the experiment by Harmon-Jones and Sigelman (2001). The experiment was designed to assess the effects of anger on asymmetrical frontal cortical activity. In addition to measuring brain activity with electroencephalography (EEG), measures of aggressive behavior and self-reported anger were included to verify that anger had indeed been evoked. To induce anger, the researchers manipulated interpersonal feedback to be either neutral or insulting. Aggressive behavior was measured by giving participants the opportunity to deliver a noxious stimulus to the person who had insulted them. However, both the anger induction and the measure of aggression needed to be disguised, because if participants knew of the researchers' interest in manipulating anger and measuring it and aggression, their responses may not have been valid.

The experiment began when the experimenter greeted the participant in a waiting room. When arriving at the door of the lab room, the experimenter pointed to a sign indicating that the room was occupied. He then said that they needed to go to another lab room because the other experimenter and participant were in this room. All of these steps were taken to assist in convincing the participant that another participant was being run through the same experiment at the same time. On arrival at the second lab room, the experimenter presented the participant with the cover story. That is, he explained that the experiment concerned personality, psychophysiology, and perception and that the study would be conducted in connection with the other participant. He then said that there would be two perception studies, the first involving person perception and the second involving taste perception. To enhance the believability of the person-perception study and make it seem plausible, the experimenter explained that people often easily form impressions of others based on articles that they have written and that this research concerned how the reader's perceptions of the writer was related to personality characteristics of both the reader and the writer. The experimenter explained that the two participants never meet each other, to obtain the most reliable and valid indicator of perception of the writer based solely on the written essay, because physical appearance can also influence perception of personality. Many of the preceding details appear very minor, and care was taken to present them in an offhanded way. Taken together, they created a convincing belief in the reality of the "other participant."

Following this oral introduction, participants read a brief written description of the experiment to further ensure that the participant understood the cover story. Participants then completed a baseline affect scale and were prepared for an EEG recording, which was followed by a baseline EEG recording. The baseline measures served three purposes: They allowed for statistical control of individual differences; they accustomed the participants to these measures, which would be assessed later as dependent variables; and they made subsequent assessment of these measures more plausible. Next, the experimenter further explained the "person perception" study by telling participants that they would be randomly assigned to either write an essay on a personally important social issue or to give their perception of the person who wrote such an essay. In fact, all participants were assigned to the role of writing the essay, but the presentation of the idea of random assignment to condition was used to make participants more likely to believe the entire cover story and not become suspicious when they were later insulted.

After they finished their one-page essay arguing for their position on a personally important social issue, the experimenter collected their essays and ostensibly took them to the other participant (who did not actually exist) for evaluation. The experimenter made sure to open and close the necessary doors and leave the participant for a reasonable amount of time. Again, all of these steps were taken to make all aspects of the experiment more believable to the participants.

Anger Manipulation. The experimenter returned and offhandedly mentioned that the participant could look at the evaluation of his or her essay. Of course, the evaluation would provide the manipulation of insult, and it was given to the participants in an envelope so that the experimenter could remain blind to condition. The evaluation was designed to be relatively positive or relatively negative in tone. The evaluation consisted of ratings ostensibly made by the other participant on a number of bipolar scales (e.g., unintelligent–intelligent). The neutral evaluation consisted of slightly positive ratings. The neutral evaluation was slightly positive because past research had revealed that most individuals view themselves as better than average (e.g., Weinstein, 1980). Indeed, this slightly positive evaluation did not cause any changes in self-reported affect. The negative evaluation consisted of fairly negative ratings. In addition, on the neutral evaluation, the other participant wrote at the bottom of the rating form, "I can understand why a person would think like this." On the negative evaluation, the other participant wrote, "I can't believe an educated person would think like this. I hope this person learns something while at the university." The person providing the evaluation was ostensibly of the same gender as the participant (to avoid any of the complexities associated with male-female interactions). Immediately after the participant finished reading this evaluation, the experimenter indicated over the intercom that he needed to collect more baseline brain wave readings. EEG was acquired for 1 minute.

Aggression Measure. Following the collection of EEG, the experimenter described the second study involving "taste perception." This "second study" was used to obtain a disguised behavioral measure of aggression. The study was supposedly concerned with the relationship between EEG and self-reported indexes of detecting slight differences in tastes.

The experimenter noted that it was very important for experimenters to remain blind to the type of tastes to which participants are exposed in taste-perception studies. He explained that one way to keep experimenters blind to the tastes is to have one participant assign the tastes to the other participant. He also explained that the participant had been randomly chosen to assign the tastes to the other participant, and that the other participant would have to drink the entire amount he or she was given. The experimenter then showed that participant six types of beverages, and each type consisted of three concentration levels (i.e., 11 oz. of water mixed with 1, 2, or 3 teaspoons of sugar, apple juice, lemon juice, salt, vinegar, or hot sauce). The experimenter indicated that most persons find the sugar water most pleasant and the hot sauce most unpleasant and that the other beverages were rated in between these two extremes, with those closer to sugar being more pleasant and those closer to hot sauce being more unpleasant. This was done to ensure that participants "knew" which beverages were noxious and which were not. The beverages were always presented on a tray and in the same order, from very pleasant to very unpleasant (see figure 6.1).

The experimenter then asked participants to select one of the six types of beverages for the other participant, to pour some of each of the three concentrations into cups, and to cover the cups with lids when done. Participants were told to label the concentration level on the bottom of each cup. To further bolster the cover story about keeping the experimenter blind to the type of beverage they chose, participants were given a black sheet to cover the unused beverages with when they were finished administering the beverages. Again, all of these steps were taken to ensure that the cover story was indeed plausible.

Figure 6.1. Experimenter explains "taste perception study," which ultimately provides a behavioral measure of aggression.

Aggression was calculated by assigning each beverage a value that corresponded to its unpleasantness. This measure of aggression is similar to a technique developed by other researchers (Lieberman, Solomon, Greenberg, & McGregor, 1999; McGregor et al., 1998). However, the aggression measure used in the Harmon-Jones and Sigelman (2001) experiment extends the past technique by giving participants more than one type of substance to administer to the other participant. The hot-sauce paradigm described previously effectively eliminates several problems associated with past laboratory aggression measures, such as the administration of electric shock. However, it does not give participants a clear opportunity to choose not to be aggressive. If they were to choose not to administer hot sauce, they might believe that the experimenter would be upset with them, because the taste perception experiment could not be completed. In contrast, the Harmon-Jones and Sigelman (2001) measure does not suffer from this limitation because participants who do not intend to behave aggressively can choose a neutral- or pleasant-tasting beverage.

Emotion Measures.   After participants finished with the administration of the beverages, they were asked to complete questionnaires designed to assess emotions they felt during the experiment. This measure was positioned after the aggression measure so as not to reduce aggressive tendencies via self-regulation (Berkowitz et al., 2000). Following the collection of this measure, participants were interviewed and debriefed, as described earlier.

Results.   As predicted, individuals who were insulted evidenced greater self-reported anger, more aggression, and greater relative left frontal activity (which has been related to approach motivation; Harmon-Jones, 2003) than individuals who were not insulted.

Using Motivationally Relevant Audiotapes to Induce Anger

The insult methodology just described works for individuals who are not preselected according to certain characteristics. Other ways of inducing anger are available but may require preselecting participants according to certain attitudes or other characteristics. For example, participants could be selected because they possess a particular attitude and then exposed to information that challenges that attitudinal position, as a large body of research has suggested that exposure to such messages evokes negative affect (for a review, see Harmon-Jones, 2000). Care will still need to be taken in designing a compelling cover story and assessing suspicion in the postexperimental interview.

As an example, consider the following experiment (Harmon-Jones, Sigelman, Bohlig, & Harmon-Jones, 2003). Participants were university students who were preselected based on their responses during a mass testing session held early in the semester. Individuals who paid at least 33% of their tuition by themselves or with student loans and who

moderately or strongly disagreed with a statement indicating that tuition should be increased by 10% at the university were invited to participate in the experiment. Such participant selection criteria ensured that the participants would find the message they would hear in the experiment emotionally arousing.

The study was described as being concerned with reactions to pilot radio broadcasts conducted by Professor Harmon-Jones as a service for WERN, an affiliate radio station of Wisconsin Public Radio, which targeted its broadcasting toward students, faculty, and staff at the University of Wisconsin-Madison. WERN was said to be considering introducing two new programs. The experimenter further explained that for several years, Professor Harmon-Jones, an expert on responses to mass media, had pilot-tested new programming ideas for WERN by trying them out on introductory psychology students at the university. He finished the introduction by explaining that the participant would be randomly assigned to listen to two brief pilot broadcasts, one for "Bulletin Board" and one for "News from the Personal Side." It was further explained that there were several tapes for each broadcast and that participants' emotional and evaluative responses to the broadcast would be assessed using questionnaires and brain wave activity. The experimenter then noted that the broadcast tape they would hear was prepared as a pilot for use in this study, so the quality was below normal broadcast standards. After hearing this introduction, participants read an introduction written on WERN letterhead that reiterated this information to ensure that they completely understood all of the details. The description of WERN, the use of WERN's letterhead, the presentation of two new programming ideas, the mention of several tapes of each program, and the fact that it was a pilot study similar to studies that had been conducted on students in the past are important features in the cover story because they make participants more likely to believe that the program is real and less likely to become suspicious when they are later emotionally aroused (i.e., to believe that it is just one of the possible broadcasts).

After baseline EEG and self-reported emotions were recorded and other instructions were delivered (irrelevant to the present discussion), participants listened to the pilot broadcast, in which a trained male speaker made persuasive arguments in favor of a 10% tuition increase. EEG was collected following the broadcast. Then participants completed questionnaires assessing their responses to the broadcast. Finally, to obtain a behavioral measure that would reflect their desire to rectify the anger-producing situation, participants were given an opportunity (in one condition) to sign a petition to protest the tuition increase and to take petitions with them to have others sign. As predicted, the counterattitudinal message caused significant increases in self-reported anger among all participants and greater left frontal activity in participants who expected to be able to rectify the anger-producing situation. Finally, the greater left frontal activity in the action-possible condition was related to being more likely to sign the petition and to taking more petitions with them for others to sign.

Joy, Sadness

Similar to other emotions, joy and sadness can be elicited effectively using social psychological methods that eliminate concerns that the effects of the emotion manipulations are due to self-presentational concerns or social desirability concerns of the participants. A study by Masters, Carlson, and Rahe (1985) elicited both happiness and sadness by using a social-comparison manipulation. The participants, who were first- and second-grade children, were told that they would be participating in a simple word game that required them to repeat aloud words printed on cards. To reduce the possibility that participants would make their own judgments of success or failure, they were told that there were no right or wrong answers and that the speed with which they said the words would not affect the outcome. Each participant was seated at a table next to a comparison peer. Over the course of the experiment, the participants were awarded plastic chips that could later be exchanged for prizes. Chips were awarded 10 times, with the relative reward outcome manipulated by the experimenter. On each of the 10 trials, participants could either receive more (positive inequality), fewer (negative inequality), or the same number of chips as the comparison peer. During this procedure, participants were videotaped, and affect was assessed using behavioral coding of facial expressions.

During the social-comparison manipulation, behavioral coding data indicated that children who experienced positive inequality appeared significantly happier than children who experienced equality or negative inequality. Similarly, children who experienced negative inequality appeared significantly sadder than those who experienced equality or positive inequality. Moreover, these manipulations of emotion affected the children's behavior, with those who experienced positive inequality giving fewer rewards to themselves and those who experienced negative inequality giving fewer rewards to others.

The authors noted that, although this study used young children as participants, there is no reason to believe that adults would not be similarly emotionally responsive to social comparison. In fact, several other studies (e.g., Forgas, Bower, & Moylan, 1991; Isen & Means, 1983) have used similar manipulations to elicit emotions in adult participants. For example, Forgas (1991; study 1) investigated the effects of mood (happy, sad, and control) on preferences in choosing a partner. Participants were first told that they would participate in two brief but unrelated experiments (ostensibly run together to save time). The first experiment was described as a test of verbal ability that involved completing as many analogies from a list as possible in 5 minutes. The instructions were manipulated to describe the task as being easy or difficult to complete in the allotted time. In the control condition, participants were told simply to complete as many as they could without worrying about difficult items. After the time period was over, participants were given the correct answers, as well as bogus performance standards that indicated that their verbal skills were either above average (positive mood group) or below average (negative mood group). Participants in the control group were simply thanked for their help. All participants then completed a series of questionnaires, including three mood scales embedded in several distracter items. Results indicated that, indeed, the participants who were told their performance was above average rated their moods as more happy than did controls and that participants who were told their performance was below average rated their moods as more sad than did controls.

Success and failure manipulations are effective methods of inducing general positive and negative affect, respectively (e.g., Nummenmaa & Niemi, 2004). However, such manipulations have yet to be demonstrated to affect discrete emotions. Moreover, they also affect self-esteem (see, e.g., Greenberg et al., 1992). Consideration of these issues by both emotion and self-esteem researchers is important in interpreting the observed findings.

Sympathy

The emotion of sympathy or empathy, which includes feelings of compassion and tenderness, has often been examined in social psychological experiments because of its importance in motivating helping behavior (e.g., Batson, 1991, 1998). The manipulation of sympathy is most cleanly accomplished by using perspective-taking instructions, and past research has revealed that the perspective-taking instructions cause significant differences in emotional arousal (e.g., Coke, Batson, & McDavis, 1978; Stotland, 1969). An experiment using the perspective-taking method of inducing sympathy is described in detail next (Harmon-Jones, Peterson, & Vaughn, 2003).

On a participant's arrival, an experimenter explained that two new programming ideas were being pilot-tested for a local public radio station. Then the participant was given two folders, which allowed the experimenter to remain blind to condition. One folder contained the listening-perspective instructions—the sympathy manipulation. The other folder contained the questionnaires that were to be completed after hearing the broadcast. It was placed next to participants at this point so that the experimenter would not have to return and interrupt or interfere with the participants' emotional experience by giving them the folder immediately after the broadcast. After placing the folders next to the participant, the experimenter left the participant to open the first folder and read the instructions within it, which were the listening-perspective instructions designed to manipulate sympathy (e.g., Batson et al., 1997; Stotland, 1969). These began with a description of the broadcast, which read:

> You will be listening to an interview with Scott Neumann, a 16-year-old and a student at Memorial High School. Recently, Scott has been rediagnosed with cancer. He had been in remission for the past three years but will be starting a two-month period of treatment in the coming weeks. His parents are struggling to make ends meet due to the additional medical expenses. They are trying to get help through private contributions of time and money. (Harmon-Jones et al., 2003, p. 71)

In the *low-sympathy condition,* participants were instructed to "be as objective as possible about what has happened to Scott and how it has affected his life" while listening to the broadcast. In the *high-sympathy condition,* participants were instructed to "imagine how Scott feels about what has happened and how it has affected his life" while listening to the broadcast.

In the broadcast, a female announcer, ostensibly from a local public radio station, introduced Scott Neumann, a boy who had cancer. Then Scott described how his illness affected his life. At the end of Scott's description, the announcer provided the radio station's phone number, which listeners could call if they wanted to help the family.

Following the broadcast, over the intercom, the experimenter instructed participants to complete the questionnaires within the folder, which assessed self-reported emotions and evaluations of the "News from the Personal Side" radio program. The emotion questionnaire was included to assess self-reported emotions, and the "News From the Personal Side" questionnaire was included to bolster the cover story. It also contained items to assess participants' evaluation of the radio program and to determine the effectiveness of the sympathy manipulation.

After participants indicated that they had completed the questionnaires, they were given a letter from the professor in charge of the research (to obtain a measure of helping), as in previous helping research (Coke et al., 1978). They were left alone to read and respond to it. The letter explained that the broadcast they had heard was not going to be aired but that the professor thought that some participants might have an interest in helping the family, anyway. A volunteer form was attached, asking participants if they were willing to help. They were informed that if they volunteered, they could help the family by watching Katie (Scott's younger sister), by running errands, or by tutoring Scott (the boy with cancer). If they were willing to help, they were asked to indicate how much time or money (to help with medical expenses) they could give. After completion of the helping form, participants were thoroughly debriefed, using methods described earlier.

Results indicated that the perspective-taking manipulation was effective. Participants in the high-sympathy condi-

tion reported feeling more sympathy, reported feeling less objective toward Scott's situation, and reported that they concentrated more on Scott's feelings than did participants in the low-sympathy condition. Moreover, participants in the high-sympathy condition offered more help than participants in the low-sympathy condition. These findings are consistent with past findings using similar manipulations (see reviews by Batson, 1991, 1998).

Guilt

The emotional experience of guilt and of self-directed negative affect more generally has played a central role in much social psychological research on racial prejudice. Theories of prejudice control (e.g., Monteith, 1993) posit that people low in prejudice but not those high in prejudice should experience guilt when they unintentionally respond with prejudice. The experience of guilt, in turn, is theorized to impel regulatory behavior aimed at preventing future unwanted prejudiced behaviors. As such, many prejudice researchers have used inductions of guilt in order to study the processes of prejudice control. A variety of induction methods have been used in the prejudice literature. Here, we describe some high-impact methods used in recent research.

Monteith, Ashburn-Nardo, Voils, and Czopp (2002) used a false physiological feedback procedure to induce guilt among participants who were low in prejudice to study the role guilt plays in promoting the inhibition of prejudiced behavior. As in most high-impact inductions of emotion, a convincing cover story was key. Thus the researchers took several steps to ensure that the feedback that participants received was believable and was interpreted as reflecting negative feelings toward black people. The experiment was introduced as a study of people's ability to control and reduce negative arousal. Participants learned that they would view a series of pictures that varied in negativity while their physiological arousal was monitored via skin-conductance response (SCR). Electrodes used for measuring SCR were then attached to participants' fingers, and these electrodes were connected to amplifiers used for physiological recording. To bolster the cover story, participants were shown a few seconds of fake SCR signal, purported to be their own, on a computer monitor. The experimenter then instructed participants to remain still during a 3-minute period of baseline recording. In continuing with the cover story, participants listened to instructions explaining the important implications of the current study for pain management, stress reduction, depression, and overall mental health. To learn how to control negative arousal, participants were told that they should read an article from *Psychology Today* that provided arousal-control strategies. Participants were then given a copy of the article, along with a summary, and encouraged to look over these materials. Participants were then prepared to view the series of pictures. After viewing each picture, the computer program would display their arousal level. It was explained that the equipment being used was sensitive only to negative forms of physiological arousal and that any increases in arousal level should be interpreted as reflecting a negative reaction to the preceding picture. The experiment began with a practice block that included neutral and highly negative pictures. After seeing the neutral pictures (e.g., leaves, pepper shaker), participants saw that their arousal levels were low. However, after the negative pictures (e.g., mutilated hand, attacking dog), the bogus display indicated that their arousal level was markedly higher. By initially providing bogus arousal feedback that matched participants' expectations, participants felt confident that the measure reflected their true responses. Finally, participants received one last set of instructions. Following from Dutton and Lake (1973), these instructions emphasized that the content of the pictures would vary considerably and that certain pictures might or might not cause negative reactions among different participants. The instructions went on to give the following example related more directly to prejudice: "Social situations can provoke intense reactions in people. These reactions can include hatred, prejudice, discomfort, and other negative states. . . . Many psychologists feel the autonomic responses are the truest measures of underlying reactions we have about social groups and situations" (Monteith et al., 2002, p. 1034). After going to great lengths to convince participants that the bogus SCR measures of arousal were valid, the experimenters proceeded to show participants a set of pictures that included neutral, negative, racial (e.g., interracial couple holding hands and smiling), and nonracial pictures (abstract art with ambiguous valence). As with the practice trials, bogus arousal feedback was provided following each picture. One group of participants received high arousal feedback following negative and racial pictures, but not neutral and nonracial pictures. The other group received high arousal feedback following the negative and nonracial pictures only. Following this procedure, all participants completed an affect checklist that included 29 different emotion words. Indices were created from these to represent self-directed negative affect (including guilt, self-disappointment, shame, regret), discomfort, positive affect, depressive affect, and other-directed negative affect. Participants who received high arousal feedback to racial pictures reported significantly higher levels of self-directed negative affect than those who received low arousal feedback to these pictures. Participants did not differ in positive, depressive, or other-directed affect (but differed in discomfort). Monteith et al. (2002) went on to show that participants' levels of self-directed negative affect predicted a pattern of more controlled behavior to race-related stimuli.

Like Monteith et al. (2003), Amodio, Harmon-Jones, and Devine (in press) used a false physiological feedback induction of guilt to examine the association of guilt with frontal cortical asymmetry and the role of guilt in producing behaviors aimed at prejudice reduction. Because their study involved several real physiological measures, it was not necessary to build such an elaborate cover story. For their study, Amodio et al. (in press) recruited participants who were high or low in prejudice and described the study simply as one that ex-

amined people's brain wave responses to different types of stimuli. On arrival, participants were prepared for several physiological measures (EEG and facial electromyography [EMG]). After baseline measures of EEG and self-reported affect were collected, participants viewed a series of faces of black, white, and Asian males and then a series of positive, negative, and neutral pictures. The primary purpose of the picture presentation portion of the study was to measure participants' startle eyeblink responses to different types of pictures, as detailed in Amodio, Harmon-Jones, and Devine (2003).

When the picture-viewing portion was completed, the experimenter entered the participant room and explained that, although they were nearly done with the session, additional measures of baseline EEG were required. The experimenter then indicated that the computer program had finished processing some of the data from the picture-viewing portion and that the participants would be able to view these results while the final EEG measures were taken. The instructions continued: "Some graphs will appear on the computer monitor. These graphs will show levels of your brainwave activity. Our measures of brain waves are very sensitive—they're used in a number of labs here—and can measure emotions that you may not consciously feel. I have the results from the second picture set ready first. When they appear, you should see that you had a negative reaction to the unpleasant pictures, and a more positive reaction to the pleasant pictures. I'll have the computer show your results from the first set with the faces after that." As in Monteith et al. (2002), it was important to first show participants a set of responses that were likely to match their expectations. That is, participants were presented with a graph that clearly indicated that they responded more negatively to the negative pictures and more positively to the positive pictures. Next, the experimenter presented the bogus reactions to the white, black, and Asian faces. The graph depicted a very negative reaction to black faces and moderately positive reactions to white and Asian faces. After viewing the feedback, the computer monitor went blank, and participants were instructed to remain still while EEG was recorded for 2 minutes. Immediately following the EEG recordings, participants completed an affect scale that included measures of guilt.

Finally, behavioral reactions to the prejudice feedback were measured. The experimenter explained that there were a few minutes remaining in the allotted time and asked whether the participant would be willing to help with the development of measures for a future study. The experimenter explained that this future study would involve having participants read various newspaper articles and that it was important to pretest the articles so that they could be equated on how interesting they were to undergraduates. All participants agreed to help. Participants were then shown a series of headlines from the articles, presented on the computer screen one at a time, for 6 s each. As indicated by the headlines, some articles were about decreasing one's prejudice level, whereas others involved justifying racial prejudice, affirming one's level of egalitarianism, or topics unrelated to racial issues. Participants rated each headline according to how interested they were in reading it.

Results indicated that the induction of guilt was successful. Self-reported levels of guilt were significantly greater than baseline following the feedback manipulation for all participants. In addition, examination of frontal EEG asymmetry indicated an increase in right frontal cortical activity compared with baseline levels, consistent with the hypothesis that the feedback would produce an avoidance-related motivational state (e.g., Amodio, Shah, Sigelman, Brazy, & Harmon-Jones, 2004; Harmon-Jones & Allen, 1998). Furthermore, higher levels of guilt predicted greater right frontal cortical activity, as well as participants' interest in reading articles about decreasing one's prejudice and affirming one's egalitarian beliefs. Guilt was not related to an interest in articles that justified prejudice or in articles not related to issues of racial prejudice.

Conclusion

Social psychological methods contribute to the study of emotion by using high-impact manipulations and deception to achieve high levels of psychological realism in the laboratory. Such methods avoid many of the pitfalls (e.g., participant awareness biases) inherent in other methodologies and allow researchers to induce some emotions that may be difficult to induce using other methods (e.g., anger). Social psychological methods of emotion induction are designed to produce emotional responses by placing research participants in psychologically involving situations. As described in this chapter, the construction of a high-impact emotion manipulation involves several important features aimed at masking the nature of the manipulation while maintaining internal validity. The examples we provided showcase just a few of the ways emotion has been induced in this way. Although some emotional processes may be examined using less immersive manipulations (e.g., using picture presentations to study automatic affective processing), we believe that high-impact social psychological methods of emotion induction are essential for investigating emotional phenomena.

Appendix A: Example Debriefing

What do you think about what we have done so far?
How did you feel when you heard the broadcast concerning tuition increase?
Did you feel like you had an opportunity to do something about the decision to raise tuition?
What do you think about the broadcast now?
Did anything seem odd or unusual?

Based on what has happened thus far, can you think of something that we might be interested in other than what I told you to begin with? [Probe carefully; if someone answers yes, find out why, when they thought this, and if it affected how they answered the questionnaires]. I ask you that because I am interested in something else. I could not tell you from the beginning because it might have affected how you responded (i.e., you might not have responded in a natural way). I will now tell you what I am interested in.

This study is a test of your emotional reactions to information that is counter to your attitude about a tuition increase. We measure these reactions through self-report (surveys) and your brain activity. Brain activity is an important response for us to analyze because the activity in the frontal lobes of your brain has been found to be associated with different motivations. It has been found that activity in the left frontal brain region is associated with approach, or "moving toward," motivation. Activity in the right frontal brain region is associated with withdrawal, or "moving away," motivation. In other studies, depressed individuals were found to have decreased left frontal brain activity, and angry individuals were found to have increased left frontal brain activity.

Previous studies support the idea anger is associated with increased approach motivation. To further test this idea, we attempted to induce the emotion of anger by exposing you to information that is emotionally relevant to you and then presenting the possibility or impossibility of changing this situation.

In this study you were randomly assigned to a condition and were then exposed to a message about a tuition increase. We created the message to make it emotionally arousing, and we worked very hard to make it convincing to you. The conditions differed in the following way. You were told that a 10% tuition increase was being considered for next year, or that a 10% tuition increase would definitely be implemented next year. We then offered people in the first group the opportunity to sign a petition against the tuition increase and ask them whether or not they would like to take some petitions with them, get them signed, and turn them back in. The other group, who is told the tuition increase is definite, will not be offered this option.

We predicted these reactions. In the group who is told that there may be a tuition increase next year, we predicted feelings of anger more than sadness. We also predicted that the students in this condition would show greater left frontal brain activity and that it would relate to signing the petition, because this condition would increase approach motivation.

In the other group, who believe that tuition is definitely increasing and is not offered the possibility of change through petitions, we expected to see less left frontal brain activation, because approach motivation should be lower.

Of course, we do not know what we will find out, and these are only our predictions. We may find that people do not respond how we think they will, and that is okay, because we, as scientists, will be interested in whatever we discover.

In the beginning of the study, we told you we wanted you to assess different radio broadcasts. But now you know we are interested in your emotions, motivations, and brain activity. We did not tell you this in the beginning because we thought you might not respond in a natural way and that the broadcasts would not be as involving for you. Do you understand why we did this?

Before you go, I need to ask a favor of you. Will you promise that you will not discuss this study with anyone [ask them to verbally promise]? We should be conducting this study for most of the semester, and the results of the study might be biased if people who participate in the study know about it beforehand. Thank you for your cooperation. Do you have any questions?

Appendix B

This is a short list of publications that report other social psychological methods of emotion induction. To obtain this list, we submitted a request to the Society for Personality and Social Psychology e-mail list. Many thanks to those who responded to our request.

Albarracín, D., & Kumkale, G. T. (2003). Affect as information in persuasion: A model of affect identification and discounting. *Journal of Personality and Social Psychology, 84,* 453–469.

Ax, A. F. (1953). The physiological differentiation between anger and fear in humans. *Psychosomatic Medicine, 15,* 433–442.

Batson, C. D. (1991). *The altruism question: Toward a social-psychological answer.* Hillsdale, NJ: Erlbaum.

Berkowitz, L., & Holmes, D. S. (1959). The generalization of hostility to disliked objects. *Journal of Personality, 27,* 565–577.

Brehm, J. W. (1999). The intensity of emotion. *Personality and Social Psychology Review, 3,* 2–22.

Burris, C. T., Harmon-Jones, E., & Tarpley, W. R. (1997). "By faith alone": Religious agitation and cognitive dissonance. *Basic and Applied Social Psychology, 19,* 17–31.

Coke, J. S., Batson, C. D., & McDavis, K. (1978). Empathic mediation of helping: A two-stage model. *Journal of Personality and Social Psychology, 36,* 752–766.

Dolinski, D., Ciszek, M., Godlewski, K., & Zawadzki, M. (2002). Fear-then-relief, mindlessness, and cognitive deficits. *European Journal of Social Psychology, 32,* 435–447.

Ensari, N., & Miller, N. (1998). Effects of affective reactions by an out-group on preferences for crossed categorization discussion partners. *Journal of Personality and Social Psychology, 75,* 1503–1527.

Fredrickson, B. L., Mancuso, R. A., Branigan, C., & Tugade, M. M. (2000). The undoing effect of positive emotions. *Motivation and Emotion, 24,* 237–258.

Griner, L. A., & Smith, C. A. (2000). Contributions of motivational orientation to appraisal and emotion. *Personality and Social Psychology Bulletin, 26,* 727–740.

Herrald, M. M., & Tomaka, J. (2002). Patterns of emotion-specific appraisals, coping and physiological reactivity during an ongoing emotional episode. *Journal of Personality and Social Psychology, 83,* 434–450.

Laird, J. D. (1974). Self-attribution of emotion: The effects of expressive behavior on the quality of emotional experience. *Journal of Personality and Social Psychology, 29,* 475–486.

Manucia, G. K., Baumann, D. J., & Cialdini, R. B. (1984). Mood influences on helping: Direct effects or side effects? *Journal of Personality and Social Psychology, 46,* 357–364.

Miller, R. S. (1987). Empathic embarrassment: Situational and personal determinants of reactions to the embarrassment of another. *Journal of Personality and Social Psychology, 53,* 1061–1069.

Schachter, S., & Singer, J. E. (1962). Cognitive, social, and physiological determinants of emotional states. *Psychological Review, 69,* 379–399.

Stotland, E. (1969). Exploratory investigations of empathy. In L. Berkowitz (Ed.), *Advances in experimental social psychology* (Vol. 4, pp. 271–314). New York: Academic Press.

Strack, F., Martin, L. L., & Stepper, S. (1988). Inhibiting and facilitating conditions of the human smile: A nonobtrusive test of the facial feedback hypothesis. *Journal of Personality and Social Psychology, 54,* 768–777.

Zanna, M. P., & Cooper, J. (1974). Dissonance and the pill: An attribution approach to studying the arousal properties of dissonance. *Journal of Personality and Social Psychology, 29,* 703–709.

Acknowledgments

We thank John Allen, Jim Coan, Cindy Harmon-Jones, and members of the Harmon-Jones Emotive Psychophysiology Lab for helpful comments on previous versions of this chapter. Preparation of this chapter was supported by grants from the National Science Foundation and the National Institute of Mental Health. Address correspondence to Eddie Harmon-Jones, Texas A&M University, Department of Psychology, 4235 TAMU, College Station, TX 77843; or via the Internet at eddiehj@gmail.com.

Notes

1. Social psychologists use a variety of methods to induce emotion (e.g., recall of past emotional episodes, guided imagery, pictures, film clips). However, the focus of this chapter is on the methodology unique to social psychological experimentation—the use of deception to evoke emotions.

2. Ideally, in pretesting, it should be ascertained that there is relatively little suspicion. If, however, several participants express suspicion, in data analyses, suspicion level can be coded and analyzed to assess whether it exerts a significant effect on the results. An interview is subject to the same participant response biases that might occur in self-report questionnaires, and these biases may contaminate the data obtained in the interview. Care should be taken to attempt to avoid such by asking relatively indirect questions (discussed later).

3. In our debriefings, we avoid use of the term *deception* and other, similar terms with negative meanings. However, we fully explain the deceptions used and the need for them (see appendix A for an example).

4. Determining whether an emotion is psychologically real is best achieved by collecting various measures—self-reports and physiological and behavioral measures. It is also important that the effects on the observed variables cannot be explained away as due to demand characteristics or other participant response biases.

References

Amodio, D. M., Devine, P. G., & Harmon-Jones, E. (in press). A dynamic model of guilt: Implications for motivation and self-regulation in the context of prejudice. *Psychological Science*.

Amodio, D. M., Harmon-Jones, E., & Devine, P. G. (2003). Individual differences in the activation and control of affective race bias as assessed by startle eyeblink responses and self-report. *Journal of Personality and Social Psychology, 84,* 738–753.

Amodio, D. M., Shah, J. Y., Sigelman, J., Brazy, P. C., & Harmon-Jones, E. (2004). Implicit regulatory focus associated with asymmetrical frontal cortical activity. *Journal of Experimental Social Psychology, 40,* 225–232.

Aronson, E., Brewer, M., & Carlsmith, J. M. (1985). Experimentation in social psychology. In G. Lindzey & E. Aronson (Eds.), *Handbook of social psychology* (3rd ed., Vol. 1, pp. 441–486). New York: Random House.

Aronson, E., & Carlsmith, J. M. (1968). Experimentation in social psychology. In G. Lindzey & E. Aronson (Eds.), *Handbook of social psychology* (2nd ed., Vol. 2, pp.1–79). Reading, MA: Addison Wesley.

Aronson, E., Ellsworth, P. C., Carlsmith, J. M., & Gonzales, M. H. (2000). *Methods of research in social psychology.* New York: McGraw-Hill.

Bargh, J. A., & Ferguson, M. J. (2000). Beyond behaviorism: On the automaticity of higher mental processes. *Psychological Bulletin, 126,* 925–945.

Batson, C. D. (1991). *The altruism question: Toward a social-psychological answer.* Hillsdale, NJ: Erlbaum.

Batson, C. D. (1998). Altruism and prosocial behavior. In D. T. Gilbert, S. T. Fiske, & G. Lindzey (Eds.), *The handbook of social psychology* (4th ed., Vol. 2, pp. 282–316). Boston: McGraw-Hill.

Batson, C. D., Polycarpou, M. P., Harmon-Jones, E., Imhoff, H. J., Mitchener, E. C., Bednar, L. L., et al. (1997). Empathy and attitudes: Can feeling for a member of a stigmatized outgroup improve attitudes toward the group? *Journal of Personality and Social Psychology, 72,* 105–118.

Berkowitz, L. (1962). *Aggression: A social psychological analysis.* New York: McGraw-Hill.

Berkowitz, L. (1993). *Aggression: Its causes, consequences, and control.* New York: McGraw-Hill.

Berkowitz, L., Jaffee, S., Jo, E., & Troccoli, B. T. (2000). On the correction of feeling induced judgmental biases. In J. Forgas (Ed.), *Feeling and thinking: The role of affect in social cognition* (pp. 131–152). Cambridge, UK: Cambridge University Press.

Coke, J. S., Batson, C. D., & McDavis, K. (1978). Empathic mediation of helping: A two-stage model. *Journal of Personality and Social Psychology, 36,* 752–766.

Dutton, D. G., & Lake, R. A. (1973). Threat of own prejudice and reverse discrimation in interracial situations. *Journal of Personality and Social Psychology, 28,* 94–100.

Epstein, S. (1994). Integration of the cognitive and the psychodynamic unconscious. *American Psychologist, 49,* 709–724.

Festinger, L., Garner, W. R., Hebb, D. O., Hunt, H. F., Lawrence, D. H., Osgood, C. E., et al. (1959). Education for research in psychology. *American Psychologist, 14,* 167–179.

Forgas, J. P. (1991). Affective influences on partner choice: Role of mood in social decisions. *Journal of Personality and Social Psychology, 61,* 708–720.

Forgas, J. P., Bower, G. H., & Moylan, S. J. (1990). Praise or blame? Affective influences on attributions for achievement. *Journal of Personality and Social Psychology, 59,* 809–819.

Greenberg, J., Solomon, S., Pyszczynski, T., & Rosenblatt, A. (1992). Why do people need self-esteem? Converging evidence that self-esteem serves an anxiety-buffering function. *Journal of personality and social psychology, 63,* 913–922.

Harmon-Jones, E. (2000). A cognitive dissonance theory perspective on the role of emotion in the maintenance and change of beliefs and attitudes. In N. H. Frijda, A. R. S. Manstead, & S. Bem (Eds.), *Emotions and beliefs* (pp. 185–211). Cambridge, UK: Cambridge University Press.

Harmon-Jones, E. (2003). Clarifying the emotive functions of asymmetrical frontal cortical activity. *Psychophysiology, 40,* 838–848.

Harmon-Jones, E., & Allen, J. J. B. (1998). Anger and frontal brain activity: EEG asymmetry consistent with approach motivation despite negative affective valence. *Journal of Personality and Social Psychology, 74,* 1310–1316.

Harmon-Jones, E., Peterson, H., & Vaughn, K. (2003). The dissonance-inducing effects of an inconsistency between experienced empathy and knowledge of past failures to help: Support for the action-based model of dissonance. *Basic and Applied Social Psychology, 25,* 69–78.

Harmon-Jones, E., & Sigelman, J. (2001). State anger and prefrontal brain activity: Evidence that insult-related relative left prefrontal activation is associated with experienced anger and aggression. *Journal of Personality and Social Psychology, 80,* 797–803.

Harmon-Jones, E., Sigelman, J. D., Bohlig, A., & Harmon-Jones, C. (2003). Anger, coping, and frontal cortical activity: The effect of coping potential on anger-induced left frontal activity. *Cognition and Emotion, 17,* 1–24.

Hass, R. G., Katz, I., Rizzo, N., Bailey, J., & Moore, L. (1992). When racial ambivalence evokes negative affect, using a disguised measure of mood. *Personality and Social Psychology Bulletin, 18,* 786–797.

Isen, A. M., & Means, B. (1983). The influence of positive affect on decision-making strategy. *Social Cognition, 2,* 18–31.

Lieberman, J. D., Solomon, S., Greenberg, J., & McGregor, H. A. (1999). A hot new way to measure aggression: Hot sauce allocation. *Aggressive Behavior, 25,* 331–348.

Masters, J. C., Carlson, C. R., & Rahe, D. F. (1985). Children's affective, behavioral, and cognitive responses to social comparison. *Journal of Experimental Social Psychology, 21,* 407–420.

McGregor, H. A., Lieberman, J. D., Greenberg, J., Solomon, S., Arndt, J., Simon, L., et al. (1998). Terror management and aggression: Evidence that mortality salience motivates aggression against worldview threatening others. *Journal of Personality and Social Psychology, 74,* 590–605.

Monteith, M. J. (1993). Self-regulation of stereotypical responses: Implications for progress in prejudice reduction. *Journal of Personality and Social Psychology, 65,* 469–485.

Monteith, M. J., Ashburn-Nardo, L., Voils, C. I., & Czopp, A. M. (2002). Putting the brakes on prejudice: On the development and operation of cues for control. *Journal of Personality and Social Psychology, 83,* 1029–1050.

Nummenmaa, L., & Niemi, P. (2004). Inducing affective states with success-failure manipulations: A meta-analysis. *Emotion, 4,* 207–214.

Rosenthal, R. (1994). Interpersonal expectancy effects: A 30-year perspective. *Current Directions in Psychological Science, 3,* 176–179.

Rosenthal, R., & Lawson, R. (1964). A longitudinal study of the effects of experimenter bias on the operant learning of laboratory rats. *Journal of Psychiatric Research, 2,* 61–72.

Schachter, S. (1959). *The psychology of affiliation: Experimental studies of the sources of gregariousness.* Stanford, CA: Stanford University Press.

Simon, L., Greenberg, J., Harmon-Jones, E., Solomon, S., Pyszczynski, T., & Abend, T. (1997). Terror management and cognitive experiential self theory: Evidence that terror management occurs in the experiential system. *Journal of Personality and Social Psychology, 72,* 1132–1146.

Stotland, E. (1969). Exploratory investigations of empathy. In L. Berkowitz (Ed.), *Advances in experimental social psychology* (Vol. 4, pp. 271–314). New York: Academic Press.

Weinstein, N. D. (1980). Unrealistic optimism about future life events. *Journal of Personality and Social Psychology, 39,* 806–820.

Nicole A. Roberts

Jeanne L. Tsai

James A. Coan

Emotion Elicitation Using Dyadic Interaction Tasks

Of all the possible elicitors of human emotion, interactions with other people may be the most powerful. Coworkers, friends, romantic partners, family members, and children can make us feel any type or intensity of emotion, ranging from mild joy to extreme frustration. Thus social interaction can be a rich source of spontaneous emotion, even in laboratory settings. By bringing two people (a *dyad*) into the laboratory and asking them to participate in an emotionally charged discussion (a *dyadic interaction*), researchers are able to observe a variety of emotions that closely resemble those that occur in everyday life. When used effectively, dyadic interaction tasks can offer researchers a wealth of information about the nature of emotion.

Overview

Dyadic interaction tasks have been used to elicit emotion in various types of dyads, including romantic partners (e.g., Cohan & Bradbury, 1997; Gonzaga, Keltner, Londahl, & Smith, 2001; Gottman, Coan, Carrere, & Swanson, 1998; Richards, 2001; Tsai & Levenson, 1997), siblings (Shortt & Gottman, 1997), peers (Gonzaga et al., 2001; Keltner, Young, Heerey, Oemig, & Monarch, 1998), and patients and therapists (Pole, 2000). This chapter primarily focuses on a task originally developed by Levenson and Gottman (1983) that has been used extensively to elicit emotion in married couples and romantic partners. In brief, the procedure consists of

dyads engaging in a series of unrehearsed, minimally structured conversations in the laboratory. Conversations are facilitated in a way that optimizes the elicitation of intense emotion, either negative (e.g., through the discussion of an area of disagreement in the relationship; Coan, Gottman, Babcock, & Jacobson, 1997) or positive (e.g., through the discussion of an enjoyable topic; Levenson, Carstensen, & Gottman, 1993). Multiple measures of emotional responding typically are obtained during and immediately after dyads' conversations. For instance, continuous measures of peripheral nervous system physiology (e.g., heart rate, skin conductance) can be obtained from each partner during the conversations (e.g., Carstensen, Gottman, & Levenson, 1995; Pole, 2000; Roberts & Levenson, 2001). Researchers also typically videotape the conversations, allowing for subsequent coding of facial, postural, and verbal behavior (see Coan & Gottman, chapter 16, this volume). In addition, immediately after each conversation, participants may be asked to rate the degree to which they experienced various emotions during the conversation (Tsai, 1996).

In this chapter, we discuss the relative advantages and disadvantages of dyadic interaction tasks, describe the specific tools recommended for carrying out such tasks, and present a detailed description of the procedure. Because dyadic interaction tasks have been used most often with married and dating couples, such couples will serve as the primary illustrative examples (and, consequently, the terms *couples* and *dyads* may be used interchangeably). Researchers are encouraged to modify the procedures according to the types of dyads studied and the research questions of interest.

Why Use Dyadic Interaction Tasks? The Advantages

Dyadic interaction tasks allow researchers to: (1) study emotion in social contexts; (2) elicit spontaneous emotion under fairly controlled conditions without compromising ecological validity; (3) capture the natural temporal course of emotion; and (4) elicit a range of emotional responses. These advantages make dyadic interaction the emotion-eliciting task of choice for many researchers.

Emotions in Social Contexts

In recent years, emotion researchers have paid increased attention to the social functions of emotion (see Keltner & Haidt, 1999, for a review). In fact, it is difficult to think of an emotion that does not have interpersonal antecedents and consequences. For example, love typically increases our contact with others, whereas disgust decreases it; anger is evoked when someone has wronged us; and embarrassment appeases others after a social transgression (Darwin, 1872/1998; Keltner & Buswell, 1997; Keltner & Haidt, 1999). Dyadic interaction tasks make it possible to examine how individuals experience and express emotions during social interactions and how emotions shape and are shaped by the reciprocal interactions between individuals (e.g., Keltner et al., 1998; Levenson & Gottman, 1985; Ruef, 2001).[1] For example, playful teasing may facilitate positive emotional exchanges, whereas aggressive teasing can lead to an escalation of negative emotion (Keltner et al., 1998). In addition, eliciting and measuring transactional emotional processes (i.e., the way emotions transpire between individuals) can yield useful information about the role emotion plays in interpersonal relationships. For example, Levenson and Gottman (1983) found that couples suffering from marital distress showed greater "physiological linkage," in which one partner's physiological arousal predicted greater physiological arousal in the other partner. Similarly, they found that when husbands displayed more negative emotion compared with positive emotion during a conflict conversation (i.e., greater ratios of negative to positive emotional displays), their wives showed more disgust and contempt during a similar conversation held 4 years later, placing couples on a trajectory toward marital dissolution (Gottman & Levenson, 1999).

Ecological Validity

Affective science's most sophisticated measures are of limited use if they are not generalizable to situations outside the laboratory. Compared with other emotion-eliciting tasks, dyadic interaction tasks may have the greatest ecological validity, because they rely on an ongoing emotional relationship between two individuals. In essence, they allow researchers to sample from an extant reservoir of feelings between two individuals. As a result, the type, intensity, and timing of emotion occurring during dyadic interaction tasks should closely resemble the emotions that occur between these two individuals in their daily lives. Anecdotally, participants often report that the only difference between the conversations they have in the laboratory and those they have at home is the fact that they are not having the conversation while engaging in another activity, such as doing the dishes or making dinner for their children. Indeed, in a study of Chinese American and European American dating couples, participants were asked to indicate how similar their laboratory conversations were to conversations they have in daily life (on a scale from 1 = *not at all* to 7 = *extremely*; Tsai, 1996). For a conversation in which partners updated each other about what they did during the day (the "events-of-the-day" conversation), the mean response was 5.5 (SE = 0.1). For a conversation in which partners discussed a disagreement in their relationship (the "conflict conversation"), the mean response was 5.2 (SE = 0.1). These ratings indicate that participants perceived conversations in the laboratory as more similar to than different from the conversations they have in their daily lives.

Moreover, whereas other emotion-eliciting tasks may emphasize standardization of content over meaning (e.g., in film-viewing tasks, all participants watch the same film, even though the subjective meaning of the film may differ for each participant), dyadic interaction tasks focus on standardizing the task's meaning rather than content. For example, when dyadic interaction tasks are used to elicit negative emotion in couples, couples are instructed to discuss the topic that they report as the greatest area of disagreement in their relationship. Thus, even though one couple may discuss communication and another may discuss jealousy, both will discuss topics that are the greatest source of disagreement in their respective relationships. This increases the likelihood that the emotions sampled in the laboratory via dyadic interaction tasks generalize to those that occur outside the laboratory.

In any case, it seems clear that the emotions elicited during dyadic interaction tasks are highly generalizable to situations outside of the laboratory, an advantage that cannot be overstated.

Emotion as a Dynamic Process

Emotions can change from one moment to the next. Dyadic interaction tasks allow researchers to capture the natural ebb and flow of emotions in the laboratory. More specifically, dyadic interaction tasks make it possible to examine the onset, offset, and duration of an emotional episode, as well as the temporal sequence of different emotional episodes (Ruef & Levenson, chapter 17, this volume). Such information can offer important clues as to the function of different emotional states. For example, positive emotions, such as amusement, appear to facilitate physiological recovery following the experience of negative emotions (Fredrickson & Levenson, 1998). Using a dyadic interaction task, Gottman and Levenson (1999) found that couples who were most satisfied with their relationships were more likely to interrupt their negative emotional exchanges with positive ones (e.g., affection, humor), suggesting that positive emotions may in part serve to soothe and repair negative interactions.

Range of Emotional Responses

Dyadic interaction tasks are ideal for studying variability in emotional responding, because the conversations employed are fairly unstructured. As a result, dyadic interaction tasks tend to generate a wider range of emotions than more tightly controlled emotion-eliciting stimuli (e.g., film clips used to elicit specific emotional states). For example, for some dyads, the task of discussing an area of conflict in their relationship may elicit large increases in physiology, frequent displays of negative emotional behavior, and intense reports of negative emotional experience. For other dyads, the same task may elicit only moderate increases in physiology, frequent displays of positive, as well as negative, emotional behavior, and reports of both positive and negative emotional experience. Thus dyadic interaction tasks leave room for researchers to explore the considerable variation in emotional responses that exist from dyad to dyad, from person to person, and even within individuals over time or in different contexts. Researchers have, in fact, already identified many correlates of variation in emotional responding during dyadic interaction tasks, such as gender, ethnicity, age, relationship history, personality, and current level of stress (e.g., Carstensen et al., 1995; Coan et al., 1997; Gottman et al., 1998; Jacobson et al., 1994; Roberts & Levenson, 2001; Robins, Spranca, & Mendelsohn, 1996; Tsai & Levenson, 1997). Finally, by measuring multiple components of emotion during dyads' conversations, it is possible to examine variation not only in the type and intensity of emotion experienced and expressed but also in the channels through which emotion is expressed (e.g., physiology, expressive behavior, subjective experience), as well as the degree to which these different channels cohere.

Why Not Use Dyadic Interaction Tasks? The Disadvantages

According to conventional wisdom, the characteristics that initially draw you to your mate are the same ones that you ultimately want to change. Unfortunately, the same can be said of any emotion-eliciting task, and dyadic interaction tasks are no exception. That is, aspects of dyadic interaction tasks that are their greatest strengths are also their greatest limitations. Disadvantages of the task are that: (1) its procedures allow considerable room for participant noncompliance and experimenter error, (2) it requires significant resources, and (3) it provides only a snapshot sampling of emotion.

Participant Noncompliance and Experimenter Error

Because dyadic interaction tasks allow considerable variability in emotional responding, they also allow participant non-

compliance. First, the task requires participants to have conversations about intimate aspects of their relationships under the scrutiny of strangers. Second, to preserve ecological validity and minimize discomfort, participants typically are left to themselves (albeit with cameras rolling) to complete this task. Thus it is not uncommon for participants to avoid discussing the topic assigned to them. For example, some romantic couples discuss an assigned area of conflict during the first minute of the allotted 15-minute conversation and then discuss a nonconflictual topic for the remainder of the time. Other couples disengage once the conversation reaches a high level of emotional intensity, such as by changing the topic or ceasing their conversation altogether. It is quite possible that these behaviors reflect how participants deal with conflict at home, but it also may be that they are avoiding the discomfort or embarrassment of discussing difficult topics in a laboratory setting.

Of course, participants are not the only source of unwanted variability. As discussed in greater detail later, the dyadic interaction task *facilitator* (i.e., the primary individual who facilitates the procedure) introduces a source of variability. Although facilitators are trained to behave in a standard manner, they still may establish different levels of rapport with each dyad. In addition, there are individual differences among different facilitators. Because facilitators not only have extensive contact with each dyad but also play the central role of facilitating dyads' emotional conversations, facilitator differences may affect how comfortable participants feel and, consequently, how much their interaction in the laboratory resembles their typical interactions outside the laboratory.

Resource Demands

Dyadic interaction tasks require significant resources from both participants and researchers. Dyadic interaction procedures can require anywhere from 2 to 4 hours to complete. Thus both members of the dyad must find and coordinate a 2- to 4-hour block of time in their schedules. Busy couples may be particularly reluctant to give up a free night together to participate in an experiment. Therefore, researchers have to make the experience convenient and rewarding enough for dyads to participate (e.g., by offering significant financial compensation, or by providing child care as needed for some couples). In addition, the dyadic interaction task typically requires two or more experimenters (one facilitator and one data collector), especially when obtaining multiple measures of emotion. If a researcher decides to collect physiological measures, the expense of data collection and data reduction expands considerably. As a result, it can be difficult for researchers to use this task without substantial personnel and financial support.

Snapshot Sampling of Emotion

As described earlier, one of the reasons that dyadic interaction tasks are such effective elicitors of emotion is that they sample from a dyad's existing reservoir of emotion, which increases the ecological validity of the task. However, as is the case with most emotion-eliciting tasks, dyadic interaction tasks are able to provide only a snapshot of participants' emotional responses. Without a full history of the dyad's relationship, we have limited understanding of *why* partners are responding to one another in the ways that they are. Similarly, the generalizability of one partner's emotional responses to interactions with other partners (i.e., other relationship partners or other people in general) is unknown. Ideally, researchers would be able to study individuals' emotional responses with different dyadic interaction partners; however, given the tremendous resources required, this usually is not a viable option.

Not surprisingly, we believe that, in most instances, the advantages of dyadic interaction tasks far outweigh their disadvantages. Moreover, because dyadic interaction tasks provide a unique window into the interpersonal functions of emotion, we believe they should be part of any emotion researcher's tool chest.

Methods

What Do You Need to Get Started?

Although dyadic interaction tasks can be intensive in terms of equipment and personnel, once the materials are obtained and the procedure is rehearsed, these tasks can be smoothly run. This section discusses the primary components involved in setting up a dyadic interaction task. We base our discussion on Levenson and Gottman's (1983) dyadic interaction procedure. Of course, as mentioned earlier, this procedure should be tailored to meet the specific needs of one's research program.

Personnel

The first issue is *whom* you need to get started. The key player in any dyadic interaction task is the *facilitator*. Facilitators have the most contact with participants and, therefore, are critical to the successful elicitation of emotional conversations. Prior to a dyad's conversation, the facilitator delivers instructions to the dyad, identifies the topic that the dyad will discuss, and reviews with each partner his or her feelings about the topic. After the conversation, the facilitator attempts to diffuse any residual feelings and then introduces subsequent parts of the task. Therefore, the ideal facilitator is someone who can put couples at ease so that they are willing to discuss their feelings openly and who at the same time is not afraid to stir up intense emotions. It is an added bonus if the facilitator is well versed in aspects of the experiment (e.g., attaching physiological sensors, collecting physiological data, recording audio and visual responses) so that he or she can assist the other experimenters.

The specific needs of the experiment should, in part, influence the selection of the facilitator. Most of our work has been with samples of romantic couples. To date, our facilitators have been women with a background or interest in psychology and in working with couples. We typically have used one or two facilitators throughout the study. Using just one facilitator has the advantage of holding this source of experimental variance constant for all dyads. It also avoids the possible confound of introducing a new facilitator midway through the study and creates continuity for couples who are followed over time. However, it can be difficult to maintain the same facilitator throughout the study, particularly with longitudinal studies or large samples. Furthermore, there are disadvantages to using just one rather than several facilitators. One disadvantage is that the facilitator is likely to mature throughout the course of the study, and, as a result, conversations facilitated at the study's start may differ from those facilitated near the study's end. In addition, using just one rather than several facilitators potentially may limit the study's replicability.

When using multiple facilitators for the same study, one approach is to match the facilitators as closely as possible, such as in terms of age, appearance, and personality. This approach may be important when comparing different types of dyads in a between-subjects design. For example, previous research has suggested that participants are more comfortable when the experimenter is of the same ethnicity (Anderson, 1989; Murphy, Alpert, Willey, & Somes, 1988). Therefore, in a study of ethnicity and emotion conducted by Tsai, Levenson, & McCoy (2006), a Chinese American facilitator was selected to interact with Chinese American couples and a European American facilitator to interact with European American couples. The two facilitators (both undergraduate psychology majors) were matched in terms of physical appearance, wore similar uniforms when conducting the study, and worked together to ensure that their demeanors were as similar as possible. An alternative approach, however, is to select different kinds of facilitators, who vary in age, appearance, and personality. In the example of the Tsai and Levenson (1997) study, this would involve using several Chinese American facilitators and several European American facilitators. This kind of approach has the advantage of randomizing any facilitator-specific error variance. In part, the decision about whether to use a few similar facilitators or many different facilitators will depend on the sample size and the questions the researchers are attempting to answer with the dyadic interaction task.

Regardless of the number of facilitators used, extensive training is important to ensure that facilitators are practiced in the logistics of the experiment and in their interpersonal responses (e.g., responding in a fairly controlled, yet sensitive and personable manner). Training typically includes watching videotapes of facilitators in previous studies, role plays, and practice with several volunteer pilot couples. Individuals with prior clinical training or training in basic interviewing skills most likely will require less training.

One experimental challenge is keeping the facilitator "blind" to the experimental conditions and hypotheses. For example, in a dyadic interaction study conducted by one of us (JLT), half of the couples engaged in conversations in the presence of a confederate (an older gentleman; Tsai, 1996). The facilitator introduced the gentleman to the couple and therefore was not blind to the manipulation. Although this approach introduces a source of bias in that it is possible that the facilitator will respond differently toward couples in the two experimental conditions (with and without the confederate), having the facilitator involved throughout the experiment is often necessary to provide continuity for couples. For example, if a confederate suddenly appeared without being introduced by the facilitator, couples might feel nervous and be reluctant to engage in an emotional conversation. In other between-subjects designs, such as studies involving older versus younger couples or couples of different ethnicities, it is almost impossible to keep the facilitator blind to these different groups. Nevertheless, standardizing the facilitator's role as much as possible and avoiding discussion of specific hypotheses with the facilitator can help preserve the integrity of the experiment.

Finally, in addition to the facilitator, it is helpful to have at least one additional person (e.g., an undergraduate research assistant or graduate student experimenter) assist with data collection, especially when videotaping sessions and collecting physiological data at the same time.

Setting

The Levenson and Gottman (1983) dyadic interaction task typically has been conducted in a comfortably furnished laboratory setting (e.g., Richards, 2001; Roberts & Levenson, 2001; Tsai & Levenson, 1997). In this setting, two chairs (i.e., one for each partner) face each other. Behind each chair is a bookshelf, and on each bookshelf are neutral objects, such as old books and other decorative items. Two tables are turned perpendicularly to the dyad, one with physiological preparatory equipment and one with a video monitor. An additional chair is situated to the side of the dyad for the facilitator. Importantly, a separate experimenter room is located adjacent to the participant room. Communication takes place via an intercom and audiovisual apparatus controlled and monitored remotely. The facilitator is able to enter the participant room quickly if needed.

Apparatus and Materials

An advantage of using dyadic interaction tasks is that multiple kinds of data can be collected, including verbal responses, facial expressions and other nonverbal behaviors, ratings of self-reported emotion, and physiology. Consequently, this procedure can be quite equipment-intensive. It should be noted, however, that the dyadic interaction procedure can be conducted without this kind of equipment-intensive data collection. For example, although this section reviews how to collect physiological data and continuous ratings of self-reported affect, conversations can just be videotaped or transcribed.

Audiovisual Apparatus

Valuable information about couples' emotional responses can be obtained by recording a frontal view of each partner's face and upper torso. Following the procedure by Levenson and Gottman (1983), we have videotaped participants continuously and unobtrusively by embedding two remotely controlled high-resolution video cameras in the respective bookshelves behind each partner's head. In addition to being embedded in bookshelves, cameras are partially concealed behind darkened glass. Thus, even though participants are told up front that they will be videotaped, they typically report not noticing or forgetting about the cameras. The two images (i.e., one of each partner) can be combined into a single split-screen image using a video special effects generator and then recorded on a VHS videocassette recorder (Levenson & Gottman, 1983). Advances in computer-mediated digital video recordings undoubtedly will continue to increase both the quality of recordings and the ease with which such data are collected.

In addition to videotaping dyads, audiotaping their conversations with a *tape recorder,* either placed in the participant room or connected in the adjacent experimenter room, allows researchers to transcribe the conversations later and to code dyads' narratives (e.g., for content and word use). A Lavaliere *microphone* can be clipped onto each partner's shirt collar to record partners' verbal responses, and a room microphone can be used to pick up the facilitator's comments (and is helpful in the event that one microphone fails during the dyad's conversation). Audio quality can be monitored from the experimenter room by a *digital audio mixer.*

An *intercom* from the experimenter room to the participant room enables the experimenter to communicate with the dyad (e.g., instructing them to sit quietly if they are talking during the baseline period) without having to enter the room and risk making participants feel self-conscious. Another useful device that reduces the number of times that the experimenter has to enter the room is a timed light indicator (the *signal light*), which receives a signal from the data collection software to indicate when the dyad can begin conversing. When this device is used, dyads are instructed to simply sit quietly until the signal light goes on, at which time they can begin their conversation.

Finally, the participant room should contain a video playback *monitor* if the researchers would like participants to watch a videotaped recording of their conversations (described later).

Rating Dials

To obtain continuous ratings of participants' subjective emotional experience during the conversations, a *rating dial* may be used. The type of dial used in previous research consists of a pointer attached to a dial, on which the pointer traverses a 180-degree arc over a 9-point scale, anchored by *very negative* at zero degrees, *neutral* at 90 degrees, and *very positive* at 180 degrees (Gottman & Levenson, 1985; see also Ruef & Levenson, chapter 17, this volume). Using this type of dial, participants can provide moment-by-moment ratings of how positive or negative they felt during their conversations. Rating dials can be configured such that participants' ratings are input directly into a computer in the experimenter room.

Self-Reported Emotion Inventories

Another option for collecting subjective emotional experience in response to the dyadic interaction task is to administer self-report emotion inventories after each conversation. For example, Tsai et al. (2006) used inventories adapted from Ekman, Friesen, and Ancoli (1980), in which participants rated how strongly they felt each of several specific emotions (e.g., disgust, contempt, shame, amusement) during their conversations. However, there are a variety of questionnaire measures that can be used for collecting self-reports of subjective emotional experience (e.g., see Gray & Watson, chapter 11, this volume).

Topic Inventories

Two self-report inventories are critical to the facilitation of emotional conversations in married or romantic couples: the Couple's Problem Inventory (Gottman, Markman, & Notarius, 1977), which has been labeled as the "Areas of Disagreement" form in participants' questionnaire booklets; Tsai, 1996) and the Enjoyable Conversations form (a list of topics developed by Lowell Krokoff and mentioned in Gottman et al., 2003). The facilitator uses these inventories to help identify topics that couples will discuss during their conversations. On the Couple's Problem Inventory, couples rate the perceived severity of 10 relationship issues (e.g., money, communication, jealousy) using a scale ranging from 0 (*Don't disagree at all*) to 100 (*Disagree very much*). We have added a question to this form asking couples to list the topic that *currently* represents the greatest area of disagreement in their relationship, which is useful in case more than one area receives a high rating (Tsai, 1996). The Enjoyable Conversations inventory follows the same format, except that couples use the 0–100 scale to indicate how much they enjoy talking about a list of 16 pleasant topics (e.g., vacations we've taken, silly and fun types of things, our plans for the future). These inventories are included in appendix A.

Although each partner may complete these inventories during the laboratory session, it might be desirable, in terms of saving time and obtaining thoughtful responses, to have partners complete the inventories at home prior to the laboratory session. Importantly, partners are instructed to complete these inventories independently, whether at home or in the laboratory. This prevents partners from being influenced by each other's responses. It also increases the likelihood that their ratings will reflect genuine sources of concern (or enjoyment), and therefore more emotion should be evoked at the time of the interaction in the laboratory (e.g., a jealous partner may be more likely to indicate *jealousy* as a strong area of disagreement if he or she completes the rating form without the other partner present).

Relationship Satisfaction

In addition to the inventories that assess couples' primary areas of disagreement and enjoyment, researchers may wish to ask couples to complete a relationship satisfaction inventory, such as the Locke-Wallace Marital Adjustment Test (Locke & Wallace, 1959) or the Locke-Williamson Test (Burgess, Locke, & Thomes, 1971; these can be adapted for use with dating couples or other types of dyads). Relationship satisfaction is likely to be a moderating variable in dyadic interaction tasks, but it also may be a predictor or outcome variable. Again, these inventories can be administered before or during the laboratory session, but they may yield more honest and thoughtful responses when completed outside the laboratory and when completed by partners independently.

Other Self-Report Questionnaires

A host of other questionnaire measures have been used in conjunction with dyadic interaction tasks, depending on the study's aims. These include measures of personality (e.g., NEO Personality Inventory; Costa & McCrae, 1992), health (e.g., Symptom Checklist-90; Derogatis & Lazarus, 1994), recent life stress (e.g., Horowitz, Schaefer, Hiroto, Wilner, & Levin, 1977), and cultural background and practices (e.g., Suinn-Lew Asian Self-Identity Acculturation Scale; Suinn, Rickard-Figueroa, Lew, & Vigil, 1987; Acculturation Rating Scale for Mexican Americans; Cuellar, Harris, & Jasso, 1980). These measures are best administered outside the laboratory and before participants engage in the dyadic interaction task.

Physiological Apparatus

Researchers have identified ways to collect autonomic and somatic nervous system physiology data in a fairly unobtrusive manner during dyads' conversations (e.g., Levenson & Gottman, 1983). For example, by attaching sensors to a participant's nondominant hand (e.g., electrodes to measure skin conductance; a thermistor to measure finger temperature; a plethysmograph to measure finger pulse transit time and finger pulse amplitude), multiple autonomic indicators can be collected while the participant's dominant hand is free to complete inventories or gesture as usual while conversing. In addition, an electromechanical transducer can be attached to a platform under each participant's chair to measure general somatic activity (bodily movement). Physiological sensors are attached at the beginning of the procedure, and physiology is monitored continuously throughout dyads' conversations. Although participants often joke in a self-conscious manner while the sensors are being attached (e.g., commenting to one another, "Look, I'm wearing earrings," while sensors are being attached to their ears), they report that they tend to forget about the sensors during the experiment. Again, the procedures for facilitating emotional conversations in the laboratory can be used even if physiological data are not collected or if different kinds of physiological measures are selected. (Also refer to Curtin, Lozano, & Allen, chapter 24, this volume, for a more thorough description of physiological data collection.)

Dyad Selection and Recruitment

As with any study, careful attention must be paid to selection criteria. When studying close relationships, there is the added consideration of evaluating factors that may influence the intimacy of the relationship, which can have implications for the quality of the interaction and the emotions elicited. For example, for married couples, it may be important to consider the length of relationship, whether the relationship is a first marriage, and whether there have been previous separations. For other types of dyads, such as dating couples, peers, or siblings, it is equally important to consider factors that could affect the nature of the relationship, such as whether or not the two individuals live together, age differences, power and status differences, and degree of commitment to the relationship (Keltner et al., 1998; Shortt & Gottman, 1997; Tsai & Levenson, 1997).

Dyads can be recruited in the same manner as single participants, such as through large survey firms, advertisements, or word of mouth. When screening potential participants who may have found out about the study through word of mouth (e.g., college-age dating couples), it is important to ask whether or not they have heard anything about the specifics of the study. In one case, we learned that couples were choosing not to participate in our study because it was gaining a reputation for "breaking up couples" (presumably by having them discuss areas of conflict in their relationships).[2] Similarly, when offering monetary compensation for study participation, careful screening should be done to ensure that participants are not "faking" their relationship to be in the experiment. In one case, due to our suspicions about the nature of the relationship of the couple, we brought partners into different rooms and asked them questions about their relationship (e.g., How did you meet? What is your partner's birthday) to assess whether or not they were actually romantically involved.

Procedure

A sample timeline for the dyadic interaction task is provided in appendix B. The procedure described in this timeline measures multiple aspects of emotional responding and has been used in various laboratories with great success. Never-

theless, researchers are urged to view this timeline as one example of a dyadic interaction task and to modify it to suit their particular scientific interests.

Prior to the Interaction Session

After telephone screening to ensure that the dyad meets criteria for the particular study, partners are mailed a set of questionnaires (e.g., demographics, relationship satisfaction) and are instructed to complete the questionnaires *independently*. Partners also are instructed not to speak to one another for at least 8 hours prior to their laboratory visit, to ensure that they have enough material to discuss during their initial conversation (about the events of their day). Couples who have spoken to each other extensively within the 8 hours prior to their laboratory session are rescheduled. If possible, contacting *both* partners before the laboratory session ensures their arrival at the appropriate time and location. In some instances, however, one partner may take responsibility for ensuring that the other partner has all of the needed logistical information.

Interaction Session: Consent and Attaching Sensors

Upon arrival at the laboratory, couples read and sign consent forms. After partners provide consent, physiological sensors are attached (i.e., if physiological data are being collected). Given that there are two participants in the room, sensors can be attached to one partner at a time (e.g., while the other partner completes "filler" questionnaires), or two experimenters (e.g., the facilitator and a research assistant) can attach the sensors to both partners simultaneously. Throughout this procedure, it is important to maintain a fairly neutral yet warm stance, to neither promote nor inhibit interaction between partners.

Initial Baseline

To obtain baseline measures of physiology before experimental instructions are given, partners are instructed to sit quietly for 5 minutes. Because partners often engage in significant nonverbal communication during this baseline period, a screen is placed between them to prevent any conversation or distraction. A card with a letter "X" is placed on the screen in front of each partner, and they are instructed to relax, watch the X, and empty their minds of any thoughts, feelings, or memories. Partners also are instructed not to close their eyes or fall asleep. Partners are asked to complete a self-report emotion inventory after the 5-minute baseline period. (Again, this baseline period may not be needed if physiological data are not being collected, or may be of a different duration to suit the needs of the particular experiment.)

Events-of-the-Day Conversation

To acclimate dyads to conversing in the laboratory, they are asked to discuss the "events of the day" or the events that occurred during the time since they were last in contact. This conversation can serve as a "control" conversation that is compared with other, more emotional conversations or as a conversation of interest in itself. To introduce this conversation, we (Tsai, 1996; Roberts & Levenson, 2001) have given the following instructions:

> We have found that couples, after not having seen each other for most of the day, typically talk about the day's events. I'd like you to have a conversation like the ones the two of you normally have at the end of the day. I'd like you to be as normal and natural as you can. Because we're interested in your normal, natural interactions, you don't need to explain who people or where places that you discuss are. The idea is to behave as naturally as you can. Do you have any questions?

If partners deny that anything has happened since they last saw each other, they are encouraged to "do the best they can" and to talk about what they normally would talk about after not having seen each other for a period of time.

Prior to the conversation, partners are asked to sit quietly and relax for a few minutes. A signal light goes on after 5 minutes, signaling to the dyad that they can begin their conversation. After 20 minutes (the 5-minute silent period and 15-minute conversation), the facilitator enters the room to signal that the conversation period is over. (Participants are not instructed beforehand how long to keep talking—they are just told to converse until the facilitator returns.) The facilitator can then administer a self-report emotion inventory to each partner.

Conflict Discussion and the Role of the Facilitator

After the events-of-the-day conversation, dyads are asked to have a conversation about an area of conflict in their relationship. Success in eliciting emotion during this dyadic interaction task largely hinges on selecting a topic that evokes the most emotion for each dyad. This is accomplished during the *conflict facilitation*. A sample conflict facilitation is provided in appendix C. There are three primary goals of the conflict facilitation: (1) to identify a topic about which partners disagree; (2) to highlight partners' differences of opinion; and (3) to draw out each partner's emotions about the disagreement, priming them to engage in conflict.

Identifying the Topic

Prior to the conflict conversation—either following the events-of-the-day conversation or before coming to the laboratory session—each partner independently completes an Areas of Disagreement form (described earlier). Before speaking with the dyad, the facilitator reviews each partner's form and identifies the two or three areas that they disagree about the most. Although this form provides a sense of the areas about which partners disagree, these self-report ratings do not necessarily reflect the topic that will elicit the strongest emotions during a dyadic interaction. For example, spouses may rate "religion" as a "100," because they have very different religious views and practices; however, they may accept these differences and therefore not become emotional when discussing them. Furthermore, there may be a discrepancy between the areas each partner rated as highest in conflict. This can make for either an emotional conversation (e.g., if partners argue about whether or not there is a disagreement) or a one-sided conversation (e.g., if only one partner becomes emotionally engaged). Therefore, rather than simply relying on partners' self-report ratings, the facilitator's task is to review systematically with the couple several areas of disagreement and to determine which topic will be most likely to generate the strongest emotions.

Approaching the Facilitation

When working with the couple to identify the primary area of disagreement, one of two approaches can be used: a long, drawn-out exploration of the topics, or a shorter, more structured approach. A slightly more "chatty" approach may convey a relaxed stance on the part of the facilitator and allow more room for building rapport with the dyad. On the other hand, a more structured approach may be advisable when length of procedure is of concern or when standardizing a dyadic interaction protocol for multiple facilitators. In either case, it is important to maintain rapport and help the couple feel comfortable by discussing the topics in a respectful manner. This is made easier when the facilitator is comfortable with the expression of negative emotion and with discussing intimate and potentially embarrassing topics (e.g., sex) with the dyad. (Again, these are important considerations when selecting the facilitator.)

Inquiring About the Disagreement

Couples typically are introduced to the facilitation with the statement, "Another thing we know about couples is that they often disagree. I'm going to ask you about a few topics that, based on your questionnaires, it looks like the two of you may disagree about."[3] A good starting point is to ask each partner, one at a time, to describe the last time they had a disagreement about the first topic.[4] For example: "One area of disagreement seems to be communication. Jane, why don't you start out by telling me when the last time was that you and John had a disagreement about communication, and how it made you feel." Asking partners to cite a specific time when they disagreed can help provide an anchor for the discussion and illustrate how the area of conflict plays out in the relationship. One thing the facilitator should keep in mind is that partners were not supposed to see one another's ratings beforehand, so it is important not to reveal these ratings or to specify which partner suggested that a certain topic was an area of disagreement. In addition, as one partner begins to tell his or her side of the story, the other partner often interrupts (e.g., to defend himself or herself). In these instances, the facilitator should tell the other partner that he or she will have a chance to tell his or her side of the story in a moment. The facilitator should prevent the couple from engaging in an argument during the facilitation; the argument itself should be saved for the interaction.

Focus on Emotions

A crucial aspect of the facilitation is identifying and highlighting the emotions underlying the disagreement. "Reflective listening" is a helpful technique the facilitator can use to draw out each partner's emotions. Reflective listening involves simply restating the participant's feelings in his or her own words (e.g., "So, when John didn't tell you why he was upset, you felt really confused and angry"). Although it sometimes may be necessary to make inferences about emotions if a participant is reluctant to say anything or is having difficulty articulating his or her feelings, it is important to avoid making judgments or assumptions about how partners feel. Incorrect assumptions could increase a participant's discomfort with the task and decrease task compliance. Asking about emotions in an open-ended fashion (e.g., "What else were you feeling when you had the sense John was ignoring you?") and sticking as closely as possible to what each partner actually said can be helpful strategies.

Deciding How Much to Probe

It is important to explore each topic enough to gain a sense of the disagreement and to bring the underlying issues and emotions to the surface. At the same time, the goal is for the couple to experience the most emotion during the conversation itself and not before. Ideally, couples should be on the verge of becoming emotional just before their conversation.

Summarize

As soon as the facilitator has a clear sense of the disagreement, including each partner's viewpoint and feelings, it is useful to make a summary statement that highlights the disagreement as much as possible. For example: "It sounds, Jane, as though you were confused about why John was upset, and you get angry thinking about how he often does not tell you why he is upset. And you, John, also felt angry and hurt, because you feel Jane should have known why you were upset, and that you shouldn't have had to tell her." The dyad should be discussing a current area of disagreement, so the summary statement should be phrased in the present tense, even though the facilitator will refer to past events. After making a summary statement, the facilitator should check with each partner to make sure his or her statement is accurate (e.g., "Does that sound about right?").

Repeat With Each Topic

Once an understanding of the first topic is achieved, the facilitator should inform the couple that they will move on to the next topic. For example: "Okay, I think I have a pretty clear sense of what the disagreement regarding communica-

tion is about. Another area it looks like the two of you may disagree about is money." The second topic then should be explored in the same manner as the first, addressing the inquiry to the other partner (e.g., "John, could you tell me about the last time you and Jane had a disagreement about money, and how it made you feel").

Choosing the Final Topic

After exploring two or three topics, it is up to the facilitator to determine which topic will be the most emotionally evocative. The following factors can be considered to assist with this decision: (1) *Is the issue current?* A recent argument is more likely to be emotionally charged than one that took place several years ago or has been resolved. (2) *Do both partners seem engaged?* Although it may be the case that one partner's refusal to engage in a discussion about a particular topic actually generates more emotion, the topic ideally will be an area that generates engagement and emotion from both partners. (3) *Is the couple comfortable?* Although it can be expected that there may be some discomfort when couples are asked to discuss an area of relationship conflict, if the couple appears too uncomfortable or distressed to even engage in a particular topic, it is advisable to select a different topic. (4) *When in doubt, ask the couple.* If the facilitator is stumped as to which topic seems to generate the most emotion, he or she may ask the couple which topic they view as the greatest area of conflict in their relationship.

Conflict Conversation

After the conflict facilitation and the selection of a conversation topic, couples are asked to have a conversation about the selected topic and are encouraged to attempt to resolve their conflict about the topic. They are instructed to follow the same format as with the first conversation. That is, they are asked to sit quietly for 5 minutes and then to begin their conversation about the selected topic when the signal light turns on. After 20 minutes have passed (the 5-minute silent period and the 15-minute conversation), the facilitator comes back into the room, and each partner completes a self-report emotion inventory.

Enjoyable Conversation

Although researchers typically have used data from conflict conversations to study emotion and intimate relationships (e.g., Levenson & Gottman, 1985; Tsai & Levenson, 1997; Gottman et al., 2003), the dyadic interaction paradigm often involves a third conversation after the events-of-the-day and conflict conversations, during which couples are asked to discuss an enjoyable topic. This conversation serves two purposes: (1) to learn more about dyads during interactions designed to elicit positive emotions and (2) to end the procedure on a pleasant note. The enjoyable conversation follows the same format as the conflict conversation. First, the facilitator uses the Enjoyable Conversations form to select the areas partners rated as the most enjoyable to discuss. Second, the facilitator systematically reviews these areas with the couple, with careful attention paid to each partner's emotions (e.g., "John, how do you feel when you and Jane are talking about vacations you've taken together?"). Third, the facilitator selects the final topic and asks couples to have a conversation about it. As with the previous conversations, partners sit quietly for 5 minutes and then begin their conversation after the signal light turns on. The facilitator returns after the 15-minute conversation, and partners complete a self-report emotion inventory.

If length of the procedure is of concern, it is possible to omit the enjoyable conversation or to randomly assign couples to engage in either a conflict conversation or an enjoyable conversation (both preceded by the events-of-the-day conversation). Based on our experience, the enjoyable conversation is less effective at eliciting intense emotion and, in many cases, is very similar to the events-of-the-day conversation.

Recall Session

To collect continuous measures of self-reported affect, after the conversations researchers can show the dyad a videotape of each conversation and ask them to use a rating dial to provide continuous ratings of how positive or negative they were feeling at each moment during the conversation (described earlier; also see Ruef & Levenson, chapter 17, this volume). Although this method is not an essential component of the dyadic interaction task, it has the advantage of enabling continuous measures of emotional experience to be collected without interrupting the procedure (and thereby interrupting the affective experience). When presented with the rating dial, partners are instructed to use the dial to provide continuous reports of how positive or negative they felt moment by moment during the preconversation silent period, as well as during the conversation. Couples should be given some time to practice using the dial; ideally, couples would learn how to make their ratings without looking down at the dial. It is important that couples understand that they should rate how they were feeling moment by moment *during the conversation itself,* not while watching the videotape during the recall session.

This "recall" portion of the experiment has been integrated into the dyadic interaction procedure in two different ways. In the original Levenson and Gottman (1983) procedure, couples engaged in three conversations during one laboratory session, and then each partner returned individually on a separate occasion for the recall session. Having two sessions is advantageous in that it minimizes fatigue and allows partners to make their ratings without the other partner present. It is problematic, however, if there is a concern about partners not returning for the second session. Moreover, with this time lag, it is possible that participants will forget how they actually felt during the conversation.

An alternative method is to have couples engage in just one or two conversations and then conduct the recall session immediately afterward (e.g., Roberts & Levenson, 2001; Tsai et al., 2006). The advantages of this method are that partners do not have to come back for an additional session and that couples are less likely to forget how they felt during their conversation. With this method, after the couple completes the conversations, partners' chairs are turned 90 degrees so that both partners are facing the video monitor. A screen is placed between them so that they cannot see one another's ratings or facial expressions while making their ratings. Headphones also are placed on each partner's head to deter them from talking and so that they cannot hear each other's verbal responses (e.g., laughing out loud).

Excerpts

One shortcoming of collecting continuous measures of affect using a rating dial is that only valence (positive and negative affect) is measured. Therefore, to capture couples' subjective experience of specific emotions, the researcher may ask them to complete self-report emotion inventories about their emotional experience at certain key moments during the conversation. For example, after couples finish rating their affect using the rating dial, the software that collects the rating dial data can be programmed to extract periods, or points in time (i.e., in minutes and seconds), that each partner rated as most positive and most negative. The videotape (or digital video file) then can be cued to these moments (e.g., most positive and most negative moment for Partner A and most positive and most negative moment for Partner B). Partners are shown these excerpts (without being informed about the significance of these particular excerpts) and asked to complete a self-report emotion inventory about how they felt during that portion of the conversation. This allows researchers to assess the specific emotions partners experienced when they were feeling negatively or positively.

Troubleshooting

As mentioned earlier, two of the strengths of dyadic interaction tasks are that they resemble naturalistic conversations and that they allow room for variability in emotional responding. However, these strengths also open the door to a number of problems that might compromise the task's ability to elicit emotion. In this section we discuss several of these potential problems and how we have attempted to address them in our own work.

What If the Couple "Has Nothing to Say"?

Some couples may explicitly state that they rarely disagree and therefore have nothing to resolve, even if they indicated on their Areas of Disagreement form that they disagree on different topics. Although some couples may in fact rarely disagree, it is more likely that couples are uncomfortable with the facilitator, lack insight about their own disagreements, and/or dislike discussing conflict. In these cases, it may be helpful for the facilitator to state explicitly that most couples experience some degree of conflict, and that this is a normal (and in many ways healthy) part of human relationships. The facilitator should also state that although some couples initially mention that they do not have conflicts, what this usually means is that they do not have intense yelling and screaming matches. Facilitators should emphasize that "conflicts" can be mild disagreements or things that irritate partners and that they rarely discuss. Facilitators should be patient and give couples more time as needed to think about and discuss possible areas of disagreement. Finally, it has been our experience that some couples who refuse to open up to the facilitator often are quite aware of the disagreement and willing to engage with one another once the facilitator leaves the room. If this appears to be the case (e.g., based on partners' nonverbal cues), summarizing the disagreement as much as possible and ending the facilitation sooner rather than later may be sufficient to ignite a discussion when the couple is alone.

What If the Couple Becomes Exceptionally Angry?

Because the primary goal of the dyadic interaction task is to elicit intense emotion, in most cases, experimenters will not intervene when the couple is arguing and is visibly angry during the conversation. In fact, at times experimenters are more uncomfortable with the conflict than the couples themselves, because, despite couples' anger, they often are relieved to have engaged in a much-needed discussion. Nevertheless, we have encountered couples who engaged in unusually heated conversations. In these instances, after the conversation, the facilitator emphasized that conflict is a normal part of relationships but that discussing an area of disagreement can lead couples to realize that they have issues that they could use help resolving. The facilitator then has given the couple a list of referrals to couples' therapists. In some studies, we have provided referral lists (e.g., addresses and phone numbers of local outpatient or community mental health clinics; toll-free crisis hotline numbers) to all participants, stating that it is in case they or a friend ever need this information. On rare occasions, couples engage in a discussion in which one partner threatens the other. This is more likely to occur when researching couples with a history of domestic violence (Jacobson et al., 1994). Researchers are advised to have a specific protocol on hand (e.g., a debriefing form; contact information for backup staff or campus police) should one partner become a threat to the other partner or to him- or herself.

What If the Couple Veers Off Topic?

As with everyday interactions, many times couples will digress during their conversations. Most times, couples who digress will eventually return to the assigned topic. To minimize the frequency with which this occurs, after the conflict facilitation and before leaving the room, facilitators should ask couples to try to stay on the topic of their disagreement as much as they can. Facilitators also can ask participants to discuss other areas of conflict should they resolve the first one, which will help ensure that couples continue discussing areas of disagreement. We have not intervened when couples veer off topic, because we want their conversations to be as natural as possible and for them to forget as much as possible that their conversations are being observed from an adjacent room.

What If the Couple Asks Questions During the Conversation?

Couples are informed at the beginning of the experiment that they are being videotaped and that they can communicate with the facilitator when he or she is not in the room by simply speaking out loud. Nevertheless, to promote the most natural interaction possible, it is important to minimize couples' sense that they are being observed. This poses a challenge when—after the facilitator has left the room—couples ask questions that either directly or indirectly address the experimenter (e.g., "Do we have to sit quietly now?" "When do we begin talking?" "Is this sensor too loose?"). Usually, one partner can answer the other partner's questions. However, there are times when neither partner knows the answer. If the couple asks these questions after the facilitator has left the room but before beginning their conversation, the facilitator should reenter the participant room and ask whether the couple has any questions (i.e., so as not to give participants the sense that someone is observing them closely). If the questions arise after the conversation period has already begun, the facilitator must decide whether or not answering the question will interfere with the effectiveness of the task. We would advise that the facilitator avoid answering the question unless it is necessary for effective completion of the task. For example, a participant may say, "I wonder how long we are supposed to talk for." By answering the question via the intercom, the facilitator may increase the couple's awareness that they are being observed and therefore may alter the nature of the interaction (e.g., Carver, 2003; Zegiob, Arnold, & Forehand, 1975). Because knowing the length of time should not matter in terms of the overall effectiveness of the task, this question is better left unanswered. However, if the couple asks, "Wait a minute—which topic are we supposed to talk about again?" the facilitator should ask participants via the intercom if they have any questions and then answer this question as succinctly and clearly as possible (e.g., "Please try to resolve your disagreement about communication").

Debriefing and Video Consent Form

Conflictual interactions can leave couples in a distressed state, particularly couples who were distressed to begin with. Therefore, immediately after the conflict conversation, it is critical to normalize the experience by saying that even though conflict is a normal part of relationships, it can be difficult to talk about areas of disagreement. The facilitator should thank couples for their openness and honesty and let them know that their ability to share their relationship openly reflects their strength as a couple. Because couples may be self-conscious about their areas of conflict, facilitators should be careful not to refer to couples' conversations in their subsequent interactions with them.

At the end of the study, the experimenter may join the couple and reiterate his or her appreciation for the couple's participation. In addition to a traditional experimental debriefing form, a referral list of mental health professionals may be provided (as discussed previously). For nonlongitudinal studies, in which participants will not be returning for subsequent sessions, more information about the details of the study can be provided. For longitudinal studies, couples are reminded that they will be contacted in the future and that their cooperation is appreciated. We also advise asking couples not to discuss the specific details of the study with others until after the study is over in order to minimize the chances that other couples will have knowledge about the study prior to participating in it.

Because of the rich behavioral data collected on videotape, couples are asked to complete, in addition to the traditional consent form, a consent form indicating where and how the videotapes can be used (e.g., to show to couples in other studies; to show at scientific meetings; to show to the popular media). The "video consent form" may be administered at the beginning or end of the session; however, in most cases, we administer the form at the end of the session so that couples can decide how they would like the videotapes to be used based on their conversations.

Uses of the Dyadic Interaction Task

In this final section, we describe some of the ways in which we and other researchers have used dyadic interaction tasks. Table 7.1 provides examples of different phenomena that have been studied with these tasks. Based on these examples, readers can determine the applicability of dyadic interaction paradigms for their research purposes.

Different Types of Relationships

This chapter primarily focused on studying spouses and romantic partners, but dyadic interaction tasks also have been used to study fraternity brothers (Keltner et al., 1998), siblings (Shortt & Gottman, 1997), parents and children (Repetti & Wood, 1997), and patients and therapists (Pole, 2000). In addition to studying intimate relationships, dyadic interaction procedures have been applied to unfamiliar dyads, such as ethnically similar and ethnically

Table 7.1

Uses of Dyadic Interaction Tasks

Study	Sample	Research Topic
Coan et al. (1997)	Domestically violent couples	Affective differences among types of violent men
Gottman et al. (1998)	Newlywed couples	Function of positive affect during marital conflict
Gottman et al. (2003)	Gay and lesbian couples	Correlates of relationship satisfaction and stability among gay and lesbian couples
Keltner et al. (1998)	Fraternity brothers (study 1); romantic couples (study 2)	Relation between teasing behavior and social status, personality, and relationship satisfaction
Kupperbusch (2003)	Middle-aged and older long-term married couples	Relation between marital satisfaction and health
Levenson & Gottman (1985)	Long-term married couples	Predictors of marital satisfaction and stability
Levenson, Carstensen, & Gottman (1994)	Middle-aged and older long-term married couples	Impact of aging on emotion and marriage
Pole (2000)	Patients and therapists	Impact of therapeutic interventions on emotion
Repetti & Wood (1997)	Mothers and preschoolers	Impact of job stress on mother-child interactions
Richards (2001)	College-age dating couples	Impact of emotion regulation on memory
Roberts & Levenson (2001)	Police officers and spouses	Impact of job stress on emotion during marital interaction
Shortt & Gottman (1997)	Young adult siblings	Predictors of emotional closeness versus distance in adult sibling relationships
Tsai & Levenson (1997)	Chinese American and European American dating couples	Impact of ethnicity and cultural context on emotion
Weis & Lovejoy (2002)	Mothers and preschoolers	Impact of emotion on mothers' perception of the parent-child relationship

dissimilar individuals (Littleford, Wright, & Sayoc-Parial, 2005) and unacquainted individuals instructed to adopt different emotion regulatory strategies (Butler et al., 2003).

Research Questions

First and foremost, dyadic interaction tasks are ideal for examining fundamental emotional processes, such as emotional reactivity, emotion regulation, and empathy. They also are ideal for examining the link between patterns of emotional responding and relationship satisfaction. However, dyadic interaction methodology can be applied to almost any research question. This paradigm lends itself to studying predictors of emotional responding, ranging from personality traits to cultural background to job stress, and is effective for studying how emotional responding predicts outcomes such as physical and psychological health. As with any study, a longitudinal approach to dyadic interaction, whereby the same dyads are studied over time, enhances the predictive power of the research.

Through studies using dyadic interaction tasks, we have learned that displays of contempt and disgust are among the most toxic for a marriage (Gottman & Levenson, 1999); that marriages are stable and happy to the degree that husbands do not avoid or escalate negative affect expressed by wives (Gottman et al., 1998); that one spouse's job stress affects the other spouse's physiology (Roberts & Levenson, 2001); that suppressing emotions, rather than reappraising a situation, takes a toll on memory (Richards, 2001); that culture exerts different effects on expressive versus physiological aspects of emotion (Tsai et al., 2006); and that when therapists make more accurate interventions, their clients show decreases in physiological arousal (Pole, 2000) and more positive emotional behavior with their partner (Roberts et al., 2006).

Conclusion

Interactions between two people can evoke a wealth of emotion. This chapter reviewed how researchers have made use of this natural reservoir of emotion to study ecologically valid emotional responses in the laboratory. In this chapter, we discussed the relative advantages and disadvantages of using dyadic interaction tasks to study emotion. We also described specific procedures and equipment that have been used in dyadic interaction studies. Finally, we briefly reviewed the various ways in which researchers have used dyadic interaction paradigms. It is our hope that this review of dyadic interaction tasks will enable both novice and seasoned researchers to decide whether or not to incorporate dyadic interaction methodology into their studies of emotion.

Appendix A: Conversation Facilitation Forms

AREAS OF DISAGREEMENT

<u>Instructions</u>: This form contains a list of topics that many couples disagree about. Please use this form to show how much you think you and your spouse disagree about each area.

In the left column, indicate how much you and your spouse disagree by writing in a number from **0 to 100**. A **zero** indicates that you don't disagree at all and a **100** indicates that you disagree very much.

In the right column, please write down the number of years, months, weeks, or days that this level of disagreement has existed.

For example:

We disagree about . . .	How much?	How long?
A. Recreation	90	2 yrs.
B. Religion	0	10 yrs.

This would indicate that recreation is something you disagree about very much and have disagreed about for two years. Religion is something you have agreed about for ten years.

We disagree about . . .	How much?	How long?
1. Money		
2. Communication		
3. In-laws		
4. Sex		
5. Religion		
6. Recreation		
7. Friends		
8. Alcohol and drugs		
9. Children		
10. Jealousy		

Please write down any other areas of disagreement.

11.		
12.		

What is currently the strongest area of disagreement in your relationship?

ENJOYABLE CONVERSATIONS

Instructions: Below is a list of topics many couples enjoy talking about. We would like to get some idea of how enjoyable each topic is to you.

Please indicate how enjoyable each topic is by assigning it a number from 0 to 100. Zero indicates that the topic is not enjoyable, and 100 indicates that it is very enjoyable.

For example:

I enjoy talking to my partner about . . .	**How enjoyable?**
1. Vacations we've taken..	85

This indicates that talking to your partner about vacations is very enjoyable.

I enjoy talking to my partner about . . .	**How enjoyable?**
1. Other people we know..	_____
2. Casual and informal types of things	_____
3. Politics and current events..	_____
4. Things that have to get done around the house	_____
5. Things happening in town	_____

6. Silly and fun types of things... _____

7. Some of the good times we've had together in the past.................. _____

8. The children (or grandchildren)... _____

9. Our views on different issues .... _____

10. Our accomplishments .... _____

11. The family pet .... _____

12. Something we've recently done together .... _____

13. Our (sleep) dreams .... _____

14. Our plans for the future .... _____

15. Things we've seen on television, heard on the radio, or read about.............. _____

16. Vacations we've taken... _____

Please feel free to write down any other conversations you find enjoyable.

17. _____ _____

18. _____ _____

Appendix B: Sample Timeline of a Dyadic Interaction Task Used With Romantic Partners

I. Prior to Laboratory Session
   a. Partners complete questionnaires independently, including Areas of Disagreement and Enjoyable Topics inventories
   b. Partners are instructed not to see or talk with each other for 8 hours prior to their session.
II. During Session*
   a. Administration of consent forms (5 minutes)
   b. Physiological sensor attachment (15 minutes)
   c. Preinstruction baseline and administration of emotion inventory (5 minutes)
   d. Instructions for events-of-the-day conversation (2 minutes)
   e. Events-of-the-day conversation
      i. Silent period (5 minutes)
      ii. Conversation (15 minutes)
      iii. Completion of emotion inventory (2 minutes)
   f. Conflict facilitation (10–30 minutes)
   g. Conflict conversation
      i. Silent period (5 minutes)
      ii. Conversation (15 minutes)
      iii. Completion of emotion inventory (2 minutes)
   h. Recall session
      i. Instructions (5 minutes)
      ii. Watch and rate events-of-the-day conversation, including preconversation silent period (20 minutes)
      iii. Watch and rate conflict conversation, including preconversation silent period (20 minutes)
      i. Sensor detachment and debriefing (10 minutes)

*Times are approximations.

Appendix C: Sample Conflict Facilitation Used With a Romantic Couple

FACILITATOR: Another thing we know about couples is that they often disagree. According to your questionnaire packets, you reported that money was an area of disagreement in your relationship. *John*, could you start out and tell me about the last time you and *Jane* had a disagreement about money. Please tell me specifically what the disagreement was and how you feel about it.

JOHN: I guess the main disagreement is about our new place; we'll be moving in together at the end of the semester. I'm not as concerned with making it look so together as Jane is. There are other things I'd rather spend money on.

FACILITATOR: So you don't feel it's as necessary to spend money on it.

JOHN: I'd like to spend money on it, but we're both graduating, so it's not as permanent as it could be, and I just don't want to have a lot of extra stuff to deal with. It's not that big of a deal. I don't want to paint it [the disagreement] as anything bigger than it is. But that's the last time we had a disagreement about money.

FACILITATOR: How does it make you feel that Jane wants to put more money into the place than you, because you feel you're graduating and it's not permanent?

JOHN: It doesn't make me feel bad, but that's not what I want to spend my money on. I'm glad she cares about our relationship, but I think we can work on the relationship without working on the place.

FACILITATOR: So you're saying that maybe Jane feels the place is a sign of your relationship, whereas you don't feel that way, so you don't want to spend money on it.

JANE: Well, that's not exactly how I. . . .

FACILITATOR: Jane, first I'd like to get a sense of the disagreement from John, and then we'll focus on your sense of the disagreement and how you feel about it.

JOHN: Yeah. The other thing is that we get money in different ways, so I can't spend money how she does. She gets it all at once, and I get a monthly allowance. That's where I feel the pressure—she wants it to all be done.

FACILITATOR: You feel you can't just spend all the money at once, because you get a monthly allowance.

JOHN: Exactly.

FACILITATOR: And you said you feel pressured.

JOHN: Yeah.

FACILITATOR: Jane, now will you tell me about the last time you and John had a disagreement about money and how you felt about it.

JANE: I consider the last disagreement we had about money to be when we were planning a vacation and deciding where we would go. We wanted to go skiing, but the cheapest place we could get was the most he was willing to spend. But he's thinking about the money he has right now, not the money he has in total. What's more important: hoarding money in a bank account, or enjoying life with it? I think sometimes it can be worth it to take an extra couple hundred dollars out of the bank. It bummed me out that we haven't been on a vacation together since last year, and we can't take a vacation together. Also, I got used to nice vacations as a kid, and he did, too, but I'm not as willing to sacrifice them as he is.

FACILITATOR: You feel that sometimes you'd like to have nicer vacations or spend more money at the time, but John hoards his money away, so even if he does have the money, he's not willing to spend it on things you would like to. And it bums you out.

JANE: Yep, that about sums it up. The other thing is that I have more money now, but come May, at the end of the semester, he'll have money and I won't, so it's kind of ironic.

FACILITATOR: Do you wonder why you're willing to spend more money on the place and on vacations than he is, when you feel he has more?

JANE: Yeah; I understand it more now, in terms of how he was brought up. It just bums me out, because I think life is more important than money. I think it's important to live at a certain standard if you're capable, or to take vacations.

FACILITATOR: John, do you have anything to add?

JOHN: No.

The facilitator would then explore two or three other topics as needed, and pick the seemingly strongest area of disagreement.

FACILITATOR: Okay, then for your next conversation, I'd like you to talk about money, and how for John [facilitator addresses him], you only have a monthly allowance right now, so you don't like to spend money in big chunks, because then you don't have any for the rest of the month—you'd rather spread it out. And instead of spending it on the new place, you feel there are more important places you can spend your money. You don't feel spending money is necessary for the relationship like Jane might, so you end up feeling pressured. But for Jane [facilitator addresses her], it bums you out that John doesn't want to put in more money for a nice vacation, or other things you feel it would be worth spending money on so you can enjoy life—instead, you feel he hoards money, and perhaps it takes away from the relationship in some way.

I'd like you to have as normal a conversation as you can, and because this is an area of conflict in your relationship, I'd like you to try and resolve your conflict about *money*. I'd like you to have as normal a conversation as you can, much like when you're normally working on a disagreement at home. Do you have any questions?

Notes

1. It is important to note that when two or more individuals engage in an interaction, their responses are intertwined. Given the reciprocal nature of emotion in dyads, readers are encouraged to refer to statistical sources such as Bakeman and Gottman (1997) and Reis and Judd (2000) for methods of analyzing the statistical "dependency" of dyadic data.

2. We did not receive any actual complaints from couples who participated, however.

3. The wording used to introduce the facilitation can be adjusted to be more collaborative and less abrupt, particularly if couples are not engaging in an events-of-the-day conversation prior to their conflict discussion. For example, in a study where couples participated in the dyadic interaction procedure (the conflict conversation only) at the beginning and end of an 8-week "relationship coaching" intervention, one of us (NAR) referred to the conflict discussion as a "problem-solving conversation," and introduced the facilitation by saying: "I'm

going to ask you to have a problem-solving conversation, but before that we'll talk for a few minutes about one or more topics, to choose the topic that it makes the most sense for you to discuss during your conversation. In looking at your questionnaires, one topic it may make sense for the two of you to talk about is . . ." (and then each partner is asked systematically about the topic; Roberts, Kanter, Manos, Rusch, & Busch, 2006).

4. A systematic approach to determining which topic to explore first is to alternate (in a randomized, between-subjects fashion) between wives' and husbands' strongest areas of conflict (per their Areas of Disagreement form ratings). The same kind of randomized, between-subjects approach can be used to determine which partner to question first.

References

Anderson, N. B. (1989). Racial differences in stress-induced cardiovascular reactivity and hypertension: Current status and substantive issues. *Psychological Bulletin, 105*(1), 89–105.

Bakeman, R., & Gottman, J. M. (1997). *Observing interaction: An introduction to sequential analysis* (2nd ed.). New York: Cambridge University Press.

Burgess, E. W., Locke, H. J., & Thomes, M. M. (1971). *The family.* New York: Van Nostrand Reinhold.

Butler, E. A., Egloff, B., Wilhelm, F. H., Smith, N. C., Erickson, E. A., & Gross, J. J. (2003). The social consequences of expressive suppression. *Emotion, 3*(1), 48–67.

Carstensen, L. L., Gottman, J. M., & Levenson, R. W. (1995). Emotional behavior in long-term marriage. *Psychology and Aging, 10*(1), 140–149.

Carver, C. S. (2003). Self-awareness. In M. R. Leary & J. P. Tangney (Eds.), *Handbook of self and identity* (pp. 179–196). New York: Guilford Press.

Coan, J., Gottman, J. M., Babcock, J., & Jacobson, N. (1997). Battering and the male rejection of influence from women. *Aggressive Behavior, 23*(5), 375–388.

Cohan, C. L., & Bradbury, T. N. (1997). Negative life events, marital interaction, and the longitudinal course of newlywed marriage. *Journal of Personality and Social Psychology, 73*(1), 114–128.

Costa, P. T., & McCrae, R. R. (1992). Normal personality assessment in clinical practice: The NEO Personality Inventory. *Psychological Assessment, 4*(1), 5–13.

Cuellar, I., Harris, L., & Jasso, R. (1980). An acculturation scale for Mexican American normal and clinical populations. *Hispanic Journal of Behavioral Sciences, 2,* 199–217.

Darwin, C. (1998). *The expression of the emotions in man and animals* (3rd ed., P. Ekman, Ed.). New York: Oxford University Press. (Original work published 1872)

Derogatis, L. R., & Lazarus, L. (1994). SCL-90-R, Brief Symptom Inventory, and matching clinical rating scales. In M.E. Maruish (Ed.), *The use of psychological testing for treatment planning and outcome assessment* (pp. 217–248). Hillsdale, NJ: Erlbaum.

Ekman, P., Friesen, W. V., & Ancoli, S. (1980). Facial signs of emotional experience. *Journal of Personality and Social Psychology, 39*(6), 1125–1134.

Fredrickson, B. L., & Levenson, R. W. (1998). Positive emotions speed recovery from the cardiovascular sequelae of negative emotions. *Cognition and Emotion, 12*(2), 191–220.

Gonzaga, G. C., Keltner, D., Londahl, E. A., & Smith, M. D. (2001). Love and the commitment problem in romantic relations and friendship. *Journal of Personality and Social Psychology, 81*(2), 247–262.

Gottman, J. M., Coan, J., Carrere, S., & Swanson, C. (1998). Predicting marital happiness and stability from newlywed interactions. *Journal of Marriage and the Family, 60*(1), 5–22.

Gottman, J. M., & Levenson, R. W. (1985). A valid procedure for obtaining self-report of affect in marital interaction. *Journal of Consulting and Clinical Psychology, 53*(2), 151–160.

Gottman, J. M., & Levenson, R. W. (1999). What predicts change in marital interaction over time? A study of alternative models. *Family Process, 38*(2), 143–158.

Gottman, J. M., Levenson, R. W., Gross, J., Fredrickson, B. L., McCoy, K., Rosenthal, L., et al. (2003). Correlates of gay and lesbian couples' relationship satisfaction and relationship dissolution. *Journal of Homosexuality, 45*(1), 23–43.

Gottman, J. M., Markman, H., & Notarius, C. (1977). The topography of marital conflict: A sequential analysis of verbal and nonverbal behavior. *Journal of Marriage and the Family, 39*(3), 461–477.

Horowitz, M., Schaefer, C., Hiroto, D., Wilner, N., & Levin, B. (1977). Life event questionnaires for measuring presumptive stress. *Psychosomatic Medicine, 39*(6), 413–431.

Jacobson, N. S., Gottman, J. M., Waltz, J., Rushe, R., Babcock, J., & Holtzworth-Munroe, A. (1994). Affect, verbal content, and psychophysiology in the arguments of couples with a violent husband. *Journal of Consulting and Clinical Psychology, 62*(5), 982–988.

Keltner, D., & Buswell, B. N. (1997). Embarrassment: Its distinct form and appeasement functions. *Psychological Bulletin, 122*(3), 250–270.

Keltner, D., & Haidt, J. (1999). Social functions of emotions at four levels of analysis. *Cognition and Emotion, 13*(5), 505–521.

Keltner, D., Young, R. C., Heerey, E. A., Oemig, C., & Monarch, N. D. (1998). Teasing in hierarchical and intimate relations. *Journal of Personality and Social Psychology, 75*(5), 1231–1247.

Kupperbusch, C. S. (2003). Change in marital satisfaction and change in health in middle-aged and older long-term married couples (Doctoral dissertation, University of California, Berkeley, 2002). *Dissertation Abstracts International, 63,* 4419.

Levenson, R. W., Carstensen, L. L., & Gottman, J. M. (1993). Long-term marriage: Age, gender, and satisfaction. *Psychology and Aging, 8*(2), 301–313.

Levenson, R. W., Carstensen, L. L., & Gottman, J. M. (1994). The influence of age and gender on affect, physiology, and their interrelations: A study of long-term marriages. *Journal of Personality and Social Psychology, 67*(1), 56–68.

Levenson, R. W., & Gottman, J. M. (1983). Marital interaction: Physiological linkage and affective exchange. *Journal of Personality and Social Psychology, 45*(3), 587–597.

Levenson, R. W., & Gottman, J. M. (1985). Physiological and affective predictors of change in relationship satisfaction. *Journal of Personality and Social Psychology, 49*(1), 85–94.

Littleford, L. N., Wright, M., & Sayoc-Parial, M. (2005). White students' intergroup anxiety during same-race and interracial interactions: A multimethod approach. *Basic and Applied Social Psychology, 27*(1), 85–94.

Locke, H. J., & Wallace, K. M. (1959). Short marital adjustment and prediction tests: Their reliability and validity. *Marriage and Family Living, 21,* 251–255.

Murphy, J. K., Alpert, B. S., Willey, E. S., & Somes, G. W. (1988). Cardiovascular reactivity to psychological stress in healthy children. *Psychophysiology, 25*(2), 144–152.

Pole, N. (2000). Client appraisals of danger and safety in psychotherapy and its physiological, facial, and subjective correlates (Doctoral dissertation, University of California, Berkeley, 2000). *Dissertation Abstracts International, 61,* 2217.

Reis, H. T., & Judd, C. M. (2000). *Handbook of research methods in social and personality psychology.* New York: Cambridge University Press.

Repetti, R. L., & Wood, J. (1997). Effects of daily stress at work on mothers' interactions with preschoolers. *Journal of Family Psychology, 11*(1), 90–108.

Richards, J. M. (2001). Emotion regulation and memory (Doctoral dissertation, Stanford University, 2001). *Dissertation Abstracts International, 61,* 5059.

Roberts, N. A., Kanter, J. W., Manos, R. C., Rusch, L., & Busch, A. (2006). *Physiological and behavioral changes in couples in response to individual relationship coaching.* Unpublished manuscript.

Roberts, N. A., & Levenson, R. W. (2001). The remains of the workday: Impact of job stress and exhaustion on marital interaction in police couples. *Journal of Marriage and the Family, 63*(4), 1052–1067.

Robins, R. W., Spranca, M. D., & Mendelsohn, G. A. (1996). The actor-observer effect revisited: Effects of individual differences and repeated social interactions on actor and observer attributions. *Journal of Personality and Social Psychology, 71*(2), 375–389.

Ruef, A. M. (2001). Empathy in long-term marriage: Behavioral and physiological correlates (Doctoral dissertation, University of California, Berkeley, 2001). *Dissertation Abstracts International, 62,* 563.

Shortt, J. W., & Gottman, J. M. (1997). Closeness in young adult sibling relationships: Affective and physiological processes. *Social Development, 6*(2), 142–164.

Suinn, R. M., Rickard-Figueroa, K., Lew, S., & Vigil, P. (1987). The Suinn-Lew Asian Self-Identity Acculturation Scale: An initial report. *Educational and Psychological Measurement, 47,* 401–407.

Tsai, J. L., & Levenson, R. W. (1997). Cultural influences on emotional responding: Chinese American and European American dating couples during interpersonal conflict. *Journal of Cross-Cultural Psychology, 28*(5), 600–625.

Tsai, J. L., Levenson, R. W., & McCoy, K. (2006). Cultural and temperamental variation in emotional response. *Emotion, 6*(3), 484–497.

Weis, R., & Lovejoy, M. C. (2002). Information processing in everyday life: Emotion-congruent bias in mothers' reports of parent-child interactions. *Journal of Personality and Social Psychology, 83*(1), 216–230.

Zegiob, L. E., Arnold, S., & Forehand, R. (1975). An examination of observer effects in parent-child interactions. *Child Development, 46*(2), 509–512.

Eric Eich

Joycelin T. W. Ng

Dawn Macaulay

Alexandra D. Percy

Irina Grebneva

Combining Music With Thought to Change Mood

Experimental methods for modifying mood are a mainstay of modern research in the area of cognition and emotion. Reflecting the popularity of this approach, a survey of *Psychological Abstracts* spanning the past three decades reveals a steady increase in the number of research reports dealing with experimentally engendered moods: from fewer than 10 between 1973 and 1977 to over 170 within the most recent 5-year period, 2001–2005.

When it comes to picking a particular method of mood induction, researchers have many candidates from which to choose (for reviews, see Gerrards-Hesse, Spies, & Hesse, 1994; Martin, 1990). One option is to have participants read and internalize a series of self-referential statements that are either positive or negative in emotional tone. Developed by Velten (1968) and revised by Seibert and Ellis (1991), this technique has been used repeatedly in research on *mood-congruent cognition*—the observation that people interpret, acquire, and retain information in a manner that concurs with their current moods. Thus, for example, several Velten-based studies (reviewed by Blaney, 1986) have shown that people recollect more happy memories from their personal pasts and retrieve fewer sad incidents when they are experiencing a positive as opposed to a negative mood.

Another option is to ask hypnotized individuals to think about things that make them feel a certain way (Friswell & McConkey, 1989). Bower, Monteiro, and Gilligan (1978) used this technique in their pioneering work on *mood-dependent memory*—the observation that events encoded in a certain state of affect or mood are most retrievable in that state. In one study (Bower et al., 1978, experiment 3), hypnotized undergraduates learned two lists of common words, one while feeling happy and the other while feeling sad. Later, the recall of both lists was tested while the students were either happy or sad. Indicative of mood dependence, the students recalled more words when their learning and testing moods matched (mean = 70%) than when their moods mismatched (mean = 46%). In other studies of either mood dependence or mood congruence, researchers have sought to instill particular moods by means of aerobic exercise (Roth, 1989), facial expression (Laird, 1989), physical posture (Riskind & Gotay, 1982), guided imagery (Wright & Mischel, 1982), task feedback (Forgas & Bower, 1987), restricted environmental stimulation (Suedfeld & Eich, 1995), and emotionally evocative music (Pignatiello, Camp, & Rasar, 1986). Various combinations of methods—music plus mood-appropriate thought, for instance (Sutherland, Newman, & Rachman, 1982)—have also been tried (see Gerrards-Hesse et al., 1994).

Notwithstanding their popularity and diversity, mood-induction techniques are neither the only way to investigate the interplay between cognition and emotion nor necessarily the best way. Many researchers, concerned about the inherent artificiality of such techniques, prefer to work with endogenous, or naturally occurring, moods—typically either normal affective states, subclinical depression, or clinical emotional disorders (see, for example, Eich, 1995a; Eich,

Macaulay, & Lam, 1997; Hasher, Rose, Zacks, Sanft, & Doren, 1985; Johnson & Magaro, 1987; Parrott & Sabini, 1990). According to Ingram (1989), the advantages of this approach are that, as a rule, endogenous affects are stronger, longer lasting, more realistically complex, and truer to life than are the exogenous affects evoked by experimental mood manipulations. Furthermore, by studying natural shifts in affective state, an investigator can largely finesse a problem endemic to research entailing experimentally induced moods—namely, that participants may claim that their moods have changed when in fact they have not in order to comply with perceived experimental demands (see Clark, 1983; Ingram, 1989; Isen, 1984; Kenealy, 1986; Martin, 1990). This problem is particularly acute for techniques, such as hypnotic suggestion or self-referential statements, that specifically require participants to "get into" a designated mood (Buchwald, Strack, & Coyne, 1981; Larsen & Sinnett, 1991; Polivy & Doyle, 1980). However, the problem may also apply to subtler methods, such as facial expression or restricted environmental stimulation, as their impact on mood is usually assessed by asking participants to verbally describe or numerically rate their current feelings. Besides making people keenly aware of their moods, the very act of assessment is apt to make them wonder what the research is really about and what the investigator is up to, thus opening the door to experimental demand (Eich, 1995b; Parrott, 1991).

Though the natural-mood approach is attractive in several respects, it is problematic in others. In the first place, this approach does not allow for random assignment of participants to mood conditions, making it difficult, if not impossible, to tease apart the experiential or state-related aspects of a mood from its dispositional or trait-related foundations. Relatedly, researchers who select and classify participants on the basis of existing mood can determine whether a given mood is correlated with a given cognitive process, but they cannot draw any causal conclusions (see Ellis, 1985; Ellis & Ashbrook, 1989). This is why experimental methods of mood induction were developed in the first place and why such methods have seen a steady rise in popularity. Assuming that this trend will continue, it makes sense to ask: What can be done to maximize the benefits of experimental mood modification, while minimizing its costs? Our answer takes the form of a wish list of six attributes, itemized in Table 8.1, that would seem attractive in any mood-induction technique.

First, the technique should have a high rate of success, operationalized in terms of the percentage of participants with demonstrably malleable moods. For most investigators, mood induction is a means to an end—such as demonstrating mood congruence or detecting mood dependence—rather than an end in itself. Consequently, the research will run smoother and faster if most participants are responsive to the selected method of mood induction. Moreover, a high success rate reduces the risk that the results will apply only to a small, select subset of the target population.

Table 8.1

Desirable attributes of a mood induction technique

- Technique has a high rate of success in altering participants' moods in predicable ways.
- Technique allows for individual differences in time taken to develop a particular mood.
- Induced moods are strong or intense.
- Induced moods are stable over time and across tasks.
- Induced moods seem real or authentic to the participants.
- One and the same mood can be reliably induced on more than one occasion.

How successful are available methods of mood induction? The question is difficult to answer, owing to a shortage of comparative studies and to the absence of a consensual standard for deciding whether or not a given mood has been successfully induced in a given individual. Still, estimates from several sources (e.g., Clark, 1983; Martin, 1990; Teasdale & Russell, 1983; Teasdale & Taylor, 1981) suggest that there are substantial differences among techniques in their rates of success: from a high of 87% for music plus ideation to a low of 15% for hypnotic suggestions. According to Clark (1983), about one-third, and perhaps as many as one-half, of all participants show little or no mood change in response to the Velten technique—a sobering statistic for such a well-known and widely used method.

Second, the technique should allow for the possibility that people may vary in the rate at which they develop a particular mood. To date, the common practice in research involving exogenous affects has been to impose an arbitrary limit on the amount of time allowed for mood induction. Though this practice makes sense from a practical standpoint, it virtually guarantees wide variability among participants in their postinduction levels of mood—variability that could easily eclipse the effects of the mood on subsequent task performance. An alternative, arguably better, strategy is to allow each individual to achieve a predetermined degree of mood at his or her own pace, thus ensuring that all participants are on the same affective plane at the start of the critical task.

Third, moods instilled by the technique should be strong. This is important not only from the standpoint of external validity—recall Ingram's (1989) claim that natural moods are typically more intense than are induced moods—but also from the perspective of demonstrating mood dependence, mood congruence, or other cognitive phenomena that depend for their expression on a clear and sharp contrast between affective states (see Bower & Forgas, 2000; Eich & Forgas, 2003).

Fourth, no less critical than the strength of induced moods is their stability over time and across tasks (see Albersnagel, 1988; Vastfjall, 2002). It is hard to see how a given mood could possibly affect the performance of a given task if, for one reason or another, the mood established at the start of the task should cease to exist at its end. In this regard, it is notable that, whereas moods elicited through hypnotic suggestions or music plus ideation seem to be robust (see Bower, 1981; Parrott, 1991), those evoked via self-referential statements appear to start strong but pale rapidly (see Chartier & Ranieri, 1989; Eich & Metcalfe, 1989; Isen & Gorgoglione, 1983). Little is known about the durability of moods induced by other techniques, for the simple—and surprising—reason that most researchers monitor mood just *before* participants begin the task of interest (as a check on the effectiveness of the mood manipulation) but seldom do so *after* the task has been completed.

In light of long-standing concerns about both the external validity of exogenous moods and their vulnerability to experimental demand, the fifth item on our wish list is that such moods should strike most, if not all, participants as feeling real (see Eich & Macaulay, 2000). Though sincerity is a strong suit of hypnotically suggested affects (see Bower, 1981), the genuineness of the moods engendered by other means is a largely unexplored matter.

Finally, it should be possible to induce the same mood on two or more occasions. This proviso is particularly important in studies of mood-dependent memory, which, by design, require that some participants be tested for retrieval in a mood that matches the one they had experienced during encoding several hours or (oftentimes) days earlier.

In the remainder of this chapter, discussion centers on a mood-modification technique, abbreviated as MCI, that seems to possess all six of the properties described here and bulleted in Table 8.1. Like the music plus ideation method that was introduced by Sutherland, Newman, and Rachman (1982) and further refined by many other researchers (see Vastfjall, 2002, for a comprehensive review), the MCI involves having participants listen to selections of merry or melancholic Music while they Contemplate elating or depressing thoughts about real or imaginary people, places, or events. Periodically, participants rate their current levels of pleasure and arousal—the two principal dimensions underlying Russell's (1980) circumplex model of mood. To advance to formal testing (which may entail a number of different cognitive tasks), participants are required to rate themselves as feeling either very pleasant or very unpleasant, irrespective of their current level of arousal. Understandably, participants are not apprised in advance of these Idiographic criteria, and, as one might expect, people differ markedly in how long it takes them to achieve the critical levels of mood. Thus, unlike other techniques (including the original music-plus-ideation method; see Vastfjall, 2002) in which mood induction lasts the same amount of time for all participants, the MCI takes an idiographic approach to mood manipulation—one that allows each person to achieve a predetermined degree of pleasure or displeasure at his or her own pace. The advantages of this approach are revealed by the results of a series of MCI studies, to which we now turn.

The MCI Method of Modifying Mood

To date, the MCI technique has been used in more than a dozen different studies. Here we focus on eight experiments that entailed a total of 536 individually tested participants, the vast majority of whom were university undergraduates. Each of these studies comprised two 45- to 90-minute sessions, spaced 1 to 7 days apart. At the start of each session, participants were induced, via the MCI technique, into either a very pleasant (P) or very unpleasant (U) mood, and they then went on to perform anywhere from one to four different cognitive tasks. To simplify discussion and aid comparison across studies, we deal exclusively with the initial task that participants undertook in either the first or second session of any given study.

All eight focal experiments used a balanced experimental design, such that participants experienced one of two MCI-induced moods (P or U) during either or both sessions. To make the results more comparable, studies using partial or unbalanced designs (e.g., Eich & Metcalfe, 1989, experiments 2–4) are excluded from consideration.

Overview of MCI Studies

As a guide to further discussion, Table 8.2 provides a synopsis of the eight MCI studies ordered here so as to ease exposition, rather than to reflect true chronology. The reference for each study is included in the note at the bottom of the table.

Studies 1 and 2 explored mood *congruent* effects in autobiographical memory. During the first session of these studies, every participant was presented with neutral nouns, such as *piano* and *pearl,* as probes for recollecting or generating specific episodes or events from their personal past. Participants were given up to 2 minutes in which to generate a given event, which they then described in detail and rated in terms of its original emotional intensity, current vividness of recollection, and other attributes. Half of the participants performed this task while in an MCI-induced P mood and half did so while in a U mood. During the second session, held 2 or 3 days later, every participant was induced into the alternative mood and then generated additional autobiographical events in response to a new set of probes. Thus, both studies 1 and 2 entailed a single-factor within-participants design (session 1 mood vs. session 2 mood).

Study 1 used a "constrained" test of autobiographical memory such that in each session participants were instructed to generate an emotionally positive event in response to certain probes and to generate an emotionally negative event in response to certain others. Using a similar task, Teasdale and Fogarty (1979) found that positive events were generated more rapidly than negative events when participants experienced pleasant moods, whereas negative events were generated more rapidly than positive events when participants experienced unpleasant moods. One of the objec-

Table 8.2
Synopsis of MCI studies

			Initial Cognitive Task				
Study Number	Chief Concern	Sample Size	Session 1	Session 2	Mood Measures	Genuineness Ratings	Thought Accounts
1	MC	36	CEG	CEG	AG	no	no
2	MC	60	UEG	UEG	AG, PANAS	yes	yes
3	MD	48	G/R	FR	AG	no	no
4	MD	64	WR	SC	AG	no	no
5	MC, MD	64	UEG	FR	AG	no	no
6	MC, MD	128	UEG	FR	AG	no	yes
7	MC, MD	72	UEG	CP	AG	no	no
8	MC, MD	64	UEG	CP	AG, PANAS	yes	yes

Note: MC = mood congruence; MD = mood dependence. Sample size = total number of participants (all experimental conditions combined). CEG (UEG) = constrained (unconstrained) autobiographical event generation; G/R = generate/read; WR = word rating; FR = free recall; SC = stem completion; CP = category production. AG = affect grid; PANAS = Positive and Negative Affect Schedule. References: Study 3 = Eich & Metcalfe, 1989, experiment 1; Studies 5, 6 = Eich et al., 1994, Experiments 2, 3; Studies 4, 7, 8 = Ryan & Eich (2000); Studies 1 and 2 as yet unpublished.

tives of study 1 was to replicate this pattern of event-generation latencies.

In contrast, study 2 entailed a test that was "unconstrained" in that the type or valence of event generated in response to a given probe was determined by the participants themselves, instead of being stipulated in advance by the experimenter. The issue of chief concern here was whether participants would generate more positive events and fewer negative ones when they were experiencing a pleasant rather than an unpleasant mood.

Studies 3 and 4 (see Table 8.2)—examined mood *dependent* effects in either explicit or implicit memory. Both of these studies entailed a 2 x 2 between-participants design, wherein the two moods (P vs. U) induced during session 1 were crossed with these same two moods during session 2. Thus participants in either study were assigned randomly, and in equal numbers, to one of four mood conditions: two matched (P/P and U/U) and two mismatched (P/U and U/P).

Study 3 was an early effort to see whether shifts in mood state have a greater adverse impact on explicit memory for internal (participant-produced) events than for external (experimenter-provided) events. During session 1, participants either read an item (such as *silver*) that was paired with a category name and a related exemplar (*precious metals: gold–silver*) or generated (with a very high probability) the same item when primed with its initial letter, in conjunction with the category name and exemplar cues (*precious metals: gold–s*). Items that had either been read or generated in session 1 were the targets of a surprise test of free recall in session 2.

Study 4 sought to secure evidence of mood dependence using an implicit measure of retention. During the second session of this study, participants were asked to name a word—any word—that starts with a particular three-letter stem (such

as *str*). Some of the stems corresponded to items (such as *street*) that participants had rated along various semantic dimensions during the first session, whereas other stems corresponded to new (unrated) items. The key question was whether participants would show significantly more priming (here operationalized as the advantage in stem completion of old over new items) when tested under matched as opposed to mismatched mood conditions.

During the first session of studies 5 through 8, equal numbers of P-mood and U-mood participants undertook an unconstrained task of autobiographical event generation, similar to the one performed by participants in study 2, thus providing additional data relevant to mood *congruence*. Unlike participants in study 2, however, participants in studies 5–8 were tested for retention of their previously generated events under either matched or mismatched mood conditions, thereby providing data relevant to mood *dependence* (above and beyond that supplied by studies 3 and 4, which also involved a 2 x 2 factorial design). Whereas retention of the previously generated events was assessed by means of an explicit test (free recall) in studies 5 and 6 , an implicit measure of memory (category production) was used in studies 7 and 8.

MCI Implementation and Mood Measurement

Session 1

At the start of the first session of every study, participants were told that the experiment was part of a research program aimed at understanding how moods affect the performance of various cognitive tasks and how the performance of these tasks in turn affects mood. Participants were also advised that their current moods would be periodically assessed by means of the matrix drawn in Figure 8.1—an adaptation of the *affect grid* developed by Russell, Weiss, and Mendelsohn (1989). It was noted that the grid was designed to measure two principal dimensions of present mood: level of pleasure (indicated along the horizontal) and level of arousal (identified by the vertical axis). It was further remarked that, reading from left to right, the columns connote a mood that is *extremely unpleasant, very unpleasant, moderately unpleasant, slightly unpleasant, neutral* (the shaded center square), *slightly pleasant, moderately pleasant, very pleasant,* and finally *extremely pleasant.* Similarly, the rows signify a state that ranges from *extremely high arousal* at the top through *neutral* at the shaded center to *extremely low arousal* at the bottom (with *slightly, moderately,* and *very* high or low levels in between). Examples of various combinations of pleasure and arousal were given, and it was stressed that the two dimensions are independent of one another, so it is possible for a person to experience any level of pleasure with any level of arousal.

After making their marks, participants were apprised that they soon would listen to a selection of classical music that should help them develop a pleasant (or unpleasant) mood. It was stressed that because music alone cannot create the desired state, they should concentrate on ideas or images that make them feel pleasant (or unpleasant). Participants were also advised to develop as intense a state as possible and that, as an aid in maintaining their moods, the music would continue to play softly in the background. Finally, participants were informed that the research assistant would return from time to time to check on their progress and to monitor their moods and that, when the assistant thought the time was right, they would advance to their initial cognitive task (as specified in Table 8.2).

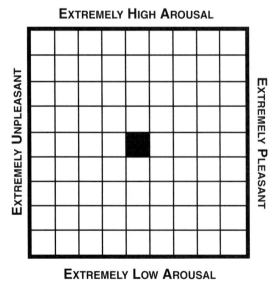

Figure 8.1. The affect grid used to measure current levels of pleasure and arousal. Russell, Weiss, and Mendelsohn (1989). Adapted with permission of the authors.

Each participant was seated in a leather lounge chair flanked by stereo speakers. Through these speakers was played, at a comfortable listening volume, one of four audio recordings, each carrying 23–28 minutes of instrumental music. Two of these recordings contained different sets of "happy" music and the other two contained different sets of "sad" pieces. Participants who were induced into the same mood (either P or U) during both the first and second sessions heard different sets of the mood-appropriate music on each occasion.

Since the MCI technique was introduced under a different name in the late 1980s—see Eich and Metcalfe's (1989) "continuous music technique"—we have tried to keep pace with changes in audio-recording technology, switching from cassettes to compact discs (CDs). At the same time, we have constantly tweaked our selections of happy and sad pieces—admittedly through intuition and guesswork rather than through hard data—so as to capture what works best in creating strong, stable, and sincere shifts in people's moods. Table 8.3 shows our most current playlists of happy and sad music (CDs are available, free of charge, from Eric Eich).

Five minutes after music onset, and every 5 minutes thereafter, participants marked their current levels of pleasure and arousal on a clean copy of the affect grid (which, once marked, was promptly collected by the assistant and never used again). The music continued to play while participants made these mood ratings and did not stop until the end of the session (which is why Eich and Metcalfe [1989] originally called this the *continuous* music technique). Because the typical session lasted 40–60 minutes, each participant heard the same recording two or three times.

As noted earlier, participants understood that cognitive testing would begin when the assistant thought the time was right. Depending on whether a pleasant or an unpleasant mood was being induced, the "right time" occurred either (1) when P-mood participants marked any of the squares included in the two rightmost columns of the affect grid, or (2) when U-mood participants checked any of the squares contained in the two leftmost columns. Thus, to proceed to their initial cognitive task, participants were required, at a minimum, to rate themselves as feeling either *very pleasant* or *very unpleasant,* irrespective of their level of arousal. Participants were not told that the start of testing was contingent on their achieving a criterion level of pleasure or displeasure, lest they try to rush matters by rating their moods as being more extreme than they really were.

In the event that participants were already at criterion when mood induction commenced, they nevertheless listened to the mood-appropriate music and pondered mood-appropriate thoughts for a minimum of 5 minutes before testing began. The maximum amount of time allowed for achieving criterion varied from 40 minutes (in studies 2 and 8) to 60 minutes (in studies 1 and 3–7), depending on the estimated duration of cognitive testing and on the ease with which the participants' class or work schedules could be accommodated. However, in every study, participants were

Table 8.3
Selections of happy and sad music used in the MCI

Music	Set	Composer	Composition	Duration (min:sec)
Happy	1	Mozart	*Eine Kleine Nachtmusik*: Allegro	5:38
	1	Mozart	*Eine Kleine Nachtmusik*: Rondo	3:01
	1	Mozart	Serenade #9: Finale	4:26
	1	Bach	*Brandenburg Concerto #3*: Allegro	4:57
	1	Tchaikovsky	*The Nutcracker*: Waltz of the Flowers	6:36
	1	Tchaikovsky	*The Nutcracker*: Trepak	1:00
Happy	2	Beethoven	Symphony #9: Presto	2:36
	2	Vivaldi	*Four Seasons*: Spring I Allegro	3:01
	2	Vivaldi	*Four Seasons*: Spring III Allegro	3:56
	2	Vivaldi	*Four Seasons*: Autumn I Allegro	4:24
	2	Vivaldi	*Four Seasons*: Autumn III Allegro	3:10
	2	Tchaikovsky	*The Nutcracker*: Dance of the Flutes	2:04
	2	Tchaikovsky	*1812 Overture* (excerpt)	2:04
Sad	1	Albinoni	Adagio in G Minor	4:52
	1	Sibelius	Violin Concerto: Adagio di Molto	3:14
	1	Lehar	Vilja-Lied	2:23
	1	Schumman	Traummeri	3:31
	1	Dvorak	Symphony #9: Largo	5:50
Sad	2	Grieg	*Peer Gynt*: The Death of Ase	5:49
	2	Tchaikovsky	*Swan Lake*: Dances des Cynges	3:00
	2	Chopin	Prelude #4 in E Minor	2:00
	2	Vivaldi	*Four Seasons*: Autumn Adagio	2:20
	2	Stravinsky	*Firebird*: Lullaby (excerpt)	3:15

dismissed earlier if they remained fixed at a particular subcriterion level (e.g., moderately pleasant or slightly unpleasant) for at least 20 minutes (or four consecutive mood-matrix assessments) and thus did not appear to be making any appreciable progress toward attaining the criterion level of pleasure or displeasure after a considerable amount of time.

On reaching the requisite level of pleasure (or displeasure), participants performed one of the initial cognitive tasks listed in Table 8.2. Immediately thereafter, participants checked their current levels of pleasure and arousal on a clean copy of the affect grid. Though participants in study 6 had only one task to do in session 1, those in the other studies went on to complete one or more additional tasks (and marked a new affect grid after each). When they had finished their final task, P-mood participants were discharged with a reminder to return at a certain time and date for a second session of testing, details of which would be divulged at that time. U-mood participants stayed longer—sharing cookies and conversation with the research assistant—so that they left the lab feeling no worse than neutral.

Session 2

Procedures involved in manipulating and measuring mood during the second session mirrored those used in the first. Thus, on returning to the lab, participants provided a baseline rating of pleasure and arousal using the affect grid. Depending on whether a P or a U mood was to be induced, participants then started listening to either merry or melancholic music, and reflecting on elating or depressing thoughts, while

checking a new affect grid every 5 minutes. When the participants reported feeling at least very pleasant or very unpleasant, irrespective of level of arousal, they undertook one of the various cognitive tasks cited in Table 8.2. Afterward, participants marked yet another affect grid. The session came to a close with a thorough debriefing oriented toward the study's aims and methods. As was the case in the earlier session, U-mood participants were not dismissed until their level of pleasure was neutral or higher.

Special Features of Select Studies

Though all eight MCI experiments adhered to the protocol outlined, certain studies differed from the others in three respects, as discussed next.

Ancillary Measures of Mood

To develop a clearer and more complete picture of how the MCI technique influences self-reported mood, participants in studies 2 and 8 (total $n = 124$) were periodically asked to complete the Positive Affect-Negative Affect Schedule (PANAS) in addition to the affect grid. The PANAS was developed by Watson, Clark, and Tellegen (1988) to assess a model of affect proposed by Watson and Tellegen (1985). Their model—like the one favored by Russell (1980) and reflected in the affect grid—holds that happiness, sadness, and other mood states can be envisaged as points in a two-dimensional "affective space." Further, both models assume that the underlying dimensions are conceptually distinct, descriptively bipolar, and psychometrically independent. Watson and Tellegen (1985) prefer to rotate these dimensions, termed *pleasure* and *arousal* by Russell (1980), 45 degrees to produce two alternative factors called *positive affect* and *negative affect*. As defined by Watson et al. (1988, p. 1063):

> Positive Affect (PA) reflects the extent to which a person feels enthusiastic, active, and alert. High PA is a state of high energy, full concentration, and pleasurable engagement [the sort of state that would be indicated by a checkmark in the upper-right corner of the affect grid drawn in Figure 8.1], whereas low PA is characterized by sadness and lethargy [as would be implied by checking the lower-left corner of the grid]. In contrast, Negative Affect (NA) is a general dimension of subjective distress that subsumes a variety of aversive mood states, including anger, contempt, disgust, guilt, fear, and nervousness [represented by the upper-left corner of the affect grid], with low NA being a state of calmness and serenity [identified with the lower-right corner of the grid].

The PANAS provides a practical means of assessing both PA and NA. It consists of 20 affect-related adjectives, 10 pertaining to PA (e.g., *active, alert*) and 10 to NA (e.g., *afraid, ashamed*). In studies 2 and 8, participants were read the items one at a time and indicated the extent to which they were experiencing the conveyed feeling "right now." Responses were made on a 5-point scale (1 = *very slightly* or *not at all*; 5 = *extremely*), then summed over the appropriate items to yield separate scores for PA and NA, each ranging from 10 to 50.

Over the course of studies 2 and 8, there were six occasions on which participants completed the PANAS moments after marking an affect grid. These occasions were: at the outsets of both session 1 and session 2 (before mood induction had begun); immediately preceding the initial cognitive task in either session (once participants had indicated on an affect grid that they felt at least very pleasant or very unpleasant); and immediately following the initial cognitive task in either session.

Ratings of Mood Genuineness

By definition, any participant who successfully completed one of the eight MCI experiments had to report feeling either *very pleasant* or *very unpleasant* at some point in each of the study's two sessions. But were these feelings genuine? Or were the participants exaggerating the true intensity of their moods just to please the experimenter or to fulfill a more self-serving goal—namely, to get on with cognitive testing or to get out of the experiment altogether?

Studies 2 and 8 (see Table 8.2) sought to address this thorny issue. Just prior to their final debriefing, participants in these studies (total *n* = 124) were asked to respond, with utmost candor, to the question: How real or genuine was the mood you experienced when you began cognitive testing today (i.e., during the second session of the study)? Responses were made on an 11-point scale ranging from 0 (*totally artificial*) through 5 (*moderately real*) to 10 (*completely genuine*). After voicing a response (which the assistant recorded in writing), participants rated (on the same scale) the genuineness of the moods they had experienced when they began cognitive testing during the study's first session (held 2 days earlier in study 8 and 2–7 days earlier in study 2).

Thought Accounts

After registering their ratings of mood genuineness, the 124 participants in studies 2 and 8 were asked to articulate the ideas or images they had entertained as an aid to developing the particular moods assigned to session 1 and to offer a similar statement with respect to session 2. The 128 participants in study 6 were asked to provide similar accounts just prior to their debriefing. Participants were assured that their commentaries (which were transcribed by the assistant) would be kept strictly confidential, and they were asked to provide only as much detail as they felt comfortable giving. Later, these "thought accounts" were examined with a view to clarifying (1) whether participants prefer to think about actual events or imaginary scenarios, (2) whether the actual events relate to issues of concern in the immediate present as opposed to the more distant past, and (3) whether participants who experience the same mood (either P or U) during session 1 and session 2 think similar or different thoughts on the two occasions.

Participant Selection and Recruitment

Participants were recruited through sign-up sheets and advertisements at the University of British Columbia (UBC) and the surrounding area. About 90% of the recruits were UBC undergraduate students, and the remaining 10% were members of the university staff or local residents.

Participants averaged 21.5 years of age and ranged from 18 to 65 years. Criteria for selection included no significant depression (assessed by means of Beck's [1967] Depression Inventory, which was administered during a preexperimental interview), fluency in English, and no prior participation in research involving either autobiographical memory (studies 1, 2, and 5–8) or experimentally induced moods (all eight experiments). In return for their participation, participants in studies 2, 6, and 8 received payment, while those in the other studies earned course credit.

Assessment of the MCI Method

Having described how the MCI studies were designed, we now turn to what they showed.

Success Rate

The first facet of results to consider concerns the success rate of the MCI technique. For seven studies (all but study 3, which was the first to use the technique), information was available on the number of participants who attempted to achieve the criterion level of pleasure or displeasure.

A total of 589 participants (390 women and 199 men) were recruited to serve in these seven studies. Twenty-nine participants were lost either because they failed to return as scheduled for the second session (12 cases) or because of technical problems encountered in testing (17 cases).

Of the remaining 560 participants, 72 were lost due to problems related to mood induction; specifically, they either became too upset in the course of U-mood induction to continue (4 cases) or they made no discernible progress toward achieving the criterion level of mood (either *very pleasant* or *very unpleasant*) within a reasonable amount of time (viz. 20 minutes or more; 68 cases). Women accounted for the majority of the mood-induction failures (41/68 = 60%), which is consistent with their majority representation among all recruits (390/589 = 66%). Irrespective of their gender, far more participants were unable (or unwilling) to meet the mood criterion in the first than in the second session (55 vs. 13 cases), and more participants had trouble developing a U rather than a P mood (48 vs. 20 cases).

Nonetheless, the vast majority of both women (331/375 = 88%) and men (157/185 = 85%) succeeded in attaining either the P-mood or the U-mood criterion during both sessions of a given study. Thus the overall success rate of the MCI technique was 87% (488/560).

Time to Criterion

Given that most participants were able to develop very pleasant or very unpleasant moods, the next issue to address is: How long did it take them to do so?

Apropos of this question, Table 8.4 shows the mean minutes that women and men needed to achieve the targeted mood in either session of all eight studies. Separate 2x2 analyses of the session 1 and session 2 data yielded similar results; specifically, a reliable effect of mood condition ($F(1, 532) > 6.86$, $p < .01$), an insignificant effect of participant gender, and an insignificant interaction ($F < 1$). On average, U moods were slower to develop than were P moods (means = 17.3 vs. 15.6 minutes in session 1; 17.7 vs. 14.9 minutes in session 2)—a difference that will be explained momentarily. For now, the important point is that the MCI technique not only works well, but it also works quickly: Just over 81% of the participants (436/536) reached the requisite level of pleasure or displeasure in 20 minutes or less in session 1, and just under 81% (433/536) did so in session 2.

Ratings of Pleasure and Arousal

Mean ratings of pleasure recorded on six occasions over the course of the eight studies are illustrated in the left panel of Figure 8.2. These ratings correspond to marks made by participants along the horizontal axis of the affect grid (shown

Table 8.4

Minutes to achieve mood criterion as a function of mood condition, participant gender, and study segment (studies 1–8 combined)

Mood Condition	Participant Gender	nS1/nS2	Study Segment	
			Session 1	*Session 2*
P	Women	185/181	15.8 (9.3)	14.5 (7.5)
P	Men	83/87	15.2 (8.1)	15.7 (9.5)
U	Women	181/185	16.7 (8.8)	17.4 (7.7)
U	Men	87/83	18.6 (8.7)	18.3 (8.3)

Note: P = pleasant mood, U = unpleasant mood. nS1/nS2 = number of participants per mean value in session 1 (S1) and in session 2 (S2). Standard deviations are enclosed in parentheses.

in Figure 8.1) and range from 4 (*extremely pleasant*) through 0 (*neutral*) to −4 (*extremely unpleasant*).

Several aspects of the data deserve comment. First, as one would expect, baseline ratings registered at the outset of either session 1 or session 2 (ratings labeled 1.1 and 2.1, respectively) were about the same, regardless of which mood (P or U) was soon to be induced via the MCI technique. The fact that P-mood and U-mood participants alike started off feeling *slightly pleasant* means that the latter participants had farther to go along the pleasure-displeasure dimension to reach criterion; accordingly, it is unsurprising that it took them longer to get there (as was noted in the previous section).

Second, in keeping with the mood criteria stated earlier, participants rated themselves as feeling, at a minimum, either *very pleasant* (3 or higher) or *very unpleasant* (−3 or lower) just before they began their initial cognitive task in session 1 or session 2 (ratings coded as 1.2 and 2.2, respectively).

Third, the impact of the mood manipulation declined over time and across tasks. More precisely, the mean differ-

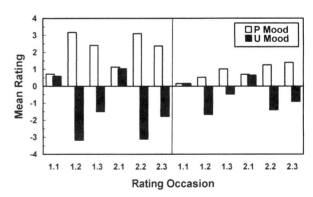

Figure 8.2. Mean ratings of pleasure (left panel) and arousal (right panel) recorded on six occasions (defined in the text) by participants in a pleasant (P) or unpleasant (U) mood.

ence in pleasure ratings made by P-mood and U-mood participants was 6.4 points when the initial cognitive task in session 1 began (rating 1.2: P-mood = 3.2, U-mood = −3.2), but only 3.9 points when the task concluded (rating 1.3: P-mood = 2.4, U-mood = −1.5). Similarly, the mean difference between mood conditions decreased from 6.2 points at the start of the initial task in session 2 (rating 2.2: P-mood = 3.1, U-mood = −3.1) to 4.2 points at its end (rating 2.3: P-mood = 2.4, U-mood = −1.8). These diminishing differences may reflect a regression to the mean, or they may be due to the tasks themselves. In any case, it should be noted that although the mood manipulation lost some of its effectiveness, it did not lose it all: Mean differences in rated pleasure between P-mood and U-mood participants were significant at the conclusion of either session's initial task ($t(534) > 26.71, p < .01$). It is also worth noting that although the posttask ratings shown in Figure 8.2 suggest that U moods faded faster than P moods, that actually was not the case. Analysis of the absolute difference between baseline and posttask ratings demonstrated that, by the end of cognitive testing in either session, U-mood participants had maintained a greater distance from their baseline ratings than had their P-mood peers (mean absolute differences in session 1: P-mood = 1.7, U-mood = 2.1; in session 2: P-mood = 1.3, U-mood = 2.8; $t(534) > 3.97, p < .01$).

Two additional points regarding pleasure ratings are worth making that are *not* obvious from the data depicted in Figure 8.2. One is that there are no consistent gender differences in pleasure ratings for either mood condition on any rating occasion. Indeed, for every combination of study, mood, and rating, the mean pleasure rating for men falls within 1 standard deviation of the corresponding mean for women.

The second point is that although the pleasure ratings registered during the first session of a given study usually mirrored those recorded in the second, this was not always so. In study 6, for example, U-mood participants had a much higher posttask pleasure rating in session 1 than in session 2 (means = −0.3 vs. −2.5). Assuming that MCI-induced moods lose their strength over time, we suspect that this disparity reflects the fact that the session 1 task lasted much longer than did the session 2 task (estimated averages = 28 minutes vs. 5 minutes). Had the tasks been more similar in duration, differences between the posttask ratings obtained under a given mood condition should have been less striking. This was indeed the case in all other experiments that entailed tasks of equal or similar length (viz., studies 1–4).

The right panel in Figure 8.2 depicts ratings of arousal, averaged over all P-mood and U-mood participants in all eight experiments. These ratings were assigned in accordance with marks made by participants along the vertical axis of the affect grid and varied from 4 (*extremely high arousal*) through 0 (*neutral*) to −4 (*extremely low arousal*).

Comparison of the two sides of Figure 8.2 suggests that the MCI led to substantial changes not only in the participants' ratings of pleasure—which is what the technique was specifically intended to do—but in their ratings of arousal, as well. More to the point, P-mood participants rated themselves as being more aroused than their U-mood peers, and this was true for all ratings taken after mood induction had begun (viz., ratings 1.2, 1.3, 2.2, and 2.3 in the right panel of Figure 8.2; $t(534) > 10.38, p < .01$). Though not apparent from the figure, differences between P-mood and U-mood levels of arousal emerged consistently across both genders and all eight MCI studies.

Ratings of Positive and Negative Affect

Earlier, we remarked that the bipolar dimensions of mood termed *positive affect* (PA) and *negative affect* (NA) by Watson and Tellegen (1985) represent rotational variants of the bipolar dimensions called *pleasure* and *arousal* by Russell (1980). Given this relation, and in view of patterns of pleasure and arousal ratings depicted in Figure 8.2, the MCI should have a marked impact on ratings of both positive and negative affect.

Results shown in Figure 8.3 support this inference. Compared to their U-mood peers, P-mood participants experienced a higher level of PA (left panel) and a lower level of NA (right panel) at all points following mood induction (i.e., ratings 1.2, 1.3, 2.2, and 2.3; ts(122) > 7.96, ps < .01). Though not shown in Figure 8.3, the patterns of PA and NA ratings made by women were similar, qualitatively and quantitatively, to those made by the men. This observation bolsters the claim, made earlier in connection with ratings of pleasure and arousal, that the MCI technique has robust, reliable, and gender-independent effects on self-reported mood.

Ratings of Mood Genuineness

Recall that shortly before final debriefing, participants in studies 2 and 8 (total n = 124) were asked to assess the authenticity of the moods they had experienced during the first and second sessions.

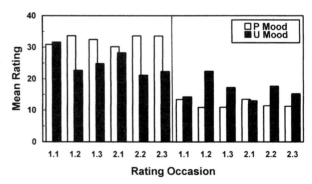

Figure 8.3. Mean ratings of positive affect (left panel) and negative affect (right panel) recorded on six occasions (defined in the text) by participants in a pleasant (P) or unpleasant (U) mood.

The overall average rating for session 1 (7.8) was equivalent to that found in session 2 (7.7). Further, in neither session was there an appreciable effect of gender, either alone or in combination with moods ($p > .05$). In both sessions, however, P moods differed reliably from U moods ($F(1, 120) > 10.57, p < .01$), the former feeling more real than the latter (means = 8.2 vs. 7.3). Conceivably, this difference may reflect the fact that the typical participant was in a good mood at the start of each session, which could make the leap to a very pleasant state seem more natural than a switch to a very unpleasant affect. Whatever the explanation, it is important not to lose sight of the fact that, in absolute terms, the overall U-mood rating (viz., 7.3) was on the high end of the 0–10 genuineness scale.

Thought Accounts

As indicated in Table 8.2, a total of 252 participants (i.e., participants in studies 2, 6, or 8) were asked to describe the specific ideas or images they had contemplated to aid in developing a particular mood during a particular session. Examination of these thought accounts yielded two sets of observations.

First, the clear majority of both P-mood and U-mood participants (women and men alike) preferred to think about prior episodes or experiences, involving themselves or others, that carried either a positive or a negative emotional charge. Such past events accounted for 77% of all 473 codable thought accounts. A relatively small number of participants found it useful to muse about imaginary scenarios having pleasant or unpleasant overtones (accounting for 17% of the usable responses), and even fewer participants focused on issues of current concern (the remaining 6% of the codable thought accounts).

Second, participants tested under matched-mood conditions (viz., P/P or U/U) were about evenly split on how best to develop the same mood on two different occasions: to stay with the same thoughts (29% of participants with codable responses); to entertain different thoughts related to the same (or similar) theme, such as academic success or failure (34%); or to switch to entirely new thoughts and themes (37%). In contrast, participants assigned to the mismatched-mood conditions (viz., P/U or U/P) had no choice but to think different thoughts, were they to feel very pleasant during one session and very unpleasant in the other.

Discussion

We began this chapter by composing a wish list of six characteristics that would seem desirable in a mood-modification technique. Based on the results reviewed herein, the MCI technique appears to possess each of these properties. In particular, the MCI offers a high rate of return at relatively low cost: About 81% of women and men alike are able to develop either a *very pleasant* or a *very unpleasant* mood in un-

der 20 minutes. Nevertheless, the MCI imposes no arbitrary limit on the amount of time allocated to mood induction—a practice common to other methods of mood induction and one that virtually ensures wide variability among participants in their postinduction levels of mood. Rather, the MCI entails an idiographic approach to mood manipulation, and thus enables each individual to achieve a predetermined level of pleasure or displeasure at his or her own pace.

Depending on how high or low these target levels are set, the strength or intensity of the participant's mood can, in principle, be controlled. In practice, we have routinely set the criteria to *very pleasant* or *very unpleasant* feelings, as these have sufficient strength and discriminability to elicit both mood-congruent and mood-dependent effects in autobiographical memory. Though this strategy requires us to rely on ratings of pleasure as the principal metric of mood strength, the MCI has robust and reliable effects on several other measures of self-reported mood (viz., arousal, positive affect, and negative affect). Moreover, all of these measures indicate that MCI moods, once induced, remain relatively stable over time and across tasks and that functionally similar moods can be instilled on at least two separate occasions—a particularly important consideration in research on mood-dependent memory. And even though the MCI is plainly an experimental contrivance, it creates moods that seem real to most participants.

This last point leads us to revisit the thorny issue of experimental demand, which was raised in the introduction. Like many other induction techniques, the MCI requires participants to play an active role in their own mood development. Though participants do not know about any specific mood criteria, they do know that they should try to get into either a pleasant or an unpleasant mood. This raises the possibility that participants are simply acceding to experimental demand and acting in a manner that is consistent with their beliefs about moods rather than experiencing an authentic alteration in their affective states (e.g., Bower, 1981; Ellis & Hertel, 1993; Vastfjall, 2002).

Two considerations argue against this possibility. First, the participants' own ratings of mood genuineness implied a high degree of affective realism, averaging 8.2 among P-mood participants and 7.3 among their U-mood peers (based on a 0–10 scale). Given that the participants were asked to be completely candid in their evaluations and that their ratings were made at the end of formal testing, we are inclined to take them at their word. Second, ratings of pleasure tend to regress toward baseline over time, and the amount of change is related to task duration (see the subsection "Ratings of Pleasure and Arousal"). It is unclear why the consistency of these ratings should be related to the time spent performing a particular cognitive task if demand is the principal force controlling the participants' self-reports.

Considered collectively, the results reviewed here show that the MCI instills moods that are reasonably strong, stable, sincere, and reproducible. These characteristics, together with the technique's high rate of success and assurance of comparability across participants (vis-à-vis pretask ratings of pleasure and displeasure), recommend the MCI as a useful tool for investigating the interplay between cognitive and emotional processes.

That said, there is still much room for improvement and no shortage of questions about ways in which the efficacy of the MCI might be enhanced, as the following examples illustrate:

- The MCI employs musical excerpts that were originally selected on the basis of intuition, guesswork, and personal preference (Eich, Macaulay, & Ryan, 1994; Eich & Metcalfe, 1989). Might a more conceptually principled approach to music selection be possible?

  Recent developments in music theory (see Juslin, 2001; Vastfjall, 2002) suggest an affirmative answer. Musicologists have identified six main elements or cues—mode (major or minor), tempo, pitch, rhythm, harmony, and loudness—that are central to the *perception* of intended emotion in musical expression. Though there is no assurance that such cues are also central to the *experience* of emotion—music that sounds happy to the ear doesn't necessarily stir the heart (see Gabrielsson, 2002; Russell, 2003)—their potential value to the MCI is worth investigating in partnership with interested musicologists.

  Another way that the selection of music might be improved is by ensuring that particular styles and ensembles complement one another. Each style (within classical music, for example) communicates emotion through unique sets of compositional techniques. Keeping styles and genres consistent (string quartet vs. solo piano, for example) not only eliminates the distraction of contrasting sounds, harmonies, keys, and meters but leads naturally to a more systematic review of the musical categories that are best suited for mood induction. Again, collaboration with music experts seems well advised.

- All participants in prior MCI studies listened to the same experimenter-selected music. Might the effectiveness of the technique be improved if, in the future, participants were free to select the music themselves? The question has been raised, but not resolved, in connection with alternative musical-mood induction procedures (MMIPs)—"alternative" meaning techniques which, unlike the MCI, reflect a nomothetic rather an idiographic approach to mood modification (see Carter, Wilson, Lawson, & Bulik, 1995; Panksepp, 1995; Vastfjall, 2002).

  Given that emotional reaction to music is a personalized process (Gabrielsson, 2002), it makes sense to compare the current MCI with at least two other conditions: one in which participants select and supply their own music (à la Carter et al., 1995) and one in which they choose from among several experimenter-provided programs that reflect different musical tastes (à la Sutherland et al., 1982).

  As a first step in that direction, we are now conducting a survey of the specific recordings or general types of music that participants would bring to our lab were they asked to develop pleasant or unpleasant moods. One thing that leaps out from the preliminary data is that although most participants favor contemporary genres (an unsurprising outcome, given that the participants are mostly young adult undergraduates), there are clear and consistent differences in the musical preferences of Asian and European American undergraduates (who comprise about 30% and 60% of our university's student body, respectively). MMIPs in general, and the MCI in particular, stand to benefit from attention to cultural differences in musical preferences, which may in turn be tied to cultural differences in emotional experience and expression.

- Although participants in past MCI studies have had no say in the selection of music, they alone have decided what they want to think about in aid of developing a particular (pleasant or unpleasant) mood. Would the MCI work just (or nearly) as well if participants were asked to read and internalize experimenter-prepared scripts describing hypothetical (but believable) positive or negative scenarios? In principle, such scripts could provide a level of experimental control over mood induction that is clearly lacking in current MCI practice.

- Self-report measures of affect have long been a fixture of experimental mood-modification methods in general and the MCI in particular. Given that the MCI induces bona fide moods in most people, it makes sense to ask: Can this high degree of affective realism also be captured using behavioral-physiological indices of emotion, such as changes in facial expressions or plasma cortisol levels (e.g., Clark, Iversen, & Goodwin, 2001; Davidson, Scherer, & Goldsmith, 2002; Krumhansl, 1997)?

This list is just a beginning. As the title of this chapter suggests, and its contents show, the MCI relies on the combination of music and thought to change mood. But how much of this change is attributable to music and how much to thought? Because prior research using MMIPs other than the MCI offers no clear answer to this question (see Vastfjall, 2002), we have recently begun a pair of "deconstructive" studies. In one of these studies, undergraduates are asked simply to listen to various selections of happy or sad music for 15 or 20 minutes, respectively (the average amount of time taken to reach criterion levels of pleasure or displeasure using regular MCI procedures.). In the other study, students are asked to entertain elating or depressing thoughts (again, for 15 or 20 minutes, respectively) in the absence of any music.

Following standard MCI practice, half of the participants in either study rate their present levels of pleasure and arousal on an affect grid both before they receive their instructions and every 5 minutes thereafter. In contrast, the remaining participants rate their current moods only once, at the very end of the (15- or 20-minute) mood-induction period. The intent here is to see whether the very act of assessing one's mood alters one's experience of that mood—an issue that arises out of Berkowitz's claim that mood awareness plays a critical role in the occurrence of mood congruence (Berkowitz, Jaffee, Jo, & Troccoli, 2000; Berkowitz & Troccoli, 1990). This is but one of several issues that need to be addressed if we are to understand why the MCI works and how it can be improved.

Acknowledgments

Preparation of this chapter was aided by grants to the first author from the (American) National Institute of Mental Health (R01-MH59636) and the (Canadian) Natural Sciences and Engineering Research Council (37335). Address correspondence to Eric Eich, Department of Psychology, University of British Columbia, Vancouver, BC/Canada V6T 1Z4 (ee@psych.ubc.ca).

References

Albersnagel, F. A. (1988). Velten and musical mood induction procedures: A comparison with accessibility of thought associations. *Behaviour Research and Therapy, 26,* 79–96.

Beck, A. T. (1967). *Depression: Clinical, experimental, and theoretical aspects.* New York: Harper & Row.

Berkowitz, L., Jaffee, S., Jo, E., & Troccoli, B.T. (2000). On the correction of feeling-induced judgmental biases. In J. P. Forgas (Ed.), *Feeling and thinking* (pp.131–152). Cambridge, UK: Cambridge University Press.

Berkowitz, L., & Troccoli, B. T. (1990). Feelings, direction of attention, and expressed evaluations of others. *Cognition and Emotion, 4,* 305–325.

Blaney, P. H. (1986). Affect and memory: A review. *Psychological Bulletin, 99,* 229–246.

Bower, G. H. (1981). Mood and memory. *American Psychologist, 36,* 129–148.

Bower, G. H., & Forgas, J. P. (2000). Affect, memory, and social cognition. In E. Eich, J. F. Kihlstrom, G. H. Bower, J. P. Forgas, & P. M. Niedenthal (Eds.), *Cognition and emotion* (pp.100–189). New York: Oxford University Press.

Bower, G. H., Monteiro, K. P., & Gilligan, S. G. (1978). Emotional mood as a context for learning and recall. *Journal of Verbal Learning and Verbal Behavior, 17,* 573–585.

Buchwald, A. M., Strack, S., & Coyne, J. C. (1981). Demand characteristics and the Velten mood induction procedure. *Journal of Consulting and Clinical Psychology, 49,* 478–479.

Carter, F. A., Wilson, J. S., Lawson, R. H., & Bulik, C. M. (1995). Mood induction procedure: Importance of individualizing music. *Behaviour Change, 12,* 159–161.

Chartier, G. M., & Ranieri, D. J. (1989). Comparison of two mood induction procedures. *Cognitive Therapy and Research, 13,* 275–282.

Clark, D. M. (1983). On the induction of depressed mood in the laboratory: Evaluation and comparison of the Velten and musical procedures. *Advances in Behaviour Research and Therapy, 5,* 27–49.

Clark, L., Iversen, S. D., & Goodwin, G. M. (2001). The influence of positive and negative mood states on risk taking, verbal fluency, and salivary cortisol. *Journal of Affective Disorders, 63,* 179–187.

Davidson, R. J., Scherer, K. R., & Goldsmith, H. H. (Eds.). (2002). *Handbook of the affective sciences.* New York: Oxford University Press.

Eich, E. (1995a). Mood as a mediator of place dependent memory. *Journal of Experimental Psychology: General, 124,* 293–308.

Eich, E. (1995b). Searching for mood dependent memory. *Psychological Science, 6,* 67–75.

Eich, E., & Forgas, J. P. (2003). Mood, cognition, and memory. In I. B. Weiner (Series Ed.) & A. F. Healy & R. W. Proctor (Vol. Eds.), *Handbook of psychology. Vol. 4: Experimental psychology* (pp. 61–83). New York: Wiley.

Eich, E., & Macaulay, D. (2000). Are real moods required to reveal mood-congruent and mood-dependent memory? *Psychological Science, 11,* 244–248.

Eich, E., Macaulay, D., & Lam, R. (1997). Mania, depression, and mood dependent memory. *Cognition and Emotion, 11,* 607–618.

Eich, E., Macaulay, D., & Ryan, L. (1994). Mood dependent memory for events of the personal past. *Journal of Experimental Psychology: General, 123,* 201–215.

Eich, E., & Metcalfe, J. (1989). Mood dependent memory for internal versus external events. *Journal of Experimental Psychology: Learning, Memory, and Cognition, 15,* 443–455.

Ellis, H. C. (1985). On the importance of mood intensity and encoding demand in memory: Commentary on Hasher, Rose, Zacks, Sanft, and Doren. *Journal of Experimental Psychology: General, 114,* 392–395.

Ellis, H. C., & Ashbrook, P. W. (1989). The "state" of mood and memory research: A selective review. *Journal of Social Behavior and Personality, 4,* 1–21.

Ellis, H. C., & Hertel, P. T. (1993). Cognition, emotion, and memory: Some applications and issues. In C. Izawa (Ed.), *Cognitive psychology applied* (pp.199–215). Hillsdale, NJ: Erlbaum.

Forgas, J. P., & Bower, G. H. (1987). Mood effects on person-perception judgments. *Journal of Personality and Social Psychology, 53,* 53–60.

Friswell, R., & McConkey, K. M. (1989). Hypnotically induced mood. *Cognition and Emotion, 3,* 1–26.

Gabrielsson, A. (2002). Perceived emotion and felt emotion: Same or different? *Musicae Scientiae,* Special Issue 2001/2002, 123–148.

Gerrards-Hesse, A., Spies, K., & Hesse, F. W. (1994). Experimental inductions of emotional states and their effectiveness: A review. *British Journal of Psychology, 85,* 55–78

Hasher, L., Rose, K. C., Zacks, R., Sanft, H., & Doren, B. (1985). Mood, recall and selectivity effects in normal college students. *Journal of Experimental Psychology: General, 114,* 104–118.

Ingram, R. E. (1989). External validity issues in mood and memory research. *Journal of Social Behavior and Personality, 4,* 57–62.

Isen, A. M. (1984). Toward understanding the role of affect in cognition. In R. S. Wyer & T. K. Srull (Eds.), *Handbook of social cognition* (Vol. 3, pp.179–236). Hillsdale, NJ: Erlbaum.

Isen, A. M., & Gorgoglione, J. M. (1983). Some specific effects of four affect-induction procedures. *Personality and Social Psychology Bulletin, 9,* 136–143.

Johnson, M. H., & Magaro, P. A. (1987). Effects of mood and severity on memory processes in depression and mania. *Psychological Bulletin, 101,* 28–40.

Juslin, P. N. (2001). Communicating emotion in music performance: A review and a theoretical framework. In P. N. Juslin & J. A. Sloboda (Eds.), *Music and emotion: Theory and research* (pp. 309–340). New York: Oxford University Press.

Kenealy, P. M. (1986). The Velten mood induction procedure: A methodological review. *Motivation and Emotion, 10,* 315–335.

Krumhansl, C. L. (1997). An exploratory study of musical emotions and psychophysiology. *Canadian Journal of Experimental Psychology, 51,* 336–353.

Laird, J. D. (1989). Mood affects memory because feelings *are* cognitions. *Journal of Social Behavior and Personality, 4,* 33–38.

Larsen, R. J., & Sinnett, L. M. (1991). Meta-analysis of experimental manipulations: Some factors affecting the Velten mood induction procedure. *Personality and Social Psychology Bulletin, 17,* 323–334.

Martin, M. (1990). On the induction of mood. *Clinical Psychology Review, 10,* 669–697.

Panksepp, J. (1995). The emotional sources of "chills" induced by music. *Music Perception, 13,* 171–207.

Parrott, W. G. (1991). Mood induction and instructions to sustain moods: A test of the subject compliance hypothesis of mood-congruent memory. *Cognition and Emotion, 5,* 41–52.

Parrott, W. G., & Sabini, J. (1990). Mood and memory under natural conditions: Evidence for mood-incongruent recall. *Journal of Personality and Social Psychology, 59,* 321–336.

Pignatiello, M., Camp, C., & Rasar, L. (1986). Musical mood induction: An alternative to the Velten technique. *Journal of Abnormal Psychology, 95,* 295–297.

Polivy, J., & Doyle, C. (1980). Laboratory induction of mood states through the reading of self-referent mood statements: Affective changes or demand characteristics? *Journal of Abnormal Psychology, 89,* 286–290.

Riskind, J. H., & Gotay, C. C. (1982). Physical posture: Could it have regulatory or feedback effects on motivation and emotion? *Motivation and Emotion, 6,* 273–298.

Roth, D. L. (1989). Acute emotional and psychophysiological effects of aerobic exercise. *Psychophysiology, 26,* 593–602.

Russell, J. A. (1980). A circumplex model of affect. *Journal of Personality and Social Psychology, 39,* 1161–1178.

Russell, J. A. (2003). Core affect and the psychological construction of emotion. *Psychological Review, 110,* 145–172.

Russell, J. A., Weiss, A., & Mendelsohn, G. A. (1989). Affect grid: A single item scale of pleasure and arousal. *Journal of Personality and Social Psychology, 57,* 493–502.

Ryan, L., & Eich, E. (2000). Mood dependence and implicit memory. In E. Tulving (Ed.), *Memory, consciousness, and the brain* (pp. 91–105). Philadelphia: Psychology Press.

Seibert, P. S., & Ellis, H. C. (1991). A convenient self-referencing mood induction procedure. *Bulletin of the Psychonomic Society, 29,* 121–124.

Suedfeld, P., & Eich, E. (1995). Autobiographical memory and affect under conditions of reduced environmental stimulation. *Journal of Environmental Psychology, 15,* 321–326.

Sutherland, G., Newman, B., & Rachman, S. (1982). Experimental investigations of the relations between mood and intrusive unwanted cognitions. *British Journal of Medical Psychology, 55,* 127–138.

Teasdale, J. D., & Fogarty, S. J. (1979). Differential effects of induced mood on retrieval of pleasant and unpleasant events from episodic memory. *Journal of Abnormal Psychology, 88,* 248–257.

Teasdale, J. D., & Russell, M. L. (1983). Differential effects of induced mood on the recall of positive, negative and neutral words. *British Journal of Clinical Psychology, 22,* 163–172.

Teasdale, J. D., & Taylor, R. (1981). Induced mood and accessibility of memories: An effect of mood state or of induction procedure? *British Journal of Clinical Psychology, 20,* 39–48.

Vastfjall, D. (2002). Emotion induction through music: A review of the musical mood induction procedure. *Musicae Scientiae,* Special Issue 2001/2002, 173–211.

Velten, E. (1968). A laboratory task for induction of mood states. *Behavior Research and Therapy, 6,* 473–482.

Watson, D., & Tellegen, A. (1985). Toward a consensual structure of mood. *Psychological Bulletin, 98,* 219–235.

Watson, D., Clark, L. A., & Tellegen, A. (1988). Development and validation of brief measures of positive and negative affect: The PANAS scales. *Journal of Personality and Social Psychology, 54,* 1063–1070.

Wright, J., & Mischel, W. (1982). Influence of affect on cognitive social learning variables. *Journal of Personality and Social Psychology, 43,* 901–914.

Edmund T. Rolls

Emotion Elicited by Primary Reinforcers and Following Stimulus-Reinforcement Association Learning

What are emotions? Why do we have emotions? What are the rules by which emotion operates? What are the brain mechanisms of emotion, and how can disorders of emotion be understood? What motivates us to work for particular rewards, such as food when we are hungry or water when we are thirsty? How do these motivational control systems operate to ensure that we eat approximately the correct amount of food to maintain our body weight or to replenish our thirst? What factors account for the overeating and obesity that some humans show? Why is the brain built to include reward and punishment systems, rather than in some other way?

In this chapter I describe an approach to these issues that leads to ways based on fundamental principles to investigate emotions by using and understanding the processing of primary (unlearned) reinforcers and how learning of associations of other stimuli to these primary reinforcers occurs. I pay special attention to analyses of the operation of these systems in nonhuman primates, because of their close relevance to understanding the function of these reward-and-punishment systems in humans.

A Theory of Emotion and Some Definitions

Emotions can usefully be defined as states elicited by rewards and punishers, including changes in rewards and punishers (Rolls, 1999a, 2005; see also Rolls, 1986a, 1986b, 1990,

2000a). A reward is anything for which an animal will work. A punisher is anything that an animal will work to escape or avoid. Some examples of emotion include happiness produced by being given a reward, such as a pleasant touch, praise, or a prize of a large sum of money, or fear produced by the sound of a rapidly approaching bus, or the sight of an angry expression on someone's face. We work to avoid such stimuli. Other examples include frustration, anger, or sadness produced by the omission of an expected reward, such as a prize, or the termination of a reward, such as the death of a loved one; or relief produced by the omission or termination of a punisher, such as the removal of a painful stimulus or sailing out of danger. These examples indicate how emotions can be produced by the delivery, omission, or termination of rewards or punishers, and they go some way to indicate how different emotions could be produced and classified in terms of the rewards and punishers received, omitted, or terminated. A diagram that summarizes some of the emotions associated with the delivery of a reward or punisher or a stimulus associated with them or with the omission of a reward or punisher is shown in Figure 9.1. It should be understood that this diagram summarizes the states that could be produced by manipulation of the reinforcement contingencies for any one reinforcer. The brain is built to have a large set of different primary reinforcers, and the reinforcer space is in this sense high dimensional.

Before accepting this approach, we should consider whether there are any exceptions to the proposed rule. Are

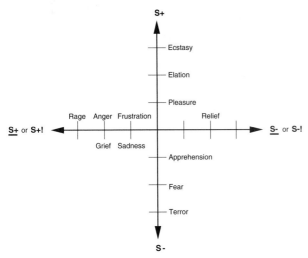

Figure 9.1. Some of the emotions associated with different reinforcement contingencies are indicated. Intensity increases on a continuous scale away from the center of the diagram. The classification scheme created by the different reinforcement contingencies consists, with respect to the action, of (1) the delivery presentation of a reward (S+), (2) the presentation of a punisher (S-), (3) the omission of a reward (S+; extinction) or the termination of a reward (S+!; time out), and (4) the omission of a punisher (S-; avoidance) or the termination of a punisher (S-!; escape). Adapted from Rolls, 1999a, Figure 3.1.

any emotions caused by stimuli, events, or remembered events that are not rewarding or punishing? Do any rewarding or punishing stimuli not cause emotions? We consider these questions in more detail later. The point is that if there are no major exceptions, or if any exceptions can be clearly encapsulated, then we may have a good working definition at least of what causes emotions, and this leads to principled ways for eliciting and studying emotion.

I next consider a slightly more formal definition than rewards or punishers, in which the concept of reinforcers is introduced, and show how there has been a considerable history in the development of ideas along this line.

The proposal that emotions can be usefully seen as states produced by instrumental reinforcing stimuli follows earlier work by Millenson (1967), Weiskrantz (1968), Gray (1975, 1987) and Rolls (1986a, 1986b; 1990). Instrumental reinforcers are stimuli that, if their occurrence, termination, or omission is made contingent on the making of an action, alter the probability of the future emission of that action (see Dickinson, 1980; Gray, 1975; Lieberman, 2000; Mackintosh, 1983). Rewards and punishers are instrumental reinforcing stimuli. The notion of an action here is that an arbitrary action, for example, turning right versus turning left, will be performed in order to obtain the reward or avoid the punisher, so that there is no prewired connection between the response and the reinforcer. Some stimuli are primary (unlearned) reinforcers (e.g., the taste of food if the animal is hungry; pain), whereas others may become reinforcing by

learning because of their association with such primary reinforcers, thereby becoming "secondary reinforcers." This type of learning may thus be called *stimulus-reinforcement association,* and it occurs via an associative learning process. A positive reinforcer (such as food) increases the probability of emission of a response on which it is contingent; the process is termed *positive reinforcement,* and the outcome is a reward (such as food). A negative reinforcer (such as a painful stimulus) increases the probability of emission of a response that causes the negative reinforcer to be omitted (as in active avoidance) or terminated (as in escape), and the procedure is termed *negative reinforcement.* In contrast, *punishment* refers to a procedure in which the probability of an action is decreased. Punishment thus describes procedures in which an action decreases in probability if it is followed by a painful stimulus, as in passive avoidance. Punishment can also be used to refer to a procedure involving the omission or termination of a reward ("extinction" and "time out," respectively), both of which decrease the probability of responses (see, further, Dickinson, 1980; Gray, 1975; Lieberman, 2000; Mackintosh, 1983).

My argument is that an affectively positive or "appetitive" stimulus (which produces a state of pleasure) acts operationally as a *reward,* which instrumentally, when delivered, acts as a positive reinforcer or, when not delivered (omitted or terminated), acts to decrease the probability of responses on which it is contingent. Conversely, I argue that an affectively negative or aversive stimulus (which produces an unpleasant state) acts operationally as a *punisher,* which instrumentally, when delivered, acts to decrease the probability of responses on which it is contingent or, when not delivered (escaped from or avoided), acts as a negative reinforcer.

The link being made between emotion and instrumental reinforcers is partly an operational link. Most people find that it is not easy to think of exceptions to the statements that emotions occur after rewards or punishers are given (sometimes continuing for long after the eliciting stimulus has ended, as in a mood state); or that rewards and punishers, but not other stimuli, produce emotional states. But the link is deeper than this, as we will see, in that the theory has been developed that genes specify primary reinforcers in order to encourage the animal to perform arbitrary actions to seek particular goals, thus increasing the probability of their own (the genes') survival into the next generation (Rolls, 1999a, 2005). The emotional states elicited by the reinforcers have a number of functions, described later, related to these processes.

This foundation has been developed (see Rolls, 1999a, 2005, 2000a, 1986a, 1986b, 1990) to show how a very wide range of emotions can be accounted for as a result of the operation of a number of factors, including the following, all of which can be manipulated to influence the elicitation of emotion:

1. The *reinforcement contingency* (e.g., whether reward or punishment is given or withheld; see Figure 9.1).

2. The *intensity* of the reinforcer (see Figure 9.1).
3. Any environmental stimulus might have a *number of different reinforcement associations.* (For example, a stimulus might be associated both with the presentation of a reward and of a punisher, allowing states such as conflict and guilt to arise.)[1]
4. Emotions elicited by stimuli associated with *different primary reinforcers* will be different.
5. Emotions elicited by *different secondary reinforcing stimuli* will be different from each other (even if the primary reinforcer is similar). For example, if two different people were each associated with the same primary reinforcer, then the emotions would be different. This is in line with my hypothesis that emotions consist of states elicited by reinforcers and that these states include whatever representations are needed for the eliciting stimulus, which could be cognitive, and the resulting mood change (Rolls, 1999a, 2005). Moods then may continue in the absence of the eliciting stimulus; or they can sometimes be produced, as in depression, in the absence of an eliciting stimulus, perhaps due to dysregulation in the system that normally enables moods to be long lasting (see Rolls, 1999a, 2005).
6. The emotion elicited can depend on whether an *active* or a *passive behavioral response* is possible. (For example, if an active behavioral response can occur to the omission of a positive reinforcer, then anger—a state that tends to lead to action—might be produced; but if only passive behavior is possible, then sadness, depression, or grief might occur.)

By combining these six factors, it is possible to account for, and also elicit, a very wide range of emotions (for elaboration, see Rolls, 1990, and Rolls, 1999a, 2005). It is also worth noting that emotions can be elicited by the recall of reinforcing events as much as by external reinforcing stimuli[2] and that cognitive processing (whether conscious or not) is important in many emotions, for very complex cognitive processing may be required to determine whether or not environmental events are reinforcing. Indeed, emotions normally consist of cognitive processing that analyzes the stimulus, determines its reinforcing valence, and elicits a mood change if the valence is positive or negative. In that an emotion is produced by a stimulus, philosophers say that emotions have an object in the world and that emotional states are intentional in that they are about something. We note that a mood or affective state may occur in the absence of an external stimulus, as in some types of depression, but that normally the mood or affective state is produced by an external stimulus, with the whole process of stimulus representation, evaluation in terms of reward or punishment, and the resulting mood or affect being referred to as emotion. The external stimulus may be perceived consciously, but stimuli that are not perceived consciously may also produce emotion. Indeed, there may be separate routes to action for conscious and unconscious stimuli (Rolls, 1999a, 2005, 2004b).

Three issues receive discussion here (see Rolls, 1999a, 2005, 2000a). One is that rewarding stimuli such as the taste of food are not usually described as producing emotional states (though there are cultural differences). It is useful here to separate rewards related to internal homeostatic need states associated with regulation of the internal milieu—for example, hunger and thirst—and to note that these rewards are not universally described as producing emotional states. In contrast, the great majority of rewards and punishers are external stimuli not related to internal need states such as hunger and thirst, and these stimuli do produce emotional responses. An example is fear produced by the sight of a stimulus that is about to produce pain.

A second issue is that some philosophers categorize fear, but not pain, in the example as an emotion. The distinction they make may be that primary (unlearned) reinforcers do not produce emotions, whereas secondary reinforcers (stimuli associated by stimulus-reinforcement learning with primary reinforcers) do. They describe the pain as a sensation. But neutral stimuli (such as a table) can produce sensations when touched. It accordingly seems to be much more useful to categorize stimuli according to whether they are reinforcing (in which case they produce emotions) or are not reinforcing (in which case they do not produce emotions). Clearly, there is a difference between primary reinforcers and learned reinforcers; but this is most precisely caught by noting that this is the difference, and that operationally it is whether a stimulus is reinforcing that determines whether it is related to emotion.

A third issue is that, as I am about to discuss, emotional states (i.e., those elicited by reinforcers) have many functions, and the implementations of only some of these functions by the brain are associated with emotional feelings, that is, with conscious emotional states (Rolls, 1999a, 2005). Indeed, there is evidence for interesting dissociations in some patients with brain damage between actions performed to reinforcing stimuli and what is subjectively reported. In this sense it is biologically and psychologically useful to consider emotional states to include more than those states associated with conscious feelings of emotion (Rolls, 1999a, 2005).

The Functions of Emotion

The functions of emotion also provide insight into the investigation, elicitation, and measurement of emotion in that different brain mechanisms may be involved in the outputs to behavior required for these different functions and that these different pathways do not always have the same activity. These functions, described more fully elsewhere (Rolls, 1990, 1999a, 2005), can be summarized as follows:

1. *The elicitation of autonomic responses* (e.g., a change in heart rate) *and endocrine responses* (e.g., the release of adrenaline). Although this is an important function of emotion, it

is the next function that is crucial in my evolutionary theory of why emotion is so important.

2. *Flexibility of behavioral responses to reinforcing stimuli.* Emotional (and motivational) states allow a simple interface between sensory inputs and action systems. The essence of this idea is that goals for behavior are specified by reward and punishment evaluation and that the innate goals are specified by genes. When an environmental stimulus has been decoded as a primary reward or punishment or (after previous stimulus-reinforcer association learning) as a secondary rewarding or punishing stimulus, then it becomes a goal for action. The animal can then perform any action (instrumental response) to obtain the reward or to avoid the punisher. The instrumental action, or "operant," is arbitrary and could consist of a left turn or a right turn to obtain the goal. It is in this sense that, by specifying goals and not particular actions, the genes are specifying a flexible route to action. This is in contrast to specifying a reflex response and is also in contrast to stimulus-response, or habit, learning in which a particular response to a particular stimulus is learned. It also contrasts with the elicitation of species-typical behavioral responses by sign-releasing stimuli (such as a baby herring gull pecking at a spot on the beak of the parent in order to be fed [Tinbergen, 1951], an action in which there is inflexibility of the stimulus and the response and which can be seen as a very limited type of brain solution to the elicitation of behavior). The emotional route to action is flexible not only because any action can be performed to obtain the reward or avoid the punishment but also because the animal can learn in as little as one trial that a reward or punishment is associated with a particular stimulus, in what is termed "stimulus-reinforcer association learning." It is because goals are specified by the genes, and not actions, that evolution has achieved a powerful way for genes to influence behavior without having to—rather inflexibly—specify particular responses. An example of a goal might be a sweet taste when hunger is present. We know that particular genes specify the sweet-taste receptors (Buck, 2000), and other genes must specify that the sweet taste is rewarding only when there is a homeostatic need state for food (Rolls, 1999a, 2005). Different goals or rewards, including social rewards, are specified by different genes, and one type of reward must not dominate the others if it is to succeed in the phenotype that carries the genes.

All of these gene-specified reinforcers are primary reinforcers. A preliminary list of these, which is subject to extension and revision but which is intended to convey the types of stimuli that may be primary reinforcers, is shown in Table 9.1.

Selecting between available rewards with their associated costs and avoiding punishers with their associated costs is a process that can take place both implicitly (unconsciously) and explicitly, using a language system to enable long-term plans to be made (Rolls, 1999a, 2005). These many different brain systems, some involving implicit evaluation of rewards and others explicit, verbal, conscious evaluation of rewards and planned long-term goals, must all enter into the selection systems for behavior (see Figure 9.2). These selector systems are poorly understood, but they might include a process of competition between all the competing calls on output and might involve structures such as the cingulate cortex and basal ganglia in the brain that receive from structures such as the orbitofrontal cortex and amygdala that compute the rewards (see Figure 9.2 and Rolls, 1999a, 2005).

3. *Emotion is motivating,* as just described. For example, fear learned by stimulus-reinforcement association provides the motivation for actions performed to avoid noxious stimuli. Genes that specify goals for action, for example, rewards, must as an intrinsic property make the animal motivated to obtain the reward; otherwise, it would not be a reward. Thus no separate explanation of motivation is required.

4. *Communication.* Monkeys, for example, may communicate their emotional states to others by making an open-mouthed threat to indicate the extent to which they are willing to compete for resources, and this may influence the behavior of other animals. This aspect of emotion was emphasized by Darwin (1872/1998) and has been studied more recently by Ekman (1982, 1993). He reviews evidence that humans can categorize facial expressions into the categories *happy, sad, fearful, angry, surprised,* and *disgusted* and that this categorization may operate similarly in different cultures. He also describes how the facial muscles produce different expressions. Many different types of gene-specified reward have been suggested by Rolls (1999a, 2005; see Table 9.1) and include not only genes for kin altruism but also genes to facilitate social interactions which may be to the advantage of those competent to cooperate, as in reciprocal altruism.

5. *Social bonding.* Examples of this are the emotions associated with the attachment of the parents to their young and the attachment of the young to their parents. The attachment of the parents to each other is also beneficial in species such as many birds and humans, in which the offspring are more likely to survive if both parents are involved in their care (Rolls, 1999a, 2005).

6. *The current mood state can affect the cognitive evaluation of events or memories* (see Oatley & Jenkins, 1996). This may facilitate continuity in the interpretation of the reinforcing value of events in the environment. A hypothesis that back projections from parts of the brain involved in emotion, such as the orbitofrontal cortex and amygdala, to higher perceptual and cognitive cortical areas implement this evaluation is described by Rolls (1999a, 2005) and is developed in a formal model of interacting attractor networks by Rolls and Stringer (2001). In this model, the weak back projections from the "mood" attractor can, because of associative connections formed when the perceptual and mood states were originally present, influence the states into which the perceptual attractor falls.

7. *Emotion may facilitate the storage of memories.* This occurs because episodic memory (i.e., one's memory of par-

Table 9.1
Some primary reinforcers and the dimensions of the environment to which they are tuned

Taste

Salt taste	+ reinforcer in salt deficiency
Sweet	+ reinforcer in energy deficiency
Bitter	− reinforcer, indicator of possible poison
Sour	− reinforcer
Umami	+ reinforcer, indicator of protein; produced by monosodium glutamate and inosine monophosphate; see Rolls, Critchley, Mason, & Wakeman, 1996
Tannic acid	− reinforcer, it prevents absorption of protein; found in old leaves; probably somatosensory rather than strictly gustatory; see Critchley and Rolls (1996c)

Odor

Putrefying odor	− reinforcer; hazard to health
Pheromones	+ reinforcer (depending on hormonal state)

Somatosensory

Pain	− reinforcer
Touch	+ reinforcer
Grooming	+ reinforcer; to give grooming may also be a primary reinforcer
Washing	+ reinforcer
Temperature	+ reinforcer if it tends to help maintain normal body temperature; otherwise −

Visual

Snakes, etc.	− reinforcer for, e.g., primates
Youthfulness	+ reinforcer, associated with mate choice
Beauty	+ reinforcer
Secondary sexual characteristics	+ reinforcers
Face expression	+ (e.g., smile) and − (e.g., threat) reinforcer
Blue sky, cover, open space	+ reinforcer, indicator of safety
Flowers	+ reinforcer (indicator of fruit later in the season?)

Auditory

Warning call	− reinforcer
Aggressive vocalization	− reinforcer
Soothing vocalization	+ reinforcer (part of the evolutionary history of music, which at least in its origins taps into the channels used for the communication of emotions)

Reproduction

Courtship	+ reinforcer
Sexual behavior	+ reinforcer (a number of different reinforcers, including a low waist-to-hip ratio, and attractiveness influenced by symmetry and being found attractive by members of the other sex, are discussed in Chapter 8)
Mate guarding	+ reinforcer for a male to protect his parental investment; jealousy results if his mate is courted by another male, because this may ruin his parental investment
Nest building	+ reinforcer (when expecting young)
Parental attachment	+ reinforcer
Infant attachment to parents	+ reinforcer
Crying of infant	− reinforcer to parents; produced to promote successful development

Other

Novel stimuli	+ reinforcers (encourage animals to investigate the full possibilities of the multidimensional space in which their genes are operating)
Sleep	+ reinforcer; minimizes nutritional requirements and protects from danger
Altruism to genetically related individuals (kin altruism)	+ reinforcer
Altruism to other individuals (reciprocal altruism)	+ reinforcer while the altruism is reciprocated in a 'tit-for-tat' reciprocation; − reinforcer when the altruism is not reciprocated

(continued)

Table 9.1

(continued)

Group acceptance	+ reinforcer (social greeting might indicate this)
Control over actions	+ reinforcer
Play	+ reinforcer
Danger, stimulation, excitement	+ reinforcer if not too extreme (adaptive because practice?)
Exercise	+ reinforcer (keeps the body fit for action)
Mind reading	+ reinforcer; practice in reading others' minds, which might be adaptive
Solving an intellectual problem	+ reinforcer (practice in which might be adaptive)
Storing, collecting	+ reinforcer (e.g. food)
Habitat preference, home, territory	+ reinforcer
Some responses	+ reinforcer (e.g. pecking in chickens, pigeons; adaptive because it is a simple way in which eating grain can be programmed for a relatively fixed type of environmental stimulus)
Breathing	+ reinforcer

Adapted from Rolls (1999a).

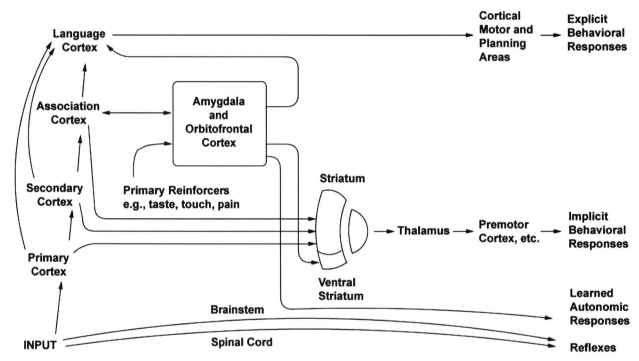

Figure 9.2. Dual routes to the initiation of action in response to rewarding and punishing stimuli. The inputs from different sensory systems to brain structures such as the orbitofrontal cortex and amygdala allow these brain structures to evaluate the reward- or punishment-related value of incoming stimuli or of remembered stimuli. The different sensory inputs enable evaluations within the orbitofrontal cortex and amygdala based mainly on the primary (unlearned) reinforcement value for taste, touch, and olfactory stimuli and on the secondary (learned) reinforcement value for visual and auditory stimuli. In the case of vision, the "association cortex," which outputs representations of objects to the amygdala and orbitofrontal cortex, is the inferior temporal visual cortex. One route for the outputs from these evaluative brain structures is via projections directly to structures such as the basal ganglia (including the striatum and ventral striatum) to enable implicit, direct behavioral responses to be made based on the reward- or punishment-related evaluation of the stimuli. The second route is via the language systems of the brain, which allow explicit (verbalizable) decisions involving multistep syntactic planning to be implemented. Adapted from Rolls, 1999a, Figure 9.4.

ticular episodes) is facilitated by emotional states. This may be advantageous in that storing many details of the prevailing situation when a strong reinforcer is delivered may be useful in generating appropriate behavior in situations with some similarities in the future. This function may be implemented by the relatively nonspecific projecting systems to the cerebral cortex and hippocampus, including the cholinergic pathways in the basal forebrain and medial septum, and the ascending noradrenergic pathways (see Rolls, 1999a, chapter 4; and Rolls & Treves, 1998). Emotion may also affect the storage of memories in that current emotional state may be stored with episodic memories, providing a mechanism for the current emotional state to affect which memories are recalled. A third way in which emotion may affect the storage of memories is by guiding the cerebral cortex in the representations of the world that are set up. For example, it may be useful for the visual system to build perceptual representations or analyzers that are different from each other if they are associated with different reinforcers and to be less likely to build these representations if they have no association with reinforcement. Ways in which back projections from parts of the brain that are important in emotion (such as the amygdala) to parts of the cerebral cortex could perform this function are discussed by Rolls and Treves (1998) and by Rolls and Stringer (2001).

8. *Another function of emotion* is that, by enduring for minutes or longer after a reinforcing stimulus has occurred, it may help to produce *persistent* and *continuing motivation* and *direction of behavior* to help achieve a goal or goals.

9. *Emotion may trigger the recall of memories* stored in neocortical representations. Amygdala back projections to the cortex could perform this for emotion in a way analogous to the way in which the hippocampus can implement the retrieval in the neocortex of recent (episodic) memories (Rolls & Stringer, 2001; Rolls & Treves, 1998). This is one way in which the memories recalled can be biased by mood states.

Reward, Punishment, and Emotion in Brain Design: An Evolutionary Approach

The implication of this approach to emotion and its evolution (Rolls, 1999a, 2005) is that operation by animals using reward and punishment systems that are tuned to dimensions of the environment that increase fitness provides a mode of operation that can work in organisms that evolve by natural selection. It is clearly a natural outcome of Darwinian evolution to operate using reward and punishment systems that are tuned to fitness-related dimensions of the environment if arbitrary responses are to be made by the animals, rather than just preprogrammed movements, such as taxes and reflexes. Is there any alternative to such a reward-punishment based system in this situation of evolution by natural selection? It is not clear that there is, if the genes are efficiently to control behavior by specifying the goals for actions. The argument is that genes can specify actions that will increase their fitness if they specify the goals for action. It would be very difficult for them in general to specify in advance the particular responses to be made to each of a myriad of different stimuli. This may be why we are built to work for rewards, to avoid punishers, and to have emotions and needs (motivational states). This view of brain design in terms of reward and punishment systems built by genes that gain their adaptive value by being tuned to a goal for action (Rolls, 1999a, 2005) offers, I believe, a deep insight into how natural selection has shaped many brain systems, and it is a fascinating outcome of Darwinian thought. This framework also provides a systematic approach to designing stimuli that elicit emotion.

Dual Routes to Action

It is suggested (Rolls, 1999a, 2005) that there are two types of routes to action performed in relation to reward or punishment in humans. Examples of such actions include emotional and motivational behavior.

The first route is via the brain systems that have been present in nonhuman primates such as monkeys and to some extent in other mammals for millions of years. These systems include the amygdala and, particularly well-developed in primates, the orbitofrontal cortex. These systems control behavior in relation to previous associations of stimuli with reinforcement. The computation that controls the action thus involves assessment of the reinforcement-related value of a stimulus. This assessment may be based on a number of different factors. One is the previous reinforcement history, which involves stimulus-reinforcement association learning using the amygdala and its rapid updating, especially in primates, using the orbitofrontal cortex. This stimulus-reinforcement association learning may involve quite specific information about a stimulus, for example, about the energy associated with each type of food by the process of conditioned appetite and satiety (Booth, 1985). A second factor is the current motivational state, for example, whether hunger is present, whether other needs are satisfied, and so forth. A third factor that affects the computed reward value of the stimulus is whether that reward has been received recently. If it was received recently but in small quantity, this may increase the reward value of the stimulus. This is known as incentive motivation, or the "salted peanut" phenomenon. The adaptive value of such a process is that this positive feedback of reward value in the early stages of working for a particular reward tends to lock the organism onto behavior being performed for that reward. This means that animals that are, for example, almost equally hungry and thirsty will show hysteresis in their choice of action, rather than continually switching from eating to drinking and back with each mouthful of water or food. This introduction of hysteresis into the reward evaluation system makes action selection a much more efficient process in a natural environment, for constantly switching between different types of behavior would be very costly if all the different rewards were not available in the same place at the same time. (For example, walking half a mile between a site where water was available and a site where food was available after every mouthful would be very inefficient.) The amygdala is one structure that may be involved in this increase in the reward value of stimuli early on in a series of presentations: Lesions of the amygdala (in rats) abolish the expression of this reward-incrementing process, which is normally evident in the increasing rate of working for a food reward early on in a meal, and amygdala lesions do impair the hysteresis normally built in to the food-water-switching mechanism (Rolls & Rolls, 1973). A fourth factor is the computed absolute value of the reward or punishment expected or being obtained from a stimulus, for example, the sweetness of the stimulus (set by evolution so that sweet stimuli will tend to be rewarding, because they are generally associated with energy sources); or the pleasantness of touch (set by evolution to be pleasant according to the extent to which it brings animals together, e.g., for sexual reproduction, for maternal behavior, and for grooming, and depending on the investment in time that the partner is willing to put into making the touch pleasurable), a sign that indicates the commitment and value for the partner of the relationship. After the reward value of the stimulus has been assessed in these ways, behavior is then initiated based on approach toward or withdrawal from the stimulus. A critical aspect of the behavior produced by this type of system is that it is aimed directly toward obtaining a sensed or expected reward by virtue of connections to brain systems, such as the basal ganglia, that are concerned with the initiation of actions (see Figure 9.2). The expectation may, of course, involve behavior to obtain stimuli associated with reward, which might even be present in a chain. This expectation is built by stimulus-reinforcement association learning in the amygdala and orbitofrontal cortex and reversed by learning in the orbitofrontal cortex, from which signals may reach the dopamine system (Rolls, 1999a, 2005).

With this first route, behavior is partly controlled by reward value of the outcome. At the same time, the animal may work for the reward only if the cost is not too high. Indeed, in the field of behavioral ecology, animals are often thought of as performing optimally on some cost-benefit curve (see, e.g., Krebs & Kacelnik, 1991). This does not at all mean that the animal thinks about the rewards and performs a cost-benefit analysis with a lot of thoughts about the costs, other rewards available and their costs, and so forth. Instead, it should be taken to mean that the system has evolved in such a way that the variations in the rewards that occur with the different energy densities or amounts of food and the delay before it is received can be used as part of the input to a mechanism that has also been built to track the costs of obtaining the food (e.g., energy loss in obtaining it, risk of predation, etc.) and then to select the current behavior that provides the most "net reward," given many such types of reward and the associated cost. Part of the value of having the computation expressed in this reward-minus-cost form is that there is then a suitable "currency," or net reward value, to enable the animal to select the behavior with currently the most net reward gain (or minimal aversive outcome).

The second route in humans involves a computation, with many "if . . . then" statements, to implement a plan to obtain a reward. In this case, the reward may actually be *deferred* as part of the plan, which might involve working first to obtain one reward and only then to work for a second, more highly valued reward, if such a strategy was thought to be optimal overall in terms of resource usage (e.g., time). In this case, syntax is required, because the many symbols (e.g., names of people) that are part of the plan must be correctly linked or bound. Such linking might be of the form: "if A does this, then B is likely to do this, and this will cause C to do this. . . ." The requirement of syntax for this type of planning implies that an output to language systems that at least can implement syntax in the brain is required for this type of planning (see Figure 9.2, and Rolls, 2004a). Thus the explicit language system in humans may allow working for deferred rewards by enabling use of a one-off, individual plan appropriate for each situation. Another building block for such planning operations in the brain may be the type of short-term memory in which the prefrontal cortex is involved. This short-term memory may be, for example in nonhuman primates, a memory of where in space a response has just been made. A development of this type of short-term-response memory system in humans to enable multiple short-term memories to be held in place correctly, preferably with the temporal order of the different items in the short-term memory coded correctly, may be another building block for the multiple-step "if . . . then" type of computation in order to form a multiple-step plan. Such short-term memories are implemented in the (dorsolateral and inferior convexity) prefrontal cortex of nonhuman primates and humans (see Goldman-Rakic, 1996; Petrides, 1996; Rolls & Deco, 2002) and may be part of the reason that prefrontal cortex damage impairs planning (see Rolls & Deco, 2002; Shallice & Burgess, 1996).

Of these two routes (see Figure 9.2), it is the second, involving syntax, that I suggested earlier is related to consciousness (see Rolls, 1999a, 2005).

The question then arises of how decisions are made in animals such as humans that have both the implicit, direct reward-based and the explicit, rational planning systems (see Figure 9.2). One particular situation in which the first, implicit, system may be especially important is a case in which rapid reactions to stimuli with reward or punishment value must be made, for then the direct connections from structures such as the orbitofrontal cortex to the basal ganglia may allow rapid actions. Another is a situation in which there may be too many factors to be taken into account easily by the explicit, rational planning system, so that therefore the implicit system may be used to guide action. In contrast, when the implicit system continually makes errors, it would then be beneficial for the organism to switch from automatic, direct action based on obtaining what the orbitofrontal cortex system decodes as being the most positively reinforcing choice currently available to the explicit, conscious control system that can evaluate, with its long-term planning algorithms, what action should be performed next. Indeed, it would be adaptive for the explicit system to regularly be assessing performance by the more automatic system and to switch itself on to control behavior quite frequently, as otherwise the adaptive value of having the explicit system would be less than optimal. Another factor that may influence the balance between control by the implicit and explicit systems is the presence of pharmacological agents such as alcohol, which may alter the balance toward control by the implicit system, may allow the implicit system to influence more the explanations made by the explicit system, and may, within the explicit system, alter the relative value it places on caution and restraint versus commitment to a risky action or plan.

There may also be a flow of influence from the explicit verbal system to the implicit system, in that the explicit system may decide on a plan of action or strategy and exert an influence on the implicit system that will alter the reinforcement evaluations made by and the signals produced by the implicit system. As an example, if a pregnant woman feels that she would like to escape a cruel mate but is aware that she may not survive in the jungle, then it would be adaptive if the explicit system could suppress some aspects of her implicit behavior toward her mate so that she does not give signals that she is displeased with her situation. (In the literature on self-deception, it has been suggested that unconscious desires may not be made explicit in consciousness—or may be actually repressed—so as not to compromise the explicit system in what it produces; see, e.g., Alexander, 1975, 1979; Trivers, 1976, 1985; and the review by Nesse & Lloyd, 1992). As another example, the explicit system might, because of its long-term plans, influence the implicit system to increase its response to, for example, a positive reinforcer. One way in which the explicit system might influence the implicit system is by setting up the conditions in which, for example, when a given stimulus (e.g. person) is present, positive reinforcers are given to facilitate stimulus-reinforcement association learning by the implicit system of the person receiving the positive reinforcers. Conversely, the implicit system may influence the explicit system, for example, by highlighting certain stimuli in the environment that are currently associated with reward to guide the attention of the explicit system to such stimuli.

However, there is often a conflict between these systems in that the first, implicit, system is able to guide behavior particularly to obtain the greatest immediate reinforcement, whereas the explicit system can potentially enable immediate rewards to be deferred and longer-term multistep plans to be formed. This type of conflict will occur in animals with a syntactic planning ability (as described earlier), that is, in humans and any other animals that have the ability to process a series of "if . . . then" stages of planning. This is a property of the human language system, and the extent to which it is a property of nonhuman primates is not yet fully clear. In any case, such conflict may be an important aspect of the operation of at least the human mind, because it is so essential for humans to correctly decide, at every moment, whether to invest in a relationship or a group that may offer long-term benefits or whether to directly pursue immediate benefits (Nesse & Lloyd, 1992).

Within this framework, we now consider the investigation of emotion using primary reinforcers, including the mechanisms by which previously neutral stimuli are associated by learning with primary reinforcers, and how this learning can be rapidly reversed.

The Use of Primary Reinforcers to Elicit Emotion

Taste Stimuli and Taste Processing in the Primate Brain

Pathways

Diagrams of the taste and related olfactory pathways in primates are shown in Figures 9.3 and 9.4. It is of particular interest that primates have a direct projection from the rostral part of the nucleus of the solitary tract (NTS) to the taste thalamus and thus to the primary taste cortex in the frontal operculum and adjoining insula, with no pontine taste area and associated subcortical projections as in rodents (Norgren, 1984; Pritchard et al., 1986). This emphasis on cortical processing of taste in primates may be related to the great development of the cerebral cortex in primates and to the advantage of using extensive and similar cortical analysis of inputs from every sensory modality before the analyzed representations from each modality are brought together in multimodal regions, as is documented later.

The Secondary Taste Cortex

A secondary cortical taste area in primates was discovered by Rolls, Yaxley, and Sienkiewicz (1990) in the caudolateral orbitofrontal cortex, extending several millimeters in front of the primary taste cortex. One principle of taste processing is that the tuning of neurons by the secondary taste cortex can become quite specific, with some neurons responding, for example, only to sweet taste. This specific tuning (especially when combined with olfactory inputs) helps to provide a basis for changes in appetite for some but not other foods eaten during a meal.

Five Prototypical Tastes, Including Umami

The primary and secondary taste cortices contain many neurons that respond best to each of the four classical prototypical tastes—sweet, salt, bitter, and sour (Rolls, 1997)—but also many neurons that respond best to umami tastants such

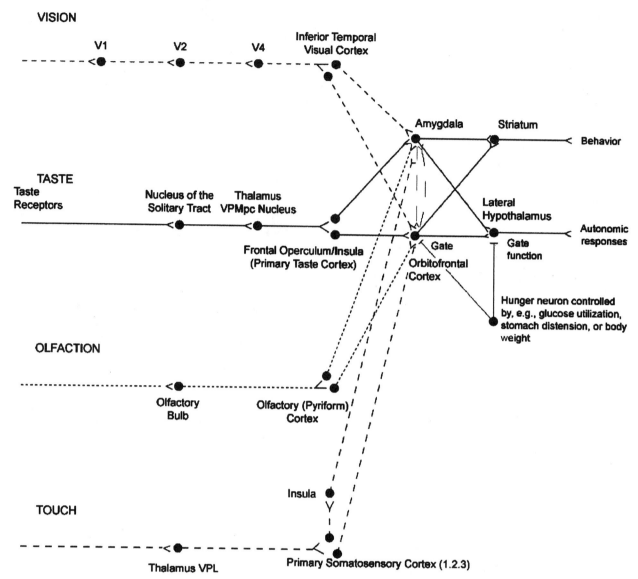

Figure 9.3. Schematic diagram showing some of the gustatory, olfactory, visual, and somatosensory pathways to the orbitofrontal cortex and amygdala and some of the outputs of the orbitofrontal cortex and amygdala. The secondary taste cortex and the secondary olfactory cortex are within the orbitofrontal cortex. V1 = primary visual cortex; V4 = visual cortical area.

as glutamate (which is present in many natural foods such as tomatoes, mushrooms, and milk; Baylis & Rolls, 1991) and inosine monophosphate (which is present in meat and some fish, such as tuna; Rolls, Critchley, Wakeman, & Mason, 1996). This evidence, taken together with the identification of a glutamate taste receptor (Chaudhari, Landin, & Roper, 2000), leads to the view that there are five prototypical types of taste information channels, with umami contributing, often in combination with corresponding olfactory inputs (Rolls, Critchley, Browning, & Hernadi, 1998), to the flavor of protein.

In humans studies using functional magnetic resonance imaging (fMRI) have shown that taste activates an area of the anterior insula/frontal operculum, which is probably the primary taste cortex, and part of the orbitofrontal cortex, which is probably the secondary taste cortex (Francis et al., 1999; O'Doherty, Rolls, et al., 2001). The orbitofrontal cortex taste area is distinct from areas activated by odors and by pleasant touch (Francis et al., 1999). It has been shown that within individual participants separate areas of the orbitofrontal cortex are activated by sweet (pleasant) and by salt (unpleasant) tastes (O'Doherty, Rolls, et al., 2001). Francis et al. (1999) also found activation of the human amygdala by the taste of glucose. Extending this study, O'Doherty, Rolls, et al. (2001) showed that the human amygdala was as much activated by the affectively pleasant taste of glucose as by the affectively negative taste of NaCl and thus provided evidence that the human amygdala is not

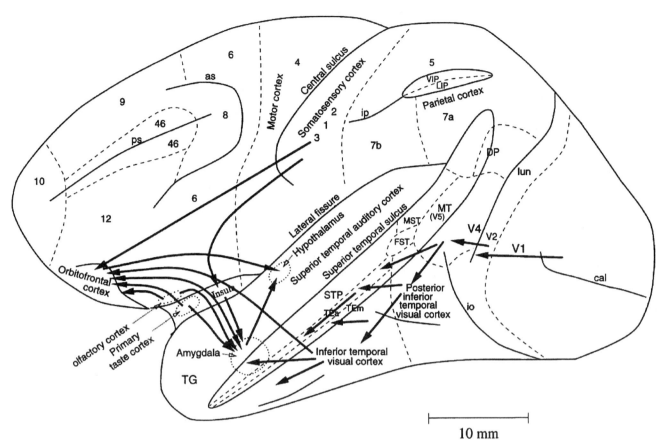

Figure 9.4. Some of the pathways involved in emotion described in the text are shown on this lateral view of the brain of the macaque monkey. Connections from the primary taste and olfactory cortices to the orbitofrontal cortex and amygdala are shown. Connections are also shown in the ventral visual system from V1 to V2, V4, the inferior temporal visual cortex, and so forth, with some connections reaching the amygdala and orbitofrontal cortex. Also shown are connections from the somatosensory cortical areas 1, 2, and 3 that reach the orbitofrontal cortex directly and via the insular cortex and that reach the amygdala via the insular cortex.

Abbreviations: as, arcuate sulcus; cal, calcarine sulcus; lun, lunate sulcus; ps, principal sulcus; io, inferior occipital sulcus; ip, intraparietal sulcus (which has been opened to reveal some of the areas it contains); FST, visual motion processing area; LIP, lateral intraparietal area; MST, visual motion processing area; MT, visual motion processing area (also called V5); STP, superior temporal plane; cortex; architectonic area including subareas (TEa and Tem) of high-order visual association cortex; TG, architectonic area in the temporal pole; V1, V2 and V4, visual areas 1, 2 and 4; VIP, ventral intraparietal area. The numerals refer to architectonic areas and have the following approximate functional equivalence: 1,2,3, somatosensory cortex (posterior to the central sulcus); 4, motor cortex; 5, superior parietal lobule; 7a, inferior parietal lobule, visual part; 7b, inferior parietal lobule, somatosensory part; 6, lateral premotor cortex; 8, frontal eye field; 12, part of orbitofrontal cortex; 46, dorsolateral prefrontal cortex.

especially involved in processing aversive as compared with rewarding stimuli. Another study has recently shown that umami taste stimuli, an exemplar of which is monosodium glutamate (MSG) and which capture what is described as the taste of protein, activate similar cortical regions of the human taste system to those activated by a prototypical taste stimulus, glucose (De Araujo, Kringelbach, Rolls, & Hobden, 2003). A part of the rostral anterior cingulate cortex (ACC) was also activated. When the nucleotide 0.005 M inosine

5'-monophosphate (IMP) was added to MSG (0.05 M), the BOLD (blood-oxygenation-level-dependent) signal in an anterior part of the orbitofrontal cortex showed supralinear additivity, and this may reflect the subjective enhancement of umami taste that has been described when IMP is added to MSG.

In neuroimaging studies of taste, it is helpful to use as a comparison in a "contrast" a tasteless solution, containing the main ionic components of saliva (e.g., 25 mM KCl + 2.5 mM

NaCO$_3$) to control for non-taste, somatosensory, inputs, as well as the single tongue movement that is made when the tastant is introduced into the mouth. The use of this was introduced in the studies described earlier and enabled us to go on to show that water in the mouth activates cortical taste areas, with the primary cortex representing taste independently of motivational state and the orbitofrontal cortex representing the reward value of taste, in that its activation by water when thirsty was decreased after water was consumed to satiety (De Araujo, Kringelbach, Rolls, & McGlone, 2003). The use of a single-event design enables subjective ratings made after every trial of the affective value of the stimulus to be correlated with the activation of different brain areas, and indeed in this study (De Araujo, Kringelbach, Rolls, & McGlone, 2003) and others (Kringelbach, O'Doherty, Rolls, & Andrews, 2003) it was found that the subjective pleasantness of the taste correlates with the activation of the orbitofrontal cortex produced by the stimulus. When brain areas such as the orbitofrontal cortex are imaged with fMRI, loss of signal may be a problem due to magnetic susceptibility introduced by the air-filled spaces in the frontal sinuses, and distortion may be introduced. We have developed a number of techniques to minimize these problems, including imaging in the coronal plane, minimizing voxel size in the plane of the imaging, using as high a gradient switching frequency as possible (960 Hz), using a short echo time of 25 ms (as described in the aforementioned studies), and using local shimming for the inferior frontal area using methods described by Wilson et al. (2002).

The Pleasantness of the Taste of Food

The modulation of the reward value of a sensory stimulus such as the taste of food by motivational state, for example, hunger, is one important way in which motivational behavior is controlled (Rolls, 1999a, 2005). The subjective correlate of this modulation is that food tastes pleasant when one is hungry and tastes hedonically neutral when one has eaten to satiety. We have found that the modulation of taste-evoked signals by motivation is not a property found in early stages of the primate gustatory system. The responsiveness of taste neurons in the nucleus of the solitary tract (Yaxley, Rolls, Sienkiewicz & Scott, 1985) and in the primary taste cortex (frontal opercular; Rolls, Scott, Sienkiewicz, & Yaxley, 1988; insular; Yaxley, Rolls, & Sienkiewicz, 1988) is not attenuated by feeding to satiety. In contrast, in the secondary taste cortex in the caudolateral part of the orbitofrontal cortex, it has been shown that the responses of the neurons to the taste of the glucose decreased to zero as a monkey ate it to satiety, during the course of which the behavior turned from avid acceptance to active rejection (Rolls, Sienkiewicz, & Yaxley, 1989). This modulation of responsiveness of the gustatory responses of the orbitofrontal cortex neurons by satiety could not have been due to peripheral adaptation in the gustatory system or to altered efficacy of gustatory stimulation after satiety was reached, because modulation of neuronal respon-

siveness by satiety was not seen at the earlier stages of the gustatory system, including the nucleus of the solitary tract, the frontal opercular taste cortex, and the insular taste cortex. The evidence that these neurons, in closely correlating with the decrease in preference for a food as it is eaten to satiety, encode the preference for a food has been supported by Schultz, Tremblay, and Hollerman (2000; see also Soelch et al., 2001).

Sensory-Specific Satiety

In the secondary taste cortex, it was also found that the decreases in the responsiveness of the neurons were relatively specific to the food with which the monkey had been fed to satiety. For example, in seven experiments in which a monkey was fed glucose solution, neuronal responsiveness decreased to the taste of the glucose but not to the taste of black currant juice (see the example in Figure 9.5). Conversely, in two experiments in which the monkey was fed to satiety with fruit juice, the responses of the neurons decreased to fruit juice but not to glucose (Rolls, Sienkiewicz, & Yaxley, 1989).

These findings provide evidence that the reduced acceptance of food that occurs when food is eaten to satiety and the reduction in the pleasantness of its taste (Cabanac, 1971; Rolls, Rolls, Rowe, & Sweeney, 1981; Rolls, Rowe, Rolls, Kingston, & Megson, 1981; Rolls, Rowe, & Rolls, 1982; B. J. Rolls, Rolls, & Rowe, 1983; Rolls & Rolls, 1997) are not produced by a reduction in the responses of neurons in the nucleus of the solitary tract or frontal opercular or insular gustatory cortices to gustatory stimuli. Indeed, after feeding to satiety, humans reported that the taste of the food on which they had been satiated tasted almost as intense as when they were hungry, though much less pleasant (E. T. Rolls, Rolls, & Rowe, 1983). This comparison is consistent with the possibility that activity in the frontal opercular and insular taste cortices, as well as the nucleus of the solitary tract, does not reflect the pleasantness of the taste of a food but rather its sensory qualities, independent of motivational state. On the other hand, the responses of the neurons in the caudolateral orbitofrontal cortex taste area and in the lateral hypothalamus (Rolls, Murzi, Yaxley, Thorpe, & Simpson, 1986) are modulated by satiety, and it is presumably in areas such as these that neuronal activity may be related to whether a food tastes pleasant and to whether the food should be eaten (see also Critchley & Rolls, 1996b; Rolls, 1996, 1999a, 2005, 2000b, 2000c; Rolls & Scott, 2003).

It is an important principle that the identity of a taste and its intensity are represented separately from its pleasantness. Thus it is possible to represent what a taste is and to learn about it even when we are not hungry.

The Representation of the Pleasantness of Odor in the Brain

It has been possible to investigate whether the olfactory representation found in the primate orbitofrontal cortex is af-

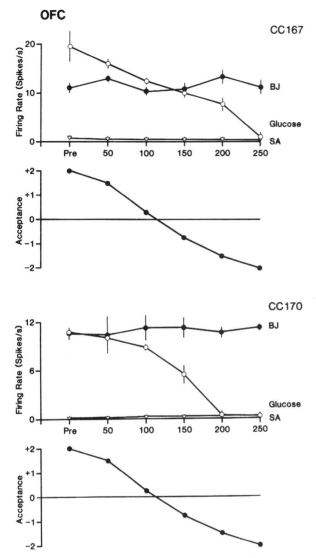

Figure 9.5. The effect of feeding to satiety with glucose solution on the responses of two neurons in the secondary taste cortex to the taste of glucose and of black currant juice (BJ). The spontaneous firing rate is also indicated (SA). The behavioral measure of the acceptance or rejection of the solution on a scale from +2 to –2 (see text) is shown below the neuronal response data for each experiment. A 20% glucose solution was used to feed to satiety. The monkey was fed 50 ml of the solution at each stage of the experiment, as indicated along the abscissa, until it was satiated, as shown by whether it accepted or rejected the solution. Pre = the firing rate of the neuron before the satiety experiment started. The values shown are the mean firing rate and its standard error. From Rolls, Sienkiewicz, & Yaxley, 1989.

fected by hunger and thus whether the pleasantness of odor is represented in the orbitofrontal cortex. In satiety experiments, Critchley and Rolls (1996b) showed that the responses of some olfactory neurons to a food odor are decreased during feeding to satiety with a food (e.g., fruit juice) containing that odor. In particular, seven of nine olfactory neurons that were responsive to the odors of foods,

such as black currant juice, were found to decrease their responses to the odor of the satiating food. The decrease was typically at least partly specific to the odor of the food that had been eaten to satiety, potentially providing part of the basis for sensory-specific satiety.

In humans, in addition to activation of the pyriform (olfactory) cortex (Poellinger et al., 2001; Sobel et al., 1998; Zald & Pardo, 1997), there is strong and consistent activation of the orbitofrontal cortex by olfactory stimuli (Francis et al., 1999; Zatorre, Jones-Gotman, Evans, & Meyer, 1992). In an investigation of where the pleasantness of olfactory stimuli might be represented in humans, O'Doherty et al. (2000) showed that the activation of an area of the orbitofrontal cortex to a banana odor was decreased (relative to a control vanilla odor) after bananas were eaten to satiety. Thus activity in a part of the human orbitofrontal cortex olfactory area is related to sensory-specific satiety, and this is one brain region in which the pleasantness of odor is represented.

We have also measured brain activation by whole foods before and after the food is eaten to satiety (Kringelbach, O'Doherty, Rolls, & Andrews, 2003). The aim is to show, using a food that has olfactory, taste, and texture components, the extent of the region that shows decreases when the food becomes less pleasant in order to identify the different brain areas in which the pleasantness of the odor, taste, and texture of food are represented. The foods eaten to satiety were either chocolate milk or tomato juice. A decrease in activation by the food eaten to satiety relative to the other food was found in the orbitofrontal cortex (Kringelbach et al., 2003) but not in the primary taste cortex. This study provided evidence that the pleasantness of the flavor of food is represented in the orbitofrontal cortex.

An important issue is whether there are separate regions of the human brain, discriminable with fMRI, that represent pleasant and unpleasant odors. To investigate this, we measured the brain activations produced by three pleasant and three unpleasant odors. The pleasant odors chosen were linalyl acetate (floral, sweet), geranyl acetate (floral), and alpha-ionone (woody, slightly food-related). The unpleasant odors chosen were hexanoic acid, octanol, and isovaleric acid. We found that they activated dissociable parts of the human brain (Rolls, Kringelbach, & De Araujo, 2003). Pleasant, but not unpleasant, odors were found to activate a medial region of the rostral orbitofrontal cortex (see Figure 9.6). The method that was used to demonstrate this utilized conjunction analysis to reveal brain regions activated by all the pleasant odors. Further, there was a correlation between the subjective pleasantness ratings of the six odors given during the investigation and activation of a medial region of the rostral orbitofrontal cortex (see Figure 9.7). This event-related approach—in which a correlation can be investigated between the BOLD signal in different brain regions and subjective ratings of its affective value—is a powerful way to investigate the neural basis of the affective states elicited by different types of stimuli. In contrast, a correlation between the subjective unpleasantness

Figure 9.6. The representation of pleasant and unpleasant odors in the human brain. *Above*: Group conjunction results for the three pleasant odors. Sagittal, horizontal, and coronal views are shown at the levels indicated, all including the same activation in the medial orbitofrontal cortex, OFC ($x, y, z = 0, 54, -12; Z = 5.23$). Also shown is activation for the three pleasant odors in the anterior cingulate cortex, ACC ($x, y, z = 2, 20, 32; Z = 5.44$). These activations were significant at $p < .05$ fully corrected for multiple comparisons. *Below*: Group conjunction results for the three unpleasant odors. The sagittal view (*left*) shows an activated region of the anterior cingulate cortex ($x, y, z = 0, 18, 36; Z = 4.42, p < .05$, S.V.C.). The coronal view (*right*) shows an activated region of the lateral orbitofrontal cortex ($-36, 27, -8; Z = 4.23, p < .05$ S.V.C.). All the activations were thresholded at $p < .00001$ to show the extent of the activations. From Rolls, Kringelbach, & De Araujo, 2003a. See color insert.

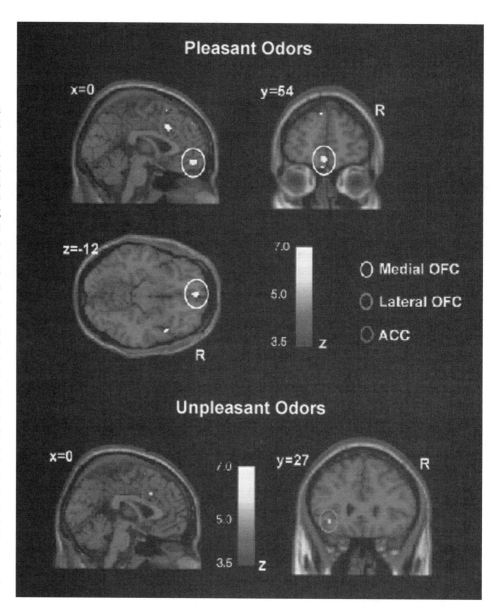

ratings of the six odors was found in regions of the left and more lateral orbitofrontal cortex. Activation was also found in the anterior cingulate cortex, with a middle part of the anterior cingulate activated by both pleasant and unpleasant odors (Figure 9.7), and in a more anterior part of the anterior cingulate cortex showing a correlation with the subjective pleasantness ratings of the odors. These results provide evidence for a hedonic map of the sense of smell in brain regions such as the orbitofrontal cortex and cingulate cortex.

The Representation of Flavor: Convergence of Olfactory and Taste Inputs

At some stage in taste processing, it is likely that taste representations are brought together with inputs from different modalities, for example, with olfactory inputs to form a rep-

resentation of flavor (see Figure 9.3). We found (Rolls & Baylis, 1994) that, of 112 single neurons in the orbitofrontal cortex taste areas that responded to any of these modalities, many were unimodal (taste, 34%; olfactory, 13%; visual, 21%) but were found in close proximity to each other. Some single neurons showed convergence, responding, for example, to taste and visual inputs (13%), taste and olfactory inputs (13%), and olfactory and visual inputs (5%). Some of these multimodal single neurons had corresponding sensitivities in the two modalities in that they responded best to sweet tastes (e.g. 1M glucose) and responded more in a visual discrimination task to the visual stimulus that signified sweet fruit juice than to the stimulus that signified saline or responded to sweet taste and, in an olfactory discrimination task, to fruit odor. The different types of neurons (unimodal in different modalities and multimodal) were fre-

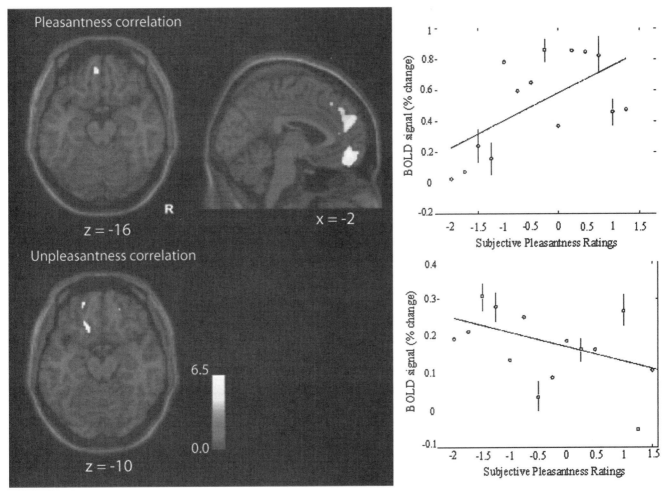

Figure 9.7. The representation of pleasant and unpleasant odors in the human brain. Random effects group analysis correlation analysis of the BOLD signal with the subjective pleasantness ratings. On the top left is shown the region of the mediorostral orbitofrontal (peak at [–2, 52, –10]; z = 4.28) correlating positively with pleasantness ratings, as well as the region of the anterior cingulate cortex in the top middle. On the far top right of the figure is shown the relation between the subjective pleasantness ratings and the BOLD signal from this cluster (in the medial orbitofrontal cortex at Y = 52), together with the regression line. The means and standard error of measurement across participants are shown. At the bottom of the figure is shown the regions of left more lateral orbitofrontal cortex (peaks at [–20, 54, –14]; z = 4.26 and [–16, 28, –18]; z = 4.08) correlating negatively with pleasantness ratings. On the far bottom right of the figure is shown the relation between the subjective pleasantness ratings and the BOLD signal from the first cluster (in the lateral orbitofrontal cortex at Y = 54), together with the regression line. The means and standard error across participants are shown. The activations were thresholded at p < .0001 for extent. From Rolls, Kringelbach, & De Araujo, 2003a. See color insert.

quently found close to one another in tracks made into this region, consistent with the hypothesis that the multimodal representations are actually being formed from unimodal inputs to this region.

It thus appears to be in these orbitofrontal cortex areas that flavor representations are built, where flavor is taken to mean a representation that is evoked best by a combination of gustatory and olfactory input. This orbitofrontal region does appear to be an important region for convergence, for

there is only a low proportion of bimodal taste and olfactory neurons in the primary taste cortex (Rolls & Baylis, 1994).

To investigate the rules underlying the affective representation of odors, many of which may not be primary reinforcers, investigations have been performed of whether the representation of odor depends on the taste (a primary reinforcer) with which it is associated during learning. Critchley and Rolls (1996a) showed that 35% of orbitofrontal cortex olfactory neurons categorized odors based on their taste association in an olfactory-to-taste-discrimination task. Rolls, Critchley, Mason, and Wakeman (1996) found that 68% of orbitofrontal cortex odor-responsive neurons modified their responses in some way following changes in the taste reward associations of the odorants during olfactory-taste discrimination learning and its reversal. In an olfactory discrimination experiment, if a lick response to one odor, the S+, is made, a drop of glucose taste reward is obtained; if incorrectly, a lick response is made to another odor, the S−, a drop of aversive saline is obtained. At some time in the experiment, the contingency between the odor and the taste is reversed, and when the "meaning" of the two odors alters, so does the behavior. It is of interest to investigate in which parts of the olfactory system the neurons show reversal, for where they do, it can be concluded that the neuronal response to the odor depends on the taste with which it is associated and does not depend primarily on the physicochemical structure of the odor. Full reversal of the neuronal responses was seen in 25% of the neurons analyzed. (In full reversal, the odor to which the neuron responded reversed when the taste with which it was associated reversed.) Extinction of the differential neuronal responses after task reversal was seen in 43% of these neurons. (These neurons simply stopped discriminating between the two odors after the reversal.) These findings demonstrate directly a coding principle in primate olfaction whereby the responses of some orbitofrontal cortex olfactory neurons are modified by and depend on the taste with which the odor is associated (Rolls, 2001, 2002a, 2002b).

It was of interest, however, that this modification was less complete, and much slower, than the modifications found for orbitofrontal visual neurons during visual-taste reversal (Rolls, Critchley, Mason, & Wakeman, 1996). This relative inflexibility of olfactory responses is consistent with the need for some stability in odor-taste associations to facilitate the formation and perception of flavors. In addition, some orbitofrontal cortex olfactory neurons did not code in relation to the taste with which the odor was associated (Critchley & Rolls, 1996a), so that there is also a taste-independent representation of odor in this region.

Imaging studies in humans are consistent with what has been discovered in macaques in that both taste and olfactory stimuli can activate parts of the orbitofrontal cortex and the adjoining most anterior part of the agranular insula but neither activates earlier cortical areas such as the taste insula (De Araujo, Rolls, Kringelbach, McGlone, & Phillips, 2003).

The Representation of the Affective Value of Somatosensory Stimuli in the Brain

Pleasant touch, pain, an environmental temperature that promotes homeostasis (Cabanac, 1971), and probably the texture of food are primary reinforcers. Some single neurons in the primate orbitofrontal cortex represent the viscosity of food in the mouth (shown using a methyl cellulose series in the range of 1–10,000 centiPoise), others encode the par-

ticulate quality of food in the mouth (Rolls, Verhagen, & Kadohisa, 2003), and others code for the texture of fat (Rolls, Critchley, Browning, Hernadi, & Lenard, 1999; Verhagen, Rolls, & Kadohisa, 2003). At least some of the neurons that encode the texture of fat encode its reward value, in that feeding to satiety with fat decreases their responses to fat to zero but not their responses to other rewards, such as glucose (Rolls et al., 1999). The temperature of oral stimuli are also represented in the macaque orbitofrontal cortex (Kadohisa, Rolls, & Verhagen, 2004). In designing investigations of the representation of temperature, it is of interest to include stimuli that are within the region transduced by different genetically identified receptor systems and to include chemical stimuli that activate the different classes of temperature receptor (Patapoutian, Peier, Story, & Viswanath, 2003).

Pleasant touch (administered in an fMRI experiment using velvet on the hand) and pain (administered using a stylus applied to the hand) produced relatively more activation of the human orbitofrontal cortex than a neutral (wood texture) stimulus, with the somatosensory cortex as a reference, providing evidence that the affective aspects of touch are represented in the orbitofrontal cortex (Rolls, O'Doherty, et al., 2003). The investigation of the brain pathways that transmit information from pain receptors is well developed (Craig, 2003), and, centrally, cingulate activation is invariably observed, but there is no full understanding of the brain regions that are crucial for the affective aspects of pain. Studies of patients with brain lesions suggest that the orbitofrontal cortex is one crucial area, as patients with lesions to this region may report that they can discriminate a stimulus as being painful, yet they do not have a strong affective response to it (Rolls, 1999a, 2005).

Visual and Auditory Stimuli That Are Primary Reinforcers

Although the majority of visual and auditory stimuli are not primary reinforcers, some, such as vocal and face expression, warning calls, and even correlates of attractiveness such as face symmetry, may be (see Table 9.1; Rolls, 1999a, 2005). To understand the neural basis of emotion, it is therefore of interest to investigate where in the brain the affective representations of these stimuli may be. It has been shown that patients with lesions of the orbitofrontal cortex can be impaired at identifying the face and/or voice expression in the absence of face or voice identity discrimination impairments (Hornak, Rolls, & Wade, 1996). This can occur even with lesions restricted to a medial and posterior part of the orbitofrontal cortex (Hornak et al., 2003) and occurs for a range of different face and voice expressions (such as happiness, sadness, anger, fear, etc.; Hornak et al., 2003; Rolls, 1999b). Face expression is encoded by neurons in the cortex in the anterior part of the superior temporal sulcus of macaques (Hasselmo, Rolls, & Baylis, 1989), but whether these neurons are perceptual analyzers that send information to the orbitofrontal cortex (Rolls, Critchley, Browning, & Inoue, 2006) and amygdala (Leonard, Rolls, Wilson, & Baylis, 1985), where the affective value is represented, or whether the affective value is represented in the cortex in the superior temporal sulcus is not yet known. The attractiveness of a face has a brain correlate in the BOLD response in orbitofrontal cortex (O'Doherty et al., 2003). Phillips and colleagues (1998) have produced evidence that activation of a part of the human insula occurs to the facial expression of disgust, although it is not clear whether this is the taste insula, as taste stimuli have not been used in the same series of experiments. It has analogously been suggested that amygdala activation occurs to fearful facial expressions and that lesions of the amygdala impair the identification of facial expressions of fear (Calder, Lawrence, & Young, 2001), although caution in ascribing particular emotions to particular brain regions is appropriate (Rolls 1999a, 2005, 1999b; Winston, O'Doherty, & Dolan, 2003).

Learning and Reversing Associations to Primary Reinforcers

Given the importance of rewards and punishers in emotion, the learning of associations from previously neutral stimuli to primary reinforcers is the type of learning that is fundamental in emotion. It is also very important that such associations can be rapidly and flexibly reversed. For example, in social interactions, even a short change in a facial expression may indicate that a change of behavior toward the person is appropriate. The processes that underlie this type of associative learning, which is stimulus-stimulus (in that the primary reinforcer is a stimulus), are therefore of considerable interest and clinical relevance.

Given the anatomical connections shown in Figure 9.3, there would not seem to be a basis in high-order visual cortical areas such as the inferior temporal visual cortex for associations between visual stimuli and primary reinforcers to be learned, as taste and somatosensory stimuli do not reach these cortical areas. This has been directly demonstrated: When the reward that a monkey normally obtains from licking a visual stimulus is altered in a visual discrimination task so that the monkey obtains only aversive salt, no alteration takes place in the responses of inferior temporal cortex neurons, which continue to fire to the physical stimulus to which they respond independently of its affective significance (Rolls, Aggelopoulos, & Zheng, 2003; Rolls, Judge, & Sanghera, 1977).

In contrast, some neurons in the macaque orbitofrontal cortex learn in as little as one trial to respond to a visual stimulus associated with a taste reward and can reverse this response when the reinforcement contingencies are reversed (Rolls, Critchley, Mason, & Wakeman, 1996; Thorpe, Rolls, & Maddison, 1983). These neurons reflect the reward (or affective) value of the visual stimulus in that they stop responding to the visual stimulus gradually as the monkey is fed to satiety (Critchley & Rolls, 1996b). Also consistent with this, lesions of the macaque orbitofrontal cortex impair stimulus-reward reversal learning and extinction (Butter, 1969; Iversen & Mishkin, 1970), and deficits in this type of learning are also found in humans after orbitofrontal cortex lesions (Rolls, Hornak, Wade, & McGrath, 1994; Hornak et al., 2004). In humans, activation of the orbitofrontal cortex can reflect quite abstract rewards, though in the end associated with primary reinforcers, such as monetary reward (medially) and loss (laterally; O'Doherty, Kringelbach, Rolls, Hornak, & Andrews, 2001). A probabilistic presentation of the magnitude of reward was used in this investigation and in a complementary investigation with the same task in patients with lesions of the orbitofrontal cortex (Hornak et al., 2004) so that the magnitude of the brain activation could be correlated in a single-event fMRI design with the amount of monetary reward or loss on each trial and to minimize the use of verbal strategies and encourage the use of implicit associative emotional learning processes. The special role of the orbitofrontal cortex in rapid reversal of stimulus-reinforcement associations is expressed also in the presence in the orbitofrontal cortex of neurons that respond when an expected reward is not obtained (Thorpe et al., 1983), and these can be called *reward error neurons* or *frustrative non-reward neurons*. They may have a special role in reversal (Deco & Rolls, 2005; Rolls, 2004a). Consistent with this evidence in macaques, Kringelbach and Rolls (2003) found activation of a lateral part of the human orbitofrontal cortex specifically when a changed facial expression was used as a cue to signal reversal in a visual discrimination task (see also Kringelbach & Rolls, 2004).

The amygdala receives information about primary reinforcers (such as taste and touch) and also about visual and auditory stimuli from higher cortical areas (such as the inferior temporal cortex) that can be associated by learning with primary reinforcers (Figure 9.3). Bilateral removal of the amygdala in monkeys produces tameness; a lack of emotional responsiveness; excessive examination of objects, often with the mouth; and eating of previously rejected items, such as meat (the Kluver-Bucy syndrome). In analyses of the bases of these behavioral changes, it has been observed that there are deficits in learning to associate stimuli with primary reinforcement, including both punishments and rewards (see Rolls, 2000c). The association-learning deficit is present when the associations must be learned from a previously neutral stimulus (e.g., the sight of an object) to a primary reinforcing stimulus (such as the taste of food). Further evidence that links the amygdala to reinforcement mechanisms includes the facts that monkeys will work in order to obtain electrical stimulation of the amygdala, that single neurons in the amygdala are activated by brain-stimulation reward of a number of different sites, and that some amygdala neurons respond mainly to rewarding stimuli and others to punishing stimuli (see Rolls, 1999a, 2005, 2000c). The association learning in the amygdala may be implemented by associatively modifiable synapses from visual and auditory neurons onto neurons that receive inputs from taste, olfactory, or somatosensory primary reinforcers (LeDoux, 1996, 2000). Consistent with this, Davis (2000) has found that at least one type of associative learning in the amygdala can be blocked by local application to the amygdala of an N-methyl-D-aspartate (NMDA) receptor blocker, which blocks long-term potentiation (LTP), a model of the synaptic changes that underlie learning (see Rolls & Treves, 1998). Davis (2000) used a fear-potentiated startle response as a measure of the conditioned fear. Consistent with the hypothesis that the learned incentive (conditioned reinforcing) effects of previously neutral stimuli paired with rewards are mediated by the amygdala acting through the ventral striatum, amphetamine injections into the ventral striatum enhanced the effects of a conditioned reinforcing stimulus only if the amygdala was intact (see also Everitt, Cardinal, Hall, Parkinson, & Robbins, 2000). In an imaging study in humans, Ploghaus et al. (2000) showed that fear conditioning produced activation of the amygdala. A difference between the amygdala and the orbitofrontal cortex in stimulus-reinforcement association learning may be that the rapid reversal of the associations may require the orbitofrontal cortex (Rolls, 1999a, 2005, 2002b), which may implement this rapid reversal at the neuronal level more efficiently (Rolls, 1999a, 2005; Rolls & Deco, 2002), perhaps because it has rule-based attractor networks that can be rapidly switched by nonreward (Deco & Rolls, 2005).

Acknowledgments

I have worked on some of the experiments described here with G. C. Baylis, L. L. Baylis, M. J. Burton, H. C. Critchley, M. E. Hasselmo, J. Hornak, M. Kringelbach, C. M. Leonard, F. Mora, J. O' Doherty, D. I. Perrett, M. K. Sanghera, T. R. Scott, S. J. Thorpe, and F. A. W. Wilson, and their collaboration and helpful discussions with or communications from M. Davies (Corpus Christi College, Oxford) and M. S. Dawkins are sincerely acknowledged. Some of the research described was supported by the Medical Research Council.

Notes

1. Rewards and punishers are generally external, that is, exteroceptive, stimuli, such as the sight, smell, and taste of food when one is hungry. Interoceptive stimuli, even when produced by rewards and punishers after ingesting foods and including digestive processes and the reduction of the drive (hunger) state, are not good reinforcers. Some of the evidence for this is that the taste of food is an excellent reinforcer, but placing food into the stomach is not. This important distinction is described by Rolls (1999a, 2005).

2. Part of the basis for this is that when memories are recalled, top-down connections into the higher perceptual and cognitive cortical areas lead to reinstatement of activity in those areas (Rolls & Deco, 2002; Treves & Rolls, 1994), which in turn can produce emotional states via onward connections to the orbitofrontal cortex and amygdala (Rolls, 1999a, 2005).

References

Alexander, R. D. (1975). The search for a general theory of behaviour. *Behavioral Sciences, 20,* 77–100.

Alexander, R. D. (1979). *Darwinism and human affairs.* Seattle: University of Washington Press.

Baylis, L. L., & Rolls, E. T. (1991). Responses of neurons in the primate taste cortex to glutamate. *Physiology and Behaviour, 49,* 973–979.

Booth, D. A.(1985). Food-conditioned eating preferences and aversions with interoceptive elements: Learned appetites and satieties. *Annals of the New York Academy of Sciences, 443,* 22–37.

Buck, L. (2000). Smell and taste: The chemical senses. In E. R. Kandel, J. H. Schwartz, & T. H. Jessel (Eds.), *Principles of neural science* (4th ed., pp. 625–647). New York: McGraw-Hill.

Butter, C. M. (1969). Perseveration in extinction and in discrimination reversal tasks following selective prefrontal ablations in *Macaca mulatta. Physiology and Behavior, 4,* 163–171.

Cabanac, M. (1971). Biological role of pleasure. *Science, 173,* 1103–1107.

Calder, A. J., Lawrence, A. D., & Young, A. W. (2001). Neuropsychology of fear and loathing. *Nature Reviews. Neuroscience, 2,* 352–363.

Chaudhari, N., Landin, A.M., & Roper, S. D. (2000). A metabotropic glutamate receptor variant functions as a taste receptor. *Nature Neuroscience, 3,* 113–119.

Craig, A. D. (2003). Pain mechanisms: labelled lines versus convergence in central processing. *Annual Review of Neuroscience, 26,* 1–30.

Critchley, H. D., & Rolls, E. T. (1996a). Olfactory neuronal responses in the primate orbitofrontal cortex: Analysis in an olfactory discrimination task. *Journal of Neurophysiology, 75,* 1659–1672.

Critchley, H. D., & Rolls, E. T. (1996b). Hunger and satiety modify the responses of olfactory and visual neurons in the primate orbitofrontal cortex. *Journal of Neurophysiology, 75,* 1673–1686.

Critchley, H. D. & Rolls, E. T. (1996c). Responses of primate taste cortex neurons to the astringent tastant tannic acid. *Chemical Senses, 21,* 135–145.

Darwin, C. (1998). *The expression of the emotions in man and animals* (3rd ed., P. Ekman, Ed.). Chicago: University of Chicago Press. (Original work published 1872)

Davis, M. (2000). The role of the amygdala in conditioned and unconditioned fear and anxiety. In J. P. Aggleton (Ed.), *The amygdala: A functional analysis* (2nd ed., pp. 213–228). Oxford, UK: Oxford University Press.

De Araujo, I. E. T., Kringelbach, M. L., Rolls, E. T., & Hobden, P. (2003). Representation of umami taste in the human brain. *Journal of Neurophysiology, 90,* 313–319.

De Araujo, I. E. T., Kringelbach, M. L., Rolls, E. T., & McGlone, F. (2003). Human cortical responses to water in the mouth, and the effects of thirst. *Journal of Neurophysiology, 90,* 1865–1876.

De Araujo, I. E. T., Rolls, E. T., Kringelbach, M. L., McGlone, F., & Phillips, N. (2003). Taste-olfactory convergence, and the representation of the pleasantness of flavour, in the human brain. *European Journal of Neuroscience, 18,* 2059–2068.

Deco, G., & Rolls, E. T. (2005). Synaptic and spiking dynamics underlying reward reversal in the orbitofrontal cortex. *Cerebral Cortex, 15,* 15–30.

Dickinson, A. (1980). *Contemporary animal learning theory.* Cambridge, UK: Cambridge University Press.

Ekman, P. (1982). *Emotion in the human face* (2nd ed.). Cambridge, UK: Cambridge University Press.

Ekman, P. (1993). Facial expression and emotion. *American Psychologist, 48,* 384–392.

Everitt, B. J., Cardinal, R. N., Hall, J., Parkinson, J. A., & Robbins, T. W. (2000). Differential involvement of amygdala subsystems in appetitive conditioning and drug addiction. In J. P. Aggleton (Ed.), *The amygdala: A functional analysis* (2nd ed., pp. 353–390). Oxford, UK: Oxford University Press.

Francis, S., Rolls, E. T., Bowtell, R., McGlone, F., O'Doherty, J., Browning, A., et al. (1999). The representation of pleasant touch in the brain and its relationship with taste and olfactory areas. *Neuroreport, 10,* 453–459.

Goldman-Rakic, P. S. (1996). The prefrontal landscape: Implications of functional architecture for understanding human mentation and the central executive. *Philosophical Transactions of the Royal Society of London: Series B. Biological Sciences, 351,* 1445–1453.

Gray, J. A. (1975). *Elements of a two-process theory of learning.* London: Academic Press.

Gray, J. A. (1987). *The psychology of fear and stress* (2nd ed.). Cambridge, UK: Cambridge University Press.

Hasselmo, M. E., Rolls, E. T., & Baylis, G. C. (1989). The role of expression and identity in the face-selective responses of neurons in the temporal visual cortex of the monkey. *Behavioural Brain Research, 32,* 203–218.

Hornak, J., Bramham, J., Rolls, E. T., Morris, R. G., O'Doherty, J., Bullock, P. R., et al. (2003). Changes in emotion after circumscribed surgical lesions of the orbitofrontal and cingulate cortices. *Brain, 126,* 1691–1712.

Hornak, J., O'Doherty, J., Bramham, J., Rolls, E. T., Morris, R. G., Bullock, P. R., et al. (2004). Reward-related reversal learning after surgical excisions in orbitofrontal and dorsolateral prefrontal cortex in humans. *Journal of Cognitive Neuroscience, 16,* 463–478.

Hornak, J., Rolls, E. T., & Wade, D. (1996). Face and voice expression identification in patients with emotional and behavioural changes following ventral frontal lobe damage. *Neuropsychologia, 34,* 247–261.

Iversen, S. D., & Mishkin, M. (1970). Perseverative interference in monkey following selective lesions of the inferior prefrontal convexity. *Experimental Brain Research, 11,* 376–386.

Kadohisa, M., Rolls, E. T., & Verhagen, J. V. (2004). Orbitofrontal cortex neuronal representation of temperature and capsaicin in the mouth. *Neuroscience, 127,* 207–221.

Krebs, J. R., & Kacelnik, A. (1991). Decision making. In J. R. Krebs & N. B. Davies (Eds.), *Behavioural ecology* (3rd ed., pp. 105–136). Oxford, UK: Blackwell.

Kringelbach, M. L., O'Doherty, J., Rolls, E. T., & Andrews, C. (2003). Activation of the human orbitofrontal cortex to a liquid food stimulus is correlated with its subjective pleasantness. *Cerebral Cortex, 13,* 1064–1071.

Kringelbach, M. L., & Rolls, E. T. (2003). Neural correlates of rapid reversal learning in a simple model of human social interaction. *NeuroImage, 20,* 1371–1383.

Kringelbach, M. L., & Rolls, E. T. (2004) The functional neuroanatomy of the human orbitofrontal cortex: Evidence from neuroimaging and neuropsychology. *Progress in Neurobiology, 72,* 341–372.

LeDoux, J. E. (1996). *The emotional brain.* New York: Simon & Schuster.

LeDoux, J. E. (2000). The amygdala and emotion: A view through fear. In J. P. Aggleton (Ed.), *The amygdala: A functional analysis* (2nd ed., pp. 289–310). Oxford, UK: Oxford University Press.

Leonard, C. M., Rolls, E. T., Wilson, F. A. W., & Baylis, G. C. (1985). Neurons in the amygdala of the monkey with responses selective for faces. *Behavioural Brain Research, 15,* 159–176.

Lieberman, D. A. (2000). *Learning* (3rd ed.). Belmont, CA: Wadsworth.

Mackintosh, N. J. (1983). *Conditioning and associative learning.* Oxford, UK: Oxford University Press.

Millenson, J. R. (1967). *Principles of behavioral analysis.* New York: Macmillan.

Nesse, R. M., & Lloyd, A. T. (1992). The evolution of psychodynamic mechanisms. In J. H. Barlow, L. Cosmides, & J. Tooby (Eds.), *The adapted mind* (pp. 601–624). New York: Oxford University Press.

Norgren, R. (1984). Central neural mechanisms of taste. In I. Darien-Smith (Series Ed.), J. Brookhart, & V. B. Mountcastle (Vol. Eds.), *Handbook of physiology: Vol. III. The nervous system: Sensory processes* (pp. 1087–1128). Washington, DC: American Physiological Society.

O'Doherty, J., Kringelbach, M. L., Rolls, E. T., Hornak, J., & Andrews, C. (2001). Abstract reward and punishment representations in the human orbitofrontal cortex. *Nature Neuroscience, 4,* 95–102.

O'Doherty, J., Rolls, E. T., Francis, S., Bowtell, R., & McGlone, F. (2001). The representation of pleasant and aversive taste in the human brain. *Journal of Neurophysiology, 85,* 1315–1321.

O'Doherty, J., Rolls, E. T., Francis, S., Bowtell, R., McGlone, F., Kobal, G., et al. (2000). Sensory-specific satiety related olfactory activation of the human orbitofrontal cortex. *Neuroreport, 11,* 893–897.

O'Doherty, J., Winston, J., Critchley, H., Perrett, D., Burt, D. M., & Dolan, J. (2003). Beauty in a smile: The role of medial orbitofrontal cortex in facial attractiveness. *Neuropsychologia, 41,* 147–155.

Oatley, K., & Jenkins, J. M. (1996) *Understanding emotions.* Oxford: Blackwell.

Patapoutian, A., Peier, A. M., Story, G. M., & Viswanath, V. (2003). ThermoTRP channels and beyond: Mechanisms of temperature sensation. *Nature Reviews. Neuroscience, 4,* 529–539.

Petrides, M. (1996). Specialized systems for the processing of mnemonic information within the primate frontal cortex. *Philosophical Transactions of the Royal Society of London: Series B. Biological Sciences, 351,* 1455–1462.

Phillips, M. L., Young, A. W., Scott, S. K., Calder, A. J., Andrew, C., Giampetro, V., et al. (1998). *Proceedings of the Royal Society of London: Series B. Biological Sciences, 265,* 1809–1817.

Ploghaus, A., Tracey, I., Clare, S., Gati, J. S., Rawlins, J. N., & Patthews, P. M. (2000). Learning about pain: The neural substrate of the prediction error for aversive events. *Proceedings of the National Academy of Sciences of the USA, 97,* 9281–9286.

Poellinger, A., Thomas, R., Lio, P., Lee, A., Makris, N., Rosen, B. R., et al. (2001). Activation and habituation in olfaction: An fMRI study. *NeuroImage, 13,* 547–560.

Pritchard, T. C., Hamilton, R. B., Morse, J. R., & Norgren, R. (1986). Projections of thalamic gustatory and lingual areas in the monkey, *Macaca fascicularis. Journal of Comparative Neurology, 244,* 213–228.

Rolls, B. J., & Rolls, E. T. (1973). Effects of lesions in the basolateral amygdala on fluid intake in the rat. *Journal of Comparative and Physiological Psychology, 83,* 240–247.

Rolls, B. J., Rolls, E. T., & Rowe, E. A. (1983). Body fat control and obesity. *Behavioral and Brain Sciences, 4,* 744–745.

Rolls, B. J., Rolls, E. T., Rowe, E. A., & Sweeney, K. (1981). Sensory specific satiety in man. *Physiology and Behavior, 27,* 137–142.

Rolls, B. J., Rowe, E. A., & Rolls, E. T. (1982). How sensory properties of foods affect human feeding behavior. *Physiology and Behavior, 29,* 409–417.

Rolls, B. J., Rowe, E. A., Rolls, E. T., Kingston. B., & Megson, A. (1981). Variety in a meal enhances food intake in man. *Physiology and Behavior, 26,* 215–221.

Rolls, E. T. (1986a). Neural systems involved in emotion in primates. In R. Plutchik & H. Kellerman (Eds.), *Emotion: Theory, research, and experience: Vol. 3. Biological foundations of emotion* (pp. 125–143). New York: Academic Press.

Rolls, E. T. (1986b). A theory of emotion, and its application to understanding the neural basis of emotion In Y. Oomura (Ed.), *Emotions: Neural and chemical control* (pp. 325–344). Tokyo: Japan Scientific Societies Press.

Rolls, E. T. (1990). A theory of emotion and its application to understanding the neural basis of emotion. *Cognition and Emotion, 4,* 161–190.

Rolls, E. T. (1996). The orbitofrontal cortex. *Philosophical Transactions of the Royal Society of London: Series B. Biological Sciences, 351,* 1433–1444.

Rolls, E. T. (1997). Taste and olfactory processing in the brain and its relation to the control of eating. *Critical Reviews in Neurobiology, 11,* 263–287.

Rolls, E. T. (1999a). *The brain and emotion.* Oxford, UK: Oxford University Press.

Rolls, E. T. (1999b). The functions of the orbitofrontal cortex. *Neurocase, 5,* 301–312.

Rolls, E. T. (2000a). Précis of the brain and emotion. *Behavioral and Brain Sciences, 23,* 177–234.

Rolls, E. T. (2000b). The orbitofrontal cortex and reward. *Cerebral Cortex, 10,* 284–294.

Rolls, E. T. (2000c). Neurophysiology and functions of the primate amygdala, and the neural basis of emotion. In J. P. Aggleton (Ed.), *The amygdala: A functional analysis* (2nd ed., pp. 447–478). Oxford, UK: Oxford University Press.

Rolls, E. T. (2001). The rules of formation of the olfactory representations found in the orbitofrontal cortex olfactory areas in primates. *Chemical Senses, 26,* 595–604.

Rolls, E. T. (2002a). The cortical representation of taste and smell. In G. Rouby, B. Schaal, D. Dubois, R. Gervais, & A. Holley (Eds.), *Olfaction* (pp. 367–388). New York: Cambridge University Press.

Rolls, E. T. (2002b). The functions of the orbitofrontal cortex. In D. T. Stuss & R. T. Knight (Eds.), *Principles of frontal lobe function* (pp. 354–375). New York: Oxford University Press.

Rolls, E. T. (2004a) The functions of the orbitofrontal cortex. *Brain and Cognition, 55,* 11–29.

Rolls, E. T. (2004b). A higher order syntactic thought (HOST) theory of consciousness. In R.J. Gennaro (Ed.), *Higher order theories of consciousness* (pp. 137–172). Amsterdam: John Benjamins.

Rolls, E. T. (2005). *Emotion Explained.* Oxford, UK: Oxford University Press.

Rolls, E. T., Aggelopoulos, N. C., & Zheng, F. (2003). The receptive fields of inferior temporal cortex neurons in natural scenes. *Journal of Neuroscience, 23,* 339–348.

Rolls, E. T., & Baylis, L. L. (1994). Gustatory, olfactory and visual convergence within the primate orbitofrontal cortex. *Journal of Neuroscience, 14,* 5437–5452.

Rolls, E. T., Critchley, H. D., Browning, A., & Hernadi, I. (1998). The neurophysiology of taste and olfaction in primates, and umami flavor. *Annals of the New York Academy of Sciences, 855,* 426–437.

Rolls, E. T., Critchley, H. D., Browning, A. S., Hernadi, A., & Lenard, L. (1999). Responses to the sensory properties of fat of neurons in the primate orbitofrontal cortex. *Journal of Neuroscience, 19,* 1532–1540.

Rolls, E. T., Critchley, H. D., Browning, A. S., & Inoue, K. (2006). Face-selective and auditory neurons in the primate orbitofrontal cortex. *Experimental Brain Research, 170,* 74–87.

Rolls, E. T., Critchley, H., Mason, R., & Wakeman, E. A. (1996). Orbitofrontal cortex neurons: Role in olfactory and visual association learning. *Journal of Neurophysiology, 75,* 1970–1981.

Rolls, E. T., Critchley, H., Wakeman, E. A., & Mason, R. (1996). Responses of neurons in the primate taste cortex to the glutamate ion and to inosine 5'-monophosphate. *Physiology and Behavior, 59,* 991–1000.

Rolls, E. T., & Deco, G. (2002). *Computational neuroscience of vision.* Oxford, UK: Oxford University Press.

Rolls, E. T., Hornak, J., Wade, D., & McGrath, J. (1994). Emotion-related learning in patients with social and emotional changes associated with frontal lobe damage. *Journal of Neurology, Neurosurgery, and Psychiatry, 57,* 1518–1524.

Rolls, E. T., Judge, S. J., & Sanghera, M. (1977). Activity of neurones in the inferotemporal cortex of the alert monkey. *Brain Research, 130,* 229–238.

Rolls, E. T., Kringelbach, M .L., & De Araujo, I. E. T. (2003). Different representations of pleasant and unpleasant odors in the human brain. *European Journal of Neuroscience, 18,* 695–703.

Rolls, E. T., Murzi, E., Yaxley, S., Thorpe, S. J., & Simpson, S. J. (1986). Sensory-specific satiety: Food-specific reduction in responsiveness of ventral forebrain neurons after feeding in the monkey. *Brain Research, 368,* 79–86.

Rolls, E. T., O'Doherty, J., Kringelbach, M. L., Francis, S., Bowtell, R., & McGlone, F. (2003). Representations of pleasant and painful touch in the human orbitofrontal and cingulate cortices. *Cerebral Cortex, 13,* 308–317.

Rolls, E. T., Rolls, B. J., & Rowe, E. A. (1983). Sensory-specific and motivation-specific satiety for the sight and taste of food and water in man. *Physiology and Behavior, 30,* 185–192.

Rolls, E. T., & Rolls, J. H. (1997). Olfactory sensory-specific satiety in humans. *Physiology and Behavior, 61,* 461–473.

Rolls, E. T., & Scott, T. R. (2003). Central taste anatomy and neurophysiology. In R. L. Doty (Ed.), *Handbook of olfaction and gustation* (2nd ed., pp. 679–705). New York: Dekker.

Rolls, E. T., Scott, T. R., Sienkiewicz, Z. J., & Yaxley, S. (1988). The responsiveness of neurones in the frontal opercular gustatory cortex of the macaque monkey is independent of hunger. *Journal of Physiology, 397,* 1–12.

Rolls, E. T., Sienkiewicz, Z. J., & Yaxley, S. (1989). Hunger modulates the responses to gustatory stimuli of single neurons in the orbitofrontal cortex. *European Journal of Neuroscience, 1,* 53–60.

Rolls, E. T., & Stringer, S. M. (2001). A model of the interaction between mood and memory. *Network: Computation in Neural Systems, 12,* 89–109.

Rolls, E. T., & Treves, A. (1998). *Neural networks and brain function.* Oxford, UK: Oxford University Press.

Rolls, E. T., Verhagen, J. V., & Kadohisa, M. (2003). Representations of the texture of food in the primate orbitofrontal cortex: Neurons responding to viscosity, grittiness, and capsaicin. *Journal of Neurophysiology, 90,* 3711–3724.

Rolls, E. T., Yaxley, S., & Sienkiewicz, Z. J. (1990). Gustatory responses of single neurons in the orbitofrontal cortex of the macaque monkey. *Journal of Neurophysiology, 64,* 1055–1066.

Schultz, W., Tremblay, L., & Hollerman, J. R. (2000). Reward processing in primate orbitofrontal cortex and basal ganglia. *Cerebral Cortex, 10,* 272–284.

Shallice, T., & Burgess, P. (1996). The domain of supervisory processes and temporal organization of behaviour. *Philosophical Transactions of the Royal Society of London: Series B. Biological Sciences, 351,* 1405–1411.

Sobel, N., Prabhakaran, V., Desmond, J. E., Glover, G. H., Goode, R. L., Sullivan, E. V., et al. (1998). Sniffing and smelling: separate subsystems in the human olfactory cortex. *Nature, 392,* 282–286.

Soelch, M., Leenders, K. L., Chevalley, A. F., Missimer, J., Kunig, G., Magyar, S., et al. (2001). Reward mechanisms in the brain and their role in dependence: Evidence from neurophysiological and neuroimaging studies. *Brain Research Reviews, 36,* 139–149.

Thorpe, S. J., Rolls, E. T., & Maddison, S. (1983). The orbitofrontal cortex: Neuronal activity in the behaving monkey. *Experimental Brain Research, 49,* 93–115.

Tinbergen, N. (1951). *The study of instinct.* Oxford, UK: Clarendon Press.

Treves, A., & Rolls, E. T. (1994). A computational analysis of the role of the hippocampus in memory. *Hippocampus, 4,* 374–391.

Trivers, R. L. (1976). Foreword. In R. Dawkins, *The selfish gene.* Oxford, UK: Oxford University Press.

Trivers, R. L. (1985). *Social evolution.* Menlo Park, CA: Benjamin Cummings.

Verhagen, J. V., Rolls, E. T., & Kadohisa, M. (2003). Neurons in the primate orbitofrontal cortex respond to fat texture independently of viscosity. *Journal of Neurophysiology, 90,* 1514–1525.

Weiskrantz, L. (1968). Emotion. In L. Weiskrantz (Ed.), *Analysis of behavioral change* (pp. 50–90). New York: Harper & Row.

Wilson, J. L., Jenkinson, M., de Araujo, I., Kringelbach, M. L., Rolls, E. T., Jezzard, P. (2002). Fast, fully automated global and local magnetic field optimisation for fMRI of the human brain. *NeuroImage, 17,* 967–976.

Winston, J. S., O'Doherty, J., & Dolan, R. J. (2003). Common and distinct neural responses during direct and incidental processing of multiple facial emotions. *NeuroImage, 20,* 84–97.

Yaxley, S., Rolls, E. T., & Sienkiewicz, Z. J. (1988). The responsiveness of neurones in the insular gustatory cortex of the macaque monkey is independent of hunger. *Physiology and Behavior, 42,* 223–229.

Yaxley, S., Rolls, E. T., Sienkiewicz, Z. J., & Scott, T. R. (1985). Satiety does not affect gustatory activity in the nucleus of the solitary tract of the alert monkey. *Brain Research, 347,* 85–93.

Zald, D. H., & Pardo, J. V. (1997). Emotion, olfaction, and the human amygdala: Amygdala activation during aversive olfactory stimulation. *Proceedings of the National Academy of Sciences of the USA, 94,* 4119–4124.

Zatorre, R. J., Jones-Gotman, M., Evans, A. C., & Meyer, E. (1992). Functional localization and lateralisation of the human olfactory cortex. *Nature, 360,* 339–340.

Robert W. Levenson

Emotion Elicitation With Neurological Patients

This chapter presents a set of issues and methods related to studying emotional functioning in neurological patients. It incorporates discussions of the advantages and disadvantages of two primary paradigms for studying neural substrates of human emotion (patient studies and activation studies); the importance of studying multiple emotion processes, emotion types, and emotion response systems; and the details of specific elicitation methods (along with modifications that may be necessary for use with patients). Throughout, there is a recounting of "lessons learned," based on our own experience taking methods that we had developed and used over several decades for studying emotion in normal individuals and adapting them to study patients suffering from focal lesions (e.g., orbitofrontal lesions), congenital brain damage (e.g., Moebius syndrome), and neurodegenerative diseases (e.g., frontotemporal lobar degeneration, Alzheimer's disease, amyotrophic lateral sclerosis).

Affective Neuroscience: Two Approaches

Affective neuroscience is concerned with understanding the neural substrates of emotional functioning. As with other areas of neuroscience, questions pertaining to localization of function loom large. On this foundation, more complex questions concerning the nature of neural circuits and the bidirectional interactions between affective and cognitive processes are built. As has been the case with cognitive neu-

roscience, research in affective neuroscience has primarily utilized two paradigms, one studying the emotional functioning of patients with damage in particular brain areas and the other studying the activation of particular brain regions during well-defined emotional activities. Although some laboratories specialize in one or the other methodology, opportunities abound for using the findings from one methodology to inform research using the other.

Patient Studies

Studies of neurological patients have been critical to advancing our understanding of the human brain. In some instances, fundamental insights were gained and doors opened to entire new areas of inquiry based on findings from a single patient. Examples include Phineas Gage and the functions of the frontal lobes (Harlow, 1848) and patient H. M. and the organization of memory (Scoville & Milner, 1957). In other instances, findings from a small group of patients were seminal, such as epileptics treated with cerebral commissurotomy and hemispheric specialization (Gazzaniga & Sperry, 1967). In addition to these spectacular advances, there has been a steady and continuing parade of findings derived from the deceptively simple strategy of identifying individuals with loss in particular brain areas of interest, determining how their abilities and functioning differ from the norm, and studying the ways that they change over time. The great power and advantage of patient studies is that the behavioral, cognitive, and emotional "dependent measures" need not be constrained. Patient studies allow use of the entire armamentarium of methods and techniques available for studying the full range of basic behavioral and social processes under both controlled and naturalistic conditions.

The great disadvantage of patient studies pertains to the localization of brain injuries. Many brain injuries are diffuse, and even focal lesions can be highly idiosyncratic. This greatly complicates attempts to assemble groups of individuals with comparable brain damage. Neurodegenerative disorders also produce quite diffuse damage and, by definition, are constantly changing. Nonetheless, damage caused by lesions and neurodegeneration can be localized and quantified using methods such as voxel-based morphometry (Ashburner & Friston, 2000) and diffusion tensor imaging (Basser, Mattiello, & LeBihan, 1994), which can then be correlated with specific behavioral, emotional, and cognitive deficits and changes. A second problem with patient studies comes into play when patients with "old" injuries are studied. Humans are masters of compensation, and even the adult brain retains considerable plasticity (Jenkins, Merzenich, & Recanzone, 1990). Over the years that ensue following injury, "work-arounds" for recovering lost functions using uninjured areas of brain can mask or alter the nature of the functional deficits associated with the original injury. Finally, brain injuries can produce ancillary damage that can make testing difficult or misleading. For example, a patient with changes in emotional behavior associated with temporal lobe damage may be much harder to test and findings much more difficult to interpret if the damage extends to language comprehension areas as well (e.g., is observed lack of emotional response to an emotion-eliciting film due to damage to the emotional production areas or lack of comprehension of the film's dialogue?).

Activation Studies

Despite the stellar history of scientific yield from patient studies, the spotlight in affective neuroscience now clearly shines most brightly on studies that use technologically sophisticated imaging methodologies (e.g., functional magnetic resonance imaging [fMRI]; positron emission tomography [PET]) that utilize hemodynamic information to quantify ongoing brain activity. Older methods that directly measure the brain's electrical activity, such as the classic electroencephalogram (EEG), have continued to evolve with changes in acquisition methodology (e.g., dense-electrode arrays), paradigms (e.g., event-related analyses), and analyses (e.g., current source localization). Magnetoencephalography (MEG) offers a promising alternative to EEG for measuring brain activity, and transcranial magnetic stimulation (TMS) offers a way to stimulate activity in particular brain areas.

The great advantage of the imaging-based methods is localization. As acquisition technologies and analytic methods have developed, both spatial and temporal resolutions have improved. At this point, it is not unreasonable to utilize fMRI (whose temporal resolution has always lagged behind the other activation methods) to study a fleeting phenomenon such as emotion. Arguably, only a fool would bet against such stunning technology (and the many talented scientists it has attracted). Nonetheless, applying these methods to study emotion engenders some serious problems and significant compromises, which are likely to plague these approaches for the foreseeable future. As a prime example, naturalistic studies of emotion in freely behaving individuals are simply impossible when participants need to be "in the magnet," lying on their backs, awash in hammering sounds, and repeatedly warned that motion (an essential part of emotion) is forbidden.

Another serious limitation with imaging-based methods is that they are typically highly solitary and isolating. Most human emotion, in contrast, occurs in social contexts, arising from interaction and communication with others. Recreating a meaningful social context is highly challenging in any laboratory environment, but even more so in the typical imaging environment. Thus, for now, social influences can be introduced only in highly diluted forms (although recent studies using "alone vs. in the company of another person" comparisons are promising).

The emotional processes studied in activation studies are often limited by the methodologies used. The implications of these limitations for interpreting findings are often not explicitly and fully considered. For example, many fMRI studies have participants make emotional judgments (e.g., identifying the emotion in photographs of faces or in paragraphs). On minimal reflection, wouldn't most agree that *identifying* an emotion conveyed in a photograph or paragraph is a very different process than *having* an emotional reaction to some significant event? Moreover, these processes are likely to involve quite different neural substrates. Thus using emotion judgment paradigms as a proxy for emotion production is highly suspect.

Last, activation studies must deal with the pervasive problem of stimulus equivalence. Stimuli such as slides and films that are typically used to elicit different emotions or emotion-related states (e.g., loneliness, sympathy) often differ greatly in other dimensions, such as familiarity, color, cognitive complexity, and movement, any of which could account for findings of differential regional brain activation between experimental conditions. Adequately controlling for these sources of variation requires great care, and there is often a dramatic trade-off between applying the experimental controls necessary to insure comparability of stimuli and preserving their ecology validity (Levenson, 2003).

Emotional Functioning: Processes, Types, and Response Systems

Modern neuropsychological testing of cognitive functioning is based on a highly differentiated model of human cognition in which deficits can appear in any of a number of processes (e.g., memory, executive function, language, computation, attention). Moreover, many of these major cognitive functions can be broken down into component processes that can also be assessed (e.g., working memory and long-term memory).

The state of affairs is much less advanced when it comes to testing emotional functioning. As with cognition, there are compelling theoretical, empirical, and anatomical reasons to consider emotion as consisting of a number of different processes and subprocesses. However, relatively few tests are available for assessing different emotional processes in neurological patients, and, for those that are available, the relationship with specific emotion processes is often not well articulated. In fact, in many neuropsychological batteries, only a single emotion process is tested (typically the ability to recognize the emotion being expressed in photos of facial expressions). Just as no one would consider a particular test (e.g., maze drawing) designed to assess a particular cognitive function (i.e., executive control) adequate for assessing overall cognitive functioning, extrapolating overall emotional functioning from a test of a single emotional process seems logically flawed and practically misguided.

What needs to be included in a comprehensive assessment of emotional functioning? Akin to many fundamental issues in emotion, significant controversy exists among emotion theorists and researchers about how best to parse emotion into its component processes, types, and indicators. There are many models of emotions, and they differ widely in their relative emphasis on biological features, cognitive features, appraisal processes, motor action patterns, expressive behavior, language, and coping. The definition we have proposed (Levenson, 1994) emphasizes the adaptive, organizing function of emotion:

> Emotions are short-lived psychological-physiological phenomena that represent efficient modes of adaptation to changing environmental demands. Psychologically, emotions alter attention, shift certain behaviors upward in response hierarchies, and activate relevant associative networks in memory. Physiologically, emotions rapidly organize the responses of disparate biological systems including facial expression, somatic muscular tonus, voice tone, autonomic nervous system activity, and endocrine activity to produce a bodily milieu that is optimal for effective response. Emotions serve to establish our position vis-à-vis our environment, pulling us toward certain people, objects, actions and ideas, and pushing us away from others. Emotions also serve as a repository for innate and learned influences, possessing certain invariant features, and others that show considerable variation across individuals, groups, and cultures. (p. 123)

Reflecting this definition of emotion, our assessment of emotional functioning focuses on brief emotional phenomena (not on longer moods) and on the activation of multiple response systems (which requires assessing multiple indicators of emotion rather than relying on a single indicator, such as verbal report of subjective emotional experience) and includes assessment of emotion in multiple contexts.

Three Emotion Processes

There are three processes that should be included in any comprehensive assessment of emotional functioning: (1) *emotional reactivity,* (2) *emotional regulation,* and (3) *emotional understanding.* Emotional reactivity refers to the type, magnitude, and duration of responses to changes in the internal and external environment that have significance for our goals and well-being. Emotional regulation refers to the adjustments in type, magnitude, and duration of emotional responses that are made to meet personal, situational, and interpersonal demands. Emotional understanding refers to the recognition of emotions in oneself and others and the knowledge of the reasons they have occurred and their consequences.

These processes capture three of the most fundamental qualities of human emotional life—having emotion, controlling emotion, and knowing what we and others are feeling. Although the evidence is far from conclusive, we hypothesize that each of these processes is subserved by somewhat different neural circuitry. Patient (and activation) studies can shed light on this hypothesis if they utilize methods that allow for studying these processes separately. The methods presented in this chapter have been designed explicitly with this goal in mind.

Emotional Reactivity

Emotional reactivity is usually operationalized in terms of the type, magnitude, and duration of response. In the laboratory, emotional reactivity is typically assessed by presenting the individual with a standardized or personally tailored emotion-eliciting stimulus and measuring the reactions in one or more response systems (discussed later).

Emotional reactivity should be assessed in vivo, that is, at the time emotions are actually produced. Procedures in which individuals are asked to indicate what emotional responses they *think* they have or would have in certain situations reflect an uncertain amalgam of additional processes (e.g., self-awareness, "emotional intelligence," cultural beliefs and norms, self-presentation biases).

Emotional Regulation

Gross (1998) defines emotional regulation as:

> the processes by which individuals influence which emotions they have, when they have them, and how they experience and express these emotions. Emotion regulatory processes may be automatic or controlled, conscious or unconscious, and may have their effects at one or more points in the emotion generative process. (p. 275)

Perhaps because the term *emotional regulation* is so closely associated with learning how to rein in emotions during childhood, it is easy to think of emotional regulation as being limited to emotional down-regulation. However, it is clear that emotional regulatory competence goes beyond this to include the ability to amplify emotion (when emotional signals need to be clear and unambiguous) and to substitute one emotion for another (e.g., when social conventions call for the display of an emotion that may be different from what is actually being felt).

Emotional reactivity and emotional regulation can be quite difficult to separate. For example, consider the case of a patient who exhibits very small facial expressive and autonomic responses to a highly emotional film. Is this patient showing a low level of emotional reactivity or a high level of emotional regulation (down-regulation, in this example)? The difficulty of making this distinction underscores the value of assessing *instructed* regulation (i.e., the person is explicitly told how to alter emotional response and the ability to comply with this instruction is assessed), in addition to *spontaneous* regulation (i.e., the person is placed in situations in which regulation would be expected but is not explicitly requested). Instructed regulation provides an indication of what the person *can* do and can be measured quite precisely; spontaneous regulation provides an indication of what the person *does* do and is always difficult to separate completely from emotional reactivity. Moreover, spontaneous regulation often depends not only on the ability to regulate emotion per se but also on other abilities, such as knowing social norms and recognizing situational demands.

Emotional Understanding

Emotional understanding takes a number of forms, ranging from the relatively simple (e.g., knowledge about whether or not we or others are experiencing emotion) to the more differentiated (e.g., knowledge about the particular emotion or emotions being experienced) to the highly complex (e.g., knowledge of cultural norms that apply to emotional expression in the current situation).

We consider the basic building block of emotional understanding to be empathic accuracy (Ickes, 1997), which is the ability to recognize what another person is feeling. In its simplest form, empathic accuracy can be assessed by having an individual identify the particular emotion being shown in a photograph or expressed in a vocalization. Two common tests of this sort are the Florida Affect Battery (Bowers, Blonder, & Heilman, 1991) and the Pictures of Facial Affect (Ekman & Friesen, 1976). More complex and arguably more ecologically valid assessments of emotional understanding utilize dynamic stimuli in which the emotional content is embedded in a meaningful social context and unfolds over time. Examples of these include recognizing and/or tracking emotions during films (Gross & Levenson, 1995) and social interactions (Levenson & Ruef, 1992).

Three Emotion Types

Three broad categories of emotion should be considered when assessing emotional functioning: (1) *negative emotions,* (2) *positive emotions,* and (3) *self-referential emotions.* Whereas early theories tended to posit a single mechanism that was thought to apply to all types of emotion (e.g., unexplained physiological arousal coupled with cognitive appraisal; Schachter & Singer, 1962), contemporary emotion theories and research are less likely to treat emotion as a monolith. Thus the assumption that what holds for one emotion holds for all emotions—whether it be antecedent conditions, appraisals, activating mechanisms, functions, or manifestations—is no longer tenable.

Negative Emotions

Negative emotions prepare the organism for dealing with conditions of threat, challenge, and opportunity. "Basic" negative emotions such as anger, disgust, fear, and sadness can be characterized as having different associated patterns of facial expression, motor action, and physiological activation (Ekman, 1992) that have been selected through evolution as being most likely to deal successfully with the modal eliciting condition most of the time (Levenson, 2003). Early theorizing about and laboratory studies of emotion focused primarily on negative emotions, emphasizing adaptive patterns such as "flight" and "fight" and attempting to document associated physiological activation (Ax, 1953; Levenson, 1992; Roberts & Weerts, 1982). Traditionally negative emotions are thought to reside in brainstem and limbic regions, with medial temporal circuitry involving the amygdala playing a critical role (LeDoux, 1992, 2000).

Positive Emotions

Until recently, positive emotions were relatively understudied and their functions less well understood. Clearly, "fight or flight" is not a good metaphor for positive emotions such as amusement and joy. In our work, the role that positive emotions play in calming, soothing, and "undoing" the physiological effects of negative emotions has been emphasized (Fredrickson & Levenson, 1998; Levenson, 1988). Others have emphasized the role that positive emotions play in broadening perspectives, increasing flexibility of response, and increasing group cohesion (Fredrickson, 1998; Isen, 1999). In contrast to long-held views that emotion is a right-hemisphere phenomenon, Davidson (e.g., Davidson & Fox, 1982) has argued that the left hemisphere is particularly important for positive emotion.

Self-Referential Emotions

Self-referential emotions arise when our behavior is evaluated against personal standards and social norms. These evaluations and the ensuing emotions can be negatively (e.g., shame, guilt, embarrassment) or positively (e.g., pride) toned. Because they require self-monitoring, complex appraisals, and knowledge of norms, self-referential emotions appear relatively late in ontogeny and phylogeny. Research with neurological patients suggests that these emotions are particularly vulnerable to injury to frontal brain regions (Beer, Heerey, Keltner, Scabini, & Knight, 2003; Sturm, Rosen, Allison, Miller, & Levenson, 2006).

Four Emotion Response Systems

Emotion researchers always have to deal with the thorny issue of how to account for the multiple emotion response systems. Even in normal individuals, the extent of coherence between different indicators of emotion (e.g., autonomic nervous system, expressive behavior, subjective experience) varies depending on person, situation, response system, and emotion (Mauss, Levenson, McCarter, Wilhelm, & Gross, 2005). In neurological patients, this problem can be compounded when central and peripheral neural systems responsible for certain emotion responses are damaged. Moreover, the kinds of disjunctions between emotion response systems that have been found with psychiatric populations (e.g., low levels of facial expression combined with high levels of subjective experience and autonomic response in schizophrenics with "blunted affect"; Kring & Neale, 1996) could prove important in neurological populations. Thus, for an adequate accounting of emotional functioning, it is important to measure multiple emotional response systems.

Self-Reported Emotional Experience

Self-reported emotional experience can be measured in several ways. In our laboratory, we ask participants to do one or more of the following: (1) describe their emotional responses in an open-ended fashion, (2) rate the intensity of discrete emotions (e.g., fear, anger, amusement) and dimensions (e.g., pleasantness), or (3) use a rating dial to indicate moment-to-moment emotional changes (see Ruef & Levenson, chapter 17, this volume). For neurological patients with language and/or memory problems, we have developed modified versions of these measures that can be used as needed (e.g., rating scales with reduced ranges, pictures rather than words, pointing rather than writing/speaking, online ratings or very short time intervals between emotional events and retrospective ratings).

Emotional Expressive Behavior

Emotional expressive behavior is typically quantified by applying objective coding systems to videotapes of participants' emotional behavior. In our laboratory, we use a number of different coding systems, including: (1) the Facial Action Coding System (FACS; Ekman & Friesen, 1978), which decomposes facial expressions into their component muscular actions and involves no inference; (2) the Emotion FACS (EMFACS; Friesen & Ekman, 1983), which provides emotion predictions for certain combinations of FACS scores; (3) the Emotional Expressive Coding System (Gross & Levenson, 1993), which includes descriptions of specific facial actions and inferential codes for different emotions; and (4) the Specific Affect Coding System (SPAFF; Coan & Gottman, chapter 16, this volume; Gottman, 1989), which is generally used for dyadic interaction and which assigns codes to emotions based on multiple indicators, including facial expression, tone of voice, and content of speech. These coding systems can all be employed with neurological patients; however, for those with language problems, SPAFF coding can be difficult because of its use of speech cues.

Peripheral Physiology

Peripheral physiology is usually quantified in terms of selected measures of cardiovascular, electrodermal, respiratory, and somatic activity. Measurement timing is very important because these systems are often under the influence of emotion for only brief periods before they return to the service of other functions (e.g., homeostasis). In our laboratory, we precede each emotion elicitation with a resting baseline period and then obtain measures continuously throughout the elicitation and during a postelicitation "cooling down" period. Analyses focus either on the times during which we attempted to stimulate emotion (e.g., while the participant watched a film) or when we have independent evidence that an emotion has occurred (e.g., when an emotional facial expression appeared during a dyadic interaction). Measures of peripheral physiology are very useful with neurological patients because they do not depend on language. However, it is important to take into account any impact that the disease process has on autonomic centers (see the section on control tasks later in the chapter) and the autonomic effects of patient medications (e.g., medications with cholinergic and/or adrenergic effects, such as antimuscarinics, phenothiazines, and beta-blockers).

Emotional Language

Emotional language can be quantified by determining the frequency or proportion of words used in different categories (e.g., all emotion words, negative emotion words, fear words). Verbatim transcripts of participant responses are prepared and processed using text-analysis computer software (e.g., Marchitelli & Levenson, 1992; Mergenthaler, 1985; Pennebaker, Francis, & Booth, 2001). To control for the paucity of language in some neurological patients, word usage in particular emotion categories of interest can be expressed as a percentage of total words spoken.

Laboratory Tests of Emotion

In this section, the laboratory tasks we use to assess emotional functioning are described, along with the modifications necessary for use with neurological patients.

Acoustic Startle Reflex

The acoustic startle reflex is a primitive, defensive response to the threat posed by a sudden loud noise (Sokolov, 1963). We use a 115 db, 100 ms burst of white noise administered through loudspeakers directly behind the patient (roughly commensurate with a close-proximity gunshot). The startle response exists on the boundary between reflex and emotion (Ekman, Friesen, & Simons, 1985). The initial response (typically occurring in the first 500 ms) consists of a stereotyped pattern of somatic and facial muscle actions (Ekman et al., 1985) and attendant activation of autonomic nervous system response (Soto, Levenson, & Ebling, 2005). This is often followed by a secondary emotional response, a "response to having been startled" that varies across individuals. As the person takes stock of what has happened (including his or her reaction to the loud noise), the secondary response can take several emotional forms, including amusement, embarrassment, anger, or fear. In our work with neurological patients, we have found this secondary response to be particularly vulnerable to frontal lobe damage (Sturm et al., 2006).

We administer the startle under three conditions (unanticipated, anticipated, inhibited), which enables us to probe different aspects of emotional functioning. In the unanticipated condition, the startle occurs without warning. This assesses emotional reactivity to a simple aversive stimulus. In the anticipated condition, the startle is preceded by a 20-s countdown. Because participants know exactly when it will occur, most use the time to try to reduce the impact of and their response to the startle. This procedure provides a good measure of spontaneous regulation (we have found deficits in this kind of regulation in patients with orbital prefrontal cortex damage; Roberts, et al., 2004). Finally, in the inhibited condition, the startle is preceded by a 20-s countdown and instructions to try to minimize the reaction. This enables us to assess participant's capacity to regulate emotion on demand and thus provides a measure of instructed regulation. A variant of the inhibited condition, in which participants are instructed to exaggerate the visibility of reactions, can also be included.

Startle Eyeblink Modulation

The acoustic stimulus described in the previous section is sufficiently loud to activate an intense defensive whole-body reflex (Sokolov, 1963). An acoustic stimulus of considerably lower amplitude (typically ranging from 95–100 db) will activate a much smaller startle reflex (Bradley, Cuthbert, & Lang, 1990) that can be quantified by electromyographic measurement of the intensity of the associated eyeblink. To put this in perspective, the 115 db acoustic stimulus used to generate the defensive reflex is more than 30 times as powerful as the 100 db stimulus used to generate the startle eyeblink. Unlike the high-amplitude startle, the lower amplitude startle does not disrupt ongoing activity and thus can be used as a repeated background "probe" stimulus while the person is engaged in other activities. The amplitude of the startle eyeblink reflects higher cortical functioning, such as attentional and emotional processing. Importantly, it is also sensitive to affective valence—with positive/approach states

attenuating the amplitude of the eyeblink and negative/avoidance states having a potentiating effect (Bradley et al., 1990). Startle eyeblink modulation can provide useful information about underlying attentional and emotional processes in ways that are relatively free of demand characteristics and reporting biases (e.g., Bradley & Vrana, 1993). These qualities are appealing for use with patient populations for whom self-report might be problematic.

Films

Carefully selected excerpts from commercial and other films can be used to elicit particular emotions (Gross & Levenson, 1995; Philippot, 1993). Emotions in real life often occur in response to dynamic external visual and auditory stimulation; thus films have a relatively high degree of ecological validity. Use of films as laboratory stimuli can be traced back to early studies of diffuse "stress" responses (e.g., Lazarus, et al., 1962). However, for assessing emotion, it is important to have films that are sufficiently thematically pure to target specific emotions (or at least specific types of emotion). Gross and Levenson (1995) describe a set of films that can be used to elicit the emotions of amusement, anger, contentment, disgust, fear, sadness, and surprise, as well as a neutral emotional state. Based on this work, it appears that anger is the most difficult emotion to elicit reliably using short film excerpts. Films can be used to assess the emotional processes of reactivity (by having participants just watch the film and measuring their responses), regulation (e.g., by instructing participants to alter their emotional responses), and understanding (by having participants indicate the emotions being experienced by characters in the film).

When using films with neurological patients, it is important to consider possible cognitive and language deficits. Films vary greatly in their thematic complexity and in the extent to which emotional cues are embedded in language, action, or situation. Thus, it is important to select films that are appropriate for the cognitive capabilities of the population. Fortunately, we have found that, even with highly impaired neurological patients, it is possible to assess emotional reactivity, regulation, and understanding with carefully selected, thematically simple films in which the emotion is embedded more in action and situation than in language.

Slides

The International Affective Picture System (IAPS; Lang, Greenwald, & Bradley, 1988) consists of more than 700 colored images of situations selected because of their ability to evoke emotion and to be internationally understandable. These pictures have been used in a large number of studies of emotional and cognitive functioning, including many activation studies. The pictures were developed to explore a dimensional model of emotion; thus normative ratings are available for pleasure and arousal for each picture rather than for specific emotions. Although in theory the full array of specific emotions could be represented, there are clear biases (e.g., pictures of contamination and mutilation, which would primarily elicit disgust, dominate the high unpleasant–high arousal quadrant).

The IAPS slides have primarily been used to assess emotional reactivity, the emotion process for which they are best suited. However, they could also be used to assess regulation, especially if the emotional impact were extended through longer times of exposure and/or viewing sequences of similarly themed slides. Emotional understanding could also be assessed using slides that portray people having emotional reactions. Because these pictures are static, cognitively simple, and do not require language processing, they can be very useful when working with impaired patients.

Relived Emotions

Recalling memories of emotionally significant events can be a powerful elicitor of emotion. Interestingly, even in patients suffering from retrograde amnesia that affects neutral and semantic autobiographical memories, emotional memories can be spared (Daum, Flor, Brodbeck, & Birbaumer, 1996). We use emotional memories of two kinds: (1) personally relevant, autobiographical emotional memories (e.g., recalling one's saddest or happiest moment; Ekman, Levenson, & Friesen, 1983), and (2) memories of shared historic or group events (e.g., flashbulb memories, such as recalling the events of September 11, 2001). Autobiographical memories can elicit intense emotion, but their idiosyncratic nature leads to differences in the characteristics of memories across individuals. Flashbulb memories provide much better comparability of the memory itself, but they still can vary greatly across individuals in personal salience and capacity to elicit emotion.

To identify personally relevant autobiographical memories, we use a semistructured interview to prompt participants to retrieve memories of a specific event that elicited a specific emotion (Ekman et al., 1983). Subsequently, participants are asked to relive those memories as strongly as possible. Emotional responses can be assessed during both the retrieval and reliving periods. We consider relived memories to be most useful for assessing emotional reactivity and less so for assessing emotional regulation and understanding. Because memory is involved, these tasks need to be used judiciously with patients who have memory impairments.

Singing

Among the self-referential emotions, embarrassment is probably the best understood (Keltner & Buswell, 1997). To elicit embarrassment, we use a singing task in which participants unwittingly become objects of attention and evaluation. Participants are seated in front of a television monitor while their expressive behavior is recorded. After sitting quietly through

a baseline period, participants are asked to sing a familiar song (e.g., we use "My Girl") while the instrumental background music is played through headphones and the lyrics are presented on the television monitor. On completion of the song, the experimenter removes the headphones and instructs participants just to watch the television for the next task. Without warning, they are then shown a recording of their just-completed singing performance. In our laboratory, participants are typically alone while watching themselves sing, but it would be possible to have an "audience" present, which might heighten the effect.

Singing tasks of this sort are effective elicitors of embarrassment and other signs of self-consciousness (e.g., amusement). Other tasks that have been used for eliciting embarrassment include posing complex facial expressions (Keltner, 1995) or having participants disclose personal, emotional experiences (Beer et al., 2003). An advantage of the singing task is that it is thematically and instructionally simple and suitable for use even with quite impaired patients (if patients have trouble reading lyrics, childhood songs such as "Twinkle, Twinkle, Little Star" can be used).

Dyadic Interaction

Most human emotions occur in interpersonal contexts. We have emotional responses to the actions of others, and our emotions serve to regulate social distance, drawing people to us in some instances and away from us in others (Levenson, 1994). Specific emotions can serve important intrapersonal functions, for example, the role that positive emotions play in establishing social bonds (Fredrickson, 1998; Panksepp, 2000) and the role that sadness plays in eliciting help from others (e.g., crying as a distress signal; Bowlby, 1969).

In our laboratory, we assess socioemotional functioning during dyadic interaction (Levenson & Gottman, 1983). Participants engage in the interaction with a spouse, family member, or caregiver. Members of the dyad sit in chairs facing each other and engage in brief conversations (typically 15 min) preceded by silent resting periods (typically 5 min). We have found that discussions of areas of relationship conflict are the most powerful elicitors of emotion. We also use more neutral topics (e.g., discussing the events of the day), positive topics (e.g., discussing things they enjoy doing together), and disease-specific topics (e.g., discussing the ways the illness has changed their relationship). Before each conversation, a facilitator helps the dyad decide on the topic for discussion.

Dyadic interaction allows us to assess emotional reactivity, emotional regulation, and emotional understanding under conditions that closely approximate the "real world." In addition to assessing these processes during the interaction (through behavioral coding, analysis of language, and measurement of physiological responding), we also assess subjective emotional experience and emotional understanding using a video recall methodology (Gottman & Levenson, 1985). After the conversation, participants view the video recording and use a rating dial to report continuously on the valence (negative-neutral-positive) of their own emotions during the interaction. An additional viewing can follow in which each participant rates the other participant's emotional state. Comparing the similarity between the two sets of ratings provides an objective measure of emotional understanding (Levenson & Ruef, 1992).

Dyadic interaction is a powerful way to study emotional functioning. It is particularly useful in revealing how patients' specific emotional (and cognitive) deficits and strengths play out in the highly demanding context of social interaction. We have found that this task can be used with even highly impaired patients (although they may not be able to do the rating dial portion).

Control Tasks

When working with neurological patients, we typically have access to a fairly complete clinical examination, neuropsychological workup, medical history, and current medications. We supplement this information with several additional tests conducted in the laboratory that are critical to subsequent interpretation of the results of our testing of emotional functioning.

Understanding Emotion Terms

Participants are asked to match a list of emotion terms (e.g., *anger*) with a list of definitions (e.g., "what you feel when someone takes something that is yours") to ensure that they are familiar with emotion semantics.

Ability to Use Rating Dial

Because we often make use of rating dials to obtain continuous emotional reports, we determine whether the person has the psychomotor skills necessary to use the device by having them move the dial to track a changing color presented on a television monitor.

Autonomic Functioning

We use an isometric handgrip task to ensure that the cardiovascular system responds normally to somatic demand and a valsalva maneuver to ensure that both parasympathetic and sympathetic influences on the heart are present. It is also important to have some test to assess whether the electrodermal system is functional, especially given that many individuals fail to show electrodermal responses to any stimulus (for reasons related to age, disease, skin coloration, calluses, medication, etc.). Electrodermal responses are afforded an important role in affective neuroscience, for example, as part of the somatic marker hypothesis (Damasio, Tranel, & Damasio, 1991). Thus it is particularly important to assess nonemotional electrodermal responding in both patients and controls. Having participants take several deep breaths provides a quick indication of the intactness of the electrodermal system. An alternative is to use a calibrated orienting stimulus such as a low intensity tone or light flash. This has the advantage of exposing all participants to the same stimulus; thus, the magnitude of the electrodermal response can be used as a nonemotional covariate in other analyses.

Facial Responding

Because emotional facial responding is an important nonverbal indicator of emotional state, it is important to know whether patients have any damage to circuitry that controls the action of the facial muscles. If not tested as part of the neurological exam, voluntary facial expression can be quickly assessed by having participants make individual facial actions (Ekman & Friesen, 1982) and simple emotional expressions. Because voluntary and spontaneous facial muscle actions reflect somewhat different neural pathways (Rinn, 1984), it is important to assess involuntary facial expression as well. This can be monitored informally during the preexperimental interactions (e.g., watching for smiles) or can be evaluated more systematically with simple stimuli that reliably elicit facial responses (e.g., acoustic startle, bad smells, sour tastes).

Utilizing Control Data

We use data obtained from these control tasks as covariates in subsequent analyses. These are supplemented by additional covariates derived from clinical and neuropsychological data, such as use of autonomically active medications and overall level of cognitive functioning (Mini-Mental State Examination; Folstein, Folstein, & McHugh, 1975). This analytic strategy reflects our interest in isolating deficits in emotional functioning above and beyond those that could be accounted for by cognitive, motor, and medication-related factors.

Summary of Elicitation Methods

In Table 10.1, the various tests of emotional processing discussed in this chapter are summarized in terms of the emotion processes, emotion types, and emotion-response systems they can assess. For each test, advantages and disadvantages are briefly noted.

Conclusions

In this chapter I have argued for the value of patient studies at a time when activation studies have become the primary coin of the realm in affective neuroscience. I have also presented a case for the importance of a comprehensive assessment of emotional functioning, which includes testing of three different emotion processes (reactivity, regulation, understanding), three different emotion types (negative, positive,

Table 10.1
Summary of various tests of emotional processing

	Emotion Processes	Emotion Types	Emotion Response Systems	Advantages	Disadvantages
Acoustic startle reflex	Reactivity Regulation (instructed) and spontaneous)	Negative Positive and self-referential in secondary reaction	Subjective Behavioral. Physiological	Requires little cognitive processing	Produces a general defensive response initially rather than specific emotions
Startle eyeblink modulation	Regulation	Negative Positive	Behavioral	Requires little cognitive processing Unobtrusive and continuous	Does not produce rich repertoire of emotional behavior
Films	Reactivity Regulation (instructed) Understanding	Negative (anger difficult) Positive Self-referential	Subjective Behavioral Physiologica	High ecological validity (dynamic, socially embedded)	High cognitive demands if thematically complex Difficult to elicit anger
Slides	Reactivity Regulation (instructed)	Negative Positive	Subjective Behavioral Physiological	Minimal cognitive and language demands	Biased toward eliciting disgust, amusement, sexual arousal
Relived emotions	Reactivity	Negative Positive Self-referential	Subjective Behavioral Physiological Language	Makes high demands on memory	Idiosyncratic stimuli— not standardized
Singing	Reactivity	Self-referential	Subjective Behavioral Physiological	Simple, effective	Need to be sensitive to patient discomfort Useful only for embarrassment
Dyadic Interaction	Reactivity Regulation (usually spontaneous, but instructed possible) Understanding	Negative Positive Self-referential	Subjective Behavioral Physiological Language	Produces highly naturalistic samples of emotional functioning High ecological validity	Responses influenced by both members of dyad

self-referential), and four different emotion response systems (self-reported experience, expressive behavior, peripheral physiology, language). Arguably, this kind of comprehensive assessment is critical for studying emotional functioning in all areas of emotion research (e.g., individual and group differences, development, social and cultural influences, emotion-cognition interactions, and impact of psychopathology and neuropathology). The methods described for testing emotional functioning are suitable for use in studies of both normal populations and, with some modifications and controls, neurological patients. Comprehensive, differentiated assessment of emotional functioning is essential for advancing our understanding of the neural substrates of emotion. Applied to patients, this approach may also help inform and improve the diagnosis and treatment of the many neurological and psychiatric disorders that affect emotional functioning.

Acknowledgments

This material is based on a recent chapter written with Elizabeth Ascher, Madeleine Goodkind, Megan McCarthy, Virginia Smith, and Kelly Werner (Levenson, et al., 2006) that described our approach to studying emotional functioning in frontal lobe patients. For this volume, I have rewritten and expanded a number of the sections, shortened others, and added several new sections, all in the hopes of making the chapter more useful to the emotion researcher interested in working with neurological patients. Still, there is much that is similar between the two chapters. My thanks to my coauthors and to the editors for agreeing to allow this material to appear in both volumes. Thanks also to my collaborators Bruce L. Miller, Howard J. Rosen, and Richard J. Perry (and to the many other members of the Memory and Aging Center) in the Department of Neurology at the University of California, San Francisco, for making this work possible, interesting, and so enjoyable.

Preparation of this chapter was supported by NIA grants AG17766 and AG19724.

References

Ashburner, J., & Friston, K. J. (2000). Voxel-based morphometry: The methods. *NeuroImage, 11*(6, Pt. 1), 805–821.

Ax, A. F. (1953). The physiological differentiation between

fear and anger in humans. *Psychosomatic Medicine, 15,* 433–442.

Basser, P. J., Mattiello, J., & LeBihan, D. (1994). MR diffusion tensor spectroscopy and imaging. *Biophysical Journal, 66*(1), 259–267.

Beer, J. S., Heerey, E. A., Keltner, D., Scabini, D., & Knight, R. T. (2003). The regulatory function of self-conscious emotion: Insights from patients with orbitofrontal damage. *Journal of Personality and Social Psychology, 85*(4), 594–604.

Bowers, D., Blonder, L. X., & Heilman, K. M. (1991). *Florida Affect Battery.* Gainesville, FL: University of Florida, Center for Neuropsychological Studies, Cognitive Neuroscience Laboratory.

Bowlby, J. (1969). Disruption of affectional bonds and its effects on behavior. *Canada's Mental Health Supplement, 59,* 12.

Bradley, M. M., Cuthbert, B. N., & Lang, P. J. (1990). Startle reflex modification: Emotion or attention? *Psychophysiology, 27*(5), 513–522.

Bradley, M. M. & Vrana, S. R. (1993). The startle probe in the study of emotion and emotional disorders. In N. Birbaumer & A. Ohman (Eds.), *The structure of emotions: Psychophysiological, cognitive, and clinical aspects* (pp. 270–287). Toronto: Hogrefe-Huber.

Damasio, A. R., Tranel, D., & Damasio, H. C. (1991). Somatic markers and the guidance of behavior: Theory and preliminary testing. In H. S. Levin, H. M. Eisenberg, & A. L. Benton (Eds.), *Frontal lobe function and dysfunction* (pp. 217–229). New York: Oxford University Press.

Daum, I., Flor, H., Brodbeck, S., & Birbaumer, N. (1996). Autobiographical memory for emotional events in amnesia. *Behavioural Neurology, 9*(2), 57–67.

Davidson, R. J., & Fox, N. A. (1982). Asymmetrical brain activity discriminates between positive and negative affective stimuli in human infants. *Science, 218,* 1235–1237.

Ekman, P. (1992). An argument for basic emotions. *Cognition and Emotion, 6*(3–4), 169–200.

Ekman, P., & Friesen, W. V. (1976). *Pictures of Facial Affect.* Palo Alto, CA: Consulting Psychologists Press.

Ekman, P., & Friesen, W.V. (1978). *Facial Action Coding System.* Palo Alto, CA: Consulting Psychologists Press.

Ekman, P., & Friesen, W. F. (1982). *The requested facial action test.* San Francisco: University of California Press.

Ekman, P., Friesen, W. V., & Simons, R. C. (1985). Is the startle reaction an emotion? *Journal of Personality and Social Psychology, 49,* 1416–1426.

Ekman, P., Levenson, R. W., & Friesen, W. V. (1983). Autonomic nervous system activity distinguishes among emotions. *Science, 221*(4616), 1208–1210.

Folstein, M. F., Folstein, S. E., & McHugh, P. R. (1975). Mini-Mental State: A practical method for grading the cognitive state of patients for the clinician. *Journal of Psychiatric Research, 12*(3), 189–198.

Fredrickson, B. L. (1998). What good are positive emotions? *Review of General Psychology, 2*(3), 300–319.

Fredrickson, B. L., & Levenson, R. W. (1998). Positive emotions speed recovery from the cardiovascular sequelae of negative emotions. *Cognition and Emotion, 12*(2), 191–220.

Friesen, W. F., & Ekman, P. (1983). *EMFACS-7: Emotional Facial Action Coding System.* San Francisco: University of California Press.

Gazzaniga, M. S., & Sperry, R. W. (1967). Language after section of the cerebral commissures. *Brain: A Journal of Neurology, 90*(1), 131–148.

Gottman, J. M. (1989). The Specific Affect Coding System (SPAFF). Unpublished manuscript. Seattle: University of Washington.

Gottman, J. M., & Levenson, R. W. (1985). A valid procedure for obtaining self-report of affect in marital interaction. *Journal of Consulting and Clinical Psychology, 53*(2), 151–160.

Gross, J. J. (1998). The emerging field of emotion regulation: An integrative review. *Review of General Psychology, 2*(3), 271–299.

Gross, J. J., & Levenson, R. W. (1993). Emotional suppression: Physiology, self-report, and expressive behavior. *Journal of Personality and Social Psychology, 64*(6), 970–986.

Gross, J. J., & Levenson, R. W. (1995). Emotion elicitation using films. *Cognition and Emotion, 9*(1), 87–108.

Harlow, J. M. (1848). Passage of an iron rod through the head. *Boston Medical and Surgical Journal, 39,* 389–393.

Ickes, W. J. (Ed.). (1997). *Empathic accuracy.* New York: Guilford Press.

Isen, A. M. (1999). *Positive affect.* New York: Wiley.

Jenkins, W. M., Merzenich, M. M., & Recanzone, G. (1990). Neocortical representational dynamics in adult primates: Implications for neuropsychology. *Neuropsychologia, 28*(6), 573–584.

Keltner, D. (1995). Signs of appeasement: Evidence for the distinct displays of embarrassment, amusement, and shame. *Journal of Personality and Social Psychology, 68*(3), 441–454.

Keltner, D., & Buswell, B. N. (1997). Embarrassment: Its distinct form and appeasement functions. *Psychological Bulletin, 122*(3), 250–270.

Kring, A. M., & Neale, J. M. (1996). Do schizophrenic patients show a disjunctive relationship among expressive, experiential, and psychophysiological components of emotion? *Journal of Abnormal Psychology, 105*(2), 249–257.

Lang, P. J., Greenwald, M. K., & Bradley, M. M. (1988). *The International Affective Picture System (IAPS) standardization procedure and initial group results for affective judgments* (Tech. Rep. Nos. 1A–1D). Gainesville: University of Florida, Center for the Study of Emotion and Attention.

Lazarus, R. S., Speisman, J. C., Mordkoff, A. M., & Davison, L. A. (1962). A laboratory study of psychological stress produced by a motion picture film. *Psychological Monographs, 76,* No. 34 (Whole No. 553).

LeDoux, J. E. (1992). Emotion and the amygdala. In J. P. Aggleton (Ed.), *The amygdala: Neurobiological aspects of emotion, memory, and mental dysfunction.* (pp. 339–351). New York: Wiley-Liss.

LeDoux, J. E. (2000). Emotion circuits in the brain. *Annual Review of Neuroscience, 23,* 155–184.

Levenson, R. W. (1988). Emotion and the autonomic nervous system: A prospectus for research on autonomic specificity. In H. L. Wagner (Ed.), *Social psychophysiology and emotion: Theory and clinical applications* (pp. 17–42). Chichester, UK: Wiley.

Levenson, R. W. (1992). Autonomic nervous system differences among emotions. *Psychological Science, 3*(1), 23–27.

Levenson, R. W. (1994). Human emotion: A functional view. In P. Ekman & R. J. Davidson (Eds.), *The nature of emotion: Fundamental questions* (pp. 123–126). New York: Oxford University Press.

Levenson, R. W. (2003). Autonomic specificity and emotion. In R. J. Davidson, K. R. Scherer, & H. H. Goldsmith (Eds.), *Handbook of affective sciences* (pp. 212–224). New York: Oxford University Press.

Levenson, R. W., Ascher, E., Goodkind, M., McCarthy, M. E., Smith, V. E., & Werner, K. (2006). Laboratory testing of emotion and frontal cortex. In B. L. Miller & J. L. Cummings (Eds.), *The human frontal lobes: Functions and disorders* (2nd ed.). New York: Guilford Press.

Levenson, R. W., & Gottman, J. M. (1983). Marital interaction: Physiological linkage and affective exchange. *Journal of Personality and Social Psychology, 45*(3), 587–597.

Levenson, R. W., & Ruef, A. M. (1992). Empathy: A physiological substrate. *Journal of Personality and Social Psychology, 63*(2), 234–246.

Marchitelli, L., & Levenson, R. W. (1992, October). When couples converse: The language and physiology of emotion. Paper presented at the meeting of the Society for Psychophysiological Research, San Diego, CA.

Mauss, I. B., Levenson, R. W., McCarter, L., Wilhelm, F. H., & Gross, J. J. (2005). The tie that binds? Coherence among emotion experience, behavior, and physiology. *Emotion, 5*(2), 175–190.

Mergenthaler, E. (1985). *Textbank systems: Computer science applied in the field of psychoanalysis.* Heidelberg, Germany: Springer.

Panksepp, J. (2000). The riddle of laughter: Neural and psychoevolutionary underpinnings of joy. *Current Directions in Psychological Science, 9*(6), 183–186.

Pennebaker, J. W., Francis, M. E., & Booth, R. J. (2001). *Linguistic inquiry and word count: A computerized text analysis program.* Mahwah, NJ: Erlbaum.

Philippot, P. (1993). Inducing and assessing differentiated emotion-feeling states in the laboratory. *Cognition and Emotion, 7,* 171–193.

Rinn, W. E. (1984). The neuropsychology of facial expression: A review of the neurological and psychological mechanisms for producing facial expressions. *Psychological Bulletin, 95*(1), 52–77.

Roberts, N. A., Beer, J. S., Werner, K. H., Scabini, D., Levens, S. M., Knight, R. T., et al. (2004). The impact of orbital prefrontal cortex damage on emotional activation to unanticipated and anticipated acoustic startle stimuli. *Cognitive, Affective, and Behavioral Neuroscience, 4*(3), 307–316.

Roberts, R. J., & Weerts, T. C. (1982). Cardiovascular responding during anger and fear imagery. *Psychological Reports, 50*(1), 219–230.

Schachter, S., & Singer, J. (1962). Cognitive, social, and physiological determinants of emotional state. *Psychological review, 69*(5), 379–399.

Scoville, W. B., & Milner, B. (1957). Loss of recent memory after bilateral hippocampal lesions. *Journal of Neurology, Neurosurgery, and Psychiatry, 20,* 11–21.

Sokolov, E. N. (1963). Higher nervous functions: The orienting reflex. *Annual Review of Physiology, 25,* 545–580.

Soto, J. A., Levenson, R. W., & Ebling, R. (2005). Cultures of moderation and expression: Emotional experience, behavior, and physiology in Chinese Americans and Mexican Americans. *Emotion, 5*(2), 154–165.

Sturm, V. E., Rosen, H. J., Allison, S., Miller, B. L., & Levenson, R. L. (2006) . Self-conscious emotion deficits in frontotemporal lobar degeneration. *Brain, 129,* 2508–2516.

Figure 2.1. The self-assessment manikin (SAM; Lang, 1980) used to acquire ratings of pleasure and arousal for pictures in the IAPS. Each dimension is represented by five graphic figures, and participants can select any of the figures or between any of the figures, making a 9-point scale.

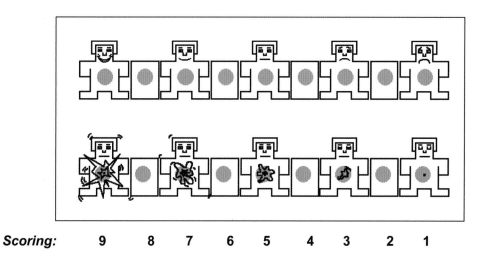

Scoring: 9   8   7   6   5   4   3   2   1

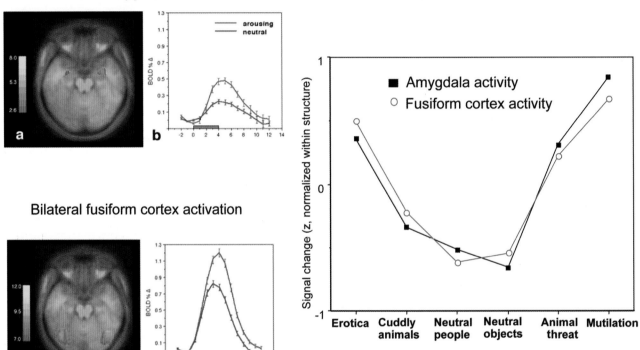

Figure 2.10. Neural activity measured in the amygdala (*top left*) and fusiform cortex (*bottom left*) using fMRI is increased when viewing emotionally arousing, compared with neutral, pictures, and both covary similarly with specific picture contents (Sabatinelli et al., 2004)

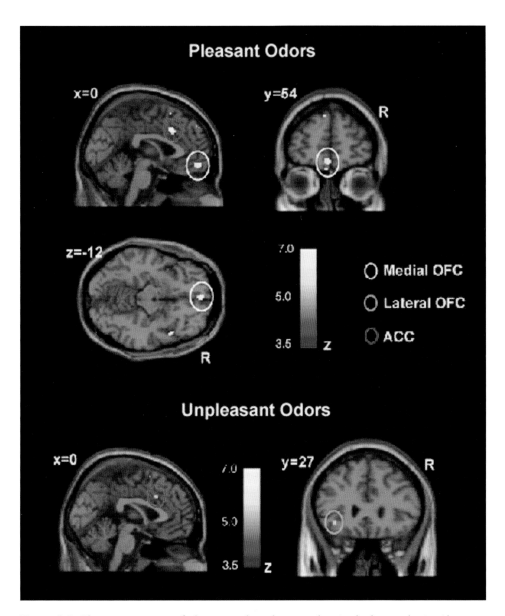

Figure 9.6. The representation of pleasant and unpleasant odors in the human brain. Above: Group conjunction results for the three pleasant odors. Sagittal, horizontal, and coronal views are shown at the levels indicated, all including the same activation in the medial orbitofrontal cortex, OFC (x, y, z = 0, 54, −12; Z = 5.23). Also shown is activation for the three pleasant odors in the anterior cingulate cortex, ACC (x, y, z = 2, 20, 32; Z = 5.44). These activations were significant at $p < .05$ fully corrected for multiple comparisons. Below: Group conjunction results for the three unpleasant odors. The sagittal view (left) shows an activated region of the anterior cingulate cortex (x, y, z = 0, 18, 36; Z = 4.42, $p < .05$, S.V.C.). The coronal view (*right*) shows an activated region of the lateral orbito-frontal cortex (−36, 27, −8; Z = 4.23, $p < .05$ S.V.C.). All the activations were thresholded at $p < .00001$ to show the extent of the activations. From Rolls, Kringelbach, & De Araujo, 2003a.

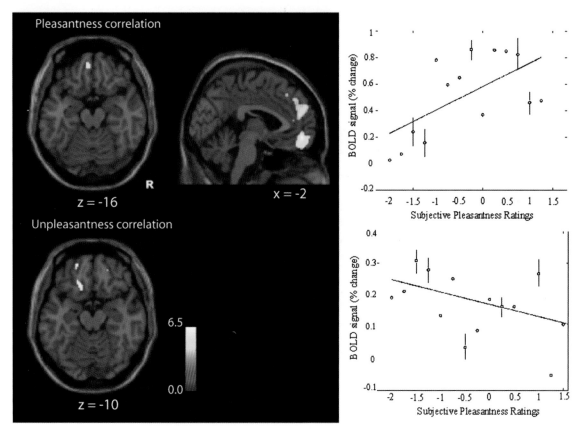

Figure 9.7. The representation of pleasant and unpleasant odors in the human brain. Random effects group analysis correlation analysis of the BOLD signal with the subjective pleasantness ratings. On the top left is shown the region of the mediorostral orbitofrontal (peak at [−2, 52, −10]; z = 4.28) correlating positively with pleasantness ratings, as well as the region of the anterior cingulate cortex in the top middle. On the far top right of the figure is shown the relation between the subjective pleasantness ratings and the BOLD signal from this cluster (in the medial orbitofrontal cortex at Y = 52), together with the regression line. The means and standard error of measurement across participants are shown. At the bottom of the figure is shown the regions of left more lateral orbitofrontal cortex (peaks at [−20, 54, −14]; z = 4.26 and [−16, 28, −18]; z = 4.08) correlating negatively with pleasantness ratings. On the far bottom right of the figure is shown the relation between the subjective pleasantness ratings and the BOLD signal from the first cluster (in the lateral orbitofrontal cortex at Y = 54), together with the regression line. The means and standard error across participants are shown. The activations were thresholded at $p < .0001$ for extent. From Rolls, Kringelbach, & De Araujo, 2003a.

Figure 24.3. Custom response button and two-button response pad. Details on their construction are provided in appendix A.

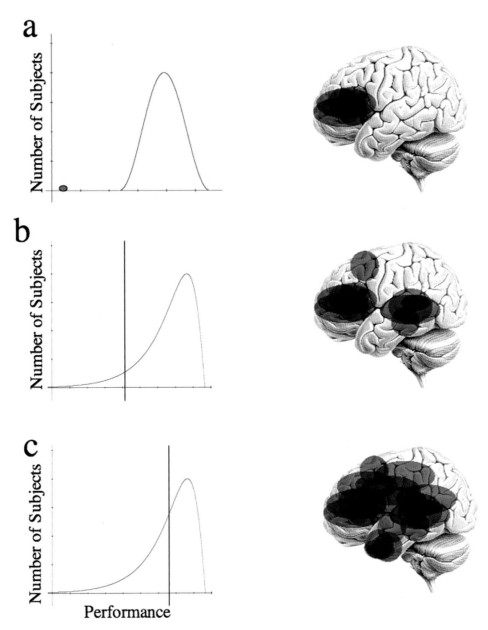

Figure 25.1. The Lesion Method. The goal of the approach is to relate covariances between brain damage and task performance: How does the location of a lesion covary with performance? The classical single-case approach is illustrated in (a): a single participant with a focal lesion (red) performs far outside the normal performance distribution (blue curve). To the extent that the lesion involves a particular brain structure and results in impairment on only a particular task, we can infer that the lesioned structure is normally involved in executing the task.

The group approach is a logical extension of the single-case approach. The performance distribution of a group of participants with brain damage differs in two respects from the normal performance distribution: Its mean is lower, and its variance is larger due to a skew toward impaired performance. One way of using this distribution is simply to compare it with that from normal participants, comparing their means. Another way is to capitalize on the variance within the distribution of participants with brain damage and ask how task performance is associated with low or high performance.

Some examples of how partitioning of the variance in the performances of participants with brain damage might be reflected in their neuroanatomy are shown in the figure. (a) Single cases with focal damage to left frontal operculum would show a severe impairment on certain language tasks and inform hypotheses about the neuroanatomy of Broca's aphasia. (b) Performance on language tests at a very low level would yield a specific set of neural structures that constitute a system in the left hemisphere for processing language. (c) Increasing the performance threshold for analysis would include many more participants, yielding the conclusion that the left hemisphere is involved in processing language.

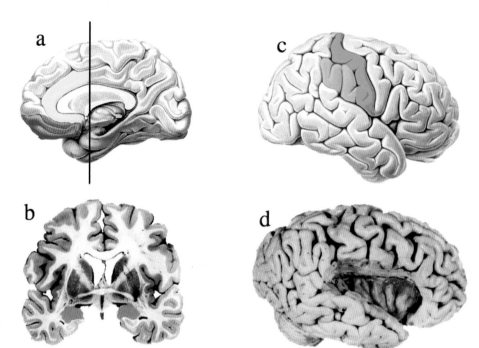

Figure 25.2. Some brain regions important for processing emotion. Shown are the regions discussed in this chapter, color coded onto views of a human brain.

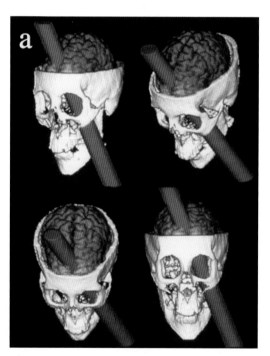

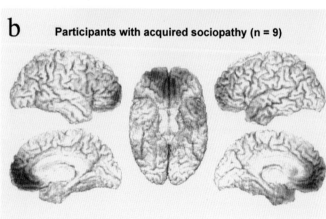

b Participants with acquired sociopathy (n = 9)

Figure 25.3. Lesions of the human orbitofrontal cortex. (a) The case of Phineas Gage, as reconstructed by Hanna Damasio. The path of the tamping iron through Gage's brain was reconstructed from the known dimensions of the iron, from measurements of Gage's skull and the hole within it, and from descriptions of the accident. From Damasio, Grabowski, Frank, Galaburda, and Damasio, 1994. (b) Overlap representation of lesions from patients with bifrontal tumor resections who all share a behavioral profile similar to that reported for Gage. In general, their lesions are more restricted than Gage's, but in all cases they include ventral and medial regions of the prefrontal cortex. Damage to these regions leads to a constellation of impaired emotional response, lack of remorse, poor planning for the future, and impulsive behavior, dubbed "acquired sociopathy." From Bechara, Tranel, and Damasio, 2002.

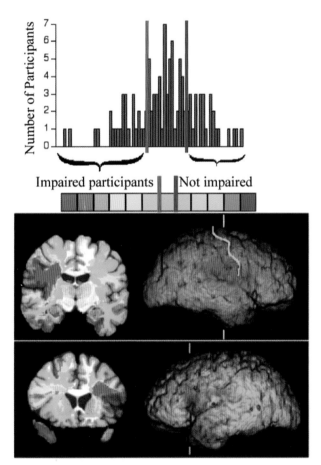

Figure 25.5. The right somatosensory cortex is necessary to judge emotions. A group lesion analysis was conducted on 108 participants with focal brain lesions, whose performance histogram is shown at the top. Color was used to encode their lesion overlaps, dependent on what partition of the performance distribution they fell in (scale). At the bottom, the brain cuts and 3-D views show superimposed overlaps of the lesions of all participants, encoded by color according to their density and performance in recognizing emotion from faces. The red regions identify locations at which a large number of lesions were associated with impaired emotion recognition. These were in right somatosensory cortex (*top images*) and in left frontal operculum (*bottom images*). From Adolphs, 2002.

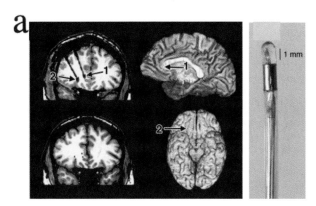

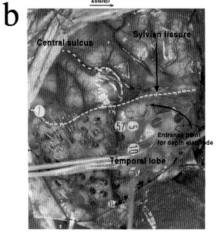

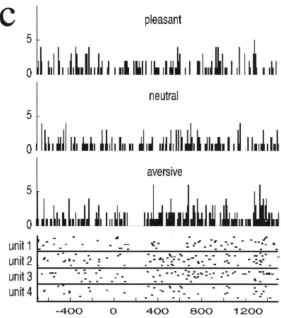

Figure 25.6. Electrophysiological recordings from intracranial electrodes. (a) MR images of a patient's brain showing location of implanted electrodes in prefrontal cortex. *Left*: At the top is an MR image with the implanted electrodes and indicated recording sites (numbers); at the bottom are the locations of those recording sites mapped onto a preimplantation scan of the patient's brain. *Right*: 3-D reconstructions of the brain with recording site locations indicated. *Inset*: micrograph of the electrodes. (b) Photograph of surface grid electrodes from which cortical field potentials can be recorded. The grid lies on the surface of cortex. (c) Single-neuron responses categorized by the emotion of the stimulus. Shown are peristimulus-time histograms (*top*) and individual rasters (action potentials from four neurons, *bottom*), in response to emotional visual pictures in three categories: pleasant, neutral, and aversive. There was a selective change in firing rate of the neurons only to aversive stimuli. The time point at zero corresponds to the onset of the visual stimuli.

Emotion Assessment

Elizabeth K. Gray
David Watson

Assessing Positive and Negative Affect via Self-Report

Affect plays a central role in human experience, providing the ongoing hedonic tone that colors the everyday lives of individuals. Not surprisingly, therefore, affect occupies an equally prominent role in the psychological and social science literature. As such, a number of different approaches exist for assessing mood and emotion. This chapter focuses on outlining and describing a variety of self-report measures that are available to affect researchers.

Defining Affect

In outlining the available means for measuring affect, we must address two central issues. First, we must be clear about the definitions of affect, emotion, and mood that will be used within this chapter. The constructs of mood and emotion are similar in that they both refer to feeling states that can be broadly characterized as pleasant or unpleasant (i.e., as positive or negative) and that reflect what is happening within the organism (Parkinson, Totterdell, Brinner, & Reynolds, 1996). It is also widely believed that they contain some common components and are controlled by similar processes (Clark & Watson, 1999; Parkinson et al., 1996). Because these constructs do share many similarities, they have often been researched together under the more general label of *affect*. Affect is a broader, more inclusive psychological construct that refers to mental states involving evaluative feelings, that is, states in which a person feels good or bad or

likes or dislikes what is happening (Parkinson et al., 1996). For the purposes of this chapter, we review measures that fit into this general framework. However, we note that although these constructs of mood and emotion are closely related, they also reflect a number of fundamental differences, including duration, frequency, intensity, and pattern of activation; these differences should be considered carefully by the researcher before choosing a specific assessment technique.

Although moods and emotions both involve subjective feeling states, mood is a much broader concept than emotion. First, moods are experienced with greater duration than emotions (Davidson, 1994; Gray & Watson, 2001; Watson & Clark, 1994b). An emotional episode may last seconds, or minutes at the most. Emotions are intense yet brief. A mood, on the other hand, can last hours or even days. For example, the experience of fear is a quick, unexpected response that can be quite intense—involving increased heart rate, sweaty palms, rapid breathing, dry mouth, and so on—but it usually waxes and wanes very quickly. In a few seconds, a person makes the decision to act or run, and then the emotion subsides. On the other hand, nervousness or anxiety (e.g., waiting for test results from your doctor, anticipating an important interview)—which involves a similar subjective experience that is much less intense—could last days or even a week.

Moods are also experienced more consistently and frequently than are emotions (Gray & Watson, 2001; Watson, 2000). True emotional reactions occur rarely. Their relative infrequency makes good evolutionary sense, as it clearly would be maladaptive to experience these high intensity states often (see Watson, 2000). In contrast, moods fill much of our everyday lives. In fact, researchers have proposed that moods are probably always present during waking consciousness, providing a continuous stream of subjective experience (what Watson, 2000, calls "the stream of affect") as an affective backdrop to our lives (Ekman, 1994; Watson & Clark, 1994b). Thus, for example, most people infrequently experience the full emotion of anger, an intense state with strong physical (e.g., clenched fists) and subjective (e.g., rage) components; in contrast, however, the milder moods of annoyance, irritability, frustration, and grouchiness are experienced much more often and form an important part of everyday life.

Finally, moods and emotions differ in the experiences and events that trigger them (Davidson, 1994; Gray & Watson, 2001). Emotions typically can be linked to a specific, defining moment that causes the response. Put differently, because emotions prompt the organism into action or decision, they must be triggered by a particular object that sets them into motion. Moods, on the contrary, are not so much a reaction that is triggered by a specific event as a summary of one's overall affective state (Watson & Clark, 1994b). As Larsen (2000) puts it, "moods do not have the 'aboutness' of emotions. That is, they often occur without reference to, nor are they directed toward, any specific object or event" (p. 130).

The second important issue in defining affect concerns the distinction between trait versus state affect. Due to the nature of affective experience, it can be studied either as a temporary, transient state or as a long-term, stable trait. State affects are defined as the experience of moods or emotions that are comparatively short-lived and follow a fluctuating course. They are transient episodes of feeling that are particularly influenced by the current situation (Tellegen, 1985; Watson, 2000). Trait affects, on the other hand, are durable dispositions or long-term, stable individual differences that reflect a person's general tendency to experience a particular affective state (Tellegen, 1985; Watson, 2000). These two types of affective constructs generally show the same underlying structure and can be measured simply in self-report instruments by altering the instructions to the participant; for instance, respondents can be asked to rate either (1) their current affect, that is, how they feel right now (state affect) or (2) their average, typical affective experiences, that is, how they generally feel (trait affect).

The Structure of Affect

Assessment instruments invariably reflect an explicit or implicit structural model. In other words, researchers attempt to create measures that capture the key constructs within the target domain. Consequently, it is important to describe the underlying structure of affect. Within this domain, the two primary approaches are the specific-affect and dimensional models. Specific-affect theories focus on discrete affect states such as fear, anger, sadness, and joy, whereas dimensional theories argue that affect is composed of a smaller number of general dimensions (Watson, 2000; Watson & Tellegen, 1985; Watson & Vaidya, 2003).

Early affect research typically adopted the discrete emotional model, focusing on specific moods and emotions. Some investigators simply assessed a single emotional state, using measures such as the Beck Depression Inventory (BDI; Beck, Ward, Mendelson, Mock, & Erbaugh, 1961). Another popular approach was to use adjective checklists that allowed one to assess several different discrete affects; among the widely used measures of this type were the Multiple Affect Adjective Checklist (MAACL; Zuckerman & Lubin, 1965) and the Profile of Mood States (POMS; McNair, Lorr, & Droppleman, 1971). The specific-affect scales in these measures (e.g., depression, anxiety, hostility) were constructed to measure separate, distinct types of mood and emotion. This approach, of course, reflects the basic assumptions of the discrete-affect model, which stresses that affective experience is characterized by a number of well-defined content factors. These multiple-affect checklists were very similar to each other, relying on a basic response scale on which participants indicated whether an adjective described their current, past, or general moods (Stone, 1995). The actual affect terms varied across these measures, depending on the technique used for scale development; nevertheless, they yielded similar structures and typically showed comparable associations with real-world outcomes. Thus, these measures yielded a common set of basic moods and emotions, including happiness, fear, anxiety, sadness, and anger; these same basic affects were found consistently across various measures and samples (Watson & Vaidya, 2003).

Unfortunately, however, these specific-affect scales usually were found to be significantly interrelated (Watson & Clark, 1997). In particular, individuals showed a strong tendency to experience moods or emotions with the same valence together. For example, when participants reported feeling anxious, they also reported experiencing other negative affects, such as sadness and hostility. This problem of high correlations between the discrete affects indicated the need for newer, better models of affective experience. These problems stimulated an intense discussion of the underlying structure of affect, which eventually led to the articulation of dimensional theories and circumplex models in the 1980s (see Diener & Emmons, 1984; Russell, 1980; Watson & Tellegen, 1985). That is, given the very broad, nonspecific nature of affective experience of affect, researchers began to adopt models that bypassed these discrete affects and posited fewer underlying dimensions.

As research accumulated using this dimensional approach, researchers eventually converged on a two-factor structure. In 1980, James Russell proposed an influential model—based largely on analyses of facial expressions and judged similarities among mood terms—arguing that "affective dimensions are interrelated in a highly systematic fashion" (1980, p. 1161). Specifically, his model provided evidence that the structure of the affective dimensions could be represented in a circumplex model. A circumplex model is a special type of two-dimensional structure in which variables can be systematically arranged around the perimeter of a circle. Russell named the dimensions that define this two-dimensional space *Pleasure-Displeasure* and *Arousal-Sleep* (Russell, 1980). In 1985, Watson and Tellegen expanded this circumplex idea through the analysis of extensive self-report affect data. In their analyses, they also discovered two robust dimensions of affect that could be arranged in a circumplex. In contrast, however, Watson and Tellegen emphasized the importance of *Positive Affect* and *Negative Affect* as the major dimensions in affective space (Watson & Tellegen, 1985). These dimensions can be viewed as rotational variants of those proposed by Russell and are located approximately 45 degrees apart from Pleasure and Arousal in a common space; consequently, these four dimensions jointly define a single circumplex structure (see Watson & Tellegen, 1985; Watson, Weise, Vaidya, & Tellegen, 1999), which therefore yields a consensual model of affect at the higher order level. The emergence of this consensual model led to an explosion of research on the basic dimensions of affect.

It should be noted, however, that these two alternative circumplex models offer opposing views on the polarity of the dimensions of affective space. Russell's model emphasizes the bipolarity of affect (see Feldman Barrett & Russell, 1998; Russell, 1979, 1980; Russell & Carroll, 1999a, 1999b), which is consistent with historical measurements of mood (see Lorr, McNair, & Fisher, 1982; Meddis, 1972). In his circumplex model, pleasant (e.g., happy, satisfied) and unpleasant (e.g., sad, gloomy) states occupy opposite ends of the same dimension, thus creating a bipolar continuum of positive versus negative feelings. In contrast, Watson and Tellegen's model focuses on two independent and largely unipolar dimensions of affective space, Positive Affect (i.e., the extent to which one is experiencing positive moods such as cheerfulness and enthusiasm) and Negative Affect (i.e., the extent to which one is experiencing negative moods such as fear, anger, guilt, and disgust; see Watson & Tellegen, 1985, 1999; Watson et al., 1999). Both models have received extensive empirical support. Moreover, they have generated an intense theoretical discussion regarding the basic structure of affect. This, in turn, has stimulated increased research on affect and has led to the creation of new mood measures.

Beginning in this period and continuing to the present, research on affective experience has flourished. The emergence of this robust and relatively simple two-dimensional structure encouraged many researchers to include affect measures in their studies. Relations were established between affect and personality, clinical psychopathology, cognitive processes, daily events, and health and organizational outcomes; more fundamentally, affective variables increasingly

were integrated into important theories in personality, clinical, social, health, organizational, and cognitive psychology (e.g., Berry & Hansen, 1996; Clark & Watson, 1988; Diener, Smith, & Fujita, 1995; Eckenrode, 1984; Meyer & Shack, 1989; Schwarz & Clore, 1983; Stone, 1981). During this resurgence of research on mood and emotion, many advances were made in the measurement of affective experience.

Starting in the late 1980s, the Watson and Tellegen model—based on the dimensions of Positive and Negative Affect—gradually emerged as the most prominent structural/assessment scheme in research on self-rated affect. Its popularity is based, in part, on its robustness: positive and negative affect are reliably found in the measurement of affect across different measures, time frames, and samples (e.g., Almagor & Ben-Porath, 1989; Mayer & Gaschke, 1988; Watson, 1988b; Watson & Clark, 1992; Watson & Tellegen, 1985; Zevon & Tellegen, 1982). Its popularity also reflects the fact that measures of positive and negative affect are weakly correlated with one another and, in empirical studies, show very different associations with personality and real-world outcomes (Clark & Watson, 1999).

The broad dimension of Positive Affect is composed of positively valenced mood states, including enthusiasm, energy, interest, pleasure, confidence, and feelings of affiliation. Trait positive affect reflects an individual's stable level of pleasurable engagement with the environment; state positive affect reflects an individual's short-term, often context-specific, experience of positive emotions such as confidence or joy. Both state and trait positive affect are reliably correlated with personality measures of extraversion (Clark & Watson, 1999). Conversely, Negative Affect assesses the experience of negative mood and emotion. It can be characterized as an individual's subjective distress and negative response to the environment, including feelings of nervousness, fear, anger, guilt, and scorn. Trait negative affect reflects an individual's general tendency to experience some type of negative mood; in contrast, state negative affect is a more temporary, situation-specific experience of negative emotion. Negative affect is consistently and strongly associated with measures of general neuroticism (Clark & Watson, 1999). The affect measures we discuss subsequently all measure some aspect of positive and negative affectivity.

Watson, Clark, and Tellegen (1988) developed the Positive and Negative Affect Schedule (PANAS) to measure these basic affect dimensions (see appendix A). The PANAS provides quick, simple, and easy assessment of positive and negative affect; it is psychometrically superior to the older adjective checklists and has become the most widely used measurement tool in affect research. In the PANAS and the later expanded form of the PANAS (PANAS-X), positive and negative affect scales are largely independent of one another (Watson & Clark, 1994a; Watson, Clark, & Tellegen, 1988) and show distinctive associations with personality, social, behavioral, and cognitive variables (e.g., Berry & Hansen, 1996; Costa & McCrae, 1980; Larsen & Ketelaar, 1991; Watson, 1988a).

A Hierarchical Synthesis

In order to reconcile these various models and ideas, we refer to a hierarchical structure that includes both specific, discrete affects and broader dimensions. We discuss self-report scales that assess multiple affects within this tradition. As many of the other chapters in this volume are concerned with the measurement of particular affects, this chapter focuses instead on the broader measurement of affective experience.

In the self-report literature, a three-level hierarchical model has been proposed to integrate all of the major approaches to affective structure (Tellegen, Watson, & Clark, 1999). In this hierarchical model, the highest level contains the general bipolar dimension of happiness versus unhappiness (i.e., Russell's dimension of Pleasure-Displeasure), the intermediate level includes the two broad general dimensional factors of Positive and Negative Affect, and the lowest level reflects the unique, distinct specific affects (Watson & Tellegen, 1985). Thus both Russell's (1980) bipolar dimension of Pleasure-Displeasure and Watson and Tellegen's (1985) Positive and Negative Affect dimensions can be accommodated (Tellegen et al., 1999) in this hierarchical scheme, which also has room for the important specific affects contained in the older discrete-emotion models.

Self-Report Measures of Affective Experience

Countless measures have been developed, tested, and used throughout the long history of research on mood and emotion. These instruments share many similar features but also have subtle differences in their instructions, response formats, and psychometric properties. This review includes the major and most widely accepted measures—emphasizing particularly those with excellent reliability and validity—as well as more recent approaches.

Five comprehensive affective measures have been particularly prominent in the mood literature: the Mood Adjective Checklist (MACL; Nowlis, 1965), the Profile of Mood States (POMS; McNair et al., 1971), the original and revised versions of the Multiple Affect Adjective Checklist (MAACL & MAACL-R; see Zuckerman & Lubin, 1965, 1985), the Expanded Form of the Positive and Negative Affect Schedule (PANAS-X; Watson & Clark, 1994a), and the Differential Emotions Scale (DES; see Izard, Libero, Putnam, & Haynes, 1993). Each has been used extensively in studies of self-rated affect. Additionally, newer scales—such as the Affect Grid (Russell, Weiss, & Mendelsohn, 1989; see appendix B, this chapter), the Current Mood Questionnaire (Feldman Barrett & Russell, 1998), and the UWIST Multiple Adjective Checklist (Matthews, Jones & Chamberlain, 1990)—have been proposed to clarify issues in the dimensional structure of affect and to improve measurement (e.g., through the elimination of response biases). We therefore consider these measures as well.

We use the hierarchical model discussed previously as a guide in discussing these measures. Most notably, we separate measures according to their classification in the hierarchy (i.e., whether they primarily were designed to assess specific affects or general dimensions).

Measures of Specific Affects

Mood Adjective Checklist

The Mood Adjective Checklist (MACL) was one of the first scales created to measure affect and was based on research done by Victor Nowlis and Russell Green in the 1950s and early 1960s (summarized in Nowlis, 1965). It was based on factor-analytic studies of 130 adjectives designed to identify the basic dimensions of mood. Additionally, the authors wanted to design a scale that could measure current mood and could reliably detect mood change (Nowlis, 1965). The MACL was very influential in mood measurement but never became widely used or popular because "much of the supporting psychometric data were buried in the Office of Naval Research technical reports and unpublished conference proceedings" (Watson & Vaidya, 2003, p. 359). Indeed, basic psychometric properties of the MACL scales—such as their internal consistency—never were clearly established.

Despite its name, the MACL is not a true checklist; rather, respondents rate each adjective on a 4-point scale with a double check (√√)for "definitely describes how you feel at the moment," a single check (√) for "only slightly applies to your feelings at the moment," a question mark (?) for "not clear or cannot decide if it applies to your feelings at the moment," or "no" if the word "definitely does not apply to your feelings at the moment" (Nowlis, 1965). Rating scales may also be substituted for these "check marks," where √√ = 3, √ = 2, ? = 1 and no = 0 (Nowlis, 1970). Twelve factors are assessed by the MACL adjectives: Aggression, Anxiety, Surgency, Elation, Concentration, Fatigue, Social Affection, Sadness, Skepticism, Egotism, Vigor, and Nonchalance (Nowlis, 1965). A short form of the instrument is also available; it contains 36 adjectives (Stone, 1995).

Multiple Affect Adjective Checklist

Developed by Zuckerman and Lubin in 1965, the Multiple Affect Adjective Checklist (MAACL) assesses several discrete affects using ratings on 132 adjectives. The scales have both state ("check how you feel now") and trait ("check how you generally feel") versions. The MAACL was developed out of an earlier measure, the Affect Adjective Checklist (AACL), that was created to measure anxiety. It was expanded to assess the multiple affects of depression, anxiety, and hostility in patients, but this measure subsequently has been used widely with many different types of samples (see Gotlib & Meyer, 1986). However, the original MAACL was plagued by very high interscale correlations and, therefore, poor discriminant validity (see Gotlib & Meyer, 1986); this situation led to a revision of the MAACL scales to remedy this problem (Zuckerman & Lubin, 1985). The Revised MAACL (MAACL-R) includes five unipolar scales: Anxiety, Depression, Hostility, Positive Affect, and Sensation Seeking. Subsequent analyses of the adjectives also has led to the identification of two higher order factors, which basically represent the familiar dimensions of Positive and Negative Affect (Gotlib & Meyer, 1986; Stone, 1995).

The MAACL has been included in hundreds of studies and has been used in a wide variety of samples (Cooper & McCormack, 1992; Gotlib & Meyer, 1986). Alpha coefficients for the scales generally are acceptable (the average is .79); moreover, the trait versions of the scales show appropriate test-retest reliability and have been validated against peer reports, clinical observations, and the MMPI (Cooper & McCormack, 1992). However, the MAACL-R negative affect scales continue to be highly correlated and to display limited convergent validity. Furthermore, internal consistency estimates for the Sensation Seeking scale vary widely (Zuckerman & Lubin, 1985) and often reflect an unacceptable level of reliability (see Watson & Vaidya, 2003).

Profile of Mood States

Originally developed as the Psychiatric Outpatient Mood Scale, the Profile of Mood States (POMS) was introduced by Douglas McNair and Maurice Lorr in 1971 (see McNair et al., 1971). The scale originally was designed to measure the potentially changing emotional condition of psychiatric patients (McNair & Lorr, 1964). In the following years the measure took on a new focus and a new name—the Profile of Mood States—although it retained the same acronym. The scale includes 65 adjectives that are rated on a 4-point scale, from *not at all* to *extremely,* based on how the participant has "felt the way described during the past week, including today." Later the rating scale was increased to 5 points. The original 1-week time frame was designed to be just long enough to emphasize a patient's typical state in his or her current life situation, while at the same time being short enough to be sensitive to changes resulting from treatment (McNair & Lorr, 1964). The instructions also have been successfully altered to reflect trait affect or current, ongoing states (e.g., "the past 3 minutes"; see Howarth & Schokman-Gates, 1981; Payne, 2001). The POMS can be used with a wide range of respondents, including healthy, physically ill, and psychiatric samples (Curran, Andrykowski, & Studts, 1995). The scale includes six factors: Anger-Hostility, Vigor-Activity, Fatigue-Inertia, Confusion-Bewilderment, Tension-Anxiety, and Depression-Dejection. Affect adjectives include easily understood terms such as *tense, cheerful, confused, unhappy,* and *angry.*

The POMS takes between 3 and 7 minutes to complete and therefore is an excellent measure if time is a constraint

within research (Curran et al., 1995; Shacham, 1983). However, individuals who are physically ill or psychologically compromised often require a much greater time to complete the measure (Shacham, 1983). Therefore, short forms with 11 to 40 adjectives are also available (Lane & Lane, 2002; Shacham, 1983). In particular, a 24-item, short version of the POMS—previously named the Profile of Mood States-Adolescent and currently referred to as the Brunel University Mood Scale—has been validated in sport research settings (Lane & Lane, 2002). Shacham (1983) also created a statistically equivalent shorter version, the POMS-SF, with 37 adjectives for assessment situations that have significant time or patient limitations (Curran et al., 1995). Finally, Cella and colleagues (1987) developed the Brief POMS, which contains only 11 adjectives from the original scale and provides only an overall distress score (Curran et al., 1995).

The available evidence indicates that the POMS scales have acceptable internal consistency reliabilities and moderate stability over short time periods in patients and are sensitive to changes due to therapy (McNair & Lorr, 1964; Payne, 2001). The POMS shows good predictive validity with patients and athletes and good to excellent concurrent validity with scales such as the BDI and Manifest Anxiety Scale (Lane & Lane, 2002; Payne, 2001). Unfortunately, the POMS negative mood scales show relatively poor discriminant validity (Watson & Clark, 1994a; Watson & Vaidya, 2003), which makes them less than optimal for researchers interested in assessing these discrete affects.

Differential Emotions Scale

The Differential Emotions Scale (DES) originally was developed by Izard and colleagues to measure the 10 basic emotions of interest, joy, surprise, sadness, anger, disgust, contempt, fear, shame/shyness, and guilt (see Izard et al., 1993; Stone, 1995). The DES has several different versions, but in each form, the participant is instructed to rate each term on a multipoint rating scale; depending on the particular instructions that are used, respondents rate their current feelings, their feelings over the past week, or their long-term trait affectivity (i.e., How frequently in daily life do you feel this particular emotion?). The DES was derived from cross-cultural research on emotion-expression labeling (Izard et al., 1993). The most recent version of this scale, the DES-IV, includes 12 scales by (1) measuring shame and shyness separately and (2) adding a new scale that assesses inner-directed hostility (Izard et al., 1993).

The DES scales show moderate to high intercorrelations. The biggest problem with the instrument, however, is that many of the scales display only low to moderate internal consistencies (see Watson & Vaidya, 2003). Izard et al. (1993, Table 1), for example, report coefficient alphas of .56 (Disgust), .60 (Shame), .62 (Shyness), and .65 (Surprise). These reliability problems are due in large part to the small number of items (typically three) that compose each scale.

Nevertheless, the scales are stable across time and are significantly correlated with personality variables and outcomes (Izard, 1991; Izard et al., 1993).

Expanded Form of the Positive and Negative Affect Schedule (PANAS-X)

As discussed earlier, Watson et al. (1988) created the original PANAS to assess the higher order dimensions of Positive Affect and Negative Affect. Watson and Clark (1994a) subsequently expanded this instrument by including 11 factor-analytically derived scales that assess specific, lower order affects. As with the PANAS, respondents rate the extent to which they have experienced each mood term on a 5-point scale (1 = *very slightly or not at all*, 5 = *extremely*); the items can be used with varying time instructions to assess either state or trait affect. Four scales assess specific negative mood states that are strong markers of the higher order Negative Affect dimension: Fear (6 items; e.g., *scared, nervous*), Sadness (5 items; e.g., *blue, lonely*), Guilt (6 items, e.g., *ashamed, dissatisfied with self*), and Hostility (6 items; e.g., *angry, scornful*). In addition, three scales assess positively valenced states that are strongly linked to the higher order Positive Affect factor: Joviality (8 items; e.g., *happy, enthusiastic*), Self-Assurance (6 items; e.g., *confident, bold*), and Attentiveness (4 items; e.g., *alert, concentrating*). Finally, four scales are less strongly and consistently related to the higher order dimensions: Shyness (4 items; e.g., *bashful, timid*), Fatigue (4 items; e.g., *sleepy, sluggish*), Serenity (3 items; e.g., *calm, relaxed*), and Surprise (3 items; e.g., *amazed, astonished*).

Watson and Clark (1994a, 1997) report extensive reliability and validity data on these scales (see also Bagozzi, 1993). For instance, Watson and Clark (1997, Table 7) present median internal consistency estimates across 11 samples (9 student samples, 1 adult sample, 1 psychiatric patient sample), with a combined sample size of 8,194; these data reflect eight different time frames. All of the longer (i.e., 5–8 item) PANAS-X scales were highly reliable, with median coefficient alphas of .93 (Joviality), .88 (Guilt), .87 (Fear), .87 (Sadness), .85 (Hostility), and .83 (Self-Assurance). As would be expected, the reliabilities of the shorter scales tended to be lower, but they still were quite good: .88 (Fatigue), .83 (Shyness), .78 (Attentiveness), .77 (Surprise), and .76 (Serenity).

Measures of Affect Dimensions

Activation-Deactivation Adjective Checklist

The Activation-Deactivation Adjective Checklist (AD-ACL) was originally developed by Thayer (1967) to measure fluctuations in activation and arousal. The instrument was developed from studies using the MACL and the existing literature on activation; it was designed to provide a measure that would be easily administered and to eliminate ap-

paratus problems to allow for maximum flexibility in affect research (Thayer, 1967). The scale includes adjectives to be rated on a 4-point scale, ranging from *definitely feel* to *definitely do not feel*. Factor analyses revealed that these items measure four general factors—General Activation (Energy), Deactivation-Sleep, High Activation, and General Deactivation (Calmness). Subsequent structural analyses revealed the presence of two higher order activation dimensions—Energy versus Tiredness and Tension versus Inactivation (Thayer, 1967, 1978).

Despite their differing labels, these factors generally are thought to be very similar to the familiar dimensions of Positive and Negative Affect, respectively (Nemanick & Munz, 1994; Watson, 1988b). In support of this idea, Yik, Russell, and Feldman Barrett (1999) established a strong level of convergence (1) between Positive Affect and Energy versus Tiredness and (2) between Negative Affect and Tension versus Inactivation (see Yik et al., 1999, Figure 5).

The AD-ACL correlates highly with physiological changes, can detect changes in activation, and predicts individual-differences variables (Thayer, 1967, 1978, 1986). The scale is rapidly and easily administered in approximately 2 minutes; a short form that requires only 20 seconds is also available (Thayer, 1978). The AD-ACL also shows excellent test-retest reliability and validity (Thayer, 1978).

Positive and Negative Affect Schedule

As discussed previously, the Positive and Negative Affect Schedule (PANAS) was introduced in 1988 by Watson, Clark, and Tellegen as a brief measure of the two major dimensions of affect (see appendix A). The PANAS can measure either state or trait affect, with a slight modification in the instructions to the participant (e.g., How do you feel right now? How have you felt in the last week? How do you generally feel?). Positive and negative affect are each measured by 10 items; sample items include *active, enthusiastic,* and *proud* for Positive Affect (PA), and *upset, afraid,* and *guilty* for Negative Affect (NA). Participants rate the extent to which they have felt each mood term using a 5-point scale on which 1 = *very slightly or not at all* and 5 = *extremely*. The general, trait versions of the scales can also be adapted for partner ratings by changing the instructions from "indicate to what extent you generally feel this way" to "indicate to what extent your partner generally feels this way." Watson, Hubbard, and Weise (2000) reported significant convergent correlations between self- and partner ratings on these scales in three different samples.

The PANAS scales were developed to address an important problem in affect assessment, namely, that then-existing measures of positive and negative affect were inadequate, often showing low reliability and/or poor convergent and discriminant validity (Watson, Clark, & Tellegen, 1988). The brief PANAS scales were developed from the 60 adjectives used by Zevon and Tellegen (1982) through factor analysis to create scales that were "pure markers of either PA or NA; that is, terms that had a substantial loading on one factor but a near-zero loading on the other" (Watson et al., 1988, p. 1064). The resulting 10-item scales show excellent internal consistency and convergent and discriminant validity (Watson & Clark, 1997; Watson et al., 1988; Watson et al., 2000).

Affect Grid

The Affect Grid is a single-item, 9 x 9 grid introduced by Russell, Weiss, and Mendelsohn (1989; see appendix B, this chapter). Participants are presented with a grid graphic with affect descriptors placed at each corner and at the midpoint on each side; they are asked to check the appropriate cell of the grid that best represents their current feelings. The Affect Grid is designed to represent affect terms in the two-dimensional space of Russell's circumplex. The affect descriptors are placed around the grid according to their relationship within the circumplex model, defining the general dimensions of Pleasure-Displeasure and Arousal-Sleepiness. These descriptors are arranged from the northwest corner of the grid in a clockwise direction—*stress, high arousal, excitement, pleasant feelings, relaxation, sleepiness, depression*, and *unpleasant feelings*—so that the two major dimensions are represented as bipolar opposites (see Russell et al., 1989, Figure 1, p. 494). This assessment technique yields a particularly quick and efficient means of assessing these higher order dimensions (Russell et al., 1989).

Studies completed primarily by Russell and colleagues show adequate interrater reliability and good convergent validity with other affect scales, such as the PANAS (Russell et al., 1989). The Affect Grid is potentially useful (1) when a very brief measure is required, (2) in detecting frequent short-term change in mood states, or (3) in studies that require a manipulation check (Russell et al., 1989). It must be noted, however, that single-item scales present problems in testing internal consistency reliability; moreover, they may be subject to larger effects of systematic or random error without the potential for aggregation of items into an overall score.

UWIST Mood Adjective Checklist

The UWIST Mood Adjective Checklist (UMACL) was created as a refinement of existing measures of mood and was designed to improve upon the psychometric deficiencies and limitations of existing instruments (Matthews et al., 1990). In particular, the designers of the UMACL sought to create an instrument that provides clearly labeled factors that model the entire affective space at the dimensional level (Matthews et al., 1990). Matthews et al. (1990) specifically designed their instrument to reconcile and synthesize the competing structural models proposed by Watson and Tellegen (1985), Russell (1980), and Thayer (1986). Accordingly, their measure includes adjectives to measure the affective dimensions of Tense

Arousal, Energetic Arousal (i.e., the basic dimensions included in the structural schemes of Thayer and of Watson and Tellegen), and Hedonic Tone (which corresponds to Russell's Pleasure-Displeasure factor); the terms also can be scored to yield a General Arousal index (Russell's second dimension). The UMACL contains mood adjectives rated on a 4-point response scale; respondents judge the extent to which these terms describe their current mood on a scale ranging from *definitely* to *definitely not*. Both a full version and short form of the scale are available (Matthews et al., 1990).

Based on seven studies presented in Matthews et al. (1990), the UMACL scales have excellent internal consistencies. The arousal scales are largely independent of one another —although they are moderately correlated with Hedonic Tone —and show appropriate associations with personality. The UMACL, although not as well known as other measures, is being utilized in the health, performance, and work literatures (e.g., Gold, MacLeod, Frier, & Deary, 1995), as well as in other countries (e.g., in a Japanese version).

Current Mood Questionnaire

Introduced in 1998, Feldman Barrett and Russell's Current Mood Questionnaire (CMQ) is a complex instrument that measures Russell's complete circumplex using multiple response formats to assess each dimension (see also Yik et al., 1999). This inventory was constructed in order to test key elements of Russell's model, most notably his assertion that the basic dimensions of affect (i.e., Pleasure vs. Displeasure; Arousal vs. Sleep) are fully bipolar in nature (see Feldman Barrett & Russell, 1998; Green, Goldman, & Salovey, 1993; Russell & Carroll, 1999a, 1999b; Tellegen, Watson & Clark, 1999; Watson & Tellegen, 1999). Consequently, the CMQ includes bipolar opposite terms in each of its scales (Feldman Barrett & Russell, 1998). The full CMQ assesses mood via three different rating methods: (1) simple adjectives rated on a 5-point Likert scale; (2) more complex mood statements rated using a 5-point agree-disagree format; and (3) trait-like descriptions rated on a 4-point according to whether it "describes me." These multiple formats were created to allow researchers to correct correlations for both random and systematic error using structural equation modeling (Feldman Barrett & Russell, 1998).

Feldman Barrett and Russell (1998) report good convergent and discriminant validities for their scales. However, although internal consistency reliabilities are acceptable for the Pleasure-Displeasure scales, they are less satisfactory for the CMQ measures of the Arousal-Sleep dimension (see Watson & Vaidya, 2003). Further, these Arousal and Sleep scales are not strongly negatively correlated, suggesting that the underlying dimension is not fully bipolar (Watson & Vaidya, 2003). These problems are not unique to the CMQ; indeed, it generally has proven much more difficult to create good measures of Arousal-Sleep than of the other major dimensions that make up the affect circumplex (see Watson

& Vaidya, 2003; Watson et al., 1999). In any event, given the complexity of this instrument, it is rather time-intensive and awkward to use; therefore, it is not often employed as a practical affect assessment instrument.

Basic Considerations in Affect Measurement

Due to the nature of the underlying construct, the measurement of affective experience involves some unusual and challenging assessment issues. When participants are asked to judge their affective conditions, they must integrate objective physiological sensations with a subjective interpretation of cues from both the body and the surrounding context in formulating their responses. More broadly, the self-report assessment of affect requires respondents to both (1) notice and quantify their affective experience and then (2) honestly and accurately report that assessment on a questionnaire (Watson, 2000). Because of the inherently subjective nature of these judgments, one could argue with some justification that measures of current affect are valid as long as participants are not deliberately distorting their assessment. Put differently, the respondents' ongoing synthesis of this physiological, situational, and cognitive information is their current mood. However, self-report measures of affect—similar to any other assessment technique—are not perfect and, in fact, are subject to both random and systematic measurement errors.

With this in mind, we briefly review some potentially important sources of error in mood measurement. Before proceeding further, however, we must emphasize that there is no evidence that self-rated affect is particularly subject to any particular type of error or distortion (Watson & Clark, 1997). Indeed, self-report affect measures display excellent construct validity in terms of their temporal stability, associations with personality, and relations with non-self-report data (e.g., Diener et al., 1995; Meyer & Shack, 1989; Watson & Clark, 1994a; Watson & Vaidya, 2003). Nevertheless, error may be introduced into affect measures in a number of predictable ways. Error is a significant concern in all types of measurement, and researchers should be aware of it and take precautions to control it whenever possible.

First, affective measurement is subject to potential accuracy problems whenever respondents are asked to make retrospective judgments in which they are asked to report on past affective experiences (e.g., how they have felt over the course of the day, or over the past few days or weeks; see Robinson & Clore, 2002). Among other things, these retrospective ratings suffer from *duration neglect* (i.e., a tendency to focus primarily on the peak or highest intensity experiences, with an accompanying insensitivity to the actual amount of time that an affect is experienced) and *recency effects* (i.e., overweighting the importance of more recent experiences relative to more distal states; see Hedges, Jandorf, & Stone, 1985; Robinson & Clore, 2002; Watson & Tellegen,

2002). Affective assessments, therefore, should provide very clear instructions to the participant; moreover, the rated time frame should be chosen carefully and should be appropriate to the study and research question.

Second, systematic measurement error may be progressively introduced into affect measures through the process of aggregation. Due to the problems associated with retrospective reports, several recent researchers have recommended aggregating current online assessments of mood to eliminate these biases. Unfortunately, however, these aggregated ratings suffer from two unique problems of their own. The first problem is that aggregated ratings produce substantially higher intercorrelations among specific affects of the same valence when compared with global ratings (see Watson & Tellegen, 2002; Watson & Vaidya, 2003). For instance, scales that assess fear, sadness, and anger are much more strongly intercorrelated in aggregated ratings than in global trait ratings; thus measures of the discrete negative and positive affects show substantially reduced discriminant validity in aggregated data. The second problem is that aggregated ratings show almost a complete lack of bipolarity (Watson & Tellegen, 2002; Watson & Vaidya, 2003). For example, ratings of happiness and sadness display near-zero correlations in aggregated data. These problems likely are due to the augmented influence of acquiescence, that is, the tendency to respond similarly to items regardless of their content. Acquiescence serves to distort observed correlations toward +1.00; thus, it may artifactually inflate the correlations among variables that naturally are positively related (i.e., fear vs. anger) same-valence measures and weaken the correlations between variables that naturally are negatively associated (e.g., sadness vs. happiness; see Watson & Tellegen, 2002; Watson & Vaidya, 2003).

Third, the response format of the scale can play a crucial role in reducing systematic error (Clark & Watson, 1995). Most of the currently available assessment techniques use an adequate response format, including a wide variety of different types of Likert scale responses. However, many older affect measures (e.g., the MAACL) used a checklist format, which is much more problematic. In particular, this response format is notoriously susceptible to systematic rating biases—such as acquiescence—that can lead to highly distorted results; because of this, measurement experts now strongly recommend that this format be avoided (see Clark & Watson, 1995; Watson & Tellegen, 1999). Investigators should consider the response format of the scale carefully when determining which assessment technique to choose for their research.

Finally, social desirability potentially may introduce another form of systematic bias into affect assessments. Because of the rather obvious, face-valid nature of affect measures (which, for example, may ask respondents to indicate whether they generally are happy, energetic, angry, and sad), it seems reasonable to argue that participants may distort their responses in order to appear socially appropriate. In order to test this hypothesis, Watson and Vaidya (2003) compared self-ratings of mood with peer ratings in four different samples (with a combined N of more than 1,000) consisting of friendship dyads, dating couples, and married couples. Peer raters should be less subject to a social desirability bias, because they are not rating themselves and, therefore, can be more objective about the true affective condition of the friend or partner they are rating. However, Watson and Vaidya (2003) found that self-ratings were not skewed toward more socially desirable responses when compared with peer ratings; these data suggest that self-enhancement does not present a significant problem in affect assessment.

Aside from systematic errors that are inherent in a test or in the testing conditions, a recent body of evidence has established that humans are relatively poor regulators of their moods. As a society, we are sleep deprived, we tend to eat too much of the wrong kinds of food, we are overweight, and we do not exercise enough (Thayer, 2001). These maladaptive patterns suggest that we are insensitive to the physiological sources of our moods. In a related vein, the contemporary research literature suggests that people also are not very good at determining the specific internal and external factors that influence affective experience (Watson, 2000). Therefore, many types of affect ratings may require knowledge and insight that respondents largely lack; in such instances, they can be expected to rely on cultural stereotypes and incorrect expectations and beliefs about the nature of affective experience. For instance, because Monday is widely perceived in our society to be the worst day of the week (the so-called "Blue Monday" phenomenon), participants tend recall that their moods were worse on that day than they actually were. Similarly, women tend to exaggerate the extent to which their moods vary as a function of the menstrual cycle (see Watson, 2000).

In order to clarify this crucial issue in affect assessment, Robinson and Clore (2002) offer an accessibility model of emotional self-report that provides insight into understanding when participants may be especially good or bad at assessing their affect. According to this model, problems of inaccuracy in affect assessment emerge from an imperfect correspondence between the reality of affective experience and beliefs about this experience (Robinson & Clore, 2002). As such, the most accurate self-ratings are reports of current mood or emotion. In order to make judgments about current affect, a participant simply reports what they are feeling; this judgment is not biased by flawed recall or beliefs (Robinson & Clore, 2002). Retrospective, prospective, and hypothetical judgments of affect, however, are influenced by (1) the rapid decay of episodic memory, (2) expectations about what affects are typical for a particular situation, and (3) beliefs about one's own characteristic emotional experience (Robinson & Clore, 2002). For example, most people believe that birthdays and vacations are particularly happy situations; accordingly, when asked to describe their affect retrospectively, their ratings match this belief. However, if

respondents are asked to rate their moods concurrently on their birthdays or while on vacation, their current moods may reflect the stress of being in a new or unfamiliar vacation location or the mundaneness of a typical adult birthday.

Given these potential problems in affective assessment, it is the responsibility of the researcher to choose an affect measure that is appropriate for the goals of his or her study, that uses an acceptable response format, and that has established reliability and validity. Moreover, investigators must take reasonable steps to limit the influence of random and systematic measurement errors in the data, following the basic considerations we have outlined here (see also Watson & Vaidya, 2003, for a more detailed discussion of measurement error).

Concluding Recommendations for Researchers

This chapter provides some general guidance regarding the self-report measures that are available to affect researchers. Given the large quantity of scales available, the absence of comparative studies using multiple instruments, the lack of consensus regarding a definitive structure of affect, and the wide range of possible uses for affect measures, it is impossible to offer specific recommendations regarding which scales should be used. Certainly, however, any scale chosen for research should have acceptable to superior psychometric properties (including both reliability and validity); should be appropriate for the sample intended in time, language, and complexity; and should provide the maximum possible information for the purposes stated in the research. (For other recommendations and evaluations of affect measures—and for further discussion of the issues involved in affect measurement—see Howarth & Schokman-Gates, 1981; Mossholder, Kemery, Harris, Armenakis, & McGrath, 1994; Stone, 1995; Watson, 1988b, 2000; Watson & Clark, 1997; Watson & Tellegen, 1999; and Watson & Vaidya, 2003.)

Appendix A: PANAS

This scale consists of a number of words that describe different feelings and emotions. Read each item and then mark the appropriate answer in the space next to that word. Indicate to what extent [INSERT APPROPRIATE TIME INSTRUCTIONS HERE]. Use the following scale to record your answers.

1	2	3	4	5
very slightly or not at all	a little	moderately	quite a bit	extremely

_____ interested	_____ irritable
_____ distressed	_____ alert
_____ excited	_____ ashamed

_____ upset   _____ inspired

_____ strong   _____ nervous

_____ guilty   _____ determined

_____ scared   _____ attentive

_____ hostile   _____ jittery

_____ enthusiastic   _____ active

_____ proud   _____ afraid

We have used the PANAS with the following time instructions:

Moment	(you feel this way right now, that is, at the present moment)
Today	(you have felt this way today)
Past few days	(you have felt this way during the past few days)
Week	(you have felt this way during the past week)
Past few weeks	(you have felt this way during the past few weeks)
Year	(you have felt this way during the past year)
General	(you generally feel this way; that is, how you feel on the average)

Reprinted with permission from Watson, D., Clark, L. A., & Tellegen, A. (1988). Development and validation of brief measures of positive and negative affect: The PANAS scales. _Journal of Personality and Social Psychology, 54,_ 1063–1070; Appendix, p. 1070.

Appendix B: Affect Grid

You use the affect grid to describe feelings. It is in the form of a square—a kind of map for feelings. The center of the square (marked by X in the grid below) represents a neutral, average, everyday feeling. It is neither positive nor negative.

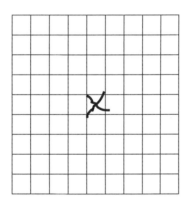

The right side of the grid represents pleasant feelings. The farther to the right, the more pleasant. The left half represents unpleasant feelings. The farther to the left, the more unpleasant.

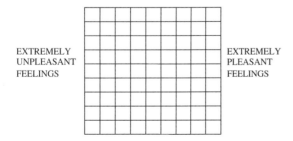

The vertical dimension of the map represents degree of arousal. Arousal has to do with how wide awake, alert, or activated a person feels—independent of whether the feeling is positive or negative. The top half is for feelings that are above average in arousal. The lower half is for feelings below average. The bottom represents sleep, and the higher you go, the more awake a person feels. So, the next step up from the bottom would be half awake/half asleep. At the top of the square is maximum arousal. If you imagine a state we might call frantic excitement (remembering that it could be either positive or negative), then this feeling would define the top of the grid.

EXTREMELY HIGH AROUSAL

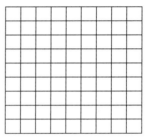

EXTREME SLEEPINESS

If the "frantic excitement" was positive, it would, of course, fall on the right half of the grid. The more positive, the farther to the right. If the "frantic excitement" was negative, it would fall on the left half of the grid. The more negative, the farther to the left. If the "frantic excitement" was neither positive nor negative, then it would fall in the middle square of the top row, as shown below.

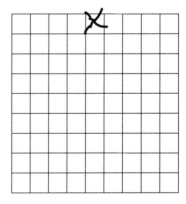

Other areas of the grid can be labeled as well. Up and to the right are feelings of ecstasy, excitement, joy. Opposite these, down and to the left, are feelings of depression, melancholy, sadness and gloom.

Up and to the left are feelings of stress and tension. Opposite these, down and to the right, are feelings of calm, relaxation, serenity.

STRESS   EXCITEMENT

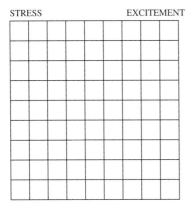

DEPRESSION   RELAXATION

Feelings are complex. They come in all shades and degrees. The labels we have given are merely landmarks to help you understand the affect grid. When actually using the grid, put an X anywhere in the grid to indicate the exact shade and intensity of feeling. Please look over the entire grid to get a feel for the meaning of the various areas.

EXAMPLE: Suppose that you were just surprised. Suppose further that the surprise was neither pleasant nor unpleasant. Probably you would feel more aroused than average. You might put your mark as shown.

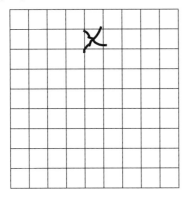

EXAMPLE: Suppose, instead, that you were only mildly surprised but that the surprise was a mildly pleasant one. You might put your mark as shown below.

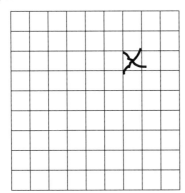

Reprinted with permission from Russell, J. A., Weiss, A. & Mendelsohn, G. A. (1989). Affect grid: A single-item scale of pleasure and arousal. *Journal of Personality & Social Psychology, 57,* 493–502; appendix, pp. 501–502.

References

Almagor, M., & Ben-Porath, Y. S. (1989). The two-factor model of self-reported mood: A cross-cultural replication. *Journal of Personality Assessment, 53,* 10–21.

Bagozzi, R. P. (1993). An examination of the psychometric properties of measures of negative affect in the PANAS-X scales. *Journal of Personality and Social Psychology, 65,* 836–851.

Beck, A. T., Ward, C. H., Mendelson, M., Mock, J., & Erbaugh, J. (1961). An inventory for measuring depression. *Archives of General Psychiatry, 4,* 561–571.

Berry, D. S., & Hansen, J. S. (1996). Positive affect, negative affect, and social interaction. *Journal of Personality and Social Psychology, 71,* 796–809.

Cella, D. F., Jacobsen, P. B., Orav, E. J., Holland, J. C., Silberfarb, P. M., & Rafla, S. (1987). A brief POMS measure of distress for cancer patients. *Journal of Chronic Diseases, 40,* 939–942.

Clark, L. A., & Watson, D. (1988). Mood and the mundane: Relations between daily life events and self-reported mood. *Journal of Personality and Social Psychology, 54,* 296–308.

Clark, L. A., & Watson, D. (1995). Constructing validity: Basic issues in objective scale development. *Psychological Assessment, 7,* 309–319.

Clark, L. A., & Watson, D. (1999). Temperament: A new paradigm for trait psychology. In L. Pervin & O. John (Eds.), *Handbook of personality: Theory and research* (2nd ed., pp. 399–423). New York: Guilford Press.

Cooper, A., & McCormack, W. A. (1992). Short-term group treatment for adult children of alcoholics. *Journal of Counseling Psychology, 39,* 350–355.

Costa, P. T., Jr., & McCrae, R. R. (1980). Influence of extraversion and neuroticism on subjective well-being: Happy and unhappy people. *Journal of Personality and Social Psychology, 38,* 668–678.

Curran, S. L., Andrykowski, M. A., & Studts, J. L. (1995). Short form of the Profile of Mood States (POMS-SF): Psychometric information. *Psychological Assessment, 7,* 80–83.

Davidson, R. J. (1994). On emotion, mood and related affective constructs. In P. Ekman & R. J. Davidson (Eds.), *The nature of emotion: Fundamental questions* (pp. 94–96). New York: Oxford University Press.

Diener, E., & Emmons, R. A. (1984). The independence of positive and negative affect. *Journal of Personality and Social Psychology, 47,* 1105–1117.

Diener, E., Smith, H., & Fujita, F. (1995). The personality structure of affect. *Journal of Personality and Social Psychology, 69,* 130–141.

Eckenrode, J. (1984). Impact of chronic and acute stressors on daily reports of mood. *Journal of Personality and Social Psychology, 46,* 907–918.

Ekman, P. (1994). Moods, emotions, and traits. In P. Ekman & R. J. Davidson (Eds.), *The nature of emotion: Fundamental questions* (pp. 56–58). New York: Oxford University Press.

Feldman Barrett, L., & Russell, J. A. (1998). Independence and bipolarity in the structure of current affect. *Journal of Personality and Social Psychology, 74,* 967–984.

Gold, A. E., MacLeod, K. M., Frier, B. M., & Deary, I. J. (1995). Changes in mood during acute hypoglycemia in healthy participants. *Journal of Personality and Social Psychology, 68,* 498–504.

Gotlib, I. H., & Meyer, J. P. (1986). Factor analysis of the Multiple Affect Adjective Check List: A separation of positive and negative affect. *Journal of Personality and Social Psychology, 50,* 1161–1165.

Gray, E. K., & Watson, D. (2001). Emotion, mood and temperament: Similarities, differences and a synthesis. In R. L. Payne & C. L. Cooper (Eds.), *Emotions at work: Theory, research and applications in management* (pp. 21–43). West Sussex, UK: Wiley.

Green, D. P., Goldman, S. L., & Salovey, P. (1993). Measurement error masks bipolarity in affect ratings. *Journal of Personality and Social Psychology, 64,* 1029–1041.

Hedges, S. M., Jandorf, L., & Stone, A. A. (1985). Meaning of daily mood assessments. *Journal of Personality and Social Psychology, 48,* 428–434.

Howarth, E., & Schokman-Gates, K. (1981). Self-report multiple mood instruments. *British Journal of Psychology, 72,* 421–441.

Izard, C. E. (1991). *The psychology of emotions.* New York: Plenum Press.

Izard, C. E., Libero, D. Z., Putnam, P., & Haynes, O. M. (1993). Stability of emotion expression experiences and their relations to traits of personality. *Journal of Social and Personality Psychology, 64,* 847–860.

Lane, A. M., & Lane, H. J. (2002). Predictive effectiveness of mood measures. *Perceptual and Motor Skills, 94,* 785–791.

Larsen, R. J. (2000). Toward a science of mood regulation. *Psychological Inquiry, 11,* 129–141.

Larsen, R. J., & Ketelaar, T. (1991). Personality and susceptibility to positive and negative emotional states. *Journal of Personality and Social Psychology, 61,* 132–140.

Lorr, M., McNair, D. M., & Fisher, S. (1982). Evidence for bipolar mood states. *Journal of Personality Assessment, 46,* 432–436.

Matthews, G., Jones, D. M., & Chamberlain, A. G. (1990). Refining the measurement of mood: The UWIST Mood Adjective Checklist. *British Journal of Psychology, 81,* 17–42.

Mayer, J. D., & Gaschke, Y. N. (1988). The experience and meta-experience of mood. *Journal of Personality and Social Psychology, 55,* 102–111.

McNair, D. M., & Lorr, M. (1964). An analysis of mood in neurotics. *Journal of Abnormal and Social Psychology, 69,* 620–627.

McNair, D. M., Lorr, M., & Droppleman, L. F. (1971). *Manual: Profile of mood states.* San Diego, CA: Educational and Industrial Testing Service.

Meddis, R. (1972). Bipolar factors in mood adjective checklists. *British Journal of Social and Clinical Psychology, 11,* 178–184.

Meyer, G. J., & Shack, J. R. (1989). Structural convergence of mood and personality: Evidence for old and new directions. *Journal of Personality and Social Psychology, 57,* 691–706.

Mossholder, K. W., Kemery, E. R., Harris, S. G., Armenakis, A. A., & McGrath, R. (1994). Confounding constructs and levels of constructs in affectivity measurement: An empirical investigation. *Educational and Psychological Measurement, 54,* 336–349.

Nemanick, R. C., Jr., & Munz, D. C. (1994). Measuring the poles of negative and positive mood using the Positive and Negative Affect Schedule and Activation-Deactivation Adjective Check List. *Psychological Reports, 74,* 195–199.

Nowlis, V. (1965). Research with the Mood Adjective Checklist. In S. S. Tompkins & C. E. Izard (Eds.), *Affect, cognition, and personality: Empirical studies* (pp. 352–389). New York: Springer.

Nowlis, V. (1970). Mood, behavior and experience. In M. B. Arnold (Ed.), *Feelings and emotions: The Loyola Symposium* (pp. 261–277). New York: Academic Press.

Parkinson, B., Totterdell, P., Brinner, R. B., & Reynolds, S. (1996). *Changing moods: The psychology of mood and mood regulation.* London: Addison-Wesley Longman.

Payne, R. (2001). Measuring emotions at work. In R. L. Payne & C. L. Cooper (Eds.), *Emotions at work: Theory, research and applications in management* (pp. 107–129). West Sussex, UK: Wiley.

Robinson, M. D., & Clore, G. L. (2002). Belief and feeling: Evidence for an accessibility model of emotional self-report. *Psychological Bulletin, 128,* 934–960.

Russell, J. A. (1979). Affective space is bipolar. *Journal of Personality and Social Psychology, 37,* 345–356.

Russell, J. A. (1980). A circumplex model of affect. *Journal of Personality and Social Psychology, 39,* 1161–1178.

Russell, J. A., & Carroll, J. M. (1999a). On the bipolarity of positive and negative affect. *Psychological Bulletin, 125,* 3–30.

Russell, J. A., & Carroll, J. M. (1999b). The phoenix of bipolarity: Reply to Watson and Tellegen (1999). *Psychological Bulletin, 125,* 611–617.

Russell, J. A., Weiss, A., & Mendelsohn, G. A. (1989). Affect Grid: A single-item scale of pleasure and arousal. *Journal of Personality and Social Psychology, 57,* 493–502.

Schwarz, N., & Clore, G. L. (1983). Mood, misattribution, and judgments of well-being: Informative and directive functions of affective states. *Journal of Personality and Social Psychology, 45,* 513–523.

Shacham, S. (1983). A shortened version of the Profile of Mood States. *Journal of Personality Assessment, 47,* 305–306.

Stone, A. A. (1981). The association between perceptions of daily experiences and self- and spouse-rated mood. *Journal of Research in Personality, 15,* 510–522.

Stone, A. A. (1995). Measurement of affective response. In S. Cohen, R. C. Kessler, & L. Underwood Gordon (Eds.), *Measuring stress* (pp. 148–171). New York: Oxford University Press.

Tellegen, A. (1985). Structures of mood and personality and their relevance to assessing anxiety, with an emphasis on self-report. In A. H. Tuma & J. D. Maser (Eds.), *Anxiety and the anxiety disorders* (pp. 681–706). Hillsdale, NJ: Erlbaum.

Tellegen, A., Watson, D., & Clark, L. A. (1999). On the dimensional and hierarchical structure of affect. *Psychological Science, 10,* 297–303.

Thayer, R. E. (1967). Measurement of activation through self-report. *Psychological Reports, 20,* 663–678.

Thayer, R. E. (1978). Factor analytic and reliability studies on the Activation-Deactivation Adjective Check List. *Psychological Reports, 42,* 747–756.

Thayer, R. E. (1986). Activation-Deactivation Adjective Check List: Current overview and structural analysis. *Psychological Reports, 58,* 607–614.

Thayer, R. E. (2001). *Calm energy.* New York: Oxford University Press.

Watson, D. (1988a). Intraindividual and interindividual analyses of positive and negative affect: Their relation to health complaints, perceived stress, and daily activities. *Journal of Personality and Social Psychology, 54,* 1020–1030.

Watson, D. (1988b). The vicissitudes of mood measurement: Effects of varying descriptors, time frames, and response format on measures of positive and negative affect. *Journal of Personality and Social Psychology, 55,* 128–141.

Watson, D. (2000). *Mood and temperament.* New York: Guilford Press.

Watson, D., & Clark, L. A. (1992). Affects separable and inseparable: On the hierarchical arrangements of the negative affects. *Journal of Personality and Social Psychology, 62,* 489–505.

Watson, D., & Clark, L. A. (1994a). *The PANAS-X: Manual for the Positive and Negative Affect Schedule—Expanded Form.* Unpublished manuscript, University of Iowa, Iowa City.

Watson, D., & Clark, L. A. (1994b). The vicissitudes of mood: A schematic model. In P. Ekman & R. J. Davidson (Eds.), *The nature of emotion* (pp. 400–405). New York: Oxford University Press.

Watson, D., & Clark, L. A. (1997). Measurement and mismeasurement of mood: Recurrent and emergent issues. *Journal of Personality Assessment, 68,* 267–296.

Watson, D., Clark, L. A., & Tellegen, A. (1988). Development and validation of brief measures of positive and negative affect: The PANAS scales. *Journal of Personality and Social Psychology, 54,* 1063–1070.

Watson, D., Hubbard, B., & Weise, D. (2000). Self-other agreement in personality and affectivity: The role of acquaintanceship, trait visibility, and assumed similarity. *Journal of Personality and Social Psychology, 78,* 546–558.

Watson, D., & Tellegen, A. (1985). Toward a consensual structure of mood. *Psychological Bulletin, 98,* 219–235.

Watson, D., & Tellegen, A. (1999). Issues in the dimensional structure of affect—Effects of descriptors, measurement error, and response formats: Comment on Russell and Carroll (1999). *Psychological Bulletin, 125,* 601–610.

Watson, D., & Tellegen, A. (2002). Aggregation, acquiescence, and the assessment of trait affectivity. *Journal of Research in Personality, 36,* 589–597.

Watson, D., & Vaidya, J. (2003). Mood measurement: Current status and future directions. In J. A. Schinka & W. Velicer (Eds.), *Comprehensive handbook of psychology: Vol. 2. Research methods* (pp. 351–375). New York: Wiley.

Watson, D., Weise, D., Vaidya, J., & Tellegen, A. (1999). The two general activation systems of affect: Structural findings, evolutionary considerations, and psychobiological evidence. *Journal of Personality and Social Psychology, 76,* 820–838.

Yik, M. S. M., Russell, J. A. & Feldman Barrett, L. (1999). Structure of self-reported current affect: Integration and beyond. *Journal of Personality and Social Psychology, 77,* 600–619.

Zevon, M. A., & Tellegen, A. (1982). The structure of mood change: An idiographic/nomothetic analysis. *Journal of Personality and Social Psychology, 43,* 111–122.

Zuckerman, M., & Lubin, B. (1965). *Manual for the Multiple Affect Adjective Checklist.* San Diego, CA: Educational and Industrial Testing Service.

Zuckerman, M., & Lubin, B. (1985). *Manual for the MAACL-R: The Multiple Affect Adjective Check List Revised.* San Diego, CA: Educational and Industrial Testing Service.

Edward Wilson
Colin MacLeod
Lynlee Campbell

The Information-Processing Approach to Emotion Research

The past two decades have witnessed a remarkable growth of interest in cognitive aspects of emotional vulnerability. Stimulated initially by the work of clinical theorists such as Aaron Beck (Beck, 1976; Beck, Emery, & Greenberg, 1985) and cognitive psychologists such as Gordon Bower (1981), much of this research has been designed to address predictions concerning the selective processing of emotional information. The general idea under experimental scrutiny most often has been that heightened levels of susceptibility to negative emotions, such as anxiety or depression, reflect idiosyncratic processing biases that operate to favor the encoding and retrieval of negative information and to yield negative interpretations of ambiguity. In order to objectively test such hypotheses, many researchers now have systematically mined the rich potential offered by cognitive-experimental psychology, drawing on and creatively adapting established methodologies for assessing selective encoding, interpretation, and memory. This line of investigation has greatly enhanced our understanding of the patterns of biased cognition that underpin individual differences in emotional vulnerability.

Of course, as is usually the case with scientific progress, these advances in understanding have been accompanied by the development of more specific questions, and addressing these new questions has, in turn, required further refinement of the original methodologies. Consequently, any contemporary investigators whose interest may newly turn to this field of study will find themselves confronted by a diverse array of experimental techniques that not only reflect differ-

ing methodological principles but that also have been designed to assess rather different aspects of cognition. Our goal in this chapter is to provide a brief overview of the information-processing tasks that have exerted the greatest influence within this research domain. In doing so, we endeavor to communicate the basic rationale that underpins each type of experimental paradigm, to illustrate each approach by describing some of the task variants employed in published studies, and to summarize both the strengths and limitations of these alternative methodologies. Although available space does not permit us to provide a complete account of the many findings that have been generated using these approaches, we also convey the general patterns of selective information processing that have been found to characterize vulnerability to anxiety and to depression. More comprehensive recent reviews of experimental findings are provided by Mathews and MacLeod (2005) and by MacLeod and Rutherford (2004).

Although we intend for this methodological review to equip the reader with a firm grasp of the types of cognitive-experimental tasks most commonly employed to investigate the patterns of selective information processing associated with emotional vulnerability, we must emphasize that good experimental design requires more than an understanding of these assessment techniques. Always, it is necessary to ensure that the specific manner in which any assessment task is employed is strictly guided by the precise hypothesis the researcher wishes to test in order that the findings can serve adequately to address this particular issue. For example, decisions concerning which stimulus materials to employ must be tightly aligned with the prediction under scrutiny. If an investigator wishes to test the hypothesis that certain types of emotional vulnerability are characterized by a heightened tendency to process negative materials, then it would be appropriate to include control materials that are equated in emotional intensity but that are not affectively negative in order to eliminate any confound between stimulus negativity and emotionality (cf. Rutherford, MacLeod, & Campbell, 2004). Similarly, decisions concerning which groups of participants to contrast must be taken in light of the hypothesis that motivates the experiment. If, for example, the study is intended to determine whether the clinical disorder major depression is characterized by a particular processing bias, then it will be important to ensure that control participants differ from the clinical patients only in terms of diagnostic status. If, instead, control participants who do not meet diagnostic status nevertheless are excluded on the basis of showing high scores on conventional depression inventories, then it will be impossible to attribute any resulting group differences to clinical status (cf. MacLeod, 2004).

Clearly, good experimental design requires the identification and elimination of such potential confounds, and their range is simply too great to exhaustively review here. However, equally clearly, good design also demands that the investigator fully appreciate the principles that underpin alternative cognitive assessment procedures and be able to select the most appropriate task from among these alternatives in light of their recognized strengths and limitations. The following review is intended to provide this knowledge, taking the reader in turn through methods of assessing the selective encoding of emotional information, the selective emotional interpretation of ambiguity, and the selective retrieval of emotional information from memory.

Methods of Assessing the Selective Encoding of Emotional Information

A number of quite different procedures have been employed to address the hypothesis that individual differences in emotional disposition are associated with biases in the selective encoding of emotional information. Some investigators have examined the ease with which emotional stimuli can be identified, whereas others have assessed how well they can be ignored. Attentional responses to affectively toned stimuli have been inferred from probe detection latencies and from more direct measures of eye gaze. In this section, we illustrate the nature of these experimental techniques, summarize some of the key findings they have generated, and consider their strengths and limitations.

Identification Tasks

In this approach, participants are directed to identify emotional stimuli presented under conditions that make such identification difficult, in order to test the prediction that anxiety or depression will be associated with enhanced identification of negatively toned information. For example, Powell and Hemsley (1984) compared clinically depressed and nondepressed participants' ability to report the identity of 30 negative and 30 neutral words, exposed in random order at brief durations individually precalibrated to permit only around 50% accuracy. The depressed participants were found to be disproportionately accurate in naming the negative words relative to the neutral words, consistent with a depression-linked encoding advantage for such information.

In other variants of this identification approach, participants have been directed to monitor input for predetermined target stimuli that are rendered difficult to detect. For instance, Burgess, Jones, Robertson, Radcliffe, and Emerson (1981) required participants with phobias and nonanxious controls to repeat aloud prose presented to one ear and ignore prose presented to the other ear, while also trying to detect certain target items among words occasionally interjected into either auditory channel. These target items could be either threatening or neutral terms, and participants indicated their detection with a manual response. Relative to the control participants, the participants with phobias detected a disproportionate number of threat, but not neutral, words presented to the unshadowed channel, consistent with the operation of an anxiety-linked encoding advantage for threat information.

One problem with this approach is that the observed effects could reflect a negative response bias rather than a selective encoding bias. Individuals with anxiety or depression may simply be more willing to guess that negative stimuli were present when exposure conditions render stimulus identity uncertain. In order to eliminate this possible interpretation, it is necessary to assess not only capacity to correctly detect emotional target stimuli but also the tendency to falsely indicate their presence (e.g., Byrne & Eysenck, 1995; Rinck & Becker, 2005). For example, Byrne and Eysenck (1995) presented participants high and low in trait anxiety with grids consisting of 12 faces, each of which depicted a particular emotional expression. On half of the 24 trials, all these faces showed a neutral expression, whereas on the other trials one random face displayed an angry expression. Participants were required to indicate which face showed a different expression from the other faces by selecting 1 of 12 response keys or to indicate that all faces displayed an equivalent emotional expression by pressing a 13th response key. Despite the absence of any group difference in the number of false alarms, the individuals high in trait anxiety were disproportionately fast to detect the presence of an angry face in such neutral arrays. This finding strengthens the conclusion that this anxiety-linked effect may reflect the selective encoding of negative information rather than the operation of a negative response bias.

Interference Tasks

A very different method of eliminating the response bias problems that potentially can compromise identification tasks is provided by those experimental approaches that explicitly direct participants simply to ignore emotional stimuli, then infer their selective encoding on the basis of the degree to which such distracters interfere with performance on a central cognitive task. In an early variant of this interference approach, Mathews and MacLeod (1986) required patients with generalized anxiety disorder (GAD) and nonanxious controls to shadow prose presented to their right ears while ignoring a list of 15 words presented to their left ears. On some trials, these words were threatening in content, whereas on others they were emotionally neutral. While ignoring these words, participants were instructed to perform the simple central task of pressing a button each time the word *press* appeared on a computer screen, which occurred three times during each word list. For the participants with GAD, but not the controls, response latency on this central task was found to be slowed when it was performed during the presentation of threatening, rather than neutral, words in the unattended channel. This suggests that the threat stimuli captured attention to a disproportionate degree in the individuals with clinical anxiety.

In other versions of this dichotic-listening-interference paradigm, shadowing performance itself has been employed as the measure of central task performance, though results have been somewhat inconsistent. For example, Trandel and McNally (1987) found no evidence that shadowing errors were disproportionately increased among patients with posttraumatic stress disorders relative to nonanxious control participants when threatening rather than neutral words were presented to the unattended ear. However, using a very similar approach, Ingram and Ritter (2000) observed that, when exposed to a depressive mood induction, participants with a history of depression displayed increased rates of shadowing errors when negative words, rather than neutral or positive words, were exposed in the unattended channel. This effect was not observed among control participants with no history of depression.

Not all interference tasks employ dichotic-listening procedures. In fact, the interference paradigm most commonly employed to assess emotional encoding biases is probably the variant that has become known as the emotional Stroop task (cf. Williams, Mathews, & MacLeod, 1996). In this approach, participants are presented with a series of colored words that differ in emotional tone and are required to perform the central task of quickly naming the color of the type used for each word, while ignoring the distracting emotional content. Slowed latencies to name the colors of the words of a given emotional tone is taken as evidence that participants experience particular difficulty ignoring the semantic content of these items.

The emotional Stroop task sometimes is delivered in an easy-to-administer card-based format, though most contemporary studies tend to employ a computer-based format (cf. MacLeod, 2004). In the card version of the task, the words associated with each experimental condition are repeated on a single card, which may thus contain around a hundred or so colored stimuli, and the dependent measure is usually the time taken to complete naming the colors of all items on each card. In contrast, computer versions of the emotional Stroop most commonly present colored words singly, often mixing the words from all conditions in a random order, and color-naming latency is assessed on every trial using a voice key.

In an early example of the computerized approach, Gotlib and McCann (1984) presented participants with and without mild depression with 50 depression-related words, 50 mania-related words, and 50 neutral words, each of which appeared singly in random order on a computer monitor. Every word could appear in any of five colors (red, yellow, green, brown, or blue), and participants were directed to name the color of each word as quickly as possible. Their latency to do so was recorded using a voice key. Compared with the nondepressed controls, the participants with mild depression were disproportionately slow in naming the colors of only the depression-related words.

Although such findings suggest that depression may be associated with the selective encoding of emotionally negative stimulus content, it is important to note that this effect has not proven consistently reliable in depression. Quite a number of subsequent studies using the emotional Stroop task have failed to observe a disproportionate slowing in naming colors of negative words either in patients with clinical depression (e.g., Bradley, Mogg, Millar, & White, 1995), or in nonclinical participants who report elevated levels of depression (e.g., Hill & Knowles, 1991). In contrast, slowness in naming colors of threatening words within this type of emotional Stroop task has consistently emerged as a robust feature of anxiety vulnerability, both within the normal population and among clinical participants suffering from anxiety disorders, whether the card-based presentation format (e.g., Mathews & MacLeod, 1985) or computer-presentation format (e.g., Mogg et al., 2000) has been employed (cf. Logan & Goetsch, 1993; Williams, Mathews, & MacLeod, 1996).

Although researchers may sometimes choose between card-based and computer-based versions of the emotional Stroop task on the basis of convenience, it is important to recognize that these two task variants may not measure precisely the same dimensions of selective encoding. Kindt, Bierman, and Brosschot (1996) calculated indices of the color-naming interference shown by participants with phobias on fear-relevant words, using both card and computer versions of the emotional Stroop task. These indices were not significantly correlated with each other. Kindt et al. (1996) suggest that in the card-based format the degree of interference may be influenced by the word stimuli physically surrounding each item that is to be color-named, whereas in the computer-based format color naming can be influenced only by the semantic content of the single presented word. This may result in more robust interference on card-based versions of the Stroop task but reduced confidence in the locus of the interference effect. An additional advantage of the computer-based version of the emotional Stroop task is that it affords a higher level of experimental control, making it possible to develop variants designed to address more specific hypotheses.

For example, methodological refinements to the computerized emotional Stroop task have made it possible to determine whether the observed patterns of emotion-linked selective interference occur automatically, in the sense that these effects are not mediated by conscious awareness of the stimulus information. To address this issue, investigators have exposed the stimulus words very briefly (typically 20 milliseconds or less) and have followed them with pattern masks, which previous research has established can preclude conscious awareness of a stimulus word without preventing its semantic processing (Turvey, 1973). In such an experiment, MacLeod and Rutherford (1992) presented colored word stimuli for 20 milliseconds and followed each with a pattern mask of the same color consisting of inverted and rotated letter fragments. A series of awareness-check trials were distributed throughout the task, each presenting either a word or a nonword under such masked exposure conditions. Participants performed at chance when requested to guess the lexical status of these items, suggesting an inability to consciously apprehend stimuli exposed in this manner. Nevertheless, when approaching a stressful examination, participants with high trait anxiety displayed disproportionately slow color-naming responses on trials that exposed negative rather than positive words. Other studies have confirmed the persistence of this effect under exposure conditions that eliminate awareness of stimuli content in patients with anxiety disorders (e.g., Becker, Rinck, Margraf, & Roth, 2001; Mogg, Bradley, Williams, & Mathews, 1993).

Although interference tasks overcome the response-bias problems that can compromise interpretation of identification task findings, they are nevertheless vulnerable to other possible criticisms. In particular, such methodologies permit only the conclusion that in the presence of negative information, participants with anxiety, and perhaps sometimes those with depression, show compromised performance on a central task. Although this finding is consistent with the possibility that such participants' attention may be drawn toward distracting negative stimuli, the interference methodology does not actually measure such an attentional shift. We now consider tasks designed to more directly assess the distribution of attention during the presentation of emotional information.

Attentional-Probe Tasks

In attentional-probe methodologies, participants usually are briefly presented with pairs of differentially valenced stimuli, each member of which appears simultaneously in different screen locations. The screen then goes blank, and a visual probe appears in either location. Participants are required to make a simple response to this probe, such as indicating its presence or its identity, and response latency is recorded. Attentional bias is inferred from these latencies, with speeding to probes in the vicinity of one valence of stimuli serving to indicate attentional orientation toward the locus of this information.

In the original implementation of this task, MacLeod, Mathews and Tata (1986) exposed patients with GAD and nonanxious controls to 288 pairs of words separated vertically on a computer screen, which were exposed for 500 milliseconds. On each of 48 critical trials, one of these words was threatening and the other was neutral, and each valence of word appeared with equal probability in either location. On a third of all trials, including all 48 critical ones, a small dot probe appeared directly following the offset of the word pair, and this too appeared with equal frequency in either location. The participants' task was to press a button as soon as they detected the probe. Unlike the control participants, the patients with GAD demonstrated faster detection latencies for probes in the vicinity of threat words, rather than in the vicinity of nonthreat words, indicating attentional orientation toward these threat words.

This general methodology has spawned a number of variants. Some have used emotional images rather than words as stimuli (e.g. Bradley, Mogg, & Millar, 2000), whereas others have used somatically related stimuli, such as mild shock or heart rate readings (e.g., Ehlers, Margraf, Davies, & Roth, 1988; Kroeze & van den Hout, 2000). More recent versions of the task often have employed two differing types of probes and required participants to discriminate probe identity rather than simply to indicate probe presence (e.g., Yiend & Mathews, 2001). Across these variants, it has remained a robust finding that anxiety is associated with speeded processing of probes in locations at which threat stimuli were recently presented. This pattern of effects has been observed not only in participants with GAD but also in other populations with anxiety, such as patients with panic disorder (Horenstein & Segui, 1997) and individuals with high trait anxiety who are under stress (e.g., Broadbent & Broadbent, 1988). In contrast to these findings with participants with anxiety, studies that have employed this probe methodology commonly have failed to observe any such speeding to probes in the vicinity of negative stimuli in participants with depression (e.g. Hill & Dutton, 1989; MacLeod et al., 1986; Musa, Lepine, Clark, Mansell, & Ehlers, 2003).

A number of researchers also have modified the attentional-probe approach to investigate the automaticity of observed effects by systematically varying the exposure duration of the initial word stimuli and/or the stimulus onset asynchrony (SOA) between the word pair and the probe. Whereas effects observed under very brief stimulus exposure conditions or at very short SOAs may reflect automatic aspects of attentional capture, those effects that emerge only with more prolonged stimulus exposure durations or more extended SOAs seem likely to reflect the impact of strategic attentional control (e.g., Bradley, Mogg, Falla, & Hamilton, 1998). Once again, the pattern of findings has differed for participants with anxiety and those with depression. When word pairs have been exposed for only 14 milliseconds and pattern masking has been used to prevent conscious awareness of these stimuli, then anxiety remains associated with the speeded processing of probes in the vicinity of threat stimuli (e.g., Bradley, Mogg, & Lee, 1997; Mogg, Bradley, & Williams, 1995), suggesting that this attentional bias operates quite automatically. Only when the word stimuli are presented for long enough to permit their conscious identification and the SOA is extended to 500–1000 milliseconds have participants with depression sometimes been observed to demonstrate a similar speeding to process probes in the vicinity of negative stimuli (e.g., Bradley et al., 1997). It seems likely, therefore, that such attentional bias in people with depression represents the influence of controlled processing and does not reflect the automatic attentional capture by negative information that is characteristic of anxiety.

Although such adaptations of attentional-probe tasks may give some insight into the temporal pattern of attentional response to emotional information, clearly the methodological constraints associated with this approach preclude the derivation of a truly continuous attentional measure. We now turn to consider eye-gaze approaches, which may more readily yield a continuous, rather than a discrete, measure of attentional allocation.

Tasks That Employ Eye-Gaze Measures

Investigators who adopt this approach have made use of two slightly different measures, each derived from eye-gaze indices. Some studies have examined the duration or proportion of eye fixations within differentially valenced stimulus regions, whereas others have recorded the direction of eye shifts relative to such regions. In an example of the former approach, Matthews and Antes (1992) examined the distribution of eye fixations shown by participants with mild depression and nondepressed individuals when viewing an image across a duration of 20 seconds. Each of the seven images used contained spatially separated happy and sad regions. For example, one of the images was a painting depicting a skull next to a flower. Matthews and Antes (1992) sampled eye fixation 60 times per second, using a Gulf and Western Eye View Monitor, which determines eye fixation on the basis of the relative location of the pupil midpoint and corneal reflection. They found that, although, in general, participants fixated happy regions for a greater proportion of presentation time than they did sad regions, this tendency was reduced in participants with mild depression. This finding suggests that individuals with mild depression may be characterized by reduction of the positive encoding bias that characterizes people without depression.

Studies that have employed eye-movement measures to assess attentional bias sometimes have also simultaneously taken reaction-time-based measures of attentional distribution. For example, Bradley et al. (2000) supplemented their examination of attentional bias using the attentional-probe methodology by employing an HVS Image Eye Tracker device, which uses reflection of an infrared beam directed at the limbus to track eye movements. In this experiment, the presented stimuli were angry, happy, and depressed facial expressions, each paired with neutral facial images of the same individuals. These researchers found that the attentional allocation toward differentially valenced facial expressions, as indicated by relative latencies to detect probes in each location, was significantly correlated with indices of eye movement toward these emotional stimuli under certain conditions. However, Bradley et al.'s (2000) study also highlights some of the difficulties associated with the use of eye movement measures, as approximately 20% of their sample ("starers") did not show readable eye movements at all.

In addition, as Bradley et al. (2000) acknowledge, although attentional allocation inferred from eye movements and from probe response latencies were sometimes correlated, this was not invariably the case. Other studies have confirmed that, under some circumstances, measures of attention derived from eye movements and from reaction times (RT) may be dissociated. For example, in a series of studies, Stelmach, Campsall, and Herdman (1997) provided evidence that under conditions of exogenous cuing, as with sudden peripheral stimulation, RT measures indicate that attention moves to the cued location in advance of eye movements. In contrast, with endogenous cues, such as symbolic directional cues, such RT measures reveal that shifts of attention may occur more slowly than eye movements, and indeed it appears that participants are able to intentionally dissociate their eye movements from their focus of attention. Thus, where practical, eye-movement and eye-fixation measures may perhaps most usefully supplement, rather than replace, other measures of attentional allocation, such as the attentional-probe approach.

As this overview has shown, each approach to the assessment of attentional selectivity has both advantages and limitations that must be considered by researchers planning to investigate individual differences in selective encoding. Undoubtedly, the easiest approach to employ, particularly within many field settings, is the card-based version of the emotional Stroop task, as this requires little in the way of technical apparatus. However, when more precise measurement is necessary, or when the experimental hypotheses under scrutiny require more rigorous control over stimulus presentation parameters, then computer-based task variants become preferable, and the attentional-probe approach probably represents the most powerful approach. Should experimental predictions concern the dynamics of attentional responses across time, then eye-gaze measures may provide a useful supplementary source of information, though at the cost of introducing considerable additional technical complexity. Across these various experimental approaches, the general pattern of findings suggests that anxiety is reliably associated with an attentional bias toward negative information that operates automatically in the sense of occurring rapidly and without the need for conscious awareness of such stimulus information. In contrast, depression is less strongly associated with attentional bias toward negative information, though individuals with depression do sometimes appear to lack the attentional bias away from negative information that characterizes nondepressed individuals. The limited evidence of depression-linked attentional orientation toward negative stimuli comes from those task variants that permit the greatest influence from strategic processing, suggesting that when this bias occurs in depression it may result from a controlled attentional strategy rather than from automatic attentional capture.

Methods of Assessing the Selective Interpretation of Ambiguity

Various methodologies have been developed to assess the degree to which vulnerability to anxiety and depression is associated with biases that favor the negative interpretation of ambiguous stimuli. Some studies have employed questionnaires that require participants to self-report their likely interpretations of ambiguous scenarios, whereas others have inferred interpretive bias from performance measures, such as the spelling of emotionally ambiguous homophones or the degree to which ambiguous primes facilitate the processing of targets related to their alternative meanings. This section outlines these different approaches, indicates the general pattern of findings they have produced, and discusses their advantages and disadvantages.

Tasks That Employ Self-Report Measures of Interpretation

One common approach to assessing interpretive bias involves presenting descriptions of hypothetical ambiguous scenarios and asking participants to self-report the interpretation that they believe themselves likely to impose on these imaginary situations. In one of the first studies to use this methodology, Butler and Mathews (1983) provided patients with clinical anxiety, patients with clinical depression, and nonclinical controls with a questionnaire booklet that contained a series of 10 hypothetical ambiguous scenarios, each permitting a threatening and a nonthreatening interpretation, such as "suppose you wake with a start in the middle of the night thinking you heard a noise but all is quiet." Participants first answered an open-ended question concerning their likely interpretation of this situation (e.g., "What do you suppose woke you up?") then rank-ordered three provided alternative interpretations that differed in emotional valence in terms

of how likely they thought it was that each would come to mind if the situation were encountered. The experimenters obtained blind ratings of the negativity of the answers to each initial question and calculated participants' rankings for the more negative provided interpretations. Analyses of both data sets revealed that the participants with anxiety and depression, relative to controls, more often reported that they would impose negative interpretations on these hypothetical scenarios. These findings are consistent with the operation of a negative interpretive bias in anxiety and depression. Using this same approach, similar findings have been obtained for other populations with clinical anxiety (e.g., Clark et al., 1997; Richards, Austin, & Alvarenga, 2001). Other work using this type of methodology also has replicated the finding that individuals with depression report themselves to be more likely than nondepressed controls to impose negative interpretations on imaginary ambiguous situations (e.g., Nunn, Mathews, & Trower, 1997).

Although this questionnaire-based assessment approach is easily administered, such findings cannot permit the firm conclusion that individuals with anxiety and depression truly are characterized by a genuine interpretive bias. In this methodology, participants indicate only how they *believe* they would interpret *hypothetical* ambiguous situations. Introspective reports of this type can be highly inaccurate (e.g., Nisbett & Wilson, 1977), and participants' subjective beliefs about their likely patterns of interpretation may well be invalid. As an alternative to having participants report the interpretations they believe they would impose on imaginary situations, other researchers have sought to investigate the interpretations that participants actually do impose on personally relevant ambiguous information. One common variant of this latter approach involves exposing participants to a social situation, such as an interaction with an experimental confederate, and then presenting a recording of this interaction and requiring participants to rate their social performance. The recording typically permits differentially valenced interpretations of the interaction to be imposed, and so participants' ratings provide an indication of their interpretive bias.

In one study of this type, carried out by Clark and Arkowitz (1975), men high and low in social anxiety individually participated in two 5-min audiotaped conversations with female confederates. Participants and independent judges subsequently rated these recordings for demonstrated social skill level, using an 11-point scale with anchoring statements at each end. Although participants low in social anxiety tended to rate their interactions as more socially skilled than did the independent judges, this pattern was reversed for the group high in social anxiety, suggesting that these participants interpreted their social interactions more negatively. Other studies that have employed this methodology to assess interpretation have yielded similar findings, both for individuals with elevated vulnerability to anxiety (e.g., Derakshan & Eysenck, 1997) and for those with elevated susceptibility to depression (e.g., Cane & Gotlib, 1985).

This latter variant of the self-report approach permits the use of genuine ambiguous stimuli with a high degree of ecological validity. In addition, instead of assessing only beliefs regarding probable future interpretations of hypothetical situations, it requires participants to directly report their actual interpretations of this personally relevant ambiguous information. Of course, the methodology is somewhat more demanding to execute than is the case when questionnaires are used to assess subjective beliefs about interpretive style. Furthermore, *all* self-report methodologies of this general type, which invite participants to introspectively access and verbally describe their interpretations to the experimenter, can readily be criticized on the basis of their inherent demand characteristics and their susceptibility to response bias effects. Such experimental approaches are likely to leave many participants fully aware of the experimenters' interest and likely hypotheses, which in turn could have an impact on their self-reports. Even when this is not the case, any general tendency to favor negative response options would be misconstrued as an interpretive bias within such tasks, as interpretations are inferred on the basis of participants' tendencies to emit negative responses within their self-reports. Alternative methods of assessing selective interpretation have sought to reduce the likelihood of experimenter demand effects, the potential influence of response bias, or both.

Homophone Spelling Tasks

To reduce the likely impact of demand effects, some experimenters have employed approaches that render both the purpose of the task and the measure of interpretive bias less salient to participants while permitting interpretations to be inferred from certain aspects of task performance. One example of this approach is the homophone spelling task. This involves auditorily presenting a series of homophones, each of which has differentially valenced alternative meanings (e.g., *dye/die*). Participants are required simply to write down each word as it is presented, and the measure of interpretation is the spelling that they employ for each homophone.

Eysenck, MacLeod, and Mathews (1987) used a variant of this task to contrast individuals who were high and low in trait anxiety. These researchers compiled a list of 56 words, half of which were unambiguous filler words and half of which were homophones that each permitted a threatening and a nonthreatening interpretation. A randomly ordered list of the words was presented auditorily in the guise of a spelling test, and participants were directed to write each presented word down. Relative to the group with low trait anxiety, the group high in trait anxiety produced a disproportionate proportion of threat spellings when writing down the homophones, consistent with the hypothesis that elevated trait anxiety is associated with a threat-oriented interpretive bias. This finding has since been replicated by researchers examining other populations of participants who were vulnerable to anxiety (e.g., Dalgleish, 1994; Mogg, Baldwin, Brodrick,

& Bradley, 2004). Surprisingly, the homophone spelling task has not yet been used to examine interpretive bias in participants selected on the basis of reporting elevated depression levels. However, correlational analyses suggest that the tendency to spell such homophones in their more negative manner is more directly related to individual differences in trait anxiety than to individual differences in depression (Eysenck et al., 1987; Mathews, Richards, & Eysenck, 1989).

Homophone spelling tasks provide an efficient method of assessing interpretive bias, because a series of homophones can be presented within a matter of 5 or 10 minutes and responses can be easily scored. Although the approach has the additional advantage of bypassing the need for introspective access to interpretive style and is less likely than self-report tasks to be contaminated by experimenter demand effects, it nevertheless remains possible that the findings could reflect the impact of an emotionally linked response bias rather than of a genuine interpretive bias. Specifically, on some occasions, participants may apprehend both homophone meanings, and those who are prone to anxiety may be biased to produce the more threatening spelling under these circumstances simply because of a preference for negative response options. This possible response bias explanation must be borne in mind when considering the findings from homophone spelling studies. In contrast, priming approaches to the assessment of selective interpretation, which we now consider, are capable of circumventing experimenter demand problems while also precluding the potential influence of response bias effects.

Priming Tasks

Priming methodologies for assessing selective interpretation present ambiguous items (e.g., words or sentences) as priming stimuli and infer interpretive bias from the degree to which such ambiguous primes facilitate the processing of subsequently presented targets related to each of their potential meanings. The relative degree of facilitation afforded the processing of targets related to the negative and nonnegative prime meanings usually is calculated in comparison with a baseline condition in which the targets are not preceded by related primes. Thus the potentially contaminating influence of response bias is controlled for.

In one example of this approach, Richards and French (1992) assessed interpretive bias in participants who were high and low in trait anxiety by presenting them with a series of 40 trials employing homograph primes that each permitted a threatening and a nonthreatening interpretation (e.g., *stroke* and *sentence*). A target letter string overwrote the prime 750 ms later. In 10 of the trials, the target word was an associate of the prime's threatening meaning, whereas in another 10 trials this target was an associate of the prime's nonthreatening meaning. These are referred to as the "primed" trials. In the other 20 trials, the target was preceded by an unrelated prime, thereby providing the baseline condition against which to compute facilitation of target processing. These are referred to as the "unprimed" trials. In addition to the 40 trials that involved word targets, an additional 40 trials using nonword targets were distributed through the test session. Participants made a lexical decision response to the target letter string on each trial, and their response latencies were recorded.

The key measure of interpretation within this paradigm was the relative degree to which participants were speeded in accurately identifying the lexical status of each category of target word under the primed condition compared with the unprimed condition, a phenomenon usually labeled the "priming effect." It was observed that for participants with high relative to low trait anxiety, the magnitude of such priming effects was disproportionately greater for targets related to the threat meanings of the preceding ambiguous primes than to the nonthreat meanings of these primes. This is consistent with the hypothesis that participants with high trait anxiety were more likely than those with low trait anxiety to selectively access the threatening meanings of the primes, leading to this greater facilitation of targets related to these negative interpretations. Thus these findings support the existence of a threat-oriented interpretive bias in anxiety.

Ambiguous sentences, rather than ambiguous words, also have been used as prime stimuli within such methodologies, and studies of this type have yielded the same basic pattern of findings. For example, in a study cited by MacLeod (1990), the priming stimuli were sentences that each permitted a threatening and a nonthreatening interpretation (e.g., "working behind bars gave Sammy a different view of life"). Target stimuli were words that, in the primed condition, were related either to the threatening or to the nonthreatening meanings of these sentences (e.g., "jails" and "pubs," for the example sentence). Participants high in both trait and state anxiety showed larger priming effects from such ambiguous sentences on threat-related than on non-threat-related target words, whereas the reverse pattern was shown by participants low in trait anxiety when they, too, were experiencing relatively high levels of state anxiety.

Some priming studies have employed more extended textual stimuli as primes. For example, Hirsch and Mathews (1997) developed a methodology for assessing interpretive bias in individuals with social anxiety, using descriptions of interview situations as priming stimuli. The descriptions were designed to include certain key junctures at which the text was ambiguous. At each of these ambiguous points, a single target word was presented, which could be related to either the threatening or the nonthreatening interpretation of the primed information. Thus, for example, the sentence, "As you go into the interview you think that all your preparation will be," could be followed by the threat target, "forgotten," or by a nonthreat target, such as "worthwhile." Participants were required to judge whether or not the target was related to the preceding primed description, and their latencies to make these judgments were recorded. Those participants who re-

ported being vulnerable to experiencing anxiety about interviews displayed disproportionately large priming effects on targets related to the threatening meanings rather than to the nonthreatening meanings of the preceding ambiguous information.

Target stimuli within such priming tasks have not been limited to single words. In some variants, interpretation is inferred from comprehension latencies for target sentences as opposed to single target words. For example, in MacLeod and Cohen's (1993) study, on each trial an initial priming sentence was presented that could be interpreted in either a threatening or a nonthreatening fashion (e.g., "working behind bars gave Sammy a new view of life"; MacLeod & Cohen, p. 246). This was followed by a second sentence (the target sentence), which represented a meaningful continuation either for the threatening interpretation of the ambiguous first sentence (e.g., "the prisoners' problems greatly affected his attitude") or for its nonthreatening interpretation (e.g., "the patrons' problems greatly affected his attitude"). Participants were required to press the button each time they finished reading a sentence in order to receive the next sentence, and so a measure of comprehension latency for each sentence could be taken without participants' knowledge. In the baseline conditions within this study, the priming sentence was disambiguated by preceding it with a threat cue suggesting its threatening interpretation (e.g., "cell") or by a nonthreat cue suggesting its nonthreatening interpretation (e.g., "pub"). The sensitivity of the paradigm to interpretation was confirmed by the finding that all participants showed speeded comprehension latencies for continuation sentences consistent with congruently valenced cues. The possibility of group differences in interpretive bias was addressed by examining relative comprehension latencies for cases in which no initial cue served to constrain interpretation of the initial ambiguous text. Under this no-cue condition, participants high in trait anxiety showed the same speeded comprehension latencies to threat continuation sentences as they had demonstrated under the threat-cue condition, suggesting that they selectively interpreted the unconstrained ambiguous sentences in a threatening manner. In contrast, the participants low in trait anxiety instead showed the same speeded comprehension latencies for nonthreat continuation sentences as they had displayed under the neutral-cue condition, indicating that these participants interpreted the unconstrained ambiguous sentences in a nonthreatening manner.

Only two published studies to date have used a priming approach to examine selective interpretation in participants who were selected on the basis of depression proneness (Lawson & MacLeod, 1999) or low positive affect (Pury, 2004). Neither experiment yielded reliable evidence that ambiguous primes disproportionately facilitate the processing of targets related to their negative meanings in participants with depression. This suggests the possibility that depression may not be characterized by a negative interpretive bias and that the elevated tendency shown by people with depression to report that they interpret ambiguity in a negative manner may instead result from a depression-linked response bias and/or from experimenter demand effects (Lawson & MacLeod, 1999).

Priming tasks are extremely adaptable, permitting investigation of many factors that may influence the expression of interpretive bias. For example, by varying the interval between prime and target presentation, it is possible to employ such methodologies to chart the temporal course of interpretive bias, permitting discrimination of automatic and strategic aspects of such selective processing (e.g., Amir, Foa, & Coles, 1998; Richards & French, 1992). The cost of this enhanced experimental rigor is in the greater technical demands that these tasks typically impose on the experimenter, for example, in terms of computing and programming resources.

Overall, then, as with tasks that measure selective encoding, choosing a particular procedure to assess interpretive bias will be informed by a number of considerations, both practical and theoretical. Questionnaire measures and homophone spelling procedures may be straightforward to administer, but computer-administered priming procedures may provide more rigor, adaptability, and flexibility and ultimately serve to better constrain the number of alternative explanations that could account for the findings. Of course, these computer-administered procedures do require considerably more technical resources and expertise. The most consistent findings from such methodologies support the proposal that individuals with anxiety are characterized by a negative interpretive bias. However, priming studies have offered less evidence for the existence of a parallel interpretive bias in depression, despite the fact that people with depression self-report that they believe themselves likely to selectively impose negative interpretations on ambiguity.

Methods of Assessing the Selective Retrieval of Emotional Information

A diverse array of approaches have been adopted to address the hypothesis that elevated susceptibility to depression or anxiety is associated with selectively enhanced memory for negative emotional information. In this section, we review the main classes of experimental methodologies, which can be divided into those tasks designed to assess bias in explicit selective retrieval and those instead designed to assess bias in implicit memory. The procedures developed to assess explicit retrieval biases have ranged from measures designed to tap autobiographical recall to procedures designed to assess recall or recognition of stimuli encoded within experimental sessions. Implicit tasks have assessed memory by examining the influence of prior stimulus presentation on ability to perceive or otherwise process subsequently presented stimuli derived from these initial stimulus items. Recently, it has been recognized that the distinction between implicit and explicit memory tasks has often been con-

founded with the degree to which these tasks assess perceptual or conceptual memory, respectively. Methodologies have been developed to break this confound in order to distinguish the patterns of selective conceptual and perceptual memory shown by participants with anxiety and depression. We now review each of these different approaches to the assessment of selective memory in turn.

Autobiographical Memory Tasks

A number of studies have assessed the ease with which individuals can explicitly retrieve emotionally toned past events from autobiographical memory. In such studies, participants are typically provided (auditorily or visually) with a series of single-word cues and are required to provide a brief description of a personal memory elicited by each cue. One variant of this approach uses word cues that are neutral in valence and assesses selective retrieval by examining the emotional valence of the memories that these cues elicit (e.g., Field & Morgan, 2004; Teasdale, Taylor, & Fogarty, 1980). For example, following the induction of negative or positive mood, Teasdale and colleagues (1980) then read participants a series of 20 neutral words. Participants were asked to briefly describe a memory related to each cue word. Memories subsequently rated as unhappy by participants were significantly more likely to be provided following the negative rather than the positive mood induction procedure, whereas the reverse was the case for memories rated as happy. Similarly, Clark and Teasdale (1982) found that individuals with clinical depression were more likely than nondepressed controls to provide unhappy rather than happy autobiographical memories in response to neutral cue words. Burke and Mathews (1992) reported a parallel pattern of findings for participants diagnosed with GAD who, compared with nonanxious control participants, reported a disproportionate number of anxiety-related autobiographical memories elicited by such neutral cues.

The use of emotionally neutral cue words may raise some difficulties for the interpretation of findings. Experimental demand alone could potentially account for the tendency of individuals with depression and with anxiety to report more negatively valenced memories. However, this demand explanation is perhaps less likely to explain the effects obtained in variants of autobiographical recall tasks in which the experimenter indicates to participants which emotional valence of memories they should retrieve on each trial through verbal instruction, for example, by providing emotionally valenced rather than neutral cue words (e.g., Williams & Broadbent, 1986). Although all participants retrieve equivalent numbers of positive and negative memories under these circumstances, the ease with which different classes of emotional memories are recalled is revealed by their relative latencies to access memories of each valence.

Using a variant of this approach that employed emotionally toned cue words, Williams and Broadbent (1986) found that a group of participants who recently had attempted suicide showed slowness in retrieving positive, relative to negative, memories in comparison with a control group. These findings were replicated in samples of patients with clinical depression (e.g., Williams & Scott, 1988). In a similar study that assessed the accessibility of anxiety-related autobiographical memories in individuals with high and low trait anxiety, Richards and Whittaker (1990) obtained parallel findings, with the group high in trait anxiety, relative to that with low trait anxiety, more rapidly retrieving anxiety-related memories. However, studies that involved individuals who are prone to anxiety have not consistently replicated these findings (e.g., Wenzel, Jackson, & Holt, 2002)

Methodologies that assess selective memory bias by investigating recall of valenced autobiographical memories may be considered to have ecological validity, because the reported memories presumably originate from real-life experiences. However, it is difficult to confidently attribute observed group differences within such studies to biases in retrieval processes, given the possibility that the actual contents of autobiographical memory may systematically differ across participant groups. As Williams, Watts, MacLeod, and Mathews (1997) note, more emotionally disturbed participants may, in reality, have experienced a greater number of emotionally negative events. Consequently, it may be that these participants demonstrate good autobiographical recall of negative events simply because they have more such events stored in autobiographical memory. In order to determine whether memory retrieval processes themselves are differentially biased across participant groups, it is necessary to control the initial encoding of emotional information more tightly. We now turn to tasks that have been designed with this goal in mind.

Tasks That Assess the Selective Recall of Emotional Experimental Stimuli

In general, studies designed to examine recall of experimentally presented stimuli first involve an encoding phase, in which the same set of valenced materials are presented to all participants. Following a fixed interval, which often involves an irrelevant filler task, participants are then asked to report as many of the items presented during the encoding phase as possible. This memory test may involve free recall, in which participants are usually given a time limit of around 3–6 minutes in which to report as many items as possible, or a cued recall task, in which participants are asked to complete target fragments to yield stimuli presented during the encoding phase.

Bradley and Mathews (1983) adopted this experimental approach to assess recall of differentially valenced word stimuli by individuals with clinical depression and by individuals without depression. Participants initially were presented with six blocks of 12 adjectives, of which 6 were negative and 6 positive in emotional tone. During this encoding phase, participants were required to rate the words with respect to whether they were self-descriptive, descriptive of a well-known other, or descriptive of someone not well known. Following a 20-second retention interval, during which participants were asked to count backward, they then were invited to recall as many of the words as possible within a 2-minute period. Compared with the nondepressed control group, the patients with depression recalled a disproportionately higher number of negative, relative to positive, words, particularly under the self-referent-encoding condition.

A great many experiments that have employed this general approach have confirmed that a recall bias favoring experimentally presented negative stimuli is indeed characteristic of heightened proneness to depression (cf. Burt, Zembar, & Niederehe, 1995; Matt, Vazquez, & Campbell, 1992). In contrast, studies that have used similar methodologies to investigate recall of emotional stimuli by individuals varying in anxiety proneness most commonly have obtained no evidence of an anxiety-linked recall advantage for such negative items. Consequently, recent reviews by Coles and Heimberg (2002) and by MacLeod and Mathews (2004) have concluded that research has not in general supported the existence of a recall advantage for anxiety-related experimental stimuli in individuals prone to anxiety.

Although people with depression do tend to demonstrate elevated recall scores for negative stimuli, it remains possible that this could result from a depression-linked response bias rather than from a genuine bias in memory retrieval. Specifically, participants with depression may simply be more inclined than participants without depression to make negative guesses during the recall phase when they are uncertain about which stimuli were presented earlier, thereby increasing the recall "hit rate" for negative items. One method of determining whether individuals with depression do demonstrate such a response is to examine the types of words falsely "recalled" at testing (i.e., intrusions). The few studies that have adopted this approach to establish whether emotionally vulnerable participants show the elevated levels of negative intrusions that would result from the operation of such a response bias have indeed found evidence of such an effect (e.g., Dowens & Calvo, 2003; Zuroff, Colussy, & Wielgus, 1983). However, such findings do not preclude the possible concomitant existence of a genuine recall bias. For this reason, it has been more common to systematically examine this issue using recognition memory tasks rather than recall tasks, as these are better suited to independently assessing memory sensitivity and response bias.

Tasks That Assess the Selective Recognition of Valenced Experimental Stimuli

In methodologies designed to assess recognition memory for emotional stimuli, participants are presented, following the initial encoding phase, with memory test lists that contain items presented in the encoding list and matched items not originally presented. Usually, participants are required to indicate whether or not each item appeared during the initial encoding phase.

Dunbar and Lishman (1984) used this approach to assess recognition memory for valenced stimuli in individuals with and without clinical depression. During the encoding phase of this study, participants were presented with a series of 36 words, each of which appeared for 1 second. Twelve of the words were negative, 12 were positive, and 12 were neutral in emotional tone. Following the subsequent completion of a short filler task, participants' recognition memory for these previously presented word stimuli was tested. The test list included the 36 words that had been presented during the encoding phase and an additional 36 emotionally matched words that had not been previously presented. Participants verbally indicated whether or not each word had been presented earlier during the encoding phase. From recorded hit rates (correct endorsements of words that had appeared earlier) and false-alarm rates (incorrect endorsements of words that had not appeared earlier), the researchers were then able to calculate a measure of memory sensitivity (i.e., d'), and a measure of response bias (i.e., β), using signal detection analysis. As predicted, the individuals with clinical depression did show disproportionately greater memory sensitivity for negative relative to positive words, though the groups also differed in response bias, with the participants with depression showing a relatively elevated tendency to endorse all negative words. Similar findings have subsequently been obtained in other groups with depression (e.g., Ridout et al., 2003). In contrast, studies using similar recognition memory procedures to compare individuals with different levels of anxiety have not revealed any evidence of group differences in memory sensitivity for threat stimuli relative to neutral stimuli (e.g., Dalgleish, 1994; Nugent & Mineka, 1994; Thorpe & Salkovskis, 2000).

Another useful feature of recognition memory tasks is that they can be adapted more easily than can recall tasks to employ stimuli other than words, as memory assessment requires only a simple discrimination response rather than the capacity to articulate stimuli. Thus, for example, researchers have recently used these procedures to assess the capacity of individuals with and without social phobia to recall images of differentially valenced facial expressions (e.g., Foa, Gilboa-Schechtman, Amir, & Freshman, 2000). Nevertheless, one must realize that the processes that underpin recognition memory and recall are likely to differ in some respects. Specifically, recall requires an initial attempt to actively search for, or generate, candidate memory items, followed by the judgment of familiarity needed to decide whether each candidate was recently presented. Recognition, on the other hand, depends only on the process of judging item familiarity, given that candidate items are provided rather than self-generated. Thus any memory bias for emotional stimuli that reflects selectivity within the active search component of recall may not reliably be observed on measures of recognition memory.

Tasks That Assess Implicit Memory for Valenced Stimulus Materials

Although recall and recognition tasks differ in important ways, they share the common requirement that participants must intentionally address their memories and must respond on the basis of their recollective experience. That is, they assess explicit memory. However, it has been clearly established that behavior can be influenced by memory traces that are unavailable to recollective experience, and much research has been diverted toward illuminating the nature of such implicit memory (cf. Bowers & Marsolek, 2003). It is not surprising, therefore, that researchers investigating the hypothesis that emotional vulnerability is characterized by selective memory advantages for negative information have sought to determine whether participants with anxiety and depression display biased implicit memory for emotional information. We now consider some of the main methodologies that have been employed for this purpose.

Methodologies designed to assess emotional bias in implicit memory often involve measuring the degree to which prior exposure to stimuli facilitates participants' capacity to subsequently identify these stimuli at very brief exposure durations or to complete degraded versions of the stimuli (such as word fragments and word stems). In either case, participants are not informed that the to-be-identified items have been previously presented, and so the influence of prior exposure to these items on performance is presumed to be implicit. Well-designed versions of these tasks typically include control conditions that involve valence-matched stimuli that were not presented during encoding in order that biases in implicit memory can be distinguished from differences in the capacity to generate valenced stimuli per se.

MacLeod and McLaughlin (1995) compared participants with GAD and nonanxious controls on an implicit memory task that was designed to assess the influence of prior exposure to valenced stimuli on subsequent ability to identify these stimuli at short exposure durations. An initial calibration stage was used to obtain an exposure duration for which each participant could be expected to accurately identify stimuli on 50% of the trials. An encoding task then followed in which participants were presented with four repetitions of 96 words, 48 of which were threatening and 48 of which were nonthreatening in content. The final stage of the experiment provided the crucial word identification measure of implicit memory. This stage involved the presentation of a series of words, each at the exposure duration derived from the initial calibration task. Half of these words were threatening and half were nonthreatening; half of each valenced subset had been presented during the encoding phase, whereas half had not previously been shown. The participant was required simply to name each word, and the accuracy of this naming response was recorded. The index of implicit memory was the degree to which perceptual identification accuracy was enhanced by previous exposure to the word stimuli. In this study, the group with GAD, compared with the nonanxious control group, showed disproportionately higher implicit memory scores for threat relative to nonthreat words. This suggests that individuals with generalized anxiety disorder may be characterized by an implicit memory advantage for threat stimuli. It is important to note, however, that MacLeod and McLaughlin's (1995) findings have not consistently been corroborated for other groups with anxiety proneness (e.g., Russo, Fox, & Bowles, 1999).

A slightly different method of measuring implicit memory involves assessing the degree to which initial exposure to stimuli subsequently facilitates the completion of word stems (or word fragments) to yield these same stimuli. Mathews, Mogg, May, and Eysenck (1989) adopted this approach to examine explicit and implicit memory for threat in participants with GAD and controls. These researchers used an encoding phase in which a series of threatening and nonthreatening words were presented within an imagery generation task. The implicit memory test then involved presenting participants with a series of word stems, half of which were derived from words previously presented and half of which were derived from valence-matched words that had not been previously presented. The participants were instructed to write down the first word that came to mind, using the word stems provided. An index of implicit memory was computed from the degree to which previous exposure to a word increased the possibility of it being generated to complete the word stem. Mathews et al. (1989) found that, compared with the nonanxious control participants, patients with GAD demonstrated disproportionately higher implicit memory scores for threatening relative to nonthreatening words. Once again, however, subsequent studies using this same methodology to examine implicit memory in other populations with anxiety have not consistently replicated this effect in individuals with high trait anxiety or in different clinical anxiety disorders (cf. Coles & Heimberg, 2002; MacLeod & Mathews, 2004).

Whereas findings concerning implicit memory bias have been inconsistent across those studies that have investigated anxiety, the results of experiments employing this type of task to assess implicit memory bias in depression have been less variable. Surprisingly, such studies have consistently failed to find evidence that participants with depression display enhanced implicit memory for negative stimuli within this type of task. Thus, despite the clear evidence that people with depression do demonstrate a selective explicit memory advantage for negative information, word-stem-completion measures reveal no parallel implicit memory bias in participants with depression (e.g., Watkins, Mathews, Williamson, & Fuller, 1992; cf. Watkins, 2002).

Some theorists have questioned the purity of the implicit memory measure provided by the word-stem-completion approach. In this type of task, one cannot ensure that participants do not consciously employ explicit memory of words presented during the encoding phase to assist in gen-

erating word-stem completions. One way of overcoming this problem may be to use the process dissociation approach, introduced by Jacoby (1991), to distinguish implicit and explicit influences on memory performance (e.g., McNally, Otto, Hornig, & Deckersbach, 2001). Another option is to assess implicit memory using tasks that do not require participants to produce or identify valenced stimuli. A good example of this latter approach is the white-noise task (Jacoby, Allan, Collins, & Larwill, 1988), within which implicit memory for previously exposed stimuli is assessed using subjective judgments of the loudness of white noise that accompanies stimuli in the final test phase.

Using this approach, Amir, McNally, Riemann, and Clements (1996) first exposed patients with panic disorder and nonanxious control participants to an audiotaped series of 12 panic-related and 12 neutral sentences. Following a short retention interval, participants then completed the implicit memory test, in which 24 panic-related and 24 neutral sentences were auditorily presented. Half of the sentences of each valence were repetitions of those presented during encoding, and half were new. Each sentence was embedded in one of three levels of white noise (60 +/– 1 dB; 64 +/– 1 dB; and 68 +/– 1 dB). Participants were asked to recite each sentence and to indicate the level of background noise. The index of implicit memory was the degree to which the white noise accompanying previously exposed sentences was perceived to be quieter than that accompanying new sentences. Particularly when noise level was low, Amir and colleagues (1996) found this index to reveal that the participants with panic disorder, compared with the nonanxious controls, displayed disproportionately greater implicit memory for the panic-related sentences relative to the neutral sentences. Subsequent studies have continued to use this approach primarily to examine implicit recall in individuals prone to anxiety rather than depression. These studies have had inconsistent success in demonstrating an implicit memory bias for threat stimuli across other populations with anxiety, with some evidence having been obtained for the presence of this bias in individuals with posttraumatic stress disorder (Amir, McNally, & Wiegartz, 1996) and with social phobia (Amir, Foa, & Coles, 2000), but not for participants with obsessive-compulsive disorder (Foa, Amir, Gershuny, Molnar, & Kozak, 1997).

The motivation behind the creation of the implicit memory tasks described in this section was to permit comparison of memory effects that occur in the absence of effortful retrieval with those effects that instead result from intentional memory search. However, more recently, it has been recognized that traditional implicit memory tasks of this type also may differ from conventional explicit memory tasks in terms of their relative sensitivity to perceptual and conceptual memory traces, respectively (cf. Watkins, 2002). This has led to the development of more refined tasks designed to break this confound and so reveal whether patterns of emotionally linked selectivity differ for conceptual and perceptual forms of memory representation. We conclude this section by briefly considering how this has been achieved.

Tasks Designed to Distinguish Biases in Conceptual and Perceptual Memory

As originally noted by Blaxton (1989), traditional explicit memory tasks, such as recall and recognition procedures, typically permit participants to use the semantic content of memory representations in order to benefit retrieval, whereas performance on traditional implicit memory tasks, such as the word-stem-completion procedures, requires the use only of structural information from such memory traces. This has led researchers to suggest that conventional explicit memory tasks may primarily assess conceptual memory, whereas conventional implicit memory tasks instead may primarily assess perceptual memory (Roediger & McDermott, 1992). Thus it may be that the differing sensitivity of such explicit and implicit memory tasks to emotionally linked patterns of selective process reflects not the differing demands they place on intentional retrieval but the differing degrees to which they assess conceptual and perceptual memory.

In order to experimentally address this issue, researchers now have developed new variants of explicit memory tasks designed to assess perceptual memory and new variants of implicit memory tasks designed to assess conceptual memory. This makes it possible to provide participants with any of four different combinations of memory instructions and memorial cues designed to encourage, respectively, (1) explicit, conceptually driven retrieval; (2) explicit, perceptually driven retrieval; (3) implicit, conceptually driven retrieval; and (4) implicit, perceptually driven retrieval. By contrasting patterns of selective processing across these conditions, it can be determined whether emotionally linked memory selectivity is influenced by the intentionality versus unintentionality of retrieval, by the conceptual versus perceptual nature of the memory test, or by both factors.

For example, in an investigation of selective memory in children with high trait anxiety, Daleiden (1998) employed all four such memory assessment conditions. During the encoding phase, participants received 10 positive, 10 negative, and 10 neutral words, each presented for a 5-second interval. Each participant then completed one of four memory tasks. One of these tasks was designed to assess explicit, conceptual memory for the valenced information presented at encoding. In this condition, participants were presented with a series of cue words that were synonyms of the targets and were instructed to write down a previously presented word that was similar in meaning to each cue word. Another task was designed to assess explicit, perceptual memory for the valenced information. In this variant, participants were presented with a series of cue words that were structurally (but not semantically) similar to target words (e.g., *moved* was the cue word for *loved*), and were instructed to write down a

previously exposed word that looked similar to each cue word. The third task was designed to assess implicit, conceptual memory for the valenced stimuli. This task involved providing participants with a series of definitions, some of which fit previously exposed words, and requiring them to write down any word that met each definition (regardless of whether or not this word had been presented earlier). The final task was designed to assess implicit, structural memory by providing participants with word fragments derived either from the valenced target words or from valence-matched distracter words and instructing them simply to complete each such fragment with the first word that came to mind (again, without regard to whether or not the word appeared in the encoding phase).

Daleiden's (1998) findings and the results of other studies employing this same experimental approach (cf. Watkins, 2002) have revealed that elevated levels of emotional vulnerability are more reliably characterized by biases in conceptual rather than perceptual memory, regardless of whether such memory is assessed using explicit or implicit tasks. This is consistent with the idea that the greater sensitivity of traditional explicit rather than implicit memory tasks to emotionally linked patterns of selective processing may reflect their tendency to assess conceptual rather than perceptual memory.

It is clear that a wide variety of tasks can be used to assess selective memory for emotional information. However, it is important to recognize that different tasks often are designed to assess quite different facets of memorial processing. Thus the specific hypothesis that an investigator wishes to address concerning memory selectivity always should be instrumental in guiding the selection of the most appropriate methodology. In general, evidence that emotional vulnerability is associated with a selective memory advantage for negative information has been most reliable when proneness to depression rather than anxiety has been examined, when explicit rather than implicit memory tasks have been employed, and when conceptual rather than perceptual memory has been assessed.

Concluding Comments

Despite the brevity of this chapter and the associated need to restrict consideration to only a sample of the many cognitive-experimental tasks that have been employed to assess the information-processing characteristics of emotional vulnerability, it nevertheless serves to illustrate the diversity of these various assessment procedures. Of course, this diversity partly reflects the fact that different tasks have been developed to assess quite separate categories of cognitive operations, and it is no surprise that the techniques employed to investigate selective encoding, interpretation, and memory are not equivalent. However, it also is the case that investigators addressing the same hypothesis concerning a given cognitive bias often have chosen to develop and employ quite dissimilar tasks, commonly because of each researcher's desire to eliminate perceived problems associated with earlier approaches. Yet there seldom have emerged universally preferred methodologies. Rather, alternative approaches are characterized by their own profiles of strengths and limitations, and researchers usually opt to adopt a given task based on whether its strengths for that particular study sufficiently outweigh its limitations.

Not uncommonly, those task variants that have the greatest capacity to permit precise measurement and to effectively exclude alternative interpretations of effects also impose the greatest technical demands on the researcher, often requiring, for example, computer-controlled delivery of stimulus presentation and the precise electronic recording of individual response latencies. Although simpler task variants that can be delivered with a minimum of equipment may yield less refined measures, this disadvantage may be offset by the capacity to more readily employ these approaches within field settings. Hence, it is perhaps best to consider these as complementary, rather than competing, approaches to the assessment of selective information processing. Indeed, recognizing that each alternative is characterized by differing strengths and limitations, the prudent investigator will draw conclusions with the greatest confidence when these are warranted by converging evidence obtained using a variety of such experimental approaches. Appendix A provides a summary of the various approaches surveyed in this chapter, with reference to the domains of processing to which they have been applied, as well some example references that describe in detail the application of these measures. In addition, a selection of stimuli that typify those used in a range of task variants to assess biases in processing are provided in appendix B. Although they are far from exhaustive, we hope that these appendices may be of some practical use to researchers wishing to choose and develop task variants to assess novel hypotheses.

As this review has indicated, considerable converging evidence now confirms that elevated levels of vulnerability to anxiety and to depression both are associated with selective biases that operate to favor the processing of negative information. However, the profiles of biases associated with each emotional disposition appear to differ. Both types of emotional vulnerability are characterized by self-reports of a tendency to selectively interpret ambiguity in a negative manner, though assessment tasks designed to minimize the influence of experimenter demand and response bias effects yield more support for the operation of such an interpretive bias in individuals with anxiety than in those with depression. Vulnerability to anxiety also is more robustly associated with the tendency to selectively encode negative information than is vulnerability to depression, and this anxiety-linked effect appears to operate automatically at a very early stage of processing. In contrast, vulnerability to depression is characterized by a more reliable memory advantage for negative information than is found to be associated with anxiety vulnerability, and this is particularly evident on those memory tasks that are sensitive to the conceptual processing of stimulus information. Such findings have led to the development of refined cognitive models that attribute anxiety vulnerability and depression vulnerability to biases in quite different cognitive mechanisms (cf. Williams et al., 1997).

The advances in understanding that have been enabled by past information-processing research into emotional vulnerability have brought contemporary investigators to the threshold of many important new issues. Researchers have more recently ventured to extend the cognitive-experimental study of anxiety and depression into other domains of negative emotion, such as anger (e.g., Putman, Hermans, & van Honk, 2004), and to positive emotions resulting, for example, from high self-esteem (e.g., Christensen, Wood, & Barrett, 2003) or from clinical mania (e.g., Lembke & Ketter, 2002), and it remains to be seen whether each distinctive emotional disposition is associated with a unique profile of processing selectivity. Also, investigators have just begun to systematically map out the types of selective processing biases that are shared across related clinical disorders, such as phobias, generalized anxiety disorders, and posttraumatic stress disorder, and those biases that distinguish these clinical conditions from one another and from nonclinical manifestations of related emotional dispositions (cf. MacLeod & Rutherford, 1998). Another important line of current work concerns determination of the causal role played by selective processing biases in the functional mediation of emotional vulnerability (cf. MacLeod, Campbell, Rutherford, & Wilson, 2004). Encouraged by the emerging evidence that biases in selective information processing can indeed causally contribute to emotional vulnerability (MacLeod, Rutherford, Campbell, Ebsworthy, & Holker, 2002; Mathews & Mackintosh, 2000), clinical researchers presently are evaluating the therapeutic impact of directly manipulating such processing biases in the treatment of emotional dysfunction (Amir, Selvig, Elias, & Rousseau, 2002; Mathews & MacLeod, 2002; Vasey, Hazen, & Schmidt, 2002).

Across all these endeavors, variants of the information-processing tasks reviewed within this chapter have continued to play a major role, and although they undoubtedly will undergo further adaptation and extension to meet the specific needs of differing research programs, the basic principles that underpin these methodologies are likely to remain constant. We very much hope that this review has communicated these principles with sufficient clarity not only to facilitate understanding of such tasks and their associated findings but also to permit fellow researchers to make practical use of these techniques within their own future investigations into the cognitive basis of emotional vulnerability.

Appendix A

Overview of common methods used to assess selective processing biases

Task	Task Description	Example Publication
Methods for assessing the selective encoding of emotional information		
Identification tasks	Stimuli varying in emotional tone are presented under conditions designed to make identification difficult. Encoding bias is inferred from comparative degree of enhanced identification of stimuli of particular emotional tone.	Byrne & Eysenck (1995); Rinck & Becker (2005)
Interference tasks	A central task is performed simultaneously with the presentation of task-irrelevant emotionally toned stimuli. Selective encoding bias is inferred from the degree to which stimuli of different emotional tone differentially interfere with central task performance.	Ingram & Ritter (2000); Mogg et al. (2000)
Attentional-probe tasks	Pairs of stimuli differing in emotional tone are briefly presented. Following stimulus offset, a probe appears in the vicinity of one member of the stimulus pair. Selective encoding bias is inferred from comparative speed to respond to probes in the vicinity of differentially toned stimuli.	Bradley et al. (2000); Kroeze & van den Hout (2000)
Eye-gaze measures	Stimuli of differing emotional tone are simultaneously presented. Eye gaze with reference to stimulus locations is continuously monitored during presentation in order to determine bias in encoding.	Bradley et al. (2000); Matthews & Antes (1992)
Methods for assessing the selective interpretation of ambiguity		
Self-report measures of interpretation	Participants report their preferred interpretations of emotionally ambiguous scenarios. Emotional tone of preferred interpretations is used to infer interpretive bias.	Richards et al. (2001); Derakshan & Eysenck (1997)
Homophone spelling tasks	A series of emotionally ambiguous homophones is dictated to participants. Emotional tone of the words written down in this supposed spelling test provides a measure of interpretive bias.	Mathews et al. (1989); Mogg et al. (2004)
Priming tasks	Emotionally ambiguous items are presented as primes, followed by targets related to one or the other of their meanings. The degree to which primes facilitate processing of targets related to their alternative meanings is used to infer interpretive bias.	Hirsch & Mathews (1997); Pury (2004)
Methods for assessing the selective retrieval of emotional information		
Autobiographical memory tasks	A series of cues is provided, to which participants respond with descriptions of personal memories. The relative probability or speed with which descriptions of differing emotional tone are provided is used to infer retrieval bias.	Richards & Whittaker (1990); Field & Morgan (2004)
Tasks assessing recall of valenced experimental stimuli	A series of items varying in emotional tone is first presented. Following a retention interval, participants' relative capacity to recall items of differential emotional tone is used to infer recall bias.	Bradley & Mathews (1983); Dowens & Calvo (2003)
Tasks assessing recognition of valenced experimental stimuli	Following initial stimulus presentation and a retention interval, as above, participants' capacity to explicitly distinguish old and new items differing in emotional tone is used to infer retrieval bias.	Foa et al. (2000); Thorpe & Salkovskis (2000).
Tasks assessing implicit memory for valenced materials	Following initial stimulus presentation and a retention interval, as above, participants' capacity to identify degraded old and new items differing in emotional tone in the absence of information that these stimuli were previously presented is used to infer implicit memory bias.	MacLeod & McLaughlin (1995); Russo et al. (1999); Amir et al. (1996)

Appendix B

Stimuli used in common assessments of selective encoding, interpretation, and retrieval

Unambiguous Words		Ambiguous Threat/ Nonthreat Words	
Threat words	*Nonthreat words*	*Homophones*	*Homographs*
Disease	Playful	Die/Dye	Arms
Injury	Hobby	Slay/Sleigh	Bark
Coronary	Reassured	Moan/Mown	Beat
Mutilated	Secure	Foul/Fowl	Blow
Fatal	Genial	Groan/Grown	Box
Ambulance	Contended	Liar/Lyre	Brood
Coffin	Carefree	Bore/Boar	Choke
Hazard	Leisure	Pain/Pane	Club
Cancer	Merriment	Weak/Week	Corn
Deathbed	Satisfaction	Skull/Scull	Die
Emergency	Cocky	Tease/Teas	Dock
Paralyzed	Overjoyed	Bury/Berry	Grave
Indecisive	Welcome	Guilt/Gilt	Graze
Pathetic	Confident	Flu/Flew	Growth
Foolish	Optimistic		Hamper
Lonely	Bold		Hang
Inferior	Capable		Incense
Criticized	Aloof		Jam
Inept	Relaxed		Lie
Hated	Windfall		Maroon
Inadequate	Entertainment		Odd
Stupid	Assured		Parting
Failure	Holiday		Patient
Embarrassed	Melody		Ram
			Rattle
			Revolution
			Sack
			Sentence
			Shady
			Sharp
			Shot
			Sink
			Stalk
			Stern
			Stole
			Strain
			Stroke
			Tank
			Terminal

Note: Threat and nonthreat word lists are frequency matched

Threat/neutral word pairs taken from Mathews & MacLeod (1985); homophones from Mathews, Richards, & Eysenck (1989); homographs from Richards & French (1992).

References

Amir, N., Foa, E. B., & Coles, M. E. (1998). Automatic activation and strategic avoidance of threat-relevant information in social phobia. *Journal of Abnormal Psychology, 107,* 285–290.

Amir, N., Foa, E. B., & Coles, M. E. (2000). Implicit memory bias for threat-relevant information in individuals with generalized social phobia. *Journal of Abnormal Psychology, 109,* 713–720.

Amir, N., McNally, R. J., Riemann, B. C., & Clements, C. (1996). Implicit memory bias for threat in panic disorder: Application of the "white noise" paradigm. *Behaviour Research and Therapy, 34,* 157–162.

Amir, N., McNally, R. J., & Wiegartz, P. S. (1996). Implicit memory bias for threat in posttraumatic stress disorder. *Cognitive Therapy and Research, 20,* 625–635.

Amir, N., Selvig, A., Elias, J., & Rousseau, G. (2002, November). Manipulation of information processing bias in anxiety: Malleability of attention and interpretation biases. Paper presented at the annual conference of the American Association of Behavior Therapy, Reno, NV.

Beck, A. T. (1976). *Cognitive therapy and the emotional disorders.* Oxford, UK: International Universities Press.

Beck, A. T., Emery, G., & Greenberg, R. L. (1985). *Anxiety disorders and phobias: A cognitive perspective.* New York: Basic Books.

Becker, E. S., Rinck, M., Margraf, J., & Roth, W. T. (2001). The emotional Stroop effect in anxiety disorders: General emotionality or disorder specificity? *Journal of Anxiety Disorders, 15,* 147–159.

Blaxton, T. A. (1989). Investigating dissociations among memory measures: Support for a transfer appropriate processing framework. *Journal of Experimental Psychology: Learning, Memory, and Cognition, 15,* 657–668.

Bower, G. H. (1981). Mood and memory. *American Psychologist, 36,* 129–148.

Bowers, J. S., & Marsolek, C. J. (Eds.). (2003). *Rethinking implicit memory.* London: Oxford University Press.

Bradley, B., & Mathews, A. (1983). Negative self-schemata in clinical depression. *British Journal of Clinical Psychology, 22,* 173–181.

Bradley, B. P., Mogg, K., Falla, S. J., & Hamilton, L. R. (1998). Attentional bias for threatening facial expressions in anxiety: Manipulation of stimulus duration. *Cognition and Emotion, 12,* 737–753.

Bradley, B. P., Mogg, K., & Lee, S. C. (1997). Attentional biases for negative information in induced and naturally occuring dysphoria. *Behaviour Research and Therapy, 35,* 911–927.

Bradley, B. P., Mogg, K., & Millar, N. H. (2000). Covert and overt orienting of attention to emotional faces in anxiety. *Cognition and Emotion, 14,* 789–808.

Bradley, B. P., Mogg, K., Millar, N., & White, J. (1995). Selective processing of negative information: Effects of clinical anxiety, concurrent depression, and awareness. *Journal of Abnormal Psychology, 104,* 532–536.

Broadbent, D., & Broadbent, M. (1988). Anxiety and attentional bias: State and trait. *Cognition and Emotion, 2,* 165–183.

Burgess, I. S., Jones, L. M., Robertson, S. A., Radcliffe, W. N., & Emerson, E. (1981). The degree of control exerted by phobic and non-phobic verbal stimuli over the recognition behaviour of phobic and non-phobic subjects. *Behaviour Research and Therapy, 19,* 233–243.

Burke, M., & Mathews, A. (1992). Autobiographical memory and clinical anxiety. *Cognition and Emotion, 6,* 23–35.

Burt, D. B., Zembar, M. J., & Niederehe, G. (1995). Depression and memory impairment: A meta-analysis of the association, its pattern, and specificity. *Psychological Bulletin, 117,* 285–305.

Butler, G., & Mathews, A. (1983). Cognitive processes in anxiety. *Advances in Behaviour Research and Therapy, 5,* 51–62.

Byrne, A., & Eysenck, M. W. (1995). Trait anxiety, anxious mood, and threat detection. *Cognition and Emotion, 9,* 549–562.

Cane, D. B., & Gotlib, I. H. (1985). Depression and the effects of positive and negative feedback on expectations, evaluations, and performance. *Cognitive Therapy and Research, 9,* 145–160.

Christensen, T. C., Wood, J. V., & Barrett, L. F. (2003). Remembering everyday experience through the prism of self-esteem. *Personality and Social Psychology Bulletin, 29,* 51–62.

Clark, D. M., Salkovskis, P. M., Ost, L. G., Breitholtz, E., Koehler, K. A., Westling, B. E., et al. (1997). Misinterpretation of body sensations in panic disorder. *Journal of Consulting and Clinical Psychology, 65,* 203–213.

Clark, D. M., & Teasdale, J. D. (1982). Diurnal variation in clinical depression and accessibility of memories of positive and negative experiences. *Journal of Abnormal Psychology, 91,* 87–95.

Clark, J. V., & Arkowitz, H. (1975). Social anxiety and self-evaluation of interpersonal performance. *Psychological Reports, 36,* 211–221.

Coles, M. E., & Heimberg, R. G. (2002). Memory biases in the anxiety disorders: Current status. *Clinical Psychology Review, 22,* 587–627.

Daleiden, E. L. (1998). Childhood anxiety and memory functioning: A comparison of systemic and processing accounts. *Journal of Experimental Child Psychology, 68,* 216–235.

Dalgleish, T. (1994). The relationship between anxiety and memory biases for material that has been selectively processed in a prior task. *Behaviour Research and Therapy, 32,* 227–231.

Derakshan, N., & Eysenck, M. W. (1997). Interpretive biases for one's own behavior and physiology in high trait anxious individuals and repressors. *Journal of Personality and Social Psychology, 73,* 816–825.

Dowens, M. G., & Calvo, M. G. (2003). Genuine memory bias versus response bias in anxiety. *Cognition and Emotion, 17,* 843–857.

Dunbar, G. C., & Lishman, W. A. (1984). Depression, recognition-memory and hedonic tone: A signal detection analysis. *British Journal of Psychiatry, 144,* 376–382.

Ehlers, A., Margraf, J., Davies, S., & Roth, W. T. (1988). Selective processing of threat cues in subjects with panic attack. *Cognition and Emotion, 2,* 201–220.

Eysenck, M. W., MacLeod, C., & Mathews, A. (1987). Cognitive functioning and anxiety. *Psychological Research, 49,* 189–195.

Field, A. P., & Morgan, J. (2004). Post-event processing and the retrieval of autobiographical memories in socially anxious individuals. *Journal of Anxiety Disorders, 18,* 647–663.

Foa, E. B., Amir, N., Gershuny, B., Molnar, C., & Kozak, M. J. (1997). Implicit and explicit memory in obsessive-compulsive disorder. *Journal of Anxiety Disorders, 11,* 119–129.

Foa, E. B., Gilboa-Schechtman, E., Amir, N., & Freshman, M. (2000). Memory bias in generalized social phobia: Remembering negative emotional expressions. *Journal of Anxiety Disorders, 14,* 501–519.

Gotlib, I. H., & McCann, C. D. (1984). Construct accessibility and depression: An examination of cognitive and affective factors. *Journal of Personality and Social Psychology, 47,* 269–288.

Hill, A. B., & Dutton, F. (1989). Depression and selective attention to self-esteem threatening words. *Personality and Individual Differences, 10,* 915–917.

Hill, A. B., & Knowles, T. H. (1991). Depression and the emotional Stroop effect. *Personality and Individual Differences, 12,* 481–485.

Hirsch, C., & Mathews, A. (1997). Interpretative inferences when reading about emotional events. *Behaviour Research and Therapy, 12,* 1123–1132.

Horenstein, M., & Segui, J. (1997). Chronometrics of attentional processes in anxiety disorders. *Psychopathology, 30,* 25–35.

Ingram, R. E., & Ritter, J. (2000). Vulnerability to depression: Cognitive reactivity and parental bonding in high-risk individuals. *Journal of Abnormal Psychology, 109,* 588–596.

Jacoby, L. L. (1991). A process dissociation framework: Separating automatic from intentional uses of memory. *Journal of Memory and Language, 30,* 513–541.

Jacoby, L. L., Allan, L. G., Collins, J. C., & Larwill, L. K. (1988). Memory influences subjective experience: Noise judgement. *Journal of Experimental Psychology: Learning, Memory, and Cognition, 14,* 240–247.

Kindt, M., Bierman, D., & Brosschot, J. F. (1996). Stroop versus Stroop: Comparison of a card format and a single-trial format of the standard color-word Stroop task and the emotional Stroop task. *Personality and Individual Differences, 21,* 653–661.

Kroeze, S., & van den Hout, M. A. (2000). Selective attention for cardiac information in panic patients. *Behaviour Research and Therapy, 38,* 63–72.

Lawson, C., & MacLeod, C. (1999). Depression and the interpretation of ambiguity. *Behaviour Research and Therapy, 37,* 463–474.

Lembke, A., & Ketter, T. A. (2002). Impaired recognition of facial emotion in mania. *American Journal of Psychiatry, 159,* 302–304.

Logan, A. C., & Goetsch, V. L. (1993). Attention to external threat cues in anxiety states. *Clinical Psychology Review, 13,* 541–560.

MacLeod, C. (1990). Mood disorders and cognition. In M. W. Eysenck (Ed.), *Cognitive psychology: An international review* (pp. 9–56). Oxford, UK: Wiley.

MacLeod, C. (2004). The Stroop task in clinical research. In A. Wenzel & D. C. Rubin (Eds.), *Cognitive methods and their application to clinical research* (pp. 41–62). New York: APA Books.

MacLeod, C., Campbell, L., Rutherford, E. M., & Wilson, E.

(2004). Causal status of anxiety linked attentional and interpretive bias. In J. Yiend (Ed.), *Cognition, emotion, and psychopathology* (pp. 172–189). Cambridge, UK: Cambridge University Press.

MacLeod , C., & Cohen., I. L. (1993). Anxiety and the interpretation of ambiguity: A text comprehension study. *Journal of Abnormal Psychology, 102,* 238–247.

MacLeod, C., & Mathews, A. (2004). Selective memory effects in anxiety disorders: An overview of research findings and their implications. In D. Reisberg & P. Hertel, (Eds.), *Memory and emotion* (pp.155–185). London: Oxford University Press.

MacLeod, C., Mathews, A., & Tata, P. (1986). Attentional bias in emotional disorders. *Journal of Abnormal Psychology, 95,* 15–20.

MacLeod, C., & McLaughlin, K. (1995). Implicit and explicit memory bias in anxiety: A conceptual replication. *Behaviour Research and Therapy, 33,* 1–14.

MacLeod, C., & Rutherford, E. M. (1992). Anxiety and the selective processing of emotional information: Mediating roles of awareness, trait and state variables, and personal relevance of stimulus materials. *Behaviour Research and Therapy, 30,* 479–491.

MacLeod, C., & Rutherford, E. M. (1998). Automatic and strategic cognitive biases in anxiety and depression. In K. Kirsner, & C. Speelman (Eds.), *Implicit and explicit mental processes* (pp. 233–254). Mahwah, NJ: Erlbaum.

MacLeod, C., & Rutherford, E. M. (2004). Information-processing approaches: Assessing the selective functioning of attention, interpretation, and retrieval. In R. G. Heimberg, C. L. Turk, & D. S. Mennin (Eds.), *Generalized anxiety disorder: Advances in research and practice* (pp. 109–142). New York: Guilford Press.

MacLeod, C., Rutherford, E., Campbell, L., Ebsworthy, G., & Holker, L. (2002). Selective attention and emotional vulnerability: Assessing the causal basis of their association through the experimental manipulation of attentional bias. *Journal of Abnormal Psychology, 111,* 107–123.

Mathews, A., & Mackintosh, B. (2000). Induced emotional interpretation bias and anxiety. *Journal of Abnormal Psychology, 109,* 602–615.

Mathews, A., & MacLeod, C. (1985). Selective processing of threat cues in anxiety states. *Behaviour Research and Therapy, 23,* 563–569.

Mathews, A., & MacLeod, C. (1986). Discrimination of threat cues without awareness in anxiety states. *Journal of Abnormal Psychology, 95,* 131–138.

Mathews, A., & MacLeod, C. (2002). Induced processing biases have causal effects on anxiety. *Cognition and Emotion, 16,* 331–354.

Mathews, A., & MacLeod, C. (2005). Cognitive vulnerability to emotional disorders. *Annual Review of Clinical Psychology, 1,* 167–195.

Mathews, A., Mogg, K., May, J., & Eysenck, M. (1989). Implicit and explicit memory bias in anxiety. *Journal of Abnormal Psychology, 98,* 236–240.

Mathews, A., Richards, A., & Eysenck, M. (1989). Interpretation of homophones related to threat in anxiety states. *Journal of Abnormal Psychology, 98,* 31–34.

Matt, G. E., Vazquez, C., & Campbell, W. K. (1992). Mood-congruent recall of affectively toned stimuli: A meta-analytic review. *Clinical Psychology Review, 12,* 227–255.

Matthews, G. R., & Antes, J. R. (1992). Visual attention and depression: Cognitive biases in the eye fixations of the dysphoric and the nondepressed. *Cognitive Therapy and Research, 16,* 359–371.

McNally, R. J., Otto, M. W., Hornig, C. D., & Deckersbach, T. (2001). Cognitive bias in panic disorder: A process dissociation approach to automaticity. *Cognitive Therapy and Research, 25,* 335–347.

Mogg, K., Baldwin, D. S., Brodrick, P., & Bradley, B. P. (2004). Effect of short-term SSRI treatment on cognitive bias in generalised anxiety disorder. *Psychopharmacology, 176,* 466–470.

Mogg, K., Bradley, B. P., Dixon, C., Fisher, S. Twelftree, H., & McWilliams, A. (2000). Trait anxiety, defensiveness and selective processing of threat: An investigation using two measures of attentional bias. *Personality and Individual Differences, 28,* 1063–1077.

Mogg, K., Bradley, B. P., & Williams, R. (1995). Attentional bias in anxiety and depression: The role of awareness. *British Journal of Clinical Psychology, 34,* 17–36.

Mogg, K., Bradley, B. P., Williams, R., & Mathews, A. M. (1993). Subliminal processing of emotional information in anxiety and depression. *Journal of Abnormal Psychology, 102,* 304–311.

Musa, C., Lepine, J.-P., Clark, D. M., Mansell, W., & Ehlers, A. (2003). Selective attention in social phobia and the moderating effect of a concurrent depressive disorder. *Behaviour Research and Therapy, 41,* 1043–1054.

Nisbett, R. E., & Wilson, T. D. C. (1977). Telling more than we can know: Verbal reports on mental processes. *Psychological Review, 84,* 231–259.

Nugent, K., & Mineka, S. (1994). The effect of high and low trait anxiety on implicit and explicit memory tasks. *Cognition and Emotion, 8,* 147–163.

Nunn, J. D., Mathews, A., & Trower, P. (1997). Selective processing of concern-related information in depression. *British Journal of Clinical Psychology, 36,* 489–503.

Powell, M., & Hemsley, D. R. (1984). Depression: A breakdown of perceptual defence? *British Journal of Psychiatry, 145,* 358–362.

Pury, C. L. S. (2004). Low positive affect and less extreme emotional encoding. *Cognition and Emotion, 18,* 149–158.

Putman, P., Hermans, E., & van Honk, J. (2004). Emotional Stroop performance for masked angry faces: It's BAS, not BIS. *Emotion, 4,* 305–311.

Richards, A., & French, C. C. (1992). An anxiety-related bias in semantic activation when processing threat/neutral homographs. *Quarterly Journal of Experimental Psychology, 45,* 503–525.

Richards, A., & Whittaker, T. M. (1990). Effects of anxiety and mood manipulation in autobiographical memory. *British Journal of Clinical Psychology, 29,* 145–153.

Richards, J. C., Austin, D. W., & Alvarenga, M. E. (2001). Interpretation of ambiguous interoceptive stimuli in panic disorder and nonclinical panic. *Cognitive Therapy and Research, 25,* 235–246.

Ridout, N., Astell, A. J., Reid, I. C., Glen, T., & O'Carroll, R. E. (2003). Memory bias for emotional facial expressions in major depression. *Cognition and Emotion, 17,* 101–122.

Rinck, M., & Becker, E. S. (2005). A comparison of attentional biases and memory biases in women with social phobia and major depression. *Journal of Abnormal Psychology, 114,* 62–74.

Roediger, H. L., & McDermott, K. B. (1992). Depression and implicit memory: A commentary. *Journal of Abnormal Psychology, 101,* 587–591.

Russo, R., Fox, E., & Bowles, R. J. (1999). On the status of implicit memory bias in anxiety. *Cognition and Emotion, 13,* 435–456.

Rutherford, E. M., MacLeod, C., & Campbell, L. W. (2004). Negative selectivity effects and emotional selectivity effects in anxiety: Differential attentional correlates of state and trait variables. *Cognition and Emotion, 18,* 711–720.

Stelmach, L. B., Campsall, J. M., & Herdman, C. M. (1997). Attentional and ocular movements. *Journal of Experimental Psychology: Human Perception and Performance, 23,* 823–844.

Teasdale, J. D., Taylor, R., & Fogarty, S. J. (1980). Effects of induced elation-depression on the accessibility of memories of happy and unhappy experiences. *Behaviour Research and Therapy, 18,* 339–346.

Thorpe, S. J., & Salkovskis, P. M. (2000). Recall and recognition for spider information. *Journal of Anxiety Disorders, 14,* 359–375.

Trandel, D. V., & McNally, R. J. (1987). Perception of threat cues in post-traumatic stress disorder: Semantic processing without awareness? *Behaviour Research and Therapy, 25,* 469–476.

Turvey, M. T. (1973). On peripheral and central processes in vision: Inferences from an information-processing analysis of masking with patterned stimuli. *Psychological Review, 80,* 1–52.

Vasey, M. W., Hazen, R., & Schmidt, N. B. (2002, November). Attentional retraining for chronic worry and GAD. Paper presented at the annual conference of the American Association of Behavior Therapy, Reno, NV.

Watkins, P. C. (2002). Implicit memory bias in depression. *Cognition and Emotion, 16,* 381–402.

Watkins, P. C., Mathews, A., Williamson, D. A., & Fuller, R. D. (1992). Mood-congruent memory in depression: Emotional priming or elaboration? *Journal of Abnormal Psychology, 101,* 581–586.

Wenzel, A., Jackson, L. C., & Holt, C. S. (2002). Social phobia and the recall of autobiographical memories. *Depression and Anxiety, 15,* 186–189.

Williams, J. M. G., & Broadbent, K. (1986). Autobiographical memory in suicide attempters. *Journal of Abnormal Psychology, 95,* 144–149.

Williams, J. M. G., Mathews, A., & MacLeod, C. (1996). The emotional Stroop task and psychopathology. *Psychological Bulletin, 120,* 3–24.

Williams, J. M. G., & Scott, J. (1988). Autobiographical memories in depression. *Psychological Medicine, 18,* 689–695.

Williams, J. M. G., Watts, F. N., MacLeod, C., & Mathews, A. (1997). *Cognitive psychology and emotional disorders* (2nd ed.). Chichester, UK: Wiley.

Yiend, J., & Mathews, A. (2001). Anxiety and attention to threatening pictures. *Quarterly Journal of Experimental Psychology: Human Experimental Psychology, 54A,* 665–681.

Zuroff, D. C., Colussy, S. A., & Wielgus, M. S. (1983). Selective memory and depression: A cautionary note concerning response bias. *Cognitive Therapy and Research, 7,* 223–231.

Jeffrey F. Cohn
Zara Ambadar
Paul Ekman

Observer-Based Measurement of Facial Expression With the Facial Action Coding System

Facial expression has been a focus of emotion research for over a hundred years (Darwin, 1872/1998). It is central to several leading theories of emotion (Ekman, 1992; Izard, 1977; Tomkins, 1962) and has been the focus of at times heated debate about issues in emotion science (Ekman, 1973, 1993; Fridlund, 1992; Russell, 1994). Facial expression figures prominently in research on almost every aspect of emotion, including psychophysiology (Levenson, Ekman, & Friesen, 1990), neural bases (Calder et al., 1996; Davidson, Ekman, Saron, Senulis, & Friesen, 1990), development (Malatesta, Culver, Tesman, & Shephard, 1989; Matias & Cohn, 1993), perception (Ambadar, Schooler, & Cohn, 2005), social processes (Hatfield, Cacioppo, & Rapson, 1992; Hess & Kirouac, 2000), and emotion disorder (Kaiser, 2002; Sloan, Straussa, Quirka, & Sajatovic, 1997), to name a few.

Because of its importance to the study of emotion, a number of observer-based systems of facial expression measurement have been developed (Ekman & Friesen, 1978, 1982; Ekman, Friesen, & Tomkins, 1971; Izard, 1979, 1983; Izard & Dougherty, 1981; Kring & Sloan, 1991; Tronick, Als, & Brazelton, 1980). Of these various systems for describing facial expression, the Facial Action Coding System (FACS; Ekman & Friesen, 1978; Ekman, Friesen, & Hager, 2002) is the most comprehensive, psychometrically rigorous, and widely used (Cohn & Ekman, 2005; Ekman & Rosenberg, 2005). Using FACS and viewing video-recorded facial behavior at frame rate and slow motion, coders can manually code nearly all possible facial expressions, which are decomposed into action units (AUs). Action units, with some qualifications, are the smallest visually discriminable facial movements. By comparison, other systems are less thorough (Malatesta et al., 1989), fail to differentiate between some anatomically distinct movements (Oster, Hegley, & Nagel, 1992), consider movements that are not anatomically distinct as separable (Oster et al., 1992), and often assume a one-to-one mapping between facial expression and emotion (for a review of these systems, see Cohn & Ekman, 2005).

Unlike systems that use emotion labels to describe expression, FACS explicitly distinguishes between facial actions and inferences about what they mean. FACS itself is descriptive and includes no emotion-specified descriptors. Hypotheses and inferences about the emotional meaning of facial actions are extrinsic to FACS. If one wishes to make emotion-based inferences from FACS codes, a variety of related resources exist. These include the FACS Investigators' Guide (Ekman et al., 2002), the FACS interpretive database (Ekman, Rosenberg, & Hager, 1998), and a large body of empirical research (Ekman & Rosenberg, 2005). These resources suggest combination rules for defining emotion-specified expressions from FACS action units, but this inferential step remains extrinsic to FACS. Because of its descriptive power, FACS is regarded by many as the standard measure for facial behavior and is used widely in diverse fields. Beyond emotion science, these include facial neuromuscular disorders (Van Swearingen & Cohn, 2005), neuroscience (Bruce & Young, 1998; Rinn, 1984, 1991), computer vision (Bartlett,

Ekman, Hager, & Sejnowski, 1999; Cohn, Zlochower, Lien, & Kanade, 1999; Pantic & Rothkrantz, 2000; Tian, Cohn, & Kanade, 2005), computer graphics and animation (Breidt, Wallraven, Cunningham, & Buelthoff, 2003; Parke & Waters, 1996), and face encoding for digital signal processing (International Organization for Standardization, 2002; Tao, Chen, Wu, & Huang, 1999).

In this chapter, we discuss the conceptual basis for FACS, the numerical listing of discrete facial movements identified by the system, the evaluative psychometrics of the system, and the recommended training requirements. We also include information on how to obtain software for computer-assisted FACS coding.

FACS has progressed through three versions: the initial version (FACS 1978), a document-based update (FACS 1992), and a new edition (FACS 2002), which includes improvements in scoring criteria and in didactic materials, extensive use of hyperlinked cross-referenced text, and embedded video links in the CD version. Throughout this chapter, we use publication date when referring to a specific version of FACS.

Conceptual Basis

Sign Versus Message Judgment

Ekman and Friesen (Ekman, 1964, 1965; Ekman & Friesen, 1969) distinguished two conceptual approaches to studying facial behavior, namely, measuring judgments about one or another message and measuring the sign vehicles that convey the message. In message judgment, the observer's task is to make *inferences* about something underlying the facial behavior—emotion, mood, traits, attitudes, personality, and the like; for this reason observers typically are referred to as "judges" or "raters." In measuring sign vehicles, observers *describe* the surface of behavior; they count how many times the face moves a certain way, or how long a movement lasts, or whether it was a movement of the *frontalis* or *corrugator* muscle. As an example, on seeing a smiling face, an observer with a judgment-based approach would make judgments such as "happy," whereas an observer with a sign-based approach would code the face as having an upward, oblique movement of the lip corners. Observers with a sign-based approach are supposed to function like machines and typically are referred to as "coders."

Though message- and sign-based approaches can sometimes answer the same questions, they can also answer different questions, for they focus on different phenomena. Message judgment research is not typically focused on the face. The face is but an input. The focus is on the person observing the face and/or on the message obtained. Questions have to do with whether a difference is detectable or accurate, whether there are individual differences among raters, reflecting skill, gender, or personality, and whether

messages obtained are best represented as dimensions or categories.

Facial sign vehicles are measured when the focus is on unearthing something fairly specific about facial behavior itself, not about the perception of the face. It is the only method that can be used to answer such questions as:

1. To what extent is the facial activity shown by newborns and infants systematic, not random, and which particular actions first show such systematic organization? To answer this question, facial behavior shown during samples taken at different developmental points or in different situational contexts can be measured. Then the probabilities of particular co-occurrences and sequential patterns of facial actions can be evaluated (Cohn & Tronick, 1983; Oster & Ekman, 1978).

2. Which particular facial actions are employed to signal emphasis in conversation? Facial actions that co-occur with verbal or vocal emphasis must be measured to determine whether there are any actions that consistently accompany any emphasis (Ekman, 1980).

3. Is there a difference in the smile during enjoyment as compared with a discomfort smile? The particular facial actions evident in smiling movements must be measured when persons are known, by means other than the face, to be experiencing positive and negative affect (Ekman, Friesen, & Ancoli, 1980; Frank, Ekman, & Friesen, 1993).

4. Are there differences in heart rate that accompany nose wrinkling and upper lip raising versus opening the eyes and raising the brows? Facial behavior must be measured to identify the moments when these particular facial configurations occur in order to examine coincident heart rate activity (Levenson et al., 1990).

The preceding examples are not intended to convey the full range of issues that can be addressed only by measuring facial sign vehicles. They should, however, serve to illustrate the variety of questions that require this approach. One might expect the measurement of sign vehicles approach to have been followed often, as it is required for study of many different problems. However, there have been only a few such studies compared with the many that have measured the messages judged when viewing the face. It is much easier to perform the latter sort of study. The investigator need not tamper with the face itself, other than by picking some samples to show. Data are obtained quickly: One can measure observers' judgments much more quickly than one can describe reliably the flow and variety of facial movement.

Until the advent of FACS, an important obstacle to research measuring sign vehicles has been the lack of any accepted, standard, ready-for-use technique for measuring facial movement. Investigators who have measured facial movement have invented their techniques in large part de novo, rarely making use of the work of their predecessors. Some have seemed to be uninformed by the previous literature. Even the more scholarly have found it difficult to build on the methods previously reported, because descriptions of facial activity are often less clear than they appear on first reading. A facial action may seem to be described in sufficient detail and exactness until an attempt is made to apply that description to the flow of facial behavior. For instance, descriptions of brow motion that omit specific appearance changes in facial lines and furrows and in the appearance of the upper eyelid omit information that may be needed to discriminate among related but different facial actions. FACS addresses the need for a comprehensive system that can be readily learned, that is psychometrically sound, and that has high utility for various research applications.

Basis for Deriving Action Units

The anatomical basis of facial action (Figure 13.1) provides the basis for deriving units of behavior. With few exceptions, all people have the same facial muscles (Schmidt & Cohn, 2001). FACS action units are based on what the muscles allow the face to do. To determine the appearance changes associated with each muscle, Ekman and Friesen began by electrically stimulating individual muscles and by learning to control them voluntarily. The result is that each action unit is associated with one or more facial muscles.

In selecting facial actions, Ekman and Friesen (1978) used the criterion that observers were capable of reliably distinguishing all appearance changes resulting from the various muscles. If two appearance changes could not be reliably distinguished, they were combined, even if different muscles were involved. Conversely, some actions proved too subtle for reliable measurement. Visemes, for instance, are visually distinguishable phonemes (Massaro, Cohen, Beskow, Daniel, & Cole, 1998); with some exceptions, they are not included as AUs in FACS.

Facial Action Units

FACS 2002 specifies 9 action units in the upper face and 18 in the lower face. In addition, there are 14 head positions and movements, 9 eye positions and movements, 5 miscellaneous action units, 9 action descriptors, 9 gross behaviors, and 5 visibility codes. Action descriptors are movements for which the anatomical basis is unspecified. Upper and lower face AUs and head and eye positions are shown in Figure 13.2. Each one has both a numeric and verbal label and a specified anatomical basis in one or more facial muscles. With some exceptions, action units are organized by region of the face in which they occur. Brow action units, for instance, have AU labels 1, 2, and 4. There is no action unit 3 in FACS, although it is used to refer to a specific brow action in a specialized version of FACS intended for use with infants (Oster,

2001). Eye region action units have action unit labels 5, 6, and 7 and 41 through 46. For each action unit, FACS 2002 provides a detailed description, instructions on how to perform the action, and instructions for intensity scoring. For many action unit combinations, FACS 2002 covers these same topics and details subtle differences among related ones (e.g., AU 1+2 versus AU 1+2+4). Reference sections give information about AUs that might affect their scoring. By convention, when more than one action unit is present, they are listed in ascending order.

Appendix A describes some of the principal changes in action unit criteria and coding that occurred between FACS 1978 and FACS 2002. This material may be of particular interest to readers who have used the earlier version and are transitioning to FACS 2002.

FACS includes codes for head and eye positions. These action units often are omitted in FACS scoring. However, there is increasing evidence of their relevance to the interpretation of facial expression. Similar facial actions, such as smiling (AU 12), often vary in meaning depending on their temporal coordination with head motion. In embarrassment, for instance, smile intensity increases as the head pitches forward, and smile intensity decreases as the head pitches back toward frontal orientation (i.e., negative correlation; Cohn et al., 2004; Keltner & Buswell, 1997). FACS 2002 adds some specific codes for particular combinations of eye or head motion and facial action units, such as eyes (gaze) to the side occurring with AU 14, which may be a sign of contempt. Unless head and eye positions are scored, such relationships cannot be found.

Combinations of AUs that occur may be additive or nonadditive. In additive combinations the appearance of each action unit is independent, whereas in nonadditive combinations they modify each other's appearance. Nonadditive combinations are analogous to coarticulation effects in speech, in which one phoneme modifies the sounds of those with which it is contiguous. An example of an additive combination in FACS is AU 1+2, which often occurs in surprise (along with AU 5) and in the brow-flash greeting (Eibl-Eibesfeldt, 1989). The combination of these two action units raises the inner (AU 1) and outer (AU 2) corners of the eyebrows and causes horizontal wrinkles to appear across the forehead. The appearance changes associated with AU 1+2 are the product of their joint actions.

An example of a nonadditive combination is AU 1+4, which often occurs in sadness (Darwin, 1872/1998). When AU 1 occurs alone, the inner eyebrows are pulled upward. When AU 4 occurs alone, they are pulled together and downward. When they occur together, the downward action of AU 4 is modified. The result is that the inner eyebrows are raised and pulled together. This action typically gives an oblique shape to the brows and causes horizontal wrinkles to appear in the center of the forehead, as well as other changes in appearance.

Several chapters from FACS 2002 are viewable online at http://face-and-emotion.com/dataface/facs/manual/TOC .html.

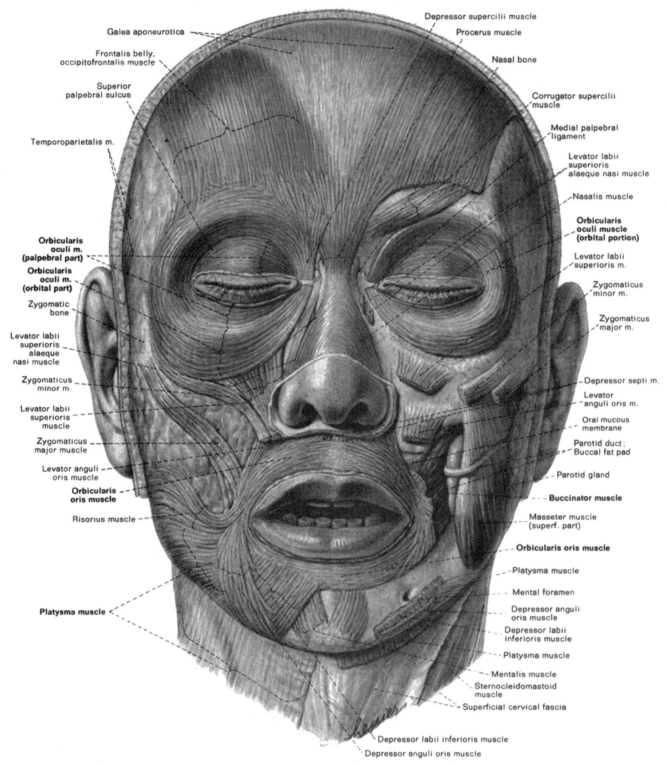

Figure 13.1. Muscles of the face (Clemente, 1997).

206

AU	Description	Facial Muscle	Example Image	Inter-rater Agreement (Kappa Coefficient) (tolerance window in seconds)			
				1/30th	1/6th	1/3rd	1/2
1	Inner Brow Raiser	*Frontalis, pars medialis*	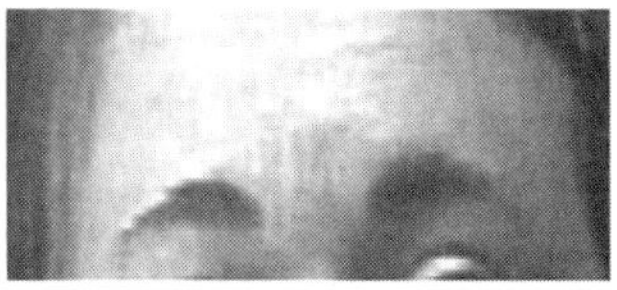	.73	.79	.81	.83
2	Outer Brow Raiser	*Frontalis, pars lateralis*	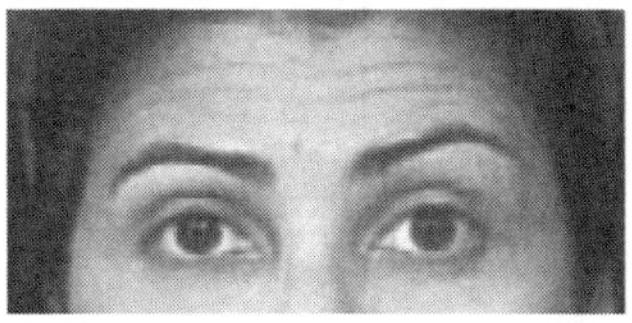	.66	.71	.74	.76
4	Brow Lowerer	*Corrugator supercilii, Depressor supercilii*	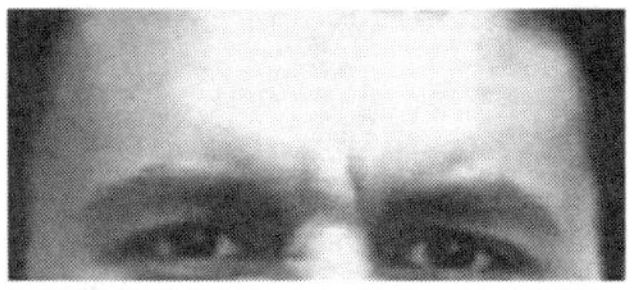	.58	.64	.67	.70
5	Upper Lid Raiser	*Levator palpebrae superioris*	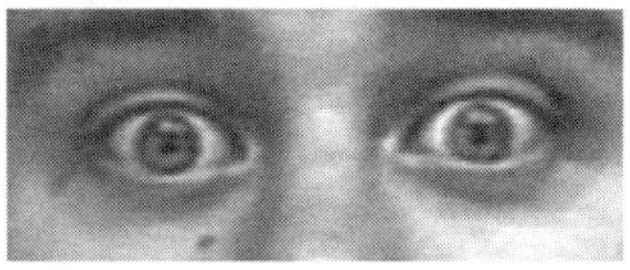	.68	.76	.79	.82
6	Cheek Raiser	*Orbicularis oculi, pars orbitalis*	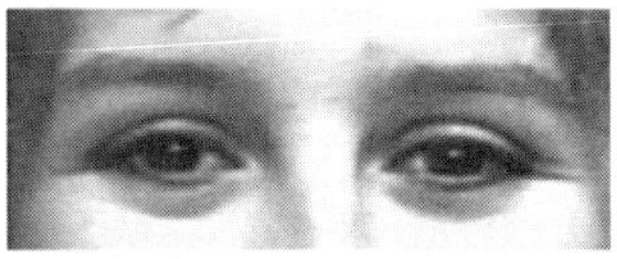	.72	.78	.82	.85
7	Lid Tightener	*Orbicularis oculi, pars palpebralis*	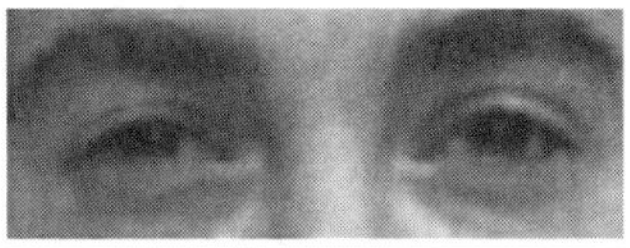	.44	.49	.53	.56
9	Nose Wrinkler	*Levator labii superioris alaquae nasi*	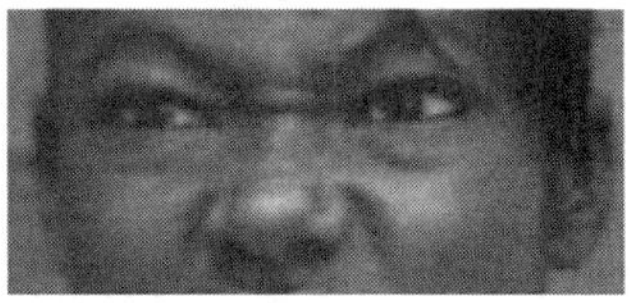	.67	.76	.81	.83
10	Upper Lip Raiser	*Levator labii superioris*	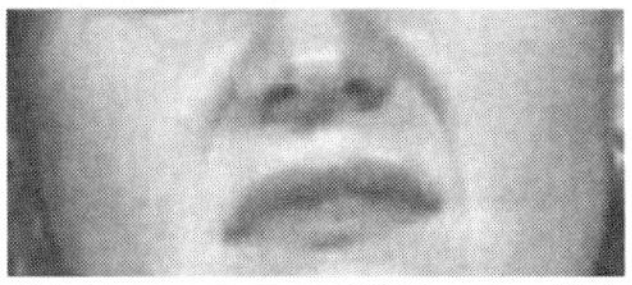	.69	.76	.79	.81
11	Nasolabial Deepener	*Zygomaticus minor*	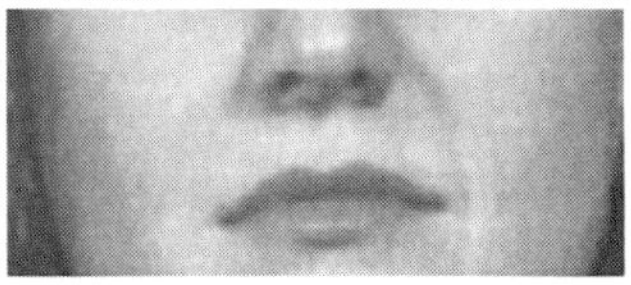	-	-	-	.97
12	Lip Corner Puller	*Zygomaticus major*	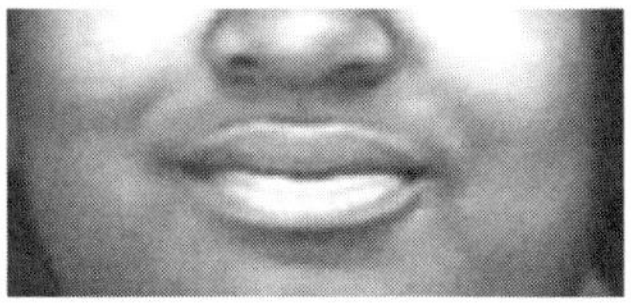	.67	.71	.74	.76

Figure 13.2. Action units of the Facial Action Coding System (Ekman & Friesen, 1978; Ekman, Friesen, & Hager, 1978). *Note:* Action units for eye position are not shown. Interrater agreement is quantified using coefficient kappa, which controls for chance agreement. All kappa statistics are for spontaneous facial behavior and are from Sayette et al. (2001) except as noted in the text. Criteria for AUs 25, 26, 27, 41, 42, and 44 differ between FACS 1978 and FACS 2002. Please see appendix A for specifics. Images are from Kanade et al. (2000) with the exceptions of AU 23 and 24, which are from Ekman, Friesen, & Hager (2002).

AU	Description	Facial Muscle	Example Image	Inter-rater Agreement (Kappa Coefficient) (tolerance window in seconds)			
				1/30th	1/6th	1/3rd	1/2
13	Cheek Puffer	*Levator anguli oris (a.k.a. Caninus)*		-	-	-	-
14	Dimpler	*Buccinator*		.59	.67	.72	.75
15	Lip Corner Depressor	*Depressor anguli oris (a.k.a. Triangularis)*		.54	.65	.69	.72
16	Lower Lip Depressor	*Depressor labii inferioris*		-	-	-	-
17	Chin Raiser	*Mentalis*		.55	.63	.66	.68
18	Lip Puckerer	*Incisivii labii superioris* and *Incisivii labii inferioris*		.65	.71	.74	.75
20	Lip stretcher	*Risorius* with *platysma*		.38	.47	.54	.60
22	Lip Funneler	*Orbicularis oris*		-	-	-	-
23	Lip Tightener	*Orbicularis oris*		.32	.41	.47	.53
24	Lip Pressor	*Orbicularis oris*		.50	.58	.62	.64
25	Lips parted	*Depressor labii inferioris* or relaxation of *Mentalis*, or *Orbicularis oris*		.57	.62	.65	.67

AU	Description	Facial Muscle	Example Image	Inter-rater Agreement (Kappa Coefficient) (tolerance window in seconds)			
				1/30th	1/6th	1/3rd	1/2
26	Jaw Drop	*Masseter*, relaxed *Temporalis* and *internal Pterygoid*		.65	.72	.76	.79
27	Mouth Stretch	*Pterygoids, Digastric*		-	-	-	.96
28	Lip Suck	*Orbicularis oris*		.61	.70	.76	.79
41	Lid droop	Relaxation of *Levator palpebrae superioris*		-	-	-	-
42	Slit	*Orbicularis oculi*		-	-	-	-
43	Eyes Closed	Relaxation of *Levator palpebrae superioris; Orbicularis oculi, pars palpebralis*		-	-	-	-
44	Squint	*Orbicularis oculi, pars palpebralis*		-	-	-	.87
45	Blink	Relaxation of *Levator palpebrae superioris; Orbicularis oculi, pars palpebralis*		-	-	-	.98
46	Wink	Relaxation of *Levator palpebrae superioris; Orbicularis oculi, pars palpebralis*		-	-	-	-
51	Head turn left	———		-	-	-	-

AU	Description	Facial Muscle	Example Image	Inter-rater Agreement (Kappa Coefficient) (tolerance window in seconds)			
				1/30th	1/6th	1/3rd	1/2
52	Head turn right	———		-	-	-	-
53	Head up	———		-	-	-	-
54	Head down	———		-	-	-	-
55	Head tilt left	———		-	-	-	-
56	Head tilt right	———		-	-	-	-
57	Head forward	———		-	-	-	-
58	Head back	———		-	-	-	-

This material conveys the thoroughness with which AUs are described, detailed information related to instruction, and subtle differences among AUs.

Scoring of Action Units

FACS provides researchers with a flexible range of options with respect to the level of detail with which action unit coding is performed. The options are not all mutually exclusive. Several may be combined, depending on the research question.

Comprehensive or Selective Coding

In comprehensive coding, each and every AU present in a chosen segment of facial behavior is coded. In selective coding, only predetermined AUs are coded; any others that appear are ignored. Each approach has its own advantages and disadvantages. The advantage of a comprehensive approach is that it allows researchers to analyze their data in more ways, to interpret null findings, and to make new discoveries. When a comprehensive approach is used, a null result can readily be interpreted as no differences between groups or conditions of interest. When a selective approach is used, the absence of differences between groups is open to question. There may be no difference between groups or conditions, or the investigator may have looked in the wrong places (i.e., chosen the "wrong" subset of actions to compare).

The primary drawback of comprehensive coding is that it is more labor intensive. A well-trained FACS coder can take about 100 minutes to code 1 minute of video data depending on the density and complexity of facial actions. The drawback of comprehensive coding is where the advantage of selective coding becomes apparent. Economy is the primary advantage of selective coding. Coding can be done more quickly because coders need to focus on only a subset of the facial actions.

Some research questions require a comprehensive approach to coding facial behavior. For example, an investigator who is interested in discovering whether there are unique facial behaviors that signal embarrassment would need to comprehensively code video segments of facial behavior during which participants reported feeling embarrassed and not embarrassed (Keltner, 1995). Keltner (1995) examined video records of people taken when they were reporting embarrassment, shame, or enjoyment. Comprehensive FACS coding of their facial expression enabled the discovery that self-reported embarrassment is uniquely associated with a particular sequence of action units: AU 12 followed by AU 24 and then by AU 51+54. Had the researcher selectively focused on only a subset of action units (for example, a smile with or without contraction of the muscle around the eye, AU 6, which is believed to distinguish between an enjoyment and a nonenjoyment smile), the discovery of the embarrassment display would not have been possible. Had a selective approach been used, they might have mistakenly concluded that there was no unique facial display of embarrassment.

Exploratory studies benefit from a more comprehensive approach to coding.

Selective coding is best used when the investigator has strong hypotheses about specific action units or is interested only in specific facial regions (Messinger, Fogel, & Dickson, 1999; Prkachin, 1992). When selective coding is used, it is important to record which facial actions (AUs) were ignored. This record allows for more precise understanding of the results, so that readers/researchers can tell whether there was no result that involved the specific AUs or whether the AUs were not considered in the first place.

Presence/Absence or Intensity

Regardless of whether comprehensive or selective coding is used, researchers can determine the level of detail in their coding method. Most rudimentary is to code whether action units are present or absent. A different approach is taken when, in addition to coding presence or absence, coders also pay attention to the intensity or strength of the actions. FACS 2002 allows for five levels of intensity coding (A, B, C, D, and E), with A being the least intense (a trace) action and E the maximum strength of the action. Guidelines for intensity coding are somewhat subjective, however, and it may require special effort to establish and maintain acceptable levels of reliability, especially in the mid-range.

The importance of assessing intensity level depends on the nature of the study and the research question. In studies of pain, for instance, differences in intensity of facial actions have been found to vary among different types of pain elicitors (Prkachin, 1992). In related work, Deyo, Prkachin, and Mercer (2004) were interested in the functional relation between intensity of pain elicitors and intensity of selected action units; it was thus essential to code action unit intensity. As another example, Messinger (Messinger, 2002) proposed that mouth opening and cheek raising increase perceived intensity of infant's smile and distress independent of the strength of other actions (i.e., actual intensity of the AU 12 and AU 20, respectively).

Individual Action Units or Events

An event is a set of action units that overlap in time (i.e., co-occur) and appear to define a perceptually meaningful unit of facial action. AU 1+2+5 is an example of action units that frequently co-occur. Whether or not one AU begins or ends in advance of the others, they appear to constitute a single display. Rather than code each action unit independently, an investigator may wish to code or define them as an event. (A variant of this approach is found in Oster, 2001, and Oster et al., 1996). The guiding assumptions are:

1. Facial behavior occurs not continuously but rather as episodes (events) that typically manifest themselves as discrete events.
2. Action units that occur together are related in some way and form an event.

Event coding can be more efficient than coding single action units. Because action units are precoded into defined patterns, data reduction is facilitated as well. It also addresses the problem that some action units may linger and merge into the background. Events then can be coded independent of these longer lasting actions (e.g., a low-intensity AU 12 that may persist for some time). For investigators who wish to use event coding, FACS includes numerous suggestions for how to delineate events. These appear in FACS 1992, FACS 2002, and the Investigator's Guide that comes with FACS 2002 (Ekman et al., 2002).

There are some limitations to event coding. An event is a higher order perceptual unit than an action unit, and the rules or bases for identifying events are not as well defined. One basis is frequency of co-occurrence: AU combinations that are known to co-occur can be considered an event. A concern here is that normative data on co-occurrence rates are lacking and could be population specific, varying, for instance, with psychopathology or cultural differences. Another basis, suggested by the Investigator's Guide (Ekman et al., 2002), is a known association between specific AU combinations and specific emotions: An AU combination that is commonly associated with an emotion can be considered an event. This basis potentially violates the sign-based logic of FACS, which is to keep description separate from inference. To code some AUs as events based on their association with emotion while omitting others is more consistent with a judgment- than a sign-based approach. Studies that have utilized event coding typically do not report the basis on which they define an event. It may well be that association with emotion is not used often or even at all. But it is important that investigators realize the nature of event coding and recognize the potential bias it may introduce. The coder may impose organization where none exists or misidentify or omit events.

A related concern is that FACS guidelines for overlapping events may prove overwhelming, as there are quite a few exceptions to the rules and little or no rationale is provided. Sometimes an increase in AU intensity is treated as a separate event, whereas at other times it is treated as a "background" AU that is not coded in the subsequent event.

Unlike action unit coding, which is well validated, little is known about the psychometrics or perception of event coding. The literature in event perception is limited to the perception of complex scenes (Avrahami & Kareev, 1994; Newtson, Rindner, Miller, & Lacross, 1978; Zacks & Tversky, 2001). Studies remain to be done about how people segment facial behavior. Do people see facial behavior as episodic and event-like? Where and how do people segment the stream of facial behavior? Are people reliable in perceiving and determining the boundaries of these events? Carefully designed empirical studies are needed to answer such questions. In the meantime, given that delineating an event to a certain extent involves subjective judgments on the part of the coders, it raises a reliability issue of event segmentation, and

hence it is important to establish and report coders' reliability on this issue. Ekman and Friesen found good reliability for event coding in developing FACS, but to our knowledge, no published studies of facial expressions that utilize the event-based approach have reported reliability for event determination, with the exception of emotion-specified aggregates, as presented subsequently.

Event coding has proven problematic when FACS coding is used for training computer algorithms in automatic FACS coding. Event coding typically ignores onset and offset times and only includes action units present at the "peak" of the event. Moreover, action units present at the peak may or may not be at their peak intensity at that moment, and event coding ignores other action units that may be present but not considered part of the event. Algorithms must learn not only to detect action units but also when to ignore ones that might also be present. The higher order, top-down decision making of event coding stands in sharp relief against the bottom-up sign-based coding of action units on which FACS is based.

Psychometric Evaluation

Reliability (Interobserver Agreement)

We report reliability, defined as interobserver agreement,[1] for individual action units in spontaneous facial behavior when that has been established. Except as noted in the following, reliability for posed facial behavior is not reported here. In general, reliability for spontaneous facial behavior is less than that for posed behavior. In spontaneous facial behavior, camera orientation is less likely to be frontal, head motion larger and more varied, and face size smaller relative to the size of the image. In spontaneous facial behavior, action unit intensity may also be lower. All of these factors make reliability more difficult to achieve (Sayette, Cohn, Wertz, Perrott, & Parrott, 2001). Thus the reliability reported here represents a conservative estimate for investigators whose interest is in posed facial behavior.

Most studies that have reported reliability for FACS report average reliability across all AUs. As a consequence, there is no way to know which AUs have been reliably coded and which have not. Low reliability, especially for AUs occurring less frequently, may easily go unnoticed. This is of particular concern because these AUs often are of special interest (e.g., when occurring as microexpressions that qualify the interpretation of smiling; Ekman, Friesen, & O'Sullivan, 1988). When specific AUs are the focus of hypothesis testing, reliability at the level of individual AUs is needed. Otherwise, statistical power may be reduced by measurement error and, as a result, negative findings misinterpreted.

For individual AUs, at least four types of reliability (i.e., agreement between observers) are relevant to the interpretation of substantive findings. These are reliability for occurrence/nonoccurrence of individual AUs, as discussed earlier; temporal precision; intensity; and aggregates. Temporal precision refers to how closely coders agree on the timing of action units, such as when they begin or end. This level of reliability becomes important when hypothesis testing focuses on questions such as response latency. Action unit intensity becomes important when hypothesis testing focuses on questions such as whether intensity is related to subjective experience or individual differences. And, finally, in many studies, investigators are interested in testing hypotheses about emotion-specified expressions or events. The reliability of emotion–specified expressions or event coding will, of course, depend on the constituent AUs. By assessing the reliability of these aggregates directly, one can more accurately estimate their reliability.

The most systematic, large-scale investigation of FACS reliability in spontaneous facial behavior is that of Sayette and colleagues (Sayette et al., 2001). They evaluated each type of reliability across three studies of spontaneous facial behavior involving 102 participants, with approximately equal numbers of men and women. The studies induced change in facial expression by using one of three emotion inductions: olfactory stimulation, cue-induced craving for nicotine, and a speech task. Action units were comprehensively coded using FACS 1978 and FACS 1992. The number of frames (at 30 frames per second) for each action unit ranged from 800 (for AU 12) to less than 48 (e.g., AU 11). Action units occurring in less than 48 frames were not analyzed. Nineteen AUs met the authors' criterion of occurring in 48 or more video frames. We report reliability for these action units based on their findings.

To increase the number of AUs for which reliability is reported, we include findings from two other sources. One is from a study of spontaneous blinks (AU 45; Cohn, Xiao, Moriyama, Ambadar, & Kanade, 2003) in video data collected by Frank and Ekman (Frank & Ekman, 1997). In this study, male participants either lied or told the truth to an interviewer in a high-stakes deception interview. Some participants wore glasses, which made coding more challenging. The other source for reliability data is the Cohn-Kanade database (Kanade, Cohn, & Tian, 2000) of posed facial behavior (i.e., directed facial action tasks). We report reliability for AU 11, 27, and 44 from this database.

A caveat is that comparison coding in these two supplemental sources was not blind to the original codes. Instead, comparison coding was used to confirm or reject the original coding. Because comparison coding was not independent in coding AU 11, 27, 44, and 45, some caution must be used in interpreting the findings for these four AUs. We do not believe that bias was a significant factor, however, because independent comparison of three of these AUs (AU 27, 44, and 45) with automatic facial image analysis has been consistently high, especially for blinks (Cohn et al., 2003; Cohn et al., 1999; Tian, Kanade, & Cohn, 2002).

In all, the action units from the primary (Sayette et al., 2001) and supplementary (Cohn et al., 2003; Kanade et al., 2000) sources include those that have occurred most frequently in studies of both spontaneous and deliberate facial behavior. Reliability was assessed using coefficient kappa to control for agreement due to chance. With the exception of AUs 11, 27, and 44, all AUs occurred in spontaneous facial behavior.

Occurrence and Temporal Precision

Reliability for occurrence/nonoccurrence is reported in Figure 13.2. For the data from Sayette et al. (2001), reliability is reported for each of four tolerance windows. These tolerance windows represent the temporal precision with which action units were comprehensively coded, that is, from beginning to end. Only a single estimate is available for the four AUs from supplemental sources.

Using a one-half-second tolerance window, all but two action units (AU 7 and AU 23) had good to excellent reliability (see Figure 13.2). As the tolerance window decreased in size, reliability decreased; however, even at the smallest window, 11 of 19 AUs had excellent reliability. One of the AUs that had consistently low reliability was AU 23, which often is confused with AU 24; pooling them into a single category can improve reliability. Reliability for AU 7 was low. The revised coding of AU 7 in FACS 2002 should result in improved reliability for this AU, as it is now combined with AU 44.

Sayette et al. (2001) did not report reliability for specific phases of AUs, such as onset, offset, peak, intensity, or change in intensity; nor to our knowledge have such data been reported by other sources. The FACS 2002 Investigator's Guide presents data from a dissertation by Ancoli on temporal precision for AU onset and offset; these data show average agreement across all AUs for two samples. Temporal precision of onset and offset for individual AUs was not reported. Percent agreement in Sample 1 was low and may have reflected inexperience of the coders. In Sample 2, percent agreement (not kappa) within a one-tenth-second tolerance for onset and offset was 65% and 61%, respectively. Using a one-half-second tolerance window, the corresponding figures were 74% and 67%, respectively. More studies of this issue are needed.

Intensity

In Sayette et al. (2001), intensity was evaluated for AU 10, 12, 15, and 20. Reliability for intensity coding was not as high as what was found for occurrence/nonoccurrence and was better for AU 10 and AU 12 than for AU 15 and AU 20 (see Table 13.1). Although FACS 2002 provides for intensity coding of all action units, the current findings suggest that reliability for intensity coding may be problematic and that further work is needed.

Aggregates

Four aggregates, or emotion-specified events, were defined: positive and negative expressions, disgust, and sadness. Re-

Table 13.1
Kappa coefficients for 5-point intensity coding

	Tolerance Window (seconds)			
Action Unit	1/30	1/6	1/3	1/2
10	0.61	0.67	0.70	0.72
12	0.57	0.61	0.63	0.66
15	0.44	0.53	0.57	0.59
20	0.31	0.39	0.45	0.49

Adapted from Sayette et al. (2001).

liability for positive and negative aggregates and disgust was acceptable (kappa > 0.60) even at the shortest tolerance window (one-thirtieth of a second; Table 13.2). Reliability for sadness was acceptable only at one-third of a second or larger. The latter is likely to be an underestimate, however, in that the sadness aggregate occurred in only 37 frames.

Validity

Concurrent Validity

The validity of a technique designed to measure facial movement entails questions on a number of levels. Most specifically, validity requires evidence that the technique actually measures the behavior it claims to measure. When a technique claims to measure brow raise, are the brows actually raised, or is it just the inner corners that are raised? If the technique claims to measure the intensity of an action, such as whether the brow raise is slight, moderate, or extreme, do such measurements correspond to known differences in the intensity of such an action? The problem, of course, is how to know what facial action occurs and what criterion to utilize independently of the facial measurement technique itself. At least five approaches have been taken:

1. Performed action criterion. Ekman and Friesen trained people to perform various actions on request. Records of such performances were scored without knowledge of the performances requested. FACS accurately

Table 13.2
Kappa coefficients for emotion-specified combinations

		Tolerance Window (seconds)			
Action Unit Aggregates	Frames	1/30	1/6	1/3	1/2
Positive emotion	335	.71	.78	.81	.83
Negative emotion	313	.64	.74	.79	.82
Disgust	103	.75	.82	.85	.86
Sadness	37	.47	.61	.67	.73

Tabled values are from Sayette et al. (2001) and are based on 3-point intensity coding. Reliability of 5-point intensity scoring was not reported for emotion-specified expressions.

distinguished the actions the performers had been instructed to make. These findings were replicated by Kanade and colleagues (2000).

2. Electrical activity criterion. Ekman and Friesen, in collaboration with Schwartz (Ekman, Schwartz, & Friesen, 1978) placed surface EMG leads on the faces of performers while the performers produced actions on request. Utilizing the extent of electrical activity observed from the EMG placements as the validity criterion, they found that FACS scoring of facial movement accurately distinguished the type and the intensity of the action.

3. Pixel-wise displacement criterion. Reed and Cohn (2003) compared maximum FACS intensity for AU 12 with automatic feature tracking of lip-corner displacement (see chapter 15, this volume, for a description of this measurement approach). Participants were young adults; spontaneous smiles occurred while they watched a video clip intended to elicit positive affect. FACS intensity for the onset phase of AU 12, measured on a 5–point scale, correlated .55 with pixel-wise lip-corner displacement, which suggests good concurrent validity.

4. Concurrent validity of FACS action units with automatic coding by computer-vision-based approaches. Concurrent validity has been demonstrated by several independent research groups. Examples from each of three separate groups include Bartlett et al. (1999), Cohn et al. (1999), and Pantic & Patras (2006).

5. Computer simulation. Work in computer graphics has shown that use of FACS action units in computer simulation can generate realistic movement of the target actions. FACS has provided an effective basis for facial animation, as well as for video encoding of facial images (Massaro et al., 1998; Parke & Waters, 1996).

Stability

Several studies have found moderate stability in FACS action units and predictive validity for a wide range of personality and clinical outcomes. Cohn, Schmidt, Gross, and Ekman (2002) found moderate to strong stability in FACS action units over a 4-month interval; stability was sufficiently robust as to suggest that facial behavior could function as a biometric. Person recognition from FACS action units was comparable to that of a leading face recognition algorithm.

Utility

The utility of FACS has been shown in a wide range of studies with infants and adults in North America, Europe, and Asia. Research has included emotion and social processes, personality, psychopathology, pain, deception, perception, and biological bases. FACS has proven to be valid and useful for facial measurement in relation to each of these areas. Harker and Keltner (2001), for example, found that FACS action units predicted adjustment to bereavement, teacher ratings of problem behaviors, and marital adjustment over periods as long as 30 years. A review of this literature is beyond the scope of this chapter. A good introduction to this literature appears in Ekman and Rosenberg (2005).

Instruction

FACS 2002 (Ekman et al., 2002), a 370-page self-instructional text, is available on compact disk (CD). It comes with an Investigator's Guide that contains suggestions on the procedure for training FACS. For each action unit, there are detailed criteria described in the text and illustrated in photographic images and video examples. Frequently occurring action unit combinations, especially those involving nonadditive combinations as defined earlier, are included. Detailed tables are available that highlight similarities and differences between closely related action unit combinations. The material is thorough and well cross-referenced.

FACS 2002 may be learned through self-instruction or in groups with or without an expert leader. Training with a partner or in a group is preferable. Each person in a learning group can benefit from looking at others performing each AU, which is likely to contain idiosyncrasies in how an AU appears on individual faces. The group can also help to monitor reliability in practice scoring and is a motivational aid. Appendix B describes an intensive 1-week training course offered by Dr. Erika Rosenberg that has been proven highly successful. Here we present general guidelines for individual and group instruction.

In learning FACS, trainees are instructed to perform each AU and AU combination. This didactic, which Ekman and Friesen followed in developing FACS, helps the trainee master the mechanics of facial action and learn the idiosyncrasies in appearance changes associated with each AU. They are able to compare their own performances with those of other trainees and with the filmed and photographed demonstrations of each AU in the manual. Later on, this skill continues to be useful in coding, specifically to help coders determine whether the AUs are needed to visually duplicate the facial action being scored.

Consistent with the sign-based approach of FACS, the trainee is discouraged from thinking or talking about the meaning of AUs or AU combinations. With practice, coders are expected to think of facial action in terms of the AU labels (e.g., AU 1 and AU 2) and to forget about their meaning entirely.

The Investigator's Guide provides detailed information about how a group of six coders progressed as they learned FACS. Trainees can use this information to compare their own performances and to guide them as they learn. For example, if a trainee makes more errors than those six coders did, then he or she may benefit from reviewing action units with which he or she experienced difficulty relative to the reference group.

Forty-six still photographs and 47 MPEG digital video clips are included for practice scoring. The answer key is provided in the Investigator's Guide, which also functions as a trainer's guide.

A computer program referred to as FACS Score Checker is provided with FACS 2002. This program serves to aid the trainee in comparing his or her scores for practice items with the criterion codes. It provides a more structured alternative to visual inspection of the correspondence between the trainee's scores and the criterion scores and contains features that help the trainee learn the scoring notation and avoid errors. It also provides a quantitative measure of success in learning to score with FACS.

FACS Score Checker can be used to save codes for the FACS Final Test, as described below. FACS Score Checker is written in Java 2 and can run on any computer on which the appropriate Java runtime is installed.

The time required to learn FACS is variable, depending on the number of hours per week that can be devoted to training, the availability of expert trainers, and individual differences among trainees. In our experience, approximately 3 months are required to become sufficiently proficient as to demonstrate mastery on the FACS Final Test. This would assume a training routine of weekly meetings and 3 to 4 days of practice per week.

FACS Final Test (Certification)

A certification test is available to demonstrate proficiency at the completion of training. Certification on this test is expected before one begins using FACS in research. The test consists of 34 short video segments in MPEG 2 format. The test items differ from the practice items provided in the FACS manual in a number of ways. The test video clips contain excerpts from actual conversations, and hence the expressions are spontaneous in nature. Head movements, speech, and nonfrontal orientation to the camera are common. These characteristics of the test items make them more difficult to code than the practice items in which speech is absent and camera orientation is frontal to the face. The test items represent the characteristics of actual facial behavior that might be typical in research materials. Following submission of the test scores, a trainee receives a reliability measure of his or her score compared with those of experts in FACS scoring. The trainee is also provided with a commentary on sources of errors in his or her scoring and suggestions for improvement. If his or her score is below criterion, retesting can be arranged. Procedures for obtaining and using the test are provided in the Investigator's Guide that accompanies FACS 2002.

Computer-Assisted FACS Coding

FACS comes with a score sheet that aids coders in organizing and recording their codes. This score sheet was designed

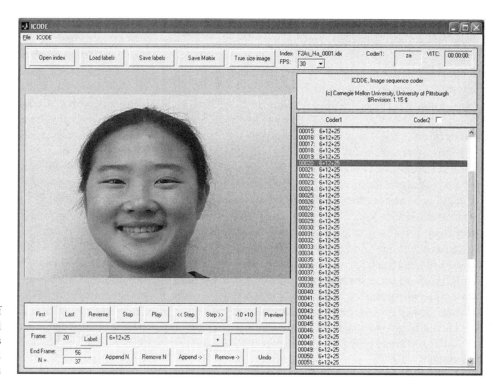

Figure 13.3. Snapshot of ICODE for computer assisted FACS coding. Available as shareware from http://www-2 .cs.cmu.edu/~face/index2.htm

for coding single images that may occur alone or as part of a longer image sequence. Much early work in facial expression research focused on single images, for which the score sheet may have been sufficient. In practice, facial expression is dynamic and occurs in time. This dynamic nature of facial expressions is important for the recognition process (Ambadar et al., 2005), as well as for making finer distinctions among facial expression categories (Frank et al., 1993; Hess & Kleck, 1990). Timing of facial expressions influences judgments of genuineness among other dimensions (Krumhuber & Kappas, 2005; Schmidt, Ambadar, & Cohn, 2006). With the growing interest in analyzing the timing of facial expressions, a more sophisticated tool for coding dynamic facial expressions is needed. Using FACS to code video recorded facial expressions by hand (e.g., using paper and pencil or manual entry into a spreadsheet) is unnecessarily laborious and susceptible to error.

Computer-assisted coding enables precise control over video and eliminates the need to manually record time stamps or frame numbers, thus increasing efficiency and eliminating transcription errors. Image sequences may be viewed at variable speed forward and backward, and time stamps can be automatically logged whenever FACS codes are entered via the keyboard or other serial input device. Many of the systems that are available for computer-assisted coding also include a number of advanced data management, analysis, and display features. (See Bakeman, Deckner, and Quera [2005] for a more thorough discussion of computer-assisted coding.) Software for computer-assisted coding is available commercially and as shareware.

Examples of commercial systems are the Observer (Noldus, Trienes, Henriksen, Jansen, & Jansen, 2000; http://www .noldus.com), the Video Coding System (James Long Company; http://www.jameslong.net/), and INTERACT (Mangold Software and Consulting; http://www.mangold.de/english/ intoverview.htm). Early versions of these and related systems are reviewed by Kahng and Iwata (1998). The most recent versions of Observer and Mangold INTERACT are well suited for complete FACS coding (all action units plus all modifiers).

Ordering Information for FACS 2002

FACS 2002 is available on CD-ROM from http://www .paulekman.com.

Appendix A: Changes in FACS 2002

FACS 2002 includes numerous changes, which are described here. The following list is not exhaustive but includes most changes.

General Changes

- FACS 2002 is available on CD and fully exploits this medium. The text is richly hyperlinked to related text, still images, and video. There are 135 still image examples and 98 video examples of single AU and AU combinations.

- General instructions for scoring intensity are presented in the introduction; criteria for specific action units are listed in corresponding sections of the manual. FACS uses conventions or rules to set thresholds for scoring action unit intensity. The criteria are set in terms of the scale of evidence of the presence of the AU. A distinction is made among a trace (A), slight (B), marked or pronounced (C), severe or extreme (D), and maximum (E) evidence.
- Change of the meaning of the notation "M." FACS 1978 listed the meaning of error messages from a Coder Check Program (CDRCHK), which came with the manual. All of these messages were numbered and had an "M" notation preceding the number. For example "M72" means "Two AU scores have been located that were not in numerical order, or a value greater than 74 has been identified. . . ." FACS 2002 does not list error messages. The notation "M" now is used to indicate "movement" of the head associated with other action units. For example "M59" indicates that the onset of 17 + 24 is immediately preceded, accompanied, or followed by an up-down head shake (nod).
- Changes in the key answer for the practice items. The Investigator's Guide of FACS 2002 includes a revision of the answer key for practice items. The revision reflects changes in scoring decisions, as well as changes in the rules (elimination of minimum requirements, reduction of co-occurrence rules, changes with AU 25, 26, 27 and 41, 42, etc).

Elimination of Action Units

- Elimination of AU 41 and 42. In FACS 1978, the numbers 41 and 42 were used to denote different actions of the same muscle in the eye region. Both AU 41 and AU 42 involve the relaxation of the muscle that, when contracted, raises the upper eyelid. With a relaxation of this muscle, the eyelid comes down, drooping (41) or almost entirely closed to just a slit (AU 42). In FACS 2002, these actions are no longer represented in different action units but are described as increasing degrees of upper eyelid lowering (AU 43b and 43d, respectively). However, the numbers 41 and 42 are used to indicate different strands of AU 4 (brow lowerer). Although only described in the Investigator's Guide, the recycling of these numbers to indicate completely different actions can create confusion and miscommunication. For this and other reasons, one should always report which version of FACS is used.
- Elimination of AU 44. In FACS 1978, AU 44 was used to denote a specific action of squinting. In FACS 2002, this action represents the maximum level of eyelid tightening as indicated by AU 7E. The number 44, however, is recycled and is used to indicate a different

strand of AU 4, which is discussed in the Investigator's Guide (Ekman et al., 2002).

Elimination and Reduction of Scoring Rules

- Elimination of minimum requirements from all action units.
- Elimination of dominance rules.
- Reduction of Co-occurrence rule. Minimum requirements and co-occurrence rules were a pervasive aspect of the original FACS, designed to make scoring more deterministic and conservative, and thus more reliable. These expected benefits, however, were outweighed by difficulties in remembering and applying complicated rules, and experienced FACS coders proved able to make finer discriminations with greater reliability than these rules assumed. For these and other reasons, most co-occurrence rules and minimum requirements are eliminated in FACS 2002.

Modification in Scoring Rules

- FACS 2002 uses five levels of intensity coding for all AUs (except for head position AUs, in which the "A" level of intensity was treated as "Unscorable"). Intensity scoring was recommended only for some AUs in FACS 1978. However, in FACS 2002, guidelines for intensity scoring for all AUs are provided. Most intensity criteria refer to the degree of an appearance change or to the number of appearance changes. The intensity score for some AUs involves a criterion in terms of time duration or some other benchmark.
- A detailed description of AU combinations AU 6+12; 7+12; and 6+7+12 is added in FACS 2002. Previously, a strong action of AU 12 required that AU 6 be coded as well. In the 2002 version, this requirement is dropped. A careful inspection of the movement, the location of the crows' feet wrinkles, and the lowering of the outer corners of the brows are listed as necessary clues to determine whether AU 12 appears with or without AU 6 in any intensity level of AU 12. The possibility of AU combination 6+7+12 is for the first time introduced and described in detail in the current (2002) version of FACS. FACS 2002 notes, interestingly, that scoring a 6+7+12 is more likely than a 6+12.
- Revised scoring of AU 25, 26, and 27. FACS 2002 includes a more extensive description to separate the degree of mouth opening due to AU 25, 26, and 27. The previous version assumed that, by default, the action of jaw drop (AU 26) and mouth stretch (AU 27) included the separation of the lips (AU 25). In the case that the jaw drop was not accompanied by lip part, the score was indicated by S26 (Shut 26), which could be scored only when a movement of the jaw dropping

was visible. With this way of coding, if an action was coded as AU 26, it was assumed that the mouth was opened simultaneously. With AU 27 (mouth stretch), it was always assumed that the lips were also parted (AU 25). In FACS 2002, each action unit code is listed in the score whenever it is present. Therefore, a jaw drop that includes parting of the lips is coded AU 25 + 26. Likewise, mouth stretch action that includes lip part is to be coded as AU 25 + 27. Under the new rule, therefore, an action coded as 26 or 27 alone holds the assumption that the mouth remains closed. This change should eliminate much ambiguity. The manual also describes in detail the rules for scoring intensity with these mouth-opening AUs (25, 26, and 27).

- Timing information is used to differentiate some AUs, including 26 versus 27 and Unilateral 45 and 46.
- Revised rule for scoring AU 28. FACS 1978 recognized that the jaw is always lowered in AU 28, but scoring AU 26 was not recommended unless the lips were not touching. In FACS 2002, however, this rule is revised, and coders are to score AU 26+28 to indicate the jaw lowering action that allows the lip sucking action. To distinguish the lips touching from the lips parted, AU 25 should be added in the lip-part condition.
- In FACS 1992, the intensity scoring of AU 43 and 45 was determined by the intensity scoring of AU 6 and/ or 7. In FACS 2002, there is no intensity scoring for AU 45 (blink), but for AU 43, the intensity-score guideline is provided; it is not determined by the intensity score of AU 6 or 7.

Addition of Action Unit or Behavior Category

- Two head movement codes are added. AU M59 (nod up and down accompanying AU 17 + 24) and AU M60 (shake side to side).
- Gross behavior codes are added. These are new codes that indicate behaviors of possible relevance to facial behavior. These new codes include: 40 (sniff), 50 (speech), 80 (swallow), 81 (chewing), 82 (shoulder shrug), 84 (head shake back and forth), 85 (head nod up and down), 91 (flash), and 92 (partial flash). No descriptions for these AUs are provided.

Appendix B: Description of Erika Rosenberg's FACS Workshop

Erika Rosenberg offers a 5-day intensive training workshop in FACS 2002.[2] The workshop takes participants through the entire manual and prepares them to take the final test for certification as a FACS coder. Traditionally, people have learned FACS via a minimum of 100 hours of self-instruction. The FACS workshop offers a dynamic group setting for learning FACS in about a week, with the benefit of guidance and feedback from an expert. FACS certification testing is done independently, after the workshop.

Basic Description of the Workshop

The 5-day workshop follows an intensive schedule of work and preparation. Participants read through the first three chapters of the FACS CD manual and do some preassigned practice scoring before coming to the workshop. This is necessary to get them thinking in terms of action units and to instill a sense of what the world of FACS is like. Part of the challenge of learning FACS is getting used to attending to feature details of the face (e.g., wrinkles, bulges, furrows, etc.) and understanding that FACS is a system of describing *movement*. She encourages students to think of themselves as "facial detectives" whose job it is to most efficiently describe observed changes in facial action.

The workshop schedule involves several activities: instruction in new actions, practicing AUs on one's own face, looking at other's faces, discussing difficulties in recognizing AUs, practicing coding with feedback, and evaluating progress daily. Rosenberg offers numerous clues to recognizing AUs—primarily by demonstrating on her own face and discussing subtleties of appearance changes included in the manual, but also by providing valuable field experience and tricks that are not available there. Part of the instruction is advice on how to use the manual most efficiently.

Daily quizzes and evening homework are an important component of the training, as they ensure that the students are staying with the class. The assignments also offer the instructor opportunity to evaluate each student's progress and problem areas. All homework and quizzes are graded.

By late in the week students have learned all AUs and head and eye positions (through chapter 9 in the manual), at which time they devote most of their time to practicing coding (with feedback), and discussion of common confusions and difficulties. Rosenberg provides real-life examples so that students can get a feel for what it is like to code spontaneous behavior in preparation for the FACS certification test. Also discussed are strategies for coding. Depending on the group, emotion interpretation may be included.

Effectiveness of the Workshop

Initial data suggested that people who train via the workshop pass the FACS final test the first time at the same rate as people who train via the traditional method. Everyone passes by the second time. Mark Frank—who has had more than 30 people trained in these workshops—reports that workshop trainees achieve intercoder agreement in his lab assessments more quickly and more often achieve reliability compared with people who have used the self-instruction method.

Contact Information

Further information may be obtained from http://www.erikarosenberg.com/.

Acknowledgments

Preparation of this manuscript was supported by NIMH grant MH 51435. The section on sign versus message judgment is from Cohn and Ekman (2005; used with permission of Oxford University Press). We thank Erika Rosenberg for her comments on an earlier version of this chapter.

Notes

1. We define *reliability* as agreement between two or more observers about the occurrence, intensity, and timing of action units. Alternatively, one might be interested in whether summary counts are consistent between coders. That is, are coders consistent in estimating the number of times an action unit occurs or its average intensity? Agreement is a more stringent measure in that coders must not only be consistent about the number of times an action unit occurs but must also agree on when each one occurred. Agreement may actually be quite low and yet reliability in the sense of consistency be quite high (Tinsley & Weiss, 1975). Agreement between coders is best quantified by coefficient kappa or a similar statistic that corrects for chance agreement. Reliability (consistency between coders) for summary counts is best quantified with intraclass correlation, which is mathematically related to kappa (Fleiss, 1981).

2. Appendix B is based on materials provided by Dr. Rosenberg and is used with her permission.

References

Ambadar, Z., Schooler, J., & Cohn, J. F. (2005). Deciphering the enigmatic face: The importance of facial dynamics to interpreting subtle facial expressions. *Psychological Science, 16,* 403–410.

Avrahami, J., & Kareev, Y. (1994). The emergence of events. *Cognition, 53,* 239–261.

Bakeman, R., Deckner, D. F., & Quera, V. (2005). Analysis of behavior streams. In D. M. Teti (Ed.), *Handbook of research methods in developmental psychology* (pp. 394–420). Oxford, UK: Blackwell.

Bartlett, M. S., Ekman, P., Hager, J. C., & Sejnowski, T. J. (1999). Measuring facial expressions by computer image analysis. *Psychophysiology, 36,* 253–263.

Breidt, M., Wallraven, C., Cunningham, D. W., & Buelthoff, H. H. (2003). Facial animation based on 3D scans and motion capture. In N. Campbell (Ed.). *SIGGRAPH '03 Sketches & Applications.* New York: ACM Press.

Bruce, V., & Young, A. (1998). *In the eye of the beholder: The science of face perception.* New York: Oxford University Press.

Calder, A. J., Young, A. W., Rowland, D., Perrett, D. I., Hodges, J. R., & Etcoff, N. L. (1996). Facial emotion recognition after bilateral amygdala damage: Differentially severe impairment of fear. *Cognitive Neuropsychology, 13,* 699–745.

Clemente, C. D. (1997). *Anatomy: A regional atlas of the human body* (4th ed.).Baltimore: Williams & Wilkins.

Cohn, J. F., & Ekman, P. (2005). Measuring facial action. In J. A. Harrigan, R. Rosenthal, & K. R. Scherer (Eds.), *The new handbook of nonverbal behavior research* (pp. 9–64). New York: Oxford University Press.

Cohn, J. F., Reed, L. I., Moriyama, T., Xiao, J., Schmidt, K. L., & Ambadar, Z. (2004). Multimodal coordination of facial action, head rotation, and eye motion. *Proceedings of the IEEE International Conference on Automatic Face and Gesture Recognition, 7,* 645–650.

Cohn, J. F., Schmidt, K. L., Gross, R., & Ekman, P. (2002). Individual differences in facial expression: Stability over time, relation to self-reported emotion, and ability to inform person identification. *Proceedings of the International Conference on Multimodal User Interfaces, 4,* 491–496.

Cohn, J. F., & Tronick, E. Z. (1983). Three-month-old infants' reaction to simulated maternal depression. *Child Development, 54,* 185–193.

Cohn, J. F., Xiao, J., Moriyama, T., Ambadar, Z., & Kanade, T. (2003). Automatic recognition of eye blinking in spontaneous facial behavior. *Behavior Research Methods, Instruments, and Computers, 35,* 420–428.

Cohn, J. F., Zlochower, A. J., Lien, J. J. J., & Kanade, T. (1999). Automated face analysis by feature point tracking has high concurrent validity with manual FACS coding. *Psychophysiology, 36,* 35–43.

Darwin, C. (1998). *The expression of the emotions in man and animals* (3rd ed.). New York: Oxford University Press. (Original work published 1872)

Davidson, R. J., Ekman, P., Saron, C. D., Senulis, J. A., & Friesen, W. V. (1990). Approach-withdrawal and cerebral asymmetry: Emotional expression and brain physiology: I. *Journal of Personality and Social Psychology, 58,* 330–341.

Deyo, K., Prkachin, K. M., & Mercer, S. R. (2004). Development of sensitivity to facial expressions of pain. *Pain, 107,* 16–21.

Eibl-Eibesfeldt, I. (1989). *Human ethology.* New York: Aldine de Gruyter.

Ekman, P. (1964). Body position, facial expression and verbal behavior during interviews. *Journal of Abnormal and Social Psychology, 68,* 295–301.

Ekman, P. (1965). Differential communication of affect by head and body cues. *Journal of Personality and Social Psychology, 2,* 725–735.

Ekman, P. (1973). Cross-cultural studies of facial expression. In P. Ekman (Ed.), *Darwin and facial expression: A century of research in review* (pp. 169–222.). New York: Academic.

Ekman, P. (1980). Facial asymmetry. *Science, 209,* 833–834.

Ekman, P. (1992). An argument for basic emotions. *Cognition and Emotion, 6,* 169–200.

Ekman, P. (1993). Facial expression and emotion. *American Psychologist, 48,* 384–392.

Ekman, P., & Friesen, W. V. (1969). The repertoire of nonverbal behavior. *Semiotica, 1,* 49–98.

Ekman, P., & Friesen, W. V. (1978). *Facial Action Coding System.* Palo Alto, CA: Consulting Psychologists Press.

Ekman, P., & Friesen, W. V. (1982). *Rationale and reliability for EMFACS.* Unpublished manuscript. University of California at San Francisco, Human Interaction Laboratory.

Ekman, P., Friesen, W. V., & Ancoli, S. (1980). Facial signs of emotional experience. *Journal of Personality and Social Psychology, 39,* 1125–1134.

Ekman, P., Friesen, W. V., & Hager, J. C. (Eds.). (2002). *Facial Action Coding System* [E-book]. Salt Lake City, UT: Research Nexus.

Ekman, P., Friesen, W. V., & O'Sullivan, M. (1988). Smiles when lying. *Journal of Personality and Social Psychology, 54,* 414–420.

Ekman, P., Friesen, W. V., & Tomkins, S. S. (1971). Facial affect scoring technique: A first validation study. *Semiotica, 3,* 37–58.

Ekman, P., & Rosenberg, E. (Eds.). (2005). *What the face reveals* (2nd ed.). New York: Oxford University Press.

Ekman, P., Rosenberg, E., & Hager, J. (1998). *Facial Action Coding System Interpretive Database (FACSAID).* Unpublished manuscript. University of California at San Francisco, Human Interaction Laboratory.

Ekman, P., Schwartz, G. E., & Friesen, W. V. (1978). *Electrical and visible signs of facial action.* San Francisco: University of California, Human Interaction Laboratory.

Fleiss, J. L. (1981). *Statistical methods for rates and proportions.* New York: Wiley.

Frank, M. G., & Ekman, P. (1997). The ability to detect deceit generalizes across different types of high-stakes lies. *Journal of Personality and Social Psychology, 72,* 1429–1439.

Frank, M. G., Ekman, P., & Friesen, W. V. (1993). Behavioral markers and recognizability of the smile of enjoyment. *Journal of Personality and Social Psychology, 64,* 83–93.

Fridlund, A. J. (1992). The behavioral ecology and sociality of human faces. In M. S. Clark (Ed.), *Emotion* (pp. 90–121) London: Sage.

Harker, L., & Keltner, D. (2001). Expressions of positive emotion in women's college yearbook pictures and their relationship to personality and life outcomes across adulthood. *Journal of Personality and Social Psychology, 80,* 112–124.

Hatfield, E., Cacioppo, J. T., & Rapson, R. L. (1992). Primitive emotional contagion. In M. S. Clark (Ed.), *Emotion and social behavior* (Vol. 14, pp. 151–177). Newbury Park, CA: Sage.

Hess, U., & Kirouac, G. (2000). Emotion expression in groups. In M. Lewis & J. M. Haviland-Jones (Eds.), *Handbook of emotion* (pp. 368–381). New York: Guilford Press.

Hess, U., & Kleck, R. E. (1990). Differentiating emotion elicited and deliberate emotional facial expressions. *European Journal of Social Psychology, 20,* 369–385.

International Organization for Standardization. (2002). *Overview of the MPEG-4 standard.* Retrieved from http://www.chiariglione.org/mpeg/standards/mpeg-4/mpeg-4.htm

Izard, C. E. (1977). *Human emotions.* New York: Plenum.

Izard, C. E. (1979). *Facial expression scoring manual (FESM).* Newark: University of Delaware Press.

Izard, C. E. (1983). Maximally discriminative facial movement coding system (MAX). Unpublished manuscript, University of Delaware, Newark.

Izard, C. E., & Dougherty, L. M. (1981). Two complementary systems for measuring facial expressions in infants and children. In C. E. Izard (Ed.), *Measuring emotions in infants and children.* Cambridge, UK: Cambridge University Press.

Kahng, S., & Iwata, B. A. (1998). Computerized systems for collecting real-time observational data. *Journal of Applied Behavior Analysis, 31,* 253–261.

Kaiser, S. (2002). Facial expressions as indicators of "functional" and "dysfunctional" emotional processes. In M. Katsikitis (Ed.), *The human face: Measurement and meaning* (pp. 235–253). Dordrecht, Netherlands: Kluwer Academic.

Kanade, T., Cohn, J. F., & Tian, Y. (2000). Comprehensive database for facial expression analysis. *Proceedings of the IEEE Conference on Automatic Face and Gesture Recognition, 4,* 46–53.

Keltner, D. (1995). Sign of appeasement: Evidence for the distinct display of embarrassment, amusement, and shame. *Journal of Personality and Social Psychology, 68*(3), 441–454.

Keltner, D., & Buswell, B. N. (1997). Embarrassment: Its distinct form and appeasement functions. *Psychological Bulletin, 122,* 250–270.

Kring, A. M., & Sloan, D. M. (1991). *The facial expression coding system: FACES.* Berkeley: University of California Press.

Krumhuber, E., & Kappas, A. (2005). Moving smiles: The role of dynamic components for the perception of the genuineness of smiles. *Journal of Nonverbal Behavior, 29,* 3–24.

Levenson, R. W., Ekman, P., & Friesen, W. V. (1990). Voluntary facial action generates emotion-specific autonomic nervous system activity. *Psychophysiology, 27,* 363–384.

Malatesta, C. Z., Culver, C., Tesman, J. R., & Shephard, B. (1989). The development of emotion expression during the first two years of life. *Monographs of the Society for Research in Child Development, 54,* 105–136.

Massaro, D. W., Cohen, M. M., Beskow, J., Daniel, S., & Cole, R. A. (1998). Developing and evaluating conversational agents. *Workshop on Embodied Conversational Characters,* 137–148.

Matias, R., & Cohn, J. F. (1993). Are MAX-specified infant facial expressions during face-to-face interaction consistent with differential emotions theory? *Developmental Psychology, 29,* 524–531.

Messinger, D. S. (2002). Positive and negative: Infant facial expressions and emotions. *Current Directions in Psychological Science, 11,* 1–6.

Messinger, D. S., Fogel, A., & Dickson, K. L. (1999). What's in a smile? *Developmental Psychology, 35,* 701–708.

Newtson, D., Rindner, R., Miller, R., & Lacross, K. (1978). Effects of availability of feature changes on behavior segmentation. *Journal of Experimental Psychology, 14,* 379–386.

Noldus, L. P. J. J., Trienes, R. J. H., Henriksen, A. H. M., Jansen, H., & Jansen, R. G. (2000). The Observer Video-Pro: New software for the collection, management, and presentation of time-structured data from videotapes and digital media files. *Behavior Research Methods, Instruments, and Computers, 32,* 197–206.

Oster, H. (2001). Baby FACS: Facial Action Coding System for infants and young children. Unpublished manuscript, New York University.

Oster, H., Camras, L. A., Campos, J., Campos, R., Ujiee, T., Zhao-Lan, M., et al. (1996). The patterning of facial expressions in Chinese, Japanese, and American infants in fear- and anger- eliciting situations. Poster presented at the International Conference on Infant Studies, Providence, RI.

Oster, H., & Ekman, P. (1978). Facial behavior in child development. In A. Collins (Ed.), *Minnesota Symposium on Child Development* (Vol. 11). Hillsdale, NJ: Erlbaum.

Oster, H., Hegley, D., & Nagel, L. (1992). Adult judgments and fine-grained analysis of infant facial expressions: Testing the validity of a priori coding formulas. *Developmental Psychology, 28*, 1115–1131.

Pantic, M., and Patras, I. (2006). Dynamics of facial expressions: Recognition of facial actions and their temporal segments from profile image sequences. *IEEE Transactions on Systems, Man and Cybernetics, Part B, 36*(2), 443–449.

Pantic, M., & Rothkrantz, M. (2000). Expert system for automatic analysis of facial expression. *Image and Vision Computing, 18*, 881–905.

Parke, F. I., & Waters, K. (1996). *Computer facial animation.* Wellesley, MA: Peters.

Prkachin, K. M. (1992). The consistency of facial expressions of pain. *Pain, 51*, 297–306.

Reed, I.L. & Cohn, J.F. (2003). Unpublished data. Affect Analysis Group, University of Pittsburgh, Pittsburgh, PA.

Rinn, W. E. (1984). The neuropsychology of facial expression. *Psychological Bulletin, 95*, 52–77.

Rinn, W. E. (1991). Neuropsychology of facial expression. In R. S. Feldman & B. Rime (Eds.), *Fundamentals of nonverbal behavior: Studies in emotion and social interaction* (pp. 3–30). New York: Cambridge University Press.

Russell, J. A. (1994). Is there universal recognition of emotion from facial expression? A review of the cross-cultural studies. *Psychological Bulletin, 115*, 102–141.

Sayette, M. A., Cohn, J. F., Wertz, J. M., Perrott, M. A., & Parrott, D. J. (2001). A psychometric evaluation of the Facial Action Coding System for assessing spontaneous expression. *Journal of Nonverbal Behavior, 25*, 167–186.

Schmidt, K. L., Ambadar, Z., & Cohn, J. F. (2006). Timing of lip corner movement affects perceived genuineness of spontaneous smiles. Manuscript submitted for publication.

Schmidt, K. L., & Cohn, J. F. (2001). Human facial expressions as adaptations: Evolutionary perspectives in facial expression research. *Yearbook of Physical Anthropology, 116*, 8–24.

Sloan, D. M., Straussa, M. E., Quirka, S. W., & Sajatovic, M. (1997). Subjective and expressive emotional responses in depression. *Journal of Affective Disorders, 46*, 135–141.

Tao, H., Chen, H. H., Wu, W., & Huang, T. S. (1999). Compression of MPEG-4 facial animation parameters for transmission of talking heads. *IEEE Transactions on Circuits and Systems for Video Technology, 9*, 264–276.

Tian, Y., Kanade, T., & Cohn, J. F. (2002). Evaluation of Gabor-wavelet-based facial action unit recognition in image sequences of increasing complexity. *Proceedings of the IEEE Conference on Automatic Face and Gesture Recognition, 5*, 229–234.

Tian, Y., Kanade, T., & Cohn, J. F. (2005). Facial expression analysis. In S. Z. Li & A. K. Jain (Eds.), *Handbook of face recognition, 247–276.* New York: Springer.

Tinsley, H., & Weiss, D. (1975). Interrater reliability and agreement of subjective judgements. *Journal of Counseling Psychology, 22*, 358–376.

Tomkins, S. S. (1962). *Affect, imagery, consciousness.* New York: Springer.

Tronick, E. Z., Als, H., & Brazelton, B. T. (1980). Monadic phases: A structural descriptive analysis of infant-mother face-to-face interaction. *Merrill-Palmer Quarterly of Behavior and Development, 26*, 3–24.

Van Swearingen, J. M., & Cohn, J. F. 2005). Depression, smiling and facial paralysis. In R. vanGelder (Ed.), *Facial palsies, 373–386.* Amsterdam: Lemma Holland.

Zacks, J. M., & Tversky, B. (2001). Event structure in perception and conception. *Psychological Bulletin, 127*, 3–21.

Jeffrey F. Cohn
Takeo Kanade

Use of Automated Facial Image Analysis
for Measurement of Emotion Expression

Facial expressions are a key index of emotion. They have consistent correlation with self-reported emotion (Ekman & Rosenberg, 2005; Keltner, 1995; Rosenberg & Ekman, 1994) and emotion-related central and peripheral physiology (Davidson, Ekman, Saron, Senulis, & Friesen, 1990; Fox & Davidson, 1988; Levenson, Ekman, & Friesen, 1990). They share similar underlying dimensions with self-reported emotion (e.g., positive and negative affect; Bullock & Russell, 1984; Gross & John, 1997; Watson & Tellegen, 1985). Facial expressions serve interpersonal functions of emotion by conveying communicative intent, signaling affective information in social referencing (Campos, Bertenthal, & Kermoian, 1992), and more generally contributing to the regulation of social interaction (Cohn & Elmore, 1988; Fridlund, 1994; Schmidt & Cohn, 2001). As a measure of trait affect, stability in facial expression emerges early in life (Cohn & Campbell, 1992; Malatesta, Culver, Tesman, & Shephard, 1989). By adulthood, stability is moderately strong, comparable with that of self-reported emotion (Cohn, Schmidt, Gross, & Ekman, 2002), and predictive of favorable outcomes in emotion-related domains, including marriage and personal well-being over periods as long as 30 years (Harker & Keltner, 2001). Expressive changes in the face are a rich source of cues about intra- and interpersonal functions of emotion (cf. Keltner & Haidt, 1999).

To make use of the information afforded by facial expression for emotion science and clinical practice, reliable, valid, and efficient methods of measurement are critical. Until recently, selecting a measurement method meant choosing one or another human-observer-based coding system (e.g., Ekman & Friesen, 1978; Izard, 1983) or facial electromyography (EMG). Although each of these approaches has advantages, they are not without costs. Human-observer-based methods are time-consuming to learn and use, and they are difficult to standardize, especially across laboratories and over time (Bakeman & Gottman, 1986; Martin & Bateson, 1986). The other approach, facial EMG, requires placement of sensors on the face, which may inhibit facial action and which rules out its use for naturalistic observation.

An emerging alternative to these methods is automated facial image analysis using computer vision. Computer vision is the science of extracting and representing meaningful information from digitized video and recognizing perceptually meaningful patterns. An early focus in automated face image analysis by computer vision was face recognition (Kanade, 1973, 1977). That area has sufficiently advanced that commercially viable applications have become available (Phillips et al., 2003). Computer vision research in facial image processing has turned increasingly toward automated facial expression recognition. In 1992, the National Science Foundation convened a seminal interdisciplinary workshop on this topic (Ekman, Huang, Sejnowski, & Hager, 1992), which brought together psychologists with expertise in facial expression and computer vision scientists with interest in facial image analysis. Since then, there has been considerable research activity, as represented by a series of six international meetings beginning in 1995 (see http://image.korea.ac.kr/FG2004).

Several automated facial image analysis systems have been developed (Cootes, Edwards, & Taylor, 2001; Essa & Pentland, 1997; Lyons, Akamasku, Kamachi, & Gyoba, 1998; Padgett, Cottrell, & Adolphs, 1996; Wen & Huang, 2003; Yacoob & Davis, 1996; Zhang, 1999; Zhu, De Silva, & Ko, 2002). They can classify a small set of emotion-specified expressions, such as joy and anger. Others (Bartlett, Hager, Ekman, & Sejnowski, 1999; Cohn, Zlochower, Lien, & Kanade, 1999; Fasel & Luttin, 2000; Pantic & Rothkrantz, 2000a; Tian, Kanade, & Cohn, 2001) have achieved some success in the more difficult task of recognizing facial action units of the Facial Action Coding System (FACS; Ekman & Friesen, 1978; Ekman, Friesen, & Hager, 2002). Action units (AU) are the smallest visibly discriminable changes in facial expression. Comprehensive reviews of the literature in automated facial expression analysis can be found in Pantic and Rothkrantz (2000b, 2003) and in Tian, Kanade, and Cohn (2005). Although many basic research issues remain (Bartlett et al., 2005; Kanade, Cohn, & Tian, 2000; Matthews, Ishikawa, & Baker, 2004; Pantic & Rothkrantz, 2003; Smith, Bartlett, & Movellan, 2001; Tian, Kanade, & Cohn, in press), applications of automated facial image analysis to emotion science have begun (e.g., Schmidt, Cohn, & Tian, 2003), with broader adoption likely to follow as methods continue to evolve.

In this chapter, we present work on, development of, and progress on the Carnegie Mellon University/University of Pittsburgh (CMU/Pitt) Automated Facial Image Analysis (AFA) system, a leading approach to automatic recognition of facial action units and quantitative analysis of their timing. We describe how we have used it to assess emotion processes and discuss prospects for its broader use in emotion science

and clinical practice. AFA has progressed through three versions. In the remainder of this chapter, we distinguish between them when referring to features that are specific to one or another version.

Automatic Facial Expression Analysis (AFA)

Figure 14.1 depicts the overall structure of the CMU/Pitt AFA system for recognition of facial action units and analysis of their dynamics. A digitized image sequence[1] is input to the system. The region of the face and location of individual facial features are delineated in the initial frame. This step is performed automatically for frontal images and adjusted manually for nonfrontal images. Head motion then is recovered automatically and used to warp (or stabilize) the face image to a standard (i.e., canonical) view. Changes in both permanent (e.g., brows) and transient (e.g., furrows) facial features are automatically detected and tracked offline throughout the image sequence. Informed by FACS, facial features are grouped into separate collections of feature parameters. These parameters include feature displacement, velocity, and appearance. The extracted facial feature and head motion trajectories are fed to a classifier for action unit recognition. In addition to action unit recognition, the system quantifies the timing of facial actions and head gesture for studies of timing of facial actions.

Face Detection and Facial Feature Localization

To locate the face and obtain the positions of facial features, AFA-I used hand initialization in the first video frame. AFA-

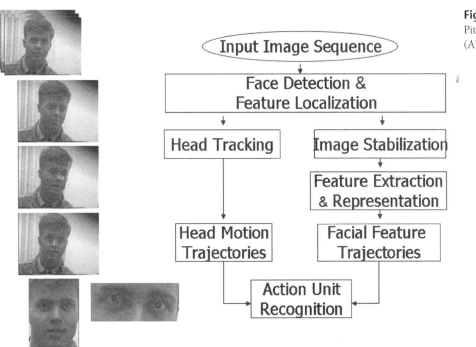

Figure 14.1. Overview of CMU/Pitt Automated Face Analysis (AFA) System.

II used a combination of automatic face detector (Rowley, Baluja, & Kanade, 1998) and manual adjustment. Recently, AFA-III uses more automatic approaches: One is a method developed by Zhou, Gu, and Zhang (2003), and the other by Matthews and Baker (2005). The method of Zhou et al. is limited to mostly frontal images (see Figure 14.2); otherwise, manual adjustment remains necessary. The Matthews and Baker method performs well for moderate out-of-plane head rotation but requires more extensive algorithm training.

Automatic Recovery of 3-D Head Motion and Image Stabilization

Expressive changes in the face often co-occur with head movement. People raise their heads in surprise (Camras, Lambrecht, & Michel, 1996) and turn toward a friend while beginning to smile (Kraut & Johnson, 1979). In a video sequence, both types of motion are likely to be present. The effects of rigid (head) motion must be measured and removed prior to extracting information about nonrigid motion (expression) so that these two types of motion are not confounded.

AFA-III uses a cylindrical head model to estimate the 6 degrees of freedom of head motion, whose parameters are horizontal and vertical position, distance to the camera (i.e., scale), pitch, yaw, and roll. A cylindrical model is fit to the initial face region, and the face image is cropped and "painted" onto the cylinder as the template of head appearance. For any given subsequent frame, the template is projected onto the image plane, assuming that the pose has remained unchanged from the previous frame. We then compute the difference between the projected image and the current frame, and the difference provides the correction on the estimate of pose. We iterate this process to further refine the estimate by using a model-based optical-flow algorithm. As new parts of the head become visible, their appearance is added to the cylinder surface for a more complete template of the head appearance (Xiao, Moriyama, Kanade, & Cohn, 2003).

An example of system output is shown in Figure 14.3. The image data are of spontaneous facial behavior from Frank and Ekman (1997). From the input image sequence (Figure 14.3A), the head is tracked and its pose recovered (Figure 14.3B). The system stabilizes the face region by transforming the image to a common orientation (Figure 14.3C) and then localizes a region of interest. Figure 14.3D shows the localized eye region. Note that even though the head pitches forward in the image sequence, size and orientation of the "stabilized" eye region remain the same.

We have tested the head tracker in image sequences that include maximum pitch and yaw as large as 400 and 750, respectively, and time duration of up to 20 minutes (Xiao et al., 2003). We compared the recovered motion with ground truth obtained by a position and orientation measurement device that used markers attached to the head (Optotrak 3020 Position Sensor). The AFA head tracker was highly consistent with ground truth measurements; for example, for 75° yaw, absolute error was 3.860 (Xiao et al., 2003).

Although a head shape is not actually a cylinder, a cylinder model is adequate for many facial actions and contributes to system stability and robustness. A cylinder model, however, does not take into account the depth variation on the face surface. This is a problem for recognizing some facial action units such as lip puckering (AU 18). An alternative is to use an anatomically based complete face model in which the exact proportions of facial features are represented (DeCarlo & Metaxas, 1996; Essa & Pentland, 1997). Although powerful, such a person-specific anatomical model requires a large number of parameters that are dependent on the exact shape of the participant's individual face, which typically is unknown. Until recently, therefore, short of laser-scanning individual faces (Wen, 2004) or making anthropometric measurements in advance of facial image analysis, use of anatomically based 3D face models was not feasible. A recently developed algorithm that is capable of extracting 3D shape and appearance parameters from a single video (Xiao, Baker, Matthews, & Kanade, 2004) may change the situation. The participant-specific shape information of the face can be obtained from the input video data to be analyzed itself (see Figure 14.4).

Feature Extraction and Representation

Contraction of the facial muscles produces changes in the appearance and shape of facial landmarks, such as the eyes and lips, and in the direction and magnitude of the motion on the skin surface, resulting in the appearance of transient facial features. Transient features include facial lines and furrows that are not present at rest but that appear with facial expressions. Some of the transient facial features, such as crow's-feet wrinkles, may become permanent with age.

Permanent Facial Features

To track permanent facial features, AFA uses several different approaches. These include optical flow, Gabor wavelets,

Figure 14.2. Example result of automatic face and facial feature detection. © J. F. Cohn

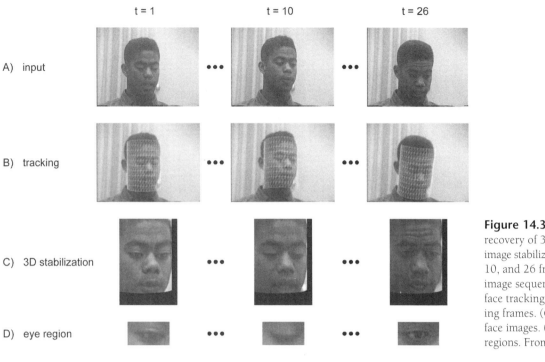

Figure 14.3. Automatic recovery of 3D head motion and image stabilization. (A) Frames 1, 10, and 26 from the original image sequence. (B) Automatic face tracking in the corresponding frames. (C) Stabilized face images. (D) Localized eye regions. From Cohn et al., 2003.

multistate models, and generative model fitting. Using multiple approaches increases the accuracy of action unit recognition (Tian, Kanade, & Cohn, 2001, 2002).

Optical Flow. In FACS, most action units are anatomically related to contraction of a specific facial muscle. AU 12 (oblique raising of the lip corners), for instance, results from contraction of the *Zygomatic major* muscle, AU 20 (lip stretch) from the *Risorius* muscle, and AU 15 (oblique lowering of the lip corners) from the *Depressor anguli* muscle (see appendix). Muscle contractions produce movement in the overlaying tissue. Optical flow quantifies the magnitude and direction of

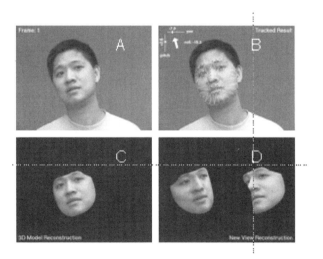

Figure 14.4. Sample results for 3D+2D AAM. (A) The input image. (B) The tracked result. (C) The 3DMM reconstruction. (D) Two new view reconstructions. From Xiao et al., 2004.

such movement. Figure 14.5 shows an example of dense flow extracted over the entire face. As the jaw drops (AU 26/27), the eyes widen (AU 5), and the brows are raised (AU 1+2), the flow captures these facial actions.

Obtaining smooth dense flow for the whole face image reliably requires incorporating a global model of motion (Wu, Kanade, Li, & Cohn, 2000), which is computationally intensive. It is more efficient to compute feature motion for localized facial regions. Tracking specific "feature points" (Figure 14.6) in these regions yields motion that is still consistent with that obtained from dense flow. Lien, Kanade, Cohn, and Li (2000) found that the two approaches to optical flow computation achieved similar high accuracy for action unit recognition.

Gabor Wavelets. Gabor wavelets are filters of varying orientations (e.g., vertical, oblique, or horizontal image gradients) and resolution. An example of Gabor filters is shown in Figure 14.7. Various orientations of the filter are shown across rows, whereas resolutions are shown across columns; each image in Figure 14.7 is referred to as a Gabor kernel. Gabor coefficients for a given image are the correlation images between the image and a set of these Gabor kernels. Figure 14.8 shows an example of Gabor coefficients in the eye region. Note that the output of the Gabor filter differs for each eye state. It was found that Gabor coefficients in the eye region could discriminate between three action units (AU 41, AU 42, and AU 45) with accuracy comparable to that of manual FACS coding (Tian et al., 2002).

Multistate Models. Facial features such as the mouth can exhibit both quantitative and qualitative changes in appearance. An example of quantitative change is the amount of

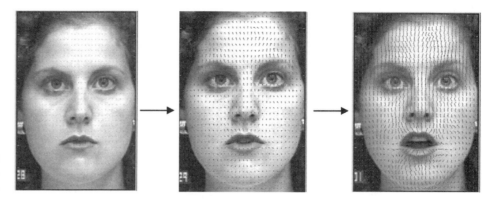

Figure 14.5. Example of dense flow extraction. From Lien et al. (2000).

displacement of the lip corner as smile intensity increases. Optical flow works well for this type of change. Qualitative change in appearance is characterized by disappearance of features and appearance of totally new features, such as the one that occurs when the lips tightly compress. Detecting this type of change is not easy with a technique such as optical flow, as it involves more than detecting movement of features. Multistate models of facial components address these issues.

Figure 14.9 shows an example of a three-state model of the lips. The model represents open, closed, and tightly closed lips. Different lip contour templates are prepared for different lip states. The open and closed lip contours are modeled by two parabolic arcs, which are described by six parameters: the lip center position (*xc, yc*), the lip shape (*h1, h2,* and *w*), and the lip orientation. For tightly closed lips, the dark mouth line connecting the lip corners represents the position, orientation, and shape.

Generative Model Fitting Approach for Eye-State Analysis. AFA-II used an eye model similar to the lip model, in which parabolic curves represent contours. The appearance of the eye region, however, is more complex than such a simple model. As Figure 14.10 illustrates, appearance of the eye varies within individuals (e.g., eye state, illumination, and orientation) and across individuals (e.g., race and gender). Asiatic and European faces, for example, differ in having single or double upper eyelids, respectively. To represent such variation, a more sophisticated model is needed. Figure 14.11a shows the structure-generative eye model that AFA-III uses. Structural individuality is represented by size and color of the iris, width and boldness of the eye cover fold,

width of the bulge below the eye, and width of the proximal illumination reflection on the bulge and furrow. Motion is represented by up-and-down positions of the upper and lower eyelids and 2D position of the iris. By matching this model with the eye region of an input image by means of an extended Lucas-Kanade (1981) algorithm and other techniques, we obtain detailed measurement of eye region appearance and eye motion (Moriyama, Xiao, Cohn, & Kanade, 2004; Figure 14.11b).

Transient Facial Features. Transient features provide crucial information for recognition of certain AUs. Wrinkles and furrows appear perpendicular to the direction of the motion of the activated muscles. Contraction of the *corrugator* muscle, for instance, produces vertical furrows between the brows, which is coded as AU 4 in FACS. Contraction of the medial portion of the *frontalis* muscle causes horizontal wrinkling in the center of the forehead (AU 1). Some of these transient features may become permanent with age. Permanent crow's-feet wrinkles around the outside corners of the eyes, which are characteristic of AU 6, are common in adults but not in children. When wrinkles and furrows become permanent, contraction of the corresponding muscles accentuates their appearance, such as deepening or lengthening.

AFA detects wrinkles and furrows in the nasolabial region, the nasal root, and the areas lateral to the outer corners of the eyes (Figure 14.12). These areas are found using the tracked locations of the corresponding permanent features. Presence or absence of wrinkles and furrows in these regions is determined by the strength and orientation of edge-like features using Gabor wavelet or edge detection technique.

Figure 14.6. Example of facial feature tracking. From Cohn et al. (1999).

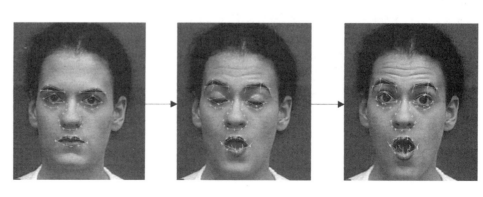

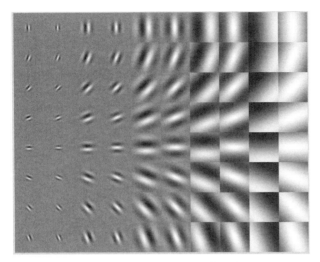

Figure 14.7. Gabor filters. Orientation of the filter systematically varies across rows, while resolution varies across columns.

The wrinkle/furrow state is classified as present if edge features increase from the neutral frame. For nasolabial furrows (Figure 14.13), the existence of vertical to diagonal connected edges is used for classification. If the length of connected edge pixels is longer than a threshold, the nasolabial furrow is determined to be present and is modeled as a line. The orientation of the furrow is represented as the angle between the furrow line and a line connecting the medial canthi (inner eye corners). This angle determines different action units. For example, the nasolabial furrow angle of AU 9 or AU 10 is larger than that of AU 12.

Facial Feature Representation and Action Unit Recognition by Pattern Recognition

Extracted features are transformed into a set of parameters for AU recognition. Upper and lower facial features are di-vided into two groups of parameters: the upper and lower faces. With a few exceptions (e.g., AU 9 effects on brow motion), facial actions in the upper and lower face have little interaction with each other. All parameters are either normalized for variation in face orientation and size (AFA-I and AFA-II) or computed from stabilized face images (AFA-III). Facial feature parameters are unaffected by variation in head position, rotation, and scale. Figure 14.13 shows the coordinate scheme and parameters used in AFA-II for the upper and lower face. We define a face coordinate system in AFA-II by using the inner corners of the eyes: the x-axis as the line connecting the two inner corners of the eyes and the y-axis as perpendicular to it pointing upward. The positions of the two inner corners of the eyes are least affected by facial muscle contraction and can be most reliably detected.

We have experimented with various approaches of classifying feature parameters into action units. These include hidden Markov models (HMM; Lien et al., 2000), discriminant analysis (Cohn et al., 1999; Lien et al., 2000), rule-based recognition (Cohn, Xiao, Moriyama, Ambadar, & Kanade, 2003; Moriyama et al., 2002), and neural networks (Tian et al., 2001, 2002).

HMM encodes extracted features into a sequence of a set of symbols. Sequences of symbols representing target action units and action unit combinations are modeled separately. These HMM models represent the most likely action units and action unit combinations and are used to evaluate encoded feature data for automatic action unit recognition (Lien et al., 2000). Discriminant analysis computes dimensions along which phenomena differ and obtains classification functions that predict class membership. Discrimination among action units is done by computing and comparing the *a posteriori probabilities* of action units. Neural networks can learn nonlinear, as well as linear, discriminants. A single network models multiple action units. We have used neural networks with three layers (with one layer hidden) and have used a

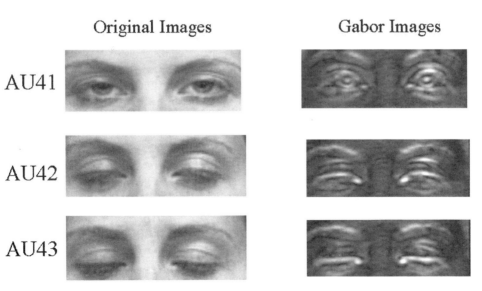

Figure 14.8. Results of Gabor filtering of the eye state (AU 41, AU 42, and AU 45). From Tian et al. (2002).

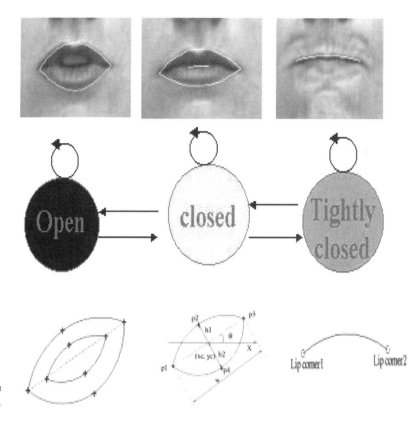

Figure 14.9. Multistate lip model. From Tian et al. (2001).

standard back-propagation method for training. When action units occur in combination, multiple output nodes are excited (Tian et al., 2001). When we have compared the classification results by various classifiers, we have found that they perform similarly (Lien et al., 2000), although others suggest there may be advantages to one or another classifier (Bartlett, Littlewort, Lainscsek, Fasel, & Movellan, 2004). More important than the choice of classifier is that the selected features be measured precisely and have high specificity for the target action units.

Use of AFA in Studies of Facial Expression of Emotion

It is known that both the configuration of facial features and the timing of facial actions are important in emotion expression and recognition (Cohn, 2005). The configuration of facial action units in relation to emotion, communicative intent, and action tendencies has been a major research topic. Less is known about the timing of facial actions because, with manual methods, timing measurement is only coarse and time-consuming. We know, however, that people are highly sensitive to the timing of facial actions (Edwards, 1998) in social settings. Slower facial actions, for instance, appear more genuine (Krumhuber & Kappas, 2003; Schmidt, Ambadar, & Cohn, 2006), as do those that are more synchronous in their movement (Frank & Ekman, 1997). Facial electromyo-

graphy (EMG) effectively quantifies the timing of covert muscle action (e.g., Dimberg & Thunberg, 1998), but the timing of observable facial action had been measured only coarsely by manual coding. AFA makes possible quantitative measurement of the timing of observable facial actions.

We have used AFA to recognize action units, to make comparisons with criterion measures of facial dynamics, and to investigate the timing of spontaneous smiles, multimodal coordination, and infant expressions of joy and distress. The first two versions of AFA (AFA-I and AFA-II) assume that head motion is mostly parallel to the image plane of the camera and is minimal in out-of-plane motion. We therefore applied AFA-I and AFA-II to images stemming from directed facial action tasks, in which participants are asked to perform deliberate facial actions with small head movement (Kanade, Cohn, & Tian, 2000) and spontaneous facial behavior in which out-of-plane motion was small (Cohn & Schmidt, 2004; Schmidt, Cohn, & Tian, 2003). Spontaneous facial behavior, however, often includes moderate to large out-of-plane head motion, for which AFA-I and AFA-II are not appropriate. A major breakthrough in AFA-III was the capability to accommodate such motion, which enabled us to expand our research in spontaneous facial behavior.

Automatic Recognition of FACS Action Units

Motivated by our interest in emotion expression and social interaction, we have focused on the action units that are most

Variance from structural individuality

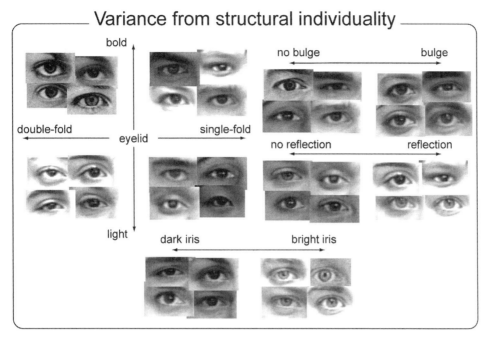

Variance from motion of a particular eye

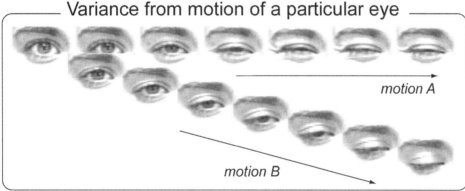

Figure 14.10. Diversity in the appearance of eye images. From Moriyama et al. (2004).

common in these contexts (e.g., Sayette, Cohn, Wertz, Perrott, & Parrott, 2001). In directed facial action tasks, AFA has shown high agreement with manual FACS coding for approximately 20 action units (AFA-I: Cohn et al., 1999; Lien et al., 2000; AFA-II: Tian et al., 2001, 2002; AFA-III: Cohn et al., 2003, Moriyama et al., 2002). In the upper face, AFA recognizes AU 1, AU 2, AU 4, AU 5, AU 6, AU 7, AU 41, AU 42, AU 43/45, and neutral (AU 0). In the lower face, it recognizes AU 9, AU 10, AU 12, AU 15, AU 17, AU 20, AU 25, AU 26, AU 27, AU 23/24, and neutral. (See appendix A for definitions of action units.) These action units include most of those that have been a focus in the literature on facial expression and emotion (Ekman & Rosenberg, 2005).

We made extensive comparisons to evaluate the AFA system's ability to generalize to new participants by training and testing in independent data sets collected and FACS coded in different laboratories using similar camera orientation (i.e., frontal pose) and lighting. Average recognition accuracy exceeded 93% regardless of what data set was used for training or testing. Accuracy was high for all action units

with the exception of AU 26 (jaw drop). This action unit is one that manual FACS coders have found troubling, as well. The recently revised FACS manual (Ekman et al., 2002) addressed this difficulty by altering the criteria for AU 25 and AU 26.

Action units can occur singly or in combination (Kanade, Cohn, & Tian, 2000; Smith et al., 2001). Recognizing action units when they occur in combination is difficult because action units may modify each other's appearance when proximal to each other, analogous to coarticulation effects in speech. Recognizing an individual action unit even when it appears in combination is important because there are thousands of possible combinations. Were each combination to be recognized separately, the task of training would become impractical. The AFA is capable of recognizing action units AU 1, AU 2, AU 4, AU 5, AU 6, AU 7, AU 9, AU 10, AU 15, AU 17, AU 20, AU 25, AU 26, AU 27, and AU 23/24 whether they occur alone or in some combinations (Tian et al., 2001).

In spontaneous facial behavior, AFA-III was tested for recognition of action unit 45 (blink) and flutter and brow

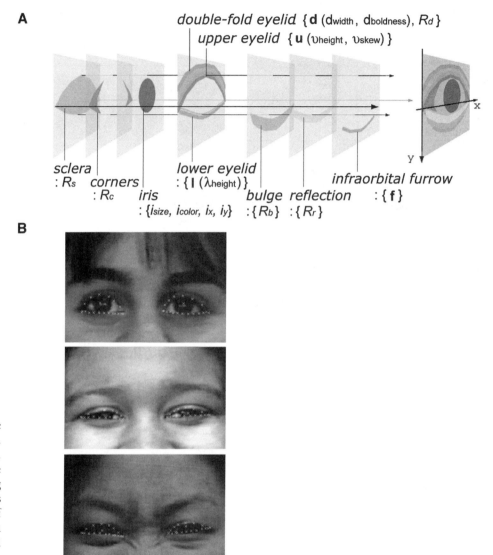

A

double-fold eyelid { **d** (d$_{width}$, d$_{boldness}$), R_d }

upper eyelid { **u** (υ$_{height}$, υ$_{skew}$) }

sclera : R_s corners : R_c iris : {i$_{size}$, i$_{color}$, i$_x$, i$_y$}   lower eyelid : { **l** (λ$_{height}$) }   bulge :{R_b}   reflection :{R_r}   infraorbital furrow :{ **f** }

B

Figure 14.11A. Generative eye model. From Moriyama et al. (2004).
Figure 14.11B. Eye state analysis including contour fitting of the upper and lower eyelids and detection of the center of the iris. Cropped images from three participants of varied ethnic background are shown.

raising and lowering (AU 1+2 and AU 4, respectively). Flutter is defined as multiple partial blinks in rapid succession. Image data used were those from a study of deception by Frank and Ekman (1997). Ethnically diverse young men, some of whom wore glasses, were video recorded while telling the truth or lying in a high-stakes situation. The video contained moderate head motion. The system achieved 98% agreement with manual FACS coding of blink, flutter, and nonblink (Cohn et al., 2003). Accuracy for brow actions was slightly lower: 89% for the two-state discrimination between brow raising and lowering and 76% for the three-state discrimination between brow raising, lowering, and neutral (Cohn, Reed, Ambadar, Xiao, & Moriyama, 2004). AU recognition in spontaneous facial behavior with nonfrontal pose, moderate head motion, and variable lighting is more challenging relative to posed facial actions performed under more controlled conditions and is a current research topic.

The FACS manual labels head orientation and gaze as "action descriptors" rather than "action units." Codes for action descriptors are late entries to the FACS manual, and, unlike action units, they lack the thorough description and differentiation. For this reason, we have not compared the AFA with FACS for action descriptors. We have instead compared the AFA results with motion-capture devices, which produce precise quantitative measurement of head motion and are considered the gold standard. AFA-III demonstrated high concurrent validity with a motion-capture device for pitch and yaw as large as 40° and 75°, respectively. Average recovery accuracy was within 3° (Xiao et al., 2003). Preliminary work with the eye-state analyzer in AFA-III indicates similar high concurrent validity for gaze (Moriyama, Xiao, Cohn, & Kanade, 2004). Together, these findings suggest that AFA produces far better measures of head motion and at least comparable measure of gaze to that of manual FACS coding.

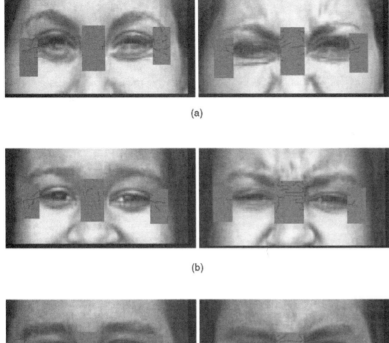

Figure 14.12. Results of Canny edge filtering of facial lines and furrows in areas of the nasal root and lateral to the outer eye corners. From Tian et al. (2001).

Comparison With Criterion Measures of Facial Dynamics

We evaluated the temporal precision of AFA by comparing it with manual measurement in digitized video and with facial EMG. AFA was highly consistent with both.

Wachtman, Cohn, Van Swearingen, and Manders (2001) compared facial feature tracking by AFA with manual marking of change in the position of facial features in directed facial action tasks in digitized video of individuals with facial neuromuscular disorder. The two methods were found highly consistent, with Pearson's $r = .96$ or higher, $p < .001$, for each of the facial actions. Differences between the methods were small—on the order of less than 1 pixel on average—and comparable to the interobserver reliability of the manual method.

Another useful comparison is between AFA results and facial EMG. Facial EMG is a gold standard for measurement of facial muscle activity. AFA output and *Zygomaticus major* EMG were compared for lip corner motion (AU 12) in Cohn and Schmidt (2004). Lip corner motion was quantified by the total displacement,

$$\Delta d = \sqrt{\Delta x^2 + \Delta y^2}$$

These two methods were in agreement for lip corner motion in 72% of cases with distinct EMG onset. Because EMG can detect occult changes in muscle activation below the threshold of visible change, this percentage agreement represents

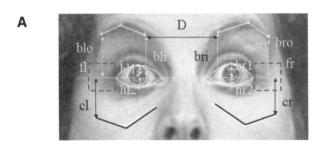

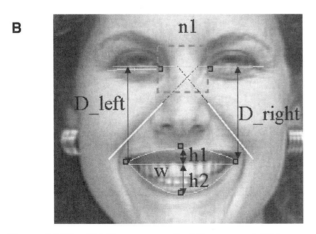

Figure 14.13. AFA-II parameters for (A) upper and (B) lower face. From Tian et al. (2001).

a conservative comparison of AFA's sensitivity to AU 12. For smiles, the two methods were highly correlated ($r = .95$, $p < .01$). Visible onset occurred an average of 0.23 seconds after the EMG onset (see Figure 14.14 for an example). This kind of relation between physiological measurement (i.e., EMG) and visible behavior (lip motion) at this level of precision became possible only by using AFA.

Timing of Spontaneous Smiles

Smiles, as one of the most important facial expressions, emerge early in development and occur throughout the life span with high frequency to express emotion and communicative intention. Whereas the configuration of smiles is well studied (e.g., Ekman, 1993; Frijda & Tcherkassof, 1997; Fridlund, 1994; Izard, 1983; Malatesta et al., 1989; Matias, Cohn, & Ross, 1989; Pantic & Rothkrantz, 2000b, 2003; Tian et al., in press), with few exceptions little is known about their timing (e.g., Frank, Ekman, & Friesen, 1993; Hess & Kleck, 1990). We used AFA to investigate the timing of the onset phase of spontaneous smiles. The onset phase provides the initial and most conspicuous change in appearance in smiling as perceived by human observers (Leonard, Voeller, & Kuldau, 1991). Viewers respond in kind either overtly or covertly as early as 0.30–0.40 s after viewing an image of a smile (Dimberg & Thunberg, 1998). Because this duration is well within the average duration of smile onsets (Bugental, 1986; Cohn & Schmidt, 2004), it is likely that this phase of smiles functions as the initial social signal.

We found that the onset phase of spontaneous smiles has highly consistent temporal characteristics, regardless of context and the occurrence of other action units, including AU 6 and masking movements. The larger the intensity of the onset phase, the faster is the peak velocity, with an average

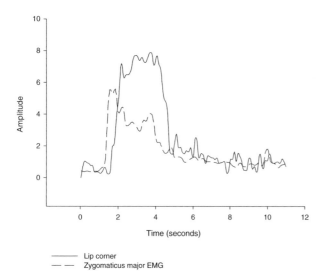

Figure 14.14. Relation between *Zygomaticus major* EMG and lip-corner displacement in a spontaneous smile. From Cohn & Schmidt (2004).

$R^2 = 0.82$. This finding that intensity and velocity of smile onsets have a strong relationship is consistent with ballistic motion. Previous attempts to examine this issue were limited to relatively gross measures, such as the duration of manually coded action units (Frank et al., 1993). The fact that AFA produces quantitative measures of rate of change —velocity in particular—allowed more rigorous kinematic analyses to test hypotheses about the timing of spontaneous smiles.

Multimodal Coordination of Facial Action, Head Motion, and Gaze

We investigated coordination among head motion, facial action, and gaze that occurs in spontaneous smiles. We focused on spontaneous smiles that occurred following directed facial action tasks. Keltner (1995) found that smiles in this context were frequently associated with embarrassment. Following Keltner, we hypothesized a pattern of coordination of head motion, gaze, and facial expression; smiles associated with embarrassment involve motion of looking down and away while beginning to smile. We found strong support for this hypothesis. Facial action, as indicated by lip-corner displacement during spontaneous smiles, was moderately correlated with all 6 degrees of freedom of head motion and with eye motion, as suggested by neuroscience literature (King, Lisberger, & Fuchs, 1976; Klier, Hongying, & Crawford, 2003). Further, the patterns of correlation we found appeared to be specific to embarrassment and part of a coordinated motor routine (Michel & Camras, 1992). Smile intensity increases as the face and gaze pitch down and move away from the experimenter, followed by decreasing intensity as the orientation of the face comes back toward the experimenter (see Figure 14.15). (For details, see Cohn, Reed, Moriyama, et al., 2004). As we did not collect self-report measures, we cannot say with certainty that the smiles we observed were related to feelings of embarrassment or to relief at the task's completion. The findings, however, provide strong quantitative support for existence of dynamic coordination of multimodal actions and suggest that the detection of such a coordination can disambiguate smiles that are otherwise morphologically similar (e.g., smiles of embarrassment vs. those of enjoyment).

Infant Expressions of Joy and Distress

Previous literature proposes that cheek raising (AU 6) increases observers' perceptions of smile intensity in infants (Messinger, 2002). This hypothesis has been difficult to test in perceptual judgment studies because infant head orientation typically is confounded with smile and distress intensity and because manual FACS coding of intensity is relatively coarse. The head tracking and face stabilization features of AFA allowed us to address these difficulties. After recovering 3D head motion, we used AFA-III to warp face images to

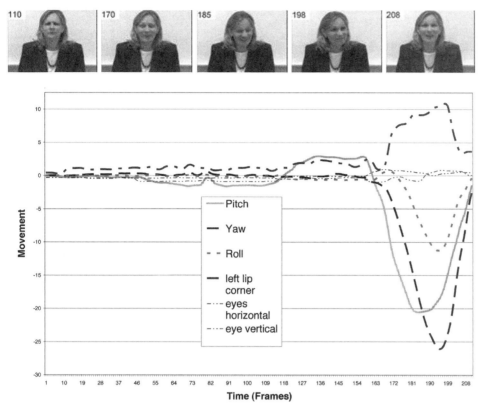

Figure 14.15. Top panel: Selected frames from image sequence showing the relation between lip-corner displacement, head rotation, and eye motion. Bottom panel: Corresponding time series for these parameters. From Cohn, Reed, Moriyama, et al. (2004).

a common orientation and precisely measure smile intensity as the lip corner displacement (described previously). We (Bolzani-Dinehart, Messinger, Acosta, Cassel, Ambadar, & Cohn, 2005) then conducted a judgment study. We found that smiles with cheek raising and greater lip corner displacement were perceived by raters as more emotionally positive than equivalent smiles without these features. In related work, we have begun to use AFA to track changes in facial expression of infants during mother-infant face-to-face interaction. Mother and infant facial expression are quantitatively measured in a way that manual coding could only approximate. As an example, Figure 14.16 shows a time series plot of mother-and-infant lip-corner displacement, a measure of smile intensity, using the next version of AFA, now under development. Precise measurement of infant and parent affective behavior during face-to-face interaction enables us to more rigorously test parent-infant bidirectional influence than previously possible (e.g., Cohn & Tronick, 1988) and provides new capability to investigate the dynamic processes in emotion and emotion regulation.

Availability of AFA

Although AFA is still in development and not yet ready for release, we anticipate that AFA will become available for initial applications by the research community within the next 2 years. Several collaborative efforts with other investigators already are in progress, including studies of emotional development and parent-infant interaction, pain, and facial neuromuscular disorders. Investigators interested in becoming involved in development efforts, testing, and application are encouraged to contact the authors.

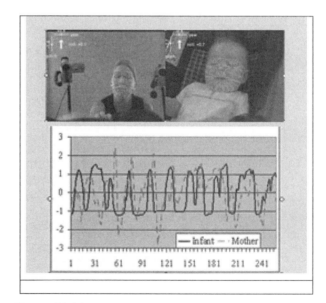

Figure 14.16. Mother-and-infant lip-corner displacement, a measure of smile intensity, as measured by AFA v.4. (Image data from Daniel Messinger, University of Miami).

Discussion

Automated facial image analysis exemplified by AFA is an emergent option for assessing facial expression of emotion. AFA has shown good agreement in action unit recognition with manual FACS coding in deliberate facial action tasks and in head motion with ground-truth measures in the more challenging case of spontaneous facial behavior. Automated face image analysis has proven especially effective in revealing the dynamics of facial action, head motion, and gaze. It affords quantitative power similar to EMG, and yet it is specific to observable facial actions and quantifies head motion and eye position, as well, without the intrusive nature of EMG. The study of emotion dynamics in facial behavior is an especially exciting domain because until now it could be studied only in a coarse way other than using facial EMG sensors.

In addition to dynamic aspects of emotion expression, a major application of automated facial image analysis will be recognition of FACS action units and emotion-specified expressions. Initial efforts with AFA have been encouraging. Nearly all of the action units prevalent in emotion expression are recognized by AFA, and similar results also were reported by several other facial image analysis systems. An important qualification, however, is that high level of performance has been demonstrated only in deliberate facial actions. Automated action unit recognition in spontaneous facial behavior is more difficult and needs more research before it becomes broadly useful. Toward that end, AFA has made a small step by demonstrating recognition of a few action units in spontaneous behavior. In a video of spontaneous facial behavior from a study of deception by Frank and Ekman (1997), AFA achieved 98% agreement with manual FACS coding for blinks (AU 45), flutter, and eyes open (Cohn et al., 2003) and 76% agreement between brows up (AU 1 + 2), brows down (AU 4), and neutral (AU 0; Cohn, Reed, Ambadar, Xiao, & Moriyama, 2004). Cohn and Schmidt (2004), in other videos of spontaneous facial behavior, found strong concurrent validity with facial EMG for continuous measurement of *Zygomatic major* intensity, which is the primary measure of positive affect in facial EMG studies (Cacioppo, Martzke, Petty, & Tassinary, 1988).

To accomplish this goal will require not only algorithm development but also use of rigorously FACS-coded image data for training and testing algorithms. For deliberate facial action tasks, we created a large representative database, the Cohn-Kanade AU-Coded Facial Expression Database (Kanade et al., 2000). A subset of the database consists of FACS-coded directed facial action tasks in about 200 adult men and women of varying ethnicity. The database has been widely distributed for research in automated facial image analysis and is serving as a test bed and benchmark for algorithm development and testing. Comparable FACS-coded data sets of spontaneous facial behavior will be required for fast progress and to explore generalizability in spontaneous facial behavior. The emotion science community can be of invaluable help in this regard by making available to researchers in this area facial expression image data with associated manual codes.

A number of technical challenges exist for AFA. Among these, the most important are how to parse the stream of behavior, prevent error accumulation, and increase automation. AFA and other facial image analysis approaches have assumed that expressions involve a single facial action or expression and that they begin and end from a neutral position. In actuality, facial expression is more complex. Action units occur in combinations or show serial dependence. Transitions among action units may involve no intervening neutral state. Parsing the stream of facial action units under these circumstances is a challenge. Human coders meet this task in part by having a mental representation of a neutral face. However, even for human coders, defining events and transitions is not a solved problem. For AFA, parsing will likely involve higher order pattern recognition than has been considered to date.

Many of the methods used in AFA so far involve dynamic templates for which estimates are continually updated. With dynamic templates, error tends to propagate and accumulate across an image sequence. So far, most AFA applications have involved relatively short image sequences—up to 10 seconds or so—for which error accumulation was not a significant problem. As we begin to process much longer sequences, an appropriate measure is required. The head tracking module in AFA overcomes this problem through a combined use of robust regression and reference images. Robust regression identifies and discounts the effects of outliers, and reference images provide a way to reinitialize estimates so as to attenuate error accumulation. For head tracking, this approach has been highly successful. The cylinder model head tracker has performed well for image sequences as long as 20 minutes. Similar capability will be needed for action unit recognition.

Current methods involve some degree of initialization, such as delimiting face regions to process, adjusting templates of facial features, or personalizing active appearance models (Matthews & Baker, 2004). For example, current active appearance models require a fair amount of manual input during the training phase. Although a fully automated system is not always necessary for all applications, increased automation will accelerate the adoption of AFA in emotion science and clinical practice.

In summary, automated facial image analysis for measurement of facial expression is advanced, its application to the study of emotion has started to inform our understanding of emotion processes, and new types of findings, such as the timing of multimodal behavior in spontaneous smiles, have begun to emerge.

Appendix: Action Units of the Facial Action Coding System

FACS Action Units

AU	Facial muscle	Description of muscle movement
1	Frontalis, pars medialis	Inner corner of eyebrow raised
2	Frontalis, pars lateralis	Outer corner of eyebrow raised
4	Corrugator supercilii, Depressor supercilii	Eyebrows drawn medially and down
5	Levator palpebrae superioris	Eyes widened
6	Orbicularis oculi, pars orbitalis	Cheeks raised; eyes narrowed
7	Orbicularis oculi, pars palpebralis	Lower eyelid raised and drawn medially
9	Levator labii superioris alaeque nasi	Upper lip raised and inverted; superior part of the nasolabial furrow deepened; nostril dilated by the medial slip of the muscle
10	Levator labii superioris	Upper lip raised; nasolabial furrow deepened, producing square-like furrows around nostrils
11	Zygomaticus minor	Lower to medial part of the nasolabial furrow deepened
12	Zygomaticus major	Lip corners pulled up and laterally
13	Levator anguli oris (a.k.a. Caninus)	Angle of the mouth elevated; only muscle in the deep layer of muscles that opens the lips
14	Buccinator	Lip corners tightened. Cheeks compressed against teeth
15	Depressor anguli oris (a.k.a. Triangularis)	Corner of the mouth pulled downward and inward
16	Depressor labii inferioris	Lower lip pulled down and laterally
17	Mentalis	Skin of chin elevated
18	Incisivii labii superioris and Incisivii labii inferioris	Lips pursed
20	Risorius w/ platysma	Lip corners pulled laterally
22	Orbicularis oris	Lips everted (funneled)
23	Orbicularis oris	Lips tightened
24	Orbicularis oris	Lips pressed together
25	Depressor labii inferioris, or relaxation of mentalis, or orbicularis oris	Lips parted
26	Masseter; relaxed temporal and internal pterygoid	Jaw dropped
27	Pterygoids and digastric	Mouth stretched open
28	Orbicularis oris	Lips sucked
41	Relaxation of levator palpebrae superioris	Upper eyelid droop
42	Orbicularis oculi	Eyelid slit
43	Relaxation of Levator palpebrae superioris; orbicularis oculi, pars palpebralis	Eyes closed
44	Orbicularis oculi, pars palpebralis	Eyes squinted
45	Relaxation of Levator palpebrae superioris; Orbicularis oculi, pars palpebralis	Blink
46	Relaxation of Levator palpebrae superioris; orbicularis oculi, pars palpebralis	Wink

Note. Entries are limited to action units that have a known anatomical basis. Action descriptors and codes for head and eye position are omitted.

Source: Ekman & Friesen (1978)

Acknowledgment

Preparation of this manuscript was supported by NIMH grant MH 51435. Correspondence should be addressed to Jeffrey F. Cohn, Department of Psychology, University of Pittsburgh, 4327 Sennott Square, 210 South Bouquet Street, Pittsburgh, PA 15260; phone: 412–624–8825; fax: 412–624–5407; e-mail: jeffcohn@pitt.edu.

Note

1. Image sequences may consist of either a continuous series of image files or a single movie file in which images are packaged. Supported formats for sequences of single images include Tiff, Bitmap, PNG, and JPG. Supported movie file formats include AVI and MPEG2. When using lossy compression, it is best to select minimal compression (typically, 5:1), because higher compression rates may compromise necessary detail and introduce artifact.

References

Bakeman, R., & Gottman, J. M. (1986). Observing behavior: An introduction to sequential analysis. Cambridge, UK: Cambridge University Press.

Bartlett, M. S., Hager, J. C., Ekman, P., & Sejnowski, T. J. (1999). Measuring facial expressions by computer image analysis. Psychophysiology, 36, 253–263.

Bartlett, M. S., Littlewort, G., Lainscsek, C., Fasel, I., & Movellan, J. (2004). Machine learning methods for fully automatic recognition of facial expressions and facial actions. Proceedings of the IEEE International Conference on Systems, Man, and Cybernetics, 592–597.

Bartlett, M. S., Movellan, J. R., Littlewort, G. C., Braathen, B., Frank, M. G., & Sejnowski, T. J. (2005). Towards automatic recognition of spontaneous facial actions. In P. Ekman & E. Rosenberg (Ed.), What the face reveals: Basic and applied studies of spontaneous expression using the Facial Action Coding System (FACS) (2nd ed.; pp. 393–426). New York: Oxford University Press.

Bolzani Dinehart, L. H., Messinger, D. S., Acosta, S. I., Cassel, T., Ambadar, Z., & Cohn, J. F. (2005). Adult perceptions of positive and negative infant expressions. Infancy, 8, 279–306.

Bugental, D. (1986). Unmasking the "polite smile:" Situational and personal determinants of managed affect in adult-child interaction. *Personality and Social Psychology Bulletin, 12*(1), 7–16.

Bullock, M., & Russell, J. A. (1984). Preschool children's interpretation of facial expressions of emotion. *International Journal of Behavioral Development, 7,* 193–214.

Cacioppo, J. T., Martzke, J. S., Petty, R. E., & Tassinary, L. G. (1988). Specific forms of facial EMG response index emotions during an interview: From Darwin to the continuous flow hypothesis of affect laden information processing. *Journal of Personality and Social Psychology, 54,* 592–604.

Campos, J. J., Bertenthal, B. I., & Kermoian, R. (1992). Early experience and emotional development: The emergence of wariness of heights. *Psychological Science, 3,* 61–64.

Camras, L. A., Lambrecht, L., & Michel, G. (1996). Infant "surprise" expressions as coordinative motor structures. *Journal of Nonverbal Behavior, 20,* 183–195.

Cohn, J. F. (2005). Automated analysis of the configuration and timing of facial expression. In P. Ekman & E. Rosenberg, *What the face reveals: Basic and applied studies of spontaneous expression using the Facial Action Coding System (FACS)* (2nd ed.; pp. 388–392). New York: Oxford University Press.

Cohn, J. F., & Campbell, S. B. (1992). Influence of maternal depression on infant affect regulation. In D. Cicchetti & S. Toth (Eds.), *Rochester Symposium on Developmental Psychopathology: Vol. 4. A developmental approach to affective disorders* (pp. 105–130). Hillsdale, NJ: Erlbaum.

Cohn, J. F., & Elmore, M. (1988). Effect of contingent changes in mothers' affective expression on the organization of behavior in 3-month-old infants. *Infant Behavior and Development, 11,* 493–505.

Cohn, J. F., Reed, L. I., Ambadar, Z., Xiao, J., & Moriyama, T. (2004). Automatic analysis and recognition of brow actions and head motion in spontaneous facial behavior. *Proceedings of the IEEE Conference on Systems, Man, and Cybernetics,* 210–216.

Cohn, J. F., Reed, L., Moriyama, T., Xiao, J., Schmidt, K., & Ambadar, Z. (2004). Multimodal coordination of facial action, head rotation, and eye motion during spontaneous smiles. *Proceedings of the Sixth IEEE International Conference on Automatic Face and Gesture Recognition (FG'04),* 129–135.

Cohn, J. F., & Schmidt, K. L. (2004). The timing of facial motion in posed and spontaneous smiles. *International Journal of Wavelets, Multiresolution, and Information Processing, 2,* 1–12.

Cohn, J. F., Schmidt, K., Gross, R., & Ekman, P. (2002). Individual differences in facial expression: Stability over time, relation to self-reported emotion, and ability to inform person identification. *Proceedings of the International Conference on Multimodal User Interfaces (ICMI 2002),* 491–496.

Cohn, J. F., & Tronick, E. Z. (1988). Mother-infant interaction: Influence is bidirectional and unrelated to periodic cycles in either partner's behavior. *Developmental Psychology, 24,* 386–392.

Cohn, J. F., Xiao, J., Moriyama, T., Ambadar, Z., & Kanade, T. (2003). Automatic recognition of eye blinking in spontaneously occurring behavior. *Behavior Research Methods, Instruments, and Computers, 35,* 420–428.

Cohn, J. F., Zlochower, A., Lien, J., & Kanade, T. (1999). Automated face analysis by feature point tracking has high concurrent validity with manual FACS coding. *Psychophysiology, 36,* 35–43.

Cootes, T. F., Edwards, G. J., & Taylor, C. J. (2001). Active appearance models. *IEEE Transactions on Pattern Analysis and Machine Intelligence,* 681–685.

Davidson, R. J., Ekman, P., Saron, C. D., Senulis, J. A., & Friesen, W. (1990). Approach-withdrawal and cerebral asymmetry: Emotional expression and brain physiology: I . *Journal of Personality and Social Psychology. 58,* 330–341.

DeCarlo, D., & Metaxas, D. (1996). The integration of optical flow and deformable models with applications to human face shape and motion estimation. *Proceedings of the IEEE Conference on Computer Vision and Pattern Recognition,* 231–238.

Dimberg, U., & Thunberg, M. (1998). Rapid facial reactions to emotional facial expressions. *Scandinavian Journal of Psychology, 39,* 39–45.

Edwards, K. (1998). The face of time: Temporal cues in facial expressions of emotion. *Psychological Science, 9*(4), 270–276.

Ekman, P. (1993). Facial expression and emotion. *American Psychologist, 48,* 384–392.

Ekman, P., & Friesen, W. V. (1978). *Facial Action Coding System.* Palo Alto, CA: Consulting Psychologists Press.

Ekman, P., Friesen, W., & Hager, J. (2002). *Facial Action Coding System* [E-book]. Salt Lake City, UT: Research Nexus.

Ekman, P., Huang, T. S., Sejnowski, T. J., & Hager, J. C. (1992). *Final report to NSF of the Planning Workshop on Facial Expression Understanding,* Washington, DC: National Science Foundation. Retrieved from http://face-and-emotion.com/dataface/nsfrept/overview.html

Ekman, P., & Rosenberg, E. (2005). *What the face reveals: Basic and applied studies of spontaneous facial expression using the Facial Action Coding System (FACS)* (2nd ed.). New York: Oxford University Press.

Essa, I., & Pentland, A. (1997). Coding, analysis, interpretation and recognition of facial expressions. *IEEE Transactions on Pattern Analysis and Machine Intelligence, 7,* 757–763.

Fasel, B., & Luttin, J. (2000). Recognition of asymmetric facial action unit activities and intensities. *Proceedings of the International Conference on Pattern Recognition, 1,* 5100.

Fox, N., & Davidson, R. J. (1988). Patterns of brain electrical activity during facial signs of emotion in ten-month-old infants. *Developmental Psychology, 24,* 230–236.

Frank, M., & Ekman, P. (1997). The ability to detect deceit generalizes across different types of high-stake lies. *Journal of Personality and Social Psychology, 72,* 1429–1439.

Frank, M., Ekman, P., & Friesen, W. (1993). Behavioral markers and recognizability of the smile of enjoyment. *Journal of Personality and Social Psychology, 64,* 83–93.

Fridlund, A. J. (1994). *Human facial expression: An evolutionary view.* New York: Academic Press.

Frijda, N. H., & Tcherkassof, A. (1997). Facial expressions as modes of action readiness. In J. A. Russell & J. M. Fernandez-Dols (Eds.), *The psychology of facial expression* (pp. 78–102). New York: Cambridge University Press.

Gross, J. J., & John, O. P. (1997). Revealing feelings: Facets of emotional expressivity in self-reports, peer ratings, and behavior. *Journal of Personality and Social Psychology, 72,* 435–448.

Harker, L. A. & Keltner, D. (2001). Expressions of positive emotions in women's college yearbook pictures and their relationship to personality and life outcomes across adulthood. *Journal of Personality and Social Psychology, 80,* 112–124.

Hess, U., & Kleck, R. (1990). Differentiating emotion elicited and deliberate emotional facial expressions. *European Journal of Social Psychology, 20,* 369–385.

Izard, C. E. (1983). The maximally discriminative facial movement coding system. Unpublished manuscript, University of Delaware.

Kanade, T. (1973). Picture processing system by computer complex and recognition of human faces. Unpublished doctoral dissertation, Kyoto University.

Kanade, T. (1977). *Computer recognition of human faces.* Stuttgart, Germany: Birkhauser Verlag.

Kanade, T., Cohn, J. F., & Tian, Y. (2000). Comprehensive database for facial expression analysis. *Proceedings of the Fourth IEEE International Conference on Automatic Face and Gesture Recognition,* 46–53.

Keltner, D. (1995). Signs of appeasement: Evidence for the distinct displays of embarrassment, amusement, and shame. *Journal of Personality and Social Psychology, 68,* 441–454.

Keltner, D., & Haidt, J. (1999). Social functions of emotions at four levels of analysis. *Cognition and Emotion, 13,* 505–521.

King, W. M., Lisberger, S. G., & Fuchs, A. F. (1976). Response of fibers in medial longitudinal fasciculus (MLF) of alert monkeys during horizontal and vertical conjugate eye movements evoked by vestibular or visual stimuli. *Neurophysiology, 39,* 1135–1149.

Klier, E. M., Hongying, W., & Crawford, J. D. (2003). Three-dimensional eye-head coordination is implemented downstream from the superior colliculus. *Journal of Neurophysiology, 89,* 2839–2853.

Kraut, R. E. & Johnson, R. (1979). Social and emotional messages of smiling: An ethological approach. *Journal of Personality and Social Psychology, 37,* 1539–1553.

Krumhuber, E., & Kappas, A. (2003, September). *Moving smiles: The influence of the dynamic components on the perception of smile-genuineness.* Paper presented at the European Conference on Facial Expression: Measurement and Meaning, Rimini, Italy.

Leonard, C. M., Voeller, K. K. S., & Kuldau, J. M. (1991). When's a smile a smile? Or how to detect a message by digitizing the signal. *Psychological Science, 2,* 166–172.

Levenson, R. W., Ekman, P., & Friesen, W. V. (1990). Voluntary facial action generates emotion-specific autonomic nervous system activity. *Psychophysiology, 27,* 363–384.

Lien, J. J. J., Kanade, T., Cohn, J. F., & Li, C. C. (2000). Detection, tracking, and classification of subtle changes in facial expression. *Journal of Robotics and Autonomous Systems, 31,* 131–146.

Lucas, B., & Kanade, T. (1981). An interactive image registration technique with an application in stereo vision. *Proceedings of the International Joint Conference on Artificial Intelligence,* 674–679.

Lyons, M., Akamasku, S., Kamachi, M., & Gyoba, J. (1998). Coding facial expressions with Gabor wavelets. *Proceedings of the International Conference on Face and Gesture Recognition,* 200.

Malatesta, C. Z., Culver, C., Tesman, J. R., & Shepard, B. (1989). The development of emotion expression during the first two years of life. *Monographs of the Society for Research in Child Development, 54,* 1–104.

Martin, P., & Bateson, P. (1986). *Measuring behavior: An introductory guide.* Cambridge, UK: Cambridge University Press.

Matias, R., Cohn, J. F., & Ross, S. (1989). A comparison of two systems to code infants' affetive expression. *Developmental Psychology, 25,* 483–489.

Matthews, I., & Baker, S. (2004). Active appearance models revisited. *International Journal of Computer Vision, 60*(2), 135–164.

Matthews, I., Ishikawa, T., & Baker, S. (2004). The template update problem. *IEEE Transations on Pattern Analysis and Machine Intelligence, 26,* 810–815.

Messinger, D. S. (2002). Positive and negative: Infant facial expressions and emotions. *Current Directions in Psychological Science, 11,* 1–6.

Michel, G. F., & Camras, L. A. (1992). Infant interest expressions as coordinative motor strutures. *Infant Behavior and Development, 15,* 347–358.

Moriyama, T., Kanade, T., Cohn, J. F., Xiao, J., Ambadar, Z., Gao, J., et al. (2002). Automatic recognition of eye blinking in spontaneously occurring behavior. *Proceedings of the International Conference on Pattern Recognition,* 78–81.

Moriyama, T., Xiao, J., Cohn, J. F., & Kanade, T. (2004). Detailed eye model and its application to analysis of facial image. *Proceedings of the IEEE Conference on Society, Man, and Cybernetics,* 629–634.

Padgett, C., Cottrell, G. W., & Adolphs, B. (1996). Categorical perception in facial emotion classification. *Proceedings of the Cognitive Science Conference, 18,* 249–253.

Pantic, M., & Rothkrantz, M. (2000a). Expert system for automatic analysis of facial expression. *Image and Vision Computing, 18,* 881–905.

Pantic, M., & Rothkrantz, M. (2000b). Automatic analysis of facial expressions: The state of the art. *IEEE Transactions on Pattern Analysis and Machine Intelligence, 22,* 1424–1445.

Pantic, M., & Rothkrantz, M. (2003). Toward an affect-sensitive multimodal human-computer interaction. *Proceedings of the IEEE, 91,* 1371–1390.

Phillips, P. J., Grother, P., Michaels, R. J., Blackburn, D. M., Tabasi, E., & Bone, J. M. (2003). Face Recognition Vendor Test 2002. Retrieved from http://www.frvt.org/FRVT2002/documents.htm

Rosenberg, E., & Ekman, P. (1994). Coherence between expressive and experiential systems in emotion. *Cognition and Emotion, 8,* 201–229.

Rowley, H. A., Baluja, S., & Kanade, T. (1998). Neural network-based face detection. *Pattern Analysis and Machine Intelligence, 20,* 23–28.

Sayette, M. A., Cohn, J. F., Wertz, J. M., Perrott, M. A., & Parrott, D. J. (2001). A psychometric evaluation of the Facial Action Coding System for assessing spontaneous expression. *Journal of Nonverbal Behavior, 25,* 167–186.

Schmidt, K. L., Ambadar, Z., & Cohn, J. F. (2006). *Timing of lip corner movement affects perceived genuineness of spontaneous smiles*. Pittsburgh: Department of Psychology, University of Pittsburgh.

Schmidt, K. L., & Cohn, J. F. (2001). Human facial expressions as adaptations: Evolutionary questions in facial expression. *Yearbook of Physical Anthropology, 44,* 3–24.

Schmidt, K., Cohn, J. F., & Tian, Y. L. (2003). Signal characteristics of spontaneous facial expressions: Automatic movement in solitary and social smiles. *Biological Psychology, 65,* 49–66.

Smith, E., Bartlett, M. S., & Movellan, J. R. (2001). Computer recognition of facial actions: A study of co-articulation effects. *Proceedings of the 8th Annual Joint Symposium on Neural Computation.*

Tian, Y. L, Kanade, T., & Cohn, J. F. (2001). Recognizing action units for facial expression analysis. *IEEE Transactions on Pattern Analysis and Machine Intelligence, 23,* 97–116.

Tian, Y. L., Kanade, T., & Cohn, J. F. (2002). Evaluation of Gabor-wavelet-based facial action unit recognition in image sequences of increasing complexity. *Proceedings of the Fifth IEEE International Conference on Automatic Face and Gesture Recognition,* 229–234.

Tian, Y., Cohn, J. F., & Kanade, T. (2005). Facial expression analysis. In S. Z. Li & A. K. Jain (Eds.), *Handbook of face recognition* (pp. 247–276). New York: Springer.

Wachtman, G. S., Cohn, J. F., Van Swearingen, J. M., & Manders, E. K. (2001). Automated tracking of facial features in facial neuromotor disorders. *Plastic and Reconstructive Surgery, 107,* 1124–1133.

Watson, D., & Tellegen, A. (1985). Toward a consensual structure of mood. *Psychological Bulletin, 98,* 219–235.

Wen, Z. (2004, January). Face processing research at the University of Illinois, Champaign-Urbana. Paper presented at the Meeting on Face Processing, Carnegie Mellon University, Pittsburgh, PA.

Wen, Z., & Huang, T.,S. (2003). Capturing subtle facial motions in 3D face tracking. *Proceedings of the International Conference on Computer Vision,* 1343–1350.

Wu, Y. T., Kanade, T., Li, C. C., & Cohn, J. F. (2000). Image registration using wavelet-based motion model. *International Journal of Computer Vision, 38,* 129–152.

Xiao, J., Baker, S., Matthews, I., & Kanade, T. (2004). Real-time combined 2D + 3D active appearance models. *Proceedings of the IEEE Conference on Computer Vision and Pattern Recognition.*

Xiao, J., Moriyama, T., Kanade, T., & Cohn, J. F. (2003). Robust full-motion recovery of head by dynamic templates and re-registration techniques. *International Journal of Imaging Systems and Technology, 13,* 85–94.

Yacoob, Y., & Davis, L. (1996). Recognizing human facial expression from long image sequences using optical flow. *IEEE Transactions on Pattern Recognition and Machine Intelligence, 18,* 636–642.

Zhang, Z. (1999). Feature-based facial expression recognition: Sensitivity analysis and experiments with multi-layer perceptron. *International Journal of Pattern Recognition and Artificial Intelligence, 13,* 893–911.

Zhou, Y., Gu, L., & Zhang, H. J. (2003, June). Bayesian tangent shape model: Estimating shape and pose parameters via Bayesian inference. *Proceedings of the IEEE Conference on Computer Vision and Pattern Recognition, 1,* 109–116.

Zhu, Y., De Silva, L. C., & Ko, C. C. (2002). Using moment invariants and HMM in facial expression recognition. *Pattern Recognition Letters, 23,* 83–91.

Michael J. Owren
Jo-Anne Bachorowski

Measuring Emotion-Related Vocal Acoustics

Recent years have seen great advances in digital-audio technology, making it much easier to incorporate work with sound as a routine component of emotions research. Where there once were, for instance, only a few programs available for sound analysis, synthesis, and editing, there now are many. These developments present unparalleled opportunities for investigating how human emotion may be reflected in both verbal and nonverbal vocal behavior. However, acoustics work is nonetheless a challenging endeavor, for it requires both care and some specialized knowledge in order to apply the analysis tools effectively. The purpose of this chapter is, therefore, to present basic information about analyzing human vocal acoustics for the purpose of extracting correlates of affect-related states, with particular emphasis on avoiding some of the fundamental errors that can occur.

In putting the chapter together, we have attempted to present the material in a conceptual and pragmatic fashion, with minimal emphasis on theoretical and mathematical aspects. Some of the latter is necessary, of course, and work in acoustics can admittedly be both difficult and time-consuming. However, our goal has been to make the material accessible to a broad spectrum of emotions researchers and to provide as much specific and concrete advice as possible. In the rest of this section, we briefly review some historical trends in the vocal acoustics of emotion, mention the acoustic features that have been of greatest interest to emotions researchers, and outline a hypothetical application as a frame for a number of the acoustic principles and measurement techniques discussed later.

In the first sections, we discuss some basics about sound and how it is produced by the human vocal apparatus. The initial technical issues are how to acquire and store sound on a computer and how to "preprocess" the resulting files to help ensure an overall level of uniformity. We then examine how to characterize both the energy source associated with a given vocalization and the filtering effects that modify this energy as it passes through the vocal-tract cavities above the larynx. Here, measures of interest include vocal-fold vibration rates, perturbations in these vibrations, and both the short- and long-term frequency distributions of the vocalizations. We also mention some issues in measuring vocal amplitude and describe a few of the so-called nonlinear phenomena that can occur in human vocalizations. After some advice about editing sounds for use as experimental stimuli, our final practical remarks concern how to describe and illustrate an acoustic analysis in a scientific publication. Several appendices are also included, providing a précis of an acoustic analysis, an overview of common scales used in psychological acoustics, a listing of useful frequencies for octave-band analyses, a table of amplitude clipping found in the first edition of a popular set of sounds developed for use in emotions experiments, and a brief bibliography of recommended readings.

Background

Everyday experience suggests that the voice carries clues to the underlying emotional state of vocalizers, an idea that has also played a prominent role in the study of human communication. Darwin (1872/1998) offered the first comprehensive description of the vocal sounds associated with emotion, which was later famously followed by Fairbanks and Pronovost's (1939) report that the fundamental frequency (F_0; commonly referred to as vocal pitch) of speech varied with simulated expressions of contempt, anger, fear, grief, and indifference. This and subsequent studies have routinely shown that F_0-related measures, such as mean F_0 and overall pitch contour, are influenced by affect-related arousal. Moreover, listeners have been found to make reasonably accurate inferences about talkers' arousal levels from hearing such cues in speech samples.

At this point, it is unclear whether the voice provides reliable cues to more detailed aspects of naturally occurring emotional experience, such as positive versus negative valence or more differentiated emotional states (cf. Johnstone & Scherer, 2000; Bachorowski & Owren, 2003). An important obstacle to resolving this issue is that most of the work conducted to date has investigated simulations of vocal emotion as portrayed by amateur or professional actors rather than examining naturally occurring episodes drawn from everyday life. Fortunately, many new experimental paradigms for testing emotion-related vocal acoustics have now been developed, which should help stimulate significant progress in this area.

Acoustic Features of Interest to Emotions Researchers

Of the numerous acoustic features that can be measured from vocal samples, those that have received the most attention have been overall speech rate, measures related to the fundamental frequency, and vocal amplitude (see Scherer, 1986). Vocal perturbation (including moment-to-moment deviations in fundamental frequency) is less often studied but shows great promise as a potential source of emotion-related cuing. Distribution of energy across the frequency range is also likely to be an important aspect of emotion-related vocal acoustics, and vocal-tract filtering effects in particular have received much less empirical attention than they likely deserve. In each case, the frequency patterns in question can be measured both from very short speech segments and as long-term averages calculated over entire utterances.

A Hypothetical Application

Although many of the technical terms used may as yet be unfamiliar, we begin by presenting a brief but full-fledged example of how emotion-related speech data might hypothetically be acquired and analyzed. The reader is encouraged to refer back to this example while working through the more detailed explanations of issues and analyses presented later in the chapter.

Data Acquisition

Consider an experiment designed to compare the effects of experimentally induced arousal and affective valence on participant voice quality. Participants with headworn microphones view emotion-evoking slides from the International Affective Picture System (IAPS; Lang, Bradley, & Cuthbert, 1999), selected so as to induce emotional responses that vary across three levels of arousal (low, medium, high) and two kinds of valence (positive vs. negative). In each case, speech samples consist of participants reading the number used to label each slide (i.e., "slide number *n*"), as well as describing out loud any reactions they have to the images presented. The procedure thus yields both standardized and free-form utterances, which are digitized using a sampling rate of 44.1 kHz and anti-alias filtering at 22.05 kHz or less. Before any further processing, the sounds are down-sampled to 11.025 kHz, with the original versions kept as an archive. The down-sampled files are then preprocessed to remove any DC or AC contamination and normalized to a common peak amplitude. No other filtering is applied. It is noted that clipping occurred in some of the highest-amplitude sounds, and these sounds are excluded from the sample. In a few cases, the input level was so high that all data from the participant had to be discarded.

Data Analysis

The duration of each word is measured and divided by its number of constituent phonemes to produce a measure of overall speech rate by condition. Pitch tracks are then computed for each phrase or sentence, using an analysis window of 0.04 s for males and 0.08 s for females, and a time step of 0.01 s. In each case the window is long enough to incorporate three pitch periods within the expected range of F_0 variation in each sex (males: 75–150 Hz; females: 150–300 Hz). F_0 values of each voiced segment are characterized using means, lowest values, highest values, and overall range. Pitch contours occurring over the course of each phrase or sentence are visually scored as being flat, rising, falling, or chevron-shaped, with the number of pitch-inflection points associated with each being scored as a continuous variable. The pitch-extraction algorithm fails for segments in which the vocal folds are not vibrating which provides a measure of the proportion of voiced versus unvoiced speech. Vocal perturbation is measured using jitter and shimmer values computed from the archived 44.1-kHz files. Harmonic-to-noise ratio is measured in each continuously voiced segment in the down-sampled files, using the same parameters as in earlier pitch extraction. Nonlinear events are also noted and are quantified as a rate of occurrence in each condition.

A long-term-average spectrum is computed over each file, with the spectrum then divided into 100 frequency bins for statistical comparison across files. Linear- predictive-coding spectra are computed around the midpoint of each phoneme and overlaid on corresponding fast-Fourier-transform representations. Both are computed using a 0.03-s Gaussian analysis window, and the number of linear coefficients used is fixed at 14 as a first pass and then varied as needed from 12–16 to produce optimal convergence in a second pass. Frequencies and amplitudes of the first four formants are recovered in each case, along with LPC coefficients themselves. Spectral moments (mean, standard deviation, skewness, and kurtosis) are computed for each Fourier spectrum. Comparison of vocal-amplitude levels in the various conditions is considered but ruled out due to the technical difficulties involved.

Hypothetical Results for High-Arousal Speech

As an example of results that might occur in one condition—comparisons with outcomes with neutrally valenced, low-arousal slides—participants who experienced high arousal in both positively and negatively valenced states tend to show increased speech rate and a number of changes in the source energy of the sounds. For example, mean F_0 and F_0 range both increase, a larger number of the high-arousal pitch contours are found to be generally rising, and the number of inflection points increases. Vocal perturbation also goes up, as reflected in higher jitter and shimmer values but lower harmonic-to-noise ratios. More nonlinear phenomena are observed, particularly in the rate of voice breaks. Each of these outcomes suggest that vocal-fold vibration has become noisier, which is confirmed in finding an upward frequency shift both in short-term spectral moments and spectral tilt and in long-term spectral outcomes. Formant locations do not show a corresponding upward shift, which means that supralaryngeal filtering effects do not account for the observed increase in high-frequency energy. However, the formants do become somewhat more uniformly spaced across various vowel sounds, suggesting that participants are not enunciating as clearly as in the neutral condition. This effect is likely due to increases in speech rate as arousal goes up. High arousal appears to be associated with higher vocal amplitude, but the apparent difference cannot be reliably quantified without a common reference or calibration of the recording equipment.

Basics of Sound and Vocal Production

Basics of Sound

Waveforms and Spectrograms

Sound consists of continuous variation in the air pressure impinging on the tympanic membrane (ear drum). In hearing sound played through a loudspeaker, for instance, the tympanic membrane moves inward and outward in close relationship to the motion of the speaker diaphragm. Mathematically, the simplest kind of sound is a *sine wave,* defined as a continuous sine (or cosine) function of a particular frequency. Figure 15.1 shows a 0.02-s segment of a 500-Hz sine wave, a frequency at which the sine function completes 500 cycles in 1 s. Each cycle consists of a continuous sweep from 0 to a positive peak, back though 0 to a negative peak, and back to 0. Frequencies are typically described in *Hertz* (Hz), which is equivalent to an older term, "cycles per second" (cps), that is no longer used. The amount of time required for completion of a single sine-wave cycle is the *period* of the waveform, with frequency and period thus being inverse quantities (i.e., frequency = 1/period; period = 1/frequency).

The 500-Hz sine wave illustrated in Figure 15.1, therefore, has a period of 0.002 s, and 10 complete cycles are shown. Any cyclical signal is referred to as *periodic,* with individual sine signals being referred to as *simple periodic* waves. Sine waves can be fully characterized based on just two other properties, namely amplitude and phase. Amplitude is measured from negative-going to positive-going peaks, whereas phase refers to the relative location of the waveform within its full (360-degree) cycle at a particular point in time. Figure 15.1 also shows a second 500-Hz sine wave that is 180 degrees out of phase with the first. Individual sine waves can be added, which in a digital signal means algebraic summation of amplitude values at corresponding points in each sound. If the two 500-Hz sine waves of Figure 15.1 are added, the result is perfect cancellation. However, if the first 500-Hz waveform is added to the 1000-Hz sine wave that is also shown in the figure, the result is a more complexly patterned but still cyclical signal referred to as a *complex periodic* wave.

Whereas individual sine waves are pure and tonal in quality, complex periodic waves take on other auditory properties, becoming fuller and richer sounding. Depending on the mix of frequencies and amplitudes involved, the sounds can range from pleasant and sonorous to quite buzzy, rough, and noxious. When many different sine waves with unrelated frequencies are present, the sound becomes noisy. Although there are many different kinds of noise, *white noise* is a variety in which waveform energy varies randomly from moment to moment. The result is an ever-changing, *aperiodic* sound with random distribution of energy across all possible frequencies. The statistical distribution of energy values in the waveform creates subtly different noise variants, including *uniform* and *Gaussian* noise. A 0.02-s segment of Gaussian noise is illustrated at the bottom of Figure 15.1.

The frequency content of several of these waveforms is shown in Figure 15.2, beginning with the 500-Hz sine wave displayed both as a single spectrum, or *spectral slice* (a frequency-energy display), and as a *spectrogram* (a time-frequency display). The spectral slice reveals the energy of each frequency component over some particular segment of the waveform and has no time dimension. In contrast, a spectrogram reveals the

Figure 15.1. A sine wave with frequency of 500 Hz is a simple periodic signal with a period of 0.002 s (*upper left*). It would be exactly canceled out if added to an identical 500-Hz signal that is out of phase by one-half cycle, or 180 degrees (*upper right*). However, when this 500 Hz sine wave is added to a 1,000-Hz signal (*middle left*), the point-by-point sum is a complex periodic signal. A white noise (*bottom center*) includes sine waves of all possible frequencies whose amplitudes at any given moment vary in accordance with a random probability function, such as a Gaussian distribution.

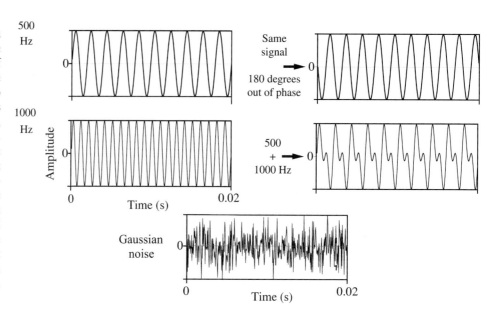

amount of energy present at each frequency component over repeated segments. In this display, the amount of energy present at any given time is represented by the darkness of shading at that point. Spectral displays are also shown for the 500 + 1000-Hz waveform and for the Gaussian noise.

Filtering and Resonance

Filtering refers to frequency-dependent energy attenuation and is a property of all media that sound passes through. Because high frequencies are more readily absorbed when passing through physical obstacles, for example, it is specifically the bass one hears through the wall when a stereo is playing loudly in an adjacent apartment. Although a variety of such effects are possible in the real world, filtering is at its most flexible in the digital domain, where waveforms are represented as a series of numerical values. In this case, filtering is simply a matter of using a particular algorithm to transform this number stream in useful ways.

Digital filters have a variety of names, often commemorating the individual who developed the algorithm used and studied its properties (e.g., *Bessel, Blackman, Butterworth, Chebychev*). It is more important to understand the terms that describe a filter's overall effects—for instance, whether it is designed to *pass* or *stop* energy at particular frequencies—and which frequency *bands* are affected (see Figure 15.3). A *lowpass* filter is meant to pass the energy below a designated *corner frequency*, while removing energy above that point. Conversely, a *highpass* filter is meant to pass energy above a particular frequency while removing energy below that point. A filter can also have *bandpass* or *bandstop* properties, meaning that it targets an intermediate frequency range and has both upper and lower corner frequencies.

Unfortunately, no filter is perfect, for instance, by uniformly removing or passing all energy in particular frequency bands or having perfectly square corners. There are always frequency-dependent heterogeneities in both passbands and stopbands (noticeable as *ripple* effects in the filter's *frequency-response function*) and a transition zone between adjacent passbands and stopbands. This *attenuation slope* or *rejection rate* is usually expressed in deciBels (dB) per *octave* (an octave is a doubling or halving of frequency). Filters are also described based on amount of attenuation in dB that occurs at a particular frequency or in a particular range of frequencies (e.g., −40 dB in the stopband).

Resonance is another important acoustical property of all physical objects, and it is related to filtering. Resonance essentially means that different objects have differentiated attenuation or damping effects across the frequency range. If one imparts a single energy pulse to a physical object (for instance, by rapping on a tabletop), the acoustic energy produced is a joint function of the frequency content of the original energy pulse (the rap) and the frequency-dependent attenuation effects of the object being impacted (the table). Those filtering effects depend on the physical properties of that object (such as density, composition, and thickness) and can shape the energy pulse in ways that are both specific and distinctive. Thus, when energy is imparted to a physical object and movement of that object sets air into motion, one can often tell from the frequency content of the resulting sound what kind of object has been struck.

This resonance property becomes particularly apparent over time when an energy source affects a *resonator* repeatedly. The wood in a guitar, for example, is repeatedly set into motion by impulse energy that the musician imparts to its strings. Each string produces a complex and nearly periodic waveform that has its own heterogeneous frequency pattern. These waves set the wood of the guitar into motion, with the wood then passing some frequencies well while attenuating others. Incident energy from the guitar strings also travels

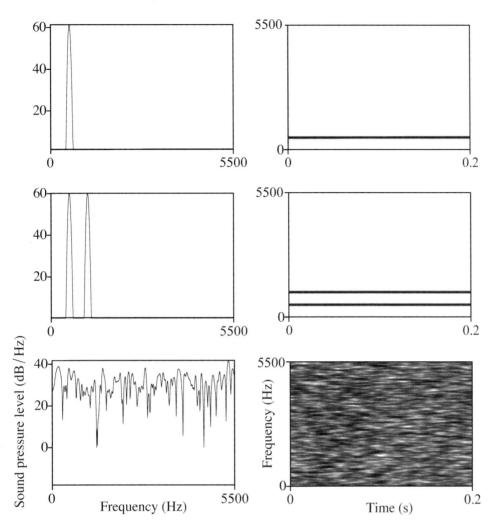

Figure 15.2. Frequency content of a 500-Hz sine wave, a 500-plus-1000-Hz complex wave, and a Gaussian noise shown through Fourier spectra (*left*) and narrowband spectrograms (*right*).

within the enclosed space of the guitar body and, when it reaches the back and sides of that space, is partially absorbed and partially reflected. The general rule for waveforms that encounter physical objects is that high-frequency energy is affected more than low-frequency energy, meaning, for instance, that higher frequencies will be more susceptible to reflection, whereas lower-frequency components are more likely to simply pass right through the barrier. In addition, waveforms that happen to be at either a positive or a negative amplitude maximum (i.e., 90° or 270°) or minimum (e.g., 0° or 360°) when encountering the barrier will reflect better than those at other phases.

The result is that, depending on the size and shape of the guitar body, energy at some frequencies will be differentially attenuated, whereas energy at others will be reflected back and forth within the guitar body. Because of this repeated reflection, energy at these frequencies will encounter the new wavefronts being produced as the strings vibrate, producing summation and cancellation effects over time. At any given moment, some energy will be passing to the outside world through the guitar's body and sound hole, but much of it will be reverberating within the instrument. The guitar is thus acting as a resonator, accumulating energy at particular frequencies over time and removing it at other frequencies. The energy passing out of the guitar at any point in time is what listeners hear, with the size, shape, and wood of a guitar combining to affect its resonance properties and hence its overall sound quality, or *timbre*.

Source-Filter Theory

The concepts of input energy and resonance effects are critical in the *source-filter* approach to understanding vocal acoustics (Fant, 1960; Stevens, 2000). Although originally developed to account for the acoustics of human vowels in particular, this model is now routinely applied both to other kinds of speech sounds and to vocal production in nonhuman mammals. Source-filter principles are therefore also critical in understanding the effects that emotional state may have on vocal production (Scherer, 1986).

Source

In the source-filter approach, vocal acoustics are treated as a linear combination of source energy and subsequent filtering

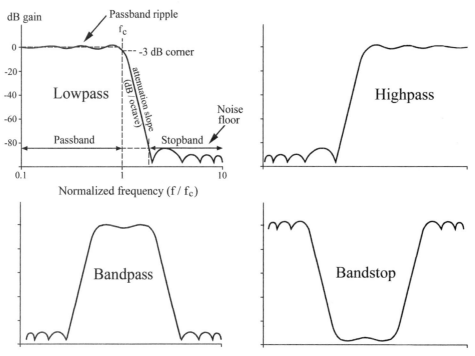

Figure 15.3. Key filter characteristics are illustrated in the top left panel, including the passband, the stopband, the corner frequency (fc; also known as the half-power point, where amplitude has been attenuated by 3 dB), the passband ripple (artifactual variation in filter response in the passband), the noise floor (noise inherent to the electronic device in the absence of input), and the attenuation slope (the rate of attenuation in the stopband, measured in dB per octave). The various panels illustrate basic features for a lowpass filter (removes energy above the corner frequency), highpass filter (removes energy below the corner frequency), bandpass filter (removes energy above and below two corner frequencies), and bandstop filter (removes energy between two corner frequencies).

effects of the pharyngeal, oral, and nasal cavities that together make up the *supralaryngeal vocal tract* (see Figure 15.4). For vowel sounds, source energy arises from air passing through the *glottis*, which is the opening between the *vocal folds* (known informally as the vocal cords). The vocal folds are in turn tissue folds enclosed in the cartilaginous *larynx* (informally referred to as the voice box). The source energy in vocal production can be either *voiced* or *unvoiced*, referring to whether or not the vocal folds are vibrating. Unvoiced sounds are noisy, including those produced by creating turbulence in the air moving through the vocal tract (e.g., "h," "s," and "th" sounds). Voiced (or *phonated*) sounds are those in which the vocal folds do vibrate, usually in a synchronized, quasi-periodic fashion. All vowels are produced this way, and it is the regular vocal-fold vibration involved that gives these sounds their relatively clear, tonal quality. The basic rate of vocal-fold vibration is referred to as the *fundamental frequency* (F_0) of a voiced sound, and this physical property is also a primary correlate of the psychological experience of pitch. F_0 properties, in particular, have figured prominently in investigations of source-related cues to vocalizer emotional state.

Filter

If the quasi-periodic energy resulting from vocal-fold vibration could be heard in isolation, it would be quite buzzy. After leaving the larynx, however, the energy of speech passes through the supralaryngeal vocal tract. Here, the resonance properties (or *formants*) of the pharyngeal, oral, and nasal cavities act as filters, with striking effects. As with any filter, the outcome is that energy in some frequency regions passes relatively unimpeded, whereas energy in other regions is strongly attenuated. Precisely which frequencies are passed or removed is determined by a number of factors, including vocal-tract length and the size and shape of each cavity. In articulate speech, human talkers execute rapid movements of the tongue and jaw specifically to change the dimensions of these cavities, alter their filtering effects, and thereby produce distinctive sounds. For example, putting the tongue at the back of the teeth during phonation has different filtering effects than raising it toward the roof of the mouth. Even facial expressions can have a measurable impact on vocal-tract filtering effects, as has been found in speech produced while smiling.

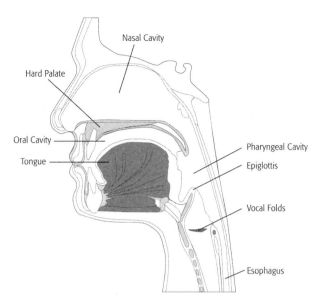

Figure 15.4. A schematic cross-sectional illustration of the basic anatomy of the human vocal tract. Vocalizations usually involve vibration of the vocal folds, enclosed in the cartilaginous larynx (not shown). Energy then passes through the pharyngeal, oral, and nasal cavities, which together make up the supra-laryngeal vocal tract. Sound emerging at the lips thus represents the combined properties of both source energy and subsequent filtering effects.

Digital Representation of Sound

Digital Signals

To represent sound digitally, continuous variation in sound-pressure levels is converted to a series of discrete values (illustrated in the top panel of Figure 15.5). This series is created by an *analog-to-digital* (*A/D*) converter and reproduced as sound by a *digital-to-analog* (*D/A*) converter. The number of bits in the converter determines the accuracy with which amplitude variation can be represented. That number has improved dramatically over time, going from 8 bits (with just 256 integer values available to cover the entire amplitude range of a sound) to 12 bits (4096 integer values ranging from –2047 to +2048) to the current standard of 16 bits (65,536 integer values ranging from –32,767 to +32,768). However, A/D-D/A *wordwidths* of 32 or even higher have also become available.

Digital Recording

Traditionally, sound data have been recorded onto an analog medium and then digitized in a separate, time-consuming step. The advent of digital recorders now allows direct recording to digitized format, including both to tape (DAT recorder) and to CD/DVD media. However, the formats used on those devices are not usually the same as those used on personal computers, and should be checked ahead of time.

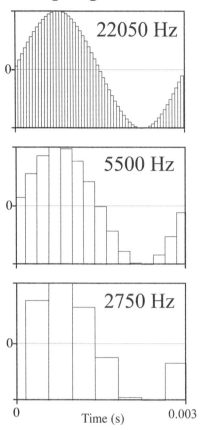

Figure 15.5. The individual samples that make up digital representations of a single cycle of a 500-Hz waveform reveal dramatic changes in quantization fidelity across sampling rates of 22050, 5500, and 2750 Hz.

Compatibility is assured for DAT recorders that can output audio data in a form that can be read bit for bit (for example, via SPDIF ports) and for CD/DVD recorders that are able to store files in computer-friendly formats like AIFF or WAV (discussed in the section on digital representation of sound). But it is never appropriate to record to compressed formats that discard part of the data, as is the case for such products as minidisc and MP3 players. These devices are able to produce greatly compressed recordings, but they do so by using algorithms that explicitly remove some elements of the sounds (those deemed to have the least effect on aesthetic enjoyment of music and intelligibility of speech). When sound is used as scientific data, it should always be recorded, archived, and analyzed in a form that remains as close to the original event as possible.

Amplitude Clipping

Digital sampling requires that the entire dynamic range of a sound be represented within the numerical range of the A/D converter. Ideally, the input level of the recording device will be set so that peak amplitudes are captured as values close to the highest number available (top panel, Figure 15.6). If the input is set too low (middle panel, Figure 15.6), only a fraction of the available values are being used, background noise levels become noticeably higher, and overall amplitude resolution suffers. However, setting the input level too high is even worse. In that case, any and all input amplitudes that exceed the available numerical range will be *clipped* and set to the same maximum digital value. The resulting representation both looks and sounds *distorted* (bottom panel, Figure 15.6). Amplitude clipping can occur either when recording onto analog or digital tape and when an analog signal is being digitized. In each case, the waveform takes on a squared-off or flattened appearance. Amplitude clipping is one of the most fundamental mistakes one can make when working with sound and should always be avoided.

Sampling Frequency (or Rate)

Sampling frequency refers to the rate at which the A/D converter reads incoming voltage values from a microphone or line-level source (e.g., tape recorder or CD recorder) and determines the range of frequencies that can be represented. Higher sampling rates produce more accurate representations

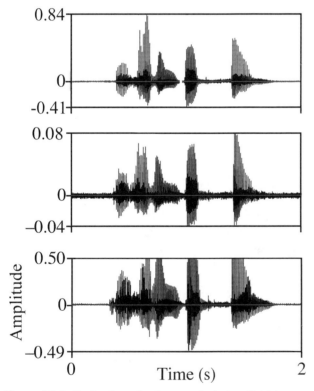

Figure 15.6. Setting input levels properly during digitizing makes a dramatic difference, as shown when the same speech signal is acquired at an appropriate level (*top*), so low that the signal-to-noise ratio suffers (*middle*), and so high that clipping occurs (*bottom*).

but also produce larger files that use more memory and take longer to process during analysis. Although sampling can occur at any frequency, the consumer electronics industry has in recent years created its own de facto standards. Two common sampling frequencies for CD and DAT recordings are 44100 and 48000 Hz (44.1 and 48.0 kHz, respectively). When working with human vocalizations, rates of 22.05 and 11.025 kHz are, therefore, now often used as readily realized fractions of 44.100 kHz. Sampling frequencies of 20.0, 16.0, 10.0, and 8.0 kHz were more typical in speech research before the spread of CD technology, and these rates are still sometimes used.

Nyquist Frequency and Aliasing

A sound wave is typically modeled as being the sum of a series of discrete frequency components, all of which have to be captured using a single, fixed sampling rate. As shown in Figure 15.5, digital representation is more accurate when the sampling rate is much higher than the frequency being modeled. Here, accuracy means having more rather than fewer sample points "mapping out" the energy at each frequency. In the figure, sampling a 500-Hz sine wave at 22.05 kHz produces a much smoother and more detailed representation of the signal than does a rate of 5500 Hz. At 2750 Hz, the representation has become quite crude.

At a bare minimum, a sine wave must be represented by at least two samples per cycle, one from the positive-going half and one from the negative-going half. For any given sampling rate, in other words, the maximum frequency that can be represented is exactly one-half that rate. Frequency content above the halfway point (referred to as the *Nyquist* or *folding frequency*) cannot be even minimally represented and therefore must be filtered out before A/D or D/A conversion. Computer sound cards therefore typically include built-in *anti-alias filters* that are automatically applied both when digitizing and playing sounds. Undersampling, or *aliasing*, occurs if energy above the Nyquist frequency is not filtered out, thereby producing spurious energy at lower frequencies in the digitized version.

Sound-File Formats

A digital sound file can take many different forms, although most are fundamentally similar. In the early days, each different manufacturer or vendor seemed to use its own unique format. Fortunately, that confusing variety has now been distilled to two predominant file types, namely *audio interchange file format* (AIFF) and *WAV* format. It is usually easy to convert from one to the other, and many sound programs can handle both. However, one can also encounter different variants within each type, particularly for WAV files. It can therefore still happen that a particular program creates WAV files that are incompatible with some of the other software being used.

Sound-File Structure

A sound file consists of two basic parts: a "header," usually located at the beginning of the file, and amplitude data. The header contains critical information about the file and its contents, such as the file name, sampling frequency, how the data are coded, number of channels (mono or stereo), file duration, and user- or program-generated comments about the file. The header is usually (although not always) of fixed length, which means that a sound program has to "know" how long that header is.

The true data that follow in the file are quite simple, being no more than a series of amplitude values. However, they can be stored in a variety of numerical formats, which is usually what causes incompatibility among sound files and programs. A mono sound file consists of a single "channel" of numbers, in which, for example, sampling at 44.1 kHz for 1 s would create a waveform file consisting of 44100 values. Details of how the values are encoded are not important here, but a few points are of interest. First is that one difference between AIFF and WAV formats lies in the "direction" of data storage. In AIFF, the convention is that the lowest-value bits are at the beginning of the file, putting the most significant bits at the end and making the file *big-endian*. WAV files are just the opposite, being *little-endian* files whose least significant bits are placed at the end. Second, no matter what encoding form the sound file uses, most programs can convert their sound files to "raw" binary form or to numerical values stored as text. In that case, the header information is discarded, which means the user must keep a separate record of the sampling rates involved. But the advantage is that once converted to binary or text format, the sound data can easily be read by other software.

Examining a sound file in text format is instructive, as the file becomes no more than a long series of numbers. The numbers themselves vary, depending on both the sound card and program used. If a 16-bit card was used, for instance, they may range from −32,767 to +32,768, or from 0 to 65,536. For the latter, the sound program is subtracting 32,767 when displaying the file, using this *offset value* to center the waveform around a midpoint of 0. Offset values can play an important role when files are converted from one format to another. Sound-file values may also be represented as generic voltages or normalized to an arbitrary but particularly useful range such as −1.0 to +1.0.

Practical Advice

Recording

Signal levels can vary dramatically in live recordings. In human speech, for example, energy levels are typically low in noisy consonants such as "f" and "s" but are much higher in vowel sounds (illustrated in Figure 15.7). Amplitude ranges can also vary dramatically in emotional speech, for instance, between calm and excited utterances. The upshot is that, although input levels should always be held constant once recording has begun, no single setting is ideal for capturing the full range of likely amplitude variation. With input levels turned up, the highest amplitude components are clipped and distorted. With input level turned down, the lowest amplitude components virtually disappear into the background noise. One useful strategy is, therefore, to split the microphone output into two input channels on the recording device, setting one channel at a lower level to accommodate higher amplitude elements and setting the other at a higher level to accommodate lower amplitude elements. Commercial "splitter" components are available for this purpose.

Digitizing

As in recording, one cannot let peak signal values exceed the maximum representable amplitude when digitizing sounds. Clipping distorts both the frequency content and the audible quality of digitized sound. Nonetheless, one should always be turning the input level up as much as possible to produce an optimal representation of the sound. This conundrum can make digitizing a laborious, time-consuming process that requires careful adjustments to input levels as the signal is acquired in relatively small chunks. Realistically, the goal should be to get the bulk of peaks in a given waveform to about halfway between 0 and the maximum representable range (either positive or negative). Achieving that outcome, one has used all but one bit of the A/D-board's representational capacity. In addition, the shorter the sound segment being captured, the easier it is to find the right input level. It is also good practice to leave a bit of room both before and after the signal of interest.

Archiving Sound Files: Sampling Rate and Format

When analyzing human vocalizations, sampling rates as low as 8.0, 11.025, or 16.0 kHz can all be acceptable and even advisable for many analyses. However, some analyses de-

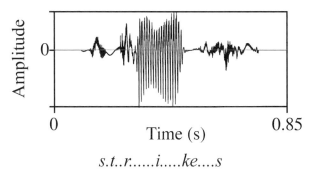

Figure 15.7. The waveform of the word *strikes* spoken by a male talker illustrates that the amplitude of noisy (fricative) sounds such as *s* are routinely quite low in comparison with harmonically structured (vowel) sounds such as *i*.

mand higher sampling rates, and the best approach is therefore to sample and archive the data at a relatively high rate, such as 44.1 kHz. One can then down-sample those files prior to analysis, for instance, by retaining every second or every fourth sample point to create rates of 22.05 and 11.025 kHz, respectively (anti-alias filtering is again required). More complex down-sampling can also be performed, but using integer fractions is best. Because storage capacity is no longer a critical constraint in digital processing, archiving sound at higher sampling frequencies has become preferable to running the risk of having to redigitize sounds that were sampled at too low a rate. For simplicity and compatibility with scientific collaborators, sound archives should probably also be based on the most common available formats, such as AIFF or WAV. These two formats are in widespread use and are likely to remain so for many years. File-format conversion capabilities have become sufficiently common that binary or text formats are rarely needed. If the need does arise, however, a generic binary format is preferred over conversion to text, as the latter creates much larger files.

Anti-Alias Filtering

When there is a choice, it is good policy to set the anti-aliasing cutoff frequency somewhat below the Nyquist frequency, thereby removing energy at the frequencies at which the digital representation is poorest. However, one cannot take the quality of filtering for granted—inexpensive sound cards and devices such as video cameras may not do a particularly good job in combating aliasing and must be checked before being used in scientific work.

The International Affective Digitized Sounds (IADS)

In addition to the IAPS image set mentioned earlier, Bradley, Lang, and colleagues have also developed a set of digitized sounds for use in emotions research (Bradley & Lang, 2000). These files are supplied with normative affective ratings (i.e., pleasure, arousal, and dominance), potentially making them a very useful tool. However, a number of these sounds are clipped, some substantially so. For research in which the sounds are used simply to induce an affective response, clipping may make little difference. On the other hand, if the nature of the sound itself is important, clipping becomes a confounding factor. This issue is therefore being addressed by the developers (Bradley, personal communication, August 2006), and, in the interim, it is advisable to take the amount of clipping in a given file into account when selecting stimuli for experimental use. To help in those decisions, we have included a table of the number of clipped peaks in the current IADS set (appendix D). If distortion is a potentially important factor in an experiment, sounds in which clipping is most likely to be audible to listeners should be excluded. As a practical strategy, we suggest avoiding the files with 50 or more clipped peaks.

Before Analysis Begins

Preprocessing

All sound files should be *preprocessed* before analysis, both to remove possible artifacts produced in recording and digitizing and to at least partially compensate for amplitude variation among the files. Preprocessing can thus make the sound files as uniform as possible before analyses and comparisons begin. The procedures involved need only be performed once on each file.

Removing DC Offset

One artifact that can be introduced into the signal either in recording or in digitizing is *direct-current* (*DC*) contamination. The resulting *DC-offset* is a constant voltage that pushes the overall waveform away from a midpoint of 0 volts (top panel of Figure 15.8). The waveform then looks normal except for being centered on a net positive or net negative value. This problem can be addressed by subtracting the overall mean of the waveform from each individual value. However, if the amount of DC offset fluctuates visibly over the course

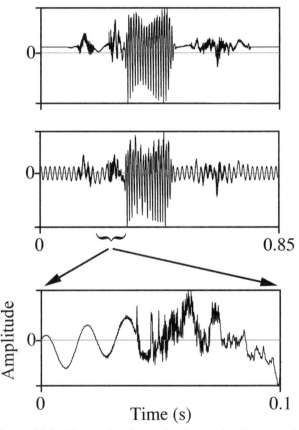

Figure 15.8. The word *strikes* spoken by a male talker is used to illustrate the effect of DC-offset (*top*) and contamination by 60-Hz AC energy (*middle*). A magnified view of a short section of the latter shows that the signal can take on the appearance of "riding on" the 60–Hz energy.

of a waveform, the problem is more difficult to remedy and is likely symptomatic of a problem in the sound card or other hardware component.

Removing 60-Hz Energy

Another kind of problem arises if *alternating current (AC)* audio components used in recording or digitizing are imperfectly grounded. When this occurs, signals can become contaminated with 60-Hz energy (the frequency of AC cyclical polarity; middle and bottom panels of Figure 15.8). The result is a signal that undulates 60 times per second, with the true signal riding on top of this slow wave. Such energy should be removed prior to further analysis, and if there is no energy of interest below 60 Hz, a highpass filter set just above 60 Hz can be used. If there is energy of interest at the lowest frequencies, a bandstop filter can be set just above and just below 60 Hz. In either case, it is also advisable to find the source of the 60-Hz contamination and to remove it, either through better grounding or by replacing the culprit component.

Amplitude Scaling

A final preprocessing step is to normalize the amplitude of each file. Because signal amplitude is sensitive even to minute changes in recording conditions, it is almost never possible to preserve reliable information about the absolute amplitude of the original sound. For example, the distance between sound source and microphone, input level on the recorder, and input level during digitizing all have marked effects on the apparent amplitude of a digitized signal. However, relative amplitude comparisons are still possible, especially within a file or across files for which one has some additional standard for comparison. Having lost the absolute amplitude information anyway, it is useful to rescale each waveform to the full amplitude range available for the file. For example, if the sound card supports 16-bit files, the representable range is from −32,767 to +32,768. A waveform can be rescaled by finding the most extreme value in the file, determining the scaling factor needed to set it to the maximum value available, and then multiplying every point in the file by that amount.

Practical Advice

In many cases, there is no DC offset or 60-Hz energy to remove from the file. However, there is little cost to routinely performing these manipulations if the process can be automated. Amplitude normalization also seems a reasonable step to always take, even though it produces only an approximation of standardization. Many other sorts of filtering techniques are also available, including a variety of "postproduction" algorithms designed to improve the aesthetics of the listening experience. Such techniques are often applied to older musical recordings, for instance in order to remove hiss, hum, clicks, and pops. We suggest being very conservative about

using such techniques in scientific analyses, in which aesthetics are much less important than the integrity of the data. Rather than relying on remedial filtering applied after the fact, researchers should focus on improving recording conditions and, if necessary, restrict their analyses to the best-quality recordings. If after-the-fact filtering is used, then the same operations should be performed uniformly on all the files included in an analysis.

Measuring Duration

The duration of a sound is one of its most basic characteristics, and measuring duration is therefore part of virtually every acoustic analysis. In theory, the procedure is quite simple—one marks the beginning and end of each segment of interest in the waveform file, retrieves those times, and calculates duration. In practice, however, even this measurement can involve some guesswork and error. Two common problems are the presence of background noise that can obscure the beginnings and endings of target events, and reverberation effects in the recording environment that make it difficult to find the end of the original sound.

A good strategy for measuring duration is to display both the waveform and a corresponding wideband spectrogram, with linked cursor placement in the two images. Signal onsets and offsets are often easier to see in the time-frequency display provided by a spectrogram than in the time-amplitude waveform display. Using a wideband spectrogram is important because its temporal resolution is superior to that of a narrowband spectrogram. However, sometimes the components of interest become visible only when using finer frequency resolution, in which case all three displays should be examined simultaneously. The event of interest can then be located in the narrowband version, with start and end times marked based on the wideband display.

The obvious approach is to simply mark signal boundaries at points at which signal energy seems to first appear (or disappear), whether in the form of visible cycles (no matter how small) or as other energy that is distinguishable from that seen in immediately preceding or following segments. This approach can nonetheless be problematic, such as when some target sounds have better signal-to-noise ratios than others. Duration measurements may then be systematically longer when the signals are better, with the beginnings and endings of the poorer ones routinely disappearing into the background noise. The converse problem can arise when signals have very high signal-to-noise ratios but trail off over a relatively extended period of time. In quasi-periodic signals such as vowel sounds, minute but unmistakable waveform cycles can be evident both well before and well after the perceptible portion of the sound. Deciding how to set the temporal boundaries, therefore, often becomes a pragmatic issue best addressed by adopting a strategy that can yield comparable results across all the sounds of interest regardless of variation in recording quality. Later, we suggest an approach of "splitting the difference" in setting beginning and ending markers.

Another issue to address is that of *reverberation*. When sounds are recorded in environments in which waveform energy is reflected from nearby surfaces, the reflected energy can meld with the ongoing source energy to produce a signal that in a spectrogram appears to have a "trailer" or "tail." Reverberation effects are inevitable in many recording environments, especially those in which emotions researchers are likely to be working. Here again, the best strategy may be one of minimizing rather than trying to eliminate measurement error. Close examination of both narrowband and wideband representations can often be helpful in determining endpoints, bearing in mind that reverberant energy will most likely mirror whatever the original signal was doing as it ended. One can therefore look for the point in the latter part of a reverberated sound at which it seems to become a static reflection or extension of immediately preceding energy.

Speech Rate

Measuring speech rate is also typically more challenging than one might imagine, in this case due to complications created by pauses, lexical content, and variability of word length. Characterizing speech rate basically requires that one can quantify the amount of speech produced, based on the number of phonemes, syllables, or words present. The simplest approach is therefore to count the number of phonemes, syllables, or words occurring over the duration of a sentence. Rate calculations can be made both with and without pauses, with the number, duration, and variability of pauses themselves also being potentially informative about the talker's emotional state. Some attempt to control for lexical content, and word-length variability should be built into the larger experimental design, where the question of what participants will be saying is an important consideration when thinking about how to measure the effect of emotional state on vocal acoustics.

Practical Advice

As noted, several factors can make it challenging to determine the beginnings and endings of target segments, including background noise and reverberation. In each case, the best advice may be to simply minimize the average error that occurs. When the onset or offset is obscured by noise or reverberation, for example, one approach is to normalize the amplitudes of the sounds and set the beginning and ending marks at points at which the target energy crosses some threshold proportion of the maximum value (e.g., 0.05 or 0.1). A simpler strategy is to find the earliest possible point at which there is some realistic possibility that the signal is starting (or ending) and then set the boundary halfway between that point and where it is certain that the sound has not started (or not ended). For simplicity and consistency, sound onsets and offsets should be marked as close to zero-crossing points as possible.

When characterizing speech rate, syllable-counting is arguably the most straightforward approach, as it obviates the need for specific knowledge of phonemic-level structure and alleviates at least some of the difficulties of variation in content and word length. In vocal-production experiments, participants should be required to produce both stock speech (e.g., standard phrases or sentences) and free-form narrative. In this way, converging evidence of speech-rate effects can be sought in utterances that are either fixed in content and length or free to vary in both dimensions.

Analyzing the Frequency Spectrum

Fourier Analysis

Fourier analysis is the most used mathematical tool in acoustic analysis, and perhaps even in all of Western science. The basic method is to *transform* data in the *time domain* to the *frequency domain,* or vice versa. The key is a theorem that any infinitely long and periodic time-series signal (time domain) can be exactly re-created as the sum of an infinitely long series of harmonically related sine (or cosine) components (frequency domain). In other words, an infinitely repeating signal, no matter how complex, can be represented as the sum of a fundamental frequency and an infinite series of additional frequencies that are integer multiples of that base frequency. By adjusting the amplitudes and phases of each component as needed, one can create an exact match to the original waveform. For many years, the immense number of calculations required by a full *discrete Fourier transform (DFT)* severely limited its usefulness. However, that barrier was lifted by Cooley and Tukey (1965), whose *fast Fourier transform (FFT)* greatly reduced the number of computations needed by restricting the number of waveform sample points involved be exactly a power of 2 (e.g., 64, 128, 256, 512, 1,024). This more tractable approach is now so widely implemented that the terms FFT and Fourier transform are often used interchangeably.

Real-world waveforms are, of course, never truly periodic —they are neither infinitely long nor perfectly cyclical. Although waveforms can thus be *quasi-periodic,* many are also noisy and aperiodic. Fourier analysis is nonetheless applied to all waveforms, by using a mathematical sleight of hand. The trick is to use a finite-length *analysis window* to transform the signal one piece at a time. Each chunk of waveform is modeled using a series of equally spaced frequency components whose amplitudes and phases are set so that the series, when summed, recreates the original piece as well as possible. This approach handles each windowed segment as an isolated event, in effect treating it as a single cycle of an infinitely long periodic waveform. In other words, even if the larger waveform is entirely aperiodic, each chunk becomes a single "cycle" of a hypothetical periodic signal. Spacing of the resulting "harmonic" components produced by the Fourier transform becomes the de facto frequency resolution of the analysis. If the sound is quasi-periodic, the energy will be largely concentrated in true harmonics, meaning the Fourier components that fall closest to the fundamental frequency and its integer multiples (visible in the top panels of Figure 15.9). Energy will be present at other frequencies as well, but their amplitudes will generally be much lower. Fourier analysis produces both amplitude and phase values at each frequency, but the latter are usually considered unimportant to human auditory perception and are therefore discarded.

Analysis Window Length

Although ubiquitous, Fourier analysis is simply a modeling technique. Like all models, a Fourier transform necessarily distorts the data in various ways, among the most important of which is the *time-frequency trade-off* or *uncertainty principle*. Specifically, short analysis windows with correspondingly good temporal resolution produce low-resolution frequency spectra, whereas achieving high-resolution frequency spectra requires long analysis windows that have requisitely bad temporal resolution (illustrated in Figure 15.9). The trade-off would not be so problematic if signals were always uniform, or *stationary* over time; analysis windows could then be made very long in order to maximize frequency resolution. However, the frequency content of human vocalizations changes constantly, particularly in speech. Because Fourier transformation treats the windowed waveform piece as an essentially static event (exactly one cycle of an infinitely repeating signal), any frequency component that changes over the course of an analysis window is being averaged. Avoiding these averaging errors in nonstationary signals thus requires using shorter analysis windows. The strategy of comparing both narrowband (longer analysis window) and wideband (shorter analysis window) spectra and spectrograms in speech analysis is a direct reflection of the inherent constraints of Fourier analysis. Each of the particular window lengths typically used represents a compromise between accuracy and time and frequency domains, and using both together is a way to negotiate this need to compromise.

Analysis Window Shape

The notion of an analysis window is actually metaphorical—"windowing" refers to analyzing the waveform one piece at a time while differentially weighting each of the sample points that make up that piece. Although each point can be treated similarly in the calculation, this *rectangular* window approach usually produces large, artifactual *side lobes* in the Fourier spectrum due to abrupt amplitude discontinuities occurring at the beginning and end of the waveform piece selected for analysis. Fourier transformation therefore relies on a tapering strategy in which points that are close to the center of the window are weighted much more heavily than are more distant points. These kinds of analysis windows, or *tapers*, are typically named for their shapes or originators, including *triangular* (Bartlett), *parabolic* (Welch), *Hanning* (the square of a half-cycle of a sine wave), and *Hamming* (a "raised" version of this sine-square window) types. A *Gaussian* window is the best choice for avoiding lobes in a Fourier spectrum,

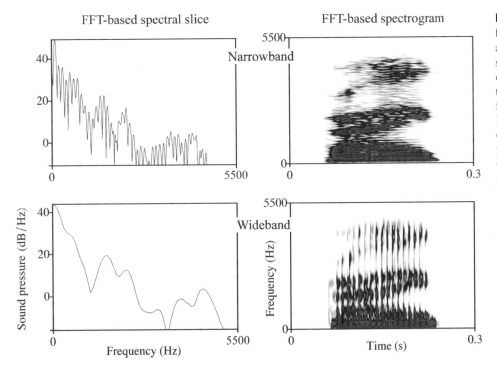

Figure 15.9. The "time-frequency" tradeoff of Fourier analysis is illustrated in both single spectra and in spectrograms of a vowel sound from a male talker whose fundamental frequency is approximately 100 Hz. Analysis using a 0.03-s Gaussian window produces narrowband representations (*top*) whose 43-Hz frequency resolution makes the individual harmonics visible. A 0.005-s Gaussian window produces wideband representations (*bottom*) whose 260-Hz resolution averages across the harmonics. However, this averaging makes it easy to see the talker's formants and provides sufficient temporal resolution to reveal vertical striations corresponding to individual glottal pulses (*left bottom*).

although it requires twice as much computation time. However, processing has now become very fast, even on personal computers, and has made Gaussian windowing the preferred approach in vocal acoustics research.

Distribution of Energy Across the Frequency Range

No matter how it is computed, a Fourier spectrum is composed of a very large number of individual points. Creating the spectrum is, therefore, only half the battle—one also has to be able to compare these spectral outcomes across sounds. Conceptually, the simplest approach might be just to treat each amplitude value as an individual data point, comparing the spectra on a point-by-point basis across sounds, individual vocalizers, and conditions. A better approach is to simplify the spectrum in any of a variety of ways before comparisons are made. For example, the spectrum can be modeled as a function defined by a much smaller number of polynomial coefficients using *linear predictive coding* techniques (discussed in detail in the later section on analyzing vocal-tract filtering effects). Alternatively, one can use some simple global measures to capture the overall shape of the spectrum, including overall tilt and the mean, standard deviation, skewness, and kurtosis of the spectral distribution. Finally, the spectrum can be summarized by integrating across the energy in adjacent frequencies to create a smaller number of *frequency bins* or *frequency bands*. Outcomes for spectral tilt, spectral moments, and frequency binning are each illustrated for both an unvoiced and a voiced speech sound in Figure 15.10.

Spectral Tilt

Measuring the overall tilt of a Fourier spectrum is a simple and widely used approach to global frequency characterization. There are a number of ways to quantify tilt; for example, using linear regression to fit a line to the individual points that make up the spectrum. The slope of this regression line is then used to characterize spectral tilt. When only voiced sounds are of interest, spectral tilt has also been measured as the difference between the first and second harmonic amplitudes, measured in dB (i.e., H1-H2, which is equivalent to F_0-H2). *Spectral emphasis* is a related measure, referring to the relative mean energy values in the lower and upper halves of the frequency spectrum.

Spectral Moments

A lesser used but very promising approach to characterizing a spectrum is to treat it as a statistical distribution to which standard measures of descriptive statistics can be applied. To do so, the amplitude of each Fourier component is first transformed from logarithmic dB values to linear pascal units (see Appendix B). Taking the inverse log changes the Fourier

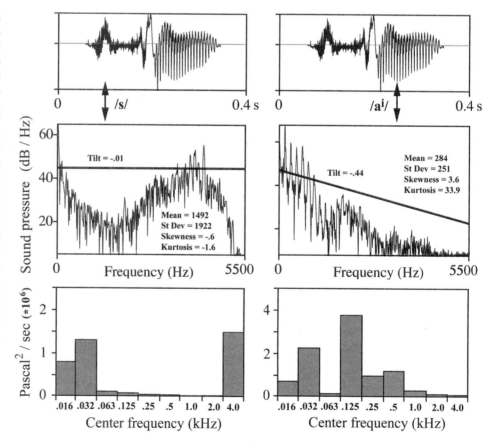

Figure 15.10. A segment from the word *strikes* as spoken by a male talker is used to illustrate global spectral differences between a noisy sound such as "s" and a vowel sound such as "i." The Fourier spectrum of a 60-ms segment of the noisy sound (*left column*) reveals a flatter overall spectral tilt than for a similarly derived spectrum from the vowel sound (*right column*). The first two spectral moments (mean and standard deviation, respectively) of the spectra are much higher for the noisy sound, whereas the third and fourth spectral moments (skewness and kurtosis, respectively) are higher for the vowel sound. Differences in overall spectral distribution are also captured in a 9-bin octave-band analysis (*bottom*).

spectrum to a *power spectrum,* with frequency and phase energies of each component then being added and squared. These outcomes are, in turn, divided by the total spectral energy summed over all components, which transforms the spectrum to a normalized distribution with an area of 1.0. Mean, standard deviation, skewness, and kurtosis values can then be computed as the first four moments of this spectral distribution.

Energy Bands

Distribution of frequency energy is often characterized by computing overall energy levels in a smaller number of *bands* (also *bins*) across the range of interest. One approach is to compute mean energy within frequency bands that are all equally wide, such as 500 or 1000 Hz. Another technique is *1/N-octave analysis,* in which energy bands are computed using a set of filters whose widths are computed as a fixed fractional ratio of each center frequency. This approach is inspired by the finding that the human frequency response is approximately logarithmic rather than linear, making loudness perception equal across octave bands (or fractions thereof) and not across bands that are equally wide in absolute terms.

Typical bandwidths are 1/1 octave and 1/3 octave, where an octave is a 2-to-1 frequency ratio and an octave band around a center frequency f_c extends from 0.707 to 1.414 f_c (center frequencies and frequency cutoffs for octave-band and 1/3-octave-band analyses in the speech range are listed in Appendix C). In octave analysis one might compute 9 or more bands (for instance, centered on 31.5, 63, 125, 250, 500, 1000, 2000, and 4000 Hz), whereas 30 or more bands could be involved in a 1/3-octave analysis. Both produce a significant decrease in the number of values characterizing the spectrum relative to using the full set of Fourier components computed over the same frequency range.

Long-Term Average Spectrum Analysis

Although spectral analysis is most often conducted on short sound segments, frequency characteristics of entire utterances can also be examined. This *long-term average spectrum* (*LTAS;* illustrated in Figure 15.11) approach is, for instance, useful when the effect of a talker's emotional state lies in its influence across multiple speech segments rather than particular component sounds. It is advisable to analyze 30-s or longer segments to achieve stable estimates of long-term energy distribution and to analyze voiced and unvoiced segments separately. Voiced and unvoiced speech can usually be readily separated using a pitch-extraction algorithm, with the software registering where reliable periodicity estimates could be made and where no periodicity was found.

A disadvantage of the long-term-average technique is that it does not pinpoint the particular segments that are most revealing of talker state. As a result, this approach is unlikely to uncover the short-term acoustic cues that listeners may actually be attending to. LTAS can nonetheless be an efficient

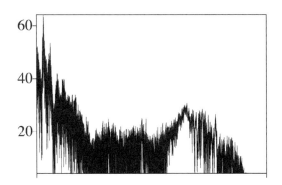

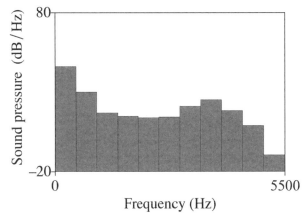

Figure 15.11. Long-term average spectra (LTAS) associated with a female talker producing 4.3 seconds of continuous speech. The raw Fourier spectrum (*top*) is processed by averaging the energy within a smaller number of frequency bins (*bottom*).

way to cover long stretches of speech, as it provides virtually immediate results and can be used to screen longer speech samples for more in-depth follow-up analyses. The output of LTAS analysis is a single Fourier spectrum whose properties can be characterized using any of the global measures just enumerated. The most common strategy has been to compute energy averages within equal and contiguous frequency bins, which is illustrated in Figure 15.11 using bin-widths of 500 Hz (see Banse & Scherer, 1996, for an application of LTAS measures and outcomes).

Practical Advice

Choosing a Window Length and Shape

To compute an FFT, one first has to select the length of the sample window. In some programs, that length is necessarily selected as a power of 2, with window lengths of 128, 256, 512, and 1,024 being common alternatives. Other programs allow window lengths to be designated in seconds (or milliseconds), automatically adding zeros at the beginning and end of the selected segment so as to bring the total number of points up to the next power of 2 (a technique called *zero-padding*). Zero-padding is arguably the better strategy, as it is virtually impossible to conceptualize segments of waveforms or spectrographic displays in terms of sample points. Additional confusion can arise given that when an analysis window is specified as being a fixed number of points in length, its absolute duration then depends on signal sampling frequency. For example, a 512-point segment is 46.4 ms long when sampling at 11.025-kHz but only 11.6 ms with a 44.1-kHz sampling rate.

However, the most important point is that in Fourier analysis, there is always a direct trading relationship between resolution in the time domain and resolution in the frequency domain. Given this trade-off, the preferred strategy in studying human vocal acoustics is to routinely use both kinds of analyses—narrowband computations for greater frequency resolution, and wideband computations either for better temporal resolution. A good approach is to use a 50-ms Gaussian analysis window to produce 43-Hz narrowband spectrograms and a 3-ms Gaussian window to produce 260-Hz wideband spectrograms (see Figure 15.9). Hanning and Hamming windows remain common, but with the faster computers that are now available, Gaussian windowing is preferred.

Energy-Distribution Measures

No one single strategy has emerged as a clear favorite for characterizing energy distribution in either short- or long-term Fourier spectra, and it can therefore be wise simply to include a variety of approaches—computing spectral tilt, comparing low versus high frequencies, and simplifying the spectrum through variable- or fixed-width frequency-band analysis. Although it has been the least used to date, the spectral-moments approach is a straightforward way to characterize a Fourier spectrum using familiar statistical tools. Its global characterizations can be particularly useful for noisy sounds, whereas harmonically structured speech sounds can often be economically captured using source-filter-based methods (discussed in the next two sections).

Analyzing Source Characteristics

The frequency-spectrum measures described in the previous section were essentially generic—applicable to any sound. However, measurements of speech as a particular kind of signal can take advantage of the source-filter model of vocal production. As noted earlier, this approach treats speech as a combination of source energy and vocal-tract filtering, with researchers suggesting that emotion-related effects can be expected in both aspects (e.g., Scherer, 1986).

Source energy that occurs during voiced speech has historically received the most attention in this regard, with features of interest occurring both at the *segmental* level (e.g., individual vowel sounds) and at the *suprasegmental* level (e.g., sentence-length utterances). Researchers typically proceed by extracting F_0 values across the speech sample of interest and compiling basic measures such as mean, minimum, and

maximum F_0 values, moment-to-moment fluctuations in F_0 over the course of the sample, and any longer-term F_0 patterns emerging across individual segments (*pitch contour*). These kinds of analyses are of particular interest in this chapter, because changes in emotional state have empirically been associated with global increases or decreases in F_0, increased variability in the periodicity of vocal-fold vibration, and changes in F_0 patterning over time (known as *prosody*). Measuring F_0 is typically referred to as *pitch extraction,* whereas various types of F_0 variability are referred to collectively as *vocal perturbation*.

Pitch Extraction

Pitch extraction can be surprisingly challenging and has generated much interest and work in speech science. Typical algorithms are based on correlating the waveform against itself, which, for a periodic signal, produces an *autocorrelation* function whose periodicity mirrors any periodicity present in the original sound. Speech analysis software always includes pitch-extraction capabilities, but actual results can be quite variable. Errors are particularly likely to be caused by noise, either occurring extraneously in the recordings or as part of the speech itself. The most common error that results is that an F_0 estimate is off by an octave, meaning that it is either too high or too low by a factor of 2.

Figure 15.12 shows pitch tracks extracted from speech produced by female and male talkers saying "when the sunlight strikes raindrops in the air" while simulating a happy tone of voice. Pitch tracks such as these can typically be edited by the user to correct for obvious errors. F_0 mean, standard deviation, and range over each segment of interest can then be easily calculated. The values can also be exported as a vector to software that can characterize the overall pattern of the pitch contour (e.g., rising, falling, bell-shaped) or to extract features such as the number of inflection points present. Many programs also show results as pulses marked in the waveform, allowing hand-editing to be used to correct obvious errors by moving, adding, or removing pulse markers.

Due to the fallibility of pitch-extraction algorithms, the user typically provides a range of acceptable outcomes, where 75–150 Hz are reasonable limits for adult male speech and 150–300 Hz are appropriate if talkers are adult females. However, high-arousal speech (or the speech produced by prepubescent children) may fall outside such ranges, requiring wider limits. If so, however, it becomes particularly important to screen the outcomes and to redo the analysis or hand edit when errors occur. Two other parameters that users may be asked to specify are the length of the window over which to calculate pitch periods and the degree of overlap between successive calculations. Practically speaking, the time window should be set so as to encompass 3–4 pitch periods in the speech being analyzed, with 25–75% overlap between adjacent windows. Including multiple pitch periods within a single analysis window helps to avoid octave errors, and

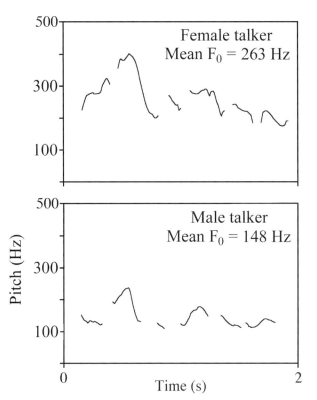

Figure 15.12. Pitch tracks extracted from 2-s segments of the same sentence spoken by a female (*top*) and a male (*bottom*) talker.

overlap between adjacent windows helps smooth the pitch contour.

If automated pitch extraction simply cannot be made to work for a particular set of samples, F_0 values can also be estimated either directly from the waveform or from a spectrographic representation. F_0 values are measured from the waveform by identifying individual cycles by eye (or marking a contiguous series of cycles), extracting their periods, and finding the corresponding frequencies (see the section on basics of sound and vocal production earlier in this chapter). However, doing pitch extraction by hand is both laborious and tedious and is therefore best used as a method of spot-checking the results of automated analysis. A better approach to use with recalcitrant segments is to identify the F_0 contour on a narrowband spectrogram and to measure its frequency value at key points. Alternatively, all the F_0 values can be extracted by setting a cursor-based "box" around the contour and recovering the frequency value associated with the highest amplitude pixel from each spectrogram column within that box. This latter technique requires programming and some flexibility on the part of the acoustics software being used.

Pitch Contour

Although standardized methods have not yet been developed, it is also of interest to characterize the patterns of the pitch contours being extracted, for instance, at the level of words, phrases, and sentences. The best known approach is to classify pitch contours either by eye or through standard curve-fitting procedures. Classification by eye has typically included categories such as *rising, falling, bell-shaped, sinusoidal,* and *complex*. Contours can also be classified depending on degree of fit by mathematical functions, creating such categories as *linear, power, decay, exponential,* and others.

Vocal Perturbation

In vocal acoustics, perturbation typically means a deviation from an expected regularity in vocal-fold vibration. No biological system can produce truly periodic oscillations, and some moment-to-moment fluctuation is therefore always expected. However, the degree of deviation can vary considerably, with high-arousal emotional states typically being associated with increased vocal perturbation. Several different measures can be used to capture such effects, including *jitter* as short-term (cycle-to-cycle) variability in F_0 frequency and *shimmer* as short-term (cycle-to-cycle) variability in F_0 amplitude. Noisiness is also often of interest, with the caveat that vocal noise can arise due either to vocal-fold perturbation or to turbulence created by incomplete glottal closure during phonation. So-called *breathy voice* is an example of the latter. Noisiness affects both jitter and shimmer values but is a specific focus of harmonic-to-noise-ratio measurement.

Jitter and Shimmer

A basic problem for both jitter and shimmer computation is the need to separate moment-to-moment variation in F_0 from longer-term patterning (meaning prosodic effects). This and associated problems have spurred the development of a large number of each kind of measure, although most are closely related. Only one of each sort is presented here.

Relative Average Perturbation

Relative average perturbation (RAP; Koike, 1973) is arguably the seminal jitter measure. It characterizes frequency perturbation as the mean absolute difference between a given pitch period and the mean of its two nearest neighbors, divided by the mean period of all three. It is also called the frequency perturbation quotient. The crucial innovation is that each period is first computed as the mean of itself and its two neighbors (known as a 3-point *moving average*), which greatly decreases the effect of slow changes in F_0 and thereby isolates fast changes as perturbation.

$$\frac{\frac{1}{n-2}\sum_{i=2}^{n-1}|P_{i-1}+P_i+P_{i-1}|}{\frac{1}{n}\sum_{i=1}^{n}P_i}$$

Shimmer calculations of moment-to-moment amplitude variation are typically based exclusively on peak amplitudes from each cycle. This approach is therefore fundamentally different from computations of waveform energy and power (see Appendix B), which are based on amplitudes of individual sample points. The *amplitude perturbation quotient* (*APQ*; Takahashi & Koike, 1975) is a prototypical measure of shimmer and is analogous to the RAP estimate of jitter. APQ is based on the average absolute difference between the peak amplitude of a given cycle and the mean peak amplitude of its nearest neighbors divided by the mean amplitude of all the cycles. The number of neighbors can vary and might include 1, 2, and 5 on each side (the last case, which includes 11 points, is shown here):

$$\frac{\dfrac{1}{n-10}\sum_{i=6}^{n-5}\left|\dfrac{A_{i-5}+A_{i-4}+\ldots+A_{i+5}}{11}\right|-A_i}{\dfrac{1}{n}\sum_{i+1}^{n}A_i}$$

Harmonic-to-Noise Ratio (HNR)

In addition to cycle-to-cycle variability, naturally occurring, quasi-periodic waveforms also inevitably exhibit at least some noisiness. HNR quantifies the degree of that noisiness by comparing the amount of energy occurring in harmonic versus nonharmonic components of the signal. A variety of such measures have also been developed, with Boersma's (1993) *harmonicity* measure arguably being the most successful. It works by first isolating the amount of energy in periodic waveform components using autocorrelation. That energy is subtracted from the normalized correlation function, making the remainder the energy that is attributable to noise components. Harmonicity is then the ratio of periodic to noise energy, expressed in dB.

Nonlinear Phenomena

Recent developments in voice science have emphasized the importance of the larynx as a nonlinear dynamical system, with the vocal folds as coupled oscillators that are theoretically capable of an infinite number of different vibration patterns. Each pattern can be modeled as an attractor state, with the vocal folds changing from one state to another through virtually instantaneous *bifurcations*. This approach makes sense of voice acoustics that are otherwise difficult to understand if vocal-fold vibration is viewed only as being either quasi-periodic or random.

The two phenomena of greatest interest here are *voice breaks* (brief cessations of vibration that are also known as *aphonia*), and *frequency jumps* (discontinuities in which F_0 changes discretely up or down). Both kinds of events would be known as *dysphonias* in classic speech science. Voice breaks can be quantified by using a pitch-extraction algorithm and recording the number of times it fails to recover an F_0 value over a voiced segment while always also checking that such failures are due to voicing anomalies rather than misbehavior by the algorithm. Further quantification

can then include the absolute number or total duration of voice breaks, the rate of occurrence or percentage of overall segment duration, or the proportion of voiced frames that include breaks. Frequency jumps can be quantified in much the same way.

Practical Advice

The most important advice concerning pitch extraction is simply that results should be carefully checked—including visual monitoring of pitch contours for octave errors and using the waveform to spot-check the results. Although hand editing introduces some subjectivity, it is common to have to adjust a pitch contour a bit. However, it is also not unusual for an unruly pitch period to reflect emotion-related vocal perturbation rather than algorithm failure. The best approach is therefore to be open to both possibilities, and to listen carefully to the speech being analyzed.

Vocal perturbation measures should be computed from signals digitized at the highest possible sampling rates. This is one reason that it is a good policy to digitize and archive the samples at 44.1 kHz, even when routinely down-sampling for most other analyses. Higher sampling rates create more detailed waveform representations (as shown in Figure 15.5), which is exactly what is required to uncover the minor deviations from perfect periodicity that are the focus when measuring vocal perturbation. Finally, we suggest that the various perturbation measures be used as a package rather than in isolation. The origin, extent, and consistency of vocal perturbation within and across different human vocalizers is not well understood in speech science. The best approach for an emotions researcher is therefore to look for converging evidence using jitter, shimmer, HNR, and the occurrence of nonlinear effects such as voice breaks and frequency jumps.

Analyzing Vocal-Tract Filtering Effects

The second aspect of the source-filter model of vocal acoustics is that the supralaryngeal vocal tract also plays a critical role in sound production by shaping the frequency characteristics of the source energy through resonance-based filtering effects. The vocal-tract filter is a central topic in speech science, with researchers being particularly interested in uncovering invariant formant patterns that differentiate linguistically significant vowel contrasts. However, that research has also tended to underscore the fact that formant patterning shows significant variation within individuals, between individuals, between sexes, and in adults versus children. Some studies have shown that talker emotional state can significantly influence those formant positions as well, making vocal-tract resonance effects potentially fertile ground for investigations of vocal emotion.

Linear Predictive Coding

The most commonly used technique for characterizing speech formants is *linear predictive coding (LPC),* a term that actually represents a family of related computational approaches. Like Fourier analysis, the goal of LPC is to create a spectral representation of time-series data. Unlike Fourier analysis, the process is explicitly one of modeling rather than transforming the data. In the LPC case, the spectrum is represented using a relatively small set of polynomial coefficients defining a function that captures only the most prominent spectral peaks. The rationale is that these global peaks in the spectral envelope most likely reflect the filtering effect of formants. In other words, whereas a Fourier representation is more or less faithful to the "raw" waveform data, the LPC spectrum is a smoothed, simplified characterization of frequency content.

Because LPC is explicitly a modeling approach, it may be found to work better for some kinds of signals than for others. It is the user who determines which spectral peaks to try to capture and who must also verify that the analysis is doing so. Verifying LPC performance usually means explicitly comparing this smoothed representation to a Fourier transform computed over the same segment (illustrated in Figure 15.13). Window lengths and shapes should be the same for both analyses, and the comparison is best made by overlaying a single LPC function on the corresponding Fourier spectrum (second panel from the bottom in Figure 15.13). Alternatively, LPC-based formant tracks can be overlaid on Fourier-based spectrograms (bottom panel in Figure 15.13). Note that LPC is not modeling the Fourier spectrum—the two representations are independent computations over time-domain data. Taken together, they can therefore provide convergent evidence about spectral properties of the sound.

LPC Theory

LPC is associated with a confusing variety of algorithms and jargon terms. Historically, this diversity is traceable to the multiple theoretical origins of LPC, wherein each approach gave rise to a particular set of methods and terminology. One is purely statistical, a *linear regression* technique that models major trends in the waveform by predicting subsequent values from earlier ones. In this case, LPC computation is an exercise in linear prediction and relies on finding a polynomial that best predicts each successive data point based on a weighted combination of previous points. The LPC model, therefore, consists of a series of *linear prediction coefficients.*

Whereas linear regression modeling is a purely statistical and generic technique applicable to any time-series data, the *inverse-filtering* approach is explicitly grounded in source-filter theory. The reasoning here was that in speech, one can begin by assuming that the source energy is either quasiperiodic vocal-fold vibration or random noise resulting from turbulent airflow. The spectrum of the source is therefore already known as the energy enters the supralaryngeal filter.

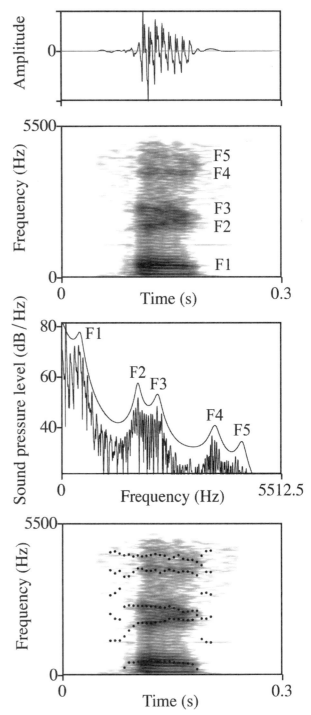

Figure 15.13. An "eh" vowel produced by a male talker is shown both as a waveform (*top*) and in a narrowband spectrogram in which the first five formants are labeled (*second from top*). These formants also appear in a smooth spectral envelope computed over a 100-ms segment from the middle of the sound (*second from bottom*). This envelope was produced through linear predictive coding (LPC) using 14 analysis coefficients and a Gaussian window. It has been overlaid on a narrowband Fourier spectrum independently computed over the same segment, also using a Gaussian window. A series of formant frequencies derived from individual LPC computations performed across the entire sounds are shown as five tracks overlaid on the spectrogram (*bottom*).

Given that the spectrum of the recorded signal is also known, one can work backward to derive the filter function that best recreates those assumed properties of the source energy. Inverting this function produces what must have been the supralaryngeal filter that was at work during production. The inverse-filtering approach also produces a polynomial model, in this case involving *filter coefficients*. Another production-based rationale gave rise to a method known as *PARCOR*. This latter approach is more sophisticated than simple inverse filtering, modeling the supralaryngeal vocal tract as a series of contiguous tubes whose boundaries create partial reflections of component frequencies of the source energy. These reflections are computed using partial correlation techniques, producing a polynomial model based on *reflection coefficients*.

Although these three theoretical perspectives are quite different, the various coefficients involved were ultimately found to be mathematical transformations of one another. Given that each type can be derived from the others regardless of theoretical approach, all are now known more generally as *LPC coefficients* and can now be computed using any number of available algorithms. *Autocorrelation, Burg, covariance,* and *modified covariance* methods are among the most common computational techniques.

LPC Parameters

Key parameters to set when doing LPC analysis are *preemphasis*, analysis window length and shape, and the number of LPC coefficients. Preemphasis is a means of changing the overall tilt of the spectrum, and is typically used to accentuate formants occurring in higher-frequency regions of a signal where overall amplitudes tend to become quite low. In speech research, preemphasis is usually set at 6-dB per octave, although many analysis programs allow users to select any of a range of preemphasis values.

Window length is set in the same way as in Fourier analysis—the window must be long enough to ensure that clear formant peaks emerge in the model, but not so long that the formants are visibly changing and hence being averaged over the course of the target segment. In other words, the analysis is most effective if the window is short enough that underlying segments can be considered stationary. Window shape is often preset in the analysis program, but the options are otherwise similar to those available for Fourier analysis.

The most important parameter to set is arguably the number of coefficients to use in the polynomial model. In the linear-regression approach, the number of coefficients selected corresponds to the number of preceding waveform sample points used to predict each successive value. In the inverse-filter approach, the number of coefficients corresponds to the filter order, whereas in PARCOR it is equivalent to the number of contiguous tubes used in the supralaryngeal vocal-tract model. Theoretical observations aside, the number of coefficients used critically determines the resolution of the LPC function. Using a small number of coefficients produces a crude model with only a few peaks in the spectral enve-

lope, whereas using a larger number of coefficients produces a more detailed model. One historical rule of thumb is that the number of coefficients should be set as the sampling frequency in kHz plus 4 (e.g., 14 coefficients should be used for a sampling rate of 10.0 kHz). Another is that the number of peaks "found" by LPC will be one-half the number of coefficients minus 1 (e.g., using 12 coefficients will produce 5 peaks). These guidelines are complicated somewhat by the fact that unvoiced sounds typically have fewer formants than voiced sounds and more so by the occurrence of intra- and inter-individual variation in formant characteristics. However, sampling rate in particular is critical in that any peaks found using LPC will be spread over the entire spectral range up to the Nyquist frequency. LPC analyses are therefore typically conducted on files that have been down-sampled to 22.05 kHz, 11.025 kHz, or even lower rates.

Formant Modeling

LPC analysis as described so far produces a single spectral slice from which one can visually locate and measure formant peaks and amplitudes (shown in the bottom panel of Figure 15.13). However, algorithms also exist to automatically derive both frequencies and bandwidths of those formant peaks. Doing so involves *peak-picking* algorithms that can identify likely candidate formants within each LPC frame. Oftentimes, the software allows a user to preselect the most likely frequency ranges for one or more formants, as well as a variety of other parameters that can affect the algorithm's "decision" process. The typical output includes a display of resulting *formant tracks* drawn as a series of dots superimposed on a spectrogram (shown in Figure 15.13). Because individual points in these tracks can sometimes go astray, it is also common for acoustics software to allow users to hand edit formant tracks in much the same was as pitch tracks.

Practical Advice

The earlier point that LPC should always be used in conjunction with FFTs bears repeating. If one were analyzing only a single spectrum from each sound or sound segment, either the midpoint or the point of maximum amplitude would be a reasonable location. Once the location is established, both FFT and LPC should be computed using the same window, with the latter then superimposed to check the "fit" (Figure 15.13 shows a good fit). If the smoothed spectral envelope of the LPC misses obvious global peaks in the FFT, the number of coefficients can be adjusted upward. If the LPC is found to be responding to minor, local peaks, coefficient number can be adjusted downward.

One caveat is that formants are typically more clearly defined in sounds produced by adult males than in those from either adult females or children. This difference can be quite striking and is traceable in part to the lower F_0s of adult male voices. Lower pitch produces decreased harmonic spacing, which in turn presents a better medium for "displaying" supralaryngeal filtering effects. Formant effects are much easier to model when at least three adjacent harmonics have been affected by each resonance, as that allows "triangulation" of the center frequency and bandwidth. Harmonics become requisitely more widely spaced as F_0s increase, which can mean that two or fewer are falling within range of any given formant in the voices of females and children. In that case, a formant cannot be as easily reconstructed based on its differential effects on adjacent harmonics, and LPC instead begins to track individual harmonics rather than formants. One alternative for these cases is to analyze both voiced and unvoiced sounds, using converging evidence from both kinds of segments to first find formant locations and then to look for emotion-related effects.

Overall, LPC is a powerful formant-modeling tool that usually works well. However, it does not provide usable results for all sounds or all voices. There are other methods, but none that we recommend for routine use. Nor do we suggest falling back on the old-fashioned approach of visually estimating formant locations from wideband spectrograms, which is too subjective. When individual formants that should be present come up missing in a given spectrum, they can either be treated as missing values in statistical analysis or replaced using one of the standard data imputation techniques developed in the field of statistics. Otherwise, the most practical alternative is to restrict analysis to the samples that do yield good formant values, accepting the limitations that this kind of restriction can create for the generalizability of results.

Measuring formants from LPC spectra means that one is inspecting the display to locate peaks and extract cursor-based measurements. If so, the data typically consist of center frequencies and amplitudes. One choice to make is whether to measure a single spectrum or to extract data from multiple spectra distributed across the segment. If formant tracks are computed, automated peak-picking typically returns center frequencies and formant bandwidths. In this case, one can extract the values associated with a single point or multiple points in the sound or compute mean values across each formant track. In both cases, it can be very handy to also recover the LPC coefficients themselves for use in statistical analysis. That might, for example, add an additional set of 12 values to the data recorded for each spectrum (coefficient values range from −1 to +1), creating a set of variables that together provide an objective encoding of the smooth spectral envelope. These generic coefficient values thus allow statistical comparison of global spectral features without intrusion of subjectivity either in human or algorithmic form.

Finally, it should be noted that, although it is arguably best to analyze all the sounds in a data set using the same number of coefficients, formant extraction often works best if this parameter is adjusted as needed for a given segment. We suggest doing the analysis both ways. In one pass, the number of coefficients is fixed, producing good models in most cases but producing a suboptimal fit in some others. In a second pass, LPC spectra are customized to each segment to produce an optimal fit, while thereby introducing an element of subjectivity to the analysis. With any luck, subsequent statistical comparisons will reveal few if any functionally important differences in the outcomes provided.

Vocal Amplitude

Only Limited Comparisons Are Possible

Signal amplitude is of obvious interest in studying emotion-related vocal acoustics, with production amplitude certainly expected to be affected by talker arousal, and perhaps valence as well. Unfortunately, measuring the actual absolute amplitude of any sound is an arduous undertaking its own right, requiring both a carefully calibrated recording system and a controlled recording environment. Emotions researchers probably do not have either, instead using off-the-shelf equipment and recording in naturalistic settings. In that case, information about absolute amplitude is lost from the very first. However, it is still possible to make comparisons of relative signal amplitudes, albeit cautiously.

The most reliable comparisons are those made entirely within a single, continuously digitized file that also represents near-invariant recording conditions. In other words, if factors such as vocalizer-to-microphone angle and distance, background noise level, recorder input level, and digitizing level all remain constant, amplitudes of some segments within the file can be compared with amplitudes of other segments in that file. Given that contemporary computer technology makes it possible to process sound files that are many minutes long, one can imagine designing a within-subject experiment that tests for condition-based amplitude effects.

Another possibility is to introduce a calibration signal into each recording, thereafter computing all amplitude values relative to the intensity of that signal. For example, sound engineers commonly use a calibrated sine-wave generator that plugs directly into the inputs of a mixing board in order to set levels on amplification equipment used in public performances. Emotions researchers may also want to consider introducing a calibration signal through the recording microphones themselves, for instance, by using a sound level meter to adjust the amplitude of a calibration signal from a speaker, and with the signal recorded at a fixed angle and distance from the microphone. However, that method is both cumbersome and approximate.

Finally, it may be possible to take advantage of the background noise produced by ventilation systems in indoor recording environments. Although often a vexing and unavoidable nuisance, that kind of noise can also be used as a calibration signal. To do so, it must first be shown that the noise is constant over time, has approximately equal intensity throughout the recording environment, and is not dramatically affected by the presence of participants in the room or their movements during an experiment. If these conditions are met, then the background noise level may be useful in normalizing recordings on a given input channel within a recording session. In this case, recording, digitizing, and subsequent amplitude-normalization procedures all have equivalent effects on the signal and background noise components of a given file. One might even go so far as to try to use this background noise as a means of making amplitude comparisons across participants and sessions, but only if one is also able to argue that factors such as microphone angle and distance were held constant.

Practical Advice

In considering using amplitude as a point of comparison, the first step is to think carefully about recording conditions. For example, headworn microphones become a necessity as the single best means of ensuring that the angle and distance between sound source (the vocalizer's mouth) and the microphone remains constant throughout the session. Another major advantage of using headworn microphones is, of course, that they yield high-quality recordings with excellent signal-to-noise ratios. Using them helps alleviate concerns about comparing amplitudes of a given talker's sounds that occur relatively close together and are acquired together as part of the same digitized file.

Whether it is legitimate to go on to compare amplitudes of sounds separated by longer periods, or even drawn from separate sessions, depends on how confident one is about the recording conditions. If there is measurable, constant, and pervasive background noise in the recording environment, it can be worth exploiting as means of signal normalization for amplitude comparison. However, those are strong preconditions that should both be confirmed through direct testing and be corroborated by whatever indirect means is afforded by data from the various sounds, talkers, and experimental conditions used. It is also sound policy to calibrate input levels, both at the microphone input and via a free-field sound source recorded through the microphones once they are placed in their final positions. These calibrations will undoubtedly be approximate, but can serve as a complementary or perhaps an alternative strategy to using background noise levels. Nonetheless, we must include the caveat that the kinds of amplitude comparisons that emotions researchers are likely to be able to make should always be interpreted with caution.

Editing Digital Sounds and Preparing Stimuli

When sounds are to be used for experimental purposes, they are typically prepared as digitized files and presented to listeners through headphones or speakers via a computer. These sounds may include digitized and edited versions of natural recordings or synthesized sounds. In each case, some simple steps should be taken to minimize events such as distracting clicks and pops during stimulus presentation and to help avoid confounding effects of amplitude variation in the sounds. For the former, good editing and using amplitude-ramping or zero-padding at the beginnings and endings of the sound files can be key. For the latter, amplitude normalization is a good tactic, and randomizing stimulus amplitude during testing should also be considered.

Editing

A basic benefit of working with digital sound is that it allows simple cut-and-paste waveform editing. Virtually any acoustic program allows the user to cut or paste pieces of waveform, set a section to zero, change relative amplitudes, and make other basic editing changes. Usually no more is required to cut or copy than to mark a target section with the cursor and apply a menu command or keyboard stroke. Pasting in a segment is just as simple. However, these maneuvers can just as easily produce amplitude discontinuities in the waveform that become audible clicks when the sound is played. In this case, discontinuity means that the difference between adjacent voltage values has become artificially large. Even a single discrepant sample point is enough to "pop" a headphone or a loudspeaker. Such effects are particularly important in emotions-related perceptual experiments because even small sudden auditory events such as these are known to be attention and arousal inducing.

Cut and Paste at Zero Crossings

Avoiding amplitude discontinuities thus becomes a basic goal in waveform editing. The most basic precaution is to always cut and paste at zero-crossing points, meaning locations at which sample points are as close as possible to 0 volts. If cuts are made at these points, values just before and just after will also be close to 0 and will form a seamless junction with one another (illustrated in the top panels of Figure 15.14). Cutting or pasting at nonzero values tends to join points of different amplitudes, which does create audible artifacts (middle panels of Figure 15.14).

Rapid reversals in amplitude trajectories at cutting and pasting points should also be avoided. For example, one can readily create a problem by making a cut that connects a positive-going trajectory to a negative-going trajectory (or vice versa), even when the cut is made at zero points (bottom panels of Figure 15.14). Bad transitions can often be seen by blowing up and inspecting the waveform, but a better strategy is often just to look at a wideband spectrogram of the sound—the wider the better. These spectrograms are maximized for temporal resolution, and transients become dramatically visible as vertical striations. Zooming in makes the artifact increasingly visible, and successful transient

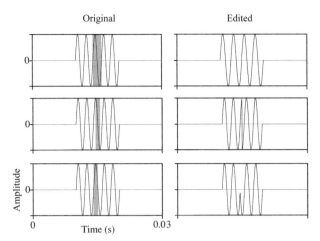

Figure 15.14. Deleting one cycle of a 500-Hz sine wave by cutting at zero crossings (*top left*) produces an artifact-free result (*top right*). However, audible transients result if a cut either joins radically different amplitude values (*middle*) or creates an abrupt change in the overall direction of voltage change (*bottom*).

removal also visibly cleans up the corresponding spectrographic image.

Avoiding Transients During Presentation

Ramping

Abrupt onset or offset is another common source of transients. Again, the problem is that a rapid amplitude change in the waveform pops the speaker. One way to solve the problem is to *ramp* the onsets and offsets of stimuli to make them more gradual. In this case, "gradual" is still very rapid—the ramp need be no longer than 10 or 20 ms. To create a 10-ms-onset ramp, one might make a file whose values change linearly or exponentially from 0.0 to 1.0 over the course of 10 ms. Values in the first 10 ms of the waveform are then multiplied by the corresponding values in the ramp file. Values in a 10-ms-offset ramp should fall linearly or exponentially from 1.0 to 0.0. Sounds whose onsets and offsets are already gradual are also less likely to create audible transients. It can nonetheless be advantageous to routinely ramp all stimuli that are long enough to allow it.

Zero-Padding

There are also cases in which ramping cannot be used; for example, because the sound may be so short that even the first and last few milliseconds must be left as is. Clicks and pops sometimes also occur in the absence of any obvious abruptness in onsets or offsets, in which case the multimedia system playing the sound may be to blame. Even more maddening is that a given stimulus may produce clicks only some of the time. If so, it can be helpful to zero-pad the file, meaning that a short segment of sample points at 0 volts are added to the beginning and end. Even a few milliseconds of silence can help significantly, and it is good practice to routinely zero-pad all stimulus files by 50 or 100 ms. If reaction times are important, one simply subtracts the zero-padding length from the latency recorded on each trial.

Noisy Files

In the earlier section titled "Before Analysis Begins," we argued against relying on filtering to clean up noisy files during analysis, a position that applies at least as much to files presented for perceptual evaluation. Noise is a problem, to be sure, particularly in recordings drawn from the naturalistic settings that are typically of greatest interest to emotions researchers. Although hand editing to remove discrete events such as clicks and pops can be quite beneficial when judiciously done, wholesale removal of ongoing background noise is risky. As an alternative to filtering, we suggest explicitly introducing a constant, quiet, but noticeable level of white noise through the headphones or speakers used in the experimental session. In human perception, this kind of pervasive background noise can be quite effective in blending with and masking background noise components occurring in stimulus sounds. Signal components typically stand out more clearly, with noisiness in the sound file becoming significantly less salient.

Amplitude

A last point to make is that the relative amplitudes of stimuli must also be considered. If amplitude per se is not being investigated, the ideal outcome is for all stimuli in an experiment to have the same physical amplitude, and for participants to hear them as all having the same psychological loudness. Unfortunately, due to the complexity of the relationship between amplitude and loudness, it is virtually impossible to achieve both outcomes simultaneously.

One strategy is to set the *root-mean-square* (RMS) amplitudes of all stimuli to the same value, such as 80 dB. However, unless all the sounds have virtually identical spectral and temporal properties, some will sound louder than others. Noisier sounds, in particular, will be noticeably louder than sounds with more purely harmonic structures, which is not desirable in a perceptual experiment. In addition, any stretches of silence occurring in longer sounds have a dramatic effect on mean values and therefore complicate the amplitude-measurement process. Another approach is to adjust RMS values on a case-by-case basis to achieve equal loudness, either by ear or based on pilot studies. The former is unacceptably subjective, however, whereas the latter becomes very cumbersome as experiments and stimulus sets multiply.

We suggest the following strategies. First, experience indicates that equating stimuli based on their peak amplitudes produces significantly less loudness variation than does relying on RMS values. Loudness differences will at least have been minimized, so if some variation can be tolerated, this approach may be the one to use. If amplitude and loudness must be entirely ruled out as potential confounds, the best approach is to first equate the stimuli (using either of the two methods) and then to systematically vary presentation amplitude across trials and stimuli. On any given trial, in other words, a stimulus may be presented at any of several amplitudes, for instance, varying quasi-randomly across a range of 6 dB or more.

What to Report and Show in Acoustic Analysis

Results of acoustic analyses do not make for scintillating reading, and therefore they cry out for judicious use of graphics. However, some essentials about the digitizing and analysis process should always be reported, particularly as pertains to hardware used for the former and parameter settings used for the latter. This information should be fleshed out graphically and there may be both waveform and frequency-domain features to illustrate.

Waveforms

When describing digitized sounds that are either analyzed or presented to listeners, important parameters to include are their sampling frequency (e.g., 44.1 kHz) and wordwidth (e.g., 16 bits). Showing waveforms is often not very informative, but it can be useful to include them in order to demonstrate that recording and digitizing was competently done—in other words, that no amplitude clipping occurred. If so, a single waveform will likely suffice, for example, being shown in conjunction with the first spectrogram. Waveforms can also be useful when illustrating particular acoustic properties that may become of interest, such as a sound's amplitude envelope or the detailed relationships between particular stretches of sound and their corresponding frequency properties.

Spectra and Spectrograms

For both Fourier and LPC analyses, descriptions of both single spectra and time-frequency spectrograms should include the method used to compute them, for example, whether they are based on Fourier transformation or LPC. In Fourier representations, computation might have been DFTs but more likely are FFTs. In LPC representations, the particular algorithm used should be mentioned (e.g., autocorrelation, covariance, or Burg method). In both cases, the length (in time or sample points) and shape of the analysis window used are also critical. Frequency resolution of FFTs should also be reported explicitly, although it can be derived from knowing the sampling frequency and window length. Parameters to report from LPC include the preemphasis set-

ting and the number of coefficients used. Although applied to both FFT- and LPC-based spectra and spectrograms, the terms *narrowband* and *wideband* do not have precise definitions in digital signal processing. They are handy descriptors, but they do not supersede the need to include more precise computational parameters. For spectrograms, one should also include the degree of overlap as the successive spectra were computed.

Both single spectra and spectrograms are typically shown in order to illustrate prototypical features of sounds. They can also be used to demonstrate acoustic variation occurring across the data set. A few carefully chosen spectrograms can be particularly helpful in conveying a sense of both prototypical and nonprototypical versions of sounds. It is a good idea to include both narrowband and wideband versions of at least some spectrograms, given the complementary nature of these displays.

Final Thoughts

In this chapter, we have tried to outline each major component of analyzing emotion-related vocal acoustics. The overview has not been comprehensive, of course, but we hope it covers enough ground to allow an acoustically inexperienced researcher to conduct a credible, professional-level analysis. Each of the topics raised in the hypothetical example discussed in the first section have been covered, including discussion of digital acquisition of recordings, selecting file formats and sampling rates both for archiving and analyzing sounds, preprocessing of files prior to analysis, and some of the measures that can be used to characterize durations of segments of interest, speech rate, pitch characteristics, vocal perturbation, short and long spectral properties, and formant characteristics.

The hypothetical results we presented in our hypothetical experiment were rather simple-minded, inspired by the intuition that elevating a vocalizer's overall arousal relative to normative levels might give rise to a suite of acoustic effects. However, this particular example was selected precisely because it would be easy both for us to present and for readers to understand. It is apparent, based on important empirical work that has already been done, that relationships between emotion and vocal acoustics are much more complex than we would want to get into in a tutorial chapter such as this one. However, only a modest amount of empirical evidence is available about those likely rich and varied relationships, especially when compared with related areas such as facial expression of emotion. Given the dramatic advances that have occurred in the technology associated with recording and processing of sound, the field of vocal expression of emotion is ripe for a corresponding explosion in substantive scientific contributions. We look forward to a steadily increasing stream of work on emotion-related vocal acoustics in the future and hope that this chapter contributes toward such an outcome.

Appendix A: Précis of an Acoustic Analysis

Recording and/or Digitizing

Set input levels for each segment as needed to avoid amplitude clipping, while trying to have most waveform peaks cross the halfway point in one or both directions. Record and digitize in mono rather than stereo. However, if the signal covers a wide amplitude range, "split" it into two channels that are set to different input levels on the recorder. Digitize at 44.1 kHz or higher, archive in AIFF or WAV format, and leave some preceding and following sound, thereby bracketing the segment of interest within each file. Record and digitize in mono rather than stereo, unless the signal input has been split. If recording on two channels with different levels, choose and archive the better of the two representations created for each sound segment.

Preprocessing (Performed in the Following Order)

Edit the archived files as needed. Down-sample the files to 22.05, 16.0, 11.025, or 8.0 kHz, selecting the lowest rate that nonetheless captures the critical frequency range of interest. Remove any DC offset, highpass- or bandstop-filter the signal to remove any 60-Hz, but perform other filtering only if absolutely necessary. Normalize amplitude to the maximum representable range.

Acoustic Measurements

Variables of interest include durations, F_0 values (e.g., mean, standard deviation, range, first, last, minimum, maximum, contour shapes), vocal perturbation (e.g., jitter, shimmer, HNR, voice breaks, frequency jumps), global spectral characteristics (e.g., spectral moments, LTAS, LPC coefficients), and formants (e.g., frequencies, relative amplitudes, bandwidths). Amplitude measurements are possible, but challenging.

Appendix B: Common Scales Used in Psychological Acoustics

Energy and Power

The strength of a sound can be expressed in many different ways, creating a bewildering variety of quantities. The physical event itself involves collisions between molecules, and each of the measures involved is ultimately about force, which can be measured in newtons.

Force in newtons: $N = m * kg/s^2$

In other words, 1 N is the amount of force needed to accelerate 1 kilogram by 1 meter per second. The pressure exerted through sound energy can then be measured in *pascals*, referring to the number of newtons being exerted over a particular area (in square meters).

Pressure in pascals: $Pa = N/m^2$

The quantity of energy involved can also be expressed in *joules*, which is the work done when a force of 1 newton causes a displacement of 1 meter.

Energy in joules: $J = N * m$

The amount of energy transferred over time is power, which can be measured in *watts*, meaning joules per second.

Power in watts: $W = J/s$

Because sound energy has both positive- and negative-going pressure components, energy and power values are based on squared pressure amplitudes. *Energy in air* is measured as sound pressure in joules per square meter (J/m^2), also taking into account air density and sound velocity in air. *Power in air* is measured as watts per square meter (W/m^2), taking the same factors into account. Both quantities are expressed in relation to time. Energy is computed per unit time, and for a discretely sampled waveform it is the sum of the squared amplitude values multiplied by the sampling period (which is a small fractional value). Power is computed over a specified time window, and for a discretely sampled waveform, it is its mean-squared amplitude over that window (meaning the sum of squared waveform amplitude values divided by the number of values). Power is thus equivalent to the variance of the amplitude values, while *root-mean-square* (*RMS*) corresponds to the (biased) standard deviation of the values.

Amplitude: The deciBel Scale

The most common measure of sound intensity is based on the Bel scale, named for the inventor Alexander Graham Bell. However, this scale consists of units so large that it is typically reported in tenths of Bels, or deciBels (dB). The dynamic range of human audition from the threshold of detection to the threshold of pain is equivalent to the ratio of air pressures of 1,400,000 to 1, which is only 12.0 steps on the Bel scale. Breaking each step into tenths to create a total of 120 steps makes this measure much more tractable. The dB scale was first developed as an attempt to create evenly sized loudness units, where loudness refers to the psychological experience that corresponds to the physical amplitude of a waveform. It was once believed that loudness increases as the log of amplitude, which is the relationship captured by the dB scale. Even though that relationship does not in fact hold, dB measurement nonetheless became widespread.

Sound represents a series of positive and negative fluctuations around some non-zero value, such as atmospheric pressure. The dB scale therefore has no true zero point. Instead, values are computed as the log of the ratio between an observed value and a reference value. There are in fact various versions of the dB scale, including electrical (power or voltage) and acoustical (intensity or pressure) units. Using a reference level designated as L_1, measurement in Bels would be computed as follows:

$$L_2 - L_1 \; (Bels) = log \; (P_2 / P_1),$$

where L_1 has average power P_1, and L_2 is a signal with average power P_2. Expressed as dB, the formula becomes the following:

$$L_2 - L_1 \; (dB) = 10 \; log \; (P_2 / P_1).$$

When real numbers are represented as logarithms, division is done by subtracting and exponentiation by multiplication. Power is defined as the square of waveform amplitude values, $P = A^2$, which can therefore be written as $log \; P = 2 \; log \; A$. The deciBel equation can therefore also be written as follows:

$$L_2 - L_1 = 2 * 10 \; log \; (A_2 / A_1) = 20 \; log \; (A_2 / A_1)$$

In other words, signal intensity (relative to a corresponding reference level) is twenty times the log of the ratio of waveform amplitude to the reference amplitude. Different versions of the dB scale can be created depending on the reference values selected, where one of the most common is dB as sound pressure level, or dB SPL. For this scale, the reference sound pressure level was designated as 20 microPa ($2 * 10^{-5}$ Pa), which was chosen as an approximation of the sound pressure needed to reach the detection threshold for a human listening for a 1000-Hz sine wave. This scale is therefore dB *re* 20 microPa.

Because it is logarithmic, the dB scale can be difficult to conceptualize. Some telling numbers to remember are that an increase of 6 dB SPL means that air pressure has doubled, whereas an increase of 20 dB SPL means a ten-fold change in air pressure.

Loudness and Pitch: Phons, Sones, Barks, and Mels

Loudness

The human ear is sensitive to an enormous range of sound intensities. The ratio of the highest amplitude that can be tolerated to the lowest amplitude that can be detected is an astonishing $10^{14}:1$ (100 billion to 1). The psychological dimension of loudness exhibits a smaller range, although it is still an impressive $10^5: 1$ (100,000 to 1). Loudness is thus significantly compressed compared to intensity, although the relationship is nonetheless monotonic. The scale has been mapped, and can be summarized as a power function:

$$L = kP^{0.6}.$$

Here, L is loudness, P is sound pressure, and k is a constant of proportionality. This relationship applies most precisely for frequencies between 500 and 4000 Hz. The subjective nature of loudness perception has given rise to several measures meant to capture this dimension of psychological experience.

Phons

Units in *phons* are not a measure of loudness per se, but rather comprise a frequency-compensated dB scale. The reference point here is 40 phons, defined as the *loudness level* of a 1000-Hz sine wave at an SPL of 40 dB. The loudness levels of other sounds are defined, relative to this value, as the SPL of an equally loud 1000–Hz tone. Since a 1000-Hz sine wave is equal in loudness to itself, its SPL and loudness level have the same values. Above approximately 30 phons, each 10-phon increase in a 1000-Hz sine wave approximately doubles its loudness. While a true measure of loudness would scale with the sensation of magnitude, the phon scale does not.

Sones

Because loudness cannot be expressed in dB (which is a physical measure), *phons* are defined in terms of another unit, namely *sones*. In this case, 1 sone is defined as the loudness of a 1000-Hz sine wave at an SPL of 40 dB, which makes it equivalent to 40 phons. Because phon values of other frequencies are tied to the 1000–Hz standard, that means that any sine wave at 40 phons has a loudness of 1 sone (regardless of absolute dB value, which could be either higher or lower than 40). The sone scale is thus meant as a true measure of loudness.

Barks

The *bark* scale is an absolute frequency scale based on critical bandwidths. It is a measure of critical-band number and was named after Heinrich Barkhausen (1881–1956), a German electrical engineer. There is no exact analytic expression for the bark scale, but bark units can be calculated from frequency.

$$z' = 26.81 \; f1(1960 + f) - 0.53$$

Here, f is frequency in Hz, and z is the critical band number in barks. Corrections must be applied below 2 bark and above 20.1 bark. The above calculation uses *Munich* critical band measurements, as opposed to the *Cambridge* version. If the latter are used, the unit is called a *Cam*, or *ERB* ("equivalent rectangular bandwidth") rather than a bark.

Mels

The *mel* scale represents an attempt to find a measure of the psychological experience of pitch similar to the sone scale for loudness. There are several mel scales, each empirically measuring pitch relationships of sine waves relative to a reference frequency. One scale is for instance defined with 1000 mels being equivalent to the pitch of a 1000-Hz sine wave at

40 dB SPL. Another scale has been referenced such that 125 mels is equivalent to the pitch of a 125-Hz sine wave, 100 mels corresponding to 1 bark and spanning a range of 2400 mels.

Appendix C: Octave and 1/3-Octave Bands

Octave bands	
f_c	f_1 and f_2
	14
16	
	22.4
31.5	
	45
63	
	90
125	
	180
250	
	355
500	
	710
1000	
	1400
2000	
	2800
4000	
	5600
8000	
	11200

1/3-octave bands	
f_c	f_1 and f_2
	14
16	
	18
20	
	22.4
25	
	28
31.5	
	35.5
40	
	45
50	
	56
63	
	71
80	
	90
100	
	112
125	
	140
160	
	180
200	
	224
250	
	280
315	
	355
400	
	450

1/3-octave bands	
f_c	F_1 and f_2
	450
500	
	560
630	
	710
800	
	900
1000	
	1120
1250	
	1400
1600	
	1800
2000	
	2240
2500	
	2800
3150	
	3550
4000	
	4500
5000	
	5600
6300	
	7100
8000	
	9000
10000	
	11200
12500	
	14000

Appendix D: Clipped Peaks in the International Affective Digitized Sounds

IADS file #	Description	# of clipped peaks	IADS file #	Description	# of clipped peaks
100	tom cat	5	358	writing	0
105	puppy cry	0	360	rollercoaster	2
106	dog growl	840	361	restaurant	0
109	carousel	57	362	football	0
110	baby laugh	0	370	court sport	0
111	music box	15	380	jackhammer	0
112	kids in park	20	400	jet	111
113	cows	290	401	applause	12
115	bees	43	403	helicopter	5700
116	wasp	553	410	helicopter	0
120	rooster	0	415	countdown	906
130	pig	0	420	car horns	0
132	chickens	847	422	tire skids	31
133	bear	63	423	injury	0
151	cardinal	0	424	car wreck	0
152	tropical	0	425	train	17
171	country night	0	500	wind	507
200	erotic couple	4	501	plane crash	15
201	erotic female	7	502	engine failure	2
202	erotic female	11	600	bike wreck	0
205	erotic female	11	601	colonial music	30
206	Shower	0	602	thunderstorm	0
210	erotic male	0	610	cowboys and indians	182
215	erotic couple	1486	625	mayday	10785
216	erotic couple	2377	626	bombs	8
220	boy laughing	59	627	howling rain	0
221	male laughing	215	699	bomb	0
225	clapping game	0	698	raging fire	14492
226	laughing	30	700	toilet flush	3
230	giggling	23	701	fan	0
251	nose blow	2	702	belch	1595
252	male snoring	1038	704	touchtone	0
254	video game	0	705	rotary dial	0
261	baby crying	26	706	war	1589
262	yawn	11	708	clock ticking	0
270	Whistling	54	709	alarm clock	12
276	female screaming	1	710	cuckoo	0
277	female screaming	70	711	sirens	39
278	child abuse	1	712	buzzer	4
279	attack	333	720	brush teeth	0
280	funeral	8	721	beer pouring	0
285	attack	8	722	walking	0
286	victim	0	723	radio	214
287	cardiac arrest	9	724	chewing	0
290	fight	7	725	soda fizz	0
291	prowler	0	726	cork	0
292	male screaming	0	730	glass break	0
310	crowd	45	802	natives	80
311	crowd	0	810	Beethoven	0
319	office	0	811	Bach	406
320	office	0	812	choir	0
322	typewriter	0	815	rock 'n roll	917
325	traffic	196	816	guitar	0
351	applause	0	820	funk music	552
352	sports crowd	14	826	bag pipes	0
353	baseball	12			

Appendix E: A Brief Bibliography

Books

Baken, R. J., & Orlikoff, R. F. (2000). *Clinical measurement of speech and voice* (2nd ed.). San Diego: Singular Thomson Learning.

Borden, G. J., Harris, K. S., & Raphael, L. J. (2002). *Speech science primer: Physiology, acoustics, and perception of speech* (4th ed.). New York: Lippincott, Williams, & Wilkens.

Fant, G. F. (1960). *The acoustic theory of speech production.* The Hague: Mouton.

Haughton, P. (2002). *Acoustics for audiologists.* New York: Academic.

Johnson, K. (2003). *Acoustic and auditory phonetics.* New York: Blackwell.

Kent, R. D. (1997). *The speech sciences.* San Diego: Singular.

Kent, R. D., & Read, C. (2001). *Acoustic analysis of speech* (2nd ed.). San Diego: Singular.

Markel, J. D., & Gray, A. H. (1976). *Linear prediction of speech.* New York: Springer-Verlag.

Ladefoged, P. (1996). *Elements of acoustic phonetics* (2nd ed.). Chicago: University of Chicago.

Ladefoged, P. (2001). *Vowels and consonants: An introduction to the sounds of the world's languages.* New York: Blackwell.

Ladefoged, P. (2003). *Phonetic data analysis: An introduction to fieldwork and instrumental techniques.* New York: Blackwell.

Pickett, J. M. (1999). *The acoustics of speech communication.* Boston: Allyn and Bacon.

Stevens, K. N. (2000). *Acoustic phonetics.* Cambridge, MA: MIT Press.

Titze, I. R. (1994). *Principles of voice production.* Englewood Cliffs, NJ: Prentice Hall.

Articles and Chapters

Acoustic theory of speech production:
Carre, R. (2004). From an acoustic tube to speech production. *Speech Communication, 42,* 227–240.

Filtering:
Stoddard, P. K. (1997). Application of filters in bioacoustics. In S. L. Hopp, M. J. Owren, & C. S. Evans (Eds.), *Animal acoustic communication: Sound analysis and research methods* (pp. 10–127). Berlin: Springer Verlag.

Linear predictive coding:
Owren, M. J., & Bernacki, R. H. (1998). Applying linear predictive coding (LPC) to frequency-spectrum analysis of animal acoustic signals. In S. L. Hopp, M. J. Owren, & C. S. Evans, (Eds.), *Animal acoustic communication: Sound analysis and research methods* (pp. 129–161). New York: Springer-Verlag.

Pitch extraction and vocal perturbation:
Boersma, P. (1993). Accurate short-term analysis of the fundamental frequency and the harmonics-to-noise ratio of a sampled sound. *Proceedings of the Institute of Phonetic Sciences Amsterdam, 17,* 97–110.

Pitch contour:
Moore, C. A., Cohn, J. F., & Katz, G. S. (1994). Quantitative description and differentiation of fundamental frequency contours. *Computer Speech and Language, 8,* 385–404.

Vocal Expression of Emotion Reviews

Bachorowski, J.-A., & Owren, M. J. (2003). The sounds of emotion: Production and perception of affect-related vocal acoustics. *Annals of the New York Academy of Sciences, 1000,* 244–265.

Banse, R., & Scherer, K. R. (1996). Acoustic profiles in vocal emotion expression. *Journal of Personality and Social Psychology, 70,* 614–636.

Cowie, R., Douglas-Cowie, E., & Schröder, M. (2000). *ISCA Workshop on Speech and Emotion: A conceptual framework for research.* Retrieved from http://www.qub.ac.uk/en/isca/

Johnstone, T., & Scherer, K. R. (2000). Vocal communication of emotion. In M. Lewis & J. Haviland (Eds.), *Handbook of emotion* (2nd ed.; pp. 220–235). New York: Guilford.

Murray, I. R., & Arnott, J. L. (1993). Toward the simulation of emotion in synthetic speech: A review of the literature on human vocal emotion. *Journal of the Acoustical Society of America, 13,* 1–15.

Russell, J. A., Bachorowski, J.-A., & Fernandéz-Dols, J.-M. (2003). Facial and vocal expressions of emotion. *Annual Review of Psychology, 54,* 329–349.

Scherer, K. R. (1986). Vocal affect expression: A review and model for future research. *Psychological Bulletin, 99,* 143–165.

Scherer, K. R. (2003). Vocal communication of emotion: A review of research paradigms. *Speech Communication, 40,* 227–256.

Acknowledgments

This work was supported by NIMH Prime Award 1 R01 MH65317-01A2, Subaward 8402-15235-X, and by the Center for Behavioral Neuroscience under the STC Program of the National Science Foundation under Agreement No. IBN-9876754. Special thanks to Paul Boersma, co-author with David Weeninck of *Praat: Doing phonetics by computer* (freeware available for PC, Mac, multiple other platforms, and as source code at http://www.fon.hum.uva.nl/praat/). The analyses discussed in this chapter are all implemented in Praat, along with many other editing, analysis, and synthesis capabilities. Chapter graphics were created using Praat's *Picture* facility.

References

Bachorowski, J.-A., & Owren, M. J. (2003). The sounds of emotion: Production and perception of affect-related vocal acoustics. *Annals of the New York Academy of Sciences, 1000,* 244–265.

Banse, R., & Scherer, K. R. (1996). Acoustic profiles in vocal emotion expression. *Journal of Personality and Social Psychology, 70,* 614–636.

Boersma, P. (1993). Accurate short-term analysis of the fundamental frequency and the harmonics-to-noise ratio of a sampled sound. *Proceedings of the Institute of Phonetic Sciences Amsterdam, 17,* 97–110.

Bradley, M. M., & Lang, P. J. (2000). Affective reactions to acoustic stimuli. *Psychophysiology, 37,* 204–215.

Cooley, J. W., & Tukey, J. W. (1965). An algorithm for the machine calculation of complex Fourier series. *Mathematics of Computation, 19,* 297–301.

Darwin, C. (1998). *The expression of the emotions in man and animals.* New York: Oxford University Press. (Original work published 1872)

Fairbanks, G., & Pronovost, W. (1939). An experimental study of the pitch characteristics of the voice during expression of emotion. *Speech Monographs, 6,* 85–105.

Fant, G. F. (1960). *The acoustic theory of speech production.* The Hague: Mouton.

Johnstone, T., & Scherer, K. R. (2000). Vocal communication of emotion. In M. Lewis & J. Haviland (Eds.), *Handbook of emotion* (2nd ed., pp. 220–235). New York: Guilford Press.

Koike, Y. (1973). Application of some acoustic measures for the evaluation of laryngeal dysfunction. *Studia Phonologica, 7,* 17–23.

Lang, P. J., Bradley, M. M., & Cuthbert (1999). *International Affective Picture System (IAPS): Technical manual and affective ratings.* Gainesville: University of Florida, Center for Research in Psychophysiology.

Scherer, K. R. (1986). Vocal affect expression: A review and model for future research. *Psychological Bulletin, 99,* 143–165.

Stevens, K. N. (2000). *Acoustic phonetics.* Cambridge, MA: MIT Press.

Takahashi, H. & Koike, Y. (1975). Some perceptual dimensions and acoustical correlates of pathological voices. *Acta Otolaryngologica, 338*(Suppl.), 1–24.

James A. Coan
John M. Gottman

The Specific Affect Coding System (SPAFF)

In 1989, Gottman and Krokoff introduced the Specific Affect Coding System (SPAFF) for the purpose of systematically observing affective behavior in the context of marital conflict. The original SPAFF conferred a host of advantages over earlier "microanalytic" coding strategies, the primary innovation being the ability to code affect at the construct level instead of at the level of extremely discrete bits of behavior, such as specific gestures or facial movements (Gottman, McCoy, Coan, & Collier, 1995).

Since its debut, the SPAFF has, in one version or another, informed dozens of published scientific findings deriving from numerous laboratories (e.g., Burman, Margolin, & John, 1993; Carstensen, Gottman, & Levenson, 1995; Coan, Gottman, Babcock, & Jacobson, 1997; Cohan & Bradbury, 1994, 1997; Jacobson et al., 1994; Notarius, Benson, Sloane, Vanzetti, & Hornyak, 1989). For example, the SPAFF has been used to study affective behavior among newlyweds (Cohan & Bradbury, 1997; Gottman, Coan, Carrere, & Swanson, 1998), domestically violent couples (Babcock, Waltz, Jacobson, & Gottman, 1993; Coan et al., 1997), couples in long-term marriages (Carstensen et al., 1995; Levenson, Carstensen, & Gottman, 1994), and, most recently, gay and lesbian couples (Gottman, Levenson, Gross, et al., 2003; Gottman, Levenson, Swanson, et al., 2003). Although initially developed for the study of emotional communication among romantic couples, the SPAFF is now used for coding interactions among children, their parents, and their peers (Joanne Wu Shortt, personal communication, April 9, 2002), and even to therapy

situations (Janine Giese-Davis, personal communication, October 11, 2003). Indeed, individuals in applied settings have expressed interest in learning the SPAFF (Coan, 1998). In a recent review of observational couples research, Heyman (2001) noted that the SPAFF has "by far the best evidence of construct and criterion validity for its constructs" of all current microanalytic coding systems (Heyman, 2001, p. 25).

History of the SPAFF

Early observational coding systems, such as the Marital Interaction Coding System (MICS; Hops, Wills, Weiss, & Patterson, 1972), and the Facial Affect Scoring Technique (FAST; Ekman, Friesen, & Tomkins, 1971), sought to identify extremely discrete bits of behavior that might prove useful in understanding how such behaviors function in the context of interpersonal relationships. Initially, Gottman followed in this tradition with the development of the Couples Interaction Scoring System (CISS; Gottman, 1979). CISS coders were instructed to hierarchically scan behaviors for specific cues, starting with the face, moving to the voice, and finally coding body movements. Notably, the CISS ignored verbal content altogether. A short while later, frustrated with perceived inadequacies in the CISS, Gottman sought a revision of his system that was heavily influenced by the Facial Action Coding System (FACS; Ekman & Friesen, 1978). Nevertheless, Gottman's frustrations mounted as his lists of discrete codable behaviors grew at an alarming rate. As he recounted in his first published SPAFF manual:

> I did not want my summary codes to read something like: "Husband shows zygomatic major contracts on face with contraction of the cheek raiser muscle, with shift downward in fundamental frequency, decrease in amplitude and voice in a major key and rapid inhalation and exhalation of breath with *hut hut* vocalizations." Instead, I wanted to say that the husband laughed. (Gottman et al., 1995, p. 3)

The point was not to ignore the identification of zygomatic major contractions or modulations of frequency and amplitude in vocal communication. Rather, the point was that modern affect coding, although informed by a thorough knowledge of discrete behaviors such as those described by Ekman, Scherer, and others (e.g., Banse & Scherer, 1996; Ekman & Friesen, 1975; Scherer, 1974), often missed the forest for the trees. Gottman sought to devise a coding system that made explicit use of discrete bits of information in the service of describing constructs representing generalizable human affective behavior. Thus Gottman reintroduced *verbal content* to the specification of those constructs.

Of course, previous microanalytic coding systems had been used to cluster codes into "macrocodes" or constructs, but these attempts had been empirical and, in any event, had often been implemented *after* the coding had been completed. Gottman (Gottman et al., 1995) sought instead to let his coders code *theoretically specified* constructs directly. This new approach assumed that coders had, or could be taught, the ability to integrate a variety of different affective cues into broader constructs both rapidly and accurately. It was hoped that such an approach would increase the speed with which such coding could be done and also that it would render such coding more reliable and externally valid.

It was from these efforts that the first major version of the SPAFF was born. The original version of the SPAFF comprised 10 gestalt behavior codes: Neutral, Humor, Affection/Caring, Interest/Curiosity, Anger, Disgust/Scorn/Contempt, Whining, Sadness, and Fear. This was later expanded to a second major version that comprised 16 such codes, adding Surprise and Validation to the positive set and expanding the negative set to include Belligerence, Dominance, Stonewalling, and Defensiveness, as well as separating Disgust and Contempt into distinct codes (Gottman et al., 1995). Since the publication of the first SPAFF manual, the SPAFF has been revised yet further. This chapter holds to a description of the SPAFF in its most current form, with a full listing of its revised and updated list of codes and their indicators. It also includes advice for training SPAFF coders, for assessing coding reliability, and for solving various data analytic issues. Recent innovations in weighting SPAFF codes for use as a continuous scale, as well as attempts to utilize SPAFF codes as separate continuous variables, are also described.

Learning to Code Behavior: The Philosophy of the SPAFF

Among the core ideas underlying the SPAFF is the uncontroversial notion that emotions are expressed in a wide variety of ways and that this variety should be respected. If there is a second major idea, it is that SPAFF coding requires the use of human beings with a personal history of interpersonal, affective communication. Such a personal history provides access to subtle cues that even many years of strict training in the identification of discrete physical features may neglect. Thus learning to observe emotional behavior means, on the one hand, learning to identify multiple discrete indicators, any one of which may or may not be present during a particular emotional episode, and, on the other hand, drawing from one's own personal history of affective communication in order to spot the complexities of behavior that remain outside the grasp of highly detailed discrete analysis. SPAFF coding means learning to integrate voice, physical features, verbal content, and more—indicators that are sometimes hard to describe (e.g., "positive energy") but that are easily grasped by most coders.

SPAFF Codes Are Latent Psychological Constructs

Figure 16.1 depicts, for the purpose of illustration,[1] a *latent variable model* (cf. Bollen, 2002) representing the SPAFF code Validation. In this model, the core, latent construct Validation (represented in the oval) is not directly observable. Rather, it is assumed to exist and to actually *cause* the expression of its various observable indicators (represented as rectangles). One would not be able to "see" Validation without directly observing at least one of its indicators. An indicator is an objective piece of evidence that any observer can see or hear directly. It is called an indicator because when it is present, it literally "indicates" the underlying construct we are interested in—it tells us that our latent construct is happening. Importantly, we are rarely interested in any one of the indicators of Validation per se. Rather, we are interested in the construct that those indicators indicate. Put another way, it is of little specific consequence to us as SPAFF coders whether we observe direct statements of agreement or apology, whether we observe summarizing behaviors, or whether we observe head-nodding behavior with eye contact. These bits of observation are merely the media through which we become aware of the thing we are *really* interested in, which is Validation. We cannot "see" Validation without the presence of one or more or its indicators, but without the construct of Validation, those indicators are by themselves of little theoretical value. This is true even when discrete and easily identified behaviors wind up predicting important outcomes, such as happens, for example, in the association between the "eye roll" and marital dissolution. The importance of a discrete behavior such as the eye roll lies in its connection to the construct of contempt (cf. Gottman, 1993b).

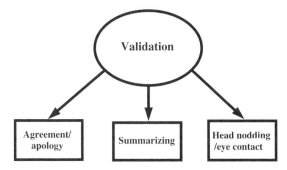

Figure 16.1. The SPAFF code Validation represented as a latent construct.

Physical Features and Cultural Informants

In the language and history of behavior coding, at least two broad approaches can be identified. These are the *physical features* and *cultural informant* approaches. Physical-features approaches hold strictly to the detailed description of physical observables, such as changes in vocal acoustic properties, facial expressions, specific gestures, and body postures. In theory, anyone, or nearly anyone, can be taught to be a physical-features coder; even computers are now becoming capable of doing so (Xiao, Moriyama, Kanade, & Cohn, 2003).

By contrast, the cultural-informant approach utilizes individuals who are, for one reason or another, sensitive observers in a specific cultural setting. They may, for example, have specific knowledge about a certain culture or group of cultures and, by virtue of this specific knowledge, be uniquely capable of decoding the *meaning* of specific behaviors within the context of that culture. Anthropologists have employed cultural informants to study cultures with which they were not intuitively familiar. Cultural informants aid researchers in the *interpretation* of specific observable events.

In SPAFF coding, both physical-features and cultural-informant approaches are utilized in the service of capturing meaningful affective constructs. In training SPAFF coders, the assumption is made that most individuals will be sensitive to subtle differences between certain instances of observable events. Take, for example, an instance in which a young woman gently rubs her cheek on her shoulder while making eye contact with her partner. A purely physical-features approach might note her cheek-shoulder distance and append that particular unit of distance to a tally of other such distances for later analysis. Such units of distance would certainly constitute a kind of information about this woman. Indeed (as was noted earlier), a computer could very probably do this kind of coding. However, it is probably still true that only a live human being with a lifetime of experience observing people interacting with each other would be able to distinguish between a cheek rubbed on the shoulder as part of an emotional display (of, say, coy affection) versus a cheek rubbed on the shoulder to relieve an itch.

Such a large and complex number of indicators are needed to distinguish these two possibilities that computer algorithms, as sophisticated as they are becoming, are probably still many years from being able to do so. On the other hand, a human being—that is, a cultural informant—could reliably note the difference in an instant, and the difference is likely to be a meaningful one.

Becoming a Cultural Informant: Seeing Versus Observing

Perhaps the most recognizable quotation of Sir Arthur Conan Doyle's literary creation Sherlock Holmes is "you saw, but you did not observe." The line was used to chastise the affable and earnest Dr. Watson, but it applies equally well to most of us, most of the time. We usually attend to only some fraction of the sensory information that is available to us. Most of our time is spent reflexively responding to a kind of social and affective rhythm, to the pitch and meter of conversation, to the style of the clothes people are wearing, to the moods implied in the ways people carry themselves and the obvious components of the looks on their faces. All of these bits of information influence our behaviors, and our behaviors in turn influence the individuals who are influencing *us*. Presumably, our brains "see" all of this information as it occurs, at least in the sense that the information is causing us to respond in certain ways, but under ordinary circumstances, we do not reflect on the information explicitly.

Becoming an effective cultural informant means learning to be an *active observer* of the kinds of information just described. The first step toward becoming an active observer simply involves learning to be mindful of the information that is available at any one moment. For example, when conversing with an office mate, it may be useful to pay close attention to how he expresses his feelings with his face and to note what he's wearing and how he typically carries himself. Such exercises prompt a number of interesting questions. What, for example, might this person be intending to communicate other than what he is explicitly saying? Perhaps one would conclude that he is interested in portraying himself as a serious and highly skilled worker but also a fun-loving and adventuresome person in other contexts. Fair enough. But what is he actually doing to convey this information? In other words, after we have come to some tentative conclusions about who this person is and what he is trying to tell us in subtle ways about himself, we can ask the next question: *How do we know?* By doing so, we are already well on the way to becoming active observers.

Three Rules of People Watching

We have found that active observation can be facilitated with some simple exercises that we refer to as the *rules of people watching* (Gottman et al., 1995). These rules are predicated on the idea that when people behave in certain characteristic ways, or even in ways that seem specific to certain situations, they are doing so *to portray themselves as a kind of character*. Further, they select behaviors for this purpose *from a set of possible choices of how to act at any one moment*. That said, it is important to recognize that we are *not* asserting that this is *actually* what people are doing most of the time, though it might be. Rather, our intention is to provide the reader with ways to approach the problem of people watching so that he or she can become a more sensitive and more accurate cultural informant. In other words, what follows are not the rules of behavior but the rules of the active observation of behavior. They are rules for becoming an active observer.

Rule 1: View a Behavior as Though It Were Chosen From a Collection of Possible Alternatives

If one imagines two different people with precisely the same mild disability, a limp for example, it is possible to imagine further that each individual will behave differently with regard to the limp he or she copes with. One of them may, for example, work to minimize the extent of the limp through a variety of movements designed to keep others from seeing it. Another may exaggerate the limp, forming it into a kind of a swagger. The obvious point is that either of them could have chosen either approach to dealing with the limp, and there may indeed be other approaches as well. There are multiple options for incorporating the disability into their day-to-day behaviors. The other point, however, and perhaps the less obvious one, is that these options could be thought of as *alternative styles* of having a mild disability.

One can imagine a multitude of behavioral styles in a variety of contexts. People watching at parties can be particularly useful for this. It is informative to note the variety of dress, the different kinds of laughter people use, the intensity of the smiles one observes, the degree of physical space that people maintain, and so forth. Any of these dimensions of behavior could, in theory, be selected by any of the people in the room. And yet, certain people "select" only certain behaviors. The question is *why* certain people select certain behaviors, and that leads to rule 2.

Rule 2: View Behavior as if It Were Designed to Portray a Character in a Play or a Film—as if It Were Written to Follow a Script

As you watch people at our hypothetical party, it is possible to imagine that everyone's role has been scripted and that one is actually observing actors working to portray certain characters. When actors begin preparing characters, they are frequently given a number of character attributes that they must then devise ways of communicating to an audience. Thus, when an individual at a party begins laughing loudly and becoming very animated, one might ask, *What is it that the actor is trying to portray about that character?* He or she may, for example, be attempting to communicate that he or she is uninhibited, spontaneous, and warm. When meeting a new individual at a party, or indeed in any setting, it can be very

useful to ask the question, *I wonder how this person is going to communicate what he or she is like?*

Rule 3: Watch a Person as if You Were an Actor Who Had to Play That Person in a Film

It is instructive to ask oneself what kinds of behaviors would be necessary to portray any individual being that one is observing. This exercise can be as simple, at first, as just trying to mirror his or her behavior. Frequently, your body will know what to do if you just try to mimic someone. Indeed, research suggests that mirroring behavior can enhance one's ability to code it (e.g., Blairy, Herrera, & Hess, 1999). Mimic the life of the party and contrast that with the feeling of mimicking the person who seemed to spend the evening in relative seclusion. Each exercise in imitation reveals a set of feelings, specific movements, props, and even attitudes that can assist in the development of active observation. In practice, the three rules of people watching can begin the process of becoming comfortable with, and deliberate about, observing rather than merely seeing. But when it comes to observational coding, being comfortable with and deliberate about observing people is only the first step.

Facial Expressions of the SPAFF

As noted in some detail previously, the SPAFF is not a strictly physical-features-based coding system. Nevertheless, more than any other such system, the SPAFF has been heavily influenced by, and indeed incorporates, the Facial Action Coding System of Paul Ekman and Wallace Friesen (Cohn, Ambadar & Ekman, chapter 13, this volume; Ekman & Friesen, 1978). We regard the FACS as the state of the art in facial coding, and in this section we describe the movements that are regarded as essential to understanding many SPAFF codes. That said, there are notable departures from official FACS protocol in the SPAFF, not the least of which is that the intensity levels of FACS codes are more or less ignored in favor of coding specific FACS codes as either present at any level of intensity or not present. Further, for the sake of brevity and specificity, many FACS codes are not included in the SPAFF at all.

Specific facial movements are covered in detail elsewhere in this volume (Cohn, et al., chapter 13, this volume). Thus we refer the reader to the chapter by Cohn, et al., and, indeed, to the FACS manual itself for detailed descriptions of the action units (AUs) described in this and subsequent sections. Figure 16.2 depicts a selection of common facial expressions associated with the SPAFF.

Action Units of the Upper Face

- Action Unit 1 (AU1)—The Inner Brow Raiser. (We sometimes refer to this as the *Woody Allen*.)

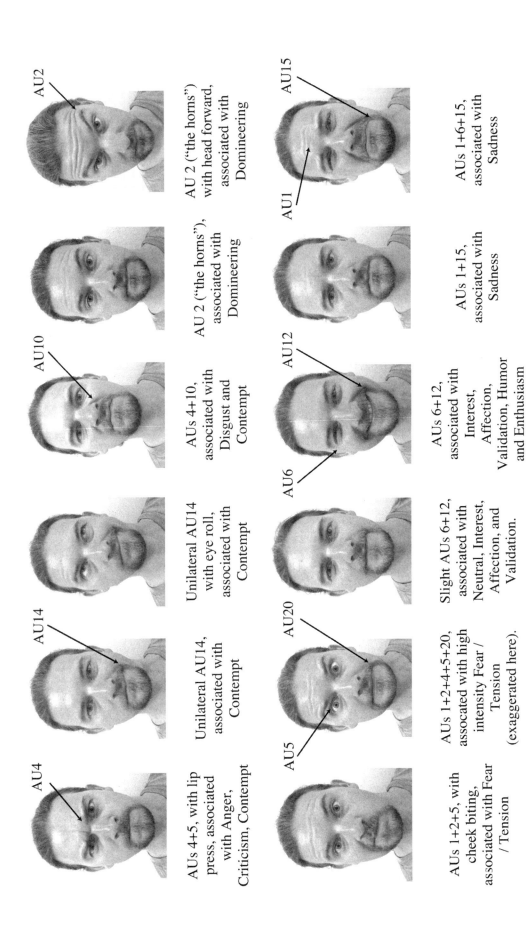

Figure 16.2. In this figure of the common facial expressions of the SPAFF, arrows highlight the major action units (AUs) involved in the different expressions. Note that although AUs are highlighted only once each, several occur in more than one expression.

- Action Unit 2 (AU2)—The Outer Brow Raiser. (We frequently refer to the bilateral manifestation of this movement as the *horns*.)
- Action Unit 4 (AU4)—The Brow Lowerer.
- Action Unit 5 (AU5)—The Upper Lid Raiser.
- Action Unit 6 (AU6)—The Cheek Raiser and Lid Compressor.
- Action Unit 7 (AU7)—The Lid Tightener. (We sometimes refer to this movement as the *Clint Eastwood*.)
- Action Unit 9 (AU9)—The Nose Wrinkler.

Action Units of the Lower Face

- Action Unit 10 (AU10)—The Upper Lip Raiser.
- Action Unit 12 (AU12)—The Lip Corner Puller.
- Action Unit 14 (AU14)—The Dimpler.
- Action Unit 15 (AU15)—The Lip Corner Depressor.
- Action Unit 17 (AU17)—The Chin Raiser.
- Action Unit 20 (AU20)—The Lip Stretcher.
- Action Unit 25/26 (AU25/26)—Lips Part/Jaw Drop

The facial action units detailed in the preceding lists may occur singly or in combination. Moreover, some action units, such as AU14, which is heavily implicated in the SPAFF code Contempt, frequently manifest on one side of the face only.

Codes of the SPAFF

As described earlier, coding the SPAFF requires that attention be paid to verbal content, facial behaviors, voice tones, and other forms of communication. What follows are detailed description of the codes that make up the current version of the SPAFF (see Table 16.1). Descriptions include subsections that detail the *function* of the code in interpersonal communication, various *indicators* of the code, *physi-*

Table 16.1
Current codes of the SPAFF

Positive Affects	Negative Affects
Affection	Anger
Enthusiasm	Belligerence
Humor	Contempt
Interest	Criticism
Validation	Defensiveness
	Disgust
	Domineering
	Fear / Tension
	Sadness
	Stonewalling
	Threats
	Whining
Neutral	

cal cues for the code, and specific *counterindicators* regarding the code. Indicators and physical cues provide information about behaviors that *probably* derive from the presence of the code, whereas counterindicators provide information about behaviors that *probably do not* derive from the presence of the code. Throughout these descriptions, reference is made to *speakers* and *receivers*. Speakers are those who are observed using the code, and receivers are those the speakers are speaking to.

Affection

Function

Affection expresses genuine caring and concern and offers comfort. Often the voice slows and becomes quieter or lower. Its function is to facilitate closeness and bonding.

Indicators

1. *Reminiscing.* The speaker shares warm memories of something she and the receiver enjoyed together.
2. *Caring statements.* Direct statements of affection or concern, such as "I love you," "I care about you," "I worry about you," and so forth.
3. *Compliments.* Statements that communicate pride in or admiration of one's partner (e.g., "you are so smart!" or "you did such a great job with the . . .").
4. *Empathy.* Empathizing individuals mirror the affect of their partners. Such mirroring need not be verbal, but however it is expressed, it should be obvious that the intent of the mirroring is to express an understanding of the partner's feelings. Importantly, empathy does more than simply validate the partner's thoughts and feelings—by mirroring the affect of the partner at the same time, it conveys a level of care that surpasses validation per se.
5. *The common cause.* An important indicator of Affection, similar to empathy, is the common cause, whereby individuals engage in virtually any affective behavior *together* as a form of building trust, closeness, consensus, or bonding. This indicator can sometimes be confusing. Insults, such as remarking that "Bob is a jerk," can be coded Affection if intended to express obvious agreement. A shared anger, a shared fear, a shared and vocalized political opinion—all of these things could be coded Affection.
6. *Flirting.* When individuals flirt, they are communicating desire for their partners. The verbal expression would be "I want you," but flirting needn't be verbal. Flirting can be playful, sweet, warm, intense, or all of the these.

Physical Cues

There are no particular AUs that indicate affection, but AUs 6 + 12 will commonly be seen.

Counterindicators

- *Defensive affection.* Occasionally, a speaker will insist that he loves the receiver as a defensive maneuver. The indicators of defensiveness (discussed later) will usually give this away. Watch for defensive voice tone, a defensive context, and a lack of warm, positive feeling underlying the affectionate message.

Anger

Function

In the SPAFF, anger functions to respond to perceived violations of the speaker's rights to autonomy and respect. It serves as a kind of "affective underlining" of displeasure and complaint, indicating that an interpersonal boundary has been transgressed. Some SPAFF coders have called the SPAFF code of Anger "angry affect without belligerence, contempt, defensiveness, disgust or attempts to dominate." This is largely true.

Indicators

1. *Frustration.* A relatively low intensity form of Anger, here facial expressions of anger become apparent at low levels and the voice may lower in pitch and tempo. The anger will appear constrained or out of the obvious awareness of the speaker. Otherwise, the person may not express anger verbally at all.
2. *Angry "I-statements."* These are verbal statements that express personal feelings, as in "I am so angry!" or "I am so frustrated right now!"
3. *Angry questions.* Questions asked with angry affect and usually with sharp exhalations, as in "Why?!"
4. *Commands.* Commands are not attempts to dominate but rather are strong, affectively intense attempts to stop a recent or ongoing violation of the speaker's autonomy or dignity. Sharp exhalations and strong angry affect frequently accompany commands. Examples include "Stop!" or "Don't speak to me like I'm a child!"

Physical Cues

AUs 4, 5, 7, 4+5, 4+5+7, 23, 24. The lips will frequently thin, with the red of the upper lip disappearing or the lips pressed together; the teeth will clench; and the muscles of the jaw and neck will tighten. The voice may suddenly increase in pitch, amplitude, and tempo and may include a kind of "growl" as when yelling.

Counterindicators

- *Blends with other codes.* Angry affect is frequently observed during moments in which indicators of other negative codes are present. In these instances, Anger is never coded.

Belligerence

Function

The function of Belligerence is to "get a rise" out of the receiver through provocation of anger. The belligerent speaker is, in a sense, looking for a fight.

Indicators

1. *Taunting questions.* These are questions whose function is to irritate or confuse the receiver. An example might include the frequent and irritating use of the question "Why?" in the context of a serious discussion. Frequently the belligerent speaker is seen struggling to suppress a smirk while asking taunting questions as the receiver becomes increasingly enraged.
2. *Unreciprocated humor.* Sometimes, the belligerent speaker appears to actually believe he or she is being funny, even though the receiver is obviously annoyed. Such moments of unreciprocated humor are neither playful, fun, and shared (as in humor) nor sarcastic, mocking, and insulting (as in contempt). Belligerent speakers do not appear to get the message that the humor is not universally funny. The fact that the jokes are annoying the receiver may increase the level of humor experienced by the speaker.
3. *Interpersonal terrorism.* Here, the belligerent speaker is posing direct challenges to the agreed-on rules or boundaries of the relationship. Frequently, such behavior takes the form of a dare, as in "What would you do if I did?" or "What are you going to do about it?"

Physical Cues

AUs 1 or 2. Jaw thrust forward.

Counterindicators

1. *Good-natured teasing.* Good-natured "jabs" at the receiver's foibles are not coded as belligerence, especially if the humor or the teasing appears to be shared.
2. *Hostile humor.* Unreciprocated humor that is obviously hostile, mocking, belittling, or insulting is coded Contempt.

Contempt

Function

The function of Contemptuous behavior is to belittle, hurt, or humiliate. Contempt can be any statement made from a superior position to the partner, such as correcting an angry person's grammar. Such behavior deliberately and forthrightly communicates an icy lack of respect, often cruelty. On theoretical and empirical grounds, we regard this behavior as extremely detrimental to interpersonal relationships (Coan et al., 1997; Gottman, 1993a; Gottman et al., 1998; Gottman & Levenson, 1992), and so the SPAFF gives it precedence over most other behaviors.

Indicators

1. *Sarcasm.* Sarcasm in conversation frequently precedes derisive laughter at the receiver's expense or manifests as a ridiculing comment regarding something the receiver has said. Frequent examples include the ironic use of such statements as "sure!" or "I'll bet you did!"
2. *Mockery.* When speakers mock, they repeat something the receiver has said while exaggeratedly imitating the receiver's manner of speech or emotional state for the purpose of making the receiver look ridiculous or stupid.
3. *Insults.* Insults are active and straightforward forms of contempt—they are shows of disrespect for the receiver through obvious verbal cruelty.
4. *Hostile humor.* Often, the contemptuous speaker uses a form of unshared humor that, though an apparent joke, utilizes sarcasm, mocking, or insults to achieve the aim of contempt. By delivering such messages as a "joke," the speaker may be attempting to leave him- or herself an "out" (as in, "hey, I was only joking"). Hostile humor can be momentarily confusing for coders and receivers alike. The contemptuous speaker may laugh heartily, and sometimes the receiver will briefly and reflexively laugh along. Such moments are not coded as Humor.

Physical Cues

AU 14 (uni- or bilateral). *Note: Eye rolls are nearly always coded as contempt.*

Counterindicators

• *Good-natured teasing.* Good-natured "jabs" at the receiver's foibles are not coded as contempt. A good indication that contempt is not occurring is that the context of the conversation appears to contradict contemptuous intentions or that the speaker and receiver appear to both experience laughter and joy as a result of the teasing.

Criticism

Function

Criticism functions as an attack on someone's character or personality in a way that is not obviously insulting, as in Contempt. It is a complaint that suggests that the partner's personality is defective. It is often accompanied by blame and is quite distinct from complaining.[2] Complaints refer to specific instances of behavior, whereas Criticisms are character-

ized by negative global assessments of a person's abilities or value as a person. Complaints accompanied by "you always" or "you never" statements are considered criticisms. Criticism may or may not make reference to a specific event.

Indicators

1. *Blaming.* In blaming, one individual assigns fault to another, along with a personal attack or global accusation, as in "the reason the engine blew up is that you *never* put oil in it."
2. *Character attacks.* Often expressed as "you never/you always" generalizations, character attacks are critical of a person's personality or abilities in very general ways. Examples include statements such as "you don't care," "you always put yourself first," and so forth.
3. *Kitchen sinking.* This is essentially a long list of complaints. Even though any particular item on the list may not fit criteria for Criticism per se, a long list functions to illustrate the incompetence or personality defects of the person on the receiving end. For example, an individual might "kitchen sink" using complaints and "I" statements, such as, "I don't feel listened to by you, and you don't touch me very often, and I asked you to do certain chores, but you didn't, and we don't do very many fun things together lately."
4. *Betrayal statements.* Similar to blaming, betrayal statements specifically reference trust and commitment, implying that the person on the receiving end is either not committed, untrustworthy, or both. "How could you?" is a question frequently indicative of Criticism.
5. *Negative mind reading.* Generally speaking, mind-reading statements express attributions about another's feelings, behaviors, or motives. They indicate Criticism when negative or accompanied by negative affect. An example of negative mind reading would be "you just don't like Tom because he smokes."

Physical Cues

There are no particular AUs that indicate Criticism.

Counterindicators

• *Insults.* Critical statements designed to inflict gratuitous emotional pain (e.g., "you're an idiot") are coded contempt.

Defensiveness

Function

Defensiveness functions to deflect responsibility or blame. It communicates a kind of innocent victimhood or righteous indignation (e.g., as a counterattack) on the part of the speaker, implying that whatever bad thing being discussed is not the speaker's fault. Defensive speakers can engage in defending themselves or friends and loved ones who may be under attack by their partners.

Indicators

1. *The "yes-but."* SPAFF coders refer to statements that start off as momentary agreements but very quickly end in disagreements as "yes-buts." They are common indicators of defensiveness.
2. *Cross-complaining.* This behavior involves meeting one complaint with an immediate countercomplaint. In this way, complaints are simply not responded to—cross-complaints deflect them by leading the conversation into a suddenly new direction.
3. *Minimization.* Defensive speakers will frequently try to minimize a complaint by asserting that the problem they are potentially responsible for was scarcely a problem in the first place. A minimizing speaker might say, for example, "You're right, I did forget to put the garbage out, but there was hardly any garbage anyway, so it really isn't a problem. It can wait until next week."
4. *Excuses.* Excuses are attempts to locate responsibility or blame in something other than the speaker, as in, "well, traffic was all backed up, there was nothing I could do."
5. *Aggressive defenses.* Oftentimes a speaker will aggressively assert things, for example, "I did *not!*" These are vehement denials of responsibility that come across as childish, as in "did not/did too" interactions.

Physical Cues

AUs 1, 2, 1 + 2, arms folded across chest. The voice will increase in pitch and amplitude.

Counterindicators

- *Invalidations.* Statements designed to directly contradict the receiver (e.g., "you are wrong" or "that's simply untrue"), spoken in a lower pitched voice tone, are more properly coded Domineering.

Disgust

Function

Disgust is a relatively involuntary verbal or nonverbal reaction to a stimulus that is perceived to be noxious. Harmful substances (e.g., feces, rotted food) reliably elicit disgust, but disgust can also occur for moral or symbolic reasons (Rozin, Lowery, & Ebert, 1994).

Indicators

1. *Involuntary revulsion.* Here the object of disgust is some obvious image of, or reference to, an aversive, noxious stimulus, as in momentary descriptions of a gruesome physical injury.
2. *Moral objection.* Here the object of disgust is an action or idea that the speaker finds repulsive for moral or other symbolic reasons, as in responses to undesirable sexual practices or even political positions.

Physical Cues

The physical cues of Disgust are robust and specific. AUs 9, 10, 4, 15, and 17 can sometimes be seen, either singly or in any combination. The tongue will sometimes protrude, and the head will sometimes turn to one side as if avoiding the noxious stimulus.

Counterindicators

1. *Mockery, insults, or belittlement.* If the function of a disgust response, whether verbal or nonverbal, appears to be to communicate obvious disrespect of the receiver, it is more properly coded as Contempt. This includes instances in which the speaker appears to be disgusted by the behavior of the receiver.
2. *Disapproval without Disgust affect.* Disapproval, absent other obvious signs of disgust, can be coded Neutral (when lacking in obvious affective tone), Domineering (when spoken in a patronizing tone), or Anger (with angry affect).

Domineering

Function

The function of Domineering behavior is to exert and demonstrate control over one's partner or a conversation. Domineering behaviors attempt to impose compliance on the receiver's responses or behaviors.

Indicators

1. *Invalidation.* Invalidation deliberately and forcefully contradicts the validity of the receiver's point of view (e.g., "that's just wrong") or expressed feelings (e.g., "oh, you are not afraid, quit exaggerating").
2. *Lecturing and patronizing.* This indicator identifies attempts to belittle or disempower a person or a person's arguments. Many "subindicators" suggest the presence of lecturing and patronizing, including pointing or wagging a finger while talking, citing authorities (e.g., "well, Dr. Phil says . . ."), speaking in platitudes and clichés, appealing to an ambiguous "everyone" (as in "everyone knows"), and so forth. A distinctly patronizing quality often accompanies these behaviors. Look for finger pointing used for emphasis.
3. *Low balling.* Low balling expresses itself in the form of questions that have predetermined answers. The questions are not merely rhetorical but also have a

manipulative quality, such as, "You want me to be happy, don't you?" Low-balling behaviors are similar to sales ploys that seek to force unwary customers to answer "yes" to very simple questions (e.g., "Do you want your children to achieve their potential?") in order to manipulate them into purchasing a product.

4. *Incessant speech.* By using incessant speech, domineering persons can ensure that the receiver is not allowed an opportunity to respond. It is a form of forcibly maintaining the floor in a conversation at all times. Incessant speech often has a repetitious, steady, almost rhythmic quality in the voice. When speaking incessantly, domineering persons often repeat or summarize their point of view while paying very little attention to the verbal content of things said by the people with whom they are speaking. Look for finger pointing used for emphasis.

5. *Glowering.* Glowering is really a kind of steady gaze, often characterized by the head tilted forward with the chin down, and the outer portions of the eyebrows raised—an eyebrow configuration we refer to as "the horns" because, when configured in this way, the eyebrows do indeed resemble horns. Thus, when glowering, the "horns" are emphasized, and the person may be leaning the head, body, or both forward.

Physical Cues

AU 2 ("the horns"), head forward, body forward, finger pointing, head cocked to one side.

Counterindicators

- *Contemptuous patronizing.* Whenever the content of patronizing becomes blatantly insulting, it should be coded Contempt.

Enthusiasm (Formerly Joy)

Function

The function of enthusiasm is to express a passionate interest in a person or activity, as well as a positive valence associated with that interest. Enthusiasm is infectious and often sudden, loud, boisterous, and energetic. Nonverbal behaviors prominently accompany verbal expressions of eagerness and joy.

Indicators

1. *Anticipation.* Anticipatory behaviors are hopeful, future-oriented, and often childlike. They may be accompanied by fidgeting and distraction.

2. *Positive surprise.* This is an emphatically happy reaction to some unanticipated event or remark. Prominent smiles and loud verbalizations characterize this indicator (e.g., AU 1+2+6+12+24, accompanied by "Really!?")

3. *Positive excitement.* Positive excitement includes expressions of joy and anticipation at very high levels of intensity.

4. *Joy.* Joyful moments reflect high levels of often suddenly felt happiness. Joy will frequently follow receipt of a compliment and will often be accompanied by broad, warm smiles and bright, alert, positive facial expressions.

5. *Expansiveness.* Expansive individuals feel creative, motivated, and inspired and convey an effervescent and elated affect.

Physical Cues

AUs 1+2, 5, 6+12, 23, 24, 25–27 will commonly be seen. Individuals will sometimes sit up or forward in their chairs, and their voices will increase in pitch and volume.

Counterindicators

- *Interest indicators.* Enthusiasm can sometimes look like Interest and vice versa. Interested questions are accompanied by positive affect but of a lower intensity than those coded Enthusiasm.

- *Negative surprise.* Surprise reactions are not unequivocally positive, and it is important to be watchful for surprise reactions that contain either a lack of positive affect or the presence of negative affect.

Fear/Tension

Function

Fear/Tension communicates, usually involuntarily, fear, worry, anxiety, nervous anticipation, or dread.

Indicators

1. *Speech disturbances.* Fearful or tense speakers will often have a difficult time expressing or even knowing what they want to say. This will manifest as incomplete or unfinished statements, stuttering, or *frequent* and *rapid* "uhs" and "ahs." Watch also for shallow, rapid breathing. (Note that the *occasional* use of "ah, "er," or "umm" can simply reflect attempts to keep the floor or turn at speech.)

2. *Shifts in fundamental frequency.* In studies of vocal quality, *chest register* refers to a lower pitch characterized by vibratory sensations felt in the sternum and trachea, and *head register* refers to a higher pitch characterized by vibratory sensations felt in the head. Either of these states can characterize a *fundamental frequency,* or the lowest frequency, of sound waves characterizing a person's speech. In fear/tension, one can often detect a shift in fundamental frequency that moves from a chest register to a head register.

3. *Fidgeting.* Fearful or tense individuals will fidget, repeatedly shifting their position in their chairs (as if in the "hot seat"), plucking at clothes or hands, rubbing their faces (especially the temple, mouth, and chin), or biting the lips or inside of their mouths.
4. *Nervous laughter.* Unshared laughter or giggling that doesn't appear to fit in the conversation and likely is a response to nervous tension (e.g., no jokes or humorous moments have occurred). Often, the fearful or tense individual will seem unable to stop. The smile will often appear "pasted on" (see "Physical Cues").
5. *Nervous gestures.* Certain gestures of the arms and face can indicate fear/tension, such as arms akimbo (folded across the chest) and hands frequently touching the face.

Physical Cues

AUs 1, 2, 4, 12, 20, 1+2+4, 1+2+4+5. Watch for frequent eye movements, frequent gulping, biting of lips and inside of mouth, and the "unfelt smile," a smile without AU6 that has been associated with neurophysiological patterns suggestive of behavioral withdrawal (Ekman & Davidson, 1993; Ekman, Davidson, & Friesen, 1990).

Counterindicators

1. *Away behaviors.* Away behaviors, such as paying attention to trivial objects in the room, looking at one's own hands or nails, and so forth, when unaccompanied by anxious affect and when in the context of high negative affect, are more properly coded as Stonewalling.
2. *Foreign object.* Sometimes individuals will become occupied with picking their teeth or removing something from their eye in the midst of a conversation. Such behaviors may be associated with increased anxiety but are more likely simply Neutral.
3. *Shared nervous laughter.* Nervous laughter that is shared among two or more individuals can quickly escalate into a shared moment of positive affect that is more properly coded as Humor.

Humor

Function

The function of humor is to share in mutual amusement and joy following a mutually recognized moment of absurdity or fun. Humor is relatively unique within the SPAFF in that it cannot be coded in isolation. The humor code requires a moment of *shared* amusement.

Indicators

1. *Good-natured teasing.* When an individual teases, she highlights qualities or behaviors in her partner that

both agree are somewhat ridiculous, cute, or otherwise funny.
2. *Wit and silliness.* Wit is expressed as an apt or clever observation that is considered by both individuals to be humorous. This could manifest as a funny observation or the straightforward telling of a joke.
3. *Private jokes.* Private jokes can include moments of shared laughter and obvious amusement that derive from coded messages or moments of sudden mutually recognized humor that are opaque to all but the two individuals who are communicating.
4. *Fun and exaggeration.* A very playful form of humor; here individuals share active, animated, and exaggerated play or imitation behavior. High energy and a deeper form of laughter often accompanies this indicator.
5. *Nervous giggling.* Occasionally, individuals will begin to chuckle with each other for no apparent reason. This could result from a private joke or may indicate a brief release of nervous tension given the experimental context. The affect underlying the giggling should be obviously positive and shared, unlike a similar form of giggling associated with the Fear/Tension code.

Physical Cues

AUs include 1, 2, 6, 12, 6 + 12, and 25–27.

Counterindicators

1. *Unshared humor.* Laughter or amusement that is not shared is never coded Humor.
2. *Tense humor.* Humor that is obviously both a nervous reaction to a high level of tension in the conversation and either lacking in any positive energy or unshared.
3. *Affectionate humor.* Sometimes a joke will be coupled with affectionate messages. Such moments are more properly coded affection.
4. *Belligerent humor.* A form of unshared humor, one individual makes jokes that are intended to "get a rise" out of the other or make the other angry.
5. *Contemptuous humor.* Jokes that are intended to be hurtful or insulting and that are unshared. This is sometimes confused with teasing. A good rule for distinguishing contemptuous humor from good-natured teasing is to attend closely to the degree to which both individuals are amused.

Interest

Function

The function of this behavior is to communicate genuine interest in one's partner through active elaboration or clarification seeking. As used in the SPAFF, Interest is characterized as a positively valenced behavior that emphasizes information gathering about the partner as opposed to minor or trivial factual information.

Indicators

1. *Nonverbal attention with positive affect.* Interested persons will frequently attempt to actively communicate their interest through nonverbal behaviors, such as leaning forward in their chairs, affecting a warm tone of voice, and making steady eye contact. The interested person will communicate focused, respectful, and active engagement with what his or her partner is saying. If cues associated with Fear/Tension are not present, the interested person will sometimes communicate low levels of excitement (not to be confused with Enthusiasm) that communicates a desire to hear more.
2. *Elaboration and clarification seeking.* Interested individuals will often ask specific questions in order to gather additional information. Frequently, such questions will be accompanied by nonverbal behaviors such as those described in indicator 1. It is important that questions that serve to elicit more information are not accompanied by nonverbal negative affect, as such affect can indicate other affective agendas. Elaboration and clarification-seeking questions can include questions about a partner's opinions and questions that serve to paraphrase what a partner has been saying. Paraphrasing questions are easy to confuse with paraphrasing statements that are coded as Validation (discussed later).
3. *Open-ended questions.* Almost any question that does not require a "yes" or "no" response and that allows the partner to express him- or herself in greater detail.

Physical Cues

AUs 1+2, 6, 12, 6+12, leaning forward, positive valence.

Counterindicators

1. *Lack of eye contact.* Eye contact is not absolutely essential for coding interest, but a lack of eye contact can indicate that interest is feigned or that questions are serving some other affective function.
2. *No pauses following questions.* When questions are frequent and no opportunity is provided for a partner to respond to them, it is unlikely that genuine interest is being observed. Relentless question asking, especially if it appears to be leading the partner to a very specific series of answers, can be a sign of Domineering behavior.
3. *Low-balling questions.* Similar to counterindicator 2, low-balling questions are those to which there is only one rational answer. An example would be, "Don't you want me to be happy?" Such a question is properly coded Domineering.
4. *Exchange of general factual information.* It is important, though sometimes difficult, to distinguish between questions that communicate an interest in the partner and those that communicate an interest in settling some minor factual issue. An example of a noninterested (per SPAFF) question might be "What time is it?"

Neutral

Function

The Neutral code represents a sort of "dividing line" between positive and negative SPAFF codes. It is relatively nonaffective and is associated with the exchange of unvalenced information. The voice will have a relaxed quality, with an even pitch and volume. It is important to become familiar with an individual's neutral behavior early on in a coding session, as facial morphology and other characterological mannerisms that are actually neutral for a given person can often seem affective to coders unfamiliar with them.

Indicators

1. *Information exchanges.*
2. *Noncodable moments.* Sometimes it will be unclear whether a behavior is affective or what a particular affective behavior represents. In the SPAFF, such moments are coded Neutral.

Physical Cues

The neutral face is apparent, though care must be taken to avoid coding baseline facial morphologies as affective facial behavior.

Counterindicators

1. *Loaded issue.* It is possible that a moment of behavior that seems to be a neutral exchange of information actually makes reference to an issue that has emotional relevance to the speaker, the receiver, or both. Such moments are not properly coded Neutral.
2. *Any codable affect.*

Sadness

Function

In the SPAFF, the Sadness code refers to behaviors that communicate loss, resignation, helplessness, pessimism, hopelessness, or a plaintive or poignant quiescence.

Indicators

1. *Sighing.* Sighs, especially deep sighs, very frequently occur in the context of Sadness. Thus sighing is nearly always considered an indication of sad feelings (note, however, "relief" as a counterindicators).
2. *Pouting/Sulking.* Sadness physical cues in the context of being rebuffed, ignored, or not getting one's way.

Pouting may cause the sad person to appear to withdraw from the conversation.

3. *Resignation.* Sad individuals will frequently behave as if resigned or hopeless. This behavior is communicated through a pattern of very low energy, slouching, long pauses between words, and so forth. In the resigned person, nearly all movement appears to require extra effort.

4. *Crying.* Nearly all instances of crying indicate sadness (but see "happy tears" as a counterindicators.) Sometimes individuals can be observed "choking back tears," or trying not to cry. Physical cues and tears welling up in the eyes will give them away.

5. *Hurt feelings.* In response to moments of high negativity, such as belligerence, contempt, or anger, individuals will sometimes report or appear to have hurt feelings. Such moments are coded as Sadness.

Physical Cues

AUs 1, 6, 15, 17, 1+6, 1+15, 1+6+15, 1+6+15+17. Shoulders may droop, and individuals may hang their heads or look down. The lips and the chin may tremble. The voice may quaver in terms of pitch and amplitude and may occasionally break.

Counterindicators

1. *No back channels.* A lack of responding that is attributable to the deliberate attempt to communicate lack of interest is not a form of pouting and is more properly coded Stonewalling.

2. *Relief.* Individuals who display a sudden decrease in energy as a result of the diffusion of tension or an escape from responsibility may be showing evidence of relief, which may be coded as Neutral.

3. *Happy tears.* Happy tears are here intended to mean one of two things. First, tears can sometimes result from intense laughter. Second, tears can sometimes result from sudden moments of shared intimacy, compliments, accomplishments, and so forth. These instances of tears are more properly coded as Humor, Enthusiasm, or Affection.

Stonewalling

Function

Stonewalling functions to communicate an unwillingness to listen or respond to the receiver.

Indicators

1. *Active away behavior.* The speaker focuses on some trivial object in order to avoid contact with the receiver. Such away behavior frequently entails the use of "automanipulation," a behavior characterized by playing with hair or hands (e.g., cleaning fingernails or looking at split ends). This behavior is "active" in Stonewalling in that it is not a function of idleness but rather purposefully communicates an unwillingness to pay attention, especially during conversational moments characterized by high levels of negative affect. The "speaker" (i.e., the stonewaller) is communicating the message, "I'd rather not be here right now, and I don't want to listen to you."

2. *No back channels.* The stonewalling person offers no vocal or nonvocal back channels such as one would find in Validation. There are no head nods, the neck is rigid, there are no vocal or verbal assents (as in "umm-hmmm," "yeah," "uh-huh," etc.), and no other verbal responses. There is little if any facial movement and certainly no facial mirroring or eye contact. The "no-back-channeling" behavior may occur very abruptly, as if intended to suddenly put up an obvious, though technically invisible, wall between the speaker and the receiver.

3. *Monitoring gaze.* Within the context of "no back channels," stonewalling individuals will occasionally steal glances at their partners, as if to remind their partners to notice their lack of listening behavior. This can appear as a intermittent glance in the partner's direction, as if the partner is an annoyance that must be endured, much as one might occasionally glance over at a noisy person in a library.

Physical Cues

In Stonewalling, the face will typically appear stiff or frozen. The jaw may be clenched, and the muscles of the neck may be obviously flexed. Other times, the face will show no obvious signs of emotion at all, deliberately arranged to appear neutral.

Counterindicators

1. *Boredom.* Individuals can sometimes become bored or otherwise run out of things to say to each other. Sometimes, this will cause them to sit quietly without interacting for seemingly long periods of time. Away behavior can characterize these moments, but they should not be confused with Stonewalling behavior. Stonewalling does not result from idleness or boredom but is rather a form of active and aggressive communication, most frequently observed during heated moments.

2. *Sleepiness.* If an individual stops offering back channels but also appears to be very sleepy (as sometimes happens), his or her behavior is more properly coded as Neutral.

3. *Resignation.* Sometimes individuals will become sad or defeated during an intense conversation. During such moments, they can appear to be Stonewalling for want of back-channeling behavior. It is important to recognize when this is occurring and to code accord-

ingly. Most often, resigned behaviors such as these are coded as Sadness.

Threats

Function

Threats are a particularly hostile form of domineering behavior in that their function is to control the behavior of the receiver by setting explicit conditions under which the receiver will be punished for behaving in ways the speaker finds undesirable.

Indicators

1. *Bans.* These are direct "if/then" statements that forbid certain behaviors and threaten to impose punitive (sometimes violent) consequences if those behaviors occur. An example might be "if you ever speak to me like that again, I'll. . . ."
2. *Ultimatums.* Ultimatums reflect demands for change within some defined context or time period. An example might include "if you don't start doing your share around here by next month, I'm moving out."

Physical Cues

AU 1, 2 ("the horns"), 1+2, 1+2+5, head forward, body forward, finger pointing, head cocked to one side.

Counterindicators

- *Good-natured teasing.* Good-natured "jabs" at the receiver's foibles and those that include humorous threats (as in "Ooh, I'm going to get you for that!") are coded as Humor.

Validation

Function

The function of validation is to communicate sincere understanding and acceptance of one's partner or of one's partner's views and opinions. In the SPAFF, Validation is considered to be a positively valenced behavior.

Indicators

1. *Back channels.* Back channels are behaviors that indicate attentive and affirmative listening through the use of paralinguistic and physical cues, such as head nods and "uh-huhs" or other physical and vocal assenting behaviors. Usually, back channels are accompanied by eye contact.
2. *Direct expressions of understanding.* Direct expressions of understanding include explicit expressions of respect or agreement (e.g., "I agree," or "that's a very good point").
3. *Paraphrasing.* In this behavior, individuals repeat back what their partners have told them, usually verbatim, but sometimes in a slightly altered style.

4. *Apologies.*
5. *Sentence finishing.* In this behavior, individuals will place endings on the sentences their partners have begun. This behavior lets partners know that both individuals are "on the same page." Importantly, sentence finishing is an indicator of validation only if it is delivered in a package of positive affect (see "Physical Cues").

Physical Cues

AUs 1+2, 6, 12, 6+12. Head nod, eye contact, nonconfrontational voice tone.

Counterindicators

1. *Lack of eye contact.* A lack of eye contact can mean that the back channels being offered are insincere, as in humoring. Back channels without eye contact can also be associated with sarcastic behavior.
2. *Bobbing heads.* "Bobbing heads" are head nods that appear so automatic and repetitive that they essentially become meaningless. Bobbing heads can also be a sign of exasperation—a kind of nonverbal request to "shut up."
3. *Affect mirroring.* Sometimes, the various indicators of validation occur in the context of strong mirroring of affect, as when an individual says, "I understand how you're feeling" while expressing facial signs of sadness in response to their crying partners. The SPAFF considers such expressions to be signs of empathy, and such signs are properly coded Affection.
4. *Interrupting.* Sentence finishing can be an important indicator of Validation, but if the sentence finishing is abrupt or is delivered with negative affect, it is likely nothing more than an interruption related to Domineering, Defensiveness, or other negative affective behaviors.

Whining

Function

Whining functions to make what might otherwise be an ordinary complaint into a plaintive or pleading form of emotional protest. Whining suggests an innocent victim stance, communicating something like "What are you picking on me for?" or "What about all the good I do?"

Indicators

- *Whiny protest.* Whining is really characterized by a quality of voice paired with a complaint or protest. This voice quality is high-pitched, nasal, "sing-songy," or otherwise annoyingly plaintive. For example, the question "why" might be expressed in a high-pitched voice and drawn out with an exaggerated "eeee" sound at the end, as in "whyyyyeeee?"

Physical Cues

AUs 1, 1 + 2, 1 + 2 + 15.

Counterindicators

- *Defensive whining.* Sometimes defensive behaviors can be expressed in a whiny voice style. Such moments are more properly coded Defensive.

The Nuts and Bolts of SPAFF Coding

Training

In our experience, SPAFF training requires some reading, some didactic exercises, and a large amount of practice. Indeed, SPAFF practice is generally ongoing in our laboratories, including weekly meetings at which confusions are clarified and practice tapes are watched collectively. In the past, we have trained SPAFF coders in steps, as follows.[3]

Step 1. *People watching and learning to think about constructs.* Following the structure of this chapter, students are encouraged to think about and practice the rules of people watching and are trained to understand the difference between constructs and indicators.

Step 2. *FACS training.* At a minimum, coders should be trained to reliably recognize those FACS codes that are commonly observed in the codes of the SPAFF. It is preferable, though not necessary, for SPAFF coders to be fully FACS certified through a process of studying the FACS manual and taking the FACS exam (see Cohn et al., chapter 13, this volume, for details).

Step 3. *Learning the SPAFF codes.* Learning the SPAFF codes requires careful explanation of the codes, in addition to frequent viewing of examples of the codes using videotapes.[4] When viewing videotapes, we start whenever possible by showing clips designed to illustrate codes that are the subject of discussion or recent reading. Eventually, longer clips are played, and students are encouraged to discuss what they see in terms of the SPAFF codes they have learned. Virtually any videotaped interaction (e.g., tapes of participants, clips from movies or television) can be useful for this. Exercises such as these serve at least two purposes. First, they train people to talk about and discuss affective behavior using SPAFF as their "language." The value of this first purpose is often underappreciated (more on this later). Second, they hone their skills in reliably identifying SPAFF codes.

Data Collection and Reliability Assessment

Video- and Audiotapes

Several pragmatic data collection considerations are important for maximizing the effectiveness of the SPAFF. For example, it is critical that audio and video are of high quality. We have found that small microphones with gated compressor mixers attached to people's shirts or collars provide the best audio quality. Many video cameras come with their own built-in microphones, but the audio quality provided by these is inconsistent. Alternatives include wall-mounted omnidirectional cardoid condenser microphones, generally aimed at the participants. For video collection, many options now exist, including sophisticated digital recorders that are quite compact and relatively unobtrusive. In any case, we recommend that two cameras are used to generate a "split screen," at least with dyads (such that both participants can be viewed simultaneously on the same monitor), and that both cameras are situated to provide full-face shots, including coverage from the top of the head to the mid-chest. To create a split screen, a special-effects generator with "wipe" capabilities will be required. A wide variety of such devices are commercially available. Profile shots should be avoided whenever possible, as they make it harder to read emotion on the face (e.g., AU14, a FACS code associated with contempt, is frequently only seen on one side of the face). Moreover, and despite the risk of participant self-consciousness, cameras should be low. We have found that cameras placed about 1 foot above the participants' eye level causes minimal self-consciousness and that, in any case, participants in emotionally charged situations habituate to the cameras rapidly. In coding the SPAFF, a time-code generator that is both visible on the video recording and readable by computer interface is imperative. Devices that accomplish this, frequently referred to as *vertical interval time code* (or "VITC") *generators*, are widely available.

Reliability Assessment

Timing is critical to the utility of the SPAFF as a measure, as well as to the assessment of reliability. Before coding begins, a number of timing decisions must be made. For example, the *unit* of time per code must be established. Due to technological limitations, early versions of the SPAFF used very little or no timing information, using "thought units" based on transcripts for coding instead. Since then, we have frequently used 1 second as the unit of time for SPAFF coding, allowing for one code per second per participant. Next, the *time window* for assessing reliability must be established. The time window refers to the amount of time relative to a target moment around which coders may agree or disagree. For example, a time window of plus or minus 1 second may be established around some target second, allowing for a total *window of agreement* of 3 seconds within which SPAFF coders may agree or disagree about how to categorize a particular behavior. The size of this window is a function of the investigator's discretion. For most coding, a 3-second window provides an adequate balance between precision and agreement.

A variety of options exist for the statistical assessment of reliability of these kinds of data (Bakeman & Gottman, 1997). We have assessed reliability by computing *confusion matrices,* which tally agreements and disagreements between two coders, allowing for the computation of *Cohen's kappa* both for each interaction and for all interactions within a sample combined. Cohen's kappa is useful for assessing the reliability of event-coded data to be used for sequential-type analyses in which agreements must be locked in time within a particular window. We have also computed Cronbach's alpha for this purpose, per Wiggins (1973). However, when reliability concerns the total *frequency* of a given code, the rank-order intraclass correlation, or *generalizability coefficient,* provides a sufficient assessment of reliability (see also Shrout & Fleiss, 1979). Figure 16.3 provides a sample confusion matrix obtained from a sample of domestically violent couples, taken from Gottman et al. (1995).

Typically, all tapes in a given study are coded twice, once each by two independent coders. Checking the reliability of every interaction in a given study is recommended for optimal data quality. Moreover, reliability should be checked continuously as a study is ongoing if those reliabilities are to remain high throughout. It is useful for coders to know that their reliability will be checked for every tape that they code. A variety of computer-based coding packages are now available, including the Long Video Coding System (VCS, available from the James Long Company; see http://www.jameslong .net/ for more information). Tape-by-tape reliability checks are augmented by weekly meetings, with all coders present. Such meetings are critical to the success of coding any given study. Because studies differ in sometimes subtle ways, it is possible that the SPAFF manual will be unclear about a particular behavior or distinction. Coding meetings cope with this in at least two ways. First, they can clarify applications of the SPAFF to particular samples (e.g., is Contempt—a latent construct—always indicated in the same ways in all samples?). Second, they contribute to clarifications within

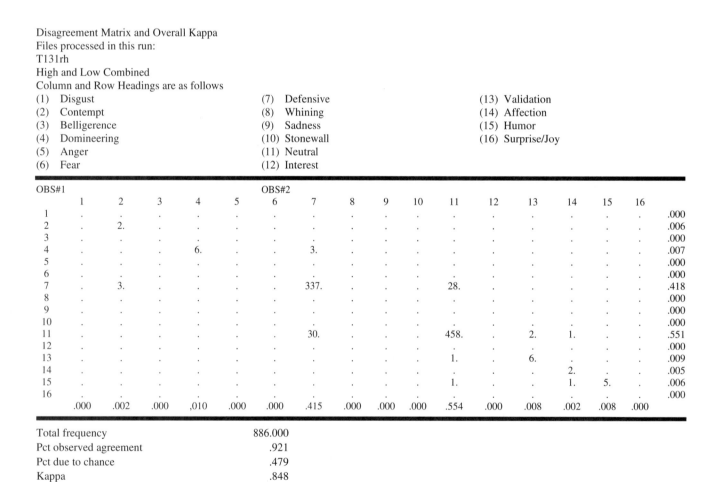

Disagreement Matrix and Overall Kappa
Files processed in this run:
T131rh
High and Low Combined
Column and Row Headings are as follows

(1) Disgust	(7) Defensive	(13) Validation
(2) Contempt	(8) Whining	(14) Affection
(3) Belligerence	(9) Sadness	(15) Humor
(4) Domineering	(10) Stonewall	(16) Surprise/Joy
(5) Anger	(11) Neutral	
(6) Fear	(12) Interest	

OBS#1 / OBS#2

	1	2	3	4	5	6	7	8	9	10	11	12	13	14	15	16	
1	.	.	.	.	.	.	.	.	.	.	.	.	.	.	.	.	.000
2	.	2.	.	.	.	.	.	.	.	.	.	.	.	.	.	.	.006
3	.	.	.	.	.	.	.	.	.	.	.	.	.	.	.	.	.000
4	.	.	.	6.	.	.	3.	.	.	.	.	.	.	.	.	.	.007
5	.	.	.	.	.	.	.	.	.	.	.	.	.	.	.	.	.000
6	.	.	.	.	.	.	.	.	.	.	.	.	.	.	.	.	.000
7	.	3.	.	.	.	.	337.	.	.	.	28.	.	.	.	.	.	.418
8	.	.	.	.	.	.	.	.	.	.	.	.	.	.	.	.	.000
9	.	.	.	.	.	.	.	.	.	.	.	.	.	.	.	.	.000
10	.	.	.	.	.	.	.	.	.	.	.	.	.	.	.	.	.000
11	.	.	.	.	.	.	30.	.	.	.	458.	.	2.	1.	.	.	.551
12	.	.	.	.	.	.	.	.	.	.	.	.	.	.	.	.	.000
13	.	.	.	.	.	.	.	.	.	.	1.	.	6.	.	.	.	.009
14	.	.	.	.	.	.	.	.	.	.	.	.	.	2.	.	.	.005
15	.	.	.	.	.	.	.	.	.	.	1.	.	.	1.	5.	.	.006
16	.	.	.	.	.	.	.	.	.	.	.	.	.	.	.	.	.000
	.000	.002	.000	.010	.000	.000	.415	.000	.000	.000	.554	.000	.008	.002	.008	.000	

Total frequency	886.000
Pct observed agreement	.921
Pct due to chance	.479
Kappa	.848
Standard Error	.031
Z-score	27.652

Figure 16.3. A sample confusion matrix (Gottman et al., 1995).

the manual. In this way, the development of the SPAFF is analogous to "open source" software, with many groups of coders, within and between labs, contributing to its development. Coding meetings are typically semistructured, with meeting facilitators bringing clips that are frequently, or recently, the source of disagreement and confusion. Such clips are often brought to the attention of the meeting facilitator by the coders themselves, but they need not be. For example, the VCS program allows for the easy identification of disagreements in the coding record that can be used for discussion. It is important to discuss specific instances, with video, during these meetings; abstract discussions of the codes are generally less helpful. In general, the agreement in a single session of coding should be above 75%, but 60% can be acceptable with particularly difficult tapes. If the percentage of agreement is lower, two different coders should recode the tape.

Table 16.2
Weighting scheme for the 16-code version of the SPAFF

Positive Affects		Negative Affects	
Joy	+ 4	Contempt	– 4
Humor	+ 4	Disgust	– 3
Affection	+ 4	Defensiveness	– 2
Validation	+ 4	Belligerence	– 2
Interest	+ 2	Stonewalling	– 2
		Domineering	– 1
		Anger	– 1
		Whining	– 1
		Sadness	– 1
		Fear / Tension	0
	Neutral	+ 0.1	

The Future of the SPAFF

The SPAFF is always in development. It can be used to quantify affective and interactive behaviors, but it can also be thought of more generally as a language for describing those behaviors. Indeed, recent applications of the SPAFF include its transformation into a continuous scale and the use of the SPAFF terminology to code higher order constructs, and even sequences of behavior, directly.

The SPAFF as a Scale

The transformation of an earlier version of the SPAFF was accomplished by using prior research to assign weights to each code (see Carrere & Gottman, 1999; Gottman, Swanson, & Murray, 1999). Thus codes more predictive of negative outcomes received more negative weights, and codes more predictive of positive outcomes received more positive weights. The weighting scheme resulted in a continuous scale running from –4 to +4 in any given second. These scores were then summed across 6-second intervals, resulting in a continuous score of –24 to +24 for any given 6-second epoch. Weights assigned to a previous version of the SPAFF code are given in Table 16.2.

The SPAFF as a Language

In new ongoing research, the language of the SPAFF is being implemented as a means of training coders to observe specific sequences of behavior across larger periods of time (e.g., 5 minutes). In this work, very specific sequences of behavior are of interest, and estimates of the frequency of such sequences are given by continuous Likert-type rating scales. For example, of particular interest is a sequence of behavior that begins with one spouse's low-level negative affect (the antecedent) and ends with the other's high-level

negative affect (the consequent). In previous research, this sequence has been interpreted as a "rejection of influence" (Coan et al., 1997; Gottman et al., 1998). Coders understand that low-level negative affect includes such SPAFF codes as Anger, Fear/Tension, Sadness, and so forth, and that high-level negative affect includes Stonewalling, Contempt, Criticism, Defensiveness, and so on. They use their knowledge of the SPAFF to code the sequence directly. Though currently in the experimental stages, this approach has dramatically increased the speed with which coding is done, with little or no apparent cost in terms of reliability. For example, the intraclass correlation coefficient (ICC) across three coders and 64 couples for the coding of husband influence rejection was .84, although the same ICC for the wife was somewhat lower, at .63. This work is still in development and awaits further testing and analysis. Nevertheless, it holds the promise of new ways to implement the SPAFF.

Conclusion

The SPAFF is a flexible, evolving, and reliable language for describing interactive affective behavior. It has informed numerous studies and enjoys ample empirical support for its constructs. The SPAFF has typically been applied to the study of married couples, but in recent years it has been applied to parent-child interactions and even to group therapy sessions. A few new codes have been introduced here, and recent new directions in the use of the SPAFF have been covered. Using the SPAFF can be labor intensive and challenging but also highly rewarding. As use of the SPAFF increases, we enthusiastically anticipate yet more innovation and development.

Notes

1. Here we are using the language of latent variable models analogously, not literally. Actual latent variable models imply a host of mathematical properties that are not necessarily true of any of our SPAFF codes. Nevertheless, many of the theoretical properties do apply. It is better, for example, to observe multiple indicators of a construct if one wishes to infer the construct's existence. This is equally true of the SPAFF. However, in mathematical latent variable modeling, it is virtually axiomatic that one is *required* to have at least three indicators (sometimes referred to as *manifest variables*) to properly model the construct. This is not true of SPAFF coding, in which, in many cases, a single indicator is sufficient.

2. For the sake of clarity, we contrast critical statements with complaint statements. These examples are taken from John Gottman's book *Why Marriages Succeed or Fail* (Gottman, 1994).

> Complaint: We don't go out as often as I'd like to.
> Criticism: You never take me anywhere.
> Complaint: It upset me when I came home and there were dirty dishes in the sink. This morning we agreed you'd wash them.
> Criticism: You left dirty dishes in the sink again. You promised me you wouldn't. I just can't trust you, can I?
> Complaint: I expected you to come home right after work. When you didn't, it made me feel like you care more about going out with your friends than spending time with me.
> Criticism: I hate that you're the type of person who never thinks to call and tell me you'll be late coming home. You always leave me hanging. You care more about your friends than you do about our marriage.

3. One of the authors (JAC) is available for SPAFF workshops.

4. Training and test tapes for the SPAFF are not currently commercially available, although new tapes may be available in the future, depending on demand. Alternatively, any tapes involving affective behavior can be used to gain practice in coding SPAFF. One of the authors (JAC) has even used movie clips to illustrate examples of SPAFF codes. Virtually any videotaped social interaction can be useful for SPAFF training, as long as the faces of the individuals are clearly visible.

References

Babcock, J. C., Waltz, J., Jacobson, N. S., & Gottman, J. M. (1993). Power and violence: The relation between communication patterns, power discrepancies, and domestic violence. *Journal of Consulting and Clinical Psychology, 61*(1), 40–50.

Bakeman, R., & Gottman, J. M. (1997). *Observing interaction: An introduction to sequential analysis* (2nd ed.). New York: Cambridge University Press.

Banse, R., & Scherer, K. R. (1996). Acoustic profiles in vocal emotion expression. *Journal of Personality and Social Psychology, 70*(3), 614–636.

Blairy, S., Herrera, P., & Hess, U. (1999). Mimicry and the judgement of emotional facial expressions. *Journal of Nonverbal Behavior, 23*(1), 5–41.

Bollen, K. A. (2002). Latent variables in psychology and the social sciences. *Annual Review of Psychology, 53,* 605–634.

Burman, B., Margolin, G., & John, R. S. (1993). America's angriest home videos: Behavioral contingencies observed in home reenactments of marital conflict. *Journal of Consulting and Clinical Psychology, 61*(1), 28–39.

Carrere, S., & Gottman, J. M. (1999). Predicting divorce among newlyweds from the first three minutes of a marital conflict discussion. *Family Process, 38,* 293–301.

Carstensen, L. L., Gottman, J. M., & Levenson, R. W. (1995). Emotional behavior in long-term marriage. *Psychology and Aging, 10*(1), 140–149.

Coan, J., Gottman, J. M., Babcock, J., & Jacobson, N. (1997). Battering and the male rejection of influence from women. *Aggressive Behavior, 23*(5), 375–388.

Coan, J. A. (1998, March). *The systematic observation of affect in therapy.* Paper presented at the Conference on Successful Relating in Couples, Families, Between Friends, and at Work, Tucson, AZ.

Cohan, C. L., & Bradbury, T. N. (1994). Assessing responses to recurring problems in marriage: Evaluation of the Marital Coping Inventory. *Psychological Assessment, 6*(3), 191–200.

Cohan, C. L., & Bradbury, T. N. (1997). Negative life events, marital interaction, and the longitudinal course of newly-wed marriage. *Journal of Personality and Social Psychology, 73*(1), 114–128.

Ekman, P., & Davidson, R. J. (1993). Voluntary smiling changes regional brain activity. *Psychological Science, 4*(5), 342–345.

Ekman, P., Davidson, R. J., & Friesen, W. V. (1990). The Duchenne smile: Emotional expression and brain physiology: II. *Journal of Personality and Social Psychology, 58*(2), 342–353.

Ekman, P., & Friesen, W. V. (1975). *Unmasking the face: A guide to recognizing emotions from facial clues.* Englewood Cliffs, NJ: Prentice-Hall.

Ekman, P., & Friesen, W. V. (1978). *The Facial Action Coding System (FACS): A technique for the measurement of facial action.* Palo Alto, CA: Consulting Psychologists Press.

Ekman, P., Friesen, W. V., & Tomkins, S. S. (1971). Facial Action Scoring Technique (FAST): A first validity study. *Semiotica, 3*(1), 37–38.

Gottman, J. M. (1979). *Marital interaction: Experimental investigations.* New York: Academic Press.

Gottman, J. M. (1993a). The roles of conflict engagement, escalation, and avoidance in marital interaction: A longitudinal view of five types of couples. *Journal of Consulting and Clinical Psychology, 61*(1), 6–15.

Gottman, J. M. (1993b). A theory of marital dissolution and stability. *Journal of Family Psychology, 7*(1), 57–75.

Gottman, J. M. (1994). *Why marriages succeed or fail.* New York: Simon and Shuster.

Gottman, J. M., Coan, J., Carrere, S., & Swanson, C. (1998). Predicting marital happiness and stability from newlywed interactions. *Journal of Marriage and the Family, 60*(1), 5–22.

Gottman, J. M., & Krokoff, L. J. (1989). Marital interaction and satisfaction: A longitudinal view. *Journal of Consulting and Clinical Psychology, 57,* 47–52.

Gottman, J. M., & Levenson, R. W. (1992). Marital processes predictive of later dissolution: Behavior, physiology, and health. *Journal of Personality and Social Psychology, 63*(2), 221–233.

Gottman, J. M., Levenson, R. W., Gross, J., Frederickson, B. L., McCoy, K., Rosenthal, L., et al. (2003). Correlates of gay and lesbian couples' relationship satisfaction and relationship dissolution. *Journal of Homosexuality, 45*(1), 23–43.

Gottman, J. M., Levenson, R. W., Swanson, C., Swanson, K., Tyson, R., & Yoshimoto, D. (2003). Observing gay, lesbian and heterosexual couples' relationships: Mathematical modeling of conflict interaction. *Journal of Homosexuality, 45*(1), 65–91.

Gottman, J. M., McCoy, K., Coan, J., & Collier, H. (1995). *The Specific Affect Coding System (SPAFF) for observing emotional communication in marital and family interaction.* Mahwah, NJ: Erlbaum.

Gottman, J. M., Swanson, C., & Murray, J. (1999). The mathematics of marital conflict: Dynamic mathematical nonlinear modeling of newlywed marital interaction. *Journal of Family Psychology, 13,* 3–19.

Heyman, R. E. (2001). Observation of couple conflicts: Clinical assessment applications, stubborn truths, and shaky foundations. *Psychological Assessment, 13*(1), 5–35.

Hops, H., Wills, T. A., Weiss, R. L., & Patterson, G. R. (1972). *Marital Interaction Coding System.* Eugene, OR: University of Oregon and Oregon Research Institute.

Jacobson, N. S., Gottman, J. M., Waltz, J., Rushe, R., Babcock, J., & Holtzworth-Munroe, A. (1994). Affect, verbal content, and psychophysiology in the arguments of couples with a violent husband. *Journal of Consulting and Clinical Psychology, 62*(5), 982–988.

Levenson, R. W., Carstensen, L. L., & Gottman, J. M. (1994). The influence of age and gender on affect, physiology, and their interrelations: A study of long-term marriages. *Journal of Personality and Social Psychology, 67*(1), 56–68.

Notarius, C. I., Benson, P. B., Sloane, D., Vanzetti, N. A., & Hornyak, L. M. (1989). Exploring the interface between perception and behavior: An analysis of marital interaction in distressed and nondistressed couples. *Behavioral Assessment, 11,* 39–64.

Rozin, P., Lowery, L., & Ebert, R. (1994). Varieties of disgust faces and the structure of disgust. *Journal of Personality and Social Psychology, 66*(5), 870–881.

Scherer, K. R. (1974). Acoustic concomitants of emotional dimensions: Judging affect from synthesized tone sequences. In S. Weitz (Ed.), *Nonverbal communication* (pp. 249–253). New York: Oxford University Press.

Shrout, P. E., & Fleiss, J. L. (1979). Intraclass correlations: Uses in assessing rater reliability. *Psychological Bulletin, 33,* 159–174.

Wiggins, J. S. (1973). *Personality and prediction: Principles of personality assessment.* Reading, MA: Addison-Wesley.

Xiao, J., Moriyama, T., Kanade, T., & Cohn, J. F. (2003). Robust full-motion recovery of head by dynamic templates and re-registration techniques. *International Journal of Imaging Systems and Technology, 13,* 85–94

Anna Marie Ruef
Robert W. Levenson

Continuous Measurement of Emotion

The Affect Rating Dial

What Is the Affect Rating Dial?

Measurement of an individual's subjective experience of emotion has long been a key component of emotion research, but it presents some unique challenges. Researchers have developed a number of different methods to assess the subjective emotional experiences of study participants, each of which has its strengths and limitations. Self-report measures such as the Positive and Negative Affect Schedule (PANAS; Watson, Clark, & Tellegen, 1988) are well established and easy to complete and provide useful information; however, administration of any written measure necessitates an interruption in the flow of an experiment and does not allow frequent or continuous sampling of affective states. More involved methods, such as interviewing, give a detailed and comprehensive picture of a person's emotions, but they are time-consuming and can provide only a retrospective report of affect. The interactive computer version of the Self-Assessment Manikin (SAM) Scales (Bradley & Lang, 1994) allows online assessment of both emotional valence and arousal levels, but it, too, does not provide a continuous record of affect.

The affect rating dial is an assessment method that was developed to measure self-reported emotion continuously in social interaction. It is unique among subjective measures of affect in allowing the measurement of the time course of an emotional experience and generating continuous data that can be viewed both normatively and ideographically. This chapter outlines the development of the affect rating dial, its strengths and limitations as a measure of subjective emotion, studies in which it has been used, construction of the device, instructions for its use, techniques for evaluating the data it generates, and, finally, possible future uses for the dial.

Development of the Affect Rating Dial

In the early 1980s John Gottman and Robert Levenson were beginning to study the emotional behavior of married couples in the laboratory. They were collecting continuous data on the physiological responses and expressive emotional behavior of their research participants, and they also wished to measure participants' subjective emotional reactions in a similar fashion. They needed to know how couples were feeling as they engaged in two conversations with one another, the first focusing on the events of the day and the second on an area of conflict in their marriage. Ideally, the investigators would obtain a measure of each spouse's subjective emotional state in the moment, as he or she was engaged in the discussion. Also, they wanted to be able to track the rapid changes in emotion they expected to observe (Gottman & Levenson, 1986).

Existing methods for obtaining self-reports of emotion throughout a social interaction required the experimenter to stop the conversation repeatedly to ask participants how they were feeling. Gottman et al.'s talk-table procedure (Gottman et al., 1976; Markman, 1979, 1981) was one such technique: The experimenter would stop the interaction after each communication to obtain spousal ratings of the intent of the message sent and the impact of the message received, each rated on a 5-point Likert scale. However, this method was highly intrusive, and the frequent disruptions resulted in less external validity with regard to real-life marital interactions. The other assessment methods then in use consisted of pre- and postintervention questionnaires and rating scales that did not allow for continuous ratings of emotion. Because the existing methods did not meet their needs, the researchers set out to develop a new procedure for obtaining self-report of affect.

The affect rating dial was a key component of this new "video recall" procedure (Gottman & Levenson, 1985; Levenson & Gottman, 1983). Research participants first came to the laboratory for an interaction session, where they engaged in the events of the day and problem area conversations. A video recording was made of these discussions, and a number of physiological measures were recorded from each spouse. Several days later, participants returned separately to the laboratory to view the videotaped recordings of the conversations, and the same physiological measures were recorded and synchronized with the data obtained previously. While viewing the tapes, participants used the affect rating dial, a type of joystick device, to give a continuous report of their emotions during each marital interaction. The dial traversed a 180° arc over a 9-point scale anchored with the legends *very negative* at 0°, *neutral* at 90°, and *very positive* at 180°. Spouses were instructed to rate how they felt when they were actually in the interaction. They were told to adjust the dial position as often as necessary while viewing, so that it always reflected their emotional state during the discussions.

The investigators hypothesized that participants watching the videotape would at least partially relive the emotions they had experienced at the time of the interactions. If this were true, the ratings obtained with this recall procedure would be as valid and reliable as if spouses' emotions had been assessed during the original session but without the associated difficulties. Five methods were used to assess the validity of the procedure, and all produced supportive data. First, participants' mean affect ratings discriminated high-conflict (problem area) interactions from low-conflict (events of the day) interactions. Second, when mean ratings for the problem-area interaction were correlated with participants' marital satisfaction scores, more dissatisfied couples were found to rate their interaction more negatively. Third, husbands' affect ratings during conversations were found, using time-series analyses, to be coherent with their wives' ratings (see the section on data-analytic approaches later in the chapter). Fourth, participants' ratings were consistent with observers' objective coding of couples' affect (discussed later). Finally, spouses in the recall session appeared to relive the emotions they experienced in the original interaction, as reflected by coherence between interaction session and recall session physiological measures.

Fredrickson and Kahneman (1993) later developed their own variation of the affect rating dial, which they called a *positive-negative affect meter.* This version consisted of a sliding knob attached to a potentiometer that controlled an array of 15 colored lights positioned above the participant's video monitor. A series of 7 green lights to the right of center represented degrees of positive feelings the participant might experience, whereas the 7 red lights to the left of center represented degrees of negative feelings. The yellow light at the center represented neutral feelings and was the only light illuminated when the sliding knob was centered. As the knob was slid to the right, the green lights came on one by one, so that all 7 green lights were illuminated when the sliding knob was set to the extreme right. Negative ratings were indicated similarly by the number of red lights illuminated. A computer recorded the mean position of the sliding knob every second. As with the affect rating dial, participants were asked to adjust this sliding scale as often as necessary so that it always reflected how positive or negative they were feeling. This light display has the advantage of allowing participants to keep their eyes trained on the video monitor while receiving continuous, synchronized feedback on their reported affect level.

Strengths and Limitations of the Method

The affect rating dial as a method of assessment has several positive attributes. First, it allows the investigator to collect online emotion ratings from participants over the time course of an experiment. Its temporal resolution allows participants to indicate rapid changes in their emotions. Second, no forced choices among rating categories are required, because the rating dial provides a continuous measure. A third strength is its ease of use. Once participants are shown how to manipulate the dial, they tend to find it fairly unobtrusive and simple to use. Most are able to make their ratings with only an occasional glance at the device. Fourth, it provides both normative and ideographic data. Finally, it is a robust method that can be validated in a number of different ways when used as part of a video recall procedure (e.g., agreement with objective coders and physiological reliving).

A limitation of the affect rating dial is its use of a single-valence dimension of emotion with two poles (very negative and very positive). Although research suggests that evaluations of positivity and negativity are often combined into a single affective or behavioral (appetitive/aversive) response (Cacioppo & Berntson, 1994; Cacioppo & Gardner, 1999), the rating dial does not allow for those instances in which an individual experiences both positive and negative emotions at the same time. For instance, a research participant who was feeling both mild sadness and mild affection would be forced to choose a dial position that indicates a neutral state, which would not do justice to the complexity of the emotional experience. In this instance, the participant would provide the same rating for that period as would a participant who chose *neutral* because he or she actually was not feeling any emotion. Another limitation is that the dial provides only a single rating at a time. It may be possible to have participants use multiple dials, but this has not been validated.

In the original studies using the dial (Levenson & Gottman, 1983, 1985), the data it generated were broken down into three categories (neutral, positive, or negative) in order to make comparisons between participants' self-ratings of affect and trained observers' ratings using the Specific Affect Coding System (SPAFF; Gottman & Krokoff, 1989). Dividing the data into categories in this manner leads to a loss of information, but this is not a necessary step in other methods of analysis, such as time-series analysis. By necessity, the rating dial originally was used to measure relived emotions, not emotions as they were actually occurring in an interaction. However, more recent studies show that the dial can be used to provide online reports of affect as it is occurring, such as in film viewing (e.g., Tsai, Levenson, & Carstensen, 2000) without unduly influencing ratings (Mauss et al., 2005). Moreover, although the original studies were limited to ratings of affective valence, a more recent study has used obtained ratings of specific emotions, such as amusement and sadness (Mauss et al., 2005).

Past Uses of the Affect Rating Dial

The affect rating dial has been utilized in a number of different ways in emotion research, for example, in single-participant and dyadic interaction studies; to obtain self-ratings and ratings of a target person's emotions; and to rate emotions online and retrospectively. The following are brief descriptions of research studies that have employed the rating dial and summaries of the results that involve subjective affect ratings obtained in this manner.

Alcohol Studies

The first version of the affect rating dial was used in a series of studies that explored the stress response-dampening effects of alcohol (Levenson, Oyama, & Meek, 1987; Levenson, Sher, Grossman, Newman, & Newlin, 1980; Sher & Levenson, 1982). Instead of reporting their general affective state, participants used the rating dial to provide online continuous ratings of their perceived levels of tension or anxiety throughout the experimental session. This anxiety rating dial was anchored by *extremely calm* (0°) and *extremely tense* (180°), but in other respects it was similar to the later version. After ingesting alcohol or a placebo, participants gave continuous ratings of their tension levels as they were exposed to two stressors, electric shock and a self-disclosing speech. In this context, ratings were reflective of online anxious feelings, not relived emotions. Anxiety dial data were used to demonstrate that alcohol consumption had a dampening effect on subjective tension levels prior to a stressor but not during the stressor.

Dyadic Interaction Studies

With the development of the previously described video recall procedure, the rating dial was adapted to measure the positive-negative dimension of emotion. This version of the dial first appeared in Levenson and Gottman's (1983) study of marital interaction. As described earlier, participants watched a videotape of a conversation with their spouses and continuously rated how they were feeling during that interaction. The dial was used in much the same manner in a series of dyadic interaction studies, both with younger and older married couples (Gottman & Levenson, 1992; Levenson, Carstensen, & Gottman, 1994; Levenson & Gottman, 1985) and dating couples (Tsai & Levenson, 1997).

In the original marital study (Levenson & Gottman, 1983), rating dial data revealed that dissatisfied marital relationships were characterized by less positive and more negative affect and greater reciprocity of negative affect than satisfied relationships; these differences were more pronounced when couples were discussing a highly conflictual topic than one low in conflict. Couples in a 5-year follow-up study (Levenson & Gottman, 1985) demonstrated the greatest decline in marital satisfaction when husbands did *not* reciprocate their wives' negative affect and when wives *did* reciprocate their husbands' negative affect (again, as measured by the rating dial). Older married couples in the long-term marriage study (Levenson et al., 1994) rated their emotions as being more positive and were less physiologically aroused when interacting with one another than were middle-aged couples. Dissatisfied couples in this study reported less positive emotion, more negative emotion, and greater negative-affect reciprocity than did satisfied pairs. Husbands reported feeling more affectively negative the more they were aroused, but wives showed no relation between subjective affect and arousal. Chinese American dating couples who used the rating dial during conversations about an area of conflict in their relationship (Tsai & Levenson, 1997) reported less variable and less positive affect than did European American couples. Rating dial data in each of these studies contributed to a greater understanding of the role of emotion in intimate relationships.

Empathy Studies

In a study of the physiological correlates of empathy, Levenson and Ruef (1992) used the affect rating dial, together with videotape viewing, but in a different manner than in the marital studies. In these studies, participants did not provide ratings of their own emotional states but instead rated how they thought strangers on videotape were feeling. They were asked to watch 15-minute videotaped interactions of married couples, focusing their attention on a designated spouse and using the rating dial to indicate continuously how they thought that spouse was feeling. These ratings were compared with the target spouse's self-ratings, obtained previously using the video recall procedure, to calculate a measure of empathic accuracy. Accuracy scores were correlated with measures of physiological linkage, or similarity in physiological responding, between the participant during the rating task and the target during the original conversation. Empathic accuracy for negative emotion was associated with a state of shared physiology between the rater and the person being rated, whereas accuracy for positive emotions was associated with a state of low cardiovascular arousal in the rater.

A study of empathy in long-term marriages (Ruef, 2001) required participants to rate both their own emotions and the emotions of their spouses. Spouses in long-term marriages engaged in a 20-minute discussion of a marital problem, then returned separately to the laboratory to view the video recording of their interaction twice. During the first viewing they used the affect rating dial to rate continuously how they had felt during the interaction. Then they were asked to watch the tape a second time and rate how they thought their spouses had felt. Autonomic and somatic physiological responses were monitored continuously during the interaction and rating sessions. As in the previous empathy study with strangers, empathic accuracy was determined by measuring the extent to which the participant's emotion ratings matched those of the spouse; physiological linkage between married partners was determined, as well. For both husbands and wives, a state of low cardiovascular arousal increased the accuracy of detecting both positive and negative emotions in their spouses. Physiological linkage also increased accuracy, but only for wives.

Emotional Responses to Films

Although the affect rating dial has been used primarily in dyadic interaction studies, it has also been utilized successfully in experimental contexts unrelated to social interaction. In a study of duration neglect in global evaluations of affective experiences, Fredrickson and Kahneman (1993) used their version of the rating dial to measure affective escalation and satiation over the course of viewing emotional film clips. They found that the duration of the viewed emotional episodes had little effect on participants' retrospective evaluations of their feelings. Later, Fredrickson and colleagues (Fredrickson & Levenson, 1998; Fredrickson, Mancuso, Branigan, & Tugade, 2000) used the rating dial to explore the "undoing" effect of positive emotions on cardiovascular arousal. The dial was used to measure participants' subjective emotional states as they watched affectively positive and negative film clips. Tsai et al. (2000) utilized the dial in a similar fashion in their study of older and younger Chinese Americans' and European Americans' responses to emotional films. Rating dial data revealed no age or cultural differences in subjective responding to the films. These uses are similar to the original use of the anxiety rating dial in the previously mentioned alcohol studies (Levenson et al., 1980; Levenson et al., 1987; Sher & Levenson, 1982). They represent a return to the online measurement of a participant's subjective feelings when presented with an emotion-inducing stimulus. Concerns about whether providing the ratings influenced the emotional reactions were addressed in a recent study (Mauss et al., 2005), which found no meaningful differences between online ratings and video recall ratings.

Implementation of the Affect Rating Dial

Construction of the Device

The affect rating dial was originally constructed in a 7.5 x 5 x 3.25-inch (19 x 12.5 x 8 cm) metal box. The box had a faceplate with the rating scale and a large knob. All of the electronics were housed inside the box. The box attached to the arm of the participant's chair, so that the participant's hand could rest comfortably on the dial and manipulate it easily. The box could be moved to either arm of the chair, depending on the handedness of the participant.

Faceplate

The faceplate consisted of an 180° arc drawn in black against a white background. Running along the arc were nine tick marks, one every 20°, labeled "1" to "9." The arc was anchored with the legends *very negative* at 0°, *neutral* at 90°, and *very positive* at 180° (see Figure 17.1). This faceplate was covered by a rectangle of clear Plexiglas or plastic.

Dial

The dial consisted of a large round plastic knob (2.4 inches, or 6 cm, in diameter) with a clear Plexiglas pointer attached. As the knob rotated clockwise, it caused the pointer to traverse the 180° arc scribed on the faceplate.

Mounting to Chair

The rating dial box was mounted atop a wooden "arm" that slid into a metal sleeve attached to the arm of the participant's chair. (Sleeves were attached to both arms of the chair to accommodate right- and left-handed participants.) When the wooden arm was slid into place, the box rested against the

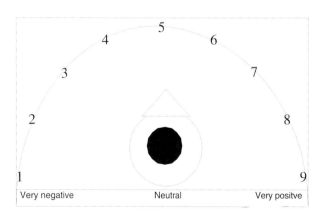

Figure 17.1. The affect rating dial faceplate.

end of the arm of the chair, so the participant's hand could rest easily on top of it to manipulate the dial (see Figure 17.2). Other methods may be used to mount the box and the dial and pointer, keeping in mind participant comfort, need for easy accessibility, and adjustment for handedness.

Electronics

The electronics for the dial consisted of 5-volt DC power applied across a 100K linear potentiometer. The dial pointer was attached to this potentiometer, with the wiper contact and ground leading to a 12-bit analog-to-digital converter on the laboratory computer. This voltage-dividing circuit provided a signal to the computer system that was proportional to the dial position. The dial was calibrated by determining what the voltage readings were when the knob was turned completely to the left and completely to the right. The linear potentiometer allowed the researcher to interpolate the readings by calculating a simple ratio.

Interface With Computer

The laboratory computer used in conjunction with the affect rating dial sampled the dial position at a rate of 30 times per second and then computed the average dial position every second. Because this same computer monitored the physiological measures, whenever rating dial and physiological measures were obtained at the same time, synchronization was ensured. Initially, to synchronize these data with the videotapes of participants' behavior, a tone was recorded on an unused audio track at the precise start of each experimental trial, and an on-screen timer was started. This tone could then be detected by the computer during the video recall session to start the timing of the rating dial and physiological data. Later, this system was replaced by one that recorded a unique number in the vertical retrace interval of every frame of the video. Whereas the older system allowed synchronization to be checked only at one point in time per trial (i.e., at the start of the trial), the new system allowed this throughout the trial.

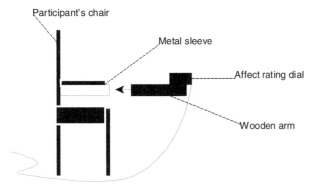

Figure 17.2. Mounting the affect rating dial. A metal sleeve is attached to the underside of the arm of the participant's chair. The dial is mounted atop a wooden arm, which slides into the sleeve.

The original rating dial was an electromechanical device. Recently, Robert Levenson's laboratory has developed a version that is implemented entirely on a computer. The participant sits at a computer screen on which the videotape being rated is played back in a large window. Below the window a horizontal "scroll bar," similar to those used in browser windows, with the numerical 9-point scale and anchor labels provides visual feedback. Participants move the bar with the computer's mouse to indicate changes in their emotional state. This method requires no external electronics at all, and we have found that participants seem quite comfortable with this approach.

Instructions for Participants

The following are sets of specific instructions for the use of the affect rating dial. Typically, the experimenter or research assistant would deliver one of these explanations in person to the participant, as a part of the general experimental instructions. These are meant to be a guide for those who plan to use the rating dial and will need to be altered depending on the experimental context.

For Dyadic Interaction Studies

I'm going to ask you to use this rating dial with this hand [indicate dominant hand] during the experiment. Please use it to give a continuous report of how you were *feeling* during the discussion with your spouse. You can choose between "extremely positive" [pointing the dial to each position as it is mentioned], "extremely negative," neither positive nor negative [pointing to "neutral"], or *any point in between;* it's a continuous scale. It's like keeping a radio station tuned in or using a steering wheel to stay on course. Just keep your hand on the dial and keep it adjusted to show how you were feeling *at the time of the interaction, not* how you feel about watching yourself on videotape. Do you have any questions about what you are supposed to do? I need to go next door now and make some more adjustments. While I'm gone, I'd like you to practice using the rating dial to get used to it. That will also help me to see if it's registering properly. I'll let you know when I'm ready to start the videotape. [Prior to starting the first video segment, the experimenter lets the participant know that the tape will be starting and reminds him or her of the task.] Please adjust the dial as often as you need to so that it indicates how you were feeling during the entire conversation.

For Empathy Studies

I'm going to ask you to use this rating dial with this hand [indicate dominant hand] during the experiment. Please use it to give a continuous report of how you think the person you are watching is *feeling* during the 20-minute tape. You can choose between "extremely positive" [pointing the dial to each position as it is mentioned], "extremely negative," neither positive nor negative [pointing to "neutral"], or *any point in between;* it's a continuous scale. It's like keeping a radio station tuned in or using a steering wheel to stay on course.

Just keep your hand on the dial and keep it adjusted to show how you think the person is feeling. *Don't* base your ratings on how *you* would feel if you were in the interaction. You should pay careful attention to the target person and try to determine how *he or she* was feeling. Do you have any questions about what you are supposed to do? I need to go next door now and make some more adjustments. While I'm gone, I'd like you to practice using the rating dial to get used to it. That will also help me to see if it's registering properly. I'll let you know when I'm ready to start the videotape. [Prior to starting the first video segment, the experimenter lets the participant know that the tape will be starting, and reminds him or her of the task.] Please concentrate on the [man/woman] in this segment and indicate with the dial how you think they are feeling during the entire 20 minutes.

For Film Viewing Studies

(The instructions for these types of studies are similar to those used in the dyadic interaction studies, but with the substitution of present-tense language, e.g., ". . . a continuous report of how you *are feeling* as you view the film clip." The following are some additional instructions used by Fredrickson and Levenson in their 1998 study.)

Negative and positive can mean a lot of different things. In this context, we'd like you to consider "Positive" as referring to any positive emotions such as amusement, contentment, happiness, or calmness and "Negative" as referring to any negative emotions, such as sadness, anger, disgust, frustration, irritation, fear, or contempt.

Data Analytic Approaches

Affect rating dial data can be analyzed in a variety of ways, depending on the nature of the experimental context in which they were gathered and the types of research questions posed. The following section briefly describes each analytic approach and gives examples of its application in past studies that utilized the rating dial.

Mean Affect Ratings

The simplest way to analyze affect rating dial data is to calculate a participant's mean emotional response over an entire interaction or stimulus exposure. In the original study that made use of the dial (Levenson & Gottman, 1983), mean rating dial scores were computed for each 15-minute marital discussion. These means were used to determine whether the study's conversation topics elicited different levels of negative affect. As the investigators had hoped, *t* tests revealed that the couples' average rating for the conflict discussion segment was significantly more negative than the average rating for the events-of-the-day segment. Simple means were also used to compare the husbands' and wives' overall affect ratings within each discussion.

In the long-term marriage study (Levenson et al., 1994), preconversation rating dial means were subtracted from conversation means to give a change score. This score was analyzed in univariate analyses of variance (ANOVAs) with age (middle-aged couples vs. older couples) and marital satisfaction (satisfied vs. dissatisfied) and correlated with spouses' mean physiological levels.

In a similar fashion, Tsai et al. (2000) used overall mean rating dial scores in their study of age and ethnic differences in responding to emotional films. They calculated mean levels of rating dial response for the one-minute prefilm baseline and means of participants' responses during the film viewing period, then subtracted the baseline means from the film means. The resultant change scores were used in later analyses to control for age differences in responsiveness during the baseline period. The investigators conducted an ANOVA for rating dial change scores to examine the effects of culture, age, and type of film on participants' subjective reports of emotion.

Fredrickson et al. (Fredrickson & Levenson, 1998; Fredrickson et al., 2000) used rating dial data to determine whether the film stimuli used in their studies induced or altered subjective emotional states the way the experimenters intended. In the first pair of studies (Fredrickson & Levenson, 1998), they calculated each participant's mean rating dial response over a prefilm baseline, then over the entire period of each stimulus film. For those participants whose means represented significant changes from baseline (determined by within-subject *t* tests), they also determined the peak response during the fear film and the latency to achieve it. An omnibus ANOVA, followed by planned comparisons, confirmed that the affective responses to several secondary films differed from each other and from the initial negative film clip. In a second pair of studies (Fredrickson et al., 2000), the researchers calculated change scores by subtracting baseline period means from film period means and then ran within-subject *t* tests to examine whether these change scores were significantly different from prefilm resting baselines. An ANOVA was used to explore sex and ethnicity differences in rating dial responses.

Although the use of mean affect ratings offers the advantage of simplicity, it does not take advantage of a major strength of rating dial data, the continuous measurement of subjective emotion over time. The following techniques make full use of data obtained from this method.

Amount-of-Affect Scores

In addition to simple means, investigators in the marital interaction studies (Levenson & Gottman, 1983; Levenson et al., 1994) calculated variables that they called "amount of affect" scores. These scores reflected the amount of negative and positive affect for each participant, taking into account the participant's own range of affect ratings. Analyzing rating dial data in this way appears to offer unique information not provided by mean dial position alone: In the 1994 study, correlations between these two types of variables suggested a sizeable amount of unshared variance (approximately 30–80%).

For the first step in computing amount-of-affect scores, means and standard deviations were calculated for each spouse's rating dial data for baseline segments and for each of the 15-minute discussions. Next, spouses' raw-score dial ratings for each 15-minute marital conversation were averaged into 90 10-s periods. Z scores were then computed for each of these 90 periods, using the mean and standard deviation for the 5-min baseline preceding that segment (Levenson & Gottman, 1983) or the mean and standard deviation of the 90 interaction periods (Levenson et al., 1994).

Once these basic computations were made, the next step involved classifying the raw-score average for each 10-s period as positive, negative, or neutral. To be coded positive, a raw-score average had to be greater than or equal to 6.0 (referenced to the 1–9 affect rating scale) and the z score had to be greater than or equal to 0.5. For a given period, a positive code meant that the pointer was actually on the positive portion of the dial (the raw-score criterion) *and* was positive relative to the participant's range of ratings (the z-score criterion). To receive a negative classification, the raw-score average had to be less than or equal to 4.0 and the z score had to be less than or equal to –0.5.

For the final step, two amount-of-affect variables were calculated for each spouse: the number of positive periods and the number of negative periods. Correlating these scores with marital satisfaction scores enabled the researchers to observe a pattern of less positive and more negative affect in dissatisfied marriages (Levenson & Gottman, 1983). Amount-of-affect scores were analyzed in a similar manner to rating dial change scores in the 1994 marital study (i.e., in ANOVAs with age and marital satisfaction and correlated with participants' mean physiological levels).

Rating dial z scores were used later to assess the validity of the rating dial/video recall procedure (Gottman & Levenson, 1985). For this analysis, dial ratings for 10-s periods were classified as positive or negative based on the z-score criterion alone, rather than on a combination of raw and z scores. Observers used the SPAFF coding system to categorize couples' speech units as positive, negative, or neutral, based on a speaker's verbal content, voice tone, context, facial expression, gestures, and body movement. Coders' data were converted to the proportion of negative affect in each 10-s period (i.e., the number of each spouse's speech units coded as negative in the period divided by the total number of that spouse's speech units in the period) and the proportion of positive affect in each period. Investigators compared the agreement between spouses' affect dial ratings for each 10-s period and observer's objective coding of the speech units for both spouses within that period. For example, if a 10-s period were rated negatively by a husband, they predicted that a greater proportion of his speech units and his wife's speech units would be coded negatively by the ob-

server, compared with 10-s periods rated positively by the husband. Repeated measures ANOVAs were used to test these hypotheses, and the relations between subjective rating dial data and objective coding were found to be significant in all cases (i.e., for each spouse and for positive and negative affect).

Lag Sequential Analysis

Lag sequential analysis is a more complex method of analyzing rating dial data that was employed in Levenson and Gottman's first (1983) marital interaction study and in the empathy study (Levenson & Ruef, 1992) described earlier. In the marital work (Levenson & Gottman, 1983) this method was used to study "affect reciprocity," or patterned exchanges of affect between spouses. The first steps in this analysis were outlined in the previous section on amount-of-affect scores; they involved classifying 10-s periods as positive or negative. In the next step, affect-reciprocity scores were calculated for positive and negative affect at lag 0 (i.e., both spouses gave the same rating in the same 10-s period) and lag 1 (i.e., one spouse's rating in a given 10-s period was matched by the other spouse's rating in the following period). A match between spouses for any given 10-s period required both to have rated the period positive or negative; neutral ratings were not counted as matching either positive or negative ratings.

Each affect-reciprocity z score was computed by subtracting the unconditional probability from the conditional probability and dividing by an estimate of the standard error. For example, the formula for the wife reciprocating the husband's positive affect at lag 0 was

$$\frac{(HWPOS/HPOS) - (HPOS/90)}{SQRT\{(HPOS/90) \times (1-[HPOS/90])/HWPOS\}},$$

where HWPOS = number of periods in which *both* the husband's and the wife's affect ratings were coded positive, HPOS = number of periods in which the husband's affect rating was coded positive, SQRT = square root, and 90 = total number of 10-s periods in the 15-min interaction. The formula for the husband reciprocating the wife's positive affect at lag 0 was

$$\frac{(WHPOS/WPOS) - (WPOS/90)}{SQRT\{(WPOS/90) \times (1-[WPOS/90])/WHPOS\}},$$

At lag of one period, the formula for the wife reciprocating the husband's positive affect was

$$\frac{(HWPOS1/HPOS) - (HPOS/90)}{SQRT\{(HPOS/90) \times (1-[HPOS/90])/HWPOS1\}},$$

where HWPOS1 = number of periods in which the husband's affect rating was coded positive and the wife's affect rating was coded positive in the *following* period. The formula for the husband reciprocating the wife's positive affect at lag 1 was

$$\frac{(WHPOS1/WPOS) - (WPOS/90)}{SQRT\{(WPOS/90) \times (1-[WPOS/90])/WHPOS1\}}.$$

Similar formulas were used to compute the z scores for negative affect reciprocity. These formulas corrected for the total number of periods that met the positive and negative coding criteria, and the resultant scores can be seen as indications of the gain in prediction of one spouse's affect by knowledge of the partner's affect (see Allison & Liker, 1982, for a discussion of the advantages of alternative algorithms). Affect-reciprocity z scores were correlated with couples' marital satisfaction scores to examine the affect patterns in distressed and nondistressed marriages.

Affect dial data was utilized similarly in the study of the physiological substrate of empathy (Levenson & Ruef, 1992). The researchers wished to measure participants' accuracy in determining the feelings of targets they viewed on videotape. Instead of computing affect-reciprocity scores, they used lag sequential analysis to compute rating accuracy scores for participants at lag 0 and lag 1. In addition, they examined lag minus 1 (participant matches target's rating for the following 10-s period) to determine whether participants' accuracy was based on actually viewing the targets' behavior, as opposed to a chance relation between the way participants and targets used the rating dial.

Formulas for deriving rating accuracy scores were adapted from the preceding affect-reciprocity formulas, with the substitution of the target's data for the spouse's. For instance, the formula for a participant's accuracy of rating positive affect at lag 1 was

$$\frac{(TSPOS1/TPOS) - (TPOS/90)}{SQRT\{(TPOS/90) \times (1-[TPOS/90])/TSPOS1\}},$$

where TSPOS1 = number of times in which the target's affect rating was positive in a given period and the participant's affect rating was positive in the following period; TPOS = number of periods in which the target's affect rating was positive; and SQRT = square root. Similar formulas were used to calculate rating accuracy for negative affect at the various lags. Rating accuracy scores were correlated with an overall index of physiological linkage, linkage z scores for individual physiological variables, mean physiological levels and variabilities, and scores on traditional empathy scales.

The researcher who uses the preceding formulas to assess affect reciprocity or rating accuracy should take care to examine the distribution of z scores computed from them. In the long-term marriage study (Levenson et al., 1994), these scores showed greater departure from normality than did the sequential probabilities themselves, so the investigators made the decision to use the latter for affect-reciprocity scores. For instance, positive affect reciprocity at lag 0 would be the number of positive periods for which the other spouse also rated the period as positive (i.e., HWPOS or WHPOS). This method has the advantage of simplicity and ease of interpretation, but it does not correct for total number of periods rated positive or negative.

Alternate Rating Accuracy Indices

Percentage Index

In their empathy study, Levenson and Ruef (1992) also used an index based on the percentage of matching ratings to estimate participants' mean overall level of rating accuracy. This was done by calculating the percentage of 10-second periods rated positive by the target person that were also rated positive by the participant in the same rating period. Similarly, a percentage was computed for participants' matching targets' ratings from the *previous* rating period (lag 1). Eight such percentages were derived (for positive or negative affect in the first or second conversation rated and at lag 0 or lag 1); each served as a simple index of rating accuracy. The mean level of this accuracy index across participants ranged from 28 to 43%, with the majority above the chance level (33%), whereas the performance of individual participants ranged from 0 to 100% accuracy. Participants' rating accuracy indices were correlated with measures of physiological linkage between participant and target and with measures of participants' cardiovascular arousal.

Mean Square Difference Index

A different rating accuracy index was used to determine which videotaped marital conversations to use as stimuli in the empathy study. The researchers wanted to avoid target spouses whose self-ratings were highly idiosyncratic, because others probably would not be able to rate them at all. They had a group of participants rate a number of conversations using the affect rating dial and then determined agreement by examining similarity between targets' and participants' ratings in two different ways. They took into account both similarity in mean affect ratings over the 15-minute conversation and similarity in second-to-second variation, using a simple index based on the mean square differences.

The researchers decided to compare ratings not only in the same time frame but also lagged by increments of 1 second. A maximum lag of 25 seconds in either direction was chosen to allow for delays in detecting the target's affect, as well as anticipation of affect. The difference between the participant's ratings and the target's ratings were calculated for each lag time, and these differences were averaged, producing a mean raw difference score for each lag. The best of *these* was called the best raw difference score. The same procedure was used with z scores to derive the best z difference score. The average closest raw difference score was obtained by comparing the participant's rating for each second with all target ratings in the corresponding 50–s window and finding the closest match; these "least differences" were then averaged. The average closest z difference score was derived in the same manner, using z scores. The sum of the preceding five variables (best raw difference + best z difference + average closest raw + average closest z + mean difference) was divided by the standard deviation of the target person's ratings to produce an index of rating accuracy. This index allowed the researchers to select for use in the empathy study those four target spouses whose self-ratings best agreed with those of the participants.

Spectral Time-Series Analysis

Another approach to making sense of affect rating dial data is spectral time-series analysis. Unlike time-series regression based on generalized least squares, spectral time-series analysis allows the researcher to consider all lags simultaneously. It produces a coherence statistic for each frequency in the overtone series; together, these measure the degree of linear association between two time series. Gottman and Levenson (1985) used this technique with marital data to support the validity of their video recall procedure. They examined the relationship between a husband's and wife's affect ratings, and in a second analysis they compared a spouse's physiological responses in the interaction session with his or her responses in the recall session. For each analysis, the two compared series were considered related if the coherence was significant only in the frequency range of maximum variance for both series.

As a first step in this analysis, affect rating dial data were processed as previously described (see the earlier section on amount-of-affect scores), then each spouse's 10-s raw-score data were transformed into a 10-s z-score time series using the mean and standard deviation for that spouse during that interaction segment. Next, spectral density functions were derived for each time series, and the frequency range that contained the maximum variance for both series was identified. The coherence spectrum within this frequency range of maximum overlap was examined to determine whether it was significant. If it was, the peak value of the coherence within this band was recorded; if not, zero coherence was recorded. The investigators then performed a binomial sign test across couples: the z score for this test determined whether the number of couples showing significant coherence for a given measure was significantly greater than chance. They made the conservative assumption that significant coherences would be found in half of the couples by chance. Finally, they reported the averages of the maximum coherence across couples (analogous to a Pearson r^2). Results of these spectral time-series analyses demonstrated coherence between the husband's and wife's self-reports of affect for a given interaction; physiological data also reflected coherence between physiological behavior in interaction and recall sessions.

Although spectral analysis is appropriate for data collected in many experimental contexts, there are certain circumstances for which it is not adequate. For example, this analysis should not be used to test for dominance (one participant's behavior influencing the responses of another) and bidirectionality (each participant's behavior exerting influence on the responses of the other) because it does not control for autocorrelation (Gottman & Ringland, 1981). In cases in which the researcher wishes to test for cross-correlation but suspects that autocorrelation may be a problem, bivariate time-series analysis is a better choice.

Bivariate Time-Series Analysis

Bivariate time-series analysis attempts to account for as much of the variance in a given series (e.g., husband's heart rate) as is possible by knowledge of its past (i.e., the autocorrelation) and then determines how much additional variance can be accounted for by adding knowledge of the past of the other series (e.g., wife's heart rate). In other words, the past of one series is used to predict the residual from the autoregression of the other series (Gottman & Ringland, 1981). In the marital and empathy studies previously described (Gottman & Levenson, 1985; Levenson & Gottman, 1983; Levenson & Ruef, 1992; Ruef, 2001), bivariate time-series analysis was used with physiological data to control for cyclicity in each participant's bodily responses. Also, this form of analysis was considered appropriate because physiological data gathered at different times from the same participant or from two participants in an interaction are not independent observations (Levenson & Ruef, 1992). Bivariate time-series analysis was not typically used with rating dial data in these studies, for two reasons: first, cyclicity is not as characteristic of rating dial output; and second, neither the partner nor the target were in the room to influence the participant's ratings during the video recall or rating session, when rating dial data were collected. However, if dyadic study participants in recall sessions are indeed reliving emotions experienced at the time of the interaction with their partners, one could make the case that partner ratings are not independent of one another and do merit a bivariate time-series approach.

This analysis uses the 10-s-period z-score averages (see the previous section on amount-of-affect scores) to produce two log-likelihood statistics for each variable obtained from the participant and the partner or target. These log-likelihood statistics, denoted Q, have approximately chi-square distributions. For each variable, the first of these statistics represents the extent to which a participant's pattern of response accounts for variance in the partner's pattern of response beyond the variance accounted for by the partner's autocorrelation. The second represents the extent to which the partner's pattern of response accounts for variance in the participant's pattern of response beyond the variance accounted for by the participant's autocorrelation. The Q values can be tested for significance, or they can be converted to z scores to allow comparison across experimental measures. For more detailed information on bivariate time-series analysis, the reader is referred to Gottman and Ringland (1981).

Future Uses of the Affect Rating Dial

Research participants have used the affect rating dial to rate their own emotions and the emotions of others in a variety of experimental contexts, as described previously. However, many other applications are possible. For instance, the dial has been utilized to study emotion in marital interaction, but it would work equally well in studies of other dyads, such as pairs of friends, therapist and client, or mother and child. Use of the dial has been limited to adult participants, but its ease of use makes it appropriate for studies that focus on the affective experiences of children or adolescents. Participants have used the dial to rate their own emotions and those of others; coders could use it in the same manner to rate the affect of participants.

Although the affect rating dial can provide useful data on its own, it is used most effectively in combination with other measures of emotional responding to allow exploration of the relationship between subjective affect and observed emotional behavior or physiological changes. Data from systems that quantify emotional behavior, such as the SPAFF or the Facial Action Coding System (FACS; Ekman & Friesen, 1978), can be paired with rating dial data for this purpose. Other methodologies that may be used with the dial are those that measure electrical activity in the brain, such as electrophysiological measures of prefrontal asymmetry or functional magnetic resonance imaging (fMRI). For example, Larson, Sutton, and Davidson (1998) have studied the relationship of differential brain activation to the time course of recovery from an emotional challenge, as measured by startle magnitude. In future studies, rating dial data collection could be added to these measures to study the time course of recovery from subjective emotional arousal, and then the patterns of recovery in different response systems could be compared for coherence. A continuous measure of subjective affect would seem a useful addition to this and other studies of "affective chronometry" (Davidson, 2000).

In addition to dyadic interaction and emotion elicitation using film clips, the rating dial could be used to evaluate the effects of other emotion elicitors. Participants could use the rating dial to give continuous ratings of affect when presented with emotionally evocative still images or sounds, such as the International Affective Picture Series (IAPS; Lang, Bradley, & Cuthbert, 1995) or the International Affective Digitized Sounds (IADS). Obtaining continuous ratings of subjective emotion also would be useful when participants are asked to vividly imagine an emotional scene, such as in personalized script-driven imagery procedures (Lang, Levin, Miller, & Kozak, 1983; Pitman & Orr, 1986; Pitman, Orr, Forgue, de Jong, & Claiborn, 1987). Another possible application of the rating dial

is in research in which participants pose emotional facial expressions and body postures. Use of the dial under such conditions may prove somewhat challenging, depending on the difficulty of the pose; in some cases the participant might not be able to give ratings without interfering with the manipulation. In contrast, the affect rating dial seems especially suited to studies that use music as an emotion elicitor, because the emotional content often varies over time in musical selections and because the aural stimuli and the visual ratings would not interfere with one another. If not too intrusive, the rating dial could easily be added to many studies, to give a more immediate and comprehensive rating of participant's subjective emotional states than could be gathered from traditional retrospective self-report measures.

Thus far, the discussion of alternate uses of the rating dial has focused on ratings of general affect, but with a few simple modifications the dial has been used to measure the level of a specific emotion such as anxiety, amusement, or sadness (Levenson et al., 1980; Mauss et al., 2005). In these uses the dial scale reflects the intensity of the single emotion rather than a bipolar measure of positive and negative affect. An example of such an application would be using the dial to rate subjective anxiety during exposure to feared stimuli in individuals with anxiety disorders, such as social phobia or posttraumatic stress disorder.

Rating more than one discrete emotion presents a different kind of challenge. As we have seen, an important aspect of rating dial application is the time frame of data collection: online versus retrospective (relived emotions). In studies in which a participant is interacting with a partner or engaged in any activity that requires a great deal of concentration, then rating dial data are best gathered retrospectively, using the video recall procedure. When the experimental task is more passive, not requiring a great deal of physical activity, speech, or interaction with others, then online emotion ratings are more feasible. Because the investigator is asking participants to rate their emotional state at the same time as they are attending to a stimulus, there are limits on how much information they can be expected to process at one time. With video recall, participants could watch the videotape of their interaction more than once, giving ratings of different discrete emotions on each pass. With online ratings, the computerized, mouse-driven affect rating dial could be programmed to toggle regularly from the measurement of one emotion to another, perhaps changing the color of the pointer (e.g., red to blue) to indicate the change. For example, the investigator could collect 1 minute of data for anger, then 1 minute for another emotion, such as sadness. However, with this kind of sampling one would lose the continuity of the data stream. There is always a balance between what a participant can reasonably attend to without becoming distracted from the experimental task at hand and the level and amount of information the experimenter wishes to gather. If the rating task is too complex, one risks distraction and intrusiveness; if too simple, one is left with a measure that offers little emotional information and no continuity of data.

The rating dial also could be modified to measure aspects of emotion other than valence, such as perceived level of physiological arousal. Dimensions of metamood (Mayer & Stevens, 1994; Salovey, Mayer, Goldman, Turvey, & Palfai, 1995), such as acceptance and comfort with one's emotional state, could be tracked over the course of an experiment and related to subjective affect ratings or physiological measures.

Conclusion

In their article demonstrating the validity of the affect rating dial and the video recall procedure, Gottman and Levenson (1985) concluded:

> We expect that the procedure will also be valid for other kinds of dyadic interaction besides marital interaction as long as the interaction produces a reasonable range of emotional responding. It is our hope that the strength of these findings will provide other researchers with sufficient confidence in these procedures to be able to adopt them when a continuous self-report of affect is needed. For those experimental paradigms that differ substantially from ours or in instances where the amplitude of emotional responding is suspect, we have provided two validational techniques—agreement with objective coders and physiological reliving—that could be utilized to validate our affective self-report procedures in other experimental contexts. (p. 159)

Since the time this statement was written the affect rating dial has continued to play a part in studies of interaction, but it also has been utilized in experimental contexts that the authors may not have anticipated. These applications were outlined in this chapter, along with possible future implementations of the measure.

The years since the affect rating dial was developed have seen a great expansion in emotion research, including techniques for emotion assessment. We hope that the information contained in this chapter will be helpful to those investigators looking for ways to continuously measure subjective emotion and will stimulate new creative applications and adaptations of the rating dial.

References

Allison, P. D., & Liker, J. K. (1982). Analyzing sequential categorical data on dyadic interaction: A comment on Gottman. *Psychological Bulletin, 91,* 393–403.

Bradley, M. M., & Lang, P. J. (1994). Measuring emotion: The self-assessment manikin and the semantic differential. *Journal of Behavior Therapy and Experimental Psychiatry, 25,* 49–59.

Cacioppo, J. T., & Berntson, G. G. (1994). Relationship between attitudes and evaluative space: A critical review, with emphasis on the separability of positive and negative substrates. *Psychological Bulletin, 115,* 401–423.

Cacioppo, J. T., & Gardner, W. L. (1999). Emotion. *Annual Review of Psychology, 50,* 191–214.

Davidson, R. J. (2000). Affective style, psychopathology, and resilience: Brain mechanisms and plasticity. *American Psychologist, 55*(11), 1196–1214.

Ekman, P., & Friesen, W. V. (1978). *The Facial Action Coding System.* Palo Alto, CA: Consulting Psychologists Press.

Fredrickson, B. L., & Kahneman, D. (1993). Duration neglect in retrospective evaluations of affective episodes. *Journal of Personality and Social Psychology, 65*(1), 45–55.

Fredrickson, B. L., & Levenson, R. W. (1998). Positive emotions speed recovery from the cardiovascular sequelae of negative emotions. *Cognition and Emotion, 12*(2), 191–220.

Fredrickson, B. L., Mancuso, R. A., Branigan, C., & Tugade, M. M. (2000). The undoing effect of positive emotions. *Motivation and Emotion, 24*(4), 237–258.

Gottman, J. M., & Krokoff, L. J. (1989). The relationship between marital interaction and marital satisfaction: A longitudinal view. *Journal of Consulting and Clinical Psychology, 57,* 47–52.

Gottman, J. M., & Levenson, R. W. (1985). A valid procedure for obtaining self-report of affect in marital interaction. *Journal of Consulting and Clinical Psychology, 53*(2), 151–160.

Gottman, J. M., & Levenson, R. W. (1986). Assessing the role of emotion in marriage. *Behavioral Assessment, 8,* 31–48.

Gottman, J. M., & Levenson, R. W. (1992). Marital processes predictive of later dissolution: Behavior, physiology, and health. *Journal of Personality and Social Psychology, 63*(2), 221–233.

Gottman, J., Notarius, C., Markman, H., Bank, C., Yoppi, B., & Rubin, M. E. (1976). Behavior exchange theory and marital decision making. *Journal of Personality and Social Psychology, 34,* 14–23.

Gottman, J. M., & Ringland, J. T. (1981). The analysis of dominance and bidirectionality in social development. *Child Development, 52,* 393–412.

Lang, P. J., Bradley, M. M., & Cuthbert, B. N. (1995). *International Affective Picture System (IAPS): Technical manual and affective ratings.* Gainesville: University of Florida, Center for Research in Psychophysiology.

Lang, P. J., Levin, D. N., Miller, G. A., & Kozak, M. J.(1983). Fear behavior, fear imagery, and the psychophysiology of emotion: The problem of affective-response integration. *Journal of Abnormal Psychology, 92,* 276–306.

Larson, C. L., Sutton, S. K., & Davidson, R. J. (1998). Affective style, frontal EEG asymmetry and the time course of the emotion-modulated startle. *Psychophysiology, 35,* S52.

Levenson, R. W., Carstensen, L. L., & Gottman, J. M. (1994). The influence of age and gender on affect, physiology, and their interrelations: A study of long-term marriages. *Journal of Personality and Social Psychology, 67*(1), 56–68.

Levenson, R. W., & Gottman, J. M. (1983). Marital interaction: Physiological linkage and affective exchange. *Journal of Personality and Social Psychology, 45*(3), 587–597.

Levenson, R. W., & Gottman, J. M. (1985). Physiological and affective predictors of change in relationship satisfaction. *Journal of Personality and Social Psychology, 49*(1), 85–94.

Levenson, R. W., Oyama, O. N., & Meek, P. S. (1987). Greater reinforcement from alcohol for those at risk: Parental risk, personality risk, and sex. *Journal of Abnormal Psychology, 96*(3), 242–253.

Levenson, R. W., & Ruef, A. M. (1992). Empathy: A physiological substrate. *Journal of Personality and Social Psychology, 63*(2), 234–246.

Levenson, R. W., Sher, K. J., Grossman, L. M., Newman, J., & Newlin, D. B. (1980). Alcohol and stress response dampening: Pharmacological effects, expectancy, and tension reduction. *Journal of Abnormal Psychology, 89,* 528–538.

Markman, H. J. (1979). Application of a behavioral model of marriage in predicting relationship satisfaction of couples planning marriage. *Journal of Consulting and Clinical Psychology, 47,* 743–749.

Markman, H. J. (1981). Prediction of marital distress: A 5-year follow-up. *Journal of Consulting and Clinical Psychology, 49,* 760–762.

Mauss, I. B., Levenson, R. W., McCarter, L. M., Wilhem, F. W., & Gross, J. J. (2005). The tie that binds? Coherence among emotion experience, behavior, and physiology. *Emotion, 5,* 175–190.

Mayer, J. D., & Stevens, A. (1994). An emerging understanding of the reflective (meta-) experience of mood. *Journal of Research in Personality, 28,* 351–373.

Pitman, R. K., & Orr, S. P. (1986). Test of the conditioning model of neurosis: Differential aversive conditioning of angry and neutral facial expressions in anxiety disorder patients. *Journal of Abnormal Psychology, 95,* 208–213.

Pitman, R. K., Orr, S. P., Forgue, D. F., de Jong, J. B., & Claiborn, J. M. (1987). Psychophysiologic assessment of posttraumatic stress disorder imagery in Vietnam combat veterans. *Archives of General Psychiatry, 44,* 970–975.

Ruef, A. M. (2001). Empathy in long-term marriage: Behavioral and physiological correlates (Doctoral dissertation, University of California, Berkeley, 2000). *Dissertation Abstracts International, 62*(01), 563B.

Salovey, P., Mayer, J. D., Goldman, S., Turvey, C., & Palfai, T. (1995). Emotional attention, clarity, and repair: Exploring emotional intelligence using the Trait Meta-Mood Scale. In J. W. Pennebaker (Ed.), *Emotion, disclosure and health* (pp. 125–154). Washington, DC: American Psychological Association.

Sher, K. J., & Levenson, R. W. (1982). Risk for alcoholism and individual differences in the stress-response-dampening effect of alcohol. *Journal of Abnormal Psychology, 91,* 350–367.

Tsai, J. L., & Levenson, R. W. (1997). Cultural influences on emotional responding: Chinese and European American dating couples during interpersonal conflict. *Journal of Cross-Cultural Psychology, 28*(5), 600–625.

Tsai, J. L., Levenson, R. W., & Carstensen, L. L. (2000). Autonomic, subjective, and expressive responses to emotional films in older and younger Chinese Americans and European Americans. *Psychology and Aging, 15*(4), 684–693.

Watson, D., Clark, L. A., & Tellegen, A. (1988). Development and validation of brief measures of positive and negative affect: The PANAS scales. *Journal of Personality and Social Psychology, 54,* 1063–1070.

Nancy L. Stein

Marc W. Hernandez

Assessing Understanding and Appraisals During Emotional Experience

The Development and Use of the Narcoder

Assessing the experience and understanding of emotion, especially in real-world situations, is a complex, daunting task. One reason for the difficulty is that information about emotion is expressed through many different modalities (Lewis & Haviland-Jones, 1993, 2000). The face (Ekman, 1977, 1992), the melody of the voice (Fernald, 1984), body posture, hand gesture (McNeill, 1992), and language (Stein, Trabasso, & Liwag, 1993) all carry information about emotion. Physiological measures of heart rate, blood pressure, and evoked response potentials (ERPs) also allow us to describe the physical and biological processes (LeDoux & Phelps, 2000) that occur during emotional experience. Information contained in one channel may be unique and not available in other channels. For example, the melodic expression of the voice carries critical information about the intent of the speaker, as well as information about the valence of the feeling states the speaker is experiencing. The simple expression, "Don't touch the plug on the wall," uttered to a 2-year-old child, can have two or three different meanings, depending on the prosodic tone and other nonverbal behaviors that accompany the utterance. Similarly, the hands can be used to gesture and convey information about valence, emphasis, intent, and mood of the moment that may or may not be expressed in other modalities. Physiological indicators, such as heart rate, blood pressure, and ERPs, can assess the intensity with which emotion is experienced, whether or not incoming information is registered in any way, and the different parts of the brain that are affected by the experience.

Talk during an emotional experience can be used to assess different types of affective feelings about an event; appraisals of the event and the meaning it carries, especially in terms of its personal significance; whether or not the emotional experience will lead to further action; and ways in which an emotion has affected the beliefs, thinking, decision making, future planning, and coping strategies of a person. Language provides speakers with the capacity to refer to states in the past, present, and future. They are not limited to the here and now. Talk further allows a description of the temporal and causal sequence of events, feelings, thoughts, and actions that precede, accompany, and follow the experience of emotion (Frijda, 1987, 1988; Johnson-Laird & Oatley, 1989, 1992; Stein & Levine, 1987, 1990). Some reporters of emotional experience may give inaccurate reports about the causes of emotion or the way in which the sequence of events unfolded. However, it is essential that we understand how a reporter represents causality and casual mechanisms, especially if we desire a change in a reporter's representation of events (e.g., in cognitive therapy).

In this chapter, we focus on the expression of emotion through thought and language and the ways in which talk indicates emotional understanding and psychological well-being. We present a small part of our computer program that was created to code all types of talk about emotional experience. We describe the thinking and cognitive evaluations that accompany emotional experience, and we show the power of different categories of language and thought to predict psychological well-being. Finally, we discuss how thoughts and language correlate with the expression of emotion in the face, body, hands, and physiological functioning during an emotion episode.

Measuring the expression of emotion across modalities with the inclusion of physiological indicators is critical if we are to achieve a deeper understanding of the organization and sequence of thinking, feeling, and behaving during the experience of emotion. Recent work on the physiology of emotion has raised many issues about the components, organization, and sequence of emotional experience (see Damasio, 1999; LeDoux & Phelps, 2000, for an example of these issues) in both humans and other animals. The physiological measures that have been used, be they MRI, ERP, heart rate, or blood pressure, often provide ambiguous results about emotion. Unless these measures are related to ongoing cognitive interpretations of events, as well as to the behavioral expression of emotion, they provide an incomplete picture of the experience of emotion.

To fully understand the nature of emotional experience, it becomes important to map out the causal sequence of an emotion episode, *going across modalities,* so that we understand both the parallel and sequential components of emotion experience, from the event that precipitated an emotion to the actions and outcomes that follow from an emotion. Thus one of our goals is to describe the cognitive and behavioral components of emotional experience that result in a more accurate understanding of the processes linked to emotion. We also point out several critical issues in emotion research that need further resolution.

The Nature of Emotional Experience

We have argued (Stein & Levine, 1987, 1990; Stein, Trabasso, & Liwag, 1993, 2000) that the experience of emotion almost always results from an interpretation and meaning analysis of ongoing events and situations. From our perspective, emotion is intimately linked to personally significant goals and to beliefs that people hold about whether or not their desired goals will be attained, maintained, or thwarted. The evocation of emotion not only involves a meaning analysis of the situation, but it is also intimately linked to problem solving, planning, and the ensuing actions that are carried out while experiencing a change in the state of a desired goal and a particular emotion.

The experience of emotion almost always occurs when a change takes place in a personally significant goal. The change can be either positive (attaining or maintaining a desired goal or avoiding an undesired goal state) or negative (failing to attain or maintain a desired goal or failing to change an undesired state). We are highlighting the significance of a change in goals to elicit an emotional response. A distinguishing characteristic of emotional experience is an effort to assimilate some type of new information into current knowledge

schemes (Mandler, 1975, 1984; Stein & Jewett, 1986; Stein & Levine, 1987, 1990; Stein & Trabasso, 1989, 1992; Stein, Trabasso, & Liwag, 1993, 2000). We contend that people constantly monitor their environment in an effort to maintain or attain their desired goals and to experience a positive state of emotion. In order to succeed at this task, procedures analogous to pattern matching and assimilation are used to analyze and compare incoming data to what is already known. When new information is detected in the input, a mismatch occurs, causing an interruption in current thinking processes. Attention then shifts to the novel or discrepant information. Along with this shift in attention comes arousal of the autonomic nervous system and a focus on the implications that the new information has for the maintenance of valued goals. Thus, from our perspective, emotional experience is almost always associated with attending to and making sense out of new information.

As a function of attending to new information, *learning* (via content and structural changes in the mental structures used to understand an emotional event) almost always results during an emotion episode. In an effort to understand the consequences of changing conditions on the status of goals, people are forced to revise and update their beliefs about two dimensions: the probability of maintaining goals under a new set of conditions and whether or not they have access to plans that will lead to successful goal maintenance. For example, when people *fail* to maintain or attain a desired goal state, they attend to the conditions that prevented them from being successful (e.g., the consequences of their failure), and they assess the probability of generating a plan of action to overcome their goal failure. This type of thought sequence characterizes children's emotional responses (Capatides, 1989; Levine, Stein, & Liwag, 1997; Liwag & Stein, 1995; Stein & Levine, 1989; Stein & Trabasso, 1989), parents' descriptions and responses to the children's emotional behaviors (Capatides, 1989; Levine, Stein, & Liwag, 1997; Stein & Albro, 2001; Stein, Trabasso, & Albro, 2001), and adult reactions to stressful events (Stein, Folkman, Trabasso, & Richards, 1997; Stein, Ross, & Fergusson, 2001; Stein et al., 2001).

In updating knowledge about the conditions that lead to goal success or failure, people may change the *value* they have imputed to a particular set of goals. That is, in attaining or failing to attain a goal, the value associated with that and other goals may increase or decrease in strength. As a result, people often *forfeit* their goals because the goals have declined in value, or they may *reinstate* their original goals and intensify their efforts to achieve them. Alternatively, they may still value failed goals at the same level, but they choose to *substitute* different goals, depending on the attainability that their original goals now possess. Thus it becomes necessary to be particularly sensitive to the types of plans that are formulated as a result of experiencing a goal failure or success in conjunction with a specific emotion. The reasons that people perceive for goal failure are intimately linked to how they formulate plans of action to overcome obstacles to attaining or maintaining a desired goal.

In privileging intentional action as a core part of our theory, we are assuming that people have a built-in mechanism that allows them to represent *goal-action-outcome* sequences in relationship to the maintenance of goals (Gallistel, 1985; Piaget, 1981; Stein & Levine, 1987, 1990; Stein et al., 1993, 2000). Individuals are able to infer and represent the causal conditions that operate to produce actions that result in certain outcomes, and they are able to use this knowledge to achieve goals. Thus, when a change in the ability to maintain or attain a goal occurs and an emotion is evoked, plans of action are generated and then mobilized in an effort to accomplish a particular goal.

The emotion that a person feels constrains the type of goal plan that is constructed. Happiness occurs when goals succeed or when negative outcomes are avoided. The plans that follow happiness are ones of *reinstatement* of the successful goal or ones of *generating new goals* as the original goal has been fulfilled. Anger and sadness occur when goals are not achieved or when negative states are continued. The plans that follow anger are ones of *reinstatement* of the original goal or ones of *substitution* of the original goal. The plans that follow sadness are ones of *goal abandonment* and sometimes *goal substitution* (Stein et al., 2000). The emotion of fear is associated with a perceived threat to a desired end state, when the end state has yet to change but the person experiencing fear believes that the end state change is clearly imminent and is most likely to occur. The plan associated with fear is one of *prevention*.

If these assertions are true, we should expect talk about emotional experience to be focused on the goal-directed action sequence that reflects emotional experience that is under way. Thus talk during an emotion episode should focus on the events that precipitated emotion; how the precipitating event changed personally significant goals; the reasons for the occurrence of the specific emotion; whether or not the change in goals is permanent; how important the change is to the person experiencing the emotion; whether a plan of action is available to reinstate, maintain, or change the goal; what should or could be done as a result of the change; and what the consequences would be if action were carried out. In other words, talk about emotion should be goal related, causal in nature, and focused on either attaining and maintaining a preferred state or getting out of or avoiding an aversive state.

Table 18.1 includes a set of questions that reflect the thoughts that reporters have when they focus their attention on describing emotional experience. These questions should be used as *pedagogical devices* for understanding an emotion episode. When reporting emotional experience, people do not include a literal recitation of these questions. However, an analysis of more than 5,000 narrative reports of either retrospective or ongoing emotional experience has shown that almost every report contains the information that answers these questions.

Although much of the thinking and planning that occurs during emotion experience is not carried out on a conscious level, critical parts of emotion experience are indeed conscious and available for further evaluation (Mandler, 1984; Pribram, 2003). We as researchers need to examine and describe the experience and expression of emotion as the sequence unfolds so that we can better understand what parts of the emotion episode are experienced in an unconscious fashion and what parts are indeed conscious and available for reflection. Analyzing the talk that occurs during an emotion episode is one way we can begin to understand more clearly which parts of the emotion episode are conscious. Linking the talk to physiology and to nonverbal behavior deepens our understanding of the process even more.

As we discuss the various types of talk that people use during emotional experience, it will become clear that a relatively small number of language and meaning categories are used during talk about emotion. Almost all of these categories correspond to some part of a problem-solving schema that is reflected in the list of questions presented in Table 18.1. Miller, Galanter, and Pribram (1960), as well as Simon and Newell (1970; Newell & Simon, 1972) first described

Table 18.1

The content and sequence of appraisals made during the experience of an emotional event

What happened?

1. What type of event occurred?
2. Have my goals been affected?
3. Which goals have changed in status?
4. How have the goals changed (have they failed or succeeded)?
5. Who or what caused the change in the status of the goal?
6. What are the consequences of the change in the goal's status?
7. What beliefs have been violated and updated due to the change?

What can I do about it?

1. What do I want to do about it?
2. Do I think the goal can (should) be reinstated?
3. Is an action plan available that would reinstate or modify the desired goal?
4. How do I feel about it?
5. What are the reasons for my emotional reactions?

What did I do and what were the results of my actions?

1. Did I carry out actions in the service of attaining or maintaining the goal?
2. What were the actions?
3. What were the outcomes?
4. Did any unintended outcomes result from goal achievement or failure?
5. Did the unintended outcomes cause a reappraisal or reevaluation of the goals at stake?
6. How will the immediate outcomes affect other desired goals?

this type of problem-solving schema. Although many well-known researchers in emotion, such as Arnold (1960, 1970), Lazarus (1982, 1984), and Frijda (1987), do not reference the basic problem-solving schema described by Miller and colleagues (1960) or by Newell and Simon (1972), the ways in which these researchers envision and theorize about emotion directly follow from the theoretical assumptions and postulates of Miller et al. (1960) and Newell and Simon (1972).

One reason for the lack of overlap between emotion theorists such as Arnold, Lazarus, and Frijda and theorists such as Miller, Galanter, and Pribram, as well as Newell and Simon, is that the latter group of scientists came from a cognitive–biological–computer science tradition, whereas Arnold and Lazarus came from a personality–clinical psychology tradition. We have found theories from both of these domains to be useful because each theory focuses on different variables, each of which is essential to the experience of emotion.

The cognitive perspective has made us more sensitive to issues involved in unfolding the emotion episode. Many of us have strongly held beliefs about the causal sequence of emotion and cognition (e.g., whether cognition always precedes emotion or whether emotion always precedes cognition). Understanding that both *parallel* and *sequential* processes occur during thinking and feeling (Stein & Levine, 1987; Stein et al., 1993, 2000) and that thinking processes occur very rapidly enables us to better describe the *sequential* and *simultaneous components* of both thought and emotion. The cognitive perspective also forces us to create a process theory that describes the *specific appraisals* and *evaluations* that make up the meaning analysis that is carried out during emotion expression, as well as the problem-solving process and plans of action that are carried out when changes occur in a desired goal state and emotion is experienced.

By taking a cognitive perspective, we are also forced to differentiate between *emotion states* and *other feeling states,* such as *mood states, general affective states,* and *mental states.* For us (Stein & Levine, 1987, 1989; Stein et al., 1993, 2000), emotion states are different from general affective states, mood states, physical states, mental states, and states of preference. Defining and making a distinction between emotion and general affective states is critical to any theory of emotion because the differences in how emotion is defined probably account for the majority of disputes that emotion researchers have with one another.

For example, Zajonc (1980) took a strong stand against the primacy of cognition in regulating emotional reactions, whereas Lazarus (1982) took a strong stand against emotion regulating cognition, advocating the primacy of cognition in determining emotions. Zajonc's main thesis was that preferences, the building blocks of emotion (e.g., liking, disliking), are innate and need no inferences. Therefore, emotion was not controlled by or regulated by cognition. In our chapter in the first *Handbook of Emotion* (Stein et al., 1993), we took issue with Zajonc on the following points.

The first was whether preferences are innate. At birth, the infant's repertoire includes a set of behaviors for responding to different types and intensities of stimulation. Many actions are reflexive in nature (e.g., the startle, orienting, blinking, and sucking reflexes). Some behaviors involve an affective reaction specific to the nature of the stimuli. For example, certain events precipitate distress responses, consisting of volatile activity, crying, and particular facial expressions. Other events elicit a quieting response, with the absence of volatile activity and expression. A few researchers have taken these responses as evidence that the infant has innate preferences for being in certain states and innate preferences for avoiding others. For example, Zajonc (1980) argues that initial preferences need no cognitive input for their elicitation and that they drive all other forms of emotional development.

We do not question the existence and importance of preferences. They are critical to the experience and expression of emotion. However, we take issue with the claim that newborns possess full-blown preferences, such as desires to be in certain states or desires to avoid others. The fact that infants experience pleasure and distress does not mean that they prefer or desire to shift from one state to another. Having preferences requires the ability to represent, remember, compare, and choose between two different states and to express a desire to orient more toward one state than toward another. In order to carry out action that corresponds to preferential thinking, a person must have acquired the ability to represent a state that does not currently exist. Although newborns can demonstrate quieting or distress in direct response to different events, they have yet to achieve the capacity to represent internal or external states different from those that currently direct their behavior. This type of representation would be necessary to say that preferences were innate.

However, for the moment, let us assume that infants do have the capacity to remember and choose between two alternatives. This ability still does not result in an emotion that has been elicited by a precipitating event. Distress, a general negative affective state in our affective taxonomy, is evoked when infants experience sensory input that creates pain. Actions following from distressful responses, such as volatility and crying that have been observed in infants (Sroufe, 1979), may indeed be innate. However, for emotion to be experienced, infants need access to knowledge in the form of beliefs that allows them to make inferences about the current aversive situation in terms of whether or not the current situation can be terminated by some type of planning and action response. In order to make these inferences, infants need to be able to access knowledge about different types of plans of action. They need to be able to represent a plan and to decide whether a specific plan contains the appropriate actions to stop the aversive situation.

If infants were able to do this, then we would probably see one of the three basic emotions experienced (fear, anger, or sadness), depending on the specific inferences that were made about the probability of stopping the aversive action. Fear would be experienced if the infant made an inference that the painful stimulation could not be stopped and that the intensity of pain might even worsen. It would be the inference about the intensity of pain worsening that would create a threat to the infant and generate a fear response.

The most probable response, however, to painful stimulation is one of anger, with infants having made the decision that the current situation is aversive and that they need to end the aversive situation. Anger is elicited when infants fail to stop the painful stimulation, given that they or other people have initiated and carried out a plan of action chosen to end the pain. Anger would be elicited when infants believe, based on their knowledge of past situations, that plans of action are available to stop the pain. Sadness would rarely be initiated, but if it were elicited, the infant would have made the inference that the aversive state could not be stopped by anything the infant or another person did. Thus, for the three basic emotions to be elicited, very specific inferences need to be made about the availability of plans of action that would stop the aversive situation or the availability of plans that would stop the situation from becoming even more aversive. What we are trying to demonstrate is that sets of very rapid inferences need to be made about the availability of plans of action to change the current situation or to prevent the current situation from getting worse.

In many situations, children and adults do not make these sets of inferences about the viability of the current situations. However, affective reactions can still be elicited and do not function the same way that emotions do. In almost all cases of emotion experience, some type of event precedes the emotion. The person who experiences the emotion makes a set of inferences about the probability that the precipitating event will change the state of a personally significant goal. To make the inference that a desired goal will be affected, the person needs to have knowledge about past situations in terms of the types of events and actions that have been successful or unsuccessful in terminating an undesired state or in achieving a desired state.

We have argued (Stein & Levine, 1987, 1990, 1999; Stein et al., 2000) that infants begin to be able to access and use this type of plan knowledge at about 3–4 months of age. Stenberg and Campos (1990) have shown that at about 3–4 months, infants begin to change their visual search strategies in terms of following human action that results in aversive stimulation to the infant. When the search strategies begin to focus on an external agent that is causing the aversive situation, anger results. Sroufe (1979) has also described the types of cognitive strategies that are necessary for basic emotions to be elicited. Until a set of core inferences are made about the probability of attaining or maintaining a desired goal, emotions such as anger, sadness, and fear will not arise.[1]

Other affective responses, however, may well be elicited. These affective responses do not require as many inferences about the availability of plans and actions. Some general af-fective responses, such as startle and distress, may be innate responses to the intensity or speed of some type of stimulation. Some affective responses focus more on the desirability of the current state and a desire to change the state without accessing any knowledge about the probability that a plan of action would indeed change the current situation.

Some general affective responses, such as surprise, are elicited when inferences have been made about the expectedness or the novelty of a precipitating event. Inferences about the novelty of events are critical to the experience of emotion and are produced by pattern recognition and pattern matching procedures that are continually carried out in states of wakefulness and sleep. Emotion responses require that recognition of the novelty of the event take place in terms of what is known, because attention to the new information, in terms of its effect on the well-being of the perceiver, is critical for an emotional response. However, attention can remain on the novelty of an event for some period of time before the perceiver tries to determine an event's impact in order to access plans of action. Surprise is usually evoked not only when the situation is unexpected but also when the perceiver cannot make inferences about the function, identity, and nature of the precipitating event (Stein et al., 2000). That is, many situations exist in which the full set of core inferences necessary to produce an emotion are not carried out. However, some of the core processes are carried out, and, depending on which processes have resulted, either general affective or emotional responses will be elicited.

Therefore, it becomes mandatory for current theories of emotion to focus on different types of affective responses, some of which are not emotions and others of which are emotions. A good example of the necessity to differentiate among the various types of affective states that can be evoked is seen in the pencil-and-paper measure of mood states called the Positive and Negative Affect Schedule (PANAS), devised by Watson, Clark, and Tellegen (1988). The PANAS measures both positive and negative "mood" states. Of some 30 items listed on the PANAS, 11 are emotions (guilty, scared, proud, ashamed, afraid, hopeful, angry, relieved, sad, happy, and worried). The remainder of the PANAS terms are classified as: general positive or negative affective states (interested, excited, distressed, upset, relaxed), mood states (nervous, jittery, irritable, hostile, content, alone), mental states (alert, attentive, inspired), and personal disposition states (active, confident, strong, enthusiastic, determined).

Table 18.2 lists all of the categories of clauses that the Narcoder recognizes. Each category is defined, and five instances appear under each category listing. Table 18.3 contains the oral report of a 3-year-old boy telling one of our interviewers about a conflict that he had with his dad, who made him angry. Each clause in Table 18.3 is scored according to one of the categories listed in Table 18.2.

The importance of distinguishing among different types of affective responses is critical if we are to build better predictors of emotional well-being and behavior in emotion

Table 18.2

Definitions of the components of an emotion-based goal-directed action episode

1. Precipitating Event

An event that is unexpected in some fashion and that challenges current beliefs about the world. Precipitating events can be physical events, human actions, or the activation of a memory of an event. In all cases, the precipitating event leads to the appraisal of current states of well-being and to an evaluation of the status of current goals. Precipitating events can be identified by the participant's answers to the questions, "What event was stressful for you this week?" or "What event made you feel (any appropriate emotion)?". Precipitating events are perceived as events that cause changes in the status of personally significant goals.

2. Emotion States

Emotions are identified using an emotion-word taxonomy that incorporates functional criteria and standardized norms (Johnson-Laird & Oatley, 1989) used to specify different emotion states. By definition, emotions are preceded by some type of precipitating event by which a valued goal is blocked, attained, under threat, or accompanied by states of uncertainty in terms of the future maintenance or attainment of the goal. By definition, emotions are short-lived in nature (generally measured in seconds) and of moderate to high intensity; they can occur in sequence (very rapidly), and they have physiological, as well as cognitive and behavioral, components. Emotions also encode an antecedent, as well as a consequence. The emotions generated so far include the positive ones of happiness, hope, pride, and relief and the negative ones of anger, anxiety, disgust, embarrassment, fear, guilt, hopelessness, jealousy, pity, and regret.

3. General Affective States

These states clearly signal some type of physiological change due to a precipitating event. Unlike emotion states, however, these states do not carry a specific belief, goal, and plan of action in conjunction with the physiological state (Stein & Levine, 1990; Stein et al., 1993). General affective states can be positive, negative, or without a valence. Positive affective states include feeling comfortable, grateful, pleasant, and nice. Negative affective states include feeling bad, distressed, bothered, concerned, and hurt. General affective states without a valence include feeling in awe, amazed, excited, shocked, stunned, and surprised. These states carry a neutral valence because they often precede both positive and negative emotion states. They encode the occurrence of an unexpected event that contains some novel aspect. However, the affective state itself does not convey whether the novelty is perceived positively or negatively. Further evaluation of the event's relationship to personally meaningful goals is necessary.

4. Mood States

Mood states are similar to emotion states in that they are physiological in nature and carry a valence. Mood states, however, are longer lasting than emotions, generally lower in intensity, and do not necessarily encode a goal plan or specific event that initiated the mood state. Feeling good, jubilant, satisfied, and calm are examples of mood states.

5. Mental States

Mental states refer to awareness of a cognitive state and can have a positive or negative valence. Mental states include being crazy, disappointed, ambivalent, and fascinated.

6. Personal Disposition States

Personal dispositions convey a person's personality attributes, which are often inferred from actions. They are generally appraisals of one's more permanent qualities. Examples include *lazy, nice, friendly, mean,* and *nasty.*

7. Beliefs

Beliefs encode knowledge about the world. Beliefs are statements that carry truth value, and they can be focused on the past, present, or future. Beliefs are often signaled by the use of a mental-state term (*think, know, remember, forget, my opinion, believe,* etc.). However, beliefs can also be stated as assertions, and these assertions often increase the certainty associated with the utterance of a statement. Assertions are given as statements of fact, such as: "He has a red Jaguar"; "He was the one who caused the trouble"; and "He was there before anyone else." Rather than telling an audience that these statements are all uttered from a particular point of view or opinion, the narrator states these beliefs as though they contain factual evidence that everyone can observe.

8. Belief Violation

Belief violations are a class of beliefs that have been challenged or violated by a precipitating event. Belief violation is scored using the linguistic criteria of violation of normality: "It wasn't supposed to happen"; "I couldn't believe what was happening"; "I hadn't expected him to get sick this fast"; "I really had to change my thinking about the situation." Explicit mention of the violation consists of two parts: mention of the change that has occurred ("He got sick really fast") and mention of the fact that this change violated what was expected ("I didn't expect him to get sick so fast").

9. Belief Revision

Belief revisions refer to the updating of beliefs. Does the participant reinstate beliefs about how things were before the beliefs were challenged by a precipitating event, or are the beliefs revised? Belief revisions are scored by examining the semantic content of a clause and the relational significance of adjacent clauses. For example, "His T4 cells took a dive. I guess he's really getting sick,"

(continued)

Table 18.2 (*continued*)

which represents a belief update in the form of a revision. "His T4 cells took a dive, but he'll bounce back. He'll be okay," represents a reinstatement of a belief prior to the event. In this latter case, a prior belief is challenged but not revised.

10. Preference

A preference is a state of liking or disliking someone or something. Statements of preference are often intensified, that is, I really like him; I love him; I really dislike him; I hate him; I can't stand him. Preferences connote the positive or negative value that something has, but they do not include a desire to attain or eliminate the particular person, object, or event. That is, they do not encode a state that is not present. Preferences simply mark the value and likeability of an object.

11. Goal

A goal is defined as a desire to go from one state to another or a desire to maintain a current state. Goals refer to any valued object, activity, or state that the participant wants to attain. Goals can be identified from stated reasons or purposes for actions that were taken. Goals motivate action and often occur in conjunction with actions or in conjunction with the completion of the goal. Statements such as: *I am going/ to get the groceries today*, and *I got the puppy/ that I really wanted* encode, respectively, (1) an attempt plus a goal and (2) an outcome plus a goal. Thus a different part of the sentence is used to code each type of category. Goals do not exist in isolation. They are related to the precipitating events that activate them and to other goals. The relationship between goals is hierarchical: Some goals are formulated in order to achieve other goals. The hierarchical order can be determined by asking "why" questions about actions or goals. The goal that is highest in a hierarchy can be considered the most important. Evidence of its importance comes from the number of goals subordinate to it and the number of times that events affect it.

12. Plans of Action

Plans are identified by the use of verbs that are either conditional or future oriented and that refer to desires: "Here's what I'd really like to do"; "Here's what I thought about doing"; "Here's how I planned to handle the disaster." Plans are normally expressed as subordinate goals to a higher order goal mentioned previously in the narrative. They usually contain goals that can be directly enacted to achieve a superordinate goal. In the initial coding of goals, the superordinate goals are not distinguished from the subordinate goals. Thus, the Narcoder will first list everything as a goal without distinguishing the superordinate from the subordinate. However, in later analyses, when we look at the causal structure and coherence of the narrative, the superordinate and subordinate dimensions of goals become very important.

13. Action (Attempt) Category

Actions are labeled as "attempts" and identified in terms of verbs of movement. Actions may be identified using Hopper and Thompson's transitivity criteria (Hopper & Thompson, 1984), according to which certain types of changes in the state of the actor or the object of action occur. Thus most actions are identified by movement from one state to another, and their identification depends on the verb used in each sentence: "I took him to the hospital"; "I changed the sheets three times that night"; "I tried to make him as comfortable as possible." Most actions are voluntary and are intended to achieve a particular goal. Actions do exist that are continuous in nature, for example, "I am running very fast." Continuous actions have no beginning and no ending. Verbs such as *talking, asking, going, saying reading, bending,* and so forth, are all considered to be "attempts." Communication verbs such as *said, told, report, repeat, recall, yelled, screamed,* and so forth, are also coded as attempts.

14. Outcomes

Outcomes result from the actions taken with respect to the attainment or maintenance of a goal. Was there goal success or goal failure? Success and failure are stated in terms of outcomes such as "I did it"; "I really accomplished a lot"; or "It just didn't happen." Outcomes generally include reference to the result of an action or to the ending of an action: "I gave him a massage *and he felt better*" or "Although I gave him the medicine, *he got worse.*"

---

episodes. As we show, *only emotion-state words* have a high predictive validity in terms of being correlated with positive and negative states of psychological well-being, such as depressive mood and positive morale (Stein, Folkman, et al., 1997; Stein et al., 2001). Categorizing emotion-state words with other affective categories, such as general affective states, mood states, mental states, and personal disposition states, to create general positive- and negative-valenced categories only lowers the correlation between online verbal reports of emotional functioning and assessments of psychological well-being.

One reason that some affective categories have little relationship to well-being is that these affective categories are not necessarily linked to the plans and actions being carried out by the person who experiences the many different nu-

ances of affective states. The use of emotion words, however, almost always includes reference to plans that have succeeded or failed and plans of action that could be used or that were used in response to the experience of some specific emotion.

Access to plans and thoughts about future states is critical to states of positive well-being. The one defining characteristic of depression across many different theories and contexts is the inability to construct plans of action or to impute positive value to any current goal that has a possibility of being enacted. Many different emotions can be evoked during depressive episodes. But the one thing that can be found across almost all episodes that lead to depression is the lack of an available plan or goal to initiate should the valued goal under consideration be lost, obstructed, or judged to be

Table 18.3
Three-year-old male's memory of a conflict with his father

Clause	Functional Category and Valence	Attribution (Self-Other)
I get *mad* from *my dad*,	Emotion, - and precipitating event	Self appraises father as cause of self-emotion
because he's a boogaloo!	Person disposition evaluation, -	Self appraises father's personal disposition
I hate my daddy!	Preference, -	Self dislike for father
He makes me mad!	Emotion, -	Self appraises father as cause of self emotion
I Don't (GET TO) go in some places	Outcome, -	Self-goal failure
and I says, "Daddy! I want to go someplace!"	Attempt & Goal, +	Self communicates to father about self-goal
He won't take me,	Outcome, -	Father blocks self-goal
He never takes me	Belief (-)	Self-appraisal of frequency of father denying self-goal
where I want	Belief (-)	Father fails to act on son's goal
so I ask my mom	Attempt,	Communicates self-goal to M
and I said, "Mom, can we go for dinner?"	Attempt & Goal, +	Communicates self-goal to M
And she says, "No, not right now."	Attempt & Outcome, -	Mother blocks self-goal
and I'll say: "Mommy what have you done to me	Attempt, Belief, -	Self attributes self-harm to mother
I want to go to McDonald's."	Goal, +	Self-goal
So, I say it to my mom and my dad,	Attempt, +	Communicates self-goal
I looove McDonald's	Preference, +	Self-preference for testaurant
But today, we're going to Tipsuda	Outcome, -, IE	Self-failure of goal
I like Tipsuda,	Preference, +	Self-preference for restaurant
but not their horseradish	Preference, -	Self-preference for food
I hate horseradish!	Preference, -	Self-preference for food
I'm angry about it,	Emotion, -	Self-emotion
because I hate horseradish!	Preference, -	Self-preference
And we always go where my dad wants	Belief, -	Self-appraisal of father success
Never where I want	Belief, -	Self-appraisal of self-failure
So I'm angry	Emotion, -	Self-emotion
It's not fair,	Belief, -	Self-belief about social justice
So I hit my mom and my dad.	Attempt, -	Self-action toward parents
'Cause I hate them!	Preference, -	Self-preference for parents
I just like my mom, not, not Rachel.	Self preference, +,-	Self-preference for mother/sister
I don't want my dad,	Goal, -	Self-goal toward father
'Cause he's a boogaloo	Person evaluation, -	Self-appraisal of father's personal disposition
and he's yucky.	Person evaluation, -	Self-appraisal of father's personal disposition
I think I'm going to throw him away in the garbage.	Belief about Future Goal, -	Self-goal for father
I'm going to make him explode!	Future Goal, -	Self-goal for father
Everyone, too!	Future Goal, -	Self-goal for family
*(In response to: You mean you're going to make your parents explode?) No, they're not parents,	Belief, -	Self-repudiation of interviewer's belief
they're my mommy and daddy.	Belief, +	Communicates correct belief to I
my parents are at grandma and grandpa.	Belief, +	Communicates correct belief to I

unattainable. References to the viability of plans of action are made throughout the reporting of stressful events; not only adults (Stein, Folkman, et al. 1997; Stein et al., 2001) but also children make the same types of appraisals when they judge themselves to be in a depressive state (Stein, Sheldrick, & Broaders, 1999).

Analyses of reports of stressful events also show that, even though many participants can nominate a series of alternative goals to substitute for a failed goal, the critical variable linked to nondepressive behavior is the ability to impute positive value to one of the new goals nominated. Thus it is not just the ability to generate alternative goals in the face of loss that lessens the probability of depression occurring; it is also the ability to impute value to new goals generated (Klinger, 1977, 1996; Stein et al., 1999). Thus the mentioning of goals and the value imputed to these goals during stressful events becomes a critical component that gives rise to positive states of well-being.

Statements of preference are also important in the analysis of emotion episodes. However, preferences, which are defined as states of liking or disliking, loving or hating, must be distinguished from goal states, which refer to states of desire or wanting. Preferences are clearly related to goals in that those goals that carry strong positive preferences are the ones that are normally activated and put into action. However, the strength of liking or disliking something does not always predict whether a goal will be activated. That is, talking about how much a goal is desired does not predict whether or not the goal will be activated and whether or not the goal will be accomplished.

In our analysis of emotion episodes, both during online processing of emotion (Stein & Albro, 2001) and in retrospective reporting of emotion experience, the most frequent reporting of preferences is found at two times: after the reporter tells about failure or success of a plan of action or immediately preceding a course of action to give legitimacy to the plan of action. An example of this type of preference talk can be found in Table 18.3, in which a 3-year-old boy is explaining why he is mad at his dad. At the beginning of the emotion report, the little boy states that he hates his dad. The reason: His dad never takes him where he would like to eat out, only where the dad would like to eat out. Thus even though the little boy's preference statement occurs close to the beginning, it is given as a reason for a failed outcome.

The little boy states another preference later in his report, right after his mother also denies his request to go to McDonald's. The little boy reports that he explicitly told his parents that he wanted to go to McDonald's because he loves McDonald's. Although preferences indeed serve as reasons to activate goals, preferences are cited mostly at the end of an episode that results in a failed goal. The fact that preferences occur after failure or success of a goal strongly suggests that anyone or anything that causes a negative outcome for the perceiver is appraised negatively in terms of liking-disliking or loving-hating. That is, the causal language of out-

comes and preferences reported in an emotion episode shows the powerful influence that outcomes have on preferences.

A second issue arises with the scoring of preferences in terms of their relationship to positive or negative well-being. At the moment, most researchers, such as Pennebaker, (1997) and those who use their computer program to score stressful or traumatic events, put positive preferences in the same category as positive emotion words. As we stated previously, clumping all positive-valenced words into the same category is a serious error, and this extends to the statement of positive preferences. The reason is that positive preferences are mostly indicative of goal failure, and the number of positive preferences stated correlates significantly with depressive mood as measured by the Center for Epidemiologic Studies Depression Scale (CES-D) and the Bradburn Affective Balance Scale (Bradburn, 1969; Stein et al.,2001). Thus the mention of positive preferences generally indicates that a person has failed to achieve goal states that are strongly valued and loved.

Similarly, positive affective words do not predict significantly whether a positive state of well-being will be present. Contentment may be expressed without feeling happy. Although contentment is a positive affective state, it may function only as a prerequisite for satisfaction or happiness. Many of our participants have expressed contentment without scoring high on paper-and-pencil measures of positive morale (Stein et al., 2001). References to feeling content, without references to happiness or satisfaction, may indicate a lack of a negative state operating at the time of the participant's report without the participant engaging in actions that would result in stronger forms of positive affect, such as happiness and pride. Thus satisfaction, happiness, and pride are mentioned when a desire or need has been fulfilled. Contentment does not require the fulfillment of a desired goal. It is related to the absence of negative states of psychological well-being.

It should be noted, then, that our three different categories of affective words (general affective reactions, emotions, and moods) vary on critical dimensions. General affective states do not necessarily require cognitive inferences, although many of them, such as surprise, come about because of the awareness of novelty in the environment. General affective states do not necessarily encode a goal and plan of action. Emotions, however, do encode an awareness of change states in regard to desired goals, plans of action formulated in an attempt to obtain the desired goal, and actions that are carried out in the service of maintaining or attaining a goal. Mood states are often derivatives of emotion states in that they frequently follow an emotional experience. A mood state is longer in duration than an emotional response and generally incorporates some awareness or reference to a specific body state. Thus feeling "nervous," "on edge," or "irritable" are lower intensity states of affect and often signal an awareness of some type of change in the environment, without the necessity of making a deeper set of inferences about the consequences of the noted environmental changes. This type of body state can last quite a long time, whereas emotion states are much shorter in duration (Levenson, 1999).

Three categories, in addition to emotions, have been shown to be predictive of either positive well-being or depression: negative and positive *disposition statements* about oneself; negative and positive beliefs about one's ability to *find a plan of action* that will eventually solve the problem at hand, no matter how stressful or traumatic the problem seems at the moment; and the absence or presence of beliefs that *something positive was learned from trauma,* despite the negative consequences that occurred.

The types of positive and negative disposition statements that we score include the following:

> *Negative:* "I thought how lazy I am"; "I'm as bad as he is"; "I was stupid—very stupid"; "I felt like I was worthless."
> *Positive:* "I really am quite good at this"; "I'm a doer"; "I was really nice to her"; "I was very kind."

Examples of beliefs that refer to oneself as being a good planner or being able to cope with stressful events are the following:

> *Negative:* "I'll never be able to find another relationship like this"; "I'm not very good at solving problems, he is"; "there will never be a solution to this problem."
> *Positive:* "I'm a planner and problem solver—it will get me through this"; "I know that I'll be able to deal with this—I had to do it several times before this one"; "I've learned to help other people, and it really helps my ability to help myself."

Examples of comments about learning from trauma are: "I grew up a lot over those 4 days and can confidently and proudly say that I've done the right thing, despite how awful it was"; "I had the upper hand now, but I wouldn't go back—I think now it is better than it was before the crisis"; "I really learned quite a bit—I was resolved positively and definitely—never had things seemed so clear—I felt as if I had suddenly emerged from religion, able to see over the tops of all the steeples."

Our analyses of talk about emotion, affective states, and goal-directed action encompass more than 5,000 reports of emotion experience with both children and adults. Some of our studies focus on the retrospective reporting of emotion experience (Levine & Stein, 2003; Levine et al., 1999; Sandhya & Stein, 2003; Stein, Folkman, et al., 1997; Stein & Levine, 1989), some on the actual experience of emotion (Liwag & Stein, 1995; Stein & Albro, 2001; Stein, Bernas, & Calicchia, 1997; Stein & Boyce, 1999), and some on the predictive validity of current talk in regard to future states of well-being (Stein et al., 2001).

We created the different categories by using both a "bottom-up" and "top down" approach, and, as such, our method is exhaustive for the protocol we have analyzed. All

language uttered during the experience and expression of emotion is recorded and described. The top-down approach came from our theoretical work on emotional understanding (Stein & Levine, 1987; Stein et al., 1993, 2000), as well as from our work on narrative comprehension (Stein & Glenn, 1979; Stein & Trabasso, 1982, 1989, 1992) and conflict resolution (Bernas & Stein, 2001; Stein & Bernas, 1999; Stein, Bernas, & Calicchia, 1997; Stein & Miller, 1993). The categorical breakdown follows the logic of a goal-directed episode that basically describes the types of events, thoughts, goals, plans, and actions that are carried out on an everyday basis. The categorical structure can be used to code talk from a single perspective or talk from face-to-face interaction.

The organization and content of these mental structures, often called narrative schemes or frames, are based primarily on our knowledge of human intentionality and goal-directed action. For the most part, human action is goal directed and purposeful, oriented toward maintaining positive states of well-being. By blocking or facilitating the attainment of well-being, external events and human actions act as precipitators in the appraisal of changes in the status of important goals. People react emotionally to perceived changes in the status of goals, and they formulate plans to deal with these changes. Formulating a plan then leads to an overt attempt to achieve, maintain, prevent, or revise a current goal. Successes or failures in actions that are carried out in the service of satisfying different goal-plans serve to start the cycle of appraisal and evaluation again. Individuals evaluate and react emotionally to the consequences of their actions. Actions become the new precipitating events, as people make further decisions to continue, reinstate, abandon, or revise the goal(s) that have either succeeded or failed.

As we noted previously, Table 18.2 lists all of the categories in a goal-directed emotion episode. Table 18.3 contains an individual emotion report and the category label for each clause in the report, as well as a description of the causal and content meaning of each statement. To score any type of oral or written report, one must first transcribe the report and parse it into clauses. Table 18.4 provides the instructions for parsing any transcribed emotion, stressful, or conflict episode. Table 18.5 includes a template that we use to summarize and quantify the data for any single report.

Purpose of the Narcoder Program

To facilitate the coding of emotion reports, we have automated much of the scoring of important information in an emotion narrative. The computer program that we use is called the *Narcoder.* The purpose of the Narcoder program is to identify and code data from any type of oral or written material that focuses on:

1. Talk about personal conflicts, problems, emotional or traumatic events that occur in a relationship with another person.

Table 18.4

Parsing rules for emotion, stressful, and conflict report

Rule: Most clauses have one verb

Our concept of a clause is verb-based. Most clauses are simple sentences. The only difficulty in parsing clauses correctly is learning to deal with the exceptions. Despite all of the exceptions that will be introduced, as a general rule, one parsed segment contains one verb.

Exceptions:

1. **Mental State Terms** (I think, I know, I remember, I forgot, I believe, it is my opinion that, I'm uncertain that, I do not know whether, I did not forget to):
    Examples: He thinks that I am lazy, // and I am lazy.
    I know he went to the store.
    I imagine that you would want me to eat that sandwich.
2. **Goals and Desires** (I want, I desire, I will decide, I am deciding, I decided not to, I have decided to, I'm not going to):
    Examples: I wish that I were a hockey player.
    I want her to stop hitting me // and [*I want her*] to be nice.
    I need your help // and [*I need*] love // to get me through the day.
    He wanted me to say no to his request.
3. **Attempt/Goals** (I went to, I am going in, I am going on, I am going to, I go in):
    Those attempts that encode a goal (went to, going to) are not separated even though both a goal and an attempt are encoded. The reason for this is that the Narcoder more easily recognizes goal words if the attempts that encode the goals are also included.
    Examples: I am going to the zoo.
    I went in the bedroom // and [*I went in*] the kitchen.
4. **Actions** (I said that, he said that, I did not say that, he did not say that):
    What was said should not be separated from who said it. When coding for accurate memory, we do separate out accurate source memory from accurate content memory. Thus the actor who is speaking is not separated from what is being said. Remember, many synonyms for *said* exist: *told, asked, explained, replied, stated, expressed, agreed that, screamed, yelled, disagreed that, promised that, gave permission to,* etc. The context of the clause is critical in making a judgment as to the meaning of the verb.
    Examples: I said that he should give me some candy. (not parsed)
    I said, "Give me some candy!" (not parsed)
    I said loudly to give me some candy. (not parsed)
    I said that I would; // I even promised. (parsed)
    I disagree, // and actually I said so. (parsed)
5. **One-word expressions of agreement or disagreement:**
    Occasions arise on which people express consent or disagreement using only one word. These terms are coded together with the statement that follows if the following statement is redundant. Thus you do not separate the first example, but the second example with agreement is parsed because the statement following the agreement contains information in addition to an agreement response:
    Examples: F: Do you want the ball?
    O: Yes, I want the ball. (not parsed)

    F: Are your pants orange?
    O: Yes, // they are very snazzy. (parsed)

    F: Do you want to come to the store with us?
    O: Okay, // I like the store. (parsed)

    Coders often have trouble with questions that have implied verbs or "to be" hard-to-spot verbs. For example, "Okay?" "You sure?" "So what?" "Don't you?" "Aren't you?" "Wasn't it?" are all distinct statements on their own and make up one clause. They should not be combined with another clause.
6. **"THAT" conjunction:**
    There are times when the word *that* should be inferred and inserted in parentheses to signal that a second clause is beginning:
    Examples: I ate the lunch meat //{THAT was} sitting in the fridge.
    I get angry // when it doesn't get done the way //{THAT} I want it to.
7. **The word "TO":**
    The word *to* is used in many ways, especially in relationship to goals. Always make sure that you can substitute *in order to* or *so that* when you are trying to identify something as a goal and the word *to* has been used. If you can replace *to* with *in order to*, then it should be parsed as a goal.
    Examples: I put on my shoes // to go out dancing.
    I went to the opera // to watch the pretty lady sing.
    I gave him my permission// to go swimming.
8. **If-then clauses:**
    Sometimes the second component of an *if-then* statement is implied. When it is possible for *then* to be implied, it is still parsed.
    Examples: If you build it, // he will come.
    If I said I would do it, // I will do it.
9. **Clause fragment:**
    If a speaker doesn't finish a clause, and the clause contains no meaning at all, it should not be parsed separately from the rest of the sentence. For coding purposes, it is not helpful to have these kinds of things on a separate line. There should be only one meaning per line.
    Examples: I get your point, but I-. . .
    I don't understand you. I mean, its totally like I want, I think, um. . .

Table 18.5
Template for functional categories and subcategories

Functional Categories	+ Val	– Val	0 Val	Where Is Clause Found?
1. Action-oriented categories				
Precipitating event				
Attempt				
Outcome				
2. Internal response categories (Not observable)				

Motivation

Preferences
Goals
   Reinstatement
   Substitution
   Abandonment
   Absence of Goal

Affective States

Emotions
Positive
   Happy
   Hope
   Pride
   Relief
Negative
   Anger
   Anxiety
   Disgust
   Embarrassment
   Fear
   Guilt
   Hopeless
   Jealousy
   Pity
   Regret
Moods
General affective states
Personal dispositions
Mental states
Lack of emotion state

Beliefs About:

Self
Other
Relationships
Events
Actions

2. Talk about positive events and the attainment of personally significant goals that occur in the course of maintaining a relationship with another person.
3. Talk about and evaluation of personal, close, or intimate relationships.
4. Talk during the negotiation and mediation of a conflict.
5. Talk about stressful events that affect psychological well-being.
6. Talk about reconstruction of the self after a loss or disruption of a relationship.

We have completed or are in the process of analyzing and coding *by hand* 16 different databases. The Narcoder contains more than 17 different "dictionaries" that correspond to the types of "talk" that people express in one of the six situations just listed. The Narcoder analyzes these different types of talk, identifies all types of appraisals, marks specific appraisals by category type, marks positive or negative valence, and marks the theme of each particular clause identified.

The Narcoder is particularly good at identifying the following: personal beliefs, emotions, affective appraisals, personal preferences, personal dispositions, plans of action, different types of initiating events that lead to a conflict, the appraisal of a personal relationship in terms of the quality of the relationship, the affective feelings that people hold regarding a relationship and another person, and the emotional impact that a relationship has on a person in terms of depressive mood and positive well-being.

The basic principles that underlie the program are word- and clause-recognition devices that literally find specific words or patterns of words in each of 12 different types of categories. The categories in the Narcoder directly correspond to the specific episodic categories in emotion reports that are described and defined in Table 18.2. Thus the Narcoder is able to code and tag all emotion and affective words in a report in a matter of seconds. The program also codes all preference and goal statements, as well as all mental state beliefs.

The Narcoder is capable of allowing a coder to add new categories to the base structure. Thus, if a coder finds that a particular category is not represented in the current existing dictionaries, she or he may add the algorithm that permits the selection of new material. We are in the process of constructing new algorithms that focus on the process of resolving a conflict in a positive, constructive fashion rather than in a destructive, negative fashion. The addition of these new categories requires the hand coding and analysis of protocol. The items that are identified in the hand coding are then entered into the Narcoder's database in order to form a new dictionary. The program is then run, with the goal of illustrating that the program has identified each instance of the new category that has been added. We then load another corpus that has been hand coded but not yet scored. After the Narcoder is run through the corpus, we determine the reliability of the new dictionary, find those instances that the Narcoder failed to identify, and include all instances that need identification into the new dictionary.

A Summary of Relevant Findings Using the Emotion Episode Coding Scheme

To date, we have carried out more than 10 studies using the Narcoder coding scheme. We present a summary of some of the most relevant findings with regard to understanding emotion and stressful events.

Predicting Psychological Well-Being

One of our aims has been to develop measures of talk and behavior that would be sensitive indicators of psychological well-being, such as depressive mood, general anxiety reactions, general anger reactions, and positive morale. We be-

gan this task by using the results of our Narcoder analysis and correlating the outcomes with subjective paper-and-pencil measures of psychological well-being such as the CES-D, the Beck Depression Inventory, the Bradburn Affective Balance Scale (Bradburn, 1969), Rosenberg's Self-Esteem Scale (Rosenberg, 1965), and measures of positive morale. The Bradburn and Rosenberg scales measure both positive and negative appraisals of the self. The CES-D and the Beck Depression Inventory focus on depressive symptoms. Horowitz's measure of positive states of mind (Horowitz et al., 1988) focuses on the expressive feeling and behaviors of positive states of mind.

In three studies (Stein & Albro, 2003; Stein, Folkman, et al., 1997; Stein, Ross, & Fergusson, 2001), we have shown the predictive power of talk about emotions, beliefs, goals, and certain types of precipitating events on positive well-being. In the Stein, Folkman, et al. (1997) study, we showed that three dimensions predicted current and future states of well-being of male caregivers who were caring for their male partners with AIDS: (1) the proportion of positive emotions expressed in two bereavement interviews, (2) the number of future-oriented goals the caregiver stated that focused on himself rather than on his terminally ill partner, and (3) the types of beliefs the caregiver expressed about himself. The dimension that predicted most of the variance in the relationship between talk and positive morale, as well as depressive mood, was the proportion of positive emotions mentioned at the 2- and 4-week postbereavement interviews. The proportion of positive emotions further predicted the degree of depression our caregivers experienced 1 year later and better predicted depression 1 year later than did the caregiver's score on depressive mood at bereavement. Thus the ability to talk about positive states close to the time that a loved one has passed away is highly predictive of current states of well-being, as well as future states of well-being.

The number of new goals and plans that our caregivers mentioned in regard to their own lives was also correlated significantly with concurrent depressive mood, as well as with positive morale 1 year later. Those caregivers who had several different goals that they wanted to accomplish with respect to *their own development* were the ones who were the least depressed. Those caregivers who generated very few goals for themselves were the most depressed. Thus generating future goals for oneself within a context of bereavement turned out to be essential for maintaining or attaining positive states of well-being. This means that even though most of these caregivers devoted the majority of their time to caring for their partners, they were still able to formulate goals important to their own well-being, and they were able to envision themselves carrying out activities that were pleasurable and that would lead to growth in the future.

In a follow-up study on the same caregivers, Stein and Albro (2003) analyzed the interviews of caregivers who entered the study at least 8 months before the deaths of their partners and then participated in an interview every 2 months until their partners passed away. The interviews with these male caregivers (before the deaths of their partners) focused on those events that were most stressful for the caregivers and the events that were most meaningful in terms of generating positive states of mind during the caregiving process. The caregivers then continued to participate in interviews after the deaths of their partners, at 2 weeks after the deaths, then at 2 months, 6 months, and 1 year later. Thus we were able to analyze longitudinal data with caregivers who went through the caregiving process, the bereavement process, and the recovery process.

We made two advances in understanding the relationship between reactions to stressful events during caregiving and subsequent feelings of psychological well-being after the death of a partner. First, we examined whether or not any one specific emotion (e.g., anger, fear, sadness, happiness, etc.) predicted psychological well-being better than the total proportion of positive or negative emotional states mentioned. We also built a taxonomy of beliefs that caregivers expressed in relation to themselves and their partners. We then examined whether or not specific types of beliefs were related to positive and negative states of psychological well-being. Table 18.6 contains the data on the relationship between emotions and psychological well-being.

Table 18.6a

Correlations between proportion of positive emotions and scores on Bradburn Positive Morale Scale

Bradburn Positive Morale Scale	N	Correlations
At bereavement	39	.27, $p < .09$
Postbereavement—2 mos.	38	.37, $p < .02$
Postbereavement—6 mos.	38	.41, $p < .01$
Postbereavement—12 mos.	20	.64, $p < .001$

Table 18.6b

Correlations between proportion of fear emotions and scores on the Bradburn Positive Morale Scale

Bradburn Positive Morale Scale	N	Correlations
At bereavement	39	$-.37$, $p < .02$
Postbereavement—2 mos.	38	$-.48$, $p < .002$
Postbereavement—6 mos.	38	$-.47$, $p < .002$
Postbereavement—12 mos.	20	$-.59$, $p < .003$

Table 18.6c

Correlations between proportion of fear emotions and scores on the CES-D Scale

CES-D Scale	N	Correlations
At bereavement	39	.30, $p < .06$
Postbereavement—2 mos.	38	.23, $p < .17$, ns
Postbereavement—6 mos.	38	.33, $p < .05$
Postbereavement—12 mos.	20	.57, $p < .004$

We found that the proportion of positive emotion states mentioned during the recall of stressful events *before* the partner's death predicted positive morale *after* the death of a partner. The correlations presented in Table 18.6A show the increasing strength in the relationship between the recall of positive emotion during stressful events and expressing positive morale *after* the death of the partner. Recalling positive emotions during descriptions of stressful events predicted whether or not caregivers were able to recover in a positive fashion after the deaths of their partners. The frequency of recalling positive emotions before the deaths of their partners was significantly correlated with the frequency of recalling positive emotions after the deaths of their partners.

When caregivers talked about positive emotions during stressful events, they almost always talked about times during the caregiving process when they and their partners found ways to have pleasurable times together, despite the partners' illnesses. Caregivers also expressed positive emotion toward family members and friends who helped them through the process. Finally, they expressed positive emotions toward their partners, whom many felt had given them or taught them invaluable lessons that they would treasure throughout their lives, and they mentioned positive emotions in relationship to being as good caregivers as possible and providing their partners with a positive environment, despite the never-ending negative events that were occurring. Thus analyzing reasons for positive emotions provided critical information about caregivers' focus of attention and the types of events that were meaningful to them and gave them pleasure.

The total proportion of negative emotions was not predictive of depression, but the specific type of emotion mentioned was critical in producing a significant relationship between emotions expressed and psychological well-being. The proportion of fear responses, calculated by taking the number of fear responses divided by the total number of negative emotion responses, was significantly related to both positive morale and to depressive mood. Table 18.6B shows the relationship between the proportion of fear responses and positive morale. Table 18.6C shows the relationship between the proportion of fear responses and depressive mood, as measured by the CES-D. The most interesting finding was that the relationship between the proportions of fear reports during stressful events and scores on the CES-D became more predictive of depression over a year's time than at the time of bereavement. The same type of relationship held for the negative correlation between the proportion of fear responses during caregiving and the scores on the Bradburn Positive Morale Scale. The Bradburn Positive Morale Scale consists of all positive items on the Bradburn Affective Balance Scale (Bradburn, 1969). The greater the proportion of fear responses, the less likely the caregiver was to obtain a high score on the Bradburn Positive Morale Scale.

The relationship between fear and depression has not been as well documented as the relationship between depression and sadness or anger. Psychologically and theoretically, however, this relationship makes sense. The evocation of fear occurs when a person perceives that a change in a valued goal is imminent and has the added problem of having difficulty formulating a new goal and plan of action to overcome the loss. When we analyzed the reasons for fear responses, 90% of all reasons focused on the fact that the caregiver was going to lose his partner and that the partner was irreplaceable. Over 70% of the caregivers who stated that they feared the loss of their partners could not generate any type of goal or plan that would substitute for the loss of their current relationship and that would help them through the difficulty of contending with the loss. Thus, again, the specific emotion of fear proved to be critical in predicting depressive mood and the absence of positive morale. The total proportion of negative emotions *did not prove to be significantly related to depression.*

The reasons for fear responses were critical in our understanding of why fear would lead to states of depression. Most of the caregivers who frequently expressed fear believed that they would not be able to generate a goal that would act as a substitute to replace the relationship they had with their dying partners. They simply could not envision themselves in another relationship, and they had difficulty envisioning anyone else being able to understand their dilemma or offer them compassion in any form. Because of these beliefs, according to caregivers' reports, few viable goals and plans of action that would bring pleasure or satisfaction could be generated.

As we illustrated previously in our first caregiver study (Stein et al., 1997), the number of future-oriented goals and plans that were generated by caregivers was significantly correlated with the degree of depression experienced by caregivers. This relationship was also found when stressful events during caregiving were analyzed. The inability to generate future goals and plans during stressful events was related to the repeated experience of fear. The relationship between generating goals and plans and other emotions was not significant. Thus it becomes important to unpack the types of emotions that make up a total positive or total negative score when analyzing the verbal protocols of people who are reporting emotional experiences during stressful events.

The three most frequent negative emotions reported by caregivers who recalled stressful events during caregiving were anger, fear, and sadness. Although other negative emotions were mentioned, none were mentioned with the frequency of these three emotions. All other negative emotions accounted for only 5% of all emotion responses. Of the three most frequent negative emotions, sadness accounted for 25%, anger accounted for 34%, and fear for 41%.

The same distribution of negative emotion reports was found when bereavement interviews were analyzed: Anger accounted for 21% of all reports, sadness for 25%, and fear and anxiety for 48%. Again, other negative emotions accounted for only 6% of all negative emotions reported. A rank-order correlation between the proportion of fear mentions during stressful events and the proportion elicited during bereavement interviews yielded a +.64 correlation. Thus those caregivers who expressed the most fear during caregiving were those who expressed the most fear after the deaths of their partners. Consequently, these caregivers were also the most depressed, especially 1 year after the deaths of their partners.

Table 18.7A presents the taxonomy of beliefs that our caregivers reported during interviews both before and after the deaths of their partners. Three classes of beliefs were reported: beliefs about the self, beliefs about the relationship with their partners, and beliefs about their partners. Only beliefs about the self were correlated with depression and

Table 18.7a

Coded belief categories for stressful event and bereavement interviews

Belief Category	Positive	Negative
Self		
Self-worth	**	**
Self-coping strategies	**	**
Self-assessment of external resources		
Self-assessment of support systems	**	**
Self-beliefs about caregiving	**	**
Self-attitude toward death	**	**
Relationship		
Quality of partner-caregiver relationship		
Existence of a continuing relationship		
Partner		
Partner internal appraisals		
Partner health		
Partner memories		

** = Categories related to psychological well-being

Table 18.7b

Correlations between proportion of positive self beliefs and Bradburn Positive Morale Scale

Bradburn Positive Morale	N	Correlations
At bereavement	39	.49, p < .001
Postbereavement—2 mos.	38	.48, p < .002
Postbereavement—6 mos.	38	.33, p < .04
Postbereavement—12 mos.	20	.46, p < .04

Table 18.7c

Correlations between proportion of positive self beliefs and CES-D Scale

CES-D Scale	N	Correlations
At bereavement	39	−.38, p < .02
Postbereavement—2 mos.	38	−.33, p < .04
Postbereavement—6 mos.	38	−.42, p < .01
Postbereavement—12 mos.	20	−.45, p < .04

positive morale. In particular, the proportion of *positive beliefs* about the self that focused on self-worth, coping skills, attitudes toward death, and caregiving skills were those that correlated significantly with both the Bradburn Positive Morale Scale and the CES-D Scale. Each of these positive self-belief categories was significantly related to psychological well-being, and thus the total score, summed over the four positive belief categories, was also significantly related to psychological well-being.

The relationship between positive beliefs about oneself and psychological well-being has proved to be significant in one of our studies on the nature of traumatic experience in college students (Stein, Ross, & Fergusson, 2001). We have shown that when college students narrate stories about traumatic experience, the beliefs that they hold about themselves and the degree to which they have learned positive strategies from the trauma predict their current levels of depression at the time of narration and 1 month later. Those students who reported the most self-derogatory beliefs were the most depressed, both at the time of the narration and 1 month later. Conversely, those students who reported that they experienced positive outcomes and learned from the trauma, despite the seriousness of the event, were those students that were the least depressed. They were also the students who had the highest self-esteem, as measured by the Rosenberg Self-Esteem Scale. Thus beliefs about self-worth, the self's ability to cope in the middle of a crisis, and the self's ability to perceive positive benefits and insight from traumatic experience are significantly related to measures of psychological well-being.

Beliefs expressed about other people and beliefs about the partner did not correlate with either scale of psychological well-being. Thus, if a total positive or total negative belief score was computed, summed over all belief categories, and correlated with measures of psychological well-being, the resulting correlations would prove to be insignificant or marginally significant. The focus on the self as a problem solver and planner, however, especially in situations that called for the construction of new goals or the use of novel strategies, was critical.

The presence of positive appraisals about themselves as planners, problem solvers, or survivors almost always led to comments about the invention of new strategies, despite the devastating loss that participants experienced. What lay behind many of these appraisals was the belief that many of these participants had experienced traumatic events previously and that they had managed to survive the trauma. Thus they compared the current trauma to those of the past and believed that they could survive their current situation, just as they survived their other traumas. Even though their current traumas might be unique and require a novel approach to overcoming the devastation, knowing that they had survived a past trauma and actually learned from the trauma provided the motivation for many participants to do the same thing in the current situation. Thus it was not the use of previous strategies that served as the motivating force. Rather, it was the appraisal of themselves as survivors and good problem solvers, able to find the appropriate strategy to survive the current situation, that was the critical factor.

Assessing the Quality of Intimate Relationships

Our studies on the nature of intimate and marital relationships (Sandhya & Stein, 2003; Stein & Bernas, 1999) also used the Narcoder to determine how appraisals of the self, partner, and marital relationship predicted marital happiness, as well as psychological well-being. We have shown, as have other researchers (Gottman, 1994a, 1994b, 1996, 2001; Gottman, Coan, Carrere, & Swanson, 1998; Gottman & Levenson, 1992; Huston, Caughlin, Houts, Smith, & George, 1999; Huston, Niehuis, & Smith, 2001; Reis, 2001), that appraisals of the marital relationship and of one's partner affect the degree of happiness and the longevity of the relationship. Appraisals of oneself predict marital happiness and psychological well-being. Thus appraisals of other people are predictive more of the quality of the relationship with another person than they are of positive morale or depressive mood per se. That is, a person can be in an unsatisfactory relationship without being depressed or relinquishing positive states of mind, especially if that person has formulated a plan of action to terminate the relationship and begin another or to go outside the relationship to fulfill important desires.

The presence of self-derogatory appraisals, however, almost always signals some type of depressive response or some type of general anxiety reaction. Thus using the Narcoder to determine the frequency and type of self-appraisal becomes an important task if the object is to assess current and future states of well-being. If the goal is to assess the quality of relationships, then the focus is on appraisals of the significant other person, as well as on appraisals of the relationship.

The reason that both types of appraisals (self and other) are important is that the types of appraisals that people make about themselves and their partners are significantly related to the beliefs they hold about themselves as well as the plans they intend to carry out. The use of the episodic categories in Table 18.2 allows us to make causal connections between beliefs, appraisals, emotions, and plans of action, as well as to assess correlations among the various components of the narratives that people construct. Thus we are able to plot the causal representation of knowledge that people report during an interview, so that we understand the nature of people's causal attributions about emotion and stress-laden events.

The report of the 3-year-old boy's narrative in Table 18.3 is a good example of the order and causal structuring of an emotional event. It is clear that even at 3 years of age, this little boy attributes the evocation of anger to something that his father did. We then learn that his father had blocked his request to go to his favorite restaurant. We also see that when the boy's goal is blocked by his father, he then makes the same request of his mother. The plans of action that the little boy develops are in direct response to having his request rejected. However, the anger that he feels about the rejection of his desire is directed mostly toward his father. We can see this clearly in the little boy's action of hitting both parents and in his desire to blow up his father. Thus the connections between precipitating events and thinking, as well as between plans of action and expressed action, become clearer as a function of using the categorical scheme of the emotion episode.

In Stein et al. (2000), we indicated the causal relationship between initiating events, goals, and plans of action. The important finding in this chapter is that children as young as 3 years of age are using the same causal understanding schema that adults use to understand emotion events. Further, children make the same types of positive and negative evaluations of family members as do adults (Stein & Levine, 1999; Stein & Trabasso, 1992; Stein et al., 2000), and these appraisals are significantly related to the quality of relationship these children have with different family members. Thus the appraisals that are made in response to emotional events, in addition to the plans and actions that go along with specific emotion responses, can easily be coded using the Narcoder program. At the moment, the program serves as a time-saving device to isolate different components of the emotion episode. Our goal in the near future is to incorporate algorithms that will allow us to code the causal structure of the episode. By doing this, we can actually test whether or not specific causal links are made between emotions and plans of action.

Assessing Face-to-Face Interaction

Finally, the types of coding that we have described can also be used to code face-to-face interaction between two or more people (Stein & Bernas, 1999). The Narcoder is capable of pulling out all of the different categories of the emotion episode when two or more people are interacting about a recent conflict, a recent good time, or whatever event they think is the most important to discuss. Categories can be added to the Narcoder that indicate how a conflict was resolved (win, loss, compromise, or standoff), the types of appraisals that each person in the dyad has made of one another, the emotions that each person expresses during the course of the conflict or good time, the types of goals and preferences that are at stake during the course of a conflict, the reasons for the conflict, the reasons that support a favored position, the reasons that go against an opponent's position, what was said during the course of the conflict interaction, and the ways in which the participants evaluate each other after the conflict is over.

Using the coding scheme of the Narcoder allows us to evaluate the causal relationships between the moves that the two individuals make during the course of an interaction. For example, we can assess the valence of the responses that each of two people make toward one another during an interac-

tion and then analyze the proportion of positive and negative moves in relation to the outcome of the conflict. When we talk about positive and negative moves during the course of an interaction, we are referring to moves such as the following. Positive moves would include augmentation of what the other person has said, agreement with the other's position or comment, collaborative overlap in constructing an evaluation of a situation, seeking more information from the other when the other's comment is not clear, providing the other person with critical information that would allow the advancement of the other's position, praising the other person, and offering to help plan the attainment of the other person's goal. Negative moves would include continuation of one's own position after a request for a response to the other's position, switching topics in response to a direct request to respond to the other person's argument, agreeing but offering a counterargument to the other person's position, disagreeing and offering a counterargument to the other person's position, threatening the other person if he or she does not adhere to a particular position, and denigrating the other person because of his or her position.

Using the Narcoder to code conflict interactions provides a complete analysis of all of the moves and interactions that take place between two people. In addition, the structure of the argumentative interaction can be coded to determine the types of reasons that two people give in support of or against a position, the point during the interaction that indicates when a positive or negative change in stances occurs such that either person responds positively or negatively to a given piece of evidence, the number and types of reasons that need to be given to persuade an opponent to accept the other point of view, and the types of moves that end in a standoff or lack of a solution to a problem. Thus the Narcoder's potential is dependent on the investigator being able to formulate an algorithm that contains critical information about specific types of moves or dimensions that would allow selection of all such components or examples.

Summary

We have presented a method for unpacking the emotion episode as it occurs in real interaction or as it is reported, retrospectively, by a person who has participated in or observed an emotion episode. The type of coding scheme we described can be used to characterize individual experience, and it can be used to characterize face-to-face interactions in which two or more people are interacting and influencing one another. The types of appraisals that occur in face-to-face interactions also occur in individual reports of an emotion situation, because the narrator is often describing a face-to-face interaction that had serious consequences. However, face-to-face interaction often evolves into the dialogue of argumentation or collaboration, and thus categories unique to face-to-face interaction need to be described, in addition to the categories of information that occur in an individual interview. In particular, face-to-face interaction encourages and often demands justification for a point of view and the explicit naming of the positive and negative consequences that will occur if a person adheres to one position versus another position.

Our past studies have indicated that both individual recall and dyadic interaction can be coded in terms of the content and causal structure of the language and talk that occurs during these two situations. What we have shown is that personal appraisals of the self and appraisals of another person are indicative of psychological well-being for a person and of the quality of relationship that the person has with another individual. We have also argued that specific types of positive or negative categories of language, rather than broad integrative categories of language, are more predictive of psychological well-being. The specificity of language predictors of psychological well-being are similar to the specific-emotion expressions of anger and disgust that occur in the married couples studied by Gottman and Levenson (1992). The repetitive expression of disgust reactions have very different outcomes in terms of predicting the quality and viability of the relationship than does the occurrence of anger expressions during a conflict interaction. Similarly, talk about different emotions results in different types of outcomes in regard to psychological well-being.

The one finding that characterizes emotional talk and conflict talk is that the type of talk that occurs during these events is highly constrained, despite the seemingly great variation that can occur across development and culture. Although the themes of conflicts might vary across culture and the importance of specific events might vary across culture and development, the content and structure of an emotion episode does not. The questions described in Table 18.1 characterize every type of emotion episode that we have seen, independent of the age and ethnicity of the narrator. Further, we have succeeded in creating a computer program to code emotion and conflict events because of the enormous constraints that occur during emotion and conflict interactions. The fact that these episodes are about the attainment or maintenance of personally significant goals and that this type of behavior can be characterized by a problem-solving schema limits the variations that occur during these types of interactions.

We have found (Stein & Trabasso, 1992) that different cultures, religions, and ethnic groups have the most effect on a participant's beliefs about what is important and what is to be valued. Cultures, religions, and ethnic groups also specify the appropriate types of strategies and interactions that should occur, as well as the specific people who are allowed to carry out and participate in specific interactions. The types of emotions that are expressed and the strategies that correspond to each specific emotion, however, have universal components, as well as universal appraisals. A major advance in cultural theories would be to test the appraisal

and planning categories that are coded by the Narcoder to determine the frequency and types of appraisals that do occur. We have begun such a task. The results of our comparisons will allow a direct test of some of the current appraisal theories. To date, the analyses that need to be done to determine the similarities and differences across different cultural and religious groups remain to be carried out.

Finally, coding the emotion episode according to our scheme has allowed us to begin analyses of the ways in which the language of emotion is interleaved with the nonverbal expressive systems of emotion, such as the face (Gottman & Levenson, 1992), the hands (McNeill, 1992), and the voice (Fernald, 1984). We have discovered that unique gestures are encoded with the different negative emotions of fear, sadness, and anger, with these gestures occurring immediately after the elicitation of a facial expression and during talk about plans of action in response to the emotion. We have also found that a unique prosodic pattern exists for fear and anger and occurs most often as the narrator puts plans of action into effect. For us, the goal is to better understand the coordination of these systems so that a fuller meaning analysis and understanding of emotion and affective states can be achieved. By providing an in-depth analysis of the language of emotion, we can begin to achieve this goal.

Acknowledgments

This research was funded by grants from the National Institute of Child Health and Human Development, Grant No. HD38895 to Nancy L. Stein and Grant No. HD 25742 to Tom Trabasso and Nancy L. Stein; and by a Provost's Grant to Nancy Stein and Tom Trabasso. We thank Valerie Photos-Kissel for suggestions on the manuscript and Tom Trabasso, Hildy Ross, and Mike Ross for input and suggestions on the Narcoder categories and dictionaries.

Note

1. We are aware of the findings in infant research that show the infant capable of generating facial patterns corresponding to emotions such as fear. The same is true of the smiling response in infancy. The smiling response, however, is endogenously driven, and this may be true for the fear face as well. What we are referring to are the smiling and fear responses that occur as a function of appraising one's environment, such that plans of action are formulated to respond to changes in the environment (Sroufe, 1979).

References

Arnold, M. B. (1960). *Emotion and personality* (2 vols.). New York: Columbia University Press.

Arnold, M. B. (1970). Perennial problems in the field of emotions. In M. B. Arnold (Ed.), *Feelings and emotions: The*

Loyola Symposium (pp. 169–186). New York: Academic Press.

Bernas, R., & Stein, N. L. (2001). Changing stances on abortion during case-base reasoning tasks: Who changes and under what conditions. *Discourse Processes, 32*(2 & 3), 177–190.

Bradburn, N. (1969). *The structure of psychological well-being.* Chicago: Aldine.

Capatides, J. (1989). Mothers' socialization of children's affect expression. Unpublished doctoral dissertation, Columbia University.

Damasio, A. R. (1999). *The feeling of what happens.* New York: Harcourt.

Ekman, P. (1977). Biological and cultural contribution to body and facial movements. In J. Blacking (Ed.), *Anthropology of the body* (pp. 34–84). London: Academic Press.

Ekman, P. (1992). An argument for basic emotions. *Cognition and Emotion, 6*(3/4), 169–200.

Fernald, A. (1984). The perceptual and affective salience of mothers' speech to infants. In L. Feagans, C. Garvey, & R. Golinkoff (Eds.) (with M. T. Greenberg, C. Harding, & J. Bohannon), *The origins and growth of communication* (pp. 5–29). Norwood, NJ: Ablex.

Frijda, N. H. (1987). Emotion, cognitive structure, and action tendency. *Cognition and Emotion, 1,* 115–143.

Frijda, N. H. (1988). The laws of emotion. *American Psychologist, 43*(5), 349–358.

Gallistel, C. R. (1985). Motivation, intention, and emotion: Goal-directed behavior from a cognitive neuroethological perspective. In M. Frese & J. Sabini (Eds.), *Goal-directed behavior: The concept of action in psychology* (pp. 48–66). Hillsdale, NJ: Erlbaum.

Gottman, J. M. (1994a). *What predicts divorce?.* Hillsdale, NJ: Erlbaum.

Gottman, J. M. (1994b). *Why marriages succeed or fail.* New York: Simon & Schuster.

Gottman, J. M. (Ed.) (1996). *What predicts divorce? The measures.* Hillsdale, NJ: Erlbaum.

Gottman, J.M. (2001). Crime, hostility, wife battering, and the heart: On the Meehan et al. (2001) failure to replicate the Gottman et al. (1995) typology. *Journal of Family Psychology, 15,* 409–414.

Gottman, J., Coan, J., Carrerre, S., & Swanson, C. (1998). Predicting marital happiness and stability from newlywed interactions. *Journal of Marriage and the Family, 60,* 5–22.

Gottman, J. M., & Levenson, R. W. (1992). Marital processes predictive of later dissolutions: Behavior, physiology, and health. *Journal of Personality and Social Psychology, 63,* 221–233.

Hopper, P. J., & Thompson, S. A. (1984). The discourse basis for lexical categories in universal grammar. *Language, 60,* 703–753.

Horowitz, M., Adler, N., & Kegeles, S. (1988). A scale for measuring the occurrence of positive state of mind: A preliminary report. *Psychosomatic Medicine, 50,* 477–483.

Huston, T. L., Caughlin, J. P., Houts, R. M., Smith, S. E., & George, L. (2001). The connubial crucible: Newlywed years as predictors of marital delight, distress, and divorce. *Journal of Personality and Social Psychology, 80,* 237–252.

Huston, T. L., Niehuis, S., & Smith, S. E. (2001). The early roots of conjugal distress and divorce. *Current Directions on Psychological Science, 10,* 116–119.

Johnson-Laird, P. N., & Oatley, K. (1989). The language of emotions: An analysis of a semantic field. *Cognition and Emotion, 3*(2), 81–123.

Johnson-Laird, P. N., & Oatley, K. (1992). Basic emotions, rationality, and folk theory. *Cognition and Emotion, 6*(3/4), 201–223.

Klinger, E. (1977). *Meaning and void: Inner experience and the incentives in people's lives.* Minneapolis: University of Minnesota Press.

Klinger, E. (1996). Emotional influences on cognitive processing with implications of both. In P. M. Gollwitzer & J. A. Bargh (Eds.), *The psychology of action* (pp. 168–192). New York: Guilford Press.

Lazarus, R. S. (1982). Thoughts on the relations between emotion and cognition. *American Psychologist, 37,* 1019–1024.

Lazarus, R. S. (1984). On the primacy of cognition. *American Psychologist, 39*(2), 124–129.

LeDoux, J., & Phelps, E. (2000). Emotional networks in the brain. In M. Lewis & J. M. Haviland-Jones (Eds.), *Handbook of emotions* (2nd ed., pp. 157–172). New York: Guilford Press.

Levenson, R. W. (1999). The intrapersonal functions of emotion. *Cognition and Emotion, 13*(5), 481–504.

Levine, L. & Stein, N.L. (2003). Young children's understanding of emotions in themselves and others. Unpublished manuscript, University of Chicago.

Levine, L., Stein, N. L., & Liwag, M. (1999). Remembering children's emotions: Sources of concordant and discordant accounts between parents and children. *Developmental Psychology, 5*(3), 210–230.

Lewis, M., & Haviland, J. M. (1993). *Handbook of emotions.* New York: Guilford Press.

Lewis, M., & Haviland-Jones, J. M. (2000). *Handbook of emotions* (2nd ed.). New York: Guilford Press.

Liwag, M.D., & Stein, N.L. (1995). Children's memory for emotional events: The importance of emotion-related retrieval cues. *Journal of Experimental Child Psychology, 60,* 2–31.

Mandler, G. (1975). *Mind and emotion.* New York: Wiley.

Mandler, G. (1984). *Mind and body: Psychology of emotion and stress.* New York: Norton.

McNeill, D. (1992). *Hand and mind: What gestures reveal about thought.* Chicago: University of Chicago Press.

Miller, G. A., Galanter, E., & Pribram, K. H. (1960). *Plans and the structure of behavior.* Cambridge, MA: Harvard University Press.

Newell, A., & Simon, H. A. (1972). *Human problem solving.* Oxford, England: Prentice-Hall.

Pennebaker, J. W. (1997). Writing about emotional experiences as a therapeutic process. *Psychological Science, 8,* 162–166.

Piaget, J. (1981). *Intelligence and affectivity.* Palo Alto, CA: Annual Reviews.

Pribram, K. H. (2003). Forebrain psychophysiology of feelings: Interest and involvement. *International Journal of Psychophysiology, 48*(2), 115–131.

Reis, H. T. (2001). Relationship experiences and emotional well-being. In C. D. Ryff & B. H. Singer (Eds.), *Emotion, social relationships and health* (pp. 57–95). New York: Oxford University Press.

Rosenberg, M. (1965). *Society and the adolescent self-image.* Princeton, NJ: Princeton University Press.

Sandhya, S., & Stein, N. L. (2003). The influence of different living arrangements on marital happiness in Hindu Indian couples. Manuscript in preparation.

Simon, H. (1967). Motivational and emotional controls of cognition. In H. Simon (Ed.), *Models of thought* (pp. 29–38). New Haven, CT: Yale University Press.

Simon, H. A., & Newell, A. (1971). Human problem solving: The state of the theory in 1970. *American Psychologist, 26*(2), 145–159.

Sroufe, A. (1979). Socio-emotional development. In J. Osofsky (Ed.), *Handbook of infant development* (pp. 462–516). New York: Wiley.

Stein, N.L, & Albro, E.R. (2001). The origins and nature of arguments: Studies in conflict understanding, emotion, and negotiation. *Discourse Processes, 32,* 113–133.

Stein, N. L., & Albro, E. R. (2003). Psychological well-being in caregivers before and after the death of their partners: From care giving to bereavement through recovery. Manuscript in preparation.

Stein, N. L. & Bernas, R. (1999) The representation and early emergence of argument understanding. In P. Coirier & J. Andriessen (Eds.), *Foundations of argumentative text processing* (pp. 97–116). Amsterdam: Amsterdam University Press.

Stein, N. L., Bernas, R., & Calicchia, D. (1997). Conflict talk: Understanding and resolving arguments. In T. Givon (Ed.), *Typological studies in language: Conversational analysis* (pp. 233–267). Amsterdam: Benjamins.

Stein, N. L., & Boyce, W. T. (1999, April). The role of physiological reactivity in responding to and remembering an emotional event. Paper presented at the meeting of the Society for Research in Child Development, Albuquerque, NM.

Stein, N. L., Folkman, S., Trabasso, T., & Richards, T. A. (1997). Appraisal and goal processes as predictors of psychological well-being in bereaved caregivers. *Journal of Personality and Social Psychology, 72*(4), 872–884.

Stein, N. L., & Glenn, C. G. (1979). An analysis of story comprehension in elementary school children. In R. O. Freedle (Ed.), *Advances in discourse processes: Vol. 2. New directions in discourse processing* (pp. 53–120). Norwood, NJ: Ablex.

Stein, N. L., & Jewett, J. (1986). A conceptual analysis of the meaning of negative emotions: Implications for a theory of development. In C. Izard & P. Read (Eds.), *Measuring emotions in infants and children* (Vol. 2, pp. 238–267). Cambridge, UK: Cambridge University Press.

Stein, N. L., & Levine, L. (1987). Thinking about feelings: The development and organization of emotional knowledge. In R. Snow & M. Farr (Eds.), *Aptitude, learning and instruction* (Vol. 3, pp. 165–197). Hillsdale, NJ: Erlbaum.

Stein, N. L., & Levine, L. (1989). The causal organization of emotional knowledge: A developmental study. *Cognition and Emotion, 3*(4), 343–378.

Stein, N. L., & Levine, L. (1990). Making sense out of emotion: The representation and use of goal structured knowledge. In N. L. Stein, B. Leventhal, & T. Trabasso (Eds.), *Psychological and biological approaches to emotion* (pp. 45–73). Hillsdale, NJ: Erlbaum.

Stein, N. L., & Levine, L. J. (1999). The early emergence of emotional understanding and appraisal: Implications for theories of development. In T. Dalgleish & M. Power (Eds.), *Handbook of cognition and emotion* (pp. 383–410). Chicester: Wiley.

Stein, N. L., & Miller, C. A. (1993). The development of memory and reasoning skill in argumentative contexts: Evaluating, explaining, and generating evidence. In R. Glaser (Ed.), *Advances in instructional psychology* (Vol. 4, pp. 285–335). Hillsdale, NJ: Erlbaum.

Stein, N. L., Ross, M. A., & Fergusson, P. (2001). Writing about psychological trauma from two different perspectives: The effects on narration and subsequent states of psychological well-being. Unpublished manuscript.

Stein, N. L., Sheldrick, R., & Broaders, S. (1999). Predicting psychological well-being from beliefs and goal appraisal processes during the experience of emotional events. In S. Goldman, P. L. Van den Broek, & A. Graesser (Eds.), *Essays in honor of Tom Trabasso* (pp. 279–301). Mahwah, NJ: Erlbaum.

Stein, N.L. & Trabasso, T. (1982). What's in a story: An approach to comprehension and instruction. In R. Glaser (Ed.), *Advances in instructional psychology: Vol. 2.* (pp. 212–267). Hillsdale, NJ: Erlbaum.

Stein, N. L., & Trabasso, T. (1989). Children's understanding of changing emotion states. In C. Saarni & P. L. Harris (Eds.), *Children's understanding of emotion* (pp. 50–77). New York: Cambridge University Press.

Stein, N. L., & Trabasso, T. (1992). The organization of emotional experience: Creating links among emotion, thinking and intentional action. *Cognition and Emotion, 6* (3/4), 225–244.

Stein, N. L., Trabasso, T., & Albro, E. R. (2001). Understanding and organizing emotional experience: Autobiographical accounts of traumatic events. *English Studies of America, 19*(1), 111–130.

Stein, N. L., Trabasso, T., & Liwag, M. (1993). The representation and organization of emotional experience: Unfolding the emotional episode. In M. Lewis & J. Haviland (Eds.), *Handbook of emotion* (pp. 279–300). New York: Guilford Press.

Stenberg, C. R., & Campos, J. J. (1990). The development of anger expressions in infancy. In N. L. Stein, B. Leventhal, & T. Trabasso (Eds.), *Psychological and biological approaches to emotion* (pp. 247–282). Hillsdale, NJ: Erlbaum.

Watson, D., Clark, L. A., & Tellegen, A. (1988). Development and validation of brief measures of positive and negative affect: The PANAS scales. *Journal of Personality and Social Psychology, 54,* 1063–1070.

Zajonc, R. (1980). Feeling and thinking: Preferences need no inferences. *American Psychologist, 35,* 151–175.

Hermann Brandstätter

The Time Sampling Diary (TSD) of Emotional Experience in Everyday Life Situations

Following the flow of a person's experiences and activities over a longer period of time in his or her daily life is not just difficult; it is virtually impossible. A person moving around all the time, pursuing simultaneously several goals, entering inaccessible private settings, protecting thoughts and feelings against unwanted detection by interaction partners or observers; all this makes observation and recording extremely cumbersome.

For many research questions, retrospective diaries—reporting in the late evening on the events, thoughts, feelings, and actions of the preceding day—are not close enough to the process to be studied. People may not remember or may not find worthwhile reporting what they remember. Thus self-report time sampling of experience in situ is an alternative that gives access to any kind of situation, provides representative data, and keeps the effort for the participant and the researcher still at a tolerable level.

I designed the time sampling diary (TSD) in the mid-1970s at the University of Augsburg (Brandstätter, 1977), at the same time that Mihalyi Csikszentmihalyi at the University of Chicago (Csikszentmihalyi, Larsen, & Prescott, 1977) independently started a similar research program. Hurlburt (1997) reminds us of his thought sampling technique (Hurlburt, 1979) and of Eric Klinger's (1984) "consciousness sampling", both developed in the late 1970s. Obviously, several researchers at that time felt the need for a close observation of people's subjective experience. Meanwhile, the number of publications on "experience sampling" has remarkably increased during the past 25 years (see Figure 19.1).

One should not forget, however, that the British psychologist and psychoanalyst John Carl Flügel (1884–1955) had published a study with 9 participants who retrospectively and "as often as possible" recorded, over a period of 30 consecutive days, their emotions during the preceding hour or so (Flügel, 1925, 1955).[1] It is also worth remembering Hersey (1929, 1932), who spent much of his time over a year with 12 workers in a public utility corporation, continuously observing their behavior and interviewing them (with a special focus on their emotional ups and downs) four times a day in three periods of 13, 10, and 13 consecutive weeks interrupted by 8 weeks and 4 weeks of "rest."

The Basic Assumptions

What should be subsumed under a scientific concept of emotion and what should be excluded has been (Reymert, 1928) and still is a quite controversial issue (cf., e.g., Lambie & Marcel, 2002; Russell, 2003). I do not go into the sophisticated debate about core characteristics, components, antecedents, and consequences of emotion in its heterogeneous theoretical and empirical perspectives. My focus is on the (conscious) subjective experience of emotions.

Emotions are conceived of as the most immediate feedback about how successful a person is in pursuing his or her goals, which are a confluence of motives, perceived opportunities (incentives), or barriers in the environment and

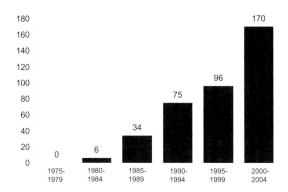

Figure 19.1. Number of publications on experience sampling according to Psychinfo, 1975–2004.

beliefs about one's capabilities. Motives are understood as a person's basic needs for survival as an organism, for establishing and maintaining essential social relationships, and for developing one's potential in a personally meaningful life, just to mention a few very broad and abstract categories (for a more comprehensive classification of human needs, see Sheldon, Elliot, Kim, & Kasser, 2001).

The quality and intensity of emotions is assumed to vary with the kind and importance, respectively, of motives affected (satisfied or frustrated) by an event and its causal attribution (cf. Weiner, 1986). Thus triumph is a strong positive emotion that indicates an extraordinary, internally attributed success of the power motive, whereas pride mirrors the fulfillment of the achievement motive.

Emotions imply both perceptual qualities (I perceive something as ugly or beautiful, as dangerous or enticing) and action tendencies (I tend to avoid the ugly or dangerous and to approach the beautiful or enticing object); thus emotions integrate perception and action. Furthermore, emotional experience can be predominantly self-focused, such as pride over a personal success, or world-focused, such as perceiving a situation as "lovely" or "dreadful" (Lambie & Marcel, 2002).

In disagreement with the majority of emotion researchers who speak of emotions as processes of shorter duration, elicited by and directed toward events, and of mood as a more enduring state without such an "intentional" orientation (e.g., Oatley & Jenkins, 1996), I conceive of emotions as transitory deflections (ups and downs) from a person's characteristic level of mood that also imply an evaluation and that have, therefore, an intentional focus but one that is more comprehensive and enduring because it relates to a person's global situation. Thus mood is not the stable background or the stage on which emotions come and go but changes all the time in shorter and longer waves. The shorter waves of mood are called emotions, elicited by events (remembered, perceived, or anticipated) that are relevant for the person's motives in the specific situation. Together with physiological processes that are connected with weather, illness, and drugs, the cumulative aftereffects of emotions contribute to the

longer waves of mood. The aftereffects of emotions are supposed to depend on their recency and intensity, as well as on a person's disposition to "ruminate" (Nolen-Hoeksema & Morrow, 1993).

The TSD focuses a person's attention on her or his feelings in the moments of randomized self-observations. It is based on the assumption that self-observation, with its special form of awareness of emotional experience (cf. Brown & Ryan, 2003; Lambie & Marcel, 2002), leaves the "original" (nonreflective) feelings essentially unchanged (for the distinction between first-order phenomenal experience and second-order awareness of it, see Lambie & Marcel, 2002). Otherwise, one could not claim good enough validity for the self-reports of emotional experience (cf. Hurlburt & Heavey, 2001).

The situations of self-observation are described by time, place, activities, persons present, and freedom of choice. In addition, the participants refer to the perceived causes of their emotions and to the motives that are satisfied or frustrated. Thus the TSD of emotional experience tells us very much about what people strive for, what kinds of situations are freely chosen or imposed, and what kinds of activities or events make them happy or unhappy and elicit the various qualities of emotions. Because characteristics of the person are assessed by traditional personality questionnaires or defined as intraindividually consistent ways of responding to certain classes of situations, one can study how characteristics of the circumstances interact with characteristics of the persons in eliciting emotional experience. The TSD technique prompts study participants to report on their momentary mood in the sense of how they feel about their present situation, in which certain objects or events might be in the foreground or in which (in the absence of personally relevant events) the person is focusing on his or her situation in general.

Method

Diary Format and Questionnaire

At the first meeting the participants are thoroughly informed of the procedure they should follow: They are told to make notes in a booklet on their momentary experience about four times a day, usually during a period of 30 days. The random time samples are different for each day and each person. There are seven questions to answer each time (for the detailed diary instructions, see appendix A):

1. Is my mood at the moment rather negative, indifferent, or rather positive?
2. How can I describe my momentary mood state using one or two adjectives?
3. Why do I feel as I have indicated?
4. Where am I?
5. What am I doing?

6. Who else is present?
7. To what extent do I feel free to choose to stay in or leave my present activity?

Before leaving the first meeting, the participants fill in Cattell's 16PF questionnaire (Schneewind, Schröder, & Cattell, 1983) or an adjective list designed in correspondence with Cattell's primary dimensions (Brandstätter, 1988). After 2 days' experience with the diary, the participants meet again with the experimenters or are called by phone to discuss their problems with the method. The following day they start the diary, which has to be kept during the consecutive 28 days or, if the study extends over a longer period of time, 10 days each in the first, second, third, and sixth month (i.e., of unemployment or adjusting to a new job or to studies at the university). At the end of the recording time period, the participants answer the personality questionnaires a second time and provide ratings of their attitudes toward the study. Except for minor modifications and some variations in the additional questionnaires, the procedure was virtually the same in all 25 studies run with the TSD up to now, partly in my research groups, partly elsewhere.

Time Sampling

The schedule for time sampling, printed on a sheet of paper and handed out to the participants, is generated by a computer program by dividing the 24 hours of the day into six segments of 4 hours each and choosing randomly one point of time within each segment, with the restriction that two consecutive signals are at least half an hour apart. In the booklet a separate page is provided for each of the 180 scheduled observation times (6 per day over 30 days). The participants have to set the alarm of a wristwatch on the next observation time.[2] Assuming 8 hours of sleep on average, the expected number of records per day is 4, resulting in a total expected number of 120 per person over 30 days. The actual number varies between days and persons owing to a variation in hours of sleeping and in frequencies of omissions. In case a scheduled time point has been forgotten, the participants are instructed to take their notes for only the moment that they become aware of their omission. Because there are also times for recording scheduled during the night, the participants have to mark those that were within their hours of sleep the next morning.

Information Technology in Collecting TSD Data

In our studies the participants were given an alarm wristwatch and a list of random times, different for each person and day of observation. Each participant was correctly reassured that nobody, neither the experimenter nor anybody else, knew which list was (randomly) chosen by him or her from a box. The only thing they had to do was to set the time of the next alarm on the watch. This inexpensive procedure worked quite well.

Meanwhile, there are, of course, various electronic devices on the market—in particular, handheld computers—for random signaling and recording the answers to the questions of interest (Barrett & Feldman Barrett, 2000; Feldman Barrett & Barrett, 2001; Bolger, Davis, & Rafaeli, 2003; Laurenceau & Bolger, 2005) and for taking "ambulatory" physiological measures (Fahrenberg & Myrtek, 1996; Hawkley, Burleson, Berntson, & Cacioppo, 2003; Räikkönen, Matthews, Flory, Owens, & Gump, 1999). Practical considerations and recommendations for various kinds of self-observation are given by Foster, Laventry-Finch, Gizzo, and Osantowski (1999). A study by Green, Rafaeli, Bolger, Shrout and Reis (2006) speaks for the equivalence of paper and electronic time sampling diaries.

Coding the Diary Records

In order to make sure that the participants trust the promise that all data will be completely anonymous and confidential and to preserve the personal structuring of experience, the diary notes are coded by the participants themselves (see the coding instructions in appendix B). The list of categories is designed or, if a prior study provides suitable categories, revised in cooperation with the participants, who then are trained in using the coding scheme. There are categories for the following aspects of situations:

1. Time of note
2. Mood state (negative, indifferent, positive)
3. Time perspective (present mood state attributed to a past, present, or future event)
4. Sources of satisfaction and dissatisfaction (e.g., other persons, objects, weather)
5. Affected motives (e.g., achievement, affiliation, power)
6. Behavior setting (e.g., living room, shop, office)
7. Activities (e.g., working, cooking, watching TV)
8. Other persons present (e.g., spouse, children, colleagues)
9. Perceived freedom
10. Adjectives that describe the mood state

In coding the sources of satisfaction and dissatisfaction, or, as we may also call them, the *causal attributions* (category 4), the participants, after looking at the specific record, have to answer the following questions for each observation time: Who or what, respectively, was the source of my mood state at that particular moment, and who or what made me feel happy or unhappy? Participants have a list of sources that comprise various classes of persons (self, husband, children, etc.) and objects (work equipment, clothes, mass media, etc.) at hand. The most important source has to be put in first place; sources of minor importance can be added in second or third place.

The list of 19 motives consists of statements indicating the frustration or satisfaction of the respective motives. For each page of their diary, corresponding to one point of time, participants have to mark at least one and no more than three (for the list of motives, see Brandstätter, 2001). Examples of those statements are as follows:

I feel rather bad because:

1. What I have achieved in my work is not good enough (achievement).
2. My surroundings are monotonous and boring (sentience).
3. I am lonely and/or have difficulties in making contacts (affiliation), and so forth.

I feel rather good because:

1. I experience success in my work (achievement).
2. I have varied and novel experiences (sentience).
3. I am enjoying the company of people I like (affiliation), and so forth.

The 19 motives were classified by the author (cf. Brandstätter, 1983, p. 876) into six broader categories: Sentience/Activity, Achievement, Physical Comfort, Affiliation, Power, and "Higher" Motives (comprising need for knowledge, order, esthetics, morality, and religion).

The adjectives used to describe the quality of mood and emotions are usually not coded by the participants but are literally transferred from the diary. In one of the studies (Kiss, Dornai, & Brandstätter, 2001), the participants, who came from different European countries and described their emotions in their native languages, did code the adjectives by indicating which of Russell's (1980) 24 adjectives that make up the affect circumplex came closest to the set of (one, two, or three) adjectives freely generated by the participant to describe the momentary mood. The adjectives of the circumplex, represented in the two-dimensional space of arousal (ordinate) and valence (abscissa), are (counterclockwise, beginning with the upper right quadrant):

- glad, pleased, happy, delighted, excited, astonished, aroused
- tense, alarmed, angry, afraid, annoyed, distressed, frustrated
- miserable, sad, gloomy, depressed, bored, droopy, tired
- sleepy, calm, relaxed, satisfied, at ease, content, serene

TSD Compared With ESM

The experience sampling method (ESM; Csikszentmihalyi et al., 1977) and the TSD, the methods used most frequently (for other variants of the technique, such as event sampling, see Wheeler & Reis, 1991), are different in some remarkable aspects. Most important is the fact that with TSD the participants do their codings of the diary entries themselves, thus structuring their experience according to their personal understanding of situations. The explicit reference to attributions (subjective explanations of emotions) and affected motives is also noteworthy as a special characteristic of the

TSD. Not less important is the free-answer format used in describing the specific qualities of emotions. Whereas most other varieties of experience sampling (cf. Hormuth, 1986; Wheeler & Reis, 1991) use prefabricated scales for rating the occurrence and intensity of emotions, the TSD asks the participants to describe their moods with a few freely generated adjectives, thus giving a more idiographic picture of the individual's emotional experience and the individual's way of speaking about emotions (for the viability of the adjective generation technique, see also Allen & Potkay, 1973). Individual or group differences in emotion language can be analyzed (cf. Brandstätter, Grossman, & Filipp, 1992) and related to personality characteristics or other individual parameters derived from the TSD data. One may find out, for example, whether persons with high scores on emotional awareness measured by questionnaires (Lischetzke, Eid, Wittig, & Trierweiler, 2001; Swinkels & Giuliano, 1995) are those who use a highly differentiated vocabulary in describing their daily emotional experience.

Hierarchical Linear Models as a Means of Analyzing TSD Data

A characteristic feature of the TSD is the fact that the data belong to at least two levels. Level 1 comprises the sequence of points in time when the self-observations are made. The units of level 2 are the persons who participate in the study. The data of level 1 are "nested" within the level 2 units. Only recently, statistical models developed decades ago within mathematical statistics and econometrics found their way into the psychological literature (Raudenbush & Bryk, 2002; Goldstein, 1995; Rasbash, Steele, Browne, & Prosser, 2005). Hierarchical linear modeling (HLM) is a promising way of analyzing TSD data simultaneously on the level of a person's repeatedly reported experiences over a longer period of time (level 1) and the level of the person (level 2) with personality measures derived from traditional questionnaires or generated by aggregating level 1 data across occasions and situations. Prior attempts at analyzing multilevel data were not able to deal properly with the dependence of level 1 data and to analyze simultaneously the effects within and across the different levels (cf. Affleck, Tennen, Zautra & Armeli, 1999). Multilevel models account for random variation (between level 2 units) of intercepts and slopes of regressions when the dependent variable belongs to level 1 and the independent variables are only level 1 variables or a mixture of level 1 and level 2 variables. For the model assumptions see Goldstein (1995) and Raudenbush & Bryk (2002). Many of the recent ESM studies have used hierarchical linear modeling (see, e.g., Oisi, Diener, Scollon, & Biswas-Diener, 2004; Swendsen, 1998).

Table 19.1 presents the results of a two-level analysis of data that I collected from 11 participants of a summer school on time sampling of emotions. Mood in situation *i* of person

Table 19.1
The results of a two-level hierarchical regression analysis

		1	2	3	4	5	6	7
								Work × Others × Extraversion
		Intercept	Activity	Social Situation	nPower	nAffiliation	Extraversion	
1		$\beta_{0j} = \beta_0 + u_{0j}$	$\beta_{1j} = \beta_1 + u_{1j}$	$\beta_{2j} = \beta_2 + u_{2j}$	$\beta_{3j} = \beta_3 + u_{3j}$			
2	u. b.	2.26	−.32	2.13	.83			
3	fixed effects	β_0 1.16 (.12)	β_1 −.64 (.14)	β_2 .63 (.22)	β_3 −.37 (.30)	β_4 .76 (.13)	β_5 .03 (.06)	β_6 .22 (.07)
4	l. b.	.06	−.96	−.87	−1.57			
5	random effects	$\sigma^2(u_{0j})$ .31 (.11)	$\sigma^2(u_{1j})$ .03 (.11)	$\sigma^2(u_{2j})$ .58 (.33)	$\sigma^2(u_{3j})$ 1.44 (.62)			
6	M (SD)	1.13 (1.94)	.28 (.45)	.80 (.40)	.17 (.38)	.27 (.44)	5.07 (1.89)	−.04 (.91)

Note: Row 6 contains means (M) and standard deviations (SD). The residual variance $\sigma^2 (e_{ij})$ = 2.83.

j (−4 = very negative, 0 = indifferent, 4 = very positive)[3] is the dependent variable (level 1). Activity (0 = leisure, 1 = work), Social Situation (0 = alone, 1 = with others), Power Actualization (0 = no, 1 = yes), Affiliation Actualization (0 = no, 1 = yes), Extraversion (derived from self-ratings on 9–point adjective scales representing the 16PF primary personality dimensions; Cattell & Johnson, 1986), and the Work x Others x Extraversion interaction are the independent variables. Extraversion is the only level 2 personality dimension included in the model:

$$mood_{ij} = \beta_{0j} + \beta_{1j}Leisure/Work_{ij} + \beta_{2j}Alone/Others_{ij} + \beta_{3j}Power_{ij}$$
$$+ \beta_4 Affiliation_j + \beta_5 Extraversion_j + \beta_6 Work$$
$$\times Others \times Extraversion_{ij} + e_{ij}$$

The independent variables are centered around the grand mean (across observations and persons). Column 1 presents in row 3 the fixed part of the intercept β_0 = 1.16 (in parentheses its standard error [SE] = .12). Row 5 contains in column 1 the random variance $\sigma^2(u_{0j})$ around the intercept β_0 and (in columns 2 to 4) the random variances around the fixed part of the slopes (the partial regression of mood on the respective independent variable, based on the pooled within-subjects variance-covariance matrix), in parentheses again the standard errors of the estimates. The figures above and below the fixed coefficients (in rows 2 and 4) show the range of random variation (between +1.96* $\sigma(u_{ij})$ as upper bound [u.b.] and −1.96* $\sigma(u_{ij})$ as lower bound [l.b.]). Within this range the intercepts and slopes of 95% of the persons are expected to vary. Although actualization of the affiliation motive can vary both within and between persons, it turned out that the random part of the slope is practically nonexistent. Therefore, it was included in the model with its fixed effect only. Each of the independent variables, except extraversion, contributes uniquely and significantly ($p < .01$) to the prediction of mood.

On the average, Work, β_1 = −.64 (.14), is less pleasant than Leisure; and being with Others makes feel better, β_2 = .63 (.22), than being alone. Whenever the affiliation motive (nAffiliation) is involved, mood is by .76 units better than in

other situations. Only in situations in which the participants work with or in the presence of others do extraverts feel better than introverts (β_6 = .22 [.07]). All these effects are highly significant ($p < .01$). Highly significant is also the random (between persons) variation of the intercept, $\sigma^2(u_{0j})$ = .31 (.11), which means (under the condition of mean-centered predictors) that people differ in their average moods after controlling for activity, social situation, power, affiliation, extraversion, and the interaction term. The *interindividual* variance of mood, $\sigma^2(u_{0j})$ is about the same before and after including the predictor variables 2 to 7 (Table 19.1) in the model. However, the *intraindividual* residual variance $\sigma^2(e_{ij})$ of mood, which in the present model is assumed to be equal for all persons, reduces from 3.46 to 2.83 (a reduction of 18%) by the fixed effects of Leisure/Work (β_1), Alone/Others (β_2), nAffiliation (β_4), and the interaction term Work x Others x Extraversion (β_6). The actualization of the power motive (nPower) contributes, with its random effect $\sigma^2(u_{3j})$ significantly to the explanation of the intraindividual variance of mood, whereas the random effects of Leisure/Work and Alone/Others are not significant.

Examples of Problems Studied With the Time Sampling Diary or the Experience Sampling Method

Examples of questions explored or hypotheses tested by myself and my associates with the TSD are reported by Brandstätter (2001). They refer to emotions in interacting with other people (example 1), motivational person-environment-fit as a condition of subjective well-being (example 2), the quality of the relationship of married couples as it appears in their TSD records (example 3), the TSD as a means of measuring organizational climate (example 4), attribution of emotional experience during the first 6 months at a new workplace (example 5), and the emotional vocabulary of women and men (example 6).

Experience sampling techniques have often been used, to mention just a few examples, for testing hypotheses about how emotions are influenced by a person's goals and life tasks (Fleeson & Cantor, 1995), motives (O'Connor & Rosenblood, 1996; Updegraff, Gable & Taylor, 2004), personality characteristics (Brandstätter, 1994; Côté & Moskowitz, 1998; Eaton & Funder, 2001; Eid & Diener, 1999; Fleeson, 2001; Moskowitz, 1994; Penner, Shiffman, Paty, & Fritzsche, 1994; Tennen, Suls, & Affleck, 1991; Tugade, Frederickson, & Feldman Barrett, 2004), adult age differences (Carstensen, Pasupathi, Mayr, & Nesselroade, 2000), and how measures of happiness and life satisfaction relate to intensity and frequency of emotions (Diener, Sandvik & Pavot, 1991). Tugade, Frederickson and Feldman Barrett (2004) relate the "granularity" of emotion language (i. e., a person's tendency to describe emotional experience with concrete and specific terms), derived from the intraindividual covariation across occasions of emotion descriptive rating scales of the same valence, to individual differences in emotion regulation and coping with stress. (See also Feldman Barrett [2004] for relating the structure of a person's emotion language to the structure of his or her reports on emotional experience. The structure in both perspectives is characterized by the relative emphasis of valence versus emphasis of arousal). Norem and Illingworth (1993) used ESM in a field experiment in which half of the participants reported only their experience, whereas the other half was prompted, in addition, to reflect on the progress made toward their goals.[4]

TSD or ESM have become valuable tools also in various fields of applied psychology: work and organizations, unemployment, family interaction, health behavior, and psychotherapy.

Peter Totterdell (Institutes of Work Psychology at the University of Sheffield, United Kingdom) and his associates have been particularly active in emotion research on the workplace (Totterdell & Holman, 2003; Totterdell, Kellett, Teuchmann & Briner, 1998; Totterdell & Parkinson, 1999; Triemer & Rau, 2001) and in sports (Totterdell, 1999). Other examples of ESM applied to the work setting are given by Ilies and Judge (2002) and Judge and Ilies (2004), who analyzed the relationship between mood and concurrent job satisfaction as dependent on personality characteristics. Brandstätter and Gaubatz (1997) studied the process of adjustment to a new workplace. Several other studies about the emotional experience during job entry are reported in Brandstätter and Eliasz (2001). Miner, Glomb and Hulin (2005) found, compared to the rather frequent positive work events, much stronger effects of the less frequent negative work events on mood; but they did not find the expected effects of mood on organizational citizenship behavior and temporary work withdrawal. Rathunde and Csikszentmihalyi (2005) proved the usefulness of ESM in comparing the effects of different types of schools on students' motivational and emotional experience.

Studies with the TSD have further been done in a high-security prison (Kette, 1991) and in a military unit (Kirchler,

1984). The effects of job loss on the emotional experience have been studied by Kirchler (1985) and Džuka (2001). Mothers' variations in self-esteem (Wells, 1988), marital couples' synchronous TSD recordings (Brandstätter & Wagner, 1994; Kirchler, 1989), the daily life of married women staying at home without paid work (Brandstätter, 1983), and the spillover of emotional experience from work to home of parents with adolescent children (Matjasko & Feldman, 2006) are examples of studies on the daily experience within the family life.

In the clinical context, among others Swendsen et al. (2000) and Hussong, Hicks, Levy, and Curran (2001) looked for the relationship between mood and alcohol consumption. Peeters, Nicolson, Berkhof, Delespaul, and deVries (2003) focused on differences between mentally healthy people and patients diagnosed with major depressive disorders in experiencing and responding to negative life events. Clinical psychologists can find out whether an attribution training (helping the participants in avoiding dysfunctional, self-esteem-undermining attributions) has a favorable impact on their daily emotional experience (cf. Swendsen, 1998).

Merits and Shortcomings of Time Sampling Techniques

The TSD technique generates very rich data sets on the emotional experience of people in everyday life situations that allow us to test a great variety of hypotheses about environmental and personal conditions of subjective well-being. The technique lends itself to the idiographic approach in studying individuals, as well as to the nomothetic approach in studying the regularities of emotional experience of people in general or of categories of people who have a specific personality structure or a specific environment in common. The technique is particularly useful in analyzing the mutual influence of mood in couples, families, or small work groups. Sticking to the basic design in a longer series of studies has the advantage that a large data set can be used for testing hypotheses on how characteristics of the person interact with characteristics of the environment in emotional experience.

The *main advantages* of time sampling techniques in studying everyday emotional experience can be summarized as:

- Immediacy of the reports
- Representativeness of sampled situations
- Idiographic accuracy
- Simultaneous statistical analysis of intra- and inter-individual variation
- Exploratory potential
- A device for measuring and comparing social welfare

Immediacy of the Reports

Answering the traditional questions about well-being and satisfaction with work, leisure, marriage, and so forth demands from the participants rather difficult categorizations and résumés of their emotional experience in ill-defined situations and time periods. In addition, people often are tempted to answer in a socially desirable way. The complete privacy of the TSD and focusing of self-observation on the current moment can be expected to improve the validity of the reports.

Representativeness of Sampled Situations

Random time sampling is the only realistic way to generate a representative description of everyday life situations. The frequencies by which the situations appear in the diary are proportional to their actual frequencies and duration if the monitoring of the random signals is efficient and if the participants perceive themselves as research partners who are responsible for high data quality. For special purposes—in particular, if a study focuses on events that occur with low frequencies—a combination of time sampling with event sampling might be the most appropriate approach.

Idiographic Accuracy

The great number of observations per person—in our TSD studies usually four observations per day over 4 weeks—allows detailed idiographic analyses of how an individual interacts with his or her environment before the data are aggregated for more or less homogeneous collectives of persons. To observe changes in the individual's way of interacting with the environment is particularly useful in studies on periods of transition (starting a new job, moving into a new neighborhood, getting married, adjusting to retirement). Time sampling diaries can provide evidence on the progress of a psychotherapeutic process, and reflecting on the daily experience can support the therapeutic intervention.

Simultaneous Statistical Analysis of Intra- and Interindividual Variation

Data generated by TSD and ESM can now be adequately analyzed by HLM, which opened a more efficient way of dealing with multilevel data. This is particularly useful, if not essential, whenever characteristics of the person and characteristics of the person's environment are drawn on to explain intra- and interindividual variation in mood and causal attributions of mood in daily life.

Exploratory Potential

Even if the TSD in its standard form is used for testing specific hypotheses, the data set provided by it is so rich that there are ample opportunities for looking at regularities in the data that originally were not thought of or to see whether additional statistical analyses support post hoc interpretations of unexpected results. It would be highly desirable to have data sets generated by various research groups that share the experience sampling methodology and are well documented and permanently saved so that they can be reanalyzed from different theoretical perspectives years or even decades later. Carefully collected and documented data might be valuable and significant well beyond the theoretical context of the original study.

A Device for Measuring and Comparing Social Welfare

At least in democratic countries, advancing social welfare is accepted as a principal goal of economic policy, although defining and measuring social welfare has been and still is a controversial issue (Sen, 1999). In particular, using the gross domestic product (GDP) as a principal indicator of social welfare, understood as an aggregate measure of people's preferences revealed by their economic choices, can be debated (Clarke & Islam, 2003). A completely different approach to social welfare would be time sampling of subjective well-being in a representative sample of people and taking the average frequency (across persons and time points of self-observation) by which people feel good as a welfare measure of a nation (Brandstätter, 1998; for similar ideas with respect to frequency and intensity of satisfaction in various life domains, assessed with ESM, see Diener, 2000).

The indifference point—feeling neither good nor bad—is supposed to have the same meaning for everybody, thus providing the reference point for interindividual and intergroup comparison of subjective well-being. Because ratings of intensity are ambiguous—we do not know how much of it represents the intensity of emotions and how much the way of speaking about emotions—the traditional attitude scales used for measuring general life satisfaction or satisfaction with specific life domains make interindividual or intergroup comparisons more problematic than comparisons of frequencies by which people feel above the indifference point irrespective of the intensity.

Of course, the TSD technique has also its shortcomings and flaws. These are mainly:

- High demands on time, money, and effort
- Changes of the observed experience by the observation technique
- Limited awareness of internal states
- Fragmentation of the continuous flow of experience
- Restriction to self-reports of emotions

High Demands on Time, Money, and Effort

The single TSD records usually do not take more than 1 minute, but the weekly coding of the diary entries needs about 2 hours for each one. In addition, the time necessary for instructing the participants, for weekly meetings of groups of participants and/or for repeated telephone contacts with individual participants, and for answering additional questionnaires at the beginning and at the end of the data collection, together with an interview, amounts to 20 to 25 hours per participant. This time investment deserves an adequate financial compensation. The researchers, too, need more time and effort for the processing of the data than they would have to invest in traditional surveys or experiments.

Changes of the Observed Experience by the Observation Technique

Observing oneself again and again and coding the diary entries result in an atypical self-awareness, the effects of which need to be studied more thoroughly. Wicklund (1975) gives some evidence that self-focused attention ("objective self-awareness") augments the effects of a perceived discrepancy between what a person wants and what he or she gets. In the case of a negative discrepancy—which, in Wicklund's view, happens most of the time—the negative affect, as well as discrepancy-reducing activities, are intensified by self-focused attention. If the perceived discrepancy happens to be positive, the positive affect is intensified. In a field experiment, a randomly chosen half of the participants in a TSD study could be told to keep the diary during the full time of 4 weeks, whereas the other half could be allowed to pause in the 2nd week. If both groups provide retrospective ratings of the frequency and intensity of emotions experienced during the 2nd week, Wicklund's hypothesis and other possible effects of self-observation could be tested.

Limited Awareness of Internal States

Even if people are willing to report sincerely on their conscious experience, one has to accept that there are many unconscious or subconscious processes that unknowingly influence a person's behavior. The assumption of unconscious but nevertheless *mental* (and not just physiological) processes is not only essential for the psychoanalytic tradition in its various ramifications but also has attracted some attention in recent experimental cognitive research (Bargh & Ferguson, 2000; Greenwald & Banaji, 1995). There are also individual differences in emotion awareness and in the ability to differentiate and label one's emotions (Lischetzke, Eid, Wittig, & Trierweiler, 2001; Swinkels & Giuliano, 1995).

Fragmentation of the Continuous Flow of Experience

Time sampling gives a series of "still photographs" cut from the continuous flow of experience. The specific processes of goal setting, action planning, and action regulation are not easily reconstructed from these time samples of experience. As a complement, interviews and narratives of how people perceive and interpret their present life situations, their pasts, and their futures are indispensable for a deeper understanding of a person's world view and self-actualization (cf. Thomae, 1988).

Restriction to Self-Reports of Emotions

Emotions are processes in which a number of conceptually and phenomenologically distinguishable components are intertwined. The TSD focuses on the subjective experience, which may be conceived as the central component of an emotion, and takes additionally into account the events that elicit the emotions. The facial expression of emotions, as well as the concurrent central and peripheral physiological processes, are outside the reach of the TSD technique. New electronic measuring and data recording devices may be used more frequently in the future in order to overcome the neglect of physiological processes, at least of the peripheral ones (Fahrenberg & Myrtek, 1996). Collecting information about a person's mood from relatives, friends, or acquaintances in addition to the TSD self-reports should help to widen the horizon of observation (Brandstätter & Wagner, 1994; Kirchler, 1989; Sandvik, Diener, & Seidlitz, 1993).

Conclusions

The time sampling diary (TSD) provides representative samples of people's emotions in everyday life situations. Emotions are conceived as a person's most "central" and most characteristic responses to failures and successes in pursuing motive satisfaction in continuously changing situations (behavior settings) qualified by certain activities under specific circumstances (time, place, persons present, freedom of choice). Thus the TSD gives a rather direct insight into a person's *real-time* experience of satisfaction and discomfort, which could be considered a validity criterion for any other global or specific life satisfaction or utility measure (cf. Kahneman, Wakker, & Sarin, 1997).

Whether maximizing not just the short-term but the lifetime balance of happiness can and should be the ultimate personal and societal goal is less a psychological than a philosophical and religious question, to which many different and controversial answers have been given throughout the cultural history of mankind until today and will be given in the future. At least, let us hope that not too many people follow or have the power to follow the principle of maximizing their personal lifetime balance of happiness at the expense of the lifetime balance of happiness of others in their neighborhood and around the world. Subjective well-being is an important criterion for evaluating one's life, but it may nevertheless not be the ultimate criterion. We can never escape the critical question behind the pursuit of happiness: whether the motives we want to satisfy and the goals we are striving for are the right ones.

Appendix A: Instructions for Keeping the Diary

What Is the Goal of the Study?

Up to now psychologists do not know much, for sure not enough, about the experiences and activities of [*refer to the specific kind of subjects under study*] in their everyday life during work and leisure, about events and circumstances which make them happy or unhappy. This study aims at a better psychological understanding of the situation of [*insert specific situation under study here*] in order to find out how the professional and private life of this important group of people could be improved. Time sampling, the method which will be explained in more detail later, is now quite frequently and successfully used in exploring what people experience and do in their ordinary life. It provides more concrete and more valid information on a person's interaction with her or his environment than any other technique.

What Will Be Done?

The study runs over 30 days and is expected to give a thorough picture of your personal experience beginning with the time when you wake up to the time when you fall asleep. You will take notes in a kind of diary about four times a day on how you feel at the moment, why you feel this way, where you are, what you are doing, who else is present, and how free you are to stay in or to leave the situation.

Note: Please be aware not to change your activities in order to accommodate to keeping the diary. The data are valuable only if you organize your day as usual.

The data are strictly confidential. Nobody can identify the source of the data, because you sign the questionnaires and the diary protocols with a code which is known only to you.

When Do You Make the Entries in Your Diary?

You will be provided with a wristwatch on which you can set the next alarm according to your time schedule. Each person has a different random time schedule, which is not known to anybody else. When the alarm goes off you complete the diary report immediately. In some exceptional situations you may go through the diary questions mentally, memorize the answers, and make the notes as soon as possible. In the diary you should record the alarm time (planned time), the time of observation (usually identical with the planned time), and the time of writing down the observations (usually identical with planned and observed time). For each day you need six sheets of paper, which you number 1.1, 1.2, . . . 1.6 for the first day, 2.1, 2.2, . . . 2.6 for the second day, and so on. Should you once miss a scheduled time, perhaps because you forgot to set the next alarm or because you didn't hear the alarm, you can take the diary notes just for the moment when you realize that you have missed a scheduled time. If a scheduled diary entry falls in your sleeping time, you mark the respective page with *S* (sleeping) the next morning.

How Do You Answer the Diary Questions?

Each diary page refers to the same seven questions:

1. **How is my mood at the moment?** Here you have to indicate whether immediately before the alarm went off your feelings were just noticeably below or above the point of indifference. The question is definitely not whether the circumstances are such that you actually should feel bad or good. What counts is how you really feel. If you feel just noticeably bad (or clearly bad), you put down a minus sign (–), if you feel just noticeably well (or clearly well), you write a plus sign (+). In some rare situations, if you really can't tell whether your mood is rather negative or rather positive, you write zero (0).

2. **How can I describe my momentary mood by (up to three) adjectives?** Imagine you have to describe the weather of a summer day. You might say, it is sunny, humid, and windy. The common language provides many different adjectives by which one can describe emotions and mood states. Please try to characterize your mood in its specific quality as precisely as possible. Adjectives like *good* or *bad* are too general to be informative.

3. **Why do I feel as I have indicated?** Here you write down your subjective explanations of your feelings, for example: Who (another person or yourself) or what (something around you or some characteristics of your personality) is the cause? Is it something that you remember from the past, or that you are experiencing just now, or that you expect for the future? Which of your more general motives or more specific goals you are presently pursuing are affected?

4. **Where am I?** Indicate the place rather precisely so that you can remember the situation later when you code your diary!

5. **What am I doing?** Characterize the private or social activities in concrete terms! Indicate what you do and with whom!

6. **Who else is present?** Persons who are particularly relevant to you in the present situation should be recorded by their names, others by generic terms (like colleagues, strangers).

7. **Do I feel free in the present situation?** If you could just leave the present situation or choose a different activity without negative consequences (being blamed by significant others or feeling personally guilty), you are rather free. Otherwise your freedom is restricted by social norms and obligations you cannot escape without breaking rules. The question here is not whether you would like to do something different, but

whether you would have the external or internal freedom to do something different.

Note: Whenever you have difficulties with the diary, use the next group meeting to discuss it or call number [Insert telephone number here] for assistance!

Can You Confide All Your Experiences, Even Very Intimate Ones, to Your Diary?

Yes, you can and you should. Please be completely open in your diary. Otherwise the data will not be very useful. Take precautions that nobody has access to your diary. You will not be asked to hand out your original diary entries to the researcher. What you deliver to the researcher for further analysis is just your anonymous codings of the diary entries. You will personally code your diary entries according to rules which are presented on the next page.

Appendix B: Instructions for Coding the Diary Entries

The time sampling diary is completely private. Since you were sure that nobody will have access to it, you have written down your very personal experience, no matter how intimate it might have been. You will not hand over your diary to any other person. Therefore, you personally have to code the diary entries before the data can be processed. This not only assures you of the unconditional privacy and anonymity of the data but is also the best way of coding the diary notes according to your personal perspective.

It is very important that you code the diary carefully. Otherwise all the efforts you have put into observing your personal experience and writing down your observations would eventually be fruitless.

Each coding sheet has 42 free rows and 25 columns [see appendix C]. Each row (line) corresponds to one time point of observations. Since each day has 6 random times of observations, a single coding sheet provides space for the 42 observations during 7 days. You need 4 sheets for the whole observation period of 28 days. Please use a separate sheet for the trial period of 2 days! On the top of each page enter your code, the date of coding, and the number of the week.

Now we go through each column in order to clarify its meaning.

Column	Label	Explanation
3	Nuob	There are six lines for each day, one for each random time of observation. 11 means first day, first observation.
4	M	Month (01 January, 02 February, etc.).
5	D	Day of observation. If the first day were October 26, you would enter 10 in column 4 and 26 in column 5.
6	Tpla	Time planned, for example, 0906, which means 6 minutes past 9 in the morning, or 2023, which means 23 minutes past 8 in the evening.
7	Tobs	Time actually observed
8	Trec	Time recorded
9	Mood	Mood (Question 1 in the diary: How is my mood at the moment?): −1 (rather bad), 00 (indifferent), +1 (rather good).
10	Adc	You look at your adjectives (Question 2 in the diary: How can I describe my momentary mood by adjectives?) and choose *one* from the Adjective List which comes closest to the meaning of your combination of adjectives.
11, 12	t1, t2	Time (1 = past, 2 = present, 3 = future) of the event (remembered, experienced just now, expected) influencing your mood.
13–15	S1–S3	Source 1 to Source 3. This is the place for causal attributions of your mood states. You ask yourself what or who is the origin (the cause) of your mood or emotion (emotion in the sense of a transitory shift of your mood elicited by an observed event or by a thought which comes to your mind (e. g. remembering a past or expecting a future event). The causes can be external (another person, a TV program, the weather, etc.) or internal (your abilities or efforts, your appearance, some other personality characteristics). You can enter up to three different sources (causes). The most important one should be entered on first place. Use *S1* if there is only one source.
16–17	M1–M3	Motive 1 to Motive 3. Select up to three motives from the list of motives. You enter an odd number, if a motive has been frustrated, and an even number, if a motive has been satisfied. The most important motive should be put on first place. Should you enter only one motive, please use the first motive column!
19	Pla	Place
20, 21	A1, A2	Activities. The code number of the primary activity is put in first place.
22–24	P1–P3	Persons present. The person (or category of persons) with the highest relevance in the present situation is put in first place. If you use only one person column, please use *P1*!
25	Fri	Write down the perceived degree of internal freedom (1 to 4), i.e., the freedom from inner obligations or self-imposed duties.
26	Fre	Write down the perceived degree of external freedom (1 to 4), i.e., the freedom from social pressure (social norms, social expectations).
27	Adt	Adjectives (literally transferred) as you have written them down in the diary.

Appendix C: Coding Schema

Coding Schema

1 Nusu	2 Code	3 Nuob	4 M	5 D	6 Tpla	7 Tobs	8 Trec	9 Mood	10 Adc	11 t1	12 t2	13 S1	14 S2	15 S3	16 M1	17 M2	18 M3	19 Pla	20 A1	21 A2	22 P1	23 P2	24 P3	25 Fri	26 Fre	27 Adt
		11																								
		12																								
		13																								
		14																								
		15																								
		16																								
		21																								
		22																								
		etc.																								
		etc.																								
		75																								
		76																								

Key:

1	Nusu	Serial number participant	9	Mood	Mood	25	Fri	Freedom (internal)
2	Code	Code of participant	10	Adc	Adjective category	26	Fre	Freedom (external)
3	Nuob	Serial number of random point of time*	11	t1, t2	Time perspective	27	Adt	Adjective transcript
4	M	Month	13	S1, S2, S3	Sources			
5	D	Day	16	M1, M2, M3	Motives			
6	Tpla	Time planned	19	Pla	Place			
7	Tobs	Time observed	20	A1, A2	Activities			
8	Trec	Time recorded	22	P1, P2, P3	Persons			

*Three-digit serial number like 275, which means the 5th random time point of the 27th day.

Note: A sample TSD data set together with SPSS commands for running basic statistical analyses are available on request from the author. E-mail: h.brandstaetter@jk.uni-linz.ac.at.

Acknowledgment

Appendices and parts of other paragraphs are from: Brandstätter, H. (2001). Time sampling diary: An ecological approach to the study of emotions in everyday life situations. In H. Brandstätter & A. Eliasz (Eds.), *Persons, situations and emotions* (pp. 20–52). New York: Oxford University Press. Reprinted with permission.

Notes

1. In a similar way, retrospective reports on emotional experience, each time concerning the previous 2 hours (four times a day, at 11 A.M., 1 P.M., 3 P.M., and 5 P.M.) were collected by Totterdell and Holman (2003).

2. The prices of electronic devices for signaling and recording are not prohibitive anymore. However, according to my experience, using the alarm of a cheap wristwatch as a reminder to make notes with paper and pencil works quite well. In any case, whenever each participant gets his or her own randomized time schedule, one has to take precautions that the researcher is not able to identify the responder.

3. In other studies, mood was rated on a 5-point scale (ranging from –2 to +2) or on a 3-point scale (–1, 0, +1).

4. Because TSD is a special type of experience sampling technique, it shares the theoretical and methodological perspectives with other ESM studies, of which only a few examples are reported here.

References

Affleck, G., Tennen, H., Zautra, A., & Armeli, S. (1999). Multilevel daily process designs for consulting and clinical psychology: A preface to the perplexed. *Journal of Consulting and Clinical Psychology, 67,* 746–754.

Allen, B. P., & Potkay, C. R. (1973). Variability of self-description on a day-to-day basis: Longitudinal use of the adjective generation technique. *Journal of Personality, 41,* 638–652.

Bargh, J. A., & Ferguson, M. J. (2000). Beyond behaviorism: On the automaticity of higher mental processes. *Psychological Review, 126,* 925–945.

Barrett, D. J., & Feldman Barrett, L. (2000). The Experience-Sampling Program (ESP). Retrieved August 24, 2006, from http://www.experience-sampling.org/esp/

Bolger, N., Davis, A., & Rafaeli, E. (2003). Diary methods: Capturing life as it is lived. *Annual Review of Psychology, 54,* 579–616.

Brandstätter, H. (1977). Wohlbefinden und Unbehagen: Entwurf eines Verfahrens zur Messung situationsabhängiger Stimmungen [Subjective well-being and uneasiness: Design of a technique for measuring situation dependent mood]. In W. H. Tack (Ed.), *Bericht über den 30. Kongress der DGfPs in*

Regensburg 1976 (Vol. 2, pp. 60–62). Göttingen, Germany: Hogrefe.

Brandstätter, H. (1983). Emotional responses to other persons in everyday life situations. *Journal of Personality and Social Psychology, 45*, 871–883.

Brandstätter, H. (1988). Sechzehn Persönlichkeits-Adjektivskalen (16PA) als Forschungsinstrument anstelle des 16PF [Sixteen Personality Adjective Scales as research instrument as substitute for 16PF]. *Zeitschrift für experimentelle und angewandte Psychologie, 35*, 370–391.

Brandstätter, H. (1994). Pleasure of leisure—pleasure of work: Personality makes the difference. *Personality and Individual Differences, 16*, 931–946.

Brandstätter, H. (1998). Wohlbefinden statt Wohlstand als Ziel der Wirtschaftspolitik [Subjective well-being instead of high living standard as goal of economic policy]. In H. Hesse & P. Welzel (Eds.), *Wirtschaftspolitik zwischen gesellschaftlichen Ansprüchen und ökonomischen Grenzen* (pp. 21–37). Göttingen, Germany: Vandenhoeck & Ruprecht.

Brandstätter, H. (2001). The time-sampling diary: An ecological approach to the study of emotions in everyday life situations. In H. Brandstätter & A. Eliasz (Eds.), *Persons, situations, and emotions: An ecological approach* (pp. 20–52). New York: Oxford University Press.

Brandstätter, H., & Eliasz, A. (Eds.). (2001). *Persons, situations, and emotions: An ecological approach.* New York: Oxford University Press.

Brandstätter, H., & Gaubatz, S. (1997). Befindenstagebuch am neuen Arbeitsplatz in differentialpsychologischer Sicht [Time-sampling diary at the new workplace: An individual difference perspective]. *Zeitschrift für Arbeits- und Organisationspsychologie, 41*, 18–29.

Brandstätter, H., Grossman, M., & Filipp, G. (1992). Gefühle im Alltag—berichtet von Frauen und Männern [Emotions in everyday life—reported by women and men]. *Zeitschrift für Sozialpsychologie, 23*, 64–76.

Brandstätter, H., & Wagner, W. (1994). Erwerbstätigkeit der Frau und Alltagsbefinden von Ehepartnern im Zeitverlauf [Employment status of the wife and marital partner's well-being in the course of time]. *Zeitschrift für Sozialpsychologie, 25*, 126–146.

Brown, K. W., & Ryan, R. M. (2003). The benefits of being present: Mindfulness and its role in psychological well-being. *Journal of Personality and Social Psychology, 84*, 822–848.

Carstensen, L. L., Pasupathi, M., Mayr, U., & Nesselroade, J. R. (2000). Emotional experience in everyday life across the adult life span. *Journal of Personality and Social Psychology, 79*, 644–655.

Cattell, R. B., & Johnson, R. C. (Eds.). (1986). Functional psychological testing: Principles and instruments. New York: Brunner/Mazel.

Clarke, M., & Islam, S. M. N. (2003). Measuring social welfare: Application of social choice theory. *Journal of Socio-Economics, 32*, 1–15.

Côté, S., & Moskowitz, D. S. (1998). On the dynamic covariation between interpersonal behavior and affect prediction from neuroticism, extraversion, and agreeableness. *Journal of Personality and Social Psychology, 75*, 1032–1046.

Csikszentmihalyi, M., Larsen, R., & Prescott, S. (1977). The ecology of adolescent activity and experience. *Journal of Youth and Adolescence, 6*, 281–294.

Diener, E. (2000). Subjective well-being: The science of happiness and a proposal for a national index. *American Psychologist, 55*, 34–43.

Diener, E., Sandvik, E., & Pavot, W. (1991). Happiness is the frequency, not the intensity, of positive versus negative affect. In F. Strack, M. Argyle, & N. Schwarz (Eds.), *Subjective well-being: An interdisciplinary perspective* (pp. 119–139). Oxford, UK: Pergamon Press.

Džuka, J. (2001). Time sampling of unemployment experiences by Slovak youth. In H. Brandstätter & A. Eliasz (Eds.), *Persons, situations, and emotions: An ecological approach* (pp. 147–162). New York: Oxford University Press.

Eaton, L. G., & Funder, D. C. (2001). Emotional experience in daily life: Valence, variability, and rate of change. *Emotion, 1*, 413–421.

Eid, M., & Diener, E. (1999). Intraindividual variability in affect: Reliability, validity, and personality correlates. *Journal of Personality and Social Psychology, 76*, 626–676.

Fahrenberg, J., & Myrtek, M. (Eds.). (1996). *Ambulatory assessment: Computer assisted psychological and psychophysiological methods in monitoring and field studies.* Seattle, WA: Hogrefe & Huber.

Feldman Barrett, L. (2004). Feelings or words? Understanding the content of self-report ratings of experienced emotions. *Journal of Personality and Social Psychology, 87*, 266–281.

Feldman Barrett, L., & Barrett, D. J. (2001). An introduction to computerized experience sampling in psychology. *Social Science Computer Review, 19*, 175–185.

Fleeson, W. (2001). Toward a structure- and process-integrated view of personality traits as density distributions of states. *Journal of Personality and Social Psychology, 80*, 1011–1027.

Fleeson, W., & Cantor, N. (1995). Goal relevance and the affective experience of daily life: Ruling out situational explanations. *Motivation and Emotion, 19*, 25–57.

Flügel, J. C. (1925). A quantitative study of feeling and emotion in everyday life. *British Journal of Psychology, 15*, 318–355.

Flügel, J. C. (1955). *Studies in feeling and desire.* Bristol, UK: Western Printing Services.

Foster, S. L., Laventry-Finch, C., Gizzo, D. P., & Osantowski, J. (1999). Practical issues in self-observation. *Psychological Assessment, 11*, 426–438.

Goldstein, H. (1995). *Multilevel models in educational and social research.* London: Griffin.

Green, A. S., Rafaeli, E, Bolger, N., Shrout, P. E., & Reis, H. T. (2006). Paper or plastic? Data equivalence in paper and electronic diaries. *Psychological Methods, 11*, 87–105.

Greenwald, A. G., & Banaji, M. R. (1995). Implicit social cognition: Attitudes, self-esteem, and stereotypes. *Psychological Review, 102*, 4–27.

Hawkley, L. C., Burleson, M. H., Berntson, G. G., & Cacioppo, J. T. (2003). Loneliness in everyday life: Cardiovascular activity, psychosocial context, and health behaviors. *Journal of Personality and Social Psychology, 85*, 105–120.

Hersey, R. B. (1929). Periodic emotional changes in male workers. *Personnel Journal, 7*, 459–465.

Hersey, R. B. (1932). Rate of production and emotional state. *Personnel Journal, 10*, 355–364.

Hormuth, S. E. (1986). The time sampling of experience in situ. *Journal of Personality, 54*, 262–293.

Hurlburt, R. T. (1979). Random sampling of cognitions and behavior. *Journal of Research in Personality, 13*, 103–111.

Hurlburt, R. T. (1997). Randomly sampling thinking in the natural environment. *Journal of Consulting and Clinical Psychology, 65*, 941–949.

Hurlburt, R. T., & Heavey, C. L. (2001). Telling what we know: Describing inner experience. *Trends in Cognitive Sciences, 5*, 400–403.

Hussong, A. M., Hicks, R. E., Levy, S. A., & Curran, P. J. (2001). Specifying the relations between affect and heavy alcohol use among young adults. *Journal of Abnormal Psychology, 110*, 449–461.

Ilies, R., & Judge, T. A. (2002). Understanding the dynamic relationships among personality, mood, and job satisfaction: A field experience sampling study. *Organizational Behavior and Human Decision Processes, 89*, 1119–1139.

Judge, T. A., & Ilies, R. (2004). Affect and job satisfaction: A study of their relationship at work and home. *Journal of Applied Psychology, 89*, 661–673.

Kahneman, D., Wakker, P. P., & Sarin, R. (1997). Back to Bentham? Explorations of experienced utility. *Quarterly Journal of Economics, 112*, 375–405.

Kette, G. (1991). *Haft: Eine sozialpsychologische Analyse* [Imprisonment: A social-psychological analysis]. Göttingen, Germany: Hogrefe.

Kirchler, E. (1984). Befinden von Wehrpflichtigen in Abhängigkeit von personellen und situativen Gegebenheiten [Subjective well-being of recruits as function of personal and situational characteristics]. *Psychologie und Praxis. Zeitschrift für Arbeits- und Organisationspsychologie, 28*, 16–25.

Kirchler, E. (1985). Job loss and mood. *Journal of Economic Psychology, 6*, 9–25.

Kirchler, E. (1989). Everyday life experiences at home: An interaction diary approach to assess marital relationships. *Journal of Family Psychology, 3*, 311–336.

Kiss, G., Dornai, E., & Brandstätter, H. (2001). Freedom as moderator of the personality-mood relationship. In H. Brandstätter & A. Eliasz (Eds.), *Persons, situations, and emotions: An ecological approach* (pp. 199–214). New York: Oxford University Press.

Klinger, E. (1984). A consciousness-sampling analysis of test anxiety and performance. *Journal of Personality and Social Psychology, 47*, 1376–1390.

Lambie, J. A., & Marcel, A. J. (2002). Consciousness and the varieties of emotion experience: A theoretical framework. *Psychological Review, 109*, 219–259.

Laurenceau, J. P., & Bolger, N. (2005). Using diary methods to study marital and family processes. *Journal of Family Psychology, 19*, 86–97.

Lischetzke, T., Eid, M., Wittig, F., & Trierweiler, L. (2001). Die Wahrnehmung eigener und fremder Gefühle: Konstruktion und Validierung von Skalen zur Erfassung der emotionalen Selbst- und Fremdaufmerksamkeit sowie der Klarheit über Gefühle [Perceiving the feelings of oneself and others: Construction and validation of scales assessing the attention to and the clarity of feelings]. *Diagnostica, 47*, 167–177.

Matjasko, J. L., & Feldman, A. F. (2006). Bringing work home: The emotional experience of mothers and fathers. *Journal of Family Psychology, 20*, 47–55.

Miner, A. G., Glomb, T. M., & Hulin, C. (2005). Experience sampling mood and its correlates at work. *Journal of Occupational and Organizational Psychology, 78*, 171–193.

Moskowitz, D. S. (1994). Cross-situational generality and the interpersonal circumplex. *Journal of Personality and Social Psychology, 66*, 921–933.

Nolen-Hoeksema, S., & Morrow, J. (1993). Effects of rumination and distraction on naturally occurring depressed moods. *Cognition and Emotion, 7*, 561–570.

Norem, J. K., & Illingworth, K. S. S. (1993). Strategy-dependent effects of reflecting on self and tasks: Some implications of optimism and defensive pessimism. *Journal of Personality and Social Psychology, 65*, 822–835.

Oatley, K., & Jenkins, J. M. (1996). *Understanding emotions*. Cambridge, MA: Blackwell.

O'Connor, S. C., & Rosenblood, L. K. (1996). Affiliation motivation in everyday experience. A theoretical comparison. *Journal of Personality and Social Psychology, 70*, 513–522.

Oisi, S., Diener, E., Scollon, C. N., & Biswas-Diener, R. (2004). Cross-situational consistency of affective experiences across cultures. *Journal of Personality and Social Psychology, 86*, 460–472.

Peeters, F., Nicolson, N. A., Berkhof, J., Delespaul, P., & deVries, M. (2003). Effects of daily events on mood states in major depressive disorder. *Journal of Abnormal Psychology, 112*, 203–211.

Penner, L. A., Shiffman, S., Paty, J. A., & Fritzsche, B. A. (1994). Individual differences in intraperson variability in mood. *Journal of Personality and Social Psychology, 66*, 712–721.

Räikkönen, K., Matthews, K. A., Flory, J. D., Owens, J. F., & Gump, B. B. (1999). Effects of optimism, pessimism, and trait anxiety on ambulatory blood pressure and mood during everyday life. *Journal of Personality and Social Psychology, 76*, 104–113.

Rasbash, J., Steele, F., Browne, W. & Prosser, B.. (2005). *A user's guide to MLwiN*. (Version 2.0). Bristol, UK: Centre for Multilevel Modelling, University of Bristol.

Rathunde, K., & Csikszentmihalyi, M. (2005). Middle school students' motivation and quality of experience: A comparison of Montessori and traditional school environment. *American Journal of Education, 111*, 341–371.

Raudenbush, S. W., & Bryk, A. S. (2002). *Hierarchical linear models* (2nd ed.). Newbury Park, CA: Sage.

Reymert, M. L. (1928). *Feelings and emotions: The Wittenberg Symposium*. Worcester, MA: Clark University Press.

Russell, J. A. (1980). A circumplex model of affect. *Journal of Personality and Social Psychology, 39*, 1161–1178.

Russell, J. A. (2003). Core affect and the psychological construction of emotion. *Psychological Review, 110*, 145–172.

Sandvik, E., Diener, E., & Seidlitz, L. (1993). Subjective well-being: The convergence and stability of self-report and non-self-report measures. *Journal of Personality, 61*, 317–342.

Schneewind, K. A., Schröder, G., & Cattell, R. B. (1983). *Der 16-Persönlichkeits-Faktoren-Test—16PF* [The 16 Personality Factors Test—16PF]. Bern, Switzerland: Huber.

Sen, A. (1999). The possibility of social choice. *American Economic Review, 89,* 349–378.

Sheldon, K. M., Elliot, A. J., Kim, Y., & Kasser, T. (2001). What is satisfying about satisfying events? Testing 10 candidate psychological needs. *Journal of Personality and Social Psychology, 80,* 325–339.

Swendsen, J. D. (1998). The helplessness-hopelessness theory and daily mood experience: An idiographic and cross-situational perspective. *Journal of Personality and Social Psychology, 74,* 1398–1408.

Swendsen, J. D., Tennen, H., Carney, M. A., Affleck, G., Willard, A., & Hromi, A. (2000). Mood and alcohol consumption: An experience sampling test of the self-medication hypothesis. *Journal of Abnormal Psychology, 109,* 198–204.

Swinkels, A., & Giuliano, T. A. (1995). The measurement and conceptualization of mood awareness: Monitoring and labeling one's mood states. *Personality and Social Psychology Bulletin, 21,* 934–949.

Tennen, H., Suls, J., & Affleck, G. (1991). Personality and daily experience: The promise and the challenge. *Journal of Personality, 59,* 331–337.

Thomae, H. (1988). Das Individuum und seine Welt [The individual and his/her world]. (2nd ed.). Göttingen, Germany: Hogrefe.

Totterdell, P. (1999). Mood scores: Mood and performance in professional cricketers. *British Journal of Psychology, 90,* 317–332.

Totterdell, P., & Holman, D. (2003). Emotion regulation in customer service roles: Testing a model of emotional labor. *Journal of Occupational Health Psychology, 8,* 55–73.

Totterdell, P., Kellett, S., Teuchmann, K., & Briner, R. B. (1998). Evidence of mood linkage in work groups. *Journal of Personality and Social Psychology, 74,* 1504–1515.

Totterdell, P., & Parkinson, B. (1999). Use and effectiveness of self-regulation strategies for improving mood in a group of trainee teachers. *Journal of Occupational Health Psychology, 4,* 219–232.

Triemer, A., & Rau, R. (2001). Stimmungskurven im Arbeitsalltag—eine Feldstudie [Mood curves at normal working days—A field study]. *Zeitschrift für Differentielle und Diagnostische Psychologie, 22,* 42–55.

Tugade, M. M., Frederickson, B. L., & Feldman Barrett L. (2004). Psychological resilience and positive emotional granularity: Examining the benefits of positive emotions on coping and health. *Journal of Personality, 72,* 1161–1190.

Updegraff, J. A., Gable, S. L., & Taylor, S. E. (2004). What makes experiences satisfying? The interaction of approach-avoidance motivations and emotions in well-being. *Journal of Personality and Social Psychology, 86,* 496–504.

Weiner, B. (1986). *An attributional theory of motivation and emotion.* New York: Springer.

Wells, A. J. (1988). Variations in mothers' self-esteem in daily life. *Journal of Personality and Social Psychology, 55,* 661–668.

Wheeler, L., & Reis, H. T. (1991). Self-recording of everyday life events: Origins, types, and uses. *Journal of Personality, 59,* 339–354.

Wicklund, R. A. (1975). Objective self-awareness. *Advances in Experimental Social Psychology, 8,* 233–275.

David Matsumoto

Seung Hee Yoo

Methodological Considerations in the Study of Emotion Across Cultures

The study of emotion across cultures has played an important role in the history of research on emotion and promises to make important contributions in the future. Conducting emotion studies in different cultures well requires care and attention to a host of methodological issues that are specific to cross-cultural research. Gone are the days when researchers can simply take what they have developed in one culture and simply "plug it in" to another. The goal of this chapter is to introduce readers to what those methodological issues are, with the ultimate goal of aiding in the conduct of methodologically sound cross-cultural studies in the future.

We begin our discussion with a brief historical review of cross-cultural research on emotion, focusing on its impact on contemporary studies of emotion today. We then turn to a discussion of the definition of culture, as we strongly believe that cross-cultural studies need to be conducted within a well-defined conceptual understanding of what culture is in the first place. We then introduce the various types of cross-cultural studies that exist and then discuss in greater depth the methodological issues that are associated with the conduct of the most common types of cross-cultural research. In a final section we focus on methodological issues that pertain to the conduct of a specific line of inquiry having to do with possible in-group advantage effects in emotion recognition. We hope that these discussions will help interested readers to improve their own future studies of emotion across cultures.

The Study of Emotion Across Cultures

Historical Perspective

Most modern-day studies of emotion and culture are rooted in the work of Darwin, who in *The Expression of Emotion in Man and Animals* (Darwin, 1872/1998) suggested that emotions and their expressions had evolved across species and were evolutionarily adaptive, biologically innate, and universal across human and nonhuman primates. According to Darwin, all humans, regardless of race or culture, possessed the ability to express emotions in exactly the same ways, primarily through their faces.

Darwin's work, although influential and provocative, was supported only by his own observations and descriptions of emotional expression in humans and other animals and lacked scientific proof. Between Darwin's original writing and the 1960s, only seven studies attempted to address this gap by conducting more systematic research on the issue. These studies, however, were methodologically flawed in a number of ways, so that unequivocal data speaking to the issue of the possible universality of emotional expression did not emerge (see Ekman, Friesen, & Ellsworth, 1972, for a review).

It was not until the mid-1960s that psychologist Sylvan Tomkins joined forces independently with Paul Ekman and Carroll Izard to conduct what have become known as the universality studies. They obtained judgments in many cultures of faces that were thought to express emotions panculturally (see Ekman, 1972, 1973; Izard, 1971, for reviews) and demonstrated the existence of six universal expressions—anger, disgust, fear, happiness, sadness, and surprise.

The judgment studies in literate cultures conducted by Ekman and Izard were not the only evidence that came to support emotion universality. Ekman and his colleague Wallace Friesen also demonstrated that judgments by members of preliterate cultures were consistent with the notion of universality, as were judgments of expressions posed by members of preliterate cultures (Ekman, 1973). They also showed that the expressions that spontaneously occurred in reaction to emotion-eliciting films were universal (Ekman, 1972). Other scientists have shown that the same expressions occur in nonhuman primates and congenitally blind individuals (Charlesworth & Kreutzer, 1973; Geen, 1992) and correspond to similarities in emotion taxonomies in different languages around the world (Romney, Boyd, Moore, Batchelder, & Brazill, 1996; Romney, Moore, & Rusch, 1997; Shaver, Murdaya, & Fraley, 2001; Shaver, Wu, & Schwartz, 1992). Since the original universality studies in the late 1960s, many studies have replicated the universal recognition of these expressions across many studies and methodologies, not only in the face (Matsumoto, 2001) but also across other channels of communication as well (Elfenbein & Ambady, 2002b). Thus the universal basis for emotional expression is no longer debated in contemporary psychology and is considered a pancultural aspect of psychological functioning.

We also know, however, that people modify their expressions on the basis of *cultural display rules* (Ekman & Friesen, 1969). These are culturally prescribed rules learned early in life that dictate the management and modification of the universal expressions depending on social circumstance. Their existence was demonstrated empirically in Ekman and Friesen's (Ekman, 1972) study of American and Japanese participants viewing stressful films alone and in the presence of an experimenter. When alone, they displayed the same expressions of disgust, anger, fear, and sadness; with the experimenter, however, there were dramatic differences. Whereas the Americans continued to show their negative feelings, many Japanese smiled to conceal their negative feelings. Ekman and Friesen reckoned that cultural display rules were operating that prevented the free expression of negative emotions in the presence of another person in the Japanese culture. Today the existence of both universality and cultural display rules is well accepted in mainstream psychology (see also the Fridlund, 1997, view of display rules).

nal of emotion, both Ekman and Izard developed methods of measuring facial behaviors validly and reliably. Ekman and Friesen's Facial Action Coding System (FACS; Ekman & Friesen, 1978) is widely recognized as the most comprehensive tool for analyzing facial movements. It involves the identification of the appearance changes associated with more than 40 separate and functionally independent anatomical units that can move in the face at any one time. Using it, researchers can code the muscles involved in any facial expression, along with their timing characteristics (onset, apex, offset), intensity, and laterality.

The development of techniques such as FACS, along with the theoretical contributions of universal emotions, has led to a plethora of new research, theory, and application in psychology in the past 30 years. Notions concerning the universality of emotion and facial measurement techniques have made enormous contributions to studies in all areas of psychology and, in particular, social, personality, neuroscience, health, abnormal, and developmental psychology (Davidson, Scherer, & Goldsmith, 2002). Universality and FACS led to much of the research on infants and children concerning the emergence of emotions and their expressions in development. Universality and FACS helped to answer age-old questions concerning the specificity of physiological responses during emotions (Coan, Allen, & Harmon-Jones, 2001; Ekman, 1992a, 1992b, 1992c, 1992d, 1999; Ekman, Levenson, & Friesen, 1983; Levenson, Ekman, & Friesen, 1990; Levenson, Ekman, Heider, & Friesen, 1992). Universality and FACS led to research documenting the universality of emotion antecedents (Scherer, 1997a, 1997b), psychological themes underlying antecedents (Ekman, 2003), and subjective experience (Scherer & Wallbott, 1994). Studies involving faces and emotions have also made substantial contributions to a number of areas of psychology, with applications in clinical, forensic, industrial, and organizational psychology. An increasing number of universities are offering programs that specialize in the study of emotion, and funding sources are increasing to provide specialized training to pre- and postdoctoral candidates to develop further research in the area. The number of books, chapters, and articles on emotion has increased tremendously over the past 30 years, as has the number of theses and dissertations, due in part to the legitimacy of emotion research. Scientific journals such as *Motivation and Emotion, Cognition and Emotion,* and most recently the APA journal *Emotion* have all emerged as a result of the coming of age of emotion research. All of this has been made possible through the contributions of the original cross-cultural research on emotional expressions.

The Impact of the Discovery of Universal Emotions on Contemporary Psychology

The discovery of the universal basis for emotional expression has had an enormous impact on contemporary psychology. Because expressions provided an objective and reliable signal

The Breadth of Cross-Cultural Research on Emotion Today

Not only have the original universality studies had a considerable impact on mainstream, contemporary psychology, but they have also served as an important platform for continued work investigating the relation between culture and emotion. For example, cross-cultural research continues to show many ways in which cultures are similar in how they judge emotions. As mentioned earlier, many studies since Ekman and Izard's original research have tested the recognition of emotion in facial expressions across cultures, replicating the universality findings. In the past decade a number of studies have reported the existence of a seventh universal facial expression of emotion, contempt (Ekman & Friesen, 1986; Ekman & Heider, 1988; Matsumoto, 1992b). A recent study (Haidt & Keltner, 1999) also raises the possibility of a universal expression of embarrassment. People of different countries agree on which is more strongly expressed when comparing expressions of the same emotion (Ekman et al., 1987; Matsumoto & Ekman, 1989) in the association between perceived expression intensity and inferences about subjective experience (Matsumoto, Kasri, & Kooken, 1999), identification of secondary emotion portrayed in an emotion (Ekman et al., 1987; Matsumoto & Ekman, 1989), and stereotypes about the expressivity of people from other countries (Pittam, Gallois, Iwawaki, & Kroonenberg, 1995).

Cultural differences in judgments have also been found. For instance, there are reliable cultural differences in the levels of agreement in emotion recognition across cultures (Biehl et al., 1997; Elfenbein & Ambady, 2002b; Matsumoto, 1992a). Cultural differences also exist in attributions of personality based on smiles (Matsumoto & Kudoh, 1993), attribution of intensity of facial expressions (Biehl et al., 1997; Ekman et al., 1987; Matsumoto et al., 2002; Matsumoto & Ekman, 1989; Matsumoto et al., 1999), and inferences about the emotional experiences that underlie external display of facial expressions of emotion (Matsumoto et al., 2002; Matsumoto et al., 1999).

Although judgment is arguably the most well-studied area of culture and emotion, other aspects of emotion have also received considerable attention. For instance, a number of recent cross-cultural studies have examined cultural differences in emotional expression and cultural display rules. Waxer (1985) examined American and Canadian cultural differences in spontaneous emotional expressions by participants in television game shows and found that Americans tended to be judged as more expressive than the Canadians, despite no differences in actual behaviors. Matsumoto and his colleagues have examined cultural display rule differences between Japan and the United States (Matsumoto, 1990); the United States, Poland, and Hungary (Biehl, Matsumoto, & Kasri, in press); the United States, Japan, South Korea, and Russia (Matsumoto, Takeuchi, Andayani, Kouznetsova, & Krupp, 1998); the United States, Japan, and Russia (Matsumoto, Yoo, Hirayama, & Petrova, 2005), and among four ethnic groups within the United States (Matsumoto, 1993). Other research has also documented cross-cultural differences in expression among five European countries (Edelmann et al., 1987).

A number of studies during the past decade have also examined the antecedents of emotions across cultures. Led

mainly by a large-scale study conducted by Scherer and his colleagues, more than 3,000 participants in 37 countries described a situation in which they experienced the universal emotions (Scherer, Summerfield, & Wallbott, 1983; Scherer & Wallbott, 1994; Scherer, Wallbott, & Summerfield, 1986). Trained raters coded the situations described by participants into general categories, such as good news and bad news, temporary and permanent separation, or success or failure in achievement situations. No culture-specific category was necessary, indicating that all categories of events generally occurred in all cultures to produce each of the emotions studied. These researchers and others (Boucher & Brandt, 1981; Brandt & Boucher, 1985; Buunk & Hupka, 1987; Galati & Sciaky, 1995; Levy, 1973) have reported evidence of considerable cross-cultural similarity in emotion antecedents. To be sure, cross-cultural differences in the differential usage of emotion antecedent categories have also been reported (Scherer, Matsumoto, Wallbott, & Kudoh, 1988; see also review by Mesquita & Frijda, 1992).

A number of studies have examined cultural similarities and differences in emotional appraisal, as well. The largest cross-cultural study on appraisal processes is Scherer et al.'s (Scherer, et al., 1983; Scherer & Wallbott, 1994; Scherer, et al., 1986) large-scale study described earlier. After describing situations in which they experienced one of seven emotions, respondents answered questions designed to assess their appraisals of the events, including questions concerning novelty-expectation, intrinsic pleasantness, goal conduciveness, fairness, coping potential, norms, and self-ideals. Two studies reporting the analyses of these data (Scherer, 1997a, 1997b) indicated that, although differences existed between both emotions and countries, the differences according to country were much smaller than the differences according to emotion. That is, there were many more cultural similarities in emotion appraisal processes than there were cultural differences. Cultural similarities in emotion appraisal processes have also been reported by others (Mauro, Sato, & Tucker, 1992; Roseman, Dhawan, Rettek, & Naidu, 1995). Cultural differences are also reported in each of these studies; Roseman et al. (1995), in fact, suggest that cultural similarities may occur on more "primitive" dimensions of appraisal, whereas cultural differences may occur on more "complex" dimensions.

Scherer et al.'s (Scherer, et al., 1983; Scherer & Wallbott, 1994; Scherer, et al., 1986) large-scale studies have also been the most comprehensive to examine cultural influences on subjective emotional experience. In their study, participants provided self-report data concerning their subjective feeling states (e.g., intensity, duration, etc.), physiological symptoms, and behavioral reactions (e.g., nonverbal behaviors, verbal utterances, etc.). Although cultural differences existed, the differences among the emotions were much larger than the differences between cultures; that is, emotions appeared to share a more or less universal experiential base across cultures (see reviews in Scherer & Wallbott, 1994; Wallbott &

Scherer, 1986). To be sure, a number of writers take a more "functionalist" approach to describing emotional experience, suggesting that emotion is a set of "socially shared scripts" composed of physiological, behavioral, and subjective components that develop as individuals are enculturated (e.g., Kitayama & Markus, 1994; Kitayama & Markus, 1995; Markus & Kitayama, 1991; Shweder, 1993; Wierzbicka, 1994). Such a view argues against notions of universality in experiential basis, as emotions *have* to be as distinct as each culture is different. In reality, however, we do not view these approaches as mutually exclusive to each other.

The topic of cultural similarities and differences in the concept of emotion has also received considerable attention in the literature. A number of writers have suggested that there are substantial differences in the concept and definition of emotion across cultures and that some cultures have no concept of emotion, as we do in the American English language (Levy, 1973, 1983; Lutz, 1982, 1983; Russell, 1991). Cultures also apparently differ in what kinds of feeling states and words they use to describe and categorize emotions, in the location of emotions, and in the meaning of emotions to people, interpersonal relationships, and behavior (see Russell, 1991, for a review). Although these notions have been used to argue against the concept of universality in emotional expression, we do not believe that these are mutually exclusive to each other. Universality in a small set of emotional expressions and their underlying feeling states can coexist with substantial cultural differences in the linguistic coding of emotion via language across cultures.

A final, relatively new area of cross-cultural research on emotion concerns the influence of culture on human physiology during emotional reactions. The specificity of physiological response in emotion is a topic that has been widely debated in psychology for decades, with views varying extremely, to suggest on the one hand that physiological responses are not necessary at all (Mandler, 1984) and on the other hand that each emotion is associated with a specific physiological response pattern (James, 1890). Using universal facial expressions as markers, Ekman and his colleagues found the first systematic evidence for a distinct autonomic response for each of the six emotions tested in a sample of American participants (Ekman et al., 1983). Levenson and his colleagues have since extended these findings to include individuals from other groups, including Chinese Americans and the Minangkabau of Sumatra (Levenson et al., 1992; Tsai & Levenson, 1997). Future research in this area promises to further extend this line of inquiry, investigating also the possibility of specific patterning of central nervous system activity, as well.

As seen from this very quick review, cross-cultural studies on emotion have spanned a wide range of topics and have contributed important information to the literature on this aspect of human functioning. In order for future cross-cultural research to continue to flourish, it is important to have a solid conceptual definition of culture, a topic to which we now turn.

Defining Culture

Human Nature

In order to understand and define culture, one must inevitably start with some assumptions about human nature. The view of human nature that provides the best platform to account for not only pancultural universals, which are an important aspect of emotion, but also culture specifics is that of evolutionary psychology. This perspective suggests that people have evolved a set of motives and strivings that are ultimately related to reproductive success (Buss, 2001). Reproductive success and other biological functions such as eating and sleeping are biological imperatives if people are to survive.

In the evolutionary psychology perspective, survival is related to the degree to which people can adapt to their environments and to the contexts in which they live. Over the history of time people must have had to solve a host of distinct social problems in order to adapt and thus achieve reproductive success. These social problems include negotiating complex status hierarchies, forming successful work and social groups, attracting mates, fighting off potential rivals for food and sexual partners, giving birth and raising children, and battling nature (Buss, 1988, 1989, 1991, 2000, 2001). In fact, we need to do these things in our everyday lives today, as well. Thus universal biological imperatives have become associated with a universal set of psychological problems that people need to solve in order to survive. All individuals and groups of individuals have a universal problem of how to adapt to their environments in order to deal with their universal biological needs and functions and the imperative of reproductive success. Thus all individuals and groups of individuals must create ways to deal with these universal problems. These ways can be very specific to each group because the context in which each group lives—the physical environment, social factors, and types and sizes of their families and communities—are different. The ways that each group develops then become each group's culture.

Culture

Culture is created as people have adapted to their environments in order to survive. In our view, culture is the product of the interaction between universal biological needs and functions, universal social problems associated with those needs, and the context in which people live (see Figure 20.1). Culture results from the process of individuals' attempts to adapt to their contexts in addressing the universal social problems and biological needs.

Social scientists have been interested in culture and how it influences people for well over 100 years, and there have been many attempts at defining exactly what those biological and social needs are and the aspects of culture that address them. For example, Malinowski suggested that all

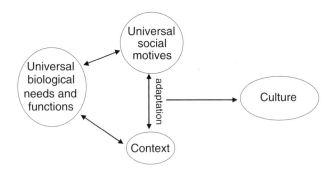

Figure 20.1. Culture as the product of the interaction between universal biological needs and functions, universal social motives to address those needs, and the contexts in which people live.

individuals had universal basic needs related to metabolism, reproduction, bodily comforts, safety, movement, growth, and health (Malinowski, 1927/1961, 1944/1960). According to Malinowski, all cultures must create ways to deal with each of these social motives, producing a cultural "response" that corresponds ultimately to the universal biological functions (see Table 20.1). Over the years there have been many different definitions of culture, with similarities as well as differences (Berry, Poortinga, Segall, & Dasen, 1992; Jahoda, 1984; Kroeber & Kluckholn, 1952/1963; Linton, 1936; Rohner, 1984; Triandis, 1972). In our work we define culture simply as *a shared system of socially transmitted behavior that describes, defines, and guides people's ways of life.*

The Characteristics of Culture

Culture touches on all aspects of our lives. It involves subjective and objective elements (Triandis, 1972). It explains differences in the types of foods we eat and how we eat them. It explains the clothes we wear and our home life. We use culture to describe our activities, values, attitudes, opinions, and beliefs and to describe our communities, religion, and even our government. We use culture to explain similarities

Table 20.1
Malinowski's conceptualization of basic needs and cultural responses

Basic Needs	Cultural Response
Metabolism	Commissariat
Reproduction	Kinship
Bodily comforts	Shelter
Safety	Protection
Movement	Activities
Growth	Training
Health	Hygiene

within and differences between groups of people (Tooby & Cosmides, 1992).

The subjective elements of culture are psychological. Culture influences many psychological processes, such as attitudes, beliefs, norms, opinions, values, and behaviors. Culture in this sense is like a syndrome, a constellation of separate but interrelated psychological components that collectively characterize a condition (Triandis, 1994).

Culture is always changing, even slowly. It is not a static entity, but a living, breathing one. What we commonly know as the "generation gap" is a cultural difference, as it refers to different ways of life and being for people who are raised in different periods of time (Pipher, 1998). Many countries around the world, including the United States, have undergone cultural changes across time and will continue to do so in the future as our ways of life change.

Culture exists on multiple levels. Individuals are part of small groups, and smaller groups are part of larger and even larger groups. Each group can have its own culture, and in this way culture can exist on many levels. This is true for different ethnic and community groups that live in a large country, such as the United States, as well as among different departments, sections, and work units of large companies.

Culture enhances survival. Cultures provide rules for living and tell people how to interact work and play with each other. Culture provides a hierarchy for decision making and sets the standards for group cooperation and divisions of labor. With culture, there is order; without culture, there is chaos. Even people who think they have no culture have a culture; it is just the culture to believe they have no culture. Culture is often difficult to perceive because we do not recognize alternative possibilities without having experienced them. That's why people learn as much about their own culture as they do about others when they travel to or live in new cultures. Of all the possible things people could do, culture helps to limit what we should do in order to survive in the environment in which we live (Poortinga, 1990).

Culture is communicated across generations. This ensures that many aspects of culture are durable. Beliefs and attitudes that become popular from time to time and that are shared by many people may be what we know of as "popular culture," but the culture we are concerned with here is more stable across time. Many elements of culture are communicated across generations, including the rules we learned when we were children, the holidays and cultural activities we celebrate, and the foods we eat at home.

Culture both enables behavior, allowing it to be created or invented, and constrains or restricts it (Adamopoulous & Lonner, 2001). On the one hand, the cultural dimension of individualism, for example, fosters uniqueness, independence, autonomy, and creativity. It provides the cultural framework within which behaviors can be invented. Jazz musicians, writers, poets, artists, rock stars, and even such disciplines as psychology can thrive and flourish in such an environment (Buss, 2001). On the other hand, culture also provides rules for constraining behavior. Laws exist in every country and culture of the world, and these laws define what is right and wrong, acceptable and not, in every land. Cultures also provide for social sanctions against inappropriate behavior. In many cultures shame is used as a powerful and important social sanction that limits behavior and keeps everyone in line. In many Asian cultures, the concept of "face" is important, and keeping and protecting one's face is as important as invention is in individualistic cultures (Oetzel et al., 2001).

Types of Cross-Cultural Studies

Now that we have defined culture, we turn our attention to issues pertaining to cross-cultural research. Because there are many different types of cross-cultural studies in the literature, it is important at the outset to elucidate them. In this section we outline five different types of cross-cultural studies. They generally describe the range of approaches to cross-cultural research. Like all research approaches, however, studies are as varied as the individuals who design and conduct them. The descriptions provided here, therefore, are not intended as exhaustive categorizations of the breadth of cross-cultural approaches; rather, they are general guidelines for the types of cross-cultural studies typically seen and conducted in the literature.

Cross-Cultural Comparisons

The first type of study to consider is the prototypical *cross-cultural comparison,* which compares two or more cultures on some psychological variable of interest, oftentimes with the hypothesis that one culture will have significantly higher scores on the variable than the other(s). In a strict experimentation sense, these studies are simply between-subject, between-group quasi-experimental designs in which specific cultures, typically operationalized by nationality, ethnicity, or race, serve as different levels of a culture factor. Thus all of the general considerations for the conduct of comparative studies of this sort apply to the conduct of cross-cultural comparisons as well.

The cross-cultural literature abounds with cross-cultural comparisons. Studies of this type document the existence of differences among cultures and are important to the psychological literature because they have tested the limitations of knowledge generated in mainstream psychological research and have helped to advance our theoretical and conceptual thinking in all areas of psychology. They have played a major role in cross-cultural psychology in the past.

Unpacking Studies

Recently there has been a call away from simple comparative research to studies that attempt to explain why cultural differences occur. These studies not only look for differences among cultures on their target variables but also include measurements of other variables that will account for those differences. These are known as *unpackaging studies,* as they unpackage the contents of the global, unspecific concept of culture into specific, measurable psychological constructs and examine their contribution to cultural differences. Poortinga and his colleagues likened these types of studies to the peeling of an onion—taking off layer after layer until nothing is left (Poortinga, van de Vijver, Joe, & van de Koppel, 1987). They viewed culture in the following way:

> In our approach culture is a summary label, a catchword for all kinds of behavior differences between cultural groups, but within itself, of virtually no explanatory value. Ascribing intergroup differences in behavior, e.g., in test performance, to culture does not shed much light on the nature of these differences. It is one of the main tasks of cross-cultural psychology to peel off cross-cultural differences, i.e., to explain these differences in terms of specific antecedent variables, until in the end they have disappeared and with them the variable culture. In our approach culture is taken as a concept without a core. From a methodological point of view, culture can be considered as an immense set of often loosely interrelated independent variables (cf. Segall, 1984; Strodtbeck, 1964). (p. 22)

These researchers suggest that culture as an unspecified variable should be replaced by more specific, measurable variables in order to truly explain cultural differences. These variables are called *context variables* and should be measured in a study to examine the degree to which they statistically account for cultural differences. Inferences about the nature of cultural differences can then incorporate the degree of contribution by the context variables. If the context variables do not account for all of the differences between cultures, then other context variables should be incorporated in subsequent research to further account for more of the differences among cultures until the differences are gone. In a strict experimentation sense, this approach is similar to that of identifying nuisance variables and using them as covariates or mediators to examine their contribution to between-group differences. In a theoretical sense, these studies play a large role in furthering knowledge of exactly what it is about cultures that produces differences in behavior.

Ecological-Level Studies

A third type of hypothesis-testing study in cross-cultural psychology involves countries or cultures as the unit of analysis. These studies are called *ecological-level studies.* Data may be obtained from individuals in those cultures, but they are often summarized or averaged for each culture, and those averages are used as data points for each culture, typically in a correlational analysis with means of other psychological variables of interest. Analyses based on this type of design are called *ecological,* or *cultural-level,* analyses, and they are different from traditional individual-level analyses in psychological research. Examples of such ecological-level analyses include Hofstede's studies of cultural values across more than 50 cultures (Hofstede, 1980, 1984), Triandis et al.'s study of the relationship between individualism and collectivism and incidence of heart attacks in eight cultures (Triandis et al., 1988), Matsumoto's study of the relationship between four cultural dimensions and incidence rates for six disease states in 28 cultures (Matsumoto & Fletcher, 1996), and Matsumoto's study of the relationship between cultural dimensions and judgments of emotion in 15 cultures (Matsumoto, 1989).

There are important differences in the interpretations that can be justified on the basis of ecological- versus individual-level research. A relationship between a cultural and a target variable on the ecological level does not necessarily mean that such a relationship exists on the individual level. For instance, demonstrating the existence of a correlation between ecological-level individualism and the incidence of heart disease does not necessarily mean that such a correlation can predict individual-level associations between the two variables. Even if such a relationship exists on the ecological level, the relationship may or may not exist on the individual level within the cultures studied and may or may not be in the same direction, even if it does exist (also see Leung, 1989). A positive correlation between culture and a psychological variable on the ecological level can be associated with a positive, negative, or no correlation between the same two variables on the individual level. Regardless of this caveat, however, ecological-level studies are important in elucidating the contribution of larger cultural systems to group-level psychological phenomena.

Cross-Cultural Validation Studies

A fourth type of cross-cultural study is that which examines the validity of a psychological test or measure across cultures. These are known as *cross-cultural validation studies.* They examine whether a measure of a psychological construct that was originally generated in a single culture is applicable, meaningful, and thus equivalent in another culture. These studies do not test a specific hypothesis about cultural differences per se; rather, they test the equivalence of psychological measures and tests for use in other cross-cultural comparative research. Although these types of studies are not as common as hypothesis-testing cross-cultural research, they serve an important purpose in investigating the cross-cultural applicability of many of the methodological techniques used in research and in establishing equivalence in measurement, which, as we discuss later, is a vital aspect of cross-cultural research.

Ethnographies

Finally, a fifth type of cross-cultural study, one that is more prevalent in psychological anthropology than in cross-cultural psychology per se, is that known as *ethnography.* These studies typically involve fieldwork, with the researchers visiting and oftentimes living together with the people they are interested in studying. Being immersed in a culture for an extended period of time, researchers learn firsthand the customs, rituals, traditions, beliefs, and ways of life of the culture to which they are exposed. Comparisons with other cultures are done on the basis of their knowledge, experience, and education about their own and other cultures. This approach is not unlike the case study of individual lives, with cultures serving as the larger unit of analysis. As such, much of the advantages of that approach, including the richness and complexity of the data obtained, are applicable, as is the disadvantage of their lack of generalizability. Ethnographies serve an important purpose in the field, complementing existing hypothesis-testing research on specific psychological variables. Important examples of such ethnographic work on emotion include Levy's work in Tahiti (Levy, 1973) and Lutz's work on the Ifaluks (Lutz, 1982, 1983).

General Issues in Cross-Cultural Research Methodology

In this section we consider methodological issues that underlie the conduct of cross-cultural research. There are many different such issues, and space limitations do not permit a full discussion of many of them; interested readers are referred to Matsumoto (2003) for a fuller discussion of the problems and possible solutions. Here we focus exclusively on cross-cultural comparisons, and on only a few issues within that topic, namely, sampling, measurement, and data equivalence. We begin with a discussion of the concept of equivalence.

Equivalence (and Bias)

In reality, there are only a few issues specific to the conduct of cross-cultural research that set it apart from general experimentation; the same problems and solutions that are typically used to describe issues concerning experimental methodology in general can and should be applied to most, if not all, cross-cultural comparisons. Most of the issues raised in this section, therefore, with the notable exception of language issues, are generally true of "good" experimentation in monocultural studies, as well. Cross-cultural research, however, has been useful in highlighting them.

One concept that is of crucial importance in the conduct and evaluation of all aspects of cross-cultural comparison is that of equivalence and its corresponding construct, bias. (Bias is generally viewed as nonequivalence and, for this reason, we will generally refer to equivalence only.) Equivalence in cross-cultural research can be defined as a state or condition of similarity in conceptual meaning and empirical method between cultures that allows comparisons to be meaningful. In a strict sense, the greater the nonequivalence (thus bias) of any aspect of a cross-cultural study in meaning or method across the cultures being compared, the less meaningful the comparison. Lack of equivalence in a cross-cultural study creates the proverbial situation of comparing apples and oranges. If, however, the theoretical framework and hypotheses have generally equivalent meaning in the cultures being compared, and if the methods of data collection, management, and analysis have equivalent meanings, only then are the results from that comparison meaningful. Of course, this is true in any between-group comparison study.

The perfectly equivalent cross-cultural study is an impossibility; there will always be some aspects of the comparison that are not perfectly equivalent to each other. Thus it is probably more accurate to suggest that for cross-cultural comparisons to be valid and meaningful, they have to be "equivalent enough." The difficult part of this concept, however, that frustrates students and researchers alike is that there is no direct method, no mathematical formula, no easy way to determine what is "equivalent enough." Sometimes a study may have a lot of little nonequivalences but still be meaningful. Sometimes a study may have one fatal nonequivalence and thus be meaningless. These issues differ from study to study, and we cannot tell you here what the fatal flaw will always be. As usual, experience and conscientiousness are probably two of the best teachers.

Sampling Equivalence

Sampling Adequacy

Researchers need to ensure that the participants in their study are adequate representatives of the cultures that they are supposed to represent. More often than not researchers assume that people who happen to fit into the categorical label of culture as operationalized (e.g., by nationality) are "good" representatives of that particular culture. Doing so often results in an unacceptable assumption of homogeneity among the participants with regard to culture that can, in its worse sense, only serve to perpetuate stereotypic impressions and interpretations based on the findings. When differences are found, researchers assume that the differences are "cultural" because they assume that the samples are representatives of culture.

Although this issue is relatively straightforward and easy to understand, in practice it is extremely difficult to achieve. In its strictest sense, proper addressing of this issue would require the following steps: (1) the researcher would have to be able to define theoretically what the cultures are that are being tested; (2) the researcher would have to be able to

access a pool of individuals from the larger population that embodied those characteristics; (3) the researcher would have to randomly sample from that larger population; and (4) the researcher would have to measure those social, cultural, and psychological characteristics in their participants and empirically demonstrate that their cultural manipulations occurred as intended.

Unfortunately, this is a tall order that is not, and perhaps cannot, be filled currently because of the limitations to our abilities to theorize about and subsequently measure culture on the individual level and our inability to randomly access all members of any given cultural population. Given that we cannot achieve this ideal, the real issue facing researchers concerns the degree to which they understand how far from this ideal they are and how much they use this information to temper their interpretations. In a practical sense, a sound cross-cultural comparison would entail the collection of data from multiple sites within the same cultural group, either in the same study or across studies, to demonstrate the replicability of a finding across different samples within the same culture.

Noncultural, Demographic Equivalence

Because of the real possibility of nonequivalence in sampling, researchers need to ensure that the differences they obtain in a study are due to culture and not to any other noncultural demographic variables on which the samples may differ. That is, researchers need to make sure that the samples they compare are equivalent on variables such as gender, age, socioeconomic status (SES), educational level, religious orientation, geographic area (e.g., rural vs. urban), and such. If they are not equivalent on noncultural, demographic variables, then those variables on which they are not equivalent may confound the comparison.

The conceptual problem that arises in cross-cultural research, which is not as apparent in monocultural studies, is that some noncultural demographic characteristics are *inextricably* intertwined with culture such that researchers cannot hold them constant across samples in a comparison. For example, there are differences in the meaning and practice of religions across cultures that oftentimes make them inextricably bound to culture. Holding religion constant across cultures does not address the issue, because being Catholic in the United States just does not mean the same thing as being Catholic in Japan or Malaysia. Randomly sampling without regard to religion will result in samples that are different not only on culture but also on religion (to the extent that one can separate the two influences). Thus presumed cultural differences often reflect religious differences across samples, as well. The same is oftentimes also true for SES, as there are vast differences in SES across cultural samples from around the world.

Despite these difficulties, researchers should take care to conduct thorough demographic assessments of their samples whenever possible, especially going beyond the standard sex and age questions. They should also then control for demographic differences in analyzing data by holding them constant or eliminating their statistical contributions to the target variables.

Measurement Equivalence

Conceptual Equivalence

Researchers need to ensure that the psychological variables being measured in their studies are conceptually equivalent across the cultures being compared. Different cultures may conceptually define constructs such as intelligence, self, personality, and emotion differently. Clearly, just because something has the same name in two or more cultures does not mean that it refers to the same thing in those cultures (Wittgenstein, 1953, cited in Poortinga, 1989). If a concept means different things to people of different cultures, then there is a lack of equivalence in the definition of the construct, and comparisons of cultures based on nonequivalent constructs will lack meaning. Researchers who wish to compare cultures on psychological constructs, therefore, have the onus of demonstrating, either empirically or conceptually, that the constructs themselves are equivalent across the cultures being compared.

Empirical Equivalence

Even if a construct is conceptually equivalent across cultures, reliable and valid measurement of it may take different forms across cultures. Concretely, this requires that researchers use measures that have been empirically demonstrated to measure the construct of interest reliably and validly in the cultures being studied. Simply taking an existing test developed in one culture and translating it for use in other cultures is not methodologically adequate, although this has often been done. Cross-cultural validations often require extensive testing in the target cultures in order to establish a reasonable number of reliability and validity parameters, especially with regard to convergent and predictive validity. Questionnaires that involve multiple scales and items will need to have been tested to establish the cross-cultural equivalence of item and scale meaning, especially concerning equivalence in factor structures and item loadings.

For example, one applied cross-cultural study examined how emotion displays of French and American political leaders on TV affect voters in France and the United States, respectively (Masters & Sullivan, 1989). The researchers showed videoclips of political leaders of participants' own countries displaying three types of emotion (happiness, anger, fear) to French and American judges and obtained ratings of the behavior of the political leaders, self-reports of their own emotional responses, and attitudes toward politics, leaders, and the media. The measures were back-translated (see the next subsection), and the French version was pretested to confirm that scales were used in the same way with French participants as they were with the American participants, offering some evidence of convergent validity. Self-reports of emotional response were factor analyzed separately for each culture and were found to have similar factor structures, providing evidence that measures and procedure in both cultures were equivalent.

Still, factor equivalence is only one step in establishing the empirical equivalence of measures across cultures. These are not easy issues to deal with, and cross-validation is not as easy as it seems. Some writers have suggested that tests of psychological abilities are inherently incomparable across cultures. Greenfield, for example, argues that constructs such as intelligence and cognitive ability are inherently symbolic products of a culture (Greenfield, 1997). As such, the constructs and tests of it presuppose a certain cultural framework in the first place in order to be valid. As these frameworks are not usually universally shared, cross-cultural comparisons of ability and intelligence therefore become meaningless. A similar argument has been raised about emotion, as well (Kitayama & Markus, 1994; Markus & Kitayama, 1991; Shweder, 1999).

Poortinga (1989) has suggested that when a measure has high content validity in all cultures being tested and when the construct being measured is in a psychological domain that is similar or identical across cultures (e.g., color schemes, pitch scale for tones), valid comparisons are generally possible. When unobservable psychological traits and attributes of individuals are being measured, comparison may be possible, as long as equivalence in the conceptual meaning of the psychological domain and its measurement in all participating cultures have been established. Other than these two situations, all other research situations, according to Poortinga (1989), preclude valid comparison across cultures.

Linguistic Equivalence

Cross-cultural research often cannot be conducted solely in one language, because the samples being tested are frequently composed of two or more distinct language groups. Researchers need to ensure that the research protocols used in their studies are linguistically equivalent across the cultures being compared. Two procedures are generally used to establish linguistic equivalence. One is known as back translation (Brislin, 1970), which involves taking the research protocol in one language, translating it to the other language(s), and having someone else translate it back to the original. The second approach is to utilize a committee approach in which several bilingual informants collectively translate a research protocol into a target-language on a consensual basis. A third approach is combines the first two approaches.

Regardless of the approach, a major caveat for researchers here is that "closest semantic equivalent" does not mean "the same." Getting protocols that are "the same" is probably impossible. Even if the words being used in the two languages are the agreed-on translations, there is no guarantee that those words have exactly the same meanings, with the same nuances, across cultures. There is also the additional problem of the difference between linguistic and cultural equivalence. That is, you can have a protocol that is linguistically equivalent to its original in another language but that just does not make sense in the target language. In this case the researcher needs to make a decision concerning whether to go with the literal translation, which may be awkward and difficult to interpret but is the closest semantic equivalent, or with the cultural translation, which will make sense but is not linguistically equivalent.

Data Equivalence

Cultural Response Sets

Cultural response sets are tendencies for members of a culture to use certain parts of a scale when responding. For example, participants of culture A in a two-culture comparison may tend to use the entire scale, whereas participants of culture B may tend to use only a part of the scale (e.g., the middle). These tendencies may exist for several reasons, including cultural differences in attitudes and values regarding self-expression of personal opinions. There have been numerous suggestions in the past that members of collectivistic cultures hesitate to use the extreme end points of a scale, in congruence with a cultural hesitation to "stick out" that results in the use of the middle of a scale. There have also been some studies that have shown tendencies for members of some cultural groups to use the end points. Bachman and O'Malley (1984), for example, found such evidence in extreme response styles among African Americans, and Marin and colleagues found similar evidence for Hispanics (Marin, Gamba, & Marin, 1992).

When analyzing data, researchers need to be aware of the possible existence of cultural response sets and, if they do exist, to deal with them. If they exist, cultural response sets may confound between-culture differences because it is difficult to know whether differences are occurring because of response sets or because of "meaningful" differences in real scores on the target variables of interest.

Effect-Size Analyses

Cultural differences in mean values on any scale do not readily predict how individuals are different between cultures. Statistical significance does not mean "practical" significance in a realistic or pragmatic sense, especially because statistical significance is so dependent on sample size. One mistake that researchers and consumers of research alike make when interpreting group differences is that they assume that most people of those groups differ in ways that correspond to the mean values. Thus, if a statistically significant difference is found between Americans and Japanese on emotional expressivity such that Americans had statistically significantly higher scores than the Japanese, people often conclude that all Americans are more expressive than all Japa-

nese. This is, of course, a mistake in interpretation that is fueled by the field's fascination and single-minded concern with statistical significance and perhaps with cultural myths that are easy to perpetuate.

In reality, statistical procedures exist that help to determine the degree to which differences in mean values reflect meaningful differences among individuals. The general class of statistics that do this is called *effect-size statistics*, and, when they are used in a cross-cultural setting, Matsumoto and his colleagues called them cultural-effect-size statistics (Matsumoto, Grissom, & Dinnel, 2001). It is beyond the scope of this chapter to present them in detail; Matsumoto et al. (2001) present four such statistics that they deemed most relevant for cross-cultural analyses, with reanalyses from two previously published studies on emotion as examples. Whether cross-cultural researchers use these or others, it is incumbent on them to include some kind of effect-size analysis when comparing cultures so that informed readers can determine the degree to which the differences reported reflect meaningful differences among people.

Dealing With Nonequivalent Data

Despite the best attempts to establish equivalence in theory, hypothesis, method, and data management, cross-cultural comparisons are often inextricably, inherently, and inevitably nonequivalent. It is virtually impossible to create any cross-cultural study that means exactly the same thing to all people in all participating cultures, both conceptually and empirically. What cross-cultural researchers often end up with are best approximations of the closest equivalents in terms of theory and method in a study.

Thus researchers are often faced with the question of how to deal with nonequivalent data. Poortinga (1989) outlined four different ways in which the problem of nonequivalence of cross-cultural data can be handled:

1. Preclude comparison. The most conservative thing a researcher could do is to not make the comparison in the first place, concluding that such a comparison would be meaningless.

2. Reduce the nonequivalence in the data. Many researchers engage in steps to identify equivalent and nonequivalent parts of their methods and then refocus their comparisons solely on the equivalent parts. For example, to compare perceptions of teacher immediacy in the United States and Japan, Neuliep (1997) asked American and Japanese university students to complete the Verbal Immediacy Behaviors Scale, the Nonverbal Immediacy Measure, and various ratings of attitudes toward content of course, attitudes toward teacher, likelihood of using behaviors taught in class, likelihood of taking another class by same teacher, and own perception of how much they learned (Neuliep, 1997). The 20-item Verbal Immediacy Behaviors Scale and the 14-item Nonverbal Immediacy Measure were

factor analyzed separately after each item was standardized within each culture to eliminate cultural differences. The factor analysis reduced the Verbal Immediacy Scale to 14 items and the Nonverbal Immediacy Measure to 9 items, and the scales with reduced items were analyzed in the study.

3. Interpret the nonequivalence. A third strategy is for the researcher to interpret the nonequivalence as an important piece of information concerning cultural differences.

4. Ignore the nonequivalence. Although this is what most cross-cultural researchers should *not* do, this is in fact what many end up doing. Poortinga (1989) suggests that the reason is that many researchers hold onto beliefs concerning scale invariance across cultures despite the lack of evidence to support such beliefs.

Obviously, how a researcher handles the interpretation of data, given nonequivalence, is dependent on experience and biases and on the nature of the data and the findings. Because of the lack of equivalence in much cross-cultural research, researchers are often faced with many gray areas in interpreting findings from their cross-cultural studies. This is, of course, to be expected, because the study of culture is neither black nor white. Culture itself is a complex phenomenon that is replete with gray, and we see that in research every day and in the journals. It is the objective and experienced researcher who can deal with the gray area in creating sound, valid, and reliable interpretations that are justified on the basis of the data. And it is the astute consumer of that research who can sit back and judge those interpretations relative to the data in his or her own mind and not be swayed by arguments alone.

Issues in Conducting Emotion Judgment Studies Across Cultures

One methodological issue that has emerged in the literature recently concerns the question of what is the most appropriate way to test for an in-group advantage in emotion recognition. The in-group-advantage hypothesis suggests that members of a cultural group are more accurate in recognizing the emotions of members of their own or similar cultural groups than of other, relatively more disparate groups. In their meta-analysis of studies involving judgments of emotion in different cultures, Elfenbein and Ambady (2002b) provided evidence for an in-group advantage in emotion recognition across all studies, as well as separately for emotion, channel of communication, cross-cultural exposure, and other potential moderators. Subsequent research by this same team has continued to build a case for the in-group hypothesis (Elfenbein & Ambady, 2003; Elfenbein, Mandal, Ambady, & Harizuka, 2002).

Matsumoto (2002) commented on Elfenbein and Ambady's original meta-analysis (Elfenbein & Ambady, 2002b) and sug-

gested that there were two methodological requirements necessary for a study to test adequately the in-group advantage hypothesis: balanced design and stimulus equivalence (see also Elfenbein & Ambady, 2002a).

Balanced Design

In a balanced design all judges of all cultures view expressions portrayed by members of all the other cultures in the study. In a two-culture design observers of cultures A and B should judge expressions of members of cultures A and B. An unbalanced design occurs in two ways. In one, judges of cultures A and B see expressions portrayed only by members of culture A; in the other, judges of only culture A see expressions portrayed by members of cultures A and B. Matsumoto (2002) argued that data from these studies cannot be used to test the in-group effect. In the first type of unbalanced design (the way in which an overwhelming number of studies have been conducted), if judges of culture B are less accurate in recognizing emotions, one cannot be sure that the same observers of culture B will be more accurate when they judge expressions portrayed by members of their own culture, because those expressions were not included in the study.

Stimulus Equivalence

The second methodological requirement for testing adequately the in-group-advantage hypothesis concerns the characteristics of the stimuli used. If stimuli that portray emotion expressed by people of two different cultural groups are to be judged by members of both those groups, then the characteristics of the stimuli specific to the emotion message must be exactly equivalent between the two expresser cultures, while only the characteristics related to cultural identification vary. For example, if faces portraying emotion expressed by people of Cultures A and B are shown to judges of both cultures, then the characteristics of the face related to emotion must be exactly the same between both cultures' expressers. This means that the same facial muscles must be innervated, with no extraneous muscle movements, and they must be at the same intensity levels. In addition, other aspects of the face related to cultural identification must be the only characteristics of the stimuli that vary systematically (facial physiognomy and morphology).

If the signals specifically related to emotion expressed by Culture A are different from those expressed by Culture B, judgments of these stimuli by observers of Cultures A and B are inherently confounded by differences in the stimuli. If, for instance, facial expressions from Culture A involve different muscle movements than those of Culture B, or if the muscles innervated are at different intensity levels, then judgment differences between Cultures A and B may be due to differences in the stimuli, not decoding processes.

The only way to address this issue adequately is to measure the actual physical properties of the stimuli related to emotion signaling to ensure that they do not vary across expresser cultures. When facial stimuli are used, such measurement can be achieved by Ekman and Friesen's Facial Action Coding System (FACS; see Ekman & Friesen, 1978). If other stimulus channels are used (e.g., voice), investigators need to demonstrate that the stimuli do not vary on the physical signal properties specific to emotion in those channels across expresser culture. If the emotion signal properties are not equivalent among the expresser cultures, the comparison of the judging cultures is inextricably confounded by stimulus differences. One could never be sure that the differences observed reflected true cultural differences in judgments or were artifacts of the differences in the stimuli.

As we have discussed earlier in this chapter, the importance and necessity of equivalence in all aspects of cross-cultural comparison studies, including in the nature of the stimuli (Leung, 1989; Poortinga, 1989; van de Vijver, 2001), have been stressed for many years by methodology experts in the area of comparisons of judgments of stimuli or ratings of items across cultures. Therefore the necessity for equivalence in cross-cultural comparisons is a well-accepted notion in cross-cultural research methodology, and thus it can and should be applied to tests of the in-group-advantage hypothesis or any hypothesis involving cultural differences, especially those involving interaction effects between participant and stimuli cultures.

Does the Evidence to Date Support the Existence of an In-Group Advantage?

Given both of these concerns, Matsumoto (2002) concluded that Elfenbein and Ambady's (2002b) original meta-analysis did not provide scientific evidence for the in-group hypothesis because they did not evaluate the studies according to whether or not they met both these requirements. Matsumoto and Choi (2003), in fact, subsequently did review the balanced studies that Elfenbein and Ambady (2002b) cited in their meta-analysis and found that of the 14 studies conducted, 5 actually provided some evidence that the physical signaling properties of the expressions used as stimuli were equivalent across the expresser ethnicities (Albas, McCluskey, & Albas, 1976; Kilbride & Yarczower, 1983; McCluskey & Albas, 1981; McCluskey, Albas, Niemi, Cuevas, & Ferrer, 1975; Mehta, Ward, & Strongman, 1992). Four of these were associated with nonsignificant interaction Fs that tested the in-group hypothesis. Two involved studies of facial expressions (Kilbride & Yarczower, 1983; Mehta et al., 1992), and both involved FACS coding of the facial muscles in the expressions. Both are important because the FACS codes were equivalent but not exactly the same across the expresser ethnicities, thus allowing minor cultural differences in the expressions to exist (perhaps corresponding to Elfenbein and Ambady's [2002a, 2003; Elfenbein et al., 2002], notion of "emotion dialects" thought to produce the supposed in-group effect). Yet they did not produce significant interaction Fs, either.

In addition, our own research program involves the use of the Japanese and Caucasian Facial Expressions of Emotion (JACFEE; Matsumoto & Ekman, 1988). The JACFEE consists of 56 expressions—8 examples of 7 emotions—portrayed by different individuals. Half are portrayed by Caucasians, the other half by Japanese; half are portrayed by males, the other half by females. All faces were reliably FACS coded to ensure that the muscles innervated in the expressions corresponded to the universal signals of emotion (as depicted by Ekman & Friesen, 1975). Within emotion the expressions include exactly the same facial muscles innervated at exactly the same intensity levels according to FACS coding, not to a group of observers. To our knowledge there is no other stimulus set in the world that reliably and validly portrays prototypic, universal expressions of emotion by two visibly different racial/ethnic groups, or for that matter any other types of emotional expressions, that are physically equivalent across expresser groups. And to date no study involving American and Japanese judgments of the JACFEE has provided any evidence for the in-group-advantage effect (Matsumoto, 2002; Matsumoto & Choi, 2003).

To be sure, Elfenbein and Ambady have argued that they have different methodological requirements (Elfenbein & Ambady, 2002a). They agreed that balanced designs "provide the strongest evidence for the in-group advantage in emotion" (p. 244) and actually employed a balanced design in a subsequent study (Elfenbein et al., 2002). They disagreed, however, with the importance of stimulus equivalence across cultures. They stated that the stimuli "should be representative and created inside that cultural context, using posers who are members of and reside in that culture, preferably with experimenters who are members of that culture"; and that "emotion itself should be elicited from participants, rather than specific expressions determined or hand-picked by the experimenter. Expressions should be as natural as possible, and not imitations of preselected theoretical models" (Elfenbein & Ambady, 2002a, pp. 243–244).

Elfenbein and Ambady (2002a) further stated that stimulus equivalence "forcibly erased" the "possibility that natural emotional expression may not be exactly equivalent across cultures" (p. 244) and that "the forcible erasing of cultural differences as a methodological requirement prevents the possibility of learning about these differences" (p. 244).

But these concerns are addressed by two studies reported in Ekman's classic report (1972) with Japanese and American participants that did involve the judgment of spontaneous expressions. In the expression condition of their experiment, American and Japanese students viewed neutral and stressful stimuli. Their spontaneous expressions of disgust, anger, fear, sadness, and happiness were comparable to each other (correlation between the coded facial behaviors of Americans and Japanese = .88) but not perfectly matched (77.44% overlap; 22.56% nonoverlap), thus providing some evidence of culture-specific responding. One-minute clips of the participants' spontaneous behaviors from both the neutral and stress film conditions were shown to different samples of both American and Japanese observers, who judged which film the participants were watching. Separate simple-effects comparisons of observer and expresser culture effects were all nonsignificant. These correspond exactly to the target interactions predicted to be significant by the in-group hypothesis. Also correlations between the Japanese and American observer responses separately for each expresser were high for both expresser cultures in both studies (ranging from .77 to .86), also arguing against the in-group hypothesis. These studies also provided no support for the in-group hypothesis.

Moreover the alternative stimulus requirements proposed by Elfenbein and Ambady (2002a) are not contradictory to Matsumoto's requirement of stimulus equivalence (Matsumoto, 2002). The necessity for stimulus equivalence is not mutually exclusive to the desirability of spontaneous and/or culture-specific expressions. Stimulus equivalence can and should be established for such stimuli. The creation of such stimuli is not a problem. In fact, it is desirable. Stimulus equivalence can and should be established for such stimuli. It would still be methodologically necessary to establish that stimuli generated in this fashion *in multiple cultures* were equivalent in their physical signaling properties. Without stimulus equivalence, judge culture differences are unavoidably confounded by stimulus differences.

We strongly feel that studies involving culture-specific expressions can and should be conducted. But we feel equally strongly that they need to be conducted within the methodological guidelines as described previously: that the stimuli and study need to be balanced for ethnicity and gender and that the stimuli need to be equivalent in the physical signaling characteristics of emotion.

How can this be done? To study culture-specific expressions expressed by people of different cultural groups, researchers will need to ensure that, in a two- group comparison, culture-specific expressions from culture A are also represented in expressions by members of culture B and vice versa and that observers of both cultures judge all examples of the expressions. Even though an expression may be specific to a culture, it is entirely possible that it exists in others but to different degrees or that it may not be labeled as such. It may be necessary to get members of culture B to pose those expressions that occur spontaneously in culture A. This is acceptable as long as the expressions that are judged do not differ in which muscles are innervated and how strongly. This would be true regardless of whether one studies spontaneous, naturally occurring expressions, imitated expressions, posed expressions, partial expressions, or any other type of expression. The key point would be for the expressions to be equivalent in their physical signaling properties related to emotion and be expressed by members of all observer cultures. Studies involving an expression from Culture A without the same expression from Culture B and an expression from Culture B without the same expression from Culture A cannot address questions about the in-group advantage be-

cause the judgments are inherently confounded by expression type. We encourage researchers interested in the in-group effect to seriously consider conducting studies that meet these requirements. The data to date, however, provide no support for it.

Conclusion

Cross-cultural research on emotion has made important contributions to the literature. With the increasing interest in culture in psychology as a whole, this area of research promises to make important contributions in the future, as well. Future cross-cultural research, however, will have to go beyond simple two-culture comparisons of the past and involve more unpacking studies that incorporate context variables that unfold the meaning of culture. Future studies will need to pay closer attention to the equivalence of methods used across cultures, taking further steps to ensure the reliability and validity of measurement across cultures engaged in the studies. Future research involving the in-group-advantage hypothesis of emotion recognition will need to do the difficult task of creating and employing stimuli that are methodologically sound and of creating methodological procedures by which in-groups can be effectively manipulated, beyond the mere matching of an observer with an unknown stimulus person who happens to share visible ethnic characteristics. Perhaps most important, future research in this area needs to tie itself to theories of culture so that findings can be integrated into ways of understanding how people live and function in the multiple milieus and contexts of the world.

References

Adamopoulous, J., & Lonner, W. J. (2001). Culture and psychology at a crossroad: Historical perspective and theoretical analysis. In D. Matsumoto (Ed.), *Handbook of Culture and Psychology* (pp. 11–34). New York: Oxford University Press.

Albas, D. C., McCluskey, K. W., & Albas, C. A. (1976). Perception of the emotional content of speech: A comparison of two Canadian groups. *Journal of Cross-Cultural Psychology, 7,* 481–490.

Bachman, J. G., & O'Malley, P. M. (1984). Black-white differences in self-esteem: Are they affected by response styles? *American Journal of Sociology, 90*(3), 624–639.

Berry, J. W., Poortinga, Y. H., Segall, M. H., & Dasen, P. R. (1992). *Cross-cultural psychology: Research and applications.* New York: Cambridge University Press.

Biehl, M., Matsumoto, D., Ekman, P., Hearn, V., Heider, K., Kudoh, T., et al. (1997). Matsumoto and Ekman's Japanese and Caucasian Facial Expressions of Emotion (JACFEE): Reliability data and cross-national differences. *Journal of Nonverbal Behavior, 21,* 3–21.

Biehl, M., Matsumoto, D., & Kasri, F. (in press). Culture and emotion. In U. Gielen & A. L. Communian (Eds.), *Cross-*

cultural and international dimensions of psychology. Trieste, Italy: Edizioni Lint Trieste S.r.1.

Boucher, J. D., & Brandt, M. E. (1981). Judgment of emotion: American and Malay antecedents. *Journal of Cross-Cultural Psychology, 12*(3), 272–283.

Brandt, M. E., & Boucher, J. D. (1985). Concepts of depression in emotion lexicons of eight cultures. *International Journal of Intercultural Relations, 10,* 321–346.

Brislin, R. (1970). Back translation for cross-cultural research. *Journal of Cross-Cultural Psychology, 1,* 185–216.

Buss, D. M. (1988). The evolution of human intrasexual competition: Tactics of mate attraction. *Journal of Personality and Social Psychology, 54*(4), 616–628.

Buss, D. M. (1989). Sex differences in human mate preferences: Evolutionary hypotheses tested in 37 cultures. *Behavioral and Brain Sciences, 12*(1), 1–49.

Buss, D. M. (1991). Evolutionary personality psychology. *Annual Review of Psychology, 42,* 459–491.

Buss, D. M. (2000). The evolution of happiness. *American Psychologist, 55*(1), 15–23.

Buss, D. M. (2001). Human nature and culture: An evolutionary psychological perspective. *Journal of Personality, 69*(6), 955–978.

Buunk, B., & Hupka, R. B. (1987). Cross-cultural differences in the elicitation of sexual jealousy. *Journal of Sex Research, 23*(1), 12–22.

Charlesworth, W. R., & Kreutzer, M. A. (1973). Facial expressions of infants and children. In P. Ekman (Ed.), *Darwin and facial expression: A century of research in review* (pp. 91–168). New York: Academic Press.

Coan, J. A., Allen, J. J. B., & Harmon-Jones, E. (2001). Voluntary facial expression and hemispheric activity over the frontal cortex. *Psychophysiology, 38,* 912–925.

Darwin, C. (1998). *The expression of emotion in man and animals.* New York: Oxford University Press. (Original work published 1872)

Davidson, R. J., Scherer, K., & Goldsmith, H. H. (2002). *Handbook of affective sciences.* New York: Oxford University Press.

Edelmann, R. J., Asendorpf, J., Contarello, A., Georgas, J., Villanueva, C., & Zammuner, V. (1987). Self-reported verbal and non-verbal strategies for coping with embarrassment in five European cultures. *Social Science Information, 26,* 869–883.

Ekman, P. (1972). Universal and cultural differences in facial expression of emotion. In J. R. Cole (Ed.), *Nebraska Symposium on Motivation, 1971* (pp. 207–283). Lincoln, NE: Nebraska University Press.

Ekman, P. (1973). *Darwin and facial expression: A century of research in review.* New York: Academic Press.

Ekman, P. (1992a). Are there basic emotions? *Psychological Review, 99*(3), 550–553.

Ekman, P. (1992b). An argument for basic emotions. *Cognition and Emotion, 6*(3–4), 169–200.

Ekman, P. (1992c). Facial expressions of emotion: An old controversy and new findings. In V. Bruce, A. Cowey, A. W. Ellis, & D. I. Perrett (Eds.), *Processing the facial image* (pp. 63–69). Oxford, UK: Clarendon Press/Oxford University Press.

Ekman, P. (1992d). Facial expressions of emotion: New findings, new questions. *Psychological Science, 3*(1), 34–38.

Ekman, P. (1999). Basic emotions. In T. Dalgleish &T. Power (Eds.), *Handbook of cognition and emotion* (pp. 45–60). Sussex, UK: Wiley.

Ekman, P. (2003). *Emotions revealed.* New York: Times Books.

Ekman, P., & Friesen, W. (1969). The repertoire of nonverbal behavior: Categories, origins, usage, and coding. *Semiotica, 1,* 49–98.

Ekman, P., & Friesen, W. V. (1975). *Unmasking the face: A guide to recognizing emotions from facial clues.* Englewood Cliffs, NJ: Prentice-Hall.

Ekman, P., & Friesen, W. V. (1978). *Facial Action Coding System: Investigator's guide.* Palo Alto, CA: Consulting Psychologists Press.

Ekman, P., & Friesen, W. V. (1986). A new pan-cultural facial expression of emotion. *Motivation and Emotion, 10*(2), 159–168.

Ekman, P., Friesen, W. V., & Ellsworth, P. (1972). *Emotion in the human face: Guidelines for research and an integration of findings.* New York: Pergamon Press.

Ekman, P., Friesen, W. V., O'Sullivan, M., Chan, A., Diacoyanni-Tarlatzis I., Heider K., et al. (1987). Universals and cultural differences in the judgments of facial expressions of emotion. *Journal of Personality and Social Psychology, 53*(4), 712–717.

Ekman, P., & Heider, K. G. (1988). The universality of a contempt expression: A replication. *Motivation and Emotion, 12*(3), 303–308.

Ekman, P., Levenson, R. W., & Friesen, W. V. (1983). Autonomic nervous system activity distinguishes among emotions. *Science, 221*(4616), 1208–1210.

Elfenbein, H. A., & Ambady, N. (2002a). Is there an ingroup advantage in emotion recognition? *Psychological Bulletin, 128*(2), 243–249.

Elfenbein, H. A., & Ambady, N. (2002b). On the universality and cultural specificity of emotion recognition: A meta-analysis. *Psychological Bulletin, 128*(2), 205–235.

Elfenbein, H. A., & Ambady, N. (2003). Cultural similarity's consequences: A distance perspective on cross-cultural differences in emotion recognition. *Journal of Cross-Cultural Psychology, 34*(1), 92–110.

Elfenbein, H. A., Mandal, M. K., Ambady, N., & Harizuka, S. (2002). Cross-cultural patterns in emotion recognition: Highlighting design and analytic techniques. *Emotion, 2*(1), 75–84.

Fridlund, A. (1997). The new ethology of human facial expressions. In J. A. Russell & J. M. Fernandez-Dols (Eds.), *The psychology of facial expression* (pp. 102–129). Cambridge, UK: Cambridge University Press.

Galati, D., & Sciaky, R. (1995). The representation of antecedents of emotion in northern and southern Italy. *Journal of Cross-Cultural Psychology, 26*(2), 123–140.

Geen, T. (1992). Facial expressions in socially isolated nonhuman primates: Open and closed programs for expressive behavior. *Journal of Research in Personality, 26,* 273–280.

Greenfield, M. P. (1997). You can't take it with you. *American Psychologist, 52,* 1115–1124.

Haidt, J., & Keltner, D. (1999). Culture and facial expression: Open-ended methods find more expressions and a gradient of recognition. *Cognition and Emotion, 13*(3), 225–266.

Hofstede, G. H. (1980). *Culture's consequences: International differences in work-related values.* Beverly Hills, CA: Sage.

Hofstede, G. H. (1984). *Culture's consequences: International differences in work-related values* (Abridged ed.). Beverly Hills, CA: Sage.

Izard, C. E. (1971). *The face of emotion.* East Norwalk, CT: Appleton-Century-Crofts.

Jahoda, G. (1984). Do we need a concept of culture? *Journal of Cross-Cultural Psychology, 15*(2), 139–151.

James, W. (1890). *The principles of psychology.* New York: Holt.

Kilbride, J. E., & Yarczower, M. (1983). Ethnic bias in the recognition of facial expressions. *Journal of Nonverbal Behavior, 8,* 27–41.

Kitayama, S., & Markus, H. R. (1994). *Emotion and culture: Empirical studies of mutual influence.* Washington, DC: American Psychological Association.

Kitayama, S., & Markus, H. R. (1995). Culture and self: Implications for internationalizing psychology. In N. R. Goldberger & J. B. Veroff (Eds.), *The culture and psychology reader* (pp. 366–383). New York: New York University Press.

Kroeber, A. L., & Kluckholn, C. (1963). *Culture: A critical review of concepts and definitions.* Cambridge, MA: Harvard University. (Original work published 1952)

Leung, K. (1989). Cross-cultural differences: Individual-level v. culture-level analysis. *International Journal of Psychology, 24,* 703–719.

Levenson, R. W., Ekman, P., & Friesen, W. V. (1990). Voluntary facial action generates emotion-specific autonomic nervous system activity. *Psychophysiology, 27*(4), 363–384.

Levenson, R. W., Ekman, P., Heider, K., & Friesen, W. V. (1992). Emotion and autonomic nervous system activity in the Minangkabau of West Sumatra. *Journal of Personality and Social Psychology, 62*(6), 972–988.

Levy, R. I. (1973). *Tahitians.* Chicago: University of Chicago Press.

Levy, R. I. (1983). Introduction: Self and emotion. *Ethos, 11,* 128–134.

Linton, R. (1936). *The study of man: An introduction.* New York: Appleton.

Lutz, C. (1982). The domain of emotion words in Ifaluk. *American Ethnologist, 9,* 113–128.

Lutz, C. (1983). Parental goals, ethnopsychology, and the development of emotional meaning. *Ethos, 11,* 246–262.

Malinowski, B. (1960). *A scientific theory of culture and other essays.* New York: Oxford University Press. (Original work published 1944)

Malinowski, B. (1961). *Sex and repression in a savage society.* Cleveland, OH: World. (Original work published 1927)

Mandler, G. (1984). *Mind and body: Psychology of emotion and stress.* New York: Norton.

Marin, G., Gamba, R. J., & Marin, B. V. (1992). Extreme response style and acquiescence among Hispanics: The role of acculturation and education. *Journal of Cross-Cultural Psychology, 23*(4), 498–509.

Markus, H. R., & Kitayama, S. (1991). Culture and the self: Implications for cognition, emotion, and motivation. *Psychological Review, 98*(2), 224–253.

Masters, R. D., & Sullivan, D. G. (1989). Nonverbal displays and political leadership in France and the United States. *Political Behavior, 11,* 123–156.

Matsumoto, D. (1989). Cultural influences on the perception of emotion. *Journal of Cross-Cultural Psychology, 20*(1), 92–105.

Matsumoto, D. (1990). Cultural similarities and differences in display rules. *Motivation and Emotion, 14*(3), 195–214.

Matsumoto, D. (1992a). American-Japanese cultural differences in the recognition of universal facial expressions. *Journal of Cross-Cultural Psychology, 23*(1), 72–84.

Matsumoto, D. (1992b). More evidence for the universality of a contempt expression. *Motivation and Emotion, 16*(4), 363–368.

Matsumoto, D. (1993). Ethnic differences in affect intensity, emotion judgments, display rule attitudes, and self-reported emotional expression in an American sample. *Motivation and Emotion, 17*(2), 107–123.

Matsumoto, D. (2001). Culture and emotion. In D. Matsumoto (Ed.), *The handbook of culture and psychology* (pp. 171–194). New York: Oxford University Press.

Matsumoto, D. (2002). Methodological requirements to test a possible ingroup advantage in judging emotions across cultures: Comments on Elfenbein and Ambady and evidence. *Psychological Bulletin, 128*(2), 236–242.

Matsumoto, D. (2003). Cross-cultural research. In S. Davis (Ed.), *The handbook of research methods in experimental psychology* (pp. 189–203). Oxford, UK: Blackwell.

Matsumoto, D., & Choi, J. W. (2003). No evidence for the ingroup advantage effect in recognizing universal facial expressions of emotions. Manuscript submitted for publication.

Matsumoto, D., Consolacion, T., Yamada, H., Suzuki, R., Franklin, B., Paul, S., et al. (2002). American-Japanese cultural differences in judgments of emotional expressions of different intensities. *Cognition and Emotion, 16*(6), 721–747.

Matsumoto, D., & Ekman, P. (1988). *Japanese and Caucasian Facial Expressions of Emotion and Neutral Faces (JACFEE and JACNeuF).* Available at http://www.paulekman.com/research_cds.php

Matsumoto, D., & Ekman, P. (1989). American-Japanese cultural differences in intensity ratings of facial expressions of emotion. *Motivation and Emotion, 13*(2), 143–157.

Matsumoto, D., & Fletcher, D. (1996). Cultural influences on disease. *Journal of Gender, Culture, and Health, 1,* 71–82.

Matsumoto, D., Grissom, R., & Dinnel, D. (2001). Do between-culture differences really mean that people are different? A look at some measures of cultural effect size. *Journal of Cross-Cultural Psychology, 32*(4), 478–490.

Matsumoto, D., Kasri, F., & Kooken, K. (1999). American-Japanese cultural differences in judgments of expression intensity and subjective experience. *Cognition and Emotion, 13,* 201–218.

Matsumoto, D., & Kudoh, T. (1993). American-Japanese cultural differences in attributions of personality based on smiles. *Journal of Nonverbal Behavior, 17,* 231–243.

Matsumoto, D., Takeuchi, S., Andayani, S., Kouznetsova, N., & Krupp, D. (1998). The contribution of individualism-collectivism to cross-national differences in display rules. *Asian Journal of Social Psychology, 1,* 147–165.

Matsumoto, D., Yoo, S. H., Hirayama, S., & Petrova, G. (2005). Validation of an individual-level measure of display rules: The Display Rule Assessment Inventory (DRAI). *Emotion, 5,* 23–40.

Mauro, R., Sato, K., & Tucker, J. (1992). The role of appraisal in human emotions: A cross-cultural study. *Journal of Personality and Social Psychology, 62*(2), 301–317.

McCluskey, K., Albas, D., Niemi, R., Cuevas, C., & Ferrer, C. (1975). Cultural differences in the perception of the emotional content of speech: A study of the development of sensitivity in Canadian and Mexican children. *Developmental Psychology, 11*, 551–555.

McCluskey, K. W., & Albas, D. C. (1981). Perception of the emotional content of speech by Canadian and Mexican children, adolescents and adults. *International Journal of Psychology, 16*, 119–132.

Mehta, S. D., Ward, C., & Strongman, K. (1992). Cross-cultural recognition of posed facial expressions of emotion. *New Zealand Journal of Psychology, 21*, 74–77.

Mesquita, B., & Frijda, N. H. (1992). Cultural variations in emotions: A review. *Psychological Bulletin, 112*, 197–204.

Neuliep, J. W. (1997). A cross-cultural comparison of teacher immediacy in American and Japanese classrooms. *Communication Research, 24*, 431–451.

Oetzel, J., Ting-Toomey, S., Masumoto, T., Yokochi, Y., Pan, X., Takai, J., et al. (2001). Face and facework in conflict: A cross-cultural comparison of China, Germany, Japan, and the United States. *Communication Monographs, 68*(3), 238–253.

Pipher, M. (1998). *Another country: Navigating the emotional terrain of our elders.* New York: Putnam.

Pittam, J., Gallois, C., Iwawaki, S., & Kroonenberg, P. (1995). Australian and Japanese concepts of expressive behavior. *Journal of Cross-Cultural Psychology, 26*, 451–473.

Poortinga, Y. H. (1989). Equivalence of cross-cultural data: An overview of basic issues. *International Journal of Psychology, 24*, 737–756.

Poortinga, Y. H. (1990, July). Towards a conceptualization of culture for psychology. Presidential Address at the meeting of the International Association of Cross-Cultural Psychology, Tilburg, the Netherlands.

Poortinga, Y. H., van de Vijver, F. J. R., Joe, R. C., & van de Koppel, J. M. H. (1987). Peeling the onion called culture: A synopsis. In C. Kagitcibasi (Ed.), *Growth and progress in cross-cultural psychology* (pp. 22–34). Berwyn, PA: Swets North America.

Rohner, R. P. (1984). Toward a conception of culture for cross-cultural psychology. *Journal of Cross-Cultural Psychology, 15*, 111–138.

Romney, A. K., Boyd, J. P., Moore, C. C., Batchelder, W. H., & Brazill, T. J. (1996). Culture as shared cognitive representations. *Proceedings of the National Academy of Sciences of the United States of America, 93*, 4699–4705.

Romney, A. K., Moore, C. C., & Rusch, C. D. (1997). Cultural universals: Measuring the semantic structure of emotion terms in English and Japanese. *Proceedings of the National Academy of Sciences of the United States of America, 94*, 5489–5494.

Roseman, I. J., Dhawan, N., Rettek, S. I., & Naidu, R. K. (1995). Cultural differences and cross-cultural similarities in appraisals and emotional responses. *Journal of Cross-Cultural Psychology, 26*(1), 23–48.

Russell, J. A. (1991). Culture and the categorization of emotions. *Psychological Bulletin, 110*, 426–450.

Scherer, K. (1997a). Profiles of emotion-antecedent appraisal: Testing theoretical predictions across cultures. *Cognition and Emotion, 11*(2), 113–150.

Scherer, K. (1997b). The role of culture in emotion-antecedent appraisal. *Journal of Personality and Social Psychology, 73*(4), 902–922.

Scherer, K., & Wallbott, H. (1994). Evidence for universality and cultural variation of differential emotion response patterning. *Journal of Personality and Social Psychology, 66*(2), 310–328.

Scherer, K. R., Matsumoto, D., Wallbott, H. G., & Kudoh, T. (1988). Emotional experience in cultural context: A comparison between Europe, Japan, and the United States. In K. R. Scherer (Ed.), *Facets of emotion: Recent research* (pp. 5–30). Hillsdale, NJ: Erlbaum.

Scherer, K. R., Summerfield, A. B., & Wallbott, H. G. (1983). Cross-national research on antecedents and components of emotion: A progress report. *Social Science Information, 22*(3), 355–385.

Scherer, K. R., Wallbott, H. G., & Summerfield, A. B. (Eds.). (1986). *Experiencing emotion: A cross-cultural study.* Cambridge, UK: Cambridge University Press.

Segall, M. H. (1984). More than we need to know about culture, but are afraid to ask. *Journal of Cross-Cultural Psychology, 15*(2), 153–162.

Shaver, P., Murdaya, U., & Fraley, R. C. (2001). The structure of the Indonesian emotion lexicon. *Asian Journal of Social Psychology, 4*(3), 201–224.

Shaver, P. R., Wu, S., & Schwartz, J. C. (1992). Cross-cultural similarities and differences in emotion and its representation. In M. S. Clark (Ed.), *Emotion: Review of personality and social psychology* (Vol. 13, pp. 175–212). Thousand Oaks, CA: Sage.

Shweder, R. A. (1993). Liberalism as destiny. In B. Puka (Ed.),*Moral development: A compendium: Vol. 4. The great justice debate* (pp. 71–74). New York: Garland.

Shweder, R. A. (1999). Why cultural psychology? *Ethos, 27*(1), 62–73.

Strodtbeck, F. L. (1964). Considerations of meta-method in cross-cultural studies. *American Anthropologist, 66*(3), 223–229.

Tooby, J., & Cosmides, L. (1992). Psychological foundations of culture. In J. Barkow, L. Cosmides, & J. Tooby (Eds.), *The adapted mind* (pp. 19–136). New York: Oxford University Press.

Triandis, H. C. (1972). *The analysis of subjective culture.* New York: Wiley.

Triandis, H. C. (1994). *Culture and social behavior.* New York: McGraw Hill.

Triandis, H. C., Bontempo, R., Villareal, M. J., Asai, M., & Lucca, N. (1988). Individualism and collectivism: Cross-cultural perspectives on self-ingroup relationships. *Journal of Personality and Social Psychology, 54*(2), 323–338.

Tsai, J. L., & Levenson, R. W. (1997). Cultural influences of emotional responding: Chinese American and European American dating couples during interpersonal conflict. *Journal of Cross-Cultural Psychology, 28*, 600–625.

van de Vijver, F. J. R. (2001). Evolution of research methods. In D. Matsumoto (Ed.), *Handbook of culture and psychology* (pp. 77–97). New York: Oxford University Press.

Wallbott, H., & Scherer, K. (1986). How universal and specific is emotional experience? Evidence from 27 countries on five continents. *Social Science Information, 25,* 763–795.

Waxer, P. H. (1985). Video ethology: Television as a data base for cross-cultural studies in nonverbal displays. *Journal of Nonverbal Behavior, 9,* 111–120.

Wierzbicka, A. (1994). Semantic universals and primitive thought: The question of the psychic unity of humankind. *Journal of Linguistic Anthropology, 4,* 23.

Heather A. Henderson
Nathan A. Fox

Considerations in Studying Emotion in Infants and Children

Many of the concerns about eliciting emotion in infants and young children are quite similar to those with adults. Developmental psychologists, like other emotion researchers, are often challenged to identify the specific responses that determine whether a particular stimulus condition has elicited emotion. Must an infant or young child display a particular facial expression in order for the researcher to state that emotion has been elicited? Can other behavioral responses, such as motor behavior (withdrawal or approach), vocal expression, or body posture, be utilized to identify the expression of emotion? The same questions may be raised with regard to physiological measures in the measurement of emotion. Is the presence of a change in physiology sufficient to determine the presence of emotion? For example, if heart rate increases or cortisol rises in response to an elicitor, does that signify the presence of emotion? In the absence of facial expression, how can we identify discrete emotion states? Or are physiological responses non-emotion-specific and thus useful only as corollaries of more specific behavioral signs of emotion? These questions are pertinent across the life span when assessing emotion.

There are, however, several unique issues to consider in the study of emotion in infants and young children. First, during infancy and early childhood, children change rapidly across several domains of development that directly or indirectly influence emotional development. Second, general issues in the elicitation of emotion, such as the importance of controlling for baseline state or the effects of contextual vari-

ables, have unique implications when studying infants and young children. Third, infants and children are a special population of research participants, as defined by the National Institutes of Health and the American Psychological Association. As such, emotions research with young children requires consideration of unique ethical issues. In this chapter we first review three specific examples of the ways in which a child's perceptual-motor, social-cognitive, and cognitive levels of functioning will affect a researcher's decisions regarding the elicitation and assessment of emotion. Next, we review a number of general considerations that are critical in emotion research with children, including the importance of assessing and controlling for baseline states, accounting for the social and physical context in which the assessment occurs, and the utility of parent reports of children's emotions. Finally, we discuss several ethical issues that are specific to conducting emotion research with young children, including the advantages and disadvantages of obtaining assent from children and the appropriateness of using deceptive techniques with young children.

The Implications of Cross-Domain Development for the Study of Emotion in Infants and Young Children

The process of emotion elicitation involves the appraisal of a stimulus within a specific context. An individual perceives and interprets a stimulus as friendly or threatening, danger-ous or interesting, engaging or aversive. The interpretation of the eliciting condition is reflected in a participant's face, voice, and motor behaviors that together signify to the ob-server the presence of an emotion. This model may be use-ful in thinking about the generation of emotion in adults and across species, as there is evidence that the evaluation of danger and threat is either innate or learned for survival in most species. However, it does not necessarily take into account the *development* of cognitive, social-cognitive, and perceptual-motor skills that underlie these appraisal and response processes and, therefore, differences in the chang-ing nature of the appraisal and experience of emotion across infancy and childhood. In what follows we summarize three examples of the ways in which different areas of development affect children's emotional appraisals and responses and, therefore, the elicitation and assessment of emotion in young children.

Motor Development and the Emergence of Fear

Between 6 and 10 months of age there is a notable increase in the frequency and intensity of infants' fear responses (e.g., Scarr & Salapatek, 1970). The early emergence of fear and other basic emotional expressions is often attributed to hardwired and preprogrammed patterns of neuromaturation that evolved to protect the infant from dangers in his or her environment (e.g., Kagan, Kearsley, & Zelazo, 1978). How-ever, several studies demonstrate the importance of experi-ences, specifically self-initiated or active experiences, for the emergence of fear reactions.

Campos and colleagues (Campos, Bertenthal, & Kermoian, 1992) conducted a series of studies that examined the asso-ciations between self-produced locomotion and the emer-gence of a fear of heights using the visual cliff paradigm. The visual cliff comprises a glass-covered table with a textured surface immediately under the glass on the "shallow" side and approximately 3.5 feet below the glass on the "deep" side. Early findings using this apparatus showed that almost all 8- and 9-month-old infants, when encouraged to cross over to the deep side of the apparatus, tended to approach fear-fully, to detour around the edges of the apparatus, or to refuse completely, a pattern of responding interpreted as reflecting a fear of heights (Campos, Hiatt, Ramsay, Henderson, & Svejda, 1978; Scarr & Salapatek, 1970). Campos and col-leagues conducted a series of studies in order to examine whether the timing of the emergence of a fear of heights sim-ply co-occurred with the onset of independent locomotion or, rather, was causally associated with independent loco-motion. In these studies, fear reactions were compared be-tween age-matched prelocomotor versus locomotor infants, and analyses were conducted to examine the associations between the duration of independent locomotion and fear of heights, controlling for age. In order to equate the task demands for age-matched prelocomotor and locomotor in-

fants, an experimenter slowly lowered each infant toward either the deep or the shallow side of the cliff while heart rate and facial expressions were recorded. Locomotor infants showed heart rate accelerations relative to baseline record-ings when lowered over the deep side of the cliff, but not the shallow side. This pattern of heart rate acceleration was in-terpreted as a defensive, fearful response. In contrast, preloco-motor infants of the same age did not show changes in heart rate relative to baseline when lowered over either side of the cliff. Thus these differences demonstrated a correlation be-tween locomotor experience and the fear of heights; how-ever, causal conclusions could not be made. In a second set of studies, self-produced locomotion experiences were ex-perimentally manipulated by providing some infants with walkers. Prelocomotor and locomotor infants were randomly assigned to receive a walker for use at home or not. When lowered over the deep side of the cliff, age-matched locomo-tor infants in both conditions and prelocomotor infants in the walker-experience condition all showed heart rate accel-erations, whereas prelocomotor infants in the no-walker-experience condition did not. These findings demonstrated that the experience of self-produced locomotion preceded the emergence of a fear of heights.

At what level are motor developments and emotional changes related? In this case, self-produced locomotion de-velops new cognitive and perceptual skills, including cali-bration of distances and the coordination of visual and vestibular stimulation (Campos et al., 1992). Once visual and vestibular information become coordinated, infants are able to detect discrepancies between the two. In the visual cliff studies, when infants are placed on the deep side of the cliff, the visual input is inconsistent with the vestibular input, creating feelings of fear (Bertenthal, Campos, & Kermoian, 1992). More generally, independent locomotion develops infants' abilities to use environmental cues as warning signs for danger and thus as cues for the expression of a fear of heights (Bertenthal & Campos, 1990).

In addition to the perceptual-cognitive changes elicited by the onset of independent locomotion, when an infant begins crawling and walking, caregivers begin more frequent and often intense emotional communications with their in-fants (Bertenthal & Campos, 1990; Campos et al., 1992). Not surprisingly, the onset of independent locomotion is associ-ated with increases in infants' expressions of other emotions, including happiness, anger, and frustration. In part, this is due to the increases in expressions of positive and negative affect between parents and their children (Biringen, Emde, Campos, & Appelbaum, 1995; Campos, Kermoian, & Zumbahlen, 1992).

The work of Campos and colleagues reviewed previ-ously is but one example of research demonstrating the in-terrelatedness of emotional development with changes in other domains of development. But it is exemplary in that it has several implications for the elicitation and assessment of emotion in infants and young children. First, at a practical level, emotional development must be considered within the context of other aspects of development, including motor development. Thus information on perceptual and motor development, including the age at which major motor milestones were reached, should be gathered on all children taking part in studies of emotional development (Biringen et al., 1995). Second, this work demonstrates that emotions do not develop in isolation but rather change as a function of the interaction between an infant and his or her physical and social environment. Therefore, assessments of individual differences and developmental change in the experience and expression of emotion need to take into consideration experiential variables that may contribute to change. As was found by Campos and colleagues (1992), the experiences a child has with his or her environment may be a much better predictor of his or her emotional reactions to various elicitors than is his or her age per se.

Social-Cognitive Development and the Emergence of Self-Conscious Emotions

In contrast to the expression of basic emotions in early infancy that are considered to be primarily genetically predetermined and preprogrammed, more complex emotions arise more gradually as a result of social-cognitive development. One example is the association between the development of an understanding of the self and the experience and expression of self-conscious emotions, including pride, shame, and embarrassment.

The development of an understanding of the self takes place gradually over the first 2 years of life (Lewis & Brooks-Gunn, 1979). Increases in self-awareness and self-reflective capacities provide children with thought processes required for self-appraisal, which in turn lays the groundwork for the emergence of a new class of emotions—self-conscious emotions (Lewis & Brooks-Gunn, 1979; Saarni, Mumme, & Campos, 1998; Stipek, 1983). Through self-appraisal, children are able to compare their own behaviors to standards and to attribute deviations from these standards to themselves. When a child recognizes that his or her behavior has met or exceeded standards, the emotion of pride is elicited. In contrast, when a child recognizes that his or her behavior has violated a standard, emotions such as shame, guilt, or embarrassment will be elicited. The ability to engage in self-appraisal depends on the understanding of the self as an object, distinct from others and open to evaluation. This objective self develops between 15 and 24 months, which corresponds to the period in which toddlers first express self-conscious emotions (Barrett, 1998; Lewis & Brooks-Gunn, 1979; Lewis, Sullivan, Stanger, & Weiss, 1989).

Measurement of the presence and intensity of basic emotions in infancy and early childhood has been well developed, based in part on identifying neuromuscular patterns of facial activity thought to reflect the presence of discrete emotions in adults (e.g., the Facial Action Coding System [FACS]; Ekman & Friesen, 1984; or the Maximally Discriminative Facial Coding System [MAX]; Izard, 1979). However, the cognitive complexity of self-conscious emotions makes it more difficult to establish consistencies between adult standard expressions and young child facial expressions (Izard & Malatesta, 1987; Stipek, 1995). As such, the empirical study of developmental changes and individual differences in the expression of self-conscious emotions has relied less on standardized elicitation procedures and more on subjective coding and interpretation. Regardless of these methodological challenges, there is a good deal of agreement that self-conscious emotions are first expressed during the second year of life and that the experience of self-conscious emotions can be quantified as long as analyses of facial responses are coordinated with measures of motor responses and verbal self-reports.

Given the importance of goal-directed behavioral outcomes of success or failure in the elicitation of both positive and negative self-conscious emotions, most empirical studies focus on observing children's reactions to actual or simulated experiences of success or failure. Kagan (1981) reported that expressions of pride were first apparent in typically developing children around 18 months of age and peaked between 20 and 26 months of age. These expressions occurred in response to the completion of a goal-directed activity, suggesting that during the second half of the second year of life, children are able not only to represent a goal state but also to evaluate whether they have successfully achieved these goals.

Because the expression of pride shares many expressive features with the expression of the basic emotion of joy, it has proven difficult to isolate purely pride-based reaction tendencies. In contrast, the expression of shame has a more universal expression pattern that consists of eyes lowered, lips rolled inward, mouth corners depressed, and the lower lip tucked between the teeth (Izard, 1977; Stipek, 1995). As well, more gross postural changes such as lowering the head and turning the face away, thought to reflect the desire to avoid social contact, are associated with the experience of shame (Izard, 1977). Children's experiences of pride and shame have most often been studied in the laboratory by manipulating success and failure outcomes to a variety of tasks, thereby modifying children's achievement experiences (e.g., Stipek, Recchia, & McClintic, 1992). In a study conducted by Stipek and colleagues (Stipek et al., 1992) of toddlers' reactions to successfully completing a task, one behavior that was identified as particularly relevant in the expression of pride was the direction of eye gaze. Toddlers were just as likely to smile when an experimenter completed the task as when they completed the task themselves, but they were significantly more likely to shift their gaze toward the experimenter after completing the task on their own. This change in gaze direction was interpreted as children showing an interest in others' reactions to their behavior, or anticipated and desired praise for their achievement.

Stipek and colleagues (1992) further examined 2- to 5-year-old children's reactions to success and failure in a laboratory task in which children were given either solvable or unsolvable problems to work on. In response to failure, children as young as 2 years of age avoided eye contact with the experimenter, turned their bodies away from the experimenter, and retained a more closed posture. Together these behaviors suggest that children as young as 2 years of age are aware of others' evaluations of them, and when they fail to meet standards children react in a way to minimize social contact. These studies emphasize the importance of combining traditional codes for facial expressions with more global codes of gross motor movement and positioning that tap into motivational systems of approaching versus withdrawing from social situations.

Given the cognitive complexity involved in experiencing self-conscious emotions, there are several issues emotions researchers must consider when working with children. First, special care must be taken to design eliciting conditions that have universal goals (i.e., it is clear to all participants what defines success vs. failure on a task). Second, self-conscious emotions require the coding of more subtle behaviors such as direction of eye gaze, in addition to traditional muscular codes that define basic emotions. Finally, because of the cognitive complexity of these emotions, researchers can expect a greater degree of variability between participants, even within a narrow age range, due to variations in factors that influence social-cognitive development, including socialization experiences, temperament, and motivation.

Attentional Control and the Regulation of Emotion

Although the study of the expression of basic emotions has been relatively well developed in infants, one factor that influences emotion elicitation and assessment beginning in the preschool years is that children experience rapid changes in neural systems that underlie attentional control, a primary process associated with the self-regulation of behavior and emotion (Posner & Rothbart, 2000; Ruff & Rothbart, 1996). With the added influence of self-regulatory skills that begin to come about in the early toddler years, researchers are faced with the increasing challenge of interpreting individual differences in emotion expression as reflecting some combination of reactive and self-regulatory processes. That is, in an emotion-elicitation paradigm, how is one to interpret the meaning of a child who does not react? Is this a child or a paradigm in which little emotion is elicited, or is this a child or paradigm that allows for a good deal of self-regulation of emotional reactions?

Over infancy and early childhood, attention becomes less under the control of external stimulus characteristics and more under internal control. The emergence of voluntary control over attention, and specifically the ability to flexibly focus and shift attention, contributes to the developing system of behaviors that allow for greater self-regulation of

thought, behavior, and emotion (Posner & Rothbart, 1998; Rueda, Posner, & Rothbart, 2004). The relation between the flexible and intentional employment of attention and the regulation of emotion is apparent early in life and characterizes many of the early interactions that take place between caregivers and infants. During adult-infant interactions, adults engage and disengage infants' attention as a way of managing the infants' level of arousal. Whereas states of engaged attention between infants and their caregivers tend to be associated with play, states of joy, and general states of positive affect, states of disengagement of attention function to dampen or reduce levels of arousal (Gottman, Katz, & Hooven, 1997). When parents respond contingently to their infants' needs to disengage and reengage interactions, infants gradually learn about the efficacy of attentional control as a means of self-regulation (Gottman et al., 1997). The relation between attentional control and self-regulation is supported by the fact that these individual differences have been associated with differences in temperamental reactivity and regulation (Johnson, Posner, & Rothbart 1991; Rothbart, Ahadi, & Hershey, 1994). These findings suggest that the development of attentional control over the first several years of life may provide children an important source of regulation over their emotional reactions. As attention comes under greater self-control across early childhood, the shifting of attention to a different aspect of a situation, or distracting oneself, may provide a strategy for dampening the experience of negative emotions such as fear and anger. Similarly, by selectively focusing attention on positive aspects of an eliciting situation, children can intentionally heighten their experiences of positive emotion.

Posner and Rothbart (1998) have postulated that the development of the anterior attention system is directly involved in the emergence of self-regulated behavior. This neural network, located within the prefrontal cortex and including structures such as the anterior cingulate cortex, has many interconnections with primary areas of brain that are involved in the expression of emotion, such as limbic and frontal motivational systems (Posner & Petersen, 1990; Posner & Raichle, 1994; Posner & Rothbart, 1998).

As a way of describing these processes at a behavioral level, Rothbart has identified a temperament factor called *effortful control* that is derived from parent-report measures of temperament and that reflects the processes involved in regulating the more reactive aspects of temperament, including positive and negative emotionality (Rothbart & Bates, 1998). These processes include inhibitory control and regulation of attention. Both of these processes appear to be related to control of emotion, particularly negative emotion. For example, in adult populations, self-reports of voluntary attentional focusing and attentional shifting correlated positively with each other but negatively with self-reports of fear, frustration, and sadness (Derryberry & Reed, 2002; Derryberry & Rothbart, 1988). Similarly, preschoolers who are able to successfully distract themselves during a delay of gratification task are reported by their parents as being generally well regulated as young adults (Shoda, Mischel, & Peake, 1990).

As young children develop and successfully utilize attention and inhibitory skills in the service of emotion regulation, it becomes necessary to examine the nature of the tasks utilized for eliciting emotion. Some contexts draw on regulatory skills and behavior more than others and tap into the combined influence of reactive and regulatory processes in emotion. For example, Kochanska and colleagues (e.g., Kochanska, Murray, & Coy, 1997) and Fox and Henderson (2000) and others have used a task in which young children must perform an uninteresting card sorting task while sitting in front of a set of attractive toys. The children are told that they are not to touch the toys but rather to keep working on the card sorting task. This task elicits a range of emotions, attention behaviors, and inhibitory skills as children attempt to ignore the tempting set of toys and comply with the experimenter's demands. Whereas coding of global affect tends to relate to children's levels of emotional reactivity, such as anger proneness, detailed coding of attentional strategies, such as purposeful distraction, better relate to children's self-regulatory skills. Similarly, Mischel and colleagues have conducted a series of classic studies on preschoolers' strategies for delaying gratification (Mischel, Ebbesen, & Zeiss, 1972; Mischel, Shoda, & Rodriguez, 1989). In this task, children sit at a table with one candy on one side and a small pile of two or three candies on their other side. They are told that if they wait while an experimenter leaves on an errand, they can have the small pile of candies when she returns. If they decide they cannot wait while the experimenter leaves the room, they can ring a small desk bell and the experimenter will return, but they will only be able to eat the one candy. Such a task elicits negative affect, primarily anger and frustration, as well as a wide range of attention and inhibitory behaviors as children attempt to wait for the experimenter's return. Children who were able to delay their gratification engaged in a variety of cognitively complex regulatory behaviors, including the verbal reframing of task conditions and demands in a more positive light, comforting self-talk, and the generation of distractions such a game playing. As such, global behavioral coding of the child's verbalizations and activities allows the quantification of both the reactive and self-regulatory strategies a child engages in during such challenging tasks.

Although such tasks and global coding schemes are informative in terms of emotional and self-regulatory processes in toddlers and preschool-age children, they are not feasible with younger participants. Very young children will not understand instructions, and toddlers generally cannot inhibit their motor responses to participate in these tasks. However, simpler eliciting conditions and more detailed coding schemes have been developed to examine the temporal dynamics of reactive and self-regulatory processes in younger children (e.g., Buss & Goldsmith, 1998; Grolnick, Bridges, & Connell, 1996; Stifter

& Braungart, 1995). For example, Buss and Goldsmith (1998) observed 6-, 12-, and 18-month-old infants in two tasks designed to elicit anger and two tasks designed to elicit fear, as described in Goldsmith and Rothbart's Laboratory Temperament Assessment Battery (Lab-TAB; Goldsmith & Rothbart, 1988). In one anger episode, the infant is allowed to play with a small, attractive toy, and then the toy is placed behind a Plexiglas barrier so that it is in sight but unreachable. In the other anger episode, the infant's arms are gently held down to his or her sides. Both fear episodes involve the approach of an unpredictable object: a fabric spider and a mechanical toy dog. Given the young age of the participants, each episode is short, lasting for approximately 1 minute. Videotapes of the sessions are then coded following standardized coding systems from the Lab-TAB, with emotional reactivity being captured by coding the peak intensity of facial expressions and vocalizations of emotion and regulatory behaviors being coded, such as gaze aversion, visual distraction, and approach/withdrawal behaviors. Using such detailed coding, Buss and Goldsmith (1998) found that infants who used visual distraction and approach responses during the anger episodes were able to reduce the intensity of or regulate their anger expressions. These behaviors did not, however, function to reduce the intensity of fear reactions.

Together, these studies demonstrate that as regulatory capacities and their underlying neural systems develop over childhood, methods for eliciting and coding reactive and self-regulatory behaviors must change as well. The age of the child and choice of task will determine whether the task will elicit both reactive emotional responses alone or in some combination with attempts at self-regulation. Similarly, the age of the child and task demands will affect the researcher's decision regarding the types of behaviors and strategies that are deemed the best indicators of reactive versus self-regulatory capacities at any given age. Although global coding schemes may capture the regulatory efforts of toddlers and preschoolers, more detailed coding of the duration and change in direction of visual orienting and engagement may be needed to capture the same processes in infants.

Specific Methodological Issues in the Study of Emotion in Children

Controlling for Baseline State

Among the issues that are of particular importance to the study of infants and young children is control over baseline state. In the literature on infant state, Prechtl (1974) described five states that vary along a dimension of sleep-wakefulness: deep sleep, slow-wave sleep, REM sleep, drowsiness, quiet alert, and crying. Infants in the first months of life often transition rapidly from one state into another, and the length of time that they spend in any one state, particularly in those associated with wakefulness, is often short. Over the first year of life, periods of wakefulness increase in duration and the abruptness of the transitions between states decreases, with patterns of sleep-wakefulness assuming a more regular schedule. However, this maturing state pattern is easily disrupted, and infants are sometimes overstimulated, in which case prolonged periods of crying or sleep may ensue. During the second and third years of life, states assume a more regular pattern, with periods of alertness now making up the majority of the child's day. Nevertheless, these alert periods are easily perturbed by alterations in sleep or feeding routines or by overstimulation.

The impact of this pattern of infant state development for assessing emotion is obvious. During the early months of life, infants may be engaged only for short periods of time when they are alert and quiet, and even then there are often abrupt changes in state, which clearly compromise the implementation and interpretation of emotion elicitation procedures. A cursory examination of the infant experimental literature finds that between 20 and 50% of infants tested in a particular paradigm (not necessarily one designed to elicit emotion) do not complete the task due to state changes during testing. By the second year of life and into the toddler period, it becomes easier to identify prolonged periods of alertness during which emotion may be elicited. Nevertheless, researchers must be cognizant of an infant's sleep-wake cycle, feeding schedule, and state prior to and during testing. Thus time of day for assessment, hours since previous feeding, and time since last nap all become critical factors in administering emotion tasks in a standard fashion across groups of infants. An example of the impact of state on young children's reactions during emotion elicitation paradigms is demonstrated in a research report by Gunnar and colleagues (Larson, Gunnar, & Hertsgaard, 1991). In this study, toddlers were screened on an emotion eliciting task and saliva was assayed to obtain a measure of cortisol. The researchers found that those children who had napped in the car on the drive into the laboratory displayed different cortisol responses relative to those who did not.

The Effects of Variations in Nonsocial and Social Context

The effect of context is as critical for developmental studies of emotion as it is for studies of emotion in adults. Where an experiment takes place, who presents the elicitor, and what the elicitor is are all research design elements that will affect a young child's emotional response. For example, brief separation from the mother in an unfamiliar laboratory setting usually evokes distress and negative affect in infants between the ages of 10 and 18 months. However, performing this same procedure in the home significantly reduces the degree of distress and negative affect infants express (Ross, Kagan, Zelazo, & Kotelchuck, 1975). Who presents the elicitor is also a factor. There are differences in infant response to physical restraint depending on whether the child's mother or an

unfamiliar adult performs the restraint. In an extreme version of the examination of the effect of the nature of the elicitor on infant response, Brooks and Lewis (1976) examined infant fear responses to an unfamiliar person by having infants exposed to either a normal-sized unfamiliar adult, a midget, or a child the same size as the midget. These authors found wariness to the normal-sized unfamiliar adult, interest to the child, and surprise expressions to the adult midget. Thus the degree of unfamiliarity and novelty of the eliciting conditions will lead not only to quantitative but also qualitative differences in the nature of the emotions that are elicited.

The issue of context also relates to a number of critical conceptual issues in emotion research with infants and young children. One assumption is that certain elicitors are specific to certain emotions and not others. That is, it is assumed that a given context or elicitor will elicit a unique set of facial and/or vocal expressions of emotion. For example, arm restraint procedures are often used to elicit anger, whereas exposure to sour tastes is used to elicit disgust. There are only a few studies, however, that have examined the specificity of the associations between eliciting conditions and emotional expressions. For example, Bennett, Bendersky, and Lewis (2002) tested 4-month-old infants with a set of elicitors and coded specific facial expressions in response to each elicitor. The eliciting conditions and the hypothesized emotion were as follows: tickling (joy), a sour taste (disgust), a jack in the box (surprise), an arm restraint (anger), and the approach of a masked stranger (fear). The data from this study were mixed in terms of supporting the specificity of the associations between elicitors and reactions. The data supported both an intraindividual position on emotion (a unique facial expression for a given context) and an interindividual position (a specific facial expression of emotion is more prevalent to a specific elicitor than to others), but only for the emotion of joy. Specifically, joy was seen to the tickle elicitor more than to any of the other elicitors. But interestingly, for the other eliciting conditions, many emotions that were not predicted were observed. For example, although the arm restraint procedure was hypothesized to elicit anger, expressions of surprise and joy were more prevalent than anger expressions. Similarly, the stranger-approach paradigm was hypothesized to elicit fear, but surprise, joy, and anger were more prevalent than expressions of fear. As such, there was little intraindividual specificity for these eliciting conditions.

Together these studies emphasize the importance of standardizing eliciting conditions when studying emotion in infants and young children. As well, it is important to examine a range of emotions to specific elicitors rather than only those thought to be elicited by the particular task. One cannot depend on a particular task to elicit only one type of emotion. Indeed, the infant's socialization and interaction history may influence the efficacy of a task to elicit a particular emotion.

The social context in which emotions take place is a specific example of the ways in which emotional displays vary by context. With an increased understanding and awareness of the impact of emotional expressions on others' behaviors and feelings, children develop the ability to strategically modify the intensity and even the valence of their emotions. In a classic example of young children's strategic use of emotions, Blurton-Jones (1967) found that 3- and 4-year-old children engaged in play were more likely to cry after a minor injury if they noticed a caregiver looking at them. This finding suggested that children's emotional expressions are tightly coupled to the social environment in which an emotion eliciting event takes place and that by early childhood children are capable of creating disparities between their internal emotional states and their external expressive behaviors. Although the preceding example demonstrates children's abilities to heighten an expression of emotion in order to gain attention, preschoolers will also dampen their emotional reactions in order to protect the feelings of others (Saarni, 1989). Discrepancies between felt and expressed emotions can also arise from children's increased understanding of culturally prescribed display rules regarding when and where emotional expressions should be managed (Saarni et al., 1998).

The ability to "mask" an emotional response requires knowledge about display rules, the ability to control skeletal muscles involved in expressions, and the motivation to enact display rules in certain situations. A paradigm that has been used extensively to study "masking" is called the *disappointment paradigm,* developed by Carolyn Saarni (1984) and Pamela Cole (1986). In this paradigm the child is first presented with a set of toys, some of which are highly desirable (e.g., a necklace, a bouncy ball) and some of which are highly undesirable (e.g., a balloon with a hole in it). The child is told to rank order the toys, indicating which toy he or she wants to have most as a prize for participation in the tasks to follow. At the conclusion of the tasks a new experimenter brings the child his or her prize, which happens to be one of the toys he or she previously ranked as highly undesirable. The child's facial and vocal affect, body posture, and verbal responses are all coded in order to assess expressions of disappointment and expressions of feigned happiness and excitement. The social context in which the child's reactions are observed is varied by having the child either sit with an unfamiliar adult experimenter or sit alone following the disappointment paradigm. Cole (1986) found that children as young as 4 years of age changed their expressions of disappointment following a lab-induced disappointment based on whether they were alone or in the company of an unfamiliar adult experimenter. Specifically, children were significantly more likely to mask expressions of disappointment in the company of the experimenter but showed a significant increase in sad and disappointed expressions once the experimenter left the child alone.

The work on children's use of display rules demonstrates the importance of considering not only the physical context in which assessments of emotion take place but also the social context. Given the increasing sensitivity of children, with age, to others' perspectives and culturally prescribed rules regarding the display of emotion, paradigms that include variations in social context (i.e., child alone vs. with an experimenter) are essential for separating out children's true emotional reactions from their use of display rules.

Validity of Parental Reports

Much of the research on emotion in adults relies on self-report measures of current emotional state, as well as more enduring emotional traits. For example, in an emotion elicitation paradigm with adults, participants might be asked to fill out a quick checklist of emotions prior to, and again following, the elicitation procedure. Given that much research on emotion in developmental psychology takes place with preverbal children, researchers tend to use parents as a primary source of information regarding their child's emotional states and traits.

Many have argued for the continued use of parental report measures simply because of the extent of knowledge and experience a parent has with his or her young child, which makes them likely to be the most reliable single source of information regarding their child's typical emotions and reactions (Carey, 1983; Rothbart & Bates, 1998). The obvious weakness in relying exclusively on parent report measures is that all parents will experience some type of bias that will influence their reporting (Goldsmith & Hewitt, 2003). Specifically, in addition to parents' objective observations and interpretations, all parent report measures will also contain a subjective component (Bates & Bayles, 1984; Goldsmith & Hewitt, 2003; Vaughn, Taraldson, Crichton, & Egeland, 1981). This subjective component derives from characteristics of the informant, including his or her own emotional biases. For example, Vaughn et al. (1981) reported that mothers' descriptions of children as difficult (negative in mood, unadaptable, intense) were more strongly related to the mothers' self-reports of anxiousness and hostility than they were to observers' ratings of the infants' actual reactions during feedings and a free-play session. One obvious interpretation of this finding is that much of the variability in parent report measures of infants' emotional and behavioral tendencies can be attributed to mothers' characteristics rather than the infant characteristics they are designed to assess. This systematic, yet difficult to quantify, measurement error may end up influencing the interpretations and conclusions drawn from these measures (Seifer, 2003). Other sources of bias in parents' reports include social desirability and a lack of experience with other infants, which gives them little to judge their own infant's behaviors against (Rothbart & Bates, 1998).

Another question these findings raise, though, is what an appropriate comparison to make in judging the validity of parent report measures is. Given the differences in context and breadth of assessment in short laboratory-based observations versus parent report measures, what is the appropriate metric with which to judge the validity of parent report measures? Several studies suggest that if parents and observers are asked to make judgments of the same behaviors over the same period of time, there is a good deal of agreement in their reports (e.g., Hagekull, Bohlin, & Lindhagen, 1984). Bates and Bayles (1984) also reported that mothers and observers showed moderate agreement in their observations of infants in both naturalistic and structured contexts.

Given the unique perspective of parents on young children's typical emotional styles, parent report measures will likely always be a part of the battery of assessment tools employed by developmental psychologists. In order to minimize the likelihood that informant bias will influence parents' responding, items must be based on sound item-writing techniques that ask parents to make specific judgments focused on the frequency of easily observable behaviors as opposed to more global judgments (e.g., Saudino, 2003). These types of items form the basis for Mary Rothbart's series of temperament questionnaires: the Infant Behavior Questionnaire (IBQ; 1981), the Infant Behavior Questionnaire—Revised (2003); the Toddler Behavior Assessment Questionnaire (TBAQ; Goldsmith, 1996), and the Children's Behavior Questionnaire (CBQ; Rothbart, Ahadi, Hershey, & Fisher, 2001), which have been extended and revised over a 25-year period.

One of the most important features in evaluating parent report measures is their validity in predicting children's actual observed responses in similar situations. Unfortunately, despite significant changes and improvements in the design and construction of parent report measures, researchers continue to find only modest associations between observational and parent report assessments of temperament (e.g., Seifer, 2003). Interpreting the meaning of these discrepancies is difficult given that they could be due to low levels of reliability and/or validity in parent reports or in lab-based observational measures. That is, all other methods of assessment are also susceptible to measurement error, including lab observations (Rothbart & Hwang, 2002).

Some ways to maximize the reliability of parental reports include structuring the environment as much as possible by having parents complete the measures in similar contexts and minimizing the amount of bias presented based on the content of other measures completed just prior to the temperament assessment. Items should address recently occurring events rather than relying on parents' memories over relatively long periods of time and should ask parents about concrete behaviors rather than asking for subjective or abstract judgments (Rothbart & Goldsmith, 1985).

Advances in the construction of parent report measures over the past two decades have led to more objective measurements. Most current parent report measures of infants' and children's temperament and emotional biases have eliminated wording that leaves questions open to interpretation and instead ask parents to report on the frequency of specific behaviors and emotional expressions within a well-

defined period of time, in an attempt to maximize the objectiveness of parents' responses. Ultimately, however, given the inherent difficulties associated with both laboratory-based assessments of emotion in infants and young children and parent report measures, the most reliable assessments of emotion likely come from using multiple measures of the same constructs.

Ethical Issues in the Elicitation and Assessment of Emotion in Infants and Young Children

Assent

In 2002, the American Psychological Association (APA) published an updated version of their Ethical Principles of Psychologists and Code of Conduct (APA, 2002). This code states that when conducting research with children (or other persons who are legally incapable of giving informed consent) researchers must (1) provide an appropriate explanation of the study, (2) seek the child's assent, (3) consider the child's preferences and best interests, and (4) obtain informed consent from a legally authorized person. Although it is standard practice to give age-appropriate explanations of research protocols to child participants, to consider children's preferences when designing research studies, and to obtain parental permission, seeking child assent is a relatively new, and controversial, requirement.

The requirement to obtain assent from child participants is vague in many ways, and the details vary from institution to institution. Specifically, there is confusion over how detailed the assent must be, how the assent is to be documented (i.e., verbal vs. written), and at what age it is required (Berenbaum, Cauffman, & Newcombe, 2004). The requirement for child assent is clearly not reasonable when children are too young to understand what is being asked. And even if children understand what they will be asked to do during the course of a study, the ethical concepts of confidentiality and research rights are more difficult to understand. Specifically, up until 12 years of age, children usually do not understand their research rights regarding confidentiality and the right to withdraw from participating, nor do they clearly understand what their participation involves or the goals of a research study, even following detailed debriefing (Hurley & Underwood, 2002). This suggests that there may be little practical or ethical utility in collecting assent from children under the age of 12 if their parents have already provided written informed consent.

In addition to describing the purpose of a study and the procedures, researchers are required to tell children that they have the right to terminate their participation in a study at any time. The practical implication of this requirement is that the first time a child protests, researchers are technically bound to discontinue the procedures. This is clearly a very difficult policy to implement, especially in the study of emotions in young children. When the purpose of a study is to elicit some negative emotion, at what point are the child's reactions considered a protest? For example, in our own research on behavioral inhibition, children are observed in unfamiliar social and nonsocial situations (e.g., Fox, Henderson, Rubin, Calkins, & Schmidt, 2001). Variables of interest in these observational paradigms are how long it takes a child to approach an unfamiliar object or person and whether the child expresses any negative emotion when confronted with the unfamiliar stimuli. If testing sessions were terminated as soon as a child hesitated before approaching and/or expressed facial or vocal signs of wariness or fear, the entire purpose of our studies would be defeated. The policy that we feel works best is to leave the decision about terminating a session up to the parents. Parents are told at the beginning of the session that if at any time they believe their child is experiencing more distress than they would in everyday situations similar to those we observe in the lab, they are free to stop the session.

Although it is important for assent to be collected, it is also important that the code be made more specific regarding the age at which assent is meaningful. For children over this age, yet under the legal age for providing consent, assent must be collected based on the child's being provided with details regarding the parameters and procedures of the study and their rights to confidentiality and to withdraw from the study at any point.

The Use of Deception

The APA code of ethics limits the use of deceptive techniques in research to situations in which deception can be justified by the study's potential scientific, educational, or applied contribution and only in situations in which it is not feasible to collect comparable information using nondeceptive procedures (APA, 2002). Also, deception is not permitted in research that is expected to cause either physical pain or severe emotional distress. Finally, when a research design includes deception, psychologists are required to explain the deception as early in the course of a study as is feasible (APA, 2002). Two paradigms that involve deception have been used in the developmental literature to elicit emotion. The first is a version of the Trier test (Kirschbaum, Pirke, & Hellhammer, 1993) and involves telling a participant that he or she is going to be videotaped or have to present in public a brief speech about his or her most embarrassing moment. In one version, a video camera is placed in front of the child, and the child is told to think about this most embarrassing event for 3 minutes and to ready him- or herself to present this orally (Schmidt, Fox, Schulkin, & Gold, 1999). The child is also told that the videotape will be played in front of other children who are his or her age peers and that he or she will be judged on the quality of his or her speech. After the 3-minute preparatory period is completed, a research assistant enters the room and checks the camera, saying to the child that the camera is broken and hence they cannot complete this task today. After the session is over, the child is debriefed regarding the task. As seen in Schmidt et al. (1999), the task elicits behavioral and physiological changes in temperamentally inhibited children. A second task that involves deception is the disappointment paradigm described earlier. The task was designed to examine children's emotion control and masking of facial expressions of disappointment. It has been used with a wide age range of children, from 3 to 9 years of age.

When researchers use either of these paradigms, it is essential that the child be fully debriefed about the fact that he or she was deceived, as well as about the reasons that the researchers needed to use deception in the study. It is important to allow children the opportunity to ask questions about the deception and to engage in dialogue about how it felt and what they were thinking during the procedure. We find that many children want to know how other children react in the same situation, and we believe it is important to explain to the participants that their response was exactly what we would expect and is in no way indicative of a weakness on their part.

Eliciting Negative Emotion

From a reading of this chapter, it should be obvious that developmental psychologists go to lengths to elicit negative emotion in infants and young children. Although the nature of the elicitors varies with age, the common element is that they are all mildly unpleasant. Example paradigms include: presenting sour tastes or odors; use of physical restraint; the approach of an unfamiliar, expressionless person; a brief separation of the infant from the mother; suspension over a visual cliff apparatus; placing attractive toys out of reach but in sight; and the approach of unpredictable mechanical toys. Even with informed consent given by parents, it is possible that some of these elicitors will produce extreme or intense degrees of upset in some infants and young children. For example, studies that assess the emotion reactions of temperamentally fearful infants or young children are likely to elicit some intense emotional reactions. In general, though, the institutional review boards of research universities have agreed to these types of research protocols based on an understanding that the nature of the eliciting conditions will be no more intense than what typically developing children experience in their everyday activities. Thus, although it is challenging to design paradigms that will serve as good general elicitors of negative emotions, researchers must always be vigilant in evaluating the intensity of the laboratory experience compared with experiences in everyday life. As is always the case in studies with children, the ultimate decision regarding participation and continuing participation once a procedure begins needs to lie with the parent for children under the age of meaningful assent and with the child who is able to provide his or her own assent.

Table 21.1

Summary of suggestions regarding emotion elicitation, assessment, and ethical considerations in research with infants and young children

Emotion elicitation	• Control for baseline state • Clearly explain goal of task to ensure comparable interpretations across participants • Vary context of elicitation to isolate effects of stimuli per se versus contextual influences
Emotion assessment	• Place assessment in developmental context by collecting developmental history for motor and language milestones • Use independent codes of reactive versus self-regulatory responses • Code presence and intensity of range of emotions, including those not intentionally elicited • Blend micro and macro codes of emotion to aid in interpretation of elicited responses • In studies of individual differences, collect multiple measures, including psychometrically sound parent report measures
Ethical considerations	• Collect assent using child-appropriate language • Use parents as primary resource regarding decisions to discontinue protocol when negative affect is elicited • Beginning at preschool age, provide full debriefing directly to children including explanation of purpose of deception if used

Conclusion

Although the study of emotion in infants and young children shares many of the challenges faced by researchers of emotion with adults, there are also many unique challenges. Infants and young children change rapidly across many domains of development in addition to emotion, including cognition, perception, and social cognition. Changes in each of these domains influence the nature of the interactions a child has with his or her environment and therefore influence his or her appraisal and reaction to emotion eliciting situations. As such, developmental psychologists interested in emotion must integrate ideas and measures from diverse areas of psychology. When working with infants and children, researchers face the challenge of working around their rapidly changing states of sleep and wakefulness and need to design paradigms that are relatively quick and easy

to administer. Although the paradigms must be relatively simple, the coding schemes used to quantify emotional reactions need to be developmentally appropriate and detailed enough to capture both reactive and self-regulatory processes that underlie emotion. Given that all measures of emotion in young children have inherent weaknesses, it is best to employ multiple measures of the same construct as a way to minimize the overall level of measurement error. Finally, when working with infants and young children, special attention must be paid to ethical issues related to child assent and research rights.

Acknowledgment

Support for this chapter was funded in part by a grant to NAF from the National Institutes of Health (HD#17899).

References

American Psychological Association. (2002). Ethical principles of psychologists and code of conduct. *American Psychologist, 57,* 1060–1073.

Barrett, K. C. (1998). The origins of guilt in early childhood. In J. Bybee (Ed.), *Guilt and children* (pp. 75–90). San Diego: Academic Press.

Bates, J. E., & Bayles, K. (1984). Objective and subjective components in mothers' perceptions of their children from age 6 months to 3 years. *Merrill-Palmer Quarterly, 30,* 111–130.

Bennett, D. S., Bendersky, M., & Lewis, M. (2002). Facial expressivity at 4 months: A context by expression analysis. *Infancy, 3,* 97–113.

Berenbaum, S., Cauffman, E., & Newcombe, N. (2004). Division 7 Task Force Report on IRB issues. As cited by Chamberlain, J. (2004). Facilitating research with children, *Monitor on Psychology, 35* (3), 74.

Bertenthal, B. I., & Campos, J. J. (1990). A systems approach to the organizing effects of self-produced locomotion during infancy. In C. Rovee-Collier & L. P. Lipsitt (Eds.), *Advances in infancy research* (Vol. 6, pp. 1–60). Norwood, NJ: Ablex.

Bertenthal, B. I., Campos, J. J., & Kermoian, R. (1992). An epigenetic perspective on the development of self-produced locomotion and its consequences. *Psychological Science, 3,* 140–145.

Biringen, Z., Emde, R. N., Campos, J. J., & Applebaum, M. I. (1995). Affective reorganization in the infant, the mother, and the dyad: The role of upright locomotion and its timing. *Child Development, 66,* 499–514.

Blurton-Jones, N. (1967). An ethological study of some aspects of social behaviour of children in nursery school. In D. Morris (Ed.), *Primate ethology* (pp. 347–368). London: Weidenfeld & Nicolson.

Brooks, J., & Lewis, M. (1976). Infants' responses to strangers: Midget, adult, and child. *Child Development, 47,* 323–332.

Buss, K. A., & Goldsmith, H. H. (1998). Fear and anger regulation in infancy: Effects on the temporal dynamics of affective expression. *Child Development, 69,* 359–374.

Campos, J. J., Bertenthal, B. I., & Kermoian, R. (1992). Early experience and emotional development: The emergence of wariness of heights. *Psychological Science, 3,* 61–64.

Campos, J. J., Hiatt, S., Ramsay, D., Henderson, C., & Svejda, M. (1978). The emergence of a fear of heights. In M. Lewis & L. Rosenblum (Eds.), *The development of affect* (pp. 149–182). New York: Plenum Press.

Campos, J. J., Kermoian, R., & Zumbahlen, M. R. (1992). Socioemotional transformations in the family system following infant crawling onset. In N. Eisenberg & R. A. Fabes (Eds.), *Emotion and its regulation in early development.* New Directions for Child Development, No. 55 (pp. 25–40). San Francisco: Jossey-Bass.

Carey, W. B. (1983). Some pitfalls in infant temperament research. *Infant Behavior and Development, 6,* 247–259.

Cole, P. M. (1986). Children's spontaneous expressive control of facial expression. *Child Development, 57,* 1309–1321.

Derryberry, D., & Reed, M. A. (2002). Anxiety-related attentional biases and their regulation by attentional control. *Journal of Abnormal Psychology, 111,* 225–236.

Derryberry, D., & Rothbart, M. K. (1988). Affect, arousal, and attention as components of temperament. *Journal of Personality and Social Psychology, 55,* 958–966.

Ekman, P., & Friesen, W. V. (1984). *Facial Action Coding (FACS) manual.* San Francisco. Consulting Psychologists Press.

Fox, N. A., & Henderson, H. A. (2000, April). Temperament, emotion, and executive function: Influences on the development of self-regulation. M. Farah & M. Moscovitch (Chairs), Life Is More Than a Delayed Saccade: Exploring the Social and Emotional Functions of Frontal Cortex. Symposium conducted at the annual meeting of the Cognitive Neuroscience Society, San Francisco, CA.

Fox, N. A., Henderson, H. A., Rubin, K. H., Calkins, S. D., & Schmidt, L. A. (2001). Continuity and discontinuity of behavioral inhibition and exuberance: Psychophysiological and behavioral influences across the first four years of life. *Child Development, 72,* 1–21.

Goldsmith, H. H. (1996). Studying temperament via construction of the Toddler Behavior Assessment Questionnaire. *Child Development, 67,* 218–235.

Goldsmith, H. H., & Hewitt, E. C. (2003). Validity of parental report of temperament: Distinctions and needed research. *Infant Behavior and Development, 26,* 108–111.

Goldsmith, H. H., & Rothbart, M. K. (1988). Manual for the Laboratory Temperament Assessment Battery, Version 1. Unpublished manuscript.

Gottman, J. M., Katz, L. F., & Hooven, C. (1997). *Meta-emotion: How families communicate emotionally.* Mahwah, NJ: Erlbaum.

Grolnick. W. S., Bridges, L. J., & Connell, J. P. (1996). Emotion regulation in two-year-olds: Strategies and emotional expression in four contexts. *Child Development, 67,* 928–941.

Hagekull, B., Bohlin, G., & Lindhagen, K. (1984). Validity of parent reports. *Infant Behavior and Development, 7,* 77–92.

Hurley, J. C., & Underwood, M. K. (2002). Children's understanding of their research rights before and after debriefing: Informed assent, confidentiality, and stopping participation. *Child Development, 73,* 132–143

Izard, C. (1977). *Human emotions.* New York: Plenum Press.

Izard, C. E. (1979). *The maximally discriminative facial action coding system.* Newark, DE: University of Delaware Press.

Izard, C., & Malatesta, C. (1987). Perspectives on emotional development: I. Different emotions theory of early emotional development. In J. Osofsky (Ed.), *Handbook of infant development* (2nd ed., pp. 494–553). New York: Wiley.

Johnson, M. H., Posner, M. I., & Rothbart, M. K. (1991). Components of visual orienting in early infancy: Contingency learning, anticipatory looking, and disengaging. *Journal of Cognitive Neuroscience, 3,* 335–344.

Kagan, J. (1981). *The second year: The emergence of self-awareness.* Cambridge, MA: Harvard University Press.

Kagan, J., Kearsley, R., & Zelazo, P. R. (1978). *Infancy: Its place in human development.* Cambridge, MA: Harvard University Press.

Kirschbaum, C., Pirke, K.-M., & Hellhammer, D. H. (1993). The "Trier Social Stress Test": A tool for investigating psychobiological stress responses in a laboratory setting. *Neuropsychobiology, 28,* 76–81.

Kochanska, G., Murray, K. T., & Coy, K. C. (1997). Inhibitory control as a contributor to conscience in childhood: From toddler to early school age. *Child Development, 67,* 490–507.

Larson, M. C., Gunnar, M. R., & Hertsgaard, L. (1991). The effects of morning naps, car trips, and maternal separation on adrenocortical activity in human infants. *Child Development, 62,* 362–372.

Lewis, M., & Brooks-Gunn, J. (1979). *Social cognition and the acquisition of self.* New York: Plenum.

Lewis, M., Sullivan, M. W., Stanger, C., & Weiss, M. (1989). Self development and self-conscious emotions. *Child Development, 60,* 146–156.

Mischel, W., Ebbesen, E. B., & Zeiss, A. R. (1972). Cognitive and attentional mechanisms in delay of gratification. *Journal of Personality and Social Psychology, 21,* 204–218.

Mischel, W., Shoda, Y., & Rodriguez, M. L. (1989). Delay of gratification in children. *Science, 244,* 933–988.

Posner, M. I., & Petersen, S. E. (1990). The attention system of the human brain. *Annual Review of Neuroscience, 13,* 25–42.

Posner, M. I., & Raichle, M. E. (1994). *Images of mind.* New York: Scientific American Books.

Posner, M. I., & Rothbart, M. K. (1998). Attention, self-regulation and consciousness. *Philosophical Transactions of the Royal Society of London: Series B. Biological Sciences, 353,* 1915–1927.

Posner, M. I., & Rothbart, M. K. (2000). Developing mechanisms of self-regulation. *Development and Psychopathology, 12,* 427–441.

Prechtl, H. F. R. (1974). The behavioral states of the new-born infant: A review. *Brain Research, 76,* 185–212.

Ross, G., Kagan, J., Zelazo, P., & Kotelchuck, M. (1975). Separation protest in infants in home and laboratory. *Developmental Psychology, 11,* 256–257.

Rothbart, M. K., Ahadi, S. A., & Hershey, K. L. (1994). Temperament and social behavior in childhood. *Merrill-Palmer Quarterly, 40,* 21–39.

Rothbart, M. K., Ahadi, S. A., Hershey, K. L., & Fisher, P. (2001). Investigations of temperament at three to seven years: The Children's Behavior Questionnaire. *Child Development, 72,* 1394–1408.

Rothbart, M. K., & Bates, J. E. (1998). Temperament. In

W. Damon (Series Ed.) & N. Eisenberg (Vol. Ed.), *Handbook of child psychology: Vol. 3. Social, emotional, and personality development* (5th ed., pp. 105–176). New York: Wiley.

Rothbart, M. K., & Goldsmith, H. H. (1985). Three approaches to the study of infant temperament. *Developmental Review, 5,* 237–260.

Rothbart, M. K., & Hwang, J. (2002). Measuring infant temperament. *Infant Behavior and Development, 25,* 113–116.

Rueda, M. R., Posner, M. I., & Rothbart, M. K. (2004). Attentional control and self-regulation. In R. F. Baumeister & K. D. Vohs (Eds.), *Handbook of self-regulation: Research, theory, and applications* (pp. 283–300). New York: Guilford Press.

Ruff, H. A., & Rothbart, M. K. (1996). *Attention in early development: Themes and variations.* New York: Oxford University Press.

Saarni, C. (1984). An observational study of children's attempts to monitor their expressive behavior. *Child Development, 55,* 1504–1513.

Saarni, C. (1989). Children's understanding of strategic control of emotional expression in social transactions. In C. Saarni & P. L. Harris (Eds.), *Children's understanding of emotion* (pp. 181–208). New York: Cambridge University Press.

Saarni, C., Mumme, D. L., & Campos, J. J. (1998). Emotional development: Action, communication, and understanding. In W. Damon (Series Ed.) & N. Eisenberg (Vol. Ed.), *Handbook of child psychology: Vol. 3. Social, emotional, and personality development* (5th ed., pp. 237–310). New York: Wiley.

Saudino, K. J. (2003). The need to consider contrast effects in parent-rated temperament. *Infant Behavior and Development, 26,* 118–120.

Scarr, S., & Salapatek, P. (1970). Patterns of fear development during infancy. *Merrill-Palmer Quarterly, 16,* 53–90.

Schmidt, L. A., Fox, N. A., Schulkin, J., & Gold, P. W. (1999). Behavioral and psychophysiological correlates of self-presentation in temperamentally shy children. *Developmental Psychobiology, 35,* 119–135.

Seifer, R. (2003). Twin studies, biases of parents, and biases of researchers. *Infant Behavior and Development, 26,* 115–117.

Shoda, Y., Mischel, W., & Peake, P. (1990). Predicting adolescent cognitive and self-regulatory competencies from preschool delay of gratification: Identifying diagnostic conditions. *Developmental Psychology, 26,* 978–986.

Stifter, C. A., & Braungart, J. M. (1995). The regulation of negative reactivity in infancy: Function and development. *Developmental Psychology, 31,* 448–455.

Stipek, D. J. (1983). A developmental analysis of pride and shame. *Human Development, 26,* 42–54.

Stipek, D. (1995). The development of pride and shame in toddlers. In J. P. Tangney & K. W. Fischer (Eds.), *Self-conscious emotions: The psychology of shame, guilt, embarrassment, and pride* (pp. 237–252). New York: Guilford Press.

Stipek, D., Recchia, S., & McClintic, S. (1992). Self-evaluation in young children. *Monographs of the Society for Research in Child Development, 57* (1, Serial No. 226).

Vaughn, B. E., Taraldson, B. J., Crichton, L., & Egeland, B. (1981). The assessment of infant temperament: A critique of the Carey Infant Temperament Questionnaire. *Infant Behavior and Development, 4,* 1–17.

Lis Nielsen
Alfred W. Kaszniak

Conceptual, Theoretical, and Methodological Issues in Inferring Subjective Emotion Experience

Recommendations for Researchers

In recent years, researchers in a variety of disciplines have outlined broad methodological strategies for approaching the scientific study of conscious experience, advocating the systematic inclusion of phenomenological data in ongoing research and the use of findings at the phenomenal level to constrain investigations at other, more objective levels of analysis (Baars, 1988; Chalmers, 1999, 2004; Flanagan, 1992; Varela, 1996). The proposals differ in the details, but they share the common theme that new and better self-report methods will be required to advance our understanding of experience. Compared with the apparent fine-grained nature of phenomenal experience, our measures of it remain crude. Varela (1996) lamented that the advancement of the field of consciousness studies may be hindered by a reticence on the part of traditional investigators to take phenomenological investigation seriously, especially when it comes to an investigation of their own conscious states.

In some respects, we find ourselves in this situation as an accident of history. Though no longer the case, the study of conscious experience was once central to psychological investigations, with elaborate methodologies developed to approach the problem. Thus in 1890, William James could write:

Introspective Observation is what we have to rely on first and foremost and always. . . . Everyone agrees that there we discover states of consciousness. . . . All people unhesitatingly believe that they feel themselves thinking, and that they distinguish the mental state as an inward activity or passion, from all the objects with which it may cognitively deal. *I regard this belief as the most fundamental of all the postulates of Psychology.* (1890/1983, p. 185)

Subsequently, behaviorism and cognitive psychology set first-person investigations on the methodological sideline, where they remained for most of the twentieth century.

Though strongly inspired by European phenomenological traditions (much of his *Principles of Psychology* is built around introspective data), James nonetheless describes the whole of the *Principles* as " a collection of illustrations of the difficulty of discovering by direct introspection exactly what our feelings and their relations are (1890/1983, p.191)." In particular, he warns that the "absence of a special vocabulary for subjective facts hinders the study of all but the very coarsest of them. . . . It is hard to focus our attention on the nameless, and so there results a certain vacuousness in the descriptive parts of most psychologies" (1890/1983, p. 194).

Conceptual Issues in the Study of Conscious Emotion

Interestingly, despite a revival of interest in the study of consciousness in psychology and neuroscience, detailed phenomenological investigation has been slow to gain a foothold,

361

with energies tending to focus on first-person—third-person correlations. Yet here lies the danger of which Varela (1996) warns. Even as our third-person methods become more sophisticated and refined and the search for the behavioral, physiological, or neural correlates of conscious experience proceeds, as long as we lack proper methods, vocabularies, and reporting schemes for first-person data, these correlations will remain extremely crude.

Within emotion research, these problems are especially salient because (1) experience plays such a central role in emotion, (2) experiences are multifaceted and subject to individual variation, and (3) experience is complexly related to the various nonconscious components of the emotional response.

Emotion, most would agree, is a nearly constant aspect of the human phenomenal experience. Over the past couple of decades, an increasing number of scholars and scientists have recognized the importance of emotion theory and research for the study of consciousness. Simultaneously, emotion researchers have grown more interested in the nature and function of conscious emotion experience (e.g., Damasio, 1994, 2003; Panksepp, 1998; Kaszniak, 2001). Some consciousness theorists (e.g., Damasio, 1999; Watt, 1999) see emotion as fundamental in the genesis of all conscious states. Others (e.g., DeLancey, 1996) have argued that the qualia of emotion experience provide a critical example for any philosophical speculation concerning the functional role of phenomenal conscious states. Within emotion research, recent developments in basic and clinical neuroscience have resulted in rapid progress toward understanding the neural bases of emotion (Lane, Nadel, Allen, & Kaszniak, 2000; LeDoux, 1996; Panksepp, 1998; Davidson, 2003). These developments also have encouraged theoretic speculation and empirical research on the neural correlates of conscious emotion experience (e.g., Kaszniak, Reminger, Rapcsak, & Glisky, 1999; Lane, 2000; Wiens, 2005). The identification of neural systems critical for the conscious experience of emotion may also provide important clues in the search for neural circuitry on which other domains of conscious experience are dependent. Meanwhile, there is lively debate among emotion researchers about the fundamental dimensions that characterize the phenomenal space of emotion experience (Cacioppo & Berntson, 1999; Feldman Barrett & Russell, 1999; Green & Salovey, 1999; Tellegen, Watson, & Clark, 1999). Individual differences in emotional awareness are also being explored using an ever-growing variety of measures (Gohm & Clore, 2000; Lane, Quinlan, Schwarz, & Walker, 1990; Salovey, Mayer, Caruso, & Lopes, 2003).

Notwithstanding this intensification of interest in conscious emotion, it remains true that, as is the case in the study of consciousness in general, one of the most difficult problems in emotion research is the measurement of subjective experience. Though many measures assume that experience reports represent actual experience, a host of theoretical and methodological issues warrant consideration by researchers interested in subjective emotion experience. How might one pursue a rigorous first-person science in a particular phenomenal domain, such as that of emotion experience, to supplement and inform our third-person investigations? Several questions can be posed about emotion experiences, all of which have methodological implications. Among these are: (1) What kinds of phenomenal content should be considered under the umbrella of emotion experience? Of all the things one may be conscious of when in an emotional state, which of them count as components of the emotion experience, and which do not? (2) What are the limits on the content of the momentary experience of emotion, that is, how many items, dimensions, or sensory modalities can we be conscious of at one time? (3) Are there distinct dimensions along which emotion experiences can vary? Are there discrete experiential types? (4) What are the relational properties of the experience to the experiencing subject (e.g., is emotion experience necessarily embodied, and if so, is it necessarily experienced as such)? Related to question 4 are: (5) What is the spatial structure of the phenomenal field during an emotion experience? (6) How is emotion experience temporally structured (how are the dynamics of emotion experienced)? and (7) Are there individual differences that result in qualitative or quantitative differences in how emotion is experienced? Finally, (8) Are there necessary relationships between the various components of an emotion experience, and on what underlying principles are these based?

These questions give rise to methodological concerns such as: (1) What are the cognitive (attentional, memory) limits on the reportability of emotion experience? (2) Does the process of reporting change the quality or content of the experience? (3) What sorts of reporting schemes are best suited to the different modalities, types, dimensions, and relational aspects of emotion experience?

The Complex Nature of Emotion

The measurement of emotion experience is further complicated by the very complexity of the phenomena we call emotions. There is no consensus among emotion theorists on the proper definition of emotion. Yet most would agree that emotions arise in separate response systems that are dynamically interrelated, including activities in central and autonomic nervous systems, changes in facial expression and posture, alterations in cognitive activity and content, activation of behavioral action tendencies, and changes in subjective experience. From an evolutionary perspective, emotions can be conceived of as solutions to the adaptive problem of how to coordinate these multiple response systems in the service of important survival goals. Emotions arise as response cascades that focus attention on important environmental stimuli, mobilize behavioral responses, and signal our emotional states to others. Evolutionary theorists Tooby and Cosmides (1990) have argued that the emotional feeling state plays a pivotal role in this process, providing the internal signal that coordinates behavior and cognition and promotes adaptive flexibility in an ever-changing environment.

Some scientists identify emotion with feeling, linking it inextricably to consciousness. Clore (1994), for example, views feeling as a necessary condition for emotion and sees conscious cognitive appraisal as preceding other emotional reactions. Some cognitive appraisal (in terms of positive or negative valuation in relation to personal goals, need states, or self-preservation) may indeed be a necessary condition for the activation of the various other emotion components (Lazarus, 1991). However, such appraisals need not necessarily be conscious (Frijda, 1993). Some of the evidence that important functions of emotion occur nonconsciously comes from nonhuman animal research. LeDoux's (1996, 2000) studies of fear in rodents have identified the amygdala as a key neural substrate for the hypothetically nonconscious generation of adaptive emotional fear responses. LeDoux proposes that early, rapid, unconscious appraisal carried out by the amygdala can activate autonomic effector systems, override ongoing cognitive processing, and bring the organism into appropriate behavioral modes, without these signals ever necessarily being represented in conscious experience or processed cortically. Human psychophysiological studies using visually masked presentations of emotional stimuli have also demonstrated that both skin conductance responses (Öhman & Soares, 1993, 1994, 1998) and facial EMG responses (Dimberg, Thunberg, & Elmehed, 2000) can be elicited when participants are not consciously aware of the eliciting stimulus. Both lines of evidence have been used to make claims about the existence of unconscious emotion.

As we discuss later, inferences about when emotion is or is not conscious depend on assumptions about the nature of conscious emotion and the necessary or sufficient conditions for its generation. Such inferences and assumptions depend, in turn, on one's conception of the interrelationships between the multiple response systems that contribute to emotional states. Although there is an empirical matter of fact about these questions, the science at present admits of multiple interpretations. For the purposes of this discussion, emotions are viewed as complex phenomena involving several distinguishable and often dissociable components, including physiological change, cognitive appraisal, action dispositions, expressive behaviors, and subjective experience. Theories of emotion differ as to whether any one or a combination of these components is necessary or sufficient to indicate the presence of an emotion.

Empirically, it has been demonstrated that certain of these components tend to operate in synchrony. For example, in paradigms involving the passive viewing of emotional pictures, the activity in certain physiological systems is significantly correlated with the experience of emotion: Electrodermal responses and electrocortical activity covary with self-reports of emotional arousal, whereas facial muscle electromyography, heart rate, and magnitude of eyeblink startle reflex covary

with self-reports along a dimension of emotional valence (Bradley & Lang, 2000; Lang, Greenwald, Bradley, & Hamm, 1993). Yet despite correlations between emotional self-report and physiology, the action in both physiological and experiential systems is multiply determined, and there are large individual differences in both the degree to which different systems are activated and the kinds of stimuli that evoke emotional responses (Bradley & Lang, 2000; Frijda, 1999; Lang, 1994).

Moreover, the various components of emotion appear to be dissociable in a number of ways. For example, a standard emotional regulatory strategy allows us to make conscious emotional appraisals and to experience emotion while inhibiting emotional behaviors and expression. As noted previously, numerous experimental studies have demonstrated that we can be physiologically aroused by emotional stimuli that we have not consciously appraised. Studies with neurological patient populations indicate that the self-reported experience of emotion can remain unchanged alongside deficits in the physiological systems that index emotional arousal and expression (Kaszniak, Nielsen, Rapcsak, & David, 2001; Reid, 2000; Burton & Kaszniak, 2006). Such findings underscore the difficulty in establishing the necessary or sufficient conditions for inferring the presence of an emotional state.

Were this situation not complex enough, it turns out that the components of emotion listed earlier also have dissociable elements. Cognitive appraisals may involve both nonconscious and conscious evaluations, with certain evaluations made prior to others (Scherer, 1999). The physiological change associated with emotion can be separated into multiple response units with separate underlying neural substrates—distinct actions in the sympathetic and parasympathetic nervous systems, as well as activity in specific central nervous system loci. Expressive behaviors have vocal, facial, and postural components. Action tendencies may include both dispositions to act and actual behaviors, with independent systems for approach and avoidance (Cacioppo & Gardner, 1999; Davidson, 2000; Davidson, Ekman, Saron, Senulis, & Friesen, 1990). Indeed, as we suggested earlier, the very feeling state that characterizes an emotion experience has multiple and dissociable components. It manifests itself in a variety of informational channels—including those that carry sensory, cognitive, and motivational information—and is complexly related to other emotion response systems.

The Subjective Experience of Emotion

Though not all theorists consider phenomenal experience a necessary feature of emotion, for most lay people, it is the most central component, adding color and meaning to events, relationships, and activities. Two independent approaches exist in the literature for classifying emotional states, and these have important implications for any analysis of emotion experience. One, the dimensional approach, conceives of emotion experiences as varying along two orthogonal dimensions of valence and arousal. Any given emotion can be located, in this view, in an affective space described by these dimensions (Bradley & Lang, 1994; Feldman Barrett & Russell, 1999). In contrast, the categorical—or "basic emotions"—approach emphasizes the unique qualities of discrete emotions such as fear, anger, joy, and sadness (Ekman, 1992; Izard, 1992; Panksepp, 1998, 2000). Proponents of the categorical approach claim that a dimensional approach obscures important features of emotional states, such as its failure to capture the differences between anger and fear, both highly arousing, negatively valenced states. Yet the two approaches may be compatible. The experience of any given basic emotion may have both intensity (arousal) and hedonic tone (valence) while simultaneously possessing unique phenomenal qualities not captured by these dimensions alone.

Neither the dimensional nor the categorical view does full justice to the rich phenomenal nature of emotion, as both fail to account for (1) the relational qualities of emotion experiences and how these are manifested in felt action tendencies or dispositions, (2) the ways perception and attention are altered by emotion and thereby alter emotion experience, or (3) the distinction between the raw "what it is like" (Nagel, 1974) phenomenal features of emotion experience and their more reflective conscious cognitive components.

Raw feelings and reflective cognitions contribute uniquely and interactively to shape current emotion experience. Because self-reports of emotion experience are generated when reflective cognition is brought to bear on these experience-constituting phenomena, these reports are, by definition, a product of the interaction of raw feeling and cognition.[1] The raw phenomenality of emotion is often the presumed target of our instruments when we seek to measure the subjective experience of emotion, that is, the nature of the raw phenomenal state that lies behind and gives rise to that report (though exceptions might include studies that explicitly target conscious emotional regulatory strategies). This distinction between raw phenomenality and reflective consciousness is fundamental to an understanding of conscious experience and has been elsewhere described as the distinction between "the immediate *feltness* of a feeling, and its perception by a subsequent reflective act" (James, 1890/1983, p. 189); between primary and secondary consciousness (Farthing, 1992; Lane, 2000); or between "first-order phenomenal experience and second-order awareness" (Lambie & Marcel, 2002, p. 228).

Although a full discussion of all aspects of emotion experience is beyond the scope of this chapter, the distinction between raw phenomenality and reflective consciousness is explored further, as it provides a useful framework for further discussion of methodological concerns in measuring conscious emotion. Issues of dimensions, discrete emotions, action dispositions, perception, and attention are addressed, where relevant, within this overall framework.

Raw Emotion Phenomenality

The "raw feel" of emotions is generally thought to consist largely in what are typically called feelings and desires, many (but by no means all) of which have a bodily or visceral component. Among the potential contributors to the raw feel of emotions are a variety of visceral and somatic changes, including the felt qualities of action tendencies and emotion expressions, somatically diffuse feelings of pleasure and displeasure, a host of bodily sensations associated with the arousal of various response systems and presumably linked to discrete physiological or neurochemical processes, as well as possibly unique physiological manifestations of discrete emotions.[2] In addition, a nonexhaustive list of *nonbodily* conscious experiences can be considered, which includes sensations of mental arousal, experiences of heightened or narrowed attention, felt changes in the temporal or relational properties of thoughts and specific perceptual imagery in any sensory channel, and cognitive phenomena such as the experience of uncertainty or conviction.[3]

In a recent analysis of emotion experience, Lambie and Marcel (2002) emphasize the error in supposing that all aspects of emotional phenomenality are grounded in awareness of states of the self. They distinguish two types of fundamental attentional focus that shape the current content of emotion experience: self-focus and world-focus. In world-focused experience, it is how things seem, rather than how one feels, that provides the experiential content. The *way things seem* to us is at the very core of the notion of raw phenomenality, and insofar as different emotional states alter perceptual, associative, and attentional processes, they are bound to influence the way in which the world is perceived. Arguing from a dimensional perspective, Fredrickson (1998) has proposed that positive emotional states engender a broader and more expansive cognitive and attentional style, in contrast to negative emotions that tend to narrow and focus attention on behaviorally relevant objects in the environment. Along these lines, one might predict that in a state of joy, the world would seem rich and full of prospects, whereas in a state of fear the salience of the feared object and of possible avenues for escape might eclipse all awareness of objects and possibilities in the periphery.

Discussions of attentional focus in emotion experience suggest that we are already talking about a more cognitive, reflective conscious experience of emotion. This is not the case, however, as Lambie and Marcel's (2002) analysis makes clear. Even raw feelings are experienced from within an attentional stance. In the case of raw feelings, however, it is a stance that is not deliberately taken but is rather a fundamental and constituting fact about the experiential state. In addition, the "degree of immersion or detachment of one's attentional attitude" can also vary, bringing variations in the content of one's experience along with it (Lambie & Marcel, 2002, p.234). In experiences of "flow" (Csikszentmihalyi, 1988), for example, awareness of the *self as object* evaporates during full immersion in an activity at which one is skilled, such as playing an instrument or cooking a meal. In contrast, more detached emotional phenomenality might result in states of striving to maintain attention on a difficult task or on controlling the expression of one's emotions, as when negotiating a raise or in an argument with colleagues.

Reflective Emotional Consciousness

The range of phenomena that constitute emotion experience is not exhausted by raw phenomenal states. Accompanying these is often a reflective cognitive overlay involving conscious thoughts and appraisals of one's state or of some aspect of the emotion-eliciting situation or environment. These reflective conscious thoughts are also "experienced" and are subject to many of the same organizing principles and distinctions as raw phenomenal states.

In self-focused emotion experience, the apprehension of a feeling state is often accompanied by a variety of reflective cognitions that contribute to shaping that experience. These include, but are not limited to, a reflective apprehension of the raw feeling state; the conscious appraisal of the eliciting stimulus in terms of one's goals, needs, and coping resources; and reappraisals of the eliciting event and the experience itself throughout the course of an emotion episode. These appraisals may be accompanied by conscious efforts to control or regulate the emotional state. Additional nonevaluative thoughts that arise in the course of an emotion episode may or may not properly constitute components of the emotion experience.

Lambie and Marcel (2002) emphasize that one's second-order attentional stance may vary along an analytic-synthetic dimension. From an analytic stance, one is aware of the constituting details of one's subjective state, such as changes in heart rate or respiration, or impulses to carry out particular behaviors. A synthetic stance involves, by contrast, an experience of an emotional state more categorically or holistically, as being afraid, for example, or as being in a diminished relationship to one's environment, whereby it is the gestalt of the experience that is in focus for the experiencing subject.

What determines the balance of reflective consciousness versus raw phenomenality in any emotion experience are factors such as how much one is "in the grip" of the emotion, or the extent to which one is regulating and reappraising the emotional state. One's degree of immersion or detachment may therefore influence the degree to which one is able to both experience and reflect simultaneously. Although we may never be able to measure raw phenomenality, unfiltered through reflective consciousness, it may be possible to cultivate states of consciousness that are simultaneously detached and immersed, allowing for a kind of minimally intrusive reflection on ongoing emotion experiences. Individuals with greater ability to enter such states might be of assistance in mapping out the relational and dimensional structure of emotion phenomenality.

Organizing Principles of Emotion Experience

Emotions, we proposed earlier, are solutions to the adaptive problem of how to coordinate multiple response systems in the service of important survival goals within one's environment. Lambie and Marcel (2002) propose two organizing principles that underlie the structure of emotion experience that are compatible with this analysis. Emotion experiences can be primarily focused on (1) the "evaluative description" of the emotion-eliciting event—"a representation (either of an event relative to a concern or of the state of the self)"—or (2) the "action attitude" adopted in responding to the event—"the bodily state itself (musculoskeletal, autonomic, and hormonal) and not a representation of it nor a plan" (p. 232–233). In the former, experience will focus on features of the world or the self as they are evaluated in light of one's current concerns, whereas in the latter, experience will be of the bodily and motivational or dispositional changes resulting from the evaluation.

For each of the components of the emotion response, there may be features of that component of which one is conscious—of physiological change, of action impulses, of thoughts and evaluations. If there is "something it is like" to be in such physiological, dispositional, or cognitive states, then this phenomenality ought to be considered constitutive of emotion experience. In addition, much of the relational structure of emotion experience arises directly from the various components of the emotional state—for example, action tendencies are directed at (or away from) objects in the world or one's own feelings and thoughts; physiological and expressive changes occur within a spatiotemporal context, within a physical body in a situated environment. These relational and contextual properties impose constraints, albeit very broad, on what constitutes a component of emotion experience, and they ought to inform the scales or dimensions along which we seek to measure that experience.

The Relation Between Raw Feelings and Reflective Consciousness

How raw feelings and reflective cognitive consciousness interact to shape emotion experience is only partly understood. As just described, cognition can shape experience by focusing attention on particular features of that experience, either deliberately or as the result of some nonconscious attentional bias. For example, cognitions can exert control over feelings in processes of deliberate emotion regulation (Gross, 2002), as when one tries to control an angry outburst by reminding oneself of the possible deleterious consequences. Conversely, feelings can influence reflective cognition and behavior, as when a positive mood state results in more flexible cognitive processing (Isen, 2000) or when a strong visceral drive leads to behaviors that would, in less heated moments, be considered unwise (Loewenstein, 1996). Interactions between feeling states and reflective cognition are also thought to lie at the root of some psychopathologies. In anxiety, automatic biases in the processing of negative environmental stimuli are believed to give rise to emotional arousal preattentively, leaving the individual in the grip of fear before the eliciting stimulus can be consciously appraised, so that evaluations of the stimulus are exaggerated by the already present bodily state (Öhman & Soares, 1998). In contrast, depression may involve a failure of selective (conscious) attention to actively disengage from negative thoughts that lead to maintenance of an already dysphoric mood state (Hertel, 2002; Joormann, 2004).

Valence and Arousal as Dimensions of Raw Phenomenality

The many possible interactions between raw and reflective conscious phenomenality pose methodological challenges to the emotion researcher. At any given moment, any one or a subset of features of emotion experience may capture attention and be available for self-report. Thus open-ended descriptions of emotion experience would tend to be unreliable indicators of the presence or absence of specific features of emotion experience, which may go unnoticed if attention is not directed to them.[4] This circumstance highlights one distinct advantage of taking a dimensional approach to the measurement of emotion experience, namely, the ability to constrain self-reports to specific dimensions along which experiences are known to vary and the ease in getting participants to attend to these dimensions. The dimensions of valence and arousal have the added advantage of being reliably correlated with physiological measures and of constituting the two factors that account for a majority of the variance in affective judgments of emotional words (Osgood, Suci, & Tannenbaum, 1957; Russell, 1980). Moreover, from a functional or evolutionary perspective, there is good reason to think that these dimensions capture features of emotion that might be functionally useful to a behaving organism. Arousal might signal the degree of importance or self-relevance of a choice or behavioral option, whereas valence might signal whether one ought to approach or avoid that option or whether a particular outcome is beneficial or harmful to one's interests. Thus, although few would maintain that the dimensions of valence and arousal are *all* there is to the experience of emotion, they nonetheless provide a useful starting point for examining its phenomenal structure and functional properties.

Despite much reliance on dimensional ratings in the study of emotion, the inferences participants use when providing reports along these dimensions are poorly understood. Do participants make ratings on valence and arousal dimensions based on a readout of their raw phenomenal states? Or are reflective processes engaged, whereby feelings are interpreted, evaluated, or inferred through a filter of cognitive appraisal before being reported? In one of the earliest psychological theories of emotion, William James (1894/1994)

proposed that emotion experience was the direct readout of physiological changes in the body. Over half a century later, Schachter and Singer (1962) proposed a modification of this view, suggesting that the valence of an emotion experience is an interpretation imposed on a raw, but perhaps undifferentiated, emotional feeling state (a state of physiological arousal) by reference to information in the stimulus context. Despite a long history of discussion of these questions within psychology, issues regarding the phenomenal and cognitive origins of reported emotion experience remain underexplored.

Methods for separately exploring the raw and reflective components of emotion experience would greatly contribute to our understanding of emotion phenomenality. One pressing research question is: Can we experimentally measure the nature of raw emotion experience? Although reported experience is always, by definition, the object of reflective cognition, is it possible, by instruction or experimental manipulation, to limit the influence of conscious appraisals on experience reports?

Approaching Raw Phenomenality in the Laboratory

A series of studies in the laboratory of Alfred Kaszniak at the University of Arizona (Kaszniak, Reminger, Rapcsak, & Glisky, 1999; Reid, 2000; Kaszniak, Nielsen, Rapcsak, & David, 2001; Burton & Kaszniak, 2006) has examined the nature of emotion experience in neurological patients and older adults and has attempted, by instruction, to encourage self-reports uncontaminated by demand characteristics and reflective appraisals. Typically, participants view a series of emotional pictures from the International Affective Picture System (Center for the Study of Emotion and Attention, 1999) and report their experiences on scales of valence and arousal using the Self-Assessment Manikin (Bradley & Lang, 1994) while physiological measures are simultaneously recorded. These simple reporting scales have several advantages. They are easily understood, and reports can, in principle, be made without engaging in much conceptual analysis. Response time is brief, as only two dimensions of experience are being tapped, minimizing the likelihood that the experience will change as a result of the reporting process.

Though emotion experiences may be rich and multifaceted, there are limits on how much one can report without altering the experience itself. The changes in attention that accompany the shift from feeling to reporting can alter the experience fundamentally. Moreover, features reported early may set up biases for or against reporting other features later on. Therefore, attempts to capture more than a few dimensions or qualities of momentary emotion experiences carry the risk that the later in the reporting inventory a dimension or quality is assessed, the less it may reflect the veridical nature of the experience it purportedly describes. Separated both temporally and cognitively from the raw experience, participants may tend to bring conceptual or schematic knowledge to bear on their ratings or reports, which can be difficult to disentangle from influences of the experience itself.[5]

A central component of our approach is an effort to engage participants as coinvestigators of their experience (Varela, 1996; Vermersch, 1999). In deference to the fact that only the participant has direct access to his or her experiences, we provide not only a framework for reporting his or her emotions but also an understanding of the research question (i.e., whether and what sort of experiences are elicited by our manipulations) and try to impart an awareness of this first-person authority. We hope thereby to elicit honest reports of experiences unbiased by presuppositions about how one believes one should feel under a given circumstance. Thus efforts are made to focus attention on the phenomenal qualities of experiences through instructions that emphasize the possibility of remaining emotionally unaffected by highly salient content while at other times experiencing strong feelings toward stimuli that are not usually considered emotional. We emphasize the reporting of actual experiences rather than of reflective evaluations of the scenes. Training participants in the use of reporting scales with a set of stimuli that spans the range of the valence and arousal dimensions facilitates greater understanding, particularly when accompanied by efforts to meaningfully anchor the scales in descriptions of everyday events that might be differently classified along these dimensions, such as winning a prize, losing a parking place to an aggressive driver, or enjoying a beautiful sunset.

Findings from several studies in our laboratory suggest that, in neurological populations with deficits in expressive or physiological emotional response systems, self-reported experience of emotion remains unchanged. Individuals with Parkinson's disease report experiencing emotions with the same intensity and hedonic quality as normal controls, despite deficiencies in the involuntary generation of emotional facial expressions (Reid, 2000). Similarly, individuals with Alzheimer's disease show abnormal patterns of facial muscle activation, but do not differ from normal controls in their self-reported emotion experience along valence and arousal dimensions (Burton & Kaszniak, 2006). Finally, patients with bilateral lesions to the ventromedial prefrontal and anterior cingulate cortices—areas believed to be central to the generation of emotional feeling states (see Lane, 2000) by virtue of their connections to circuitry for the elicitation of emotional arousal—also report emotion experiences in the normal range, despite failure to generate measurable skin-conductance responses (SCRs) to the emotional stimuli (Kaszniak et al., 2001; see also Tranel & Damasio, 1994). These latter results are surprising when viewed in the light of case study findings that suggest that lesions to these areas simultaneously abolish the feelings associated with viewing such pictures (Damasio, Tranel, & Damasio, 1990).

With lesions to these crucial prefrontal areas that are thought to mediate the experience of emotion, why do the patients studied by Kaszniak and colleagues (2001) still report emotion experiences in the normal range? Is this yet another example of the dissociability of emotion components? Or are there alternative explanations? Perhaps instructional manipulations alone are insufficient to reduce or remove the influence of reflective cognition on emotional self-report. Vivid emotional scenes evoke an "accepted meaning" that may provide a coloring to subjective reports that is not truly "experiential," though participants unsophisticated at reporting on emotion experiences might not easily make this distinction. Even in the absence of genuine feelings, these emotional knowledge schemes may be automatically accessed and used to inform ratings on the valence and arousal scales (as true for normal controls as for patients). If patients' reports fail to reveal underlying experiential deficits, perhaps the reason is that social convention often calls on us to endorse feelings congruent with accepted emotional meanings, and patients may not experience reports derived exclusively from these knowledge schemes as lacking in emotional quality. It is also possible that patients lack awareness of their experiential deficit and no longer can distinguish between emotional knowledge and emotion experience.

The Preattentive and Nonreflective Elicitation of Emotion

If instructional manipulations are insufficient at eliciting reports based on raw emotional phenomenality, perhaps experimental manipulations offer a solution. A number of studies have employed the visual masking paradigm to eliminate conscious cognitive evaluation of an emotional stimulus in order to explore the properties of unconsciously elicited emotion. In visual masking paradigms, an emotional stimulus (typically a picture or a word) is presented very briefly (usually for less than 50 ms) and is followed—and sometimes also preceded—by a visual mask that blocks the conscious perception of the target stimulus. Without conscious awareness of the stimulus, its brief presentation may nonetheless allow for "preattentive" analysis of its emotional significance, triggering further emotional processes. This paradigm removes the primary contextual cues that might lead to evaluations of emotional meaning based on knowledge or past experience. Therefore, any measurable effects of the stimulus are assumed to be mediated by processing that occurs outside awareness.

There are at least two ways in which preattentive emotional processes might influence emotional processing and subsequent behavior. First, this influence could occur entirely without awareness of either the stimulus or the subsequent emotional response, for example, a nonconscious physiological change results in an emotional bias on behavior. Alternatively, unconscious processing of an emotional stimulus could give rise to a feeling state, which is then referenced when performing a task. Evidence that unconsciously processed stimuli can give rise to emotion experiences is limited but suggestive of an important role for the visual masking procedure and similar manipulations in the exploration of raw feeling states, as self-reports of those experiences should be relatively unbiased by conscious emotional knowledge or appraisal. Two lines of research have explored the properties of unconsciously elicited emotion. The first involves work on the primacy of affect in judgment, whereas the second explores the unconscious foundations of anxiety.

Affective Primacy

According to the *affective primacy hypothesis* (Zajonc, 1980), affective stimulus properties are rapidly processed and can exert global effects on judgment and behavior without the intervention of cognitive inferences or conscious awareness. Tests of the affective primacy hypothesis have tried to block conscious awareness of affective influences in two primary ways. The first involves repeatedly exposing participants to novel stimuli without their awareness of the degree of exposure. This manipulation results in increased liking of stimuli to which one has been repeatedly exposed—an effect aptly termed the *mere-exposure effect*. Typically, large numbers of random polygons or other unfamiliar stimuli are presented. Participants, though unable to accurately recognize stimuli as old or new, nonetheless prefer old to new items. The mere-exposure effect has survived a number of replications using different classes of stimuli and different cultural populations. It has also been demonstrated when initial exposures to stimuli were subliminal (Kunst-Wilson & Zajonc, 1980). Monahan, Murphy, and Zajonc (2000) reported that mere repeated subliminal exposure to neutral pictures elevates subjective mood, which may, in turn, be responsible for the observed effects on preference judgments.

Very brief (subliminal) stimulus presentations have been the key manipulation in the second series of studies testing the affective primacy hypothesis. Murphy and Zajonc (1993) asked participants to rate a series of neutral Chinese ideographs that were preceded by 4-ms exposures of negative and positive facial expressions. Under these presentation parameters, positive facial expressions increased liking and negative expressions decreased liking for the ideographs. In a later study, Murphy, Monahan, and Zajonc (1995) demonstrated that such nonconsciously elicited affect additively combines with influences of repeated mere exposure in biasing preference judgments. Murphy and colleagues (1995) proposed that both sorts of manipulations (priming and mere exposure) give rise to valenced affect for which there is no awareness of the source, affect that is "diffuse" and nonspecific, that is, that has no dedicated object and that arises without cognitive appraisal of the eliciting stimulus. As such, it may, under certain circumstances, come to be attached to other objects in the environment.

It is one thing to say that emotional states are valenced and quite another to say that emotional feelings have hedonic tone (Lambie & Marcel, 2002). Valenced states may give rise to dispositions, influence attention, or alter cognition fully outside of awareness. States with hedonic tone (pleasurable or unpleasant states, or felt impulses to approach or avoid) have, by definition, an experienced quality. Do subliminal affective primes give rise to experiences or merely to valenced dispositions? Because participants studied by Murphy and colleagues (Murphy & Zajonc, 1993; Murphy et al., 1995) were not queried about their ongoing experiences, they fail to provide an answer.

The idea that emotion does its decision-biasing work through the feeling state is a core component of the *feelings-as-information hypothesis* (Clore & Parrott, 1991; Schwarz & Clore, 1983). According to this hypothesis, emotion experience—like other types of experience (bodily or cognitive)—provides specific information to decision making. Emotion experience is the output of our appraisal system, indicating the significance that events hold for us. Although we may be mistaken about the causes of our experience (e.g., if the appraisals are unconscious or if we attribute our experiences to the wrong features of the environment), as long as the experiences are deemed relevant to the decisions that need to be made, they will influence those decisions (Clore & Parrott, 1991).

Tests of the feelings-as-information hypothesis have shown that participants will disregard the influences of irrelevant feelings on judgment when they are made aware of the actual causes of those feelings (for review, see Clore & Ortony, 2000). Capitalizing on these findings, Winkielman, Zajonc, and Schwarz (1997) pitted the feelings-as-information hypothesis (that the conscious feeling of emotion informs judgment) against the affective primacy hypothesis (that unconscious emotional biases, not consciously accessible, bias judgment) in two studies, using adaptations of the subliminal affective priming paradigm of Murphy and Zajonc (1993). In one study, when participants were told that subliminal primes might lead them to have pleasant or unpleasant experiences, the researchers found no evidence of correction of liking judgments, as would have been predicted by the feelings-as-information hypothesis. In the second study, a more salient misattribution manipulation—the playing of mood music (explicitly labeled positive or negative)—was used. In both studies, preference judgments of neutral stimuli were still influenced by affective primes, even when participants thought that their feelings were being manipulated. Moreover, after the experiments, participants reported that they hadn't noticed any feelings.

Though these findings suggest that the affective primes were not eliciting feelings, there are several reasons that this conclusion may be unwarranted. First, it is not clear that any conscious affect elicited by 4-ms primes would be strong enough to survive the kind of reappraisal needed when discounting one's feelings. For example, in the first study, participants were sometimes pitting influences of negative primes against expectations of positive experiences. As the authors note, "even if subjects discerned their affective reactions, they may have felt confused or overwhelmed by the attributional arithmetic required from them" (p. 450). Alternatively, subliminal affective stimuli might influence conscious emotion experience in subtle ways that naïve participants are not used to noticing. Such subtle influences on feelings might not be easily detectable against the background noise of the music manipulation in the second study. Notably, participants in the Winkielman et al. (1997) study reported only on whether or not they had noticed any emotion experiences *after* the experiment was completed. Had they been asked to assess their experiences trial by trial and been given scales on which to rate those experiences, they might have demonstrated greater sensitivity to any experiences that might have been present. Indeed, one should not assume that memory for a subtle experience is long-lived. It may be abolished well before the end of the experiment.

In sum, tests of the affective primacy hypothesis have demonstrated the ability of preattentively processed stimuli to bias emotional judgment in both a positive and negative direction. Although it remains unknown whether subliminal affective priming does its work by altering feeling states, there is good evidence that repeated exposure to a stimulus may increase positive mood. This univalent effect of repeated exposure on emotion experience is suggestive and presents a useful counterpoint to the related findings from studies that use visual masking paradigms to demonstrate the ability to preattentively process *negative* emotional material.

Unconscious Mechanisms for Threat Detection

In an elegant series of studies, Arne Öhman and colleagues employed a visual masking paradigm to demonstrate the ability of fear-relevant stimuli to evoke phobic responses preattentively (see Öhman, Flykt, & Lundqvist, 2000, for a review). Taking Seligman's (1970) notion of "biological preparedness"—the idea that a species' phylogenetic evolutionary history results in innate dispositions to develop strong conditioned responses to certain classes of stimuli—into the clinical laboratory, Öhman and colleagues sought to explore the unconscious mechanisms that underlie phobia and anxiety.

In one study, Öhman and Soares (1994) exposed participants who scored high on measures of snake or spider phobia to backwardly masked and nonmasked pictures of snakes and spiders. In people with snake phobia, masked snake pictures elicited larger SCRs compared with masked spider or neutral pictures, mirroring responses in the non-masked condition (for participants who scored high in spider phobia, this pattern was reversed). In another study (Öhman & Soares, 1993), people without phobias who had been aversively conditioned to one or the other class (snakes or spiders) of fear-relevant stimuli showed a similar pattern of responding. In a third study (Öhman & Soares, 1998), aversive shocks were associated with *masked* presentations of the fear-relevant stimuli in the *acquisition phase* of the experiment, and, despite no awareness of the conditioned stimulus–unconditioned stimulus contingency, SCRs to aversively conditioned stimuli presented masked during the extinction phase were larger than to unconditioned stimuli, in line with earlier findings (Öhman & Soares, 1993, 1994).

These studies nicely demonstrate how the physiological aspects of a phobic response can be engaged before conscious stimulus processing begins, resulting in the kind of lack of voluntary control that is so typical of phobias (Öhman & Soares, 1993). Öhman and colleagues (2000) propose that masked fear-relevant stimuli rapidly elicit these fear-like responses by accessing the "quick and dirty" routes, identified by LeDoux (1996) in studies on rats, that involve direct projections from the thalamus via the amygdala to fear-response effectors, bypassing cortical circuits for conscious stimulus evaluation.

Yet the absence of conscious appraisal does not imply that the participants in these studies have no conscious experience of emotion when exposed to the masked stimuli. Indeed, participants in experiments by Öhman and Soares (1994, 1998) also rated their experienced arousal and valence to both masked and nonmasked stimuli. Participants were able to discriminate between neutral and emotional (negative, fear-eliciting) stimuli on both valence and arousal dimensions in both conditions. Unfortunately, because these studies employed only negative and neutral stimuli, valence information is confounded with arousal information, and it is impossible to determine whether participants were really experiencing unpleasantness or just heightened arousal. Moreover, in the context of a study in which electric shocks are administered, arousing states might always be interpreted as aversive or unpleasant.

In the 1998 study, Öhman and Soares also had participants rate their "shock expectancy" in the acquisition phase of the experiment, when stimuli were visually masked. Participants were, on average, able to predict shock above chance levels, presumably using feedback from their physiological conditioned responses. Though some participants were better than others at predicting shocks, these good shock anticipators had neither larger SCRs to conditioned stimuli nor greater physiological differentiation between conditioned and unconditioned stimuli than poor shock anticipators. This finding raised the question of whether some independent participant characteristic predicted sensitivity to impending shock. Perhaps, the researchers speculated, good shock predictors were just better at detecting subtle physiological change. Indeed, in a replication of the Öhman and Soares (1998) study, Katkin, Wiens, and Öhman (2001) found that participants who were better at visceral perception (as assessed by performance on a heartbeat detection task) made more accurate shock expectancy ratings. The researchers proposed that heartbeat detection ability might index greater precision in awareness of "gut feelings" of impending negative consequences. These findings highlight the important issue of individual differences in emotion awareness and its influence on experience reports, discussed in more detail in the next section.

Although the visual masking paradigm creates a highly artificial environment for the elicitation of emotional responses, it enables one to experimentally control the influences of conscious cognition on the measurements of interest. With little or no possibility for reflective, conscious, cognitive appraisal of the emotional stimulus, any change in physiological responding, judgment, or emotion experience that arises as a function of the stimulus can be assumed to arise from the nonconscious activation of emotional processes based on a rough, preattentive analysis of stimulus features. Obviously, this methodology has limited application in the study of emotion experience and will be of little use in exploring questions about the spatial and temporal structure of the phenomenal field during emotion experience or about how emotion experience changes as a function of attentional focus or emotion regulation. Its advantages nonetheless highlight some of the difficulties in interpreting the content of experience reports elicited using more complex, evocative stimuli. By emphasizing the difficulties inherent in taking even a very simple dimensional approach to the measurement of emotion experience, we hope to shed some light on the question of when one is or is not justified in inferring veridical phenomenal emotion experience from self-reports. The issues raised here apply equally to other dimensional rating schemes, as well as to those that use discrete emotion labels. The latter pose additional challenges due to the difficulty in accessing the subjective meanings participants invoke when applying categorical labels to their emotion experiences and to the fact that these categorical emotions can, in principle, be decomposed into more fine-grained components (see Lambie & Marcel, 2002, for a discussion of categorical emotion experience).

Individual Differences in Emotion Experience

As suggested earlier, individual differences in sensitivity to various aspects of emotion experience might result in variability in experience reports. Individual differences in experience may be quantitative or qualitative. The former are less methodologically challenging and arise from differences in access as a function of attentional focus or discriminatory sophistication rather than being indicative of underlying difference in the very structure of the phenomenal field. Thus Feldman's (1995) finding that individuals differ in whether they exhibit more of a valence or an arousal focus in their reports of emotion experiences could be interpreted as evidence of quantitative differences in access. Coan and Allen's (2003) recent finding that tendencies to report physical sensations or behavioral action tendencies in emotion experience reports were related, respectively, to scores on personality measures of trait negative affectivity (Positive and Negative Affect Schedule [PANAS]; Watson, Clark, & Tellegen,

1988) and behavioral activation (Behavioral Inhibition Scales/Behavioral Activation Scales [BISBAS]; Carver & White, 1994) can be similarly interpreted, suggesting that underlying personality dimensions may serve as determinants of attentional focus during emotion experiences. More challenging is the possibility that individuals have a fundamentally different qualitative experience of the same emotions, which would prohibit cross-individual comparisons of feeling states. Although a discussion of the methodological challenges raised by the possibility of fundamental qualitative differences is beyond the scope of this chapter, we should note that a functional interpretation of emotion renders the latter possibility less likely (DeLancey, 1996), particularly if emotions are conceived of as embodied and relational.

If we assume that *fundamental* differences in emotion experiences are quantitative rather than qualitative, and if we are interested in mapping the phenomenal field of emotion experience, we might wish to enlist research participants who can provide richer or more discriminate experience reports. Just as good heartbeat detectors may have heightened visceral perception abilities (Katkin et al., 2001), a variety of other factors might render participants better reporters of their emotion experiences. These include: formal training in attending to emotion experience, differences in everyday emotional awareness, and differences in the ability to regulate one's emotional states. Although we suggest the advantages of enlisting research participants who are better at making certain kinds of experiential discriminations, we are not suggesting that reports of "poor" reporters are less veridical but rather proposing that they may admit of less nuance, be less complex, and less likely to distinguish different emotional states from one another. But, as we note subsequently, this approach has its own perils.

Attentional Training and Emotion Experience

It is often only in poetry and literature that we find descriptions of emotional phenomenality that truly resonate with our own experience. These rare literary encounters give us pause, eliciting both awe and gratitude at the writer's ability to express the inexpressible. Unlike poets, the average person usually lacks expertise in describing the fine phenomenal detail of his or her emotions. Everyday discussion of emotion typically serves a functional purpose, rendering vivid descriptions of discrete phenomenal characteristics superfluous. Emotions tend to be described as motives—for seeking restitution, facilitating social bonding, expressing sympathy—dispositional states that serve to justify thoughts and behaviors. A bit of phenomenal description can be useful for emphasis (e.g., "I was so angry at him, I thought I would explode"), but excursions into the poetic are likely to raise eyebrows and may even be considered pathological.

These considerations raise concerns about the ability of research participants to report on emotion experiences to which they may not typically attend and for which they have no ready vocabulary. There is a group of individuals, however, who, as part of their long-term meditation practice, regularly engage in exercises that focus their attention on subtle changes in the stream of consciousness, including changes in bodily states, images, and thoughts that accompany emotional episodes (Young, 1999). Two traditions of Buddhist meditation practice fit this characterization to differing extents. Possibly the most emotion-focused tradition is the Vipassana, or "mindfulness," tradition, in which practitioners are trained to identify the discrete components of their feelings and experiences and to attend to the way that these components combine to produce emotional reactions (Nyanaponika, 2000). Zen meditation practitioners do not share this specific focus on emotion, but their training typically involves similar practices, such as breathing meditations, which draw attention to the body, and attentional training techniques, which aim to heighten the precision and focus of awareness. Long-term meditation practice might enhance skill in discriminating emotion experiences particularly associated with physiological change and with changes in the content of the ongoing stream of consciousness. Such discriminations might be difficult for nonmeditators, who typically do not attend to subtle shifts in their emotional or conscious states.

Individual Differences in Emotion Awareness and Emotion Regulation

Individuals also differ in the degree to which they are aware of their emotions and in the kinds of emotional regulatory processes they employ. Recently, Gohm and Clore (2000) provided evidence, based on hierarchical cluster analyses of data collected from a sample of 151 college students, that individual differences in four trait dimensions of emotion experience can be reliably assessed by a number of standardized personality inventories. These dimensions include: *attention to emotion,* defined as "the extent to which individuals monitor their emotions, value their emotions, and maximize their experience of emotion" (p. 684); *clarity,* or "the ability to identify, distinguish, and describe specific emotions" (p. 686); *intensity,* or "the strength with which individuals tend to experience emotions" (p. 687); and *expression,* or "the extent to which individuals express their feelings and their attitudes toward expressing their feelings" (p. 688). Such individual differences in emotion awareness, assessed by self-report, might reflect a tendency to focus on emotional aspects of everyday life. Such a tendency might, in turn, result in a greater ability to discriminate among one's emotion experiences.

The alternative possibility must be considered, however: that beliefs about one's emotional awareness might distort reports, leading either to confabulation (in the case when one feels one *should* be feeling something) or to inhibition of reporting (when the feelings elicited don't match one's presuppositions about what constitutes an emotion experience). Conversely, although individuals low in self-reported emotional awareness may fail to notice subtle changes in their experiences, they may, alternatively, be more willing than "high awareness" participants to naively report experiences on whatever scales or inventories the researcher has provided. What is true about self-reported emotional awareness is just as true about training in attending to emotion, and similar considerations ought to apply in the latter case.

A related issue concerns the ways in which beliefs about emotional awareness can interact with conscious emotional regulatory strategies. Emotional regulatory processes consist in both conscious strategies (suppressing, amplifying, or dampening the experience and expression of emotion) and unconscious processes (autonomic reactivity and control of emotional response). Depending on one's experiential preferences, high emotional awareness combined with good strategic control of emotion might lead to different phenomenal profiles. In individuals with higher emotional awareness and a preference for equanimity, conscious regulation of emotion experience may result in a more placid phenomenal profile and a reduction of emotional intensity as the result of the engagement of coping mechanisms that dampen affect. Alternatively, for those who prefer to feel life more intensely, the ability to successfully tolerate the vicissitudes of feeling may lead to a more dynamic and turbulent emotional life.

Although conscious control of emotion may play a large role in determining an individual's phenomenal profile, underlying physiological regulatory mechanisms may determine whether one develops the regulatory abilities required for implementing strategic control over emotional states. One proposed psychophysiological index of emotional regulatory ability is respiratory sinus arrhythmia (RSA), a measure of parasympathetic influences on heart rate variability. Vagal control is an adaptation unique to mammals for the regulation of emotional state, with high cardiac vagal tone proposed to index an adaptive emotion regulatory style that modulates emotional reactivity to arousing stimuli, facilitating coping (Porges, 1997). Vagal tone can reflect both inherited and acquired characteristics, and individuals who are higher in cardiac vagal tone, as measured by various indices of RSA, are hypothesized to have better emotional regulatory ability (Porges, Doussard-Roosevelt, & Maita, 1994; Beauchaine, 2001). These individuals may be more emotionally reactive to emotional stimuli and, at the same time, possess the ability to be aware of changes in their emotional states. The phenomenal consequences of such abilities are open to speculation. Regulating may make the experience of emotion less intense, as coping mechanisms are quickly brought on line to modulate and contain the emotional response, or it may result in emotions being felt more intensely, because systems are in place that do not disrupt adaptive responding even when in the grip of strong emotion.

The Vocabulary of Emotion Experience

Like the expert wine tasters whose discrimination abilities led to the creation of the wine aroma wheel (Noble et al.,

1987) for guiding olfactory judgments, participants with expertise in attending to emotion may be able to assist in the development of better maps of the phenomenal affective space. Yet expertise is also associated with changes in knowledge structures and attitudes, as well as the automatization of once effortful processes, all of which can result in changes in emotion experience, placing the reports of experts at some distance from those of more naïve observers. But just as one can learn to smell the hint of clove or asparagus in a newly opened wine, reporting schemes derived from the observations of experts may be a genuine aid to the novice who struggles to put words to experiences for which he or she has no ready vocabulary without compromising the veridicality of his or her self-report.

The use of open-ended formats that allow participants to report their experiences in whatever words come most easily to them might also be of particular use in developing new reporting schemes. Though the reports collected by these means are likely to be informed by emotional knowledge schemes, they provide, at the same time, clues to the dimensions individuals use when structuring lived experiences that may suggest new dimensions and reporting vocabularies that can be adapted for laboratory studies. This approach can be taken with experience sampling methods that ask participants to report on experiences in their natural environments, as well as experiences recalled under more controlled conditions. Rosenberg and Ekman's (1994) cued review method, whereby participants first experience an emotional event (typically a film) and then, under a subsequent repeated stimulation, pause to indicate the experiences they had on the original viewing, provides one example of the latter technique.

Conclusion

More ink has been spilled on cataloguing the number of ways in which self-reports might be unreliable (e.g., the reconstructive nature of memory for experience [Bartlett, 1935; Hasher & Griffin, 1978; Kahneman, 1999; Loftus, 2003; Mitchell & Johnson, 2000; Roediger & McDermott, 2000], the influence of attentional biases on reports [McNally, 1996; Wells & Matthews, 1994], demand characteristics [Marlow & Crowne, 1961], and the distorting effects of implicit causal theories and personal motives [Nisbett & Wilson, 1977; Wilson & Dunn, 2004]), than attention has been paid to the phenomenality of emotion itself and to validating our standard measures of emotion experience based on participants' reports. As interest in mapping the neural and physiological correlates of emotion experience continues to grow, there is a pressing need to develop better first-person methods for measuring the rich phenomenality of emotion. Our inclination has been to take emotion experience reports at face value, while simultaneously taking steps to ensure their completeness and accuracy by training participants in the use of re-

porting schemes and striving where possible to incorporate direct measures of momentary experience. We adopt a broad conception of emotion experience as including all that is present in phenomenal consciousness when one is in an emotional state, including thoughts and perceptions that in themselves may not have an arousing or valenced quality but that constitute a part of what it is like to have an emotion. Despite the complexity of emotional phenomenality, we believe that an expansion of the simple dimensional approach (going beyond valence and arousal to incorporate dimensions of motivational, perceptual, or cognitive awareness and employing alternative topologies and reporting methods, such as analog scales [Fredrickson & Kahneman, 1993] and mappings of bodily sensations) is likely to bear more fruit than methods that try to simultaneously measure multiple discrete basic emotions. The latter obscure important functional features of emotion experience, which may be essential to their phenomenality. Finally, we believe it is important to consider all possible contributions to self-reports of emotion experiences—the raw experience, the reflective awareness, emotional knowledge, and differences in emotional awareness —when drawing inferences from self-reports.

Notes

1. Typically, when asked to report on emotion experiences, people do not make these kinds of distinctions and will report on thoughts and feelings, as well as on thoughts about feelings and feelings about thoughts.

2. Panksepp (1998) has outlined discrete neurochemical circuits that, he argues, differently combine to create the feeling states associated with particular basic emotions. The extent to which the feeling states that these give rise to are experienced as bodily sensations or as nonbodily qualia has not, to our knowledge, been explored.

3. Nonbodily feelings will likely have features of being embodied, as when auditory imagery feels as if it is experienced in the ear or in the head, but these embodied features should be distinguished from bodily sensations that have a clear visceral component, such as a pounding heart, a quickening of the breath, and so forth.

4. Such reports can, however, provide a window onto individual differences in attentional focus, the salience of particular aspects of experience for specific discrete emotions, and the amenability of different aspects of experience to self-report.

5. This may be equally true of structured reporting schemes and of open-ended reports. In structured inventories, the participant is asked to adopt the perspective of the experimenter and actively shift focus to specific aspects of experience, with the associated risk that immediate phenomenal awareness is distorted by these reporting demands. In open-ended reports, although the experience can be reported as it is lived, ostensibly allowing for reporting of more dimensions and features, there is an associated risk that schematic knowledge may overly contribute to shaping the response. We wish to note that there are costs in veridicality associated with both structured and open-ended approaches. It has been argued (Vermersch, 1999)

that unpracticed participants may benefit from semistructured probing of experience that encourages attention to aspects of experience that may otherwise go unnoticed. We agree that careful attention to training of participants in the use of reporting schemes and to the potential for interference of reporting demands with experience will be important in assuring veridicality of self-reports.

References

Baars, B. J. (1988). *A cognitive theory of consciousness.* Cambridge, UK: Cambridge University Press.

Bartlett, F. C. (1935). Remembering. *Scientia (Bologna), 57,* 221–226.

Beauchaine, T. (2001). Vagal tone, development, and Gray's motivational theory: Toward an integrated model of autonomic nervous system functioning in psychopathology. *Development and Psychopathology, 13,* 183–214.

Bradley, M. M., & Lang, P. J. (1994). Measuring emotion: The Self-Assessment Manikin and the semantic differential. *Journal of Behavior Therapy and Experimental Psychiatry, 25,* 49–59.

Bradley, M. M., & Lang, P. J. (2000). Measuring emotion: Behavior, feeling, and physiology. In R. D. Lane, L. Nadel, G. A. Ahern, J. J. B. Allen, A. W. Kaszniak, S. Z. Rapcsak, & G. E. Schwartz (Eds.), *Cognitive neuroscience of emotion* (pp. 242–276). New York: Oxford University Press.

Burton, K. W., & Kaszniak, A. W. (2006). Emotional experience and facial expression in Alzheimer's disease. *Neuropsychology, Development and Cognition, Section B. Aging, Neuropsychology and Cognition. 13,* 636–51.

Cacioppo, J. T., & Berntson, G. G. (1999). The affect system: Architecture and operating characteristics. *Current Directions in Psychological Science, 8,* 133–137.

Cacioppo, J. T., & Gardner, W. L. (1999). Emotion. *Annual Review of Psychology, 50,* 191–214.

Carver, C. S., & White, T. L. (1994). Behavioral inhibition, behavioral activation, and affective responses to impending reward and punishment: The BIS/BAS scales. *Journal of Personality and Social Psychology, 67,* 319–333.

Center for the Study of Emotion and Attention. (1999). *The International Affective Picture System: Digitized photographs.* Gainesville: University of Florida, Center for Research in Psychophysiology.

Chalmers, D. J. (1999). First-person methods in the science of consciousness. Retrieved on August 19, 2006, from http://www.u.arizona.edu/~chalmers/papers/firstperson.html

Chalmers, D.J. (2004). How can we construct a science of consciousness? In M.S. Gazzaniga (Ed.), *The cognitive neurosciences III.* Cambridge, MA: MIT Press.

Clore, G. L. (1994). Why emotions are never unconscious. In P. Ekman & R. J. Davidson (Eds.), *The nature of emotion: Fundamental questions* (pp. 285–290). New York: Oxford University Press.

Clore, G. L., & Ortony, A. (2000). Cognition in emotion: Always, sometimes, or never? In R. D. Lane, L. Nadel, G. L. Ahern, J. J. B. Allen, A. W. Kaszniak, S. Z. Rapcsak, & G. E. Schwartz (Eds.), *Cognitive neuroscience of emotion* (pp. 24–61). New York: Oxford University Press.

Clore, G. L., & Parrott, W. G. (1991). Moods and their vicissitudes: Thoughts and feelings as information. In J. P. Forgas (Ed.), *Emotion and social judgments* (pp. 107–123). Oxford, UK: Pergamon Press.

Coan, J. A., & Allen, J. J. B. (2003). Varieties of emotional experience during voluntary emotional facial expressions. *Annals of the New York Academy of Sciences, 1000,* 375–379.

Csikszentmihalyi, M. (1988). The flow experience and its significance of human psychology. In M. Csikszentmihalyi & I. S. Csikszentmihalyi (Eds.), *Optimal experience: Psychological studies of flow in consciousness* (pp. 15–35). Cambridge, UK: Cambridge University Press.

Damasio, A. R. (1994). *Descartes' error: Emotion, reason, and the human brain.* New York: Putnam.

Damasio, A. R. (1999). *The feeling of what happens: Body and emotion in the making of consciousness.* New York: Harcourt Brace.

Damasio, A. R. (2003). *Looking for Spinoza: Joy, sorrow, and the feeling brain.* New York: Harcourt.

Damasio, A .R., Tranel, D., & Damasio, H. (1990). Individuals with sociopathic behavior caused by frontal damage fail to respond autonomically to social stimuli. *Behavioral Brain Research, 41,* 81–94.

Davidson, R. J. (2000). Emotion, plasticity, context, and regulation: Perspectives from affective neuroscience. *Psychological Bulletin, 126,* 890–909.

Davidson, R. J. (2003). Affective neuroscience and psychophysiology: Toward a synthesis. *Psychophysiology, 40,* 655–65.

Davidson, R. J., Ekman, P., Saron, C. D., Senulis, J. A., & Friesen, W. V. (1990). Approach/withdrawal and cerebral asymmetry: Emotional expression and brain physiology: I. *Journal of Personality and Social Psychology, 58,* 330–341.

DeLancey, C. (1996). Emotion and the function of consciousness. *Journal of Consciousness Studies, 3,* 492–499.

Dimberg, U., Thunberg, M., & Elmehed, K. (2000). Unconscious facial reactions to emotional facial expressions. *Psychological Science, 11,* 86–89.

Ekman, P. (1992). Are there basic emotions? *Psychological Review, 99,* 550–553.

Farthing, G. W. (1992). *The psychology of consciousness.* Englewood Cliffs, NJ: Prentice Hall.

Feldman, L. A. (1995). Valence focus and arousal focus: Individual differences in the structure of affective experience. *Journal of Personality and Social Psychology, 69,* 153–166.

Feldman-Barrett, L., & Russell, J. A. (1999). The structure of current affect: Controversies and emerging consensus. *Current Directions in Psychological Science, 8,* 10–14.

Flanagan, O. J. (1992). *Consciousness reconsidered.* Cambridge, MA: MIT Press.

Fredrickson, B. L. (1998). What good are positive emotions? *Review of General Psychology, 2,* 300–319.

Fredrickson, B. L., & Kahneman, D. (1993). Duration neglect in retrospective evaluations of affective episodes. *Journal of Personality and Social Psychology, 65,* 45–55.

Frijda, N. H. (1993). Moods, emotion episodes, and emotions. In M. Lewis & J. M. Haviland (Eds.), *Handbook of emotions* (pp. 381–404). New York: Guilford Press.

Frijda, N. H. (1999). Emotions and hedonic experience. In D. Kahneman, E. Diener, & N. Schwarz (Eds.), *Well-being: The foundations of hedonic psychology* (pp. 190–210). New York: Russell Sage Foundation.

Gohm, C. L., & Clore, G. L. (2000). Individual differences in emotional experience: Mapping available scales to processes. *Personality and Social Psychology Bulletin, 26,* 679–697.

Green, D. P., & Salovey, P. (1999). In what sense are positive and negative affect independent? A reply to Tellegen, Watson, & Clark. *Psychological Science, 10,* 304–306.

Gross, J. J. (2002). Emotion regulation: Affective, cognitive, and social consequences. *Psychophysiology, 39,* 281–291.

Hasher, L., & Griffin, M. (1978). Reconstructive and reproductive processes in memory. *Journal of Experimental Psychology: Human Learning and Memory, 4,* 318–330.

Hertel, P. T. (2002). Cognitive biases in anxiety and depression: Introduction to the special issue. *Cognition and Emotion, 16,* 321–330.

Isen, A. (2000). Positive affect and decision making. In M. Lewis & J. M. Haviland-Jones (Eds.), *Handbook of emotions* (2nd ed., pp. 417–435). New York: Guilford Press.

Izard, C. E. (1992). Basic emotions, relations among emotions and emotion-cognition relations. *Psychological Review, 99,* 561–565.

James, W. (1983). *The principles of psychology.* Cambridge, MA: Harvard University Press. (Original work published 1890)

James, W. (1994). The physical basis of emotion. *Psychological Review, 101*(2), 205–210. (Original work published 1894)

Joormann, J. (2004). Attentional bias in dysphoria: The role of inhibitory processes. *Cognition and Emotion, 18,* 125–147.

Kahneman, D. (1999). Objective happiness. In D. Kahneman, E. Diener, & N. Schwarz (Eds.), *Well-being: The foundations of hedonic psychology* (pp. 3–25). New York: Russell Sage Foundation.

Kaszniak, A. W. (Ed.). (2001). *Emotions, qualia, and consciousness.* Singapore: World Scientific.

Kaszniak, A. W., Nielsen, L., Rapcsak, S. Z., & David, B. (2001, February). *Emotion experience and physiology following frontal vs. temporal lobe damage.* Paper presented at the annual meeting of the International Neuropsychological Society, Chicago, IL.

Kaszniak, A. W., Reminger, S. L., Rapcsak, S. Z., & Glisky, E. L. (1999). Conscious experience and autonomic response to emotional stimuli following frontal lobe damage. In S. R. Hameroff, A. W. Kaszniak, & D. J. Chalmers (Eds.), *Toward a science of consciousness: III. The third Tucson discussions and debates* (pp. 201–213). Cambridge, MA: MIT Press.

Katkin, E. S., Wiens, S., & Öhman, A. (2001). Nonconscious fear conditioning, visceral perception, and the development of gut feelings. *Psychological Science, 12,* 366–370.

Kunst-Wilson, W. R., & Zajonc, R. B. (1980). Affective discrimination of stimuli that cannot be recognized. *Science, 207,* 557–558.

Lambie, J. A., & Marcel, A. J. (2002). Consciousness and the varieties of emotion experience: A theoretical framework. *Psychological Review, 109,* 219–259.

Lane, R. D. (2000). Neural correlates of conscious emotional experience. In R. D. Lane, L. Nadel, G. L. Ahern, J. J. B. Allen, A. W. Kaszniak, S. Z. Rapcsak, & G. E. Schwartz (Eds.), *Cognitive neuroscience of emotion* (pp. 345–370). New York: Oxford University Press.

Lane, R. D., Nadel, L., Allen, J. J. B., & Kaszniak, A. W. (2000). The study of emotion from the perspective of cognitive neuroscience. In R. D. Lane, L. Nadel, G. L. Ahern, J. J. B. Allen, A. W. Kaszniak, S. Z. Rapcsak, & G. E. Schwartz (Eds.), *Cognitive neuroscience of emotion* (pp. 3–11). New York: Oxford University Press.

Lane, R. D., Quinlan, D. M., Schwartz, G. E., & Walker, P. A. (1990). The Levels of Emotional Awareness Scale: A cognitive-developmental measure of emotion. *Journal of Personality Assessment, 55,* 124–134.

Lang, P. J. (1994). The varieties of emotional experience: A meditation on James-Lange theory. *Psychological Review, 101,* 211–221.

Lang, P. J., Greenwald, M. K., Bradley, M. M., & Hamm, A. O. (1993). Looking at pictures: Affective, facial, visceral, and behavioral reactions. *Psychophysiology, 30,* 261–273.

Lazarus, R. S. (1991). *Emotion and adaptation.* New York: Oxford University Press.

LeDoux, J. E. (1996). *The emotional brain.* New York: Simon & Schuster.

LeDoux, J. E. (2000). Cognitive-emotional interactions: Listen to the brain. In R. D. Lane, L. Nadel, G. L. Ahern, J. J. B. Allen, A. W. Kaszniak, S. Z. Rapcsak, & G. E. Schwartz (Eds.), *Cognitive neuroscience of emotion* (pp. 129–155). New York: Oxford University Press.

Loewenstein, G. (1996). Out of control: Visceral influences on behavior. *Organizational Behavior and Human Decision Processes, 65,* 272–292.

Loftus, E. F. (2003). Make-believe memories. *American Psychologist, 58,* 867–873.

Marlow, D., & Crowne, D. P. (1961). Social desirability and response to perceived situational demands. *Journal of Consulting Psychology, 25,* 109–115.

McNally, R. J. (1996). Cognitive bias in the anxiety disorders. In D. A. Hope (Ed.), *Nebraska Symposium on Motivation, 1995: Perspectives on anxiety, panic, and fear* (pp. 211–250). Lincoln: University of Nebraska Press.

Mitchell, K. J., & Johnson, M. K. (2000). Source monitoring: Attributing mental experiences. In E. Tulving & F. I. M. Craik (Eds.). *Oxford handbook of memory* (pp. 179–195). London: Oxford University Press.

Monahan, J. L., Murphy, S. T., & Zajonc, R. B. (2000). Subliminal mere exposure: Specific, general, and diffuse effect. *Psychological Science, 11,* 462–466.

Murphy, S., Monahan, J., & Zajonc, R. (1995). Additivity of nonconscious affect: Combined effects of priming and exposure. *Journal of Personality and Social Psychology, 69,* 589–602.

Murphy, S. T., & Zajonc, R. B. (1993) Affect, cognition, and awareness: Affective priming with optimal and suboptimal stimulus exposures. *Journal of Personality and Social Psychology, 64,* 723–739.

Nagel, T. (1974). What is it like to be a bat? *Philosophical Review, 83,* 435–450.

Nisbett, R. E., & Wilson, T. D. (1977). Telling more than we can know: Verbal reports on mental processes. *Psychological Review, 84,* 231–259.

Noble, A. C., Arnold, R. A., Buechsenstein, J., Leach, E. J., Schmidy, J. O., & Stern, P. M. (1987). Modification of a standardized system of wine aroma terminology. *American Journal of Enology and Viticulture, 38,* 143–146.

Nyanaponika, T. (2000). *The vision of Dhamma.* BPS Pariyatti Editions.

Öhman, A., Flykt, A., & Lundqvist, D. (2000). Unconscious emotion: Evolutionary perspectives, psychophysiological data and neuropsychological mechanisms. In R. D. Lane, L. Nadel, G. A. Ahern, J. J. B. Allen, A. W. Kaszniak, S. Z. Rapcsak, & G. E. Schwartz (Eds.), *Cognitive neuroscience of emotion* (pp. 296–327). New York: Oxford University Press.

Öhman, A., & Soares, J. J. F. (1993). Backward masking and skin conductance responses after conditioning to nonfeared but fear-relevant stimuli in fearful subjects. *Psychophysiology, 30,* 460–466.

Öhman, A., & Soares, J. J. F. (1994). Unconscious anxiety: Phobic responses to masked stimuli. *Journal of Abnormal Psychology, 103,* 231–240.

Öhman, A., & Soares, J. J. F. (1998). Emotional conditioning to masked stimuli: Expectancies for aversive outcomes following nonrecognized fear-relevant stimuli. *Journal of Experimental Psychology: General, 127,* 69–82.

Osgood, C. E., Suci, G. J., & Tannenbaum, P. H. (1957). *The measurement of meaning.* Urbana: University of Illinois Press.

Panksepp, J. (1998). *Affective neuroscience: The foundations of human and animal emotions.* New York: Oxford University Press.

Panksepp, J. (2000). Emotions as natural kinds within the mammalian brain. In M. Lewis & J. M. Haviland-Jones (Eds.), *Handbook of emotions* (2nd ed., pp. 137–156). New York: Guilford Press.

Porges, S. W. (1997). Emotion: An evolutionary by-product of the neural regulation of the autonomic nervous system. In C. S. Carter, I. I. Lederhendler, & B. Kirkpatrick (Eds.), *The integrative neurobiology of affiliation* (pp. 62–77). New York: New York Academy of Sciences.

Porges, S. W., Doussard-Roosevelt, J. A., & Maita, J. K. (1994). Vagal tone and the physiological regulation of emotion. *Monographs of the Society for Research in Child Development, 59,* 167–186.

Reid, S. A. (2000). The experience of emotion in Parkinson's disease and normal aging: Assessing the roles of facial expressiveness and cognitive functioning. *Dissertation Abstracts International, Section B. The Sciences & Engineering, 60* (9–B), 4905.

Roediger, H. L., & McDermott, K. B. (2000). Tricks of memory. *Current Directions in Psychological Science, 9,* 123–127.

Rosenberg, E. L., & Ekman, P. (1994). Coherence between expressive and experiential systems in emotion. *Cognition and Emotion, 8,* 201–229.

Russell, J. A. (1980) A circumplex model of affect. *Journal of Personality and Social Psychology, 39,* 1161–1178.

Schachter, S., & Singer, J. (1962). Cognitive, social and physiological determinants of emotional state. *Psychological Review, 69,* 379–399.

Scherer, K. R. (1999). On the sequential nature of appraisal processes: Indirect evidence from a recognition task. *Cognition and Emotion, 13,* 763–793.

Salovey, P., Mayer, J. D., Caruso, D., & Lopes, P. N. (2003). Measuring emotional intelligence as a set of abilities with the Mayer-Salovey-Caruso Emotional Intelligence Test. In S. J. Lopez & C. R. Snyder (Eds.), *Positive psychological assessment: A handbook of models and measures* (pp. 251–265). Washington, DC: American Psychological Association.

Schwarz, N., & Clore, G. (1983). Mood, misattribution, and judgments of well-being: Informative and directive functions of affective states. *Journal of Personality and Social Psychology, 45,* 513–523.

Seligman, M. E. P. (1970). On the generality of the laws of learning. *Psychological Review, 77,* 406–418.

Tellegen, A., Watson, D., & Clark, L. A. (1999). On the dimensional and hierarchical structure of affect. *Psychological Science, 10,* 297–303.

Tooby, J., & Cosmides, L. (1990). The past explains the present. *Ethology and Sociobiology, 11,* 375–424.

Tranel, D., & Damasio, H. (1994). Neuroanatomical correlates of electrodermal skin conductance responses. *Psychophysiology, 31,* 427–438.

Varela, F. (1996). Neurophenomenology. *Journal of Consciousness Studies, 3,* 330–349.

Vermersch, P. (1999). Introspection as practice. *Journal of Consciousness Studies, 6,* 17–42.

Watson, D., Clark, L. A., & Tellegen, A. (1988). Development and validation of brief measures of positive and negative affect: The PANAS scales. *Journal of Personality and Social Psychology, 54,* 1063–1070.

Watt, D. F. (1999). At the intersection of emotion and consciousness: Affective neuroscience and the extended reticular thalamic activating system (ERTAS) theories of consciousness. In S. R. Hameroff, A. W. Kaszniak, & D. J. Chalmers (Eds.), *Toward a science of consciousness: III. The third Tucson discussions and debates* (pp. 215–229). Cambridge, MA: MIT Press.

Wells, A., & Matthews, G. (1994). *Attention and emotion: A clinical perspective.* Hillsdale, NJ: Erlbaum.

Wiens, S. (2005). Interoception in emotional experience. *Current Opinion in Neurology, 18,* 442–447.

Wilson, T. D., & Dunn, E. W. (2004). Self-knowledge: Its limits, value and potential for improvement. *Annual Review of Psychology, 55,* 493–518.

Winkielman, P., Zajonc, R. B., & Schwarz, N. (1997) Subliminal affective priming resists attributional interventions. *Cognition and Emotion, 11,* 433–465.

Young, S. (1999, July). *Using mindfulness meditation in working with emotions: Theory and practice.* Paper presented at the Annual Consciousness Studies Summer Institute on Facilitating Emotional Awareness, Kalamazoo, MI.

Zajonc, R. B. (1980). Feeling and thinking: Preferences need no inferences. *American Psychologist, 35,* 151–175.

Methods for Understanding the Biological

Bases of Emotion

Lisa A. Parr

Katalin M. Gothard

Studying Emotion in Animals

Methods, Materials, and Training

What Can Animals Teach Us About Emotion?

Emotion has long been viewed as an important phenomenon underlying mammalian evolution. It is not only critically involved in mate choice, reproduction, predator avoidance, and parental care but it also provides a common currency for initiating and regulating social communication, aids in structuring early development, particularly in altricial species, and plays a pivotal role in maintaining social cohesion.

Despite its important promise for understanding human emotion and in providing animal models for affective disorders, research on animal emotion has been a controversial topic. This is based, in part, on the outdated assumption that animals are devoid of emotional feelings and respond to the environment with strict, genetically determined stimulus-response behaviors. Additionally, animals cannot talk, and their emotions cannot be validated through self-report questionnaires. Self-report remains a widely used measure of emotionality despite the fact that research has directly shown that humans often unwittingly invent explanations for their feelings that are inconsistent with their actual causes (Schachter & Singer, 1962). More recently, researchers have returned to the Darwinian view that animals and humans share basic emotions and that, by studying animal behavior, science can elucidate the ancestral conditions that led to the evolution of modern human emotion (Davis & Whalen, 2000; Lang, Davis, & Öhman, 2000; Panksepp, 1998).

The use of animals to model human emotion relies on two important and related premises. The *first premise* is that phylogenetically related species share a similar basic neural architecture that coordinates the brain-body systems critical for the production, perception, and regulation of emotional processes. As such, an animal that encounters a predator, for example, exhibits a cascade of neural, physiological, and behavioral responses that collectively help that individual to survive the encounter. These experiences activate a set of genetically encoded, dedicated brain circuits that enabled our ancestors to avoid danger in the environment, find appropriate food and shelter, and engage in reproductive activities. The neural architecture of these circuits is identical or similar to the subcortical circuits of the human brain. In humans, however, a highly developed and specialized layer of gray matter, the neocortex, is superimposed on this primitive subcortical framework. The neocortical component is more elaborated in mammals than in other taxa, and is more elaborate in primates than other mammals (Byrne & Corp, 2004; Kaas, 1996; Keverne, Martel, & Nevison, 1996; Northcutt & Kaas, 1995). In humans, after subcortical systems become active in response to potential danger, cortical inputs can provide an additional level of evaluation and even inhibitory control of responses that might be inappropriate given the context. The subcortical framework is automatically activated in all mammals and ensures that primary emotions arise in relation to the same basic drives and induce similar autonomic, hormonal, and somatic responses.

The cortical component provides the organism with an additional layer of analysis that helps adjust emotional responses to the ever-changing context of social life and, in humans, to the cultural, moral, and artistic dimensions of emotionally valent stimuli.

The *second premise* for the use of animals to model human emotion is that the expression of emotional behavior is similar among closely related species, both in terms of its structural appearance, or morphology, and of the contexts in which the emotion can be evoked; that is, fear engages similar behaviors (e.g., fight or flight), and all fear systems become activated by similar or equivalent stimuli (e.g., predators). In the seminal book, *Expression of the Emotions in Man and Animals* (1872), Charles Darwin discusses the principle of antithesis, in which habitual movements associated with a basic state of mind, or feeling, have a specific form, whereas movements associated with the opposite state of mind appear antithetical. A well-known example is that of a threatening dog. This creature exhibits piloerection, its ears are oriented forward and are alert, its body posture is erect and leaning forward, and the tail is raised and stiff. These behaviors are associated with aggression and can be viewed as threatening. A dog that is expressing submission or fear, however, adopts an opposite posture. It hunches down with its hindquarters in the air, tail tucked between the legs, its ears lay flat against the head, the hair is flat, and the head bends upward. Although the behavioral repertoires of related species are clearly not identical and exhibit numerous species-specific patterns of expression, many behaviors, particularly those associated with basic drives and motivations, do appear similar and can be used to reliably predict basic emotional patterns and provide useful end points for comparisons of emotion in humans and related species.

Although these two premises appear to be reasonable approaches for comparing emotion in animals and humans, it should be noted that such approaches are not without difficulty and/or controversy. One can, for example, understand the difficulty and concern that arises when attempting to study a subjective state in organisms that cannot tell us how they feel. Two related organisms may produce similar behavioral movements, but how can we as scientists be sure that the experience of these two creatures is in any way comparable? The fact that a behavior appears similar in related species does not mean it has homologous origins; it may have evolved through analogous evolutionary processes, as in the well-known example of the wings of bats and insects. Both structures appear similar and share a similar function in providing flight, but they do not share a common ancestry. Determining homology in behavior can be guided by examining its origin at multiple levels, including its genetic origin, ontogeny, neural underpinnings, physical structure, and function, although it is not always possible to conduct such an exhaustive set of analyses in a single experiment. Researchers should be cautious about interpreting behavior that is similar in appearance as being homologous, even when the two species share a recent common ancestry.

In light of these principles, selection of the appropriate species is an extremely important step for studies of emotion in animals. Although some emotional "primitives" are part of the behavioral repertoire of all animals, including nonspecific arousal (exploration, seeking), aggression, fear, sex attraction, maternal behavior, separation distress, and play, considerable species differences are present in the organization and expression of these behaviors that are important to consider when designing an experiment and formulating hypotheses. Despite these generalities, it is clear that not all emotions, their neural underpinnings, or biological implementation can be addressed in a single organism. If one is interested in studying fear, for example, numerous species both in the field and in the laboratory could be used. If, however, one were interested in studying empathy, a primate species that exhibits greater cortical elaboration of brain systems that regulate social behavior might be a better model. Many of these issues related to the relevance of animal research for human emotions can be overcome through the use of rigorous controlled experimental approaches, the selection of the most appropriate species, and, whenever possible, the use of methodologies applicable to both humans and animals. Therefore, the goals of this chapter are to highlight some of the current issues and controversies surrounding emotion research on nonhuman primates, including training and specific testing methodologies, selection of species, and ethical considerations.

Methodology

An exhaustive list of methods used for emotion elicitation and measurement in all laboratory animals exceeds the confines of this chapter. We opted, therefore, to focus on studies of nonhuman primates, omitting the most common procedures used for rodents (e.g., fear conditioning, inhibitory avoidance, conflict tests, etc.) that are widely described in the literature. A valuable resource for standard laboratory procedures that can be used to elicit and measure emotions in animals is the *Current Protocols in Neuroscience* (Crowley et al., 2003). Both field and laboratory work with nonhuman primates share many principles and methods in common with human studies, the outcome of which can then be compared with both normal and pathological human populations. There is the added advantage that in laboratory populations environmental and genetic factors that are known to significantly complicate and potentially confound research conducted on human populations can be controlled. Researchers have access to data on early environmental histories of the subject or can directly control these variables by setting standardized rearing and housing conditions. No matter what the specific topic or approach, animal research can be divided into three basic categories: observation, controlled experimentation, and direct manipulation.

Observation

Developing an Ethogram

Before embarking on behavioral research with animals, the experimenter should learn as much as possible about the species to be studied. Most animals that are candidates for laboratory research have been studied in the wild for many years, and there are numerous resources that carefully describe their species' typical behavioral repertoire, natural ecology, development, and communication. Even though the specific research may take place in an artificial laboratory environment, where animals live in conditions that do not match the social conditions in the wild, a complete understanding of the species' natural pattern of behavior and communication is critical for designing meaningful experiments. Moreover, monitoring the subject for any signs of stress, anxiety, or other abnormal behavior might (and most likely will) affect the outcome of a carefully planned (and probably expensive) series of experiments (see the later section on ethical considerations). If the results of those experiments cannot be extrapolated to the species as a whole, it is even less likely that the results will provide anything truly meaningful or relevant for comparing human and animal emotions and behavior. Table 23.1 provides a list of some of the more well-known ecological and behavioral surveys of common laboratory species of nonhuman primates.

Table 23.1

A brief list of sources describing the behavioral repertoires of common species of laboratory primates

Coelho, A. M., & Bramblett, C. A. (1989). Behavior of the genus *Papio*: Ethogram, taxonomy, methods, and comparative measures. In P. K. Seth & S. Seth (Eds.), *Perspectives in primate biology* (Vol. 3, pp. 117–140) New Delhi, India: Today and Tomorrow's Printers and Publishers.

De Vore, I. (Ed). 1965. Primate Behavior: Field studies of Monkeys and Apes, New York: Holt; Rinehart & Winston.

De Waal, F. (1988). The communicative repertoire of captive bonobos (*Pan paniscus*) compared to that of chimpanzees. *Behaviour, 106*, 183–251.

Goodall, J. v. L. (1968). The behaviour of free-living chimpanzees in the Gombe Stream Reserve. *Animal Behavior Monographs, 1*, 165–311.

Hinde, R. A., & Rowell, T. E. (1962). Communication by postures and facial expressions in the rhesus monkey (*Macaca mulatta*). *Proceedings of the Zoological Society of London, 138*, 1–21.

Sade, D. S. (1973). An ethogram for rhesus monkeys: I. Antithetical constraints in posture and movement. *American Journal of Physical Anthropology, 38*, 537–542.

Smuts, B. B., Cheney, D. L., Seyfarth, R. M., Wrangham, R. W., & Struhsaker, T. T. (Eds.). (1987). *Primate societies*. Chicago: University of Chicago Press.

Van Hooff, J. A. R. A. M. (1967). The facial displays of the Catarrhine monkeys and apes. In D. Morris (Ed.), *Primate ethology* (pp. 7–68). Chicago: Aldine.

In addition to reading about the species in question, researchers are encouraged to spend a few hours observing a social group of the species in question. If this is not possible at a local zoo or at the institution sponsoring the work, other sources might include one of the eight National Primate Centers across the United States. These include the Yerkes National Primate Research Center in Atlanta, Georgia; the Wisconsin National Primate Research Center in Madison, Wisconsin; the New England National Primate Research Center in Southborough, Massachusetts; the Washington National Primate Research Center in Seattle, Washington; the California National Primate Research Center in Davis, California; the Oregon National Primate Research Center in Beaverton, Oregon; the Southwest National Primate Research Center in San Antonio, Texas; and the Tulane National Primate Research Center in Covington, Louisiana. In addition, a local library might possess a video archive, in which case a documentary of the species in question might be available. Finally, another wonderful resource is the Wisconsin Primate Research Center Library, which carries a detailed audiovisual library that can be searched online (http://pin.primate.wisc.edu).

Once the researcher has consulted several texts and learned about the natural ecology and emotional behavior of the species to be studied, she or he is ready to construct a behavioral ethogram. An ethogram is a detailed description of the behaviors of interest that can be used by both experienced and naïve observers to help reliably identify behaviors of interest. Traditionally, an ethogram describes the entire repertoire of the behavior of a species, but for the purposes of this chapter, an ethogram simply describes the behaviors that are of interest for a specific study. Depending on the research question, the ethogram may be very specific and detailed, if one were interested in the motor patterns that occur during play behavior, or more general, if one were interested in the overall activity patterns of a group such as feeding, grooming, sleeping, and so forth. Table 23.2 lists a portion of an ethogram used to study chimpanzee social communication, recently published by Parr, Cohen, and de Waal (2005). With the advent of multimedia technology, modern ethograms can now include short video clips of the behaviors, an audio file if the behavior is acoustic, and descriptions of the same behaviors published by other researchers. The key is that all researchers involved in studying that behavior should agree as to what the behavior looks like and be able to identify it reliably.

An ethogram is also useful in that it provides an objective description of behavior that may then be qualified in a different manner. For example, if one were interested in fearful behavior in rhesus monkeys in response to snake videos, fear could be objectively identified from a list of behaviors described in the ethogram. Fear responses, for example, may consist of showing the silent bared-teeth facial expression (commonly referred to as the fear grin), urination or defecation immediately following the presentation of the video, crouching or recoiling from the video monitor, turning the

Table 23.2

A portion of a ethogram used to study chimpanzees behavior (Parr, Cohen, & de Waal, in press).

Code	Behavioral Description
AP	*Approach neutral:* One individual approaches another within 2 m with no contact. This is coded only when the approach is observed.
NO	*Neutral behavior:* Sitting, ignore others without contact or response. This is coded if a facial expression is made with no obvious accompanying behavior, or within a dyadic interaction as a neutral response category.
NC	*Neutral contact:* Ambiguous contact by one individual toward another. The contact is not easily defined as play or aggression, i.e., touching.
P1	*Play:* Two individuals wrestling, tickling, or chasing one another in nonantagonistic ways. Code in each direction if the play is mutual. Only the initiator receives the code if the play attempts is unsuccessful. If the play is solitary, the recipient is n/a.
P2	*Rough play:* Play that includes restraining, or biting, or otherwise behavior that would be considered antagonistic. This is also coded if the response of the partner is antagonistic.
KI	*Kiss:* Mouth contact on the mouth or body of another individual. If mutual, note for both individuals.
EM	*Embrace:* Gentle contact to another individual using the arms or another body part. Note in addition to kissing if these occur together.
OV	*Avoid/displaced:* When the approach of another individual leads the focal subject to move immediately away > 1m.
sc0	*Silent scream face:* The mouth is wide open, eyes open. Top and bottom teeth are exposed. Mouth corners are withdrawn to expose teeth and lips are fully withdrawn. Either none or very quiet raspy hisses are issued.
bt1	*Silent bared-teeth display:* The mouth may be slightly open or closed, lips withdrawn and mouth corners retracted laterally, and the teeth fully exposed. Eyes may be open or squinted. The lack of vocalizations help define this from the other bared-teeth expressions.
sc1	*Low-intensity scream:* This is a category of display that includes all forms of scream that are of a lower intensity than the bared-teeth scream faces, but not clearly definable as any in the yelping/squealing, squeaking categories. The calls are highly variable, take many different facial forms where the teeth may or may not be exposed, and the mouth may or may not be open. The calls are not of a high intensity or of a prolonged duration.

head away to avoid the stimulus, or making scream vocalizations. Thus fear may objectively identified according to a set of behaviors that have been operationally defined in the study's ethogram. The behaviors themselves were identified from published data on the natural behavioral repertoire of the species.

Observational Data Collection Methods

Once the ethogram has been constructed and the research staff has understood it and demonstrated competence in identifying each behavior pattern of interest (interrater reliability statistics are usually conducted), data collection may begin. One of the seminal papers that is a "must read" for any student or scientist interested in observational research is Jeanne Altmann's (1974) "Observational Study of Behavior: Sampling Methods" or a recent textbook published by Karen Strier (1999), *Primate Behavioral Ecology*. These resources, among others, provide comprehensive descriptions of animal behavior, sampling methods, and relevant species differences that will be invaluable in helping to construct a well-designed observational protocol and to choose the correct data collection methods for the questions of interest. The three main methods that are most commonly used include scan sampling, focal sampling, and the one-zero method. These methods provide different end points for data analysis but are not mutually exclusive. They are described briefly here, but readers are encouraged to read the texts previously named for more detail.

Scan Sampling. In scan sampling, the observer creates a list of clearly identifiable behaviors, and, at periodic time intervals (to be determined by the investigator), he or she quickly surveys the entire social group and records whether the behavior is occurring or not. Typically, the identity of the individual who is performing the behavior and the individual receiving the behavior is also noted, but this is not always done. For example, if one were interested in the frequency of morning play behavior in a group of rhesus monkeys, scan sampling would be an efficient data collection method. Scan sampling is adequate for obtaining general patterns of behavior, but it does not provide detailed information about who initiated the behavior, who broke off contact, why contact was broken off, the duration of the play bout, or other behaviors. The technique is also not sufficient for measuring point behaviors that have relatively short durations, as these are too rapid for scan sampling to be an effective method. Scan sampling is more efficient for monitoring state behaviors that last for some duration, such as grooming, play, feeding, locomotion, proximity, and sleeping.

One-Zero Sampling. In one-zero sampling, the researcher identifies a few behaviors and, during set time intervals, notes whether the behavior is occurring within the social group or by a particular individual. In this case, the data are even simpler than in scan sampling. The observer, for example, might be interested in whether two individuals are grooming after feeding. Within 30-second blocks, if the behavior is ongoing, the observer enters a 1 on the data sheet; if the behavior is not present during the 30-second interval, he or she enters a 0. This gives gross estimates of the duration and/or frequency of a behavior.

Focal Sampling. Focal sampling provides the most detailed observational data during real-time sampling. Depending on the complexity of the ethogram, focal sampling can range from very straightforward to something more akin to calling the play-by-play during a highly energetic sports event. The investigator selects an individual from the social group, the focal individual, and for a set duration of time he or she records every activity performed by the focal subject that is described in the ethogram, including who the subject interacts with and who interacts with the subject. Because there is not always time to write these behaviors or interactions down without the risk of missing something, investigators typically speak the observations into a tape recorder so as not to lose visual contact with the focal subject and then transcribe the recordings at a later time. Thus focal sampling provides details about who initiates behavior, who terminates behavior, and the duration of the behaviors and their frequency during the entire sampling period; it also provides detailed data on both point and state behaviors. Depending on the complexity of the ethogram, considerable training and experience may be required in order to conduct focal animal sampling research.

Advantages and Tradeoffs

There are several advantages to studying emotional behavior in free-ranging animals using observational methods. First, what is being recorded is naturally occurring, unprovoked behavior initiated according to the motivation of the individual. Thus the data reflect typical responses to social and environmental conditions, much in the same way behavior would be observed in a wild population. Second, behavior is observed within a complex social environment. Therefore, the subject's behavior expresses more than just a response elicited by a particular environmental stimulus; rather, the behavior is expressed within a complex, fluid social environment in which interactions occur with multiple individuals with multiple consequences. Finally, the range of social individuals present in a larger group provides the opportunity to address numerous questions, such as the nature of mother-infant behavior, interactions with kin versus nonkin, interactions between aged and younger individuals, and ongoing dominance relationships that may involve coalitions and alliances among multiple group members.

Drawbacks are also apparent, however. First, behavioral data are not elicited artificially, and it takes many hours of patient observation to collect sufficient sample sizes to address questions pertaining to social and emotional behavior. Fights among group members may occur only once or twice per day, if that, so to obtain 500 data entry points would require almost a year of continuous observation. Second, a researcher can ask questions only about naturally occurring behavior. Thus the opportunity to replicate specific situations to see whether particular behaviors or outcomes would be likely to happen again is not possible. Additionally, small changes in behavior—such as increased respiration, micro changes in facial expressions or social gaze direction, or very quiet vocalizations—are not likely to be detectable at a distance and are better studied in more closely observable situations. Finally, it is difficult to control for the range of events that might, and most likely do, contribute to specific behavioral responses when observing free-ranging animals. These may include social interactions or events that occurred before the observer arrived for the daily observations. The morning may have produced a huge dominance fight between the alpha male and his rival, yet without directly knowing the details of this conflict, the observer can only wonder why the two spent the entire afternoon grooming one another.

Experimentation

In addition to behavioral observation techniques, methods used for studying animal emotion commonly involve some form of experimentation, through which scientists manipulate variables and measure desired outcomes. There are too many experimental manipulations for us to cover them exhaustively in this chapter, but we highlight some procedures that have broad applications for studies of emotion in humans and other animals. These include the use of operant tasks, playback techniques, viewing paradigms, intruder challenges, and measuring autonomic indicators of emotion.

Operant/Computerized Tasks

In operant tasks animals are trained to make a particular response, which becomes the primary dependent variable. Animals, for example, can be trained to press a lever in response to certain stimuli. A series of intriguing studies on animal emotion that used this methodology were performed in the 1960s by Robert Miller. These studies were some of the first to demonstrate that monkeys acquire affective information about conspecifics solely from their facial expressions. Miller, Murphy, and Mirsky (1959) exposed monkeys to a photograph of a *familiar monkey* with a neutral expression. The presentation of this conditioned stimulus (CS) was paired with a shock, which subjects could avoid by pressing a lever in their test cage. Subjects reduced lever-pressing when novel photographs of *unfamiliar monkeys* with neutral expressions were added to the test stimuli, indicating that they were able to discriminate the CS monkey from other neutral portraits. Response to the original CS was then extinguished by ceasing the shock, and a final experiment was performed: Subjects were shown a photograph of the same animal that was presented as the CS, but this time with a fearful expression. When subjects were shown this new stimulus, they produced significantly more lever presses, or avoidance responses, than during the original CS phase, when the same monkey displayed a neutral expression. Therefore, subjects not only generalized their avoidance responses to novel photographs of a familiar individual, but their rate of responding spontaneously increased according to the emotional valence of the expression depicted in the photograph.

Other operant paradigms used by Parr and colleagues at the Yerkes Primate Center involve a computerized joystick-testing paradigm. The results of many of these studies and their implications for understanding animal emotion have recently been reviewed (Parr, 2003), so the details of the results are not given here. The basic testing situation involves a computer that is wheeled to the subject's home cage. Testing in the home cage has both advantages and disadvantages when it comes to subject's participation. On the one hand, subjects do not have to be habituated to a novel testing room or apparatus, which can take time and produce anxiety in animals not used to novel environments. The subject would need to be separated from any cage mates during the testing period, which can be particularly stressful for nonhuman primates. Furthermore, reintroducing animals back into their home cages can produce increased aggression as individuals reestablish their dominance hierarchies. On the other hand, testing in the home cage requires cooperation among cage mates so that one does not steal the food reinforcers of the other or cause interference during testing. Home cages can be noisy, as other animals are likely to be nearby. However, with chimpanzees, we find that testing in the home cage has more advantages than disadvantages for most of our studies.

Once the computer has been moved to the front of the home cage, a joystick is positioned vertically through the mesh. Using a training battery developed at the Language Research Center (Richardson et al., 1990), subjects have been trained to control the movements of a cursor on the computer screen by manipulating the joystick. Our research at the Yerkes Primate Center has focused on social cognition and presents tasks to chimpanzees and rhesus monkeys using a matching-to-sample (MTS) procedure. This is another extremely rich and versatile paradigm for understanding animal emotion and is comparable to studies in humans and other animals (Brown, Brown, & Poulson, 1995; D'Amato, Salmon & Colombo, 1985; Hashiya & Kojima, 2001; Herman, Hovancik, Gory, & Bradshaw, 1989; Kastak & Schusterman, 1994; Malone, Tolan, & Rogers, 1980; Neiworth & Wright, 1994). The basic format of the MTS task is that subjects first see one image on the computer monitor. This is the sample, or the image they have to match. Typically, subjects orient to this image by contacting it with the joystick-controlled cursor. If the task is a touch-screen task, they simply touch the image. After this, they are presented with two comparison images, one of which matches the sample. They must contact this image in order to receive reinforcement, after which the next trial is presented.

A slight variation of this paradigm used in research on monkeys and human infants reinforces subjects for selecting the nonmatching, or novel, image (DNMS; delayed nonmatch-to-sample). This is based on the finding that monkeys and young children are attracted to novelty, and numerous experimental cognition paradigms take advantage of these biases; some of these are described later. However, we believe that for the study of emotion, MTS provides greater flexibility and control of specific experimental questions than DNMS procedures. This is because MTS allows one to assess whether the subject detects similarity between the correct pair of images presented, whereas DNMS provides only an assessment of which stimulus is novel. The flexibility of the MTS is that the basis of stimulus similarity can be quite abstract, as described later, and this provides a greater degree of stimulus and experimental control than is possible in DNMS.

Parr, Winslow, Hopkins, and de Waal (2000) presented both chimpanzees and rhesus monkeys with the task of matching identical faces of unfamiliar conspecifics (Figure 23.1a). This was immediately followed by a study of individual recognition, in which the correct pair of faces consisted of two different photographs of the same individual. Thus, in order to perform this task correctly, subjects were required to detect similarities in the facial configuration of that individual, not novelty among the photographs (Figure 23.1b). Thus the basis of matching in the first task was recognizing similar photographs, whereas the basis of matching in the second task was recognizing the identity of the individual presented in the photographs.

An extension of this procedure was used to assess facial expression categorization (Parr, Hopkins, & de Waal, 1998). Subjects were presented with an unfamiliar conspecific making one of five facial expressions as the sample image: bared-teeth display, hoot face, scream face, relaxed-lip face, and relaxed–open mouth display. The correct comparison was another individual making the same type of facial expression, whereas the nonmatching face was a third individual making another facial expression. Figure 23.2 provides an example using the play face (correct expression on the left side). The basis of matching was the type of expressions being made, not the identity of the individuals making them.

Finally, in a unique derivation of this paradigm, Parr (2001) presented chimpanzees with the task of discriminating images according to their emotional content. The sample image was a 5-second video clip showing an emotional situation familiar to the subject, such as hypodermic needles (negative image) and preferred food items (positive image). The goal of the task was for subjects to categorize the videos according to their emotional valence by selecting one of two facial expressions that matched the emotional content of the videos. Figure 23.3 shows an example of a hypodermic needle as the sample and a bared-teeth expression (on the right side) as the correct choice. Thus, in order to perform this task, subjects were required to detect something similar between the emotional content displayed by the sample video and comparison facial expressions, not something perceptually similar or something novel. In these examples, it is easy to see how MTS affords greater experimental flexibility than do novelty-detection tasks, because all the photographs in these studies—individual discrimination (Figure 23.1b), expression categorization (Figure 23.2), and emotional matching (Figure 23.3)—were novel. However, the goal of the task, to match the sample, remains consistent despite differences in the perceptual and/or conceptual bases for matching these images—that is, recognizing the same individual, recogniz-

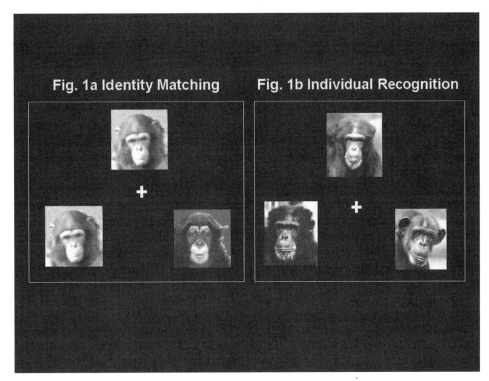

Figure 23.1. Two versions of the matching-to-sample paradigm. The image on top is the sample and represents the image to match. The cross is the joystick controlled cursor, and the two images laterally displaced on the bottom left and right sides of the monitor are the two comparison images. One resembles the sample, the other is different. (a) Example of an identity matching trial where subjects must match the sample by moving the cursor to contact the face on the left, an identical image as that presented in the sample. (b) Example of an individual recognition trial where subjects must match the sample by moving the cursor to contact the image that looks most like the sample. The correct response is to select the image on the bottom left, which shows a different photograph of the same individual that is portrayed in the sample. Therefore, this trial is one based on recognizing the same individual presented in two different photographs.

ing the same facial expression, or recognizing an emotional similarity, respectively.

Playback

Playback experiments take advantage of the naturally occurring behavior of the organism and can be used to probe for consistencies in how individuals respond to particular social and environmental situations. Thus they provide an advantage over most strictly observational studies in that social and environmental situations can be controlled experimentally while monitoring the naturally occurring response of specific individuals to these situations. Most well-known playback experiments have involved presenting known vocalizations to group members and measuring their responses as a means to assess the meaning of these acoustically distinct calls. Cheney and Seyfarth describe numerous examples of playback experiments in their 1990 publication, *How Monkeys See the World*. We give two examples here. In one experiment, the authors recorded naturally occurring alarm calls from known, wild vervet monkeys while they were in the presence of specific predators. Vocalizations were recorded in response to avian

predators, such as eagles, and ground predators, such as leopards and snakes. At a later time point, these calls were played back to the group through a hidden speaker when neither the individual who made the specific recorded call nor the specific class of predator was present. The behavioral response of group members was then measured. In these classic studies, Seyfarth and colleagues discovered that the behavioral response of vervet monkeys differed in reliable ways depending on the type of alarm call that was presented (Seyfarth, Cheney, & Marler, 1980). If the call was recorded in response to an avian predator, monkeys typically moved to the interior portion of the tree they were in, presumably to avoid being snatched from exterior branches, or under a bush if there were at a distance from a tree. If the call was one given to a ground predator, such as a leopard, individuals immediately ran into a tree. If the alarm call was one recorded in the presence of a snake, individuals typically looked on the ground or stood up on their hind legs to scan the area. The authors concluded that the different alarm calls must signal something specific about the class of predator, producing different patterns of behavior in response to their playback in the absence of the actual stimulus.

Figure 23.2. An example of a facial expression matching trial. The image on top, the sample, shows a chimpanzee making a play face. Subjects must move the cursor to contact the same facial expression as presented in the sample. In this example, the two comparison images show another chimpanzee making a play face on the left side and a third individual chimpanzee making a bared-teeth expression on the right. Thus, the correct response is to select the face on the left, the play face.

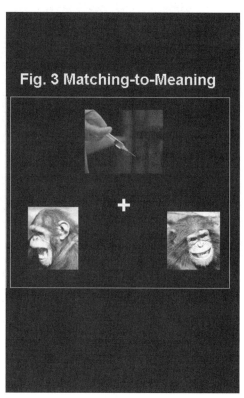

Figure 23.3. An example of an emotion matching trial. The image on top, the sample, shows a hypodermic needle. Subjects must match this by selecting the facial expression comparison image that represents a similar emotional valence as presented in the sample. In this example, the image on the left is a play face and the right shows a bared-teeth face. Bared-teeth expressions are also referred to as fear-grins, and this expression shares a negative emotional valence with the sample and represents the correct response for this trial.

In a similar study, playback experiments were used to inquire whether vervet monkeys recognize the identity of familiar group members from their intergroup vocalizations, of which there are several that are acoustically distinct (Cheney & Seyfarth, 1990). In an elegant experiment, experimenters habituated wild vervet monkeys (*Cercopithecus aethiops*) to one familiar group member's intergroup call by playing this call repeatedly until the typical pattern of behavioral responses ceased. When a second distinct intergroup call was played from the same individual, group members continued to show habituation, suggesting that group members recognized the identity of the individual making the call. When group members were subsequently played the first intergroup call given this time by another group member, they showed behavioral responses characteristic of intergroup vigilance, that is, subjects dishabituated to this intergroup call, demonstrating that they discriminated the identity of the individuals making the calls. Thus playback techniques can provide a rich paradigm for assessing social cognition and emotional behavior in different species.

Viewing Paradigms

Viewing paradigms are typically used in a laboratory setting as one of the more accessible methods for assessing cogni-

tion and emotion in nonhuman primates. These paradigms are simple and do not require training, because they rely on a natural attentional bias toward novel and/or emotional images.

Preferential Looking Tasks. Nonhuman primates, like humans, are more drawn toward novel stimuli and look at them longer when they are displayed concomitantly with familiar stimuli. An attentional bias, or viewing preference, has been demonstrated not only for novel stimuli but also for emotionally significant stimuli compared with neutral ones (Bachevalier, Brickson, & Hagger, 1993; McKee & Squire, 1993; Pascalis & Bachevalier, 1999). Such biases are particularly obvious for face stimuli that can be novel or familiar but also neutral or emotional (Gothard, Erickson, & Amaral 2004; Nemanic, Alvarado, & Bachevalier, 2004). Kyes and Candland (1987), for example, examined the viewing patterns of four baboons when looking at the face of the group's dominant male with various combinations of facial features masked. All subjects showed significantly longer viewing duration for the slides in which the eyes of the stimulus animal were visible, supporting the contention that the eyes are the most important feature for maintaining visual attention in this species. In a study designed to measure cross-modal integration of emotionally relevant expressions, Ghazanfar and Logothetis (2003), for example, reported that monkeys looked longer at one of two facial-expression videos that matched a simultaneously played vocalization. Thus monkeys were able to recognize the correspondence between the auditory and visual components of their calls.

Visual paired comparison (VPC) is another version of a preferential looking task that takes advantage of the inherent attentional bias of humans and other animals for novelty. First, subjects are shown a single stimulus for a specific duration of time. Initially, subjects visually orient and examine this image, but depending on how interesting or meaningful it is, this interest quickly habituates. When the looking time decreases, subjects are presented with the same image and a novel image. A reliable finding in these cases is that subjects immediately orient to the novel image and look at it for longer durations than they look at the previously viewed image. The VPC task has some advantages in that, once subjects are habituated to the first image, even if emotionally salient, the emotional content of the second image can be specifically chosen to address a particular question. The limitation of the VPC task is that it relies on the habituation effect and thus requires the use of stimulus images that are entirely novel. It remains, however, one of the more widely used and easily implemented methods for studies of emotion and cognition in animals.

Eye-Tracking Methods.   Eye tracking determines where an animal looks on an image and provides data on the absolute and relative duration of each fixation in a sequence of eye movements used to scan an image. These methods allow extremely detailed observations of how animals gather emotionally relevant information from the visual world. Eye-tracking methods can be noninvasive, using infrared devices that track the position of the pupil and the corneal reflection, or invasive, using surgically implanted scleral coils that are tracked with a magnetic field generated around the subject's head. With either of these methods, the sequence in which visual attention is allocated to various regions of a stimulus can be used as a dependent measure of the emotional salience of the image.

The most advanced methods are able to measure the precise target and duration of fixations but also individual saccades, smooth pursuit motion, and miniature eye movements, such as tremor, drift, and microsaccades. Fixations are periods of approximately 100–400 ms when the eye rests on a detail of the image, whereas saccades are fast eye movements (approximately 30–60 ms) used to locate the target of subsequent fixations. The sequence of fixations and saccades constitutes a scanpath. When superimposed on the image, a scanpath shows which elements of the image were most intensely explored and the order in which fixations and saccades were performed (Figure 23.4). It is instantly clear looking at these scanpaths that the eye-tracking methodology provides a rich and elaborate set of data for understanding which features of emotionally relevant stimuli are more interesting or salient for subjects.

Conventional noninvasive eye tracking involves the use of a high-speed digital video camera surrounded by a series of infrared light-emitting diodes (LEDs) that produce an infrared beam aimed at the eye. Part of the beam is absorbed though the pupil, and part is reflected by the cornea. The pupil and/or the corneal reflection are captured by the camera, and their x-y position is transmitted to a computer according to preset sampling frequency. These are either converted by an A/D converter and further processed or directed via digital interface to a data acquisition card.

In a more invasive eye-tracking method, a fine coil of wire is attached to a contact lens or implanted directly in the sclera

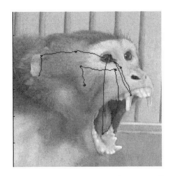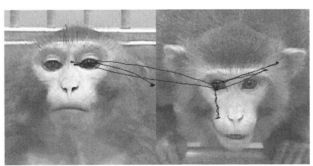

Figure 23.4. Scanpaths recorded an adult monkey viewing images of conspecific facial expressions. The lines indicate the eye movements (saccades) while the small "knots" correspond to the fixations. The image on the left shows the scanpath on a yawning face. The fixation in the middle of the cheek is the initial fixation on the monitor before the image was displayed. Note that the eye is the most explored region, followed by the mouth (canines) and the ear. The two images on the right show the same monkey with a neutral (left) and a threatening (right) facial expression. The scanpath indicates that the viewer explored only the eyes of the neutral face, whereas the threatening face elicited repeated saccades to the ears and the mouth.

of the eye, and the head of the subject is placed within horizontally and vertically oriented alternating magnetic fields (Robinson, 1963). The signal induced in the eye coil depends on the orientation of the eye within the two fields. For example, in the eye-tracking system made by DNI (northmor@udel .edu), the two fields are of different frequencies so that the eye coil's signal can be separated into horizontal and vertical components by synchronous demodulation. The result is a high-resolution reconstruction of eye position (to within a few minutes of arc or less). Researchers interested in eye tracking will find extensive information in a recent (2003) book by Andrew T. Duchowski, *Eye Tracking Methodology: Theory and Practice,* that surveys various noninvasive eye-tracking devices and gives a detailed introduction to the technical requirements for installing and using various eye-tracker systems. In addition, the second edition of *Psychophysiological Recording,* by Robert M. Stern, William J. Ray, and Karen S. Quigley (2001), provides detailed methodological information that compares several eye-tracking systems.

Almost all eye trackers require precise calibration for the eye position measures to be meaningful. This is done by requesting the subject to look at specific locations on a presentation surface, such as a computer monitor, and adjusting the gain and the output of the system to the actual distance between the calibration points. To eliminate head movements and compensate for fatigue in the subject, the infrared systems most often employ a chin rest. More advanced eye-tracking systems, such as those available from Applied Science Laboratories (http://www.a-s-1.com), use a magnetic tracking device and sophisticated algorithms, in addition to infrared corneal reflection technology, to compensate for head motion without loss in resolution or accuracy of data monitoring and to allow for long-lasting calibrations. This device consists of a small magnetic sensor, approximately 2.5 cm^3, that can be mounted to a hat that the subject wears.

Head movements are not tolerated by magnetic eye coil systems. Temporal resolution of these systems is high, and even slight movements such as those produced by voluntary positioning in a chin rest can cause problems. Therefore, this system works best when the head is immobilized. The most common procedure for head fixation requires surgically implanting small metal posts into the skull using orthopedic bone screws and bone cement. During the period in which head immobilization is necessary, these metal posts lock into a rigid bar and frame. The advantage of this type of system over training the animal to sit in a chin rest is that the system needs to be calibrated only once (provided the monkey can be placed in exactly the same position in the head fixation device).

After recovery from the implantation surgery, the animals are habituated to the apparatus and trained to tolerate head fixation through the use of positive reinforcement. Most head fixation systems use a single head post, which provides a safe and solid attachment to the rigid frame and does not cause discomfort to the animal. Several of these devices are commercially available (e.g., from Crist Instruments, http://www .cristinstrument.com). Newer head fixation systems are based on multiple small head posts that connect to a head ring locked into a holder (Thomas Recording, http://www .thomasrecording .com). The advantage of the multiple post system is that the forces generated by head fixation are distributed across the skull, minimizing potential complications or physical stress to the animal.

Once the animals are habituated to head fixation, they are trained to perform a task necessary for calibrating the tracker. The initial training takes advantage of the natural orienting reflex of the monkey. The monkey is seated in front of a computer monitor placed 57 cm from the eyes. At this distance, 1 cm on the monitor corresponds to 1 degree of visual angle. To reduce distractions and maximize visual attention to the task, it is desirable to place the monkey and the display monitor in a sound-attenuated enclosure in dim light. A surveillance camera (infrared is preferable because of the low illumination) can be directed toward the face and eyes of the animal to allow the experimenter to monitor spontaneous eye movements and the alertness of the monkey during the training. When the monkey is habituated to the dark screen, a small bright dot or fixation icon is displayed on the monitor. The monkey automatically saccades to this spot, a movement that is detected by the eye tracker and is visible to the experimenter via the surveillance camera. Looking at the fixation icon is rewarded with a drop of fruit juice delivered into the monkey's mouth. As the animal learns that reward can be obtained by looking at the icons on the monitor, the size of the icon can be gradually reduced, and the icon can be displayed at various locations on the monitor. Failure to look at the fixation icon should be followed by a time-out period (2–3 s), when the monitor remains blank. When the monkey looks reliably at the fixation icons, the eye tracker can be calibrated by displaying the fixation icon at known vertical and horizontal distances from the center of the monitor.

In a recent experiment performed by Gothard and colleagues (Gothard, Erickson, & Amaral, 2004), eye movements were monitored using the scleral eye coils during a VPC task. Monkeys were shown simultaneously a novel and familiar image of conspecific facial expressions. As the subject was trained to maintain gaze within the joint boundary of the two images, the eye was continually exploring either the novel or the familiar side of the stimulus. The precise quantification of scanpaths allowed the authors to conclude that monkeys, like humans, explore novel images for significantly longer durations than familiar images. Regardless of the novelty or familiarity of face image, the eyes are the most explored feature in a neutral face. Images of facial expressions elicit exploration patterns that involve not only the eyes but also those facial features that are the most characteristic for a particular expression. For example, monkeys explore to the same extent the eyes and the mouth on threatening facial expressions, whether a threat or a yawn. On yawning faces, the saccades to the mouth area are directed precisely to the canines in about 50% of scanpaths (an example is shown in Figure 23.4). Canines are sexually dimorphic and signal important information about the sex, age, health, and possibly status of the displaying animal. Scanpaths can be used, therefore, to determine the more salient, biologically relevant components of a stimulus image. This methodology has considerable advantages over other cognitive/operant task formats as subjects do not have to be trained to perform a discrimination task.

Intruder Paradigms

The stranger-intruder paradigm was designed by Kalin and Shelton (1989) as an objective measure of anxious temperament in infant and adult rhesus monkeys. Anxious monkeys display excessive defensive behaviors in response to a social challenge, such as a human intruder in the immediate vicinity of their home cage. Kalin and colleagues (Kalin, Larson, Shelton, & Davidson, 1998; Kalin, Shelton, & Davidson, 2000) have identified asymmetries in the pattern of cortical electrical activity in rhesus monkeys that can be correlated with basic emotional processes. Monkeys with strong right prefrontal asymmetries show higher basal cortisol levels and secrete higher levels of corticotropin-releasing hormone than control animals or those displaying left-side prefrontal asymmetries. In humans, these asymmetry patterns correlate with self-reported negative feelings on a number of emotion surveys, suggesting a biological disposition toward certain affective styles (Davidson, 1992).

Four challenges of increasing intensity have been included in the stranger-intruder paradigm. Behavioral responses of the monkeys to these challenges are typically coded by a rater who is blind to the specific intensity of the challenge and temperament group of the subject. Monkeys are tested alone in their cage, but they should be familiar with the surroundings so as not to produce anxiety before testing. Before the onset of the challenge, baseline behavior is recorded for a specific period of time, typically around 9 minutes, with each challenge period lasting approximately the same duration so that rates of behavior can be compared across conditions. The test starts with the intruder entering the room, stopping 2.5 meters from the subject's cage, and presenting his or her profile to the subject while avoiding eye contact. Halfway through the 9-minute test period, the human intruder makes a step toward the cage but remains in profile orientation. The human leaves the room and reenters after 10 minutes to stand in the same position, but this time facing the cage and staring at the subject with a neutral face. Again, halfway through this test, the intruder makes one step toward the monkey. At the conclusion of the test, postchallenge baseline behaviors are recorded for 9 minutes. Ideally, the behaviors and vocalizations are videotaped, and the tape is scored by two experienced observers blind to the specific conditions; that is, the posture of the intruder is not visible on the tape.

In a behavioral study, Kalin, Shelton, and Davidson (2004) used the human-intruder paradigm to compare anxiety-related defensive responses in monkeys that underwent selective lesions of the central nucleus of the amygdala. They found significant differences between normal monkeys and lesioned monkeys in that the lesioned monkeys produced more coos, barks, and freezing behavior during the first phase of the test (intruder in profile) and more defensive hostility during the second phase (intruder staring). These data indicate that the central nucleus of the amygdala has an important role in regulating the expression of defensive and anxious behaviors in monkeys. In general, the strange-intruder paradigm is a simple yet robust method for eliciting anxiety-based behavior in rhesus monkeys, does not require any training, and adopts a series of species-typical behaviors and independent measures of anxiety.

Recording Autonomic Indicators of Emotion

Autonomic variables are arguably the most objective measures for evaluating an individual's response to an emotion-eliciting stimulus, and they provide robust and valuable methods for measuring and comparing subjective emotional states both within and across species. Autonomic changes that are generated in response to an emotional stimulus are tightly coupled with overt, voluntary behaviors, yet are independent of voluntary control. Voluntary commands that arise in higher neural centers can influence autonomic centers, but the autonomic centers remain functional even when the cerebral hemispheres are removed (Blessing, 1997). For example, the voluntary command signal to the muscles to execute a movement is coupled to pathways that send concomitant signals to autonomic centers. These centers alter the contraction of the vascular smooth muscles and the heart, preparing the organism for physical effort. In contrast, the autonomic signals that arise in the body and feed back to the homeostatic regulatory centers are coupled to pathways that connect to higher centers, where sensations from the body, such as accelerated heart rate, are integrated in a perception of arousal and excitation. The most accessible autonomic measures that can be studied with minimal invasiveness in animals include heart rate, blood pressure, skin conductance, and temperature. When attempting to measure these variables, researchers are encouraged to review the guidelines for data measurement and interpretation published in the *Handbook of Psychophysiology* (Cacioppo, Tassinary, & Berntson, 2000; see also Lykken & Venables, 1971; Stern et al., 2001; Turner, Girdler, Sherwood, & Light, 1990).

Heart Rate and Blood Pressure.   Cardiac activity and its associated measures provide a sensitive index of autonomic self-regulation in that the chronotropy of the heart is regulated by a combination of sympathetic and parasympathetic activity (Berntson et al., 1997). Generally speaking, sympathetic activity accelerates heart rate, whereas parasympathetic activity decelerates the heart. The electrocardiogram (ECG) is easily monitored in animals using either surface electrodes or implantable telemetric transmitters. Animals are typically conditioned to sit in a restraining chair while disposable Ag-

AgCl surface electrodes are placed in various configurations on the limbs and/or torso (Andreassi, 1989; Stern et al., 2001). The electrical signal generated by the heart is then recorded, and these data transmitted to a computer for post-acquisition processing. An excellent package for postacquisition analysis is available from Mindware Technology, Inc. (http://www.mindwaretech.com).

The disadvantage of the noninvasive surface recording method, or ECG, is that it requires handling and restraining the animal, which can be stressful initially and which requires additional training and equipment to facilitate the restraint. This restraint also minimizes the ability of the researcher to acquire naturally occurring behavior from a freely moving individual. The impact of restraint, however, can be minimized by habituating monkeys to the chair restraint and electrode attachment procedures. Baseline heart rate should stabilize within a few minutes of the experimental setup, providing independent confirmation that the animal is comfortable. The number of training sessions required for habituation depends on the personality of the monkey, but optimally the acclimation training is performed by the same person, at the same time of the day, and follows a rigorous routine. When the animal is fully habituated to all the procedures involved, the stress response (cardiovascular or hormonal) is reduced to a minimum (Hassimoto & Harada, 2003; Ruys, Mendoza, Capitanio, & Mason, 2004).

Paradoxically, invasive methods involving telemetric transmitters might actually be less stressful for the animals because, although they require a single anesthetized surgical procedure at the beginning of the experiment when sensors and telemetric transmitters are implanted under the skin, the animal does not have to be restrained during the recording. An advanced telemetry device (Data Sciences Int., St. Paul, Minnesota) described by Schnell and Gerber (1997) consists of a transmitter (AM unit, model PA-D70, for rhesus macaques), a radio receiver placed in the vicinity of the animal (the observation cage or the laboratory wall), and a computerized data acquisition and storage system. This system measures ECG via the transmitter implanted subcutaneously and blood pressure via a catheter placed usually in the femoral artery. The surgical procedure for implanting this device has been described in detail by Brockway and Hassler (1992). Blood pressure (BP) is expressed in millimeters of mercury (mmHg), and ECG can be expressed either as heart rate, typically in beats per minute, or as heart period, which corresponds to the interbeat interval, or time between R-wave peaks, expressed in ms. Although heart rate and heart period are inversely related to one another, their relationship is not linear, particularly when baseline levels are varied. Recommendations for reporting heart rate or heart period have been made by Berntson and colleagues (Berntson, Cacioppo, & Quigley, 1995).

Several studies have used heart rate to assess the emotional significance of social stimuli in nonhuman primates using both surface electrode and telemetric recording devices.

Using a surface electrode recording technique, Berntson and colleagues (Berntson, Boysen, Bauer, & Torello, 1989) combined playback techniques with autonomic measurements to show significant changes in heart rate in captive chimpanzees in response to conspecific vocalizations. Heart rate was acceleratory in response to conspecific laughter, whereas responses to screams were primarily deceleratory. In a second study, Boysen and Berntson (1998) showed heart rate acceleration in chimpanzees viewing a photograph of an animal that had a history of being aggressive toward the subject, indicating a defensive response, but heart rate deceleration in response to an unfamiliar individual, suggestive of an orienting response to a novel stimulus. Rhesus monkeys implanted with telemetric transmitters showed heart rate acceleration when approached by a dominant animal compared with a subordinate individual or the individual's kin (Aureli, Preston, & de Waal, 1999). These responses are characteristic of emotional responses in humans. Parr and colleagues (Parr, Winslow, & Davis, 2002) measured cardiac response to acoustic startle in rhesus monkeys using surface electrodes in chair-restrained subjects. Heart rate was significantly faster in response to acoustic startle probes compared with baseline conditions, characteristic of the cardiac startle response in humans and other mammals (Gautier & Cook, 1997; Turpin, Schaefer, & Boucsein, 1999; Young & Leaton, 1994).

Electrodermal Activity.   The two main methods for measuring electrodermal activity (EDA) include the exosomatic technique, in which a small current of electricity is passed through the skin and the resistance to the passage of current is recorded, and the endosomatic technique, which measures the electrical activity at the surface of the skin when no external current is applied. The former method is most widely used today during psychological studies and is referred to as skin conductance; specific responses to environmental variables are known as skin conductance responses (SCRs).

The skin conductance response is mediated by the sympathetic nervous system and has proven to be a useful biological marker of general arousal (Lykken & Venables, 1971). There has been much debate over the psychological relevance of SCRs, but, in principle, skin conductance provides a measure of general arousal that reflects the state of the organism within the environment. When an individual encounters a novel stimulus, for example, skin conductance measures typically increase, indicating that the individual has detected the psychological relevance of the stimulus (e.g., Bauer, 1998; Lang et al., 1998; O'Gorman, 1979). These response properties led to the use of skin conductance measures for lie detection. Researchers should be cautioned, however, that although the emotional relevance of the stimulus may be detected by changes in skin conductance, these changes do not provide certification that the stimulus was appetitive or aversive; hence the use of SCR for general-arousal differences across well-controlled conditions.

The success of these measurements in monkeys depends on being able to record while the animal is relatively motionless. Direct immobilization is not sufficient, however, to obtain interpretable skin conductance data. The monkey has to be trained to remain relaxed while tolerating the electrodes for extended periods of time. For best results, the animal's palms should be washed with soapy water and the electrodes attached and taped to the hand. The animal should be grounded via a ground lead attached to the back of the hand or to the other palm. An additional electrode is attached to the forearm to detect electromyographic signals from the underlying muscles. These signals serve to identify SCR changes that coincide with arm or hand movements. These can later be filtered or removed from the analyses. Skin conductance recorded in conjunction with heart rate provides a good indicator of the salience of a stimulus. For example, images of conspecific facial expressions are more likely to elicit skin conductance responses in monkeys than abstract images (Figure 23.5). Skin conductance can also be used as a marker for the acquisition of aversive conditioning (Öhman, Fredrikson, Hugdahl, & Rimmo, 1976). Recently, skin conductance has been associated with many other psychological and psychiatric states (Stevens & Gruzelier, 1984; Ward & Doerr, 1986).

Temperature.   The autonomic aspects of thermoregulation, such as sweating, shivering, panting, and vasomotor activity, are prominent responses during basic emotional arousal and are controlled by the anterior and lateral hypothalamus (e.g., Rinn, 1984; Satinoff & Shan, 1971). Peripheral temperature may be recorded from probes placed directly on the skin, whereas central temperature is measured from the brain itself, that is, the hypothalamus, and core body measurements can be derived from the tympanic membrane. A number of experiments have demonstrated a predictable relationship between brain temperature and behavioral states in animals (Hull, Buchwald, Dubrovsky, & Garcia, 1965; Kawamura & Sawyer, 1965; Kovalzon, 1973). Some behavioral activities in monkeys—that is, sleeping, feeding, and aroused behaviors—corresponded to specific changes in hypothalamic temperature measured directly from the brain. Awake and aroused animals show higher temperatures, whereas sleeping and feeding animals showed decreases in temperature.

Directionally similar changes in tympanic membrane temperature (Tty) were simultaneously recorded during these activities, suggesting that it may be used as a noninvasive marker for changes in central temperature.

Electrophysiological studies have demonstrated the presence of thermosensitive neurons in the preoptic area of the anterior hypothalamus. These neurons are associated with the central control of thermoregulatory processes (Nakayama, Eisenman, & Hardy, 1961). Recently, however, Hori and colleagues have demonstrated that these thermosensitive neurons may also respond to nonthermal, emotional stimuli (Hori et al., 1986). This is particularly interesting considering the relationship between thermoregulatory and autonomic responses such as shivering, sweating, and piloerection, previously described. These authors recorded electrical activity from the medial preoptic area in two macaques (*M. mulatta, M. fuscata*). Animals were restrained and provided with either a variety of rewarding food items, that is, juice, raisins, or bread, or aversive items that were negatively conditioned with a puff of air, that is, a syringe, a toy snake, or hypertonic saline. Overall, the results demonstrated that thermosensitive neurons in the medial preoptic area responded similarly to the sight of the rewarding and aversive stimuli; no distinction could be made regarding the emotional valence of the stimuli. At best, these neurons may be critical to understanding the relationship between temperature and behavioral arousal that has been previously described. At the least, they demonstrate that the most anterior area of the hypothalamus is not simply involved in thermoregulatory processes but is also sensitive to emotional processing.

In a recent study, Parr and Hopkins (2001) used Tty to measure changes in physiological arousal in chimpanzees as they viewed 5-minute videos of emotional scenes, such as conspecifics engaged in aggression, play, or neutral activities. Changes in Tty were used to index sympathetically mediated changes in brain temperature, as described previously. The authors reported significant increases in right Tty in response to the negative emotional videos and increases in left Tty in response to the positive emotional videos, although this ef-

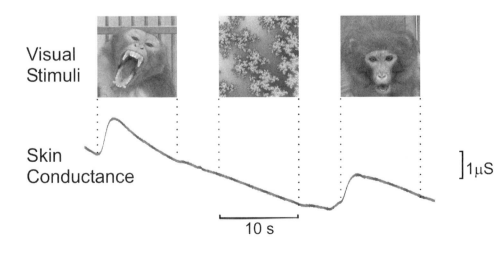

Figure 23.5. Skin conductance responses elicited by facial expressions and abstract images. Each image (top row) was presented for 10 s. Skin conductance increased when a yawning face and a threatening face were presented but remained unchanged when an abstract image was shown.

fect was not as strong as that found for right Tty. Results of this study were some of the first to support the lateralization of emotional processing in a nonhuman species in that the right hemisphere showed greater arousal in response to negative emotional scenes, consistent with findings in humans (Davidson, 1992; Kagan, Snidman, & Peterson, 2000; Zajonc, Murphy, & McIntosh, 1993).

Manipulation

Fear Conditioning

Modulation of the acoustic startle response is a simple and objective indicator of emotionality and attention in rodents and humans (Davis, 1984). This finding has proven extremely valuable for analysis of neural systems associated with fear and anxiety (Davis, 1998; Lang et al., 2000). Until recently, there have been few efforts to develop acoustic startle measurement in nonhuman primates. These initial studies revealed that the amplitude of whole-body startle in monkeys, as in rodents and humans, is directly proportional to acoustic stimulus intensity and gradually habituates with repeated exposures (Parr et al., 2002). Presentation of a weak acoustic stimulus 45–2020 ms before a startle stimulus reduces startle amplitude by 40–50% depending on interstimulus interval length, a phenomenon known as prepulse inhibition (Winslow, Parr, & Davis, 2002). More interestingly, startle amplitude can be attenuated or potentiated if the preceding stimulus is an emotional photograph or audio clip, a phenomenon referred to as affective modulation of startle. In humans, for example, preceding a startle probe with a negative photograph potentiates the startle response (measured in humans using a blink response), whereas preceding the probe with an emotionally positive photograph attenuates startle (Cuthbert, Bradley, & Lang, 1996). In monkeys, significant potentiation of the startle amplitude can be achieved through a process known as fear conditioning. Monkeys are first conditioned to an inescapable pulse of pressurized air associated with a light. The air burst serves as an unconditioned stimulus (US) eliciting fear, whereas the light serves as the conditioned stimulus (CS). After conditioning, the light alone potentiates the startle response in monkeys (Winslow et al., 2002), which, in combination with findings that startle is associated with heart rate acceleration, suggests a common mechanism arising in the central nucleus of the amygdala (Parr et al., 2002; Young & Leaton, 1994). These studies demonstrate that acoustic startle in nonhuman primates successfully bridges rodent and human research in two broad areas: stimulus-response relationships and behavioral plasticity, represented by habituation, prepulse inhibition, and fear potentiation.

Neurophysiological Methods

One of the main goals of neuroscience research has been to explain the relationship between neural circuitry and its associated behavioral and physiological outcomes. These neural circuits integrate incoming environmental signals, evaluate the significance of these signals, and orchestrate appropriate behavioral responses. A direct approach to determining the functional organization of these neural circuits is to record the discharge patterns of their component neurons in response to various stimuli. This method has the temporal and spatial resolution to determine what aspect of the stimulus or of the task is processed by the neurons in a particular circuit. Compared with functional imaging techniques that scan the entire brain and infer neural activity from haemodynamic and metabolic changes, the neurophysiological approach employs microelectrodes implanted directly into the brain tissue to determine the specific cellular correlates of information processing.

In early neurophysiological studies, a single electrode was lowered through a craniotomy to a target area, and the discharge of a single neuron was correlated with either a stimulus presented to the animal or with the ongoing behavior generated in response to a stimulus. Although these techniques were extremely influential in helping to identify the neural processes that underlie perceptual, motor, and cognitive functions, the broad implications of these observations were severely constrained in that complex behaviors could not be reduced to the activity of a single neuron. It was clear that in order to understand the neural mechanisms involved in even the simplest behavior, the activity pattern of larger neuronal populations must be recorded and analyzed.

In the late 1990s, multichannel electrodes and multielectrode probes were developed that allowed investigators to record the activity of small groups of 10–120 neurons from a single area or from multiple brain areas simultaneously (Gothard, Skaggs, Moore, & McNaughton, 1996; Hoffman & McNaughton, 2002; Wilson & McNaughton, 1994). With this technological advance, it was possible to determine the information contained in the conjoint firing of neurons, in addition to that obtained from each neuron separately. For example, with just two neurons, low-order and one high-order parameters can be considered: (1) the firing rate of the first neuron, (2) the firing rate of the second neuron, and (3) the level of interaction between them. When the number of recorded neurons grows arithmetically, the interaction parameters grow exponentially, generating a pattern of complexity commensurable with the complexities of neural ensemble activity inferred from behavioral experiments and theoretical reasoning. The concept of neural ensemble activity as the basis of all mental operations is, in fact, a more powerful concept than that of a neural circuit because it is not based on anatomy alone but on the dynamic interaction of neurons located across multiple brain areas.

Two main techniques are used in behavioral neurophysiology: (1) In acute recordings, one or more electrodes are inserted into the brain, positioned precisely to record the discharge of one or more neurons; and at the end of the experiment the electrodes are removed from the brain. (2) In chronic techniques, a single electrode, or an electrode array, is affixed to the skull and left in the brain for extended periods of time. Most advanced techniques involve a precision electrode drive that can be used to adjust the position of the indwelling electrodes. Using such precise electrode positioning devices and an acute penetration with a fine microelectrode, Gothard, Battaglia, Erickson, Spitler, and Amoral (2006) recorded the responses of small groups of neurons in the monkey amygdala. The activity of the neuron shown in Figure 23.6 was recorded from the lateral nucleus of the amygdala during the presentation of a large array of images of human faces. Note that the neuron in Figure 23.6 responded selectively to the face of a single caretaker (interestingly, the subject monkey often showed overt fear of this caretaker). From such neurophysiological recordings, human researchers have mapped out the neural circuits underlying social cognition that encompass the visual cortex of the temporal lobe, the amygdala, and the orbitofrontal cortex (Haxby, Hoffman, & Gobbini, 2000, 2002). Together, these areas form a circuit that processes social signals with special emotional significance, including facial expressions. Neurophysiological studies in monkeys suggest that the role of the visual cortex in this circuit is to identify individuals and discriminate among facial expressions (Desimone, 1991; Desimone, Albright, Gross, & Bruce, 1984; Gross, Rocha-Miranda, & Bender, 1972; Perrett, Rolls, & Caan, 1982), whereas the

amygdala appears to organize the inputs from these cortical areas in relation to the learned or inherent emotional significance of a particular stimulus (Fuster & Uyeda, 1971; Gothard et al., 2002; Ono, Fukuda, Nishino, Sasaki, & Muramoto, 1983; Sanghera, Rolls, & Roper-Hall, 1979). The outcome of this evaluative process is translated in the amygdala into commands sent to autonomic and somatic effectors to generate behavioral responses (Kaada, 1951; Kapp, Gallagher, Underwood, McNall, & Whitehorn, 1982; Pascoe & Kapp, 1985). The role of the orbitofrontal cortex might be to provide context information and signal to the amygdala the incentive value of the intended behaviors (Barbas, 2000; Gallagher & Shoenbaum, 1999).

The choice of behavioral task is perhaps the most important factor that conveys significance to neural recordings, because the cognitive state of the animal and the ongoing behaviors are factors in brain activity that are just as important as the incoming sensory signals. Ignoring the cognitive demands imposed by the physical and social environment of the species leads not only to missed results but also to misleading results. Animals use multiple strategies to solve complex problems, and a good neurophysiological experiment has to take into account and control for all possible strategies. Ideally, the animal is required to report with an overt and quantifiable behavior on various task variables, much like those described earlier (e.g., Hampton, 2001; Parr

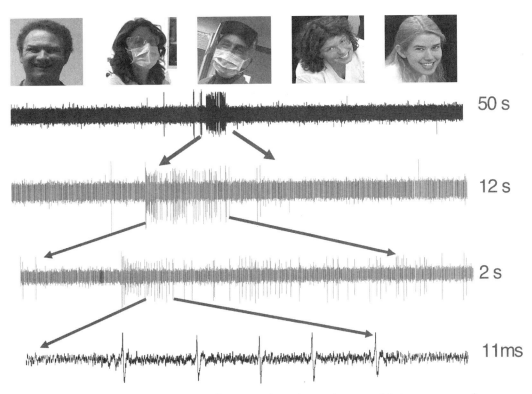

Figure 23.6. The discharge pattern of a neuron from the monkey amygdala in response to the presentation of multiple, familiar human faces (top row). The same recording trace is shown with a different time scale to illustrate that the burst of activity shown in the top trace, consists of precisely timed individual action potentials (bottom trace).

et al., 2000). The training and task design have to take into account that reliable results require many repetitions and that, throughout the experiment, the level of motivation and participation of the animal has to be kept within narrow limits. This is an excellent example of how one approach to studying emotion is not always sufficient for understanding the phenomenon. Wherever possible, multiple approaches should be used together to provide converging information to support or refute specific hypotheses.

Ethical Considerations

General Requirements and Regulatory Mechanisms

The use of animals for research requires special housing facilities and trained animal care and veterinary personnel. In the United States, two government documents contain guidelines for animal research: the *Public Health Service Policy on Humane Care and Use of Laboratory Animals* (Office of Laboratory Animal Welfare, 2002), and the *Guide to the Care and Use of Laboratory Animals* (Institute of Laboratory Animal Resources, 1996). Additionally, the facility requirements, cage sizes, and procedures for the husbandry of nonhuman primates are mandated by the United States Department of Agriculture (USDA). Surgical preparation of nonhuman primates for neurobehavioral experiments requires special facilities, skilled animal-care and veterinary personnel, and thorough training and skill on the part of the investigators. All procedures should be in full compliance with federal laws and regulations for the use the nonhuman primates in biomedical research. The Animal Welfare Act of 1966 and its amendments regulate the transportation, purchase, sale, housing, care, and handling of primates used in research and teaching. Finally, all the specific experimental procedures used in the laboratory are described in detailed protocols approved by the Institutional Animal Care and Use Committee (IACUC). This committee typically consists of scientists and veterinary personal who review research protocols that must be submitted for every experimental procedure performed at a given institution. The protocols must include methods for minimizing the pain, discomfort, and distress of research subjects, documentation that less stressful procedures are not available, justification of species and subject numbers for specific experiments, and verification that animals will be given psychological enrichment.

Ethical Considerations

The ethical considerations for the use of animals in laboratory research will undoubtedly be an issue of ongoing debate. Emotion elicitation and the behavioral and biological methods for assessing emotionality can, in and of themselves, be stressful. Just as in human health care, researchers should be continuously seeking methods to reduce stress and pain in

research subjects. This effort serves multiple purposes. Not only is it advantageous for the organism and ethically more conscientious, but also the research itself will benefit from having physically healthy and psychologically happy subjects. The personal responsibility of the investigators, who obviously differ in their own subjective ethical standards, is reinforced by institutional control mechanisms that require strict adherence to experimental protocols approved by the IACUC.

Some general practices, however, can significantly improve well-being and performance of research subjects without implementing new procedures. No matter how minimal the interaction between the investigator and the animal, the behavior of the animal will always be influenced by this interaction. It is critical to reduce the number of people with whom the animals come in contact and to avoid any changes in animal care personnel during the experimental period. Animals are creatures of habit, and they quickly learn to expect certain regular daily events such as feeding, cleaning, and health checks in the colony. A disorganized colony schedule violates these expectations and can unnecessarily stress subjects. The best results are obtained by keeping to a routine schedule for training, testing, and interacting with the animals. Changes in some details, such as the clothing of the experimenter or cosmetics (especially perfumes), are often sensed by the animals. Fluctuating rules and behavioral demands lead to inconsistencies in the animals' expectations that will ultimately affect their behavior. Finally, animal handling can be dangerous for both humans and animals. To prevent accidents, investigators should be trained by experienced handlers before they start to handle animals or lead them to a restraint chair. Personal protective gear should be worn where appropriate and is mandated by governmental and institutional agencies. An important resource in this regard is the 2003 manual of the National Research Council, *Occupational Health and Safety in the Care and Use of Nonhuman Primates.*

Author's Note

Beyond the philosophical debate pertaining to the scientific value of animal models and the use of animals in research for human benefits, researchers are often faced with an additional struggle. As a result of the time and effort invested in rearing, training, and caring for research animals, investigators become often attached to them and are faced with a constant struggle between strict scientific endeavors and the effort to protect the animals and offer them a comfortable life. As caretakers, guardians, and often the biggest champions of conservation efforts for the animals we study, there can be only one conclusion: Not only must we ensure that the experimental questions we address are the most important for the scientific questions we study, but we must also conduct the best and most ethical research we can, for the sake of the subjects we study.

References

Altmann, J. (1974). Observational study of behavior: Sampling methods. *Behaviour, 49,* 227–265.

Andreassi, J. L. (1989). *Psychophysiology: Human behavior and physiological response.* Hillsdale, NJ: Erlbaum.

Aureli, F., Preston, S. D., & de Waal, F. B. (1999). Heart rate responses to social interactions in free-moving rhesus macaques (*Macaca mulatta*): A pilot study. *Journal of Comparative Psychology, 113,* 59–65

Bachevalier, J., Brickson, M., & Hagger, C. (1993). Limbic-dependent recognition memory in monkeys develops early in infancy. *Neuroreport, 4,* 77–80.

Barbas, H. (2000). Complementary roles of prefrontal cortical regions in cognition, memory, and emotion in primates. *Advances in Neurology, 84,* 87–110

Bauer, R. M. (1998). Physiologic measures of emotion. *Journal of Clinical Neurophysiology, 15,* 388–396.

Berntson, G. G., Bigger, J. T., Jr., Eckberg, D. L., Grossman, P., Kaufmann, P. G., Malik, M., et al. (1997). Heart rate variability: Origins, methods, and interpretive caveats. *Psychophysiology, 34,* 623–648.

Berntson, G. G., Boysen, S. T., Bauer, H. R., & Torello, M. S. (1989). Conspecific screams and laughter: Cardiac and behavioral reactions of infant chimpanzees. *Developmental Psychobiology, 22,* 771–787.

Berntson, G. G., Cacioppo, J. T., & Quigley, K. S. (1995). The metrics of cardiac chronotropism: Biometric perspectives. *Psychophysiology, 32,* 162–171.

Blessing, W. W. (1997). *The lower brainstem and bodily homeostasis.* New York: Oxford University Press.

Boysen, S. T., & Berntson, G. G. (1989). Conspecific recognition in the chimpanzee (*Pan troglodytes*): Cardiac responses to significant others. *Journal of Comparative Psychology, 103,* 215–220.

Brockway, B., & Hassler, C. (1992). Cardiovascular measurements in pharmacology and toxicology. In H. Salem & S. Baskin (Eds.), *New technologies and concepts for reducing drug toxicities* (pp. 109–132). Boca Raton, FL: CRC Press.

Brown, A. K., Brown, J. L., & Poulson, C. L. (1995). Generalization of children's identity matching-to-sample performances to novel stimuli. *Psychological Record, 45,* 29–43.

Byrne, R. W., & Corp, N. (2004). Neocortex size predicts deception rate in primates. *Proceedings of the Royal Society of London: Series B. Biological Sciences, 271,* 1693–1699.

Cacciopo, J. T., Tassinary, L. G., & Berntson, G. G. (2000). *Handbook of psychophysiology.* Cambridge, UK: Cambridge University Press.

Cheney, D. L., & Seyfarth, R. M. (1990). *How monkeys see the world.* Chicago: University of Chicago Press.

Crowley, J. N., Gerfen, C. R., Rogawski, M. A., Sibley, D. R., Skolnick, P., & Wray, S. (Eds.). (2003). *Current protocols in neuroscience.* New York: Wiley.

Cuthbert, B. N., Bradley, M. M., & Lang, P. J. (1996). Probing picture perception: Activation and emotion. *Psychophysiology, 33,* 103–111.

D'Amato, M. R., Salmon, D. P., and Colombo, M. (1985). Extent and limits of the matching concept in monkeys (*Cebus apella*). *Journal of Experimental Psychology, 11,* 35–51.

Darwin, C. (1872). *The expression of the emotions in man and animals.* London: Murray.

Davidson, R. J. (1992). Emotion and affective style: Hemispheric substrates. *Psychological Science, 3,* 39–43.

Davis, M. (1984). The mammalian startle response. In R. C. Eaton (Ed.), *Neural mechanisms of startle behavior* (pp. 287–351). New York: Plenum Press.

Davis, M. (1998). Are different parts of the extended amygdala involved in fear versus anxiety? *Biological Psychiatry, 44,* 1239–1247.

Davis, M., & Whalen, P. J. (2000). The amygdala: Vigilance and emotion. *Molecular Psychiatry, 6,* 13–34.

Desimone, R. (1991). Face-selective cells in the temporal cortex of monkeys. *Journal of Cognitive Neuroscience, 3,* 1–8.

Desimone, R., Albright, T. D., Gross, C. G., & Bruce, C. (1984). Stimulus-selective properties of inferior temporal neurons in the macaque. *Journal of Neuroscience, 4,* 2051–2062.

Duchowski, A. T. (2003). *Eye tracking methodology: Theory and practice.* New York: Springer Verlag.

Fuster, J. M., & Uyeda, A. A. (1971). Reactivity of limbic neurons of the monkey to appetitive and aversive signals. *Electroencephalography and Clinical Neurophysiology, 4,* 281–293.

Gallagher, M., & Schoenbaum, G. (1999). Functions of the amygdala and related forebrain areas in attention and cognition. *Annals of the New York Academy of Sciences, 877,* 397–411.

Gautier, C. H., & Cook, E. W. I. (1997). Relationships between startle and cardiovascular reactivity. *Psychophysiology, 34,* 87–96.

Ghazanfar, A. A., & Logothetis, N. K. (2003). Neuroperception: Facial expressions linked to monkey calls. *Nature, 423,* 937–938.

Gothard, K. M., Battaglia, F. P., Erickson, C. A., Spitler, K. M., & Amoral, D. G. (2006). Neural responses to facial expressions and face identity in the monkey amygdala. *Journal of Neurophysiology,* PIMD, 17093126.

Gothard, K. M., Erickson, C. A., & Amaral, D. G. (2004). How do rhesus monkeys (*Macaca mulatta*) scan faces in a visual paired comparison task? *Animal Cognition, 7,* 25–36.

Gothard, K. M., Skaggs, W. E., Moore, M. K., & McNaughton, B. L. (1996). Binding of hippocampal CA1 neural activity to multiple reference frames in a landmark-based navigation task. *Journal of Neuroscience, 16,* 823–835.

Gross, C. G., Rocha-Miranda, C. E., & Bender, D. B. (1972). Visual properties of neurons in inferotemporal cortex of the Macaque. *Journal of Neurophysiology, 35,* 96–111.

Hampton, R. R. (2001). Rhesus monkeys know when they remember. *Proceeding of the National Academy of Sciences of the USA, 98,* 5359–5362.

Hashiya, K., & Kojima, S. (2001). Acquisition of auditory-visual intermodal matching-to-sample by a chimpanzee (*Pan troglodytes*): Comparison with visual-visual intramodal matching. *Animal Cognition 4,* 231–239.

Hassimoto, M., & Harada, T. (2003). Use of a telemetry system to examine recovery of the cardiovascular system after excitement induced by handling stress in a conscious cynomolgus monkey (*Macaca fascicularis*). *Journal of Medical Primatology, 33,* 175–186.

Haxby, J. V., Hoffman, E. A., & Gobbini, M. I. (2000). The distributed human neural system for face perception. *Trends in Cognitive Science, 4,* 223–233.

Haxby, J. V., Hoffman, E. A., & Gobbini, M.I. (2002). Human neural systems for face recognition and social communication. *Biological Psychiatry, 51,* 59–67.

Herman, L. M., Hovancik, J. R., Gory, J. D., & Bradshaw, G. L. (1989). Generalization of visual matching by a bottlenosed dolphin (*Tursiops truncatus*): Evidence for invariance of cognitive performance with visual and auditory materials. *Journal of Experimental Psychology, 15,* 124–136.

Hoffman, K. L., & McNaughton. B. L. (2002). Coordinated reactivation of distributed memory traces in primate neocortex. *Science, 297,* 2070–2073.

Hori, T., Kiyohara, T., Shibata, M., Oomura, Y., Nishino, H., Aou, S., et al. (1986). Responsiveness of monkey preoptic thermosensitive neurons to non-thermal emotional stimuli. *Brain Research Bulletin, 17,* 75–82.

Hull, C. D., Buchwald, N. A., Dubrovsky, B., & Garcia, J. (1965). Brain temperature and arousal. *Experimental Neurology, 12,* 238–246.

Institute of Laboratory Animal Resources. (1996). *Guide for the care and use of laboratory animals.* Washington, DC: National Academy Press.

Kaada, B. R. (1951). Somatomotor, autonomic and electrophysiological responses to electrical stimulation of "rhinencephalic" and other structures in primates, cat and dog. *Acta Physiologica Scandinavica, 24*(Suppl. 1951), 1–262.

Kaas, J. H. (1996). What comparative studies of neocortex tell us about the human brain. *Reviews of Brasilian Biology, 56*(Suppl. 1, Pt. 2), 315–322.

Kagan, J., Snidman, N., & Peterson, E. (2000). Temperature asymmetry and behavior. *Developmental Psychobiology, 37,* 186–193.

Kalin, N. H., Larson, C., Shelton, S. E., & Davidson, R. J. (1998). Asymmetric frontal brain activity, cortisol, and behavior associated with fearful temperament in rhesus monkeys. *Behavioral Neuroscience, 112,* 286–292.

Kalin, N. H., & Shelton, S. E. (1989). Defensive behaviors in infant rhesus monkeys: Environmental cues and neurochemical regulation. *Science, 243,* 1718–1721.

Kalin, N. H., Shelton, S. E., & Davidson, R. J. (2000). Cerebrospinal fluid corticotropin-releasing hormone levels are elevated in monkeys with patterns of brain activity associated with fearful temperament. *Biological Psychiatry, 47,* 579–585.

Kalin, N. H., Shelton, S. E., & Davidson, R. J. (2004). The role of the central nucleus of the amygdala in mediating fear and anxiety in the primate. *Journal of Neuroscience, 24,* 5506–5515.

Kapp, B. S., Gallagher, M., Underwood, M. D., McNall, C. L., & Whitehorn, D. (1982). Cardiovascular responses elicited by electrical stimulation of the amygdala central nucleus in the rabbit. *Brain Research, 234,* 251–262.

Kastak, D., & Schusterman, R. J. (1994). Transfer of visual identity matching-to-sample in two California sea lions (*Zalophus californianus*). *Animal Learning and Behavior, 22,* 427–435.

Kawamura, H., & Sawyer, C. H. (1965). Elevation of brain temperature during paradoxical sleep. *Science, 150,* 912–913.

Keverne, E. B., Martel, F. L., & Nevison, C. M. (1996). Primate brain evolution: Genetic and functional considerations.

Proceedings of the Royal Society of London: Series B. Biological Sciences, 263, 689–696.

Kovalzon, V. M. (1973). Brain temperature variations during natural sleep and arousal in white rats. *Physiology and Behavior, 10,* 667–670.

Kyes, R. C., & Candland, D. .K. (1987). Baboon (*Papio hamadryas*) visual preferences for regions of the face. *Journal of Comparative Psychology, 101,* 345–348.

Lang, P. J., Bradley, M. M., & Cuthbert, B. N. (1998). Emotion, motivation and anxiety: Brain mechanisms and psychophysiology. *Biological Psychiatry, 44,* 1248–1263.

Lang, P. J., Davis, M., & Öhman, A. (2000). Fear and anxiety: Animal models and human cognitive psychophysiology. *Journal of Affective Disorders, 61,* 137–159.

Lykken, D. T., & Venables, P. H. (1971). Direct measurement of skin conductance: A proposal for standardization. *Psychophysiology, 8,* 656–672.

Malone, D. R., Tolan, J. C., & Rogers, C. M. (1980). Crossmodal matching of objects and photographs in the monkey. *Neuropsychologia, 18,* 693–697.

McKee, R. D, & Squire, L. R. (1993) On the development of declarative memory. *Journal of Experimental Psychology: Learning, Memory, and Cognition, 19,* 397–404.

Miller, R. E., Murphy, J. V., & Mirsky, I. A. (1959). Relevance of facial expression and posture as cues in communication of affect between monkeys. *Archives of. General Psychiatry, 1,* 480–488.

Nakayama, T., Eisenman, J. S., & Hardy, J. D. (1961). Single unit activity of anterior hypothalamus during local heating. *Science, 134,* 560–561.

National Research Council. (2003). *Occupational health and safety in the case and use of nonhuman primates.* Washington, DC: National Academy Press.

Neiworth, J. J., & Wright, A. A. (1994). Monkeys (*Macaca mulatta*) learn category matching in a nonidentical same-different task. *Journal of Experimental Psychology, 20,* 429–435.

Nemanic, S., Alvarado, M. C., & Bachevalier, J. (2004). The hippocampal/parahippocampal regions and recognition memory: Insights from visual paired comparison versus object-delayed nonmatching in monkeys. *Journal of Neuroscience, 24,* 2013–2026.

Northcutt, R. G., & Kaas, J. H. (1995). The emergence and evolution of mammalian neocortex. *Trends in Neuroscience, 18,* 373–379.

Office of Laboratory Animal Welfare. (2002). *Public health service policy on humane care and use of laboratory animals.* Washington, DC: U.S. Government Printing Office.

O'Gorman, J. G. (1979). The orienting reflex: Novelty or significance detector? *Psychophysiology, 16,* 253–262

Öhman, A., Fredrikson, M., Hugdahl, K., & Rimmo, P. (1976). The premise of equipotentiality in human classical conditioning: Conditioned electrodermal responses to potentially phobic stimuli. *Journal of Experimental Psychology: General, 105,* 313–337.

Ono, T., Fukuda, M., Nishino, H., Sasaki, K., & Muramoto, K. (1983). Amygdaloid neuronal responses to complex visual stimuli in an operant feeding situation in the monkey. *Brain Research Bulletin, 11,* 515–518.

Panksepp, J. (1998). *Affective neuroscience.* New York: Oxford University Press.

Parr, L. A. (2001). Cognitive and physiological markers of emotional awareness in chimpanzees, *Pan troglodytes*. *Animal Cognition, 4,* 223–229.

Parr, L. A. (2003). The discrimination of facial expressions and their emotional content by chimpanzees (*Pan troglodytes*). *Annals of the New York Academy of Sciences, 1000,* 56–78.

Parr, L. A., Cohen, M., & de Waal, F. B. M. (2005). Influence of Social Context on the Use of Blended and Graded Facial Displays in Chimpanzees. *International Journal of Primatology, 26,* 73–103.

Parr, L. A., & Hopkins, W. D. (2001). Brain temperature asymmetries and emotional perception in chimpanzees, *Pan troglodytes. Physiology and Behavior, 71,* 363–371.

Parr, L. A., Hopkins, W. D., & de Waal, F. B. M. (1998). The perception of facial expressions in chimpanzees (*Pan troglodytes*). *Evolution of Communication, 2,* 1–23.

Parr, L. A., Winslow, J. T., & Davis, M. (2002). Rearing experience differentially affects somatic and cardiac startle responses in rhesus monkeys (*Macaca mulatta*). *Behavioral Neuroscience, 116,* 378–386.

Parr, L. A., Winslow, J. T., Hopkins, W. D., & de Waal, F. B. M. (2000). Recognizing facial cues: Individual recognition in chimpanzees (*Pan troglodytes*) and rhesus monkeys (*Macaca mulatta*). *Journal of Comparative Psychology, 114,* 47–60.

Pascalis, O., & Bachevalier, J. (1999). Neonatal aspiration lesions of the hippocampal formation impair visual recognition memory when assessed by paired-comparison task but not by delayed nonmatching-to-sample task. *Hippocampus, 6,* 609–616.

Pascoe, J. P., & Kapp, B. S. (1985). Electrophysiological characteristics of Amygdaloid Central nucleus neurons in the awake rabbit. *Brain Research Bulletin, 14,* 331–338.

Perrett, D. I., Rolls, E. T., & Caan, W. (1982). Visual neurones responsive to faces in the monkey temporal cortex. *Experimental Brain Research, 47,* 329–342.

Richardson, W. K., Washburn, D. A., Hopkins, W. D., Savage-Rumbaugh, E. S., & Dumbaugh, D. M. (1990). The NASA/LRC computerized test system. *Behavior Research Methods, Instruments and Computers, 22,* 127–131.

Rinn, W. E. (1984). The neuropsychology of facial expression: A review of the neurological and psychological mechanisms for producing facial expressions. *Psychological Bulletin, 95,* 52–77.

Robinson, D. A. (1963) A method of measuring eye movements using a scleral search coil in a magnetic field. *IEEE Transactions on Biomedical Engineering, 10,* 137–145

Ruys, J. D., Mendoza, S. P., Capitanio, J. P., & Mason, W. A. (2004). Behavioral and physiological adaptation to repeated chair restraint in rhesus macaques. *Physiology and Behavior, 82,* 205–213.

Sanghera, M. K., Rolls, E. T., & Roper-Hall, A. (1979). Visual responses of neurons in the dorsolateral amygdala of the alert monkey. *Experimental Neurology, 63,* 610–626.

Satinoff, E., & Shan, S. Y. (1971). Loss of behavioral thermo-regulation after lateral hypothalamic lesions in rats. *Journal of Comparative and Physiological Psychology, 77,* 302–312.

Schachter, S., & Singer, J. E. (1962). Cognitive, social, and physiological determinants of emotional state. *Psychological Review, 69,* 379–399.

Schnell, C. R., & Gerber, R. (1997). Training and remote monitoring of cardiovascular parameters in non-human primates. *Primate Report, 49,* 61–70.

Seyfarth, R. M., Cheney, D. L., & Marler, P. (1980). Vervet monkey alarm calls: Semantic communication in a free-ranging primate. *Animal Behavior, 28,* 1070–1094.

Stern, R. M., Ray, W. J., & Quigley, K. S. (2001). *Psychophysiological recording* (2nd ed.). New York: Oxford University Press.

Stevens, S., & Gruzelier, J. (1984). Electrodermal activity and auditory stimuli in autistic, retarded, and normal children. *Journal of Autism and Developmental Disorders, 14,* 245–260.

Strier, K. B. (1999). *Primate behavioral ecology.* Boston: Allyn & Bacon.

Turner, J. R., Girdler, S. S., Sherwood, A., & Light, K. C. (1990). Cardiovascular responses to behavioral stressors: Laboratory-field generalization and inter-task consistency. *Journal of Psychosomatic Research, 34,* 581–589.

Turpin, G., Schaefer, F., & Boucsein, W. (1999). Effects of stimulus intensity, risetime, and duration on autonomic and behavioral responding: Implications for the differentiation of orienting, startle, and defense responses. *Psychophysiology, 36,* 453–463.

Ward, N. G., & Doerr, H. O. (1986). Skin conductance: A potentially sensitive and specific marker for depression. *Journal of Nervous and Mental Disease, 174,* 553–559.

Wilson, M. A., & McNaughton, B. L. (1994). Reactivation of hippocampal ensemble memories during sleep. *Science, 265,* 676–679.

Winslow, J. T., Parr, L. A., & Davis, M. (2002). Acoustic startle, prepulse inhibition, and fear-potentiated startle measured in rhesus monkeys. *Biological Psychiatry, 51,* 859–866.

Young, B. J., & Leaton, R. N. (1994). Fear potentiation of acoustic startle stimulus-evoked heart rate changes in rats. *Behavioral Neuroscience, 108,* 1065–1079.

Zajonc, R. B., Murphy, S. T., & McIntosh, D. N. (1993). Brain temperature and subjective emotional experience. In M. L. J. M. Haviland (Ed.), *Handbook of emotions* (pp. 209–220). New York: Guilford Press.

John J. Curtin
David L. Lozano
John J. B. Allen

24

The Psychophysiological Laboratory

Psychophysiological measures have come out of the closet. A half century ago, psychophysiological tools were used by a highly specialized a group of scientists with specialized training and esoteric laboratories that resembled an electronics parts emporium. Today, however, such measures are used widely by nonspecialists as just one of many tools, in much the way they would select an implicit attitudes test, a behavioral coding scheme, or even a hierarchical linear model to address their research questions. In emotion research, the range of psychophysiological measures available is vast, including, as examples, skin conductance responses as measures of arousal (e.g., Hare, 1965) or fear conditioning (e.g., Öhman & Soares, 1994); myriad cardiovascular correlates of emotion (e.g., Chambers & Allen, 2002; Shalev et al., 1998); facial muscle activity as subtle measures of emotional valence (e.g., Cacioppo, Petty, Losch, & Kim, 1986); emotion-modulated startle responses (e.g., Curtin, Lang, Patrick, & Stritzke, 1998; Vrana, Spence, & Lang, 1988); electroencephalographic activity as a moderator or mediator of emotional response (e.g., Coan & Allen, 2004; Harmon-Jones, Sigelman, Bohlig, & Harmon-Jones, 2003); and event-related brain potentials to index various aspects of emotional stimulus processing (e.g., Curtin, Patrick, Lang, Cacioppo, & Birbaumer, 2001; Schupp, Cuthbert, Bradley, Cacioppo, Ito, & Lang, 2000).

Advances in electronics and computer technology have made psychophysiological tools far more accessible to nonspecialists, which is generally a very positive development. However, many potential users of psychophysiological measures still may find themselves wondering what equipment and expertise is required to become a competent user of these tools. The aim of this chapter is to provide a pragmatic overview of how to set up a psychophysiological laboratory and to provide references to aid in gaining competence and expertise in using psychophysiological measures.

Basic Considerations

Before you embark on the journey toward using psychophysiological measures, a candid assessment of your abilities and interests may spare later aggravation. You might reasonably assess your preferences on a variety of dimensions:

- Would you prefer to invest in your own psychophysiology laboratory or to work collaboratively with an investigator who already has a psychophysiology laboratory?
- Would you prefer to develop into an independent psychophysiological investigator or work in collaboration with or receive consultation from established researchers?
- Assuming you wish to have psychophysiological capabilities in your laboratory, would you prefer to have a dedicated psychophysiology laboratory or a multipurpose space in which psychophysiological recording is possible?

- Would you make use of a laboratory that allows for the recording of many different measures or does your research require that you record from only a small set of physiological response systems?

In this chapter, we present a wide variety of psychophysiological laboratory options, allowing you to assess your level of technical savvy and willingness to futz with things, and then providing a set of options that range from "low-tech plug and play" to "high-tech do-it yourself" solutions.

Basic Laboratory Desiderata

A basic psychophysiology laboratory for collecting data consists of a place that is free of electrical and ambient noise, a set of equipment for presenting stimuli and collecting responses, a set of hardware for amplifying physiological signals and saving them in digitized form, and software for reducing the physiological signals to a format suitable for statistical analysis. Although rather simple by way of overview, a generic schematic is provided in Figure 24.1 to help in organizing your thoughts about the various components that are included in most psychophysiological laboratories. Many considerations exist for each of these components, and each is discussed in separate sections, with section headings noted in the figure.

Participant and Observation Rooms

Although not strictly required, it is often desirable to separate the participant recording area from the control room where the experimenter controls the recording equipment and stimulus presentation. By separating the participant from the experimenter and the experimental control equipment, it is less likely that distracting noises and activities will elicit physiological responses, and it is less likely that the participant will feel self-conscious about being observed during the recording session or that physiological responses will be otherwise altered by observation (e.g., Drummond & Mirco, 2004; Kline, Blackhart, & Joiner, 2002). Participant rooms, however, tend to make some participants uneasy, especially those individuals with claustrophobic tendencies. It is thus a good idea to ensure that such spaces are not unduly small (e.g., no smaller than 6 feet by 6 feet), that participants can easily communicate with experimenters via an intercom, and that participants are aware that they can easily exit the space if required.

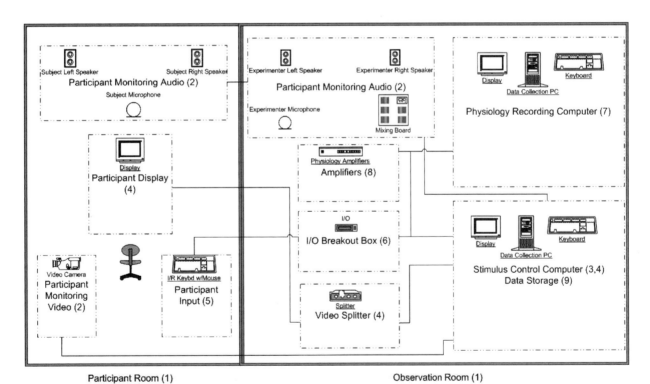

Figure 24.1. A schematic overview that includes the primary components present in most psychophysiological laboratories. Parenthetical numbers are provided for each component to indicate the section heading for relevant discussion in the text. *Section headings*: 1. Participant and observation rooms; 2. Participant monitoring; 3. The stimulus control computer; 4. Participant and experimenter displays; 5. Measuring behavioral response; 6. Digital input and output; 7. The physiology-recording computer; 8. Physiology amplifiers; 9. Data storage.

Although decades ago the separation of participant and experimenter often took the form of an electrically shielded room that was necessary to record clean signals free of ambient electrical noise, modern amplifiers are much better at recording in typical office settings, and such elaborate shielded chambers are seldom necessary from an electrical standpoint. These chambers, however, also provided a sound-dampened environment in which participants could easily attend to the tasks and stimuli at hand, free of other acoustic and visual distractions. This latter benefit can still be obtained by selecting a separate participant room and using sound insulating foam (such as that by Illbruck) to deaden noise.

If you are renovating an existing space by subdividing a room, pay attention to electrical and lighting locations to ensure that each room has separate a lighting control and contains electrical outlets. In a participant room, few outlets are needed, but often an outlet for a monitor and possibly a computer may be useful. On the other hand, if the renovation budget is limited, running high-quality grounded extension cables from the control room is an adequate option and may be preferred in that one can ensure that all equipment shares a common ground.

Another consideration in renovation is ensuring a means to pass necessary cabling between the participant room and the control room. If you are renovating a lab, you can ask that a PVC pipe or two be installed in the wall just a few inches above the floor allowing for cables to pass. The PVC diameter must exceed the largest cable end, and allowing for additional cables in the future is a wise strategy. A 2- or 3-inch diameter PVC pipe is likely to be suitable. Stuffing foam in the pipe after passing cables will provide sound buffering.

Of course, not everyone will have the luxury of a separate room for participants and experimenters. A single room can be made more suitable for psychophysiological recording by creating a separate space for the participant using room dividers such as a tri-fold screen (sometimes called Shoji screens) or by using one or two sides of an office cubicle divider. If you have a single-room setup, giving special attention to eliminating other noises—such as keyboards with loud clicks, loud computer fans, sound themes on computers, squeaky chairs, and other such nuisances—might reduce the extent to which sharing a room with the experimenter is distracting for the participant.

Adequate control of ambient temperature is another consideration in the psychophysiological laboratory. This is of special concern when recording autonomic signals, as peripheral physiological response systems may adaptively respond to help keep participants cool or warm, potentially confounding the recording of the signals of interest. Thus it would be desirable to have room-level control of the temperature, or at least control of the recording suite independent of the rest of the building. Finally, if you have an option, you may wish to consider locating the psychophysiology laboratory away from highly trafficked corridors or other sources of building noise. Similarly, selecting a location away from other large electrical equipment (e.g., HVAC units, elevator motors) in the building is desirable from the standpoint of reducing or eliminating electrical noise in your recorded signals.

Participant Monitoring

In designing the laboratory, it is important to implement audio and video capabilities for monitoring and interacting with the participant during an experiment. This will eliminate the need for the experimenter to physically enter the participant room to relay instructions or answer questions. Entering the participant room during an experiment is not only disruptive to the flow of the session but can possibly induce behavioral or movement artifact.

The laboratory audio system should provide for two-way communication between the participant and observation rooms. Off-the-shelf intercom systems are available, but care should be taken when selecting among these systems. Many only provide for one-way communication (e.g., baby monitors) or require users on both ends to press a button to be heard (e.g., "walkie-talkie" systems). Although it is reasonable for the experimenter to "push-to-talk," this is often not possible on the participant's end. Some two-way systems are not "full duplex," which means that they do not allow two-way communication simultaneously but only in sequence. These systems prevent the participant from being heard when the experimenter is talking, and vice versa, which may lead to awkward communication problems. Finally, problems may arise if the experiment itself includes audio stimuli. The experimental audio stimuli will likely be presented through a higher quality independent audio system (e.g., headphones), necessitating some redundancy, and in some configurations these two audio systems may interfere with each other. For example, if experimental stimuli are presented over headphones, the headphones may interfere with the participant's ability to hear task instructions presented via intercom speakers.

One easy and relatively low-cost way to achieve full-duplex, two-way communication that includes passive monitoring of the participant (i.e., no push-to-talk on participant's end) is to combine two systems. Passive-participant audio monitoring can be achieved with many one-way communication intercoms (and also many video monitoring systems, such as a Radio Shack 2.4GHz Black & White Wireless Surveillance System, catalog # 49-2534, or any number of systems from companies such as SmartHome). In the observation room, a push-button microphone for the experimenter can be input to the stimulus-control computer sound card, with the sound card output presented to the participant via attached computer speakers in the participant room. The audio system built into the computer can allow you to mix the sound of the microphone and that coming from the computer (e.g. MP3 files or CD or DVD) in such a way that both are at a comfortable level. Some sound cards also allow for both a microphone and "line" input so that sound from another source, such as a VCR or external source, can be mixed with experimenter-initiated instructions and other communication.

Alternatively, an integrated and flexible system for audio monitoring, recording, and presentation of experimental stimuli can be built using a good quality multichannel audio mixer-amplifier (e.g. Mackie 1202-VLZ Pro) connected to push-button (e.g., Shure MX412) and "always on" (e.g., Audio-technica PR044) microphones and speakers/headphones. This configuration will allow the presentation of computer-generated audio stimuli or video playback and experimenter instructions without requiring redundant speakers/headphones or switching wires between the computer and video player. Moreover, the audio-mixer amplifier can provide amplification of the sound card output if needed to achieve the required sound intensity for some stimuli (e.g., noise probes to elicit the startle reflex are often presented at or above 102dB, an intensity that many sound card/headphone combinations may not be able to achieve without addition of an amplifier). Another advantage to this is that all of the audio within the study can be sent from the output of the mixer into an audio or video recorder if recording of participant's verbal responses is required. A typical configuration for this integrated system is presented in Figure 24.2. Speakers/headphones in the participant room allow for the experimenter (or experimental stimuli) to be heard. A participant microphone picks up the audio from the observation room. Conversely, the speaker in the observation room allows the participant to be heard and the observation room microphone picks up task instructions and other communication from the experimenter. When selecting your microphones, it may be advantageous to select devices that do not require an internal battery to power the condenser element so as to avoid problems associated with a failed battery during a session. For example, one attractive option is to select dynamic condenser microphones that use phantom power (48vdc) supplied from the audio mixer.

When considering video monitoring systems, there exists quite a range in cost and features. For example, the Radio Shack wireless surveillance system mentioned earlier provides for static viewing of the participant in low light (via infrared technology) on a small black-and-white monitor that can be flexibly located in the observation room with wireless connection to the camera in the participant room. As mentioned, this system also provides for passive, one-way audio communication. In a more elaborate instance, some systems include a motorized camera to allow remote control of panning and tilting of the camera body, as well as lens adjustments of focus, telephoto–wide angle, and iris settings (e.g., Panasonic WV-NS324 Hybrid Unitized Network Color

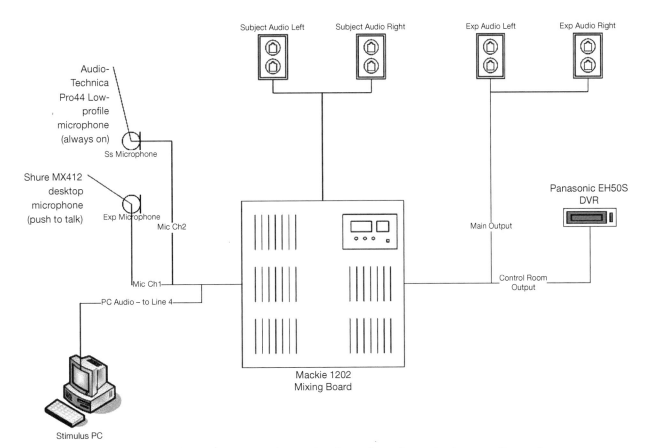

Figure 24.2. A schematic overview of a sample solution for audio monitoring, recording, and presentation of experimental stimuli.

Dome Camera with Pan, Tilt, Zoom; Sony SNC-RZ30N Network Camera). In addition, the signal from many video monitoring systems can be input to video recording devices (VHS, or digital video recorder) if subsequent coding of participant responding (e.g., facial display) is necessary.

Stimulus-Control and Physiology-Recording Computers

Although many configurations are possible, the most common configuration for display of stimuli with simultaneous recording of behavioral and physiological responding involves the use of two computers. The *stimulus-control computer,* described in this section, controls presentation and timing of the various stimuli (text, images, sounds, tactile stimuli, etc.) required by the task or paradigm used in the experiment. A second, *physiology-recording computer,* monitors and records the participant's physiology. In this configuration, communication between computers is typically unidirectional, from stimulus-control computer to physiology-recording computer. This communication is accomplished via parallel digital input-output (I/O) ports associated with each computer. In other words, specialized stimulus-control software running on the stimulus-control computer provides the overall control of the experimental events and informs the physiology-recording computer (by sending an event marker) each time an important event occurs (e.g., the presentation of a specific stimulus to the participant). Simultaneously, specialized physiology data acquisition software running on the physiology-recording computer passively records the participant's physiology continuously and saves event markers received from the stimulus-control computer into the physiology data record to indicate where in the physiology data stream various stimulus events occurred.

When configuring the stimulus-control and physiology-recording computers, you must make decisions about various issues, including operating system, CPU processing speed, amount of RAM, hard disk size, brand/model of video card(s), brand/model of sound card (if audio stimuli or sound recording will be used), method of I/O, type(s) of input devices (keyboard, mice, buttons, joysticks, etc), and type of case. However, personal computers are continually evolving, decreasing in cost, while at the same time being configured with more robust processor power, larger memory caches, and faster peripheral devices. It is the case now that features once found only in the costly, high-end, commercial work stations are now standard options in consumer-level personal computers of today. Thus the psychophysiologist interested in setting up a laboratory is faced with the choice between spending large sums of money for the top-of-the-line, high-end commercial work station versus finding low-cost machines on sale at local computer store or online retailer. The arguably best solution will address the specific functionality that is currently needed but also allow for the system to be flexibly upgraded as needs expand or as peripheral costs decrease. Given this, general

guidelines can be offered on some of these decisions. For example, when selecting the computer case, make choices that support future upgrades. Select the minitower case over the cute, small footprint case. The former will more likely provide the option to add internal cards to communicate with peripheral hardware, a second hard drive to expand your storage needs, and perhaps a faster 1GB Ethernet card as your building network grows. Don't commit to a system that can't grow. When selecting CPU speed and memory size, it is certainly true that as software applications evolve, their demands for memory and processor speed increase. Therefore, it may make sense to spend a little extra for a faster CPU and increased memory. As you consider upgrades for these components, the relationship with price is nonlinear, with a large increase observed for the current fastest processes and largest memory options. The ideal cost-to-function ratio is often achieved by selecting an option just below the top one or two processor options.

It is not necessarily bad design to have different computers set up in the laboratory, each configured differently for the task at hand. In fact, it is recommended that data collection machines (both stimulus-control and physiology-recording computers) be dedicated to this use only, if possible. Installation of additional software or hardware for other purposes can often degrade the stability of the machine and increase system crashes that result in costly data loss. In contrast, the fastest computers are often not used for data collection but instead are dedicated to data reduction and processing. As these machines age and are no longer on the cutting edge, their role can be switched to tasks that require less power (for example, some stimulus-control software packages run quite effectively on older, slower computers) to save money. It is typically best to keep the operating system constant across computers, if possible, to ease transition from computer to computer and maintenance of security and other operating system patches. Moreover, consistent with stability concerns cited earlier, if a computer acquires a new role as a data collection machine, you should reinstall the operating system once any hardware changes have been completed.

Finally, before considering additional configuration options that are most relevant for the stimulus-control computer (sound card, video card, I/O cards, etc.), the most critical decision is the software used for control and timing of stimulus presentation. Many of these other decisions about stimulus-control computer configuration will be dictated by the requirements of the stimulus-control software.

Stimulus-Control Software

Stimulus-control software packages provide the psychophysiologist with control over the presentation and timing of the various stimuli presented to the research participant during an experiment. Typically, this software also monitors, measures, and records participants' behavioral responses. Numerous commercial stimulus-control software packages are available, and it is beyond the scope of this chapter to provide a comprehensive review of features included in these various packages and their relative advantages and disadvantages. As a starting point, however, contact information for many commonly used packages are listed in the section on software vendors in Table 24.1. Software packages can be broadly categorized into three groups: (1) stand-alone or independent stimulus-control programs (e.g., DMDX, E-Prime), (2) stimulus-control software that is bundled within a "turn-key" or integrated system that also includes physiological amplifiers and software for physiology recording (e.g., Acknowledge as part of Biopac system; Digital Media Player as part of Mindware system, Stim as part of Neuroscan system), and (3) general-purpose programming languages (e.g., C/C++, Pascal, Visual Basic) used to control stimulus and timing. Given that commercial packages specifically designed for stimulus control (preceding categories 1 and 2) are now widely available, relatively inexpensive, and quite flexible and have rigorously addressed complicated issues related to the precision of stimulus timing, it is typically not recommended to use a general programming language for stimulus control. Moreover, it is possible to substitute a stand-alone stimulus-control software package for the stimulus-controls software bundled within the integrated system if desired. In fact, with only moderate technical skills, most stimulus-control software packages can be integrated with any of the available physiology amplifiers and data acquisition packages. In the remainder of this section, we outline some of the more important criteria to consider when selecting between specific stand-alone or integrated stimulus-control software packages.

The first important criterion to consider when selecting a stimulus-control software package is its ease of use. The overall weight you assign to this dimension may depend on the programming expertise in your laboratory. For example, researchers who are familiar with software development in any general-purpose programming language will not find it difficult to master task development in any of the commercially available stimulus-control software packages. However, ease of use should still be considered if you intend to train graduate or undergraduate students with varied programming backgrounds to develop their own tasks without significant involvement from you. Software packages that support "visual" development procedures are often easier for nonprogrammers to learn to use. Visual development procedures typically involve arranging a set of objects or events (e.g., an image file, text on the screen, collection of a participant response) in a time line to represent the flow of the experiment across trials. The availability of precoded routines for common experimental tasks will also speed up and simplify development if your lab regularly relies on a small set of previously developed tasks. In some instances, software developers provide these "canned" routines themselves (e.g. Neuroscan's Stim) For other packages, sample tasks can be obtained from other users via a user listserv (e.g. DMDX) or Web-based archives (e.g., Presentation).

A second, but comparably important, criterion is the flexibility or power of the software with respect to creating diverse experimental tasks or paradigms. Unfortunately, this criterion is often inversely related to ease of use. Software that relies on canned routines or on only visual development procedures to construct tasks will be easy to use but not very flexible with respect to developing novel tasks. Of course, if your research typically involves only these well established paradigms (e.g., well-known cognitive tasks such as the Stroop test, common emotion elicitation tasks such as the slide viewing paradigm, etc.), flexibility may not be as important an issue. However, if you often develop your own tasks or paradigms, it is important that your choice of stimulus-control software does not limit your development options. In general, software packages that use a scripting language (i.e., writing code vs. visually constructing the task) will tend to allow more flexibility when developing tasks. For the most flexibility, the software's features should include various options for conditional branching, looping, and the definition of macros or other forms of subroutines. Such features will make programming easier and will increase the degree to which the stimuli presented can be tailored to specific needs; for example, adjusting the presentation of stimuli based on a participant's responses. In addition, the software should include variables that can be user defined and manipulated based on participant responding while the task executes.

Another important criterion to consider is user support. User support can take many forms, ranging from direct phone, e-mail, or onsite support from software providers to user listservs, detailed embedded or online help files. Of course, each type of support has advantages and disadvantages, and therefore preference should be given to software packages that provide the most comprehensive set of user support options. That said, user listservs are particularly helpful because of the "community building" nature of this type of support, which makes it possible to share scripts for common experimental tasks or paradigms among users. Moreover, open discussion among users may increase the probability of detecting and correcting "bugs" in the software package. The most helpful listervs are also moderated by the software developer (e.g., DMDX, Presentation). Another support factor to consider is the software developer's potential responsiveness to user requests for modifications. Regardless of how flexible or powerful the software package, occasionally the limits of a package will be reached when it is attempting to implement a novel task. In these instances, it is comforting to know that the developers will consider modifying their software to accommodate your need, often for an additional cost, of course. With respect to cost, it is also important to note that user support is not universally free for all software packages. Some packages charge yearly maintenance fees to provide users with continued support and access to software upgrades. Clearly, these maintenance fees must be considered when comparing overall cost across

Table 24.1

Commercially available hardware and software for psychophysiology applications

Vendor Name	Address	Phone & Fax	Web Address	Description Instrument Types
ANS Physiology Systems Vendors				
AD Instruments	2205 Executive Circle Colorado Springs, CO 80906	P: 719-576-3970 F: 719-576-3971	adinstruments.com	Data acquisition and analysis. General biopotential (ECG, EEG, EMG) and specialty amplifiers (EDA, impedance), analysis capabilities. ANS/CNS, Animal/Human.
Biopac Systems	42 Aero Camino Goleta, CA 93117	P: 805-685-0066 F: 805-685-0067	Biopac.com	Data acquisition and analysis. General biopotential (ECG, EEG, EMG,) and specialty amplifiers (EDA, impedance), telemetry, analysis capabilities. ANS/CNS, Animal/Human.
Bio Impedance Technology, Inc.	88 VilCom Campus Suite 165 Chapel Hill, NC 27514	P: 919-960-7799 F: 919-960-6864	Microtronics-nc.com/ BIT/Home.html	Data acquisition and analysis for cardiac function.
Contact Precision Instruments	P.O. Box 425605 Kendall Square Cambridge, MA 02142	P: 617-661-7220 F: 617-661-8224	Psylab.com	Data acquisition and analysis. General biopotential (ECG, EEG, EMG,) and specialty amplifiers (EDA, impedance), analysis capabilities. ANS/CNS, Animal/Human.
Coulborn Instruments	7462 Penn Drive Allentown, PA 18106	P: 610-395-3771 F: 610-391-1333	Coulbourn.com	Data acquisition and analysis. General biopotential (ECG, EEG, EMG,) specialty amplifiers (EDA, impedance), analysis capabilities. ANS/CNS, Animal/Human.
James Long Company	335 Kasson Drive Caroga Lake, NY 12032	P: 518-835-3734 F: 518-835-8436	Jameslong.net	Data acquisition and analysis. General biopotential (ECG, EEG, EMG,) and specialty amplifiers (EDA, impedance), analysis capabilities. ANS/CNS, Animal/Human.
Lafayette Instrument Company	3700 Sagamore Parkway North PO Box 5729 Lafayette, IN 47903	P: 800-428-7545 765-423-1505 F: 765-423-4111	lafayetteinstrument.com	Data acquisition and analysis. General biopotential (ECG, EEG, EMG,) and specialty amplifiers (EDA), analysis capabilities. ANS/CNS, Animal/Human.
Mindware Technologies	1110 Beecher Crossing North, Suite D Gahanna, OH 43230	P: 888-765-9735 614-933-9735 F: 614-933-9736	Mindwaretech.com	Data acquisition and analysis. General biopotential (ECG, EEG, EMG,) and specialty amplifiers (EDA, impedance), telemetry, analysis capabilities. ANS/CNS, Animal/Human.

CNS Physiology Systems and Supplies Vendors

Company	Address	Phone/Fax	Website	Description
Biopac Systems	42 Aero Camino Santa Barbara, CA 93117	P: 805-685-0066 F: 805-685-0067	Biopac.com	Data acquisition and analysis. General biopotential (ECG, EEG, EMG,) and specialty amplifiers (EDA, impedance), telemetry, analysis capabilities. ANS/CNS, Animal/Human.
Brain Products	Stockdorfer Strasse 54 Munich, D-81475 Germany	P: 49-89-744-244-50 F: 49-89-745-244-544	Brainproducts.com	CNS data acquisition and analysis. EEG, EMG, EOG (ECG, EEG, EMG), and analysis capabilities. CNS, Animal/Human.
Cortech Solutions	208 Princess Street Suite E Wilmington, NC 28401	P: 910-362-1143 F: 910-362-1147	Cortechsolutions.com	EEG data acquisition, analysis, and mapping
Electrical Geodesics, Inc.	1600 Millrace Dr. Suite 307 Eugene, OR 97403	P: 541-687-7962 F: 541-687-7963	Egi.com	EEG data acquisition, analysis, and mapping
Lafayette Instrument Company	3700 N. Sagamore Pkwy Lafayette, IN 47904 Spring Gardens	P: 800-428-7545 F: 765-423-4111	lafayetteinstrument.com	Data acquisition and analysis. General biopotential (ECG, EEG, EMG), and specialty amplifiers (EDA), analysis capabilities. ANS/CNS, Animal/Human.
Magstim Company Ltd.	Carmarthenshire, Whales, UK SA34 OHR	P: 44 (0)1994 240798 F: 44 (0)1994 240061	Magstim.com	Nerve Monitors, nerve stimulators, and mapping
MedCare, Inc.	55 Pineview Drive, # 100 Buffalo NY 14228-2101	P: 716-691-0718 888-662-7632 F: 716-691-1004	Medcare.com	Data acquisition and analysis. Bioamplifiers for sleep research.
Mindware Technologies	1110 Beecher Crossing N., Suite D Gahanna, OH 43230	P: 614-933-9735 F: 614-933-9736	Mindwaretech.com	Data acquisition and analysis. General biopotential (ECG, EEG, EMG), and specialty amplifiers (EDA, impedance), telemetry, analysis capabilities. ANS/CNS, Animal/Human. Laboratory integration.
Neuroscan/ Compumedics	5700 Cromo Dr. Suite 100 El Paso, TX 79912	P: 915-845-5600 800-814-8890 F: 915- 845-2965	Neuro.com	EEG data acquisition, analysis, and mapping; recording supplies
SAM Technology, Inc.	425 Bush St, Fifth Floor San Francisco, CA 94108	P: 415-837-1600 F: 415-274-9575	Eeg.com	EEG data acquisition and integration with fMRI imaging.
Sensorium, Inc.	617 Dorset St. Charlotte, VT 05445	P: 802-425-2161 F: 802-425-2171	Sensoriuminc.com	EEG data acquisition
Thought Technology	8396 Route 9 West Chazy, NY 12992	P: 514-489-8251 800-361-3651 F: 514-489-8255	Thoughttechnology.com	General psychophysiological recording systems, biofeedback systems

(continued)

Table 24.1
(continued)

Ambulatory Vendors

Vendor Name	Address	Phone & Fax	Web Address	Description Instrument Types
Ambulatory Monitoring	731 Saw Mill River Road Ardsley, NY 10502-0609	P: 800-341-0066 F: 914-693-6604	Ambulatory-monitoring.com	General purpose physiological data and activity/motion monitors.
Mindware Technologies	1110 Beecher Crossing N., Suite D Gahanna, OH 43230	P: 614-933-9735 F: 614-933-9736	Mindwaretech.com	Ambulatory impedance cardiograph, ANS/CNS data acquisition, wi-fi capable.
SunTech Medical	507 Airport Blvd., #117 Morrisville, NC 27560	P: 919-654-2300 800-421-8626 F: 919-654-2301	Suntechmed.com	Ambulatory blood pressure monitors
Mini Mitter / Respiroincs	20300 Empire Ave. Bldg. B-3 Bend, OR 97701	P: 541-598-3800 800-685-2999 F: 541-322-7277	Minimitter.com	ANS/CNS ambulatory monitoring and telemetry, animal and human, actigraphs
UFI	545 Main C-2 Morro Bay, CA 93442	P: 805-772-1203 F: 805-772-5056	Ufiservingscience.com	General purpose signal and data loggers.
Vivo Metrics	121 N. Fir St. Suite E Ventura, CA 93001	P: 805-667-2225 F: 805-667-6646	Vivometrics.com	Ambulatory biopotential monitors, including the lifeshirt
VU-Ambulatory Monitor	Prof. Dr. E. J. C. de Geus or Dr. G. Willemsen Vrije Universiteit Department of Biological Psychology Van der Boechorststaat 1 1081 BT Amsterdam The Netherlands	P: +31 (0)20 598 8787 F: +31-(0)20-598 8832	vu-ams@psy.vu.nl for sales	Ambulatory impedance cardiovascular monitor

Physiology Instruments Vendors

Vendor	Address	Phone/Fax	Website	Description
Beckman Coulter, Inc.	4300 N. Harbor Blvd P.O. Box 3100 Fullerton, CA 92834-3100	P: 714-993-5321 800-526-3821 F: 714-961-4165	Beckman.com	General purpose and medical instruments and supplies
Finapres Medical Systems	Paasheuvelweg 34a NL-1105 BJ Amsterdam ZO The Netherlands	P: +31 20 609 09 74 F: +31 20 609 06 77	Finapres.com	Blood pressure monitors
Grass Telefactor	Astro-Med Industrial Park 600 East Greenwich Ave. West Warwick, RI 02893	P: 401-828-4000 877-472-7779 F: 401-822-2430	Grass-telefactor.com	Measurement instruments, with focus on EEG and polysomnography systems and supplies
Keithley-Metrabyte, Inc.	28775 Aurora Rd. Cleavland, OH 44139	P: 440-248-0400 800-552-1115 F: 440-248-6168	Keithley.com	Measurement instruments, interface cards
National Instruments Corporation	11500 N Mopac Expwy Austin, TX 78759-3504	P: 800-531-5066 888-280-7645 F: 512-683-8411	Ni.com	Measurement instruments, interface cards, development software.
MedWave/ Vasotrac Inc.	435 Newbury St. Suite 206 Danvers, MA 01923-1065	P: 978-762-8999 F: 978-762-8908	Vasotrac.com	Blood pressure monitors
NelCor Inc.	4280 Hacienda Dr. Pleasanton, CA 94588	P: 800-280-7645	Nellcor.com	Pulse oximetry
NIMS, Inc.	1666 Kennedy Causeway Suite 400 North Bay Village, FL 33141	P: 305-861-0075 F: 305-861-0669	http://www.ctech.net/ nims/products.html	Noninvasive respiratory monitoring
Polar	1111 Marcus Ave., Suite M15 Lake Success, NY 11042-1034	P: 800-290-6330 ext. 3073 F: 516-364-5454	Polar.fi Polarusa.com	Heart rate monitors
Texas Instruments	13532 N. Central Expressway M/S 3807 Dallas, TX 75243-1108	P: 972-644-5580 F: 972-927-6377	ti.com	Amplifiers and signal processors

(continued)

Table 24.1
(continued)

Vendor Name	Address	Phone & Fax	Web Address	Description Instrument Types
ANS/CNS Recording Supplies Vendors				
Biopac Systems	42 Aero Camino Santa Barbara, CA 93117	P: 805-685-0066 F: 805-685-0067	Biopac.com	Data acquisition and analysis. General biopotential (ECG, EEG, EMG,) and specialty amplifiers (EDA, impedance), telemetry, analysis capabilities. ANS/CNS, animal/human.
ElectroCap International	1011 West Lexington Rd. P.O. Box 87 Eaton, OH 45320	P: 937-456-6099 800-527-2193 F: 937-456-7323	Electrocap.com	EEG caps, electrodes, gel, sterilant, general supplies
Easy Cap	Steingrabenstrasse 14 D-82211 Herrsching-Breitbrunn Germany	P: 49-0-8152-3722-24 F: 49-0-8152-3722-29	easycap.de/easycap/	EEG caps and electrodes
Discount Disposables	PO Box 111 St. Albans, Vermont 05478	P: 802-527-8331 F: 802-527-5095	discountdisposables.com	Disposable and reusable electrodes, gels, general supplies
Lafayette Instrument Company	3700 N. Sagamore Pkwy Lafayette, IN 47904	P: 800-428-7545 F: 765-423-4111	lafayetteinstrument.com	ANS/CNS, animal/human.
Mindware Technologies	1110 Beecher Crossing N., Suite D Gahanna, OH 43230	P: 614-933-9735 F: 614-933-9736	Mindwaretech.com	ANS/CNS, animal/human.
Neuroscan/Compumedics	5700 Cromo Dr., Suite 100 El Paso, TX 79912	P: 915-845-5600 800-814-8890 F: 915-845-2965	Neuro.com	EEG data acquisition, analysis, and mapping; recording supplies
Animal Behavior and Monitoring Vendors				
Lafayette Instrument Company	3700 N. Sagamore Pkwy Lafayette, IN 47904	P: 800-428-7545 F: 765-423-4111	lafayetteinstrument.com	Animal behavior
Med Associates, Inc.	PO Box 319 St. Albans, VT 05478	P: 802-527-2343 F: 802-527-509	Med-associates.com	Animal behavior
Mini Mitter / Respiroincs	20300 Empire Ave. Bldg. B-3 Bend, OR 97701	P: 541-598-3800 800-685-2999 F: 541-322-7277	Minimitter.com	ANS/CNS ambulatory monitoring and telemetry, animal and human
Eye Tracking, Motion Measurement Vendors				
Applied Science Laboratories	175 Middlesex Turnpike Bedford, MA 01730	P: 781-275-4000 F: 781-275-3388	a-s-l.com	Eye tracking
Arrington Research	27237 N. 71st Place Scottsdale AZ 85262	P: 480-985-5810 866-222-3937 F: 425-984-6968	arringtonresearch.com	Eye tracking
Charnwood Dynamics	Unit 2, Victoria Mills, Fowke Street, Rothley, Leicestershire, LE7 7PJ, United Kingdom.	P: +44 0 116 230 1060 F: +44 0 116 230 1857	charndyn.com	Motion capture
Innovision Systems	3717 Peters Rd. Columbiaville, MI 48421	P: 810-793-5530 F: 810-793-1714	innovision-systems.com	Motion capture

Vendor	Address	Phone/Fax	Website	Description
Seeing Machines	Level 3, Innovations Building Corner Garran and Eggleston Rd Canberra ACT 2600 AUSTRALIA	P: + 61 2 6125 6501 F: + 61 2 6125 6504	Seeingmachines.com	Motion capture, gaze, head, and eye tracking
Tobii Technology	2050 Ardmore Boulevard, Suite 200 Pittsburgh, PA 15221-4610	P: 412-271-5040 F: 412-271-7077	Pstnet.com	Eye tracking
Software Vendors				
Biopac Systems	42 Aero Camino Santa Barbara, CA 93117	P: 805-685-0066 F: 805-685-0067	Biopac.com	ANS/CNS acquisition and analysis
CMET	University of Arizona		www.u.arizona.edu/~jallen	Freely available software for computing metrics of cardiac variability
DMDX Software	University of Arizona		www.u.arizona.edu/~kforster/dmdx/dmdx.htm	Freely available stimulus presentation and control
EEGLAB Software	University of California San Diego		www.sccn.ucsd.edu/eeglab	Open-source-based Matlab toolbox for CNS analysis
E-Prime; Psychology Software Tools	2050 Ardmore Boulevard, Suite 200 Pittsburgh, PA 15221-4610	P: 412-271-5040 F: 412-271-7077	Pstnet.com	Stimulus presentation and control
EMSE: Source Signal Imaging, Inc	2323 Broadway Suite 102 San Diego, CA 92102	P: 619-234-9935 F: 619-234-9934	Sourcesignal.com	EMSE: an EEG/MEG/fMRI imaging analysis suite
ERTS Software: BeriSoft Corporation	Wildenbruchstr. 49 60431 Frankfurt Germany	P: +49 69 524248 F: +49 69 524218	www.erts.de	Stimulus presentation and control
INTERACT Software; Margold Software & Consulting	Mangold Software & Consulting Graf von Deym Str. 5 94424 Arnstorf Germany	P: +49 0 8723 9 78 33 0 F: +49 0 8723 9 78 33 3	http://www.mangold.de/english/index.htm	Data processing of physiological signals, video recordings, and live observations
Labview Software; National Instruments	11500 N. Mopac Expwy Austin, TX 78759-3504	P: 800-531-5066 888-280-7645 F: 512-683-8411	Ni.com	Measurement instruments, interface cards, development software
MATLAB; The MathWorks, Inc.	3 Apple Hill Drive Natick, MA 01760-2098	P: 508-647-7000 F: 508-647-7001	www.mathworks.com	General purpose data analysis, with toolboxes for statistics and signal processing
MediaLab/Direct RT; Empirisoft Corporation	Empirisoft Corporation 28 W 27th St, Fl 5 New York, NY 10001	P: 212-686-8229 888-519-9758 F: 212-202-4536 877-474-1218	empirisoft.com	Stimulus presentation and control
Mindware Technologies	1110 Beecher Crossing N., Suite D Gahanna, OH 43230	P: 614-933-9735 F :614-933-9736	Mindwaretech.com	ANS/CNS acquisition and analysis, integrated stimulus presentation and control
Octave Software			Octave.org/	Free software for numerical computations
Pendragon Software	1580 S. Milwaukee Ave Suite 515 Libertyville, IL 60048	P: 847-816-9660 F: 847-816-9710	pendragon-software.com	PDA-based form sampling

(continued)

Table 24.1
(continued)

Vendor Name	Address	Phone & Fax	Web Address	Description Instrument Types
Presentation Software	Neurobehavioral Systems, Inc. 828 San Pablo Avenue Suite 216 Albany, CA 94706	P: 510-527-9231 F: 775-628-6773	nbs.neuro-bs.com/	Stimulus presentation and control
PsyLab: Contact Precision Instruments	P.O. Box 425605 Kendall Square Cambridge, MA 02142	P: 617-661-7220 F: 617-661-8224	www.psylab.com	ANS/CNS acquisition and analysis
SciLab Software		Scilab@inria.fr	www.scilab.org	Free development application for data acquisition and analysis
SuperLab: Cedrus Corporation	Cedrus Corporation P.O. Box 6309 San Pedro, CA 90734	P: 310-548-9595 800-233-7871 F: 310-548-9537	www.superlab.com	Stimulus presentation and control; experimental lab software and experiment generator
VivoLogic Software: Vivo Metrics	121 N. Fir St. Suite E Ventura, CA 93001	P: 805-667-2225 F: 805-667-6646	Vivometrics.com	ANS/CNS analysis
VPM Software	Ed Cook Campbell Hall/Suite 415 1300 University Blvd University of Alabama Birmingham, AL 35294		Ecook@uab.edu	DOS-based data collection and stimulus control program
Windaq Software: DataQ Instruments	241 Springside Drive Akron, OH 44333	P: 330-668-1444 F: 330-666-5434	www.dataq.com	ANS/CNS acquisition and analysis

the various software packages. In fact, total cost for stimulus-control software packages (initial purchase, license for additional work stations, maintenance fees) varies significantly, from totally free (DMDX) to well over $10,000 (Neuroscan's Stim).

Ease of setup is another criterion to consider when selecting among stimulus-control software packages. However, it may arguably be less important than the previously considered criteria because it applies primarily only when setting up your first lab (i.e., once you determine how to configure the software in one lab, setup of future labs is typically trivial). The primary challenge involves synchronization of the stimulus-control software with the software that acquires and records participants' physiology. Stimulus-control software included in turnkey systems obviously is easiest to set up, as these systems are typically preconfigured with the necessary cabling, I/O cards, and other hardware to facilitate synchronization "out of the box." However, as mentioned previously, almost any stimulus software package can be synchronized with physiology-recording software with proper information about the organization of the I/O ports on the stimulus-control and physiology-recording computers or amplifiers. Further information about I/O ports and commercially available terminal boards to facilitate setting up the physical connection between computers is described later, in the section on digital input and output.

Participant and Experimenter Displays

Many possible configurations must be considered when setting up stimulus-control computer displays for the participant and experimenter. However, the most common and important decisions include: (1) selection of type of participant display (cathode-ray tube [CRT] , liquid crystal display [LCD] panel, data or slide projector with mechanical shutter); and (2) selection among two common display options for experimental control (simply mirroring the participant display or having independent yet simultaneous participant and experimenter views). Each of these two issues is considered briefly here. Wiens and Öhman (chapter 5, this volume) extensively review many of the issues related to participant displays in the context of research involving subliminal presentation of stimuli to investigate unconscious emotion processing, a research area that requires stringent control of stimulus presentation onset and duration. Rather than reproduce that material, we direct the reader to that chapter and simply provide a broad outline here.

Currently, the most common option for participant display is to attach a CRT monitor to the stimulus-control computer and place this monitor in the participant room. This provides the simplest, most cost-efficient method for participant display and is adequate for the vast majority of experimental tasks. However, this approach is not without limitations relative to other options. Perhaps the most critical issue results from limitations surrounding the refresh rate

of the video card/CRT monitor combination. Display of an entire image on a CRT monitor does not occur instantaneously. Instead, the display is "drawn" by a CRT beam that moves rapidly across the screen (typically left to right within a line and line by line from top to bottom) and activates a thin phosphor layer on the screen. Changes in luminance as the CRT beam passes over a particular location on the screen occur quickly (typically less than a few milliseconds). However, the time required for the passage of this beam across the entire screen to change a display, referred to as the refresh cycle, is longer. Specifically, the duration of one refresh cycle is dependent on the current refresh rate, such that:

Refresh cycle duration (in ms) = 1000/Refresh rate (in Hz).

Given that currently available hardware (i.e., CRT monitors and video cards) supports refresh rates between 60 and 160 Hz, refresh cycles range from approximately 6.3 ms (at 160 Hz) up to 16.7 ms (at 60 Hz). The time required for one refresh cycle will dictate the time necessary to fully display an image that fills the entire screen. Moreover, both the duration of image presentation and the time between images must be multiples of the refresh cycle.

An obvious, but perhaps less critical, limitation of the CRT method relates to the size of the display. The largest widely available CRT displays do not currently exceed 20 viewable inches. Very expensive CRTs of up to 32 inches are available, but to achieve this size they are limited in both resolution and refresh rate (e.g., maximum resolution of 1024 × 768 at 60 Hz). In contrast, use of a data projector (or slide projector) allows presentation on vastly larger projection screens. Although we know of no systematic examination of the impact of image size on responding (e.g., whether image size affects emotional response intensity to IAPS images), subjectively we all know that we would prefer to see the latest blockbuster movie on the "big screen" in a movie theatre than on the largest CRT monitor we could fit in our laboratory. As the size of the CRT display is increased, the desk or table space required to support it (and the heat it puts outs) increases rapidly. In some instances, researchers have considered LCD panel displays to be attractive for use as a participant display in smaller participant chambers. However, operating characteristics of the LCD panels (e.g., pixel response times for dark to light, light to dark, etc.) are quite variable across manufacturers, and no standard indices for comparing these characteristics across LCD panels have been developed to date. Therefore, use of LCD panels for participant displays is not recommended for any experiment that requires timing precision for stimulus presentation.

For experiments that require the most rigorous control of stimulus onset/duration or very brief presentation times or interstimulus intervals for visual stimuli (e.g., visual stimuli followed immediately by masks), Wiens and Öhman recommend the use of data projectors with mechanical shutters (see figures 5.6 and 5.7, chapter 5, this volume). In their example, the setup includes two computers dedicated to stimulus presentation, each connected to a separate data projector. This setup provides for:

a. Instantaneous onset of the entire visual stimulus (vs. top-to-bottom drawing of the stimulus over the refresh cycle, as with CRT presentation).
b. Very brief (e.g., 1 ms) presentation duration (vs. minimum duration of approximately 6 ms with CRT, dependent on refresh cycle limitations).
c. Very brief interstimulus intervals between two different visual stimuli, as in tasks involving target followed by mask (vs. minimum times of approximately 6 ms with CRT, dependent again on refresh cycle).
d. Complete control over the choice of interstimulus interval times (vs. limitation to multiples of the refresh cycle).

Similar but simpler setups that involve only a single stimulus-control computer and a data projector with shutter are possible if experimental demands require instantaneous onset of full stimulus and/or very brief presentation duration (but not including c and d). In general, the shuttered-data-projector approach to stimulus presentation will cost more, will require more time to set up, and may lead to more complex experimental scripts to control stimulus presentation than with the use of a single CRT for participant display. However, as Wiens and Öhman review (chapter 5, this volume), these obstacles are not insurmountable if this level of precision is required for stimulus presentation.

After determining the method of stimulus presentation for the participant display, decisions must be made about the experimenter display. As described earlier, the experimenter is typically physically separated from the participant during the experiment. However, it is often advantageous for the experimenter to be able to observe the stimuli that are being presented to the participant to verify that the paradigm is executing correctly. To this end, commercially available dual-port video splitters are available (e.g., Belkin ExpandView) that can split output from the video card between the participant display (e.g., CRT or data projector in participant room) and a second monitor in the experimenter room. Some video cards also offer this dual-port option to create two identical displays. In addition, some stimulus-control software packages provide a second configuration option that includes two experimenter displays. With this configuration, one experimenter monitor duplicates the participant display, whereas the second experimenter monitor contains ongoing information about various aspects of the experiment, including participant responding (accuracy, response times), stimulus counts, and other task-related information. Typically, this will require the installation of either a dual-port video card or two independent video cards in the stimulus-control computer, but details vary across the stimulus-control software packages that support this two-display option. When available, this additional information is often useful and can save valuable data collection time. For example, providing ongoing information about participant responding can help to quickly identify participants' confusion about task instructions that could otherwise result in the loss of those participants' data if not detected until after the experiment is complete.

Sound Card

Not all psychophysiological experiments require that a sound card be available in the stimulus-control computer. However, if your stimulus-control software does support the presentation of digital sound (e.g., wav files or mp3 files), inclusion of a sound card can be advantageous with little additional cost (basic sound cards can be purchased for $15–30). Inclusion of a sound card allows you to digitize and present task instruction orally in a standardized fashion via the stimulus-control computer. Thus it is possible for participants to simultaneously read and hear instructions to facilitate training on the experimental task. The sound card can also be used by some stimulus-control software packages (e.g., DMDX) to record verbal responses and measure verbal response latency. Not all sound cards will work with every stimulus-control package, so it is worthwhile to check whether a given card is supported prior to purchase.

In some instances, presentation of auditory stimuli may be a critical component of the experimental task. For example, auditory oddball tasks require the presentation of tones or other, more complex sound stimuli. Measurement of the acoustic startle reflex requires the presentation of white noise probes to elicit the reflex. Other tasks make use of auditory stimuli to provide feedback to participants on task performance. In the past, presentation of auditory stimuli was typically accomplished by controlling peripheral hardware via an I/O port in the stimulus-control computer. Specifically, the stimulus-control computer directly controlled a gated audio mixer amplifier, with white noise or tone generators serving as inputs to the audio mixer amplifier. This setup allowed for precise control of the onset and offset of the audio signal. More recently, researchers have begun to digitize these task-related auditory stimuli and present them via the sound card within the stimulus-control computer. These sound files are created with third-party shareware (e.g., Audacity, Wavepad) or commercial (e.g., Adobe Audition) audio editing software. Control and timing of presentation of these digital sounds is then accomplished via the stimulus-control software, much like the presentation of digital images or other stimuli in the experiment. This approach facilitates the presentation of more complex sounds (e.g., International Affective Digitized Sounds; Bradley & Lang, 1999) and reduces the need to purchase somewhat costly additional audio hardware (e.g., audio mixer amplifier and various tone or noise signal generators). However, if precise timing of the presentation of sound stimuli is necessary, you must verify this for your hardware configuration. With all sound cards, there is a delay between the request from the stimulus-control software to present a digital sound file and the actual execution of that request. This delay can range from a few to 20 or more milliseconds. Perhaps more troublesome, this delay has been observed to be variable for some sound cards. This variability in the onset of the sound stimulus may be acceptable for some experiments and physiological measures (e.g., recording tone-elicited skin conductance response in a fear-conditioning task). However, such latency jitter would be unacceptable when measuring ERPs, latency of the startle reflex, or any other measure that requires a high degree of temporal precision. We have found that high-end "gamers" sound cards produce the shortest and most consistent delays (< 4 ms delay with no measurable variation). The performance of any particular sound card can be verified by recording the output of the sound card as an analog signal with your physiological amplifiers. Mark each sound presentation with an event marker and then treat the sound signal channel as you would any analog physiology signal that you can process and measure for response onset latency.

Calibrating the output of the sound card to a decibel level is sometimes required. The simplest way to do this is to contact a colleague who has a sound-level meter that fits like an ear in audiometric headphones and determine the settings that will yield the desired decibel output using a sound file typical of the stimulus you will use. Alternatively, one can find handheld sound-level meters to measure ambient decibel level, which would be used when headphones are not used, placing the meter where the participant's head will be. Once the desired decibel output is obtained, making notes about the settings on the computer software mixer is necessary, but not sufficient. One should measure the AC voltage output coming from the sound card using a standard volt-ohm meter and make note of the voltage that corresponds to the desired decibel level. One can then calibrate the decibel level on a regular or periodic basis simply by measuring the voltage output with the volt-ohm meter. Note also that sound intensity associated with a digital sound file may vary based on the application used to play it. Therefore, regardless of the calibration method, you should use the stimulus-control software package to present the sound during the calibration procedure.

Measuring Behavioral Response

In addition to measuring physiological signals, many psychophysiological experiments also involve collecting information on participants' behavioral responding. In some instances, information about simultaneous physiological and behavioral response is necessary for the reduction and processing of the physiological measure. For example, trials involving incorrect behavioral response are often excluded from the calculation of average stimulus-locked ERP waveforms. Similarly, information about trial-by-trial response time is necessary to calculate average response-locked ERPs such as the error-related negativity (Gehring, Goss, Coles, Meyer, & Donchin, 1993). In other instances, additional posttask information

is collected from participants to aid interpretation of physiological responding. For example, in emotional picture viewing tasks, it is common to present the emotionally evocative pictures a second time to collect information about viewing time, interest value, and self-reported affective response (e.g., self-assessment manikin [SAM] ratings of valence and arousal). Finally, in some experiments, both physiological and behavioral response may be central dependent measures of interest.

A range of options are available for measuring participants' behavioral responding during an experiment. The most common options include the keyboard, a mouse, handheld buttons, or a fabricated response box. Some experiments may involve the use of a joystick (e.g., for SAM ratings), a voice-activated switch (e.g., for verbal response in Stroop tasks), or other, less common input options (e.g., touch screen). Several factors must be considered to determine which option is most appropriate for any specific experimental use. Obviously, the type of response required of the participant will dictate the selection among input options. In addition, as with many of the other issues related to the stimulus-control computer, the selection of stimulus-control software may narrow the range of behavioral input options available to you, or at least the ease with which these options can be readily configured. For example, DMDX supports input via the keyboard (when response-time precision is not critical), serial or USB mouse, joystick connected to a game port, or microswitches (e.g., response buttons) attached to an 8255 parallel digital I/O port. It does not support input via the LPT printer port, nor does it support other serial input devices.

The next issue to consider when selecting among options for behavioral response is the need for precision with respect to the timing of the behavioral response. Input devices can vary significantly in how reliably they measure response time. For example, Forster and Forster (2003) tested the precision of the array of input devices that are supported by DMDX. When test hardware was constructed to produce a series of events with known response times, the response buttons, or microswitches, connected to the parallel digital I/O port provided the most accurate timing, with all recorded responses within ±1 ms of the actual event. The joystick and specific Microsoft serial mouse tested proved to be reasonably accurate as well (range of errors: ±1.5 ms and ±3 ms, respectively). In contrast, large variation was seen in the measurement of response time across keyboards from various manufacturers, with the worst keyboard displaying timings errors of ±18 ms! This poor performance of the keyboard relative to the other input devices is the result of a standard keyboard polling effect that is part of all keyboard hardware, and therefore keyboards should be avoided as input devices if response-time precision is critical. Of course, in some instances information about the exact time of the response may not be necessary. For example, if the behavioral data is limited to self-reported ratings of valence and arousal (as in the picture-viewing task described earlier), information about response time is not recorded, and the keyboard may be more than adequate as an input device.

Various configurations of response buttons and multi-button response pads are available commercially from many of the same companies that have developed stimulus-control software. For example, Psychology Software Tools, Inc. (the developers of E-Prime stimulus-control software), provides a response pad that can be customized to support five to eight buttons. Cedrus (the developer of Superlab) provides standard response pads in various configurations. Cedrus also provides response pads that are constructed entirely of plastic with fiber-optic cable suitable for use in an fMRI environment. A range of fiber-optic behavioral input devices suitable for USB, serial, or TTL input (transistor-to-transistor logic; suitable for connection to a parallel digital I/O port) are also available from Current Designs (http://www.curdes.com).

If available, it is often easiest to purchase the response pad directly from the company that provides your stimulus-control software. This will guarantee that the response pad is compatible with the capabilities and requirements of the software. For instance, the Psychology Software Tools response pad connects to the stimulus-control computer via a serial port, as this is the preferred behavioral interface method for E-Prime stimulus-control software. However, this pad would not function for input if you were using DMDX software for stimulus control, as DMDX uses a commercially available parallel digital I/O port (e.g., PCI DIO24 from Measurement Computing) instead of the serial port for input of participant responses. As a second example, the response pad from Cedrus includes a hardware timer within the box itself to provide millisecond resolution for response times. Superlab stimulus-control software appears to require this timer to provide accurate response timing, and therefore problems with response timing might occur if a different response pad were used with Superlab software. In addition, some features of the more complex response pads may be available only if you use the software for which it was designed. Again, the Cedrus response pad provides six additional digital I/O lines (with the purchase of an accessory cable), but only if used with Superlab software. Finally, it should be noted that, for the more technically inclined psychophysiologist who fully understands the requirements and capabilities of his or her stimulus-control software, construction of a simple input button or multibutton response pad is not difficult and can prove attractive both for cost considerations and for design flexibility (e.g., number and location of buttons, size of box, etc.). Appendix A and Figures 24.3 and 24.4 provide the necessary information to build an input button or response pad. If you're not one to relish the thought of constructing one yourself, often there are shops on university campuses where such devices can be easily constructed for you with the information provided in the figures and appendix.

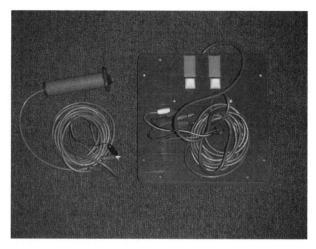

Figure 24.3. Custom response button and two-button response pad. Details on their construction are provided in appendix A. See color insert.

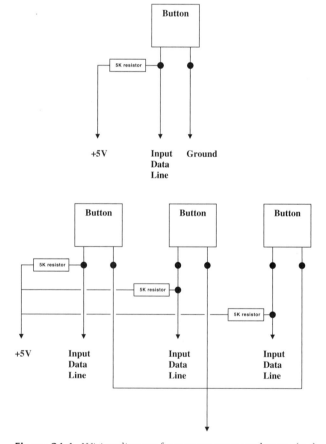

Figure 24.4. Wiring diagram for custom response button (*top*) and multibutton response pad (*bottom*). Details on their construction are provided in appendix A.

Digital Input and Output

Many stimulus-control software packages (e.g., DMDX, E-Prime, Mindware, Superlab, VPM) use parallel digital I/O ports to facilitate communication between the stimulus-control computer and the rest of the world. A parallel I/O port is an interface to the computer that allows data to be transferred in or out in parallel, that is, on more than one wire. A parallel port transfers one bit on each line, which provides for higher transfer rates than would be obtainable over a single cable (e.g., a serial port). There are also several extra lines on the port that are used for control and status signals and on some ports to provide access to the computer's power supply.

The most well-known parallel port is the standard IEEE printer port, which is used by many stimulus-control software packages (e.g., E-Prime, VPM) for digital I/O needs. However, on many modern computers, especially notebook computers, the parallel port is considered to be a "legacy port" and is omitted for cost savings. Therefore, if your software package requires this port, you should verify that the computer you purchase will include a printer port (also called an LPT port or a parallel port). The printer port has 25 independent lines (see Table 24.2 for printer port pin-out) and is accessed via a DB25 connector (a D-shaped connector on the back of the computer). In its most common configuration, 8 data lines are available for output (pins 2–9; although this can be increased to 12 lines if your software can configure the port appropriately) and 8 data lines for input (pins 10–17).

Parallel I/O ports of various configurations can also be purchased and installed. For example, one popular series of parallel digital I/O ports based on the 8255 standard is provided by Measurement Computing (http://www.measurementcomputing.com) and used for I/O by DMDX (and other) software packages. Specifically, DMDX uses the DIO24 series, with options available for installation in the PCI bus (PCI-DIO24) or PCMCIA type II/III slots (PC-CARD-D24/CTR3; ideal if using a notebook as the stimulus-control computer). These I/O cards provide 24 data lines, which are configurable in varying combinations for input or output. In addition, it provides access to +5V, +12V and ground from the computer's internal power supply to power external devices. These latter lines are convenient to provide power peripheral devices (e.g., response buttons).

The parallel I/O port is used by the stimulus-control software to accomplish three different categories of tasks:

1. *Measuring behavioral response.* Response pads/buttons are often connected to input data lines on a parallel port to precisely measure the participant's behavioral responding.
2. *Control of external devices.* The output data lines on the parallel port are often used to control external devices necessary for the experimental task. For instance, our

Table 24.2
Pin-out for standard LPT printer port

Pin	Signal
1	Strobe
2	Data Bit 0 (output)
3	Data Bit 1 (output)
4	Data Bit 2 (output)
5	Data Bit 3 (output)
6	Data Bit 4 (output)
7	Data Bit 5 (output)
8	Data Bit 6 (output)
9	Data Bit 7 (output)
10	Acknowledge (input)
11	Busy (input)
12	Paper end (input)
13	Select (input)
14	Auto Feed (input)
15	Error (input)
16	Init (input)
17	Select in (input)
18	Ground
19	Ground
20	Ground
21	Ground
22	Ground
23	Ground
24	Ground
25	Ground

laboratory has used the parallel port to control intensity and onset of administration of electric shocks (eight data lines are used to set the intensity of the shock, which provides 255 intensity settings; 2^8 minus 1 setting for "off") from a peripheral shock generator (Curtin et al., 2001) to control the onset and offset of light stimuli used as conditioned stimuli (Curtin et al., 1998), to control digital gates to present sound stimuli (e.g., startle probes for measuring acoustic startle response; Curtin et al., 2001), and to control a regulator to present noxious air blasts (an alternative to electric shock for fear-conditioning experiments; Verona & Curtin, in press).

3. *Output event markers to synchronize stimulus presentation with recording of psychophysiological response.* Each time the stimulus-control software presents a stimulus (text, bitmap image, etc), it will use the output data lines on the parallel port to send a digital event marker that is received by the data acquisition software (via a parallel port in the physiology-recording computer or associated physiology amplifier). These event markers denote both the onset time and the identity of the stimulus (typically, different event codes are used to

indicate different stimuli; e.g., in a slide viewing task, event codes might be: 1 = onset of unpleasant image; 2 = onset of neutral image; 3 = onset of pleasant image). The number of output data lines dedicated to event code markers will dictate the number of discrete event types that can be recorded.

Regardless of the type of parallel port, it is often quite helpful to purchase or construct terminal boards for easy access to the data and other lines on these ports. For example, Measurement Computing sells a relatively inexpensive 37-pin screw terminal board (CIO-MINI37) that can be connected to their PCI or ISA bus parallel I/O port. Use of this terminal board simplifies the task of attaching and/or switching configurations of buttons, response pads, and other input devices that may be used in different experiments. Similarly, other peripheral devices (e.g., lights, stimulus generators, I/O cards in physiology-recording computers) can be easily connected to the output lines of the parallel port through this terminal board. Similar terminal boards are also available for 25-pin connectors used by printer ports (e.g., Measurement Computing's CIO-MINI25 terminal board). Custom terminal boards are also not that difficult to construct. For example, one of us (JJC) has built a dual-input terminal board for use in his lab. The left side of the board has 25 female banana plugs that are wired with ribbon cable to a 25-pin connector and attached to the parallel port in our physiology amplifiers. The right side of the board has 37 female banana plugs that are wired with ribbon cable to a 37-pin connector and attached to the parallel port in our stimulus-control computer (Measurement Computing's PCI-DIO24 card).

Amplifiers and Data Collection System

One of the most important decisions when designing the laboratory is which hardware and software platform to use for collecting and analyzing your physiological data. There are numerous systems from which to choose, with a wide variety of topologies. Similar to deciding which computer to use, you want to make sure that you choose a system that fits your current needs yet offers growth in terms of channel density and signal type, as well as performance capabilities.

For example, you may be currently interested in measuring only EKG, respiration, and skin conductance, but you want to allow yourself to add additional amplifiers, such as EMG and EEG. An important consideration in this regard is not only having the ability to add the required amplifiers into your configuration but also ensuring that the performance is available to handle the increased channel count, data size, and sampling rates. Luckily, this is seldom an issue with the availability of Ethernet, USB, and PCI-based analog-to-digital (a/d) cards.

Most of the commercially available recording systems offer similar capabilities for acquiring the various physiologi-cal signals, but some may provide specific amplifiers with particular advantages for specific signals, whereas others use a more general approach in which a given amplifier can handle a wide variety of signals. Amplifiers can be classified into three general categories: biological, transducer, and specialty amplifiers.

Biological amplifiers, such as those designed to measure ECG, EMG, or EEG, can measure a voltage directly from the skin using surface electrodes. These amplifiers can increase the small electrical voltages from microvolt levels at the input to many volts. Provided that such amplifiers have the appropriate amplification and filter settings, a given amplifier may be used to record a variety of signals characterized by voltage oscillations over time (e.g., ECG, EMG, EEG). Transducer amplifiers, such as those used to measure respiration or pulse plythesmography, convert one type of energy, typically light or movement, to another. For instance, in the case of a piezoelectric respirometer belt, a small voltage is produced from the mechanical flexing on the crystal worn around the chest during inhalation and exhalation. This voltage is then magnified to a usable level by the amplifier. Photoplethysmographic devices similarly convert the amount of reflected infrared light to an electrical voltage.

Specialty amplifiers have features specifically required to measure physiological phenomena and will provide source energy, as well as measure voltages. Devices in this category would include a skin conductance amplifier or an impedance cardiograph. Both of these devices provide a small, constant current into the body and measure the amount of change to the return signal. These signals are modulated by autonomic activity, such as activation of the sweat glands or the amount of blood flow through the chest.

Just as there are basic differences between the amplifier types, there are also similarities. These would include programmable gain, input coupling, and filter settings. Gain(A), for a biological amplifier, is simply the amount an incoming signal is amplified before being output and is calculated as A = output/input. With respect to a transducer or specialty amplifier, these are typically scaled a bit differently to a voltage per unit of measure. For instance, when using a skin conductance amplifier, the gain setting is adjustable for a set amount of voltage per uSiemen of conductance. Similarly, an impedance cardiograph is adjustable for a defined voltage per every ohm of change.

Input coupling refers to how the signal is connected into the input of the internal instrumentation amplifier. There are two choices here: DC (direct current) or AC (alternating current) coupled. A DC-coupled amplifier connects the inputs directly to the instrumentation amplifier. Any DC level (essentially a baseline offset) present on the input is reflected on the output. You would use this setting when measuring skin conductance, as you are interested in the absolute level and in the slow-moving changes around that level. Conversely, an AC-coupled amplifier blocks DC by placing a capacitor at the input of the instrumentation amplifier. In AC-coupled mode, only the changes in the input signal are passed through the capacitor, and DC levels are blocked. This would be common in an amplifier configured to collect ECG, when you are primarily interested in the QRS complex, but not in the baseline level around which these features oscillate; in fact, in this example, a slow-moving DC shift can actually be problematic for detecting the R peak.

Lastly, filter selections vary among low-pass, high-pass, and notch filters. Low-pass filters, as the name illustrates, pass only frequencies present in the input signal that are lower than a specific settings. The low-pass filter is commonly used to remove higher frequency noise that lies outside of the range of interest and to make sure that you can adequately sample your signal in digital form without the problem of aliasing. Aliasing occurs when signals are sampled at a rate too slow for the highest frequencies that appear in the signal. Nyquist's (1928) theorem states that one must sample at a rate twice as fast as the highest signal frequency in order to adequately capture that signal; stated differently, the highest frequency that can be accurately represented is one-half of the sampling rate and has come to be known as the Nyquist frequency.

Conversely, high-pass filters pass frequencies that are higher than the stated setting. You might use these to remove any slow-moving component, such as the DC signal in ECG, or slow signals not of myogenic origin (e.g., movement, blinks) for the EMG. Filter settings must be chosen carefully, as incorrect settings may remove the signal of interest rather than the irrelevant noise, which could render an experiment useless.

Notch filters are different in that they stop or remove an unwanted specific frequency from the input signal. This can also be referred to as a band-stop filter. These are typically used as 60 Hz (or 50 Hz outside North America) notch filters when you want to remove noise generated from the AC power line or radiated in the ambient environment.

Another important consideration is the flexibility and features of the data-acquisition software that accompanies the hardware. Most software packages are designed to work specifically with their own hardware platform and generally will not work across systems. Generally, these software systems all have similar features, such as naming each channel, setting sampling rate (samples/second) and gain, selecting and programming digital filters, and defining the overall collection period, or epoch.

More advanced features might include the ability to synchronize data collection to an external trigger and enabling synchronous collection of digital input/output. These features are very important considerations when integrating data collection with stimulus presentation, as you are interested in physiological activity as it pertains to specific external stimuli. As discussed previously, you would likely link the parallel I/O port of your stimulus computer to your data collection system's trigger input or digital input port. The ability to send event markers via the parallel port is a common feature in most stimulus packages, such as DMDX, E-Prime, or MediaLab.

When integrating data collection and stimulus presentation systems, you must consider how best to keep timing synchronized. You may choose to collect your physiological data in a continuous fashion while storing the digital triggering information. This is often referred to as *continuous data collection*. This method is preferred when you are interested in the participant's physiological state immediately before and after a stimulus event or when timing is such that it cannot be predefined. As the data are continuous from start to end, you have a recording of all physiological activity throughout the experimental protocol, and most sophisticated analysis packages allow indexing through these data in a pre- or post-stimulus fashion. Recording in continuous mode will result in a larger data file, but it ultimately provides the greatest flexibility after data collection. Given that storage capacity has increased so rapidly, continuous mode has become the preferred method of data collection for most applications.

In cases in which you have an experimental protocol with clearly defined blocks, such as a 5-minute baseline task followed by 2-minute tasks and then a recovery period, you may prefer to collect in epoch mode. In epoch mode, you define tasks by set time periods and either randomize the order of the task or follow a sequential time line. This scenario may be better implemented by connecting the output port of the stimulus computer to the trigger input of the data collection system, allowing data collection to be controlled in start/stop fashion. The advantage of this scheme is smaller data files; however, you will have multiple files with varying names. You also need to keep a record of the order of the task, as this will likely be important. It is also possible to collect data in a single file with many different epochs, such as might occur in an ERP experiment, but one would need to carefully consider the timing of the epoch; continuous data formats may likely be preferred for such experimental designs.

Physiology Data Processing and Reduction Software

Once physiological data are collected, the raw binary signals must then be processed to accommodate the gain or scaling of the amplifiers, converted to physiological units (e.g., uSiemens/volt, ohms/volt), and then analyzed using accepted methodologies. Most physiological collection systems will have a basic means for physiological analysis (i.e., Biopac, Psylab), or these data can be analyzed using sophisticated third-party applications that can read various data formats (i.e., Mindware Technologies, Matlab)

Unfortunately, there is no universally accepted output data format used by equipment manufacturers, and each will define its own idiosyncratic format. Most manufacturers, however, will provide their file format specifications or will have a utility to output this data to a standard but space-consuming format such as ASCII.

There are standard references and textbooks that detail accepted methods for physiological data analysis. To go into this in detail is beyond the scope of this chapter; however, helpful texts and guideline articles are provided in table 24.3 as a starting point for instruction and recommendations on these topics.

Data Storage

Files created in psychophysiological research may range from rather small, in the case of a single channel of data sampled at a slow rate (e.g., skin conductance), to startlingly large, in the case of multichannel recordings sampled at a high rate. Small single-channel files may be unremarkable in size (e.g., 200 kilobytes), whereas high-density EEG arrays sampled at a high rate can easily consume over 20 megabytes per minute of recording. Digital video is similarly costly in terms of storage requirements. Thus the storage needs of the psychophysi-

Table 24.3
Guidelines articles appearing in *Psychophysiology*

Berntson, G. G., Bigger, J. T., Eckberg, D. L., Grossman, P., Kaufmann, P. G., Malik, M., et al. (1997). Heart rate variability: Origins, methods, and interpretive caveats. *Psychophysiology, 34,* 623–648.

Blumenthal, T. D., Cuthbert, B. N., Filion, D. L., Hackley, S., Lipp, O. V., & van Boxtel, A. (2005). Committee report: Guidelines for human startle eyeblink electromyographic studies. *Psychophysiology, 42,* 1–15.

Fowles, D. C., Christie, M. J., Edelberg, R., Grings, W. W., Lykken, D. T., & Venables, P. H. (1981). Publication recommendations for electrodermal measurements. *Psychophysiology, 18,* 232–239.

Fridlund, A. J., & Cacioppo, J. T. (1986). Guidelines for human electromyographic research. *Psychophysiology, 23,* 567–589.

Jennings, J. R., Berg, W. K., Hutcheson, J. S., Obrist, P., Porges, S., & Turpin, G. (1981). Publication guidelines for heart rate studies in man. *Psychophysiology, 18,* 226–231.

Picton, T. W, Bentin, S., Berg, P., Donchin, E., Hillyard, S. A., Johnson, R., Jr., et al. (2000). Guidelines for using human event-related potentials to study cognition: Recording standards and publication criteria. *Psychophysiology, 37,* 127–152.

Pivik, R. T., Broughton, R. J. H., Coppola, R., Davidson, R. J., Fox, N., & Nuwer, M. R. (1993). Guidelines for the recording and quantitative analysis of electroencephalographic activity in research contexts. *Psychophysiology, 30,* 547–558.

Putnam, L. E., Johnson, R., Jr., & Roth, W. T. (1992). Guidelines for reducing the risk of disease transmission in the psychophysiology laboratory. *Psychophysiology, 29*(2), 127–141.

Ritz, T., Dahme, B., Dubois, A. B., Folgering, H., Fritz, G. K., Harver, A., et al. (2002). Guidelines for mechanical lung function measurements in psychophysiology. *Psychophysiology, 39,* 546–567.

Shapiro, D., Jamner, L. D., Lane, J. D., Light, K. C., Myrtek, M., Sawada, Y., et al. (1996). Blood pressure publication guidelines. *Psychophysiology, 33,* 1–12.

Sherwood, A., Alen, M. T., Fahrenberg, J., Kelsey, R. M., Lovallo, W. R., & van Doornen, L. J. P. (1990). Methodological guidelines for impedance cardiography. *Psychophysiology, 27,* 1–23.

Note: All articles are available at http://www.sprweb.org/journal.html

ologist may range from an ordinary system that includes simple data redundancy to a specialized system that handles gargantuan files.

Data Redundancy

No matter what the file size is, a wise practice is to protect data against several nemeses: (1) failure of the drive or disk on which it is stored; (2) failure or theft of the computer on which it is stored; (3) corruption during subsequent storage or processing. Good security against all three nemeses will involve: (1) fault-tolerant storage of original data, preferably beginning at the moment of recording; (2) regular off-site backup of the fault-tolerant storage media; and (3) off-site backup of original files. Table 24.4 provides an overview of the different methods of data storage and backup, with a brief list of advantages and disadvantages of each method. Reviewing the table and reading the ensuing sections may be insufficient to allow readers to set up their own data redundancy system, but this overview should provide the reader with a good grasp of the issues and options and provide a vocabulary that will prove helpful in decoding the acronym soup encountered when consulting with the local computer guru.

Primary Data Storage

Digitized data files can be stored on any conventional computer during the participant session or stored on a more elaborate medium that protects against media failure. Hard drives in desktop machines purchased in 2005 can exceed 400 gigabytes, more than adequate space to store files from multichannel psychophysiology sessions for hundreds of participants. Such storage is vulnerable to a single-drive failure, however, necessitating other protections against data loss. A simple solution is known as RAID, or a redundant array of inexpensive disks (Patterson, Gibson, & Katz, 1988). In its simplest form, this involves the installation of a second drive in the machine, with data redundantly and immediately and automatically written to this second drive, a process known as mirroring (or RAID-1, explained in appendix B). Mirroring can be handled by software in some operating systems (know as software RAID), but hardware devoted to the task is preferred in terms of speed and reliability. Many motherboards have onboard RAID controllers that allow for mirroring of drives, or a dedicated PCI card can be purchased and installed for this purpose (see table 24.4). Other options for primary storage that protect against drive failure include direct attached storage in the form of a RAID tower or network attached storage, both of which are described here.

RAID Systems for Handling Very Large Files or Very Many Very Large Files

By combining more than one drive, it is possible to create rather impressively large data storage arrays. A RAID provides this, with the additional benefit of allowing data re-

Table 24.4

Relative advantages and disadvantages of various data storage hardware solutions

Storage Method	Uses	Sample Vendors	Advantages	Disadvantages
Single hard drive	• Store primary data temporarily during or following collection • Store second copy of data at remote location	• Maxtor, Western Digital, Seagate, others	• Inexpensive • Already available in all computers • Easy to add another single drive to most computers	• No data redundancy
Mirrored hard drives (also termed RAID-1)	• Store primary data with protection against single-drive failure	• Built into motherboards such as AOpen, ASUS, Gigabyte, Shuttle, Tyan • Specialized cards such as those by Promise Techologies, Adaptec	• Small additional cost over single drive • Works under any OS • Used like a single drive so users have nothing new to learn	• Space limited by currently available drives • No external indicators that mirroring is functional; need to check software utility to ensure mirroring is working • Need to purchase one duplicate drive for every used drive
RAID tower (also termed direct attached storage)	• Store primary data with protection against single drive failure • Store second copy of data at remote location	• Promise technologies, IBM, HP, FantomDrives, StorCase, SnapAppliance, Sun, Mac (XServe)	• Only need to purchase one additional drive to ensure data redundancy for remaining drives (if using RAID-3 or RAID-5) • Hot-swappable spare drives possible • Will work with any OS (Windows, Unix, Mac) • Dual power supplies available to prevent downtime • Can be accessed over net if connected to a computer that shares this resource, often a server	• To share over a network, one must know how to share network resources and, ideally, use a server • Towers can be pricey
Network attached storage (NAS)	• Store primary data with protection against single-drive failure • Store second copy of data at remote location	• Buffalo, Adaptec, Dell, Iomega	• Usually works with multiple OS (Windows, Unix, Mac) • Remote management made simple • Accessed over net from virtually anywhere without need for a server	• Cost is higher than a RAID tower • Some do not have data redundancy (RAID) • Some less expensive models have small capacity
Digital tape	• Backup of data	• Dell, Iomega, Sony, HP, Quantum, Exabyte	• Inexpensive media • Incremental backups possible	• Slow access • For larger data sets, requires human intervention to switch tapes or investment in more expensive unit with autoloading capabilities • Backups must be scheduled; not immediate redundancy

(continued)

Table 24.4

(*continued*)

Storage Method	Uses	Sample Vendors	Advantages	Disadvantages
				• Technology changes fairly quickly, requiring one to retain old tape drives • Shelf life can be short if storage environment not well controlled or media accessed frequently
CD-R, CD-RW, DVD±R, DVD±RW	• Backup of data	• Sony, Teac, NEC, LG, Pioneer, myriad others	• Inexpensive hardware • Inexpensive media • Virtually universal format that is easily read by many machines and operating systems • Format not likely to become obsolete in near future • Shelf life of many decades likely	• "Burning" can be time-consuming • While "burning," machine may be unusable for many other purposes • May require many disks to back up data sets or large drives • Organizing and retrieving disks can be challenging, although carousels (e.g., that by Dacal Technology) can make this easy
USB-connected one-touch backup drive	• Backup of data	• Maxtor, Hitachi	• Ease of use—plug and press • Relatively inexpensive • Portable	• Only a single drive; if it fails, there is no protection against data loss
Remote storage on university or commercial server	• Store primary data with protection against single-drive failure • Store second copy of data at remote location	• Your university! • U.S. DataTrust, IBackup, LiveVault, myriad others	• Ease of use—mapped as a drive or automated and continuous backup • Your data are under an expert's control	• Can be prohibitively expensive for commercial vendors • Your data are under someone else's control
Distributed file system across servers	• Store primary data with protection against single-drive failure • Store second copy of data at remote location	• Most cost-effectively accomplished by building two servers with RAID towers	• Instantaneous or virtually real-time data backup to remote location	• Cost, as two duplicate systems required • Technical expertise required to set up server systems and manage them

dundancy to protect against a single-hard-drive failure. RAID towers thus house multiple same-sized drives (e.g., anywhere from 2 to 48 or more drives) that are then accessed as if there were one single very large drive by the user, connected to a computer by an interface card (e.g., SCSI card) or USB-2 cable or firewire cable. Different configurations of RAID, termed *levels*, control how those drives are combined and what strategy for data redundancy is employed. For the technophile, RAID has many levels that may hold technological appeal, but only the most commonly used and potentially pragmatic levels are reviewed in appendix B and depicted in Figure 24.5.

RAID Towers and Network Attached Storage

RAID towers provide hardware to house multiple drives that are then connected to a host computer, often a server but quite possibly a work station. Many commercially available RAID arrays can utilize the less expensive ATA drives or sometimes the newer and cost-effective serial ATA drives rather than the more expensive high-performance SCSI drives. These RAID towers are then connected via an interface cable, either a SCSI cable, a USB-2 cable, or a firewire cable, to the host computer. If the host computer lacks the particular interface port, a card must be purchased to create a SCSI, USB-2, or firewire connection as appropriate for that

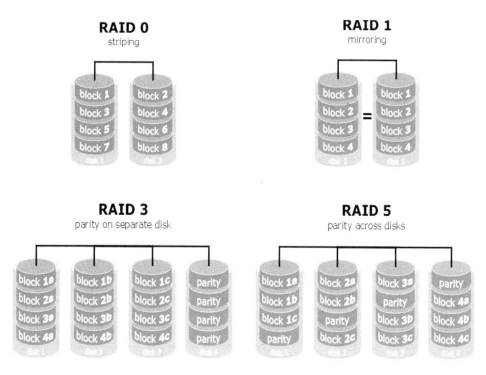

RAID 0
striping

RAID 1
mirroring

RAID 3
parity on separate disk

RAID 5
parity across disks

Figure 24.5. RAID configurations. Blocks with different numbers are entirely independent data. Blocks with identical numbers are identical data. For RAID-3, blocks with the same number but different letters are different pieces of data that are yoked together as part of a parity set, with their sum determining the parity bit for that set. For RAID-5, blocks within a "row" (e.g., 1a, 2a, and 3a) are different pieces of data yoked together as part of a parity set, with their sum determining the parity bit for that set. Adapted from the Promise Technology UltraTrak Series User Manual.

RAID tower. After installing the drives of the user's choosing, recalling that they must all be the same size, these RAID towers are easily configured to a RAID-0, 1, 3, 5 (appendix B) or other level configuration as desired. Many of these towers also allow the user to install an extra drive that is not configured as part of the array but rather is sitting there as a spare to be inserted into the array should one of the existing drives fail. When an existing drive fails, all data are safe with RAID-1, 3, or 5, but the data are then vulnerable should a second drive fail. By having such a "hot" spare, you can quickly return to having data redundancy while replacing what was previously the hot spare with a new drive.

RAID towers attached to work stations or servers can be accessed over a network from other computers, provided the host machine shares the drive for network access. An alternative is to purchase a network attached storage (NAS) device, which often is a RAID tower with its own operating system so that it need not be connected to any computer. NAS devices thus can offer all the advantages of a RAID tower but do not require the user to configure a server or work station to share files over a network. NAS devices have net-accessible interfaces that allow you to configure file access and security. Two considerations worth keeping in mind with respect to NAS devices are that (1) not all NAS devices have RAID arrays, as some are just a single drive without redundancy, and (2) NAS devices can be pricey, so it pays to shop around. NAS devices are especially helpful when data need to be accessed by machines that use different operating systems.

Archival Data Backup

In addition to a primary storage system, data backup can further protect against unforeseen catastrophe. As with pri-

mary data storage systems, these backup systems can range from very simple and inexpensive to rather expensive and sophisticated. The simplest technology is one with which most readers have experience, burning data to CD or DVD media and then storing them in cases or folders or storage carousels. CDs or the higher capacity DVDs make an excellent permanent archival copy of original data that ideally should be stored offsite at a location other than where the primary storage is housed. Because this system of archiving data is not automatic, researchers need to ensure that data backup to CD or DVD becomes a regular part of the participant-running and data-collection procedures.

Tape backup provides another option, although one that can be slow and frustrating unless you invest in a system that automatically loads tapes and conducts backups. Tape backups provide a good and inexpensive method for archiving data that one hopes to seldom have need to access (e.g., completed studies). Tape backup systems also can provide for incremental backups, backing files that have changed since a prior complete backup. In addition to backing up original participant data, such backup systems are useful for backing up operating systems and also for backing up drives that contain files that are created in the process of data scoring and data reduction. Retrieving data from tapes, however, is relatively slow and sometimes involves inserting multiple tapes to find the required file(s) to restore.

Newer USB-connected one-touch backup systems have become an appealing option. These relatively inexpensive systems will easily backup data to a single drive, and one that is easily ported to another machine or to offsite storage.

The most elaborate and expensive system of backup involves another large drive space in a separate location, whether that be another RAID tower, a NAS device, or a university or commercial server space and an automated routine that can back up data from the primary to the separate location (e.g., Cordes Development's "Backer" is very reasonable and powerful; http://www.cordes-dev.com). RAID towers and NAS devices provide another set of redundant storage that could immediately replace the main storage should a computer or device fail, thus allowing secure data storage with data redundancy. University or commercial storage provides a simple remote location for storing data, but commercial solutions are likely to be cost-prohibitive for large amounts of data. Many universities, however, provide large blocks of storage for faculty and students that could be used for backup storage.

Other Laboratory Paraphernalia

Electrodes, Caps, Gel, Wires, and More

Depending on the signals you will be recording, you will require specific electrodes, caps, transducers, conductive gels, and more. Most recording-system vendors also have catalogues of such supplies, and other vendors provide similar equipment (e.g., Discount Disposables provides disposable and reusable electrodes, gels and other accessories; www.discountdisposables.com). Some systems will have proprietary connectors (e.g., the Geodesic Sensor Net from EGI connects only to the amplifiers from the same company), whereas other connectors (e.g., those on single electrodes) are typically somewhat standard and easily utilized by a variety of systems. Appropriate gels also need to be utilized for the recording of some signals; not all gels are appropriate for all signals, although the reader is referred to the relevant articles in Table 24.3 for more details.

Most signals also require some degree of skin preparation, and for this purpose gauze pads, mildly abrasive exfoliating scrubs, and rubbing alcohol may be useful. For EEG recording, we have adopted a recommendation from Scott Smith (of Compumedics Neurscan) to use a hairbrush prior to electrode cap placement, as it will dramatically reduce the time required to obtain adequate impedance. We purchase a gross of brushes on line for less than a dollar a brush (e.g., Dollardays.com), give one to each participant, and ask them to spend a few minutes brushing their hair while ensuring that the plastic bristles brush over the scalp. (Note that we also ask bald or balding participants to do the same, as it reduces their scalp impedance as well!)

Finally, although many data acquisition systems can test impedance, having a stand-alone impedance checker can also be useful. Such devices pass a small alternating current through the electrodes and index the extent to which the signal is impeded. In contrast to a volt-ohm meter, which can check resistance using a DC signal, these impedance meters use signals that are quite similar in frequency characteristics to the signals you will be recording.

Essential Paraphernalia and Other Gadgetry

The psychophysiology laboratory may also benefit from a few additional items or conveniences. Although not essential, it can be very helpful to have a sink in the psychophysiological research space or a nearby sink dedicated for use by the psychophysiological researcher for cleaning and sanitizing electrodes and for storing electrodes and caps during the drying process. Disposable electrodes exist that are of fine quality, thus obviating the need for a cleaning and sanitizing method, although such electrodes may be more costly or may not be available for particular applications. If you need to clean electrodes, a water jet (e.g., the one by WaterPik) can be used for cleaning the gels from the electrodes.

Another essential tool is a volt-ohm meter, or at least a simple continuity tester. Volt-ohm meters are most often used to check whether there is a break in a wire, but they are also handy for checking whether batteries are charged, for calibrating sound decibel output, and for determining whether the proper voltage is being emitted by equipment.

Some additional tools may also be useful to have around the psychophysiological laboratory. A small set of screwdrivers, needle-nosed pliers, and an adjustable wrench can all be useful in attaching or wrestling with various pieces of equipment. And for simple wire fixes, a small soldering iron may be helpful.

Finally, it is worthwhile to invest in items to help keep the experimenter, the participant, and the lab clean and presentable. White lab coats are handy to keep gel off experimenters while lending a professional appearance. Wet wipes are useful for spontaneous cleanup of gel when exuberance or clumsiness results in recording gel ending up in unfortunate places on the participant or lab furniture.

Patient Safety and Comfort

Psychophysiological recording poses few risks to participants, and careful lab procedures can virtually eliminate any risk. A pragmatic overview of risks and how to drastically reduce or eliminate them is provided by Greene, Turetsky, and Kohler (2000). The main risks stem from the possibility of disease transmission and from unintentional electrical flow.

For detailed coverage of procedures to reduce the risk of disease transmission in the psychophysiological laboratory, the guidelines of the Society for Psychophysiological Research (Putnam, Johnson, & Roth, 1992; available from www.sprweb.org) are an excellent resource. These guidelines reiterate that psychophysiological recording is a very low-risk procedure in terms of the possibility of disease transmission but that, in cases in which skin must be abraded to obtain adequate signal quality (e.g., many EEG or EMG applications), a few key procedures can dramatically curtail the risk of disease transmission. Such procedures include wearing protective gloves during skin preparation, using single-use sterilized electrodes, or ensuring adequate high-level disinfection of reusable electrodes. Adequate disinfectants are available from many purveyors of electrodes and EEG caps.

Risk involving electrical flow stems primarily from the fact that during preparation for recording participants often have the top dead dry layer of skin removed and conductive gel applied in order to reduce the interference to the tiny electrical signals that originate from the participant. This reduced interference, however, not only allows signals within the participant to pass relatively unimpeded to the electrode but also allows electrical signals of external origin to pass quite easily to the participant. To appreciate this phenomenon, consider the rather common childhood antic of placing a 9-volt battery on one's tongue. When it is placed on skin, such as on the arm, one feels nothing, but when it is placed on the tongue, devoid of the protective layer and additionally coated in conductive saliva, one can feel the unmistakable and unpleasant sensation of electricity flowing across the tongue. Considering that such a sensation is produced with a mere 9-volt battery, one can appreciate the danger of the 110V or 220V electrical outlet. Procedures for minimizing the risk (see also Greene et al., 2000) of electrical current reaching the participant include: (1) proper grounding of all equipment; (2) using a ground fault interrupt circuit (such as those commonly found in bathrooms and kitchens); (3) keeping participants away from sources of electricity and ensuring that exposed electrodes are carefully wrapped in insulating material should a participant need to exit the laboratory (e.g. to use the lavatory); (4) using battery-powered equipment whenever possible; and (5) powering any equipment that must contact the participant (e.g., amplifiers, response buttons) with an isolation transformer.

Helpful Resources

Many resources exist to assist the investigator who wishes to undertake psychophysiological recording. Excellent basic handbooks that cover many aspects of psychophysiological research exist, including those by Cacioppo, Tassinary, and Berntson (2000), Andreassi (2000), Hugdahl (1996), and Stern, Ray, and Quigley (2000), as well as an older but useful compendium by Coles, Donchin, and Porges (1986). A basic primer in electricity can also help to demystify and unmuddle electrical concepts. Various primers are available on the Web or in self-paced readers such as that by Ryan (1986).

Articles that detail the guidelines for recording, analyzing, and reporting specific psychophysiological measures have been compiled by committees of the Society for Psychophysiological Research (SPR) and published in *Psychophysiology*. Table 24.3 lists these guideline articles, almost all of which are available for download from the SPR website (http://www.sprweb.org). SPR itself is a tremendous resource for nascent and experienced psychophysiologists alike, and attendance at an annual meeting (information available on the SPR website) is likely to be a tremendously helpful and stimulating experience. In addition to the opportunity to discuss psychophysiological research with other interested investigators, annual meetings often feature preconference workshops that provide pragmatic and didactic training on the recording and analysis of various psychophysiological signals. The SPR website has a variety of resources in addition to the standards articles, but especially helpful is the "teaching" page, with links to syllabi for courses in psychophysiology, as well as links to various software programs that may be of assistance.

To assist with your search for systems, software, hardware, and supplies, Table 24.1 provides a list of vendors and contact information, with a brief description of what items each vendor provides. Additionally, the instrumentation project undertaken by Dick Jennings and Pete Gianaros surveyed providers of psychophysiological systems to determine the capabilities of various systems. The results are available at http://www.pghmbc.org under Resources, Core E, Biological and Biomedical Measurement. The results of their project also greatly influenced the construction of Table 24.1.

Finally, other psychophysiologists are often excellent resources and can serve as consultants or collaborators for various projects. Phone consultations, site visits, and e-mail consultations are all potentially helpful, as is taking a semester's leave to sit in on a psychophysiology course taught .by one of the many psychophysiologists listed on the teaching page of the SPR website.

Conclusion

Psychophysiology has become a mainstream research tool, one that is utilized increasingly in a wide variety of research domains. Whereas a half-century ago, choosing to embark on a program of research that utilized psychophysiological measures demanded custom fabrication of equipment and custom programming using specialized modules linked together with an impressively intimidating mass of wires, contemporary emotion researchers have at their disposal a wide variety of software and hardware that greatly simplifies the integration of psychophysiological measures into a research protocol. Although there remain many considerations in competently integrating psychophysiological measures into a program of research, it is indeed possible for such measures to be used by nonspecialists for whom psychophysiology is just one of many tools that can help in the effort to comprehensively address their research questions. This chapter is offered in the hopes of promoting this trend.

Appendix A. Building Response Buttons and Pads

A handheld response button (see Figure 24.3) can be constructed easily from PVC tubing and momentary input buttons available from Radio Shack or other similar electronics shops. Purchase an approximately 4-inch piece of PVC tubing (choose a diameter that fits comfortably in a participant's hand) and two PVC end caps from any hardware or plumbing store. Purchase a momentary push button or switch (e.g., Radio Shack catalog #275–609), a 4.7K resistor, and some 3-conductor wire (e.g., intercom wire from Radio Shack). Drill a hole in the first end cap to allow the wire to pass through. Drill a hole in the second end cap to fit the button. Strip the ends of the three wires and feed them through one end cap (from the outside in), then through the PVC tube, the hex nut for the button, and finally the other end cap (from the inside out). Next, solder the three wires to the two tabs on the push button, as depicted in the top panel of Figure 24.4. Finally, screw on the hex nut to secure the button in the end cap and secure the two end caps on the PVC tube. This simple button is now ready for use. The respective wires will be connected to an input data line, +5V, and ground on your I/O card as depicted in the figure. A multibutton response pad (see Figure 24.3) can be constructed similarly by wiring multiple push buttons into a box, as depicted in the bottom panel of Figure 24.4.

Appendix B: RAID Demystified

RAID-0 provides no data redundancy but merely increases performance as data are "striped" across multiple drives, allowing data to be stored and retrieved faster. Imagine that 24 blocks of data need to be written to save a file. One option is to write the 24 blocks to a single drive, but a speedier option would be to write 12 to one drive and simultaneously write 12 to another, potentially cutting in half the time required to save the file. Thus the file is now split intentionally across drives in order to decrease the time required to save (and read) the file. (Such a dramatic improvement in speed is seldom realized, because other factors also determine the write speed.) The biggest disadvantage to RAID-0 is that, if any drive fails, all data, including the data on the good drive, are useless. RAID-0 has gained some popularity among computer gaming enthusiasts, but for the psychophysiologist, such modest gains in performance are far outweighed by the risk of data loss.

RAID-1 is mirroring: Identical data packets are written to two separate drives, with one drive thus providing a "mirror" of the other. The mirror analogy is not entirely apt in that a reversed image is not created; instead, an identical copy is created every time data are written. Should one of the drives fail, the hardware will then access the good drive as a single drive, and all data will continue to be accessible provided the second drive does not fail. It is advisable to have a spare drive available should one fail so that the dead drive can be replaced and the mirror can be "rebuilt." RAID-1 systems are somewhat commonly found in desktop computers, or they can be found in external RAID towers.

RAID-5 provides data redundancy using striping that enhances performance (see the preceding RAID-0 discussion) and a concept termed *parity* that allows redundancy, with fewer drives required to accomplish this redundancy. Perhaps the simplest way for behavioral scientists to understand parity is by way of analogy to degrees of freedom, a concept that refers to the number of values in the final calculation of a statistic that are free to vary. Imagine four hard drives, three of which contain blocks of data and the fourth containing a piece of data that is determined by a combination of those first three drives. Now, because computers write only 1s or 0s, a parity bit can be written based on the sum of the bits on the other drives (or the exclusive "or" function, XOR). If the sum is even, the parity is set to 0, and if the sum is odd, the parity is set to 1. Thus during normal operation, with all drives working, the degrees of freedom are $n - 1$, because data on all drives are free to vary, but the parity bit will then be determined given the data on those drives. If any one of the three data drives fails, however, there are no degrees of freedom; in other words, one can uniquely determine the value that must have existed on the failed data drive by examining the data on the other good drives in addition to the parity bit. When the parity bits are all located on a single drive, as in the preceding example, this is the seldom-used RAID-3 configuration; and when instead parity bits themselves are striped across drives, this is the more commonly used RAID-5 configuration. The biggest advantage to RAID-3 and RAID-5 systems are that they provide data redundancy without such a high overhead in terms of additional drives needed for the redundancy. With RAID-1, 50% of the drives are devoted to redundancy, whereas with a four-drive RAID-5 system, only 25% are devoted to redundancy. With larger arrays, the proportion devoted to redundancy is even smaller (e.g., 10% in a 10-drive RAID-5 array).

Finally, many drive arrays also allow for the "just a bunch of disks" (JBOD) option. Unlike the RAID options that require drives to be the same size, the JBOD option just combines any size drives you have, and the resultant single storage drive is the size of the sum of the drives you combine. This option provides no drive efficiency or data redundancy advantages, but it does use all available drive space. And a big disadvantage, like that of RAID-0, is that if any drive fails, all data, including the data on the remaining good drive(s), are useless.

References

Andreassi, J. L. (2000). *Psychophysiology: Human behavior and physiological response* (4th ed.). Mahwah, NJ: Erlbaum.

Bradley, M. M., & Lang, P. J. (1999). International Affective Digitized Sounds (IADS): Stimuli, instruction manual and affective ratings (Tech. Rep. No. B-2). Gainesville, FL: University of Florida, Center for Research in Psychophysiology.

Cacioppo, J. T., Petty, R. E., Losch, M. E., & Kim, H. S. (1986). Electromyographic activity over facial muscle regions can differentiate valence and intensity of affective reactions. *Journal of Personality and Social Psychology, 50,* 260–268.

Cacioppo, J. T., Tassinary, L. G., & Berntson, G. G. (2000). *Handbook of psychophysiology* (2nd ed.). Cambridge, UK: Cambridge University Press.

Chambers, A. S., & Allen, J. J. (2002). Vagal tone as an indicator of treatment response in major depression. *Psychophysiology, 39*(6), 861–864.

Coan, J. A., & Allen, J. J. B. (2004). Frontal EEG asymmetry as a moderator and mediator of emotion. *Biological Psychology, 67,* 7–50.

Coles, M. G. H., Donchin, E., & Porges, S. W. (1986). *Psychophysiology: Systems, processes, and applications.* New York: Guilford Press.

Curtin, J., Lang, A., Patrick, C., & Stritzke, W. (1998). Alcohol and fear-potentiated startle: The role of competing cognitive demands in the stress-reducing effects of intoxication. *Journal of Abnormal Psychology, 107,* 547–557.

Curtin, J. J., Patrick, C. J., Lang, A. R., Cacioppo, J. T., &. Birbaumer, N. (2001). Alcohol affects emotion through cognition. *Psychological Science, 12,* 527–531.

Drummond, P. D., & Mirco, N. (2004). Staring at one side of the face increases blood flow on that side of the face. *Psychophysiology, 41*(2), 281–287.

Forster, K. I., & Forster, J. C. (2003). DMDX: A Windows display program with millisecond accuracy. *Behavior Research Methods, Instruments, and Computers, 35,* 116–124.

Gehring, W. J., Goss, B., Coles, M. G., Meyer, D. E., & Donchin, E. (1993). A neural system for error detection and compensation. *Psychological Science, 4,* 385–390.

Greene, W. A., Turetsky, B., & Kohler, C. (2000). General laboratory safety. In J. T. Cacioppo, L. G. Tassinary, & G. G. Berntson (Eds.), *Handbook of psychophysiology* (2nd ed., pp. 951–977). Cambridge, UK: Cambridge University Press.

Hare, R. D. (1965). Temporal gradient of fear arousal in psychopaths. *Journal of Abnormal Psychology, 70*(6), 442–445.

Harmon-Jones, E., Sigelman, J. D., Bohlig, A., & Harmon-Jones, C. (2003). Anger, coping, and frontal cortical activity: The effect of coping potential on anger-induced left frontal activity. *Cognition and Emotion, 17,* 1–24.

Hugdahl, K. (1996). *Psychophysiology: The mind-body perspective.* Cambridge, MA: Harvard University Press.

Kline, J. P., Blackhart, G. C., & Joiner, T. E. (2002). Sex, lie scales, and electrode caps: An interpersonal context for defensiveness and anterior electroencephalographic asymmetry. *Personality and Individual Differences, 33*(3), 459–478.

Nyquist, H. (1928). Certain topics in telegraph transmission theory. *Transactions of the American Institute of Electrical Engineers, 47,* 617–644.

Öhman, A., & Soares, J. J. (1994). "Unconscious anxiety": Phobic responses to masked stimuli. *Journal of Abnormal Psychology, 103*(2), 231–240.

Patterson, D. A., Gibson, G., & Katz, R. H. (1988). A case for redundant arrays of inexpensive disks (RAID). *Proceedings of the 1988 ACM SIGMOD International Conference on Management of Data* (pp. 109–116). New York: Association for Computing Machinery.

Putnam, L. E., Johnson, R., Jr., & Roth, W. T. (1992). Guidelines for reducing the risk of disease transmission in the psychophysiology laboratory. *Psychophysiology, 29*(2), 127–141.

Ryan, C. W. (1986). *Basic electricity: A self-teaching guide* (2nd ed.). New York: Wiley.

Schupp, H. T., Cuthbert, B. N., Bradley, M. M., Cacioppo, J. T., Ito, T., & Lang, P. J. (2000). Affective picture processing: The late positive potential is modulated by motivational relevance. *Psychophysiology, 37*(2), 257–261.

Shalev, A. Y., Sahar, T., Freedman, S., Peri, T., Glick, N., Brandes, D., et al. (1998). A prospective study of heart rate response following trauma and the subsequent development of posttraumatic stress disorder. *Archives of General Psychiatry, 55*(6), 553–559.

Stern, R. M., Ray, W. J., & Quigley, K. S. (2000). *Psychophysiological recording* (2nd ed.). Cambridge, UK: Oxford University Press.

Verona, E., & Curtin, J. (2006). Gender differences in the negative affective priming of aggressive behavior. *Emotion, 6,* 115–124.

Vrana, S. R., Spence, E. L., & Lang, P. J. (1988). The startle probe response: A new measure of emotion? *Journal of Abnormal Psychology, 97*(4), 487–491.

Ralph Adolphs

Investigating Human Emotion With Lesions and Intracranial Recording

It is somewhat ironic that the classic and dramatic studies of emotion in the early twentieth century all used methods that are rarely or never applicable in humans. Kluver and Bucy, and before them Bard, Cannon, and others, gained insights into the regions of the brain important for the elicitation of emotional responses by experimentally introducing large lesions in animals. Olds, Milner, and Hess, in their classic studies, used another invasive method, direct electrical stimulation of the brain, to evoke emotional behaviors. And a third, more modern, common method for investigating emotion in animals is intracranial recordings. All of these methods are commonly used in animals; the reasons none is in common usage for the investigation of human emotions is obvious. Instead, modern cognitive neuroscience approaches to investigating emotion draw on a different set of techniques, notably functional imaging and scalp-evoked potential studies, among others.

One might thus have thought that modern imaging methods would simply replace wholesale the older invasive approaches. However, this is not the case, for two reasons: first, it in fact turns out to be entirely feasible to apply the lesion method in humans, provided that the lesions themselves are not an experimental variable but accidents of nature; and second, the lesion method is absolutely essential in forging a causal link between the function of specific neural structures and emotion, a link that no other method can provide. Similar observations apply to intracranial recording and stimulation—although these are indeed much more rarely carried out in humans, they can be done, and the informa-

tion they yield is an extremely important complement to that obtained with other methods.

An important feature of lesions and electrical stimulation is that they can provide a causal role for specific structures. This point has recently been emphasized even by those who have championed functional imaging techniques. In an important review article, Price and Friston (2002) explain why data from functional imaging have basic logical limitations in their interpretation. These limitations are independent of other difficulties in the design and technical execution of the studies and reflect the fact that data from functional imaging are always correlative and that neural systems feature an often high degree of degeneracy. The degeneracy of neural systems refers to a one-to-many mapping of global function to neural tissue. Cognitive processes, including those involved in emotions, are distributed across several spatially distinct neural regions that interact in order to implement the function in question. Moreover, the contribution of each component to such a distributed system is not fixed but depends on its interactions with other components of the system, on dynamic reorganization that is driven by task demands or executive influences, or on long-term reorganization due to pathology or, indeed, environmental factors in healthy brains. All of this conspires to make the data that functional imaging studies yield overinclusive: They reveal more than we want, and in so doing make it difficult to assign functions to single structures and to constrain information-processing models.

The Lesion Method in Humans

The basic approach of the lesion method is straightforward enough: If a specific, focal region of the brain is necessary in order for the brain to implement a specific cognitive function, then selective damage to that region of the brain should result in a selective impairment of that function (Figure 25.1). However, this logic depends on assumptions regarding the nature of the lesion and the nature of the cognitive process.

A caveat is that lesions in humans, unlike what experimentalists strive for with, say, ibotenic acid lesions in animals, are not selective for cell bodies but also involve axons. Thus, in addition to thinking about the processing deficits that might result from damage to neurons within a structure, we need to think about the deficits that might result from disconnection between structures. And finally, as already mentioned, plasticity and reorganization must be taken into account. There are several ways of approaching this topic, but for purposes of stability and to minimize distal effects of the lesion, research often focuses on chronic nonprogressive lesions.

Although a consideration of all the aforementioned issues is important, it is no less critical to have the participants in the first place. Obtaining some participant with damage to the brain is not difficult; obtaining a number of them who are neuroanatomically and neuropsychologically well characterized, stable, chronic, and willing to return for research participation over what often turns out to be years of testing is another matter. One of the best examples of such a resource can be found at the University of Iowa, where the Department of Neurology's Cognitive Neuroscience Registry includes several thousand such research participants (Damasio & Damasio, 1989). In the following sections I review some of the different approaches to using the lesion method and summarize examples of what it has told us about the neuroscience of emotion, drawing on data from the registry at the University of Iowa.

The infrastructure of the Iowa registry is important enough to warrant further comment. There are two key components to it: one neuroanatomical, the other neuropsychological. Neuroanatomically, it is, of course, most important to have precise information about the extent of the lesion; these data are obtained from magnetic resonance (MR) scans of the participants' brains. As described in more detail later, this anatomical information can be translated into a common format, permitting direct calculations on multiple participants' lesions (e.g., an examination of their shared lesion overlap; (Damasio & Frank, 1992). Neuropsychological information is provided from a neuropsychology clinic (Tranel, 1996). This information is also essential and is often incomplete in many published lesion studies because of its time-intensive nature. Ideally, one would like to have all possible background information that could have an effect on the participant's performance of an experimental task. Some typical categories are general intelligence, attention, alertness, visual acuity and perception, ability to understand and speak English, memory, planning, motivation, affect, and personality. This information can be used in one of two ways: A participant with a lesion and a given neuropsychological profile can be matched with a control participant who has a similar profile but no lesion (or a lesion in a different location), or the neuropsychological information can be used as covariates in statistical analyses involving larger numbers of participants. In broad scope, we are interested in partitioning the sources of variance that can contribute to performance on an experimental task: Some of the variance on the task can be due to variables such as age, gender, IQ, perception, memory, personality, and so on, and some can be attributed to the location of the brain lesion. We want to isolate the effect of the latter from all the possible influences that might impinge on it from the other factors.

Single-Case Lesion Studies

The classical neuropsychological approach has been to study rare and informative single lesion cases. Famous examples are Broca's patient Tan, Phineas Gage, and H.M., all of whom have contributed profoundly to modern cognitive neuroscience (to our understanding of language, social behavior, and declarative memory, respectively). The approach has been informative also in emotion research, as described in detail later: Focal damage to the prefrontal cortex or to the amygdala can result in specific dissociations of emotion processing from other processes.

Two approaches can be taken by single-case studies. One is specificity in performance impairment, in the ideal case requiring a double dissociation. Such a finding need not also be anatomically specific in order to be informative. For instance, many neuropsychiatric impairments have featured dissociations that have informed models of information-processing architecture, regardless of where in the brain those processes might actually be implemented (Halligan & David, 2001; Langdon & Coltheart, 2000). In the case of a double dissociation, a comparison between two participants is required. One shows worse performance on Task A than on Task B, the other worse performance on Task B than on Task A. Provided that the effect is so large that it cannot be attributed just to normal variation in task performance, we can conclude that the processes engaged by the two tasks are functionally independent. Often, this functional independence is reflected in some degree of anatomical independence, but it need not be.

The second case-study approach is neuroanatomical: Following focal damage to one particular brain region, the participant shows a particular performance impairment. This implicates the damaged structure in the processes normally essential for performing the task. In this case, like the first one, we also want some comparison with other participants so that we can exclude the possibility that the impairment might result from nonspecific brain damage anywhere. These

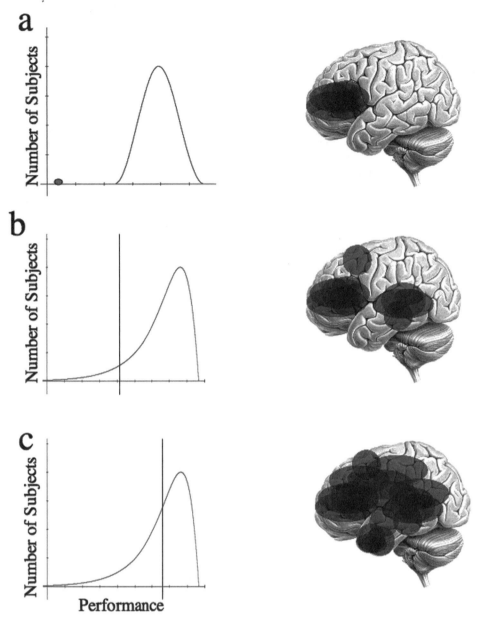

Figure 25.1. The Lesion Method. The goal of the approach is to relate covariances between brain damage and task performance: How does the location of a lesion covary with performance? The classical single-case approach is illustrated in (a): a single participant with a focal lesion (red) performs far outside the normal performance distribution (blue curve). To the extent that the lesion involves a particular brain structure and results in impairment on only a particular task, we can infer that the lesioned structure is normally involved in executing the task.

The group approach is a logical extension of the single-case approach. The performance distribution of a group of participants with brain damage differs in two respects from the normal performance distribution: Its mean is lower, and its variance is larger due to a skew toward impaired performance. One way of using this distribution is simply to compare it with that from normal participants, comparing their means. Another way is to capitalize on the variance within the distribution of participants with brain damage and ask how task performance is associated with low or high performance.

Some examples of how partitioning of the variance in the performances of participants with brain damage might be reflected in their neuroanatomy are shown in the figure. (a) Single cases with focal damage to left frontal operculum would show a severe impairment on certain language tasks and inform hypotheses about the neuroanatomy of Broca's aphasia. (b) Performance on language tests at a very low level would yield a specific set of neural structures that constitute a system in the left hemisphere for processing language. (c) Increasing the performance threshold for analysis would include many more participants, yielding the conclusion that the left hemisphere is involved in processing language. See color insert.

are comparison participants who have brain damage that spares the structure of interest.

The first approach gives us specificity with respect to the processes; the second, specificity with respect to the anatomy. In general, we want both, and so most studies use both brain-damaged comparison participants (giving anatomical specificity to the reported impairment) and comparison tasks (giving process specificity to the reported impairment). A good example in the domain of emotion are the studies of Patient S.M., described in more detail later. This participant has selective damage to one structure, the amygdala, and a selective impairment in her ability to recognize one emotion, fear. Other brain-damaged participants with lesions elsewhere do not show this same impairment. The conclusion that has been drawn from this one patient (and both corroborated and extended by additional studies) is that the amygdala is necessary to recognize fear. (However, there are additional complexities to the story, gathered from recent data, that make this finding somewhat less specific than it seems.)

Group Lesion Studies

Studies of groups of participants with brain lesions can proceed similarly, by defining the groups in one of two ways: by lesion location or by task performance. The former is the most common. In this approach, it is typically the case that there are some prior data, perhaps from single-case studies or from functional imaging studies, that suggest a neuroanatomical hypothesis to the effect that a particular region of interest is important for performing normally on a particular task. The hypothesis is then tested by comparing the performances given by a group of participants whose lesions include the region of interest and by a group of participants whose lesions do not. The prediction is that the group whose lesions include the hypothesized structure will perform at a lower level on the task in question than the group whose lesions spare that structure (Damasio & Damasio, 1989).

An alternative approach is to define the participant groups not by lesion location but by task performance (see Figure 25.1b,c). This approach has the potential to reveal new regions of the brain as important to task performance, regions that one might not have hypothesized a priori. Thus one could simply perform a median-split analysis: Put all participants with low performance scores in one group and all participants with high performance scores in a second group. The groups could also be defined in relation to normal performance, as "impaired" or "normal" performing. In either case, the aim is to investigate possible covariation between lesion location and task performance.

There are multiple ways to analyze and quantify such possible covariation. One way is as just noted: to separate participants on the basis of their performance scores and to examine where their lesions fall. This can be done, for

example, by summing all the lesions of participants with low performance scores, separately summing all the lesions of participants with high performance scores, and examining the differences in these lesion overlap sets (Damasio, Tranel, Grabowski, Adolphs, & Damasio, 2004; Adolphs, Damasio, Tranel, Cooper, & Damasio, 2000). A second way is to do calculations that are voxel-based rather than lesion-based. One can thus take a particular voxel and ask how many lesions included it in participants who had impaired scores and how many in participants who had normal scores. If there is a systematic difference, such that, for example, many more impaired participants' lesions included that voxel than normal participants' lesions did, a statistical test could show that the voxel is differentially associated with impaired rather than normal performance (Adolphs et al., 2000). Continuous calculations on performance data are also possible. Thus we could simply compute the mean performance score of all participants whose lesions included a given voxel, or we could calculate a *t*-statistic describing the difference between the mean performances of those participants whose lesions included the voxel and those whose lesions did not (Bates et al., 2003). Such mean scores or *t*-statistics can then be assigned to the voxel, and a voxel-based map of mean overall performance, or of *t*-values, can be generated across all those brain regions sampled in the experiment.

All these approaches are limited by the sampling density and homogeneity of the underlying participant groups. If no participant has a lesion in a certain brain region, nothing can be concluded about that brain region. Even within those regions sampled, some regions will be sampled much more densely (contain lesions much more frequently) than others, resulting in an uneven statistical power distribution over different brain regions. Another problem is that there will be individual differences in the precise neuroanatomical locations of specific functional regions. This is also a problem in functional neuroimaging studies that average over subjects on the basis of neuroanatomical coregistration.

At present, there is no single accepted way of analyzing group lesion data, and, indeed, there is no clearly best way to do so. The reason is that the raw data available are complex: they are never based on single voxels but on lesions containing thousands of voxels; they depend on the volume of the lesion and its precise shape and boundaries; they depend on the extent to which grey or white matter is involved; and they fundamentally violate assumptions of statistical comparisons in that the participants can never be randomly assigned to one condition ("lesion") or another ("control"). These considerations do not make the lesion method impossible, but they prevent a rigorous statistical treatment, such as the voxel-based statistic maps that can be derived from functional imaging data. Ultimately, summary figures or statistics from group lesion data must always be compared with the individual cases from which the group was derived.

Lesion Studies of Human Emotion

General Methodological Considerations

Before I review some of the findings, I think it is useful to outline some guidelines for studying specific aspects of emotion in lesion patients. These are made most clear in regard to emotion perception, but similar comments apply to investigations of emotion psychophysiology or emotional experience in participants with brain damage.

1. *Control tasks should be included to control for nonspecific impairments.* Such nonspecific impairments would include general perceptual impairments not restricted to emotion perception or general impairments in behavioral performance of a task for some other reason (e.g., failure to comprehend certain rating scales). For instance, when using visual stimuli such as facial expressions as target stimuli, it is important to obtain a measure of basic visual perception. There are several such tasks: the Judgment of Line Orientation and the Facial Recognition Task are in common use (Benton, Hamsher, Varney, & Spreen, 1983). A measure of visual acuity is also standard. Ideally, however, the experiment can be designed so that the control tasks are precisely matched to the target tasks with respect to the perceptual properties of the stimuli, as well as the behavioral demands. For example, some stimuli of the same category (or, in fact, exactly the same stimuli) as the target emotional stimuli might be used, but questions may be asked about them that do not require recognition of the emotion (such as same-different judgments or recognition of other information, such as gender of the face). Examples are given later from our studies with patient S.M.

2. *Target tasks should avoid floor and ceiling effects.* This issue should be obvious, but it is especially important to keep in mind when testing a variety of participants with brain damage, some of whose performances may be very close to normal, and others whose performances may be at chance. In order to have sufficient sensitivity to distinguish patients who perform close to either end of the scale, the task should be designed so as to avoid floor or ceiling effects. In some of our studies, for instance, we have used morphed facial expressions that show a range of emotional intensity and can construct a performance curve with such graded stimuli.

3. *The errors produced by participants should be analyzed in further detail.* Some studies of emotion in participants with brain damage have reported impairments without analyzing the pattern of errors. This is unfortunate, because the pattern of errors made is in fact quite important—it can tell us whether the participant simply makes more of the same errors that normal participants make or whether the errors are different. A common finding on some tasks of emotion recognition, for instance, has been that participants tend to mistake fear for surprise and disgust for anger. If surprise and anger are eliminated as possible responses on a task, performance can be dramatically improved (Adolphs, 2002). Care-

ful design of the response options available to participants, and a detailed analysis of the pattern of errors they might produce, can be extremely informative in telling us about the nature of the impairment.

Both single-case and group lesion approaches have yielded important new data for the cognitive neuroscience of emotion. Across the literature, three brain regions have yielded the most consistent results, and these are reviewed in the following sections: the orbitofrontal cortex, the amygdala, and cortex in the right hemisphere (see Figure 25.2).

Orbitofrontal Cortex

The studies of orbitofrontal cortex began with a famous historical case, that of Phineas Gage (Damasio, 1994). Gage, a foreman working on the railway in Vermont, sustained a traumatic brain injury due to a tamping iron that exploded through his head. It was amazing that he survived the accident at all, but no less amazing were the specific cognitive changes that ensued. His basic intellect appeared unchanged, but long-term behaviors and dispositions relating to emotional responses to his environment and to other people had been dramatically altered. Whereas before the accident he was a respected, well-liked, courteous, and amiable person, after the accident he became uncaring, rude, and profane and exhibited a gross disregard both for his own personal future and for other people. What had changed were emotional processes that contribute substantially to our concept of a personality.

Gage's case was notably resurrected in recent times by a further analysis of his likely brain lesion (Figure 25.3a) and by supplementation with data from modern patients who had sustained similar damage—typically because of tumor resections of the frontal lobe or aneurysms of the anterior communicating artery (Damasio, 1994). These modern case studies permitted more controlled experimental investigations of the impairment and eventually accrued to comprise a group of participants who shared damage to ventral and medial sectors of the prefrontal cortex, all of whom exhibited a remarkably similar constellation of findings (Figure 25.3b). They failed to show emotional psychophysiological responses to stimuli (Damasio, Tranel, & Damasio, 1990), they failed to show such responses in anticipation of future punishment (Bechara, Tranel, Damasio, & Damasio, 1996), and they failed to guide their behavior so as to avoid future punishment (or seek future reward; Bechara, Damasio, Damasio, & Anderson, 1994). Their behavior was driven by what was immediately present and did not take into account planning for the future. One of the major current theories of the function of this region of prefrontal cortex, Antonio Damasio's somatic marker hypothesis, draws on these findings and proposes that they are causally related (Damasio, 1994). In real life, all these patients fail to maintain lasting social relationships or jobs, a reflection of their dysfunction in this particular mechanism.

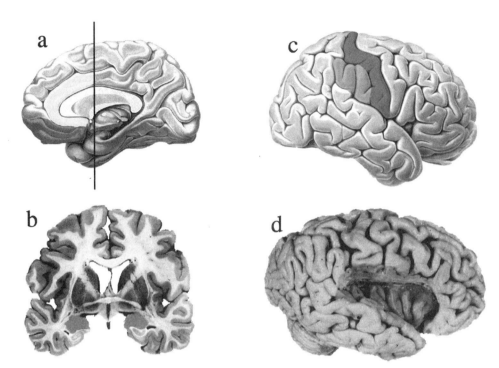

Figure 25.2. Some brain regions important for processing emotion. Shown are the regions discussed in this chapter, color coded onto views of a human brain. See color insert.

As the investigations of orbitofrontal cortex have produced a sufficient number of cases, they have permitted some further specification of the neuroanatomy and the processes. For instance, dissociations have been found between damage in dorsolateral and ventromedial prefrontal cortex in relation to working memory and decision making, respectively (Bechara, Damasio, Tranel, & Anderson, 1998). Damage to the right prefrontal cortex has been shown to result in more severe impairments in emotion processing than damage to left (Tranel, Bechara, & Denburg, 2002). A recent study has shown that this depends further on gender: whereas right prefrontal lesions impair emotions more than left in men, left prefrontal lesions impair emotions more than right in women (Tranel, Damasio, Denburg, & Bechara, 2005). And the impairments following damage to ventromedial prefrontal cortex have been shown to be distinct from any impairment in IQ, language function, or perception. Further parcellations of the orbitofrontal cortex have come from functional imaging studies, suggesting that reward and punishment may draw differentially on medial and lateral sectors, and that, perhaps, complex reinforcing stimuli activate regions that are more anterior than those activated by more biologically basic reinforcing stimuli (Kringelbach, 2005).

The previously summarized findings are consistent with what is known about the connectivity of this region of the brain. Medial and ventral sectors of prefrontal cortex have been shown to constitute a densely interconnected network that obtains polysensory information, taste and smell information, and visceral information and that projects to autonomic control structures, such as the hypothalamus and periaqueductal grey (Öngür & Price, 2000). They are consistent also with other data from functional imaging studies in humans, as well as from lesion and electrophysiological studies in animals. Given this backdrop—information about the circuitry in which the orbitofrontal cortex is embedded and information from other techniques about its role in emotional information processing—the data from lesion studies have supported specific hypotheses.

The interpretation of lesion data can take place only in the context of a particular information-processing model and is consequently limited by the processes that are postulated to exist in the first place. It should thus come as no surprise that not everyone interprets the data the same way. In particular, there is a tension between data derived from animal studies and those from humans: The animal data clearly implicate orbitofrontal cortex in basic stimulus-reward associations (Rolls, 1999); the human data point to more complex social functions (Damasio, 1994; Wood & Grafman, 2003). Perhaps these are related (typically, people tend to try to reduce the latter to the former), perhaps they reflect differences in the kinds of tasks used, and perhaps they reflect genuine phylogenetic differences; at this stage we simply do not know. However, it does seem to be the case that, although the human lesion data are not inconsistent with the idea that orbitofrontal cortex stores reward associations, this idea also cannot explain all the findings in humans. To some extent, the findings from lesion studies have indeed hinted that our initial conceptions of the processes will need to be revised, an issue I return to at the end of the chapter and that is more perspicuous in regard to a second well-studied structure in emotion: the amygdala.

The Amygdala

The amygdala plays a complex and ubiquitous role in emotion and in social behavior (Aggleton, 2000). The mechanisms that underlie this role are best understood in animals, especially rodents, in which they have been shown to draw on the amygdala's ability to modulate a large variety of response components and cognitive processes based on the emotional significance of the stimulus. Thus the amygdala

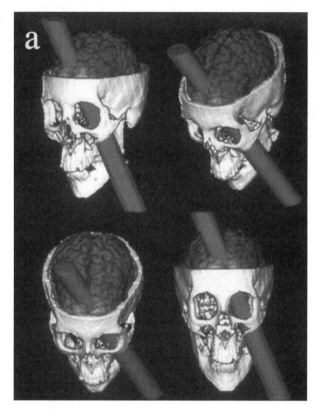

Figure 25.3. Lesions of the human orbitofrontal cortex. (a) The case of Phineas Gage, as reconstructed by Hanna Damasio. The path of the tamping iron through Gage's brain was reconstructed from the known dimensions of the iron, from measurements of Gage's skull and the hole within it, and from descriptions of the accident. From Damasio, Grabowski, Frank, Galaburda, and Damasio, 1994. (b) Overlap representation of lesions from patients with bifrontal tumor resections who all share a behavioral profile similar to that reported for Gage. In general, their lesions are more restricted than Gage's, but in all cases they include ventral and medial regions of the prefrontal cortex. Damage to these regions leads to a constellation of impaired emotional response, lack of remorse, poor planning for the future, and impulsive behavior, dubbed "acquired sociopathy." From Bechara, Tranel, and Damasio, 2002. See color insert.

modulates attention, memory, and decision making, as well as many components of an emotional response (including behavioral, autonomic, and endocrine components). Specific nuclei within the amygdala are involved in certain subsets of these processes, as well as in processing certain classes of stimuli, further complicating the picture. Shared in common by all these diverse mechanisms is the ability to associate stimuli with their emotional/social value. The representations required for such an association draw on visual neocortex (for representing the stimuli) and on brainstem and hypothalamic nuclei (for representing and implementing the emotional value).

The amygdala's functional complexity is mirrored in its vast array of connections with other brain structures: High-level sensory neocortices provide information about the stimulus, primarily to the lateral nucleus, and the amygdala projects back to much of the neocortex, as well as to the basal forebrain, hippocampus, and basal ganglia to modulate cognition and to hypothalamic and brainstem nuclei to modulate emotional response (Amaral, Price, Pitkanen, & Carmichael, 1992). It is precisely because of the complexity of the various processes in which the amygdala participates that it can effect a concerted change in cognition and behavior that plays out as an organized emotional reaction.

Several recent lesion studies reported rare patients with bilateral damage to the amygdala. Most of the impairments found were not seen in the more common unilateral cases, typically patients with neurosurgical temporal lobectomy for the treatment of epilepsy. The patients with bilateral amygdala damage fell into three classes: most common (albeit still rare) were those who had complete bilateral amygdala damage, as well as damage to surrounding structures from encephalitis. Yet more rare were those with bilateral but incomplete damage relatively restricted to the amygdala. A single case to date, participant S.M., has complete bilateral damage that is relatively restricted to the amygdala (Adolphs, Tranel, Damasio, & Damasio, 1994; Figure 25.4).

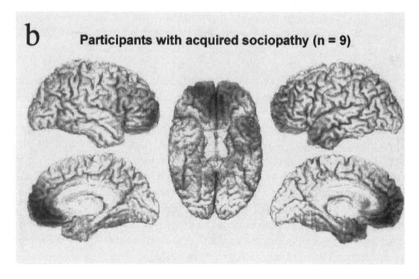

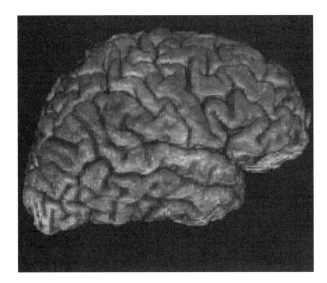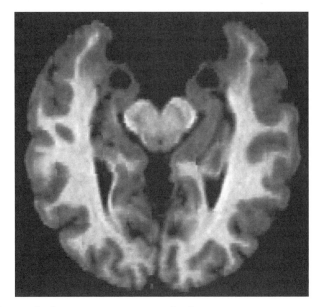

Figure 25.4. Lesions of the human amygdala. The panels show magnetic resonance (MR) scans of the brain of participant S.M., who has selective and complete bilateral amygdala damage due to Urbach-Wiethe disease. *Left*: Three-dimensional reconstruction of S.M.'s brain from serial MR images. *Right*: Coronal plane through S.M.'s brain showing the lesioned amygdala, most clearly visible as the two black holes near the top. From Adolphs, 2002.

S.M. also shows the most selective constellation of impairments. We found that she has a specific deficit in the ability to make certain judgments about faces, despite normal general intelligence, memory, perception, and language. Her impairment has been best studied in regard to judging basic emotions from facial expressions, for which she shows a very selective impairment in the ability to judge the intensity of fear and of some instances of the related emotions of surprise and anger. Like patients with damage to the orbitofrontal cortex, S.M.'s impairment translates into impaired social judgment: Not only is she impaired in judging fear from faces, but she also cannot judge whether someone looks untrustworthy or unapproachable. The findings from this valuable single case have been corroborated by other patients with similar lesions (Adolphs et al., 1999) and by functional imaging studies (Morris et al., 1996).

In establishing the specificity of S.M.'s impairment, it was important to consider control tasks. As noted earlier, basic visuoperception needs to be established as normal, and a variety of established tasks are available. Even better are control tasks that actually use the same stimuli as the target tasks. In our experiments we thus used the same emotional facial expressions that S.M. is impaired in rating. For the control tasks, we asked questions that did not involve rating the emotion. A basic visuoperceptual task asked S.M. to discriminate faint shades of emotions presented side by side; we did this study using morphed facial expressions and obtained sensitivity curves for each participant. S.M.'s threshold of morphing, at which she was just able to discriminate emotions in faces, was entirely normal for all emotions. In an-

other task, we showed her exactly the same stimuli as used in the emotion rating task but asked her to rate the degree of masculinity or femininity of the face—this task uses the same stimuli, the same measure (ratings), but requires judgments of gender, not of emotion. Again, she performed entirely normally on this task. If at all possible, such designs, in which different questions are asked about the same stimuli, provide the most powerful controls.

The studies of other patients with bilateral amygdala damage, as well as further considerations of data from S.M. alone, raised important additional questions. One puzzling finding was that some patients who had complete, nonselective bilateral amygdala damage nonetheless appeared to perform normally on the same tasks that S.M. failed. This was puzzling because the lesions of these other patients included all of the lesions present in S.M. along with additional tissue. Several explanations could be entertained: First, it is important to note that S.M.'s lesion was likely acquired developmentally, likely early in life, whereas the lesions of the other participants were acquired in adulthood. Second, it is certainly possible to construct a model whereby additional brain damage actually improves performance due to a primary lesion (Kapur, 1996). Third, the patients differed in other respects, so that performance differences might be due to other neuropsychological or demographic differences. In the end, although any of these possibilities might still be important, it turned out that (1) participants perform somewhat variably from trial to trial and (2) when data were reanalyzed, general impairments in emotion recognition were found to be present in all the participants, although they did not appear to show up in exactly the same way (Schmolck & Squire, 2001). The picture that emerged should not have been unexpected, as it is the standard picture for thinking about how risk factors contribute to pathology: Lesions of the amygdala interfere with certain basic emotional processes and hence compromise recognition of fear from faces. But this effect interacts with damage to any other parts of the brain, with age of acquisition of the lesion, with background neuropsychology and personality of the participant, and, indeed, with the particular context and task used to assess emotion recognition.

These data have highlighted the sophistication required to interpret lesion data, certainly when they concern higher cognitive functions. It is hardly ever the case that damage to a single structure completely and neatly abolishes a cognitive process. That would indeed be phrenological. Not only will a cognitive process be implemented by a plastic, interacting network of structures, but the same process also may be implemented somewhat differently in different participants on different testing occasions and may be recruited differentially by different tasks (Adolphs, 2002).

A curious tension is also generated by in-depth explorations of lesion data. On the one hand, we would like to achieve something very similar in spirit to the cognitive subtraction that functional imaging aims to achieve: We want to isolate a cognitive process by clever design of an experimental task and associated control tasks. That is certainly a good goal, but it presumes that the process that the experimenter has in mind is in some sense the right way to carve up the mind in the first place. One could start in reverse and ask: What does the amygdala (for instance) do? The answer is unlikely to map cleanly onto any of our preconceived processes. We could take this as evidence that the cognitive processes we postulate do not map one-to-one onto brain structures. Or we could revise the processes we postulate so that they do so map. The latter approach might push us toward constructing an information-processing model of the mind that is constrained not just by our interpretation of task performances but also by the data from cognitive neuroscience (Adolphs, 2003).

One upshot of these considerations is that cognitive neuroscience need not be entirely hypothesis driven. It can also be data driven, at least to some extent (namely, to the extent required to reveal to us new hypotheses that we might not have conceived a priori). Such data-driven approaches have been in use for some time, and they typically require large amounts of data. The next set of lesion studies highlights one such approach.

Right Somatosensory Cortices

Despite the consensus that the right hemisphere plays a key role in emotion processing, there has been debate regarding the details. Two main theories have been put forth: that the right hemisphere participates in processing all emotions (the *right-hemisphere hypothesis*) or that the right hemisphere is relatively specialized to process negative emotions, whereas the left hemisphere is relatively specialized to process positive emotions (the *valence hypothesis*; see Borod et al., 1998; Canli, 1999). Some modifications propose that the valence hypothesis may indeed hold for the experience and perhaps the expression of emotions but that the perception of emotion is better described according to the right-hemisphere hypothesis. Given, then, the right hemisphere's strong involvement in emotion perception, recognition, and judgment, a remaining open question has been neuroanatomical: Just which regions of the right hemisphere are important here? Most stroke patients with right-hemisphere damage have large lesions that encompass several cortical regions, as well as white matter and subcortical structures, and most studies have failed to find anatomical specificity.

We pursued this question using groups of patients with lesions in the right hemisphere. In two studies, the overlaps of lesions of participants were analyzed on the basis of their performance in recognizing emotion from facial expressions (Adolphs et al., 2000; Adolphs, Damasio, Tranel, & Damasio, 1996); in a third, the analysis was done on the basis of performance in recognizing emotion from prosody (Adolphs, Tranel, & Damasio, 2002). Two ingredients that distinguished these studies were the relatively large sample sizes of participants with lesions and the exploration of lesion-performance covariances in the absence of a prior neuroanatomical hypothesis.

In one study, we tested 108 participants with focal lesions (Adolphs et al., 2000). All 108 lesions were mapped onto a single normal reference brain so that the lesions could be directly compared and lesion-density-overlap images could be constructed. When we examined the participants who had the lowest performance scores on each emotion, regardless of absolute performance, a consistent pattern emerged for all emotions: Lesions in the right ventral parietal cortex were systematically and significantly associated with impaired recognition of emotion (see Figure 25.5). The sites within which lesions systematically resulted in impaired emotion recognition focused on ventral S-I and S-II, with a lesser involvement in insula and anterior supramarginal gyrus. Initially, the finding came as a surprise: After all, the task involved recognition of the emotion shown in a visual stimulus, yet lesions of somatosensory cortex were associated with impairment on the task. One interpretation of the findings has been as support for a recent theory of how we come to know the emotions of other people: We construct central images of the body state that would be associated with the visually observed emotion; that is, we imagine how the other person would feel. Just as the brain recruits visual cortex both during visual perception and during visual imagery, it recruits somatosensory cortex both during perception of one's own body state and during imagining the feelings of someone else. Together with the aforementioned findings on the amygdala and orbitofrontal cortex, all these data from lesion studies

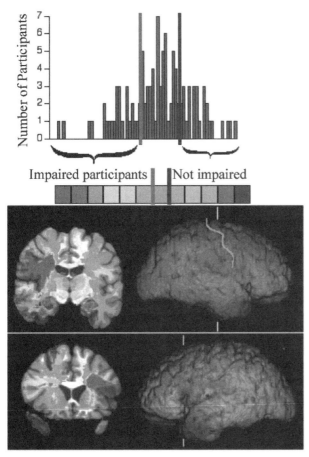

Figure 25.5. The right somatosensory cortex is necessary to judge emotions. A group lesion analysis was conducted on 108 participants with focal brain lesions, whose performance histogram is shown at the top. Color was used to encode their lesion overlaps, dependent on what partition of the performance distribution they fell in (scale). At the bottom, the brain cuts and 3-D views show superimposed overlaps of the lesions of all participants, encoded by color according to their density and performance in recognizing emotion from faces. The red regions identify locations at which a large number of lesions were associated with impaired emotion recognition. These were in right somatosensory cortex (top images) and in left frontal operculum (bottom images). From Adolphs, 2002. See color insert.

have informed a model of how we construct social knowledge about other people (Adolphs, 2002).

Intracranial Recordings and Stimulation in Humans

As with the lesion method, the opportunity to record and/or stimulate intracranially depends on an existing clinical infrastructure. At the University of Iowa, the Department of Neurosurgery, led by Dr. Matthew Howard, provides such a resource. Patients who are undergoing intracranial clinical monitoring for epilepsy can elect to participate in research at

the same time they are being monitored. Because the clinical protocol already involves the implantation of electrodes, our research studies do not introduce an additional risk beyond that due to simply presenting stimuli for research purposes.

As with functional imaging data, intracranial recordings can show only correlations between neuronal activity and task performance. In this respect, they differ fundamentally from data obtained with the lesion method. However, they are special in terms of the spatiotemporal resolution: We can record activity from single neurons (as well as from field potentials that represent hundreds of neurons) and can do so with millisecond resolution (Engel, Moll, Fried, & Ojemann, 2005). This information has placed further constraints on models of information-processing architectures.

We have recorded from each of the structures listed previously, as well as others, and have carried out electrical stimulation studies in them as well. A detailed description of neurophysiological recording techniques is beyond the scope of this chapter, but I sketch here some of the approaches we have taken and some of the data obtained (for further details, see Adolphs, Kawasaki, Oya, Howard, in press).

Three distinct types of recordings are possible: single-unit recordings from high-impedance contacts on depth electrodes (Figure 25.6a); field potential recordings from the same electrodes, either from high- or low-impedance contacts; and electrocortigram recordings, which are field potentials obtained from a grid (typically, 8 x 8 cm) of contacts that lie on the surface of the cortex (Figure 25.6b). The design of the depth electrodes varies between different labs, whereas the surface grids are more standard. In our research, we have used a hybrid clinical-depth electrode, which contains along its shaft multiple high- and low-impedance contacts for research and clinical recordings, respectively (Figure 25.6a; Howard et al., 1996).

In one study, we recorded single-neuron activity from human orbitofrontal cortex, a study carried out by Hiroto Kawasaki in our group (Kawasaki et al., 2001). The participant was shown pictures that varied in their emotional content, the well-known International Affective Picture System (Lang, Oehman, & Vaitl, 1988), while we recorded from an electrode in the orbitofrontal cortex (Figure 25.6a). Action potentials from neurons were summed into peristimulus time histograms, as shown in Figure 25.6c, for each of three different emotion categories. The vertical line at 0 corresponds to onset of the visual stimulus, and a clear modulation of neuronal response can be seen that is selective for the aversive stimulus category. The study showed two things: first, neurons in human orbitofrontal cortex can encode information about the emotion category shown in a visual stimulus, and, second, they can do so with an extremely short latency: The initial inhibitory response began about 120 ms after stimulus onset. In the human brain, this is just barely enough time for visual information processing to reach these neurons; it is not enough time for any feedback processing. At least some important information about emotion thus can

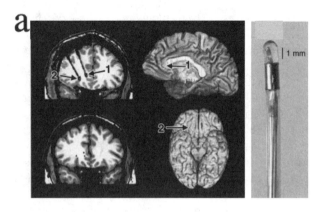

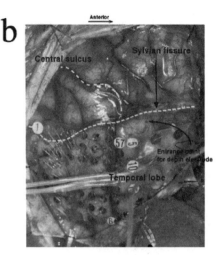

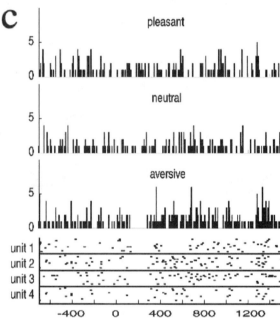

Figure 25.6. Electrophysiological recordings from intracranial electrodes. (a) MR images of a patient's brain showing location of implanted electrodes in prefrontal cortex. *Left*: At the top is an MR image with the implanted electrodes and indicated recording sites (numbers); at the bottom are the locations of those recording sites mapped onto a preimplantation scan of the patient's brain. *Right*: 3-D reconstructions of the brain with recording site locations indicated. *Inset*: micrograph of the electrodes. (b) Photograph of surface grid electrodes from which cortical field potentials can be recorded. The grid lies on the surface of cortex. (c) Single-neuron responses categorized by the emotion of the stimulus. Shown are peristimulus-time histograms (top) and individual rasters (action potentials from four neurons, bottom), in response to emotional visual pictures in three categories: pleasant, neutral, and aversive. There was a selective change in firing rate of the neurons only to aversive stimuli. The time point at zero corresponds to the onset of the visual stimuli. See color insert.

be extracted by the brain very rapidly, a mechanism that would make ecological sense for detecting potentially threatening or harmful stimuli.

Another study, carried out by Hiroyuki Oya, measured neuronal responses to the same IAPS pictures from depth electrodes within the amygdala (Oya, Kawasaki, Howard, & Adolphs, 2002). This time, the analysis used time-frequency decomposition of signals recorded from field potentials, a method that has a much better signal-to-noise ratio than do the single-neuron recordings. The data are similar to those obtained in evoked-potential studies, with a key difference in their analysis: Instead of temporally aligning all the stimulus responses and simply averaging them (as ERPs do), each stimulus response was mapped onto a time-frequency space using wavelet filtering. As in orbitofrontal cortex, we found evidence of responses in the amygdala that were rapidly able to encode information about aversive visual stimuli.

In both studies, we took care to control for possible effects of simple visual properties of the stimuli on neuronal responses, a worry similar in many respects to controlling for basic visual impairments in lesion studies. Specifically, we measured the mean luminance and luminance in different color channels and had participants rate the visual complexity of the stimuli. We wanted to avoid the possibility that emotion categories might differ systematically in terms of these basic properties. For instance, if all aversive stimuli were simply brighter than stimuli in the other emotion categories, this could explain the neuronal responses we observed. Another way in which we controlled for this possibility was to use a large variety of stimuli that were heterogeneous in all respects. For instance, the aversive category included pictures of snakes and spiders, scenes of war, and mutilations. One would be hard pressed to say what they all had in common perceptually—they were just all recognized to be aversive.

As with the design of stimuli for lesion studies of emotion perception, it is a good idea to use as large a variety of stimuli as possible.

We are now collecting data also from contacts that lie on the cortical surface (Figure 25.6b), an approach that has yielded important electrophysiological information about social information processing in the human brain (McCarthy, 1999). Current studies involve recording from multiple contacts simultaneously: for instance, from both amygdala and orbitofrontal cortex or from different regions within orbitofrontal cortex. Some of these data permit inferences about the flow of information between different brain regions. We are also undertaking intracranial recordings in some patients who have preexisting lesions. What would be the effect of the response recorded in orbitofrontal cortex, for example, if the amygdala were lesioned? By combining such approaches, we can begin to dissect the causal contributions made by individual neural structures as they participate in a distributed system.

Future Extensions

Both lesion and electrophysiological studies are now being extended in many ways, in part with technical advances, in part with conceptual advances. I list here only a few of the new directions.

Better Spatial Resolution

The preceding survey of lesion studies in human emotion brings up an important limitation of the lesion method in humans: It is macroscopic. Both orbitofrontal cortex and amygdala are highly complex, heterogeneous structures that are known to encompass many different cytoarchitectonic and functional subdivisions. For instance, the human amygdala consists of more than a dozen distinct nuclei, each of which contains multiple cell populations. At least three ways to improve on this situation within the lesion method are: detailed testing of rare participants with small, focal lesions; inclusion of participants with certain diseases that disproportionately affect certain neuronal populations; and large-group studies that examine lesion overlaps.

Within-Participant Studies

One obvious improvement in the statistical power of lesion studies is to conduct studies within the same participant, before and after lesion. This is difficult, because in those cases in which we know that a lesion will occur, a preexisting condition complicates the issue. For instance, one can study participants pre- and postneurosurgery—but the presurgery situation is already pathological, and in many cases the finding is that task performances actually improve after surgery.

Focal Transient Lesions With Intracranial Stimulation

More feasible are within-participant studies that involve a transient focal lesion by electrical microstimulation. We and others have taken this approach, but it is technically difficult, because we are limited in the location, duration, and amplitude of current that can be injected and the spread of the effect is often not very confined.

Transient Lesions With Transcranial Magnetic Stimulation

This coarser analogous approach has recently gained popularity because it can be done in normal individuals. It is also technically challenging and not without some risks, but it has tremendous potential to confirm data obtained from other methods, as well as to introduce a precise temporal dimension onto lesion data.

Developmental Studies

There is a great interest in developmental lesion studies, as they may be models of some disorders that have a developmental basis, such as autism or psychopathy. At the University of Iowa, Steven Anderson is currently accruing a registry of participants who sustained lesions in childhood, and the data from these cases is already informing comparable data obtained from adult-onset cases (Anderson, Bechara, Damasio, Tranel, & Damasio, 1999).

Combining Methods

Ultimately, of course, it is meaningless to describe any technique as better than any other; they all have their strengths and weaknesses. The aim should be to use all of them and to consider the data they provide in combination. Each of them helps to constrain our theories and can rule out competing hypotheses. Finally, it is also important to consider data from multiple species. Because the bulk of data on emotion from nonhuman animals comes from lesion or intracranial recording studies, an application of these techniques in humans provides the opportunity for direct comparisons. Conversely, functional imaging studies in animals will be an important complement to those studies that are being carried out in humans.

Acknowledgments

The research summarized here was supported by grants from the J. S. McDonnell Foundation and the National Institutes of Health.

References

Adolphs, R. (2002). Recognizing emotion from facial expressions: Psychological and neurological mechanisms. *Behavioral and Cognitive Neuroscience Reviews, 1,* 21–61.

Adolphs, R. (2003). Investigating the cognitive neuroscience of social behavior. *Neuropsychologia, 41,* 119–126.

Adolphs, R., Damasio, H., Tranel, D., Cooper, G., & Damasio, A. R. (2000). A role for somatosensory cortices in the visual recognition of emotions as revealed by three-dimensional lesion mapping. *Journal of Neuroscience, 20,* 2683–2690.

Adolphs, R., Damasio, H., Tranel, D., & Damasio, A. R. (1996). Cortical systems for the recognition of emotion in facial expressions. *Journal of Neuroscience, 16,* 7678–7687.

Adolphs, R., Kawasaki, H., Oya, H., & Howard, M. A. (in press). Intracranial electrophysiology of the human orbitofrontal cortex. In D. H. Zald & S. L. Rauch (Eds.), *The Orbitofrontal Cortex.* New York: Oxford University Press.

Adolphs, R., Tranel, D., & Damasio, H. (2002). Neural systems for recognizing emotion from prosody. *Emotion, 2,* 23–51.

Adolphs, R., Tranel, D., Damasio, H., & Damasio, A. (1994). Impaired recognition of emotion in facial expressions following bilateral damage to the human amygdala. *Nature, 372,* 669–672.

Adolphs, R., Tranel, D., Hamann, S., Young, A., Calder, A., Anderson, A., et al. (1999). Recognition of facial emotion in nine subjects with bilateral amygdala damage. *Neuropsychologia, 37,* 1111–1117.

Aggleton, J. (Ed.). (2000). *The amygdala: A functional analysis.* New York: Oxford University Press.

Amaral, D. G., Price, J. L., Pitkanen, A., & Carmichael, S. T. (1992). Anatomical organization of the primate amygdaloid complex. In J. P. Aggleton (Ed.), *The amygdala: Neurobiological aspects of emotion, memory, and mental dysfunction* (pp. 1–66). New York: Wiley-Liss.

Anderson, S. W., Bechara, A., Damasio, H., Tranel, D., & Damasio, A. R. (1999). Impairment of social and moral behavior related to early damage in human prefrontal cortex. *Nature Neuroscience, 2,* 1032–1037.

Bates, E., Wilson, S. M., Saygin, A. P., Dick, F., Sereno, M. I., Knight, R. T., et al. (2003). Voxel-based lesion-symptom mapping. *Nature Neuroscience, 6,* 448–450.

Bechara, A., Damasio, A. R., Damasio, H., & Anderson, S. W. (1994). Insensitivity to future consequences following damage to human prefrontal cortex. *Cognition, 50,* 7–15.

Bechara, A., Damasio, H., Tranel, D., & Anderson, S. W. (1998). Dissociation of working memory from decision making within the human prefrontal cortex. *Journal of Neuroscience, 18,* 428–437.

Bechara, A., Tranel, D., & Damasio, A. (2002). The somatic marker hypothesis and decision-making. In J. Grafman (Ed.), *Handbook of neuropsychology* (Vol. 7, pp. 117–143). Amsterdam: Elsevier.

Bechara, A., Tranel, D., Damasio, H., & Damasio, A. R. (1996). Failure to respond autonomically to anticipated future outcomes following damage to prefrontal cortex. *Cerebral Cortex, 6,* 215–225.

Benton, A. L., Hamsher, K., Varney, N. R., & Spreen, O. (1983). *Contributions to neuropsychological assessment.* New York: Oxford University Press.

Borod, J. C., Obler, L. K., Erhan, H. M., Grunwald, I. S., Cicero, B. A., Welkowitz, J., et al. (1998). Right hemisphere emotional perception: Evidence across multiple channels. *Neuropsychology, 12,* 446–458.

Canli, T. (1999). Hemispheric asymmetry in the experience of emotion. *Neuroscientist, 5,* 201–207.

Damasio, A. R. (1994). *Descartes' error: Emotion, reason, and the human brain.* New York: Grosset/Putnam.

Damasio, A. R., Tranel, D., & Damasio, H. (1990). Individuals with sociopathic behavior caused by frontal damage fail to respond autonomically to social stimuli. *Behavioural Brain Research, 41,* 81–94.

Damasio, H., & Damasio, A. R. (1989). *Lesion analysis in neuropsychology.* New York: Oxford University Press.

Damasio, H., & Frank, R. (1992). Three-dimensional *in vivo* mapping of brain lesions in humans. *Archives of Neurology, 49,* 137–143.

Damasio, H., Grabowski, T., Frank, R., Galaburda, A. M., & Damasio, A. R. (1994). The return of Phineas Gage: Clues about the brain from the skull of a famous patient. *Science, 264,* 1102–1104.

Damasio, H., Tranel, D., Grabowski, T., Adolphs, R., & Damasio, A. (2004). Neural systems behind word and concept retrieval. *Cognition, 92,* 179–229.

Engel, A. K., Moll, C. K. E., Fried, I., & Ojemann, G. A. (2005). Invasive recordings from the human brain: Clinical insights and beyond. *Nature Reviews Neuroscience, 6,* 35–47.

Halligan, P. W., & David, A. S. (2001). Cognitive neuropsychiatry: Towards a scientific psychopathology. *Nature Reviews. Neuroscience, 2,* 209–215.

Howard, M. A., Volkov, I. O., Granner, M. A., Damasio, H. M., Ollendieck, M. C., & Bakken, H. E. (1996). A hybrid clinical-research depth electrode for acute and chronic in-vivo microelectrode recording of human brain neurons. *Journal of Neurosurgery, 84,* 129–132.

Kapur, N. (1996). Paradoxical functional facilitation in brain-behavior research. *Brain, 119,* 1775–1790.

Kawasaki, H., Adolphs, R., Kaufman, O., Damasio, H., Damasio, A. R., Granner, M., et al. (2001). Single-unit responses to emotional visual stimuli recorded in human ventral prefrontal cortex. *Nature Neuroscience, 4,* 15–16.

Kringelbach, M. L. (2005). The human orbitofrontal cortex: Linking reward to hedonic experience. *Nature Reviews Neuroscience, 6,* 691–702.

Lang, P. J., Oehman, A., & Vaitl, D. (1988). *The International Affective Picture System.* Gainesville: University of Florida.

Langdon, R., & Coltheart, M. (2000). The cognitive neuropsychology of delusions. In M. Coltheart & M. Davies (Eds.), *Pathologies of belief* (pp. 183–216). Oxford, UK: Blackwell.

McCarthy, G. (1999). Physiological studies of face processing in humans. In M. S. Gazzaniga (Ed.), *The new cognitive neurosciences* (pp. 393–410). Cambridge, MA: MIT Press.

Morris, J. S., Frith, C. D., Perrett, D. I., Rowland, D., Young, A. W., Calder, A. J., et al. (1996). A differential neural response in the human amygdala to fearful and happy facial expressions. *Nature, 383,* 812–815.

Öngür, D., & Price, J. L. (2000). The organization of networks within the orbital and medial prefrontal cortex of rats, monkeys, and humans. *Cerebral Cortex, 10,* 206–219.

Oya, H., Kawasaki, H., Howard, M. A., & Adolphs, R. (2002). Electrophysiological responses in the human amygdala discriminate emotion categories of complex visual stimuli. *Journal of Neuroscience, 22,* 9502–9512.

Price, C. J., & Friston, K. J. (2002). Degeneracy and cognitive anatomy. *Trends in Cognitive Science, 6,* 416–420.

Rolls, E. T. (1999). *The brain and emotion.* New York: Oxford University Press.

Schmolck, H., & Squire, L. R. (2001). Impaired perception of facial emotions following bilateral damage to the anterior temporal lobe. *Neuropsychology, 15,* 30–38.

Tranel, D. (1996). The Iowa-Benton school of neuropsychological assessment. In I. Grant & K. M. Adams (Eds.), *Neuropsy-chological assessment of neuropsychiatric disorders* (2nd ed., pp. 81–101). New York: Oxford University Press.

Tranel, D., Bechara, A., & Denburg, N. (2002). Asymmetric functional roles of the right and left ventromedial prefrontal cortices in social conduct, decision-making, and emotional processing. *Cortex, 38,* 589–612.

Tranel, D., Damasio, H., Denburg, N., & Bechara, A. (2005). Does gender play a role in functional asymmetry of ventromedial prefrontal cortex? *Brain, 128,* 2872–2881.

Wood, J. N., & Grafman, J. (2003). Human prefrontal cortex: Processing and representational perspectives. *Nature Reviews Neuroscience, 4,* 139–147.

Catherine J. Norris

James A. Coan

Tom Johnstone

26

Functional Magnetic Resonance Imaging and the Study of Emotion

Functional magnetic resonance imaging (fMRI) technology has had both intentional and unintentional influences on the study of emotion. Brain imaging techniques have on one hand provided psychologists and neuroscientists access to brain-behavior relationships undreamed of only 20 years ago. On the other hand, the striking images produced by fMRI can convey a sense of "objectivity" that is unwarranted by the method (Olson, 2005), and critics have expressed concerns about the risk (and tendency) of too readily inferring the isolation of specific causal brain mechanisms that underlie extremely complex psychological phenomena (cf. Cacioppo, et al., 2003; Kahn, 2004).

Although such errors of inference are, in fact, a problem, overstating the extent of such issues may well be a growing problem of its own. In fact, the history of fMRI research can now boast a sizable and growing number of methodological inquiries into the measure's sensitivity, generalizability, and utility. In recent years, fMRI researchers have been concerned about issues such as the relationship between fMRI signal change and neural activity (e.g., Logothetis, 2003; Logothetis & Wandell, 2004), the degree to which different brain regions are equally conducive to hemodynamic signal detection (e.g., LaBar, Gitelman, Mesulam, & Parrish, 2001), how artifacts in rapid imaging can be minimized or corrected for (e.g., Jezzard, Matthews, & Smith, 2001), the amount of inter-session variability in fMRI and how to minimize it (McGonigle et al., 2000; Smith et al., 2005), the test-retest reliability of fMRI (Genovese, Noll, & Eddy, 1997; Johnstone

et al., 2005), and so on. This work has set the stage for increasingly reliable and useful results—results that, apart from indicating which areas of the brain "light up" under one condition or another, can provide access to processes that overt behavior and self-report measures cannot. Ultimately, such results can move us toward the identification of, yes, the causal brain mechanisms that underlie important and complex psychological phenomena. In short, neuroimaging is making real and important methodological progress; it is no longer a field that can be characterized as being "in its infancy." Whatever inferential overreaching may or may not have occurred in the history of fMRI research, the growing database of associations among specific brain structures and corresponding (and specific) emotional events is rapidly and richly expanding our nomological network of emotion-related structures, functions, and processes, and that is a very good thing.

The practical consequence of all this is that contemporary emotion researchers can no longer afford to be unaware of the methods and language of neuroimaging generally and of fMRI in particular. That said, this chapter will not prepare researchers to commence fMRI research. Doing so would require a book of its own. In the past few years, a number of such entry-level fMRI textbooks have been published; readers should consult these additional resources for detailed information regarding fMRI design and analysis (cf. Buxton, 2001; Huettel, Song, & McCarthy, 2004; Jezzard et al., 2001). If we are successful, this chapter will prepare researchers unfamiliar with many of the details of fMRI research to (1) become competent consumers of fMRI research and (2) gain a knowledge of the training and resources researchers must seek out should their interests lead them toward conducting fMRI research of their own. In the service of these goals we address problems ranging from causal inference in the identification of associations between psychological and physiological events to a number of technical and pragmatic realities related to fMRI as a measure. Table 26.1 outlines some of the basic problems and concerns encountered by fMRI researchers, as well as some suggested solutions, and is meant to be a helpful resource for the beginning investigator.

The Interdisciplinary Tradition in Emotion Research

Historically, psychologists have approached the study of emotion from a multilevel, interdisciplinary perspective. Emotion researchers from as long ago as Darwin (1872), James (1884), and Cannon (1927) emphasized the multifaceted nature of emotional processes—processes that included observable behaviors such as facial expressions; physiological processes such as changes in heart rate, respiration, or blood pressure; and even unique qualities of subjective experience. James (1890) captured this idea when he stated that "no shade of emotion, however slight, should be without a bodily reverberation as unique, when taken in its totality, as is the mental mood itself" (p. 450). The recognition that emotional experiences corresponded with specific physical events opened the door for the inclusion of psychophysiological measures of the motor system, autonomic nervous function, neuroendocrine responses, and brain function.

The importance of psychophysiological measures is further emphasized in critiques of self-report (or introspective) measures. In their seminal paper, Nisbett and Wilson (1977) argued that verbal reports of mental processes are based on a priori theories of behavior or stimulus-response contingencies, not direct observations of individuals' cognitive processes. Although Nisbett and Wilson (1977) are often wrongly attributed with providing evidence for the general unreliability and inaccuracy of self-report measures, their argument that such measures do not necessarily provide accurate insight into the process of interest to the experimenter has had important consequences for the study of emotion. Reports of emotional experience are subject not only to a priori causal theories (e.g., "I'm sad because I saw pictures of a funeral") but also to strong response biases (e.g., "I saw pictures of a funeral, thus I ought to report feeling sad"), social demands and norms (e.g., gender differences in self-reported sadness), contextual influences (e.g., effects of the presence of another person on reported sadness), and cultural display rules (e.g., "I shouldn't express my glee at the misfortune of my opponent"). Furthermore, certain aspects of emotion are plainly inaccessible to introspection. For example, individuals are

unable to accurately detect and report as to whether the physical or psychological aspects (i.e., "feelings") of an emotion arise first. Psychophysiological methods have offered indirect, continuous, objective measures with which to probe and track emotional processes.

As a measure of brain responses to psychological events, fMRI holds great promise. We emphasize, however, that fMRI measurements are beholden to the same concerns as any other measure collected by psychologists. To this end, we first discuss some of the overarching principles and inherent problems in relating physiological events to psychological ones. We then discuss (1) a number of technical and pragmatic considerations in fMRI measurement, (2) a number of inferential and interpretive considerations in fMRI measurement, and (3) on a related note, the problem of using fMRI to investigate high-level psychological constructs. Finally, we turn to a brief discussion of the importance of integrating fMRI with converging measures in the pursuit of more coherent, complete, and causal models of the neural processes that underlie emotion.

The Doctrine of Multilevel Analysis

In a series of articles written over the past 15 years, Cacioppo and colleagues (e.g., Cacioppo & Berntson, 1992; Cacioppo et al., 2003; Cacioppo, Berntson, Sheridan, & McClintock, 2000; Cacioppo & Tassinary, 1990; Sarter, Berntson, & Cacioppo, 1996) have described the problems inherent in making inferences about psychophysiological data and, more generally, in performing studies that cross levels of analysis (e.g., neural, cognitive, social). As brain imaging techniques are prone to the same concerns as psychophysiological data, and as any study that utilizes fMRI to shed light on a psychological process or phenomenon necessarily crosses levels of analysis, the *doctrine of multilevel analysis* applies to neuroimaging studies of emotion. We begin with a detailed discussion of the first basic principle of the doctrine of multilevel analysis, along with its corollary and related errors, and with a special focus on using brain imaging techniques to study emotion.

The Principle of Multiple Determinism

Given the importance of behavior in survival and reproduction, functional redundancy for approach/withdrawal responses is evident at multiple levels of the nervous system (Berntson & Cacioppo, 2003). This redundancy is not limited to motor control but extends throughout the central nervous system (CNS). Two implications of this organization are that the same behavioral function (e.g., approach, withdrawal) may be achievable by different CNS processes and that the same nucleus, whether alone or in combination with other loci (circuits), may be involved in different behavioral functions. The *principle of multiple determinism* states

Table 26.1

Common concerns and potential solutions in the design, execution, and analysis of fMRI studies

Concern	Possible Solution(s)
Hemodynamic responses are an indirect measure of neuronal activity; a more direct index is required.	Single cell recordings and alternative neuroimaging methods (e.g., perfusion-based fMRI) are more direct measures that can be used to answer similar questions.
Temporal resolution of fMRI is inadequate to address the question of interest.	Use EEG to collect ERPs. Use source localization techniques (e.g., BESA, LORETA) to examine potential neural generators of EEG activity or ERPs. Use MEG.
Excessive participant movement.	Provide more support for participants (e.g., cushions under knees, elbows; vacuum pillow under head). Provide extensive relaxation instructions before scan session. Require participation in a simulation scanner session to acquaint participants with environment and reduce anxiety, fear, and claustrophobia. Examine fMRI time series visually to identify spikes and sudden signal changes indicative of motion, and exclude these time points from analysis. Include motion estimates as covariates of no interest in individual-level GLM analyses to account for residual motion.
Problem of multiple comparisons (i.e., conducting many simultaneous statistical tests).	Use Monte Carlo simulations, permutation techniques, or random field theory to determine a combination of (1) cluster size threshold, (2) voxelwise α level, and (3) connection radius that controls for the number of statistical tests conducted. Use a multivariate analysis approach (currently in development). Conduct an ROI analysis, thereby limiting the number of statistical tests to the number of regions selected according to theoretical predictions.
Insufficient CNR (whole brain).	Increase magnet field strength (e.g., scan at 3T instead of 1.5T). Include more trial repetitions. Use a block design instead of an event-related design.
Insufficient SNR (specific regions) and/or excessive signal dropout in regions of interest.	Generate SNR maps to assess signal strength separately for each participant; include only participants with sufficient SNR in the region of interest in group analyses. Change acquisition sequence (i.e., spiral-in/out has been shown to increase coverage and maintain SNR; Glover & Law, 2001; Preston et al., 2004). Signal dropout is worse at high magnetic fields; decrease magnet field strength (e.g., scan at 1.5T instead of 3T). Record cardiac and respiratory signals and use to correct for associated BOLD signal changes (currently in development).
"Lateralized" activity is observed—i.e., activation is apparent at a chosen thresholded level in only one hemisphere.	A direct comparison between hemispheres MUST be run to conclude that neural activity is lateralized. Unthresholded images can be presented, with contours depicting regions that exceed threshold.
Understanding participants' strategies for performing the task.	Use converging methods (e.g., skin conductance, eye tracking, heart rate, RTs, stimulus ratings, or categorization). Provide a thorough, structured debriefing interview.
Understanding participants' responses to the scanner environment; especially limiting anxiety and claustrophobia.	Screen for previous experience of claustrophobia. Conduct simulation scanner sessions. Collect pre- and post-scanner mood and state anxiety measures. Provide a thorough, structured debriefing interview (including direct questions about comfort, estimated time spent in the scanner, etc.).
Understanding the processes involved in performing the task and how they map onto neural activation.	Design the study carefully to control for confounding variables and to isolate processes of interest. Perform behavioral pilot testing to verify that behavioral results align with predictions. Consider the modality, duration, and nature of stimuli (e.g., dynamic or static; long or short; easy or difficult). Use participant responses (e.g., ratings, RTs) to understand performance. Consider patterns of observed neural activation across the entire brain. Perform multiple contrasts, both tight (i.e., isolating a single process) and loose (i.e., allowing a general understanding of the neural signature of the task as a whole).

Note. Solutions may span multiple phases of an fMRI study; for example, to correct for excessive movements, both preventive (e.g., extra support, training or simulation sessions) and corrective (e.g., inspection of data, inclusion of motion parameters in individual-participant GLMs) measures may be taken.

that an event at one level of organization may have multiple antecedents within or across levels. Therefore, creating an antecedent condition at one level of analysis (A) and subsequently observing the event of interest (E) does not necessarily lead to the conclusion that E is caused only by A or that observing E implies A.[1]

To illustrate, imagine that in a simple fMRI study in which participants view color images that differ in emotional content, the experimenter reports that pictures with unpleasant or negative content (i.e., those with low normative pleasantness ratings) elicit greater activation of the amygdala than do pictures with neutral content (i.e., those with middling pleasantness ratings). (Note that this pattern of amygdala activation is a common finding in the neuroimaging literature; cf. Anders, Lotze, Erb, Grodd, & Birbaumer, 2004; Irwin et al., 1996; Sabatinelli, Bradley, Fitzsimmons, & Lang, 2005). This pattern of results is frequently interpreted as indicating that, all else being equal, the amygdala is involved in negative affect. Although this may be the case, it does not follow that amygdala activation is therefore a *marker* of negative affect. That is, one cannot assume that a processing state (e.g., negative affect) has been indicated by the activation of a specific brain region just because that brain region (e.g., the amygdala) has been observed to vary with that processing state. This error is termed *affirmation of the consequent* (cf. Cacioppo et al., 2003). The amygdala may be involved in generating or in processing related to a particular negative affect, but it also may contribute independently (or interactively) to other neural circuits, such as those implicated in face processing (Blonder et al. 2004), theory of mind abilities (Siegal & Varley, 2002), or novelty detection (Wright et al., 2003). Moreover, the amygdala might not always be involved in the generation of negative affect. For example, the perception of disgusting stimuli, such as noxious odors, might engage other brain circuitry, such as prefrontal areas and the insula, but not the amygdala. Thus interpreting amygdala activation as an indicator of state negative affect is assuming that activation of the amygdala has a single antecedent condition and that negative affect always engages the amygdala, both of which are incorrect. This example is particularly striking when considering the breadth and depth of existing knowledge regarding the amygdala, one of the most frequently studied structures of the brain. Note that we do not mean to suggest that the amygdala is not a critical structure for many types of negative affect or emotion; indeed, meta-analyses have clearly demonstrated a role of the amygdala during negative emotion induction (Murphy, Nimmo-Smith, & Lawrence, 2003; Phan, Wager, Taylor, & Liberzon, 2002). Rather, the amygdala may be one neural mechanism for the generation of negative affect and yet not be an index of any of several particular negative emotional states.

A second implication of multiple determinism is that the way in which cognitive phenomena can be described most parsimoniously as operating at the behavioral level may not map in a one-to-one fashion at the level of neural operations

or substrates. The *category error* (Ryle, 1949; see also Cacioppo et al., 2003) refers to the assumption that organization or description at one level of analysis (e.g., of cognitive phenomena) can be directly mapped to organization at another level of analysis (e.g., of underlying neural substrates). In neuroimaging research on emotion and affect, examples of the category error would be assuming that a specific emotion (e.g., disgust) can be explained by localized function of a single spot in the brain (e.g., the anterior insula) or that the amygdala constitutes "the emotional brain" (i.e., that emotion is localized to a single "emotion center" in the brain).

Consider another example in which researchers conduct an fMRI study examining patterns of neural activity generated as participants view pictures with negative and neutral content. In one such study, Ueda and colleagues (2003) reported a larger blood oxygenation level dependent (BOLD) response to negative than to neutral pictures in regions of right inferior and right medial prefrontal cortex, the right amygdala, the left anterior cingulate cortex, and bilaterally in the visual cortex. These results suggest that negative affect cannot be localized to one single location in the brain. However, it would also be incorrect to assume that each of these regions is a neural substrate for negative affect. Complementary studies involving patients with lesions, transcranial magnetic stimulation (TMS; a method of creating a temporary "lesion" of a localized portion of cortex), or cellular recordings may show, for example, that a lesion encompassing ventromedial prefrontal cortex (PFC) would not disrupt the ability to experience negative affect. Indeed, the case study of Phineas Gage, a railroad worker who acquired a large brain lesion centered in ventromedial PFC, provides such evidence, as Mr. Gage was clearly still able to experience negative affect after the accident that caused his lesion (Damasio et al., 1994).

In sum, there are many possible mappings of elements across different domains (e.g., psychological, physiological, neural), including a null relation (i.e., no mapping), as well as one-to-one, one-to-many, many-to-one, and many-to-many mappings between antecedents and consequents (for a more detailed discussion of possible mappings, see Cacioppo & Tassinary, 1990). Furthermore, in addition to examining the *specificity* of relationships across levels of analysis (e.g., the mapping between psychological and neural events), researchers also need to consider the *generality* of such relations across different individuals, populations, situations, and contexts. The relationship between a psychological event (negative affect) and a neural event (activation of the amygdala) can be invariant across individuals and contexts, or it can be dependent on, for example, a personality dimension that varies across individuals (e.g., neuroticism) or the current context (e.g., viewing only negative and neutral pictures; performing the task in an anxiety-producing environment such as an fMRI scanner). An illustration of these possibilities is provided by Canli and his colleagues (2001) in their investigation of the relationship between the personality dimensions of neuroticism and extraversion and neural reactivity to emotional stimuli. One interesting finding from this study concerns activation of the amygdala when participants viewed positive pictures; this pattern has not been robustly observed in the past, as some studies show an increase in amygdala activation to positive pictures relative to neutral, and others do not. Canli et al. (2001) found that extraversion positively correlated with increased activation to positive (vs. negative) pictures, suggesting that the relationship between amygdala activation and positive affect is not invariant; rather, it varies across individuals as a function of individual differences in extraversion.

The Corollary of Proximity

Finally, the principle of multiple determinism has a corollary (the *corollary of proximity*) stating that the mapping between events becomes more complex as the number of levels crossed increases. This corollary can be demonstrated by a consideration of the relationship between a behavioral pattern (e.g., social anxiety) and neural activity. Socially anxious behavior may have a multiplicity of antecedents at the cognitive level (e.g., biased attention toward social agents; selective memory retrieval for negative social interactions), which in turn may have a multiplicity of antecedents at the neural level (e.g., increased activation of the amygdala in affectively ambiguous or neutral contexts; greater basal activation of networks involved in person perception). Thus, higher level emotional constructs, such as romantic love, moral decision making, or loneliness and depression will likely have a many-to-many mapping to neural activity that is both individualistic and context-bound, whereas lower level sensory processes, such as visual perception of simple objects, may have more general (i.e., invariant) and less complex mappings to neural activity. In fact, one way in which brain imaging coupled with thoughtful and precise experimental designs is of potential use to emotion researchers is in identifying the separate and multiple mechanisms that underlie a single psychological construct—for example, separating out early visual perceptual biases from later cognitive biases. For example, it might be possible to identify different subgroups of socially anxious individuals—some who demonstrate exaggerated responses in early visual areas, others who show increased amygdala activation, and a third group that exhibits a different pattern of activation in prefrontal cortex. Such observed differences in neural activation, combined with suitable behavioral measures, might permit a more detailed understanding of the different mechanisms that underlie social anxiety.

This brief overview of the doctrine of multilevel analysis is not meant to be an exhaustive survey of the principles of causal logic but is rather intended to lay out some of the basic principles that should guide multilevel or interdisciplinary research. In addition, we have attempted to provide illustrations of these principles from the perspective of an emotion researcher using functional neuroimaging methods. Now we turn to three discussion points concerning the design and interpretation of studies that use brain imaging techniques to investigate emotional processes.

Basic Issues in fMRI Measurement

The advent of human brain imaging has provided researchers with a tool that has the potential to extend our knowledge of brain-behavior relationships beyond what most could have imagined only 20 years ago. Its potential sets it apart from the other tools of emotion research, but without a well-equipped "methodological toolbox" to accompany it, its power cannot be fully realized. What follows is an introduction to basic issues in fMRI measurement with which consumers of fMRI research should be familiar, which researchers intent on exploring their own work in fMRI can use as an introduction, and which researchers already working in fMRI can use as a review.

Hemodynamic Responding, Not Neuronal Activity

FMRI is a procedure for measuring changes in hemodynamic events in the brain. Current thought suggests that the hemodynamic response is the result of a transient increase in neuronal activity within a region of the brain that begins to consume additional oxygen in the blood proximal to these cells (cf. Heeger & Ress, 2002; Jezzard et al., 2001). Following this reduction of the oxygen level in the blood, oxygen delivery to the region increases. Combined with local vasodilation, this increase in oxygen delivery produces a higher concentration of oxygenated hemoglobin in blood near a site of neuronal activity than in locally inactive areas. BOLD fMRI provides a measure of these hemodynamic adjustments and—by inference—the transient changes in neuronal activity in the proximal brain tissue (cf. Buckner, 1998; Heeger & Ress, 2002; Liao et al., 2002; Raichle, 2000). Importantly, however, the BOLD signal is only a relative measure and cannot be used to derive an estimate of absolute hemodynamic change. This characteristic of the BOLD signal, however, makes it challenging (if not impossible) to provide a valid comparison between different parts of the brain in single subjects or between the same parts of the brain in different subjects. In sum, fMRI provides a direct but relative measure of localized changes in levels of oxygenated hemoglobin in the brain and an inferential measure of neuronal activity (for more thorough coverage of the relationship between the BOLD fMRI signal and neural activity, see Logothetis, 2003; Logothetis & Wandell, 2004).[2]

Temporal Resolution

As with any other psychophysiological signal, knowledge of its physical basis can inform our use of the measure. The temporal resolution of fMRI is limited by the time course of the hemodynamic response—specifically, the rate at which oxygen is utilized in a region of interest and oxygen delivery is increased to that region—as well as other factors. Typically, the onset of a hemodynamic response occurs approximately 1–2 s after a stimulus is presented (i.e., after the actual electrical signal from the neuron population), with the peak occurring about 6 s after stimulus onset and the entire response lasting 12–14 s for a brief stimulus—although the exact timing can vary across brain regions (Buckner et al., 1996). Importantly, the hemodynamic response does not track activity on a millisecond-by-millisecond basis; the blood flow response is influenced by activity levels over some time interval (a few hundred milliseconds or more). Combined, the base rate of blood flow changes and sampling time intervals can swamp other temporal factors, such as slight delays in onset times of the hemodynamic response as a function of brain region or psychological process. The slowness of the BOLD response affects experimental design, making the rapid sequential presentation of stimuli impractical. Fortunately, the BOLD response appears to be approximately linear and additive over periods greater than about 3–4 s (e.g., Glover, 1999). Using randomized presentation of stimuli with a varying intertrial interval (ITI), stimuli can thus be presented at a more rapid rate than the 12–14 s response duration (average ITIs of 3–4 s are attainable) and analyzed using linear modeling techniques (e.g., *deconvolution;* Glover & Law, 2001).

At the other end of the temporal scale, problems exist when using fMRI to measure slow changing brain responses; for example, in studies of sustained mental activity. Partly because of the relative nature of the BOLD response, fMRI BOLD signals drift slowly over time. Such baseline drift effects make it difficult to reliably measure hemodynamic changes corresponding to neural activity over periods of minutes rather than seconds. Techniques such as arterial spin labeling (ASL) have the potential to be used as measures of long-term hemodynamic changes, with stability over periods of hours or even days (Wang et al., 2003).

The temporal nature of the task, therefore, is one factor to weigh carefully when evaluating or considering the use of fMRI versus other measures, such as event-related brain potentials (ERPs). If the primary research question concerns the time course of an event or the unfolding of a set of psychological processes, ERPs are potentially a more informative measure; if the study focus concerns the neural substrates of a particular process, fMRI may be a more appropriate approach. Ultimately, some combination of ERPs and fMRI may provide the most complete picture of the relationship between behavior and neural activity by maximizing both temporal and spatial resolution; new methods are available for this purpose, including dipole source modeling programs that use fMRI data to constrain solutions (e.g., brain electrical source analysis [BESA], http://www.besa.de; low resolution brain electromagnetic tomography [LORETA]; Pascual-

Marqui, Michel, & Lehmann, 1994), as well as equipment (e.g., MagLink; http://www.neuro.com) and post-processing techniques (e.g., Goldman, 2005; Negishi, Abildgaard, Nixon, & Constable, 2004; Allen, Josephs, & Turner, 2000) that will allow simultaneous recording of ERPs and the BOLD response in the scanner environment. In fact, a recent study has successfully demonstrated the relationship between behavior (reaction times; RTs), simultaneously recorded scalp electroencephalography (EEG) and neural activation during a task designed to study performance monitoring (Debener et al., 2005). This study provides a striking illustration of the difficulties presented by concurrent EEG and fMRI (e.g., removal of MR gradient and ballistocardiac artifacts from the raw EEG; necessary analysis of single-trial ERPs using independent component analysis [ICA]; time-locking ERPs to the delayed hemodynamic response), as well as the tremendous promise that this approach holds for understanding higher order brain function. However, complications remain in the interpretation of fMRI and ERP data collected simultaneously or even separately while participants perform the same task. In particular, differences in patterns of brain activity collected by fMRI and ERPs need to be considered in light of constraints imposed by the physical basis of the measures. For example, the presence of an ERP component with a known source dipole (e.g., the error-related negativity [ERN] is widely acknowledged to be generated by the anterior cingulate cortex [ACC]; Holroyd, Dien, & Coles, 1998) and the absence of neural activity in the corresponding cortical tissue using fMRI during the same task does not directly lead to the conclusion that the data are inconsistent. As mentioned before, the BOLD response as assessed with fMRI is influenced by neural activity over an extended time period; if the ACC was active briefly but quickly inhibited, it may not show significant BOLD activity. Thus, although ERPs collected in tandem with fMRI hold promise for better understanding the neural activity concomitant with emotional processes, combining the two measures remains no small feat.

In addition to limitations imposed by the physical basis of the BOLD signal, technical issues in the acquisition of the signal also provide some limitations to the temporal resolution of fMRI (see Cacioppo & Tassinary, 1990, for a general discussion of such issues in psychophysiological research). Acquisition times, and therefore sampling rates, are limited by the amount of time required to fully excite protons in slices, as well as ideal decay times for acquiring the signal (Jezzard et al., 2001). These limitations are amplified by the number of slices (i.e., 2-dimensional images of brain activity) collected in a study; up to (and potentially more than, depending on the acquisition plane) thirty 5-mm slices are required to attain full brain coverage. The temporal resolution of fMRI is therefore constrained not only by the rate of blood flow changes but also by the time it takes to acquire a full set of images. In practice, a 2–3 s sampling period is typical for whole-brain fMRI experiments.

Spatial Resolution

One unique contribution of neuroimaging techniques is the spatial resolution that they afford; fMRI allows the assessment of neural activity in four dimensions, including the time course of the response, with a spatial resolution of mere millimeters.[3] Although the fine-grained spatial resolution of fMRI is a major advantage, participant movement within the scanner can be a significant problem and requires both precautions in data collection and corrections in data processing (Jezzard et al., 2001; Johnstone et al., 2006). In addition, some spatial resolution is sacrificed via spatial blurring in order to more appropriately compare data across participants with different brain anatomies and functional localization. Spatial blurring is accomplished by applying a spatial filter (essentially a local averaging function), most commonly of a Gaussian (or normal) form, to the dataset in one, two, or three dimensions. The width of the filter (e.g., 6 mm full-width half-maximum [FWHM]) determines the amount of smoothing; a larger width will result in more smoothing. Spatial blurring (or filtering) also has the positive effect of increasing the signal-to-noise ratio, as "noise" values will tend to cancel each other out while true signal will remain (Smith, 2001). Even with no explicit spatial blurring, individual participant data are typically co-registered (i.e., warped) to a standardized anatomical brain template to allow for group analysis, a process that inherently introduces a degree of spatial smoothing at the group level (though see Thirion et al. [2006] for an alternative method of combining whole brain fMRI data from multiple participants). The effects of co-registration vary for different brain regions (e.g., brain regions typically showing greater interindividual anatomical variability, such as the cortical surface, will be blurred the most) and for different methods of co-registration (e.g., warping to the Talairach atlas will result in greater distortion of regions farthest from subcortical structures and the corpus callosum; Talairach & Tournoux, 1988). Despite the spatial resolution sacrificed by blurring, fMRI allows a precision in the localization of task-related changes in neural activity that was previously impossible to attain in humans.

Alpha Slippage

The sheer power of fMRI to perform tests simultaneously across the entire brain imparts a mixed blessing to brain imaging researchers. FMRI is a powerful tool that allows researchers to concurrently track parallel processes in the brain. However, the number of statistical tests performed in a single fMRI study presents some challenges for interpreting results—specifically, researchers must both control for the number of false positives (i.e., a voxelwise α level of .05 is not appropriate when conducting upward of 100,000 voxelwise t-tests) and test a set of hypotheses. In typical brain imaging studies, the Bonferroni correction (i.e., dividing the desired overall α level by the total number of comparisons

conducted and using this modified p-value as a threshold for voxelwise significance) would be inappropriately conservative, as each voxelwise test is not independent due to substantial correlations between activation of neighboring voxels. Other techniques include using Monte Carlo simulations, permutation techniques (Hayasaka & Nichols, 2003; Holmes, Blair, Watson, & Ford, 1996), or random field theory (Worsley et al., 1996) to determine corrected voxelwise thresholds or a minimum cluster size (i.e., the minimum number of contiguous voxels that exceed a given, uncorrected, voxelwise threshold such that the cluster of active voxels meets a corrected α level of .05). The assumption in the latter case is that noise will be randomly distributed in the dataset, so one can determine the extent of contiguous activation that is unlikely to be the result of chance. As these techniques take the spatial correlation within datasets into account, each will result in a more accurate corrected threshold than the Bonferroni correction.

It is important that whatever technique is used to correct for multiple comparisons in voxelwise statistical tests can be properly justified. Numerous published studies have chosen seemingly arbitrary minimum cluster sizes to control for multiple comparisons that on more careful examination turn out to be little better than performing no correction at all. For example, for a whole brain analysis of typical fMRI data using a voxelwise threshold of $p < .01$, a minimum cluster size of 120 2 mm^3 voxels might correspond to a corrected α as high as .5, clearly unacceptably high. Figure 26.1 shows how the corrected α varies as a function of cluster size for a range of voxelwise thresholds and data smoothness, based on Monte Carlo simulations.[4] It is clear from Figure 26.1 that unless the correction for multiple comparisons is precisely specified, no conclusions regarding the overall likelihood that a given activation might have occurred due to chance can be made. In addition to explaining the justification for use of a particular method of correcting for multiple comparisons, as well as the parameters selected (e.g., voxelwise threshold, cluster size), authors ought to include the volume of the search space (i.e., the number of voxels in the dataset, directly corresponding to the number of tests performed). Indeed, one way to minimize the number of contrasts performed is to limit the search space to gray matter, as only contrasts for voxels in gray matter are of interest. Using a gray-matter mask can greatly reduce the number of simultaneous statistical tests, thereby requiring a smaller cluster size to correct for multiple comparisons.

One criticism of the methods described here is that in controlling for the chance of at least one false positive over the entire dataset (termed controlling the familywise error rate; FWE), they are too conservative, particularly when at least some true activations are likely. The false discovery rate (FDR) is designed to control for the proportion of false positives among those voxels deemed to be activated, as opposed to FWE methods that control the probability of a false positive among all voxels (Benjamini & Hochberg, 1995;

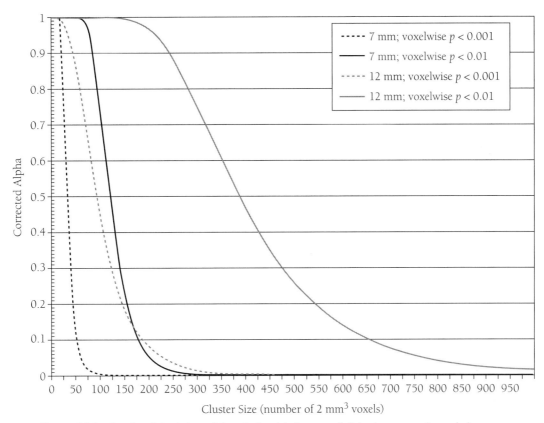

Figure 26.1. Graphical depiction of the relationship between full-brain corrected α and cluster size, voxelwise threshold, and degree of spatial smoothness for a whole-brain analysis. Estimates were derived using Monte Carlo simulations. Dashed lines correspond to a voxelwise threshold of $p < .001$; solid lines correspond to a voxelwise threshold of $p < .01$. Black lines indicate 7 mm of spatial smoothness in the data set; gray lines indicate 12 mm of spatial smoothness. Note that the cluster size required to attain an acceptable corrected α of .05 varies widely: from 59 2 mm^3 voxels (i.e., 472 μL) for a dataset with 7 mm of spatial smoothing and a voxelwise threshold of $p < .001$ to 762 $2mm^3$ voxels (i.e., 6096 μL) for a data set with 12 mm of spatial smoothing and a voxelwise threshold of $p < .01$—appropriate cluster volume for the two analyses differs by a magnitude of over 10.

Genovese, Lazar, & Nichols, 2002). The FDR is an example of weak control over Type I error in that it allows conclusions to be made about the Type I error probability over all "activated" voxels but does not allow conclusions of significance to be made about any particular voxel. Nevertheless, its increased power over FWE methods makes it a viable alternative that might become more prevalent in future research.

In addition to null-hypothesis voxelwise tests for determining which voxels show greater activation in one condition than in another, recently suggested methods for thresholding images include spatial mixture modeling, which attempts to spatially subdivide different brain regions according to the entire distribution of voxel values (as opposed to just the null distribution; Everitt & Bullmore, 1999; Salli, Visa, Aronen, Korvenoja, & Katila, 1999; Woolrich, Behrens, Beckmann, & Smith, 2005), as well as multivariate and model-free approaches (e.g., Beckmann & Smith, 2005;

Benali, Mattout, & Pelegrini-Issac, 2003). These approaches may ultimately provide more powerful and statistically appropriate techniques for analyzing fMRI data.

The problem of multiple statistical tests can be also addressed by using a hypothesis-driven approach to the data; for example, conducting a *region-of-interest (ROI) analysis* to examine patterns of activation within a particular neural region predicted to covary with the task of interest. The ROI approach allows for a powerful test of a specific hypothesis and often eliminates (or at least greatly diminishes) the need to correct for multiple comparisons.[5] ROIs can be defined in numerous ways. If brain structures are well delineated, individual ROIs may be constructed on the basis of each individual's brain anatomy, using a high-resolution anatomical scan. This process can be very time-consuming, although increasingly automated methods of brain segmentation are becoming practical (e.g., FreeSurfer; http://surfer.nmr.mgh .harvard.edu/). Alternatively, ROIs can be defined based on group-average brain anatomy or on the basis of a standardized anatomical template (e.g., the ICBM 152 template brain from the Montreal Neurological Institute; Evans et al., 1993; the Talairach Daemon atlas; Lancaster et al., 2000). When using either of these techniques, care must be taken to consider the limits of localization of ROIs; given the large variation between brain anatomies, it is often impossible to specify fine-grained distinctions between adjacent brain structures on the basis of averaged templates.

Rather than defining ROIs purely on the basis of anatomy, another possibility is to define ROIs based on the functional data per se. This is a valid approach when the contrast used to define the ROI is orthogonal to the contrast that is subsequently tested. For example, Kanwisher, McDermott, and Chun (1997) adopted a *functional ROI* approach, in which a functional region of interest is defined individually for each participant as a region of cortex (e.g., the fusiform gyrus) that is selectively responsive to the process of interest (e.g., face perception). They found that 12 of 15 participants exhibited greater activation of a portion of the fusiform gyrus to faces than to objects. They defined this ROI for each participant separately, then tested additional conditions specifically within the face-selective ROI (e.g., three-quarter faces, inverted grayscale faces; Kanwisher, Tong, & Nakayama, 1998) to examine the generalizability of the face effect. In a procedure conceptually similar to the functional ROI approach but conducted initially on group data, *statistical ROIs* can be identified as a statistical function of one specific contrast within a normative sample and then used to test orthogonal hypotheses across conditions or groups (e.g., Salomons, Johnstone, Backonja, & Davidson, 2004). For example, a group-level analysis may reveal a set of clusters showing significantly greater activation under conditions of threat (e.g., anticipated shock) than under conditions of safety; signal change within these clusters can then be analyzed as a function of different conditions (e.g., presence or absence of a romantic partner; Coan, Schaefer, & Davidson, 2006).

It is worth noting that issues of multiple statistical comparisons and their consequent effects on interpretation of study results have been addressed both by researchers in the field (e.g., http://www.sph.umich.edu/~nichols/Nipub) and by developers of statistical packages (e.g., http://en.wikibooks.org/wiki/SPM-Information_to_include_in_papers), who have begun to lay down guidelines for the acceptable analysis and presentation of results—guidelines that may be adopted by neuroimaging journals in the future but that will be of immediate benefit to reviewers and readers of fMRI literature.

Statistical Power and Signal-to-Noise Ratio

Whereas the problem of multiple comparisons in fMRI analysis lies with controlling for Type I error, an equally problematic issue with most fMRI studies is Type II error, indicative of a lack of statistical power. FMRI data is inherently noisy; repetitions of a given trial condition are typically few due to

scanning time restraints; and the number of participants included in many studies is small. Therefore, signal-to-noise ratio (SNR) is clearly of much concern in fMRI research. SNR in fMRI is affected by field strength, movement artifact, physiological artifacts such as those caused by respiration and cardiac pulsatile motion, tissue densities, and cavities such as the sinuses. Imaging certain parts of the brain (e.g., amygdala, orbitofrontal cortex [OFC]) presents particular difficulties due to signal dropout caused by intravoxel dephasing, which is a function of large differences in magnetic susceptibility between brain matter and proximal sinuses. Signal dropout leads to a generally lower SNR. Furthermore, the simple fact that signal dropout (and, consequently, SNR) varies as a function of the proximity of neural tissue to sinus cavities implies that SNR will differ across brain regions within a single participant, as well as across individual participants—and can even vary across scan sessions for the same individual if his or her head is placed at a slightly different angle. The result is that a group statistical map showing no activation in OFC or the amygdala may be due to high signal loss in that region for the majority of participants and not, in fact, to lack of neural activity.

New methods are being developed to allow experimenters to take such factors into consideration when drawing conclusions about neuroimaging data. For example, LaBar and his colleagues (2001) used computer simulations to determine the SNR value required to detect a 1% signal change in the amygdala, then generated BOLD maps depicting actual SNR values at each voxel and used these maps to assess the signal strength for each participant. The authors found that a majority of participants did not have sufficient SNR in the medial aspect of the amygdala to allow a test of the hypotheses (i.e., most participants showed significant signal loss in the medial amygdala). In addition, hemispheric asymmetries in participants' SNR maps mirrored asymmetries in activation patterns, suggesting that observed lateralized activation of the amygdala (or other neural regions with low SNR) may be due to differences in SNR and not to true hemispheric asymmetries. Using such methods, it is possible to determine on an individual-participant basis whether signal coverage and SNR are sufficient in the primary areas of interest to include a participant's data in group analyses. Although the reporting of SNR values is not yet common in the fMRI literature, reviewers might consider requesting such numbers in cases in which signal dropout is problematic (e.g., failure to replicate amygdala activation to negative stimuli).

Rather than utilizing a post hoc analysis to determine which participants have acceptable SNR to detect the signal of interest, many researchers prefer the use of *block designs,* in which the hemodynamic response is allowed to pool over multiple successive trials of the same condition, as a method of increasing statistical power. However, block designs are often not appropriate when studying psychological constructs that can be influenced by expectations, context, or habituation, such as emotion or affect. Methods for developing *event-related designs* have been established using selective averaging techniques (e.g., Buckner et al., 1996) and multiple regression analysis (e.g., deconvolution; Glover, 1999; Ward, 2001). With a sufficient number of trials, these event-related designs can attain acceptable statistical power while allowing for randomization of conditions. However, the number of trial repetitions for event-related designs is limited by scanning time restraints (e.g., the amount of time participants can remain in the scanner with some degree of comfort; the size of the data files generated); too few repetitions can also lead to inadequate SNR.

Ultimately, the result is that many experiments do not have sufficient statistical power to detect differences in hemodynamic responses between conditions. This issue is complicated by the fact that SNR varies greatly between different brain regions, with those regions of most interest to emotion researchers having some of the lowest SNRs. There is thus a risk that much real brain activation is missed in fMRI research. Furthermore, technological advances that appear to address issues such as low SNRs in fMRI research often come with additional costs. For example, SNR tends to be better in higher field magnets, resulting in a general trend for fMRI research laboratories to upgrade their 1.5 T magnets to 3 T or stronger magnets. However, stronger magnetic fields also result in increased signal dropout due to inhomogeneities in magnetic susceptibility (i.e., signal loss in OFC, amygdala). Ironically, SNRs for these difficult-to-image neural regions may be better in lower-field magnets. In sum, issues of statistical power and SNR remain largely unsolved (though not unaddressed), and the neuroimaging researcher is faced with multiple decisions regarding study design, data acquisition, and analysis—each of which can have strong effects on statistical power.[6]

Thresholding Issues

Unfortunately, a sizeable number of published studies have treated lack of significant activation as evidence of no activation, and articles are often cited as having found no activation in particular brain regions to support claims of functional localization. In addition to issues of statistical power and signal loss discussed earlier, this tendency is most probably due to the manner in which thresholded statistical maps are presented, showing only regions of significant activation in color overlaid on anatomical images. It is easy for the reader to infer that activation in such studies is localized to those areas that show suprathreshold activation. However, no evidence for functional localization exists without testing activation in one region directly against that of other brain regions—and because fMRI data is a relative rather than an absolute measure, there is no straightforward way to compare estimated activation across different brain regions. It is thus entirely possible that large areas of the brain are activated at levels falling just below statistical threshold and that these regions are not significantly differently activated than

are regions that show suprathreshold activation. Some researchers have suggested that, instead of publishing thresholded images, statistical images should be unthresholded, with contour lines overlaid to depict regions that exceed statistical threshold. Other researchers believe this would encourage the interpretation of nonsignificant activations, thus increasing Type I error. At present, it is up to the reader of fMRI literature to realize that areas that appear to show no activation in thresholded images might just as easily represent regions in which there is a lack of statistical power (and, possibly, true activation that fails to reach threshold). This issue is particularly relevant for discussions of lateralization of neural activity, as the presence of significant activation in only one hemisphere cannot be taken for evidence of laterality unless an explicit statistical contrast is performed.

Limitations in fMRI imposed by technical aspects of signal acquisition have the advantage of being mitigated as progress is made in the field. With the advent of faster spin-echo techniques, acquisition of a whole-brain volume can be accomplished in as little as 2 s; if only a subset of the brain is sampled, this time can drop dramatically. Although signal loss remains an important obstacle to drawing inferences from the BOLD signal and is of extreme importance for emotion researchers (as neural regions affected often include regions strongly implicated in emotion processing; e.g., OFC, amygdala), the researcher can employ a number of tools to maximize SNR and/or to quantify the degree of signal loss for each participant (e.g., LaBar et al., 2001). Thus the field of neuroimaging continues to make methodological advances that will only further the utility and reliability of fMRI. In sum, fMRI provides a method for noninvasive, powerful tests of questions concerning neural mechanisms with a very fine spatial resolution, while sacrificing some temporal resolution and presenting a few problems that can be addressed by careful attention to measurement conditions, design, and data analysis (e.g., SNR maps, appropriate control for multiple comparisons).

Inference and Interpretation in fMRI

In the preceding section we reviewed fMRI measurement. In this section, we assume the competent measurement and analysis of the hemodynamic response in association with some experimental task and consider the interpretation of those results.

The Whole (Picture) Is More Than the Sum of Its Parts

Although necessary for complete and thorough presentation of data, simply reporting laundry lists of voxel clusters that differentiate between experimental conditions is no more helpful to the emotion researcher than a list of available building materials would be to an architect. In other words, voxel clusters may constitute the building blocks of an fMRI data set, but they do not describe the meaning of the results. The locations of clusters can be considered along with the known functional significance of active neural regions, as well as knowledge of cytoarchitecture and anatomical connections between regions, to better inform the conclusions drawn from any fMRI study. Therefore, it is important to consider results as a whole in order to more accurately derive a description of the underlying neural mechanisms of a psychological event. We begin this discussion of problems of interpretation by addressing two common assumptions in the neuroimaging literature (amended slightly from Cacioppo et al., 2003):

1. When a brain structure is active during a task, this brain region is a neural substrate for that task.
2. When a brain structure is not active during a task, this brain region is not a neural substrate for that task.

At first glance, these two statements appear to be the very foundation of cognitive neuroimaging; however, it is easy to demonstrate that both statements are false under certain circumstances. Consider a study in which investigators are interested in the experience of sadness in different social contexts—when individuals are alone, in the presence of a loved one, or in the presence of a stranger. Imagine that bilateral amygdala activation is observed during sad films in the first two contexts, but not when participants are in the presence of a stranger (when a stranger enters and remains in the scanner room). However, the medial prefrontal cortex (mPFC) is active when participants are in the presence of a stranger, but not when alone or with a loved one. The researcher concludes that the neural mechanisms that underlie the experience of sadness differ across social contexts; specifically, that the mPFC rather than the amygdala is associated with sad feelings when participants are in the presence of an unknown other.

Although this may appear to be an appropriate interpretation of the study results, evidence from previous studies on the effects of social context on emotion suggests that individuals may regulate their emotions more in the presence of unknown others (e.g., Kleck et al., 1976; Kraut, 1982), and particularly that they may mold their feelings to be consistent with social norms (e.g., Jakobs, Manstead, & Fischer, 2001). In addition, the PFC has often been implicated in the conscious, purposeful regulation of emotion (e.g., Ochsner, Bunge, Gross, & Gabrieli, 2001; Ochsner et al., 2004). Thus activation of the PFC when participants are in the presence of a stranger could reflect increased cognitive control of emotional experience and not the experience of sadness itself (i.e., violating assumption 1). Similarly, lack of amygdalar activation to a sad movie in the presence of a stranger could be due to PFC inhibition of the amygdala (i.e., violating assumption 2). In other words, results from this study could indicate that the amygdala is involved in feelings of sadness, whereas the PFC is associated with inhibiting or controlling

those feelings of sadness. Only by considering patterns of activation across the brain in terms of the existing literature examining both the behavioral effects of social context on emotion and the functional significance of PFC activation, and with a comparison across different social contexts, does the true structure of the data emerge.

Our hypothetical study on experienced sadness in different social contexts illustrates one situation in which both assumptions may be incorrect: Specifically, a region activated in a task may be involved in inhibiting other regions that are neural substrates for the process of interest, and a region not activated in a task may be inhibited but remain a neural substrate for the process of interest. However, there are other instances in which one or both of these assumptions may be false. For example, even though extended areas of the visual cortex are often active when participants view emotional pictures (e.g., Lane et al., 1997; Lang et al., 1998), no emotion researcher would claim that these results indicate in and of themselves that the visual cortex is specifically involved in emotion. To make this point, researchers turn to contrasts of experimental conditions that isolate emotional processing from visual processing (e.g., emotional pictures–neutral pictures; emotional pictures–emotional sounds). This example indicates that regions that are active during a task may not be neural substrates for the process of interest, such as emotional processing, but for other processes that may be operating in parallel, such as visual processing.

Using Other Measures to Track What Participants Are Doing

It is also important to recognize that participants' strategies for performing tasks may differ across conditions or over time, among other possibilities. The need for fMRI researchers to know how participants are completing their experimental tasks is probably underappreciated. One means of accomplishing this goal is to collect behavioral data while participants are in the scanner. Doing so allows the researcher (1) to verify that participants are paying attention and not disengaging from the task, (2) to maintain some control over how participants perform the task, and (3) to directly examine whether the scanner environment affects participants' performance of the task. Furthermore, behavioral data collected as participants perform the task in the scanner can be used to test for differences in effort and attention across conditions.

Unfortunately, a few recent studies have indicated that asking participants to perform a task in the scanner, such as rating emotional pictures rather than just passively viewing them, alters patterns of neural activity. Taylor, Phan, Decker, and Liberzon (2003) showed decreased activation in brain structures known to be involved in emotional networks (e.g., amygdala) when participants performed a rating task, suggesting that processing of the pictures changed as a function of the imposed task. Taylor et al. (2003) argued that asking participants to make a categorical judgment about each picture in their study (e.g., to categorize the content of each picture as negative, neutral, or positive) decreased emotional and increased cognitive processing of the pictures. However, in a second study, Liberzon et al. (2000) reported greater limbic activity (using positron emission tomography [PET]) when participants rated emotional pictures than when they performed a recognition task during picture presentation (i.e., "Have you seen this picture before?"). Combined, the results from these two studies suggest that activation of the amygdala is strongly affected by the nature of the imposed task, such that highly cognitive tasks (e.g., picture recognition) elicit the least activation; making a cognitive judgment (e.g., rating or categorization) about the emotional content of the stimuli elicits middling activation; and simple passive viewing elicits the most activation. However, the question remains as to why this pattern of activation was observed—the assumption is that passive viewing of pictures elicits the most emotional processing, but in the absence of data supporting this conclusion, alternative explanations remain.

Thus, although a methodological challenge, it is still necessary to try to understand participants' behavior in the absence of an explicit task. Fortunately, many options other than self-report or overt responses exist. In the aforementioned study, Liberzon and his colleagues (2000) collected psychophysiological measures (i.e., skin conductance, heart rate) in addition to PET scans while participants viewed negative and neutral pictures and performed either a rating or memory task. Skin conductance showed an interaction between the stimulus type (i.e., negative, neutral pictures) and the explicit task (i.e., rating, memory), such that negative pictures always elicited a larger increase in skin conductance response (SCR) than did neutral pictures, but this effect was stronger when participants performed the rating task than the memory task. These data support the conclusion that the rating task produced more emotional arousal than did the memory task and they also mitigate the possibility that results could be due to greater difficulty of the memory task (which would arguably increase arousal and SCR). In a different set of studies, Williams and her colleagues have (1) employed skin conductance as an index of arousal by averaging fMRI data separately for trials that elicited SCR responses from those that did not (Williams et al., 2001); and (2) used the pattern of SCRs observed over the course of a study (i.e., U-shaped function: large at first, decreased in the middle, large again at the end) to investigate the time course of emotional responding in different neural regions (Williams et al., 2004). In addition to skin conductance, measures of heart rate and blood pressure can currently be effectively collected simultaneously with fMRI, and they hold additional promise for future studies that may provide convergent evidence for our understanding of the processes underlying emotion, mood, and affect. As mentioned previously, methods and equipment for collecting EEG simultaneously with fMRI are currently available (e.g., MagLink, from Neuroscan; www.neuro.com) and have great potential for furthering our knowledge on neural mechanisms and the time course of underlying processes. In sum, psychophysiological measures collected in real time during an fMRI study may provide indirect measures of participants' behavior in the scanner, as well as shed light on converging emotion processes (e.g., visceral, psychological) and their neural mechanisms.

One exciting and underappreciated option for monitoring participant behavior during task performance in fMRI research is the tracking of eye movements and pupil diameter as participants perform visual tasks in the scanner environment. Eye tracking allows the experimenter to assess effort (i.e., via pupil diameter; Kahneman & Beatty, 1966; Beatty & Lucero-Wagoner, 2000; Siegle, Steinhauer, Stenger, Konecky, & Carter, 2003), as well as both global (e.g., wakefulness, gaze aversion) and local (e.g., focus on a person vs. the background of an emotional picture) aspects of attention. In fact, eye-tracking data can provide interesting insights into how different individuals perform a task and how processing differs across conditions. For example, in a picture-viewing study, we might expect individual differences in the degree to which participants regulate negative affect even when not instructed to do so (as in "automatic emotion regulation"; Jackson et al., 2003). Participants also might differ in the strategies they employ in automatic emotion regulation, such that some individuals may visually disengage from negative pictures, whereas others may remain focused on a center point and fail to explore negative pictures. Pupil diameter may also indicate individual differences in the effort required to automatically regulate negative affect that potentially relate to personality dimensions, such as extraversion and neuroticism (e.g., Urry, van Reekum, Greischar, Thurow, & Davidson, 2003). Thus eye tracking may shed light on mechanisms that underlie differences in brain activation across conditions or individuals. A striking example is in the processing of faces by individuals with autism. Previous neuroimaging research has shown that when looking at pictures of faces, individuals with autism show reduced activation in the fusiform gyrus (Hubl et al., 2003), suggesting a deficit in the neural circuitry that underlies face perception. By using eye tracking in combination with fMRI, however, Dalton, Nacewicz, and Johnstone (2005) showed that reduced activation in the fusiform correlated with the tendency of individuals with autism to avert their gaze from the face, particularly the eye region. Thus an alternative explanation is that, for individuals with autism, faces may be aversive social cues and that reduced activation in the fusiform region does not necessarily imply dysfunction in that region of the brain. In summary, eye-tracking data allow the fMRI researcher to better assess how participants are completing the task and how processes differ across conditions and individuals without instituting a response that may detract from emotional processes.

Another undervalued method of examining how participants perform a task is a detailed debriefing interview. We acknowledge that conducting a debriefing interview is often a required element of an experimental protocol (e.g., when deception or a cover story is used; when participants are given course credit for participation) and that researchers must, therefore, have extensive experience with providing participants with a debriefing of sorts. However, it is possible to use a debriefing interview not only to disclose information regarding the true purpose of the study but also to assess participant behavior. Although it is widely accepted that individuals do not necessarily have access to the processes that underlie their judgments or behaviors (Nisbett & Wilson, 1977), a good debriefing interview can allow participants to express any concerns or problems they experienced during the experiment, as well as any explicit strategies that they employed to complete the task. Such conscious, deliberate, and reportable strategies can and often will have an effect on observed patterns of brain activation. Debriefing interviews may also shed light on mechanisms previously not considered by the experimenter, as participants describe their experience of the study. Studies of emotion regulation may particularly benefit from more elaborate debriefing interviews, as often experimenters do not provide extensive instruction on how participants ought to regulate their emotions but simply state that they should "increase" or "decrease" their negative emotions (Ochsner et al., 2002), or describe possible strategies for decreasing emotional experience but do not manipulate such strategies (e.g., Phan et al., 2005). In such cases, debriefing may provide insight into multiple strategies of emotion regulation, their relative efficacy, and their underlying neural mechanisms.

The Scanner Environment

On a somewhat related note, emotion researchers in particular ought to be sensitive to feelings of claustrophobia and anxiety experienced by fMRI participants, as such changes in mood may affect variables of interest in studies of emotion and affect. Importantly, it may not be enough to simply prescreen participants on previous experiences of claustrophobia, as the scanner environment may elicit such feelings even in those individuals who have never before experienced claustrophobia. Furthermore, the scanner environment may produce different results in groups of participants who vary on an important dimension; for example, depressed participants may experience a mood lift in the scanner (potentially due to personal attention and concern expressed by the experimenter), whereas control participants may show no change. Many labs have begun to require a mock scanner session before participation in an fMRI study in order to both habituate individuals to the scanner environment and familiarize participants with experimental instructions and procedures.

Stimulus Materials and Presentation

The type, modality, and duration of stimuli used to elicit emotion can have strong effects on observed neural activity, as underlying processes will frequently differ as a function of each of these factors. For example, emotion researchers often use facial stimuli to manipulate emotional experience, as these stimuli reliably engage some of the neural regions most often implicated in emotion, such as the amygdala, and are easy to match on other dimensions (e.g., contrast, complexity). However, it is important to consider how participants process facial stimuli in any fMRI study, as participants can simply perceive the emotional expression, automatically mimic the expression (Dimberg, Thunberg, & Elmehed, 2000), or experience a similar emotion (Esteves, Dimberg, & Öhman, 1994). In addition, facial expressions can be ambiguous—the perception of an angry face may, for example, generate not anger but fear in the perceiver, as anger may be a threatening stimulus. This problem is potentially confounded by individual differences in dimensions such as social anxiety and loneliness, as individuals who are less socially well-adjusted may have different interpretations of facial stimuli. Furthermore, recent evidence suggests that networks that underlie social and emotional processing, though partially distinct, are also interactive (Norris, Chen, Zhu, Small, & Cacioppo, 2004). Using stimuli that are both social and emotional (e.g., facial expressions) may result in problems separating underlying social and emotional processes.

Similarly, stimulus modality and duration may have effects on underlying mechanisms. Auditory stimuli, such as narrated imagery scenarios, nonverbal sounds with emotional content, or spoken behavioral statements that vary in emotionality, differ in at least one important dimension from visual stimuli: Auditory stimuli are dynamic and may require maintained attention to process, whereas visual stimuli are static and attention may be diverted once the content is determined, thus giving rise to differences in selective exposure and attentional focus. One potential solution to this problem is to present visual stimuli for a shorter amount of time to prevent attentional shifts later in exposure. However, some research suggests that emotional processing differs as a function of awareness—disgust and fear faces that were presented overtly (i.e., for 170 ms) showed a double dissociation of activation in the anterior insula and amygdala, respectively; when faces were presented covertly (i.e., for 30 ms), this pattern was not observed, but instead disgust elicited activation of the amygdala (Phillips et al., 2004). Vuilleumier, Armony, Driver, and Dolan (2001) have also shown that processing of fear faces is affected by attentional focus in some neural regions (e.g., fusiform gyrus was active only when faces were attended to) but not in others (e.g., amygdala was activated regardless of attentional focus). Finally, in their meta-analysis of PET and fMRI studies of emotion induction, Phan et al. (2002) found effects of induction method (visual, auditory, recall/imagery) on neural activity during the experience of a variety of emotions. In sum, it is important to consider the nature of the stimuli employed in an fMRI study and how processing might change as a function of stimulus type, modality, or even length of exposure.

Inadequate consideration of such issues as the nature of stimulus materials, the strategies employed by participants, and even differences in required effort or knowledge across conditions can lead to inappropriate (or incomplete) conclusions regarding observed patterns of neural activity. For example, a recent PET study conducted by Dickhaut et al. (2003) aimed to investigate choice behavior for gains and losses in risky (i.e., variable outcome; equal probability of winning either $50, $6, or $4) and certain (i.e., identical outcome; all outcomes result in a win of $20) contexts. The authors reported that choice behavior did not differ as a function of context but that contextual influences emerged when the authors examined both reaction times and cerebral blood flow (CBF). The authors concluded that choices made by participants did not provide a complete account of decision making and that different neural networks were active in risky as opposed to certain contexts. In a response to this article, Cacioppo and Nusbaum (2003) argued that decisions made in certain versus risky contexts differ in other important ways. First, decisions made in certain contexts are less cognitively taxing, as all outcomes are identical. Second, decisions made in risky contexts may produce both positive and negative affect, consistent with data from decision affect theory indicating that obtained outcomes (e.g., winning $6) are interpreted in comparison with unobtained outcomes (e.g., winning $50; Larsen, McGraw, Mellers, & Cacioppo, 2004; Mellers, Schwartz, Ho, & Ritov, 1997). Taking these differences into consideration, both reaction times and CBF data conformed to predictions. Specifically, decisions made in risky contexts compared with those made in certain contexts produced longer reaction times and greater CBF in areas associated with planned motor behavior (cerebellum, as well as frontal, premotor, presupplementary motor, and motor areas), mental calculation (precuneus, central sulcus, parietal cortex), and abstract rewards and punishments (medial OFC). Cacioppo and Nusbaum (2003) concluded that "choices emerge from the use of calculation, affective evaluation, and motor processes, and apparent differences reflect the nature of the task and not of the mechanism itself." (p. 3017). Thus only when the parts are considered together (i.e., when the whole picture is viewed at once, in light of performance demands and nature of the task) do the data truly reflect the underlying neural organization.

High-Level Constructs and the Problem of Multiple Underlying Processes

The advent of neuroimaging methodology, combined with the misleading perception that brain images reveal aspects of our true selves that other forms of data do not (Fitzpatrick & Landers, 2005), has given rise to a recent abundance of studies investigating high-level psychological constructs such as moral decision making (Greene, Sommerville, Nystrom, Darley, & Cohen, 2001), social rejection (Eisenberger,

Lieberman, & Williams, 2003), and romantic love (Bartels & Zeki, 2000, 2004; Aron et al., 2005). Because of their intuitive nature and broad appeal, such studies often receive a great deal of attention and generate much discussion among researchers, as well as the general public. Unfortunately, the contributions of these studies to understanding the psychological processes that underlie such high-level concepts are quite often minimal, due to complications arising from interactions among multiple levels of analysis (recall the corollary of proximity, which states that mapping across levels becomes more complex as a function of the number of intervening levels), as well as issues with interpretation of fMRI data. Specifically, fMRI is most helpful when the psychological variable of interest can be made sufficiently circumspect as to allow for inferences regarding highly specific processes.

It is important to remember that fMRI measures *task-related* changes in levels of oxygenated hemoglobin in the brain; often this is accomplished through a subtractive contrast between the condition of interest and some comparison condition. The assumption that underlies this experimental design is that BOLD differences between the two conditions reflect processing differences between them—much like the basic assumption of many attention-based reaction time studies. But high-level constructs contain multiple underlying processes, and comparison conditions are likely to differ on more than one of these. Therefore, it is often unclear how patterns of neural activation attributed to high-level social and emotional constructs ought to be interpreted.

A recent fMRI study, conducted to examine the neural substrates of grief following the dissolution of a romantic relationship, illustrates this problem. Najib and colleagues (Najib, Lorberbaum, Kose, Bohning, & George, 2004) scanned nine females, each of whom reported ruminative grief following the loss of a relationship in the previous 4 months. While in the scanner, these participants were at different times asked to engage in either a sad, ruminative thought about their loss or a neutral thought about another individual they had known as long as they had known their past relationship partner. As predicted, the authors report altered brain activity during rumination (as compared with recollection of a neutral thought) in neural areas that the authors associated with sadness, such as the cerebellum, anterior temporal cortex, insula, anterior cingulate, and prefrontal cortex. Importantly, however, some of these regions showed *more* activity during rumination (e.g., the cerebellum), whereas the remainder showed *less* activity during rumination.

This and other issues raise difficult questions, many of which the authors both recognize and attempt to address. First, the two conditions (ruminative vs. neutral thoughts) differ on multiple dimensions, including the nature of the relationship with the target individual; the importance, familiarity, and frequency of their thoughts; and even the specificity of the thoughts, as many of the neutral thoughts were event specific (e.g., "eating crab legs" with the other person), whereas many of the ruminative thoughts were more general (e.g., "our mutual dreams—not a shared dream anymore"). Any of these factors, or even some additive or multiplicative combination of them, could have contributed to the observed differences in neural activity. Moreover, although subjective ratings verified that participants felt more sad during the ruminative condition, they also indicated that participants felt more angry, anxious, and negative overall during the ruminative condition. Partially as a means of addressing this, Najib and colleagues (2004) correlated the rumination/neutral contrast in brain activation with both baseline grief and average sadness ratings during the rumination condition. As hoped, observed differences in neural activation between the rumination and neutral conditions were related to the experience of baseline grief and task-related sadness. (This goes some distance toward emphasizing our earlier point about the importance of assessing participant feelings and behaviors throughout an experiment.)

However, it is still unclear how in this study one should distinguish between and interpret increased versus decreased brain activation as a function of ruminative grief. Indeed, despite the best efforts of the researchers in question, the psychological construct of interest—in this case, grief—is not sufficiently circumspect to allow confident inferences to be drawn regarding its underlying neural organization. To their credit, Najib et al. (2004) did attempt to control for many factors that have been previously ignored in studies of sadness. For example, they required the eliciting event to be the end of a romantic relationship; the length of time since the eliciting event was limited to 16 weeks; the sex of the participant was held constant (only females were studied); and even symptoms of sadness and grief were somewhat controlled, as participation was limited to individuals who reported having ruminative thoughts about the relationship. However, sadness, let alone grief, comprises multiple cognitive, affective, and physiological processes, including but not limited to experienced negative affect, appraisal of a goal obstruction or loss, evaluation of potential actions to remedy the situation, and expression of the emotional state (facial expression, crying, dejected body posture). Recall of a past sad event adds several dimensions, such as imagery, active construction of the memory, working memory to maintain the emotional state, and knowledge of successive events. Rumination is additionally complicated by frequency of past thoughts about the event, as well as other processes.

Furthermore, differences in neural activity between recall of a ruminative thought and recall of a neutral thought, even after attempting to control for processes specific to their recall, remain ambiguous, because they simply indicate the neural correlates of ruminative grief, a multifaceted construct. In the final accounting, we've learned nothing new about ruminative grief as a construct and precious little about the functional neuroanatomy of the brain. Similarly, without considering and separately testing the constituent processes that underlie the construct of recalled ruminative grief, differences between the Najib et al. (2004) study and other studies that have examined recalled general sadness fall short of informing theory regarding either construct.

The Method of Subtraction

FMRI studies often use *subtractive designs* to make inferences regarding a series of information-processing stages, with the basic assumptions that two conditions differ in one and only one information-processing stage and that all stages are arranged linearly and additively. Subtracting one condition from the other (e.g., neural activation to negative pictures minus neural activation to neutral pictures), therefore, isolates the processing stage of interest. If two conditions differ on a multiplicity of levels, however, it will be difficult to understand how differences in neural activity across conditions map specifically onto differences in processing across conditions. For example, greater activation of the occipital cortex during recall of a sad versus a neutral thought, as in the Najib et al. (2004) study, could be due to any number of differences between the two conditions, including imagery vividness, relative importance, past frequency, salience, or level of emotional arousal. This problem is further complicated by the fact that the subtractive method assumes that processes are additive, not interactive. For example, the subtraction between recall of a sad and of a neutral thought aims to eliminate neural activity due to processes involved in recollection. However, recall of sad, ruminative (i.e., frequent) thoughts may be easier than of neutral ones, therefore producing differences in neural activity as a function of effort. Thus differences in neural activity may have nothing whatever to do with the experience of "grief," per se.

One possible approach to the problem of interpreting contrasts is to perform multiple contrasts that are both "tight" (i.e., that differ in only one information-processing stage) and "loose" (i.e., that allow a basic understanding of the neural signature associated with a psychological task; Donaldson & Buckner, 2001). Consider again a simple study in which participants view negative, neutral, and positive emotional pictures that are matched on other physical (e.g., luminance, color) and psychological (e.g., content, complexity, arousal) dimensions. The tight contrast between negative and positive pictures will produce clusters of voxels that indicate a *negativity bias,* such that, all else being equal, negative pictures elicit greater neural activation than do positive pictures. However, this contrast does not contribute to our understanding of how negative and positive pictures are processed in general. In fact, regions that are equally activated by both types of stimuli will not emerge at all in the tight contrast. By performing loose contrasts between a rest period (i.e., fixation point) and both negative and positive pictures, we may better understand the neural networks involved in emotional picture processing.

In sum, fMRI studies that investigate high-level constructs such as social behaviors or the experience of specific emotions need to be based on a foundation of existing results and theory. If little is known about the psychological processes that underlie the phenomena of interest, and if the central question lacks the definition necessary for an answer, fMRI (or any other measure, for that matter) will not produce interpretable or informative results. Contrast conditions should be considered in light of the specific processes thought to underlie the construct.

Integration of fMRI with Other Methods

On a final note, just as the fMRI researcher ought to integrate findings with and interpret results in consideration of existing psychological theory, the full value of fMRI will be realized only when it is integrated with results from other modalities of brain imaging and complementary research domains. For example, PET can provide details of the state or engagement of different neurotransmitter systems, as well as an absolute and quantifiable measure of brain metabolism both during tasks and at rest. EEG can provide a temporal breakdown of the subprocesses involved in performing different tasks or even a bridge between behavioral results and patterns of neural activation (Debener et al., 2005). Magnetoencephalography (MEG) offers the features of EEG with the additional benefit of localization of activation in 3-dimensional space.

As an example of how these features might prove useful, consider a study that focuses on the neural mechanisms that underlie responses to emotional stimuli in anxiety disorders. Whereas it would be possible to directly compare stimulus-locked changes in activation between a group of participants with anxiety disorder and a control group, the sensitivity of such a comparison would be compromised by the relative, nonquantifiable nature of the BOLD response. Additionally, one might expect that differences in baseline neural activity, particularly within the scanning environment, might exist between the two groups. If this were the case, then true differences in brain responses to emotional stimuli might not be apparent, due to ceiling effects in the patient group. Moreover, within-group variability in fMRI signal change might be due in part to differences in baseline brain metabolism. A measure of resting baseline activity as provided by PET would not only be valuable in its own right but would help in the interpretation of such fMRI signal differences. Likewise, EEG or MEG techniques might provide evidence that the brains of patients with anxiety disorders respond faster or that neural processes unfold in a different temporal sequence for patients and controls.

Of course, it is not possible with most studies to include multiple imaging modalities. But researchers should seek to use imaging techniques other than fMRI when the scientific questions of interest are better addressed by them, and they should attempt to consider results from studies that use complementary imaging modalities when interpreting fMRI results and formulating hypotheses for future fMRI experi-

ments. There is always the risk when a new, more "glamorous" technology becomes available that older techniques get ignored—to some extent one might say that the use of PET and, to a lesser extent, EEG has suffered in this manner, which is a great pity because for many research questions they remain the most appropriate imaging tools.

On a related note, there is an extensive literature in neuropsychology and animal neurophysiology that should be tightly integrated with fMRI studies. Chatterjee (2005) and Fellows, Heberlein, and Morales (2005) have shown that within the field of cognitive neuroscience, neuroimaging studies are cited far more than neuropsychological studies, primarily due to the greater number of neuroimaging studies published in high-impact journals. Furthermore, the citation of neuropsychological studies in the published neuroimaging research is lower than the converse (Chatterjee, 2005). Yet there is little reason to believe that imaging studies provide us with more or better information than well-conducted neuropsychological investigations. Indeed, neuropsychology and neurophysiology often allow causal interpretations of data where brain imaging studies would not. A balanced approach to the study of brain and behavior would seek to integrate findings from across these different neuroscientific fields. The different research techniques provide complementary information that can be useful either within the scope of a single investigation (e.g., Price, Mummery, Moore, Frackowiak, & Friston, 1999) or across different studies. The challenge for researchers is to keep up-to-date with the latest developments in one's own scientific specialty, while remaining open to and aware of parallel developments in related fields, as well as emerging methodologies (e.g., TMS) that may also contribute to a better understanding of brain-behavior relationships.

Conclusion

FMRI and other neuroimaging methods hold great promise for unraveling the mysteries of emotion experience, regulation, and dysfunction. The few principles we have outlined in this chapter are meant to be introductory, nonexhaustive guidelines for the use of fMRI to better understand the neural underpinnings of emotional life. The history of emotion research reveals a tradition of interdisciplinary design, careful implementation, and context-bound, theory-based interpretation of results. Emotion researchers are well equipped to continue in this tradition as they incorporate fMRI and other neuroimaging techniques into their work. We are confident they will.

Notes

1. In a well-designed experiment of the A → E format, one should be able to conclude that A caused E, but one cannot conclude that A is the only possible cause of E. Of course, the causal route from A to E might be indirect and involve a

number of different circuits. It might also be specific to the particular experimental context—which is the reason it is vital to broaden the contexts in which one looks for A-to-E connections (e.g., via conceptual replications).

2. New methods that allow a more direct assessment of neural activity are being developed. For example, perfusion-based fMRI using arterial spin labeling (ASL) both provides a more direct index of neural activity (i.e., requiring fewer assumptions regarding the physical basis of the signal) and has the potential to provide better functional localization as compared to BOLD fMRI (Liu, Wong, Frank, & Buxton, 2001; Wong, Buxton, & Frank, 1997).

3. Note that the basic unit of fMRI research is the *voxel*, a volume element representing a value in three dimensional space that is analogous to a pixel, which represents 2D image data. Thus, a researcher may report the resolution of her dataset as containing 3 mm x 3 mm x 3 mm, or 27 mm^3, voxels. Voxel dimensions are determined by the slice thickness and matrix size, which are parameters set by the experimenter; but are often resampled during post-processing.

4. A more exact corrected α for various cluster sizes would be obtained from the actual data using permutation tests or random field theory with localized smoothness estimates.

5. However, the results from an ROI analysis conducted in the absence of a full-brain test can also be misleading. Consider a study in which the researcher is interested in amygdala activation as a function of viewing negative pictures. An ROI analysis focusing on the amygdala may confirm the researcher's hypotheses; whereas a full brain analysis might reveal that viewing negative pictures elicits more activation not only of limbic structures, but throughout the entire brain. This pattern of results could affect the conclusions drawn from such a study. The obvious point is that one cannot draw conclusions about localization of activation on the basis of one or two ROIs.

6. Note that this discussion of issues related to statistical power in fMRI is not exhaustive. For example, the slice prescription and acquisition sequence chosen to collect functional data can have strong effects on both signal coverage and SNR (e.g., Glover & Law, 2001; Chen et al, 2003). Even basic parameters of fMRI data collection, such as the echo time (i.e., TE), can affect signal coverage, with the ideal TE varying across neural regions. For a thorough discussion of such issues, refer to Jezzard et al. (2001).

References

Allen, P. J., Josephs, O., & Turner, R. (2000). A method for removing imaging artifact from continuous EEG recorded during functional MRI. *NeuroImage, 12,* 230–239.

Anders, S., Lotze, M., Erb, M., Grodd, W., & Birbaumer, N. (2004). Brain activity underlying emotional valence and arousal: A response-related fMRI study. *Human Brain Mapping, 23,* 200–209.

Aron, A., Fisher, H. E., Mashek, D. J., Strong, G., Li, H.-F., & Brown, L. L. (2005). Reward, motivation, and emotion systems associated with early-stage intense romantic love. *Journal of Neurophysiology, 94,* 327–337.

Bartels, A., & Zeki, S. (2000). The neural basis of romantic love. *Neuroreport, 11,* 3829–3834.

Bartels, A., & Zeki, S. (2004). The neural correlates of maternal and romantic love. *NeuroImage, 21,* 1155–1166.

Beatty, J., & Lucero-Wagoner, B. (2000). The pupillary system. In J. T. Cacioppo, L. G. Tassinary, & G. G. Berntson (Eds.), *Handbook of psychophysiology* (2nd ed.). Cambridge, UK: Cambridge University Press.

Beckmann, C. F., & Smith, S. M. (2005). Tensorial extensions of independent component analysis for multisubject fMRI analysis. *NeuroImage, 25,* 294–311.

Benali, H., Mattout, J., & Pelegrini-Issac, M. (2003). Multivariate group effect analysis in functional magnetic resonance imaging. *Information Processing in Medical Imaging, 18,* 548–559.

Benjamini, Y., & Hochberg, Y. (1995). Controlling the false discovery rate: A practical and powerful approach to multiple testing. *Journal of the Royal Statistical Society: Series B. Statistical Methodology, 57,* 289–300.

Berntson, G. G., & Cacioppo, J. T. (2003). A contemporary perspective on multilevel analyses and social neuroscience. In F. Kessel, P. L. Rosenfeld, & N. B. Anderson (Eds.), *Expanding the boundaries of health and social science: Case studies in interdisciplinary innovation* (pp. 18–40). New York: Oxford University Press.

Blonder, L. X., Smith, C. D., Davis, C. E., Kesler-West, M. L., Garrity, T. F., Avison, M. J., et al. (2004). Regional brain response to faces of humans and dogs. *Cognitive Brain Research, 20,* 384–394.

Buckner, R. L. (1998). Event-related fMRI and the hemodynamic response. *Human Brain Mapping, 6,* 373–377.

Buckner, R. L., Bandettini, P. A., O'Craven, K. M., Savoy, R. L., Peterson, S. E., Raichle, M. E., et al. (1996). Detection of cortical activation during averaged single trials of a cognitive task using functional magnetic resonance imaging. *Proceedings of the National Academy of Sciences of the USA, 93,* 14878–14883.

Buxton, R. B. (2001). *Introduction to functional magnetic resonance imaging: Principles and techniques.* Cambridge, UK: Cambridge University Press.

Cacioppo, J. T., & Berntson, G. G. (1992). Social psychological contributions to the decade of the brain. *American Psychologist, 47,* 1019–1028.

Cacioppo, J. T., Berntson, G. G., Lorig, T. S., Norris, C. J., Rickett, E., & Nusbaum, H. C. (2003). Just because you're imaging the brain doesn't mean you can stop using your head: A primer and set of first principles. *Journal of Personality and Social Psychology, 85,* 650–661.

Cacioppo, J. T., Berntson, G. G., Sheridan, J. F., & McClintock, M. K. (2000). Multilevel integrative analyses of human behavior: Social neuroscience and the complementing nature of social and biological approaches. *Psychological Bulletin, 126,* 829–843.

Cacioppo, J. T., & Nusbaum, H. S. (2003). Component processes underlying choice. *Proceedings of the National Academy of Sciences of the USA, 100,* 3016–3017.

Cacioppo, J. T., & Tassinary, L. G. (1990). Inferring psychological significance from physiological signals. *American Psychologist, 45,* 16–28.

Canli, T., Zhao, Z., Desmond, J. E., Kang, E., Gross, J., & Gabrieli, J. D. (2001). An fMRI study of personality influences on brain reactivity to emotional stimuli. *Behavioral Neuroscience, 115,* 33–42.

Cannon, W. B. (1927). The James-Lange theory of emotions: A critical examination and an alternative theory. *American Journal of Psychology, 39,* 106–124.

Chatterjee, A. (2005). A madness to the methods in cognitive neuroscience? *Journal of Cognitive Neuroscience, 17,* 847–849.

Chen, N. K., Dickey, C. C., Yoo, S. S., Guttmann, C. R., & Panych, L. P. (2003). Selection of voxel size and slice orientation for fMRI in the presence of susceptibility field gradients: Application to imaging of the amygdala. *NeuroImage, 19,* 817–825.

Coan, J. A., Schaefer, H. S. & Davidson, R. J. (2006). Lending a hand: Social regulation of the neural response to threat. *Psychological Science, 17,* 1032–1039.

Dalton, K. M., Nacewicz, B. M., & Johnstone, T. (2005). Gaze fixation and the neural circuitry of face processing in autism. *Nature Neuroscience, 8,* 519–526.

Damasio, H., Grabowski, T., Frank, R., Galaburda, A. M., & Damasio, A. R. (1994). The return of Phineas Gage: Clues about the brain from the skull of a famous patient. *Science, 264,* 1102–1105.

Darwin, C. (1872). *The expression of the emotions in man and animals.* London: Albemarle.

Debener, S., Ullsperger, M., Siegel, M., Fiehler, K., von Cramon, D. Y., & Engel, A. K. (2005). Trial-by-trial coupling of concurrent electroencephalogram and functional magnetic resonance imaging identifies the dynamics of performance monitoring. *Journal of Neuroscience, 25,* 11730–11737.

Dickhaut, J., McCabe, K., Nagode, J. C., Rustichini, A., Smith, K., & Pardo, J. V. (2003). The impact of the certainty context on the process of choice. *Proceedings of the National Academy of Sciences of the USA, 100,* 3536–3541.

Dimberg, U., Thunberg, M., & Elmehed, K. (2000). Unconscious facial reactions to emotional facial expressions. *Psychological Science, 11,* 86–89.

Donaldson, D. I., & Buckner, R. L. (2001). Effective paradigm design. In P. Jezzard, P. M. Matthews, & S. M. Smith (Eds.), *Functional MRI: An introduction to methods* (pp. 177–195). Oxford, UK: Oxford University Press.

Eisenberger, N. I., Lieberman, M. D., & Williams, K. D. (2003). Does rejection hurt? An fMRI study of social exclusion. *Science, 302,* 290–292.

Esteves, F., Dimberg, U., & Öhman, A. (1994). Automatically elicited fear: Conditioned skin conductance responses to masked facial expressions. *Cognition and Emotion, 9,* 99–108.

Evans, A. C., Collins, D. L., Mills, S. R., Brown, E. D., Kelly, R. L., & Peters, T. M. (1993). 3D statistical neuroanatomical models from 305 MRI volumes. *Nuclear Science Symposium and Medical Imaging Conference, 3,* 1813–1817.

Everitt, B. S., & Bullmore, E. T. (1999). Mixture model mapping of brain activation in functional magnetic resonance images. *Human Brain Mapping, 7,* 1–14.

Fellows, L. K., Heberlein, A. S., & Morales, D. A. (2005). Method matters: An empirical study of impact in cognitive neuroscience. *Journal of Cognitive Neuroscience, 17,* 850–858.

Fitzpatrick, S., & Landers, E. (2005, February). *Brain imaging and the "cognitive paparazzi": Viewing snapshots of mental life out of context.* Symposium conducted at the annual meeting of the American Association for the Advancement of Science, Washington, DC.

Genovese, C. R., Lazar, N. A., & Nichols, T. E. (2002). Thresholding of statistical maps in functional neuroimaging using the false discovery rate. *NeuroImage, 15,* 870–878.

Genovese, C. R., Noll, D. C., & Eddy, W. F. (1997). Estimating test-retest reliability in functional MR imaging: I. Statistical methodology. *Magnetic Resonance in Medicine, 38,* 497–507.

Glover, G. H. (1999). Deconvolution of impulse response in event-related BOLD fMRI. *NeuroImage, 9,* 416–429.

Glover, G. H., & Law, C. S. (2001). Spiral-in/out BOLD fMRI for increased SNR and reduced susceptibility artifacts. *Magnetic Resonance in Medicine, 46,* 515–522.

Goldman, R. (2005, June). Simultaneous EEG and fMRI for event related studies. S. Marrett (Chair), *Imaging and modeling.* Symposium presented at the annual meeting of the Organization for Human Brain Mapping, Toronto, Ontario, Canada.

Greene, J. D., Sommerville, R. B., Nystrom, L. E., Darley, J. M., & Cohen, J. D. (2001). An fMRI investigation of emotional engagement in moral judgment. *Science, 293,* 2105–2108.

Hayasaka, S., & Nichols, T. E. (2003). Validating cluster size inference: Random field and permutation methods. *NeuroImage, 20,* 2343–2356.

Heeger, D. J., & Ress, D. (2002). What does fMRI tell us about neuronal activity? *Nature Reviews: Neuroscience, 3,* 142–151.

Holmes, A. P., Blair, R. C., Watson, J. D. G., & Ford, I. (1996). Nonparametric analysis of statistic images from functional mapping experiments. *Journal of Cerebral Blood Flow and Metabolism, 16,* 7–22.

Holroyd, C. B., Dien, J., & Coles, M. G. (1998). Error-related scalp potentials elicited by hand and foot movements: Evidence for an output-independent error-processing system in humans. *Neuroscience Letters, 242,* 65–68.

Hubl, D., Bölte, S., Feineis-Matthews, S., Lanfermann, H., Federspiel, A., Strik, W., et al. (2003). Functional imbalance of visual pathways indicates alternative face processing strategies in autism. *Neurology, 61,* 1232–1237.

Huettel, S. A., Song, A. W., & McCarthy, G. (2004). *Functional magnetic resonance imaging.* New York: Sinauer Associates.

Irwin, W., Davidson, R. J., Lowe, M. J., Mock, B. J., Sorenson, J. A., & Turski, P. A. (1996). Human amygdala activation detected with echo-planar functional magnetic resonance imaging. *Neuroreport, 7,* 1765–1769.

Jackson, D. C., Mueller, C. J., Dolski, I., Dalton, K. M., Nitschke, J. B., Urry, H. L., et al. (2003). Now you feel it, now you don't: Frontal brain electrical asymmetry and individual differences in emotion regulation. *Psychological Science, 14,* 612–617.

Jakobs, E., Manstead, A. S., & Fischer, A. H. (2001). Social context effects on facial activity in a negative emotional setting. *Emotion, 1,* 51–69.

James, W. (1884). What is an emotion? *Mind, 9,* 188–205.

James, W. (1890). *Principles of psychology* (Vol. 2). New York: Holt.

Jezzard, P., Matthews, P. M., & Smith, S. M. (2001). *Functional MRI.* Oxford, UK: Oxford University Press.

Johnstone, T., Ores Walsh, K. S., Greischar, L. L., Alexander, A. L., Fox, A. S., Davidson, R. J., et al. (2006). Motion correction and the use of motion covariates in multiple-subject fMRI analysis. *Human Brain Mapping, 27,* 779–788.

Johnstone, T., Somerville, L. H., Alexander, A. L., Oakes, T. R.,

Davidson, R. J., Kalin, N. H., et al. (2005). Stability of amygdala BOLD response to fearful faces over multiple scan sessions. *NeuroImage, 25,* 1112–1123.

Kahn, J. (2004). If you secretly like Michael Bolton, we'll know. *Wired, 12.* Retrieved October 4, 2004, from http://www .wired.com/wired/archive/12.10/brain.html

Kahneman, D. & Beatty, J. (1966). Pupil diameter and load on memory. *Science, 154,* 1583–1585.

Kanwisher, N., McDermott, J., & Chun, M. M. (1997). The fusiform face area: A module in human extrastriate cortex specialized for face perception. *Journal of Neuroscience, 17,* 4302–4311.

Kanwisher, N., Tong, F., & Nakayama, K. (1998). The effect of face inversion on the human fusiform face area. *Cognition, 68,* B1–11.

Kleck, R. E., Vaughan, R. C., Cartwright, S. J., Vaughan, K. B., Colby, C. Z., & Lanzetta, J. T. (1976). Effects of being observed on expressive, subjective, and physiological responses to painful stimuli. *Journal of Personality and Social Psychology, 34,* 1211–1218.

Kraut, R. E. (1982). Social presence, facial feedback, and emotion. *Journal of Personality and Social Psychology, 42,* 853–863.

LaBar, K. S., Gitelman, D. R., Mesulam, M. M., & Parrish, T. B. (2001). Impact of signal-to-noise on functional MRI of the human amygdala. *Neuroreport, 12,* 3461–3464.

Lancaster, J. L., Woldorff, M.G., Parsons, L. M., Liotti, M., Freitas, C. S., Rainey, L., et al. (2000). Automated talairach atlas labels for functional brain mapping. *Human Brain Mapping, 10,* 120–131.

Lane, R. D., Reiman, E. M., Bradley, M. M., Lang, P. J., Ahern, G. L., Davidson, R. J., et al. (1997). Neuroanatomical correlates of pleasant and unpleasant emotion. *Neuropsychologia, 35,* 1437–1444.

Lang, P. J., Bradley, M. M., Fitzsimmons, J. R., Cuthbert, B. N., Scott., J. D., Moulder, B., et al. (1998). Emotional arousal and activation of the visual cortex: An fMRI analysis. *Psychophysiology, 35,* 199–210.

Larsen, J. T., McGraw, A. P., Mellers, B. A., & Cacioppo, J. T. (2004). The agony of victory and thrill of defeat: Mixed emotional reactions to disappointing wins and relieving losses. *Psychological Science, 15,* 325–330.

Liao, H., Worsley, K. J., Poline, J. B., Aston, J. D., Duncan, G. H., & Evans, A. C. (2002). Estimating the delay of the fMRI response. *NeuroImage, 16,* 593–606.

Liberzon, I., Taylor, S. F., Fig, L. M., Decker, L. R., Koeppe, R. A., & Minoshima, S. (2000). Limbic activation and psychophysiologic responses to aversive visual stimuli: Interaction with cognitive task. *Neuropsychopharmacology, 23,* 508–516.

Liu, T. T., Wong, E. C., Frank, L. R., & Buxton, R. B. (2002). Analysis and design of perfusion-based event-related fMRI experiments. *NeuroImage, 16,* 269–282.

Logothetis, N. K. (2003). The underpinnings of the BOLD functional magnetic resonance imaging signal. *Journal of Neuroscience, 23,* 3963–3971.

Logothetis, N. K., & Wandell, B. A. (2004). Interpreting the BOLD signal. *Annual Review of Physiology, 66,* 735–769.

McGonigle, D. J., Howseman, A. M., Athwal, B. S., Friston, K. J., Frackowiak, R. S. J., & Holmes, A. P. (2000). Variability in

fMRI: An examination of intersession differences. *Neuro-Image, 11,* 708–734.

Mellers, B. A., Schwartz, A., Ho, K., & Ritov, I. (1997). Decision affect theory: Emotional reactions to the outcomes of risky options. *Psychological Science, 8,* 423–429.

Murphy, F. C., Nimmo-Smith, I., & Lawrence, A. D. (2003). Functional neuroanatomy of emotions: A meta-analysis. *Cognitive, Affective, and Behavioral Neuroscience, 3,* 207–233.

Najib, A., Lorberbaum, J. P., Kose, S., Bohning, D. E., & George, M. S. (2004). Regional brain activity in women grieving a romantic relationship breakup. *American Journal of Psychiatry, 161,* 2245–2256.

Negishi, M., Abildgaard, M., Nixon, T., & Constable, R. T. (2004). Removal of time-varying gradient artifacts from EEG data acquired during continuous fMRI. *Clinical Neurophysiology, 115,* 2181–2192.

Nisbett, R., & Wilson, T. (1977). Telling more than we can know: Verbal reports on mental processes. *Psychological Review, 84,* 231–259.

Norris, C. J., Chen, E. E., Zhu, D. C., Small, S. L., & Cacioppo, J. T. (2004). The interaction of social and emotional processes in the brain. *Journal of Cognitive Neuroscience, 16,* 1818–1829.

Ochsner, K. N., Bunge, S. A., Gross, J. J., & Gabrieli, J. D. (2002). Rethinking feelings: An FMRI study of the cognitive regulation of emotion. *Journal of Cognitive Neuroscience, 14,* 1215–1229.

Ochsner, K. N., Ray, R. D., Cooper, J. C., Robertson, E. R., Chopra, S., Gabrieli, J. D., et al. (2004). For better or for worse: Neural systems supporting the cognitive down- and up-regulation of negative emotion. *NeuroImage, 23,* 483–499.

Olson, S. (2005). Brain scans raise privacy concerns. *Science, 307,* 1548–1550.

Pascual-Marqui, R. D., Michel, C. M., & Lehmann, D. (1994). Low resolution electromagnetic tomography: A new method for localizing electrical activity in the brain. *International Journal of Psychophysiology, 18,* 49–65.

Phan, K. L., Fitzgerald, D. A., Nathan, P. J., Moore, G. J., Uhde, T. W., & Tancer, M. E. (2005). Neural substrates for voluntary suppression of negative affect: A functional magnetic resonance study. *Biological Psychiatry, 57,* 210–219.

Phan, K. L., Wager, T., Taylor, S. F., & Liberzon, I. (2002). Functional neuroanatomy of emotion: A meta-analysis of emotion activation studies in PET and fMRI. *NeuroImage, 16,* 331–348.

Phillips, M. L., Williams, L. M., Heining, M., Herba, C. M., Russell, T., Andrew, C., et al. (2004). Differential neural responses to overt and covert presentations of facial expressions of fear and disgust. *NeuroImage, 21,* 1484–1496.

Preston, A. R., Thomason, M. E., Ochsner, K. N., Cooper, J. C., & Glover, G. H. (2004). Comparison of spiral-in/out and spiral-out BOLD fMRI at 1.5 and 3 T. *NeuroImage, 21,* 291–301.

Price, C. J., Mummery, C. J., Moore, C. J., Frackowiak, R. S. J., & Friston, K. J. (1999). Delineating necessary and sufficient neural systems with functional imaging studies of neuropsychological patients. *Journal of Cognitive Neuroscience, 11,* 371–382.

Raichle, M. E. (2000). A brief history of human functional brain mapping. In A. W. Toga & J. C. Mazziotta (Eds.), *Brain mapping: The systems* (pp. 33–77). San Diego, CA: Academic Press.

Ryle, G. (1949). *The concept of mind.* Chicago: University of Chicago Press.

Sabatinelli, D., Bradley, M. M., Fitzsimmons, J. R., & Lang, P. J. (2005). Parallel amygdala and inferotemporal activation reflect emotional intensity and fear relevance. *NeuroImage, 24,* 1265–1270.

Salli, E., Visa, A., Aronen, H. J., Korvenoja, A., & Katila, T. (1999). Statistical segmentation of fMRI activations using contextual clustering. In C. Taylor & A. Colchester (Eds.), *Proceedings of the 2nd International conference on Medical Image Computing and Computer-Assisted Intervention* (pp. 481–488). Berlin: Springer-Verlag.

Salomons, T. V., Johnstone, T., Backonja, M. M., & Davidson, R. J. (2004). Perceived controllability modulates the neural response to pain. *Journal of Neuroscience, 24,* 7199–7203.

Sarter, M., Berntson, G. G., & Cacioppo, J. T. (1996). Brain imaging and cognitive neuroscience: Toward strong inference in attributing function to structure. *American Psychologist, 51,* 13–21.

Siegal, M., & Varley, R. (2002). Neural systems involved in "theory of mind." *Nature Reviews. Neuroscience, 3,* 463–471.

Siegle, G. J., Steinhauer, S. R., Stenger, V. A., Konecky, R., & Carter, C. S. (2003). Use of concurrent pupil dilation assessment to inform interpretation and analysis of fMRI data. *NeuroImage, 20,* 114–124.

Smith, S. M. (2001). Preparing fMRI data for statistical analysis. In P. Jezzard, P. M. Matthews, & S. M. Smith (Eds.), *Functional MRI: An introduction to methods* (pp. 229–241). Oxford, UK: Oxford University Press.

Smith, S. M., Beckmann, C. F., Ramnani, N., Woolrich, M. W., Bannister, P. R., Jenkinson, M., et al. (2005). Variability in fMRI: A re-examination of inter-session differences. *Human Brain Mapping, 24,* 248–257.

Talairach, J., & Tournoux, P. (1988). *Coplanar stereotaxic atlas of the human brain: 3D proportional system: An approach to cerebral imaging.* New York: Georg Thieme Verlag.

Taylor, S. F., Phan, K. L., Decker, L. R., & Liberzon, I. (2003). Subjective rating of emotionally salient stimuli modulates limbic activity. *NeuroImage, 18,* 650–659.

Thirion, B., Flandin, G., Pinel, P., Roche, A., Ciuciu, P., & Poline, J.-B. (2006). Dealing with the shortcomings of spatial normalization: Multi-subject parcellation of fMRI datasets. *Human Brain Mapping, 27,* 678–693.

Ueda, K., Okamoto, Y., Okada, G., Yamashita, H., Hori, T., & Tamawaki, S. (2003). Brain activity during expectancy of emotional stimuli: An fMRI study. *Neuroreport, 14,* 51–55.

Urry, H. L., van Reekum, C. M., Greischar, L. L., Thurow, M. E., & Davidson, R. J. (2004, October). Working hard when feeling bad: Pupil dilation indexes resource allocation during effortful regulation of negative affect. S. R. Steinhauer (Chair), *Pupil dilation, psychopathology, and development.* Symposium conducted at the meeting of the Society for Psychophysiological Research, Santa Fe, NM.

Vuilleumier, P., Armony, J. L., Driver, J., & Dolan, R. J. (2001). Effects of attention and emotion on face processing in the human brain: An event-related fMRI study. *Neuron, 30,* 829–841.

Wang, J., Aguirre, G. K., Kimberg, D. Y., Roc, A. C., Li, L., & Detre, J. A. (2003). Arterial spin labeling perfusion fMRI with very low task frequency. *Magnetic Resonance in Medicine, 49,* 796–802.

Ward, B. D. (2001). *Deconvolution analysis of FMRI time series data* (Tech. Rep.). Milwaukee: Medical College of Wisconsin Biophysics Research Institute.

Williams, L. M., Brown, K. J., Das, P., Boucsein, W., Sokolov, E. N., Brammer, M. J., et al. (2004). The dynamics of cortico-amygdala and autonomic activity over the experimental time course of fear perception. *Cognitive Brain Research, 21,* 114–123.

Williams, L. M., Phillips, M. L., Brammer, M. J., Skerrett, D., Lagopoulos, J., Rennie, C., et al. (2001). Arousal dissociates amygdala and hippocampal fear responses: Evidence from simultaneous fMRI and skin conductance recording. *NeuroImage, 14,* 1070–1079.

Wong, E. C., Buxton, R. B., & Frank, L. R. (1997). Implementation of quantitative perfusion imaging techniques for functional brain mapping using pulsed arterial spin labeling. *NMR in Biomedicine, 10,* 237–249.

Woolrich, M. W., Behrens, T. E. J., Beckmann, C. F., & Smith, S. M. (2005). Mixture models with adaptive spatial regularisation for segmentation with an application to fMRI Data. *IEEE Transactions on Medical Imaging, 24,* 1–11.

Worsley, K. J., Marrett, S., Neelin, P., Vandal, A. C., Friston, K. J., & Evans, A. C. (1996). A unified statistical approach for determining significant signals in images of cerebral activation. *Human Brain Mapping, 4,* 58–73.

Wright, C. I., Martis, B., Schwartz, C. E., Shin, L. M., Fischer, H. H., McMullin, K., et al. (2003). Novelty responses and differential effects of order in the amygdala, substantia innominata, and inferior temporal cortex. *NeuroImage, 18,* 660–669.

Name Index

Subject Index

AACL (Affect Adjective Checklist), 174
acoustic stimuli. *See* auditory stimuli
action attitudes, as organizing structure, 365
action units, Facial Action Coding System
  automatic recognition approach, 228–230, 234, 235
  described, 205–211, 217
  scoring procedures, 211–212, 217–218
  and SPAFF system, 270–272
Activation-Deactivation Adjective Checklist (AD-ACL), 176
activation studies. *See* functional magnetic resonance imaging (fMRI)
AD-ACL (Activation-Deactivation Adjective Checklist), 176
A/D converters, 245–246
adjective checklists, as assessment approach, 172, 174–175, 178
affect, generally, 171–174
  See also emotions, generally
Affect Adjective Checklist (AACL), 174
Affect Grid, 177, 180–181
affection, in SPAFF system, 272–273
affective primacy hypothesis, 368–369
affective science, overview, 3–6
  See also specific topics, e.g., anger; facial *entries*; Narcoder program; theory foundations
affective space, in IAPS rating studies, 32–35, 36
affect rating dial
  overview, 286–289, 296
  construction guidelines, 289–290

data analysis, 291–295
in dyadic interaction tasks, 111, 115, 165, 288, 291
future uses, 295–296
with neurological patients, 165
procedural guidelines, 290–291
affirmation of the consequent error, defined, 443
age-related patterns
  facial action tasks, 48
  IAPS ratings, 34
aggregation errors, with self-reports, 178
Alaska's Wild Denali (film), 19*t*, 24
alcohol studies, affect rating dial, 288
aliasing, defined, 246, 417
alpha slippage, fMRI studies, 446–448
alrynx, sound production, 244
ambiguity interpretation, assessment methods, 189–192
amplifiers, laboratory guidelines, 416–417
amplitude
  comparison issues, 259–260
  deciBel scale, 263–264
  digital reproduction, 245–246, 247, 249
  in sine waves, 241
  in spectrum analysis, 250–259
  stimuli editing guidelines, 260–262
  voice acoustics studies, 240–241
amputation film, 18, 19*t*, 24
amusement elicitation, films, 19*t*, 21, 23
amygdala
  animal fear study, 363
  backward masking studies, 83–84

in error example, 443
facial expressions, 152–153, 393
in fMRI research examples, 448, 450, 451, 456*n*5
and IAPS rating studies, 41–42
image *vs.* label study, 81
individual differences effect, 444
intracranial recording studies, 436
and learning of reinforcers, 153–154
in lesion-based studies, 429, 432–434
in reinforcer theory, 143–144
taste pathways, 146–147
analog-to-digital converters, 245–246
analysis windows, in frequency spectrums, 250–252, 253–255, 257, 258
anger
  in caregiver study, 312
  catharsis hypothesis, 61
  complex nature, 10
  in dyadic interaction tasks, 116
  in goal-emotion theory, 300
  infants, 302, 353
  in masking study, 83
  in SPAFF system, 273
  as universal emotion, 333
anger elicitation
  behavior manipulation, 56, 58, 61
  children, 354
  facial action tasks, 47–48, 49
  films, 19*t*, 21, 23–24
  IAPS stimuli, 32
  posture manipulation, 60
  social psychological methods, 96–99